Central America
on a shoestring

Nancy Keller

Rob Rachowiecki

Barbara Reioux

Carolyn Hubbard

Tom Brosnahan

Central America

3rd edition

Published by
Lonely Planet Publications
Head Office: PO Box 617, Hawthorn, Vic 3122, Australia
Branches: 150 Linden St, Oakland, CA 94607, USA
10a Spring Place, London NW5 3BH, UK
1 rue du Dahomey, 75011 Paris, France

Printed by
Colorcraft Ltd, Hong Kong

Photographs by

Jeffery Becom	Marc Dupee	Dave Houser
Nancy Keller	Craig Lovell	Suzanne Murphy
Kevin Schafer		

Front cover: Joel Rogers, Tony Stone Images, woman near Lake Atitlan, Guatemala

First Published
February 1992

This Edition
September 1997

Although the authors and publisher have tried to make the information as accurate as possible, they accept no responsibility for any loss, injury or inconvenience sustained by any person using this book.

National Library of Australia Cataloguing in Publication Data

Central America.

3rd ed.
Includes index.
ISBN 0 86442 418 3.

1. Central America – Guidebooks. I. Hubbard, Carolyn, 1966-.
II. Keller, Nancy J. III. Reioux, Barbara, 1955-.
(Series: Lonely Planet on a shoestring).

917.280453

text & maps © Lonely Planet 1997
photos © photographers as indicated 1997
climate charts compiled from information supplied by Patrick J Tyson, © Patrick J Tyson, 1997

Nancy Keller

Born and raised in Northern California, Nancy worked in the alternative press for several years. She returned to university to earn a master's degree in journalism, finally graduating in 1986 after many breaks for extended stays on the west coast of Mexico. Since then she's been traveling around the world and has written or co-authored several Lonely Planet books, including *Mexico, Rarotonga & the Cook Islands, New Zealand, California & Nevada* and *Guatemala, Belize & Yucatán – La Ruta Maya*. Nancy updated the Guatemala, Honduras and Panama chapters of this edition and was the book's coordinating author.

Rob Rachowiecki

Born near London, Rob spent most of the 1980s in Latin America, traveling, teaching English, visiting national parks and working for Wilderness Travel, an adventure travel company. He is the author of Lonely Planet's guides to Costa Rica, Ecuador, Peru and Southwest USA and has contributed to Lonely Planet's shoestring guides to South America. Rob has a master's degree in biology from the University of Arizona. When not traveling, he lives in Arizona with his wife, Cathy, and their three children: Julia, Alison and David. Rob updated the Costa Rica chapter for this edition, based on his research for *Costa Rica*.

Barbara Reioux

Originally from San Diego, California, Barbara got her first taste of foreign travel at age 19 on a bus trip to Mexico and Guatemala. In 1980 she joined the US Foreign Service, serving in US embassies in Bolivia, Italy and Indonesia. She left the Foreign Service in 1991 and currently lives with her husband and daughter in Managua, where she is working on a business degree at the University of Mobile, Latin American campus. Barbara updated the Nicaragua chapter for this edition.

Carolyn Hubbard

Usually working behind the scenes at Lonely Planet, Carolyn took a break to experience travel writing, squelch a biting travel bug and reawaken her interest in the history of and social change in Central America. She has hit all the main continents in her travels and hopes to explore Central America further. Carolyn updated the El Salvador chapter for this edition.

Tom Brosnahan

Tom was born and raised in Pennsylvania, went to college in Boston and then traveled in Europe. He saw Mexico for the first time as part of a Peace Corps training program and later worked with the Corps in Turkey. This whetted his appetite: After graduate school, he traveled throughout Mexico, Guatemala and Belize writing travel articles and guidebooks, and since then he has written over 20 travel guides. Tom updated the Belize chapter for this edition, based on his research for *Guatemala, Belize & Yucatán – La Ruta Maya*.

From the Authors

From Nancy Thanks to everyone whose talented work made this 3rd edition what it is. Thanks to all the co-authors, all of whom did a great job.

Special thanks to the editors, Kate Hoffman and Michelle Gagné-Ballard, for their consummate editorial magic, and to Alex Guilbert and crew for cartographical skill and resourcefulness. Great thanks also to Caroline Liou at LP's California office for her helpfulness throughout the project, especially as the 'contact with home' for the authors out in the field.

Thanks to everyone in Honduras, Guatemala and Panama, the three countries I visited for this edition, who were helpful with the project. The national tourist offices of all three countries assisted me greatly when I was doing research. Thanks especially to Erasmo Sosa of the new ecotourism section of the Instituto Hondureño de Turismo (Tegucigalpa) and Jaime Troyano (Panama City) and Julia Culiolis (Bocas del Toro) of IPAT.

Many people offered invaluable assistance and also showed much friendliness and brought much joy to the author. In Guatemala, thanks to Real Desrosiers of the Adventure Travel Center, the folks at the Rainbow Reading Room and to Juan Francisco Sic (all of Antigua), David and Flori of the Desarrollo del Pueblo Spanish school (Quetzaltenango), Ashley de Acuña and family (Cobán), Ricardo Pocorny, Alexandra and Carlos (Flores), Carole DeVine (Poptún), Eugene at Hacienda Tijax (Río Dulce), María 'La Mexicana' and Julio Raúl Chew (Lívingston) and Antonio 'Maharishi' (San Pedro La Laguna).

In Honduras, thanks to Jan and María Zaal of Amsterdam 2001 (La Ceiba), Tyll Sass and crew, Helen Sykes, 'Doc' Radawski, Marion Seaman, Jimmy and Lenora, Rudy and JC (all on Roatán), Bernd Birnbach (Utila), Natalie and the Brinkleys (Trujillo), Alessandro and Aura, Agustino and Carla, Mario, Lucy and Tati (Tela), René and Darla, Suzanne and William, Howard, Jorge Barraza and the family at Los Gemelos (all of Copán Ruinas), Warren Post (Santa Rosa de Copán), Miguel García (San Pedro Sula), Don Jim and Doña Araceli, Gustavo, Alan, Lola, Ana, Maribel and Tom Taylor (all of Tegucigalpa), Guillermo Yuscarán and many others.

In Panama, thanks to Gerasimos (Gerry) Kanelopulos and the friendly staff at Librería Argosy (Panama City), and to Frank Glavas, Lorenza and family (Boquete).

Thanks also to travelers met along the way who made the journey brighter, especially Tara Ryan and Thomas the German doctor.

Thanks also to TACA and Rosa Castro and María Ng of Central America Corp for their assistance.

From Rob Many people in Costa Rica helped me see the country through their eyes – their conversations, suggestions, hospitality and help were greatly appreciated. Michael and Yolanda Kaye of Escazú opened their hearts and home to me, providing me with a relaxing place to stay between my furiously paced forays around the country. Randy Galati, road-traveler extraordinaire, provided me with insider information about the central Pacific and southern Caribbean coastal areas. In Barra del Colorado, Ray Barry and Shawn Feliciano were super hosts and lent me a boat to check out the entire area. Others who helped hugely include Susan and Mike Kalmbach in Drake Bay, Thomas Douglas in San José, Mauricio Jurado Fernández and Milvia Cornacchia Grossi in San Pedro, Jeff Crandall in Nuevo Arenal, Jim Damalas in Manuel Antonio, Jack Ewing in Dominical, Leta Moores in Puerto Jimínez, Thea Gaudette and Ron Deletetsky near Guápiles, Jan and Pilar Westra near San Isidro de El General, Ronald Esquivel in San José, Gail Hewson de Gómez in San Vito and Francisco Chamberlain of San José.

I also thank the following for reviewing some of my work and emailing me with last-minute changes, corrections or updates: Rick and Lori, Susan and Andrew from Zancudo, Anita Myketuk from Manuel Antonio, Haymo Heyder of Arco Iris in Monteverde, Carol Chapman from Playa de Coco, the folks at The Canopy Tour, Rob Hodel of Tico Travel, Carol Weir and Charles Stratford of *The Tico Times*, Vernon Bell of Bellís Home Hospitality, Humberto Brenes of the Instituto Costarricense de Turísmo, Richard Stern, PhD, with Triangulo Rosa in San José, John Aspinall of Costa Rica Sun Tours, Elizabeth Agnew of the Canadian Worldwide Fund for Nature, Richard Krug and Todd Staley of Americana Fishing Services, William Porcher of Tamarindo Vista Villas, Lenny of El Sano Banano in Montezuma and Karen Delahaye for Fortuna restaurant reviews.

Finally, my dear wife and children tolerated with equanimity my time-consuming and ongoing love/hate relationship with the word processor. Thanks for making it all possible.

From Barbara I am especially grateful to my husband, John Naland, whose unflagging enthusiasm and support made my travel research more like a holiday than a work assignment. I'd like to thank Mireya Lopez, Marcos Antonio Menocal, Carolina Briones and Regina Hurtado of the Ministry of Tourism, Telma Prego of the Foreign Ministry, Carolina Rodriguez, Bob Blohm, Jerry Bauer, Margaret Harritt and John Dorman. Thanks also to the many people we met during our travels who shared their experiences and to the Lonely Planet readers who wrote in.

From Carolyn Many thanks to the staff at CISPES in San Francisco, CIS in San Salvador, and the former ISTU office in San Salvador. To intrepid backpacker Sylvia Bück, the readers who wrote, and to the many volunteers I met while there, thanks for your suggestions and opinions. To traveling companions Marc Dupee and Joanna Harrison, your insights, support and humor added focus and meaning to the trip – I am truly indebted to you.

This Book
The 1st edition of this book was researched and written by Nancy Keller, Tom Brosnahan and Rob Rachowiecki. The 2nd edition was researched and written by Mark Honan, Tom Brosnahan, Rob Rachowiecki and Stephen Schwartz.

From the Publisher
Various hardy souls helped weave together the many disparate pieces of this book. Kate Hoffman edited and coordinated the book through production under Carolyn Hubbard's guidance. Michelle Gagné-Ballard patiently edited and helped with the juggling through production. Don Gates helped with editing and proofing text and maps. Jeff Campbell proofread text with his usual dedication to detail. Sacha Pearson stoically proofed batch after batch of maps. Fresh from Australia, Brigitte Barta pored over the book in layout.

Hayden Foell, Rini Keagy, Cyndy Johnsen, Scott Noren and Diana Nankin drew and tweaked the maps, with subtle prodding from Alex Guilbert. Hayden also laid out the book, incorporating Scott Summer's suggestions, and designed the chapter end. Hugh D'Andrade designed the cover.

A special thanks to Tom Brosnahan for timely help polishing the Guatemala chapter.

Thanks
A special thanks to those readers who took the time and energy to write to us from places large and small all over the region. These people's names appear at the back of the book on page 819.

Warning & Request
Things change – prices go up, schedules change, good places go bad and bad places go bankrupt – nothing stays the same. So, if you find things better or worse, recently

opened or long since closed, please tell us and help make the next edition even more accurate and useful.

We value all of the feedback we receive from travelers. A small team reads and acknowledges every letter, postcard and email, and ensures that every morsel of information finds its way to the appropriate authors, editors and publishers. Everyone who writes to us will find their name in the next edition of the appropriate guide and will also receive a free subscription to our quarterly newsletter, *Planet Talk*. The very best contributions will be rewarded with a free Lonely Planet guide.

Excerpts from your correspondence may appear in updates (which we add to the end pages of reprints); new editions of this guide; in our newsletter; or in the Postcards section of our Website – so please let us know if you don't want your letter published or your name acknowledged.

Contents

INTRODUCTION **15**

FACTS ABOUT CENTRAL AMERICA **17**

History 17	Ecology & Environment 22	Population & People 27
Geography 20	Flora & Fauna 23	Arts 28
Geology 21	Government & Politics 25	Society & Conduct 28
Climate 21	Economy 26	Religion 30

REGIONAL FACTS FOR THE VISITOR **31**

Planning 31	Photography 47	Travel with Children 65
Suggested Itineraries 33	Time 48	Dangers & Annoyances 65
Highlights 33	Electricity 48	Legal Matters 68
Visas & Documents 36	Weights & Measures 48	Activities 69
Customs 38	Laundry 48	Language Courses 69
Money 38	Health 48	Work 69
Post & Communications 42	Toilets 62	Accommodations 70
Traveling with a Laptop 44	Useful Organizations 63	Food 71
Books 44	Women Travelers 63	Drinks 72
Media 46	Gay & Lesbian Travelers 64	

GETTING THERE & AWAY **74**

Air 74	Sea 83	Warning 84
Land 81		

GETTING AROUND CENTRAL AMERICA **85**

Air 85	Car & Motorcycle 88	Boat 93
Bus 86	Bicycle 92	Organized Tours 94
Train 88	Hitchhiking 93	

GUATEMALA **95**

Facts about Guatemala **95**	Books 112	**Antigua Guatemala** **134**
Geography 101	Newspapers & Magazines . . . 112	Around Antigua Guatemala . 148
Climate 101	Radio & TV 113	**Highlands – Lago de**
Ecology & Environment 101	Laundry 113	**Atitlán** **149**
Flora & Fauna 102	Health 113	Tecpán Guatemala 150
Government & Politics 105	Women Travelers 113	Sololá 151
Economy 105	Gay & Lesbian Travelers . . . 113	Panajachel 151
Population & People 105	Dangers & Annoyances 113	Santa Catarina Palopó
Education 106	Business Hours	& San Antonio Palopó 159
Arts 106	& Public Holidays 114	San Lucas Tolimán 159
Society & Conduct 106	Special Events 114	Santiago Atitlán 159
Religion 107	Activities 115	San Pedro La Laguna 161
Language 107	Language Courses 115	San Marcos La Laguna 162
Facts for the Visitor **108**	Work 115	Santa Cruz La Laguna 163
Highlights 108	Accommodations 116	**Highlands – Quiché** **164**
Tourist Offices 108	Food 116	Chichicastenango 164
Visas & Documents 108	Drinks 116	Santa Cruz del Quiché 170
Embassies 109	Things to Buy 117	Nebaj 172
Customs 109	**Getting There & Away** **117**	Uspantán 172
Money 109	**Getting Around** **118**	**Southwestern Highlands** . . **173**
Post & Communications 110	**Guatemala City** **119**	Cuatro Caminos 173

San Miguel Totonicapán 173
Quetzaltenango 174
Around Quetzaltenango 182
Huehuetenango 186
Around Huehuetenango. 190
La Mesilla 190
Todos Santos Cuchumatán . . 190
Pacific Slope. 191
Ciudad Tecún Umán 191
El Carmen 191
Coatepeque 192
El Zarco Junction 192
Retalhuleu 192
Abaj Takalik 194
Champerico 194
Mazatenango 194
Santa Lucía Cotzumalguapa . 195
La Democracia 198
Around La Democracia 199

Escuintla 199
Puerto San José,
Likín & Iztapa 199
Monterrico. 200
Lago de Amatitlán. 201
**Central & Eastern
Guatemala. 201**
Salamá. 202
Around Salamá 203
Biotopo del Quetzal. 203
Cobán 204
Around Cobán 208
Río Hondo 209
Estanzuela 210
Zacapa 211
Chiquimula 211
Padre Miguel Junction
& Anguiatú 213
Esquipulas 213

El Florido 216
Quiriguá. 217
Lago de Izabal. 219
The Road to Flores 221
Poptún 221
Puerto Barrios 222
Lívingston 226
Around Lívingston 230
El Petén. 231
Flores & Santa Elena. 233
El Remate 240
Around the Lake 241
Tikal 241
Uaxactún 249
Eastward to Belize. 250
From El Petén to
Chiapas (Mexico) 251
Sayaxché & Ceibal 252

BELIZE 255

Facts about Belize 255
Geography. 257
Climate 257
Flora & Fauna 257
Government & Politics 258
Economy 259
Population & People 259
Education. 260
Society & Conduct 260
Religion. 260
Language. 260
Facts for the Visitor 260
Highlights 260
Tourist Offices. 260
Visas & Documents. 261
Embassies & Consulates 261
Money 261
Post & Communications 262
Media. 262
Weights & Measures. 263
Disabled Travelers 263
Dangers & Annoyances. 263

Business Hours
& Public Holidays. 263
Activities. 263
Accommodations. 263
Food. 263
Drinks 264
Entertainment 264
Getting There & Away 264
Getting Around. 264
Belize City. 265
The Cayes. 274
Caye Caulker. 274
Ambergris Caye. 278
Northern Belize. 282
Bermudian Landing Community
Baboon Sanctuary 282
Altun Ha 282
Crooked Tree
Wildlife Sanctuary 283
Lamanai. 283
Orange Walk Town 284
Corozal Town 286

Crossing the Border
to Mexico. 288
Western Belize 289
Belize Zoo. 289
Guanacaste National Park . . . 289
Belmopan 289
San Ignacio (Cayo) 291
Cayo District 294
Xunantunich 296
Benque Viejo del Carmen . . . 297
Crossing the
Guatemalan Border 297
Southern Belize 298
The Hummingbird
Highway 298
Dangriga 299
Southern Highway 301
Placencia 302
Punta Gorda. 304
Around Punta Gorda 306

HONDURAS 309

Facts about Honduras 310
Geography. 316
Climate 316
Ecology & Environment 316
Flora & Fauna 317
Government & Politics 320
Economy 320
Population & People 320
Education. 321
Arts 321

Society & Conduct 321
Religion. 322
Language. 322
Facts for the Visitor 322
Highlights 322
Tourist Offices. 323
Visas & Documents. 323
Embassies 323
Customs. 324
Money. 324

Post & Communications 325
Books. 326
Media. 327
Photography & Video 328
Electricity 328
Laundry 328
Health 328
Women Travelers 328
Gay & Lesbian Travelers 329
Dangers & Annoyances. 329

Business Hours
& Public Holidays 329
Special Events 330
Activities 330
Language Courses 331
Accommodations 331
Food 332
Drinks 332
Entertainment 333
Spectator Sports 333
Things to Buy 333
Getting There & Away **334**
Getting Around **335**
Tegucigalpa **338**
Around Tegucigalpa 351
Western Honduras **355**
Tegucigalpa to
San Pedro Sula 355
Comayagua 356
Around Comayagua 358
Siguatepeque 359
Around Siguatepeque 360
La Esperanza 360
Cuevas de Taulabé 360
Lago de Yojoa 361
Pulhapanzak 361
Balneario Bahr 362

Santa Bárbara 362
San Pedro Sula 362
Parque Nacional Cusuco 369
Carretera de Occidente 370
La Entrada 370
Copán Ruinas 371
Around Copán Ruinas 375
Copán Archaeological Site . . 376
Santa Rosa de Copán 381
Around Santa Rosa
de Copán 383
Gracias 383
Around Gracias 386
Parque Nacional Celaque . . . 386
Nueva Ocotepeque 387
El Poy & Agua Caliente 388
Northern Honduras **388**
Puerto Cortés 389
Travesía & Baja Mar 391
Omoa 392
Tela 393
Around Tela 397
La Ceiba 400
Around La Ceiba 406
Parque Nacional
Pico Bonito 408
Amaras 409

Trujillo 410
Around Trujillo 415
Santa Rosa de Aguán 417
Limón 418
Bay Islands **418**
Roatán 423
Utila 435
Guanaja 441
Cayos Cochinos
(Hog Islands) 443
Eastern Honduras **444**
La Unión 444
Around La Unión 445
Parque Nacional La Muralla . 445
Juticalpa 445
Catacamas 447
The Mosquitia 447
Southern Honduras **450**
Tegucigalpa to Nicaragua . . . 451
Tegucigalpa to the Pacific . . . 451
Golfo de Fonseca 451
Choluteca 452
San Marcos de Colón 455
Border Crossing
to Nicaragua 455
Border Crossing
to El Salvador 455

EL SALVADOR 457

Facts about El Salvador . . **457**
History 457
Geography 461
Climate 461
Ecology & Environment 461
Flora & Fauna 462
Government & Politics 462
Economy 462
Population & People 463
Education 463
Arts 463
Society & Conduct 463
Religion 464
Language 464
Facts for the Visitor **464**
Planning 464
The Best & the Worst 465
Tourist Offices 465
Visas & Documents 465
Embassies 466
Customs 466
Money 466
Post & Communications 467
Books & Films 467
Media 468
Laundry 468
Health 468

Toilets 468
Useful Organizations 468
Women Travelers 469
Gay & Lesbian Travelers . . . 469
Dangers & Annoyances 469
Business Hours
& Public Holidays 469
Activities 470
Accommodations 470
Food 471
Drinks 471
Things to Buy 472
Getting There & Away **472**
Getting Around **474**
San Salvador **475**
East of San Salvador 490
West of San Salvador 490
South of San Salvador 491
Western El Salvador **493**
La Libertad 493
La Costa del Bálsamo 495
Lago de Coatepeque 495
Cerro Verde
& Volcán Izalco 496
Santa Ana 497
Lago de Güija 500
Metapán 500

Parque Nacional
Montecristo-El Trifinio 500
Ruinas de Tazumal 501
Ahuachapán 502
Apaneca 502
Santa Ana to Sonsonate 503
Sonsonate 503
Acajutla 503
Parque Nacional
El Imposible 504
Eastern El Salvador **504**
The Interamericana 504
Carretera del Litoral 505
Isla Montecristo 506
Usulután 506
San Miguel 506
El Cuco 509
La Unión 510
El Tamarindo 511
Santa Rosa de Lima 512
Ciudad Segundo Montes 512
Perquín 512
El Mozote 513
Northern El Salvador **513**
Chalatenango 513
Dulce Nombre de Maria 514
La Palma 514

NICARAGUA 517

Facts about Nicaragua. . . . 517
History. 517
Geography. 524
Climate 525
Ecology & Environment 525
Government & Politics 526
Economy 526
Population & People 526
Education. 527
Arts 527
Religion. 527
Language. 527
Facts for the Visitor 527
Planning. 527
Highlights 528
Tourist Offices. 529
Visas & Documents. 529
Embassies 529
Customs. 530
Money 530
Post & Communications 531
Books. 531
Media. 532
Photography & Film 532
Time 532
Weights & Measures. 532
Health 532
Women Travelers 532

Gay & Lesbian Travelers . . . 532
Dangers & Annoyances. 533
Business Hours
& Public Holidays. 533
Special Events 533
Activities. 533
Language Courses. 534
Work 534
Accommodations. 534
Food. 534
Drinks 535
Entertainment 535
Things to Buy 535
Getting There & Away . . . 535
Getting Around. 537
Managua 538
Around Managua 548
Parque Nacional
Volcán Masaya 548
Volcán Momotombo 550
León Viejo. 550
Pochomil 550
Other Beaches 550
North of Managua. 551
Matagalpa 551
Jinotega. 554
Lago de Apanás. 555
Estelí 555

North to Honduras. 558
Northwest of Managua. . . . 559
León. 560
Poneloya 564
Northwest from León 564
South of Managua 565
Masaya 565
Around Masaya 568
Granada 569
Around Granada 573
Rivas 574
Rivas to Costa Rica. 575
San Juan del Sur 575
Lago de Nicaragua. 577
Isla de Ometepe. 578
Archipiélago de
Solentiname. 581
San Carlos 582
Río San Juan & El Castillo . . . 582
The Caribbean Coast 583
Managua to the Caribbean. . . 584
Juigalpa 584
Rama 584
Bluefields. 585
Laguna de Perlas 587
Puerto Cabezas 587
Corn Islands 588

COSTA RICA. 589

Facts about Costa Rica . . . 589
Geography. 593
Climate 593
Ecology & Environment 594
Flora & Fauna 594
Government. 597
Economy 597
Population & People 598
Education. 598
Arts 598
Society & Conduct 598
Religion. 599
Language. 599
Facts for the Visitor 600
Highlights 600
Tourist Offices. 600
Visas & Documents. 601
Embassies 601
Customs. 602
Money 602
Post & Communications 604
Books. 604
Newspapers & Magazines. . . 605
Radio & TV. 605

Film & Photography 605
Time 605
Electricity 605
Laundry 605
Health 606
Women Travelers 606
Gay & Lesbian Travelers . . . 606
Dangers & Annoyances. 606
Business Hours
& Public Holidays. 607
Special Events 607
Activities. 607
Language Courses. 608
Accommodations. 608
Food. 609
Drinks 609
Entertainment 610
Spectator Sports 610
Things to Buy 610
Getting There & Away . . . 610
Getting Around. 611
San José 613
**Central Valley
& Highlands 628**

Alajuela. 629
Sarchí. 629
Parque Nacional
Volcán Poás. 632
Heredia 632
Barva 633
Parque Nacional
Braulio Carrillo 633
Rain Forest Aerial Tram 634
Coronado. 634
Cartago 634
Turrialba 636
Monumento Nacional
Guayabo 637
**Northwestern
Costa Rica. 638**
Monteverde & Santa Elena . . 638
Cañas. 643
Parque Nacional
Palo Verde 644
Reserva Biológica
Lomas Barbudal 644
Liberia 644

Parque Nacional
Rincón de La Vieja 646
Parque Nacional
Santa Rosa. 647
Parque Nacional
Guanacaste 648
Peñas Blancas 648
Ciudad Quesada. 648
Fortuna & Volcán Arenal . . . 649
Tilarán 650
Northern Lowlands 651
Los Chiles 651
Puerto Viejo de Sarapiquí . . 651
Caribbean Lowlands 652
Puerto Limón 652
Parque Nacional Tortuguero . 654
Tortuguero. 655
Barra del Colorado 656
Cahuita 657
Parque Nacional Cahuita. . . . 660
Puerto Viejo de Talamanca . . 661
East of Puerto Viejo 664
Sixaola. 665
Southern Costa Rica 665

San Isidro de El General 666
San Gerardo de Rivas 667
Parque Nacional Chirripó . . . 667
Palmar Norte & Palmar Sur . 669
Sierpe. 669
Bahía Drake. 669
Golfito 669
South of Golfito. 672
Puerto Jiménez 672
Parque Nacional Corcovado . . 673
Neily 673
San Vito. 673
Paso Canoas. 675
Central Pacific Coast. 675
Puntarenas. 675
Reserva Biológica Carara . . . 678
Jacó 679
Quepos. 680
Manuel Antonio. 682
Parque Nacional
Manuel Antonio. 683
Dominical 686
Uvita 687

Parque Nacional
Marino Ballena 687
Península de Nicoya 687
Playa del Coco. 688
Playa Tamarindo 691
Parque Nacional Marino
Las Baulas de Guanacaste. . . 692
Playa Avellana 693
Playa Junquillal 693
Santa Cruz. 693
Nicoya 694
Parque Nacional
Barra Honda 694
Playa Nosara 694
Refugio Nacional de Fauna
Silvestre Ostional 695
Playa Sámara. 695
Playa Naranjo 696
Paquera 696
Montezuma 696
Malpaís 697
Reserva Natural
Absoluta Cabo Blanco. 698

PANAMA 699

Facts about Panama 699
Geography. 707
Climate 707
Ecology & Environment 708
Flora & Fauna 708
Government & Politics 709
Economy 710
Population & People 710
Education. 711
Arts 711
Society & Conduct 711
Religion. 712
Language. 712
Facts for the Visitor 712
Highlights 713
Tourist Offices. 713
Visas & Documents 714
Embassies & Consulates 714
Customs. 715
Money 715
Post & Communications 715
Books. 716
Media. 717
Photography & Film 717
Time 717
Electricity 717
Laundry 717
Weights & Measures 717
Health 717

Dangers & Annoyances. 717
Business Hours 718
Public Holidays
& Special Events. 718
Activities. 718
Work 720
Accommodations. 720
Food. 720
Drinks 721
Entertainment 721
Spectator Sports 721
Things to Buy 721
Getting There & Away . . . 722
Getting Around. 723
Panama City 725
Around Panama City 740
Panama Canal 740
Canal Area. 742
Isla Barro Colorado 743
Cerro Azul. 743
Baha'i & Hindu Temples . . . 743
Beaches 744
El Valle 744
Isla Taboga 746
Archipiélago de Las Perlas
& Isla Contadora 748
Veraguas Province. 748
Colón & Around 748
Colón 748

Fuerte San Lorenzo 749
Portobelo. 750
Isla Grande 750
Península de Azuero 751
Chitré. 753
Villa de Los Santos 755
Guararé 755
Las Tablas 755
Chiriquí 756
David. 757
Around David 761
Golfo de Chiriquí 761
Playa Las Lajas 761
Boquete 762
Los Pozos de Caldera 765
Parque Nacional
Volcán Barú. 765
Around Volcán Barú 766
Volcán 766
Bambito 768
Cerro Punta 768
Guadalupe 769
Parque Internacional
La Amistad 769
Río Sereno. 770
Puerto Armuelles. 771
Bocas del Toro 771
Parque Nacional
Marino Isla Bastimentos 771

Bocas del Toro 771
Isla Bastimentos 777
Other Islands 777

Chiriquí Grande
& Almirante. 778
Changuinola 779

Eastern Panama 780
Archipiélago de San Blas . . . 780
Darién 782

GLOSSARY **793**

SPANISH FOR TRAVELERS **797**

ONLINE RESOURCES **804**

INDEX **809**
Map 809   Text 810

Map Legend

BOUNDARIES

---·---·---·--- International Boundary

---··---··---·· Provincial Boundary

AREA FEATURES

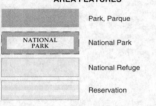

Park, Parque

National Park

National Refuge

Reservation

HYDROGRAPHIC FEATURES

Water
Reef
Coastline
Beach, Playa
Swamp
River, Waterfall
Mangrove, Spring

ROUTES

Freeway

Primary Road

Secondary Road

Tertiary Road

Poorly Maintained Road

Trail

Ferry Route

Railway, Train Station

ROUTE SHIELDS

1️⃣ Central American Highway

9️⃣ National Highway

11 Provincial/State/Department Highway

SYMBOLS

✪ NATIONAL CAPITAL	✈ Airfield	Gas Station	)(Pass
◉ Provincial Capital	✈ Airport	Golf Course	Picnic Area
● City	∴ Archaeological Site, Ruins	⊙ Hospital, Clinic	★ Police Station
● City, Small	❽ Bank, ATM	❶ Information	Pool
● Town	Baseball Stadium	🎋 Lighthouse	Post Office
	Beach	☀ Lookout	Public Toilets
	Bus Station, Bus Stop	Mine	Shopping Mall
■ Hotel, B&B	Cathedral, Catedral	Monument	Skiing, Cross-country
▲ Campground	Cave	▲ Mountain	Skiing, Downhill
⌂ Hostel	✝ Church, Iglesia	🏛 Museum	🏛 Stately Home
RV Park	Dive Site	Music, Live	☎ Telephone
⌂ Shelter, Refugio	Embassy, Consulate	Observatory	Tomb, Mausoleum
▼ Restaurant	Footbridge	← One-Way Street	Trailhead
Bar (Place to Drink)	Fort	Park, Parque	Winery
Cafe	Garden	Parking	Zoo

Note: Not all symbols displayed above appear in this book.

Introduction

Central America is a small region – its seven countries together have a land area about a quarter the size of Mexico. Nevertheless, it is a remarkably varied part of the world, with attractions ranging from the ruins of ancient Maya cities to the Panama Canal, one of the engineering triumphs of the 20th century.

Central America's attractions draw visitors from all over the world. The Maya ruins are probably the best-known sites, but off the coast of Honduras and Nicaragua visitors find idyllic Caribbean islands with waving palms and white sandy beaches that offer a chance to kick back or to scuba and snorkel. Belize boasts the second largest coral reef in the world. Costa Rica's pristine national parks, several in tropical rain forests, attract international scientists and visitors interested in wildlife watching and the natural environment. Guatemala is known for the vibrant indigenous Maya culture that still thrives there despite encroachments. Guatemala's

beautiful Lago de Atitlán, ringed by mountains, enchants visitors, as does the old Spanish colonial city of Antigua Guatemala, known worldwide for its language schools.

You can see mountain mining villages, vast wilderness areas, unusual wildlife and ecological systems ranging from large Caribbean lagoons to high-altitude cloud forests. The landscapes can be spectacular – from almost any spot in El Salvador a volcano is within sight, some of them still active. Away from these well-known highlights, however, many places are so rarely visited that the arrival of a foreigner is quite an event.

Central America has been making international newspaper headlines for decades, not so much for its tourist attractions as for its volatile politics. But peace has recently been spreading in Central America; civil wars that raged for decades have drawn to a close and the hard work of peace has begun. Apprehensions about traveling in

the region have lessened, allowing visitors to gain a personal knowledge of the Central Americans and a greater understanding of the conditions they face today.

This is a fascinating part of the world. It's also compact, accessible, easy to travel in and not expensive. All in all, it's a great place for traveling on a shoestring.

A: CRAIG LOVELL

B: MARC DUPEE

C: NANCY KELLER

D: DAVE HOUSER

A: Stela at Copán, Honduras
B: Tres amigos, El Salvador

C: Garífuna elder, La Ensenada, Honduras
D: Kuna Indian woman, Panama

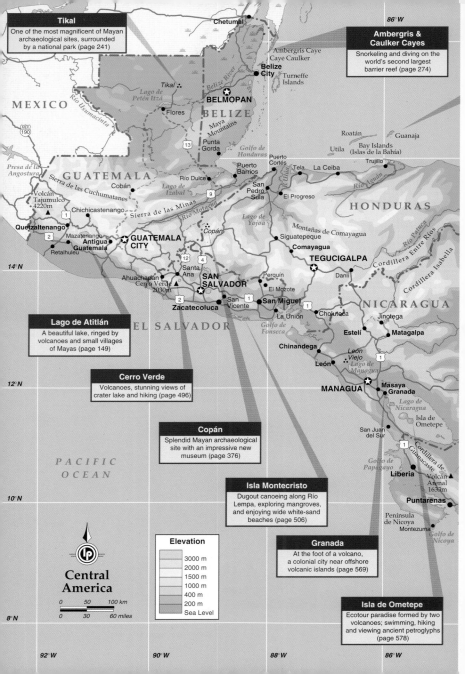

Tikal
One of the most magnificent of Mayan archaeological sites, surrounded by a national park (page 241)

Ambergris & Caulker Cayes
Snorkeling and diving on the world's second largest barrier reef (page 274)

Lago de Atitlán
A beautiful lake, ringed by volcanoes and small villages of Mayas (page 149)

Cerro Verde
Volcanoes, stunning views of crater lake and hiking (page 496)

Copán
Splendid Mayan archaeological site with an impressive new museum (page 376)

Isla Montecristo
Dugout canoeing along Río Lempa, exploring mangroves, and enjoying wide white-sand beaches (page 506)

Granada
At the foot of a volcano, a colonial city near offshore volcanic islands (page 569)

Isla de Ometepe
Ecotour paradise formed by two volcanoes; swimming, hiking and viewing ancient petroglyphs (page 578)

Central America

Elevation
3000 m
2000 m
1500 m
1000 m
400 m
200 m
Sea Level

0   50   100 km
0   30   60 miles

PACIFIC OCEAN

MEXICO

GUATEMALA

BELIZE

HONDURAS

EL SALVADOR

NICARAGUA

Chetumal
Ambergris Caye
Caye Caulker
Belize City
Turneffe Islands
BELMOPAN
Tikal
Lago de Petén Itzá
Flores
Maya Mountains
Punta Gorda
Golfo de Honduras
Puerto Cortés
Puerto Barrios
Roatán
Guanaja
Utila
Bay Islands (Islas de la Bahía)
Trujillo
Tela
La Ceiba
San Pedro Sula
El Progreso
Río Dulce
Cobán
Lago de Izabal
Sierra de las Minas
Volcán Tajumulco 4220m
Chichicastenango
Quetzaltenango
Mazatenango
Retalhuleu
Antigua Guatemala
GUATEMALA CITY
Copán
Lago de Yojoa
Montañas de Comayagua
Siguatepeque
Comayagua
TEGUCIGALPA
Cordillera Entre Ríos
Río Patuca
Cordillera Isabella
Santa Ana
Ahuachapán
Cerro Verde 2030m
SAN SALVADOR
Zacatecoluca
San Vicente
Perquín
El Mozote
San Miguel
La Unión
Golfo de Fonseca
Danlí
Choluteca
Jinotega
Estelí
Matagalpa
Chinandega
León
León Viejo
Lago de Managua
MANAGUA
Masaya
Granada
Lago de Nicaragua
Isla de Ometepe
San Juan del Sur
Cordillera de Guanacaste
Liberia
Volcán Arenal 1633m
Puntarenas
Península de Nicoya
Montezuma
Golfo de Papagayo
Golfo de Nicoya
Presa de la Angostura
Sierra de las Cuchumatanes
Río Usumacinta
Belize River
Río Motagua
Río Ulúa
Río Aguán

MEX 190

86° W
92° W
90° W
88° W
86° W
14° N
12° N
10° N
8° N

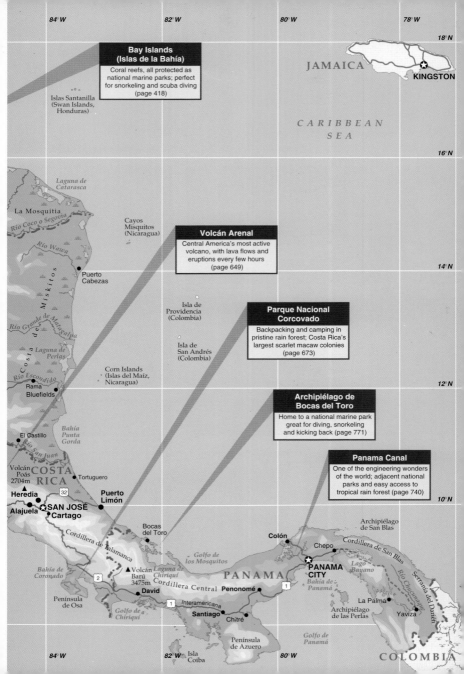

**Bay Islands
(Islas de la Bahía)**

Coral reefs, all protected as
national marine parks; perfect
for snorkeling and scuba diving
(page 418)

JAMAICA

★ KINGSTON

CARIBBEAN
SEA

18° N

16° N

Islas Santanilla
(Swan Islands,
Honduras)

Laguna de
Catarasca

La Mosquitia

Río Coco o Segovia

Río Wawa

Cayos
Misquitos
(Nicaragua)

Volcán Arenal

Central America's most active
volcano, with lava flows and
eruptions every few hours
(page 649)

14° N

Puerto
Cabezas

Isla de
Providencia
(Colombia)

**Parque Nacional
Corcovado**

Backpacking and camping in
pristine rain forest; Costa Rica's
largest scarlet macaw colonies
(page 673)

Río Grande de Matagalpa

Isla de
San Andrés
(Colombia)

Costa de Mosquitos

Laguna de
Perlas

Corn Islands
(Islas del Maíz,
Nicaragua)

12° N

Río Escondido

Rama
Bluefields

**Archipiélago de
Bocas del Toro**

Home to a national marine park
great for diving, snorkeling
and kicking back (page 771)

El Castillo

Bahía
Punta
Gorda

Río San Juan

Panama Canal

One of the engineering wonders
of the world; adjacent national
parks and easy access to
tropical rain forest (page 740)

10° N

Volcán
Poás
2704m

Tortuguero

COSTA
RICA

32

Puerto
Limón

Archipiélago
de San Blas

Colón

HEREDIA

Chepo

Cordillera de San Blas

Alajuela

★ SAN JOSÉ
Cartago

Bocas
del Toro

Golfo de
los Mosquitos

★ PANAMA
CITY

Lago
Bayano

Cordillera de Talamanca

Volcán
Barú
3475m

Laguna de
Chiriquí

PANAMA

Bahía de
Panamá

Río Chucunaque

Serranía del Darién

Bahía de
Coronado

Cordillera Central

Penonomé

2

David

Interamericana

1

La Palma

Península
de Osa

Golfo de
Chiriquí

1

Santiago

Chitré

Archipiélago
de las Perlas

Yaviza

Golfo de
Panamá

Isla
Coiba

Península
de Azuero

COLOMBIA

84° W

82° W

80° W

A: JEFFERY BECOM – PHOTO 20/20

B: DAVE HOUSER

C: NANCY KELLER

E: SUZANNE MURPHY

D: DAVE HOUSER

F: KEVIN SCHAFER

G: DAVE HOUSER

A: Painted house façade, Petén, Guatemala
B: Mercado Central, Guatemala City
C: Mural, Jinotega, Nicaragua
D: Ambergris Caye, Belize

E: Schoolgirls, Antigua Guatemala
F: Toucan, Costa Rica
G: Ox cart, Costa Rica

Facts about Central America

HISTORY

Early Human Settlement

Central America has been heavily populated for many thousands of years. Archaeologists and anthropologists have traced the origins of the Native American peoples to Asia. These peoples migrated across the Bering Strait from Siberia to Alaska during ice ages that caused an increase in polar ice and a consequent fall in sea levels, leaving a land bridge between the two continents.

A major migration occurred between 20,000 and 25,000 years ago, with populations then fanning out over the North American continent, passing down through Central America and into South America all the way to Tierra del Fuego. The Bering Strait land bridge was inundated by rising sea levels for the last time around 7000 BC.

Some speculate that there could also have been migrations, or at least contact, between the Americas and parts of Africa, particularly Egypt. The pyramids, sculptures, and many other ancient artifacts found in America have been cited as evidence of such a contact.

Native American Civilizations

Central America is not only a geographical bridge between North and South America; historically it has also been an intermediate region between North and South American cultures. The lowlands of Nicaragua and Costa Rica seem to have formed a very loose boundary between the overlapping cultures of indigenous Central and South American peoples.

South of this area were a number of tribes that had cultural contacts ranging into Colombia, Ecuador and down to the Inca empire of Peru. The languages of these tribes are related to linguistic groups of South America.

Tribes living to the north of this intermediate region were more influenced by Mexican cultures, particularly that of the Maya, whose empire stretched through Guatemala, Belize, Chiapas, the Yucatán and into the western parts of modern Honduras and El Salvador.

The Maya are among the three great ancient civilizations of the Americas, along with the Inca of Peru and the Aztec of Mexico. They left behind stone pyramids, sculptures, ceramics and ceramic art and a hieroglyphic writing that has yet to be deciphered. They had a well-established religious and social structure, and they traded throughout their large area of influence. Their architecture, agriculture, mathematics and astronomy were advanced, and they had an accurate calendar that was later adopted by the Aztec.

Though the history of the Maya can be traced back over 4000 years, the Classic Period of more advanced Maya civilization actually began around the 3rd century AD and reached its height around the 6th to 8th centuries.

After this came a period of decline, but between the 10th and 11th centuries they experienced a renaissance under the influence of the Toltec from Mexico. There was also some cultural blending between the Maya and the Aztec.

The Maya were once again in a period of decline by the 14th century, and at the time of the Spanish arrival many of the Maya cities were deserted. (See the Guatemala chapter for more about the Maya.)

European Contact & Colonization

Christopher Columbus is recognized as the first European to 'discover' America, though his first landfall in 1492 was actually on one of the Caribbean islands, Guanahaní in the Bahamas. It was not until his fourth and final voyage (1502 – 1504) that he reached mainland Central America, exploring the Caribbean Coast from present-day Honduras to Panama. Meanwhile, the north coast may have been visited by Alonso de Ojeda in 1499, and Rodrigo de Bastidas certainly sighted Central America when making exploratory trips out from the Gulf of Venezuela in 1501.

Cristobal Colón, as Columbus is known in Spanish, was not Spanish but Italian. He had unsuccessfully sought Portuguese support for his explorations before Spain's Queen Isabella finally agreed, after six years, to sponsor his voyage. He left Europe looking for a sea route for the spice trade with Asia, and at first he thought he had found it; when he landed in the Bahamas, he believed he had reached the Indies, that is, the East Indies. To this day, the Native American peoples are called 'Indians' due to his significant geographical miscalculation.

The first Spanish settlement on the American maifnland was on the east side of the Golfo de Urabá near the present-day border between Colombia and Panama. The settlement was founded in 1509 but was moved the following year to Santa María de la Antigua del Darién, which was an important base for Spanish exploration.

In 1513 Vasco Nuñez of Balboa scaled the mountains of the Isthmus of Panama and became the first European to sight the Pacific Ocean. The Indians, of course, had known about it for a long time. Panama City was founded on the Pacific side in 1519 by Pedro Arias de Avila (also known as Pedrarias Dávila). The port on the Caribbean side was first located at Nombre de Dios in the Darién but later was moved to Portobelo, which had been explored and named by Columbus. These cities and the isthmus between them became vitally important to the Spanish.

In 1519, the same year that Panama City was founded, Hernán Cortés was beginning his invasion of Mexico. The Spanish conquest of Central America then radiated outwards, from Panama in the south and Mexico in the north.

From the Panama City base, Spanish exploration branched out into the Pacific. The Central American Indians had traded with the Inca, and the Spanish were attracted to Peru by the gold they saw arriving from the south. After Pizarro's conquest of the Inca Empire in 1532, gold, pearls and other wealth from Peru began to pass across the isthmus from Panama City to Portobelo, headed for the treasuries of Spain.

Spanish Expansion

From Panama, the Spanish bypassed Costa Rica and pushed northward to the lowlands of Nicaragua. Two large Indian towns stood on the banks of Lago de Managua and Lago de Nicaragua, where Managua and Granada are today.

These cities had also attracted the Spanish forces sent down from Mexico by Cortés. The two Spanish forces, meeting on the plains of Nicaragua, battled against one another. Also in Nicaragua, León was established in 1524 by Fernández de Córdoba. Costa Rica was settled later, in the latter half of the century, mostly by missionary and agricultural Spaniards.

Cortés had also sent his lieutenant, Pedro de Alvarado, out to conquer Guatemala. Alvarado's bloodthirstiness as well as the bitter fighting between his forces and the Indians of Guatemala matched the savagery of the Mexican conquest. Alvarado, accompanied by Aztec warriors, crossed the Isthmus of Tehuantepec in 1522, and the decisive battle occurred in the area around Quetzaltenango in 1524. From there, Alvarado went on to conquer all of present-day Guatemala and a good deal of El Salvador.

Honduras, which had been initially claimed for Spain by Columbus, was also conquered by one of Cortés' warriors. Cristóbal de Olid was sent from Mexico at around the same time as Alvarado. He arrived on the Honduran coast and established a base near present-day Trujillo. From there the Spanish invaded the area of present-day Honduras and established settlements at Gracias a Dios, Comayagua, Olancho and Naca.

The Colonial Period

Under the Spanish, the region called Guatemala, which included all of Central

America except Panama, was designated a part of the viceroyalty of Mexico, then called Nueva España (New Spain).

Though under Mexico, Guatemala became a captaincy-general, reporting directly to the Spanish crown. A capital was established very briefly at an initial location, but in 1527 it was soon moved to a site on the flanks of the large Volcán Agua. The city was destroyed in 1541 when the aptly named Volcán Agua loosed a flood of water pent up in its crater, burying the city under tons of rock and mud.

The capital was moved to the nearby Valle de Panchoy, where La Muy Noble y Muy Leal Ciudad de Santiago de los Caballeros de Goathemala (today called Antigua) was founded as capital on March 10, 1543. The capital flourished there for 233 years until it was destroyed by a great earthquake on July 29, 1773. The capital was moved again, this time to Valle de la Ermita, the present site of Guatemala City, in hopes of escaping further destruction. On September 27, 1775, King Carlos III of Spain signed a royal charter for the founding of La Nueva Guatemala de la Asunción, and Guatemala City was officially born. The former capital became known as La Antigua Guatemala ('the Old Guatemala').

Panama continued to be an important part of the Spanish empire throughout the colonial period. The rest of Central America was no great producer of wealth, so it was not of such vital interest to the Spanish.

The colonial period lasted until 1821, by which time both Mexico and Guatemala had declared their independence from Spain. In the same year Colombia, including Panama, also became independent. Panama was a region of Nueva Andalucía, Nueva Granada and finally Colombia until 1903.

Independence

In 1810, a rising tide of disaffection with Spanish rule first erupted into rebellion in Mexico, under the leadership of a parish priest, Miguel Hidalgo. The following year

another priest, José Matías Delgado, together with liberal leader Manuel José Arce, organized a revolt in San Salvador, but it was quickly suppressed by forces from Guatemala City.

The will for independence sprang almost entirely from the Creoles – those born locally of Spanish ancestry – and local business people frustrated by Spain's trade restrictions on its dependencies. Together they formed a home-grown middle class, united by their resentment at being excluded from the colony's positions of power, which were reserved for Spaniards (those born in Spain).

Napoleon's invasion of Spain in 1812 boosted the drive for reform in the colonies. In 1821 Mexico's viceroy, Agustín de Iturbide, defected to the rebels and shortly became the self-styled emperor of independent Mexico. In the same year, the last of Guatemala's conservative captains general, Brigadier Don Gabino Gainza, was obliged to sign the first of several acts of independence. The link with Spain was forever severed, but Central America's political tumult had only begun.

The moment Guatemala declared independence, Iturbide sent his troops from Mexico to annex the states of the fledgling republic. Conservatives in many of the smaller states supported union with Mexico. El Salvador, however, under the leadership of Arce and Delgado, held out for months before its defenses were finally broken down by the invaders.

In many respects the forces for change were fiercely divided. A political chasm yawned between the liberals, who sought a more egalitarian state, and the powerful conservatives, who wanted to retain essentially the same kind of authoritarian society but under their control. This made any smooth political change impossible.

The Central American Federation

Iturbide's empire was short-lived. The following year he was overthrown by Mexican republicans, and in 1823 the Central American states declared their independence again, this time from Mexico. They formed a loose federation, the Provincias Unidas del Centro de América, with five constituent states – Guatemala, Honduras, El Salvador, Nicaragua and Costa Rica – and a constitution modeled on that of the United States. Slavery was abolished.

General Arce became the first federation president in 1825, but he had difficulty asserting his authority and finding the right executives. In his home state he was embroiled in conflict with fellow liberals. Ultimately, he set himself up as a dictator until he was overthrown by an alliance of liberals under Francisco Morazán, a Honduran general. Morazán became the new leader of the federation in 1830. Like Arce before him, his grip on power was tenuous.

In Guatemala, too, the liberal leader was under threat. A cholera epidemic raged and an unpopular new penal code was introduced. The underclass – a vast group of the dispossessed for whom middle-class freedoms meant little – grew increasingly restive.

Under the leadership of the young, charismatic Rafael Carrera, a largely Indian mob marched on Guatemala City in 1837. An unlikely alliance formed between Carrera, the Church and the conservatives, and Carrera was installed as dictator. His victory signaled the end of the liberal era and thus of the federation.

In 1838, the congress passed a resolution permitting states to leave the federation. By 1839, El Salvador was the only state left. Regional rivalries between the now separate countries persisted, but from this moment they pursued their own courses. The modern history of each of the Central American republics is covered in the corresponding chapters of this guide.

GEOGRAPHY

Because of the region's political history, the term 'Central America' is sometimes used to mean only the five states of the former federation, which did not include Belize and Panama, but in recent years it has usually been used to refer to all the land between Mexico and Colombia. Central America covers only a small area – the seven countries together comprise around 544,700 sq km, about a quarter the size of Mexico. Nevertheless, Central America is a strategically important part of the world as it separates the Pacific Ocean from the Caribbean Sea and the Atlantic Ocean, and it also forms a bridge, or a barrier, between North and South America.

The dominant geographical features of Central America are its mountains and volcanoes and its long coastlines. The region has 2379 km of Caribbean Coast and 3287 km of Pacific Coast, separated by a land mass that is 280 km wide at its widest point (near the border of Honduras and Nicaragua) but only about 60 km wide at its narrowest point (the isthmus of Panama).

The relatively narrow strip of land that forms Central America is primarily volcanic in origin, with over 100 major volcanoes and 150 minor ones. Several separate mountain chains (cordilleras) stretch for hundreds of kilometers down through this strip of land. The result is a pattern of mountain ranges and volcanoes, broken by valleys and basins with large, fertile areas of rich volcanic soil.

It may seem strange to find cities at the feet of giant volcanoes, where they are repeatedly threatened by eruptions and earthquakes. In the last 300 years major cities have been destroyed by such natural disasters: Antigua Guatemala in 1773, Guatemala City in 1917 – 1918 and 1976, Managua in 1931 and 1972, and San Salvador in 1854 and 1986. Another major quake, 7.4 on the Richter scale, rocked Costa Rica and the northwestern corner of Panama in April 1991. Despite these perils there is a compelling motive behind this pattern of settlement – the volcanic soil is excellent for all types of agriculture and can support the greatest concentrations of agricultural people.

A narrow plain runs along both coasts. In most places it's no more than a 15- to 40 km-wide strip between the sea and the mountains. The coastal plain is also fertile, and in some areas there are large, flat plantations of export crops (for example, bananas and pineapples) close to the ports from which the produce is shipped to overseas markets, principally the USA.

GEOLOGY

The surface of the earth consists of a number of huge tectonic plates that slowly move over millions of years, changing the character of the earth's surface slowly but constantly. With its volcanoes and earthquakes, Central America is obviously a geologically volatile area.

Four tectonic plates are in the Central America region. The two most significant are the Cocos and Caribbean Plates. The Cocos Plate, the northeastern edge of which parallels the Pacific Coast about 60 to 120 miles offshore, borders the southwestern edge of the Caribbean Plate. The Cocos Plate is moving northeast and crashing into the Caribbean Plate at a rate of around 10 meters per century – a thundering speed, geologically speaking. The point of impact between plates is called a subduction zone; in the case of Central America, this zone is where the Cocos Plate is sliding underneath and forcing the edge of the Caribbean Plate to break up and become uplifted, causing earthquakes and volcanic activity.

This process began underwater and has been going on for about five million years. Long ago, North and South America were separated by 3000 km of open sea. Animals and plants developed on the two continents quite independently of one another. Around three million years ago at the end of the Pliocene age, the volcanic activity and uplifting of land caused by the collision of the tectonic plates raised the land bridge that united North and South America, and plants and animals began to spread across.

Central America is the most active volcanic zone in the Americas. Although half the volcanoes are dormant and a quarter are extinct, the rest are still active. Guatemala's Pacaya and Santiaguito Volcanoes, and Costa Rica's Arenal, Poás, Irazú and Rincón de la Vieja Volcanoes are all glowing and smoking away. Occasionally some flare up, sometimes necessitating evacuation of nearby villages. Other vol-

canoes classified as still active include Fuego and Santa María in Guatemala, Izalco in El Salvador, and Concepción and Las Pilas-Cerro Negro in Nicaragua. Panama's sole volcano, Volcán Barú, is classified as inactive.

CLIMATE

All of Central America is within the tropics, but there's a lot of variation in climate within this small region. The land rises from sea level to over 4000 meters, dividing the region into three primary temperature zones according to altitude, but there is little variation in temperature throughout the year.

The lowlands (from sea level to about 1000 meters) are the hottest zone; daytime temperatures range from 29°C to 32°C (84°F to 90°F), night temperatures from 21°C to 23°C (70°F to 74°F).

The temperate zone (from around 1000 to 2000 meters) has a pleasant, springlike climate, with daytime temperatures ranging from 23°C to 26°C (74°F to 79°F) and nighttime temperatures from around 15°C to 21°C (59°F to 70°F).

The cold zone (above 2000 meters) has similar daytime temperatures to the temperate zone but is colder at night, around 10°C to 12°C (50°F to 54°F). The very few areas over 4000 meters have an alpine climate.

The main seasons are characterized not by temperature but amount of rainfall. The rainy season, which runs from around April to November in most of Central America, is called *invierno* (winter). The dry season, from around November to April, is called *verano* (summer). Thus the seasons are, in name at least, the reverse of what they are in the rest of the Northern Hemisphere. There are some regional variations to the general rule – Panama, for instance, has only a three-month dry season from January to mid-April.

The Caribbean side of Central America gets much more rainfall than the Pacific side – often more than twice as much. In Panama, the Caribbean side has around 3200 mm of rainfall annually, whereas the

Pacific side, less than 100 km away, receives only about 1800 mm. The Caribbean Coast receives a lot of rainfall all year round and is always green. On the Pacific side, the landscape dries out and browns in the dry season, and the air can be dusty and smoky with burning vegetation.

Even during the rainy season, it's a rare day when the sun doesn't shine; a typical pattern is sun during the morning, clouding over later in the day, and a downpour that might last for an hour or so in the late afternoon or evening. But don't bank on it: It can rain any time of day, and if a tropical storm hits (most likely in September and October on the Caribbean Coast), it can rain solidly for days at a time. In most places the rainy season doesn't interfere much with travel, but there are a few notable exceptions. It is too hazardous to go overland through the Darién Gap during the rainy season, and occasional flooding can impede travel on the Caribbean Coast of Honduras from December to February. Traveling anywhere on dirt roads can be a thrill in the rainy season, but most of the main routes in Central America are paved.

The hurricane season for the region runs from June to November.

ECOLOGY & ENVIRONMENT
Deforestation in Central America

Deforestation is happening at such a rate that most of the world's tropical forests will have disappeared by early in the 21st century; loss of other habitats is a less publicized but equally pressing concern. Deforestation is taking place in every Central American country. In some places, the forests have been stripped for export timber. Elsewhere the native forest has been cleared for subsistence slash-and-burn agriculture, for grazing land, or for the planting of crops for export.

In 1950, about 60% of Central America was forested. Today, approximately 30% of Central America is covered by some form of tropical forest (the notable exception is densely populated El Salvador where less than 5% of the land is forested). Sparsely settled Belize, with less population pressure, has about 40% of its land under forest.

Almost a million known species live in tropical rain forests, and scientists predict that millions of additional plant and animal species remain to be discovered in the world's remaining rain forests. This incredible array of plants and animals cannot exist unless the forest that they inhabit is protected – deforestation is resulting not only in the loss of the rain forest but in countless extinctions as well.

Tropical forests, and their variety, are vitally important for pharmaceutical purposes and as a source of genetic diversity in our increasingly monocultural forms of agriculture. In the event of a crop epidemic, scientists look in the forests for disease-resistant wild strains to breed into the commercially raised crops. Deforestation leads not only to species extinction but also to loss of the genetic diversity that may help species adapt to a changing world.

Rain forests are important on a global scale because they moderate climatic patterns worldwide. Destruction of the rain forests is a major contributing factor to global warming. Gases exuded by the great masses of plants in the rain forest are also important in maintaining the delicate balance of gases in the earth's atmosphere.

The rain forest is also important to the indigenous peoples who survive within it. Miskitos in Honduras and Nicaragua, Bribris in Costa Rica and the Chocóes of Panama are some of the indigenous groups that still live in the rain forest in a more or less traditional manner, practicing shifting agriculture, hunting and gathering.

However, any discussion of the rain forests must take into consideration the point of view of the developing nations within whose borders they lie. Clearing of rain forests provides lumber, pastureland, and possible mineral wealth in the short term. Efforts are now under way to show that the long-term economic value of the standing rain forest as a resource of biodiversity, genetic variation and pharmaceutical wealth is greater than the quick profits realized by deforestation.

One proposal for making the tropical forest an economically productive resource is protecting it in national parks and preserves and making it accessible to the public. 'Ecotourism' is an increasingly important element of the economies of all of the Central American countries. More people are likely to visit a tropical country to see monkeys in the forest than to see cows in the pasture. All the Central American countries have national parks and reserves, and both government and non-government organizations are devoted to conserving and protecting the natural environment. An increasing number of tour companies are offering ecotourism excursions including jungle treks, bird watching, river rafting and other adventures.

Other innovative projects for sustainable development of tropical forests are being developed on private reserves, especially in Costa Rica and Belize. One example is butterfly farming on the Rara Avis Reserve in Costa Rica and also the Shipstern Reserve in Belize. Another project, developed in Panama and now continuing in Costa Rica, is the harvesting of the green iguana, which is a traditional food in forested areas.

Despite the deforestation, Central America still has some wilderness areas where the forests are largely unexplored. These include parts of Belize, the Mosquitia region of Honduras and Nicaragua, and the Darién region of Panama.

The 30% of Nicaragua that is covered by forest has been inadvertently protected by the protracted civil war and Sandinista/Contra hostilities that occurred at a time when deforestation was rampant elsewhere. Some remote areas are still mined (with bombs), which discourages potential settlers, and the wildlife here is prolific.

Other Environmental Issues

Smog is a problem in most Central American cities, particularly Guatemala City, Tegucigalpa, San Salvador and Managua. It's frustrating to see that there are no controls on emissions from vehicles – it's very common to be engulfed in a cloud of oily black exhaust when a bus passes by, and when driving on a highway you can be stuck for miles behind a vehicle billowing a trail of smoke, a choking and unnecessary experience in an otherwise clean and beautiful countryside.

Trash is another problem. It's normal practice for people to throw trash out the windows of vehicles, and often the land along roadsides is used for impromptu trash dumps. People in boats casually toss trash over the side into lakes, rivers and the sea.

FLORA & FAUNA

Central America's flora and fauna are exceptionally rich and diversified, with tens of thousands of species represented. Much of the diversity arises from the region's location bridging the North and South American continents. Hundreds of plant and animal species from both continents spill into Central America, and there are also endemic species found only in specific areas. Costa Rica has probably the greatest range of accessible flora and fauna in Central America (see that chapter for more details).

Flora

Central America's geographical position, its varying altitudes, wet and dry climates and differing soil types all contribute to the wide variety of plant species found in Central America.

There are five major types of vegetation. On the Caribbean coastal plain, up to about 850 meters, there is tropical rain forest with a canopy of tall trees, a layer of medium-size trees and a lush ground cover of smaller plants.

The Pacific coastal strip and the northern lowlands of Belize are covered with tropical dry forest and savanna. Deciduous trees and shrubs are parched and brown during the dry season but spring into green during the rainy season.

Higher up, at around 850 to 1650 meters, there's a cooler climate with a mixed upland forest of evergreen trees and pines, deciduous oaks and broadleaf trees, and a ground cover of shrubs, herbs, grasses and flowering plants.

At around 1650 meters and above is one of Central America's loveliest terrains, the cloud forest. With close to 100% humidity and a cool climate year round, the cloud forests are bathed in either clouds or rain so they never dry out. The canopy of high trees means that direct sunlight rarely reaches the forest floor, which is covered by herbs, ferns and mosses.

Only very small areas of Central America, at elevations over 3000 meters, have alpine vegetation, with short, coarse grasses, ferns, mosses and flowering herbs. But even at such high elevations there is regional variety. For example, the Andean *páramo* is found in Costa Rica, while the North American bunchgrass landscape occurs in the Guatemala highlands above the tree line.

A walk through a tropical forest is very different from a stroll through the temperate forests familiar to many readers. Temperate forests tend to have little variety. Tropical forests, on the other hand, have great variety. If you stand in one spot and look around, you'll see scores of different species of trees, and you often have to walk several hundred meters to find another example of any particular species.

This biodiversity is one of the reasons why biologists and conservationists are calling for a halt to the destruction of tropical forests.

Fauna

Central America has thousands of species of mammals, birds, insects, reptiles, amphibians and fishes. Costa Rica and Belize are known for abundant wildlife.

Mammals include jaguars, pumas, ocelots and other cats; spider monkeys, howler monkeys, white-faced capuchin monkeys and squirrel (tití) monkeys; agoutis, coatis, kinkajous, and tapirs; two species each of deer, peccary, armadillos and sloths; several species of anteaters and squirrels; and scores of bat species. Manatees live in some coastal waters, and dolphins and whales in the sea.

Fish are also abundant in rivers and lakes, and along the Pacific and Caribbean Coasts. Reptiles and amphibians include sea, river and land turtles (Costa Rica has some famous nesting sites); crocodiles; frogs (such as tree frogs and the colorful poison-arrow frog); iguanas; and many others. There are many species of snakes, including the boa constrictor, but only a few are poisonous, notably the tiny coral snake and the large *barba amarilla* or fer-de-lance.

Central America is a bird-watcher's dream – around 900 species of birds have been recorded in Panama alone. A number of factors combine to account for the incredible diversity of birds. Part of it is due to Central America's geographical position – North American, South American and Caribbean birds are all found here. Migrating birds tend to funnel and concentrate in Central America. Another factor behind the diversity of species is the geographical diversity – everything from coastal wetland birds to mountain forest birds are all represented.

The famous, resplendent quetzal (ket-SAL) is the national bird of Guatemala and an often-used symbol of Central America. Quetzals are about 35 cm long, but the male has a very long tail that may add another 60 cm, brilliantly plumed with bright green, red and white feathers. It lives in high-altitude forests all the way from southern Mexico to Panama, but unfortunately, as the forests become threatened, the bird is also endangered. Quetzals can only survive in the wild – they die in captivity. Locals may know where to find one; good places to look are Monteverde and various areas in Southern Costa Rica. The March to June breeding season is the easiest time to see them. At other times, they are less active and quite wary.

Other beautiful birds of the region include toucans, macaws, many species of parrots, hummingbirds, hawks, harpy eagles and doves. Striking but common birds are motmots, jacamars, trogons, chacalacas, woodcreepers, puffbirds, manakins, oropendolas and tanagers. It's a rich field for bird watchers.

Not only the quetzal but also many other species are endangered and may be facing extinction. Hunting takes a large toll, but even more critical is the destruction of the forest environments on which so many creatures depend.

National Parks

Central America's ecosystems and habitats include tropical rain forests, cloud forests, jungle river systems, lagoons and coastal wildlife preserves, just to name a few. Many of these are represented in the region's national parks, where visitors find thousands of species of wildlife and tropical plants.

A few of the best-known national parks and nature reserves are listed below, but many others are also worth visiting – see the country chapters for details.

Guatemala
   Tikal is much more than just the ruins. Its national park, a lush tropical jungle full of wildlife, covers the entire north and central portions of El Petén Province.
Belize
   Mountain Pine Ridge, in the Maya Mountains, is dotted with waterfalls and teeming with exotic flora and fauna.
Honduras
   National parks protecting beautiful high-altitude cloud forests include La Tigra, Celaque, La Muralla and Cusuco. Punta Sal, a coastal national park near Tela, is also popular and accessible. The Río Plátano Biosphere Reserve in the remote and sparsely populated Mosquitia region is the first biosphere reserve in Central America, and it's a World Heritage Site as well.
El Salvador
   Bosque Montecristo, a cloud forest at the border of three countries, is shared by Guatemala, Honduras and El Salvador. It's most easily reached from the El Salvador side, but it's still very remote.
Nicaragua
   Volán Masaya National Park is still considered active and you can walk to the summit.
Costa Rica
   Península Corcovado on the southern Pacific Coast, Caño Negro in the northern lowlands, Santa Rosa on the northern Pacific Coast and Tortuguero on the northeastern coast all have magnificent wildlife. Tortuguero is the most

important nesting area in the western Caribbean for thousands of green turtles, and it's also a great place for river trips to see exotic birds, crocodiles, caymans, lizards, monkeys and toads weighing up to a kilogram.
Panama
   In western Panama there's the Parque Internacional La Amistad, a World Heritage Site shared by Panama and Costa Rica. Also in western Panama, Parque Nacional Volcán Barú contains the 3475-meter Barú volcano, and the Parque Nacional Marino Isla Bastimentos conserves marine and coastal ecosystems. Near the Panama Canal area are the Soberanía, Camino de Cruces, Chagres and Interoceánico de las Américas national parks. The Parque Nacional Metropolitano is a tropical rain forest park right in Panama City. On the north coast, Parque Nacional Portobelo is another World Heritage Site, as is the Parque Nacional Darién, which has the largest tropical rain forest wilderness area in Central America.

GOVERNMENT & POLITICS

All seven Central American countries are members of the United Nations (UN) and the Organization of American States (OAS), which was formed in 1948 to link North, Central and South America in a common defense agreement.

Guatemala, Honduras, El Salvador, Nicaragua and Costa Rica are members of the Organization of Central American States (ODECA), established in 1951 in an effort to bring unity to the region. The organization includes the Central American Court of Justice and executive, legislative and economic councils.

Central American politics are notoriously volatile, not only within the various countries but also occasionally among them. Tensions have eased in recent years, though. Conflict between Honduras and El Salvador, which erupted into the 'football war' in 1969, festered for over two decades until a continuing land dispute between the two countries was finally settled by the International Court of Justice in 1992. In the 1980s, the contra war in Nicaragua and the civil wars in El Salvador and Guatemala affected neighboring countries, as soldiers, rebels and refugees crossed borders. The USA used Honduras and (to a more limited extent) Costa Rica as bases of military operations in the region, increasing tensions with neighboring countries. The US military presence has decreased with the end of various civil wars, and tensions arising from US involvement has eased.

ECONOMY

Each Central American country has its particular economic structure. By and large this is not a 'developed' part of the world, but some countries are doing much better than others. Per capita GNP figures (in US dollars) for 1994 were:

Guatemala	3080
Belize	2750
Honduras	1820
El Salvador	1710
Nicaragua	1570
Costa Rica	5050
Panama	4670

While most countries are improving economically (particularly Belize, Costa Rica and Panama), Honduras and Nicaragua are moving backwards. Honduras appeared to have turned the corner in 1993, with the economy growing again, but then slipped backwards, as evidenced by the 30% rate of inflation in 1995. Nicaragua is still struggling, but at least it now has inflation more under control; its annual inflation rate was around 20% in 1995, compared to annual levels above 1000% a few years ago. The lowest inflation rates are enjoyed by Panama with 1.3% and Belize with 3.2% (both figures are a seven-year annual average from 1985 to 1992).

Agriculture is the most important part of the economy of every Central American country except Panama, where it's surpassed by the services industry. In addition to basic subsistence crops, such as maize, beans, vegetables and fruits, several countries also produce export crops including coffee, sugar cane, cotton, tobacco, bananas, citrus fruits, pineapples, and coconuts. Forestry and timber industries are important in some countries.

Fishing, including catches of shrimp and lobster, is also important, especially on the Caribbean Coast but also on the Pacific Coast, and in the lakes and rivers.

The manufacturing industry is developing, especially in certain places. San Pedro Sula in Honduras, for example, is becoming a center where clothing, shoes and other goods are made in hundreds of *maquiladoras* (factories). Panama has additional sources of income from the Panama Canal and from duty-free trade and offshore banking. Tourism is economically important in many parts of Central America.

The commencement of the North American Free Trade Agreement (NAFTA) on January 1, 1994, is expected to have a negative effect on Central American economies as the USA diverts its trading links more towards Mexico, a cosignatory. In the longer term, Central American countries may themselves join NAFTA. In the meantime, ways are being sought to improve trading links between the Central American economies.

In 1960 ODECA established the Central American Common Market (CACM), with all the five ODECA countries as members. The purpose of the CACM was to promote regional economic development, free trade and economic integration. In 1985 an agreement was signed between CACM and the European Community (EC), providing for economic cooperation and European aid. Overall the improvements fostered by CACM have been rather limited, but the pact was revived during the 1990s.

The great disparity of the distribution of wealth is a problem in all of these countries, some more than others. It's not uncommon for the top 5% to 10% of the population to possess over half the country's wealth, while the greatest part of the population lives in dire poverty.

This great gap between the very rich and the very poor is the source of much of the strife and civil conflict that has beset some of the Central American countries for many years, especially Guatemala, El Salvador and Nicaragua.

POPULATION & PEOPLE

The majority of the population of Central America is mestizo, that is, of mixed Indian and Spanish descent. Mestizos who speak Spanish are often called *ladinos*. Each country has its own particular mixture of peoples and cultures.

The Spanish-Indian mixture ranges from almost pure Indian to almost pure European. In Guatemala well over half of the population is Maya Indian, and many mestizos are of predominantly Indian descent. On the other hand, over 95% of Costa Ricans are of wholly or predominantly European descent. Fewer than 1% of the population is Indian; the native populations were almost completely wiped out by European diseases. In El Salvador there are very few Indians, less than 5% of the population, but Honduras, Nicaragua and Panama all have significant Indian tribes. Belize has mostly people of African descent along the coast often mixed with the British and known as Creole. Most of the people in the interior of Belize are either Maya or mestizos.

Native Americans

Before the Spanish conquest, Central America had many different groups of native peoples, and all the Central American countries still have groups, larger or smaller, of Native Americans. The largest surviving groups are the Maya in Chiapas, the Yucatán (both of Mexico), Belize and Guatemala. The Guatemalan areas around Chichicastenango, Lago de Atitlán and Todos Santos Cuchamatán are particularly known for the colorfully dressed, traditional Maya Indians who live there.

In Honduras, and spilling over into Nicaragua, are Tolupanes (Jicaque), Pech (Paya), Tawahka (Sumo), Lenca, Chorti and Miskito. Nicaragua also has Rama Indians. El Salvador has small numbers of Izalco and Pancho Indians, descended from the Pipil. Costa Rica has very few Indians, but they include Bribri, Boruca, Cabecar, Terraba and Guatuso. In Panama there are significant groups of Guaymí, Chocó and Kuna Indians.

After five centuries of contact with the Spanish, the Indian groups vary in the extent of their assimilation into ladino society. On one end of the spectrum are traditional Indians who wear traditional dress, maintain traditional social and economic systems and speak only their native language. Even these groups may have been affected by the Spanish influence. For example, they may mix Catholicism with their traditional religious practices. At the other extreme, many Indians are assimilated into modern Central American society, speak only Spanish, and are indistinguishable from the mestizo populations around them.

In between are groups of varying degrees of assimilation. In some, the men wear Western dress and speak Spanish in addition to their Indian language, while the women, more sheltered, still wear traditional dress and speak only their Indian language. In some groups the older people are more traditional, while the young people are becoming more modernized, attending school and learning Spanish.

Social distinctions are often more connected to these visible social factors than to actual bloodlines. People who observe the traditional Indian ways are called Indians, but those of Indian ancestry who speak Spanish and live and work in the towns are often called ladinos. Thus, in some places, the percentage of Indians in census figures seems to be declining, but this may be because fewer people are identifying themselves as Indians.

Blacks

All along the Caribbean Coast of Central America there are blacks, most of them descended from Africans brought to the West Indies (primarily Jamaica) as slaves. Some slaves were brought to the region by the Spanish, especially to Panama, but most blacks came to Central America from the Caribbean islands in the 19th century, not as slaves but as laborers, largely to work on agricultural (especially banana) plantations. Another large group of West Indian blacks came to Panama to work on the canal early this century.

In many places these blacks speak a Caribbean-accented English. In the countries bordering the Caribbean, blacks form a majority in some coastal areas, though only a small proportion of the total population. In Belize, however, about 40% of the people are blacks. In the past, blacks often interbred with Europeans, especially the British, and their descendants are known as black Creoles. (Note that in most of Latin America 'Creole,' from the Spanish *criollo*, means someone of European parentage born in the Americas.)

Garífuna Along the Caribbean Coast is another group of blacks, the Garífuna, who are descended from West Africans and Carib Indians. In 1797 the latter were brought by the British from the Caribbean island of St Vincent to the island of Roatán, off the coast of Honduras. From there they spread out and established communities which still thrive on the coasts of Honduras, Nicaragua, Belize and Guatemala. (For more about the Garífuna, refer to the Honduras and Belize chapters.)

ARTS

The arts of Central America correspond to the cultures of the various places. Music, poetry, literature (especially stories and legends), dance, theater, painting and sculpture are found throughout the region.

The innovative Nicaraguan poet Rubén Darío (1867 – 1916) was a prime influence in the development of modernism in Spanish literature. The literary tradition is still strong in Nicaragua (see the Nicaragua chapter).

La Palma in northern El Salvador and the Archipiélago de Solentiname in southern Nicaragua each have an artistic tradition with its own distinctive style.

Music on the Caribbean Coast has a strong reggae influence, and some of the reggae bands in Nicaragua's Bluefields area have an international reputation. Punta is a percussion-based style of music and a shuffling, hip-swinging dance performed by the Garífuna people. You can see and dance the Punta with Garífuna

people in many places along the north coast of Honduras, including Tela, La Ceiba and Trujillo.

Handicrafts *(artesanías)* are produced in every country and some are world famous, especially the weaving and embroidery of Guatemala. Also common throughout most parts of Central America are ceramics, woodcarving, leatherwork, basketry, jewelry, hammocks, musical instruments and many other handicrafts (see the Arts and Things to Buy sections in the country chapters).

SOCIETY & CONDUCT
Traditional Cultures

Most countries of Central America have agrarian economies and cultures tied to the traditions of the land. The family, usually a large, extended one, is the basic unit of society and the most important thing in the lives of most people.

Though Central America remains primarily rural, there is in many places a migration from the countryside to the cities. People come to the cities seeking education, employment, money and a more modern 'better life.' Even in the cities, though, there are holdovers from rural life – the family remains the principal social unit, and there are neighborhood churches and large open-air markets just as you would find in the country.

Religion is important in Central America and much of the culture revolves around it. Every city, town and village has its patron saint, and the annual festival or fair on the saint's day is usually the most important local celebration of the year. *Semana Santa* (Holy Week, the week before Easter) is the most important general holiday, with church services, processions through the streets, dramas, dances, fiestas, special foods and other celebrations. Semana Santa is also the time when most people get a weeklong holiday from work. For Semana Santa, people often take a trip to the beach or a resort, or visit faraway family. Often this is the only time of the year they can do this, so it's a special holiday for secular as well as religious reasons.

Navidad (Christmas), often celebrated not on Christmas Day but on the evening of December 24, is another important holiday. It is celebrated in different ways in different locales. In Tegucigalpa, for example, lots of people get drunk and many set off fireworks at midnight. After a midnight mass, people may stay up all night long, visiting from house to house and having parties, and then spend Christmas Day resting and recovering.

The many ethnic groups of Central America all have their own distinct cultures. In some countries, especially Guatemala and Panama, a number of Indian groups maintain their own language, type of dress and traditional customs. The mestizos are not only racially, but also culturally, a mixture of Spanish and Indian. The Garífunas and other blacks of the Caribbean Coast, the small groups of immigrant Chinese, North Americans, Europeans and other groups also all have their own distinctive cultural features, making Central America a patchwork rather than a uniform cultural fabric.

The USA also has a significant influence on Central American life. It's a rare place where you won't find Coca-Cola and Pepsi, blue jeans, mass-produced clothes (often second-hand from the USA), and radios and cassette tape recorders. TV stations from the USA come in by satellite. Many Central Americans have gone north to the USA to work, and many more dream of doing so.

All the Central American countries have radio and TV, and in many rural areas, homes might have a TV before they have running water. This can lead to some strange sights. For example, in a remote Garífuna fishing village you might see young men with flat-top haircuts. Ask why they wear their hair like that and they'll tell you, 'That's how they wear it in New York!' 'How do you know?' 'We saw it on television!'

Dos & Don'ts

Politeness is a very important in social interactions in Central America. When beginning to talk to someone, even in such routine situations as in a store or on the bus, you should preface your conversation with a greeting to the other person – a simple *Buenos días* or *Buenas tardes* and a smile, answered by a similar greeting on the other person's part, gets a conversation off to a positive start. When you enter a room, even a public place such as a restaurant or waiting room, it's polite to make a general greeting to everyone in the room – a simple *Buenos días* or *Buenas tardes* will do. Handshakes are another friendly gesture and are used frequently here.

Pay attention to your appearance when traveling in Central America. Latin Americans on the whole are very conscious of appearance, grooming and dress; it's difficult for them to understand why a foreign traveler, who is naturally assumed to be rich, would go around looking scruffy when even poor people in Latin America do their best to look neat. Your relations with locals will be smoother if you try to present as clean an appearance as possible. This is especially true if you're dealing with officialdom (police, border officials, immigration officers), when it's a good idea to look not only clean, but also as conservative and respectable as possible.

In recent years standards of modesty in dress have been relaxing somewhat; you may see local women wearing miniskirts though just a few years ago this would have been unthinkable. Nevertheless, not everyone appreciates this type of dressing – many local people still find it offensive. As a foreigner, it's a good idea for you to take particular care not to offend local people with your attire. A general rule of thumb is to notice what the people around you are wearing and dress accordingly.

Shorts are usually worn by both sexes only at the beach and in coastal towns; if you do wear shorts, be sure they are modest. Beach wear should be worn only at the swimming pool or the beach. You'll notice that many local women swim with T-shirts over their swimming suits, and you may want to do the same, or be prepared to receive a lot of male attention. See the

Women Travelers section in the following chapter for tips specifically for women travelers.

Dress modestly when entering churches, as this shows respect for local people and their culture. Some churches in heavily touristed areas will post signs at the door asking that shorts and singlets (tank tops) not be worn in church, but in most places it's assumed that everyone knows not to do this.

Also think about safety in connection with your appearance. In many places in Central America, especially the capital cities, the locals will warn you against wearing wedding bands or even cheap imitation jewelry: You could be mugged for it. If you have any wealth, take care not to flaunt it. See the Dangers & Annoyances section in the following chapter for basic traveling safety.

RELIGION

Roman Catholicism, brought by the Spanish, is the principal religion of Central America. In Caribbean areas that were influenced by the British, Protestant sects are predominant.

Against the background of Catholicism, however, there are many different religions and sects. Evangelical and Pentecostal Christian denominations have gained wide followings in many areas. Other religious sects include Baptists, Mennonites, Mormons and Seventh-Day Adventists.

In addition, the Indian peoples and other ethnic groups still preserve their traditional religions, often mixed and blended with Catholicism. An example is the religion of the Maya of Guatemala. The Garífuna peoples continue to practice their traditional African-related religion, focusing on ancestral spirits, in addition to Christianity.

Regional Facts for the Visitor

PLANNING
When to Go

You can have a good trip to Central America at any time of year. On the whole, Central America's busiest tourist seasons are during the dry season from around mid-December to April and again during the North American summer holidays, mostly July and August. Certain areas do have their busier times – the Caribbean islands have more 'fun and sun' enthusiasts during the North American and European winter, for obvious reasons.

The seasons are defined not by temperature but by rainfall. *Invierno* (winter), the rainy season, runs roughly from April to November, and *verano* (summer), the dry season, runs from November to April. Invierno tends to be hot and humid, verano hot, dry and dusty, but the primary climate differences throughout the region depend on elevation (see Climate in Facts about Central America). You can travel practically anywhere in Central America regardless of the season with just a few exceptions – for instance, it's too hazardous to hike the Darién Gap in the rainy season.

You might want to plan to be in a certain place at a certain time to catch a festival; *Semana Santa* (Holy Week) in Antigua Guatemala, for example, is an unforgettable spectacle. Holy Week is also holiday week all over Central America; beach resorts and other holiday spots will be packed at this time. This makes it great for meeting and partying with the locals, but not so good if you wanted the beach all to yourself.

The airlines serving Central America have high-season and off-season rates. High-season (more expensive) rates may occur around Christmas, Easter, and the North American winter or summer holiday seasons but may vary from airline to airline. Flying just a day or two earlier or later might save you a tremendous amount.

What Kind of Trip?

The kind of trip you take will be determined by how long you plan to travel, your reasons for going, and your budget (see Costs under Money below).

Central America is a small area of the world, but it's incredibly rich and diverse. If you're just rushing through on buses between North and South America, you do so in a few days. Or you could stay for six months and still feel that you'd barely scratched the surface. Look at the Highlights section later in this chapter to get an idea of what the region has to offer.

Travelers go to Central America for many reasons. Many are en route between North and South America. Others come to pursue special interests: exploring the Maya pyramids and other ruins, visiting the Caribbean islands off the coast of Central America with their famous diving and snorkeling possibilities, or studying Spanish, particularly in Antigua Guatemala, where there are some of the best and cheapest language courses in the world. Nicaragua and El Salvador draw international visitors interested in the politics there. Other people come connected with church groups or the Peace Corps. Others work on agricultural or social projects.

Ecotourism is very popular in Central America. The rain forests with their abundant wildlife are a particular attraction. They're just as interesting as those in the Amazon and a lot more accessible for most people. Equally worth exploration are mountains, cloud forests, volcanoes, coastal lands, river systems and, of course, the beautiful Caribbean beaches and islands. Every country in Central America has national parks that preserve natural features and environments. Costa Rica is probably the best known for its ecotourism possibilities, but ecotourism is quickly becoming more popular and more accessible in all of the Central American countries.

Then there are travelers who are in Central America not on any particular mission, but simply because it is a beautiful, diverse, inexpensive and fascinating part of the world.

Maps

The best map of Central America is the 1:1,800,000 map produced by Kevin Healey for International Travel Map Productions (ITM); it is map No 156 in its series of excellent maps on South and Central America. ITM also publishes separate maps covering each of the Central American countries and various regions of Mexico as well as several maps of South America. They show national parks, nature reserves, archaeological sites, geographical features, roads and much more, and have legends in four languages.

ITM maps are often available in travel shops, but if you can't find them, contact World Wide Books and Maps (☎ (604) 687-3320, fax (604) 687-5925, 736A Granville St, Vancouver, BC, Canada V6Z 1G3). They will send you a complete list of available titles; new ones are coming out all the time.

ITM maps are also available in the USA through the South American Explorers Club (see Useful Organizations) or through Map Link (☎ (805) 692-6777, fax (805) 962-0884, fax (800) 627-7768, 30 S La Patera Lane, Unit 5, Santa Barbara, CA 93117). Both of these organizations also have a variety of other maps of Central and South America. Map Link has all kinds of maps for worldwide destinations; contact them to request a catalog. In Britain ITM maps are available from Bradt Publications (☎ /fax (1494) 873 478, 41 Nortoft Rd, Chalfont St Peter, Bucks, SL9 0LA, UK).

The American Automobile Association (AAA) publishes a decent road map called *Mexico & Central America*; it's free for AAA members or members of other motor clubs with reciprocal arrangements with AAA. Texaco and Esso also publish road maps for Central America and for individual Central American countries.

What to Bring

Travel light. Most things you need can be bought along the way, often more cheaply than at home. Do be sure to bring insect repellent, something to purify water and antimalarial pills (though chloroquine is sold in many Central American pharmacies if you run out). If you use contraceptives or contact-lens solution, bring these along, too. Tampons are available in the larger cities, but bring some with you anyway as often you won't be able to find the kind you prefer.

A flashlight (torch) will come in useful for walking around at night and in case there is a power failure. During the rainy season, carry an umbrella. If you want to trek in rain forests at any time of year, you'll need water-resistant boots and decent rain gear.

If you have a special interest, such as snorkeling, bird watching or fishing, bring your own equipment with you. You may find it available in certain places, but there are some great snorkeling and birding places where no gear is available locally.

Central America is not cold, so there's no need to load up with clothing – a medium or heavy sweater is necessary in the mountains and should be warm enough for any time of year unless you plan on camping in the high-altitude cloud forests. If you'll be in the highlands of Guatemala in December or January, you will need warmer clothes. Remember that where it's cold, the locals wear warm clothing, so you can buy something locally rather than carrying around bundles of warm clothing for your entire trip.

If you'll want to do reading in any language besides Spanish, bring your own books with you. Bookstores with good books in English are few and far between, and it's even more rare to find books in any other language. Also, bring along a Spanish-English dictionary and possibly a Spanish grammar and phrasebook.

Then there are all the normal things you would take with you when traveling anywhere in the world: pocket knife, sewing kit, cord for clothesline, padlocks for your pack and so on. A short-wave radio is useful for keeping in touch with world events, and nowadays they're small and light enough to fit in a pocket. If you don't already have such a radio, Panama City is a very cheap place to buy one.

SUGGESTED ITINERARIES

This small region is so diverse, with such a variety of interesting places to visit and things to see and do, that it's difficult to suggest an itinerary – you won't be able to 'see it all' unless you have a lot of time. The following Highlights section will give you a good start in planning your trip.

People prefer to organize their travels in a different ways. You might want to pick just one or two countries and stay long enough to become familiar with them, though some folks prefer to travel in a mad dash, seeing as many highlights as possible.

You might want to focus on having a representative variety of experiences, choosing one or two cities or towns, one or two Maya ruins, one or two islands, one or two volcanoes, one or two national parks (how about one cloud forest and one marine park?), one or two handicrafts markets and so on.

If you don't know Spanish and you want to do much traveling here (or in any other Spanish-speaking countries), it's an excellent idea to plan some time for studying the language at the beginning of your journey. Courses can be taken a week at a time, usually starting every Monday. Two of the best places to study are at Antigua and Quetzaltenango, both pleasant Guatemalan towns with many schools to choose from.

Lonely Planet's USA publisher suggests the following itinerary, which she took on a 2½ week visit to Central America: Roatán (where she did a four-day diving certification course)/Tela/Copán/Antigua/Panajachel/ Chichicastenango. This itinerary might also include a trip to Tikal, the most magnificent of Central America's Mayan archaeological sites and a great place for birding. To do this itinerary, you could fly into Roatán, travel by bus the rest of the way, take a flight one (or both) ways to/from Tikal, and fly out of Guatemala City.

HIGHLIGHTS
Manmade Wonders

Mayan Archaeological Sites The stone pyramids, temples, hieroglyphics, statues, stone carvings, artwork and mysteriously abandoned cities of the Maya rank them as one of the great ancient civilizations of the world. Tikal in Guatemala is the most well-known and spectacular Maya archaeological site in Central America, followed closely by Copán in Honduras.

There are also a number of lesser known, lesser visited but still interesting sites, including Quiriguá and Uaxactún in Guatemala and El Puente at La Entrada, Honduras.

A number of other magnificent Maya sites are found in southern Mexico, including the Chichén Itzá and Uxmal sites in the Yucatán region and Palenque in Chiapas.

Panama Canal The more you learn about this engineering wonder, the more interesting it gets. It has locks where you can observe how the ships pass through, national parks beside it, the Isla Barro Colorado nature preserve in it, the graceful Bridge of the Americas over it and an impressive lineup of ships waiting at either end.

Antigua Guatemala This is among the prettiest and best-preserved colonial cities in Latin America. Semana Santa (Holy Week) is an unforgettable spectacle here.

Chichicastenango Handicrafts This picturesque, traditional Guatemalan mountain town has been famous for centuries for its traditional Maya market on Sunday and Thursday. Colorful woven cloths and textiles, wooden masks (carved and painted, still used in fiestas), pottery and many other beautiful handicrafts are sold. Sololá, near Lake Atitlán, has a Friday market day just as colorful but with fewer handicrafts (and fewer tourists).

Natural Wonders

National Parks & Wilderness Central America has some of the richest natural beauty on earth, and includes a variety of ecosystems with tropical rain forests, cloud forests, jungle river systems, lagoons and coastal wildlife preserves. Thousands of species of wildlife and tropical plants attract visitors, scientists and bird watchers from around the world. National parks have been set up in all the countries to preserve the natural wonders. Costa Rica's national park system is one of the most advanced in Latin America. For a list of the best known parks, see the National Parks section in Facts about Central America.

There are a number of real wilderness areas, like the Mosquitia region of Honduras, Darién Province in Panama and the less accessible national parks and wildlife sanctuaries of Costa Rica. These areas can offer unforgettable wilderness experiences.

Caribbean Islands Several islands off the coast of Central America are wonderful for diving, snorkeling, swimming, fishing and just enjoying sunny, palm-lined, white-sand beaches. Many of these places are designated as national marine parks to preserve and protect the coral reefs and dozens of species of fish and other marine life. The many shipwrecks from the colonial era make diving in the Caribbean additionally exciting.

The barrier reef off the coast of Belize is the second largest in the world, after Australia's Great Barrier Reef. Caye Caulker and Ambergris Caye are the two islands to visit.

Visitors go to all three Bay Islands (Islas de la Bahía) off the coast of Honduras, but Roatán is most people's favorite. Neighboring Utila, known for being the cheapest place in the world to get an open-water diving certificate, attracts lots of shoestring travelers. (A four-day PADI certification course costs around US$125 on Utila or US$195 on Roatán – still an excellent price.) Both islands have extensive protected reef areas and are great places for diving.

Nicaragua has the Corn Islands (Islas de Maíz).

The San Blas Islands – over 365 of them spread along Panama's Caribbean Coast

almost all the way to Colombia – are famous for the Kuna Indians, who live here traditionally as they have for centuries. The Bocas del Toro archipelago in western Panama is another blissful place protected by a national marine park. The people are friendly, and diving and snorkeling are fine.

Volcanoes Central America has hundreds of volcanoes, some dormant and some active. In several places you can climb them and look right into the craters; some even have roads right up to the top.

Two of the best volcanoes to see are the Poás and the Irazú, both in Costa Rican national parks that can be visited as day trips from the capital. Also in Costa Rica is Volcán Arenal, which is constantly in a state of eruption and is easily visited from nearby Fortuna, and Parque Nacional Rincón de la Vieja, which is a little less accessible but great for hikers and campers.

In Guatemala, perhaps the most famous volcano views in all of Central America are those from Lago de Atitlán and Antigua. Several volcanoes are popular for climbing, including Agua (near Antigua), Pacaya (a little farther from Antigua), San Pedro (beside Lake Atitlán) and Santa María (near Quetzaltenango). Highest of all is Volcán Tajumulco (4220 meters), accessible on a two-day trip from Quetzaltenango. At this writing, Pacaya and Santiaguito (on the flanks of Santa María) are smoking in the daytime and glowing at night.

El Salvador has a couple of magnificent volcanoes. Boquerón ('big mouth') is the deep crater of the volcano that towers over San Salvador. It's a good day trip from the city. You can also climb Volcán Izalco in the west of the country, known for over a century as 'the lighthouse of the Pacific' and now a dark cone on the landscape.

In Nicaragua, Parque Nacional Volcán Masaya can easily be visited on a day trip from Managua. The Laguna de Xiloá, also near Managua, is a beautiful volcanic crater lake.

Panama has one volcano, Volcán Barú, which is protected as a national park.

Lago de Atitlán This amazingly beautiful Guatemalan mountain lake is ringed by volcanoes and surrounded by villages of colorfully dressed traditional Maya Indians.

People & Culture

The people you meet and interact with can be the highlight of any journey, but this is especially true in Central America. As Rob Rachowiecki explains of Costa Ricans, 'Ticos always seem to have a ready smile and a helping hand for the inquisitive visitor.'

In Nicaragua, you can get an interesting discussion going with almost anyone you meet – just ask them to tell you about the revolution and the many events since. Nicaraguans have a variety of opinions on political issues, all strongly held and eloquently expressed. The many regional and ethnic groups also provide a wealth of possibilities for conversation and cultural exchange. In El Salvador, especially in the repopulated communities, you can hear hair-raising stories about the recent civil war.

And then there are your fellow travelers. Most parts of Central America are not overrun with foreign travelers, but those you do meet are often interesting and memorable characters.

Plazas, Parks & Picnics Go to places where the locals go and just hang out. In Tegucigalpa, be sure to spend one sunset sitting in the central plaza in front of the cathedral. People go in and out of the cathedral, catch buses on the sides of the plaza, stroll or rush past and watch the other people, while all around is the din of a thousand birds emanating from the trees. For a few cents you can get a little bag of crispy banana chips with lime, salt and hot sauce, and spend a sublime hour.

Another place where locals throng is Parque Balboa outside San Salvador. On Sundays the townspeople come to stroll in the park, let the children play, hear wandering musicians and eat in the many little outdoor cafes. In Guatemala, have a picnic at El Baúl near Santa Lucía Cotzumalguapa, where locals come to worship at a thousand-year-old Mayan idol. The Fuentes Georginas hot springs are an idyllic retreat near Quetzaltenango, popular with Guatemalans but relatively unfrequented by tourists.

Markets The large open-air *mercados* (markets) and *artisanías* (handicraft) markets in Central America are always interesting. It's great to eat a meal at a table set up in a marketplace amid all the activity.

Food Eating and drinking new and unusual things is a joy, and you'll discover some wonderful treats. Try the seafood soups and coconut bread along the Caribbean Coast; the strong, hot coffee in Costa Rica; the shaved ice with sweet fruit syrup from street stands in Panama City; the odd little vegetarian restaurant, like Todo Rico in Tegucigalpa; chicken, barbecued outdoors; and unfamiliar tropical fruits.

Ethnic Cultures Cultural events of the many and diverse ethnic groups of Central America are fascinating; if you get a chance to see one, don't miss it. In Honduras you may see a Garífuna music or dance performance; April 12, the anniversary of the arrival of the Garífuna people in Honduras in 1797, is a joyful occasion celebrated in all the Garífuna communities. In Belize, Garífuna Settlement Day (November 19) celebrates the arrival of the Garífuna in Belize in 1828. In Panama, the Kuna Indians perform wonderful music and dance.

Fiestas & Celebrations Town fairs, annual celebrations, Carnaval and saints' days are magnificent occasions. Some of the more famous ones are Semana Santa (Holy Week) in Antigua Guatemala; Carnaval in Panama City or the much smaller Carnaval in La Ceiba on the Caribbean Coast of Honduras; and Corpus Christi in Las Tablas, Panama. The celebrations on the anniversary of the July 19 revolution are a big event in Managua. Religious pilgrimages attracting throngs of participants take place on such occasions as the day of the Virgen de Suyapa (patron saint of Honduras) at the Suyapa Cathedral near Tegucigalpa (February 3) and on the day of the Virgen de Fátima (May 13) at the Virgin's grotto outside Cojutepeque (El Salvador).

Every city, town and village has its annual celebration and fair. These are not always big or famous occasions, but celebrations in small places, where the presence of a foreigner is an event in itself, are often the best. For example, in tiny towns in Guatemala's highlands the *cofradías* (religious brotherhoods) hold street processions on saints' days and festival Sundays, accompanied by a ragtag assortment of drums, trumpets, firecrackers and incense. The repopulated communities in northern El Salvador usually have a celebration on the anniversary of the return of the villagers after the civil war.

Theaters Some cultural events are enjoyable as much for the venue as for the event. Don't miss seeing the national theaters in San José (Costa Rica), San Salvador and Panama City, and catch a performance at any of these if you can. Built around the turn of the century, these theaters have tiered seating and lush decorations of velvet and gold.

Adventurous Side Trips
Famous Journeys There are several famous journeys that you can make within Central America:

Río Dulce Boat Trip
This one-day trip, starting at Lívingston on Guatemala's Caribbean Coast, passes up the Río Dulce through tropical jungle to El Golfete, a small gulf with a reserve for manatees, which are endangered, and other wildlife, and on to the Castillo de San Felipe, an old Spanish fort on the shores of the Lago de Izabal. Nowadays many people are doing the trip in the other direction, too, starting from the village of Río Dulce.
Bluefields
In Nicaragua, you can make a relaxing two-day journey from Managua to Bluefields on the Caribbean Coast: one day by land from Managua to Rama, a small river town on the

Río Escondido, and the next day by boat down the river to Bluefields. Bluefields itself isn't so remarkable, but it's a fine trip to get there.
Río San Juan
The San Juan forms the eastern part of the border between Nicaragua and Costa Rica. Boat trips on this river depart from San Carlos on Lago de Nicaragua and travel through the jungle to Castillo Viejo, another old Spanish fort.
Darién Gap
The Interamericana does not go straight through from Central to South America. At the border between Panama and Colombia lies an extensive wilderness area known as the Darién, where the road gives way to jungle – hence the name 'Darién Gap.' Travelers wishing to go overland all the way to (or from) South America can get through here on foot and river boat, as do the local Indians. This demanding trip (not to be taken lightly) requires at least several days, and it is becoming more dangerous by the year.

Backroads Rides In rural areas it's common for a driver (usually in a dusty diesel pickup truck) to stop for anyone he sees hitchhiking. Be sure to offer to pay something for your ride, since this is the local custom. Riding through the wilds of Central America in the back of a pickup with the wind in your hair is a marvelous feeling. Riding the backroads on the roof of a bus is a similar joy – though the bus may be stuffed to overflowing with women, children and old people, you can sometimes get on top with the boys and the big round baskets of produce being brought back from market.

Walks Simple walks in out-of-the-way places can be what you'll remember most. This includes not only scaling volcanoes and visiting magnificent national parks, but just walking around wherever you happen to be – to the other side of an island, to the top of a hill at sunset or down a long stretch of beach.

VISAS & DOCUMENTS
Passports
Before you start out, be sure your passport will be valid for a reasonable period:

Some countries will not let you in if your passport is about to expire. Six months' validity is the usual minimum requirement. Also be sure your passport has plenty of free space for visa stamps: If it fills up, you may have to get it replaced or have more pages added. This is easiest done while you are still in your home country, though in a pinch you can also get it done at an embassy or consulate of your home country.

Having a photocopy of the first page of your passport makes it much faster and easier to get a replacement from your consulate if the passport is lost or stolen. Memorizing your passport number is also a good idea.

Visas

A visa is an endorsement in your passport, usually a stamp, permitting you to enter a country and stay there for a specified period of time. It is obtained from a foreign consulate or embassy of the country you want to visit. You can get all your visas before you set out on your trip or get them at consulates and embassies during your trip. It is very important to find out how long your visas are valid; typically they are good for entry into a country within three or six months of the date of issue, but regulations vary.

A country may have a number of consulates and embassies in various places, and these may have different conditions for issuing visas. At some, you simply fill out your application, pay your money and have your passport stamped. Others may take your application and passport and have you pick them up in a few days. Still others may require one or more passport-size photos (always have some extra ones with you), or evidence of the amount of money you're planning to take into the country. You can learn a lot from fellow travelers about which consulates along the way are the easiest for obtaining visas.

Visa requirements – which nationalities need a visa and which don't – are different for each country and may change at any time. Always be sure to double-check each country's visa and onward-ticket requirements before you get there. If you need a visa and don't have it, you will be turned back at the border if you're coming overland. If you're coming by air, you will not be allowed to board the plane without having your visa in order.

The amount of time you are given on a visa is usually standard, but occasionally you may be given less time for some reason, such as not having much money ('insufficient funds') or coming across as a bit 'suspicious.'

Extensions Once you are inside a country, you can always apply for an extension at the country's immigration office. Usually there is some limit on how many extensions you can receive; if you leave the country and reenter, your time starts over again.

Photocopies

Make photocopies of vital documents and keep them in one or more places. Copy passport data pages (including the first page of your passport and any relevant visas), airline tickets and other travel documents, your driver's license and international driving permit, international certificate of vaccination, credit cards and a list of traveler's-check serial numbers. You might also want to make a copy of your birth certificate, employment documents and education qualifications. Also leave a copy of all these things with someone at home.

Onward Tickets

Some Central American countries have laws requiring you to have a ticket out of the country (onward or return) before they will let you enter. Costa Rica, Panama and Belize all have such laws on the books, though the only time they enforce them is if they think you look suspicious for some reason and they're trying to keep you out. See the chapters on Getting There & Away and Getting Around and the individual countries for suggestions on how to satisfy these requirements.

If you're continuing south, note that several South American countries, including Colombia, Venezuela, Peru and Guyana also have onward-ticket requirements. So you can't, for example, just buy a one-way ticket from Central America to one of these countries and keep on going. It's a little more complicated than that.

The only way to avoid the onward-ticket requirement altogether in countries that demand it is to enter the country by private rather than public transport. If you enter by private vehicle, either your own or one that has picked you up, no onward ticket is required.

Travel Insurance
A travel insurance policy to cover theft, loss and medical problems is a wise idea. See the Health and Theft sections for more details.

Driver's License
Before you start out, check to see if your driver's license from your home country is honored in all the countries you plan to visit. A driver's license and possibly an International Driving Permit are good to have along even if you're not driving your own vehicle (see Car & Motorcycle in the Facts for the Visitor chapter).

Hostel Card
A Hostelling International membership card is not as useful in Central America as elsewhere. Only a couple of youth hostels and other places in all of Central America give cardholders a discount.

Student Cards
The International Student Identity Card (ISIC) is another useful document, entitling you to discounts on travel (airfare, tours and so on) at student travel agencies around the world (see Useful Organizations) and to various discounts within countries. You must be a full-time student to qualify for an official ISIC card, which costs about US$19. The normal place to buy ISIC cards is at student travel agencies around the world. STA Travel is the main agency in

Europe, Australia, New Zealand and the USA. Council Travel is also big in the USA.

Some 'bucket shop' ticket agencies will sell you an 'ISIC card' when you book a 'student' flight with them. In some places where travelers congregate there's a black market in fake ISIC cards, but be wary of this – it's been going on so much for so long that the bona fide ISIC card is defending itself against phonies by incorporating a magnetic strip. A fake card won't carry any of the insurance or other benefits of the real thing.

International Health Card
Several other documents are useful to have with you. An international health certificate listing the type and date of all your vaccinations and immunizations is a good idea any time you travel internationally. You can get one from the physician who vaccinates you, your doctor back home or any government health department. Be sure to keep it up to date noting all immunizations.

CUSTOMS
Any time you enter a country, your belongings are subject to a customs check. Prohibited items may include weapons, explosives, illegal drugs, and animal or agricultural products. There's a limit for dutifiable items: usually two liters of alcoholic beverages and 200 cigarettes, 100 cigars or half a kilogram of tobacco.

MONEY
The best currency to bring with you to Central America is US dollars; they can be exchanged everywhere in Central America. Other currencies will be impossible to exchange on any consistent basis, if at all.

In Panama City, which is a center for international banking, there is one *casa de cambio* (exchange house) that will exchange currency from just about anywhere on earth with a convertible currency, so if you do have some unusual bank notes, it might be worth going there. The US dollar is the national currency of Panama (it's called a 'Balboa' but it's exactly the same money). Several international banks in Panama City exchange the currency of their home country for dollars, though if they are overstocked with foreign currency, they may refuse to do so.

You can usually manage to exchange Central American currencies from one country to the next, though it's easier when you're at or near the border. If you wait until you're far into the next country, you may not find anyone willing to change the leftover money. If you're crossing at land borders, change all your currency from the country you're leaving into either the currency of the country you're entering or US dollars. It's a good habit, though, to use up all your local money while you're in the country, and start changing dollars again when you get to the next country.

Costs

Looking through the prices in the country chapters of this book, you get a good idea of costs. (Prices are more likely to go up than down.) An inexpensive hotel can cost anywhere from US$3 to US$10 a night for two people sharing a room and will not be much cheaper for a single traveler. A meal in an inexpensive restaurant or in the outdoor market costs only about US$1 or US$2, and if you buy your own fresh fruit and other food in the market, you can eat even cheaper. Traveling on buses is cheap, and it's a fine way to get around Central America – all the countries have good (or at least adequate) bus systems.

This book focuses on the cheapest ways to get around and have an enjoyable visit to Central America, but we have adhered to some minimum standards of hygiene and comfort. If a place was too wretched, we didn't include it in the book. And for the times when you do want to spend a little more, you'll find that a few extra dollars can translate to a huge jump up in quality. The difference between a US$5 and US$10 hotel room can be great.

Carrying Money

Everyone has a preferred way to carry their money. For a few suggestions on carrying it

safely, see the Dangers & Annoyances section later in this chapter.

Cash

You should always carry some money in US dollars cash. Small bills are best: They can be changed almost anywhere. It's especially useful to have cash for times when you can't change traveler's checks – in remote places, or where no bank will change the type of checks you have, or when the banks are closed, or when the casa de cambio changes cash but not checks. If there's a black market, you might get a better rate for cash, or you may not be able to change checks at all. It's also useful to be able to change just a few dollars when you're about to leave a country. If you have to change a US$20 traveler's check to local currency and then cross a border, you will have to change most of that once again into the currency of the new country, and you lose a little with every currency exchange.

In some places you'll get the same exchange rate for traveler's checks or cash, but often you'll get a slightly better rate for cash. Banks may offer about a 4% higher rate for cash.

Traveler's Checks

Take most of your money in traveler's checks, since they can be refunded if they are lost or stolen. American Express and Visa are the most widely recognized checks and the easiest to exchange (you may have difficulty cashing other brands). American Express has offices in all the Central American capitals. Most banks and casas de cambio that change checks at all will change American Express checks. You can cash Visa checks at any bank with Visa affiliation, though this is not every bank.

Keep an up-to-date record of check numbers and the original bill of sale in a safe, separate place. If your checks are lost or stolen, you'll need to know the numbers of the missing checks to get them replaced. Sometimes banks want to see the bill of sale before they'll cash your checks.

Carry plenty of checks in small denominations. US$20 or US$50 will last a long time in many countries, and you don't want to get stuck with large amounts of a country's currency when you are about to leave.

Note that in Nicaragua, you may find it impossible to change traveler's checks anywhere outside Managua; details are given in the Nicaragua chapter. In the other countries there's usually no problem finding a bank that will change them.

Credit Cards

American Express, Visa and MasterCard are the most widely accepted credit cards in Central America. There are a couple of other types of credit cards issued by banks in Central America, but travelers should stick to the big, internationally known ones.

A credit card is a wonderful thing to have when traveling. It acts as insurance against emergencies and enables you to obtain cash or enjoy a little unexpected luxury somewhere along the way. It can also be useful if you're asked to demonstrate 'sufficient funds' when you enter a country. Some cards offer free insurance if you use the card when buying airline tickets or renting a car. This can sometimes save you up to half the cost of a car rental. Also, if you rent a car using a credit card, you don't have to pay a cash deposit.

You can take out money on your credit card and use it to buy traveler's checks in US dollars, even in countries where the only hard currency you can buy with the card is the local one (both American Express and Visa allow you to do this). Often, you can simply get your cash advance in US dollars cash. Visa and MasterCard cash advances can be transacted at branches of Credomatic and at some banks.

Some travelers rely on cash advances to reduce the need for traveler's checks, but inquire about transaction charges; for example, there's usually no charge in Honduras, but in Guatemala you may be charged between 10% and 25%. Even if there's no charge at the Central American end, however, there may be a transaction fee charged by the card company; if you're planning to make a lot of cash advances on your card, check the policy before leaving home.

Another advantage to having a credit card is that it enables you to use an ATM, where you can get cash from accounts at home 24 hours a day.

Of course you have to make the monthly payments on the bill you run up, and there are the interest charges to pay on your statement back home, but there are even ways of getting around this. You can pay a sum into your credit card account *before* you take off on your trip, so the money is already in there. When you use your card it's just like taking money out of your own bank account, and you won't have to make any payments or incur any interest until you've used up your initial deposit.

If you have an American Express card, requiring full payment each month, you can use a personal check to pay your bill at any American Express office, and then use your card to obtain cash or traveler's checks. It's like being able to cash personal checks in any country.

If you need more money on your travels, you could ask someone back home to put some into your credit card account rather than sending it by bank transfer. This might save you a lot of anxiety while you're waiting for the money to show up!

One American traveler wrote to tell us that when he returned home from Central America, he discovered his Citibank MasterCard had routinely charged him 16% more than the charges should have been each time he used his card in Honduras and 6% more than they should have for every charge he made in the Dominican Republic. Citibank had used a much less favorable rate of exchange than the official exchange rate that had been in effect when he made his purchases.

The traveler said that after much contention with Citibank, in which he was unable to prove what the official rates of exchange were on the days he had made the charges, he eventually realized travelers are likely to be hit with high surcharges when touring smaller countries for which official rates of exchange are not listed in the *Wall Street Journal*.

International Transfers

If you don't have a credit card, Western Union can quickly forward money to you while you're traveling, though the fee is expensive. For instance, you can get money within 15 minutes from the USA, but the surcharge is significant (10% or more in El Salvador). Western Union has offices in many places in Central America.

Other than Western Union, direct bank transfers are the most reliable way of having money sent to you. To do this, make sure you specify the city, the bank and the branch that you want the money sent to. It's best to make all the arrangements at the receiving bank, find out everything that should be done, request the transfer from your home bank and have them follow the instructions exactly.

Be sure to find out in advance what the policy of the receiving bank will be when your money does arrive. Can you take all or part of it in dollars or buy traveler's checks with it in dollars? Or do you have to take all of it in the currency of the country you're in? If so, at what rate of exchange? Can you pick it up the same day, or if not, how long must you wait? Will the bank charge you a service fee? How much? Different banks may have different policies, so check around.

Even though wiring money directly from bank to bank should go smoothly and be easily accomplished within a couple of days, a surprising number of technical complications and delays can arise. For example, your home bank might wire the money to the main office of the receiving bank and have it available there in hours, but it could take weeks for it to get from there to the branch where you're waiting for it. Or the transaction may be lost in a pile of paper, so the bank on your end tells you they haven't received it while the bank back home assures you it was sent days ago.

It's best to allow as much time as you can for bank transfers, rather than waiting until you're down to your last centavo before starting the process. You might ask your consulate how to send money reliably to wherever you are; the consulate may deal with a certain bank or have some other helpful hint.

Despite the problems, it's still better to have money transferred through a bank or by Western Union than to trust it to the mail. It's a fact of life that anything sent through the mail to Central America may disappear.

Currency Exchange

Exchange rates can vary quite a bit, depending where you change your money. Always ask about the going rates before you change any large amount. Usually hotels offer the worst rates of exchange. Casas de cambio may offer the same rate as banks, but sometimes it's better or worse depending on whether you're changing cash or traveler's checks. The exchange rate at a bank for cash advances on a credit card may differ from the rate for changing cash or traveler's checks.

Black Market

In some places there's a black market, and it may offer a better rate for your dollar, but sometimes the difference is very small; occasionally it's actually worse. Usually only US dollars cash can be changed on the black market. If you do decide to patronize the black market, remember that it's illegal. You could get into big trouble if you get caught, though in some places it's very common to change money this way and right out on the street at that. It's your decision whether to use the black market, but if you do, be aware of the risks.

Crossing land borders, you may find that the black market is your only way to obtain the local currency and unload your excess from the country you're leaving. Make sure you know the correct *current* rate or you could be easily ripped off. If in doubt, change only enough to last you until you can get to a bank.

If you change money on the street, be as discreet about it as possible, and be alert. Always be sure to count out the money you're receiving carefully before you hand over your dollars. If there's any mistake in what you're given the first time, be sure to count the whole lot all together, all over again, to see it's correct before you give them your money. It's remarkably easy to be caught by sleight-of-hand tricks. Have the exact amount of dollars you want to change ready to avoid fumbling around with them on the street or showing more of them than you need to. Also be aware that when you change money on the street and then put it in your pocket or wherever, you will be showing everyone in view where you keep your money.

Tipping & Bargaining

Tipping practices vary a bit throughout the region, but here are some general guidelines. In restaurants, tipping (from a little spare change up to 10% of the bill) is common in establishments frequented by foreign tourists and not so common in places patronized mostly by locals. A small tip left for the cleaning staff at any type of hotel is not necessary, but it's a warm gesture much appreciated by people who are paid very little. Taxi drivers are not usually tipped; porters at airports receive a small tip.

Bargaining is essential in some situations and not acceptable in others. Bargaining is very common at outdoor markets, but in supermarkets or other indoor shops it isn't done. Bargaining is practically universal at handicrafts markets, where the first price you're told will often be double or triple what sellers really expect to receive.

Bargaining definitely requires a technique; indeed, it's almost an art. If you're not used to it, you'll probably start to feel more comfortable and develop your own style and strategies with practice. Of course, the object is to arrive at a price agreeable to both you and the seller. Remember that bargaining is not a fight to the death; be friendly about it, keep your sense of humor and have patience.

It's important when bargaining not to succumb to the all-too-common 'ugly tourist' attitude. Surprisingly often, travelers who expect to be well paid for their jobs back home do not recognize that those they encounter when traveling have similar expectations. As a foreigner, you represent enormous wealth to local people, and your business may be one of their few opportunities to earn an income. In most Central American countries, the economy makes it almost impossible for many people to make a decent living, no matter how long or hard they work. It's great to bargain, but always do it with an attitude of respect, and don't expect to come away with something for nothing.

Aside from bargaining in markets, you can sometimes bargain for better rates at hotels and guesthouses, especially at times when business is slow. From the hotelier's point of view it's better to rent a room for a cheaper price than to have it stand empty, but there's no reason to do so if another customer is likely to show up and pay the full price. Often you can get a discount off the nightly rate if you take the room for a few days or a week; ask about this at the time you check in.

Taxes

Several Central American countries have sales taxes that are added onto the price of all purchased items; see the individual country chapters for details. Some countries also have a hotel tax. In Guatemala, the sales tax is 10% and the INGUAT (national tourist office) tax is another 10%, adding a hefty 20% onto the price of hotel rooms. Large, expensive hotels always charge this, but smaller, less expensive hotels or guesthouses often do not. In this book, we've already calculated the taxes into the room prices we quote. When you ask prices, be sure to clarify whether the price includes tax.

POST & COMMUNICATIONS
Post

Sending and receiving mail between Central America and other parts of the world sometimes goes without a hitch, but it can be a very uncertain business. Because many Central Americans go to the USA to work and send money back home to their families, often through the mail, there's a high rate of mail theft in many places. The mail simply 'disappears.'

This primarily happens to mail sent from the USA to points in Central America, but it can also occur to mail coming from other countries or even with mail being sent out from Central America to other parts of the world. Mail going more locally, within or between the Central American countries, is not as likely to disappear.

Mail is most likely to reach its destination when it looks like there is no way it could contain money or anything else of value, as with a postcard or a fold-up aerogram.

Sending Mail Sending letters is a straightforward business. If you want something to arrive within a reasonable time, be sure to specify that you want air mail (*correo aéreo* or *por avión*). Surface mail sent to other parts of the world, whether letters or packages, usually takes several months to arrive.

If you want to send a package home, check with the post office first. Don't arrive with your parcel all wrapped for mailing – you may have to have the contents approved by customs officials first, or there may be particular wrapping requirements.

Receiving Mail The poste restante (or general delivery) service is known as Lista de Correos. To receive mail at a post office, it must be addressed to you like this:

> Your Name
> Lista de Correos
> Correo Central
> City, Department
> Country
> Central America

It will be sent to the main post office in the city and held there, usually for up to 30 days. (Remember that mail sent to Panama must be addressed 'República de Panamá,' as specifying only 'Panama' can cause the mail to be returned.) Most of the time there's no charge for the service, but occasionally it costs a few cents (paid upon pickup). Often you'll be required to present your identification (a passport will do) when you claim your mail.

In larger cities, Lista de Correos mail will probably be separated into alphabetical order. In small town post offices, you may find all the mail in one box. Be sure to check every conceivable letter your name could be filed under – not only your surname, but also your first name and even titles, such as 'M' for Mr, Mrs, Miss or Ms, or 'S' for Señor (Sr), Señora (Sra) or Señorita (Srta). To minimize confusion, it's best to use no titles and to underline the surname.

Other alternatives for picking up mail include having it sent care of your country's embassy, but check in advance whether they offer this service. If you have either an American Express credit card or American Express traveler's checks, you can have mail sent to you at any American Express office, but there may be a fee for the service.

Telephone, Fax & Telex
Local, long-distance and international telephone, fax and telex services are available at national telephone offices in every city and town. See the individual country chapters for details. Note that it is *not* possible to make collect (reverse-charge) calls to many countries from Central America; you usually can place them to the USA. Special numbers allow you to dial and reach an operator in your home country; the USA's three main long-distance companies (AT&T, MCI and Sprint) all have 'direct-connect' numbers in the Central American countries, and some other countries have similar arrangements (for example, Canada Direct).

Online Services
All the Central American countries now have some form of Internet access, and it's becoming easier all the time. You can find out about access from the national telephone office in each country's capital city, or ask around to find someone who is connected and ask them. In places with plenty of international travelers, private computer and communications offices provide services.

For Internet-savvy readers, we've gathered all email and Web site addresses in the Online Resources appendix. As you read this guide, 'net' denotes an organization or business with an Internet address.

TRAVELING WITH A LAPTOP

Following some basic rules will insure the safety of your computer.

Always carry your computer by hand in a suitable carrying case. Don't check it in as luggage, especially on international flights, where it will be thrown around. It's also best not to pile heavy things on top of it.

Keep it and all disks away from magnetic fields and heat – they should not be exposed to temperatures below 0°C (32°F) or above 50°C (122°F). Metal detectors (such as the kind you walk through at the airport) may damage a computer's hard drive. In airports insist that the computer and disks be physically inspected, not passed through metal detectors or X rays. Security often asks that the computer be turned on to verify its use as a computer (and not a means of smuggling contraband).

Before traveling to another country, always check that the local AC voltage and the AC power cord specifications are compatible. If not, buy a power cord compatible with local voltage – using a converter kit designed for appliances can be risky. A good surge protector is also advisable, as current may be irregular. If your computer uses batteries, it's wise to bring along a spare. If you have a modem, check to see whether it will be compatible with the telecommunications system of the country you'll be visiting.

Before starting your trip, check to see whether your computer is covered by international warranty and/or your travel insurance. Some policies specifically exclude computers or provide an upper limit of baggage insurance that would not cover the replacement cost of the computer. You might want to phone to the company that manufactured your computer and ask if they have a service center in the country you'll be visiting, just in case.

BOOKS

Central America is a small area geographically, but it is an important and much-studied part of the world for a variety of reasons. Hundreds of books have been written about Central America as a region and about the various countries. There are history books, books about the Maya and the Maya ruins, books on modern social and political developments, books on the relationship between the USA and Central America, books about nature, tropical rain forests, wildlife and more. The following suggested titles relate to the region as a whole; books about individual countries are mentioned in the country chapters.

It's a good idea to do some reading before your trip, but Central America will probably still surprise you. Reading too much about political problems might put you off going there!

If you don't read Spanish, bring some books with you. It's hard to find books in English or any other language than Spanish. You might find some in the gift shops of luxury hotels, but they'll be expensive.

Lonely Planet

Lonely Planet publishes in-depth guidebooks for several Central American countries. Look for *Guatemala, Belize & Yucatán: La Ruta Maya*, a detailed guide to the Maya lands including the Yucatán Peninsula and Chiapas, and *Costa Rica*.

If you're heading north, there's the comprehensive guide to Mexico. If you're continuing south, *South America on a Shoestring* is that region's counterpart to this book, and LP also publishes individual guides for nearly all the countries of South America. In the Caribbean, check out Lonely Planet's guides to Cuba, Jamaica, the Bahamas and Eastern Caribbean.

Lonely Planet's *Latin American Spanish Phrasebook* includes pronunciation and is pocket-size.

General Guides

Mexico & Central American Handbook. This guide contains excellent information, though its format and style is something of an acquired taste. It also has companion volumes covering the Caribbean and South America.

People's Guide to Mexico by Carl Franz. This is mostly about Mexico, but it does venture into Central America. It makes delightful, humorous, informative and useful reading for shoestring travelers. It was first published in 1972 and has been revised several times. If you've never seen this book, you're missing something.

Central America by Chicken Bus by Vivien Lougheed (Repository Press, Prince George, BC, Canada). Recommended more for its friendly and entertaining style than for its practical travel information.

Hiking & Backpacking

Backpacking in Central America by Tim Burford (Bradt Publications, England). If you want to get out and explore the many natural wonders of Central America, this excellent guide gives detailed information for long and short treks all over the region (except Belize).

Bicycle Touring

Latin America on Bicycle by J P Panet. Has chapters on Costa Rica, Guatemala and a few other Latin American countries.

Latin America by Bike: A Complete Touring Guide by Walter Sienko (The Mountaineers; or Cordee, Leicester, UK). Covers all the Central American countries except El Salvador.

Wildlife Watching

A Field Guide to the Birds of Mexico and Central America by L I Davis (University of Texas Press).

Neotropical Rainforest Mammals: A Field Guide by Louise H Emmons.

Ancient & Maya History

Breaking the Maya Code by Michael D Coe. Tells the inside story of the deciphering of the ancient Maya hieroglyphs, a great achievement of recent years.

A Forest of Kings: The Untold Story of the Ancient Maya by Linda Schele and David Freidel. This readable history brings the ancient Maya to life. It's based on recent interpretations of the Maya glyphs, written by two of the central figures in the decoding effort.

Popol Vuh. The sacred book of the ancient Quiché Maya, telling their history from the time of creation. This is believed to be the oldest text in the Americas.

The Maya by Michael D Coe. Hundreds of books have been written about the Maya, but this is the best general introduction to their life and culture.

General History

A Brief History of Central America by Hector Perez-Brignoli. A short, readable history of the region.

Modern Politics

The Inter-Hemispheric Education Resource Center guides (Box 4506, Albuquerque, NM 87916 USA). Paperback guides on each of the seven Central American countries, covering politics, institutions, the economy, the environment, international relations and so on. The 1993 edition of *Honduras: A Country Guide* is called *Inside Honduras*; all the other country guides will eventually be similarly re-released and retitled. You can get a discount if you order the whole set. The same people publish a number of other books about Central America; write for a free catalog.

Central America Fact Book by Tom Barry and Deb Preusch. Examines the economic, political and military role of the USA in Central America, and other issues.

Cocaine Politics: Drugs, Armies and the CIA in Central America by Peter Dale Scott and Jonathan Marshall. Well researched and documented, it focuses on the contra-drug connection and provides a new perspective on the US 'war on drugs.'

Inevitable Revolutions: The United States in Central America by Walter LaFeber.

Roots of Rebellion: Land and Hunger in Central America by Tom Barry.

Turning the Tide: US Intervention in Central America and the Struggle for Peace by Noam Chomsky. A classic of the 1980s.

Nature & Rain Forests

Life above the Jungle Floor: A Biologist Explores a Strange and Hidden Treetop World by Donald Perry (Don Perro Press, San José, Costa Rica).

A Neotropical Companion: An Introduction to the Animals, Plants, and Ecosystems of the New World Tropics by John C Kricher.

Tropical Nature: Life and Death in the Rain Forests of Central and South America by Adrian Forsyth and Ken Miyata.

Travel Literature

Around the Edge by Peter Ford. The story of the author's travels along the Caribbean coast from Belize to Panama, on foot and by boat.

Incidents of Travel in Central America, Chiapas & Yucatán by John L Stephens, illustrated by Frederick Catherwood (Century, one volume; or Dover, two volumes). Originally published in 1841, this book caused an international sensation with its descriptions and drawings of the Maya ruins and many other things Stephens and Catherwood discovered in their explorations. A famous book, still widely read and enjoyed after 150 years. (Also look for *Incidents of Travel in Yucatán* by the same author.)

The Old Patagonian Express: By Train through the Americas by Paul Theroux. Theroux went by train from a suburb of Boston all the way to Patagonia. Several interesting Central American train rides are included; sadly, some of the trains he took are no longer operating, but it's still a great book.

So Far from God: A Journey to Central America by Patrick Marnham. A vivid, entertaining book describing a modern overland journey from California to Nicaragua, including Mexico, Guatemala, El Salvador and Honduras.

Sweet Waist of America by Anthony Daniels (Arrow/Hutchinson). Primarily about Guatemala, but also touches on Honduras, El Salvador and Nicaragua.

Tekkin a Waalk by Peter Ford (Flamingo). An entertaining and informative account of a trip by foot and boat along the Caribbean Coast from Belize to Panama, including negotiating the Mosquitia jungle in the dying days of the Contra-Sandinista war. Historical anecdotes and personal experiences are combined with insights into the culture of Garífuna and Miskito communities.

Through the Volcanoes: A Central American Journey by Jeremy Paxman. The story of a journey through the region in the early 1980s.

Time among the Maya: Travels in Belize, Guatemala, and Mexico by Ronald Wright (Weidenfeld & Nicolson). Describes a number of recent journeys among the modern Maya people; gives a good feel for Maya culture.

Literature

All the following books by Central American writers are translated into English:

And We Sold the Rain: Contemporary Fiction from Central America, edited by Rosario Santos (FWEW). Twenty short stories by Central American writers.

Beyond the Border: A New Age in Latin American Women's Fiction, edited by Nora Erro-Peralta & Caridad Silva-Nuñez (Cleis Press).

Clamor of Innocence: Central American Short Stories, edited Barbara Paschke and David Volpendesta (City Lights Books). Thirty-one short stories by Central American writers.

When New Flowers Bloomed: Short Stories by Women Writers from Costa Rica & Panama, edited Enrique J Levi (Latin American Literary Review Press).

MEDIA

International newspapers and magazines such as the *International Herald Tribune*, *Time* and *Newsweek* are often available in bookstores of large luxury hotels, but they may be expensive, around US$3 or so. In Panama, these and other English-language newspapers and magazines are also available at all Gran Morrison department stores.

All the Central American countries have a wide selection of radio stations and TV channels to choose from. In addition to the local TV channels, cable brings in a number of channels from the USA and even a German channel.

Periodicals

Central America Bulletin, Central America Research Institute, Box 4797, Berkeley, CA 94704, USA. Monthly in English.

Central America Report, Inforpress Centroamericana, Guatemala City. Weekly in English.

Latin American Travel Advisor, PO Box 17-17908, Quito, Ecuador (fax (593) (2) 562-566 for free sample). Quarterly guide of travel advice for the region.

NACLA Report on the Americas, North American Congress on Latin America, 9th floor, 151 W 19th St, New York, NY 10011, USA. Bimonthly, in English.

National Geographic. Excellent articles on Central American countries, including 'La Ruta Maya' and related articles in the October 1989 issue (Vol 176, No 4).

South American Explorer, South American Explorers Club. Quarterly, in English. (See the entry on Useful Organizations for more information about this club.)

The Tico Times, Apdo 4632, San José, Costa Rica or Dept 717, PO Box 025216, Miami, FL 33102, USA. Weekly English language newspaper published in Costa Rica on Fridays. It covers Costa Rica news in detail and has a page on Central America.

PHOTOGRAPHY
Film & Equipment
Film is available throughout the region, though if you want a particular type of film apart from the standard Kodak, Fuji or Agfa color print film, you might do well to bring your favorite from home. The larger cities have specialized camera and photography stores and one-hour processing.

Taking Good Photos
The best times of day for photography are usually in the early morning or late afternoon, when natural light is softest; photos taken at midday can look harsher and flatter. If your interest is wildlife photography, early morning is when you'll spot the most birds and other wildlife.

For the best quality photos, you might consider carrying a couple of different speeds of film: 100 ASA is best for outdoor photography on bright days; 200 ASA is a good all-around speed for varying conditions; and 400 ASA is best for night or dim light situations. If you'll be doing any photography in forests, consider bringing both 400 ASA film and a tripod – there's surprisingly little light on the forest floor.

A good telephoto or zoom lens is an invaluable tool for travel photography, making it possible to take close-up photos of people, wildlife, outdoor markets and innumerable other subjects even from a distance. Nowadays even pocket-size automatic 35 mm cameras come with good zoom lenses. You'll find the extra cost a good investment.

Photographing People
Local people can sometimes be touchy about being photographed by camera-happy tourists. This is particularly true of indigenous people wearing traditional clothing. While the tourist may find indigenous people a great exotic photo opportunity, indigenous people may feel rudely infringed upon by being made a spectacle by a tourist. They may feel the tourist is literally 'taking' their photo from them, and they may feel (often rightly) that the tourist sees them only as odd curiosities, not as human beings worthy of respect. Keep this in mind when you want to take people's photographs. It's polite to ask permission before shoving a camera into their face. Often people will agree to be photographed, but if they say no, respect their wishes.

Of course, if you have asked someone's permission to take his or her photograph, it becomes difficult to get a natural-looking photo. Even if they're not grinning into the camera lens, people are rarely as 'natural' when they know they're being photographed. A good telephoto or zoom lens can come in very handy for this. (Of course one could still ponder the issue of whether it's ethical to take people's photos without their knowing it.)

In some places, indigenous people may ask for a small payment from you for permission to photograph them. The Kuna Indians of Panama often do this; the usual amount to give them is around US$0.25 per photo. Some travelers balk at doing this, feeling they should get it for free. Others willingly give a small amount, reasoning that local people often have few ways of making money and that this is an exchange in which each participant gives the other something of value.

Another way of making it an equal exchange is to make a copy of the photo and give one to them. Many locals may not have a camera, and a photo can be a meaningful gift.

Airport Security
Although airports always assure you that their X-ray machines will not damage film, most photographers prefer to protect their film from these potentially harmful rays. One way to do this is to carry your film in a lead-lined bag; another is to separate your film from the rest of your luggage and

insist that it be physically inspected rather than passed through the rays.

TIME

All the Central American countries are six hours behind Greenwich mean time (GMT), except for Panama, which is five hours behind GMT.

ELECTRICITY

Electric current almost everywhere in Central America is 110 volts AC, 60 cycles, the same as in the USA, Canada and Mexico. Plugs are the same flat two-prong style as in these countries. It's rare to see a socket with three holes, so if your appliance has the third prong on it, you should bring an adapter.

There is, however, the occasional place in Honduras and Panama that has 220 volt current, as in Europe, Australia and New Zealand. If you use an electric appliance, always ask about the current first, just to be on the safe side. If you're using a delicate appliance such as a computer, be sure to use a surge protector, as current is often very uneven.

WEIGHTS & MEASURES

All of the Central American countries use some combination of metric and imperial measures. Conversion information is given inside the back cover of this book.

Lengths and distances are metric (meters, kilometers). The regional *vara* (0.825 meters or 33 inches) is also used in some places.

Land areas are often measured in hectares (a metric measurement), but local measurements are also used, including the *manzana* (0.7 hectare or 1.73 acres) in Honduras and the *cuadra* (about a quarter acre) in Guatemala.

Weights are often measured in pounds, but sometimes in kilograms. Gasoline is measured in US gallons.

LAUNDRY

Most guesthouses and less expensive hotels have a *lavadero* where you can wash your own clothes and lines where you can hang

them out to dry, all for no charge. Otherwise, laundries are plentiful and convenient: Drop off your laundry for wash, dry and fold, and pick it up after a few hours. Fees are usually very reasonable, around US$1 to US$4 for a week's laundry, though it varies from place to place – one laundry we saw was charging US$1 per pound.

HEALTH

Travel health depends on your predeparture preparations, your day-to-day health care while traveling and how you handle any medical problem or emergency that does develop. While the list of potential dangers can seem quite frightening, with a little luck, some basic precautions and adequate information, few travelers experience more than upset stomachs.

Travel Health Guides

A number of books on travel health are available. These include:

Staying Healthy in Asia, Africa & Latin America. Probably the best all-round guide to carry, as it's compact but very detailed and well organized.
Travelers' Health by Dr Richard Dawood. Comprehensive, easy to read, authoritative and also highly recommended, although it's rather large to lug around.
Where There Is No Doctor by David Werner. A very detailed guide intended for someone such as a Peace Corps worker who is going to work in an underdeveloped country.
Travel with Children by Maureen Wheeler (Lonely Planet Publications). Includes basic advice on travel health for younger children.

Predeparture Preparations

Health Insurance A travel insurance policy to cover theft, loss and medical problems is a wise idea. There are a wide variety of policies and your travel agent will have recommendations. The international student travel policies handled by STA Travel or other student travel organizations are usually a good value. Some policies offer lower and higher medical-expense options, but the higher coverage is chiefly for countries like the USA where medical costs are extremely high. Check the small print (below and on your insurance form):

• Some policies specifically exclude 'dangerous activities,' which can include scuba diving, motorcycling, even trekking. If such activities are on your agenda, you don't want that sort of policy.
• A locally acquired motorcycle license may not be valid under your policy.
• You may prefer a policy that pays doctors or hospitals direct rather than you having to pay on the spot and file a claim later. If you do have to make a claim later, make sure you keep all documentation. Some policies ask you to call back (reverse charges) to a center in your home country where an immediate assessment of your problem is made.
• Check if the policy covers ambulances or an emergency flight home. If you have to stretch out, you will need two seats and somebody has to pay for them! Some policies are designed specifically to cover the cost of emergency medical evacuation in the case of serious injury or illness.

Medical Kit A small, straightforward medical kit is a wise thing to carry. A kit should include:

• Aspirin, Panadol, ibuprofen or similar drugs, for pain or fever.
• Antihistamine (such as Benadryl), useful as a decongestant for colds and allergies, to ease the itch from insect bites or stings and to help prevent motion sickness.
• Antibiotics, useful if you're traveling well off the beaten track, but they must be prescribed and you should carry the prescription with you. See the paragraph below about using antibiotics.
• Kaolin preparation (Pepto-Bismol), Imodium or Lomotil, for stomach upsets.
• Rehydration mixture, for treatment of severe diarrhea. This is particularly important if you're traveling with children, but it is recommended for everyone.
• Antiseptic such as Betadine, which comes as impregnated swabs or ointment, and an antibiotic powder or similar 'dry' spray, for cuts and grazes.
• Calamine lotion, for bites or stings.
• Bandages, for minor injuries.
• Scissors, tweezers and a thermometer (note that mercury thermometers are prohibited by airlines).
• Insect repellent, sunscreen, suntan lotion, lip balm and water purification tablets.
• A couple of syringes, in case you need

injections in a country with medical hygiene problems. Ask your doctor for a note explaining why they have been prescribed.
• Motion sickness medication.
• Throat lozenges.
• First-aid booklet.

Antibiotics are quite specific to the infections they can treat. Ideally antibiotics should be administered only under medical supervision and should never be taken indiscriminately. Take only the recommended dose at the prescribed intervals and continue using the antibiotic for the prescribed period, even if the illness seems to be cured earlier. Stop immediately if there are any serious reactions, and don't use the antibiotic at all if you are unsure that you have the correct one.

Planning Ahead Make sure you're healthy before you start traveling. If you are embarking on a long trip, make sure your teeth are OK; there are lots of places where a visit to the dentist would be the last thing you'd want. The quality of dentistry varies – in Panama City it's as good as anywhere in the world. But in the country pulling a bad tooth would be about all they could do for you.

If you wear glasses, take a spare pair and your prescription. Losing your glasses can be a real problem, although in many places you can get new spectacles made up quickly, cheaply and competently.

If you require a particular medication, take an adequate supply, as it may not be available locally. Take the prescription or, better still, part of the packaging that shows the generic rather than the brand name (which may not be locally available), as it will make getting refills easier. It's a wise idea to have a legible prescription with you to show you legally use the medication – it's surprising how often over-the-counter drugs from one place are illegal without a prescription or even banned in another.

Immunizations Vaccinations provide protection against diseases you might be exposed to along the way.

It is important to understand the distinction between vaccines recommended for travel in certain areas and those required by law. Essentially, the number of vaccines subject to international health regulations has been dramatically reduced over the last 10 years. Currently yellow fever is the only vaccine subject to international health regulations. Vaccination as an entry requirement is usually only enforced when travelers are coming from an infected area.

On the other hand a number of vaccines are recommended for travel in certain areas. These may not be required by law but are recommended for your own personal protection.

All vaccinations should be recorded on an international health certificate, which is available from your physician or government health department.

Plan ahead for getting your vaccinations: Some of them require an initial shot followed by a booster, while some vaccinations should not be given together. It is recommended you seek medical advice at least six weeks prior to travel. Be prepared for some soreness and other side effects from immunizations – don't leave them for the day you are packing for the trip. Ask your doctor about your choice of vaccines and their various possible side effects.

Most travelers from developed countries will have been immunized against various diseases during childhood, but your doctor may still recommend booster shots against diphtheria-tetanus, measles or polio. The period of protection offered by vaccinations differs widely, and some are contraindicated if you are pregnant.

In some countries immunizations are available from airport or government health centers. Travel agents or airline offices will tell you where. Vaccinations include:

Cholera
Not required by law, but occasionally travelers face bureaucratic problems on some border crossings. Protection is poor and it lasts only six months. It is contraindicated in pregnancy.
Infectious hepatitis
The most common travel-acquired illness that can be prevented by vaccination. Protection can be acquired in two ways – either with the antibody gamma globulin or with a new vaccine called Havrix. (In the US this is called Hepatitis A vaccine.) Havrix is more expensive and must be taken at least three weeks before departure, but it is recommended because it provides up to 10 years of immunity. Gamma globulin lasts only six months and may interfere with the development of immunity to other diseases, so careful timing is important.
Tetanus & diphtheria
Boosters are necessary every 10 years and protection is highly recommended.
Typhoid
Available either as an injection or as oral capsules. Protection lasts from one to three years and is useful if you are traveling for long periods in rural, tropical areas.
Yellow fever
Protection lasts 10 years. You usually have to go to a special yellow-fever vaccination center. Vaccination is contraindicated during pregnancy, but if you must travel to a high-risk area, it is probably advisable.

Basic Rules
Care in what you eat and drink is the most important health rule. Stomach upsets are the most likely travel health problem (between 30% and 50% of travelers in a two-week stay experience this), but the majority of these upsets will be relatively minor. Don't become paranoid; after all, trying the local food is part of the travel experience.

Water The number one rule is *don't drink the water* and that includes ice. If you don't know for certain that the water is safe, always assume the worst. Reputable brands of bottled water or soft drinks are generally fine. Take care with fruit juice, particularly if water may have been added. Tea or coffee should be OK, since the water should have been boiled.

Water Purification The simplest way of purifying water is to boil it thoroughly. Vigorously boiling the water for five minutes should be satisfactory; however, at high altitudes water boils at a lower temperature, so germs are less likely to be killed.

Water filters may or may not remove all dangerous organisms, so read the manufacturers literature carefully before purchasing one. If you cannot boil water, chemical treatment may be more reliable than a filter. Chlorine tablets (Puritabs, Steritabs or other brands) will kill many but not all pathogens, including giardia and amoebic cysts. Iodine is very effective in purifying water and is available in tablet form (such as Potable Aqua), but follow the directions carefully and remember that too much iodine can be harmful.

If you can't find tablets, tincture of iodine (2%) or iodine crystals can be used. Four drops of tincture of iodine per liter (or quart) of clear water is the recommended dosage; the treated water should be left to stand for 20 to 30 minutes before drinking.

Food Salads and fruit should be washed with purified water or peeled when possible. Ice cream is usually OK if it is a reputable brand name, but beware of street vendors and of ice cream that has melted and been refrozen. Thoroughly cooked food is safest but not if it has been left to cool or if it has been reheated. Shellfish such as mussels, oysters and clams should be avoided, as should undercooked meat, particularly minced or ground beef. Steaming does not make bad shellfish safe for eating.

If a place looks clean and well run and if the vendor also looks clean and healthy, then the food is probably safe. In general, places that are packed with travelers or locals will be fine, while empty restaurants are questionable. The food in busy restaurants is cooked and eaten quite quickly and is probably not reheated.

Nutrition If your food is poor or limited in availability, if you're traveling hard and fast and therefore missing meals, or if you simply lose your appetite, you can soon start to lose weight and place your health at risk.

Make sure your diet is well balanced. Eggs, tofu, beans (especially soybeans),

lentils and nuts are all safe ways to get protein. Mixing legumes (beans, peanuts, peas or lentils) with grains (rice, corn, wheat) results in a complete protein that can be substituted for meat in the diet; throughout Central America the most common meal of beans and rice, or beans and corn tortillas, is an excellent way to get complete protein and avoid questionable meat. Other complete protein combinations include legumes with seeds (sunflower or sesame), and grains with milk products.

Fruits you can peel (bananas, oranges or mandarins, for example) are always safe and a good source of vitamins. Try to eat plenty of grains and bread. Remember that although food is generally safer when it is cooked well, overcooked food loses much of its nutritional value. If your diet isn't well balanced or if your food intake is insufficient, it's a good idea to take vitamin and iron pills on a long trip.

In hot climates make sure you drink enough – don't wait until you're thirsty to drink. Not needing to urinate or very dark yellow urine is a danger sign. Always carry a water bottle with you on long trips. Excessive sweating can lead to loss of salt and therefore muscle cramping. Salt tablets are not a good idea as a preventative, but in places where salt is not already used, adding some to your food can help.

Everyday Health Normal body temperature is 37°C (98.6°F); more than 2°C (4°F) higher indicates a 'high' fever. The normal adult pulse rate is 60 to 80 per minute (children 80 to 100, babies 100 to 140). You should know how to take a temperature and a pulse rate. As a general rule the pulse increases about 20 beats per minute for each degree Celsius rise in fever.

Respiration (breathing) rate is also an indicator of illness. Count the number of breaths per minute: Between 12 and 20 is normal for adults and older children (up to 30 for younger children, 40 for babies). People with a high fever or serious respiratory illness (like pneumonia) breathe more quickly than normal. More than 40 shallow breaths a minute usually means pneumonia.

Illnesses ranging from the common cold to cholera have been proven to be easily transmitted through physical contact. Try not to put your hand to your mouth and wash your hands before meals. Clean your teeth with purified water rather than straight from the tap. Avoid climatic extremes: Keep out of the sun when it's hot, dress warmly when it's cold. Avoid potential diseases by dressing sensibly. You can get worm infections by walking barefoot. Avoid insect bites by covering bare skin when insects are around, by screening windows or beds, and by using insect repellents. Seek local advice: If you're told the water is unsafe due to jellyfish, piranhas or schistosomiasis, don't go in. In situations where there is no information, discretion is the better choice.

Medical Problems & Treatment
Self-diagnosis and treatment can be risky, so wherever possible seek qualified help. Drug dosages given in this section are for emergency use only.

An embassy or consulate can usually recommend a good place to go for medical advice. So can the best hotels, although they often recommend doctors with the highest prices. (This is when that medical insurance really comes in useful!)

Climatic & Geographical Considerations
Sunburn In the tropics, in the desert or at high altitude, you can get sunburned surprisingly quickly, even through clouds. Use a sunscreen (SPF 15 minimum) and take extra care to cover areas that don't normally see sun – for example, your feet. Use a hat for extra protection, and also use zinc cream or some other barrier cream for your nose and lips. Calamine lotion is good for mild sunburn.

Prickly Heat Prickly heat is an itchy rash caused by excessive perspiration trapped under the skin. It usually strikes people who have just arrived in a hot climate and whose pores have not yet opened sufficiently to cope with greater sweating. Keeping cool

but bathing often, using a mild talcum powder or even resorting to air conditioning may help until you acclimatize.

Heat Exhaustion Dehydration or salt deficiency can cause heat exhaustion. Take time to acclimatize to high temperatures and make sure you get sufficient liquids. Wear loose clothing and a broad-brimmed hat. Do not do anything too physically demanding.

Salt deficiency is characterized by fatigue, lethargy, headaches, giddiness and muscle cramps, and in this case salt tablets may help. Vomiting or diarrhea can deplete your liquid and salt levels.

Heat Stroke This serious – sometimes fatal – condition can occur if the body's heat-regulating mechanism breaks down and the body temperature rises to dangerous levels. Long, continuous periods of exposure to high temperatures can leave you vulnerable to heat stroke. Avoid excessive alcohol or strenuous activity when you first arrive in a hot climate.

The symptoms of heat stroke are feeling unwell, not sweating very much or not at all and a high body temperature (39°C to 41°C, 102°F to 106°F). Skin becomes flushed and red where sweating has ceased. Severe, throbbing headaches and lack of coordination will also occur, and the sufferer may be confused or aggressive. Eventually the victim will become delirious or convulse. Hospitalization is essential, but meanwhile get the victim out of the sun, remove their clothing, cover them with a wet sheet or towel, and then fan continually.

Fungal Infections Hot weather fungal infections are most likely to occur on the scalp, between the toes or fingers (athlete's foot), in the groin (jock itch or crotch rot) and on the body (ringworm). You get ringworm (which is a fungal infection, not a worm) from infected animals or by walking on damp surfaces, like shower floors.

To prevent fungal infections, wear loose, comfortable clothes, avoid artificial fibers, wash frequently and dry carefully. If you do get an infection, wash the infected area daily with a disinfectant or medicated soap and water, and rinse and dry well. Apply an antifungal powder like the widely available Tinaderm or Tinactin. Try to expose the infected area to air or sunlight as much as possible. Wash all towels and underwear in hot water and change them often.

Cold Too much cold is just as dangerous as too much heat, as it may cause hypothermia. You're more likely to encounter too much heat than too much cold in Central America, but at higher elevations temperatures can be much chillier than you'd expect. While the lowlands are baking, nighttime temperatures at high altitudes can drop below freezing. The effects of low temperatures are exacerbated by wind, rain or dampness. If you are trekking at high altitudes or simply taking a long bus trip over mountains, particularly at night, be prepared.

Hypothermia occurs when the body loses heat faster than it can produce it and the core temperature of the body falls. It is surprisingly easy to progress from very cold to dangerously cold due to a combination of wind, wet clothing, fatigue and hunger, even if the air temperature is above freezing. It is best to dress in layers; silk, wool and some of the new artificial fibers are all good insulating materials. A hat is important, as a lot of heat is lost through the head. A strong, waterproof outer layer is essential because keeping dry is vital. Carry basic supplies, including food containing simple sugars, to generate heat quickly, and lots of drinks. A space blanket is something all travelers in cold environments should carry.

Symptoms of hypothermia are exhaustion, numb skin (particularly toes and fingers), shivering, slurred speech, irrational or violent behavior, lethargy, stumbling, dizzy spells, muscle cramps and violent bursts of energy. Irrationality may take the form of sufferers claiming they are warm and trying to take off their clothes.

To treat mild hypothermia, first get the person out of the wind and/or rain, remove their clothing if it's wet and replace it with dry, warm clothing. Give them hot liquids – no alcohol – and some high-calorie, easily digestible food. Do not rub victims; instead, allow them to slowly warm themselves. This should be enough to treat the early stages of hypothermia. The early recognition and treatment of mild hypothermia is the only way to prevent severe hypothermia, which is a critical condition.

Altitude Sickness Acute mountain sickness (AMS) occurs at high altitudes and can be fatal. The lack of oxygen at high altitudes affects most people to some extent.

A number of measures can be adopted to prevent acute mountain sickness:

• Ascend slowly – have frequent rest days, spending two to three nights at each rise of 1000 meters. When you first arrive at high altitude, try not to overexert yourself.
• Drink extra fluids. The mountain air is dry and cold, and moisture is lost as you breathe.
• Eat light, high-carbohydrate meals for more energy.
• Avoid alcohol as it may increase the risk of dehydration.
• Avoid sedatives.

Even with acclimatization you may still have trouble adjusting. Breathlessness, a dry cough (which may progress to the production of pink, frothy sputum), a severe headache, loss of appetite, nausea and sometimes vomiting are all danger signs. Increasing tiredness, confusion and lack of coordination and balance are real danger signs. Any of these symptoms individually, even just a persistent headache, can be a warning. Mild altitude sickness (*soroche*) will generally abate after a day or so, but if the symptoms persist or become worse, the only treatment is to descend – even 500 meters can help.

There is no hard and fast rule as to how high is too high: AMS has been fatal at altitudes of 3000 meters, although 3500 to 4500 meters is the usual range. (The highest point in Central America is Volcán Tajumulco in Guatemala, at 4220 meters

(13,840 feet); Chirripo in Costa Rica is also high, at 3819 meters (12,525 feet).) It is always wise to sleep at a lower altitude than the greatest height reached during the day.

The prescription drug Diamox (acetazolamide) has been shown to help with acclimatization if taken the day before the ascent and during the first few days at high altitude. There are some mild side effects, such as increased urination and tingling sensations in the extremities. It also makes fizzy drinks taste funny. If you are interested in trying Diamox, talk to your doctor.

Motion Sickness Eating lightly before and during a trip will reduce the chances of motion sickness. If you are prone to motion sickness, try to find a place that minimizes disturbance – near the wing on aircraft, close to midship on boats, near the center on buses. Fresh air usually helps; reading and cigarette smoke make it worse. Looking at the horizon or far into the distance, rather than at your immediate surroundings, is also helpful. Commercial motion-sickness preparations, which can cause drowsiness, have to be taken before the trip commences; when you're feeling sick, it's too late. Ginger is a natural preventative and is available in capsule form.

Jet Lag Jet lag occurs when a person travels by air across more than three time zones. Many of the functions of the human body are regulated by internal 24-hour cycles called circadian rhythms. When we travel long distances rapidly, our bodies take time to adjust to the 'new time' of our destination, and we may experience fatigue, disorientation, insomnia, anxiety, impaired concentration and loss of appetite. These effects will usually be gone within three days of arrival, but there are ways of minimizing the impact of jet lag:

• Rest for a couple of days prior to departure; try to avoid late nights and last-minute dashes for traveler's checks, passport and so on.
• Try to select flight schedules that minimize sleep deprivation; arriving late in the day means you can go to sleep soon after you arrive. For very long flights, try to organize a stopover.

• Make yourself comfortable by wearing loose-fitting clothes and perhaps bringing an eye mask and ear plugs to help you sleep.
• Avoid excessive eating and alcohol during the flight. Instead, drink plenty of noncarbonated, nonalcoholic drinks such as fruit juice or water.
• Avoid smoking – it causes greater fatigue.

Diseases of Poor Sanitation
Diarrhea A change of water, food or climate can all cause the runs; diarrhea caused by contaminated food or water is more serious. Despite all your precautions you may still have a mild bout of traveler's diarrhea, but a few rushed trips to the toilet with no other symptoms does not indicate a serious problem. Moderate diarrhea, involving half a dozen loose bowel movements in a day, is more of a nuisance.

Dehydration is the main danger with any case of diarrhea – children dehydrate particularly quickly. Fluid replacement remains the mainstay of management. Weak black tea with a little sugar, soda water, or soft drinks allowed to go flat and diluted 50% with water are all good. With severe diarrhea a rehydrating solution is necessary to replace minerals and salts. Commercially available ORS (oral rehydration salts) are very useful; add the contents of one packet to a liter of boiled or bottled water. In an emergency you can make up a solution of eight teaspoons of sugar to a liter of boiled water; drink that and eat salted cracker biscuits at the same time. You should stick to a bland diet as you recover.

Lomotil or Imodium can be used to bring relief from the symptoms, although they do not actually cure the problem. Only use these drugs if absolutely necessary – that is, if you *must* travel. For children Imodium is preferable, but under all circumstances fluid replacement is the most important thing to remember. Do not use these drugs if the person has a high fever or is severely dehydrated.

Antibiotics may be needed to treat diarrhea that lasts for more than five days, or that is severe, or for watery diarrhea accompanied by fever and lethargy or discharge of blood and mucus (gut-paralyzing drugs like Imodium or Lomotil should be avoided in this situation).

The recommended drugs (adults only) are either 400 mg norfloxacin or 500 mg ciprofloxacin twice daily for three days. Bismuth subsalicylate may be useful; two tablets for adults and one for children can be taken every hour up to eight times a day. (Pepto-Bismol, which comes in tablet or liquid form, is a common brand name.) Recommended drugs for children are co-trimoxazole (Bactrim, Septrin, Resprim) with dosage dependent on weight.

Giardiasis The parasite causing this intestinal disorder is present in contaminated water. The symptoms are stomach cramps, nausea, a bloated stomach, watery, foul-smelling diarrhea and frequent gas. Giardiasis can appear several weeks after you have been exposed to the parasite. The symptoms may disappear for a few days and then return; this can go on for several weeks. Tinidazole, known as Fasigyn, or metronidazole (Flagyl) are the recommended drugs for treatment. Either can be used in a single treatment dose. Antibiotics are of no use.

Dysentery This serious illness is caused by contaminated food or water and is characterized by severe diarrhea, often with blood or mucus in the stool. There are two kinds of dysentery. Bacillary dysentery is characterized by a high fever and rapid onset; headache, vomiting and stomach pains are also symptoms. It generally does not last longer than a week, but it is highly contagious.

Amoebic dysentery is often more gradual in the onset of symptoms, with abdominal pain and vomiting less likely; fever may not be present. It is not a self-limiting disease: It will persist until treated and can recur and cause long-term health problems.

A stool test is necessary to diagnose which kind of dysentery you have, so you should seek medical help quickly. In an emergency the recommended drugs for bacillary dysentery are 400 mg norfloxacin,

500 mg ciprofloxacin or 160/800 mg co-trimoxazole (Bactrim, Septrin, Resprim) twice daily for seven days. Co-trimoxazole is also the recommended drug for children.

For amoebic dysentery, the recommended adult dosage of metronidazole (Flagyl) is one 750- to 800-mg capsule three times daily for five days. Children ages eight to 12 years should have half the adult dose; the dosage for younger children is one-third the adult dose. An alternative to Flagyl is Fasigyn, taken as a two-gram daily dose for three days. Alcohol must be avoided during treatment and for 48 hours afterwards.

Cholera Cholera vaccination is not very effective. The bacteria responsible for this disease are waterborne, so attention to the rules of eating and drinking should protect the traveler.

The disease is characterized by a sudden onset of acute diarrhea with 'rice water' stools, vomiting, muscular cramps and extreme weakness. You need medical help – but first begin treatment for dehydration, which can be extreme, and if there is considerable delay in getting to a hospital, then begin taking 250 mg of tetracycline four times daily. It is not recommended for children ages eight years or under nor for pregnant women. An alternative drug is ampicillin (those allergic to penicillin should not take ampicillin). Remember that while antibiotics might kill the bacteria, it is a toxin produced by the bacteria that causes the massive fluid loss. Fluid replacement is by far the most important aspect of treatment.

Cholera has been on the increase in Central America in recent years. Several countries have started public health education projects to combat the spread of the disease. You may, for example, see signs or TV commercials advising people to boil their drinking water and to wash their hands frequently, especially before eating and after using the toilet.

Viral Gastroenteritis This is caused not by bacteria but, as the name suggests, by a virus. It is characterized by stomach cramps, diarrhea and sometimes by vomiting or a slight fever. All you can do is rest and drink lots of fluids.

Hepatitis Hepatitis A is a very common problem among travelers to areas with poor sanitation. With good water and adequate sewage disposal in most industrialized countries since the 1940s, very few young adults from those areas now have any natural immunity and must be protected. Protection is through the new vaccine Havrix (Hepatitis A vaccine) or the antibody gamma globulin.

The disease is spread by contaminated food or water. The symptoms are fever, chills, headache, fatigue, feelings of weakness, and aches and pains, followed by loss of appetite, nausea, vomiting, abdominal pain, dark urine, light-colored feces, jaundiced skin and the whites of the eyes possibly turning yellow. In some cases you may feel unwell, tired, have no appetite, experience aches and pains and be jaundiced. You should seek medical advice, but in general there is not much you can do apart from resting, drinking lots of fluids, eating lightly and avoiding fatty foods. People who have had hepatitis must forgo alcohol for six months after the illness, as hepatitis attacks the liver and it needs that amount of time to recover.

Hepatitis B, which used to be called serum hepatitis, is spread through contact with infected blood, blood products or bodily fluids – especially through sexual contact, unsterilized needles and blood transfusions. Other risk situations include having a shave or tattoo in a local shop, or having your ears pierced. The symptoms of type B are much the same as type A except that they are more severe and may lead to irreparable liver damage or even liver cancer.

Although there is no treatment for hepatitis B, an effective prophylactic vaccine is readily available in most countries. The immunization schedule requires two injections at least a month apart followed by a third dose five months after the second. Persons who should receive a hepatitis B vaccination include anyone who anticipates contact with blood or other bodily secretions, either as a health care worker or through sexual contact with the local population. Those who intend to stay in the country for a long period of time should definitely be immunized.

Hepatitis non-A non-B is a blanket term formerly used for several different strains of hepatitis, which have now been separately identified. Hepatitis C is similar to B but is less common. Hepatitis D (the 'delta particle') is also similar to B and always occurs in concert with it; its occurrence is currently limited to IV drug users. Hepatitis E, however, is similar to A and is spread in the same manner (by water or food contamination).

Tests are available for these strains but are very expensive. Travelers shouldn't be too paranoid about this apparent proliferation of hepatitis strains; they are fairly rare (so far) and following the same precautions as for A and B should be all that's necessary to avoid them.

Typhoid Typhoid fever is another gut infection that travels the fecal-oral route – contaminated water and food are responsible. Vaccination against typhoid is not totally effective, and it is one of the most dangerous infections, so medical help must be sought.

In its early stages typhoid resembles many other illnesses: Sufferers may feel like they have a bad cold or the initial stages of a flu, as early symptoms are a headache, a sore throat and a fever that rises a little each day until it is around 40°C or more. The victim's pulse is often slow relative to the degree of fever present and gets slower as the fever rises – unlike a normal fever where the pulse increases. There may also be vomiting, diarrhea or constipation.

In the second week the high fever and slow pulse continue and a few pink spots may appear on the body; trembling, delirium, weakness, weight loss and dehydration are other symptoms. If there are no further complications, the fever and other symptoms will slowly diminish during the third week. Still, you must get medical help since pneumonia (acute infection of the lungs) or peritonitis (perforated bowel) are common complications, and typhoid is very infectious. The fever should be treated by keeping the victim cool and dehydration should also be watched for.

The drug of choice is ciprofloxacin at a dose of 1 gram daily for 14 days. It is quite expensive and may not be available. The alternative, chloramphenicol, has been the mainstay of treatment for many years. In many countries it is still the recommended antibiotic, but there are fewer side affects with ampicillin. The adult dosage is two 250-mg capsules, four times a day. Children ages eight to 12 years should have half the adult dose; younger children should have one-third the adult dose. People who are allergic to penicillin should not take ampicillin.

Worms These parasites are most common in rural, tropical areas, so a stool test when you return home is not a bad idea. They can be present on unwashed vegetables or in undercooked meat, and you can pick them up through your skin by walking in bare feet. Infestations may not show up for some time, and although they are generally not serious, if left untreated they can cause severe health problems. A stool test is necessary to pinpoint the problem and medication is often available over the counter.

Diseases Spread by Animals & People
Tetanus This is a potentially fatal disease. It is difficult to treat but is preventable with immunization. Tetanus occurs when a wound becomes infected by a germ that lives in the feces of animals or people, so clean all cuts, punctures or animal bites. Tetanus is also known as lockjaw, and the first symptom may be discomfort in swallowing or stiffening of the jaw and neck; this is followed by painful convulsions of the jaw and whole body.

Rabies Rabies is caused by a bite or scratch by an infected animal. Dogs are noted carriers, as are monkeys and cats. Any bite, scratch or even lick should be cleaned immediately and thoroughly. Scrub with soap and running water, and then clean with an alcohol solution. If there is any possibility that the animal is infected, medical help should be sought immediately. Rabies takes at least five days and sometimes several weeks to develop, but once it develops it is always fatal. A vaccination after the bite occurs but before rabies appears generally results in complete recovery. Even if the animal is not rabid, all bites should be treated seriously as they can become infected or can result in tetanus. A rabies vaccination is now available and should be considered if you are in a high-risk category – particularly if you intend to explore caves (bat bites can be dangerous) or work with animals.

Meningococcal Meningitis This rare but very serious disease attacks the brain and can be fatal. A scattered, blotchy rash, fever, severe headache, sensitivity to light and neck stiffness that prevents forward bending of the head are the first symptoms. Death can occur within a few hours, so immediate treatment is important.

Treatment is large doses of penicillin given intravenously, or, if that is not possible, intramuscularly (in the buttocks). Vaccination offers good protection for over a year, but you should also check for reports of current epidemics.

Tuberculosis Although TB is widespread in many developing countries, it is not a serious risk to travelers. Young children are more susceptible than adults, and vaccination is a sensible precaution for children under 12 traveling in endemic areas. TB is commonly spread by coughing or by unpasteurized dairy products from infected cows.

Schistosomiasis Also known as bilharzia, this disease is carried in slow-moving water (especially behind dams) by minute worms. The worms attach themselves to your intestines or bladder, and then produce large numbers of eggs. The worm enters through the skin, and the first symptom may be a tingling and sometimes a light rash around the area where it entered. Weeks later, when the worm is busy producing eggs, a high fever may develop. A general ill feeling may be the first symptom; once the disease is established abdominal pain and blood in the urine are other signs.

Don't swim in fresh water where bilharzia is present. Even deep water can be infected. If you do get wet, towel off quickly as the worms supposedly burrow into the skin as the water evaporates. Dry your clothes as well. Seek medical attention if you have been exposed to the disease and tell the doctor your suspicions, as schistosomiasis in the early stages can be confused with malaria or typhoid.

If you cannot get medical help immediately, praziquantel (Biltricide) is the recommended treatment. The recommended dosage is 40 mg/kg, and should be taken in divided doses over one day. Niridazole is an alternative drug.

Diphtheria Diphtheria can be a skin infection or a more dangerous throat infection. It is spread by contaminated dust contacting the skin or by the inhalation of infected cough or sneeze vapor. Frequent washing and keeping the skin dry will help prevent skin infection. A vaccination is available to prevent the throat infection.

Sexually Transmitted Diseases STDs are spread through sexual contact with an infected partner. Abstinence is the only 100%-effective preventative; using condoms is also effective. Gonorrhea and syphilis are common STDs; sores, blisters or rashes around the genitals; discharges; or pain when urinating are common symptoms. Symptoms may be less marked or not observed at all in women. Syphilis symptoms eventually disappear completely, but the disease continues and can cause severe problems in later years. The treatment of gonorrhea and syphilis is by antibiotics. There is no cure for herpes

(which causes blisters but is not normally very dangerous) or for AIDS.

HIV/AIDS HIV (human immunodeficiency virus) may develop into AIDS (acquired immune deficiency syndrome). Any exposure to blood, blood products or bodily fluids may put an individual at risk. AIDS (SIDA is its Spanish acronym) is common in parts of Central America and is becoming more widespread, so it's very important to protect yourself.

In Central America transmission is predominantly through heterosexual sexual activity. This is quite different from industrialized countries where transmission is mostly through sexual contact with homosexual or bisexual males, or via contaminated needles shared by IV drug users. Apart from abstinence, the most effective preventative is to practice safe sex using condoms. It is impossible to detect the HIV-positive status of an otherwise healthy-looking person without a blood test.

HIV can also be spread through infected blood transfusions; if you need a blood transfusion, go to the best clinic you can find – these normally will screen blood for transfusions. HIV can also be spread by dirty needles – vaccinations, acupuncture, tattooing and ear or nose piercing can potentially be as dangerous as intravenous drug use if the equipment is not clean. If you do need an injection, ask to see the syringe unwrapped in front of you, or better still, take a needle and syringe pack with you overseas – it is a cheap insurance package against infection with HIV. Or you can buy a new syringe from a local pharmacy and ask the doctor to use it. Syringes can be effectively sterilized with chlorine bleach, but unless you do this yourself you may not be able to ascertain whether it has been done or done properly.

Fear of HIV should never preclude treatment for serious medical conditions. The risk of infection remains very small.

Insect-Borne Diseases
Malaria This serious disease is spread by mosquito bites. If you are traveling in

endemic areas, it is extremely important to take malarial prophylactics. All of Central America is considered a risk area, except for the high-altitude central highlands of Guatemala and Costa Rica. The disease has been stamped out in Panama City, but in general if you're traveling in Central America, it's a good idea to get onto an antimalarial regimen and stay on it.

Symptoms include headaches, fever, chills and sweating, any of which may subside and recur. These symptoms can show up as early as eight days after initial exposure to the disease or as late as several months or even years after leaving the malarial area. Keep this in mind if you should become ill later; be sure to inform your physician that you may have been exposed to malaria, especially once you are back in a part of the world where malaria doesn't exist. Delays in correct diagnosis can be dangerous to your health or even fatal. Without treatment, malaria can develop more serious, potentially fatal effects.

Also note that it is possible to contract malaria *even if you have correctly followed an antimalarial regimen*. Your chances of catching malaria will be greatly reduced but that doesn't mean it's impossible.

Antimalarial drugs do not prevent you from being infected but kill the parasites during a stage in their development. Chloroquine is the usual malarial prophylactic; you take a tablet once a week for two weeks before arriving in an infected area, continue taking them the whole time you're there and then for six weeks after you leave.

There are several types of malaria. In recent years the malaria parasite has become increasingly resistant to commonly used antimalarials like chloroquine, maloprim and proguanil. Newer drugs such as mefloquine (Lariam) and doxycycline (Vibramycin, Doryx) are often recommended for travelers to areas with chloroquine- and multidrug-resistant strains.

In most parts of Central America, chloroquine is considered the antimalarial of choice. Chloroquine is quite safe for general use; side effects are minimal and it can be taken by pregnant women. However, chloroquine-resistant strains are present in eastern Panama (east of the Canal Zone, including the San Blas and Darién regions) and in the Bocas del Toro region of western Panama. Chloroquine resistance can change over time: The first edition of this guide noted that chloroquine resistance had developed only in eastern Panama, but by the third edition, it had spread into Bocas del Toro. Be sure to check for current advice on what types of malaria are present in which parts of Central America before you begin your trip.

Seek expert advice, as there are many factors to consider when deciding on the type of antimalarial medication, including the area to be visited, the risk of exposure to malaria-carrying mosquitoes, your current medical condition, and your age and pregnancy status. It is also important to discuss the side-effect profile of the medication, so you can weigh the level of risk against the benefits. It is also very important to be sure of the correct dosage of the medication prescribed to you. Some people have inadvertently taken weekly medication (chloroquine) on a daily basis, with disastrous effects. It is often advisable to pack the dosages required for treatment, especially if your trip is through a high-risk area that would isolate you from medical care.

To minimize the risk of infection, remember these points:

• The mosquitoes that transmit malaria bite from dusk to dawn, so during this period wear light-colored clothing; wear long pants and long-sleeved shirts; use mosquito repellents containing deet on exposed areas; avoid highly scented perfumes or aftershave, which may attract mosquitoes; be sure windows are screened and/or use a mosquito net – it may be worth carrying your own. Burning mosquito coils and spraying with a pyrethrum-based insect spray are also protective measures. Mosquitoes can bite you right through thin fabrics or on any small part of your skin not covered by repellent.
• While no antimalarial is 100% effective, taking the most appropriate drug significantly reduces the risk of contracting the disease.

• No one should ever die from malaria. It can be diagnosed by a simple blood test. Contrary to popular belief, once a traveler contracts malaria, he or she does not have it for life. Malaria is curable, as long as the traveler seeks medical help when symptoms occur.

The most effective insect repellent is called deet (diethyl toluamide); it is an ingredient in many commercially available insect repellents. Buy your repellent before you arrive in the risk area, and look for one with at least a 28% concentration of deet. Some repellents contain up to a 95% concentration; these are greasier on the skin, may smell unpleasant, and have been associated with toxic side effects, but you might consider them if you're heading to a heavily infested area. Deet breaks down plastic and synthetic fabrics, so be careful what you touch after using it. It poses no danger to natural fiber fabrics.

If you can't get hold of insect repellent, kerosene mixed with coconut or vegetable oil is also effective, though smelly.

Dengue Fever Dengue fever is on the rise in Central America. There is no prophylactic available for this mosquito-spread disease; the main preventative measure is to avoid mosquito bites. A sudden onset of fever, headaches and severe joint and muscle pains are the first signs before a rash starts on the trunk of the body and spreads to the limbs and face. After a few days, the fever subsides and recovery begins. Serious complications are not common, but full recovery can take up to a month or more.

Yellow Fever This is a viral disease transmitted to humans by mosquitoes; the initial symptoms are fever, headache, abdominal pain and vomiting. There may appear to be a brief recovery before the disease progresses to more severe complications, including liver failure. There is no medical treatment apart from keeping the fever down and avoiding dehydration, but yellow fever vaccination gives good protection for 10 years.

Chagas' Disease This parasitic disease is transmitted by an insect called a *vinchuca* (a reduviid bug or an assassin bug, in English), which hides in crevices and palm fronds and often takes up residence in the thatched roofs of huts. The vinchuca is a smooth, oval-shaped, brownish-colored insect with a long, narrow cone-shaped head and two antennae curving under the head. The insect comes out to feed at night, sucking a victim's blood for up to 20 minutes and usually defecating at the same time. The disease is caused by a protozoan, *Trypanosoma cruzi*, which is present in the feces of the infected insect and enters through the bite wound. The trypanosomes invade internal organs such as the brain, heart, liver and spleen. A hard, violet-colored swelling appears at the site of the bite in about a week.

Usually the body overcomes the disease unaided, but it is important to seek immediate medical attention if you suspect you are infected. If it progresses, it can take one of two forms. Symptoms of the acute form of Chagas' disease are fever, vomiting and shortness of breath, proceeding to convulsions and stiffness of the neck; you could die within three months of being bitten. In the slower, chronic form of the disease, symptoms are acute at first but then subside. The trypanosomes continue to live in your body, however, weakening your organs and finally destroying them over a period of years.

Chagas' disease can be treated in its early stages, but it is best to avoid the insect in the first place. The vinchuca lives only at elevations up to 1500 meters in Central America (up to 3600 meters in South America). Beware of sleeping in thatch-roofed huts or old buildings, and of camping under palm trees. Sleep under a mosquito net, use insecticides and insect repellents, and check for hidden insects, especially in bedding. If you do get a suspicious bite, especially on your face, seek medical attention. The disease is relatively uncommon and predominantly affects children under two years of age.

However, Chagas' disease is more prevalent in some places than others. In 1997, Honduran health officials estimated that 65,000 people in that country were in the late stages of the disease and would die from it during the next few years. They estimated that around 300,000 out of Honduras' 5.8 million people, or over 5% of the population, were infected with this disease.

Typhus Typhus is spread by ticks, mites or lice. It begins as a bad cold, followed by a fever, chills, headache, muscle pains and a body rash. There is often a large, painful sore at the site of the bite, and nearby lymph nodes are swollen and painful.

Tick typhus is spread by ticks. Seek local advice on areas where ticks pose a danger, and always check your skin carefully for ticks after walking in a high-risk area such as a tropical forest. A strong insect repellent can help, and serious walkers in tick areas should consider having their boots and trousers impregnated with benzyl benzoate and dibutylphthalate.

Cuts, Bites & Stings
Cuts & Scratches Skin punctures can easily become infected in hot climates and may heal slowly. Treat any cut with an antiseptic such as Betadine. When possible, avoid bandages and Band-Aids, which can keep wounds wet.

Bites & Stings Bee and wasp stings are usually painful rather than dangerous. Calamine lotion gives relief, and ice packs reduce the pain and swelling. There are some spiders with dangerous bites, but these are not usually fatal and antivenins are usually available. Scorpion stings are notoriously painful but are very rarely fatal. Scorpions, spiders, ants and other biting creatures often shelter in shoes or clothing. Develop the habit of shaking out your clothing before putting it on, especially in the lowlands. Check your bedding before going to sleep. Don't walk barefoot, and when reaching to a shelf or branch, look before you place your hands.

Snakes To minimize your chances of being bitten, always wear boots, socks and long trousers when walking through undergrowth where snakes may be present. Don't put your hands into holes and crevices, and be careful when collecting firewood.

Central America has dozens of species of snakes, but most are not poisonous. The most poisonous snake of all is the tiny coral snake, which is actually a land snake. It is brightly colored with bands of red, yellow and black. Coral snakes are nocturnal and not aggressive. The large fer-de-lance is much more of a danger. Called *barba amarilla* (yellow chin) in Central America, it's recognizable by its lance-shaped head and the diamond markings on its back. It is often encountered in undergrowth and cane fields, and sometimes comes out at night to lie on warm roads and trails. Its venom is extremely toxic. Rattlesnakes are also found in Central America.

Snake bites do not cause instantaneous death and antivenins are usually available. If bitten, keep calm and still, wrap the bitten limb tightly, as you would for a sprained ankle, and then attach a splint to immobilize it. Seek medical help, if possible with the dead snake for identification. Don't attempt to catch the snake if there is even a remote possibility of being bitten again. Tourniquets and sucking out the poison are now widely discredited as treatments for snake bites.

Jellyfish Local advice is the best way of avoiding contact with these sea creatures, which have stinging tentacles. The stings from most jellyfish are rather painful but not lethal. Dousing skin in vinegar will get rid of the sting and deactivate any stingers that have not 'fired'; this is also useful if you touch fire coral, which causes a stinging skin reaction. Calamine lotion, antihistamines and analgesics may reduce the reaction and relieve the pain.

Bedbugs & Lice Bedbugs live in various places but particularly in dirty mattresses and bedding. Spots of blood on bedclothes or on the wall around the bed are good cause for finding another hotel. Bedbugs leave itchy bites in neat rows. Calamine lotion may help.

All lice cause itching and discomfort. They make themselves at home in your hair (head lice), your clothing (body lice) or in your pubic hair (crabs). You catch lice through direct contact with infected people or by sharing combs, clothing and the like, or from bedding where they are present. Medicated powder or shampoo treatment will kill the lice; wash infected clothing in very hot water.

Leeches & Ticks Leeches may be present in damp rain-forest conditions; they attach themselves to your skin to suck your blood. Trekkers often get them on their legs or in their boots. Salt or a lighted cigarette end will make them fall off. Do not pull them off because the bite is then more likely to become infected. An insect repellent may keep them away.

Petroleum jelly, alcohol or oil will persuade a tick to let go. You should always check your body if you have been walking through a tick-infested area, as they can spread typhus (see Typhus section above).

Women's Health
Gynecological Problems Poor diet, lowered resistance due to the use of antibiotics for stomach upsets and even contraceptive pills can lead to vaginal infections when traveling in hot climates. Wearing skirts or loose-fitting trousers and cotton underwear helps to prevent infections.

Yeast infections, characterized by a rash, itch and discharge, can be treated with a vinegar or lemon-juice douche, or with yogurt. Nystatin suppositories are the usual medical prescription.

Trichomoniasis is a more serious infection; symptoms are a discharge and a burning sensation when urinating. Male sexual partners must also be treated, and if a vinegar-and-water douche is not effective, medical attention should be sought. Metronidazole (Flagyl) is the prescribed drug.

Pregnancy Women travelers often find that their periods become irregular or even cease while they're on the road. Remember that a missed period in these circumstances doesn't necessarily indicate pregnancy. A simple urine test takes a few minutes and will determine whether you are pregnant or not; you can probably get these at hospitals in Central America's major cities.

Most miscarriages occur during the first three months of pregnancy, so this is the most risky time to travel as far as your own health is concerned. Miscarriage is not uncommon and can occasionally lead to severe bleeding. The last three months should also be spent within reasonable distance of good medical care. A baby born as early as 24 weeks stands a chance of survival but only in a good modern hospital. Pregnant women should avoid all unnecessary medication, but vaccinations and malarial prophylactics should still be taken where possible. Take additional care to prevent illness and pay particular attention to diet and nutrition. Alcohol and nicotine, for example, should be avoided.

TOILETS

Toilets are the same in Central America as most readers probably have at home – flush, sit-down varieties. However, in Central America you should always deposit used toilet paper into the wastebasket, not into the toilet bowl. There's usually a wastebasket provided for this purpose; if not, most people just toss the paper onto the floor beside the toilet, rather than into the toilet bowl (and risk clogging up the toilet). Occasionally you will see a sign asking you to deposit the paper into the toilet bowl; this is the only time it's advisable to do so.

Carry toilet paper with you when traveling – it's usually not provided in public places. Occasionally, a public toilet will have an attendant offering paper for a small tip.

Most towns and cities have public toilets, which you can use for a few *centavos*. Alternatively you can duck into a fancy hotel, a fast-food restaurant or a gas station.

USEFUL ORGANIZATIONS
South American Explorers Club
This club has long been a favorite of travelers to South America, and due to repeated requests from members it has now branched out to cover all of Latin America. The club is probably the most comprehensive source of information for travelers to Latin America. It sells maps, books and guidebooks and publishes a free catalog (members get a substantial discount). Members have submitted thousands of practical reports on trips they've made. As a member, you can request information on virtually anything having to do with traveling in Latin America, and, for a small copying fee, staff will send you copies of members' trip reports as well as articles culled from magazines, books and other sources.

The information available through the club covers a wide range of interests, not just 'exploring' in the sense of tramping through tropical jungles (though it has plenty on that). Other topics include scientific research, archaeology, working on digs, scuba diving, child adoption, retiring in Costa Rica, volunteer programs, driving through Latin America, bicycling, discount airfares and much more. It has information on Honduras' 'lost city' of Ciudad Blanca, and a whole file on the Darién Gap, including entries on bicycling or motorcycling through it.

Other services include expedition planning, connecting with exploring or traveling partners, linking members for scientific and other purposes and an informative quarterly magazine, the *South American Explorer*. Their offices in Lima (Peru) and Quito (Ecuador) offer other services, such as luggage storage, mail holding and email connections for members.

Annual membership costs US$40 a year for an individual or US$60 for a couple – or ask about the special 'afterlife membership'! You can become a member or get more information about this nonprofit organization by contacting the US office (☎ (607) 277-0488, fax (607) 277-6122, net; 126 Indian Creek Rd, Ithaca, NY 14850). The European agent is Bradt Publications (☎ /fax (1494) 873 478; 41 Nortoft Rd, Chalfont St Peter, Bucks, SL9 0LA, UK).

Latin American Bureau
Based in London, LAB is a nonprofit organization engaged in research and publishing on Latin America and the Caribbean. It is a good source of information and has extensive library facilities (access by arrangement). Many useful publications are available by mail order; for the book catalog write or call the Latin America Bureau (☎ (0171) 278 2829, fax (0171) 278-0165, net; 1 Amwell St, London EC1R 1UL, UK).

Tourist Offices
There is a tourist office in the capital city of each country; some countries have them in outlying towns as well. They can be good sources of information for travelers.

Student Organizations
There are student travel agencies in the capital cities of Costa Rica and Panama. If you have the International Student Identity Card (ISIC), you can get discounted airfares, tours and other travel services, and find out about other student bargains. Discount fares are only offered on particular flights.

American Express
American Express has offices in all of Central America's capital cities; there's an office in San Pedro Sula (Honduras) as well. You can buy American Express traveler's checks, get cash advances on your card if you have one, get refunds on lost or stolen checks or have mail sent to you at all of these offices.

Hostelling International
HI membership is not particularly useful in Central America: There are very few hostels, and they are no cheaper than other types of budget accommodations.

WOMEN TRAVELERS
Three of the authors of this book are women, and all of us had a great time traveling in

Central America. No harm came to us, and we encountered no particular dangers. This isn't a difficult part of the world for women to travel in. Having some understanding of what is going on around you and behaving with a good dose of common sense will help to smooth your way and insure your safety.

Attitudes about Women

The 'Madonna versus whore' mentality, which classifies every woman as 'good' or 'bad,' and therefore worthy of respect or not, is a well-known principle of *machismo* – the exaggerated masculine pride of the Latin American male. Evidence of this widespread mentality is obvious in many everyday situations in Latin America. While the 'bad' woman is fair game for any type of treatment, the 'good' woman is protected and treated with much more respect. You may be considered a 'loose woman,' or fair game, simply because you are foreign. Anything you can do with your personal appearance and demeanor to dispel that impression can only help you.

Women traveling alone can expect plenty of attempts by men to chat them up. It's up to you whether you wish engage in conversations – there's no need to be intimidated. You can have some very interesting conversations with locals. Just use your common sense.

More irritating can be catcalls, hisses and the like. It's a fact of life that in some parts of Latin America, this is what men do when they see a female. Do what the local women do – ignore it completely.

What to Wear

Women travelers will get on much better if they dress conservatively. A good general rule is to watch how the local women dress and behave, and follow their example. In places where there's a lot of international tourism, standards of dress tend to be more relaxed.

Technicalities of what type of dress is appropriate vary depending where you are. Wearing modest shorts is fine at the beach and in most beachside communities, but they convey a sleazy impression and bring you a lot of unwanted attention in cities or up in the mountains, where women virtually never wear them. Long pants are OK everywhere but can be hot unless you're in the mountains. Many women travelers find that loose cotton skirts with hemlines below the knee and a T-shirt or similar modest blouse are the most convenient traveling clothes.

Wherever you are and whatever else you're wearing, always wear a bra, whether or not it's your usual custom. Not doing so in this part of the world is regarded as provocative.

When swimming, many local women wear T-shirts over their swimsuits or shorts. You might want to do the same to avoid stares.

Safety Precautions

While there's no need to be paranoid, you must be aware that the possibility of rape, mugging and so on does exist. It happens more in some places than others. Use your normal traveler's caution – avoid walking alone in isolated places or through city streets late at night, avoid hitchhiking and don't camp alone. Don't wear even cheap imitation jewelry – you could be mugged for it.

Central America has a high rate of AIDS. When it's possible, be very certain that you don't do anything that could expose yourself to the virus. See the Health section for further advice on this, and the Dangers & Annoyances section for more tips on safety.

GAY & LESBIAN TRAVELERS

No Central American country has laws criminalizing homosexual behavior between consenting adults except for Nicaragua. However, this does not prevent official and police harassment, particularly in Guatemala. Central America as a whole is not only 'in the closet,' it's somewhere behind the closet. There are probably as many gays and lesbians here as anywhere, but homosexuality is not openly discussed, and there's little public support for gay rights.

Several of the larger cities (for instance, San José and Tegucigalpa) have a gay bar that acts as a meeting place and community center for local gays and lesbians. These are mentioned in the appropriate city sections.

AIDS has had devastating consequences for gays here, as everywhere. See the Health section for more on AIDS.

Organizations

Gay and lesbian travelers may want to contact the International Gay Travelers Association (☎ (800) 448-8550, Box 4974, Key West, FL 33041) to locate a travel agent familiar with gay and gay-friendly tours and lodgings.

TRAVEL WITH CHILDREN

Children and family are the primary joys of most people's lives in Central America, and children are generally adored. Traveling with children presents no special problems; in fact, you may find quite the opposite – doors may fly open for you, and your children will be warmly welcomed almost everywhere.

Of course there are the usual things to contend with when traveling with children – keeping them interested and amused, taking care of their health and so on.

Lonely Planet's book *Travel with Children* is a good resource for those traveling with small children. It's written by Maureen Wheeler, cofounder of Lonely Planet, who has plenty of experience to draw upon!

DANGERS & ANNOYANCES
Political Turmoil

Unless you have been to Central America and seen what it's like, there is a tendency to overestimate the amount of danger that the average traveler will encounter from political conflicts. This is especially true if you are coming from the USA, where news stories of unstable politics, CIA activities, guerrilla warfare and economic

catastrophes have been in the media for many years.

The good news is that peace has been emerging all over Central America in recent years. The lengthy civil wars in El Salvador and Nicaragua are now over, and the signing of the peace accords in Guatemala in December 1996 brought an end to 36 years of armed conflict there. Though political conflict could break out again, as of this writing all of the conflicts that grabbed the news for so many years are now over.

Still, you might want to check for the latest information before traveling.

The Citizens Emergency Center of the US State Department offers a 24-hour telephone recording (☎ (202) 647-5225) with travel advisories on current conditions in various countries. The advisories usually pertain to civil unrest, natural disasters or outbreaks of serious diseases, and they also offer current information on visa requirements for US citizens. Call from a touch-tone phone, since the recording gives you a number of choices. It also has a computer bulletin board (☎ (202) 647-9225), automated fax system (☎ (202) 647-3000) and a Web site (see Online Resources appendix).

In Britain, telephone the Foreign Office Consular Advice Unit (☎ (071) 270 4129), Monday to Friday from 9:30 am to 4 pm.

You can also check with your embassy or consulate. A short-wave radio is useful for keeping abreast of current affairs.

Theft

The risk of theft is greater than danger from political turmoil. It's much more likely in some places than others, major cities being the worst. The more poverty and economic problems an area has, the more you have to watch out. It's a good idea to develop the habit of being alert and doing things in such a way that you don't make yourself an easy target, no matter where you are, as thieves look for an easy mark. To some degree you are a target just because you're a foreigner, but you certainly don't have to make it easy for them.

This does not mean you should be paranoid; it's quite possible to travel for months in Central America and have no problem at all. We're just suggesting you should develop habitual, healthy awareness. You're much more likely to get ripped off if you're not paying attention – sometimes you're less likely to get robbed at the beginning of your journey when you're most alert than after you've been traveling a while, feel more secure and fail to take precautions.

Most theft in Central America is not openly confrontational robbery but rather sneak thievery of one kind or another. This sort of theft occurs most often in busy public places such as crowded buses, bus stations, markets and fiestas. Frequently the thieves work in pairs or groups to distract your attention. A 'fight' can break out, or someone can drop something in front of you, bump into you or spill something on you. Before you realize what has happened, your bag has been slashed or your pocket picked. Pay attention.

Bag slashing is one of the most common forms of theft. They do it with a razor blade, and you don't feel a thing. They can also slit your pocket, which you won't feel either. Razor thieves are especially common on crowded buses, especially urban buses where lots of people are standing pushed together.

The best protection from this is to keep your bag where you can see it. In capital cities, a local would never wear a pack on their back while riding a bus or walking in the market or on city streets. Wear your pack on your chest instead. If you have a shoulder bag, make sure it is in front of you and the strap is across your body, not just hanging on one shoulder. Even then, the strap can be slashed, enabling the thief to make off with your whole bag.

A larger pack can also be slashed or snatched while you are wearing it or when it is left unguarded, such as on a bus while you're sleeping. If you always keep moving while wearing your pack, it's harder for thieves to slash without you knowing it. Be aware of how you hold a bag when you carry one, and be especially conscious of putting things down in busy places. If you put your bag down by your feet in a bus station or market while you fumble for change, it can disappear amazingly quickly. At least keep your foot on it!

If you don't have much to carry, you may not need to have a bag at all; just use an inside pocket. If you do have to carry a bag, it's better to have one that looks like a common plastic shopping bag, not a cloth bag that looks like it contains valuables.

Snatchers are also attracted to cameras, watches, sunglasses and jewelry. It's obviously best not to go around in poor countries wearing jewels, but even a cheap brass chain can attract a thief who thinks that, if a foreigner is wearing it, it just might be gold. Locals in many parts of Central America will warn you against wearing any type of jewelry, but you can wear something obviously cheap, made of wood, thread or plastic. A US$2 plastic wristwatch (common in Central America) will usually keep time just as well as an expensive one, and not attract a problem.

Thieves can also spirit your pack off a long-distance bus. Always be sure you know where your pack is; it's best to keep it where you can see it. Some travelers carry a small padlock to lock their packs to a luggage rack, especially on long journeys where they might want to sleep. This is a good idea, but also remember the razor-blade artists.

Finally, picking pockets is one of the most common forms of theft, occurring in all the places already mentioned. The city bus routes of Managua are so famous for pickpockets that it's practically a cliché. Central America has some real professionals, but you can protect yourself by knowing what you might encounter and taking appropriate precautions.

There are many ways to protect yourself, and all of them can become good traveling habits that you do automatically. Most important is how you carry things. Obviously you shouldn't walk around with your wallet hanging out of your back pocket. Fanny packs – pouches worn on a belt around the waist and on the outside of the clothing – are another obvious target.

Everyone has a preferred way to carry money. Some carry it in a money belt under their clothing, worn with the money in front, behind, under their jeans, or wherever. Some keep it in a strong leather pouch on their belts, or in a leather belt with a secret zippered compartment. A pouch worn round the neck is pretty obvious and not so safe; if you do this, be sure to sew a guitar string through the strap so it can't be slashed. You can tuck money under your hat, into your socks, into a bra or into your underwear, in a spot where a thief won't find it, at least not without your noticing. Some travelers sew extra pockets inside their clothes, sew money into the hem or lining of a garment, or make a pocket that they can safety-pin into the clothes they're wearing. Some keep it in a front pants pocket, with a handkerchief on top just in case, so the thief gets the handkerchief instead of the money.

Don't carry all your money with you in the same spot; have separate places for your long-term traveling money and your everyday change.

It may be safer not to carry everything around with you. Many hotels, even small ones, have safes or locked drawers, and will store valuables and extra luggage for you. If you know you're going to be coming back to a place, you can leave all but what you know you'll be using – as long as the hotel is trustworthy! When leaving valuables at a hotel desk, leave them in a signed, sealed envelope, and if you break the seal to take something out, use a new freshly sealed envelope. You can take along a stash of envelopes to use for this purpose, or buy them as you go along.

Unfortunately, pilfering from hotel rooms can also be a problem. Some travelers always lock their packs or luggage when they go out to limit this possibility. In basic places, you may want to use your own padlock to lock the door instead of the hotel's.

Don't even assume your pack is safe on an airline. One traveler forgot to lock his pack when traveling by air in Guatemala, and stuff was stolen from inside; he felt all the more aggrieved because the airline had charged him to check in his luggage! Use a type of luggage that can be locked. For example, many duffel bags nowadays have zippers with two zipper heads that meet, enabling you to slip a small padlock through the holes on both ends.

Try not to take valuables to the beach. It couldn't be easier for a thief to take unattended belongings from a deserted beach while the owner is swimming or snorkeling. Stagger your swims if you're traveling with friends.

The most important things to protect are your long-term traveling money (traveler's checks), your passport and your airline tickets. Carry these in the safest way possible, but as an extra precaution make a list of check numbers, passport information and airline ticket details, take one or two photocopies of the essential documents, and carry them in a separate place from the originals.

Travel insurance is also strongly recommended (see Health for more details about travel insurance). In case of theft, be sure to get a police report – not because the police will get your things back, but because you'll need one for the insurance company.

Traveling with a friend can be good protection because you can watch out for one another. (I took a pickpocket's hand from the pocket of my traveling companion on a bus from Managua to León.) Unfortunately you can't always depend on strangers to help you, as they may be afraid to (one man showed me a knife scar over his ribs, a souvenir of his helping a young female tourist who had been pickpocketed in Managua). Locals say it's dangerous to interfere in crimes, so usually they don't get involved.

Remember to be wise but not paranoid. If you're careful and aware of what you're doing, it is perfectly possible to travel almost anywhere in Central America with no problems at all.

Health Risks

In many parts of Central America, malaria-carrying mosquitoes and microscopic organisms in the water are much more of a danger to you than other humans might be. See the Health section for tips on staying healthy.

Swimming Safety

Hundreds of people drown each year at Central America's beaches – about 200 drownings are recorded annually at Costa Rica beaches alone. Of these, 80% are caused by rip tides, which are strong currents that pull the swimmer out to sea. They can occur even in waist-deep water. The best advice of all: Ask about local conditions before entering the water.

Many deaths are caused by panicked swimmers struggling to the point of exhaustion. Remember that rip tides will pull you *out but not under*. If you're caught in a rip tide, float and do not struggle. You are unlikely to be able to swim against a rip tide, but if you do try, swim parallel to the beach, not directly back in. If you are carried out beyond the breakers, the rip tide will dissipate – it won't carry you out for miles. Then you can swim back in to shore at a 45° angle to avoid being caught by the current again.

If you feel a rip tide while wading, try and come back in sideways so the current hits less body surface, and walk parallel to the beach to get out of the rip tide. Attract attention by waving your arms and calling for help.

The Environment

Although awareness about environmental issues is growing in Central America, the message hasn't really filtered down to the majority of the people. On every bus journey you'll see passengers casually throwing rubbish out of the window, both in the city and in the countryside. Discarded cartons, wrappings and plastic bags are a depressing feature along every roadside. Try not to add to the collection.

More generally, don't undermine what you have come to see; ecosystems and indigenous cultures are very vulnerable to the effects of tourism. Treat the human and physical environment with respect, or you may end up being a danger and annoyance yourself.

LEGAL MATTERS

You don't want to get in trouble with the law here.

Marijuana and a number of other drugs are illegal. If police find you with them, you could be in big trouble. Don't become a modern-day *Midnight Express* story.

Relations with police may not be as straightforward as they are back home. To cite one example of something so common it's become a cliché: On our last trip we met a Canadian gentleman who had rented a car for a couple of days. Before he got out of the capital city, he was stopped by a police officer, who claimed he had run a traffic light where in fact there was no light. The police officer declared, 'We have a big problem here,' and announced that he would have to take the man in to the police station and confiscate the car! After a long argument in which the Canadian insisted that there was no traffic signal, that all his papers were in order and he had done nothing wrong, the police officer suddenly announced that he could 'be his friend' and look the other way if the Canadian were to give him a 'gift.' He asked for US$300, which the Canadian man was eventually able to whittle down to US$80.

A German reader wrote to tell us of an experience in which police planted marijuana on his traveling companion and then extorted money from both of them in exchange for letting them go.

Unfortunately, these are not isolated incidents. Often it's best to try to avoid the police altogether.

If you do find yourself in trouble, use your wits and your intelligence. Usually the police have the power, not you. You may end up having to part with some money in order to get out of the situation, even if you have done nothing wrong. If you can't get away, it may be a good idea to contact your consulate, though there isn't a lot they can do to help you – they can locate an attorney for you, but they won't pay for it, and they can't perform miracles.

ACTIVITIES
Hiking & Backpacking

Possibilities for hiking are infinite in Central America. An avid hiker could tramp around here for years and never get bored. The pristine natural environments and the abundant wildlife are most impressive. Terrains include mountains, cloud forests, rain forests, lowland jungles, river trails, tropical islands, palm-lined beaches, lagoons full of wildlife and dozens of volcanoes, often with natural hot springs. There are remote wilderness areas, national parks and wildlife preserves, and also the less remote trails that link rural villages to one another.

Central America has hundreds of areas close to cities and towns where you can take simple day walks and see many of the natural features. Hardier backpackers and campers will find more challenging tramps that can last for days or weeks. This part of the world is a hiker's paradise.

Snorkeling & Diving

The string of reefs off the Caribbean Coast of Central America, especially off Belize and the Bay Islands of Honduras, and some of the Caribbean islands as far east as Panama are magnificent for snorkeling and diving. Combined, this reef is the second largest in the world (after Australia's Great Barrier Reef) and has every kind of feature you could dream of, including shipwrecks from the pirate days. The reef attracts divers from all over the world and the fishing is also fantastic.

The Bay Islands of Honduras are among the cheapest places in the world to take a PADI scuba-diving course; even travelers on the most threadbare of shoestrings take advantage of the opportunity.

For diving tips, see How to Choose a Dive Shop & Guidelines for Safe Diving in the Bay Islands section of Honduras.

Surfing

The Pacific Coast has several surf breaks that enjoy an international reputation, and each country with a Pacific coastline has its own famous spots. International surfing competitions are held at some of them, notably at Zunzal in El Salvador.

LANGUAGE COURSES

Antigua Guatemala is famous for its Spanish language courses. The town has many schools and provides total immersion teaching. Students come here from all over the world and live in the homes of local families, becoming familiar with the culture as well as living with the language 24 hours a day. Quetzaltenango, also in Guatemala, is also becoming famous for its Spanish language schools.

A number of other Spanish language schools are being established in many parts of Central America. Many language schools are listed in the country chapters, or refer to *Say Sí!* (Legal Assistance Resource Center of Connecticut), a guide to Spanish language programs around the world, with extensive sections on Guatemala and Costa Rica.

WORK

Central America is an economically depressed region, so there's little casual work available for travelers. Most of the countries have a huge unemployment problem among their own citizens, and wage levels are extremely low by European or North American standards.

Various foreign-aid organizations such as the USA's Peace Corps and Australia's Overseas Service Bureau send volunteers to Central America. They usually want people with skills that are in short supply locally.

You're most likely to find work as an English teacher – the USA is, of course, influential in the region, and a lot of Central Americans go to the USA to work, so learning English is seen as desirable. It's also in big demand for those wishing to find work in the tourism industry. Bilingual schools are becoming common in many places, and there may also be private tutoring work available.

In Panama you can sometimes get work as a line handler (deckhand) on yachts passing through the canal. Last we heard, the pay was US$30 for two days of work, but you had to be lucky to land a job.

With the economy in most of Central America being what it is, it's far better to have enough money so you won't have to look for work there.

Volunteering

During the Sandinista years, Nicaragua hosted international volunteer brigades coming to pick coffee and do many other things to assist the revolution. This came to a screeching halt with the 1990 change of government. The Nicaraguan people can still use plenty of help, though. The Movimiento Comunal Nicaraguense operates community projects all over the country and welcomes foreign volunteers.

A number of Spanish language schools located in Quetzaltenango, Guatemala, are involved with social programs benefiting the local Maya Indian communities. You can easily arrange to volunteer with one of these programs.

Other volunteering opportunities involve working with nature. In Panama, for example, ANCON has volunteer programs in the Darién and other national parks, and a program in the Bocas del Toro region to protect endangered sea turtles and their eggs during nesting season. You can volunteer with ANCON for anything from a week up to several months and receive room and board for the duration. A couple of other organizations in Bocas del Toro also work to protect sea turtles.

Details on volunteer programs are given in the various country chapters.

ACCOMMODATIONS
Camping

Camping as a form of cheap accommodations is not common in Central America. Going camping is not a local custom. Only in Costa Rica, where travelers and naturalists from all over the world camp in the many national parks, is the idea of camping starting to catch on with local people. In most of Central America, anyone with a tent, sleeping bag and portable stove is an oddity.

It is recommended that you camp only in the official camping areas of national parks, in very remote wilderness areas or on someone's land with their permission.

Most national parks in Central America do not have facilities for camping; you're allowed to camp, but you need to take care of all your own needs. In Costa Rica, some national parks have organized camping grounds. The facilities are nothing fancy by international standards, but they have drinking water on tap, fire pits, latrine toilets, cold showers and so on. They charge a very small nightly fee. Some national parks in Costa Rica and other countries also offer basic indoor accommodations, such as in dorms at the ranger station.

If you want to camp in a wilderness area or on an isolated stretch of beach or other isolated area, be very aware of your surroundings. There are people living in some remarkably remote regions of Central America – you may think you're the only person around, but you could be quite mistaken. Also, if you camp in wilderness areas, be sure you know everything about local animals, insects and snakes, so that you won't have any unpleasant surprises.

In sparsely settled rural areas, it's best to camp on private land with the permission of the owner. The fact that the owner knows you are there gives you some security. Around cities and towns, indoor accommodations are so cheap and so much safer than camping that they're a much better option.

Be sure not to leave anything you would mind losing in your tent when you're not there. People have been ripped off even when they're *in* their tent – someone quietly cuts the tent with a razor blade, sticks in their hand and gets what they can reach, and the sleeping camper finds out in the morning. This has happened more than once.

If you leave things unattended in your tent, you're asking to get ripped off. People might assume that if you're a rich foreigner who can afford to leave your belongings unguarded, you can certainly afford to lose them.

Hospedajes & Hotels

In most Central American countries you can get a roof over your head for around US$5 to US$10 a night. Often the difference in price between a single and a double room is negligible, so if you're sharing with someone else the price per person can drop considerably. Since Latin American families tend to be large, most hotels also have at least a couple of rooms for up to six people, which are even cheaper per person.

The cheapest places to stay are the *hospedajes* or *casas de huespedes* (guesthouses). Often, the same establishment will have a variety of rooms at a variety of prices or rooms of widely varying quality all at the same price. There may be a choice of rooms, some with private bathrooms, others with a communal bathroom shared among several rooms. Some rooms may have one double bed while others have two singles, and so on. You might get in the habit of asking *¿ Hay algo mas barato?* ('Is there anything cheaper?'), no matter what price you're quoted at first, since often the management assumes a foreign tourist would prefer the most expensive room in the house.

Always ask to see a room, or a few rooms, before you say you'll take one. This is a perfectly legitimate request. If you don't like the first room they show, you can ask to see another; if you don't like any of the rooms, you can thank them politely and go somewhere else. Don't be shy about asking to have the sheets changed if they look dirty.

This book describes rooms as being with or without private bath *(baño)*; this means there's a bathroom with a shower (but not an actual bathtub), a sink and a toilet. Note that you should place used toilet paper in the receptacle provided, as the plumbing can't handle the paper.

Most places you'll stay will have cold water showers; this is what people in Central America use. You'll only see hot water showers in cool mountain areas or in more expensive hotels catering to foreign tourists.

When you do run into a place with hot showers, the mechanism for heating the water might be an electric device attached to the shower head. Try not to touch anything metal while taking a shower under one of these things or you could get an electric shock. It probably won't kill you, but it could be pretty uncomfortable.

As a rule, breakfast is *not* included in the overnight rate, though it may sometimes be available on the premises.

FOOD

Lunch is the big meal of the day in Central America. It is also usually the cheapest; most cafes and restaurants offer a *comida corrida* set meal at lunchtime for around US$1 to US$3. Typically it will include rice, beans, eggs or meat (usually chicken, beef or fish), cheese or a dollop of cream, a small salad, tortillas and a cold drink. It may also include soup and a dessert. If you make a habit of eating this for your main meal of the day, you can get by with a small snack in the morning and evening. This is the way the local people eat.

A *comida típica* or *comida corriente* is a typical meal of local food. It usually consists of a combination of the foods mentioned above, and it's usually the cheapest option on any menu. Other meals may cost double or more. Though great for nutrition and protein, and very filling, you might get very tired of rice, beans and tortillas. Make a point of varying your diet.

Each country has its own specialties and diet staples, and these are a way to eat cheaply. In El Salvador, for example, a *pupusa* (a hot corn tortilla stuffed with cheese, beans or sausage) costs about US$0.25, and two or three of them with a soft drink make a light meal. On the north coast of Honduras, the seafood soups and stews made with coconut milk are inexpensive but magnificent. Make a point of trying the local food specialty wherever you are.

If you can't do without a taste of home, fast-food joints – burger and pizza places – are found in most Central American cities nowadays.

Eating Cheaply

The cheapest places for a meal are the markets *(mercados)* in every city and town. You'll find fresh fruit, vegetable and tortilla stalls, and you can buy ingredients to make your own meals. There are also usually several small kitchens where food is cooked and served at tables. Take a look at the cleanliness of the kitchen before you sit down to eat, and beware of food that is cooked and then left out waiting to be served; bacteria can multiply quickly in a warm climate, and there may be many flies around. It is possible to eat in markets without ill effects in the places with good standards of cleanliness.

Meat in markets is especially suspicious if it is not properly refrigerated (it seldom is) and if flies can get to it. Many travelers avoid eating meat altogether or eat it only at better restaurants where refrigeration and cleanliness standards are higher.

A step up from eating in markets is eating in the small restaurants and cafes where the local people eat. They are not much more expensive than market kitchens, but the atmosphere is usually more peaceful. There are Chinese restaurants in every city and in most towns, and these are another good option for eating fairly cheaply, as are bakeries. Apart from these, you have to get into the larger cities before you'll find much variety in food.

Vegetarian Food

Vegetarians have no trouble finding something healthy to eat in Central America. Beans and rice, or beans and tortillas, are good sources of protein, which can be supplemented with eggs and dairy products. If you want to avoid red meat, chicken is available everywhere and seafood is also common. If you go into a restaurant, cafe or market stall and say you want a meal with no meat *(No como la carne* – 'I don't eat meat'), it's very rarely a problem.

Most larger cities have vegetarian restaurants, offering a wide variety of dishes. They often serve delicious food, and they can be among the cheapest restaurants in town.

There's something of a movement in Central America to educate the public about the benefits of soy protein. It hasn't quite caught on yet, but you will usually find soya dishes served in vegetarian restaurants.

DRINKS
Nonalcoholic Drinks

With the wide variety of tropical fruits in Central America, you'll probably find unfamiliar fruit juices. Small fruit juice places are common, and it's not unusual to see a dozen or even 20 kinds of fruit juices listed on the wall. If the local water isn't safe to drink, be sure that the juice doesn't get mixed with water. They often blend the juice with water or milk and sugar; eggs can be added for extra protein.

Soft drinks are everywhere in Central America. Coca-Cola and Pepsi are the predominant brands, but you'll also find a host of local varieties and flavors, including apple, banana, grape, orange, strawberry and pineapple. They are sometimes very sweet, tasting more like syrup or a chemical than fruit, but sometimes you'll hit on a good one. Some people delight in seeking out obscure and garish-colored concoctions in the perverse hope of experiencing an unearthly, artificial mixture that even Dr Jekyll would hesitate to consume.

Asking for *agua mineral* (mineral water) or *soda* (soda water, club soda) might get you a cold drink without the sugar. Squeeze some lime into it and it's very refreshing.

A lot of coffee is grown in Central America, but the good stuff might not be as easy to find as you'd expect – a lot of places serve instant coffee! Most of the top quality coffee is exported to places like the USA and Europe. In Costa Rica and Guatemala, where there's a lot of international tourism, some places make a point of serving 'export quality' coffee.

Never assume that water is OK to drink unless you know for sure it is safe (see the Health section for tips on drinking water safety). You can usually find bottled water for sale – or get into the habit of filling your own bottle when you stay somewhere that has a purified supply.

Alcoholic Drinks

Beer is very popular in Central America. Each country brews its own brand(s) of beer. These always cost much less than imported beers. Sometimes there's a selection of beers to choose from.

Stronger spirits, including rum, are also manufactured in some countries. *Aguardiente*, also sometimes called *vino*, is a clear firewater made from sugar cane. It has an alcohol content even higher than vodka and will destroy your brain cells at a remarkable rate – it may make you feel like a rabid pit bull. Nonetheless, it is popular stuff.

Getting There & Away

AIR

Central America has eight international airports: Guatemala City (Guatemala), Belize City (Belize), Tegucigalpa (Honduras), San Pedro Sula (Honduras), San Salvador (El Salvador), Managua (Nicaragua), San José (Costa Rica) and Panama City (Panama).

The island of Roatán, off the north coast of Honduras, also receives direct international flights, but services are limited to one flight a week from Miami, one from New Orleans and one from Houston (all on TACA).

Buying Tickets

How much you pay for a ticket will depend on a number of factors, including where you fly from, which airport you fly into, what travel agencies you have access to, whether you buy your ticket in advance, how long you want to stay, how flexible you can be with your traveling arrangements, what time of year you travel, how old you are (it can be to your advantage to be 26 years old or under) and whether you have an ISIC student card.

When shopping around for tickets, be sure to ask about any restrictions on the fare, including cancellation fees, refund policies, replacement for lost tickets, advance-purchase requirements, and the policies on making date or route changes once you've purchased the ticket. Tickets bought using an ISIC card carry an excellent free insurance policy and are among the cheapest tickets you'll find.

A good source of information about cheap fares is the travel section of newspapers, especially the Sunday edition.

In addition to the official ticket structure, there are unofficially discounted tickets available through certain travel agents. These are known in the UK as 'bucket shops' and in the USA as 'consolidators.' The practice is more widespread in Europe than the USA.

These agencies have contracts with airlines to get tickets at a discount in exchange for selling high volumes. Some agencies specialize in student and youth fares; others simply sell great volumes of cheap tickets. You fly on regularly scheduled flights on regular airlines but at a cheaper price.

Generally bucket-shop tickets cost less than advance-purchase tickets, but they don't have the advance-purchase requirements or cancellation penalties (though they often have their own set of restrictions or cancellation penalties). Most bucket shops are well established and scrupulous, but it's not unknown for fly-by-night operators to set up office, take money and then disappear without issuing any tickets, or after issuing invalid or unusable tickets. Check carefully what you are buying before handing over your money.

Ticket Options

A number of different types of discount air tickets are available.

Advance Purchase These tickets must be bought at least 21 days in advance and are usually only available for return trips. There are minimum and maximum stay requirements (usually four and 180 days respectively), no stopovers are allowed and cancellation charges apply.

Air Passes The Mayan Airpass, or Visit Central America Program, is an air pass handy for discounted travel within Central America on any combination of the Central American national airlines. You must purchase it before you arrive in Central America. Details are given in the Air section of the Getting Around chapter.

Budget Fares These can be booked at least three weeks in advance, but the actual travel date is not confirmed until seven days prior to travel. There are cancellation charges.

Courier Fares Some courier firms require people to accompany urgent documents through customs and will offer very low fares for someone to act as a 'courier.' You may be required to surrender all your baggage allowance for the use of the courier company (though you can take carry-on luggage), and there are sometimes dress codes. To Central America, courier flights are more common from the USA than from Europe. More information on these flights is given in the USA section, below.

Economy Class Symbolized by 'Y' on the airline ticket, this is the full economy fare. Tickets are valid for 12 months.

Excursion Fares These are priced midway between advance-purchase and full economy fares. There are no advance booking requirements, but a minimum stay abroad is often obligatory. The advantage over advance-purchase tickets is that you can change your bookings and/or stopovers without surcharge.

Miscellaneous Charges Order An MCO is a voucher that looks like an airline ticket but has no destination or date on it. It is exchangeable with any IATA airline for credit on a specific flight. Its principal use for travelers is as an alternative to an onward ticket, though MCOs are becoming less acceptable for this purpose. For entering those countries that demand an onward ticket it's obviously much more flexible than a ticket for a specific flight, but check first to be sure they will accept an MCO.

Open Jaw Returns This enables you to fly into one country and fly out from somewhere else; for example, flying into Panama City on the first leg and out of Guatemala City on the return leg. It needn't cost more than a normal budget return ticket and can meet the problematic onward-ticket requirement.

Point-to-Point This is a discount ticket offered on some routes to passengers who waive their stopover rights.

Round-the-World RTW tickets can be a cheap way of traveling. There are some excellent deals available, and you may well pick one up for less than the cost of a return excursion fare. You must travel around the world in one direction and you cannot backtrack; you are usually allowed from five to seven stopovers.

Standby This can be one of the cheapest ways of flying. You simply turn up at the airport or at an airline's city terminal, and if there are spare seats on the flight you want, you can get them at a considerable discount. It's become so common that many airline counters now have a special standby section. To give yourself the best possible chance of getting on the flight you want, get there early and have your name placed on the waiting list. It's first-come, first-served.

Stopover Options Extensive stopover options are common on flights to and within Central America. Whether originating outside Central America or within it, air routes usually stop at more than one airport in the region. This often means you can visit extra countries at no extra cost; usually the fare is the same whether you pick up the next leg of the journey at a later date or continue on immediately. If you would like to visit a few countries, be sure to check the stopover options before you buy your ticket.

Different airlines will have stopovers scheduled at different places, even on flights between the same two points. All the Central American national airlines schedule transfers through the international airports in their home countries and may offer stopovers in other countries as well.

Student Fares You can get up to 50% off regular fares by getting a student fare. Usually you must have an ISIC (International Student Identity Card) to get these fares and buy your ticket from a special student travel agency.

Youth Fares Youth fares, for travelers ages 26 or under, are often available at student travel agencies, whether or not you're a student.

Onward-Ticket Requirements

Costa Rica, Panama and Belize all officially have an onward-ticket requirement; that is, you cannot enter the country unless you already have an onward ticket to another destination. This requirement is satisfied by a return ticket, a ticket continuing to another country or even a ticket out of a nearby country. A ticket for any means of transport, whether by air or land, counts; the object is simply to be sure that you won't stay in the country indefinitely.

Many travelers have reported not being asked to show any sort of ticket when entering any of these countries; immigration officials almost never ask for it at either land borders or international airports. However, officially it is a requirement; although it's rarely asked for, it can be.

Though immigration officials may not enforce the onward-ticket requirement, airlines often do. If you are aiming to fly into one of these countries but you don't have a ticket out, it's likely the airline will not even let you board the plane. These are simply carriers' preventive measures: If you arrive in a country and are refused entry, the airline is responsible for flying you back out again, so they make sure you have the necessary passport, papers and tickets before you board. An open jaw ticket (see Ticket Options) will suffice.

A bus ticket also suffices as an onward ticket. However, if you are flying in, you won't have a chance to buy a bus ticket before arrival, so you'll need an airline ticket. If you do indeed want to fly out of the country, this is no problem; if, however, you plan to continue overland, the onward-ticket requirement can be a drag.

If you have to buy a ticket simply to meet this requirement, consider getting a miscellaneous charges order (MCO, see Ticket Options), which you can use later to buy a ticket for any flight with any IATA airline. Otherwise, you'll want to get a refund on the ticket, so check the refund policy carefully to be sure you can do it. Sometimes there are restrictions on refunds, such as refunds being issued only at the office where you bought the ticket – impossible if you're not going back that way.

The USA

The major gateway cities for flights to Central America are Miami, New Orleans, Houston, Los Angeles, Washington, DC, and New York. Flights do originate from a few other places, but generally if you fly from the USA, it will be through one of these airports.

The cheapest flights to Central America from the USA are those from Miami, though occasionally Houston has equivalent fares. If you're coming from some other part of the USA, your travel agent can arrange a discounted 'add-on' fare to get you to the city of departure.

The easiest way to get a cheap airfare from the USA is through a travel agency selling discounted fares. The Sunday travel sections of some major newspapers have advertisements from many such agencies; the *New York Times*, the *Los Angeles Times* and the *San Francisco Chronicle-Examiner* are all good ones to check. Even if you don't live in these areas, you can have the tickets sent to you by mail. Charter flights are another possibility.

Two of the most reputable discount-travel agencies in the USA are CIEE/Council Travel Services and STA Travel. Both of these are international travel agencies with a number of offices throughout the USA and in other countries. Both started out as student travel agencies. Although they both still specialize in student travel, honoring and selling the International Student Identity Card (ISIC), they also offer discount tickets to nonstudents of all ages. You can contact their national head offices to ask about prices, find an office near you, purchase tickets by mail or buy an ISIC card.

CIEE/Council Travel Services
  205 E 42nd St, New York, NY 10017
  ☎ (212) 822-2600, (800) 226-8624,
  fax (212) 822-2699

STA Travel
   6560 N Scottsdale Rd, Suite F100,
   Scottsdale, AZ 85253
   ☎ (800) 777-0112, fax (602) 922-0793

Council Travel has 52 offices throughout the USA. STA has offices in Berkeley (CA), Boston, Cambridge, Chicago, Gainesville, Los Angeles, Miami, New York, Philadelphia, San Francisco, Santa Monica, Seattle, Tampa and Washington, DC.

All five of the Central American airlines have offices in the USA, and they all have toll-free telephone numbers that you can call to ask about services from the USA or within Central America:

Aviateca (Guatemala)	☎ (800) 327-9832
COPA (Panama)	☎ (800) 359-2672
LACSA (Costa Rica)	☎ (800) 225-2272
Nica (Nicaragua)	☎ (800) 831-6422
TACA (El Salvador)	☎ (800) 535-8780

The Central American airlines cooperate on routing and tickets; you may find you'll take different legs of your flight on different airlines. Other airlines, such as American, Continental and United, also have toll-free numbers and fly to Central America. Note that US airports charge an airport security tax that is not included in the ticket – about US$35 for international departures from Los Angeles and Miami, less from some other cities.

Don't overlook the possibility of flying to Mexico first and then traveling overland to Central America. Travel agents and discount houses frequently offer special airfares to Mexico or package tours at very reasonable prices; ask if you can take the return portion of the ticket at a later date. You can sometimes buy a package tour for less than it would cost you for a simple airfare. Ask the travel agent if you can purchase it 'airfare only': This is sometimes possible, though the reduction may be minimal.

Courier Flights Flying as an air courier can be a handy way to get a cheap flight. Businesses pay courier companies to ensure the arrival of urgent freight without excessive customs hassles. Courier companies hire the couriers, who commit to carrying packages from one airport to another on particular dates, and the company uses their baggage allowance. Details vary, but typically you get a hefty discount on airfare in exchange for letting the courier company use all or part of your check-in baggage allowance – you retain your carry-on baggage allowance for your own needs.

Most courier flights to Central America operate from Miami. They go to a variety of destinations in Central America, including Guatemala City, San Salvador, Managua and Panama City. Two of the major courier services in Miami offering flights to Central America include Line Haul Services (☎ (305) 477-0651, fax (305) 477-0659) and Trans Air Systems (☎ (305) 592-1771, fax (305) 592-2927).

Note that you can take the flight originating at either the Miami or the Central America end. Line Haul Services can be contacted in Guatemala City (☎ (502) 362-3727, fax (502) 331-2086; no English spoken); alternatively, contact either company at their Miami offices from Central America.

A wide variety of international courier flight possibilities are listed in the *Air Courier Bulletin*, a bimonthly magazine published for the International Association of Air Travel Couriers (IAATC). Subscriptions to the magazine cost US$20 per year for IAATC members. Contact IAATC at 8 South J St, PO Box 1349, Lake Worth, FL 33460-1349 (☎ (561) 582-8320, fax (561) 582-1581, net). Courier flights for several destinations in Central America are listed, all originating from Miami.

Travel Unlimited (PO Box 1058, Allston, MA 02134), a monthly newsletter, gives details of cheap airfares and courier possibilities for destinations all over the world from the USA. Send US$5 for the current edition or you can purchase a one-year subscription for US$25.

Canada

Charter flights are sometimes available from Canada to various Central American destinations including Costa Rica, Honduras and Panama. These can be significantly cheaper than normal airline rates. As mentioned in the USA section, you can also sometimes get a good deal by buying a package tour to Mexico and then setting off from there. Flights from Canada to Central America transfer through one of the USA's gateway cities.

In Canada, the student and discount agency is Travel CUTS/Voyages Campus, which has 46 offices around Canada and two in the UK (both in London). They specialize in discounted student and youth flights and other services; special fares are available with a valid ISIC or GO25 card. They also offer the free *Student Traveller* magazine and information on the Student Work Abroad Programme (SWAP). Once again, you don't have to be a student to use their services. The national head office is at 187 College St, Toronto, ON M5T 1P7 (☎ (416) 979-2406, (416) 798-CUTS, fax (416) 979-8167, net).

South America
Panama to Colombia The shortest and cheapest way to fly between Central and South America is between Panama and Colombia. Within these countries, the cheapest routes are between Panama City and Cartagena, Barranquilla or Medellín. Flights from Panama City to Bogotá and Cali are slightly more expensive.

Another and even cheaper option is to fly from Panama City to Puerto Obaldía, cross by land to Capurganá on the Colombian side, and then fly on to Medellín, or take the boat to Turbo. See the Darién section of the Panama chapter.

Via San Andrés If you're flying from anywhere in Central America besides Panama, the cheapest way to reach South America is to fly to Colombia via the town of San Andrés on Isla de San Andrés, which is off the coast of Nicaragua (though it belongs to Colombia). San Andrés has an international airport and is a hub for flights between South America, Central America and the USA.

The only direct flights between San Andrés and Central America are on Colombia's SAM airline, which has one flight between San Andrés and Panama City, and another between San Andrés and San José (Costa Rica), which continues on to Guatemala City. From other Central American airports, you'll have to transfer at one of these places, usually San José, which will involve paying for two separate legs of travel.

It is cheaper to buy two separate tickets (one from Central America to San Andrés and another on a Colombian airline from San Andrés to mainland Colombia) than it is to buy one ticket all the way through. The same applies in the opposite direction, coming up from South America. Avianca, SAM and Aces have flights from San Andrés to all the major Colombian cities. You can buy these tickets from Central America, but you may get a cheaper fare if you wait until you arrive at San Andrés to buy your ticket.

Once you're at San Andrés, there are a couple of other cheap ways to get to the mainland. Aerosucre has one or two cargo flights weekly to Barranquilla (Monday or Tuesday, US$40) and Bogotá (Friday or Saturday, US$50). They usually take passengers, and their passenger fares are about half the commercial fare. Inquire in the Aerosucre office near the passenger terminal. It's in the green-roofed building next to the building with the Marlboro cowboy advertisement on top. The entrance is on the right side, not at the front.

Another way is to fly with Satena. They have irregular noncommercial passenger flights to Bogotá, usually around once a month, and they're very cheap: it was US$60, and though the price will probably rise, it's still a lot less than the commercial airlines. The Satena flights are heavily booked, but there is always a chance – just go to the airport before the flight and try your luck.

Cargo ships run between San Andrés and Cartagena, so you could fly in and boat out (see Sea below).

Colombia enforces an onward ticket

requirement policy wherever you enter the country, including San Andrés. This is a hassle if you want to continue to the mainland on a domestic Colombian airline. Consequently San Andrés has something of a black market in the return portions of tickets from Central America. Travelers buy a return ticket from Central America to San Andrés and then sell the return portion to another traveler coming up from South America. The return portions of the tickets are usually sold for about half their face value, and the buyers will obviously expect you to cooperate in getting them on the plane. (Remember that Costa Rica, Panama and Belize also have onward-ticket requirements to contend with.)

You can't get a refund on return portions of tickets from the airline offices in San Andrés, but you may be able to in their offices on the mainland. If you're planning to get a refund on the return portion later on, check the refund policy carefully when you buy your ticket.

San Andrés itself is a pleasant little island, about 12 km long and two km wide, covered with coconut palms – not a bad place to hang out for a few days while you're making your travel arrangements.

A lot of visitors come to San Andrés. In addition to being a transport hub, the island is one of Colombia's prime tourist attractions, mostly for its natural beauty but also for its duty-free shopping. Snorkeling and diving are good here, and equipment can be rented easily. The island has many banks, shops and places to stay and eat. Panama, Costa Rica, Honduras and Guatemala all have consulates here.

The island has only one major town, also called San Andrés but locally known as 'El Centro.' El Centro has a pretty good beach, and there are a few other things to see and do around the island. You can try snorkeling on Johnny Cay; Acuario Cay and Haynes Cay off the east coast are even better and not as crowded. Take buses or a bicycle around the island to visit the villages and see the blowhole; scooters, motorcycles and cars can also be rented.

The best place to stay for those on a

shoestring is the *Hotel Restrepo* (☎ (9811) 26744), on the opposite side of the runway from the airport terminal; rooms are US$5 per person. Meals are also served. It's a popular congregating place for international travelers.

Australasia
Coming from Australia or New Zealand, the cheapest and easiest way is to fly first to Los Angeles or Miami and then fly south from there. They are both good places to get cheap flights to Central America. Or you could go overland from Los Angeles, but it's a long way south through Mexico to Central America.

STA Travel is one agency that has student and youth airfares, and it's worth checking their deals. You don't have to be a student to use their services. In Australia, STA has offices in Sydney, Melbourne, Brisbane, Adelaide, Canberra, Cairns, Darwin and Perth. In New Zealand, STA has offices in Auckland, Christchurch and Wellington. Contact their national headquarters for the address of a branch close to you (☎ (3) 9349-2411, fax (3) 9349-2537, 222 Faraday St, Carlton, Melbourne, Victoria 3053; ☎ (9) 309-0458, fax (9) 309-2059, 10 High St, Auckland).

The UK
The cheapest fares to Central America are from London, where there are numerous bucket shops selling discount tickets. Their prices are well advertised in publications such as *Time Out* and the *Evening Standard*, both widely available in London. The best choice is in *TNT*, London's free weekly magazine for entertainment, travel and jobs, available at some London underground stations or ring ☎ (0181) 244-6529 for details of the nearest pickup points. Of the national papers the *Sunday Times* has the best selection. Before you buy a ticket, note whether the ticket vendor is 'bonded' (that is, affiliated with ABTA, ATOL or AITO), which gives you protection if the vendor goes bankrupt.

Apart from the bucket shops, there are four other agencies worth trying. Council

Travel and STA Travel are both excellent organizations specializing in both student and budget travel, but many of the cheapest fares are only available to students, academics and those under 26 years old. Trailfinders has low fares and regional branches in Manchester, Bristol, Glasgow, Birmingham and Dublin. Journey Latin America (JLA) specializes in travel from the UK to Central and South America, and they're particularly helpful. They can make travel arrangements over the phone and can arrange itineraries for both independent and escorted travel. JLA and Trailfinders both produce a free magazine.

Council Travel
    28a Poland St, Oxford Circus,
    London W1V 3DB (☎ (0171) 437-7767)
JLA
    14-16 Devonshire Rd, Chiswick,
    London W4 2HD (☎ (0181) 747-3108,
    fax (0181) 742-1312)
STA Travel
    117 Euston Rd, London NW1 2SX;
    86 Old Brompton Rd, London, SW7 3LQ
    (☎ (0171) 361-6123,
    fax (0171) 938-4755, net)
Trailfinders
    194 Kensington High St, London W8 7RG
    (☎ (0171) 937-5400 for 'longhaul' queries;
    (0171) 938-3939 for transatlantic queries,
    fax 937-0555)

There is a great variety of fares to Central America, many with complicated restrictions, conditions and dates of availability. The cheapest airline is usually Continental; an overnight stop in Houston may be necessary, with attendant hotel costs. Iberia is more expensive, but the hotel is included if a stopover is necessary in Madrid.

At the time of writing, STA quoted fares of £558 plus £10 airport tax for low-season return tickets from London to either Guatemala City or Panama City on KLM, valid for three months. Continental came in at £546 with airport tax of £33 to the above destinations for low-season dates. One travel agent suggested flying to Mexico City, which is much cheaper (£391 plus £24 airport tax). This was not a special price but a standard low-season fare on Lufthansa.

JLA quoted a fare of £439 plus £13 airport tax for a low-season three-month return ticket on KLM (London to Panama City) with price subject to availability; the high-season price was approximately £640.

Continental Europe

Amsterdam has lots of bucket shops, and in continental Europe it is probably the best place to buy tickets to Central America. Frankfurt, Brussels and Athens are also places to look for cheap fares. Depending on where you are, it may be cheaper to fly to London first and then seek a cheap ticket. Apart from the bucket shops, STA and Council Travel have a number of offices in Europe. Check these travel agencies for flights to Central America:

France
    STA Travel, c/o Voyages Decouvertes,
    21 rue Cambon, 75001 Paris
    (☎ 01-42-61-00-01)
    Council Travel, 22 rue des Pyramides,
    75001 Paris (☎ 01-44-55-55-44)
    Intairline, 28 rue Delambre, 75014 Paris
    (☎ 01-43-20-90-46)
    Maison des Ameriques, 4 rue Chapon,
    75003 Paris (☎ 01-42-77-50-50)
    Iberia, 1 rue Scribe, 75009 Paris
    (☎ 01-40-47-80-90)
    Uniclam, 11 rue du 4-Septembre,
    75002 Paris (☎ 01-40-15-07-07)
Germany
    Council Travel, 64 Graf Adolf St,
    Dusseldorf 1 (☎ 211-36-30-30)
    STA Travel, c/o Kilroy, Berger Strasse
    118, 6000 Frankfurt 1 (☎ 69-70-30-35)
Belgium
    Connections, Av Adolphe-Buyl 78,
    1050 Bruxelles (☎ 2-647-06-05)
    Eole, chaussee Haecht 43, 1210 Bruxelles
    (☎ 2-219-48-70)
Switzerland
    SSR, 20 bd de Grancy, 1006 Lausanne
    (☎ 21-614-6030)

Most flights from Europe originate from Paris, Brussels, Amsterdam, Frankfurt, Zurich, Madrid or London. They generally fly via Madrid, New York, Miami, Houston or Mexico. The major airlines with flights to Central America are American, Continental, Iberia and KLM. Return fares from

Europe typically range from around US$750 to US$950.

Also investigate the option of flying to Mexico; the fares are cheaper, and there are even charter flights. Once in Mexico you can easily fly or take a bus to Guatemala or Belize.

LAND
The Canada, the USA & Mexico
Going to Central America overland from the USA or Canada means traveling through Mexico. It's a long trip that will take at least several days, whether you do it by bus, train or car. If you fall in love with Mexico, though, it could take months to cross that fascinating country. (See Lonely Planet's *Mexico – a travel survival kit*.)

Bus Mexico has an excellent system of long-distance buses, with first- and second-class buses as well as more luxurious options. Buses cover Mexico all the way from the US border to the borders of Guatemala and Belize, and from there you change buses and continue into Central America.

Train Mexico has an extensive rail transport system, but the quality of the trains ranges from some of the best in the world to some of the worst. Take the best class of train you can afford in Mexico, and avoid those in Yucatán. Trains run as far south as Tapachula near the Guatemalan border.

Bringing Your Own Vehicle If you bring your own vehicle from the USA, you'll have to obtain Mexican car insurance and a permit to bring your vehicle into the country. These are easily obtained at the border.

If your vehicle uses unleaded fuel, you will have to change the catalytic converter so it can run on regular (see the Getting Around chapter for details). In Mexico and Central America, the only fuels commonly available are regular leaded, super leaded, and diesel (though unleaded is becoming increasingly available in Mexico). Diesel is cheaper, so it's the favorite in this region. If

you're buying a vehicle in the USA to take you to Mexico and Central America, consider buying one with a diesel engine.

South America
Via the Darién Gap The Interamericana does not go all the way through Panama but terminates in the middle of the jungle in a vast wilderness region called the Darién. This transport gap between Central and South America is known to travelers as the Darién Gap.

There are basically two ways through the Darién Gap. The first skirts the northern coast via the San Blas Archipelago and Puerto Obaldía, making use of boat services and involving a minimum of walking. The second goes through the jungle from Yaviza (Panama) to the Río Atrato in Colombia's Parque Nacional Los Katíos, and you have to walk most of the way. Either of these routes can be done in as little as a week, but you should allow twice this time, especially for the jungle route.

For details on the routes, see the Darién section in the Panama chapter.

Shipping Your Own Vehicle If you are in a private vehicle and want to travel between Central and South America, you will have to ship the vehicle around the Darién Gap. Usually this means shipping it between Panama and Colombia. The discontinued *Crucero Express* ferry, which once ran daily service between Colón (Panama) and Cartagena (Colombia), made this very easy; you could check with the IPAT tourist office in Panama City to see whether a similar service has been instituted. One was due to begin in 1997. If not, you will have to figure out another way to ship the vehicle. This is neither cheap nor easy, but people do it. There is a lot of cargo traffic between the two countries, so you can get almost anything shipped. It will involve a lot of paperwork on both sides and will require investigation, time, money and patience.

Basically your choices are shipping the vehicle by boat or by air. Air cargo planes do have size limits, but a normal car, or even a Land Rover, can fit. If you have a motorcycle, air is probably the easiest option. You may be able to get a special rate for air cargo if you are also flying with the same airline; you could start by asking the cargo departments of the airlines that fly there (like COPA), or at the cargo terminal at Tocumen International Airport in Panama City. Travel agents can sometimes help.

To mainland Colombia the options are the port of Buenaventura on the Pacific side, or either Cartagena or Barranquilla on the Caribbean side. Most people find it easier to go to a Caribbean port. To find a cargo boat heading that way, go to the docks in Colón and ask what ships are going. You'll come up with many options, some better than others.

Smaller cargo vessels depart from Coco Solo pier in Colón. They may offer you the best price but may not be able to help you with the paperwork you need to enter Colombia. These smaller vessels are sometimes contraband boats, and their service is probably the most risky and uncomfortable, but also the cheapest. Prices are very negotiable; they might start out asking US$1500 and come down to half that. You might feel it's better to go with a more established shipper. As a general rule, you might expect to pay a minimum of about US$700 to ship a vehicle from Colón to Cartagena or Barranquilla; it could easily cost US$1000 or more. Prices are extremely variable.

Another option is to go first to the Colombian island of San Andrés (see Via San Andrés under Air for a description of this island) and then on to the mainland. Expect to pay at least US$1000 for the combined fare and allow a week or so wait in San Andrés for the connecting boat. This option has worked out in the past, but of late people have experienced difficulties in doing this. Contact the South American Explorers Club (see Useful Organizations in the Facts for the Visitor chapter) for advice if you are considering this route.

There are alternatives to shipping the vehicle to Colombia. Some travelers have come upon equally good deals shipping to Venezuela, Ecuador or even Chile. It all depends on your luck and what cargo ships are leaving at the time you're asking.

After taking their vehicle through Central America and into South America, one couple said that it would have been easier and cheaper to ship their car from Miami to Caracas (the easiest way of shipping a vehicle directly from the USA to South America) or to buy a car in South America and sell it again before leaving. But they also said they wouldn't have missed Central America for anything and were glad they'd come through that way.

If you're taking a vehicle to South America, you may need a *carnet de passage* ('Libreta de Pasos por Aduana' in Spanish) in addition to the customs, shipping and other paperwork. The carnet is a bond guaranteeing that you won't sell your vehicle in South America – you post a bond to get the carnet, and it's partly refunded when you get back and show that you still have the vehicle.

You don't need the carnet for travel in Central America, but you may need it the minute you arrive on South American soil. You should arrange it before you arrive in South America. If you don't have a carnet, you and your vehicle could be halted and refused admission at any border in South America.

According to several travelers, the best way to obtain a carnet is through the Venezuelan Automobile Association, where it costs US$350, with US$100 of that refundable. Contact the Touring & Automobile Club de Venezuela in Caracas (☎ (58) (2) 794-1032, fax (58) (2) 781-9787); in San Cristóbal (☎ (58) (76) 44-2664, fax (58) (76) 43-9182); or in Maracaibo (☎ (61) 97-0350, (61) 98-1858). It may be better to get the carnet here than in your home country, not only because it will be thousands of dollars cheaper, but also because it will be issued by a South American country, and the documents will be in Spanish and thus more easily recognized and accepted throughout South America.

It may be possible to arrange a carnet through the Automobile Association in either Canada or the UK, but it is very expensive: Travelers have had to post bonds for more than the full value of their vehicle, coming to thousands of dollars.

In the USA, the American Automobile Association (AAA) formerly issued the carnet, but no longer. Don Montague at the South American Explorers Club in the USA (see Useful Organizations in the Facts for the Visitor chapter) has some information on carnets, and his most recent advice was to go through the Venezuelan Automobile Association. (If you find a way to get a carnet de passage in the USA, please let him, and us, know.)

When you ship the vehicle, you can expect that something will be stolen from it if you cannot stay with it every minute. Stealing from vehicles being shipped is a big business. If you ship the vehicle with all your worldly belongings in it, take every precaution and even then don't be surprised if thieves get your stuff. Remove everything removable (hubcaps, wipers, mirrors, etc) and take everything visible out of the interior. Camper vans are a special target – seal off the living area from the driving compartment, double-lock the living area, cover the windows so no one can see inside, and double-lock your possessions *again* inside the cabinets.

Shipping a Motorcycle Some travelers have had horrendous experiences when taking vehicles, especially motorcycles, from Panama to South America without the carnet de passage.

In Panama, Nancy met Pat, a Kiwi biker coming north from Colombia, who related some experiences of foreign bikers going the other way. He told us of one who had air-freighted his bike to Bogotá, where it took him four weeks and several hundred dollars in bribes to get it out of customs. When he did get it, they made him go straight to the Ecuadorian border. The authorities there made him pay US$50 and go straight on to the Peruvian border, accompanied by a policeman on the back of his bike!

Another biker air-freighted his machine to Colombia but never did get it out of customs – he had to air-freight it straight on to Ecuador, which was very expensive.

Pat, having himself experienced various South American scenes, stored his bike in Panama when he went to Colombia.

These are just a couple of the many unfortunate experiences bikers have encountered. Apparently some South American officials don't take kindly to long-haired foreign bikers. On the other hand, travelers with their own vehicle and a carnet de passage were getting through smoothly with no trouble at all. Pat urged Nancy to let people know about the carnet de passage, and to warn bikers about the problems they may face. Thanks, bro!

SEA

If you don't mind roughing it, there are many possibilities for getting to/from Central America by sea. Having your own yacht would, of course, make it much easier, but there are other options.

On the Caribbean side, boats are continually coming and going between all the Central American countries, the Caribbean islands, Mexico, the USA and the north coast of South America. You might be able to get on to a cargo ship, fishing boat, yacht or other vessel.

Sailing times are short in this region – for example, it's only a two-day voyage from New Orleans to the north coast of Honduras – so it's possible to make informal arrangements to get a ride on a boat. This requires luck and good timing, and it's difficult to plan in advance. Probably the best strategy is simply to ask around the docks at every port you come to. Also try at yacht marinas: Boat owners may have space for a hitchhiker or willing helper.

In the San Blas Archipelago in northeastern Panama, you may be able to catch a ride with a merchant ship heading for Colombia; see the Eastern Panama section of the Panama chapter for information on traveling in this area.

Cargo ships run between San Andrés (Colombia) and Cartagena, and they sometimes take passengers. The trip takes two to three days and costs about US$35, including food. From San Andrés you could fly out (see Air section above).

There is less sea traffic along the Pacific Coast. Most of the boats are larger vessels on defined schedules, so they're less willing to pick up the stray traveler.

The Panama Canal, one of the world's major shipping crossroads, is a sure place to encounter sea traffic. Yachts pass through the canal on certain days, traditionally on Tuesdays and Thursdays, though of late they've also been going through on Saturdays. While waiting to cross, they anchor at yacht clubs on both sides of the canal: the Balboa Yacht Club on the Pacific side, the Panama Canal Yacht Club on the Atlantic side. Check at these clubs to contact a passing yacht; both clubs have bulletin boards full of notices by people offering and seeking crew positions (paid or unpaid), or simply passage through the canal. It's not easy to make contact with larger ships, which pass through the canal without ever pulling up to a dock.

For many months, a ferry called *Crucero Express* operated daily between Colón (Panama) and Cartagena (Colombia), carrying passengers, vehicles and freight. This was a very convenient way to travel between Central and South America. However, the *Crucero Express* ceased operation in 1996. Another ferry service was due to start up in 1997, but at the time of writing, operation had still not begun.

You could check with the IPAT tourist office in Panama City to see if such a service has resumed; if it has, you can get information there.

If you arrive or depart from any country by sea, be sure to have your exit and entry stamps correctly registered into your passport at the first opportunity.

WARNING

The information in this chapter is particularly vulnerable to change: Prices for international travel are volatile, routes are introduced and canceled, schedules change, special deals come and go, and rules and visa requirements are amended. Airlines and governments seem to take a perverse pleasure in making price structures and regulations as complicated as possible. You should check directly with the airline or a travel agent to make sure you understand how a fare (and ticket you may buy) works. In addition, the travel industry is highly competitive and there are many pitfalls and perks.

The upshot of this is that you should get opinions, quotes and advice from as many airlines and travel agents as possible before you part with your hard-earned cash. The details given in this chapter should be regarded as pointers and are not a substitute for your own careful, up-to-date research.

Getting Around Central America

The Central American countries are small. Getting around is usually easy in this part of the world: Distances are short, highways are mostly good, and there are adequate bus services and other means of transport. Most travelers enjoy traveling through Central America and have no problems.

AIR

All the Central American countries except Belize and Honduras have their own international airlines. They operate cooperatively with one another to avoid overlap of routes; if you buy a ticket with more than one leg on it, you may find you'll be scheduled on different airlines for the various legs. Most of these airlines make stops at all of Central America's international airports, and others stop farther afield, particularly in the USA.

These are the Central American airlines:

> Aviateca (Guatemala)
> COPA (Panama)
> LACSA (Costa Rica)
> Nica (Nicaragua)
> TACA (El Salvador)

Considering the short distances, flights among the various Central American countries tend to be quite expensive. A half-hour flight can easily cost around US$100 or more (but could also save you a lot of travel time).

You can get at least one free stopover on many of the Central American airlines' international routes, whether they originate within or outside Central America.

If you fly between Central American countries, this can be an easy way to visit extra countries at no extra cost. It usually makes no difference in the price whether you stop for a couple of hours or a couple of weeks between flights.

International

Buying Air Tickets Unlike flights from some other parts of the world, which have complicated price options, airfares in Central America are straightforward. There are three categories of ticket: economy class, business class, and first class. Most travelers use economy class.

The governments regulate airfares so all the airlines charge the same prices for the same routes within Central America. There are no advance-purchase, length-of-stay or other requirements; you simply go to an airline office or travel agent, check when a flight is leaving, pay your money and go. Often you can go the same day or the next day – the only exception is at busy flying times, especially around Easter, when the entire region goes on holiday. Some flights may fill up, but this is generally not a region where you have to book all your tickets far in advance.

If you do have reservations on a Central American airline, be sure you find out the procedure for reconfirming your flight. Usually you must reconfirm 72 hours before the flight departs. It's not a bad idea to check once again to be sure your seat has in fact been confirmed.

If you buy any type of airline ticket in Central America, pay attention to the currency-exchange rate the airline is using. Often you can pay for the ticket in either the local currency or in US dollars (cash, traveler's checks or credit card). Check the difference between the price quoted in dollars and the price in the local currency – paying in one currency or the other can sometimes make a difference in the cost.

Air Passes The Mayan Airpass, also called the Visit Central America Program, can be a handy way of flying among several destinations within Central America for a discount – you can save up to 35% on your tickets if you buy them this way. The air pass is offered by the alliance of the five Central American airlines and is good for travel on any of these airlines.

When you buy the Mayan Airpass, you receive a packet of air coupons, with each coupon good for one segment of the journey. The pass must be bought outside Central America at least three days in advance of travel. Minimum stay is three days, maximum stay is 60 days (an extra US$100 can extend the length of stay to 90 days). You must buy a minimum of three coupons, and a maximum of 10.

Fares depend on the number of coupons you buy, your starting and ending points and the season. All the listed starting and ending points are in the USA, Mexico, South America and the Caribbean; you must start and end your travel outside Central America.

Domestic

Each country also has domestic air services within its borders. They can often save a whole day's travel on an uncomfortable bus or boat, as well as providing a bird's-eye view of the country.

Prices for domestic flights can be very reasonable; prices are given in the country sections of this book. Note, however, that fares are changeable and may be much higher than those listed. During the time we were researching the Honduras chapter for this edition, for example, domestic airfares doubled overnight in response to a surge in the price of fuel.

Student Travel Agencies Costa Rica and Panama have student travel agencies where you can use an International Student Identity Card (ISIC) to obtain discounts on airfares, tours and other travel services. If you have an ISIC card, it's worth contacting these offices to see what they're offering.

They do not offer the vast range of discounted airfares that are available at student travel agencies in, for example, the USA or Europe, but you can get discounted airfares on a few routes. (You might get the discounts even if you aren't a student!)

The offices are OTEC (☎ 256-0633, fax 233-8678, Calle 3, Avenida 3, San José, Costa Rica) and Turismo Joven Panamá (☎ 225-2356, Calle 46 & Calle 50, Bella Vista, Panama City, Panama).

BUS

It is quite easy to bus all through Central America, as all the countries have adequate bus systems. Some have notorious problems of one kind or another, particularly Nicaragua (pickpockets), but in general you can get almost anywhere by bus. By local standards it's very expensive to buy and operate your own vehicle, so buses are the principal means of transit for most people.

On both local and long-distance routes, the first bus of the day usually departs very early in the morning, around 5 am or even earlier. Often there will be many people taking the morning buses but far fewer on the afternoon buses. Buses may run every few minutes, on the half hour, hourly, or only once or twice a day, depending on the route.

With just a few exceptions, night buses are rare. Sometimes the last bus of the day is scheduled to reach its destination before or just after dark. The few night bus routes that do exist are usually in places with excellent roads and no danger of violence from bandits or guerrillas.

Buses in Central America range from decrepit, round-fendered models to modern, air-conditioned Mercedes-Benzes. Many were formerly school buses in the USA. Luggage may go in a lower compartment or be piled on the roof. Since buses are the principal means of transport, people carry anything and everything by bus: goods to sell at the market, produce bought at the market, even small farm animals.

Whether new or old, buses in Central America are rarely the monotonous, uniform and impersonal transport they can be elsewhere. A bus driver typically has his own bus to drive, and it's usually done up with bright decoration inside and out – stickers, slogans, pictures of Jesus and the Virgin Mary, names of girlfriends written all over the windows and fringes over the windscreen. Often the buses have a radio or cassette player; you can bring along your own cassettes and ask the driver to play them.

Don't assume bus departure times listed are correct, as schedules are particularly vulnerable to change. Sometimes buses only leave once there are enough passengers.

Bus Stations

Bus stations vary greatly in size, location and in the facilities they offer. In some places, all the buses arrive and depart from the same bus station. These can be large, hectic and crowded, but they're the most convenient because you know you can get the bus you want from that bus station.

In other cities such as San Salvador and Managua, different bus stations serve routes for different directions; all the westbound buses come and go from one bus station, while all the eastbound buses come and go from another. If you are just passing through the city, you will have to take a local bus between the two stations.

In still other cities such as Guatemala City, Tegucigalpa and San Pedro Sula, each bus company has its own station. When this is the case, all the major bus stations are listed in this book and shown on the city maps where possible. If the bus stations are spread out like this, try asking a taxi driver which station has the buses going to your destination.

You can almost always buy food at bus stations, and soft drinks will be sold in plastic bags to take on the bus. It is also quite common for food to be available along the way, with crowds of people running up to sell snacks and drinks through the bus windows at every stop. This is a sight to behold; a pack of these determined vendors could easily take on the average American football team. Bring your own toilet paper for bus station toilets, as it will never be provided.

Safety & Hassles

Always keep an eye on your luggage on bus trips, wherever it is stored for the journey – it's easy for things to disappear. Try to keep your stuff with you, if possible. Also watch out for pickpockets, which are notorious in some places.

Nicaragua is one of the bus rip-off centers of the world. The local buses in Managua are famous for pickpockets, but the long-distance buses have pickpockets, too, along with bag slashers, purse snatchers and, of course, the many honest people who also travel by bus.

International Buses

For international bus trips, the normal procedure is to take a bus to the border, get off, go through customs and board another bus on the other side. Most border stations are open every day from around 7 am to 5 pm, possibly with a couple of hours off for lunch, but it's best to arrive early in the day.

Some international buses will carry you across the border. For example, Tica Bus has direct express buses between all capital cities in Central America (except Belize), traveling from one capital to the next during the day, stopping overnight there and continuing on to the next capital the following day. Of course you can't stop and visit other places in between, and a direct express bus will cost more than taking two or more separate buses. There can also be delays at borders, as you have to wait while the whole busload of people goes through customs. But this is a quick and easy way to get through Central America.

Other bus companies that do international routes are also appearing. Panaline now provides direct express service between Panama City and San José (Costa Rica), in spiffy air-conditioned buses with video and free sodas. Another direct bus provides a connection between San José and Changuinola near Bocas del Toro (Panama).

Several luxury bus lines are also now operating international routes. The Crucero del Golfo operates daily between Tegucigalpa and San Salvador; other luxury buses operate daily between Guatemala City and San Salvador. So it's now possible to bus all the way between Guatemala City and Tegucigalpa, via San Salvador, in one day. Details about all the international buses are given in the various country chapters.

Tourist Minibuses

Some countries now have a growing network of tourist minibuses offering fast, convenient, door-to-door transport to tourist sites. This is especially true in Guatemala, where many tourists congregate in certain places, distances are relatively short, and the normal buses are often crowded, uncomfortable and slow. Tourist minibuses typically carry eight to 10 passengers, cost significantly more than the regular bus services, pick you up and deliver you to your hotel of choice, and provide faster service than regular buses.

TRAIN

Unfortunately, train services have been disappearing, and it is not possible to get around Central America by train.

CAR & MOTORCYCLE

Central America is easy to get around by private vehicle. Taking your own car is more expensive than taking the bus, however, and there are various hassles involved. Roads vary greatly in quality. Most major transport routes are good, paved, two-lane roads, but backcountry roads are often unpaved, making for much slower travel. Dirt roads can be dusty in the dry season and muddy in the rainy season.

Depending on which country you're from, your driver's license may be honored in the countries you'll be visiting; automobile associations have information on which licenses honor which licenses. If your home-country license is not accepted in the countries you'll be visiting, you should have an International Driving Permit even if you don't plan to drive your own vehicle. You never know when an opportunity to drive or a need to rent a car might arise. All the Central American countries honor this permit, which is issued at automobile associations around the world. To get one, simply present your valid driver's license and one or two passport-size photos, and pay a small fee (usually around US$5).

Taking Your Own Vehicle

There are many things to consider when deciding whether to bring a vehicle with you to Central America. If your intention is

---

Land Borders & Fees

Crossing land borders can sometimes present special problems. There are rarely signs telling you at which window or building you should present yourself, but fortunately children or moneychangers are usually on hand to help out. A greater pitfall is the fees demanded by border officials. These can vary from crossing to crossing, let alone country to country. Sometimes it is clearly an official fee (for example, the 75 colones ticket in your passport when leaving Costa Rica; at other times you can be fairly sure the money is just going into the guards' pockets. Charges are typically US$2 or less, but occasionally you won't be charged a thing.

Entering Honduras normally costs US$0.70 or US$1.40, but when I crossed at Las Manos the guard demanded 50 lempiras (US$7); coincidentally, the exact sum I had just changed at the moneychanger's window. I refused to pay without an official receipt, at which point she backed down and I got in for nothing. Going the other way at the same crossing a traveler was charged US$4.50 by the Nicaraguans, in addition to the normal US$1.50 or US$2.25. This, he was told, was an 'overtime' payment for crossing on the weekend after 1 pm on Saturday. Another traveler wrote that when crossing from Honduras to Nicaragua he was asked for US$20; he refused to pay and was eventually charged the usual amount.

The best policy is to pay up if the sum demanded is small to ensure a smooth passage (though some travelers have successfully argued against even minimal fees). If the fee seems too high, seek confirmation of the amount, either from written documentation, from the official in charge, or from other people crossing the border. You could refuse to pay; if there seems no option but to pay, at least insist on an official receipt. ■

Border Crossings
* indicates major crossing

BELIZE—GUATEMALA
Benque Viejo del Carmen—
   Melchor de Mencos
Punta Gorda—Lívingston (Sea route)
Punta Gorda—Puerto Barrios (Sea route)

BELIZE—MEXICO
*Santa Elena—Subteniente López,
   near Chetumal
Blue Creek Village—La Unión

COSTA RICA—NICARAGUA
*Peñas Blancas—Peñas Blancas
   (On Interamericana)
Near Los Chiles—near San Carlos,
   on Río Frío

COSTA RICA—PANAMA
Sixaola—Guabito
*Paso Canoas—Panama
   (On Interamericana)
Near San Vito—Río Sereno

EL SALVADOR—GUATEMALA
*Near Las Chinamas—near Valle Nuevo
*La Hachadura—Ciudad Pedro de Alvarado
*San Cristóbal—San Cristóbal Frontera
   (On Interamericana)
Anguiatú—Anguiatú

EL SALVADOR—HONDURAS
Citalá/El Poy, near La Palma—El Poy, near
   Nueva Ocotepeque (Honduran and
   Salvadoran buses both depart for El Poy.)
*El Amatillo, near Santa Rosa de Lima—
   El Amatillo (On Interamericana; Honduran
   and Salvadoran buses both depart for
   El Amatillo.)
Perquín—Sabanetas (Not an official border
   crossing. No public transport; difficult to
   access.)

GUATEMALA—BELIZE
Melchor de Mencos—Benque Viejo
   del Carmen
Lívingston—Punta Gorda (Sea route)
Puerto Barrios—Punta Gorda (Sea route)

GUATEMALA—EL SALVADOR
*San Cristóbal Frontera—San Cristobal
   (On Interamericana)
*Near Valle Nuevo—near Las Chinamas
*Ciudad Pedro de Alvarado—La Hachadura
Anguiatú—Anguiatú

GUATEMALA—HONDURAS
*El Florido—Copán Ruinas
*Agua Caliente—Agua Caliente
El Chinchado—Corinto
Puerto Barrios—Puerto Cortés (See Honduras)

GUATEMALA—MEXICO
*La Mesilla—Cuauhtémoc
   (On Interamericana)

*El Carmen—Tuxtla Chico, near Tapachula
Ciudad Tecún Umán—Ciudad Hidalgo
El Naranjo—La Palma (Route involves
   boat ride on Río San Pedro.)
Bethel—Frontera Corozal (Route
   involves boat ride on Río Usumacinta.)
Sayaxché—Benemerito
   (Route requires negotiating ride on
   cargo boat for eight-hour ride on
   Río de la Pasión.)

HONDURAS—EL SALVADOR
El Poy, near Nueva Ocotepeque—
   Citalá/El Poy, near La Palma (Honduras and
   El Salvador buses both depart for El Poy.)
*El Amatillo—El Amatillo, near Santa Rosa
   de Lima (On Interamericana)
Sabanetas—Perquín
   (See El Salvador regarding difficulty.)

HONDURAS—GUATEMALA
*Copán Ruinas—El Florido
*Agua Caliente—Agua Caliente
Corinto—El Chinchado
   (On foot trails; difficult.)
Puerto Cortés—Puerto Barrios (AKA the
   Jungle Trail. Route crosses land and
   water via Finca La Inca and El Límite,
   Guatemala, and Cuyamelito, Honduras.)

HONDURAS—NICARAGUA
Las Manos, near El Paraíso—
   Las Manos, near Ocotal
*Near San Marcos de Colón—El Espino,
   near Somoto (On Interamericana)
El Triunfo—Guasaule, near Somotillo

NICARAGUA—COSTA RICA
*Peñas Blancas—Peñas Blancas
   (On Interamericana)
Near San Carlos (on Río Frío)—
   near Los Chiles

NICARAGUA—HONDURAS
Guasaule, near Somotillo—El Trifuno
El Espino, near Somoto—San Marcos
   de Colón (On Interamericana)
Las Manos, near Ocotal—El Paraíso

PANAMA—COLOMBIA
Puerto Obaldía—Sapzurro
Palo de las Letras—near Cristales
   (This is a footpath.)

PANAMA—COSTA RICA
*Panama—Paso Canoas
   (On Interamericana)
Río Sereno—near San Vito
Guabito—Sixaola

to travel from North to South America, or vice versa, don't forget the Darién Gap – as noted in the previous chapter, you'll have to ship your vehicle around it.

If you plan simply to travel around Central America, there are various advantages and disadvantages to taking your own vehicle. On the positive side, it makes it easy to stop and see anything that catches your eye (the very things the bus whizzes past). You can go at anytime and at any pace – you're not tied to bus routes or schedules. Driving also allows you to stay in more remote places. You can do more traveling in less time with your own vehicle than you could on buses, which might be an important consideration if time is limited.

On the other hand, bringing your own vehicle does have certain drawbacks. There are a number of expenses: *gasolina* (petrol) costs around US$2 a US gallon (US$0.50 a liter) in Central America. Diesel fuel costs significantly less than regular or premium grades and is available practically everywhere. Because of this, diesel-run vehicles (especially the new, small pickups) are among the most common vehicles in Central America.

When calculating costs, take everything into account. If you bring your own vehicle, will you be camping and thus saving on hotel bills? Consider insurance costs: Some countries require insurance and others don't, but you should definitely have it when driving in a foreign country.

It can take a long time (sometimes hours) to cross borders with a vehicle. The law may require that the vehicle be fumigated when passing from one country to another, and a fee will be charged for this. The vehicle may be rigorously searched.

Then there is the paperwork. As a rule, Central American countries require a lot of it for any vehicle brought within their borders. There are forms to fill out at the border, more fees to pay, and then there is continuing paperwork once you're inside the country. In some places you may be given a 30-day visa for yourself, but only a 10-day permit for your vehicle! You'll then have to re-register your vehicle at the trans-port department every 10 days you stay there, and after a month they might require you either to pay a hefty import duty tax on the vehicle or to remove it from the country. Rules vary between countries.

When carrying all your belongings in a vehicle, you must be careful how and where you leave it. In some places theft from vehicles is common, and a foreign license plate naturally attracts extra attention. At night, you'll have to find a safe place not only for yourself but also for your vehicle.

Then there's the matter of meeting people. When you travel by public transport or hitchhike, you get closer to the people and culture. You meet people all along the way, buy tacos through bus windows, and do a million other things that you couldn't if you were insulated in the privacy of your own vehicle.

Catalytic Converters If you are bringing a vehicle from the USA that is less than 20 years old, it will have a catalytic converter, which enables it to run on unleaded fuel. This is required by law in the USA. In Mexico and most Central American countries, however, unleaded fuel may be unavailable so you'll have to use regular, premium, or diesel fuel. (This may not be uniform throughout the region, however – for example, we've heard that unleaded fuel is now widely available in Nicaragua.)

If your car normally requires unleaded fuel, you can modify it simply by taking off the catalytic converter and replacing it with a straight piece of exhaust pipe. It will then be able to run on regular fuel. Just be sure to reinstall the catalytic converter when you return to the USA. Workshops in Mexico, just south of the US border, will remove and reinstall catalytic converters, but it's illegal to do this in the USA.

Rental
Renting a vehicle provides many of the advantages of having your own transport and eliminates many of the disadvantages. When you rent a car, you're not stuck with it; you get it just for the time you want, make a special trip or two, and then take it

back. You can take the vehicle anywhere within the country where you rent it, but you cannot cross any borders.

Renting is expensive but there are several things you can do to mitigate the cost. The most effective is to get a group of people to share the expense. You can usually drum up four or five people by going around to the budget hotels and proposing a trip.

Ring around and ask the rates for the cheapest available cars at every agency in town. In any capital city, look in the yellow pages of the telephone directory under 'Alquiler de Automóviles' and 'Renta de Automóviles' to find a score of agencies. Some other towns may have agencies, too. The big international companies (Avis, Budget, Hertz) are represented in Central America, but the small local operators usually have the best prices. Car-rental costs at airports can be inflated; you often get much better prices by taking the airport transport into town and renting a car from an agency there.

When you phone agencies, be sure they understand that you want to hire a vehicle as cheaply as possible. Ask about special deals, and be as flexible as possible with your plans. Often you'll find a bargain: three days for the price of two, discounts during a particular month, and so on. Weekend prices are frequently lower than weekday prices, and the longer you keep the car, the lower the daily rate. It can be cheaper to hire a car for seven days than for six, as it knocks you up into the weekly rate. Compare the rate for unlimited kilometers with the per-kilometer rate, and consider the distance you intend to drive; sometimes one rate will suit your purpose much better than the other.

Many agencies have 4WD vehicles, including jeeps and pickups, as well as regular cars. Sometimes 4WDs are cheaper to rent than cars, and they're great for getting off the beaten track. Determine in advance whether you'll need a 4WD vehicle to get to your destination.

One of the best ways to save money on rentals is to have a credit card that provides free insurance when you charge the cost. Check the coverage and conditions of the insurance provided by your card. If you want to rent a car from time to time, it can be worth getting a card like this before you set off on your trip: It can save you as much as half the cost.

Whenever you rent a vehicle, particularly from a cheaper, local operator, always ask about your liability in the event of an accident or breakdown. Some travelers have been faced with big bills for damage that wasn't necessarily their fault.

Buying & Selling

You can buy a car anywhere in Central America, but prices are high; most of the Central American countries have amazingly high import duties on cars, which raises their prices sky high. If you are coming from the USA, you could buy a car there for about a quarter of what the same car would cost you in Central America.

Travelers used to make money buying used vehicles in the USA, driving them to Central America and selling them there, but recent reports on this kind of venture vary. One Central American, now living in New York, does it every couple of years. He said he wouldn't make a lot of money on any sale, but it would be enough to pay for the trip and, of course, he had the car for getting around in the meantime. An Englishman pays for his trips by bringing merchandise down from the USA and selling it out of the trunk of his car before selling the car itself.

We've heard, however, that it is getting much more difficult to do this kind of thing. Central American governments levy substantial taxes on car sales, hence all the required paperwork for bringing a private vehicle into these countries. If you sell your car privately, the government still wants its cut. Any local who buys a car from you will have to pay a large import tax before the car can be registered. This additional cost reduces the amount you can expect to get when you sell the car. You, for your part, will have to present documents to show why you no longer have your vehicle and what happened to it.

If you want to try your luck selling a vehicle in Central America, you should consider it as a possible way to subsidize your trip rather than as a big money-making venture. Probably the easiest kind of vehicle to sell is a small Japanese diesel pickup truck (a Toyota or Suzuki, for example). In rural areas this is about the only kind of vehicle anyone wants. A 4WD pickup would probably be best.

Whether you're buying or selling, be sure all the paperwork is in order, or you could be in serious trouble.

Here are a few comments on the subject that we've received recently from travelers:

A couple of French travelers wrote to us saying they bought a car in the cheap California market and drove it to Central America, intending to sell it there – only to find it virtually impossible to find a buyer, as they had bought an American rather than a Japanese car. 'Don't forget,' they wrote, 'Japanese car!' After spending weeks placing ads in newspapers, visiting car dealers and so on, they finally managed to sell it privately, but then had to pay hefty taxes.

A couple of British travelers wrote to tell us they had planned to drive through Central and South America, and then fly out to Africa. However, they said all the South American countries had made it illegal to enter with a vehicle and leave without it. In the end they decided to leave their vehicle in storage in Central America while they were traveling through South America; when they wrote to us they were preparing to make the long drive back from Central America to the USA, where they had bought the vehicle.

BICYCLE

There aren't many foreign cyclists pedaling through Central America, but it can be done (see Books in the Facts for the Visitor chapter for helpful guides). Locals don't usually bicycle long distance either.

If you try it, be sure to cycle extremely defensively; drivers in Central America are not expecting to come upon a cyclist on the road. Central American highways are often very narrow. There are plenty of drivers who are speeding along like maniacs and won't have a chance to avoid hitting you if you're in their way.

Be sure to bring with you any spare parts you might need, or you could be stuck for a very long time waiting for a replacement part to be sent to you.

The biggest drawback to cycling through Central America might be the heat. Temperatures are cooler in the highlands (though even there it can still be quite warm in the daytime), but in the flat low-lands the heat can be brutal. Be sure to drink enough water, possibly taking salt so your body will retain moisture, and avoid cycling during the heat of the day.

If you're planning a cycling trip, consider the seasons. It usually doesn't rain all day long even in the rainy season, so you won't be slogging through rain day after day, but dirt roads in the more remote areas will be very muddy. Remember that the rainy season is very humid as well as hot, causing you to feel the heat more.

In Panama City we met a game English chap who had pedaled down from the USA. He said that cycling through Central America really isn't that difficult and that more cyclists are doing it all the time. However, he would suggest bringing US$100 or US$200 to Central America and buying a local bike, which the locals would be able to deal with or fix if need be, rather than spending US$3000 on a state-of-the-art machine back home that would attract attention in Central America and might get stolen. He said he'd also recommend using a mirror, so you can see what's coming up behind you on the road.

At a cafe overlooking Lago de Atitlán in Guatemala, we met Martin, a New Yorker who was cycling throughout Latin America – he had cycled south from Texas and was heading for Tierra del Fuego. He was the kind of guy who cycles up volcanoes for his before-breakfast entertainment – no kidding!

He recommends that cyclists carry everything they need to be self-sufficient, and be prepared to spend the night out in the boonies sometimes. Map distances can be deceptive, and you must be prepared to spend the night outdoors. He had just cycled up to the lake from Chicacao, a distance that he had judged would take a couple of hours based on the map. He left in early afternoon and by nightfall had gotten only about a third of the way. He cycled on all the following day, finally reaching the lake at Santiago Atitlán that night. He said it was one of the most grueling days of cycling he'd ever had, and he would not recommend that route to anyone.

Rental

There aren't many places to rent a bicycle in Central America; you'll find a few mentioned in this book. If you plan to do any serious cycling, you should have your own bike, gear and spare parts.

HITCHHIKING

Hitchhiking is never entirely safe in any country in the world, and we don't recommend it. Travelers who decide to hitch should understand that they are taking a small but potentially serious risk. However, many people do choose to hitch, and the advice that follows should help to make their journeys as fast and safe as possible.

It's pretty easy to hitchhike around Central America. In many rural areas, where the bus comes infrequently and few people have private vehicles, hitchhiking is a recognized form of transport. Someone may pull up in a pickup truck and load up all the walkers along the road.

The custom in Central America is that hitchhikers should offer to pay for their ride (¿Cuanto le debo?, 'What do I owe you?'). It never costs much, usually less than the bus fare. It's quite likely that the driver will say you owe nothing, but don't expect a free ride – at least give a little something. Gasoline is very expensive for locals, and someone who gets a lift will usually contribute something.

All the usual commonsense hitchhiking rules of the road apply here. Hitching is much easier in the daytime than after dark. Make sure you stand in a spot where you can be easily seen and where the driver can pull over safely. Be aware of how you look – you don't want to look so grubby that nobody would want you in their car, but you don't want to look too rich either. You can use your thumb to indicate you want a lift.

Hitching is difficult in cities and populated areas; the best hitching spots are usually on major highways or roads on the outskirts of towns, where drivers will be heading out. Leaving a city, you'll find that it's often worth paying a few cents to take a local bus to a good hitching spot on the outskirts.

Two or three people hitchhiking together are safer than one person alone; women in particular should be very cautious about hitchhiking alone. In many countries it can be difficult for groups of two or more people (particularly males) to get a lift, but in Central America, three or four travelers can often successfully hitch together because of the prevalence of trucks, both large and small.

Use your instincts, and don't get into a car that seems suspicious for any reason – or even for no reason. You can always wait for another ride, but once you're in a car it might not be so easy to get out again.

BOAT

Central America has extensive coastlines on both the Caribbean and Pacific sides, hundreds of sea islands, thousands of kilometers of rivers and the Panama Canal, one of the world's most important waterways. There are plenty of options for getting around by boat within the various countries, between different countries, and from Central America to other parts of the world.

Boat travel within each country is described in the individual country chapters. Some of the more famous boat trips include journeys on the Río Dulce in Guatemala, the Río Plátano in Honduras, the trip from Rama to Bluefields in Nicaragua, various trips on the Río San Juan on the Nicaragua/Costa Rica border and crossings of the Panama Canal. Boats also serve various islands in Lago de Nicaragua, including Ometepe, the Archipiélago de Solentiname and Las Isletas near Granada. White-water rafting is becoming popular in many countries, too.

Boat trips on the Caribbean include those between Lívingston and Puerto Barrios in Guatemala, between La Ceiba and the Bay Islands in Honduras, between Bluefields and the Corn Islands in Nicaragua, and along the hundreds of islands of the Archipiélago de San Blas of eastern Panama.

Passenger boats offer transport among various Central American countries. These include boats between Punta Gorda (Belize) and Puerto Barrios (Guatemala), between Dangriga (Belize) and Puerto Cortés (Honduras), and between Lívingston (Guatemala) and Omoa (Honduras). Boats also operate on less regular schedules between Honduras' Bay Islands and places on the mainland of Honduras, Guatemala and Belize.

Aside from the scheduled passenger services, all kinds of boats ply the coasts all the time. If you're lucky, if you look like you wouldn't be too much trouble to take along, if you could pitch in with the work, and especially if you can pay for your passage, you might be able to catch a ride. The more flexible you can be, the better chance you'll have, whether on a fishing boat, a cargo vessel, a smaller boat taking supplies to coastal villages, or a sailing yacht making coastal hops. The best way to catch one of these is to go to a port and ask around the docks or yacht marinas. There's a lot more small boat traffic on the Caribbean Coast than on the Pacific. Even so, you might have to wait a while for the right boat to come along.

ORGANIZED TOURS

Throughout this book we provide information on a great variety of tours. They're mentioned in the Organized Tours sections of each country chapter and under many cities, towns and regions. It's easy to travel independently in Central America and take a tour here and there to enjoy some special attraction.

It's also possible to arrange tours before you arrive in Central America. You can phone ahead to tour and travel agencies mentioned in this book; travel agents in your home country should also have information on tours.

Organized tours can range from two-hour outings for bird watching, snorkeling or diving to extensive journeys of a week or longer focusing on a special interest – visits to remote Mayan ruins, for example, or a 14-day crossing of Panama's Darién Province, reenacting the journey Balboa took across the isthmus in 1519 when he became the first European to sight the Pacific Ocean.

Tours are a good way to visit certain places. Although you can visit natural and wilderness areas on your own, you can enrich your experience immensely by going with a knowledgeable guide familiar with the plants, animals, birds and other interesting features as well as the lay of the land. Many national parks offer guide services; the US$3 or so you spend for a guide is well worth it, as you will see more wildlife and learn more about the natural environment than if you go on your own.

Guides familiar with the history of Maya ruins, colonial cities and so on can make the old stones come to life. Some sites such as remote archaeological sites or trails are so remote that a guided tour is almost the only practical way to get there.

Some tours originate outside the region. For example, Green Tortoise, based in California, offers several budget tours to Central America. Green Tortoise has long been known for its trips and tours in North America, in which young-at-heart travelers sleep on bunks in the bus (a sort of communal home-on-wheels) and join in preparing communal meals. Most of their Central America trips operate during Central America's dry season, but some go during the green season as well. For example, their 17-day Southern Migration from San Francisco to Guatemala goes once a year, usually in December; the cost is US$599 plus US$121 for meals. Another tour, an 18-day Central America Expedition from Antigua Guatemala to Costa Rica, costs the same and usually leaves in January. Then there's their 'Language School on Wheels,' a 15-day ramble around Costa Rica with Spanish lessons included, starting and ending in San José. Contact Green Tortoise at 494 Broadway St, San Francisco, CA 94133 USA (☎ (415) 956-7500, (800) 867-8647, fax (415) 956-4900, net).

Guatemala

Guatemala is the heart of the Maya world, a beautiful, fertile land with a tragic history.

The Maya who live in the highlands amid breathtaking mountain scenery guard their ancient customs and way of life. Holidays and ceremonies are filled with ancient pageantry, and the weekly markets are ablaze with the vivid colors of traditional handmade costumes.

At the same time, the modern world is penetrating Maya culture, bringing good things and bad. Money from tourism is helping the Maya to improve their quality of life, education and health, but it is luring the younger generation away from their traditions and toward the raucous, bustling cities.

The distinction between indigenous and 'European' blood, between traditional and modern culture and commerce, has been felt strongly here since the days of the Conquistadores. Today the distinction divides Guatemalan society in two, and has often led to oppression and bloody conflict.

Traditional life and modern values also clash when local farmers and ranchers clear the rain forest to provide for their families. The need is for a livelihood; the method is the traditional one of slash-and-burn; the result is ecological disaster.

The paradoxes of Guatemala are part of its fascination.

Facts about Guatemala

HISTORY

For colonial Guatemalan history, see the regional History section in Facts about Central America.

The history of the country since independence has been one of rivalry and struggle between the forces of left and right. The Liberals have historically wanted to turn backward Guatemala into an enlightened republic of political, social and economic progress. The Conservatives hoped to preserve the traditional verities of colonial rule, with a strong Church and a strong government. Their motto might have been 'power must be held by those with merit, virtue and property'. Historically, both movements have benefited the social and economic elites and disenfranchised the people of the countryside, mostly the Maya.

Morazán & the Liberals

The Liberals, the first to advocate independence, opposed the vested interests of the elite Conservatives, who had the Church and the large landowners on their side.

During the short existence of the United Provinces of Central America, Liberal President Francisco Morazán (1830 – 1839) instituted reforms aimed at correcting three persistent problems: the great economic, political and social power of the Church; the division of society into a Hispanic upper class and an Indian lower class; and the region's powerlessness in world markets. This Liberal program was echoed by Guatemalan Chief of State Mariano Gálvez (1831 – 1838).

But unpopular economic policies, heavy taxes and a cholera epidemic in 1837 led to an Indian uprising which brought a Conservative pig farmer, Rafael Carrera, to power. Carrera held power until 1865, and undid much of what Morazán and Gálvez had achieved. The Carrera government allowed Great Britain to take control of Belize in exchange for construction of a road between Guatemala City and Belize City. The road called for in the treaty was never built, and Guatemala's claims for compensation were never resolved.

Liberal Reforms of Barrios

The Liberals came to power again in the 1870s, first under Miguel García Granados,

95

Map Index

```
0        30      60 km
0     20      40 miles
```

OTHER MAPS
• Guatemala
  pgs 98-99
• Parks & Protected Areas
  pg 103

MEXICO

Tikal
pgs 242-243

BELIZE

Lago de
Petén Itzá
pg 233

Flores pg 234
Santa Elena pg 236

Golfo de
Honduras

Lívingston
pg 227

Puerto
Barrios
pg 223

El Petén
pg 232

Cobán
pg 205

Huehuetenango
pg 187

Chichicastenango
pg 165

Chiquimula
pg 211

Quetzaltenango
pg 175
Central Quetzaltenango
pg 178

Panajachel
pg 152

Guatemala City
pgs 120-121

HONDURAS

Retalhuleu
pg 192

Lago de
Atitlán
pg 150

Antigua Guatemala
pgs 136-137

Santa Lucía
Cotzumalguapa
pg 195

EL SALVADOR

PACIFIC OCEAN

next under Justo Rufino Barrios, a rich young coffee *finca* owner who held the title of president and ruled as a dictator (1873 – 1879). With Barrios at its head the country made great strides toward modernization with construction of roads, railways, schools and a modern banking system. To boost the economy, everything possible was done to encourage coffee production. Peasants in good coffee-growing areas (up to 1400 meters altitude on the Pacific Slope) were forced off their lands to make way for new fincas, and those living above 1400 meters (mostly Indians), were forced

to contribute seasonal labor, as on plantations during colonial times. Idealistic Liberal policies, championed by the British and often meant to benefit the common people, ended up oppressing them. Most of the policies of the Liberal reform movement benefited finca owners and urban merchants.

Succeeding governments generally pursued the same policies. Economic control of the country was by a small group of land-owning and commercial families, foreign companies were given generous concessions, opponents of the government were censored, imprisoned or exiled by the extensive police force, and the government apparatus was subservient to economic interests despite a liberal constitution.

Dictators & Presidents, 1898 to 1960

Manuel Estrada Cabrera Estrada Cabrera ruled from 1898 to 1920, and his dictatorial style, while bringing progress in technical matters, placed a heavy burden on all but the ruling oligarchy. He styled himself as the 'Teacher and Protector of Guatemalan Youth.'

He sponsored Fiestas de Minerva in the cities, inspired by the Roman goddess of wisdom, invention and technology, and ordered the construction of temples, some of which still exist (as in Quetzaltenango). Guatemala was to become a 'tropical Athens.' At the same time he looted the treasury, ignored the schools, and spent millions on the armed forces.

Jorge Ubico When Estrada Cabrera was overthrown, Guatemala entered a period of instability which ended in 1931 with the election of General Jorge Ubico as president. Ubico ruled as Estrada Cabrera had, but more efficiently. Though his word was law, he insisted on honesty in government, and he modernized the country's health and social welfare infrastructure. Debt peonage was outlawed; but a new servitude of labor contributions to the government road-building program was established in its place. Other public works projects included the construction of the vast presidential palace on the main plaza in Guatemala City.

In the 1940s Ubico dispossessed and exiled the great, German coffee-finca owners, and otherwise assumed a pro-Allied stance during the war, but at the same time he openly admired Spain's dictator Generalissimo Francisco Franco. In 1944 he was forced to resign and go into exile.

Juan José Arévalo Just when it appeared that Guatemalan politics were doomed to become a succession of well-intentioned but harsh dictators, the elections of 1945 brought a philosopher to power. Arévalo

established the nation's social security system, a government bureau to look after Indian concerns, a modern public health system, and liberal labor laws. During his six years as president there was an average of one coup attempt every three months.

Jacobo Arbenz Guzmán Arévalo was succeeded by Colonel Jacobo Arbenz Guzmán in 1951. Arbenz continued the policies of Arévalo, instituting an agrarian reform law that was meant to break up the large estates and foster high productivity on small individually owned farms. He also expropriated vast lands conceded to the United Fruit Company during the Estrada and Ubico years, but now held fallow. Compensation was paid at the value which they had declared for tax purposes, which was below its actual value, and he announced that the lands were to be distributed to peasants and put into cultivation for food.

But the expropriation, supported by the Guatemalan Communist Party, set off alarms in Washington, in support of the interests of United Fruit. In 1954 the USA orchestrated an invasion from Honduras led by two exiled Guatemalan military officers, and Arbenz was forced to step down. The land reform never took place.

After Arbenz, the country had a succession of military presidents elected with the support of the officers' corps, business leaders, compliant political parties and the Church. Violence became a staple of political life. Opponents of the government regularly turned up dead. The land reform measures were reversed, voting was made dependent on literacy (which disenfranchised around 75% of the population), the secret police force was revived, and military repression was common.

The poor majority was not happy, and their grievances went unaddressed. In 1960 guerrilla groups began to form.

The 1960s & 1970s

During the 1960s and 1970s, Guatemalan industry boomed. Most profits flowed upwards, labor union organization put more stresses on the political fabric and migration from the countryside to the cities, especially the capital, produced urban sprawl and slums.

As the pressures in society increased so did the violence of protest and repression, which led to the total politicization of society. Everyone took sides, usually the poorer classes in the countryside versus the power elite in the cities. By 1979, Amnesty International estimated that 50,000 to 60,000 people had been killed during the political violence of the decade.

Another devastation: in 1976 a severe earthquake killed about 22,000 people and left about a million people homeless. Most of the aid sent to help the people in need never reached them.

The 1980s

In the early 1980s the military suppression of antigovernment elements in the countryside reached a peak, especially under the presidency of General José Efraín Ríos Montt, an evangelical Christian who came to power in a coup in March 1982. Alarming numbers of people, mostly Indian men, were killed in the name of anti-insurgency, stabilization and anticommunism.

The policy behind these killings was known as 'scorched earth.' The government did not know the identities of the rebels, but it was aware which areas were bases of rebel activity; the governement decided to exterminate the general populations of those areas to kill off the rebels. The government also hoped such tactics would dissuade the peasantry from joining or supporting the guerrillas. Over 400 villages were razed, and most of their inhabitants massacred (often tortured as well). The survivors were herded into remote, newly constructed 'model villages' surrounded by army encampments. It was later estimated that 15,000 civilian deaths occurred as a result of counter-insurgency operations during Ríos Montt's term of office.

Despite these heavy-handed tactics, perhaps half a million people, mostly peasants in the western and central highlands and in the northern El Petén region,

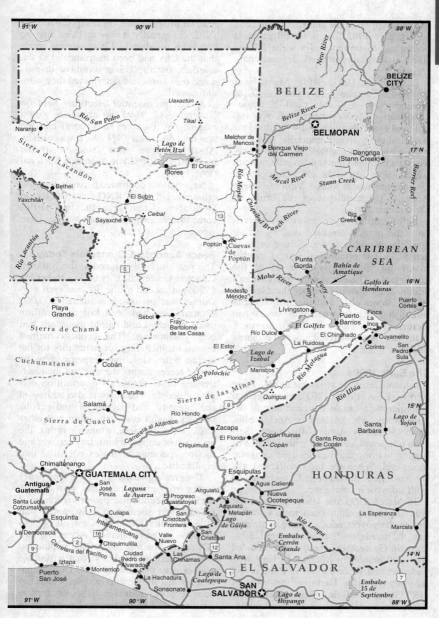

actively supported the guerrilla movement. In February 1982 four powerful guerrilla organizations united to form the URNG (the Guatemalan National Revolutionary Unity).

In August 1983, Ríos Montt was deposed by a coup led by General Oscar Humberto Mejía Victores, and the abuses continued – it was estimated that over 100 political assassinations and 40 abductions occurred every month under his rule. The bloodbath led to a cutoff of US military assistance to the Guatemalan government, which led in turn to the 1985 election of a civilian president, Marco Vinicio Cerezo Arévalo, the candidate of the Christian Democratic Party.

Before turning over power to the civilians, the military ensured that its earlier activities would not be examined or prosecuted, and it established formal mechanisms for the military control of the countryside. There was hope that Cerezo's administration would temper the excesses of the power elite and the military and establish a basis for true democracy. When Cerezo's term ended in 1990, however, many people wondered if any real progress had been made.

The Early 1990s

President Cerezo was succeeded by Jorge Serrano Elías (1990 – 1993), an evangelical Christian who ran as the candidate of the conservative Movimiento de Acción Solidaria (Solidarity Action Movement). Serrano re-opened a dialogue with the URNG, hoping to bring the decades-long civil war to an end. When the talks collapsed, the mediator from the Catholic Church blamed both sides for intransigence.

In March 1995 the USA announced it was suspending aid to Guatemala yet again due to the government's failure to investigate the murder or disappearance of US citizens in Guatemala. These cases included the 1990 murder of Michael Devine, who had operated Finca Ixobel in Poptún. US attorney Jennifer Harbury, the wife of URNG leader Efraín Bámaca Velásquez, has been conducting an internationally-renown protest since his disappearance in 1992. (Eventually it was revealed that he had been murdered.) Charges were made that the CIA had been instrumental in the murders, but the US government investigated the claims and determined they were unfounded.

At the presidential elections held on November 12, 1995, no candidate won a majority of the vote, so a runoff election was held on January 7, 1996. It was won by Álvaro Enrique Arzú Irigoyen of the middle-right Partido de Avanzada Nacional (PAN) party.

Negotiations continued between the government and the URNG, and finally, in December of that year, the two parties came to agreement and peace accords were signed.

Peace Accords & Guatemala Today

The peace accords, signed at the National Palace in Guatemala City on December 29, 1996, put an end to the 36 year civil war. During that period an estimated 200,000 Guatemalans had been killed, a million made homeless and untold thousands had been 'disappeared.' The accords contained provisions including accountability for the human rights violations perpetrated by the armed forces during the war and the resettlement of Guatemala's one million displaced people. The accords also addressed the identity and rights of indigenous peoples, health care, education and other basic social services, women's rights, the abolition of obligatory military service, and the incorporation of the ex-guerrillas into civilian life.

The greatest challenge to a lasting peace stems from great inequities in the basic social and economic power structure of Guatemalan society. It's estimated that 70% of cultivable land is owned by less than 3% of the population. According to a UN report, the top 20% of the population has an income 30 times (that's 3000%) greater than the bottom 20%. Discrimination against indigenous people, which has been deeply ingrained in the society for five centuries, is still present and manifests in poverty and misery for a large percentage of the population.

Both sides acknowledged that the signing of the peace accords was not a conclusion but a beginning. As one guerrilla representative told us, 'The peace accords will be signed on December 29. Our most challenging work will begin on December 30.'

GEOGRAPHY

Guatemala covers an area of 109,000 sq km with mountainous forest highlands and jungle plains.

The western highlands linked by the Interamericana are the continuation of Chiapas' Sierra Madre, and include 30 volcanoes reaching heights of 3800 meters in the Cuchumatanes range northwest of Huehuetenango. Land that has not been cleared for Maya *milpas* (cornfields) is covered in pine forests. Many of the volcanoes are active which signals that this is an earthquake area as well. Major quakes struck in 1773, 1917 and 1976.

The Pacific Slope of Guatemala is the continuation of Chiapas' Soconusco, with rich coffee, cacao, fruit and sugar plantations along the Carretera al Pacífico (Pacific Highway). Down along the shore the volcanic slope meets the sea, yielding vast beaches of black volcanic sand in a sweltering climate that is difficult to bear. Grass grows profusely in this climate, and it's fed to cattle.

South and east along the Interamericana the altitude decreases to about 1500 meters at Guatemala City.

North of Guatemala City the highlands of Alta Verapaz gradually decline to the lowland of El Petén, which is the continuation of southern Yucatán. To the southeast of Petén is the valley of the Río Motagua, dry in some areas, moist in others. Bananas thrive in the Motagua Valley.

CLIMATE

In the Guatemalan highlands, temperatures can get down to freezing at night in the mountains. Days can be dank and chill during the rainy season, but in the dry season from October to May they're warm and delightful. Guatemala's coasts are tropical, rainy, hot and humid, with temperatures often reaching 32°C to 38°C (90°F to 100°F), and almost constant high humidity, abating only slightly in the dry season. While the rainy and dry seasons are distinct on the Pacific Coast and in the highlands, on the Caribbean side rain is possible anytime. Cobán has only about one month of dry weather (in April).

The vast jungle lowland of El Petén has a climate and topography like that of Yucatán: seasonally hot and humid or hot and dry. December and January are the coolest months; March and April are the hottest.

ECOLOGY & ENVIRONMENT

As elsewhere in Central America, deforestation is a problem in Guatemala, especially in the Petén region, where jungle is being felled at an alarming rate to make way for cattle ranches. Only a few years ago, the government required anyone buying tracts of land in the Petén to clear a certain portion of it – presumably in the name of 'progress.'

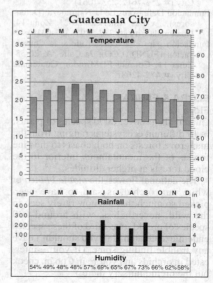

Guatemala City

Temperature

Rainfall

Humidity
54% 49% 48% 48% 57% 69% 65% 67% 73% 66% 62% 58%

Most of the Petén region is now officially designated as a protected area; in addition to the 575-sq-km Tikal National Park, there's the nearly two million-hectare Maya Biosphere Reserve, which includes most of the northern Petén region. Though these parks signify advances in conservation, the forest is still being ravaged by people illegally harvesting timber on a massive scale. Where the government has so far not acted, conservation organizations are trying to document offenses.

On the Pacific side of the country, where most of the population of Guatemala lives, the land is mostly agricultural.

The following organizations are good resources for finding out more about Guatemala's natural and protected areas:

Centro de Estudios Conservacionistas de la Universidad de San Carlos (CECON), Av La Reforma 0-63, Zona 10, Guatemala City (☎ 331-0904, 334-6064, 334-7662)

Comisión Nacional del Medio Ambiente (CONAMA), 5a Av 8-07, Zona 10, Guatemala City (☎ 334-1708, 331-2723)

Consejo Nacional de Areas Protegidas (CONAP), 8a Av 3-72, Zona 1, Guatemala City (☎ 253-7612, 253-7061)

Fundación Defensores de la Naturaleza (Defensores), Av Las Américas 20-21, Zona 14, Guatemala City (☎ 337-3897, 337-0319)

Fundación para el Ecodesarrollo y la Conservación (FUNDAECO), 7a Calle 'A' 20-53, Zona 11, Colonia El Mirador, Guatemala City (☎ 472-4268)

FLORA & FAUNA
Flora
Guatemala has over 8000 species of plants, in 19 different ecosystems ranging from the mangrove forests on both coasts to the pine forests of the mountainous interior to the cloud forests at higher altitudes.

The national flower, the *monja blanca* or white nun orchid, is said to have been picked so much that it's now rarely seen in the wild; nevertheless, with around 600 species of orchid (one-third of these species endemic to Guatemala), you shouldn't have any trouble finding some. (If you're interested in orchids and you're in Cobán, check out the orchid nursery there.)

Fauna
With its 19 ecosystems, Guatemala also has an abundance of animals. So far, estimates point to 250 species of mammals, 600 species of birds, 200 species of reptiles and amphibians, and many species of butterflies and other insects.

The national bird, the quetzal, is often used to symbolize Central America as well. (The national monetary unit, the quetzal, is named for the bird.)

Other interesting birds in Guatemala include the toucans, the macaws and the parrots. If you visit Tikal you will probably see the ocellated turkey, also called the Petén turkey, a large, impressive, multicolored bird reminiscent of a peacock. There are also large white herons, hawks, woodpeckers, hummingbirds, harpy eagles (rare), waterfowl and a plethora or other resident and migratory birds.

Notable mammals include jaguars, ocelots, pumas, howler and spider monkeys, tapirs, kinkajous, koatimundis, pizotes, tepezcuintles, white-tailed deer, armadillos and manatees. Reptiles and amphibians include at least three species of sea turtles (the leatherback, the olive Ridley and the *tortuga negra)* and at least two species of crocodile (one found in the Petén, the other in the Río Dulce).

National Parks & Protected Areas
Guatemala has more than 30 protected areas, including national parks and *biotopos* (biological reserves). Over 40 more areas have been proposed for protection. Many of the protected areas are remote; the ones mentioned here are some of the most easily accessible and interesting to visitors.

Reserva de la Biósfera Maya (Maya Biosphere Reserve)
Covering the northern half of the Petén region, this 1,844,900-hectare reserve is Guatemala's largest protected area. Within its boundaries are a number of important Mayan archaeological sites, including Tikal, Uaxactún, El Mirador, El Zotz and Piedras Negras.
Reserva de la Biósfera de Sierra de Las Minas (Sierra de las Minas Biosphere Reserve)
In the eastern part of the country, Guatemala's most important cloud forest reserve protects a

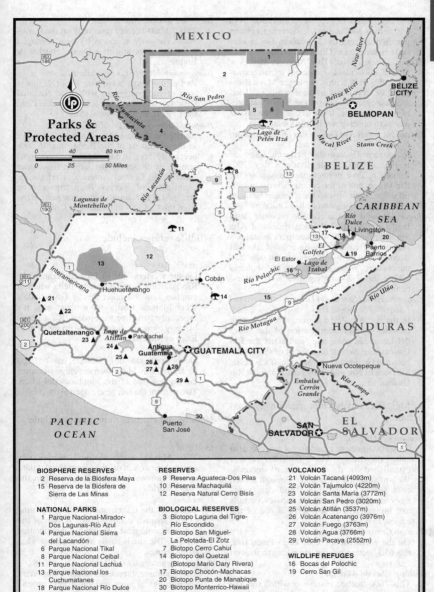

BIOSPHERE RESERVES
2 Reserva de la Biósfera Maya
15 Reserva de la Biósfera de
   Sierra de Las Minas

NATIONAL PARKS
1 Parque Nacional-Mirador-
   Dos Lagunas-Río Azul
4 Parque Nacional Sierra
   del Lacandón
6 Parque Nacional Tikal
8 Parque Nacional Ceibal
11 Parque Nacional Lachuá
13 Parque Nacional los
   Cuchumatanes
18 Parque Nacional Río Dulce

RESERVES
9 Reserva Aguateca-Dos Pilas
10 Reserva Machaquilá
12 Reserva Natural Cerro Bisís

BIOLOGICAL RESERVES
3 Biotopo Laguna del Tigre-
   Río Escondido
5 Biotopo San Miguel-
   La Pelotada-El Zotz
7 Biotopo Cerro Cahuí
14 Biotopo del Quetzal
   (Biotopo Mario Dary Rivera)
17 Biotopo Chocón-Machacas
20 Biotopo Punta de Manabique
30 Biotopo Monterrico-Hawaii

VOLCANOS
21 Volcán Tacaná (4093m)
22 Volcán Tajumulco (4220m)
23 Volcán Santa María (3772m)
24 Volcán San Pedro (3020m)
25 Volcán Atitlán (3537m)
26 Volcán Acatenango (3976m)
27 Volcán Fuego (3763m)
28 Volcán Agua (3766m)
29 Volcán Pacaya (2552m)

WILDLIFE REFUGES
16 Bocas del Polochic
19 Cerro San Gil

mountainous area ranging in elevation from 150 to over 3000 meters. Visitors must obtain permission from the Fundación Defensores de la Naturaleza in Guatemala City.

Parque Nacional Tikal (Tikal National Park)
One of Guatemala's principal tourist attractions, this park within the larger Maya Biosphere Reserve contains the magnificent Tikal archaeological site as well as 57,600 hectares of pristine jungle. It's also one of the easiest places to observe wildlife in Guatemala.

Parque Nacional Río Dulce (Río Dulce National Park)
In eastern Guatemala, between Lago de Izabal and the Golfo de Honduras, this 7200-hectare reserve protects the canyon of the Río Dulce, one of the country's most beautiful rivers. Boat trips on the river can be taken from either Lívingston or Río Dulce.

Parque Nacional Lachuá (Lachuá National Park)
In the northeast of the department of Alta Verapaz, this 10,000-hectare park contains a beautiful, circular turquoise-colored lake that is only five km in surface area but over 220 meters deep, with a great variety of fish. It has hiking trails, a camping area and visitors' center.

Parque Nacional Sierra del Lacandón (Sierra del Lacandón National Park)
In the western Petén region, this large park includes the southern portion of the Sierra del Lacandón mountains and abuts the Río Usumacinta, which forms part of the border between Guatemala and Mexico. It's accessible from El Naranjo or by boat along the Río Usumacinta.

Biological reserves *(biotopos protegidos)* include:

Biotopo del Quetzal
This 1000-hectare cloud forest reserve, also called the Biotopo Mario Dary Rivera, was established for the protection of quetzals. Well-maintained trails snake through a lush, cool forest of broad-leaf and coniferous trees, climbing plants, ferns, mosses, orchids and bromeliads. This reserve is one of the easiest to access.

Biotopo Cerro Cahuí
On the northeast shore of Lago Petén Itzá, this 650-hectare reserve has hiking trails with fine views.

Biotopo Chocón-Machacas
This 7600-hectare reserve is within the Río Dulce National Park, on the north bank of the river.

Biotopo Punta de Manabique
This 50,000-hectare reserve is on the Caribbean. The only access is by boat, arranged from the piers at either Puerto Barrios or Lívingston.

Biotopo San Miguel-La Pelotada-El Zotz
Part of the Maya Biosphere Reserve, this is west of and contiguous with Tikal National Park. It protects a dense forest, bat caves and the El Zotz archaeological site.

Biotopo Laguna del Tigre/Río Escondido
Situated within the Maya Biosphere Reserve in the northwest of the Petén, this 46,300-hectare reserve is one of Guatemala's most remote. It conserves the largest freshwater wetlands in Central America, a refuge for countless bird species. Boat trips can be arranged at El Naranjo, with prior permission from the CECON in Guatemala City.

Wildlife refuges include:

Bocas del Polochic
On the western side of Lago de Izabal, the Río Polochic forms a marshy delta where it empties into the lake; this is Guatemala's second-largest freshwater wetland area. It's especially attractive for birders. It's accessible only by water; boats can be arranged at El Estor or Mariscos.

Cerro San Gil
On the south side of El Golfete, east of Lago de Izabal, this lush, diverse refuge occupies the highest part of the Montañas del Mico. Two parts of the refuge are open to the public.

Natural and cultural monuments include:

Quiriguá
This Mayan archaeological site, easily accessible two km off the Carretera al Atlántico, is famous for the tallest stelae in the Maya world.

Iximché
Capital of the Cakchiquel Maya at the time of the Spanish conquest, this is one of the few archaeological sites with a documented history. The site is easily accessible, two km from Tecpán.

Ceibal y Aguateca-Dos Pilas
This monument protects several important archaeological sites and the forest around them. It's in the Río La Pasión valley, in the southwest of the Petén, in the municipality of

Sayaxché. It's accessible from Sayaxché, or by tour from Flores/Santa Elena.

Semuc-Champey
On the Río Cahabón in the municipality of Lanquín, Alta Verapaz, Semuc-Champey is a series of pristine pools surrounded by rain forest. It's accessible by 4WD vehicle, or by tour from Cobán.

GOVERNMENT & POLITICS

Guatemala is a republic with 22 departments. Executive power is held by a president who is elected by direct universal adult suffrage to a term of four years. He is assisted by a vice president and an appointed cabinet. The unicameral national congress consists of 80 members (64 departmental representatives and 16 national seats) also elected to four-year terms. Judicial power rests in a Supreme Court and associated courts.

Always a constitutional democracy in form, Guatemala has been ruled by a succession of military strongmen ever since Pedro de Alvarado came and conquered the Maya in the 1500s. With a few notable exceptions, Guatemala's government has been controlled for the benefit of the commercial, military, landowning and bureaucratic classes of society (see History, above).

One Guatemalan writer summed up his society this way: a bourgeoisie which doesn't invest in its country, but rather stashes its capital abroad; an incompetent, inept and corrupt political class; a left-leaning intellectual class which keeps to the realm of theory and which refuses to participate in politics because it equates politics with corruption; a political left wing which won't make peace or participate in the mainstream because it knows it has little chance of popular approval; a military class, divided into factions more or less rightist, which sees civil peace and democracy as endangering its claims to impunity, privilege and economic benefits; and a demoralized people who believe in neither their leaders nor the political process as means to make their country prosper.

ECONOMY

The Guatemalan highlands are given over to agriculture, particularly corn, with some mining and light industry around the larger cities. The Pacific Slope has large coffee, citrus and sugar cane plantations worked by migrant labor from the highlands, and the Pacific Coast has cattle ranches and some fishing villages. Coffee is the country's biggest export crop, followed by beef, cotton, cocoa, corn, beans, bananas, sugarcane, vegetables, flowers and fruits.

Guatemala City is the industrial and commercial center of the country, a copy in miniature of Mexico City, including its social problems.

Guatemala's Motagua Valley has some mining, but agriculture is most important here, with vast banana plantations. In the lush green hills of Alta Verapaz there are dairy farms, cardamom plantations and forests for timber.

El Petén depends upon tourism and farming for its livelihood. The rapid growth of agriculture and cattle farming is a serious threat to the ecology of Petén, a threat that will have to be controlled if the forests of this vast jungle province are to survive. Tourism, on the other hand, is a positive factor here, providing alternative sources of income in jobs which depend upon the preservation of the ecology for success.

POPULATION & PEOPLE

In Guatemala's population of 10 million people, the division between Maya and Spanish descent is much stricter than in Mexico. Under Spanish rule, most of highland Guatemala was administered by the friars who came to convert the Maya. The friars did a great deal to protect the indigenous people from exploitation, and to preserve traditional Maya society (though not Maya religion). But the region around Guatemala City was directly administered by the colonial government without the softening effect of the friars' intervention, and the traditional life of the Maya was largely replaced by a hybrid culture that was neither Maya nor strictly Hispanic.

Interrelations produced a mestizo population known as *ladinos*, who had abandoned their Maya traditions to adopt the Spanish ways, but who were not accepted into white Spanish society.

And so today the society is divided between the ladino and Maya peoples, both pursuing pathways that are sometimes convergent but often at odds. While the ladino culture is proceeding into the modern world, in many ways the Maya, who are the majority, are holding on tight to their traditional culture and identity despite five centuries of European domination and occupation of their land.

Maya culture expresses itself in many ways. The most noticeable to visitors is the beautiful traditional clothing worn by Maya women. In most parts of Guatemala the men now wear western clothing, but in some places, such as Sololá and Todos Santos Cuchumatán, the men also still wear traditional *trajes*. Each village has its own unique style of dress, and within the village style there can be variations according to social status; when all of the variations are taken into account, there are something like 500 distinctive forms of design, each with its own significance.

Various traditional arts, such as the weaving, embroidery and other textile arts practiced by Maya women. Others include basketry, ceramics, wood carving and music played on traditional instruments. Maya languages are still in use everyday for most Maya, with 21 different languages spoken from different regions of the country. Maya religion, firmly based in nature, is also still practiced by Maya people.

Guatemalans of European blood are proud of their ancestry as well; they form the elite of the modern commercial, bureaucratic and military upper classes. Ladinos fill in the middle ground between the Old Guard White Hispanic, European and North American elite and the Maya farmers and laborers. Ladinos are often shopkeepers, merchants, traders, administrators, bureaucrats and especially politicians.

EDUCATION

Education in Guatemala is free and compulsory between the ages of seven and 14. Primary education lasts for six years; it's estimated that only 79% of children of this age are actually in school. Secondary education begins at age 13 and lasts for up to six years, with two cycles of three years each; it's estimated that only 23% of children of the relevant age group are in secondary school. Guatemala has five universities.

Adult literacy is around 65%; the average rate of adult illiteracy is 37% for males, 53% for females, the second highest rate in the Western Hemisphere. There's a big variation in literacy rates among different groups, however. A Guatemalan organization specializing in Maya women's concerns estimates that 95% of rural women (who are mostly Maya) are illiterate. Maya children who do seasonal migrant work with their families find it difficult to get an education, as the time the families go away to work falls during the normal school year.

ARTS

Chief among the many traditional arts are the handicrafts Guatemala is famous for, especially the colorful textiles, and also basketry, ceramics and wood carving.

The Maya also have other distinctive arts, notably music played on their own traditional instruments. A number of well-known Maya painters work in a distinctive primitivist style depicting daily life.

The architecture of the ancient Maya ruins and the Spanish colonial architecture in Antigua are both impressive to see.

SOCIETY & CONDUCT

Today the Maya people are being pushed further and further into the background of society. Travelers may be surprised to learn that in Guatemala, the Maya (who are the majority of the population) are viciously and often violently discriminated against. While some are going to universities, working in the business world and joining modern society, those who preserve the traditional way of life are the poorest sector of Guatemalan society. The focus of international attention upon the plight of the Maya people has brought it to light.

Travelers can help the Maya by buying their traditional handicrafts. Fair prices help to make this trade an economically viable occupation.

Dos & Don'ts

Note that many Maya children speak only their indigenous language. Where this is the case, it's futile to try to engage them in conversation in Spanish. In recent years, stories circulated through Guatemala that some foreign visitors were kidnapping Maya children, perhaps for the grisly purpose of selling their bodily organs. Be aware that some people are extremely suspicious of foreigners who make friendly overtures towards local children. Many Maya women prefer to avoid contact with foreign men; in their culture, talking to strange men is not appropriate.

Guatemala has been attracting foreign 'hippies' for decades now, but you will still find that your relations with locals will go smoother if you try to present as clean an appearance as possible. This is especially true if you're dealing with officialdom (police, border officials, immigration officers), when it's a good idea to look not only clean, but also as conservative and respectable as possible.

An interesting paradox is that while Maya women are extremely eager to sell their traditional clothing to foreign visitors, especially the beautiful embroidered *huipiles* (blouses), it is considered very bad form for a visitor to wear these things in Guatemala.

Also think about safety in connection with your appearance. Particularly in the capital, locals will warn you against wearing even cheap imitation jewelry: you could be mugged for it. If you have any

wealth, take care not to flaunt it. See the Dangers & Annoyances section earlier in the Facts for the Visitor chapter for basic dos & don'ts of traveling safety.

RELIGION

Roman Catholicism is the predominant religion in Guatemala, but it is not the only religion. Since the 1980s, evangelical Protestant sects, around 75% of them Pentecostal, have surged in popularity and now it is estimated that about 30% of Guatemalans are of this faith.

When Catholicism was instituted here, it did not wipe out the traditional Maya religion, and it still has not today. Many aspects of Catholicism easily blended with traditional Maya beliefs (see the Facts about the Region chapter), and still do. When you see Maya people make offerings of candles, coins, cigarettes, liquor, flowers, pine needles and even sacrificing chickens before an image of the cross, the crucifixion is only one of the things that it symbolizes for them. Mayas still worship at a number of places where they have worshipped since ancient times, bringing offerings and making sacrifices to gods that predate the arrival of the Spanish.

Various Catholic saints hold a double meaning for the Maya people; often the Catholic identity of the saint was superimposed over a deity or saint the Maya people already had when the Spanish arrived. Mayas also have some of their own saints, which are quite independent of the Catholic church: two of these are Maximón (venerated in Santiago Atitlán) and San Simón (venerated in Zunil).

LANGUAGE

Spanish is the official national language, but in practice, 23 different languages are spoken in Guatemala, including Spanish, Garífuna and 21 Maya languages. Many Maya people speak Spanish, but you can't assume for sure that they do; many Maya women and children do not. Maya children often start to learn Spanish only after they start school.

Facts for the Visitor

PLANNING
When to Go
See the Climate section in the Regional Facts for the Visitor chapter and the Special Events section, below.

Maps
International Travel Maps (ITM) publishes a good 1:500,000 scale map of Guatemala. INGUAT, the Guatemalan national tourist office, publishes a tourist map with the country on one side and street maps of the larger cities and towns on the other. Pick it up for US$1 from any INGUAT office.

In Guatemala, the Instituto Geográfico Militar, Av las Américas 5-76, Zona 13, Guatemala City (☎ 332-2611) publishes a number of useful maps, including a series of 1:50,000 maps. You can buy them there at the Institute. In Antigua, you may be able to find some of their maps at the Casa Andinista bookstore.

HIGHLIGHTS
World-class highlights in Guatemala include Tikal, Lago de Atitlán, Antigua and the Thursday and Sunday markets at Chichicastenango. If you only have a few days to visit Guatemala, these are the 'must sees.'

If you have more time, climbing volcanoes is a highlight for many travelers, as is the boat trip on the Río Dulce. If you're there at the right time of year, the Saturday evening race of baby sea turtles to the sea in Monterrico is a low-key but memorable event. If you visit Guatemala City, check out the Museo Popol Vuh.

TOURIST OFFICES
The main office of Instituto Guatemalteco de Turismo (INGUAT), the national tourist office, is in Guatemala City. Branch offices are in Antigua, Panajachel, Quetzaltenango, and at the international airports in Guatemala City and Flores/ Santa Elena.

Guatemalan tourist offices abroad have been closed. However, Guatemalan embassies can provide tourist information.

VISAS & DOCUMENTS
Visa regulations were changed in October 1996, and citizens of many countries can now enter Guatemala without a visa. Regulations do change, so check with a Guatemalan consulate before heading there. If you need a visa and arrive at the border without one, you will be turned back; if you're flying into Guatemala, you probably won't be allowed to board the plane without having the visa you need for entry.

As of late 1996, citizens of the following countries need no visa or tourist card, and receive 90 days in Guatemala upon arrival: Andorra, Argentina, Austria, Belgium, Chile, Denmark, Finland, Germany, Israel, Italy, Japan, Liechtenstein, Luxembourg, Monaco, Norway, the Netherlands, Sweden, Switzerland, Uruguay and USA.

Citizens of the following countries need no visa or tourist card, and recieve 30 days in Guatemala upon arrival: Australia, Belize, Brazil, Canada, Costa Rica, El Salvador, France, Greece, Honduras, Ireland, Mexico, Nicaragua, New Zealand, Panama, Paraguay, Portugal, San Marino, Spain, Taiwan, UK, the Vatican and Venezuela.

Citizens of the following countries can enter either with a visa or a tourist card, which can be obtained at the time of entry: Bahrain, Czech Republic, Iceland, Kuwait, the Philippines, Poland, Saudi Arabia, Slovakia and South Africa.

Citizens of all other countries must obtain a visa from a Guatemalan consulate.

If you want to extend your visit, contact an immigration office within Guatemala for current requirements.

If you have a tourist card and you want to cross into Honduras on a day pass to visit Copán, the Guatemalan Migración official will usually allow you to return to Guatemala and continue your journey using the same Guatemalan tourist card. For information on this procedure, refer to the section on Copán.

Minors Traveling Alone

If you are under 18 years of age and traveling alone, technically you must have a letter of permission signed by both your parents and witnessed by a Guatemalan consular official in order to enter Guatemala.

EMBASSIES & CONSULATES
Guatemalan Embassies Abroad

Some of the consulates mentioned here are actually honorary consuls or consular agencies. These posts can issue tourist cards and visas, but they refer more complicated matters to the nearest full consulate or to the embassy's consular section. All the listings are for embassies unless noted.

Australia
    Guatemala does not maintain an embassy in Australia; contact the Guatemalan Embassy in Tokyo.

Belize
    See Embassies in Belize City.

Canada
    130 Albert St, Suite 1010, Ottawa, Ontario K1P 5G4 (☎ (613) 233-7188, 233-7237, fax 233-0135). Consulate in Toronto.

Costa Rica
    See Embassies & Consulates under Costa Rica's Facts for the Visitor.

El Salvador
    See Embassies under El Salvador's Facts for the Visitor.

France
    73 rue de Courcelles, 75008 Paris (☎ (1) 42-27-78-63, fax 47-54-02-06). Consulates in Ajaccio, Bordeaux, Le Havre, Strasbourg & Marseilles.

Honduras
    See Embassies in Tegucigalpa and San Pedro Sula.

Japan
    38 Kowa Bldg, Room 905, 4-12-24 Nichi-Azabu, Tokyo 106 (☎ (3) 3400-1830, fax 3400-1820). Consulate in Osaka.

Mexico
    Embassy, Av Explanada 1025, Lomas de Chapultepec, 11000 México 4, DF (☎ (5) 540-7520, fax 202-1142). Consulate, Calle Héroes de Chapultepec No 354 at Cecilio Chi, Chetumal, Q Roo (☎ (983) 2-85-85). Consulate, 3 Calle Poniente and 10 Av

Norte, Ciudad Hidalgo, Chiapas (☎ (962) 8-01-84, fax 8-01-93). Consulate, Av 2 Pte Sur at Calle 1 Sur Pte, Comitán, Chiapas (☎ (963) 2-26-69). Consulate, Mango 1440, Colonia del Fresno, Guadalajara (☎ (36) 11-15-03, fax 10-12-46). Consulate, Luis G Urbina 1208, Colonia Terminal, Monterrey (☎ (8) 372-8648, fax 374-4722). Consulate, 2 Calle Oriente No 33, Tapachula, Chiapas (☎ (962) 6-12-52).

Nicaragua
    See Foreign Embassies in Managua.

Panama
    See Embassies in Panama City.

South Africa
    Greenmarket Place, Greenmarket Square 54, Shortmarket St, 5th Floor, Cape Town 8001 (☎ (21) 22-57-86, fax 418-1280).

UK
    13 Fawcett St, London SW 10 (☎ (171) 351-3042, fax 376-5708).

USA
    Embassy, 2220 R St NW, Washington DC (☎ (202) 745-4952, fax 745-1908.) Consulates in Atlanta, Baltimore, Chicago, Houston, Fort Lauderdale, Leavenworth, Los Angeles, Memphis, Miami, Minneapolis, Montgomery, New Orleans, New York, Philadelphia, Pittsburgh, Providence, San Antonio, San Diego, San Francisco, Seattle.

Foreign Embassies in Guatemala

Foreign embassies are in Guatemala City; see that section.

CUSTOMS

Customs limits are the usual two cartons of cigarettes and three liters of alcohol. Tourists are allowed an exemption of US$100 in customs duty.

MONEY
Costs

Prices here are among the best in the region. Beds in little pensions may cost US$6 per person in a double, and camping places charge less. Elaborate markets sell fruits and snacks for pennies, cheap eateries called *comedores* offer one-plate meals for US$2 or less, and bus trips cost less than US$1 per hour. If you want a bit more comfort, you can readily move up to rooms with private showers and meals in nicer restaurants, and still pay only US$25 per day for room and two – or even three – meals.

Currency & Exchange

The Guatemalan quetzal (Q) is named for the country's national bird; the quetzal is divided into 100 centavos. There are coins of one, five, 10 and 25 centavos, and bills (notes) of 50 centavos, one, five, 10, 20, 50 and 100 quetzals.

Currency exchange rates at the time of writing were:

Australia	A$1	=	Q5
Canada	C$1	=	Q4.35
Germany	DM1	=	Q3.50
New Zealand	NZ$1	=	Q4.50
United Kingdom	UK£1	=	Q9.45
United States	US$1	=	Q6

US dollars are the currency to bring to Guatemala. Any other currency – even the currencies of Honduras, El Salvador and Mexico, Guatemala's neighboring countries – will probably prove impossible to exchange. The bank exchange desks at the airports in Guatemala City and Flores/Santa Elena are among the few places that exchange other currencies.

Many establishments accept cash dollars instead of quetzals, usually at the bank exchange rate, or even better, but sometimes worse. Even so, you'll need quetzals because shopkeepers, restaurateurs and hotel desk clerks may not want to deplete their supplies of ready quetzals and take on dollars, which they must then take to the bank.

Black Market

There's a healthy unofficial exchange market for dollars, but it pays only about the same as the bank rate. The national hotbed of this activity is around the main post office in Guatemala City. At most border crossing points you may find yourself buying quetzals unofficially as there are no banks; at the airports, the bank exchange desks are open only during certain hours, and you may find yourself buying your first quetzals (or your last, to pay the US$10-equivalent departure tax) at a shop in the terminal.

Credit Cards

Visa and MasterCard are accepted at all airline and car rental companies, and at the larger hotels and restaurants. American Express cards are often accepted at the fancier and larger places, and at some smaller ones.

ATMs (automatic teller machines, called *cajero automático*) are appearing in the major cities, usually on bank premises. Many banks give cash advances on Visa cards, fewer on MasterCard. Credomatic branches in Guatemala City and Quetzaltenango give cash advances on both.

Tipping & Bargaining

A 10% tip is expected at restaurants. In small *comedores* tipping is optional, but it's still polite to leave at least a little spare change.

For details about bargaining, see the regional Facst for the Visitor chapter.

Taxes

Guatemala's IVA (a value-added tax) is 10%, and there's also a 10% tax on hotel rooms to pay for the activities of the Guatemala Tourist Commission (INGUAT), so a total tax of 20% will be added to your hotel bill. (In this book, we have included the tax in the prices we quote.) The very cheapest places usually charge no tax.

A departure tax equivalent to about US$10 is levied on travelers departing Guatemala by air.

POST & COMMUNICATIONS
Sending & Receiving Mail

Most post offices are open during business hours from Monday to Friday.

The Guatemalan postal system is notoriously unreliable – mail coming into the country, or even going out, disappears so frequently that it's practically the norm.

Many Guatemalans rely on private courier services for important mail. These courier services (which often have the word 'express' in their names) are in many towns. Some are trustworthy, some are not. Express Mail Service (EMS) is more reliable than the regular post; it often has an office in or near the regular post office. Services such as Federal Express, DHL and United Parcel Service (UPS) have offices in Guatemala City and Antigua.

Try trusting the mail system for non-urgent mail. (We sent postcards to many countries when we were in Guatemala, and they all got through.) Mark air mail from Guatemala with the words 'Por Avión'. An air-mail letter sent to Canada or the USA may take anywhere from four to 14 days; to Europe anywhere from one to three weeks. It costs only a few cents to send mail anywhere in the world, US$0.03 to the USA, for example.

To receive mail, have it addressed to you care of Poste Restante, and take along your passport when you pick it up.

Telephone

Guatel, the Guatemalan telephone company, offers domestic and international telephone, fax, telex and telegraph services. There's a Guatel office in virtually every city and town. Often the Guatel office is open long hours, from around 7 am to around 10 pm, but it varies. Coin phones are usually situated outside the Guatel office (see below).

Local and domestic long-distance calls are very cheap; international calls are extraordinarily expensive.

In August 1996, every telephone number in Guatemala was changed. Now all telephone numbers have seven digits, and city codes have been abolished. Guatel offices have a handy conversion chart to help you find the new number.

If you are calling from outside the country, Guatemala's country code is 502.

International Calls & Online Services

Guatel's international tolls are frightfully expensive. Your best bet, as in Mexico, is to have the person call you back.

Guatel charges for a minimum of three minutes, whether or not you talk that long.

Interestingly, though, they don't do so with faxes; for example, while a telephone call to the USA costs US$9 with Guatel, it costs only US$1.56 per page to send a fax.

In places where there are plenty of tourists, private businesses offer telephone and fax services, and some also offer email and Internet connections. It often works out cheaper to telephone with these services than with Guatel, since they do not charge a three-minute minimum.

Collect/reverse-charge calls may be made from Guatemala *only* to the following places: Central America, Mexico, USA, Canada, Japan, Italy, Spain and Switzerland.

To place an international direct call, dial the international prefix '00,' then the country code, area or city code, and local number. Rates vary according to the time of day of the country you're calling. A full rate schedule is published in the introductory section of the Guatemalan telephone directory.

For semi-automatic (operator-assisted) calls, dial 171. The minimum call period is three minutes, and thus the minimum charge to the USA or Canada is about US$9; to countries overseas (outside the Western Hemisphere), the minimum charge is about US$22.50.

There are also numerous 'direct line' services, such as AT&T's *USADirect*: dial 190 and you will be connected with an AT&T operator in the USA who will complete your collect or credit card call. Here are the direct line numbers (Directory Assistance 124):

Canada Directo 198
Costa Rica Directo 196
España Directo 191
Intercity Long Distance Calls 121
International Calls (by Operator) 171
MCI Call USA189
Italia Directo 193
Sprint Express 195
USADirect (AT&T) 190

Coin Phones Coin phones (*teléfonos monederos*) accept coins of 10 or 25 centavos. Local calls cost 10 centavos per minute, places in other parts of the country can cost twice that. Once your alotted time is up, you'll be given a short warning tone and then if you don't insert another coin in time, your call will be cut off. Some coin phones have a slanted slot so that you can put in several coins, which will drop one by one as your time requires.

Some telephones have a button on the face of the phone, underneath the handset. On this type of phone, when the person you're calling to answers, you must press the button in order for them to start hearing you.

BOOKS

I, Rigoberta Menchú: An Indian Woman in Guatemala by 1992 Nobel Peace Prize laureate Rigoberta Menchú tells the story of her early life, the life among the highland Quiché Maya people, and the birth of her social consciousness. Menchú brought the plight of Guatemala's Mayan Indians to the attention of the world. In Guatemala, where the position of the Maya in society is a continuing issue, she is a controversial figure. This book is controversial, too. Highly recommended. The same book is published in Spanish as *Me Llamo Rigoberta Menchú y Así Me Nació La Conciencia* (Siglo XXI, 1985).

Unfinished Conquest: The Guatemalan Tragedy by Victor Perera explores the current situation of the Maya in their homeland, and the long history that has led to it. *Between Two Armies* by David Stoll shows the position that the Maya people have often felt themselves in, between government and guerrilla armies.

Jennifer Harbury's *Searching for Everardo: A Story of Love, War and the CIA in Guatemala* tells how she attracted the attention of the world when she conducted three hunger strikes, two in front of Guatemala's National Palace and one in front of the White House in Washington, DC, demanding information on her husband, a URNG commander who disappeared mysteriously in 1992. Her earlier book, *Bridge of Courage: Life Stories of the Guatemalan Compañeros and Compañeras* (Common Courage Press) focuses on a number of people who fought in the Guatemalan guerrilla movement.

Time and the Highland Maya by Barbara Tedlock is an anthropological book about Momostenango and the Quiché Maya people who live there.

Bird of Life, Bird of Death by Jonathan Evan Maslow, subtitled 'A naturalist's journey through a land of political turmoil,' tells of the author's travels in Guatemala, where he went to see the resplendent quetzal (the 'bird of life') and found it increasingly endangered, while the vulture or *zopilote* (the 'bird of death') was flourishing.

Birds of Guatemala by Hugh C Land (Lívingston, 1970) is a field guide to bird watching in Guatemala. Other more localized field guides for bird watching are available at Tikal and at the Biotopo del Quetzal.

Guatemala Handbuch by Barbara Honner is a German-language guidebook in the Reise Know-How series.

NEWSPAPERS & MAGAZINES

Guatemala has a number of daily newspapers to choose from, including the *Prensa Libre, El Gráfico, La República, Siglo Veintiuno, El Periódico* and *Al Día*. The *Prensa Libre* is the most widely read. There's also a weekly paper, *El Regional*, written in both Spanish and Maya languages; it's read by many Maya people.

Newspapers in English include the *Guatemala Weekly* and the *The Siglo News*, both free weeklies published in Guatemala City and distributed in major hotels and tourist spots around the country. The *Revue* is Guatemala's English-language magazine, published monthly. Subscriptions are available by mail, and the two newspapers also have Web sites. Contact:

Guatemala Weekly, 14 Calle 3-27, Zona 10, Local 8, Guatemala City (☎ 337-1061, fax 337-1076, net). In the USA: PO Box 591999-F-69, Miami, FL 33159-1999.

The Siglo News, 11 Calle 0-65, Zona 10, Edificio Vizcaya, 4th floor, Guatemala City (☎ 332-8101/2/3, fax 332-8119, net). In the USA: NotiNET SA, Worldbox Gu-0147, PO Box 379012, Miami, FL 33137-9012 USA (☎ (888) 287-4921).

Revue, 4a Calle Oriente No 23, Antigua Guatemala (☎ /fax 832-0767, net).

CERIGUA is an independent Guatemalan news agency producing reports and offering research services in English and Spanish. Subscriptions to their English-language 'Weekly Brief' cost US$40 per year for an individual and are available by regular mail, email or fax. Address orders to: ANI, PO Box 578191, Chicago, IL 60657-8191, USA. For all other services, contact their Guatemala City office: 9a Calle 'A' 3-49, Zona 1 (☎ /fax 232-5519, net).

Central America Report is the English-language publication of Inforpress Centroamericana, providing weekly news analysis. Subscriptions cost US$225 per year. Their office in Guatemala City (☎ /fax 232-9034, net) is open to visitors; find them at 7a Av 2-05, Zona 1. Send foreign correspondence or subscription requests to their American office: Inforpress Centroamericana, Section 23, PO Box 52-7270, Miami, FL 33152-7270 USA.

The Guatemala News and Information Bureau (GNIB) publishes *Report On Guatemala*, and other publications of the Network in Solidarity with the People of Guatemala (NISGUA). Subscriptions are around US$20. They also maintain a list of Guatemalan Web sites. Contact: GNIB, PO Box 28594, Oakland, CA 94604 USA (☎ /fax 510-835-0810, net).

RADIO & TV
Guatemala has 11 radio stations and five TV stations. A number of stations from the USA, including CNN news, come in by cable. Not all hotels have TV but when they do have it, it's usually cable TV.

LAUNDRY
Laundries are everywhere in Guatemala, offering wash, dry and fold service for around US$2 per load; drop it off and pick it up a few hours later. Cheaper lodgings usually have a *lavadero* where you can wash your clothes by hand, and a line where you can hang it.

HEALTH
Tap water is not safe to drink in Guatemala, so you must either purify water yourself or drink bottled water. Bottled water is widely available; it's what most locals drink.

Malaria is present in Guatemala, especially in lowland rural areas, but there is no malaria risk in the central highlands. Chloroquine is the recommended anti-malarial. Dengue fever is also present, as is cholera. See the Health section in the introductory Facts for the Visitor chapter for more about protecting your health while traveling.

WOMEN TRAVELERS
Women should encounter no special problems traveling in Guatemala. To make it easy for yourself while traveling here, dress modestly; most Guatemalan women do. Modesty in dress is regarded highly here, and if you practice it you will usually be treated with respect.

The catcalls, hisses and the like that are so frequently directed at women in some other parts of the region seem to be less common in Guatemala. Still, it can happen. Do what the local women do – ignore it completely.

See the Women Travelers section in the regional Facts for the Visitor chapter and more importantly the Society & Conduct section above for more on conduct that will help to smooth your way.

GAY & LESBIAN TRAVELERS
Guatemala is still very much in the closet. The only specifically gay place we heard about in Guatemala is *Pandora's*, a gay bar in Guatemala City, which is said to have been there for years and be 'the' place for gay people to meet.

DANGERS & ANNOYANCES
See the Facts for the Visitor chapter for general comments on theft and other crimes.

The greatest danger is from armed thieves who roam the highlands and the streets of Guatemala City. Don't wander around in Guatemala City late at night. You should avoid empty streets in Antigua at night, and don't wander to the outskirts of that town except in a large group. Avoid stopping by the roadside in lonely places in the highlands. In general, ask around for information on where it is safe to go.

If you are threatened by armed bandits, it's usually best to give up your belongings (and your vehicle) without a struggle as most do not hesitate to use their weapons.

There have been incidents of purse-snatching and car-jacking in Guatemala City. If you drive in the city, keep valuables out of sight, and keep the car windows rolled at least half way up at all times. (This discourages thieves from lunging through the window to grab a purse, watch or necklace.) If you are approached by armed car-jackers, embassies suggest that you give up your vehicle without resistance, rather than risk injury or worse.

Guatemala has been the scene of anti-government insurgent activity for a century or so. The signing of the peace accord in December 1996 is expected to stop guerrilla activity.

BUSINESS HOURS & PUBLIC HOLIDAYS

Banks are generally open from 8:30 or 9 am to around 6 pm on weekdays (until 7 or 8 pm in some places), and on Saturdays from around 9 am to 1 pm. Shops open about 9 am and close for lunch around 12:30 or 1 pm, reopening an hour or so later, and remaining open till about 6 pm, Monday to Friday; on Saturday many shops close for the day at 12:30 or 1 pm. Government office hours are officially Monday to Friday from 8 am to 4 pm, though there's some absenteeism around lunchtime.

Public holidays are:

January 1
New Year's Day
March/April
Holy Thursday and Friday before Easter Sunday
May 1
Labor Day
June 30
Army Day
August 15
Guatemala City

September 15
Independence Day
October 20
Revolution of 1944
November 1
All Saints' Day
December 24
Christmas Eve
December 25
Christmas Day
December 31
New Year's Eve

SPECIAL EVENTS

A number of special events throughout the year are worth attending. **Semana Santa** (Holy Week, the week before Easter) in Antigua is an unforgettable spectacle. Intricate, colorful carpets made of dyed sawdust are created in the street where later on, a solemn procession of Christ on the cross, borne on a large, heavy litter by a robed *cofradía* (religious brotherhood), bears the image over the carpet, accompanied by swinging incense burners and music. The events leading up to Christ's crucifixion and resurrection are re-enacted in impressive ceremonies.

Semana Santa is celebrated in other places, too – each of the indigenous peoples have their own religious and folkloric traditions. Huehuetenango and Totonicapán also have processions and enactments of the passion of Christ, held on Wednesday through Easter Sunday.

Traditional celebrations also take place on **All Saints' Day** (November 1) and **All Souls' Day** (November 2). Since it's believed that this is the time of year when the souls of the dead come closest to the living, throughout Guatemala people in every city, village and town spruce up the graveyards in preparation for this time, pulling weeds and painting the tombs. Families bring flowers and a picnic to the tombs of their loved ones and spend the day there. It's not a sad occasion; they are visiting with those they miss.

On November 1, giant, colorful kites (*barriletes*) are flown in the cemetery at Santiago Sacatepéquez, 24 km from Antigua. Traditionally, it's believed that the kites rising into the atmosphere provide communication with dead loved ones. Thousands of visitors come to witness the spectacle, and food, especially the traditional *fiambre*, is sold under tents.

On the same day, in Todos Santos Cuchumatán, local men dressed in traditional costumes hurtle through the town in a festive horse race – the culmination of a week of festivities (October 21 through November 1) and usually an all-night drinking spree the night before. Traditional foods are served throughout the day.

Each town celebrates the day of its patron saint with fiestas including social, cultural and sporting events. A famous fiesta is the one in Chichicastenango, celebrated from December 13 to 21, honoring the town's patron saint, Santo Tomás. The fiesta begins with traditional celebrations, including a *palo volador*, in which a very tall pole is set up in the plaza and costumed *voladores* (flyers) swing around the top of it.

Perhaps the most impressive festival of Indian traditions takes place in Cobán, where there's the folkloric festival of **Rabin Ajau**, with its traditional dance of the Paabanc. It's celebrated throughout the region by the Kekchi Indians, who wear traditional costumes and eat traditional foods. It takes place in the latter part of July, approximately July 21 to 26.

ACTIVITIES

There are many possibilities for hiking in Guatemala. Climbing volcanoes is a highlight of many a traveler's trip. People climb volcanoes around Antigua, Lago de Atitlán and Quetzaltenango; see those sections for details. Mountain bikes can be rented in Panajachel and Antigua; a place in Panajachel also rents off-road motorcycles.

Swimming is popular in the sea and in rivers and lakes. ATI Divers in Santa Cruz La Laguna, on Lago de Atitlán, offers diving courses, including the four-day PADI open-water diving course and advanced courses including a high altitude diving course.

White-water rafting is practiced year round by a rafting company based in Antigua.

Bird watching is good in Tikal National Park, on the Río Ixpop that flows into Lago Petén Itzá near El Remate, at Santiago Atitlán on Lago de Atitlán, along the Río Dulce, in Monterrico and in many other places.

Weaving courses are offered in Quetzaltenango and Zunil.

LANGUAGE COURSES

Many people from around the world come to study Spanish in Guatemala. Antigua has had a high reputation for its many language schools for many years. Nowadays, Quetzaltenango's schools are also gaining a reputation. Other places with a school or two include Panajachel, San Pedro La Laguna (on Lago de Atitlán), San Andrés (on Lago Petén Itzá), Huehuetenango, Todos Santos Cuchumatán, Monterrico, Lívingston, Guatemala City and Copán (Honduras).

In Momostenango schools offer classes in the Quiché language and Maya calendar and culture. One school in Quetzaltenango offers courses in the Quiché and Mam languages, as well as in Spanish. *K'iche'*, by Kermit Frazier, who lives in Momostenango, is a Quiché Maya language kit which includes a phrasebook, an English/Quiché cassette tape, and a Maya calendar booklet, all for US$20 (Happy Camper Publications, 1997). To order one, contact Kermit in Momostenango through the Kuinik Ta'ik Language School (net).

Virtually all language schools offer the option of homestays with local families, typically costing around US$50 per week for your own private room and three meals a day. This 'total immersion' is an excellent way to learn the language.

WORK

Work is hard to come by. You might teach English, but don't count on it; if you did wages will not be high. However, volunteer opportunities are many and what follows hardly conveys the variety. INGUAT, the national tourist office, may be able to help you with a specific interest.

ADIFAM provides education for working Quiché children in Momostenango.

Volunteer teachers, who instruct the children in their own Quiché language, receive around US$14 a month. Also, anyone in the medical, veterinary, organic gardening and computer fields can find volunteer work here. ADIFAM can also coordinate work with other volunteer organizations including a reforestation crew and UNICEF. Some knowledge of Spanish or Quiché is essential (there's a Quiché language school in Momostenango). Contact: ADIFAM, Hotel Ixchel, 1a Calle 4-15, Zona 1, Momostenango (☎ 736-5036, net).

Quetzaltenango has several social organizations working with the local Quiché Maya; see Quetzaltenango for more details.

Casa Guatemala (☎ 232-5517), 14a Calle 10-63, Zona 1, Guatemala City, helps abandoned, orphaned and malnourished children. In Guatemala City it has a clinic and food distribution program. It also has an orphanage on the Río Dulce, in eastern Guatemala.

Proyecto Ak' Tenamit, working with the Kek'chi Maya people of eastern Guatemala, has a medical volunteer project, a school, potable water projects and a women's cooperative. Contact Proyecto Ak' Tenamit (☎ /fax (502) 251-1136), Apdo Postal 2675, Guatemala City, or in the USA, the Guatemalan Tomorrow Fund (☎ (407) 747-9790, fax 747-0901), PO Box 3636, Tequesta, FL 33469.

ARCAS (the Asociación de Rescate y Conservación de Vida Silvestre; the Wildlife Rescue and Conservation Association), operates two wildlife rescue stations. One is near Flores; the other is a sea turtle hatchery on the beach eight km east of Monterrico. See the Monterrico and Flores sections for further details. ARCAS also has education and health projects. Contact: ARCAS, 1a Calle 50-37, Zona 11, Colonia Molino de las Flores, Guatemala City (☎ / fax 591-4731, net). Their mailing address is in the USA: ARCAS, Section 717, PO Box 52-7270, Miami, FL 33152-7270.

The GNIB (see Magazines & Newspapers above), based in California, has information on long-term volunteer work in Guatemala (over three months).

ACCOMMODATIONS

All levels of accommodations are available in Guatemala, from simple hotels and pensions up to luxury five-star hotels and resorts. If you'll be studying Spanish, you may prefer a homestay with a local family, which costs less than a hotel; virtually all Spanish language schools offer this option.

FOOD

When it comes to cuisine, Guatemala is the poorer cousin to the more elaborate cuisines of Mexico and the USA. You can find a few Mexican standards such as *enchiladas*, *guacamole* and *tamales*.

But mostly you will encounter *bistec*, tough grilled or fried beef; *pollo asado*, grilled chicken; *chuletas de puerco*, pork chops and lighter fare such as *hamburguesas*, hamburgers; and *salchichas*, sausages like hot dogs. Of the simpler food, *frijoles con arroz*, beans and rice, is cheapest and often best.

One of the unexpected and surprising things about Guatemala, however, is the omnipresence of Chinese restaurants. All the cities and some large towns have at least one Chinese eatery, usually small and not overly authentic, but cheap and good for a change of scene.

DRINKS

Guatemalan coffee is savored all around the world, and not surprisingly, it's one of the delights of traveling in Guatemala. Restaurants that cater to international travelers tend to serve magnificently rich (export grade) coffee. At more out-of-the-way places, though, the coffee may not be as tasty.

As elsewhere throughout the region, sweetened fruit juice mixed with water is a popular and refreshing beverage.

Gallo is Guatemala's most popular light beer. *Moza*, a dark beer, is what some travelers prefer. *Dorado* is lighter than Gallo.

Guatemala grows plenty of sugar cane, and rum is also made here. *Ron Zacapa Centenario*, a dark rum which comes in a bottle with a wicker basket around it, is said to be the best. *Ron Botrán Añejo*, another dark rum, is also good. Then there's *Quetzalteca*, a white firewater made of sugar cane, that comes in a tiny bottle.

THINGS TO BUY

Guatemalan handicrafts, especially the brilliantly colorful weavings and textiles, are world famous. Wall hangings, clothing, especially the beautiful embroidered *huipiles* (blouses) and the *cortes* (skirts), purses, belts, sashes, friendship bracelets, tablecloths, bedspreads and many other woven items are almost irresistible.

Other notable handicrafts include the blankets made in Momostenango, the wood carvings of El Remate and the ceramics of Antigua.

The largest handicrafts markets are the Thursday and Sunday markets in Chichicastenango and the permanent market in Panajachel. If you're serious about buying handicrafts, they're worth a trip. Many fine examples are also available in Antigua, but the prices are higher.

Each village also has market days, which may or may not include handicrafts; often the village markets for locals are full of more mundane items like vegetables and household goods, but sometimes you can find worthwhile things.

When buying handicrafts, it's normal practice to bargain until buyer and seller arrive at a mutually agreeable price.

Getting There & Away

AIR

Guatemala has two places served by major airlines: Guatemala City (Aeropuerto Internacional La Aurora), and Flores, near Tikal in El Petén Department. See those sections for details.

LAND

There are two highway routes and three road-and-river routes from Chiapas (Mexico) to Guatemala; one road and one sea route from Belize; and numerous routes to and from Honduras and El Salvador.

For the road-and-river routes, see the Petén chapter in the Guatemala section; for the routes from Belize, see the Western Belize and Southern Belize chapters in the Belize section.

Main crossings include El Florido, near Chiquimula and Copán Ruinas (Honduras), and Agua Caliente (Guatemala and Honduras).

There's a remote crossing at El Cinchado (Guatemala) and Corinto (Honduras), in eastern Guatemala.

An even more remote overland route that some travelers take between Puerto Barrios (Guatemala) and Omoa or Puerto Cortés (Honduras), via Finca La Inca (Guatemala), El Límite (on the Río Motagua) and Cuyamelito (Honduras). This route is covered in the Central & Eastern Guatemala chapter and is known as the Jungle Trail. It isn't an official border crossing, but people do go this way.

Bus

Several Guatemalan lines run comfortable passenger buses on long-distance routes between Guatemala City and the Mexican and Salvadoran borders, and to Puerto Barrios on the Gulf of Honduras.

For bus information on most of Guatemala, see Getting There & Away in the Guatemala City chapter.

For details on the special direct bus between Flores, Petén (near Tikal) and Chetumal (Mexico), see Flores in the Petén chapter.

RIVER & SEA

There are three routes between Palenque (Chiapas) and Flores (Petén) through the jungle. Most travel is by road, but each route entails a boatride on the Río Usumacinta. For details, see the Petén chapter.

There are regular boat services between the Guatemalan town of Puerto Barrios on the Gulf of Honduras and the southern Belizean town of Punta Gorda. There's a twice-weekly route between Lívingston and Punta Gorda, and another between Lívingston and Omoa (Honduras). There's also a sailboat that makes a trip from Utila (one of Honduras' Bay Islands) to Lívingston twice a month or so. See these towns' sections for details.

Be sure to get your exit and entry stamps at the immigration offices at both ends of the journey if you're arriving or departing the country by water.

Getting Around

AIR

Daily flights between Guatemala City and Flores save you from a torturous 15-hour bus ride. See those sections for details.

BUS

Fares are very cheap and buses are plentiful (though they're like old American schoolbuses). See Bus under Getting There & Away in Guatemala City for extensive route information.

SHUTTLE MINIBUS

Realizing that normal bus transport poses challenges to foreigners, various companies offer tourist minibus services on the main tourist routes between Guatemala City, Aeropuerto La Aurora, Antigua, Panajachel and Chichicastenango. Shuttle minibuses depart from La Aurora International Airport every hour or so, bound for Antigua; the same buses offer door-to-door transport between Antigua and Guatemala City. Other shuttles operate between Guatemala City, Panajachel and Chichicastenango.

Most of these operators have their offices in Antigua; check that section for contact information. TURANSA has an office in Guatemala City (☎ 595-3574, fax 595-3583), in the Supercentro Metro, Carretera Roosevelt Km 15, Zona 11, Local 68-69.

CAR

Traffic in Guatemala City is very heavy. Major roads in the highlands are free of heavy traffic. The Carretera al Atlántico has a moderate amount of heavy vehicle traffic.

Buy a Guatemalan liability policy on sale at border posts and in the major towns near the borders.

If you see the branch of a tree, bushes or some other unusual object in the road, slow down – this is the signal that something unexpected is just ahead, whether a broken-down vehicle or a washout in the road.

Because of these and many other hazards, including armed bandits who stop vehicles and rob the occupants under cover of darkness, many drivers in Guatemala never drive at night.

Car Rental

Most companies offer several types of vehicles, including 4WD vehicles and mini-vans. Most have offices in Guatemala City, both in town and at the airport; a few have offices in other cities as well.

Cost is high for renting a vehicle, about US$60 to US$95 per day total (including rental charges, insurance, charges per km and fuel) for even the cheapest car. Insurance does not protect you from all losses by collision or theft. You will usually be liable for US$600 to US$1500 or more of damage, after which the insurance covers any loss. Drive safely and park in a secure area at night.

You must show your passport, driver's license and a major credit card when you rent, and you must normally be 25 years or older. If you do not have a valid credit card for the rental, a very large cash deposit may be required; check in advance to avoid disappointment.

As Guatemala grows in popularity as a tourist destination, rental cars become scarcer during the busiest times of year. Reserve a car ahead of time if possible. Sometimes you'll get a better deal if you reserve from your home country.

Note that if you wish to drive a Guatemalan rental car to Copán in Honduras, you must obtain an official letter of permission from the car rental agency to give to the Guatemalan customs official at the border. Without such a letter, you must leave the car at the border and proceed by public transport.

BICYCLE

Bicycling can be a way to get around in Guatemala, if you don't mind the hills or the bandits. Mountain bikes can be rented in some places, notably Antigua and Panajachel.

HITCHHIKING

It's extremely unusual to see people hitchhiking a ride in Guatemala. It's not safe.

WALKING

Unfortunately, long walking trips are not recommended due to the threat from robbers.

BOAT

Passenger boats run frequently between Lívingston and Puerto Barrios, and along the Río Dulce between Río Dulce village and Lívingston. Boats also form the major way to get around on some lakes, notably Lago de Atitlán, and to a lesser extent on Lago de Izabal and Lago Petén Itzá.

A few of Guatemala's natural parks and reserves and archaeological sites are accessible only – or preferably – by water (see National Parks & Protected Areas, above).

LOCAL TRANSPORTATION

Local buses in larger cities and towns provide inexpensive transportation in town and to the nearby suburbs and villages. Most routes operate very frequently and cost very little.

With only a couple of exceptions, taxis in Guatemala are not metered, so it's important to agree on a fare before you climb into the cab.

ORGANIZED TOURS

Organized tours can be among the best ways to reach certain places. For instance, if you want to stay in a hotel at Tikal, a package tour could include accommodations, some meals, a guided tour of the ruins and airfare. Tours may also be advantageous for accessing certain remote places in the Petén region and around Cobán. Tours in Antigua can take you to some interesting places in the area that you probably would never find on your own, and they are a must for climbing many of Guatemala's volcanoes. Specialized tours include horseback tours, bicycle tours, white-water rafting tours and more.

In this chapter, tours are mentioned in all the following sections: Antigua Guatemala, Chichicastenango, Cobán, Flores, Lívingston, Panajachel, Quetzaltenango, El Remate, Santa Elena, Totonicapán and Tikal.

Guatemala City

Population 2 million

Guatemala's capital city, the largest urban agglomeration in Central America, sprawls across a range of flattened mountains (altitude 1500 meters), scored by deep ravines.

At first, this city may remind you of Mexico City, its great Latin sister to the north. But the superficial resemblances soon give way to purely Guatemalan impressions. There's the huge and chaotic market, typically colorful and disorganized. There are the ramshackle city buses which trundle citizens about with surprising efficiency, though hardly in comfort. And there are the thousands of guards in blue clothing carrying very effective-looking firearms. Wherever there's money or status – banks, offices, private clubs, even McDonald's – there are armed guards.

Guatemala City today has few colonial buildings to beautify its aggressive urban sprawl. The colonial buildings are all in nearby Antigua Guatemala, the former capital. Buildings are mostly concrete, but at least they're generally only five or six stories high, allowing light to flood the narrow streets.

The few interesting sights in Guatemala City may be seen in a day or two. Nowadays many travelers are avoiding the city altogether, preferring to make Antigua their base. Still, you may need to know your way around the capital because this is the hub of the country, where all transportation lines meet and where all services are available.

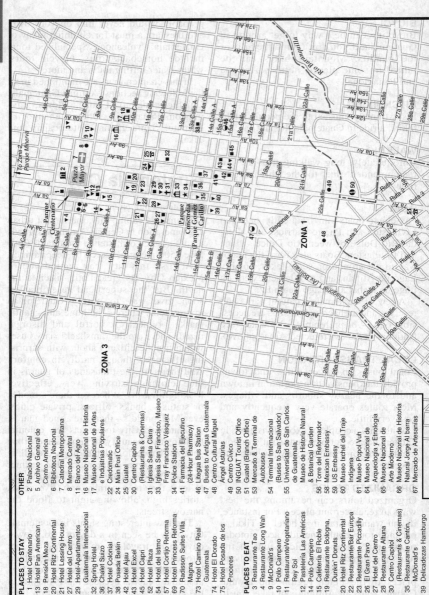

PLACES TO STAY
1   Hotel Centenario
13 Hotel Pan American
18 Pensión Meza
20 Hotel Ritz Continental
21 Hotel Lessing House
26 Hotel del Centro
29 Hotel-Apartamentos
      Guatemala Internacional
32 Spring Hotel
36 Chalet Suizo
37 Hotel Colonial
38 Posada Belén
42 Hotel Ajau
43 Hotel Excel
45 Hotel Capri
52 Hotel Plaza
54 Hotel del Istmo
57 Hotel Cortijo Reforma
69 Hotel Princess Reforma
70 Radisson Suites Villa
      Magna
73 Hotel Camino Real
      Guatemala
74 Hotel El Dorado
75 Hotel Posada de los
      Proceres

PLACES TO EAT
3   Restaurante Tao
4   Restaurante Long Wah
9   McDonald's
10 Pollo Campero
11 RestauranteVegetariano
      Rey Sol
12 Pastelería Las Américas
14 Pollo Campero
15 Cafetería El Roble
19 Restaurante Bologna,
      Dunkin' Donuts
20 Hotel Ritz Continental
22 Restaurante/Bar Europa
23 Restaurante Piccadilly
26 El Gran Pavo
27 Restaurante Altuna
28 Centro Capitol
35 Restaurante Cantón,
      McDonald's
39 Delicadezas Hamburgo

OTHER
2   Palacio Nacional
5   Archivo General de
      Centro América
6   Biblioteca Nacional
7   Catedral Metropolitana
8   Mercado Central
11 Banco del Agro
16 Museo Nacional de Historia
17 Museo Nacional de Artes
      e Industrias Populares
22 Credomatic
24 Main Post Office
25 Guatel
30 Centro Capitol
      (Restaurants & Cinemas)
31 Iglesia Santa Clara
33 Iglesia San Francisco, Museo
      Fray Francisco Vásquez
34 Police Station
41 Farmacia del Ejecutivo
      (24-Hour Pharmacy)
46 Litegua Bus Station
47 Buses to Antigua Guatemala
48 Centro Cultural Miguel
      Ángel Asturias
49 Centro Cívico
50 INGUAT Tourist Office
51 Guatel (Branch Office)
53 Mercado & Terminal de
      Autobuses
54 Terminal Internacional
      (Buses to San Salvador)
55 Universidad de San Carlos
      de Guatemala,
      Museo de Historia Natural
      & Botanical Garden
56 Torre del Reformador
58 Mexican Embassy
59 US Embassy
60 Museo Ixchel del Traje
      Indígena
61 Museo Popol Vuh
64 Museo Nacional de
      Arqueología y Etnología
65 Museo Nacional de
      Arte Moderno
66 Museo Nacional de Historia
      Natural Jorge Al barra
67 Mercado de Artesanías

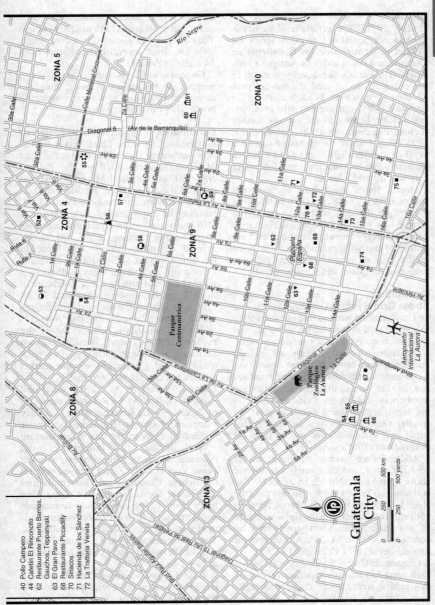

40 Pollo Campero
44 Cafetín El Rinconcito
62 Restaurante Puerto Barrios,
    Gauchos, Teppanyaki
63 El Gran Pavo
68 Restaurante Piccadilly
70 Sinacos
71 Hacienda de los Sánchez
72 La Trattoria Veneta

History

On July 29, 1773, a terrible *temblor* struck the Spanish capital of Central America, La Ciudad de Santiago de los Caballeros de Guatemala, known today as Antigua Guatemala. The earthquake destroyed much of the colonial capital, and the government decided to move its headquarters to La Ermita Valley, the present site of Guatemala City, hoping to escape any further such terrible destruction. On September 27, 1775 King Carlos III of Spain signed a royal charter for the founding of La Nueva Guatemala de la Asunción, and Guatemala City was officially born.

Hopes for a quakeless future were shaken in 1917, 1918 and 1976 as temblors did major damage to buildings in the capital – as well as in Antigua. The city's comparatively recent founding and its history of earthquakes have left little to see in the way of grand churches, palaces, mansions, or quaint old neighborhoods.

Orientation

Street Grid System Guatemala City, like all Guatemalan towns, is laid out according to a street grid system which is logical and easy to use. Avenidas run north-south; Calles run east-west. Streets are usually numbered from north and west (lowest) to south and east (highest); building numbers run in the same directions, with odd numbers on the left-hand side and even on the right as you head south or east. In smaller Guatemalan cities and towns this street grid system allows you to pinpoint destinations effortlessly.

Addresses are given in this form: '9a Av 15-12, Zona 1,' which means '9th Avenue above 15th Street, No 12, in Zone 1'. The building you're looking for (in this case the Hotel Excel), will be on 9th Avenue between 15th and 16th Streets, on the right-hand side as you walk south. Short streets may be numbered 'A,' as in 14 Calle A, a short street running between 14 Calle and 15 Calle.

Guatemala City is divided into 15 *zonas*; each zona has its own separate version of this grid system. Some major thoroughfares, such as 6a Av and 7a Av, cross through several zones maintaining the same name. Yet most zones have unique systems: Thus 14 Calle in Zona 10 is a completely different street several miles distant from 14 Calle in Zona 1.

Guatemala City's street grid has a number of anomalies as well: diagonal streets called *rutas* and *vías*, wandering boulevards called *diagonales*.

Landmarks The ceremonial center of Guatemala City is the Plaza Mayor (sometimes called the Parque Central) at the heart of Zona 1, surrounded by the Palacio Nacional, the Catedral Metropolitana and the Portal del Comercio. Beside the Plaza Mayor to the west is the large Parque Centenario, the city's central park. Zona 1 is also the retail commercial district, with shops selling clothing, crafts, film and a myriad of other things. The Mercado Central, a market selling lots of crafts, is behind the cathedral. Most of the city's good cheap and middle-range hotels are in Zona 1. 6a Av running south and 7a Av running north are the major thoroughfares which connect Zona 1 with other zonas.

Zona 4, south of Zona 1, holds the modern Centro Cívico (Civic Center) with various government buildings. In southwestern Zona 4 is the city's major market district and chaotic bus terminal.

Zona 9 (west of Av La Reforma) and Zona 10 (east of Av La Reforma) are south of Zona 4; Av La Reforma is the southerly extension of 10a Av. These are the fancier residential areas of the city, also boasting several of the most interesting small museums. Zona 10 is the poshest, with the Zona Viva (Lively Zone) arrayed around the deluxe Camino Real Guatemala and Guatemala Fiesta hotels. The Zona Viva holds many of the city's better restaurants and nightclubs. In Zona 9, convenient landmarks are the mini-Eiffel Tower called the Torre del Reformador at 7a Av and 2 Calle, and the Plazuela España traffic roundabout at 7a Av and 12 Calle.

Zona 13, just south of Zona 9, has the large Parque Aurora, several museums, and the Aeropuerto Internacional La Aurora.

Maps The INGUAT tourist office sells a useful tourist map for US$1, with the country on one side and the cities and towns on the other. It has a map of greater Guatemala City, as well as a close-up of the downtown area.

Information

Tourist Offices The tourist office is in the lobby of the INGUAT headquarters (Guatemalan Tourist Commission; ☎ 331-1333, fax 331-8893 or 332-2881), 7a Av 1-17, Centro Cívico. Look for the blue-and-white sign with the letter 'i' on the east side of the street, next to a flight of stairs a few meters to the south of the railway viaduct which crosses above 7a Av. Hours are Monday to Friday from 8 am to 4 pm, Saturday 8 am to 1 pm, closed Sunday. Staff are friendly and helpful.

INGUAT also has an office at the La Aurora International Airport (☎ 331-8392), open every day from 6 am to 9 pm.

Immigration Office If you need to extend your visa or tourist card for a longer stay, contact the Dirección General de Migración (☎ 475-1302, 475-1404, fax 475-1289), 41 Calle 17-36, Zona 8, one block off Av Castellana. It's open Monday to Friday, 8 am to 4 pm.

Foreign Embassies & Consulates There are many more embassies and consulates than are listed here. You can find them in the blue section of the Guatemalan telephone directory. Remember that embassies *(embajadas)* and their consular sections *(consulados)* often have strange, short working hours, so call ahead. Unless otherwise noted, the places listed below are embassies.

Belize
　Av La Reforma 1-50, Zona 9, Edificio El Reformador, Office 803 (☎ 334-5531, 331-1137, fax 334-5536).
Canada
　Embassy & Consulate, 13a Calle 8-44, Zona 10, Edificio Plaza Edyma (8th floor) (☎ 333-6102, 363-4348).

Costa Rica
　Embassy & Consulate, Av La Reforma 8-60, Zona 9, Edificio Galerías Reforma, Office 702 (☎ 331-9604, ☎ /fax 332-1522).
El Salvador
　Embassy & Consulate, 18a Calle 14-30, Zona 13 (☎ 334-3942, 334-8196, fax 360-1312).
France
　Embassy & Consulate, 16a Calle 4-53, Zona 10, Edificio Marbella (☎ 337-3639, 337-4080).
Germany
　Embassy & Consulate, 20 Calle 6-20, Zona 10, Edificio Plaza Marítima (☎ 337-0028).
Honduras
　Embassy & Consulate, 13a Calle 12-33, Zona 10, Colonia Oakland (☎ 337-4337, tel/fax 337-4344).
Mexico
　Embassy, 15a Calle 3-20, Zona 10, Edificio Centro Ejecutivo (7th floor) (☎ 333-7254 to 333-7258); Consulate, 13a Calle 7-30, Zona 9 (☎ 331-8165, 331-9573).
Nicaragua
　Embassy & Consulate, 10a Av 14-72, Zona 10 (☎ 368-0785, fax 337-4264).
Panama
　Embassy & Consulate, 5a Av 15-45, Zona 10, Edificio Centro Empresarial, Torre II, Offices 708 & 709 (☎ 333-7182/3, 337-2445, fax 337-2446).
UK
　Embassy & Consulate, 7a Av 5-10, Zona 4, Edificio Centro Financiero, Torre II (7th floor) (☎ 332-1601/2/4, fax 334-1904).
USA
　Embassy & Consulate, Av La Reforma 7-01, Zona 10 (☎ 331-1541 to 331-1555).

Money Banco del Agro (☎ 230-5506), on the south side of Parque Centenario, changes US dollars cash and traveler's checks; it's open Monday to Friday from 9 am to 8 pm, Saturday 10 am to 2 pm. ATMs are also appearing around town.

Credomatic (☎ 251-4185) in the tall building at the corner of 5a Av and 11a Calle, Zona 1, gives cash advances on Visa and MasterCard. It's open Monday to Friday from 8 am to 7 pm, Saturday 9 am to 1 pm. Inside, you can withdraw a maximum of US$500; their 24-hour ATM gives a maximum of US$100 per transaction, but there's no limit to the number of transactions.

The airport terminal office of Banco del Quetzal is open Monday to Friday from 7 am to 8 pm, Saturday and Sunday 8 am to 6 pm. Here you can change US dollars cash or traveler's checks into quetzales, change European currencies into US dollars, and buy US-dollar traveler's checks.

American Express is represented in Guatemala by Banco del Café (☎ 331-1311), in the Edificio Torre del País, Av La Reforma 9-30, Zona 9, 1st floor. Opening hours are Monday to Friday, from 8:30 am to 4:30 pm.

Post & Communications The city's main post office is at 7a Av 12-11, Zona 1, in the huge pink building – by the racks of postcards shall ye know it. It's open from 8 am to 7 pm on weekdays, 8 am to 4:30 pm on Saturday, closed Sunday. The philatelic department is open Monday to Friday, 9 am to 5:30 pm.

EMS, in the rear of the post office building, is open weekdays, 9 am to 5 pm.

Guatel's main office is on the corner of 12 Calle and 8a Av, Zona 1, a block from the main post office. Domestic and international telephone and fax services are available here every day from 7 am to midnight. Several smaller Guatel branches are found around the city.

At the La Aurora International Airport there's a post office (open Monday to Friday from 7 am to 3 pm) and a Guatel office (open every day, 7 am to 7 pm).

Bookstores The Arnel bookshop is at No 108 in the Edificio El Centro, at the corner of 9a Calle and 7a Av, Zona 1, a block from Parque Central. It has a variety of books in English and French, including general fiction, Latin American literature in translation, travel guides, books about the region, Maya civilization and Spanish language learning.

Geminis Bookshop (☎ 366-1031, fax 366-1034) in the Edificio Casa Alta at 3a Av 17-05, Zona 14, has a good selection of international books, but it's farther from the center.

The Europa bar/restaurant (see Places to Eat) has a shelf of used books in English for sale or trade.

Library The Biblioteca Nacional (National Library; ☎ 232-2443), on the west side of Parque Centenario, is open Monday to Friday, 9 am to 6 pm.

Medical Services This city has many private hospitals and clinics. One is the Hospital Centro Médico (☎ 332-3555, 334-2157) at 6a Av 3-47, Zona 10; another is Hospital Herrera Llerandi, (☎ 334-5959, emergencies 334-5955), 6a Av 8-71, Zona 10, which is also called Amedesgua. The Guatemalan Red Cross (☎ 125) is located at 3 Calle 8-40, Zona 1.

Guatemala City uses a duty-chemist *(farmacia de turno)* system with designated pharmacies remaining open at night and weekends. Ask at your hotel for the nearest farmacia de turno, or consult the farmacia de turno sign in the window of the closest chemist/pharmacy. The Farmacia del Ejecutivo, on 7a Av at the corner of 15 Calle, Zona 1, is open 24 hours; it accepts Visa and MasterCard.

Emergency Guatemala City's emergency telephone numbers are:

Police,	☎ 120, 137, 138
Fire,	☎ 122, 123
Ambulance,	☎ 125, 128

Dangers & Annoyances Street crime is increasing in downtown Guatemala City. Use sensible caution – don't walk down the street with your wallet hanging out of the back pocket of your jeans, and avoid walking downtown late at night. It's safe to walk downtown in early evening, as long as you stick to streets with plenty of lighting and people. 18 Calle in Zona 1, an area with many bus stations is notoriously dangerous at night; if you are arriving by bus at night, or must go someplace on 18 Calle at night, take a taxi.

The more affluent sections of the city – Zona 9 and Zona 10, for example – are much safer.

Zona 1

Plaza Mayor Most of what you'll want to see is located in Zona 1 near the Plaza Mayor, bounded by 6 and 8 Calles and 6a and 7a Avs.

To appreciate the Plaza Mayor, you've got to visit it on a Sunday when it's thronged with thousands of citizens who have come to stroll, lick ice cream cones, play in the fountains, take the air, smooch on a bench, listen to *salsa* music on boomboxes, and ignore the hundreds of trinket vendors. If you can't make it on a Sunday, try for lunchtime or late afternoon.

Palacio Nacional On the north side of the Plaza Mayor is the country's magnificent Palacio Nacional, built during the dictatorial presidency of General Jorge Ubico (1931 – 1944) at enormous cost. It's the third palace to stand here.

The Palacio Nacional is being restored, and will house a museum of the history of Guatemala. (The national government offices, which have been here till now, are being decentralized throughout the city.)

Free tours are given Monday to Friday from 9 am to 5:30 pm, Saturday and Sunday 9 am to 3 pm. The tour takes you through a labyrinth of gleaming brass and polished wood, carved stone, and frescoed arches painted by Alberto Gálvez Suárez. Notable features include the two-ton gold, bronze and Bohemian-crystal chandelier in the reception salon, and the two Arabic-style inner courtyards.

Catedral Metropolitana Built between 1782 and 1809 (the towers were finished later, in 1867), the Catedral Metropolitana has survived earthquake and fire (much better than the site of the Palacio Nacional) though the quake of 1917 did a lot of damage, and that of 1976 did even more. All has been restored. It's not a particularly beautiful building, inside or out. Heavy proportions and spare ornamentation make it look severe, though it does have a certain stateliness. The cathedral is supposedly open every day from 8 am to 7 pm, though you may find it closed, especially at siesta time.

Mercado Central Until it was destroyed by the quake of 1976, the central market on 9a Av between 6 and 8 Calles behind the cathedral was a place to buy food and other necessities. Reconstructed in the late 1970s, the modern market specializes in tourist-oriented items such as cloth (hand-woven and machine-woven), carved wood, worked leather and metal, basketry and other handicrafts. Necessities have been moved aside to the streets surrounding the market. When you visit the Plaza Mayor, you should take a stroll through here, though there are better places to buy crafts. Market hours are 6 am to 6 pm Monday to Saturday, 9 am to noon Sunday.

The city's true 'central' food market is in Zona 4.

Museums In Zona 1 these include **Museo Fray Francisco Vasquez** (☎ 232-3625), Iglesia San Francisco, at the corner of 6a Av and 13 Calle. It houses the belongings of this Franciscan friar. The museum is open every day, 9 am to noon and 3 to 6 pm.

The **Museo Nacional de Artes e Industrias Populares** (☎ 238-0334), 10a Av 10-72, is the national popular arts museum, and it displays paintings, ceramics, masks, musical instruments, metalwork and gourds. It's open Monday to Friday, 9 am to 5 pm.

The collection of the **Museo Nacional de Historia** (☎ 253-6149), 9a Calle 9-70, corner of 10a Av, is a jumble of historical relics. It's open every day, 10 am to 4 pm. This museum may be moved to the National Palace after it's restored.

Zona 2

Zona 2 is north of Zona 1. Though mostly a middle-class residential district, its northern end holds the large **Parque Minerva**, itself surrounded by golf courses, the rod-and-gun club, sports grounds and the buildings of the Universidad Mariano Gálvez.

Minerva, goddess of wisdom, technical skill and invention, was a favorite of President Manuel Estrada Cabrera (1898-1920, see History).

The Parque Minerva is a pretty place, good for relaxing, strolling among the eucalyptus trees and sipping a soft drink. Be on the alert for pickpockets, purse-snatchers and other such types, who look especially for tourists.

The prime sight in Zona 2 is the Relief Map of Guatemala, called simply the **Mapa En Relieve** in Parque Minerva. Constructed in 1904 under the direction of Francisco Vela, the map shows the country at a scale of 1:10,000, but the height of the mountainous terrain has been exaggerated to 1:2000 for dramatic effect. Little signs indicate major towns and topographical features. Viewing towers afford a panoramic view. This place is odd but fun, and costs only a few centavos for admission; hours are 8 am to 5 pm every day. Nearby are carnival rides and gmes for children.

The Mapa En Relieve and Parque Minerva are two km north of the Plaza Mayor along 6a Av, but that street is one-way heading south. Catch a northbound bus (No 1, 45 or 46) on 5a Av in Zona 1 and take it to the end of the line.

Zona 4

Pride of Zona 4 is the Centro Cívico, constructed in the 1950s and '60s. (The complex of buildings actually stretches into Zona 1 and Zona 5 as well.) Here you'll find the Palace of Justice, the headquarters of the Guatemalan Institute of Social Security (IGSS), the Banco del Quetzal, the city hall, and the headquarters of INGUAT. The Banco del Quetzal building bears high-relief murals by Dagoberto Vásquez depicting the history of his homeland; in the city hall is a huge mosaic by Carlos Mérida completed in 1959.

Behind INGUAT is the Ciudad Olímpica sports grounds, and across the street from the Centro Cívico on a hilltop are the Centro Cultural Miguel Ángel Asturias (the national theater, chamber theater, open-air theater and a small museum of old armaments). The Centro Cívico is hardly a tourist attraction, though the useful INGUAT tourist office is here.

Zona 4 is known mostly for its markets and its bus stations, all thrown together in the chaotic southwestern corner of the zona near the railway.

Zona 10

Lying east of Av La Reforma, Zona 10 is the upscale district of posh villas, luxury hotels, embassies, and two of the city's most important museums.

The **Museo Ixchel del Traje Indígena** (☎ 331-3638, 331-3739) is named for Ixchel, wife of Maya sky god Itzamná and goddess of the moon, women, reproduction and textiles, among other things. Photographs and exhibits of Indian costumes, textiles and other village crafts show the incredible richness of traditional arts in Guatemala's highland towns. If you enjoy seeing Guatemalan textiles at all, you must make a visit to the Museo Ixchel.

Just behind this is the **Museo Popol Vuh**, where well-chosen polychrome pottery, figurines, incense burners, burial urns, carved wooden masks and traditional textiles fill several exhibit rooms. Others hold colonial paintings, gilded wood and silver objects. A faithful copy of the Dresden Codex, one of the precious 'painted books' of the Maya, is among the most interesting pieces. If you're at all interested in Maya and Spanish colonial art, you must make a visit to this museum.

Both museums are in large, new buildings at the Universidad Francisco Marroquín, on the east end of 6a Calle in Zona 10, about six blocks east of Av La Reforma. They're open Monday to Friday from 8 am to 6 pm, Saturday 9 am to 1 pm; admission is US$1.65.

The biology department at the Universidad de San Carlos de Guatemala (☎ 476-2010) at Calle Mariscal Cruz 1-56 has a natural history museum and a large botanical garden open to the public Monday to Friday from 8 am to 4 pm.

Zona 13

The major attraction in the southern reaches of the city is the **Parque Aurora** with its zoo, children's playground, fairgrounds and several museums.

The Moorish-looking **Museo Nacional de Arqueología y Etnología** (☎ 472-0489) has a collection of Mayan archaeological finds from all over Guatemala, including stone carvings, jade, ceramics, statues, stelae, a tomb, and models of the ruins at Tikal and Zaculeu. Exhibits in the ethnology section show the distribution of all the various indigenous peoples and languages throughout Guatemala, with exhibits on their traditional costumes, dances and implements of daily life.

Facing the Museo Nacional de Arqueología y Etnología is the **Museo Nacional de Arte Moderno** (☎ 472-0467), with a collection of 20th-century Guatemalan art, especially painting and sculpture.

Hours at these museums are Tuesday to Friday from 9 am to 4 pm, Saturday and Sunday from 9 to noon and 1:30 to 4 pm (closed Monday). Admission is free.

Several hundred meters east of the museums is the city's official handicrafts market, the **Mercado de Artesanías** (☎ 472-0208), on 11a Av, just off the access road to the airport. Like most official handicrafts markets it's a sleepy place in which shopkeepers display the same items available in hotel gift shops. It's open 9 am to 6 pm Monday to Saturday, 9 am to 1 pm Sunday.

The **Zoológico La Aurora** (☎ 472-0507) is pleasant. It's open Tuesday to Sunday from 9 am to 5 pm. Admission is US$0.85 for adults, half price for children.

Kaminaljuyú

Several kilometers west of the center lie the extensive ruins of Kaminaljuyú (☎ 253-1570, 232-5948), a Late Preclassic/Early Classic Maya site displaying both Mexican and Mayan influences.

Unfortunately, much of Kaminaljuyú, located in Colonia Kaminaljuyú, Zona 7, has been covered by urban sprawl. Though you can visit from 9 am to 4 pm daily, your time would be better spent looking at the artifacts recovered here which are on display in the city's museums. Buses No 35 and 37 come here from 4a Av, Zona 1.

Places to Stay

Guatemala City has a good range of lodgings in all price ranges. Those at the very bottom end of the price scale, as well as those at the very top, often fill up, but there are usually plenty of rooms to be had at prices in-between.

Budget Perhaps the greatest concentration of low-budget hotels in the city is about eight blocks south of the Plaza Mayor near the Policia Nacional (National Police Headquarters) and the correos (post office), in the area bounded by 6a Av 'A' and 9a Av, and 14 and 16 Calles. There are at least a dozen decent hotels to choose from, and several handy little restaurants as well. It's very important to keep street noise in mind as you search for a budget room. All the places listed below are in Zona 1.

Spring Hotel (☎ 230-2858, 230-2958, fax 232-0107), 8a Av 12-65, is a clean and pleasant old hotel that's often *completo* (full) because the location is good, the 43 rooms presentable, the courtyard sunny, and the price right. Singles/doubles with shared bath are US$10/14.50; rooms with private bath and color cable TV are US$14.50/19, and fancier rooms in the new *anexo* are US$22/28. A cafeteria serves meals from 7 am to 2 pm.

Hotel Lessing House (☎ 251-3891), 12a Calle 4-35, offers eight tidy rooms, all with private bath. Rooms can accommodate one to four people (US$8/14/20/28).

Hotel Ajau (☎ 232-0488, 251-3008, fax 251-8097, net), 8a Av 15-62, is fairly clean, somewhat cheaper, and a lot quieter than many 9a Av hotels. Singles/doubles are US$7/9 with shared bath, US$12/14 with private bath. All rooms have color cable TV. Laundry service and coffee are available, and guests are welcome to use the email.

Hotel Chalet Suizo (☎ 251-3786, 230-2930), 14a Calle 6A-82, has been a favorite of adventurous travelers for decades. The 47 rooms around plant-filled courtyards are pleasant and exceptionally clean. Rates are US$14/17 a single/double with shared bath, or US$24/30 with private bath. Book in advance.

Hotel Excel (☎ 253-2709, 230-0140, fax 238-4071), 9a Av 15-12, is a bright, modern place with 17 rooms on three levels around an L-shaped court used as a car park. It has a 2nd-floor cafeteria. Rooms with bath and cable TV are US$20/25/30 a single/double/triple. In the same block are several cheaper hotels, including the *Capri*, the *España* and the *Gran Central*.

Pensión Meza (☎ 232-3177, 253-4576), 10a Calle 10-17, is drab and beat-up but busy with international budget travelers who like the sunny courtyard, the camaraderie, the helpful proprietor, and the low prices. With shared bath, singles/doubles are US$5.50/6 with one bed, US$7.50 with two beds, or US$2.50 per person in a dormitory. One room with private bath costs US$9 for one to three people. The restaurant serves cheap meals.

If you're arriving by bus from San Salvador, the *Hotel del Istmo* (☎ 332-4389) at the Terminal Internacional bus terminal, 3a Av 1-38, Zona 9, is clean, comfortable and convenient. Rooms with private hot bath are US$11/14 a single/double, and there's an inexpensive cafeteria.

Middle Guatemala City's midrange lodgings are good values. All are comfortable, some quite charming. All these places are in Zona 1.

Posada Belén (☎ 232-9226, 253-4530, fax 251-3478), 13a Calle 'A' 10-30, is on a quiet side street. A converted colonial home, the Belén is a charming hostelry with 11 rooms with bath, a dining room serving all meals, and laundry service. Rooms accommodate one (US$36), two (US$43), three (US$48) or four (US$53) people.

Hotel Colonial (☎ 232-6722, 232-2955, fax 232-8671), 7a Av 14-19, is a large old city house converted to a hotel with heavy colonial decor. The covered interior court is pleasant, the 42 rooms clean. Singles/doubles in four rooms with general bath are US$18/24; the rest, all with private bath, are US$24/32.50. A restaurant serves meals from 6:30 am to 2 pm.

Hotel-Apartamentos Guatemala Internacional (☎ 238-4441), 6a Av 12-21, offers 27 furnished units, each with fully-equipped kitchen, TV and telephone. The location is convenient, and the prices are good. Furnished studios are US$22/25 for singles/doubles; one/two-bedroom apartments are US$30/36 single, US$36/42 double, and US$42/48 triple or quad. Larger apartments can sleep six.

Hotel Centenario (☎ 238-0381, fax 238-2039), 6a Calle 5-33, on the north side of the Parque Centenario, has 42 rooms, many with a double and a single bed, plus well-worn but clean showers. Prices for this central location are US$25/30 a single/double.

Places to Eat

Budget It is not difficult to find cheap eats. Fast-food and snack shops abound. But to really save money, head for Parque Concordia, bound by 4a and 5a Avs and 14a and 15a Calles in Zona 1. The west side of the park is lined with little open-air food stalls serving sandwiches and snacks at rockbottom prices from early morning to late evening. A meal for US$2 is the rule here.

Delicadezas Hamburgo, 15a Calle 5-34, Zona 1, on the south side of Parque Concordia, provides a long list of sandwiches at lunch and dinner. It's open every day.

Restaurante Cantón (☎ 251-6331), 6a Av 14-29, Zona 1, facing the park on its east side, is the place to go for Chinese food, at US$5 to US$8 per platter; it's open daily.

There are numerous other Chinese restaurants near the corner of 6a Av and 14a Calle, Zona 1. The city's other rich concentration of Chinese restaurants is in the blocks west of the Parque Centenario along 6a Calle, where you'll find the *Restaurante Long Wah* (☎ 232-6611), 6a Calle 3-70, Zona 1, along with several other places such as the *Palacio Real*, *Palacio Dorado* and the *Jou Jou*.

6a Avenida between 10a and 15a Calles has dozens of restaurants and fast-food shops of all types: hamburgers, pizzas, pasta, Chinese, fried chicken. You'll have no trouble eating well for US$3 to US$4. The *Pastelería Las Américas*, 6a Av 8-52, half a block south of Plaza Mayor, is a good place to stop for a coffee and a European-style pastry or cake while you're out sight-seeing.

9a Avenida between 15a and 16a Calles, in the midst of the cheap hotel area, has several good little restaurants. There's the *Cafetín El Rinconcito*, 9a Av 15-74, facing the Hotel Capri, which is good for tacos and sandwiches, where breakfast, lunch and dinner each cost around US$1.50 to US$2. The restaurant in the Hotel Capri itself, 9a Av 15-63, Zona 1, serves more substantial meals.

You might also want to try the *Cafetería El Roble*, 9a Calle 5-46, Zona 1, facing the entrance to the Hotel Pan American. This clean little cafe is very popular with local office workers who come for lunch (US$1.65) as well as for breakfast and dinner (US$1.15).

Europa (☎ 253-4929), 11a Calle 5-16, next door to Credomatic, is a comfortable restaurant, bar and gathering place for locals and foreigners alike. A sign on the door says 'English spoken, but not under-stood.' It has international cable TV, a book exchange and good, inexpensive food; it's open Monday to Saturday, 8 am to 1 am.

Pollo Campero (Country Chicken) is the name of Guatemala's Kentucky Fried Chicken clone. You can find branches of the chain on the corner of 9a Calle and 5a Av, at 6a Av and 15a Calle, and at 8a Calle 9-29, all in Zona 1. Two pieces of chicken, french fries, and a soft drink or coffee costs US$2.50.

Many branches of American fast-food chains such as *McDonald's, Wendy's, Burger King* and *Pizza Hut* are all around the city. They're open long hours, often from 7 am to 10 pm. Pizza Hut offers free delivery (☎ 230-3490 in Zona 1, ☎ 332-0939 in Zona 9).

The *Restaurante Vegetariano Rey Sol*, 8a Calle 5-36, on the south side of Parque Centenario, has a long cafeteria line with a good selection: whole grain breads and baked goods, sandwiches, soya products, fruit and vegetable salads,

hot foods and more. It's open for every meal daily except Sunday.

Middle Most middle-range hotels in Zona 1 offer excellent set-price lunches for US$6 to US$10. Try the *Hotel Del Centro, Hotel Pan American*, and *Hotel Ritz Continental*. My favorite for ambiance is definitely the Pan American, 9a Calle 5-63, Zona 1.

Restaurante Bologna (☎ 251-1167), 10a Calle 6-20, Zona 1, just around the corner from the Hotel Ritz Continental, is very small but attractive, serving tasty pizza and pasta dishes for US$3 to US$4 per plate. It's open every day but Tuesday.

Several other good restaurants have their main establishments in Zona 1, and branches in Zona 9 or 10.

El Gran Pavo (The Big Turkey; ☎ 232-9912), 13a Calle 4-41, Zona 1, is a big place just to the left (west) of the Hotel del Centro's entrance. The menu seems to include every Mexican dish imaginable. The birria, a spicy-hot soup of meat, onions, peppers and cilantro, served with tortillas, is a meal in itself for US$3.75. The Big Turkey is open seven days a week from 10 am to midnight, with mariachi music on Friday and Saturday nights start-ing around 10 pm. There's another branch (☎ 331-3976) at 12a Calle 5-54, Zona 9, and a few others around town.

Restaurante Piccadilly (☎ 230-2866, 253-9223), 6a Av 11-01, Zona 1, is among the capital's most popular eateries, with a multinational menu that might have come from the United Nations cafeteria. Most main courses cost US$3 or less. There's another branch of the Piccadilly on the Plazuela España, 7a Av 12-00, Zona 9.

Entertainment

Wining and dining the night away in the Zona Viva is what many visitors do. If that's beyond your budget, take in a movie at one of the cinemas along 6a Av between the Plaza Mayor and Parque Concordia. Tickets sell for about US$1.50. Or check out the cultural events at the Centro Cul-tural Miguel Ángel Asturias (☎ 232-4041, 253-1743) in Zona 4.

Getting There & Away

Air International air routes to Guatemala arrive and depart from the La Aurora International Airport in Guatemala City and from the international airport at Flores/Santa Elena, near Tikal.

International air routes to Guatemala usually go through Dallas/Fort Worth, Houston, Los Angeles, Miami, Mexico City or San Salvador. If you begin your trip in any other city, you will probably find yourself stopping in one of these 'hub' cities. There are a few exceptions, which are mostly flights from cities in the region operated by smaller local airlines. The following list indicates the cities with direct and nonstop flights to and from Guatemala City, and the airlines that fly them:

Amsterdam – KLM (via Mexico City)
Belize City – Aerovías (via Flores), TACA (via El Salvador), Tikal Jets (via Flores)
Cancún – Aerocaribe, Aviateca
Chetumal (Mexico) – Aeroméxico (via Flores)
Flores, Petén (for Tikal) – Aviateca, Mayan World, Tikal Jets
Havana – Aviateca
Houston – Aviateca, Continental, TACA (via El Salvador and Belize City)
Huatulco – Mexicana
Los Angeles – Aviateca, Mexicana (via Mexico City), TACA, United
Madrid – Iberia (via Miami)
Mérida – Aviateca
Mexico City – Aviateca, KLM, Mexicana
Miami – American, Aviateca, Iberia, TACA (via El Salvador)
New Orleans – TACA (via El Salvador)
New York – TACA (via Washington, DC)
San Francisco (USA) – TACA
San José (Costa Rica) – Avianca (Guatemala City-San José-San Andrés Island-Bogotá), Aviateca, COPA, LACSA, SAM, TACA, United
San Salvador – Aviateca, COPA, TACA
Washington, DC – TACA

Many airlines have offices in Guatemala City. If you don't see one in the list below, consult a phone directory:

Aerocaribe – see Mexicana.
Aeroméxico – see Mexicana.
Aerovías, a Guatemalan regional carrier. La Aurora International Airport (☎ 332-7470, 361-5703, fax 334-7935).

American Airlines, Hotel El Dorado, 7a Av 15-45, Zona 9 (☎ 334-7379).
Avianca, the Colombian national airline. Av La Reforma 13-89, Local 1, Zona 10 (☎ 334-6801/02/09, ☎ /fax 334-6797).
Aviateca, Guatemala's national airline – see TACA.
Continental Airlines, 12a Calle 1-25, Zona 10, Edificio Géminis 10, Torre Norte, 12th Floor, Office 1210 (☎ 335-3341, fax 335-3444); also, La Aurora International Airport (☎ 331-2051/52/53/54, fax 331-2055).
COPA (Compañía Panameña de Aviación), Panama's national airline, 1a Av 10-17, Zona 10 (☎ 361-1567, 361-1607, fax 331-8314).
Iberia, Spain's national airline. Av La Reforma 8-60, Zona 9, Edificio Galerías Reforma, Local 204 (☎ 332-0911, 331-1012, fax 334-3715); also, La Aurora International Airport (☎ 332-5517/18, fax 332-3634).
KLM Royal Dutch Airlines, 6a Av 20-25, Zona 10, Edificio Plaza Marítima (☎ 337-0222/23/24/25/26, fax 337-0227).
LACSA (Líneas Aereas Costarriquenses), Costa Rica's national airline – see TACA.
Mayan World, 7a Av 6-53, Zona 4, Edificio El Triángulo, 2nd Floor (☎ 334-2070, 334-2077).
Mexicana, a Mexican international airline. 13a Calle 8-44, Zona 10 (☎ 333-6048); also, La Aurora International Airport (☎ 332-1924, 331-3291).
SAM, Colombian national airline – see Avianca.
TACA, El Salvador's national airline. Main office, Av Hincapie 12-22, Zona 13. (☎ 331-8222, reservations ☎ 334-7722, fax 334-2775); Hotel Ritz Continental, 6a Av 'A' 10-13, Zona 1 (☎ 238-1415, 238-1479); Centro de Servicio, 7 Av 14-35, Zona 9 (☎ 332-2360, 332-4640); Plaza Biltmore, 14 Calle 0-20, Zona 10 (☎ 331-2520, 337-3462); La Aurora International Airport (☎ 361-5784).
Tikal Jets, La Aurora International Airport (☎ 334-5631, 334-5568, fax 334-5631).
United Airlines, Av La Reforma 1-50, Zona 9, Edificio El Reformador, 2nd Floor (☎ 332-2995, fax 332-3903); La Aurora International Airport (☎ 332-1994/95, fax 332-2795).

Bus Guatemala City has no central bus terminal, even though many Guatemalans talk about the Terminal de Autobuses, in Zona 4. Ticket offices and departure points are different for each company. Many are near the huge and chaotic market in Zona 4. If the bus you want is one of these, go to the market and ask until you find the bus.

Here is bus route information for most of Guatemala:

Amatitlán (25 km, 30 minutes, US$0.30) Buses depart from 20a Calle and 2a Av, Zona 1, every half-hour from 7 am to 7 pm. Also see Puerto San José.

Antigua Guatemala (45 km, one hour, US$0.50) Transportes Unidos (☎ 232-4949, 253-6929), 15 Calle 3-65, Zona 1, makes the trip every half-hour from 7 am to 7 pm, stopping in San Lucas Sacatepéquez. Other buses depart more frequently, every 15 minutes from around 4 am to 7 pm, from the corner of 18a Calle and 4a Av, Zona 1. Several shuttle minibus companies also offer services; see the section below.

Autosafari Chapin (88 km, 1½ hours, US$1) Delta y Tropical, 1a Calle and 2a Av, Zona 4; buses every 30 minutes, via Escuintla.

Biotopo del Quetzal (160 km, three hours, US$2.20) Escobar y Monja Blanda, 8a Av 15-16, Zona 1; hourly buses, 4 am to 5 pm, via El Rancho and Purulhá. (Any bus heading for Cobán will stop here.)

Chichicastenango (146 km, 3½ hours, US$1.70) Veloz Quichelense, Terminal de Autobuses, Zona 4, runs buses every half-hour from 5 am to 6 pm, stopping in San Lucas, Chimaltenango and Los Encuentros.

Chiquimula (169 km, three hours, US$3) Rutas Orientales (☎ 253-6714, 251-2160), 19 Calle 8-18, Zona 1, runs buses via El Rancho, Río Hondo and Zacapa to Chiquimula every 30 minutes from 5 am to 6 pm. If you're heading for Copán, Honduras, change buses at Chiquimula to continue to the border. See El Florido.

Cobán (219 km, four hours) Escobar Monja Blanca (☎ 238-1409), 8a Av 15-16, Zona 1, has buses hourly from 4 am to 5 pm, stopping at El Rancho, the Biotopo del Quetzal, Purulhá, Tactic and San Cristóbal.

Copán (Honduras) – see El Florido

El Carmen/Talismán (Mexican border; 278 km, five to six hours, US$6) Transportes Galgos (☎ 232-3661, 253-4868), 7a Av 19-44, Zona 1, runs direct buses along the Pacific Slope road to this border-crossing point, stopping at Escuintla (change for Santa Lucía Cotzumalguapa), Mazatenango, Retalhuleu and Coatepeque, at 5:30 and 10 am, 3 and 4:30 pm. They also operate buses going

all the way to Tapachula (Mexico); see Tapachula.

El Florido/Copán (Honduras) – Bus to Chiquimula, where you change buses to continue on to the border at El Florido, a remaining 58-km, 2½-hour trip via Jocotán and Camotán.

Escuintla (57 km, one hour, US$1.15) See Autosafari Chapin, El Carmen/Talismán, La Democracia, Monterrico, Puerto San José and Tecún Umán.

Esquipulas (222 km, four hours, US$3.50) Rutas Orientales (☎ 253-7882, 251-2160, 253-6714), 19a Calle 8-18, Zona 1, has buses departing every half-hour from 4 am to 6 pm, with stops at El Rancho, Río Hondo, Zacapa and Chiquimula.

Flores (Petén; 506 km, 12 hours, US$12) Fuentes del Norte (☎ 238-3894, 251-3817), 17a Calle 8-46, Zona 1, runs buses departing from the capital at 7:30 am, 11 am, noon, 1, 3, 5 and 10 pm. Máxima (☎ 232-2495, 238-4032), 9a Av 17-28, Zona 1, has buses departing at 6:30 pm and 8 pm. La Petenera (☎ 232-9658), 16a Calle 10-55, Zona 1, operates one luxury bus daily, the Linea Dorada, departing at 7:30 pm and arriving at 7 am (US$22.50). Buses make stops at El Rancho, Teculután, Río Hondo, Los Amates, Quiriguá, Morales, Río Dulce, San Luis and Poptún. Buses usually leave Guatemala City and Santa Elena full; anyone getting on midway stands, or rides on the roof.

Huehuetenango (270 km, five hours, US$4) Los Halcones, 7a Av 15-27, Zona 1, runs two buses a day (7 am and 2 pm) up the Interamericana to Huehue, stopping at Chimaltenango, Patzicía, Tecpán, Los Encuentros, and San Cristobal and Totonicapán. Buses to La Mesilla also stop here; see La Mesilla.

La Democracia (92 km, two hours, US$1) Chatia Gomerana, Muelle Central, Terminal de Buses, Zona 4, has buses every half-hour from 6 am to 4:30 pm, stopping at Escuintla, Siquinalá (change for Santa Lucía Cotzumalguapa), La Democracia, La Gomera and Sipacate.

La Mesilla/Ciudad Cuauhtémoc (Mexican border; 380 km, seven hours, US$4.50) Transportes Velásquez, 20a Calle and 2a Av, Zona 1, has buses going to La Mesilla, on the Interamericana at the border with Mexico, hourly from 8 am to 4 pm. Stops are at Los Encuentros, Totonicapán and Huehuetenango.

Monterrico (124 km, 4½ hours, US$1.50) Transportes Cubanita, Muelle Central, Terminal de Buses, Zona 4, has buses departing at 10:30 am, 12:30 and 2:30 pm, stopping at Escuintla, Taxisco and La Avellana.

Panajachel (147 km, three hours, US$1.70) Transportes Rébuli (☎ 230-2748, 251-3521), 21a Calle 1-34, Zona 1, departs for Lake Atitlán and Panajachel hourly from 6 am to 4 pm, stopping at Chimaltenango, Patzicía, Tecpán Guatemala (for the ruins at Iximché), Los Encuentros, and Sololá.

Puerto Barrios (307 km, five hours, US$6) Transportes Litegua (☎ 232-7578, 253-8169), 15a Calle 10-40, Zona 1, has 'especial' (direct) buses at 6:30, 7:30, 10 and 10:30 am, 12:30, 2, 4, 4:30 and 5 pm, with stops at El Rancho, Teculután, Río Hondo, Los Amates and Quiriguá. Regular buses take longer, around six to nine hours.

Puerto San José (58 km, one hour) Transportes Esmeralda, Trebol, Zona 12, operates buses every 10 minutes from 5 am to 8 pm, stopping at Amatitlán, Palín and Escuintla.

Quetzaltenango (206 km, four hours, US$4.20) Transportes Alamo (☎ 253-2105), 21a Calle 1-14, Zona 1, has buses at 8 am, 3 and 5:45 pm. Líneas América (☎ 232-1432), 2a Av 18-47, Zona 1, has buses departing at 5 and 9 am, noon, 3:15, 4:40 and 7:30 pm. Transportes Galgos (☎ 253-4868, 232-3661), 7a Av 19-44, Zona 1, makes this run at 5:30, 8:30 and 11 am, and 2:30, 5 and 7 pm. All of these buses stop at Chimaltenango, Los Encuentros and San Cristobal.

Quiriguá – see Puerto Barrios.

Retalhuleu (186 km, three hours, US$3.65) See El Carmen and Tecún Umán.

Río Dulce (220 km, five hours) – see Flores.

Río Hondo – see Chiquimula, Esquipulas and Puerto Barrios.

San Pedro La Laguna, on Lago de Atitlán (170 km, three to four hours, US$2.65) Ruta Méndez, 21a Calle and 5a Av, Zona 1, operates buses at 10 and 11 am, noon and 1 pm.

San Salvador (El Salvador; 268 km, five hours) Melva Internacional (☎ 331-0874, 331-6323), 3a Av 1-38, Zona 9, runs buses from Guatemala City via Cuilapa, Oratorio and Jalpatagua to the Salvadoran border at Valle Nuevo and onward to San Salvador hourly from 5 am to 4 pm (US$6.65). Tica Bus (☎ 361-1773, 331-4279), 11a Calle 2-72, Zona 9, has a bus leaving daily at 12:30 pm (US$8.50 one-way, US$17 roundtrip). From San Salvador, buses continue to all the other Central American capitals except Belize City. Comfort Lines (☎ 361-2516, 361-2493), based at the Hotel Gran Plaza Las Américas, Av Las Américas 9-08, Zona 13,

has luxury buses departing daily at 8 am and 2 pm (US$15 one-way, US$25 roundtrip). From the same place, King Quality luxury buses depart at 6:30 am and 3:30 pm (US$20 one-way, US$35 roundtrip). Pulmantur (☎ 332-9797) has one luxury bus daily, departing at 3:15 pm from the Radisson Suites Villa Magna hotel, 2a Av 12-43, Zona 10 (US$23 one way, US$45 roundtrip).

Santa Elena – see Flores.

Santa Lucía Cotzumalguapa – see El Carmen, La Democracia and Tecún Umán.

Tapachula (Mexico; 295 km, five hours, US$19) Transportes Galgos, (☎ 253-4868, 232-3661), 7a Av 19-44, Zona 1, has direct buses from Guatemala City to Tapachula at 7:30 am and 1:30 pm. (From Tapachula they depart for Guatemala City at 9:30 am and 1:30 pm.) These buses cross the border at El Carmen/Talismán and keep on going into Mexico, as far as Tapachula, where they connect with Mexican buses.

Tecún Umán/Ciudad Hidalgo (Mexican border; 253 km, five hours, US$5) Transportes Fortaleza (☎ 230-3390, 220-6372), 19 Calle 8-70, Zona 1, has hourly buses from 1:30 am to 6 pm, stopping at Escuintla (change for Santa Lucía Cotzumalguapa), Mazatenango, Retalhuleu and Coatepeque.

Tikal – see Flores.

Shuttle Minibus Minibus companies capitalize on the difficulty most travelers have navigating the bus system. While their routes are very limited, they do serve the airport and connect Guatemala City and Antigua. See the Getting Around chapter above for more details.

Car Rental Major international rental companies have offices both at La Aurora International Airport and in the city center (see Car Rental in Getting Around above for details). Rental offices in Guatemala City include:

Ahorrent (☎ 332-0544, 332-7515, fax 361-5621), Boulevard Liberación 4-83, Zona 9; Hotel Cortijo Reforma, Av La Reforma 2-18, Zona 9 (☎ 332-0712, ext 180); La Aurora International Airport (☎ 332-6491, ext 115).

Avis (☎ 331-2750, fax 332-1263), 12a Calle 2-73, Zona 9; La Aurora International Airport (☎ 331-0017, 361-5620).

Budget (☎ 331-6546, 331-2788, fax 331-2807), Av La Reforma 15-00, Zona 9; Hotel El Dorado, 7a Av 15-45, Zona 9 (☎ 360-9725); La Aurora International Airport (☎ 331-0273, 361-5613).

Dollar (☎ 232-3446), Hotel Ritz Continental, 6a Av 'A' 10-13, Zona 1; La Aurora International Airport (☎ 331-7185).

Hertz (☎ 331-5374, 332-2242, fax 331-7924), 7a Av 14-76, Zona 9; Hotels Camino Real and Princess Reforma; La Aurora International Airport (☎ 331-1711).

National (Interrent-Europcar-Tilden) (☎ 366-4670, 368-0175, fax 337-0221), 14a Calle 1-42, Zona 10; La Aurora International Airport (☎ 331-8218, 331-8365).

Tabarini (☎ 331-9814, 334-5907, fax 334-1925), 2a Calle 'A' 7-30, Zona 10; La Aurora International Airport (☎ 331-4755).

Tally (☎ 232-0421, 232-3327, fax 253-1749), 7a Av 14-60, Zona 1; La Aurora International Airport (☎ 332-6063, fax 334-5925).

Thrifty (☎ 332-1130, 332-1220, fax 332-1207), Av La Reforma and 11a Calle, Zona 9; La Aurora International Airport (☎ 332-1306, 332-1230, fax 332-1273).

Tikal (☎ 232-4721, 361-0247), 2a Calle 6-56, Zona 10.

Getting Around

To/From the Airport La Aurora International Airport (☎ 334-7680, 331-7243) is in Zona 13, the southern part of the city, 10 or 15 minutes from Zona 1 by taxi, half an hour by bus. Car rental offices and taxi ranks are outside, down the stairs from the arrivals level.

For the city bus stop you must go upstairs to the departures level and walk across the airport parking lot to the bus stop. Bus No 83 comes by every 15 minutes, 6 am to 9 pm, costs US$.15, and will take you through Zonas 9 and 4 to Zona 1. Going from town to the airport, No 83 goes south through Zona 1 on 10a Av, south through Zona 9 on 6a Av, passes by the zoo and the museums on 7a Av, and stops right in front of the international terminal.

Taxi fares to various points in the center are supposedly set rates, but are actually negotiable, and still quite high: from the airport to Zona 9 or 10, US$5; to Zona 1, US$7. A tip is expected. Be sure to establish the destination and price before getting into the taxi.

Several companies offer direct shuttle service between the airport and Antigua, with door-to-door service on the Antigua end. The shuttles depart from the airport about every hour or so, take an hour to reach Antigua, and cost around US$10. Coming from Antigua to the airport, competition among the many shuttle services keeps prices a little lower, around US$7 (see Shuttle Minibus under Getting Around above).

Bus & Jitney Guatemala City buses are cheap, frequent, and though often very crowded, they're useful. They are not always safe, however. Theft and robbery are not unusual; there have even been incidents of rape. *Preferencial* buses are newer, safer, not as crowded and more expensive at about US$0.20 per ride. Ordinary buses cost US$0.15 per ride.

6a Avenida (southbound) and 7a Av (northbound) in Zona 9 are loaded with buses traversing the city; in Zona 1 these buses tend to swing away from the commercial district and travel along 4a, 5a, 9a and 10a Avs. The most useful north-south bus routes are Nos 2, 5 and 14. Note that modified numbers (such as 2A or 5-Bolívar) follow different routes, and may not get you where you expect to go. Any bus with 'Terminal' in the front window stops at the intercity bus terminal near the market in Zona 4.

City buses stop running at about 9 pm, and jitneys *(ruteleros)* begin to run up and down the main avenues. The jitneys run all night, until the buses resume their rattling rides at 5 am. Hold up your hand as the signal to stop a jitney or bus.

Taxi Taxis are quite expensive, around US$5 for a normal ride – even a short one – within the city. Be sure to agree on the fare before entering the cab, as most taxis do not have meters.

In Guatemala City you rarely see taxis cruising. Usually you'll have to phone for one. Taxi Amarilla (☎ 332-1515) charges about half the price of most other taxi companies, and their taxis are metered.

Antigua Guatemala

Population 30,000
Antigua Guatemala (1530 meters) is among the oldest and most beautiful cities in the Americas. Its setting is superb, amidst three magnificent volcanoes named Agua, Fuego and Acatenango. Fuego (Fire) is easily recognizable by its plume of smoke and – at night – by the red glow it projects against the sky. Experienced Guatemala travelers spend as little time in Guatemala City as possible, preferring to make Antigua their base.

On weekends a long stream of cars and buses brings the citizens of Guatemala City up the serpentine route into the mountains for a day of strolling, shopping and sipping in the former capital. On Sunday evening, traffic jams Antigua's cobbled streets as the day trippers head home.

If you have the opportunity to be in Antigua during Holy Week – especially on Good Friday – seize it; but make your hotel reservations months in advance – this is the busiest week of the year for tourism. Other busy tourist seasons are July and August; from November to April there's a steady flow; May/June and September/October are much quieter. In winter, Antigua can be cold after sunset, so bring warm clothes; you might even consider bringing a sleeping bag, or buying a blanket or two.

Residents of Antigua are known by the nickname *panza verde* (green belly) because they are said to eat lots of avocados, which grow abundantly here.

History
Antigua was founded on March 10, 1543, as La muy Noble y muy Leal Ciudad de Santiago de los Caballeros de Goathemala, after the capital at what is now called

The Highlands
The highlands, stretching from Antigua to the Mexican border northwest of Huehuetenango, are Guatemala's most beautiful region. The verdant hills are clad in carpets of emerald-green grass, fields of tawny maize (corn) and towering stands of pine. All of this lushness comes from the abundant rain that falls between May and October. If you visit during the rainy season, be prepared for some dreary, chilly, damp days. But when the sun comes out, this land is glorious.

Highlights of the region include Antigua, Guatemala's most beautiful colonial city (see above); Lago de Atitlán, a perfect mirror of blue surrounded by Fuji-like volcanoes; Chichicastenango, where traditional Maya religious rites blend with Catholic ones; Quetzaltenango, the commercial and market center of the southwest; and Huehuetenango, jumping-off place for the cross-border journey to Comitán and San Cristóbal de las Casas in Chiapas, Mexico.

Every town and village in the highlands has a story to tell, which usually begins more than a thousand years ago. Most towns here were already populated by the Maya when the Spanish arrived. The traditional values and ways of life of Guatemala's indigenous peoples are strongest in the highlands. Mayan is the first language, Spanish a distant second.

The age-old culture based on maize is still alive; a sturdy cottage set in the midst of a thriving *milpa* (field of maize) is a common sight, one as old as Maya culture itself. On every road one sees men and women carrying loads of *leña* (firewood) to be used for heating and cooking.

Each highland town has its own market and festival days. Life in a highland town can be *muy triste* (sad, boring) when there's not a market or festival going on, so you should try to visit on those special days.

If you have only three or four days to spend in the highlands, spend them in Antigua, Panajachel and Chichicastenango. With more time you can make your way to Quetzaltenango and the sights in its vicinity, such as Zunil, Fuentes Georginas, San Francisco El Alto, Momostenango and Totonicapán.

Ciudad Vieja (see Around Antigua Guatemala), on the flanks of Volcán Agua, was flooded in 1541. The capital was moved to Antigua's present site, in the Valle de Panchoy, in 1543 and remained here for 233 years. The capital was transferred again, to present-day Guatemala City, in 1776, after the great earthquake of July 29, 1773, destroyed the city, which had already suffered considerable damage from earlier earthquakes.

After the 1773 earthquake Antigua was repopulated, but only very slowly, and without losing its traditional character, architecture and cobblestoned streets. In 1799 the city was renamed La Antigua Guatemala (the Old Guatemala). In 1944 the Legislative Assembly declared Antigua a national monument, and in 1979 UNESCO declared it a World Heritage Site.

Most of Antigua's buildings were constructed during the 17th and 18th centuries, when the city was a rich Spanish colonial capital, and it seems no expense was spared in the city's magnificent architecture. Many handsome, sturdy colonial buildings remain, and several impressive ruins have been preserved and are open to the public.

Orientation

Volcán Agua is southeast of the city and visible from most points within it; Volcán Fuego is southwest, and Volcán Acatenango is to the west. These three volcanoes (which appear on the city's coat of arms) provide easy reference points.

Antigua's street grid uses a modified version of the Guatemala City numbering system. (For details on that system, see Orientation in under Guatemala City.) In Antigua, compass points are added to the avenidas and calles. The central point is the northeast corner of the city's main plaza, the Parque Central. Calles run east-west, so

---

Huehuetenango and the ruins nearby at Zaculeu are worth a visit only if you're passing through or if you have lots of time; the towns and villages high in the Cuchumatanes mountains north of Huehuetenango offer wonderful scenery and adventures for intrepid travelers.

Warning Though most visitors never experience any trouble, there have been some incidents of robbery, rape and murder of tourists in the highlands. These have occurred on trails up the volcanoes, on the outskirts of Antigua and Chichicastenango, and at lonely spots along country roads. Attacks happen at random. If you use caution and common sense, and don't do much roaming or driving at night, you should have a fine time in this beautiful region.

Before you travel in the highlands, contact your embassy or consulate in Guatemala City for information on the current situation and advice on how and where to travel in the highlands. Don't rely on local authorities for safety advice, as they may downplay the dangers. For embassy phone numbers, see the Guatemala City chapter.

Getting Around Guatemala City and the Guatemalan/Mexican border station at La Mesilla are connected by the Interamericana. It is a curvy mountain road that must be traveled slowly in many places. Driving the 266 km between Guatemala City and Huehuetenango can take five hours, but the time passes pleasantly amid the beautiful scenery. (The Carretera al Pacífico, CA-2, via Escuintla and Retalhuleu is straighter and faster, and it's the better route to take if your goal is to reach Mexico as quickly as possible.)

Many buses rumble up and down the highway; refer to specific destinations under Getting There & Away in the Guatemala City chapter. As most of the places you'll want to reach are some distance off the Interamericana, you may find yourself waiting at major highway junctions such as Los Encuentros and Cuatro Caminos to connect with the right bus. Travel is easiest on market days and in the morning. By mid or late afternoon, buses may be difficult to find, and all short-distance local traffic stops by dinner time. You should, too. ■

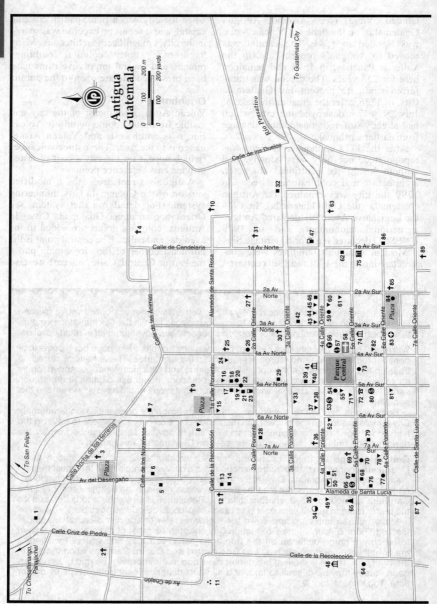

Antigua Guatemala

0   100   200 m
0   100   200 yards

To Guatemala City

To San Felipe

To Chimaltenango, Panajachel

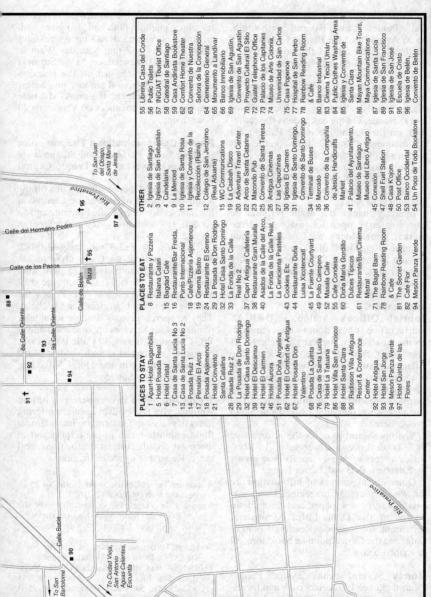

PLACES TO STAY
1 Apart-Hotel Bugambilia
5 Hotel Posada Real
6 Hotel Cristal
7 Casa de Santa Lucía No 3
13 Casa de Santa Lucía No 2
14 Posada Ruiz 1
17 Pensión El Arco
18 Posada Asjemenou
21 Hotel Convento
Santa Catalina
28 Posada Ruiz 2
29 La Posada de Don Rodrigo
32 Hotel Casa Santo Domingo
39 Hotel El Descanso
42 Hotel El Carmen
46 Hotel Aurora
51 Posada Doña Angelina
62 Hotel El Confort de Antigua
67 Hotel Posada Don
Valentino
68 Posada La Quinta
76 Casa de Santa Lucía
79 Hotel La Tatuana
86 Hotel Villa San Francisco
88 Hotel Santa Clara
90 Radisson Villa Antigua
Resort & Conference
Center
92 Hotel Antigua
93 Hotel San Jorge
94 Mesón Panza Verde
97 Hotel Quinta de las
Flores

PLACES TO EAT
8 Restaurante y Pizzería
Italiana Catari
15 Bagdad Café
16 Restaurante/Bar Freida,
Punto Internacional
18 Café/Pizzería Asjemenou
19 Cinema Bistro
24 Restaurante El Sereno
29 La Posada de Don Rodrigo
32 Hotel Casa Santo Domingo
33 La Fonda de la Calle
Real No 2
37 Capri Antigua Cafetería
38 Restaurante Gran Muralla
40 Asados de la Calle del Arco,
La Fonda de la Calle Real,
La Cenicienta Pasteles
43 Cookies Etc
44 Restaurante Doña
Luisa Xicotencatl
45 La Fuente Courtyard
49 Pollo Campero
52 Masala Cafe
55 Cafe Condesa
60 Doña María Gordillo
Dulces Típicos
61 Restaurante/Bar/Cinema
Mistral
71 The Bagel Barn
78 Rainbow Reading Room
& Cafe
81 The Secret Garden
84 Cafe Flor
94 Mesón Panza Verde

OTHER
2 Iglesia de Santiago
4 Iglesia de San Sebastián
4 Candelaria
9 La Merced
10 Iglesia de Santa Rosa
11 Iglesia y Convento de la
Recolección (Ruins)
12 Colegio de San Jerónimo
(Real Aduana)
15 WC Communications
19 La Casbah Disco
20 Adventure Travel Center
22 Arco de Santa Catalina
23 Macondo Pub
25 Convento de Santa Teresa
26 Antigua Cinemas
27 Las Capuchinas
30 Iglesia El Carmen
31 Iglesia de Santo Domingo,
Convento de Santo Domingo
35 Terminal de Buses
35 Mercado
36 Convento de la Compañía
de Jesús, Handicrafts
Market
41 Palacio del Ayuntamiento,
Museo de Santiago,
Museo del Libro Antiguo
45 Conexión
47 Shell Fuel Station
48 Casa K'ojom
50 Post Office
53 Banco Occidental
54 Un Poco de Todo Bookstore
55 Librería Casa del Conde
56 Public Toilets
57 INGUAT Tourist Office
58 Catedral de Santiago
59 Casa Andinista Bookstore
62 Comfort Home Theater
63 Convento de Nuestra
Señora de la Concepción
64 Cementerio General
65 Monumento a Landívar
66 Banco Inmobiliario
69 Iglesia de San Agustín,
Convento de San Agustín
70 Proyecto Cultural El Sitio
72 Guatel Telephone Office
73 Palacio de los Capitanes
74 Museo de Arte Colonia,
Universidad de San Carlos
75 Casa Popenoe
77 Hospital de San Pedro
78 Rainbow Reading Room
& Cafe
80 Banco Industrial
83 Cinema Tecún Umán
84 Public Clothes Washing Area
85 Iglesia y Convento de
Santa Clara
86 Mayan Mountain Bike Tours,
Maya Communications
87 Iglesia de Santa Lucía
89 Iglesia de San Francisco
91 Iglesia de San José
95 Escuela de Cristo
96 Iglesia de Belén,
Convento de Belén

To San Juan del Obispo, Santa María de Jesús

Río Pensativo

Calle del Hermano Pedro

Calle de los Pasos

Calle de Belén

Plaza

8a Calle Oriente

9a Calle Oriente

Río Pensativo

Calle Sucia

To Ciudad Vieja, San Antonio Aguas Calientes, Escuintla

To San Bartolomé

4a Calle west of the Parque Central is 4a Calle Poniente; avenidas run north-south, so 3a Av north of the Parque Central is 3a Av Norte. The city is thus divided into quadrants by 4a Av and 4a Calle.

The old headquarters of the Spanish colonial government, called the Palacio de los Capitanes, is on the south side of the plaza; you'll know it by its double (two-story) arcade. On the east side is the cathedral, on the north side is the Palacio del Ayuntamiento (Town Hall) and on the west side are banks and shops.

The Arco de Santa Catarina (Arch of St Catharine), spanning 5a Av Norte between 1a Calle and 2a Calle, is another famous Antigua landmark.

Intercity buses arrive at the Terminal de Buses, a large open lot just west of the market, four blocks west of the Parque Central along 4a Calle Poniente. Buses serving towns and villages in the vicinity leave from the terminal as well, or from other points around the market.

Information

Tourist Offices Antigua's INGUAT tourist office is next door to the cathedral, on the east side of the Parque Central. (If you don't find it there, check in the Palacio de los Capitanes on the south side of the plaza.) It's open from 8 am to 6 pm, seven days a week. They offer free city maps and plenty of helpful advice. You can pick up a schedule of Semana Santa events here.

Visitors should look for the informative little book *Antigua Guatemala: An illustrated history of the city and its monuments* by Elizabeth Bell and Trevor Long.

Other useful sources of information are the *Revue* monthly magazine, the *Guatemala Weekly* newspaper, and the bulletin boards at the Doña Luisa Xicotencatl restaurant, the Rainbow Reading Room & Cafe, and the Casa Andinista bookstore, all described below.

Money Several banks around Parque Central change US dollars cash and traveler's checks. Banco Occidental, on 4a Calle Poniente just off the northwest corner of the plaza, changes both and also gives cash advances on Visa cards; it's open weekdays from 8:30 am to 7 pm, Saturday 9 am to 2 pm. Banco Industrial, on 5a Av Sur next to the Guatel office, just off the plaza, is open weekdays from 8 am to 7 pm, Saturday 8 am to 5 pm, and has an ATM where you can get cash advances on Visa cards 24 hours a day.

Post & Communications The post office is at 4a Calle Poniente and Alameda de Santa Lucía, west of the Parque Central near the market.

The Guatel telephone office is just off the southwest corner of the Parque Central, at the intersection of 5a Calle Poniente and 5a Av Sur. It's open every day and offers fax service.

Conexión (☎ 832-3768, fax 832-0082, 832-0602, net) at 4a Calle Oriente 14, inside the La Fuente courtyard, will send and/or receive phone, fax, electronic mail and telex messages for you. Prices for sending are fairly high; receiving is cheap. They're open every day. International telephone and fax services are also available at WC Communications, 1a Calle Poniente 9, opposite La Merced church, and at Maya Communications in the Hotel Villa San Francisco, 1a Av Sur 15.

Travel Agencies Everywhere you turn in Antigua, you'll see travel agenices offering tours to places in Guatemala, international flights, shuttle buses to the airport and to the most popular tourist destinations, and more. Reputable agencies include:

Adventure Travel Center, 5a Av Norte No 25-B, near the arch (☎ /fax 832-0162)
Agenicia de Viajes Tivoli, upstairs over the Un Poco de Todo bookshop on the west side of Parque Central (☎ /fax 832-3041, 832-0892)
Servicios Turísticos Atitlán, 6a Av Sur No 7 (☎ 832-0648, or 832-3311 after 8 pm)
TURANSA, 9a Calle and Salida a Ciudad Vieja, in the Hotel Radisson Villa Antigua (☎ /fax 832-2928); 5a Calle Poniente No 11-B (☎ /fax 832-3316)

Bookstores & Library The Rainbow Reading Room & Cafe, at the corner of 7a Av Sur and 6a Calle Poniente, has thousands of used books in English and Spanish for sale, rent or trade. Un Poco de Todo and the Librería Casa del Conde, both on the west side of Parque Central, and the Casa Andinista at 4a Calle Oriente No 5, opposite the Doña Luisa Xicotencatl restaurant, are other excellent bookstores. All carry both new and used books in several languages, and all are open every day.

La Biblioteca Internacional de Antigua (The International Library of Antigua), 5a Calle Poniente 15 in the Proyecto Cultural El Sitio building, has a good collection of books, with temporary or long-term memberships available.

Laundry Laundries are everywhere. They all seem to charge the same price – US$1.65 for wash, dry and fold of seven pieces of laundry.

Medical Services Hospital de San Pedro (☎ 832-0301) is at 3a Av Sur and 6a Calle Oriente.

Toilets Public toilets are on 4a Calle Oriente, near the northeast corner of Parque Central.

Dangers & Annoyances Antigua seems like such a tranquil town that you wouldn't think any misfortune could ever befall you. Not so. Though you probably will never have a problem, be wary of walking the deserted streets late at night, as robberies have been known to take place. Armed robberies (and even murder) have also occurred on Cerro de la Cruz and Volcán Pacaya (see Around Antigua Guatemala, below).

Parque Central
This plaza is the gathering place for citizens and foreign visitors alike. On most days the periphery is lined with villagers who have brought their handicrafts to sell to tourists; on Sunday it's mobbed with marketeers, and the streets on the east and west sides of the parque are closed to traffic in order to give them room. The best prices are to be had late on Sunday afternoon, when the market is winding down.

The plaza's famous fountain was built in 1738.

Palacio de los Capitanes Built in 1543, the Palacio de los Capitanes has a stately double arcade on its façade which marches proudly across the southern extent of the parque. The façade is original, but most of the rest of the building was reconstructed a century ago. From 1543 to 1773, this building was the governmental center of all Central America, in command of Chiapas, Guatemala, Honduras and Nicaragua.

Catedral de Santiago The Catedral de Santiago, on the east side of the parque, was founded in 1542, damaged by earthquakes many times, badly ruined in 1773, and only partially rebuilt between 1780 and 1820. In the 16th and early 17th centuries, Antigua's churches had lavish baroque interiors, but most lost this richness when they were rebuilt after the earthquakes. The present cathedral, stripped of its expensive decoration, occupies what was the narthex of the original edifice. In a crypt lie the bones of Bernal Díaz del Castillo, historian of the Spanish conquest, who died in 1581. Restoration work is being carried out on other parts of the cathedral, but it will never regain its former grandeur. If the front entrance is not open, you can enter from other entrances in the rear of the building and on the south side.

Palacio del Ayuntamiento On the north side of the parque stands the Palacio del Ayuntamiento, Antigua's town hall, which dates mostly from 1743. In addition to town offices, it houses the **Museo de Santiago**, which exhibits a collection of colonial furnishings, artifacts and weapons. Hours are 9 am to 4 pm Tuesday to Friday, and 9 am to noon and 2 to 4 pm on Saturday and Sunday (closed Monday); admission costs US$0.05.

Next door (and with the same hours) is the **Museo del Libro Antiguo** (Old Book

Museum), which has exhibits of colonial printing and binding, and the colonial prison.

Universidad de San Carlos

The Universidad de San Carlos was founded in 1676, but its main building (built in 1763) at 5a Calle Oriente No 5, half a block east of the parque, now houses the **Museo de Arte Colonial** (same hours as the Museo de Santiago).

Casa K'ojom

In 1984, Samuel Franco Arce began photographing Maya ceremonies and festivals, and recording their music on audio tape. By 1987 he had enough to found Casa K'ojom ('House of Music'), a museum of Maya music and the ceremonies in which it was used.

Some visitors to Guatemalan towns and villages are lucky enough to witness a parade of the *cofradías*, or some other age-old ceremony. But lucky or not, you can experience some of the fascination of the culture in a visit to Casa K'ojom. Besides the fine collection of photographs, Franco has amassed musical instruments, tools, masks and figures. These have been arranged to show scenes of traditional Maya life; recordings of the music play softly in the background. Be sure to see the exhibit featuring Maximón, the evil folkgod venerated by the people of several highland towns.

The museum is at Calle de Recoletos 55, a block west of the bus station. It's open Monday to Friday from 9:30 am to 12:30 pm and 2 to 5 pm (till 4 pm on Saturday), and is closed on Sunday. Admission costs US$0.85, including an audiovisual show.

Churches

Once glorious in their gilded baroque finery, Antigua's churches have suffered indignities from both nature and humankind. Rebuilding after earthquakes gave the churches thicker walls, lower towers and belfries, and unembellished interiors; and moving the capital to Guatemala City deprived Antigua of the population needed to maintain the churches in their traditional

richness. Still, they are impressive. Most are open daily 9 am to 5 pm; entrance costs under US$2. In addition to the churches noted below, you'll find many others scattered around town.

La Merced

From the parque, walk three long blocks up 5a Av Norte, passing beneath the Arco de Santa Catarina, built in 1694 and rebuilt in the 19th century. At the northern end of 5a Av is the Iglesia y Convento de Nuestra Señora de La Merced, known simply as La Merced – Antigua's most striking colonial church.

La Merced's construction began in 1548. Improvements continued to be made until 1717, when the church was ruined by earthquakes. Reconstruction was completed in 1767, but in 1773 earthquake struck again and the convent was destroyed. Repairs to the church were made from 1850 to 1855; its baroque façade dates from this period. Inside the ruins of the convent is a fountain said to be the largest in Central America; entering the convent costs US$0.05 and is well worth it.

San Francisco

The next most notable church is the Iglesia de San Francisco, 7a Calle Oriente and 1a Av Sur. It dates from the mid-1500s, but little of the original building remains. Rebuilding and restoration over the centuries has produced a handsome structure; reinforced concrete added in 1961 protected the church from serious damage in the 1976 earthquake. All that remains of the original church is the Chapel of Hermano Pedro, resting place of Hermano Pedro de San José Betancourt, a Franciscan monk who founded a hospital for the poor and earned the gratitude of generations. He died here in 1667; his intercession is still sought by the ill, who pray fervently by his casket.

Las Capuchinas

The Iglesia y Convento de Nuestra Señora del Pilar de Zaragoza, usually called Las Capuchinas, 2a Av Norte and 2a Calle Oriente, was a convent founded in 1736 by nuns from Madrid. Destroyed repeatedly by earthquakes, it is now a museum, with exhibits of the religious life in colonial times. The building has many unusual features, including a circular building of 18 concentric nuns' cells around a circular patio. Guided tours are available.

La Recolección The Iglesia y Convento de la Recolección, a massive ruin at the west end of 1a Calle Poniente, is among Antigua's most impressive monuments. Built between 1701 and 1708, the church was inaugurated in 1717, but suffered considerable damage from earthquake in that same year. The buildings were destroyed in the earthquake of 1773.

Colegio de San Jerónimo (Real Aduana) Near La Recolección, at the corner of Alameda de Santa Lucía and 1a Calle Poniente, this church was built in 1757 by friars of the Merced order. However, because it did not have royal authorization, it was taken over by Spain's Carlos III in 1761. In 1765 it was designated for use as the Real Aduana (Royal Customs House), but was destroyed in the earthquake of 1773. The construction includes the hermitage of San Jerónimo. Guided tours are available for around US$8.

Santa Clara The Iglesia y Convento de Santa Clara, 2a Av Sur 27, at the corner of 6a Calle Oriente, was built in 1715 and destroyed by earthquake two years later, in 1717. The present construction was inaugurated in 1734 but was destroyed by the earthquake of 1773. The dome of the church, which had remained standing, was destroyed by earthquake in 1874.

In front of the church is a public washing area, where Indian women still come today to do their wash, spreading their laundry out on the lawn to dry.

Casa Popenoe
At the corner of 5a Calle Oriente and 1a Av Sur stands this beautiful mansion built in 1636 by Don Luis de las Infantas Mendoza y Venegas. Ruined by the earthquake of 1773, the house stood desolate for about

1½ centuries until it was bought in 1931 by Dr and Mrs Popenoe. The Popenoes' painstaking and authentic restoration yields a fascinating glimpse of how the family of an important royal official (Don Luis) lived in Antigua in the 1600s. The house is open Monday to Saturday from 2 to 4 pm; the guided tour costs US$0.85.

Monumento A Landívar
At the western end of 5a Calle Poniente is the Monumento a Landívar, a structure of five colonial-style arches set in a little park. Rafael Landívar, an 18th-century Jesuit priest and poet, lived and wrote in Antigua for some time. Landívar's poetry is esteemed as the best of the colonial period, even though much of it was written in Italy after the Jesuits were expelled from Guatemala. Landívar's Antigua house was nearby on 5a Calle Poniente.

Mercado
At the west end of 4a Calle Oriente, on the west side of Alameda de Santa Lucía, sprawls the market – chaotic, colorful and always busy. Morning, when all the village people from the vicinity are actively buying and selling, is the best time to come. (See also Things to Buy, below.)

Cementerio General
Take the opportunity to stroll through Antigua's large cemetery, west of the market and bus terminal. Hints of ancient Maya beliefs are revealed in the lavishly decorated tombs, many of which also have homey touches, and often fresh flowers or other evidence of frequent visits.

Activities
Horseback Riding Several stables in Antigua rent horses and arrange for day or overnight tours into the countryside. Establo Santiago has been recommended; contact them through the Adventure Travel Center (☎ /fax 832-0162), 5a Av Norte No 25-B, near the arch.

Several readers have recommended the Ravenscroft Riding Stables, at 2a Av Sur No 3, San Juan del Obispo, 3.2 km south of

Antigua, on the road to Santa María de Jesús (buses leave every half-hour from the bus station behind the mercado). They do English-style riding, with scenic rides of three, four or five hours in the valleys and hills around Antigua. Reservations and information are available through the Hotel San Jorge (☎ 832-3132), 4a Av Sur No 13.

R Rolando Pérez (☎ 832-2809), San Pedro El Panorama No 28, also offers horseback riding.

Bicycling Bicycles are available for hire at several places in Antigua, including:

Alquiler de Bicicletas San Vicente, 6a Av Sur No 6 (☎ /fax 832-3311)
Aviatur, 5a Av Norte No 27, just north of the arch (☎ /fax 832-2642)
Servicios Turísticos San Vicente, 6a Calle Poniente No 28 (☎ /fax 832-3311)

Prices are around US$1.35 an hour, US$4.15 a half-day, US$6 to US$8.35 a day, US$25 a week or US$35 for two weeks. Prices vary, so it pays to shop around.

Mayan Mountain Bike Tours (☎ 832-3383), 1a Av Sur No 15, offers a variety of mountain bike tours of different levels around the area. Tours usually last around four or five hours and cost around US$19, including all gear. They also do hike/bike tours to Volcanoes Agua (10 hours, US$25) and Acatenango (12 hours, US$39). They also rent bicycles, and can arrange longer tours for up to 15 days.

White-Water Rafting Area Verde Expeditions (☎ /fax 832-3863, in the USA ☎ /fax (719) 539-7102), 4a Av Sur No 8, offers a variety of white-water rafting tours lasting from one to five days. Different rivers are rafted at different times of year, making it possible to raft all year round.

Language Courses

Antigua is famous for its Spanish language schools, which attract students from around the world. There are many schools to choose from – around 70 at last count.

Price, quality of teaching and satisfaction of students varies greatly from one school to another. Often the quality of the instruction depends upon the particular instructor, and thus may vary even within a single school. Visit several schools before you choose one. If possible, ask for references and talk to someone who has studied at your chosen school recently – you'll have no trouble running into lots of Spanish students in Antigua. The INGUAT tourist office also has a list of reputable schools. They include:

Academia de Español Sevilla, 1a Av Sur No 8 (☎ /fax 832-0442)
Academia de Español Tecún Umán, 6a Calle Poniente No 34 (☎ /fax 832-2792)
AmeriSpan Guatemala, 6a Av Norte No 40 (☎ / fax 832-0164). In the USA: AmeriSpan USA, PO Box 40513, Philadelphia PA (☎ (215) 985-4522, (800) 879-6640, fax (215) 985-4524)
Centro de Español Don Pedro de Alvarado, 1a Calle Poniente No 24 (☎ /fax 832-4180)
Centro Lingüístico Maya, 5a Calle Poniente No 20 (☎ 832-0656)
Christian Spanish Academy (CSA), 6a Av Norte No 15 (☎ 832-3922, fax 832-3760)
Don Quijote Spanish Academy, Portal del Ayuntamiento No 6, in the Museo del Libro Antiguo, on the north side of Parque Central (☎ 832-2868)
Escuela de Español San José el Viejo, 5a Av Sur No 34 (☎ 832-3028, fax 832-3029, net)
Proyecto Lingüístico Francisco Marroquín, 4a Av Sur No 4 (☎ /fax 832-0406)

Classes start every Monday at most schools, though you can usually be placed with a teacher any day of the week. Cost for four hours of classes daily, five days a week, ranges from around US$45 to US$95 per week, usually for one-to-one instruction; you can also sign up for up to seven hours a day of instruction. Most schools offer to arrange room and board with local families for around US$40 to US$60 per week, giving you the chance for total immersion in the language.

Some students have reported that the main difficulty with studying Spanish in Antigua is the number of foreigners in town, making it a temptation to socialize in your own language rather than sticking to Spanish!

Organized Tours

Elizabeth Bell, author of books on Antigua, offers cultural tours of the town (in English and/or Spanish) on Mondays, Tuesdays, Wednesdays, Fridays and Saturdays. The walking tours take two hours and cost US$12. Information is available at the Adventure Travel Center (☎ /fax 832-0162), 5a Av Norte No 25-B, near the arch, where her books are also sold. (See Entertainment for information on her weekly slide shows.)

A variety of tours take you further afield. The Adventure Travel Center offers an interesting three-hour Villages & Farm Tour for US$25.

Numerous travel agencies offer tours to many places further afield, including Tikal, Copán, Quiriguá, Río Dulce, Monterrico, Chichicastenango and Panajachel. See Getting There & Away – Bus, below.

Semana Santa

By far the most interesting time to be in Antigua is during Semana Santa (Holy Week) celebrations, when hundreds of people dress up as pseudo-Israelites, in deep purple robes, to accompany daily religious processions in remembrance of the Crucifixion. Streets are covered in breathtakingly elaborate and colorful *alfombras* (carpets) of colored sawdust and flower petals. These beautiful but fragile works of art are destroyed as the processions shuffle through them, but are recreated the next morning for another day.

Traditionally, the most interesting days are Palm Sunday, when a procession departs from La Merced (see Churches) in midafternoon; Holy Thursday, when a late afternoon procession departs from the Iglesia de San Francisco; and Good Friday, when an early morning procession departs from La Merced, and a late afternoon one from the Escuela de Cristo. Have ironclad hotel reservations well in advance of these dates, or plan to stay in another town or in Guatemala City and commute to the festivities.

The booklet *Lent and Easter Week in Antigua* by Elizabeth Bell gives explanations and includes a day-by-day schedule of processions, *velaciones* and other events taking place throughout the Lenten season, the 40 days before Easter.

Warning On a secular note, beware of pickpockets. It seems that Guatemala City's entire population of pickpockets (numbering perhaps in the hundreds) decamps to Antigua for Semana Santa. In the press of the emotion-filled crowds lining the processional routes, they target foreign tourists especially.

Places to Stay

Budget When checking a pension or small hotel, look at several rooms, as some are much better than others.

Posada Ruiz 2, 2a Calle Poniente 25, is a good deal for the price, with small singles/doubles for US$2.85/5, all with shared bath, opening onto a central courtyard. Lots of young international travelers stay here, congregating in the courtyard in the evening.

Pensión El Arco (☎ 832-2701), 5a Av Norte 32, just north of the Santa Catarina arch, is clean, friendly and small, and the smiling señora makes you feel safe and welcome. Singles/doubles are US$4/6 with shared bath, US$10 with private bath. The only drawback is the Disco El Casbah, two doors away, which is incredibly loud on Friday and Saturday nights.

Not as attractive, but acceptable for the price, *Posada La Quinta*, 5a Calle Poniente 19 near the bus station, is a basic place with rooms for US$8.35/10 with shared/private bath. The *Posada Doña Angelina*, nearby at 4a Calle Poniente 33, has singles/doubles for US$4/7 with shared bath, US$9/14 with private bath.

The *Hotel Cristal* (☎ 832-4177), Av El Desengaño 25, is great for the price, with 10 clean rooms around a beautiful central garden. Singles/doubles are US$6/8.35 with shared bath, US$8.35/12.50 with private bath. Discounts are given for students, and for stays of five days or more. Meals are available.

Hotel Villa San Francisco (☎ 832-3383), 1a Av Sur No 15 at the corner of 6a Calle Oriente, is simple but pleasant. Singles/

doubles are US$7/9.50 with shared bath, US$10/12.50 with private bath. An upstairs terrace, a courtyard garden, a telephone and fax service, and bicycle rental are all here.

Casa de Santa Lucía, Alameda de Santa Lucía No 9, between 5a and 6a Calles Poniente, has dark rooms with pseudo-colonial atmosphere for US$10/12 a single/double with private bath; ring the bell to the left of the door. There's parking.

More attractive are the two newer establishments operated by the same people. They are the *Casa de Santa Lucía No 2*, Alameda de Santa Lucía Norte 21, and *Casa de Santa Lucía No 3*, 6a Av Norte 43-A, near La Merced church. Both have clean, pleasant, attractive rooms with ample windows and private hot bath for US$10/12 a night, rooftop terraces with views of Antigua, and parking. Neither place has a sign.

Hotel La Tatuana (☎ 832-0537), 7a Av Sur No 3, has good, clean rooms with private bath for US$10/17 for singles/doubles.

A step up in quality, *Hotel Posada Don Valentino* (☎ 832-0384), 5a Calle Poniente No 28, has a nice patio and garden, with bright and clean rooms for US$10/15 a single/double with shared bath, US$12/20 with private bath. They have a parking lot one block away.

Hotel El Confort de Antigua (☎ 832-0566), 1a Av Norte No 2, is clean and beautifully kept. The five rooms share two baths, and cost US$15/20/25 a single/double/triple, including continental breakfast.

Posada Asjemenou (☎ 832-2670), 5a Av Norte No 31, just north of the arch, is a beautifully renovated house built around a grassy courtyard with a fountain. Its prices of US$13/19/26 for singles/double/triples with shared bath, US$19/25/29 with private bath, make it the best value for money in town. The Cafe/Pizzería Asjemenou is also here, and there's a pay parking lot nearby.

Apart-Hotel Bugambilia (☎ 832-2732, 832-7767), Calle Ancha de los Herreros 27, has 10 apartments, each with fully equipped kitchen, two or three double beds, cable TV and private hot bath. Daily rates are US$20 (US$24 with three beds,

US$120 per week, or US$420 per month). It has sitting areas, a beautiful patio garden, a fountain and a rooftop terrace.

Middle Antigua's mid-range hotels allow you to wallow in the city's colonial charms for a very moderate outlay of cash.

Hotel El Descanso (☎ 832-0142), 5a Av Norte 9, '50 steps from the central parque' in the building facing the restaurant called Café Café, is clean and convenient. Its five rooms are US$20/24/30/40 for one to four people with shared bath, or US$20/24 for singles/doubles with private bath. There's a private upstairs terrace in the rear.

Hotel Santa Clara (☎ 832-0342), 2a Av Sur No 20, is quiet, proper and clean, with a pleasant garden and some large rooms with two double beds. Singles/doubles with bath are US$21/25, less in low season.

Hotel Posada Real (☎ 832-3396), Av El Desengaño 24, is a beautiful colonial homey hotel new in 1996. Its 10 rooms and suites, all with private bath, are lovely and many have fireplaces. Singles/doubles/triples are US$25/35/42.

Hotel San Jorge (☎ /fax 832-3132), 4a Av Sur No 13, is in a modern building where all 14 rooms have fireplace, cable TV and private bath with tub. Parking and laundry are also here, and the guests (mostly older couples from the USA) may use the swimming pool and room service facilities of the posh Hotel Antigua nearby. Rooms are US$30/35/40 a single/double/triple, with possible discounts in low season. Credit cards are accepted.

Hotel Convento Santa Catalina (☎ 832-3080, fax 832-3079), 5a Av Norte No 28, just south of the arch, is a nicely renovated convent around a courtyard. Large singles/doubles with bath are reasonably priced at US$25/30 most of the year, US$35/45 from November to April.

Places to Eat
Budget Eating cheaply is easy, even in touristy Antigua.

Probably the cheapest food in town is the good, clean, tasty food served from stands set up under the arches on the west side of the Parque Central every day from around 11:30 am to 7:30 pm. You can also eat cheaply and well at the mercado.

Capri Antigua Cafetería, 4a Calle Poniente 24, near the corner of 6a Av Norte, is a simple, modern place that's very popular with younger diners and budget travelers. They usually fill its little wooden benches and tables, ordering soup for US$0.70, sandwiches for US$1.35 to US$2.65, or *platos fuertes* (substantial platters with meat or chicken served with salad and fries) for US$1.65 to US$3. Nearby, *Restaurante Gran Muralla*, 4a Calle Poniente 18, is a simple, inexpensive place serving a Guatemalan highland version of Chinese food.

Antigua's best known restaurant is probably the *Restaurant Doña Luisa Xicotencatl*, 4a Calle Oriente No 12, 1½ blocks east of Parque Central. A small central courtyard is set with dining tables, with more dining rooms on the upper level. The menu lists a dozen sandwiches made with Doña Luisa's own bread baked on the premises, as well as yogurt, chili, burgers, stuffed potatoes, cakes and pies, all priced under US$4. Alcoholic beverages are served, as is excellent Antigua coffee. The restaurant is open every day, 7 am to 9:30 pm, and it is usually busy. The bakery here sells many kinds of breads, including whole grain.

Rainbow Reading Room & Cafe, 7a Av Sur and 6a Calle Poniente, is a lending library, bookstore, travelers' club and restaurant all in one. Healthy vegetarian dishes are a specialty, as is close camaraderie. The cafe is open every day from 9 am to 11 pm.

Cafe Condesa, in an opulent courtyard on the west side of the plaza (walk through the Librería Case del Conde book shop to the courtyard in the rear) is a beautiful restaurant in the patio of an opulent Spanish mansion built in 1549. On the menu are excellent breakfasts, coffee, light meals and snacks. The Sunday buffet from 10 am to 2 pm, a lavish spread for US$6, is an Antigua institution. It's open every day.

La Fuente, 4a Calle Oriente No 14, is another beautiful restaurant, in the court-yard of a beautiful old Spanish home. It has lots of vegetarian selections, good coffee and desserts. It's open every day, 7 am to 7 pm. The *Bagdad Cafe*, 1a Calle Poniente No 9, opposite La Merced church at the corner of 6a Av Norte, is a smaller, simpler, inexpensive patio restaurant.

A rich concentration of restaurants is on 5a Av Norte, north of Parque Central. *Asados de la Calle del Arco*, just off the Parque Central, has a simple but beautiful atmosphere, with candlelight in the evening and tables both inside and in the rear patio. It serves grilled meats and Tex-Mex food, though portions are small. It's open every day, 7 am to 10 pm.

La Fonda de la Calle Real, 5a Av Norte No 5, appears to have no room for diners, but that's because all the tables are upstairs. The menu is good and varied. The house specialty *caldo real* (hearty chicken soup) for US$3.50 makes a good lunch. Grilled chicken and meats, *queso fundido* (melted cheese), *chiles rellenos* (stuffed peppers) and nachos are priced from US$3 to 8. It's open every day, 7 am to 10 pm. Around the corner, the *La Fonda de la Calle Real No 2*, 3a Calle Poniente No 7, has the same menu and is open every day from noon to 10 pm.

La Cenicienta Pasteles, next door at 5a Av Norte 7, serves mostly cakes, pastries, pies and coffee, but the blackboard menu often features quiche lorraine and quiche chapín (Guatemalan-style), yogurt and fruit as well. A slice of something and a hot beverage cost less than US$2. It's open every day. *Cookies Etc*, 3a Av Norte at the corner of 4a Calle Oriente, is another good place for a sweet; it's open every day. *The Bagel Barn*, on 5a Calle Poniente just off the Parque Central, is popular for bagels, soups, candies and coffee.

Also on 5a Av Norte, at No 29 near the arch, *Restaurante/Bar Freida* serves good Mexican and it's a popular gathering spot in the evening, sometimes with live music. Nearby at No 35, the *Punto Internacional* has been recommended by readers.

Cafe Flor, 4a Av Sur No 1, serves huge portions of delicious food including Thai, Indonesian, Chinese and Indian dishes, each for around US$5, which can easily feed two people. They also offer take-out. It's open Tuesday to Saturday, noon to 2:30 pm and 6 to 9 pm. The *Masala Cafe*, 6a Calle Norte 14, near the corner of 4a Calle Poniente, has been recommended by readers for its Thai and Japanese food. It's open every day except Wednesday.

The Secret Garden, a block south of Parque Central at the corner of 5a Av Sur and 6a Av Poniente, is a good vegetarian restaurant. Also here are a gym, sauna, massage, table tennis and natural therapies.

For Italian food there's the *Restaurante y Pizzería Italiana Catari*, 6a Av Norte 52, opposite La Merced church, run by well-known chef Martedino Castrovinci. From noon to 4 pm the enormous lunch special including beverage is US$3. It's open daily.

Mistral, a restaurant/bar upstairs at 2a Av Norte 6-B between 4a and 5a Calle Oriente, serves a good selection main dishes from US$2.35 to US$6. The bar is a popular gathering place. News and sports in English are shown on satellite TV, and downstairs is a video cinema with movies in English.

Middle The dining room in the *Posada de Don Rodrigo* (☎ 832-0291, 832-0387), 5a Av Norte 17, is one of the city's most pleasant and popular places for lunch or dinner. Order the house favorite, the Plato Chapín, a platter of Guatemalan specialties for US$11. A marimba band plays every day from noon to 4 pm and 7 to 9 pm.

Doña María Gordillo Dulces Típicos, 4a Calle Oriente 11, across the street from the Hotel Aurora, is filled with traditional Guatemalan sweets for take-out, and there's often a crowd of antigüeños lined up to do just that. Local handicrafts are for sale here as well.

Entertainment

Elizabeth Bell gives fascinating slide shows about the town on Tuesdays from 6 to 7 pm at the Christian Spanish Academy (CSA; ☎ 832-3922), 6a Av Norte No 15; admission is US$2.50.

Proyecto Cultural El Sitio (☎ 832-3037), 5a Calle Poniente No 15, presents a variety

of cultural events including live theater, concerts, video films and art exhibitions. Stop to check the schedule, or look in the *Revue* monthly magazine.

Bars for music and dancing open and close frequently. The *Macondo Pub*, 5a Av Norte at 2a Calle Poniente, just south of the arch, is a trendy favorite. In the same block, *La Casbah Disco* is popular; it can get rough on weekends, when there's a lot of hard drinking and city folks up from Guatemala City.

The *Rainbow Reading Room & Cafe* and *Mistral* (see Places to Eat) are popular spots to congregate in the evening.

One of Antigua's most pleasant forms of entertainment is video-watching at cinema houses, where you can see a wide variety of international films. These include:

Antigua Cinemas, 2a Calle Oriente No 2 at the corner of 4a Av Norte
Cinema Bistro, 5a Av Norte 28
Cinema Tecún Umán, 6a Calle Poniente 34-A
Comfort Home Theater, 1a Av Norte No 2
Mistral, 2a Av Norte 6-B
Proyecto Cultural El Sitio, 5a Calle Poniente No 15

Most show several films daily, and films change daily, with admission around US$1.50. Check their posted schedules at the door, or look for schedules posted around town.

Things To Buy

Lots of vendors come to cater to tourists' desires for colorful Guatemalan woven goods and other handicrafts. Wherever there is an open space to spread their wares, you'll find villagers selling. The mercado, on the west side of town by the bus station, has plenty to choose from. A number of shops are on 4a Calle Poniente, in the blocks between the Parque Central and the mercado. Also look for the outdoor markets at the corner of 6a Calle Oriente and 2a Av Sur, and at 4a Calle Poniente at 7a Av Norte. Vendors may also approach you in the Parque Central.

Be aware, though, that prices for handicrafts tend to be much higher in Antigua than elsewhere in Guatemala. If you will be traveling to other regions, you might want to wait; prices will be cheaper, for example, at the markets in Chichicastenango, Panajachel and even Guatemala City. Whenever buying handicrafts, be sure to bargain for a decent price.

In 1958 an ancient Maya jade quarry near Nebaj, Guatemala, was rediscovered. When it was shown to yield true jadeite equal in quality to Chinese stone, the mine was reopened. Today it produces jade (pronounced HAH-deh) both for gemstone use and for carving.

Beautiful well-carved stones can cost US$100 or much more. Look for translucency, purity and intensity of color, and absence of flaws. Ask the merchant if you can scratch the stone with a pocket knife; if it scratches, it's not true jadeite but an inferior stone.

Antigua has two shops specializing in jade: La Casa de Jade, 4a Calle Oriente 3, and Jades, SA (HAH-dess), 4a Calle Oriente 34. At both places you can have a free tour of the jade factories in the rear of the showrooms. Jades, SA has interesting exhibits about jade. Both places are open every day.

Galería El Sitio, 5a Calle Poniente 15 at the Proyecto Cultural El Sitio, specializes in paintings by modern Guatemalan artists. Ring the bell on the gate for admission. A number of other interesting galleries are along 4a Calle Oriente, in the blocks east of the Parque Central.

Kashlan Pot, a shop in the La Fuente courtyard at 4a Calle Oriente 14, is worth a visit to see its dozens of top-quality huipiles, the embroidered women's blouses made in distinctive designs for each region of Guatemala.

Getting There & Away

Bus Buses arrive and depart from a large open lot to the west of the market, on the west side of town. Bus connections with Guatemala City are frequent, and there's one direct bus daily to Panajachel. To reach other highland towns such as Chichicastenango, Quetzaltenango and Huehuetenango, or Panajachel at any other time of day, take one of the frequent buses to Chimaltenango, on the Interamericana, and catch an onward bus from there. Or take a bus heading towards Guatemala City, get off at San Lucas Sacatepéquez and change buses there – this takes a little more time, but it's a good road and since you'll be boarding the bus closer to the capital you're more likely to get a seat (important if you want to avoid standing for possibly several hours).

Buses to outlying villages such as Santa María de Jesús (half-hour, US$0.25) and San Antonio Aguas Calientes (25 minutes, US$0.20) also depart from the bus area west of the market. It's best to make your outward trip early in the morning and your return trip by mid-afternoon, as services drop off dramatically as late afternoon approaches.

Chimaltenango (19 km, one hour, US$0.30)
  Buses every 15 minutes, 5:30 am to 6 pm.
Escuintla (102 km, 2½ hours, US$0.85) Two
  buses daily, 7 am and 1 pm.
Guatemala City (45 km, one hour, US$0.50)
  Buses every 15 minutes, 4 am to 7 pm, stopping in San Lucas Sacatepéquez.
Panajachel (80 km, two hours, US$2.85) One bus
  daily, 7:15 am. Or, take a bus to Chimaltenango and change buses there, taking a bus
  bound for Los Encuentros, Sololá or Panajachel. One of these buses passes by Chimaltenango every 20 minutes or so.

Shuttle Minibuses Numerous travel agencies and tourist minibus operators offer frequent and convenient shuttle services to places tourists go, including Guatemala City, La Aurora International Airport, Panajachel and Chichicastenango. They also go less frequently (usually on weekends) to places further afield such as Río Dulce, Copán Ruinas (Honduras) and Monterrico. These services cost a lot more than ordinary buses (for example, US$5 to US$10 to Guatemala City, as opposed to US$0.50 on a normal bus), but they are comfortable and convenient, with door-to-door service on both ends.

It seems there are dozens of these agencies in Antigua; you certainly won't have any trouble finding one. For recommendations, see Travel Agencies above.

Car Rental Rental car companies in Antigua include:

Ahorrent, La Fuente, 4a Calle Oriente No 14 (☎ 832-3768)
Avis, 5a Av Norte No 22 (☎ 832-2692)
Tabarini, 2a Calle Poniente 19-A (☎ 832-3091)

Getting Around
Several shops rent bicycles (see Activities above). Taxi stands are at the bus station and on the east side of Parque Central. A ride in town costs US$1.65.

AROUND ANTIGUA GUATEMALA
Cerro de la Cruz
Overlooking Antigua on the northeast side of town is a hill called Cerro de la Cruz (Hill of the Cross). The fine view over town looks out south towards Volcán Agua. However, we urge you not to go there, as this hill is famous for lurking muggers, waiting to prey on unsuspecting visitors. Accounts of armed robberies on Cerro de la Cruz have been so numerous that few people go there, yet in 1996 a large group of Spanish students and their teachers decided there was safety in numbers. When they were robbed by a group of armed bandits, one of their party was shot and killed. Don't go.

Ciudad Vieja & San Antonio Aguas Calientes
Six and a half km southwest of Antigua along the Escuintla road (the one which passes the Radisson Villa Antigua Resort) is Ciudad Vieja (Old City), which was the site of the first capital of the Captaincy General of Guatemala. Founded in 1527, it was destroyed in 1541 when the aptly named Volcán Agua loosed a flood of water that had been penned-up in its crater. Cascading down the steep volcano's side, the water carried tons of rock and mud over the city, leaving only a few ruins of the Church of La Concepción. There is little to see today.

Past Ciudad Vieja, turn right at a large cemetery on the right-hand side; the unmarked road takes you through San Miguel Dueñas to San Antonio Aguas Calientes. In San Miguel Dueñas, take the first street on the right – between two houses – after coming to the concrete-block paving; this, too, is unmarked. If you come to the Texaco station in the center of San Miguel, you've missed the road.

The road winds through coffee fincas, little fields of vegetables and corn, and hamlets of farmers to San Antonio Aguas Calientes, 14 km from Antigua. As you enter San Antonio's plaza, you will see that the village is noted for its weaving. Market stalls in the plaza sell local woven and embroidered goods, as do shops on side streets (walk to the left of the church to find them). Bargaining is expected.

Volcanoes
Climbing the volcanoes around Antigua is exciting in more ways than one. In recent years robbers have intercepted groups of foreigners from time to time on Volcán Pacaya, relieving them of all their goods (including clothing). There have been incidents of rape and murder as well. Still, many visitors take their chances in return for the exhilaration and the beauty of the view.

Because Pacaya is the only volcano near Antigua that is active, it's the one that attracts the most tourists, and consequently the bandits that prey on them. The volcanoes nearer Antigua (Agua, Fuego and Acatenango) are not active, they attract fewer tourists, and consequently, they haven't been attracting bandits (as of this writing). Climbing one of these won't let you see the glow, but is still very impressive, offering magnificent views.

Get reliable advice about safety before you climb. Check with your embassy in Guatemala City, or with the tourist office in Antigua, or with some of Antigua's reputable tourist and travel agencies. If you do decide to go, make sure you go with reputable guides, through an established agency. (Some 'freelancers' may be in cahoots with the robbers!)

Take sensible precautions. Bring adequate footwear, warm clothing (it's colder up there) and, in the rainy season, some sort of rain gear. Carry a flashlight, partly because you may be climbing down after dark, and also in case the weather changes; it can get as dark as night when it rains on the mountain. Also take water and snacks.

Various agencies operate tours up **Volcán Pacaya** for about US$15 per person, including a 1½-hour bus ride to the trailhead followed by a two-hour trek to the summit.

Volcán Agua is the large volcano looming over Antigua, on the south side of town. To get there, follow 2a Av Sur or Calle de los Pasos south toward El Calvario (two km), then continue onward via San Juan del Obispo (another three km) to Santa María de Jesús, nine km south of Antigua. This is the jumping-off point for treks up the slopes of Volcán Agua (3766 meters), which rises dramatically right behind the village.

Santa María (2080 meters, population 11,000) is a village of unpaved streets and bamboo fences. The main plaza is also the bus terminal. *Comedor & Hospedaje El Oasis*, a tidy little pension, offers a meal or a bed for the night.

Various outfitters in Antigua can furnish details about the Volcán Agua climb.

You could also climb the other two volcanoes near Antigua, **Volcán Acatenango** and **Volcán Fuego**. Various companies offer guided tours on Acatenango, and Mayan Mountain Bike Tours (see Activities in Antigua Guatemala) does hike/bike tours on Acatenango and Agua.

Chimaltenango

The road westward from Antigua makes its way 17 km up to the ridge of the Continental Divide, where it meets the Interamericana at Chimaltenango, capital of the department of Chimaltenango. This was an old town to the Cakchiquel Maya when the conquistadores arrived in 1526, but today is mostly just a place to change buses, with little to detain you.

Highlands – Lago de Atitlán

TO LAGO DE ATITLÁN

Westward 32 km along the Interamericana from Chimaltenango, you pass the turnoff for the back road to Lago de Atitlán via Patzicía and Patzún. The area around these two towns has been notable for high levels of guerrilla activity in recent years, and the road is often in poor condition, so it's advisable to stay on the Interamericana to Tecpán Guatemala, the starting point for a visit to the ruined Cakchiquel capital city of Iximché.

If you travel another 40 km westward along the Interamericana from Tecpán, you will come to the highway junction of **Los Encuentros**. There is a nascent town here, basing itself on the presence of a lot of people waiting to catch buses. The road to the north (right) heads to Chichicastenango and Santa Cruz del Quiché. From this intersection, the Interamericana continues three km north, where a road south descends 12 km to Sololá, which is the capital of the department of the same name, and then eight km more to Panajachel, on the shores of Lago de Atitlán.

If you are not on a direct bus to these places, you can always get off at Los Encuentros and catch another bus or minibus, or even hitch a ride from here down to Panajachel or up to Chichicastenango; it's a half-hour ride to either place.

The road from Sololá descends more than 500 meters through pine forests in its eight-km course to Panajachel. All of the excellent sights and views are on your right, so try to get a seat on the right-hand side of the bus.

Along the way the road passes Sololá's colorful cemetery and a Guatemalan army base. The guardpost by the main gate is in the shape of a huge helmet resting upon a pair of soldier's boots. Soon the road turns to snake its way down the mountainside to

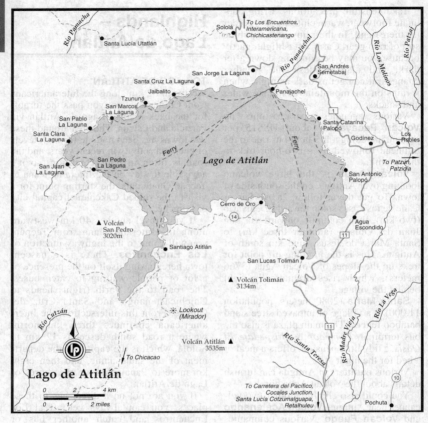

Lago de Atitlán

Santa Lucía Utatlán
Río Pamacha
Sololá
To Los Encuentros, Interamericana, Chichicastenango
Río Panajachel
San Andrés Semetabaj
Río Los Molinos
Río Patzaj
San Jorge La Laguna
Santa Cruz La Laguna
Jaibalito
Tzununá
San Marcos La Laguna
San Pablo La Laguna
Panajachel
1
Santa Catarina Palopó
Santa Clara La Laguna
Godínez
Los Robles
Ferry
Lago de Atitlán
San Pedro La Laguna
To Patzún, Patzicía
San Juan La Laguna
Ferry
San Antonio Palopó
Cerro de Oro
14
Agua Escondido
▲ Volcán San Pedro 3020m
11
Santiago Atitlán
San Lucas Tolimán
Río La Vega
▲ Volcán Tolimán 3134m
Río Cutzán
☀ *Lookout (Mirador)*
Volcán Atitlán ▲ 3535m
Río Madre Vieja
Río Santa Teresa
To Chicacao
LP
Lago de Atitlán
0   2   4 km
0   1   2 miles
To Carretera del Pacífico, Cocales Junction, Santa Lucía Cotzumalguapa, Retalhuleu
Pochuta
10

the lakeshore, offering breathtaking views of the lake and its surrounding volcanoes.

TECPÁN GUATEMALA

Founded as the Spanish military headquarters during the conquest, Tecpán Guatemala today is a small, somewhat dusty town with numerous handicrafts shops, two small hotels and, nearby, the ruins of the Cakchiquel Maya capital of Iximché.

Tecpán's market day is Thursday. The annual festival in honor of the town's patron saint, Francis of Assisi, is held in the first week of October.

Iximché

Set on a flat promontory surrounded by steep cliffs, Iximché (founded in the late 1400s) was well suited to be the capital city of the Cakchiquel Maya. The Cakchiquels were at war with the Quiché Maya, and the city's natural defenses served them well.

When the conquistadors arrived in 1524, the Cakchiquel formed an alliance with them against their enemies, the Quiché and the Tzutuhil. The Spaniards set up their headquarters right next door to the Cakchiquel capital at Tecpán Guatemala, but Spanish demands for gold and other loot soon put an end to the alliance, and in the ensuing battles, the Cakchiquels were defeated.

As you enter Tecpán you will see signs pointing to the unpaved road leading through fields and pine forests to Iximché, less than six km to the south. You can walk the distance in about an hour, see the ruins and rest (another hour), then walk back to Tecpán – a total of three hours. If you're going to walk, it's best to do it in the morning so that you can get back to the highway by early afternoon, as bus traffic dwindles by late afternoon.

After you enter the archaeological site and pass the small museum on the right, you come to four ceremonial plazas surrounded by grass-covered temple structures and ball courts. Some of the structures have been cleaned and maintained; on a few the original plaster coating is still in place, and there are even some traces of the original paint.

The site is open daily from 9 am to 4 pm.

Places to Stay & Eat

Should you need to stay the night in Tecpán, *Hotel Iximché*, 1a Av 1-38, Zona 2, will put you up in basic rooms for US$3 per person, as will *Pensión Doña Ester*, 2a Calle 1-09, Zona 3. There are various small eateries.

Getting There & Away

Transportes Poaquileña runs buses to Guatemala City (87 km, 1½ hours) every half-hour from 3 am to 5 pm. From Guatemala City to Tecpán, buses run just as frequently, from 5 am to 7:30 pm.

SOLOLÁ
Population 9000

Though the Spaniards founded Sololá (2110 meters) in 1547, there once was a Cakchiquel town (called Tzoloyá) here before they came. Sololá's importance comes from its geographic position on trade routes between the Tierra Caliente (hot lands of the Pacific Slope) and Tierra Fría (the chilly highlands). All the traders meet here, and Sololá's Friday market is one of the best in the highlands.

On market days, the plaza next to the cathedral is ablaze with the colorful costumes of people from a dozen surrounding villages and towns. Displays of meat, vegetables and fruit, housewares and clothing are neatly arranged in every available space, with tides of buyers ebbing and flowing along the spaces in between. Several elaborate stands are well stocked with brightly colored yarn and sewing notions for making the traditional costumes you see all around you. This is a market serving locals, not tourists.

Every Sunday morning the officers of the traditional religious brotherhoods (*cofradías*) parade ceremoniously to the cathedral for their devotions. On other days, Sololá sleeps.

You can make a very pleasant walk from Sololá down to the lake either on the highway to Panajachel or on the walking track to Santa Cruz La Laguna.

Places to Stay

Virtually everyone stays in Panajachel, but if you need a bed in Sololá, try the six-room *Posada del Viajero*, 7a Av 10-45, Zona 2, or the *Hotel Tzolojya* (☎ 762-1266), 11a Calle 7-70, Zona 2. *Hotel Santa Ana*, 150 meters uphill from the church tower on the road that comes into town from Los Encuentros, is even simpler.

PANAJACHEL
Population 5000

Nicknamed Gringotenango (Place of the Foreigners) by locals and foreigners alike, Pana has long been known to tourists. In the hippie heyday of the 1960s and '70s, it was crowded with laid-back travelers in semipermanent exile. When the civil war of the late 1970s and early '80s made Panajachel a dangerous – or at least unpleasant – place to be, many moved on. But in recent years the town's tourist industry has boomed again.

There is no notable colonial architecture in this town, which is a small and not particularly attractive place that has developed haphazardly according to the demands of the tourist trade. The reflections of clouds

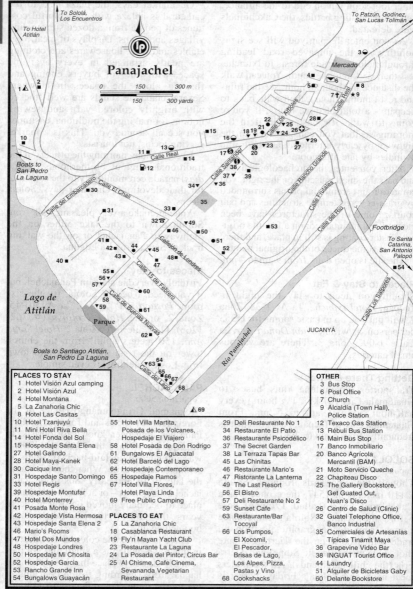

Panajachel

To Sololá,
Los Encuentros

To Hotel
Atitlán

To Patzún, Godínez,
San Lucas Tolimán

Mercado

Calle Real

Calle Los Árboles

Calle Santander

Boats to
San Pedro
La Laguna

Calle Real

Calle del Embarcadero

Calle El Chalí

Calle Rancho Grande

Calle Frutales

Calle del Río

Footbridge

To Santa
Catarina,
San Antonio
Palopó

Callejón de Londres

Calle 15 de Febrero

Calle de Buenas Nuevas

Lago de
Atitlán

Parque

Boats to Santiago Atitlán,
San Pedro La Laguna

Río Panajachel

JUCANYÁ

Calle Los Salpores

Calle del Lago

0   150   300 m
0   150   300 yards

PLACES TO STAY
1 Hotel Visión Azul camping
2 Hotel Visión Azul
4 Hotel Montana
5 La Zanahoria Chic
8 Hotel Las Casitas
10 Hotel Tzanjuyú
11 Mini Hotel Riva Bella
14 Hotel Fonda del Sol
15 Hospedaje Santa Elena
27 Hotel Galindo
28 Hotel Maya-Kanek
30 Cacique Inn
31 Hospedaje Santo Domingo
33 Hotel Regis
39 Hospedaje Montufar
40 Hotel Monterrey
41 Posada Monte Rosa
42 Hospedaje Vista Hermosa
43 Hospedaje Santa Elena 2
46 Mario's Rooms
47 Hotel Dos Mundos
48 Hospedaje Londres
50 Hospedaje Mi Chosita
52 Hospedaje Garcia
53 Rancho Grande Inn
54 Bungalows Guayacán

55 Hotel Villa Martita,
   Posada de los Volcanes,
   Hospedaje El Viajero
58 Hotel Posada de Don Rodrigo
61 Bungalows El Aguacatal
62 Hotel Barceló del Lago
64 Hospedaje Contemporaneo
65 Hospedaje Ramos
67 Hotel Villa Flores,
   Hotel Playa Linda
69 Free Public Camping

PLACES TO EAT
5 La Zanahoria Chic
18 Casablanca Restaurant
19 Fly'n Mayan Yacht Club
24 Restaurante La Laguna
24 La Posada del Pintor, Circus Bar
25 Al Chisme, Cafe Cinema,
   Sevananda Vegetarian
   Restaurant

29 Deli Restaurante No 1
34 Restaurante El Patio
36 Restaurante Psicodélico
37 The Secret Garden
38 La Terraza Tapas Bar
45 Las Chinitas
46 Restaurante Mario's
47 Ristorante La Lanterna
49 The Last Resort
51 El Bistro
57 Deli Restaurante No 2
59 Sunset Cafe
63 Restaurante/Bar
   Tocoyal
66 Los Pumpos,
   El Xocomil,
   El Pescador,
   Brisas de Lago,
   Los Alpes, Pizza,
   Pastas y Vino
68 Cookshacks

OTHER
3 Bus Stop
6 Post Office
7 Church
9 Alcaldía (Town Hall),
   Police Station
12 Texaco Gas Station
13 Rébuli Bus Station
16 Main Bus Stop
17 Banco Inmobiliario
20 Banco Agrícola
   Mercantil (BAM)
21 Moto Servicio Queche
22 Chapiteau Disco
25 The Gallery Bookstore,
   Get Guated Out,
   Nuan's Disco
26 Centro de Salud (Clinic)
32 Guatel Telephone Office,
   Banco Industrial
35 Comerciales de Artesanías
   Típicas Tinamit Maya
36 Grapevine Video Bar
38 INGUAT Tourist Office
44 Laundry
51 Alquiler de Bicicletas Gaby
60 Delante Bookstore

and volcanoes on the lake surface may help you ignore the village lad strolling along the lakeshore with an armful of newspapers shouting 'Miami Herald! Miami Herald!'

Lago de Atitlán, which is protected multiple-use area, is often still and beautiful early in the day, which is the best time for swimming. By noon the Xocomil, a southeasterly wind, may have risen to ruffle the lake's surface. Note that the lake is a caldera (collapsed volcanic cone) and is more than 320 meters deep. The land drops off sharply very near the shore. Surrounding the lake are three volcanoes: Volcán Tolimán (3158 meters), due south across the lake from Panajachel; Volcán Atitlán (3537 meters), also to the south; and Volcán San Pedro (2995 meters), to the southwest.

Six different cultures mingle on the dusty streets of Panajachel: The ladino citizens operate the levers of its tourist industry. The Cakchiquel and Tzutuhil Maya from surrounding villages come to sell their handicrafts to tourists. The lakeside villa owners drive up on weekends from Guatemala City. Group tourists descend on the town from buses for a few hours, a day or an overnight. And there are the 'traditional' hippies with long hair, beards, bare feet, local dress and Volkswagen minibuses.

Orientation
As you near the bottom of the long hill descending from Sololá, a road on the right leads to the Hotel Visión Azul, Hotel Atitlán and those obtrusive white high-rise buildings. The main road then bears left and becomes the Calle Real (also called Calle Principal), Panajachel's main street.

The geographic center of town, and the closest thing it has to a bus station, is the intersection of Calle Real and Calle Santander, where you will see the Banco Agrícola Mercantil (BAM). Calle Santander is the main road to the beach. All kinds of tourist services line Calle Santander in the few blocks from the bus stop and bank at the top of the street down to the lake.

Northeast along Calle Real are more hotels, restaurants and shops; finally, at the northeastern end of town you come to the town's civic center, with the post and telegraph offices, church, town hall, police station and market (busiest on Sunday and Thursday, but with some activity on other days, from 9 am to noon).

Calle Rancho Grande is the other main road to the beach; it's parallel to, and east of Calle Santander. A beautiful green park stretches along the lakeside between Calle Santander and Calle Rancho Grande. It's a wonderful place for strolling, day and night.

The area east of the Río Panajachel is known as Jucanyá (Across the River).

Information
Tourist Office The INGUAT tourist office (☎ 762-1392) is in the Edificio Rincón Sai on Calle Santander. It's open every day from 8 am to 1 pm and from 2 to 5 pm. Bus and boat schedules are posted on the door.

Money Banco Industrial on Calle Santander changes US dollars cash and traveler's checks, gives cash advances on Visa and has a 24-hour ATM. Banco Inmobiliario on the corner of Calle Santander and Calle Real also changes money, and it's open longer hours. BAM, on the same corner, changes money and is an agent for Western Union.

Apart from the banks, several other businesses offer financial services. You can change cash and traveler's checks at the INGUAT tourist office and at the Hotel Regis, both on Calle Santander. Cash advances on Visa and MasterCard are available from the Hotel Regis and from Servicios Turísticos Atitlán, both on Calle Santander, for a 10% commission.

Post & Communications The post office is next to the church.

The Guatel office on Calle Santander is open every day. Many other places along Calle Santander offer the same services.

Get Guated Out (☎ /fax 762-2015), at the Gallery Bookstore in the Centro Comercial on Calle Los Arboles, can ship your important letters and parcels by air freight or international courier. They will also buy handicrafts for you and ship them for export – handy if you can't come to Panajachel yourself.

Bookstores The Delante Bookstore, down a pathway off Calle de Buenas Nuevas (follow the signs), has an excellent collection of used books in English and other languages. They sell, trade and rent books (rental US$0.15 per day), and they have six rooms for rent.

The Gallery Bookstore (☎ /fax 762-2015) is upstairs in the Centro Comercial on Calle Los Arboles. It offers new and used books for sale, a telephone/fax service and travel and ticket sales.

Travel Agencies There are quite a few full-service travel agencies along Calle Santander. Most of them offer trips, tours and shuttle bus services to other places around Guatemala.

Comerciales de Artesanías Típicas Tinamit Maya
This is one of Guatemala's most extensive handicrafts markets, with dozens of stalls. You can get good buys here if you bargain and take your time. The market is open every day from 7 am to 7 pm.

Activities
Various lakeside villages, reachable by foot, bicycle, bus or passenger boat, are interesting to visit. The most popular destination for day trips is Santiago Atitlán, directly across the lake south of Panajachel, but there are others. Most of the villages have places to stay overnight.

You can walk from Panajachel to Santa Catarina in about an hour, continuing to San Antonio in about another hour; it takes only half as long on bicycle (see Getting Around for rental). Or take the bike by boat to Santiago, San Pedro or another village to start a tour of the lake.

Boat tours are another possibility (see Getting There & Away below).

Language Courses
There are two Spanish-language schools in Panajachel: Panatitlán (fax 762-1196), at Calle de la Navidad 0-40, Zona 1, and the Escuela de Español Panajachel (fax 762-1196).

Places to Stay – budget
Camping There's a free public campground on the beach on the east side of the Río Panajachel's mouth in Jucanyá. Safety can be a problem here. A safer but more expensive alternative is the campground on the spacious lakeside lawn at the Hotel Visión Azul (☎ /fax 762-1426), on the western outskirts of town. It has electrical and water hookups for campers and caravans; cost is US$1.65 per person, plus US$5 per tent, plus US$2.50 per vehicle.

Hospedajes & Hotels Luckily for low-budget travelers, Panajachel has numerous little family-run hospedajes. They're very simple – perhaps just two rough beds, a bedside table and a light bulb in a room of bare boards – but quite cheap. Most provide clean toilets and hot showers.

The first place to look for hospedajes is along Calle Santander midway between Calle Real and the beach. Follow signs along the main street for the various hospedajes down narrow side streets and alleys.

The cheapest place in town is the *Hospedaje Londres*, down one of these pathways, Callejón de Londres (follow the sign). It's very basic, with six rooms around a covered courtyard sharing a hot bath; cost is US$1.50/1.85/2.50 for a single/double/triple. The owner speaks English and Spanish.

Hospedaje Santa Elena 2, Calle 15 de Febrero 3-06, off Calle Santander on the road to the Hotel Monterrey, is tidy and typical of Pana's hospedajes. Singles/doubles with shared bath are US$3/4. The original *Hospedaje Santa Elena* is down a pathway off Calle Real, farther from the lake; it's a simple family-run place which has rooms sharing cold showers for US$2.40/3.65/4.35.

Hospedaje Vista Hermosa, Calle 15 de Febrero 3-55, is a friendly place with simple rooms on two levels around a small, pretty courtyard. There are hot showers in the daytime only, with very little water at night. Rooms with general bath are US$2.50 per person, or US$6.65 for two people with private bath. Next door, *Posada Monte Rosa* is a pleasant new hotel with five comfortable single/double rooms for US$11/20.

Hospedaje Santo Domingo is a step up in quality but a few steps off the street; follow the road toward the Hotel Monterrey, then follow signs along a shady path. It's well away from the noise on Calle Santander. Rooms with general bath are US$2.50/4.50 for simple wooden rooms, or US$7.50 for more attractive upstairs rooms. Singles/doubles with private bath are US$9.15/13.35.

Mario's Rooms (☎ 762-1313) on Calle Santander is popular with young, adventurous travelers. Singles/doubles with shared hot bath are US$5.50/6.50; with private cold bath they are US$9.15/12. The restaurant here serves economical meals. *Hospedaje Mi Chosita*, on Calle El Chali (turn at Mario's Rooms), is tidy, quiet and costs US$4.15/5.15/6.15 for a single/double/triple with shared bath. *Hospedaje García* (☎ 762-2187), 4a Calle 2-24, Zona 2, farther east along the same street toward Calle Rancho Grande, charges US$5.25/6/7.50 for a single/double/triple.

Hotel Villa Martita, on Calle Santander half a block from the lake, is a friendly family-run place with singles/doubles with general bath for US$6/8.35. The rooms are around a quiet courtyard, set back from the street. Next door, the more upmarket *Posada de los Volcanes* (☎ /fax 762-2367), Calle Santander 5-51, is a beautiful new place where all the rooms have private bath and cable TV; rooms are US$20/25.

Next door again, *Hospedaje El Viajero* is perhaps the best value in town. It's a new place, pleasant and clean, with just five rooms with private bath set about 40 meters back from the street. It's quiet and peaceful, yet you're near everything, including

the lake. Singles/doubles are US$9/12, and there's laundry service and parking.

Another clean, new place is the *Hospedaje Montufar*, down a pathway off Calle Santander. Rooms with shared bath are US$7/12/12/19 for one/two/three/four people.

La Zanahoria Chic (☎ 762-1249, fax 762-2138), Calle Los Arboles 0-46, has seven clean rooms opening onto a communal upstairs sitting area with two shared baths. The rooms are simple but comfortable and the whole place has a cozy, friendly feeling. Downstairs is the pleasant La Zanahoria Chic video-cafe. Singles/doubles/triples are US$4.15/6/8.35.

Near the beach and the Hotel Playa Linda are several more places. *Hospedaje Ramos* has simple rooms with private bath for US$6/10. Fifty meters behind it, the *Hospedaje Contemporaneo* (☎ 762-2214) is a newer place with simple but clean rooms with private bath for US$7.50/12. Also along here, the *Hotel Villa Flores* (☎ 762-2193), next door to the Hotel Playa Linda, is even newer. Many restaurants along here are convenient for meals.

Moving up in comfort, *Hotel Las Casitas* (☎ 762-1224), opposite the market near the church and town hall, rents little brick bungalows with private bath and tile roofs for US$6.65/13.35/15 for a single/double/triple.

Hotel Fonda del Sol (☎ 762-1162), Calle Real 1-74, Zona 2, is a two-story building on the main street, west of the intersection with Calle Santander. The 25 simple rooms on the upper floor are well used but fairly decently kept; they cost US$6/11 with shared bath, US$11/17 with private bath. Larger, nicer rooms are US$16/23 for a single/double. Downstairs is a restaurant.

Hotel Maya-Kanek (☎ 762-1104), Calle Real just down from the church, is a motel-style hostelry. Rooms face a cobbled court with a small garden; the court doubles as a secure car park. The 20 rooms, though simple, are a bit more comfortable than at a hospedaje, and they cost US$7/11 with shared cold bath or US$10/15 with private hot bath. It's quiet here.

Hotel Galindo (☎ /fax 762-1168), on Calle Real northeast of the Banco Agricola Mercantil, has a surprisingly lush garden surrounded by modest rooms that rent for US$12 for smaller rooms, US$14 for larger rooms (some with fireplace), US$20 for triple rooms with fireplace. Look at the room before you rent.

Down an alleyway from the church, the *Hotel Montana* (☎ /fax 762-2180) has 15 clean, bright, single/double rooms with private bath, cable TV and parking for US$15/27.

The *Delante Bookstore* (see Bookstores above) has six pleasant rooms for rent around a tranquil, quiet courtyard. The room rate includes use of the communal kitchen and having your laundry and dishes washed. You can also read all the books in the bookstore for free. Such a deal!

Places to Stay – middle
Midrange lodgings are busiest on weekends. From Sunday to Thursday you may get a discount. All of these lodgings provide private hot showers in their rooms.

Rancho Grande Inn (☎ 762-1554, 762-2255, fax 762-2247), Calle Rancho Grande, has 12 perfectly maintained German country-style villas in a tropical Guatemalan setting amid emerald-green lawns. Some bungalows sleep up to five people. Marlita Hannstein, the congenial owner, charges a very reasonable US$30/40 to 60 for a single/double, including tax and a full delicious breakfast. This is perhaps Pana's best place to stay. It's a good idea to reserve in advance.

Bungalows El Aguacatal (☎ 762-1482), Calle de Buenas Nuevas, is aimed at weekenders from the capital. Each modern bungalow has two bedrooms, is equipped with kitchen, bath and salon, and costs US$42 for one to four people Sunday to Thursday, US$52 on Friday and Saturday. Bungalows without kitchen are cheaper, costing US$10 per person Sunday to Thursday, US$45 on weekends.

Mini Hotel Riva Bella (☎ 762-1348, 762-1177, fax 762-1353), Calle Real, is a collection of neat two-room bungalows, each

with its own parking place, set around pleasant gardens. The location is convenient, and the price is US$27/32 for a single/double. The same owners also operate *Bungalows Guayacán*, just across the river, with six apartments, each with kitchenette, one bedroom, living room and garden, for US$42 for up to three people.

Hotel Dos Mundos (☎ /fax 762-2078), Calle Santander 4-72, is an attractive place with 16 bungalows, all with cable TV and nice decor, in a walled compound of tropical gardens for US$30/40/50 for a single/double/triple. The compound is set well back from the street. Also here are a swimming pool and a good Italian restaurant.

Hotel Monterrey (☎ /fax 762-1126), Calle 15 de Febrero, an unpaved road west from Calle Santander (look for the sign), is a blue-and-white, two-story motel-style building facing the lake across lawns and gardens that extend down to the beach. The Monterrey offers 29 clean and cheerful single/double rooms opening onto a terrace with a beautiful lake view for US$30/40.

Places to Eat – budget
The cheapest places to eat are crude cookshacks, down by the beach at the mouth of the Río Panajachel. The food stands around the parking lot cost only a bit more. Then there are the little restaurants just inland from the parking lot, with names such as *Los Pumpos, El Xocomil, El Pescador, Brisas de Lago* and *Los Alpes*. Not only is the food inexpensive (US$4 for a fill-up), but the view of the lake is a priceless bonus. *Pizza, Pastas y Vino* along here is open 24 hours.

At the lake end of Calle Santander, the open-air *Sunset Cafe* has a great view of the lake. Meat or vegetarian meals are US$3 to US$5, snacks are less, and there's a bar and live music on weekends. It's open every day from 11 am to 10 pm.

Nearby on Calle Santander, the *Deli Restaurante 2* is a tranquil garden restaurant serving a good variety of healthy, inexpensive foods to the strains of soft classical music. It's open every day except Tuesday from 7 am to 5:45 pm; breakfast is served all day. *Deli Restaurante No 1*, on Calle Real next to the Hotel Galindo, has the same menu and hours; it closes on Thursday.

El Bistro, on Calle Santander half a block from the lake, is another lovely, relaxing restaurant with tables both inside and out in the garden. There's candlelight in the evening and sometimes live music. It's open every day from 7 am to 10 pm.

Las Chinitas, on Calle Santander very near the Hotel Dos Mundos, is a tiny outdoor restaurant with delicious, inexpensive Chinese food. Ling, the friendly owner, is from Malaysia via New York and has been in Panajachel for many years. *Restaurante Mario's*, on Calle Santander beside Mario's Rooms, is another good spot for economical meals.

Restaurante Psicodélico, on Calle Santander, is a pleasant open-air restaurant with candlelight in the evening. Meals are ample and economical: Grilled meat or chicken (US$3.35) and fish or shrimp (US$5) come with soup, guacamole, French fries, salad and dessert. Alcohol is served, and the Grapevine Video Bar is upstairs.

The Last Resort restaurant/bar, just off Calle Santander on Calle El Chali, is small, pleasant and famous for its good, economical food. A buffet breakfast is served for US$2; a good variety of complete meals are US$3.35 to US$5. Alcohol is served, there's table tennis in the rear, and on cool evenings the fireplace is a welcome treat. It's open every day.

Al Chisme (The Gossip), on Calle Los Arboles, is a favorite with regular foreign visitors and residents, with its shady streetside patio. Breakfasts of English muffins, Belgian waffles and omelettes cost US$2 to US$4. For lunch and dinner, Al Chisme offers a variety of meat and vegetarian dishes, including Tex-Mex specialties. It's open every day except Wednesday. *Cafe Cinema* is upstairs in the rear.

Next door in the Centro Comercial complex on Los Arboles is *Sevananda Vegetarian Restaurant*, offering sandwiches and plates for US$2 to US$4. It's open every day except Sunday. *The Secret Garden*, down a pathway off Calle Santander (follow the signs), is another good vegetarian restaurant,

with tables set around a beautiful, quiet garden. It's open every day from 10 am to 3 pm for brunch and lunch.

La Posada del Pintor and its *Circus Bar*, on Calle Los Arboles, is a restaurant, pizzería and bar with walls hung with old circus posters and a vast menu. There's live music every night from 8 pm on; it's open every day, noon to midnight. This is one of Pana's most popular places.

Restaurante La Laguna, on Calle Real at the intersection of Calle Los Arboles, has a pretty front patio and garden with umbrella-covered tables. There's live music in the garden Tuesday to Sunday nights.

At the *Fly'n Mayan Yacht Club*, near the intersection of Calle Real and Calle Santander, the pizzas (US$3.50 to US$6.50) have a good reputation. It's open daily except Thursday.

Restaurante/Bar Tocoyal, opposite the big Hotel Barceló del Lago, at the beach end of Calle Rancho Grande, is a tidy, modern thatch-roofed place serving good, moderately priced meals (including fish) for about US$8.

Places to Eat – middle

Ristorante La Lanterna at the Hotel Dos Mundos, set back from the street on Calle Santander, is a good, authentic Italian restaurant with both inside and garden tables; you're welcome to use the swimming pool if you come to eat here. It's open every day, from 7 am to 3 pm and 6 to 10 pm.

Upstairs in the same building with the INGUAT tourist office, *La Terraza Tapas Bar* is a lovely, upmarket open-air restaurant/bar that's open every day. *Restaurante El Patio*, also on Calle Santander, is another good but more expensive place, as is the *Casablanca Restaurant* (☎ 762-1015), at the intersection of Calle Santander and Calle Real.

Entertainment

Strolling along the path at the lakeside park, greeting the dawn or watching the sunset behind the volcanoes across the lake, are unsurpassable entertainment.

Live music is presented at the *La Posada del Pintor/Circus Bar*, the *Restaurante La Laguna*, the *Sunset Cafe* and *El Bistro* (see Places to Eat).

Chapiteau and *Noan's*, both on Calle Los Arboles, are Pana's two discos. They open around 9 or 10 pm.

Video films are shown at the *Grapevine Video Bar*, on Calle Santander upstairs from the Restaurante Psicodélico, and at *Cafe Cinema*, on Calle Los Arboles upstairs in the rear from Al Chisme; both show several films nightly and have schedules posted out front. At *La Zanahoria Chic* video cafe on Los Arboles, you can choose from a list of over a hundred films. All of these are pleasant places with food and drink available.

Getting There & Away

Bus The town's main bus stop is where Calle Santander meets Calle Real, across from the Mayan Palace Hotel and the Banco Agricola Mercantil. Rébuli buses depart from the Rébuli office on Calle Real. For destinations off the Interamericana, you may find yourself waiting at major highway junctions such as Los Encuentros and Cuatro Caminos to connect with the right bus.

Antigua (80 km, three hours, US$2) Rébuli runs one direct bus daily, except Sunday, at 11 am. Or take any bus heading for Guatemala City and change buses at Chimaltenango.

Chichicastenango (29 km, 1½ hours, US$1.65) Nine buses daily, 7 am to 4 pm. (These buses may run only on Thursday and Sunday, Chichi's market days.) Or take any bus that is heading to Los Encuentros and change buses there.

Cocales (Carretera al Pacífico; 56 km, 2½ hours, US$1)

El Carmen/Talismán (Mexican border) Via the Pacific route, bus to Cocales and change buses there. Via the highland route, bus to Quetzaltenango and change buses there.

Guatemala City (147 km, three hours, US$2) Rébuli has buses departing from its office on Calle Real nine times daily, 5 am to 2:30 pm. Or take a bus to Los Encuentros and change there.

Huehuetenango (159 km, 3½ hours) Bus to Los Encuentros and wait there for a bus bound for Huehue or La Mesilla (see Getting There &

Away in the Guatemala City section for a schedule of these buses). Or catch a bus heading to Quetzaltenango, get out at Cuatro Caminos, and change buses there.

La Mesilla (Mexican border; 241 km, seven hours) See Huehuetenango.

Los Encuentros (20 km, 35 minutes, US$0.50) Take any bus heading toward Guatemala City, Chichicastenango, Quetzaltenango or the Interamericana.

Quetzaltenango (99 km, two hours, US$2) Four buses daily, 5:30, 6:15 and 7:30 am and 2 pm. Or, take a bus to Los Encuentros and change there.

San Antonio Palopó (nine km, one hour, US$0.50) Daily buses, via Santa Catarina Palopó.

San Lucas Tolimán (24 km, 1½ hours, US$1) Two buses daily, 6:45 am and 4 pm. Or, take any bus heading for Cocales, get off at the crossroads to San Lucas and walk about one km into town.

Santa Catarina Palopó (four km, 30 minutes, US$0.50) Daily buses.

Sololá (eight km, 10 minutes, US$0.15) Frequent direct local buses, or take any bus heading to Guatemala City, Chichicastenango, Quetzaltenango, or Los Encuentros.

Shuttle Minibus A number of travel agencies on Calle Santander offer convenient shuttle buses to popular tourist destinations, including Guatemala City, Antigua, Chichicastenango, Quetzaltenango and the Mexican border.

Car & Motorcycle Dalton Rent A Car (☎ /fax 762-1275, 762-2251) has an office on Calle Los Arboles. Moto Servicio Queche (☎ 762-2089), at the intersection of Calle Los Arboles and Calle Real, rents bicycles and off-road motorcycles.

Boat Passenger boats depart from the public beach at the foot of Calle Rancho Grande. The boat schedule is posted outside the door of the INGUAT tourist office, or stop by the dock to see when boats are leaving. You usually don't have to wait long for a boat.

The trip to Santiago Atitlán takes about an hour (or a little longer, depending upon the winds) and costs US$1.25 each way.

Another boat route heads to Santa Catarina Palopó (US$1.25)-San Antonio Palopó

(US$2.50)-San Lucas Tolimán (US$3.35), returning to Panajachel.

Another route connects Panajachel and San Pedro (1¼ hours); departing from Panajachel, these boats stop (in order) at Santa Cruz La Laguna (20 minutes), Jaibalito, Tzununá, San Marcos La Laguna (one hour) and San Juan La Laguna. They depart Panajachel from the Calle Rancho Grande docks and then stop at another dock at the foot of Calle del Embarcadero before heading out of town (vice versa, when arriving at Panajachel). Fare is US$1.25 for any destination for tourists, US$0.50 for locals.

Another option is to take a boat tour of the lake, which includes various towns. For example, the INGUAT tourist office in Panajachel makes bookings for a boat tour departing Panajachel at 8:30 am, visiting San Pedro (one hour), Santiago (1½ hours) and San Antonio (one hour) for US$6.65, arriving back in Panajachel at 3:30 pm. Advance booking is suggested.

Getting Around
Several places along Calle Santander rent bicycles, as do Moto Servicio Queche (see above) and Alquiler de Bicicletas Gaby, on Calle El Chali between Calle Santander and Calle Rancho Grande.

SANTA CATARINA PALOPÓ & SAN ANTONIO PALOPÓ
Four km east of Panajachel along a winding, unpaved road lies the village of Santa Catarina Palopó. Narrow streets paved in stone blocks, and adobe houses with roofs of thatch or corrugated tin huddled around a gleaming white church: that's Santa Catarina. Chickens cackle, dogs bark and the villagers go about their business dressed in their beautiful traditional costumes. Except for exploring village life and enjoying views of the lake and the volcanoes, there's little in the way of sightseeing. For refreshments, there are several little comedores on the main plaza, one of which advertises 'Cold beer sold here.'

If your budget allows, head to *Villa Santa Catarina* (☎ 762-1291), the village's best hotel, for a drink or a meal.

The road continues past Santa Catarina 5 km to San Antonio Palopó, a larger but similar village. Three km along the way you pass the *Hotel Bella Vista* (☎ 762-1566), 8 km from Panajachel. Fourteen little bungalows, each with TV, private bath and lake view, share gardens with a swimming pool and a restaurant. The bungalows are US$45/48/50 a single/double/triple. In San Antonio there's also the *Hotel Terrazas del Lago*, a beautiful place with a lovely lake view and singles/doubles/triples for US$20/26/32.

Getting There & Away
See the Panajachel section for details on buses and passenger or tour boats. From Panajachel, you can also walk to Santa Catarina in about an hour, continuing to San Antonio in about another hour.

SAN LUCAS TOLIMÁN
Farther around the lake from San Antonio, and reached by a different road, San Lucas Tolimán is busier and more commercial than most lakeside villages. Set at the foot of the dramatic Volcán Tolimán, San Lucas is a coffee-growing town and a transport point on the route between the Interamericana and the Carretera al Pacífico. Market days are Monday, Tuesday, Thursday and Friday. From San Lucas, a rough, badly maintained road goes west around Volcán Tolimán to Santiago Atitlán, then around Volcán San Pedro to San Pedro La Laguna.

See the Panajachel section for details on buses and passenger boats.

SANTIAGO ATITLÁN
South across the lake from Panajachel, on the shore of a lagoon squeezed between the towering volcanoes of Tolimán and San Pedro, lies the small town of Santiago Atitlán. Though it is the most visited village outside Panajachel, it clings to the traditional lifestyle of the Tzutuhil Maya. The women of the town still weave and wear huipiles with brilliantly colored flocks of birds and bouquets of flowers embroidered on them. The best day to visit is market day (Friday and Sunday, with a

lesser market on Tuesday), but in fact any day will do.

Santiago is also a curiosity because of its reverence for Maximón (MAH-shee-MOHN), a local deity who is probably a blend of ancient Maya gods, Pedro de Alvarado (the fierce conquistador of Guatemala) and the biblical Judas. Despised in other highland towns, Maximón is revered in Santiago Atitlán, and his effigy with wooden mask and huge cigar is paraded triumphantly during Semana Santa processions. The rest of the time, Maximón resides in a different house every year, receiving offerings of candles, beer and rum. Local children will offer to take you to see him for a small tip.

Children from Santiago greet you as you disembark at the dock, selling clay whistles and little embroidered strips of cloth. They'll be right behind, alongside and in front of you during much of your stay here.

Orientation & Information

Walk to the left from the dock along the shore to reach the street into town, which is the main commercial street. Every tourist walks up and down it between the dock and the town, so it's lined with shops selling woven cloth, other handicrafts and souvenirs.

Information

Near the dock is the office of the Grupo Guías de Turismo Rilaj Maam, a tourist guide cooperative offering trips to many nearby places, including the Atitlán, Tolimán and San Pedro volcanoes, the Chutinamit archaeological site and other places. The office is open every day from 8 am to 5 pm.

Santiago has a post office, a Guatel telephone/fax office and a bank where you can change US dollars cash and traveler's checks.

Things to See & Do

At the top of the slope is the main square, with the town office and huge church, which dates from the time, several centuries ago, when Santiago was an important commercial town. Within the stark, echoing church are some surprising sights. Along the walls are wooden statues of the saints, each of whom gets new clothes made by local women every year. On the carved wooden pulpit, note the figures of corn (from which humans were formed, according to Maya religion), of a quetzal bird reading a book and of Yum-Kax, the Maya god of corn. There is similar carving on the back of the priest's chair.

The walls of the church bear paintings, now covered by a thin layer of plaster. A memorial plaque at the back of the church commemorates Father Stanley Francis Rother, a missionary priest from Oklahoma; he was beloved by the local people but despised by ultra-rightist 'death squads,' who murdered him right here in the church during the troubled year of 1981.

There's a bird refuge near Santiago; the Posada de Santiago (see Places to Stay below) can give you directions.

Places to Stay & Eat

Near the dock, the *Hotel Chi-Nim-Yá* (☎ 721-7131) is a pleasant, simple hotel with 22 rooms around a central courtyard. Clean singles/doubles with shared bath are US$3.35/6.65; with private bath they are US$8.35/10. The nicest room in the place is No 106, large and airy, with lots of windows and excellent lake views. Nearby, the *Restaurante Regiomontano* is open every day from 6:30 or 7 am to 7 pm.

Hotel y Restaurante Tzutuhil (☎ 721-7174), about three blocks uphill on the road coming up from the dock, is a modern five-story building, an anomaly in this little town. Many of the rooms have large windows to the outside, with fine views, and some have cable TV. Clean rooms are US$2.50 per person with shared hot bath, or US$4.15 per person with private bath. It's a good place and a great deal for the price. Go up on the rooftop for a fine view. The restaurant here is open every day from 6 am to 10:30 pm

Restaurant Santa Rita, a few steps from the northeast corner of the plaza past Distribuidor El Buen Precio, boasts 'deliciosos pays' (delicious pies).

One of the most charming hotels around the lake, or in all Guatemala for that matter, *Posada de Santiago* (☎ 702-8462, net) has six free-standing bungalows and two suites, all with stone walls, fireplaces, porches and hammocks, set around beautiful gardens stretching up the hill from the lake. Rates are US$30/40/50/66/80 for a single/double/triple/quad/suite. It's one km from the town center; to get there, walk out of town on the road past the Hospedaje Rosita, and keep walking along the lakeside road.

The restaurant at the Posada de Santiago is special, too, with famous gourmet food and a very pleasant ambiance.

Getting There & Away

Boats between Santiago and San Pedro La Laguna take about 45 minutes to make the crossing.

SAN PEDRO LA LAGUNA

Perhaps the next most popular lakeside town to visit, after Santiago, is San Pedro La Laguna. Its number-two ranking means that fewer flocks of *muchachos* will swirl around you as you stroll the narrow cobblestone streets and wander to the outskirts for a dip in the lake.

When you arrive by boat from Panajachel, boys will greet you, asking if you want a guide to ascend the San Pedro volcano, by hiking or horseback. It's worth it to go with a guide; cost is US$2.50 per person for the whole trip by hiking, or US$1.65 per hour on horseback.

Coffee is grown in San Pedro. You'll see coffee being picked and spread out to dry on wide platforms at the beginning of the dry season.

Orientation & Information

San Pedro has two docks. The one on the south side of town serves boats going to/from Santiago Atitlán. Another dock, around on the east side of town, serves boats going to/from Panajachel. At either dock, walk straight ahead a few blocks on the road leading uphill from the dock to reach the center of town.

San Pedro has a post office, a Guatel

telephone/fax office and a casa de cambio where you can change US dollars cash and traveler's checks.

None of the hotels, restaurants or other businesses here have private telephones. To reach them, you can phone to the community telephone at Guatel (☎ 762-2486) and give them a time you expect to call back; the business will send someone over to receive your return call.

Thermal Waters

Thermal Waters has open-air solar-heated pools right on the lakeshore between the two docks; there's a great view. Come in the afternoon or evening, after the water has had a chance to warm up; a reservation is a good idea, as it's a popular spot. Cost is US$3.35 for the first person, US$1.65 for each additional person. Antonio from California, the eccentric horticulturist inventor who built and operates Thermal Waters, also has an organic vegetarian restaurant here and an underground solar steam sauna. Health retreats are offered each weekend.

Language Courses

Casa Rosario, a Spanish-language school, is operated by Professor Samuel Cumes, a well-known San Pedro teacher. It's more economical than most Spanish schools; cost is US$45 per week for instruction and lodging (food not available).

Places to Stay & Eat

When you arrive at the dock serving boats to/from Panajachel, turn right and walk along the lake for about 75 meters to reach the *Hotel & Restaurante Valle Azul*, right on the lakeshore. It's a new, beautiful, simple hostelry, supremely relaxing and tranquil, with hammocks on balconies, a great view across the lake and a pleasant, small lakeside restaurant. Rooms with shared bath are US$1.65 per person (plus US$0.50 per shower); singles/doubles with private bath are US$3.35/5. The restaurant is a great, inexpensive little place; it's open every day, 7 am to 10 pm.

Several other little restaurants are also near here, including the *Restaurante El*

Viajero, right beside the dock, and the *Restaurante/Bar El Mesón* and *Restaurante El Fondeadero* to the right of it.

Hospedaje Casa Elena, on the lakeshore 50 meters to the left of the dock, is a pleasant, simple, little family-run pension where singles/doubles with shared bath are US$2.50/3.35.

Over by the dock serving boats to/from Santiago are several more places to stay. *Ti Kaaj*, on the lakeside road near the dock, is popular and inexpensive, with hammocks around the gardens and single/double/triple rooms with shared bath for US$1.65/3/4.35. There is a restaurant, disco and bar, and cayucos (canoes) are for rent. Next door, the *Comedor Ranchón* is an open-air restaurant known for its good food.

Along and just off the road leading uphill from the Santiago dock are several more good places to stay. *Hospedaje Villa Sol*, with 45 simple rooms around a grassy courtyard, charges US$5/6 per room with shared/private bath. Next door, the *Hotel San Pedro* also has rooms around a courtyard; singles/doubles are US$6.65 with shared bath, or US$4.50/8.35 with private bath.

Just off this road, *Hospedaje San Francisco* is a pleasant, new little place up on the hill. The rooms have small outdoor kitchens, a great view of the lake from their tiny patios and hammocks in the garden. Rooms with general bath are US$3.35 per person, and rooms with private bath are being built. Nearby, *Hospedaje El Balneario* is the cheapest place in town, with 14 basic rooms, each opening onto a balcony with a lake view; single/double rooms with shared bath are US$1.33/2.50.

Cafe Arte, on the road leading uphill from the Santiago dock, is a good, inexpensive cafe serving meat, fish and vegetarian dishes. It's operated by the family of internationally known primitivist artist Pedro Rafael González Chavajay; his paintings, and those of many of his students, are exhibited at the cafe. It's open every day from 7 am to 11 pm.

If you have a chance, check out the organic vegetarian restaurant at *Thermal Waters*, on the lakeshore road between the two docks. Choose your pleasure from the extensive menu and Antonio will run out to the garden to gather the ingredients. Next door, *Kolibrí Pizza* is another good little lakeside restaurant.

Getting There & Away

Bus & Car Buses to Guatemala City depart from San Pedro at 3, 3:30, 4, 4:30 and 5 am; see the Guatemala City section for return buses. The trip takes three to four hours and costs US$2.65.

The rough road from San Lucas Tolimán to Santiago Atitlán continues 18 km to San Pedro, making its way around the lagoon and the back side of Volcán San Pedro.

A rough road connects San Pedro with the Interamericana; the turnoff is at Km 148. The road meets the lake at Santa Clara La Laguna and turns right to San Pedro, left to San Marcos. From San Pedro it continues to Santiago Atitlán and San Lucas Tolimán. From San Marcos it continues to Tzununá, but beyond that it's a walking trail only, which continues to Santa Cruz La Laguna.

Unless you want to bring a vehicle, it's easier to reach San Pedro by boat.

Boat Passenger boats come here from Panajachel (see that section for details). Boats also come come here from Santiago.

SAN MARCOS LA LAGUNA

San Marcos is a very peaceful little place, with houses set among shady coffee plants near the lakeshore. The lakeshore is beautiful here, with several little docks you can swim from.

San Marcos' greatest claim to fame is **Las Pirámides** meditation center (fax 762-2080), on the path heading inland from the Posada Schumann. A one-month spiritual course called the Curso Lunar de Meditación (lunar meditation course for spiritual and human development) begins every full moon. It covers four elements of human development (physical, mental, emotional and spiritual), with one week for each. If you can stay for a month to do the whole course, come in time for full moon.

If you can only stay a week, the week just before full moon is best, when there's a special meditation retreat program. Or come for the channeling sessions, held on the new and full moon.

Other things done here include yoga, channeling, aura work, Tarot and regression.

Every structure on the property is built in the shape of pyramids and oriented to the four cardinal points. Accommodations are available in little pyramid-shaped houses, which cost US$8.35/7.50/6.65 per day by the day/week/month. Included in this price is the meditation course, use of the kitchen and sauna, and access to a fascinating library with books in several languages.

Places to Stay & Eat

There are several places to stay in San Marcos. The Posada Schumann is 400 meters to the left of the dock, walking along the lakeside path. When you reach Posada Schumann, turn inland and walk up the pathway to reach all the rest of the places listed here.

Posada Schumann, right on the lakeside, has three stone bungalows, each with kitchen and private bath; there's also a restaurant and sauna. Singles/doubles are US$9/17, cheaper by the week or month. For reservations, you can contact them in Guatemala City (☎ 360-4049, 339-2683, fax 473-1326).

Hotel Paco Real (fax 762-1196) has beautiful gardens and rooms that are simple but beautiful and tastefully decorated; all in all it's a very artistic place. Rooms with shared bath are US$6/10/14 for a single/double/triple. Also here is a pleasant restaurant, open every day from 7 am to 9 pm.

Hotel La Paz (☎ 702-9168) has three beautiful little bungalows, each with sleeping loft and private bath; cost is US$17 for one to four people. There's also a vegetarian restaurant and a sauna. Camping is allowed.

Unicornio Rooms is another attractive place, with beautiful gardens, a sauna and a communal kitchen (but no electricity). Three small, thatch-roofed A-frame bungalows with shared cold bath are US$2.50/3.65 for a single/double. One large two-story bungalow with private kitchen and bath is US$6.65 per day for one or two people, US$10 for three.

Hotel San Marcos is another option here; it's not as beautiful as the other places. Rooms with shared cold bath are US$3.35 per person.

Getting There & Away

See Panajachel for details on passenger boats.

You can drive to San Marcos from the Interamericana, where there's a turnoff at Km 148. See the San Pedro section.

SANTA CRUZ LA LAGUNA

Santa Cruz La Laguna is another peaceful little village beside the lake. The main part of the village is up the hill from the dock; the hotels are on the lakeside, right beside the dock.

Diving

ATI Divers (fax 762-1196) operates a diving school and does underwater archaeology dives and special projects. A four-day PADI open-water diving certification course costs US$150; they also offer a PADI high-altitude advanced diving course and fun dives. It's based at the La Iguana Perdida hotel.

Hiking

You can make some good walks starting at Santa Cruz. A beautiful walk is along the lakeside walking track between Santa Cruz and San Marcos; it takes about 2½ hours. Or you can walk up the hill to Sololá, a three- to 3½-hour walk.

Places to Stay & Eat

Three pleasant lakeside hotels, all right beside the dock, provide accommodations and meals. There's electricity up the hill in town, but not down here, where the hotels are. So in the evening, you eat by candlelight and lantern-light.

None of these hotels has a telephone, but you can fax them at 762-1196. It can take a few days to hear back from them.

Arca de Noé has been known for its excellent food and friendly managers, but the management has recently changed.

La Iguana Perdida also has a restaurant and a variety of accommodations. The charge is US$2.50 per person for a dorm bed, US$3.35/5 for a single/double in 'massage room,' or US$6/8 for single/double rooms with shared bath. Here, too, meals are served family-style, with everyone eating together; dinner is US$5. There's also a sauna. The friendly managers, Deedle Denman (from the UK) and Mike Kiersgard (from Greenland), also operate ATI divers.

The *Posada Abaj Hotel*, also here on the lakefront, is a nice, big place that also has a restaurant. Rooms with shared bath are US$8.35/12/15 for a single/double/triple; bungalows with private bath are US$20 for up to three people. Spanish classes are offered here.

Getting There & Away

See Panajachel for details on passenger boats.

Highlands – Quiché

QUICHÉ

The Departamento del Quiché is famous mostly for the town of Chichicastenango, with its bustling markets on Thursday and Sunday. Beyond Chichi to the north is Santa Cruz del Quiché, the capital of the department. On its outskirts lie the ruins of K'umarcaaj (or Gumarcaah), also called Utatlán, the last capital city of the Quiché Maya.

The road to Quiché leaves the Interamericana at Los Encuentros, winding its way through pine forests and cornfields, down into a steep valley and up the other side. Women sit in front of their little roadside cottages weaving yet another gorgeous piece of cloth on their simple back-strap looms. From Los Encuentros, it takes half an hour to travel the 17 km north to the town of Chichicastenango.

CHICHICASTENANGO

Population 8000

Surrounded by valleys, with nearby mountains looming overhead, Chichicastenango (2030 meters) seems isolated from the rest of Guatemala. When its narrow cobbled streets and red-tiled roofs are enveloped in mists, as they often are, it can seem magical. Chichi is a beautiful, interesting place; not the many shiny tour buses parked near the market nor even the gaggles of camera-toting tour groups can change that. If you have a choice of days, come for the Sunday market rather than the Thursday one, as the cofradías (religious brotherhoods) often hold processions on Sunday.

Though isolated, Chichi has always been an important market town. Villagers from throughout the region would walk for many hours carrying their wares to participate in the commerce here – and that was in the days before good roads.

Today, though many traders come by bus, others still arrive on foot. At dawn on Thursday and Sunday they spread out their vegetables, fruits, chunks of chalk (ground to a powder, mixed with water and used to soften dried maize), balls of wax, handmade harnesses and other wares and wait for customers.

Many ladino business types also set up fairly touristy stalls in the Sunday and Thursday markets. Somehow they end up adding to the color and fascination, not detracting from it.

Besides the famous market, Masheños (citizens of Chichicastenango) are famous for their adherence to pre-Christian religious beliefs and ceremonies. You can readily see versions of these old rites in and around the church of Santo Tomás and at the shrine of Pascual Abaj on the outskirts of town.

Chichi has two religious and governmental establishments. The Catholic Church and the Republic of Guatemala appoint priests and town officials to manage their interests, but the local people elect their own religious and civil officers to deal with local matters.

The Indian town government has its own council, mayor and deputy mayor, and it

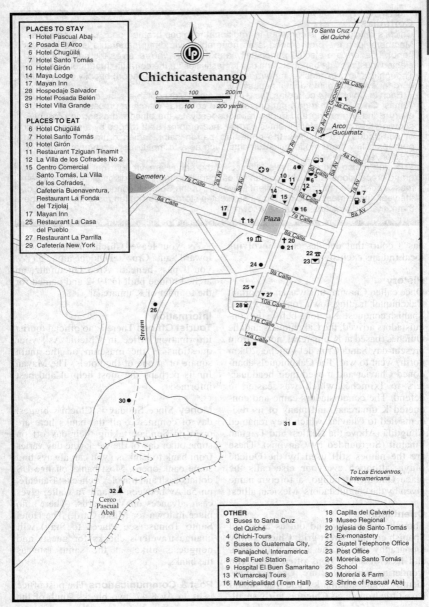

Chichicastenango

PLACES TO STAY
1 Hotel Pascual Abaj
2 Posada El Arco
6 Hotel Chugüilá
7 Hotel Santo Tomás
10 Hotel Girón
14 Maya Lodge
17 Mayan Inn
28 Hospedaje Salvador
29 Hotel Posada Belén
31 Hotel Villa Grande

PLACES TO EAT
6 Hotel Chugüilá
7 Hotel Santo Tomás
10 Hotel Girón
11 Restaurant Tziguan Tinamit
12 La Villa de los Cofrades No 2
15 Centro Comercial
     Santo Tomás, La Villa
     de los Cofrades,
     Cafetería Buenaventura,
     Restaurant La Fonda
     del Tzijolaj
17 Mayan Inn
25 Restaurant La Casa
     del Pueblo
27 Restaurant La Parrilla
29 Cafetería New York

OTHER
3 Buses to Santa Cruz
    del Quiché
4 Chichi-Tours
5 Buses to Guatemala City,
    Panajachel, Interamerica
8 Shell Fuel Station
9 Hospital El Buen Samaritano
13 K'umarcaaj Tours
16 Municipalidad (Town Hall)
18 Capilla del Calvario
19 Museo Regional
20 Iglesia de Santo Tomás
21 Ex-monastery
22 Guatel Telephone Office
23 Post Office
24 Morería Santo Tomás
26 School
30 Morería & Farm
32 Shrine of Pascual Abaj

To Santa Cruz
del Quiché

Arco
Gucumatz

Cemetery

Plaza

Stream

Cerco
Pascual
Abaj

To Los Encuentros,
Interamericana

Cofradías

Chichi's religious life is centered in traditional religious brotherhoods called cofradías. Membership in the brotherhood is an honorable civic duty; leadership is the greatest honor. Leaders are elected periodically, and the man who receives the honor of being elected must provide banquets and pay for festivities for the cofradía throughout his term. Though it is very expensive, a *cofrade* (member of the brotherhood) happily accepts the burden, even going into debt if necessary.

Each of Chichi's 14 cofradías has a patron saint. Most notable is the cofradía of Santo Tomás, Chichicastenango's patron saint. The cofradías march in procession to church every Sunday morning and during religious festivals, the officers dressed in costumes showing their rank. Before them is carried a ceremonial staff topped by a silver crucifix or sun-badge that signifies the cofradía's patron saint. Indian drum and flute, and perhaps a few more modern instruments such as a trumpet, may accompany the procession, as do fireworks.

During major church festivals, effigies of the saints are brought out and carried in grand processions, and richly costumed dancers wearing the traditional carved wooden masks act out legends of the ancient Maya and of the Spanish conquest. For the rest of the year, these masks and costumes are kept in storehouses called *morerías*; you'll see them, marked by signs, around the town. ■

has a court that decides cases involving local Indians exclusively.

History

Once called Chaviar, this was an important Cakchiquel trading town long before the Spanish conquest. Not long before the conquistadors arrived, the Cakchiquels and the Quichés (based at K'umarcaaj, not far from present-day Santa Cruz del Quiché, 20 km north) went to war. The Cakchiquels abandoned Chaviar and moved their headquarters to Iximché, which was easier to defend. The conquistadors came and conquered K'umarcaaj, and many of its residents fled to Chaviar, which they renamed Chugüilá (Above the Nettles) and Tziguan Tinamit (Surrounded by Canyons). These are the names still used by the Quiché Maya, although everyone else calls the place Chichicastenango, a foreign name given by the conquistadors' Mexican allies.

Orientation

Though supposedly laid out as a typical Spanish colonial street grid, Chichi's hilly topography defeats the logic of the plan, and lack of street signs often keeps you wondering where you are. Use our map, identify some landmarks, and you should have little trouble, as Chichi is fairly small.

As you leave Chichi heading north toward Santa Cruz del Quiché along 5a Av, you'll pass beneath Arco Gucumatz, an arched bridge built in 1932 and named for the founder of K'umarcaaj.

Information

Tourist Offices There is no official tourist information office in Chichi. Ask your questions at the museum on the main square or at one of the hotels. The Mayan Inn is perhaps the most helpful and best informed.

Money Since Sunday is Chichi's biggest day of commerce, all the banks here are open on Sunday, taking their day off on some other day of the week (the day varies from bank to bank, so you can always find some bank open). Most banks change US dollars cash and traveler's checks; Bancafé, on 5a Av between 6a and 7a Calle, gives cash advances on Visa cards. (There's no place in town for MasterCard.) The Hotel Santo Tomás (see Places to Stay) will change traveler's checks for guests and nonguests alike, at the same rate as the banks.

Post & Communications The post office is at 7a Av 8-47, two blocks south of the

Hotel Santo Tomás on the road into town. Very near it is the Guatel telephone office, at 7a Av 8-21, on the corner of 8a Calle.

Market

Years ago, intrepid travelers made their way to this mountain-bound fastness to witness Chichi's main square packed with Indian traders attending one of Guatemala's largest indigenous markets. Today the market has stalls aimed directly at tourists, as well as those for local people.

On Wednesday and Saturday evenings you'll see men carrying bundles of long poles up the narrow cobbled streets to the plaza, then stacking them out of the way. In the evening the arcades around the plaza are alive with families cooking supper and arranging their bedding for a night's sleep out of doors.

Between dawn and about 8 or 9 am on Sunday and Thursday, the stacks of poles are erected into stalls, hung with cloth, furnished with tables and piled with goods for sale. In general, the tourist-oriented stalls selling carved wooden masks, lengths of embroidered cloth and garments are around the outer edges of the market in the most visible areas. Behind them, the center of the square is devoted to things that the villagers want and need: vegetables and fruit, baked goods, macaroni, soap, clothing, spices, sewing notions and toys. Cheap cookshops provide lunch for buyers and sellers alike.

Most of the stalls are taken down by late afternoon. Prices are best just before the market breaks up, as traders would rather sell than carry goods away with them.

You may want to arrive in town the day before market day to pin down a room and a bed and to be up early for the market. One traveler wrote to say it's worth being here on Saturday night to attend the Saturday night mass. Otherwise, you can always come by bus on market day itself, or by shuttle bus: market day shuttle buses come over from Antigua, Panajachel and Guatemala City, returning in late afternoon. The market starts winding down around 3 or 4 pm.

Iglesia de Santo Tomás

Though dedicated to the Catholic rite, this simple church, dating from about 1540, is more often the scene of rituals that are only slightly Catholic and more highly Maya. The front steps of the church serve much the same purpose as did the great flights of stairs leading up to Maya pyramids. For much of the day (especially on Sunday), the steps smolder with incense of copal resin, while indigenous prayer leaders called *chuchkajaues* (mother-fathers) swing censers (usually tin cans poked with holes) containing *estoraque* incense and chant magic words in honor of the ancient Maya calendar and of their ancestors.

It's customary for the front steps and door of the church to be used only by important church officials and by the chuchkajaues, so you should go around to the right and enter by the side door.

Inside, the floor of the church may be spread with pine boughs and dotted with offerings of maize kernels, bouquets of flowers, bottles of liquor wrapped in corn husks and candles – candles everywhere. Many local families can trace their lineages back centuries, some even to the ancient kings of Quiché. The candles and offerings on the floor are in remembrance of the ancestors, many of whom are buried beneath the church floor just as Maya kings were buried beneath pyramids.

On the west side of the plaza is another little whitewashed church, the Capilla del Calvario, which is similar in form and function to Santo Tomás, but smaller.

Museo Regional

In the arcade facing the south side of the plaza is the Museo Regional. In the two large rooms of the museum you can see ancient clay pots and figurines, arrowheads and spearheads of flint and obsidian, copper axe-heads and *metates* (grindstones for maize).

The museum also holds the Rossbach jade collection, with several beautiful necklaces, figurines and other objects. Ildefonso Rossbach served as Chichi's Catholic priest for many years until his death in 1944.

The museum is open every day but Tuesday, from 8 am to noon and 2 to 5 pm.

Shrine of Pascual Abaj

Before you have been in Chichi very long, some village lad will offer to guide you (for a tip) to a hilltop on the outskirts to have a look at Pascual Abaj (Sacrifice Stone), which is the local shrine to Huyup Tak'ah (Mountain Plain), the Mayan earth god. Said to be hundreds – perhaps thousands – of years old, the stone-faced idol has suffered numerous indignities at the hands of outsiders, but local people still revere it. Chuchkajaues come here regularly to offer incense, food, cigarettes, flowers, liquor and Coca-Cola to the earth god, and perhaps even to sacrifice a chicken. The offerings are in thanks and hope for the earth's continuing fertility.

Sacrifices do not take place at regular hours. If you're in luck, you can witness one. The worshipers will not mind if you watch, and some (but not all!) won't mind if you take photographs, though they may ask if you want to make an offering (of a few quetzals) yourself. If there is no ceremony, you can still see the idol and enjoy the walk up to the pine-clad hilltop and the views of the town and valley.

There have been some incidents of robbery of tourists walking to visit Pascual Abaj, so the best plan is to join with others and go in a large group.

You don't really need a juvenile guide to find Pascual Abaj. Walk down the hill on 5a Av from Santo Tomás church, turn right onto 9a Calle and continue downhill along this unpaved road, which bends to the left. At the bottom of the hill, when the road turns sharply to the right, bear left and follow a path through the cornfields, keeping the ditch on your left. Signs mark the way. Walk to the buildings just ahead, which include a farmhouse and a morería. Greet the family here. If the children are not in school, you may be invited to see them perform a local dance in full costume on your return from Pascual Abaj (a tip is expected).

Walk through the farm buildings to the hill behind, and follow the switchback path to the top and along the ridge of the hill, called Turukaj, to a clearing in which you will see the idol in its rocky shrine. The idol looks like something from Easter Island. The squat stone crosses near it have many levels of significance for the Maya, only one of which pertains to Christ. The area of the shrine is littered with past offerings; the bark of nearby pines has been stripped away in places to be used as fuel in the incense fires.

Organized Tours

Two shuttle bus companies in Chichi offer shuttle services to and from Panajachel, Antigua, Guatemala City and Quetzaltenango: Chichi-Tours (☎ 756-1134, 756-1008), at the corner of 5a Calle and 5a Av Arco Gucumatz, Zona 1; and K'umarcaaj Tours (☎ 756-1226), 6a Calle 5-70, Local 1, Zona 1. With a minimum of three passengers (or an equivalent payment), Chichi-Tours will make trips to anyplace else you have in mind, including to the ruins at K'umarcaaj (near Santa Cruz del Quiché).

Places to Stay

Chichi does not have a lot of accommodations, and most places are in the higher price range. As rooms are scarce, it's a good idea to arrive early on Wednesday or Saturday if you want to secure a room for the Thursday and Sunday markets. Safe car parking is available in the courtyard of most hotels.

Budget *Hotel Girón* (☎ 756-1156, fax 756-1226), 6a Calle 4-52, Zona 1, is a pleasant, clean hotel; a good value. Singles/doubles are US$6/10 with shared bath, US$9.15/15 with private bath, or US$11/19 with private bath and cable TV.

Hotel Pascual Abaj (☎ 756-1055), 5a Av Arco Gucumatz 3-38, Zona 1, is a clean little place one long block north downhill from the Arco Gucumatz, an arched bridge over the road on the north of town. Rooms-with-bath cost US$7.50/10 for a single/double.

Of the cheap hotels, *Hospedaje Salvador* (☎ 756-1329), 5a Av 10-09, Zona 1, two blocks southwest of the Santo Tomás church, is the biggest. This large mazelike white-and-yellow building has 48 rooms on three floors. Singles/doubles/triples are US$4.15/6.65/10 with shared bath, or US$5/10/15 with private bath. You can get a discount if you come on your own, without children bringing you.

Hotel Posada Belén (☎ /fax 756-1244), 12a Calle 5-55, Zona 1, is up on a hill with a fine view. Rooms here are US$5/8.35/12.50 for a single/double/triple with shared bath, US$8.35/12/15 with private bath. You can pay US$1.65 more to get cable TV, and there's laundry service. Upstairs is the *Cafetería New York*; the owner is a Guatemalan who spent 14 years in New York and speaks English.

Posada El Arco (☎ 756-1255), 4a Calle 4-36 near the Arco Gucumatz, is a pleasant guesthouse where you will feel at home with the family. You can sit in the lawn chairs in the rear garden and enjoy a great view northwards toward the mountains of Quiché. All five rooms are spotless and have attractive decor. The three rooms with shared bath are US$10 for one or two people (US$7.50 if you stay two nights or more); two larger rooms with private bath are US$14 for two or $US17 for three people. The friendly owners, Emilsa and Pedro Macario, speak English and Spanish.

Middle *Hotel Chugüilá* (☎ 756-1134, fax 756-1279), 5a Av 5-24, is charming. Most of the 36 colonial-style rooms have private bath, some have a fireplace, and there are even a few two-room suites and a restaurant. For what you get, the price is very reasonable – US$15/19/24 for a single/double/triple without bath, US$31/36/41 with private bath.

Maya Lodge (☎ 756-1167), in the main plaza, has 10 rather dark rooms with clean add-on showers in the very midst of the market. Fairly plain despite some colonial touches, it is comfortable nonetheless, though overpriced. Rooms with shared bath are US$17/27 for a single/double; with private bath they are US$24/32.

Places to Eat

Budget On Sunday and Thursday, eat where the marketers do – at the cookshops set up in the center of the market. These are the cheapest in town. On other days, look for the little comedores near the post office and Guatel office on the road into town (7a Av).

Restaurant La Fonda del Tzijolaj, upstairs in the Centro Comercial Santo Tomás on the north side of the plaza, has everything: good views, nice decor, decent food and reasonable prices – US$2 to US$3 for breakfast, twice that for lunch or dinner. It's closed Tuesday. There are several other restaurants with portico tables in the Centro Comercial. At *La Villa de los Cofrades* you can while away the hours with checkers (draughts), backgammon and the best coffee in town. It's a popular place, with breakfast for around US$2.50, lunch or dinner around US$4.

The inner courtyard of the Centro Comercial Santo Tomás is a vegetable market on market days, a basketball court the rest of the time. Upstairs inside the courtyard, overlooking the vegetable market, *Cafetería Buenaventura* is clean, pleasant and one of the most economical places in town.

La Villa de los Cofrades No 2, upstairs overlooking the street at the corner of 6a Calle and 5a Av (enter from 6a Calle), has tables out on the balcony, overlooking the market street, as well as inside. It's run by the same owners as the original La Villa de los Cofrades, has the same good coffee and serves delicious food. An ample lunch or dinner with several courses and big portions costs around US$4 to US$6; simpler meals cost less.

Restaurant Tziguan Tinamit, across the street, takes its name from the Quiché Maya name for Chichicastenango. It's popular with locals and foreigners and is open all day every day.

Restaurant La Parrilla, at the corner of 5a Av Arco Gucumatz and 10a Calle, catty-corner from Hospedaje Salvador, is a good, economical little restaurant specializing in charcoal-grilled meats. Hearty meals are US$3 to US$5; breakfasts are cheaper. Half a block away, *Restaurant La Casa del*

Pueblo, at 5a Av Arco Gucumatz 9-81, is another popular little restaurant.

Pensión Chugüilá (see Places to Stay) is one of the most pleasant places to eat, and there are always a few other travelers to talk with about life on the road. Main-course plates are priced at US$5.

Middle The three dining rooms at the *Mayan Inn*, 8a Calle A and 3a Av on a quiet street one long block west of the plaza, have pale yellow walls, beamed ceilings, red-tiled floors, stocky colonial-style tables and chairs and decorations of colorful local cloth. Waiters wear traditional costumes, which evolved from the dress of Spanish farmers of the colonial era: colorful head-dress, sash, black tunic with colored embroidery, half-length trousers and squeaky leather sandals called *caïtes*. The daily set-price meals are the best way to order here; they cost US$6 for breakfast and US$12 for lunch or dinner, plus drinks and tip.

The *Hotel Santo Tomás*, 7a Av 5-32, has a good dining room, but it's often crowded with tour groups. Try to get one of the pleasant courtyard tables, where you can enjoy the sun and the marimba band, which plays at lunchtime on market days.

Getting There & Away

Bus Chichi has no bus station. Buses heading south to Guatemala City, Panajachel, Quetzaltenango and all other points reached from the Interamericana arrive and depart from 5a Calle at the corner of 5a Av Arco Gucumatz, Zona 1, which is one block south of the arch. Buses heading north to Santa Cruz del Quiché arrive and depart from around the corner on 5a Av Arco Gucumatz. Any bus heading south can drop you at Los Encuentros, where you can catch a bus to your final destination.

Antigua (170 km, 3½ hours) Take any bus heading for Guatemala City and change buses at Chimaltenango.

Guatemala City (144 km, 3½ hours, US$2.50) Buses every 20 minutes, 3:30 am to 6 pm.

Los Encuentros (17 km, 30 minutes, US$0.50) Take any bus heading for Guatemala City, Panajachel, Quetzaltenango and so on.

Nebaj (103 km, 4½ hours, US$2.50) Two buses daily, or take a bus to Santa Cruz del Quiché and change buses there.

Panajachel (37 km, 1½ hours, US$1.65) 11 buses daily (approximately hourly), 4:30 am to 2:30 pm; or take any bus heading south and change buses at Los Encuentros.

Quetzaltenango (94 km, three hours, US$6) Seven buses daily, mostly in the morning; or take any bus heading south and change at Los Encuentros.

Santa Cruz del Quiché (19 km, 30 minutes, US$0.50) Buses every 20 minutes from 6 am to 9 pm.

Minibus On market days, minibuses arrive around midmorning *en masse*, bringing tourists from Panajachel, Antigua, Guatemala City and Quetzaltenango. They park in front of the Hotel Santo Tomás and depart for the return trip around 2 pm. If you're in Chichi, you can usually catch a ride out on one of these (see Organized Tours).

SANTA CRUZ DEL QUICHÉ
Population 13,000

The capital of the department of Quiché (2020 meters) is 19 km north of Chichicastenango.

Without the bustle of the big market and the big tourism buses, Santa Cruz – which is usually called 'El Quiché' or simply 'Quiché' – is quieter and more typical of the Guatemalan countryside than is Chichi. The town is small and easy to navigate. There aren't many tourists here, but those who do come are treated well; the locals are friendly and will direct you anywhere you need to go.

Travelers who come to Quiché usually do so as a side trip from Chichi, or on their way to or from more remote places in the highlands (such as Nebaj, or the remote mountain route between Huehuetenango and Cobán), or to visit the K'umarcaaj ruins (Utatlán). A visit to the ruins is best done early in the morning, as you may have to walk to the ruins and back (or taxi from town).

Orientation

Everything you need is within a few short blocks of the church, which is on the east side of the central plaza, called Parque

Central. The bus station is about five blocks south and two blocks east of the church. The open-air market is one block east of the church.

Banco Industrial, on the northwest corner of the plaza, changes US dollars traveler's checks and cash and gives cash advances on Visa and MasterCard.

K'umarcaaj

The ruins of the ancient Quiché Maya capital are three km west of El Quiché along an unpaved road. Start out of town along 10a Calle and ask the way frequently. No signs mark the way and there is no regular transport, unless you hire a taxi in town. Consider yourself very lucky if you succeed in hitching a ride with other travelers who have their own vehicle. Admission to the site costs a few pennies.

The kingdom of Quiché was established in Late Post-Classic times (about the 1300s) from a mixture of indigenous people and Mexican invaders. Around 1400, King Gucumatz founded his capital at K'umarcaaj and conquered many neighboring cities. During the long reign of his successor Q'uikab (1425-1475), the kingdom of Quiché extended its borders to Huehuetenango, Sacapulas, Rabinal and Cobán, even coming to influence the peoples of the Soconusco region in Mexico.

The Cakchiquels, a vassal people who once fought alongside the Quichés, broke away from their former overlords and established their capital at Iximché during the 1400s.

Pedro de Alvarado led his Spanish conquistadors into Guatemala in 1524, and it was the Quichés, under their king, Tecún Umán, who organized the defense of the country. In the decisive battle fought near Quetzaltenango on February 12, 1524, Alvarado and Tecún found one another and locked in mortal combat. Alvarado won. The defeated Quichés invited the victorious Alvarado to visit their capital, where they secretly planned to kill him. Smelling a rat, Alvarado, with the aid of his Mexican auxiliaries and anti-Quiché Cakchiquels, captured the Quiché leaders instead, burned them alive, took K'umarcaaj (called Utatlán by his Mexican allies) and destroyed the city.

The history is more interesting than the ruined city, of which little remains but a few grass-covered mounds. Of the hundred or so large structures identified by archaeologists, only half a dozen are somewhat recognizable, and these are uninspiring. The site itself is a beautiful place for a picnic, shaded by tall trees and surrounded by defensive ravines, which failed to save the city from the conquistadors. Local prayer-men keep the fires of ancient Quiché burning, so to speak, by using the ruined K'umarcaaj as a ritual site. A long tunnel (cueva) beneath the plaza is a favorite spot for prayers and chicken sacrifices.

Places to Stay & Eat

Hotel San Pascual (☎ 755-1107), 7a Calle 0-43, Zona 1, a block south of the church, is a pleasant, clean hotel run by a dynamo señora who also runs a typing school for local children in a room off the lobby. It's a friendly place, with guests gathering to watch TV in the evening. Rooms are US$4/6/8 for a single/double/triple with shared bath, or US$6/10/14 with private bath.

The clean, modern Hotel Rey K'iche, 8a Calle 0-39, Zona 5, is between the bus station and the plaza, about two blocks from each. New in 1996, it has five rooms with shared bath for US$6.65 per person, and 20 rooms with private bath (some with color TV) for US$10 per person.

Comedor Fliper, 1a Av 7-31, 1½ blocks south of the church, is inexpensive, pleasant, small, clean and friendly. Guests from the Hotel San Pascual often walk around the corner to eat here. It's open every day, 7 am to 9 pm.

Restaurante El Torito Steak House, on 4a Calle half a block west of the plaza, serves breakfast for US$2; burgers or sandwiches are the same. The house specialty, filet mignon, is US$4.50 for breakfast, US$6 for a full dinner with soup and more. It's open every day. La Casona, on 2a Calle between 4a and 5a Avs, a few blocks northwest of the church, is another popular restaurant.

Getting There & Away

Many buses from Guatemala City to Chichicastenango continue to El Quiché (look for 'El Quiché' or just 'Quiché' on the signboard). The last bus from El Quiché headed south to Chichicastenango and Los Encuentros leaves midafternoon, so don't tarry too long here unless you want to spend the night.

El Quiché is the transport point for the sparsely populated and somewhat remote reaches of northern Quiché, which extends all the way to the Mexican border.

The bus station is about five blocks south and two blocks east of the plaza. Buses include:

Chichicastenango (19 km, 30 minutes, US$0.50) Take any bus heading for Guatemala City.

Guatemala City (163 km, 3½ hours, US$1.65) Buses every 20 minutes, 3 am to 4 pm.

Nebaj (84 km, four hours, US$1.65) Buses at 8 and 10 am, 12:30, 1 and 3:30 pm. Or take a bus to Sacapulas and change there.

Sacapulas (50 km, 1½ hours, US$1.15) Hourly buses, 9 am to 4 pm; or take any bus heading for Nebaj or Uspantán.

Uspantán (90 km, six hours, US$2) Buses at 10 and 11 am, noon and 1 pm; or take a bus to Sacapulas and change there.

NEBAJ
Population 9000

High among the Cuchumatanes lie the Ixil Maya village of Nebaj and its neighboring villages of Chajul and Cotzal. The scenery is breathtakingly beautiful, and the local people, remote from the cultural influences of TV and modern urbanity, proudly preserve their ancient way of life. Nebaj women wear very beautiful huipiles, and they make excellent handicrafts, mostly textiles.

Nebaj's location in this mountain fastness has been both a blessing and a curse. The Spaniards found it difficult to conquer, and they wreaked destruction on the inhabitants when they did. In recent years guerrilla forces made the area a base of operations, and the army took strong measures to dislodge them. Many small villages were destroyed, with their surviving inhabitants being herded into 'strategic hamlets,' as in the Vietnam War.

Travelers come to Nebaj for the scenery, the local culture, the excellent handicrafts, the market (Thursday and Sunday) and, during the second week in August, the annual festival.

If you're in Nebaj, consider taking this pleasant walk. Leave Nebaj on the road heading to Chajul. After walking 10 or 15 minutes, you'll reach a bridge over a small river. Just before the bridge, turn left onto a gravel road and follow the river. Walking downriver for 45 minutes to an hour, you'll pass several small waterfalls before reaching a larger waterfall about 25 meters high.

Places to Stay & Eat

Pensión Las Tres Hermanas is the best-known lodging, charging US$1 for a bed and the same price for a meal. There's no sign, but local children will bring you here from the bus. The *Hospedaje de la Esperanza* charges US$2.50 per night, but they also charge extra for bathroom tissue, hot water and so on. A new hotel in Nebaj is more expensive but very pleasant. Other alternatives include the *Pensión Las Gemelitas* and the *Hotel Ixil*.

Getting There & Away

Buses come to Nebaj from Santa Cruz del Quiché, Huehuetenango, Sacapulas and Cobán. Pickup trucks also provide transport, at a fare equivalent to that of the bus.

Coming from the Cobán side, you have to change buses several times – it's about five hours from Cobán to Uspantán, three hours from Uspantán to Sacapulas, and 2½ hours from Sacapulas to Nebaj. It's easier to reach Nebaj from Huehuetenango or from Santa Cruz del Quiché, going via Sacapulas, as buses are more frequent.

USPANTÁN
Population 2800

Uspantán is a small village on the road between Sacapulas and Cobán. Rigoberta Menchú, the 1992 Nobel Peace Prize laureate, grew up in the mountains around Uspantán; travelers who have read her works might be interested to spend some time here. If you travel this way by bus, you may find yourself spending the night here.

Pensión Galindo, about three blocks from the church and the plaza, charges US$2.50 and is a fine place to stay. On the same street, *Comedor Central* is basic but good.

Two buses a day leave Uspantán for Sacapulas, at 3 am and 9 pm. It's a bad road, taking three hours to cover about 40 km between the two towns.

Southwestern Highlands

The departments of Quetzaltenango, Totonicapán and Huehuetenango are more mountainous and less frequented by tourists than regions closer to Guatemala City. The scenery here is just as beautiful and the indigenous culture just as colorful and fascinating. Travelers going to and from the border post at La Mesilla find these towns welcome breaks from long hours of travel, and there are some interesting possibilities for excursions as well.

Highlights of a visit to this area include Quetzaltenango, Guatemala's second-largest city; the pretty nearby town of Zunil, with its Fuentes Georginas hot springs; Totonicapán, a department capital noted for its handicrafts; the Friday market at San Francisco El Alto; the blanket-makers of Momostenango; and the restored Maya city of Zaculeu near Huehuetenango. Quetzaltenango is achieving a reputation for its Spanish-language schools, which attract students from around the world.

CUATRO CAMINOS

Following the Interamericana westward from Los Encuentros, the road twists and turns ever higher into the mountains, bringing still more dramatic scenery and cooler temperatures. After 58 km you come to another important highway junction known as Cuatro Caminos (Four Roads). The road east leads to Totonicapán

(12 km), west to Quetzaltenango (13 km) and north (straight on) to Huehuetenango (77 km). Buses pass through Cuatro Caminos, shuttling to/from Totonicapán and Quetzaltenango, about every half hour from 6 am to 6 pm.

SAN MIGUEL TOTONICAPÁN
Population 9000

If you want to visit a pleasant, pretty Guatemalan highland town with few other tourists in sight, Totonicapán (2500 meters) is the place to go. Buses shuttle into the center of town from Quetzaltenango (passing through Cuatro Caminos) frequently throughout the day.

The ride from Cuatro Caminos is along a beautiful pine-studded valley. As you approach the town you pass a large hospital on the left. Turn around the enormous Minerva fountain and enter town along 17a Av.

Totonicapán's main plaza has the requisite large colonial church as well as a municipal theater, built in 1924 in the neoclassical style and recently restored. Buses go directly to the parque (as the plaza is called) and drop you there.

Market days are Tuesday and Saturday; it's a locals' market, not a tourist market, and it winds down by late morning.

Two km from the parque are the Agua Caliente hot springs, a popular bathing place for local people.

Casa de la Cultura Totonicapense
This cultural center (☎ /fax 766-1575), 8a Av 2-17, Zona 1, to the left of the Hospedaje San Miguel, has displays of indigenous culture and crafts. The museum administers a wonderful 'Meet the Artisans' program to introduce tourists to artisans and local families.

In 1991, artisans of the local Quiché community proposed to Señor Carlos Umberto Molino, director of the Casa de la Cultura Totonicapense, a program to interest tourists in visiting local handicrafts workshops. The program is now the most interesting activity in town. Starting at 10 am and lasting till about 4 pm, you meet local artisans, toymakers, potters, carvers of wooden masks and musical instruments, weavers and musicians – watch them work, listen to their music, see their dances, experience their living conditions and eat a homecooked lunch. Cost for the program depends on the number of people in the group, with prices ranging from US$42 per person for four people to US$20 per person for 15 people or more, and the money goes directly to the artisans and musicians involved. An extended program includes a one-night stay with a local family, for US$15 per person including meals.

The Casa de la Cultura also offers other, less expensive but equally interesting and worthwhile programs, including a tour of Totonicapán town (US$4 to US$8 per person) and a rural tour of the local Quiché region (US$5 to US$12.50 per person, depending on the number of people in the group).

Special Events

Totonicapán celebrates the Fiesta de Esquipulas on January 15 in Cantón Chotacaj, three km from the parque.

The festival of the Apparition of the Archangel Michael is on May 8, with fireworks and traditional dances. More dances follow on the last Sunday in June, with the Festival of Traditional Dance held in the Plaza Central from 9 am to 2 pm. There's also the Feria Titular de San Miguel Arcángel (Name-Day Festival of the Archangel St Michael) from September 24 to 30, with the principal celebration being on the 29th.

Places to Stay

On the way into town, one block before the parque, the *Hospedaje San Miguel* (☎ 766-1452) is on the left at 3a Calle 7-49, Zona 1. It's a tidy place, not what you'd call Swiss-clean but good for the price. Singles/doubles are US$5/10 with shared bath, or US$6/11 with private bath. The rooms with private bath tend to be larger, with three beds. Flash heaters provide the hot water, which is thus fairly dependable.

QUETZALTENANGO

Population 90,000

Quetzaltenango (2335 meters) is the commercial center of southwestern Guatemala. It is Guatemala's second-largest city and the center of the Quiché Maya people. It's called Xelajú or simply Xela (SHAY-lah) by its Quiché Maya citizens, who still use the original Quiché name for the site where the Spanish conquistadors built their town. Towering over the city to the south is the 3772-meter Santa María volcano, with the active 2488-meter Santiaguito volcano on its southwestern flank.

Xela's good selection of hotels in all price ranges makes it an excellent base for excursions to the nearby towns and villages, which are noted for their handicrafts and hot springs. In recent years, Xela has built a good, worldwide reputation for its Spanish-language schools.

History

Quetzaltenango came under the sway of the Quiché Maya of K'umarcaaj when they began their great expansion in the 1300s. Before that it had been a Mam Maya town. For the story of Tecún Umán, the powerful leader of the Quichés, and Pedro de Alvarado, see the K'umarcaaj section of Santa Cruz del Quiche.

In the mid-1800s, when the Federation of Central America was founded, Quetzaltenango initially decided on federation with Chiapas and Mexico instead of with Central America. Later changing its mind, the city joined the Central American Federation and became an integral part of Guatemala in 1840.

With the late 19th-century coffee boom, Quetzaltenango's wealth increased. This is where the finca owners came to buy supplies and where the coffee brokers had their warehouses. Things went along fine, with the city getting richer and richer, until a dual calamity – an earthquake and a volcanic eruption – brought mass destruction and an end to the boom.

The city's position at the intersection of the roads to the Pacific Slope, Mexico and Guatemala City guarantees it some degree

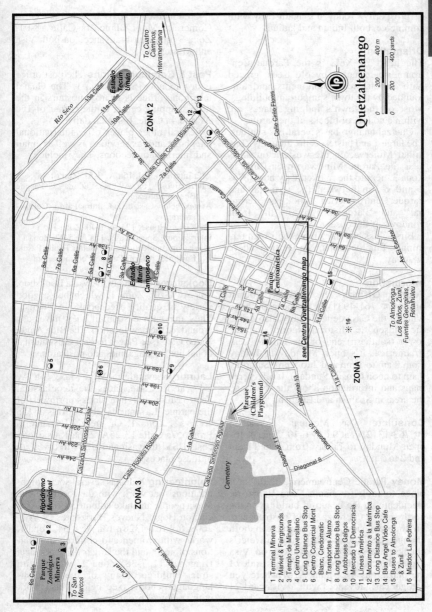

Quetzaltenango

ZONA 2

ZONA 1

ZONA 3

Río Seco

Estadio Tecún Umán

Estadio Mario Camposeco

Parque Centroamérica

see Central Quetzaltenango map

Hipódromo Municipal

Parque Zoológico Minerva

Cemetery

Parque (Children's Playground)

To Cuatro Caminos, Interamericana

To San Marcos

To Almolonga, Los Baños, Zunil, Fuentes Georginas, Retalhuleu

1   Terminal Minerva
2   Market & Fairgrounds
3   Templo de Minerva
4   Centro Universitario
5   Long Distance Bus Stop
6   Centro Comercial Mont
    Blanc; Credomatic
7   Transportes Alamo
8   Long Distance Bus Stop
9   Autobuses Galgos
10 Mercado La Democracia
11 Líneas América
12 Monumento a la Marimba
13 Long Distance Bus Stop
14 Blue Angel Video Cafe
15 Buses to Almolonga
    & Zunil
16 Mirador La Pedrera

GUATEMALA

of prosperity. Today it's again busy with commerce, both Indian and ladino.

Orientation
The heart of Xela is the Parque Centroamérica, shaded by old trees, graced with neoclassical monuments and surrounded by the town's important buildings. Most of the town's lodging places are within a couple of blocks of the parque.

Quetzaltenango has several bus stations. The largest and busiest is the 2nd-class Terminal Minerva, on the western outskirts near the Parque Minerva on 6a Calle in Zona 3, next to the market. City buses Nos 2 and 6 run between the terminal and Parque Centroamérica – look for 'Terminal' and 'Parque' signs in the front windows of the buses.

First-class bus lines have their own terminals. For locations, see Getting There & Away.

Information
Tourist Offices The INGUAT tourist office (☎ 761-4931) is in the right-hand wing of the Casa de la Cultura (also called the Museo de Historia Natural), at the lower (southern) end of the Parque Centroamérica. It's open Monday to Friday from 8 am to 1 pm and 2 to 5 pm, Saturday 8 am to noon (closed Sunday). It offers free maps and information about the town and the area, in Spanish and English.

Consulate The Mexican Consulate (☎ 763-1312) is at 9a Av 6-19, Zona 1. It's open Monday to Friday from 8 to 11 am and 2 to 3 pm.

Money Parque Centroamérica is the best place to look for banks. The Banco de Occidente, in the beautiful building on the north side of the plaza, and Construbanco, on the east side of the plaza, can both change US dollars cash and traveler's checks and give cash advances on Visa cards. Banco Industrial, on the east side of the plaza, has a 24-hour ATM where you can get cash advances with a Visa card 24 hours a day.

Credomatic (☎ 763-5722), in the Centro Comercial Mont Blanc, 4a Calle 18-01, Zona 3, gives cash advances on both Visa and MasterCard.

Post & Communications The post office is at 4a Calle 15-07, Zona 1. The Guatel telephone office is nearby, upstairs in the little shopping center at the corner of 15a Av and 4a Calle. It's open daily.

Several other places offer international telephone and fax services, as well as email and Internet connections. They include:

Alfa Internacional, 15a Av 3-51, Zona 1
Alternativos, 16a Av 3-35, Zona 3, Parque Benito Juárez
Arytex, below Casa de la Cultura, Parque Centroamérica
The Green House, 12a Av 1-40, Zona 1
International Speed Calls, 15a Av 5-22, Zona 1
Maya Communications, Bar/Salon Tecún, Pasaje Enriquez, just off Parque Centroamérica

Bookstores Check out the Vrisa Bookshop, 15a Av 0-67, Zona 1, which has a good variety of quality used books in English. They may move soon; if they have, ask around for the new location. The Blue Angel Video Cafe (see Places to Eat) sells international books, magazines and postcards.

Laundry Lavandería Mini-Max, 14a Av C47, at 1a Calle, faces the neoclassical Teatro Municipal, five blocks northwest of the parque. Lavandería El Centro is at 15a Av 3-51, Zona 1. Or there's Lavandería Pronto, 7a Calle 13-25A, Zona 1. One load costs US$1 to wash and US$1 to dry at all of these places.

Volunteering Xela has several social organizations that work with the local Quiché Maya people and take volunteers. The Asociación Hogar Nuevos Horizontes (☎ 761-2608, fax 761-4328), 13a Av 8-34, Zona 1, works with women and children in situations of need, and the Hogar de Esperanza, Diagonal 11 7-38, Zona 1, works with street children. Many of the Spanish-language schools (see below) also work with volunteer programs.

Parque Centroamérica

The parque and the buildings surrounding it are pretty much what there is to see in Xela. Start your tour at the southern (lower) end and walk around the square counter-clockwise. The Casa de la Cultura holds the **Museo de Historia Natural**, which holds exhibits on the Maya, on the Liberal revolution in Central American politics and on the Estado de Los Altos, of which Quetzaltenango was the capital. Marimbas, the weaving industry, stuffed birds and animals, and other local lore all claim places here. It's fascinating because it's funky. It's open Monday to Friday, 8 am to noon and 2 to 6 pm, Saturday 9 am to 1 pm; admission is US$1.

Just off the southeastern corner of the parque is a small **market** devoted largely to handicrafts and daily necessities, a convenient spot for a little shopping.

The once-crumbling **cathedral** has been rebuilt in the last few decades. The façade of the colonial building was preserved, and a modern sanctuary built behind it.

The city's Town Hall, or **Municipalidad**, at the northeastern end of the parque, follows the grandiose neoclassical style so favored as a symbol of culture and refinement in this wild mountain country.

On the west side of the parque between 4a and 5a Calles is the palatial **Pasaje Enriquez**, built to be lined with elegant shops, but as Quetzaltenango has few elegant shoppers, it has suffered decline.

At the southwest corner of the parque, on the corner of 12a Av and 7a Calle, is the **Museo del Ferrocarril de los Altos**, a museum focusing on the railroad that once connected Xela and Retalhuleu. Upstairs is an art museum, with mostly modern art, and schools of art, dance and marimba. Hours and admission are the same as at the Museo de Historia Natural.

Other Sights

Walk north on 14a Av to 1a Calle to see the impressive neoclassical **Teatro Municipal**, which holds regular performances. Inside are three tiers of seating, the lower two of which have private boxes for prominent families; each box is equipped with a vanity for the ladies.

Mercado La Democracia, in Zona 3, is about 10 blocks northwest of the Parque Centroamérica. To get there, walk along 14a Av to 1a Calle (to the Teatro Municipal), turn left, turn right onto 16a Av, cross the major street called Calle Rodolfo Robles, and the market is on your right. It's an authentic Guatemalan city market with fresh produce and meat, foodstuffs and necessities for city dweller and villager alike.

Less than a kilometer northwest of the Parque Centroamérica, near the Terminal Minerva, is the **Parque Minerva** with its neoclassical Templo de Minerva, built to honor the classical goddess of education and to inspire Guatemalan youth to new heights of learning.

Near the Templo de Minerva is the Parque Zoológico Minerva, a zoo with a children's playground and carnival rides; it's open Tuesday to Sunday, 9 am to 5 pm. A large outdoor market is also nearby.

The Mirador La Pedrera, a 15-minute walk from the center, offers a fine view over the city.

Courses

Language Studies In recent years, Xela has built a good reputation for its Spanish-language schools, which attract students from around the world. Unlike Antigua, which has had a similar reputation for a lot longer, Xela is not overrun with foreigners; there is a small student social scene.

Most of the Spanish schools here in Xela are somehow involved in social action programs working with the local Quiché Maya people, providing students opportunities to get involved. Prices for the schools vary a little, but not much; the standard is US$100/110/120 per week for four/five/six hours of instruction per day, from Monday to Friday, including room and board with a local family, or around US$85 per week without homestay. Reputable schools (there are more!) include:

GUATEMALA

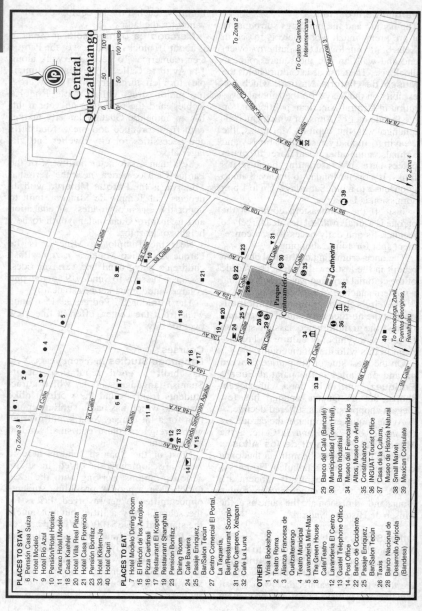

PLACES TO STAY
6   Pensión Casa Suiza
7   Hotel Modelo
9   Hotel Río Azul
10 Pensión/Hotel Horiani
11 Anexo Hotel Modelo
18 Casa Kaehler
20 Hotel Villa Real Plaza
21 Hotel Casa Florencia
23 Pensión Bonifaz
33 Hotel Kiktem-Ja
40 Hotel Capri

PLACES TO EAT
7   Hotel Modelo Dining Room
15 El Rincón de los Antojitos
16 Pizza Cardinali
17 Restaurant El Kopetín
19 Restaurant Shanghai
23 Pensión Bonifaz
     Dining Room
24 Cafe Baviera
25 Pasaje Enríquez,
     Bar/Salón Tecún
27 Centro Comercial El Portal,
     La Taquería,
31 Pollo Campero, Xelapan
     Bar/Restaurant Scorpio
32 Cafe La Luna

OTHER
1   Vrisa Bookshop
2   Teatro Roma
3   Alianza Francesa de
     Quetzaltenango
4   Teatro Municipal
5   Lavandería Mini-Max
8   The Green House
     Cafe/Teatro
12 Lavandería El Centro
13 Guatel Telephone Office
14 Post Office
22 Banco de Occidente
25 Pasaje Enríquez,
     Bar/Salón Tecún
26 Taxis
28 Banco Nacional de
     Desarrollo Agrícola
     (Bandesa)
29 Banco del Café (Bancafé)
30 Municipalidad (Town Hall),
     Banco Industrial
34 Museo del Ferrocarril de los
     Altos, Museo de Arte
35 Construbanco
36 INGUAT Tourist Office
37 Casa de la Cultura,
     Museo de Historia Natural
38 Small Market
39 Mexican Consulate

Centro de Estudios de Español Pop Wuj – 1a Calle 17-22, Zona 1 (Apdo Postal 68) (☎/fax 761-8286, net)

Desarrollo del Pueblo (Progress of the People) – a good, small school; 20a Av 0-65, Zona 1 (☎ 761-2932, 763-1190, ☎/fax 761-6754)

English Club International Language School – classes in Spanish, Quiché and Mam languages; Diagonal 4 9-71, Zona 9 (☎ 763-2198)

Escuela de Español Sakribal – 10a Calle 7-17, Zona 1 (Apdo Postal 164) (☎/fax 761-5211, net)

Guatemalensis Spanish School – 19a Av 2-14, Zona 1 (fax 763-2198)

Instituto de Estudios de Español y Participación en Ayuda Social (INEPAS) – English, French and Spanish spoken; 15a Av 4-59 at 5a Calle, Zona 1 (☎/fax 765-2584, 765-1308)

Juan Sisay Spanish School – 15a Av 8-38, Zona 1 (Apdo Postal 392) (fax 763-1684, net)

Kie-Balam Spanish School – Diagonal 12 4-46, Zona 1 (☎ 761-1636, fax 761-0391)

Weaving La Escuela de Tejer (The Weaving School) offers the opportunity to learn weaving from master weavers from various different cooperatives. Classes are two hours per day; cost is US$50 per week. If you want, they can arrange a homestay with a local family, probably a traditional Maya home in which weaving is practiced, for less than US$5 per night. The school is based at Casa Argentina, Diagonal 12, No 8-37, Zona 1. For further information you can telephone Bethania in Guatemala City (☎ 361-2470) or Mark Camp in the USA (☎ (508) 433-9831).

Weaving lessons are also offered at the Cooperativa Santa Ana in Zunil; see the Around Quetzaltenango section.

Organized Tours
Thierry Roquet, the Frenchman-turned-Guatemalan who runs the restaurant El Rincón de los Antojitos (see Places to Eat), organizes a variety of tours around the region. Contact him at the restaurant, or at the INEPAS language school, for details. The folks at the Casa Kaehler (see Places to Stay) also offer tours.

Two-day weekend climbs up Volcán Tajumulco – at 4220 meters the highest volcano (and indeed the highest point) in Central America – are organized by the Casa Argentina, Diagonal 12, No 8-37, Zona 1.

Places to Stay
Budget Cheap hostelries are concentrated at the northern end of the Parque Centroamérica along 12a Av and south of the parque more or less behind the Casa de la Cultura.

Pensión/Hotel Horiani (☎ 763-0815), officially at 12a Av 2-23 though you enter on 2a Calle, is a simple but clean little family-run hospedaje with six rooms. Singles/doubles are US$3.35/4.20 with shared hot bath.

Hotel Capri (☎ 761-4111), 8a Calle 11-39, Zona 1, a block from the Parque Centroamérica and behind the Casa de la Cultura, has rooms for US$4.20 per person with private bath. It's a basic place, and some of the rooms are quite dark; ask to see a room before you pay.

Pensión Casa Suiza (☎ 763-0242), 14a Av 'A' 2-36, Zona 1, has 18 basic rooms grouped around a big courtyard. Singles/doubles are US$5/7.50 with shared bath, US$11/13 with private bath, and there's a cheap comedor. Some readers have complained of noise and brusque management here.

Casa Kaehler (☎ 761-2091), 13a Av 3-33, Zona 1, is an old-fashioned European-style family pension with seven rooms of various shapes and sizes. Room 7, with private bath, is the most comfortable; it's US$8/10 for one/two people. Otherwise, rooms with shared bath are US$7/8/9 for a single/double/triple. This is an excellent, safe place for women travelers; ring the bell to gain entry. Ask them about tours in the region. Avoid the *Hotel Radar 99*, next door, which has many problems.

The *Rincón de los Antojitos* (see Places to Eat) has a room in the rear with private bath and cable TV for US$5/6, or US$6/9.35 with breakfast. They also rent two spacious apartments, about a 10-minute walk from the town center, for US$8.35/59/200 by the day/week/month; each has two bedrooms, fully-equipped kitchen, living room, courtyard and cable TV. They also arrange homestays with local families and provide tours and other services for travelers. French, English and Spanish are spoken.

Southwest of the parque is the huge old *Hotel Kiktem-Ja* (☎ 761-4304), in the Edificio Fuentes, a colonial-style building at 13a Av 7-18, Zona 1. The 20 rooms, all with private bath and eight with fireplace, are on two levels around the courtyard, which also serves as a car park. Rooms hold one to eight people; singles/doubles are US$10/13.35.

Hotel Río Azul (☎ /fax 763-0654), 2a Calle 12-15, Zona 1, offers luxury compared to its neighbors. All of the rooms have private bath, and some have color TV. Prices are pretty good for what you get: US$11/14/16 for a single/double/triple. Breakfast and dinner are served, and there's a car park.

Middle If you want to spend a little more for a lot more comfort, head straight for the family-run *Hotel Modelo* (☎ 761-2529, 763-0216, fax 763-1376), 14a Av A 2-31, Zona 1. Pleasant small rooms with bath, cable TV and phone are US$28/32 in the main hotel (three rooms with fireplace are the same price), US$18/22 in the equally comfortable annex. The hotel's good dining room serves breakfast (7:15 to 9:30 am), lunch (noon to 2 pm) and dinner (6 to 9 pm) daily.

Hotel Casa Florencia (☎ 761-2326), 12a Av 3-61, Zona 1, just a few steps from the plaza, is run by a pleasant señora who keeps everything spotless. The nine spacious rooms, all with bath, cable TV and carpet, are US$21/25/30 for a single/double/triple. Breakfast is served in the dining room, and there's parking.

Places to Eat

As with hotels, Quetzaltenango has a good selection in all price ranges. Cheapest are the food stalls in and around the small market near the Casa de la Cultura, where snacks and substantial main-course plates are sold for US$1 or less.

Cafe Baviera, at the corner of 13a Av and 5a Calle, is a pleasant European-style cafe. It has good coffee and is a great place for breakfast. Other meals, pastries, snacks and alcoholic beverages are also served. It's open every day.

A popular spot with good food is the tiny *El Rincón de los Antojitos*, 15a Av at 5a Calle, Zona 1. The menu is mostly Guatemalan, with a few concessions to international tastes and a variety of vegetarian dishes. The specialty of the house is pepian (chicken in a special sesame sauce), a typical indigenous Guatemalan dish, for US$5. English, Spanish and French are spoken.

Cafe La Luna, at the corner of 8a Av and 4a Calle, Zona 1, is a pleasant little place to hang out, drink coffee, write letters and socialize with friends.

Blue Angel Video Cafe, 7a Calle 15-22, Zona 1, is popular with Spanish-language students. Prices are very economical, and there's a good variety of excellent, healthy foods to choose from. All the salads and veggies are sterilized. Alcohol is served. It's open every day, 2 to 11:30 pm (see Entertainment).

The *Bar/Salon Tecún* in Pasaje Enriquez, on the west side of the parque, is another popular spot for foreigners to gather in the evening. Good Italian food is served, and there's plenty of drinking and socializing. It's open every day, noon to 3 pm and 5 pm to 1 am.

Pizza Cardinali, 14a Av 3-41, Zona 1, serves tasty pizza and pasta dishes. In the same block, *Restaurant El Kopetin*, at No 3-51, has red tablecloths, natural wood, a family atmosphere and a long menu ranging from hamburgers to Cuban-style sandwiches to filet mignon. An average full meal costs around US$5; alcohol is served. Both are open every day.

A couple of other pleasant restaurants are in the Centro Comercial El Portal, 13a Av 5-38, Zona 1. *La Taquería* is a bright, cheerful Mexican restaurant with excellent prices: full meals are US$2 to US$4. Also here, the *Bar/Restaurant Scorpio* has lunch specials or burgers for US$2.65, main dishes for US$4. The big fireplace is pleasant in the evening. Both have tables inside and out on the patio.

Restaurant Shanghai, 4a Calle 12-22, Zona 1, is convenient to the parque. The cuisine is Guatemalan Chinese: pato (duck), camarones (shrimp) and others for about US$3.35 to US$5 per plate.

Pollo Campero, 5a Calle half a block east of the parque, serves inexpensive fried chicken, burgers and breakfast every day. Next door, *Xelapan* is a decent bakery open every day from 5:15 am to 8 pm.

The dining room of the *Hotel Modelo*, 14a Av 'A' 2-31, serves breakfast and has good set-price lunches and dinners (US$5.50).

The dining room of the *Pensión Bonifaz*, (☎ 761-2182, 761-2279, fax 761-2850), 4a Calle 10-50, Zona 1, at the northeast corner of the parque, is the best in town. This is where the local social set comes to dine and be seen. Food is good, and prices, though high by Guatemalan standards, are low when compared to those even in Mexico. Soup, main course, dessert and drink can run to US$12, but you can spend about half that much if you order only a sandwich and a beer.

Entertainment

It gets very chilly when the sun goes down, so you won't want to sit out in the Parque Centroamérica enjoying the balmy breezes – there aren't any. Nevertheless, it's softly lit and still a pleasant place for an evening stroll.

The *Green House Cafe/Teatro* (☎ /fax 763-0271), 12a Av 1-40, Zona 1, is a pleasant venue for concerts, live theater, poetry readings, films and open-mike nights. It also has billiards, chess, backgammon and other games and a restaurant/bar. It's open Tuesday to Saturday, 4 pm until around midnight.

Performances and cultural events are also presented at the beautiful Teatro Municipal on 1a Calle, and at the Casa de la Cultura (☎ 761-6427) on the south side of the parque. The *Teatro Roma*, on 14a Av 'A', facing the Teatro Municipal, sometimes plays interesting movies.

The *Alianza Francesa de Quetzaltenango* (☎ 761-4076), 14a Av A, No A-20, Zona 1, opposite the Teatro Municipal, offers free French films with Spanish subtitles once a week and other activities.

Videos are shown every night at 8 pm at the *Blue Angel Video Cafe* (see Places to Eat); the US$0.85 admission includes a bowl of popcorn. The video schedule is posted on the door, or you can choose a video from the list on the back of the menu and play it before 6 pm. The cafe here is popular for socializing in the evening, as is the *Bar/Salon Tecún* in Pasaje Enriquez (see Places to Eat).

The bar at the four-star *Pensión Bonifaz* (see Places to Eat) is the place for more high-class socializing.

Getting There & Away

Bus For 2nd-class buses, head out to the Terminal Minerva, near the Parque Minerva, on 6a Calle in Zona 3, next to the market. City bus Nos 2 and 6 run between the terminal and Parque Centroamérica (look for 'Terminal' and 'Parque' signs in the front window of the bus). You can catch the city bus (US$0.10) to the terminal from 8a Calle at 12a Av or 14a Av in the town center.

The busy Terminal Minerva has almost hourly buses to many highlands destinations.

Buses that depart from Terminal Minerva and head for the Interamericana pick up passengers at bus stops at the corner of 20a Av and 7a Calle, as well as at the corner of 14a Av and 4a Calle, and at the corner of 7a Av (Calzada Independencia) and 8a Calle (Calle Cuesta Blanca) as they head out of town. You can board them at any of these stops, though you may have a better chance of getting a seat if you board at the terminal.

Transportes Alamo, Líneas América and Autobuses Galgos, three 1st-class lines operating buses between Guatemala City and Quetzaltenango, each have their own terminals. Transportes Alamo (☎ 761-2964) is at 14a Av 3-60, Zona 3. Líneas América (☎ 761-2063, 761-4587) is at 7a Av 13-33, Zona 2. Autobuses Galgos (☎ 761-2248) is at Calle Rodolfo Robles 17-83, Zona 1.

All the following buses depart from Terminal Minerva, unless otherwise noted.

Almolonga (for Los Vahos; six km, 10 minutes, US$0.35) Buses every 15 minutes from 5:30 am to 5 pm, departing from Terminal Minerva, with a possible stop for additional passengers in Zona 4 southeast of the parque.

Chichicastenango (94 km, 2½ hours, US$1.35) Buses at 6, 8:30, 9:30, 10:15 and 11 am, 12:30, 1:30, 2:30 and 4 pm. If you don't get one of these, change at Los Encuentros.

Ciudad Tecún Umán (Mexican border; 129 km, 2½ hours, US$1.65) Buses every half hour, 5:30 am to 4:30 pm.

El Carmen/Talismán (Mexican border) Take a bus to Coatepeque, and change there to a direct bus to El Carmen. From Coatepeque it's two hours to El Carmen (US$1.65).

Guatemala City (206 km, four hours, US$4.20) 1st-class buses with Transportes Alamo three or four times daily, with Líneas América six times daily, and with Autobuses Galgos six times daily, each departing from their own terminals (see above). First-class buses stop at Totonicapán, Los Encuentros (change for Chichicastenango or Panajachel) and Chimaltenango (change for Antigua). Second-class buses depart from Terminal Minerva every half-hour, 3 am to 4:30 pm, but make many stops on the way, so take longer to get there.

Huehuetenango (90 km, two hours, US$1) Buses every half hour, 5:30 am to 5:30 pm.

La Mesilla (Mexican border; 170 km, 3½ hours, US$3.35) Buses every half-hour, 5:30 am to 5:30 pm. Or, bus to Huehuetenango and change there.

Momostenango (35 km, 1½ hours, US$0.50) Hourly buses, 6:30 am to 5 pm.

Panajachel (99 km, 2½ hours, US$2) Buses at 5:30, 6:30, 8 and 10 am, noon, 1, 2 and 4 pm. Or, take any bus bound for Guatemala City and change at Los Encuentros.

Retalhuleu (67 km, one hour, US$0.85) Buses every 20 minutes, 4:30 am to 6 pm. (Look for 'Reu' on the bus, 'Retalhuleu' won't be spelled out.)

San Francisco El Alto (17 km, one hour, US$0.50) Buses every 15 minutes, 6 am to 6 pm.

Totonicapán (30 km, one hour, US$0.35) Buses every 15 minutes, 6 am to 5 pm, departing from the Parque Central Rotonda.

Zunil (10 km, 15 minutes, US$0.25) Buses every half-hour, 7 am to 7 pm, departing from Terminal Minerva, with a possible additional pick-up in Zona 4, southeast of the parque.

Shuttle Minibus Pana Tours (☎ /fax 765-1209, 763-0606), 12a Av 7-12, offers shuttle service to Guatemala City, Antigua, Chichicastenango, Panajachel and other places around Guatemala, including places nearby such as Fuentes Georginas, Zunil and so on.

Car Rental car companies in Xela include Geo Rental (☎ 763-0267), 13a Av 5-38, Zona 1, Comercial El Portal, and Tabarini (☎ 763-0418), 9a Calle 9-21, Zona 1.

AROUND QUETZALTENANGO
The beautiful volcanic countryside around Quetzaltenango has numerous possibilities for outings. The natural steam baths at Los Vahos are very primitive, but the outing into the hills surrounding the city can be fascinating whether you take a steam bath or not. The steam baths at Almolonga are basic but also cheap and accessible. The hot springs at Fuentes Georginas are idyllic.

Take note of the market days: Sunday in Momostenango, Monday in Zunil, Tuesday and Saturday in Totonicapán and Friday in San Francisco El Alto.

Buses from Quetzaltenango to Almolonga, Los Baños and Zunil depart several times per hour from Terminal Minerva; some buses stop at the corner of 9a Av and 10a Calle, Zona 1, to take on more passengers.

Los Vahos
If you're a hiker, and if the weather is good, you might enjoy a trip to the rough-and-ready sauna/steam baths at Los Vahos (The Vapors), 3.5 km from Parque Centroamérica. Take a bus headed for Almolonga and ask to get out at the road to Los Vahos, which is marked with a small sign reading 'A Los Vahos.' From here it's a 2.3-km uphill walk to Los Vahos. Views of the city on a clear day are remarkable.

If you're driving, follow 12a Av south from the parque to its end, turn left, go two blocks and turn right up the hill; this turn is 1.2 km from the parque. The remaining 2.3 km of unpaved road is steep and rutted, with a thick carpet of dust in the dry season, mud in the rainy season (when you may want a 4WD vehicle). Take the first turn along the dirt road (it's an unmarked sharp right). At the second bear left (this is badly marked).

The road ends at Los Vahos, where you can have a sauna/steam bath for only a few quetzals and (if you've brought food with you) a picnic. Los Vahos is open every day, 8 am to 6 pm; admission is US$1.

Zunil
Population 6000

Zunil (2076 meters) is a pretty agricultural and market town in a lush valley framed by steep hills and dominated by a towering volcano. As you approach it along the road from Quetzaltenango, you will see it framed as if in a picture, with its white colonial church gleaming above the red-tiled and rusted tin roofs of the low houses.

On the way to Zunil the road passes Almolonga, a vegetable-growing town four km from Quetzaltenango. Just over a kilometer beyond Almolonga, on the left side of the road, is Los Baños, an area with natural hot sulfur springs. Several little places along here have bath installations; most are quite decrepit, but if a hot bath at low cost is your desire, you may want to stop. Tomblike enclosed concrete tubs rent for a few quetzals per hour. (Thierry, the Frenchman at the El Rincón de los Antojitos restaurant, likes El Manantial the best.)

Winding down the hill from Los Baños, the road skirts Zunil and its fertile gardens on the right side before intersecting the Cantel to El Zarco road. A bridge crosses a stream to lead into the town; it's one km from the bridge to the plaza.

Zunil, founded in 1529 as Santa Catarina Zunil, is a typical Guatemalan country town. The things that make it so beautiful are its setting in the mountains and the indigenous agriculture practiced here. The agricultural plots, divided by stone fences, are irrigated by canals; you'll see the farmers scooping up water from the canals with a shovel-like instrument and throwing it over their plants. Women wash their clothes near the river bridge, in pools of hot water that come out of the rocks.

Things to See & Do Another attraction of Zunil is its particularly pretty church. Its ornate façade, with eight pairs of serpentine columns, is echoed inside by a richly worked altar of silver. On market day (Monday) the plaza in front of the church is bright with the predominantly red traditional garb of the local Quiché Maya people buying and selling.

Half a block downhill from the church plaza, the Cooperativa Santa Ana is a handicrafts cooperative in which over 500 local women participate. Handicrafts are displayed and sold here, and weaving lessons are offered. It's open Monday to Saturday from 8:30 am to 5 pm, Sunday 2 to 5 pm.

While you're in Zunil, visit the image of San Simón, an effigy of a local Maya hero venerated as a saint (though not of the church) by the local people, who bring him offerings of rum, cigarettes, flowers and candles. The effigy, propped up in a chair, is moved each year to a different house; ask any local where to find San Simón, everyone will know (local children will take you for a small tip). You'll be charged a couple of quetzals to see him.

The festival day of San Simón is held each year on October 28, after which he moves to a new house. The festival of Santa Catarina Alejandrí, official patron saint of Zunil, is celebrated on November 25. Almolonga celebrates its annual fair on June 27.

Getting There & Away From Zunil, which is 10 km from Quetzaltenango, you can continue to Fuentes Georginas (nine km), return to Quetzaltenango via the Cantel road (16 km), or alternately, take the jungle-bound toll road down the mountainside to El Zarco junction and the Pacific Slope Highway. Buses depart every 10 minutes, 6 am to 6:30 pm, for the return trip to Quetzaltenango (one hour, US$0.25).

Fuentes Georginas

Imagine a steep, high wall of tropical verdure – huge green leaves, ganglions of vines, giant ferns, spongy moss and profusions of tropical flowers – at the upper end of a lush mountain valley. At the base of this wall of greenery is a limpid pool of naturally warm mineral water. A pure white statue of a Greek goddess gazes benevolently across the misty water as families happily splash and play, clambering out for a drink or a snack at a rustic restaurant right at the pool's edge. This is Fuentes Georginas, the prettiest spa in Guatemala. Though the setting is intensely tropical, the mountain air currents keep it deliciously cool all day.

Besides the restaurant, there are three sheltered picnic tables with cooking grills (bring your own fuel). Down the valley a few dozen meters are seven rustic but pleasant cottages for US$7/9/11 for a single/double/triple. Each cottage has a shower, a BBQ area and a fireplace to ward off the mountain chill at night (wood and matches are provided).

Trails here lead to two nearby volcanoes: Volcán Zunil (three hours, one way) and Volcán Santo Tomás (five hours, one way). Going with a guide is essential, so you don't get lost. Guides are available (ask at the restaurant) for US$10 for either trip, whatever the number of people in the group.

Fuentes Georginas is open every day from 8 am to 6 pm; admission is US$1. Bring a bathing suit, which is required.

Getting There & Away Take any bus to Zunil, where pickup trucks wait to give rides the eight km up the hill to the springs, a half-hour ride. Negotiate the price for the ride. It's very likely they'll tell you it's US$4 roundtrip, and when you arrive at the top, tell you it's US$4 *each way* – this is an irritating game the pickup drivers play. If there are many people in the group, they may charge US$1 per person. Unless you want to walk back down the hill, arrange a time for the pickup driver to return to pick you up.

You can walk from Zunil to Fuentes Georginas in about two hours. If you're the mountain goat type, you may enjoy this; it's a strenuous eight-km climb.

Hitchhiking is not good on the Fuentes Georginas access road, as there are few cars

and they are often filled to capacity with large Guatemalan families. The best days to try for a ride are Saturday and Sunday, when the baths are busiest.

If you're driving, walking or hitching, go uphill from Zunil's plaza to the Cantel road (about 60 meters), turn right and go downhill 100 meters to an unpaved road on the left marked 'Turicentro Fuentes Georginas, 8 km.' (This road is near the bus stop on the Quetzaltenango-Retalhuleu road – note that there are three different bus stops in Zunil.) This unpaved road heads off into the mountains; the baths are nine km from Zunil's plaza.

You'll know you're approaching the baths when you smell the sulfur in the air.

San Francisco El Alto
Population 3000

High on a hilltop (2610 meters) overlooking Quetzaltenango (17 km away) stands the market town of San Francisco El Alto. Six days a week it's a sleepy sort of place, but on Friday it explodes with activity. The large plaza, surrounded by the requisite church and Municipalidad and centered on a cupola-like mirador (lookout), is covered in country goods. Stalls spill into neighboring streets, and the press of traffic is so great that a special system of one-way roads is established to avoid monumental traffic jams. Vehicles entering the town on market day must pay a small fee.

San Francisco's market is not heavy with handicrafts as are those in Chichicastenango and Antigua. (One reader asked us to pass on the tip, beware of pickpockets in the market!)

Great views can be had from the roof of the church. The caretaker will let you go up.

The annual festival day is October 5.

Places to Stay & Eat Most people come to San Francisco as a day trip from Quetzaltenango. This is just as well, since the lodging and eating situation in San Francisco is dire. If you're in need of a bed, you'll have to suffer the *Hotel y Cafetería Vista Hermosa*, 3a Av 2-22, Zona 1. Its 25 rooms are ill-kept (though a few on the front enjoy good views), service is nonexistent and the cafeteria rarely has any food to serve. Doubles cost US$4 with shared bath, US$5.50 to US$7.50 with private shower.

As for eating, *Comedor San Cristóbal*, near the Hospedaje San Francisco de Assis, may be your best bet, but that's not saying much.

Momostenango
Population 7500

Beyond San Francisco El Alto, 22 km from Cuatro Caminos (35 km from Quetzaltenango) along a fairly rough unpaved country road, this village in a pretty mountain valley is Guatemala's famous center for the making of *chamarras*, thick, heavy woolen blankets. The villagers also make ponchos and other woolen garments. As you enter the village square after an hour of bashing over the bad road, you will see signs inviting you to watch the blankets being made and to purchase the finished products. The best time to do this is on Sunday, which is market day; haggle like mad. A basic good blanket costs around US$10, perhaps twice as much for an extra-heavy 'matrimonial.'

You might also want to hike three km north to the hot springs of Pala Chiquito, where the blankets are washed and the dyes fixed. It has a cool water swimming pool and private hot bath rooms; admission is US$1 or less.

Momostenango is also noted for its adherence to the ancient Maya calendar and for observance of traditional rites. Hills about two km west of the plaza are the scene of these ceremonies, coordinated with the important dates of the calendar round. Unfortunately, it's not as easy to witness these rites as it is to visit the Shrine of Pascual Abaj at Chichicastenango.

Picturesque diablo (devil) dances are held here in the plaza a few times a year, notably on Christmas Eve (December 24) and New Year's Eve (December 31). The homemade devil costumes can get quite elaborate: all have masks and cardboard wings, and some go whole hog with fake fur suits, heavily sequined outfits and more.

Dance groups gather in the plaza and dance to a five-to-13-piece band, drinking alcoholic refreshments during the breaks. For entertainment sake, they are at their best around 3 pm, but the festivities go on late into the night.

The annual fair, Octava de Santiago, is celebrated from July 28 to August 2.

Courses The Kuinik Ta'ik Language School (see Online Resources appendix) offers instruction in the Quiché (sometimes spelled K'iche') language; US$75 a week covers 12 hours of instruction, room and board with a local Quiché family and a weekly day trip. Their office is in the Hotel Ixchel.

The Teklib'al Maya Cultural School offers classes in the Maya calendar and culture. Its director, Rigoberto Itzep Chanchavac, is a day-keeper and traditional Sacerdote Maya (Maya priest), which involves advising the community on special days of the Maya calendar and natural medicine. Class size is limited to three or four, and a solid knowledge of Spanish is required. The office is on 2a Calle (also called Calle Morazán), about 300 meters east of Hotel Paclom. Neither school has a telephone. Of you need to call them, you might try to contact them through the ADIFAM office.

Volunteering ADIFAM, a nongovernmental agency, works with educating the local Quiché children in 46 communities within the municipality of Momostenango. Most of these children are seasonal laborers, and thus they cannot attend normal school on a regular basis. Volunteers of any nationality are welcome to help out, especially anyone who has experience working with children or with organic gardening. The villagers are quite enthusiastic about ADIFAM, and it's a meaningful volunteer effort. The ADIFAM office (☎ /fax 736-5036, net) is in the Hotel Ixchel. UNICEF also does projects here.

Places to Stay & Eat New in 1997, the *Hotel Ixchel*, 1a Calle 4-15, Zona 1, has eight rooms sharing two large communal bathrooms for US$2.50 per room, plus two large rooms with private bath (one with a shower, the other a tub) for US$3.50 per room. It's 150 meters west of the Hotel Paclom on the same street, across the river.

Other places to stay in Momostenango are none too pleasant. *Casa de Huéspedes Paclom* charges US$5 for a bare double room; water to the toilets is shut off at night, there is no shower in the hotel and the food is no treat. *Hospedaje Roxana*, on the plaza, charges US$1, which may be too much. There are several basic comedores on the plaza.

Getting There & Away Catch an early bus from Quetzaltenango's Terminal Minerva, or at Cuatro Caminos, or at San Francisco El Alto. There are five or six buses daily, the last one returning from Momostenango by about 2:30 pm.

Another bus route departs from the west side of the plaza and goes through Pologua, which might be an advantage to travelers heading for Huehuetenango or La Mesilla. The road is basically in the same condition; same bumps, different scenery.

HUEHUETENANGO
Population 20,000

Separated from the capital by mountains and a twisting road, Huehuetenango (1902 meters) has that self-sufficient air exuded by many mountain towns. Coffee-growing, mining, sheep-raising, light manufacturing and agriculture are the main activities in this region.

The lively Indian market is filled daily with traders who come down from the Sierra de los Cuchumatanes, the mountain range (highest in Central America) that dominates the department of Huehuetenango, and which is now also protected by national park status. Surprisingly, the market area is about the only place you'll see colorful traditional costumes in this town, as most of its citizens are ladinos who wear modern clothes.

For travelers, Huehuetenango is usually a stage on the journey to or from Mexico. After leaving San Cristóbal de las Casas or Comitán in Mexico, and then crossing the border, Huehuetenango is the logical place to spend your first night in Guatemala. It's a good introduction to Guatemalan highlands life.

History
Huehuetenango was a Mam Maya region until the 1400s when the Quichés, expanding from their capital at K'umarcaaj near present-day Santa Cruz del Quiché, pushed them out. Many Mam fled into neighboring Chiapas, which still has a large Mam-speaking population near its border with Guatemala. In the late 1400s, the weakness of Quiché rule brought about civil war, which engulfed the highlands and provided a chance for Mam independence. The troubles lasted for decades, coming to an end in the summer of 1525 after the arrival of Gonzalo de Alvarado, brother of Pedro, who conquered the Mam capital of Zaculeu for the king of Spain.

Orientation
The town center is five km north of the Interamericana. The bus terminal and new market are located three km from the highway along the road to the town center (6a Calle).

Almost every service of interest to tourists is in Zona 1 within a few blocks of the plaza. The old market, bordered by 1a and 2a Avs and 3a and 4a Calles in Zona 1, is still the busy one, especially on Wednesday, which is market day. Four blocks west of the market on 5a Av between 2a and 3a Calles is the main plaza, called the parque central, the very center of town and the reference point for finding any other address. Hotels and restaurants are mostly near the parque, except for one or two small hotels near the bus station and one motel out on the Interamericana.

Information
The post office is at 2a Calle 3-54, next to the Guatel telephone office opposite the Hotel Mary, half a block east of the plaza. If you don't find the Guatel office here, look for it at 4a Av 6-54, four blocks south

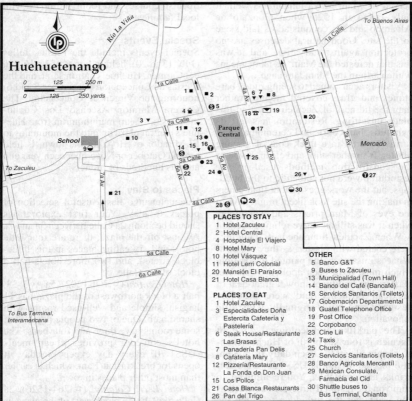

Huehuetenango

0   125   250 m
0   125   250 yards

School

To Zaculeu

To Bus Terminal,
Interamericana

Río La Viña

To Buenos Aires

1a Calle

Parque Central

Mercado

PLACES TO STAY
1 Hotel Zaculeu
2 Hotel Central
4 Hospedaje El Viajero
8 Hotel Mary
10 Hotel Vásquez
11 Hotel Lerri Colonial
20 Mansión El Paraíso
21 Hotel Casa Blanca

PLACES TO EAT
1 Hotel Zaculeu
3 Especialidades Doña
   Estercita Cafetería y
   Pastelería
6 Steak House/Restaurante
   Las Brasas
7 Panadería Pan Delis
8 Cafatería Mary
12 Pizzería/Restaurante
   La Fonda de Don Juan
15 Los Pollos
21 Casa Blanca Restaurants
26 Pan del Trigo

OTHER
5 Banco G&T
9 Buses to Zaculeu
13 Municipalidad (Town Hall)
14 Banco del Café (Bancafé)
16 Servicios Sanitarios (Toilets)
17 Gobernación Departamental
18 Guatel Telephone Office
19 Post Office
22 Corpobanco
23 Cine Lili
24 Taxis
25 Church
27 Servicios Sanitarios (Toilets)
28 Banco Agrícola Mercantil
29 Mexican Consulate,
   Farmacia del Cid
30 Shuttle buses to
   Bus Terminal, Chiantla

of the Parque Central; this is its temporary address while their regular office is being remodeled.

There is a Mexican consulate on 5a Av 4-11, near the corner of 4a Calle, in the same building as the Farmacia Del Cid; it's open Monday to Friday, 9 am to noon and 3 to 5 pm.

Town-operated *servicios sanitarios* (toilets) are on 3a Calle between 5a and 6a Av, only a few steps west of the plaza; and 4a Calle near the intersection with 2a Av. Farmacias (chemists) and banks are dotted around the center.

Parque Central

Huehuetenango's main plaza is shaded by nice old trees and surrounded by the town's imposing buildings: the Municipalidad (with its band shell on the upper floor) and the huge colonial church. The plaza has its own little relief map of the department of Huehuetenango.

Zaculeu

Surrounded by natural barriers – ravines and a river – on three sides, the late Post-Classic religious center of Zaculeu occupies a strategic defensive location that served its Mam Maya inhabitants well. It only failed in 1525 when Gonzalo de Alvarado and his conquistadors laid siege to the site. Good natural defenses are no protection against starvation, and it was this that defeated the Mam. Its name means white earth in the Mam language.

Visitors accustomed to seeing ruddy bare stones and grass-covered mounds rather than the tidiness of Zaculeu may find this place unsettling. Restoration has left its pyramids, ball courts and ceremonial platforms covered in a thick coat of graying plaster. It's rather stark and clean. Some of the construction methods used in the restoration were not authentic to the buildings, but the work goes farther than others in making the site look like it might have to the eyes of Mam priests and worshipers when it was still an active religious center.

When Zaculeu flourished, its buildings were coated with plaster, as they are now. What is missing is the painted decoration, which must have been applied to the wet plaster. The buildings show a great deal of Mexican influence and were probably designed and built originally with little innovation.

The parklike archaeological zone of Zaculeu is four km north of Huehuetenango's main plaza. It's open daily from 8 am to 6 pm; admission is US$0.20. Cold soft drinks are available. You're allowed to climb on the restored structures as much as you want, but it's forbidden to climb the grassy mounds that await excavation.

From the Parque Central, you can reach Zaculeu by several routes. Jitney trucks and vans depart from in front of the school, on 2a Calle near the corner of 7a Av; they depart every 30 minutes (or possibly hourly), 7:30 am to 7:30 pm, and cost US$0.10 for the 20-minute ride to the ruins. Or you can take a taxi from the central plaza for US$5 roundtrip, with a half-hour to spend at the ruins. To walk all the way from the main plaza takes about 45 minutes.

Language Courses
The Xinabajul Spanish Academy (☎ /fax 964-1518), 6a Av 0-69, offers one-to-one

Spanish courses and room and board with local families.

Special Events
Special events include the Fiestas Julias (July 13 to 20), held in honor of La Virgen del Carmen, Huehue's patron saint, and the Fiestas de Concepción (December 5 and 6) honoring the Virgen de Concepción. The Carrera Maratón Ascenso Los Cuchumatanes, a 12-km marathon run from Huehue's central plaza up into the mountains to El Mirador overlooking the town, is held around October or November each year and attracts hundreds of runners.

Places to Stay
Huehuetenango has a useful selection of places to stay. Your first explorations should be along 2a Calle between 3a and 7a Av, just off the plaza; there are four little hotels and six eating places in this three-block stretch, and two more hotels half a block off 2a Calle.

Hotel Central (☎ 764-1202), 5a Av 1-33, half a block northwest of the plaza, has 11 largish, simple and well-used rooms with shared bath. One or two people pay US$4; some rooms have three and four beds. The hotel's comedor provides cheap meals (US$1.70) every day except Sunday. It opens for breakfast at 7 am, which is earlier than most other places in town.

Hotel Lerri Colonial (☎ 764-1526), 2a Calle 5-49, half a block west of the plaza, is another tidy, convenient place, with 21 rooms around a courtyard. Rooms for one or two people are US$2.50/3.35 per person with shared/private bath. In the courtyard is a comedor and parking.

Across the street, *Hospedaje El Viajero*, 2a Calle 5-30, is not as good, but it's cheap, with rooms for US$1.65 per person sharing bathrooms with cold showers. The *Mansión El Paraíso* (☎ 764-1827), 3a Av 2-41, is a similar place with the same prices.

Hotel Mary (☎ 764-1618, fax 764-1228), 2a Calle 3-52, is a block east of the plaza facing Guatel. It's a cut above the other places: the 25 small rooms have bedspreads and other nice touches. The ground-floor *Cafetería Mary* is handy, as is the *Panadería Pan Delis* bakery/cafe next door. Rooms for one or two people are US$6/7.50 with shared bath, or US$12 with private bath and cable TV.

Hotel Vásquez (☎ 764-1338), 2a Calle 6-67, has a car park in the front and 20 small, fairly cheerless but very clean rooms at the back. Singles/doubles/triples are US$3.50/5.70/7.50 with shared bath, or US$4.20/6.65/9.30 with private bath.

Hotel Zaculeu (☎ 764-1086, fax 764-1575), 5a Av 1-14, half a block northwest of the plaza, is a colonial-style place with a lovely garden courtyard, a good dining room, laundry service and 37 rooms, all with private bath and cable TV. In the older downstairs section, rooms near the hotel entrance open onto the courtyard and are preferable to those at the back of the hotel; these are US$15/24/32 for singles/doubles/triples. Rooms in the newer upstairs section are US$31/40 for singles/doubles.

Hotel Casa Blanca (☎ /fax 764-2586), 7a Av 3-41, is such a bright, pleasant hotel that it's tempting to say it's the best place in town. The 15 rooms, all with private bath and cable TV, are US$18/26 for singles/doubles. There's private parking, too, and two lovely restaurants are open daily from 6 am to 10 pm.

On the Interamericana, two km northwest of the turn-off to Huehuetenango and about seven or eight km from the center of town, are several motels.

Places to Eat
Especialidades Doña Estercita Cafetería y Pastelería, on 2a Calle west of the plaza, is a tidy, cheerful place serving pastries as well as more standard dishes. The *Cafetería Mary* and *Panadería Pan Delis* (see Places to Stay, above) are next door to each other at 2a Calle 3. Another good bakery is the *Pan del Trigo*, 4a Calle 3-24, which usually has whole-grain breads; the cafeteria here, open every day, offers economical breakfasts and dinners for US$2.

The *Pizzería/Restaurante La Fonda de Don Juan*, 2a Calle 5-35, a few steps from the Parque Central, is a clean, pleasant place. It's open every day.

Los Pollos, 3a Calle between 5a and 6a Av, half a block west of the plaza, is open 24 hours a day. Two pieces of chicken with salad, chips and a soft drink cost US$2.85. Burgers and smaller chicken meals are even cheaper.

One of Huehue's best restaurants is the *Steak House/Restaurante Las Brasas*, on 4a Av just off 2a Calle, half a block from the Parque Central, where a full meal of Chinese food or steak (the specialties here) should cost no more than US$7 or so. Alcohol is served, and it's open every day.

For lovely surroundings, you can't beat the two restaurants at the *Hotel Casa Blanca* (see Places to Stay), one inside and another outdoors in the garden. Breakfasts are around US$3.35, burgers or sandwiches no more than US$1.65, and steaks (try filet mignon or cordon bleu) are under US$6. Both are open every day from 6 am to 10 pm.

Getting There & Away
Bus The bus terminal is in Zona 4, two km southeast of the plaza along 6a Calle. Buses serving this terminal include:

Cuatro Caminos (74 km, 1¾ to two hours, US$1) Take any bus heading for Guatemala City or Quetzaltenango.
Guatemala City (270 km, five hours, US$4.20) Buses at 2, 3, 8:30, 9:30 and 10 am.
La Mesilla (Mexican border; 84 km, 1½ to two hours, US$1) Buses every half-hour, 6 am to 5 pm.
Quetzaltenango (90 km, two hours, US$1) Hourly buses, 4 am to 6 pm.
Sacapulas (62 km, four hours, US$2) Buses at 11:30 am and 1 pm.
Todos Santos Cuchumatán (40 km, 2½ hours, US$1.20) 11:30 am, 12:30, 1 and 4 pm.

Shuttle buses between the bus terminal and the center of town depart from 4a Calle at the corner of 4a Av from 2 am to 11 pm, running every five minutes in daytime, every half hour at night; cost is US$0.10. A taxi between the bus terminal and the center of town costs US$1.65.

Car Tabarini Rent A Car (☎ 764-1951) has an office here.

AROUND HUEHUETENANGO

El Mirador is a lookout point up in the Cuchumatanes mountains, overlooking Huehuetenango, 12 km from town. On a sunny day it offers a great view of the entire region and its many volcanoes. A beautiful poem, *A Los Cuchumatanes*, is mounted on plaques here. This is the destination for annual marathon races (see Special Events in Huehuetenango). Getting to El Mirador is easiest with a private vehicle; a taxi roundtrip from town is expensive (around US$30).

LA MESILLA

There is a distance of four km between the Mexican and Guatemalan immigration posts at La Mesilla/Ciudad Cuauhtémoc, and you must take a collective taxi (US$1). There is no bank on either the Guatemalan or Mexican side, but moneychangers will do the deal – at a good rate if you're changing dollars, a terrible one for pesos or quetzales. There are good onward connections from Huehuetenango and Comitán, so just take the next bus from the border post to either of these cities.

TODOS SANTOS CUCHUMATÁN
Population 2000

If you're up for a trek into the Cuchumatanes, four buses per day depart from Huehuetenango on the 40-km ride to Todos Santos Cuchumatán. The road is rough, the mountain air chilly and the journey slow, but the scenery is spectacular.

The picturesque town of Todos Santos Cuchumatán (2450 meters) is one of the few in which the traditional Maya calendar is still remembered and (partially) observed, and where both men and women still wear their traditional clothing. Saturday is market day, with a smaller market on Wednesday.

It's possible to take some vigorous treks from the town into the mountains and to rejuvenate in the traditional Mam sauna. From Todos Santos you can ride a horse or walk (all day) to San Juan Atitán village.

Todos Santos is famous for the annual horse races held on the morning of November 1, which culminate a week of festivities and an all-night drinking spree the night before. Traditional foods are served throughout the day, and there are mask dances. Christmas posadas are held on each of the 10 days leading up to Christmas, with locals making processions through the streets, recreating the peregrinations of Joseph and Mary, leading up to the birth of Jesus.

If you're coming to Todos Santos in winter, bring warm clothes, as it's cold at this high altitude, especially at night.

Language Courses

La Hermandad Educativa, Proyecto Lingüístico offers Spanish classes for US$100 per week, including room and board with a local family. You can just show up, or contact them in the USA (PO Box 205-337, Sunset Park, NY 11220-0006).

Places to Stay & Eat

Hospedaje Casa Familiar, 30 meters south of the plaza, was built in 1995. It's clean but rustic, and there's hot water and a sauna. The rooms have plenty of blankets, windows and a fine view; cost is US$2.50 per person. Breakfast is available. It's upstairs over a handicrafts shop, which is next door to the Comedor Katy. Todos Santos is very cold in winter, so you'll need those blankets.

Otherwise, accommodations consist of two primitive, cheap hospedajes: *Tres Olguitas* and *La Paz*. There are also rooms in private homes. People with rooms to rent will probably solicit your business as you descend from your bus, and charge US$1 per person. Try the house attached to the cafe and shop *Ruinas de Tecumanchun*.

A few small comedores provide food; *Comedor Katy* is perhaps the best. Another comedor, on the plaza, is cheaper than the Katy and is also good.

Getting There & Away

Buses operate between Huehuetenango and Todos Santos four times daily (40 km, 2½ hours, US$1.20). Buses, which are run to take villagers into Huehue for shopping and then home again, start early in the morning, around 4 am, and the last bus of the day departs in early afternoon. Ride on the top of the bus, if you like – the bus goes slow and the views are spectacular.

Pacific Slope

A lush, humid region of tropical verdure, Guatemala's Pacific Slope is the southeasterly extension of Mexico's Soconusco, a hot, fertile coastal plain. The volcanic soil is rich, good for growing coffee at the higher elevations, and palm oil seeds and sugar cane at the lower. Vast fincas exploit the land's economic potential, drawing seasonal workers from the highland towns and villages, where work is scarce. Along the Pacific shore are endless stretches of beaches of dark volcanic sand. The temperature and humidity along the shore are always uncomfortably high, day and night, rainy season and dry. The few small resorts attract mostly local – not foreign – beachgoers.

A fast highway, the Carretera al Pacífico (CA-2), runs from the border crossings at Ciudad Hidalgo/Tecún Umán and Talismán/El Carmen to Guatemala City. The 275 km between the Mexican border at Tecún Umán and Guatemala City can be covered in about four hours by car, five by bus – much less than the 342 km of the Interamericana through the western highlands between La Mesilla and Guatemala City, which takes seven hours. If speed is your goal, the Pacific Slope is your route.

Most of the towns along the Carretera al Pacífico are muggy, somewhat chaotic and hold little of interest for travelers. The beach villages are worse – unpleasantly hot, muggy and dilapidated. There are exceptions, though. Retalhuleu, a logical stopping place if you're coming from the Mexican border, is pleasant and fun to visit. Nearby is the active archaeological dig at Abaj Takalik. The pre-Olmec stone carvings at Santa Lucía Cotzumalguapa, eight km west of Siquinalá, and those at La

Democracia, nine km south of Siquinalá, are unique.

The small beach resort village of Monterrico, with its nature reserve and wildlife preservation project, is becoming popular with foreigners who come from Antigua and Guatemala City on weekends. Otherwise, the port town of Iztapa and its beach resort of Likín are fine if you simply must get to the beach. South of Guatemala City, Lago de Amatitlán is the citified version of the more beautiful Lago de Atitlán.

CIUDAD TECÚN UMÁN

This is the preferable and busier of the two Pacific Slope border-crossings, with a bridge linking Ciudad Tecún Umán (Guatemala) with Ciudad Hidalgo (Mexico). The border posts are open 24 hours a day. Basic hotels and restaurants are available, but you'll want to get through the border and on your way as soon as possible.

Minibuses and buses run frequently between Ciudad Hidalgo and Tapachula, 38 km to the north. From Ciudad Tecún Umán there are frequent buses heading east along the Carretera al Pacífico, stopping at Coatepeque, Retalhuleu, Mazatenango and Escuintla before climbing into the mountains to Guatemala City. If you don't find a bus to your destination, take any bus to Coatepeque or, preferably, Retalhuleu, and change buses there.

EL CARMEN

Though you can cross at El Carmen, you will encounter much less hassle and expense if you cross at Tecún Umán.

A toll bridge across the Río Suchiate connects Talismán (Mexico) and El Carmen (Guatemala). The border-crossing posts are open 24 hours every day. Minibuses and trucks run frequently between Talismán and Tapachula, a half-hour (20 km) away.

There are few services at El Carmen, and those are very basic. There is good bus service from El Carmen to Malacatán, on the San Marcos-Quetzaltenango road, and to Ciudad Tecún Umán, 39 km to the south. Fairly frequent 1st-class buses run to

GUATEMALA

Guatemala City along the Carretera al Pacífico (278 km, five to six hours, US$6). Transportes Galgos (☎ 232-3661, 253-4868), 7a Av 19-44, Zona 1, Guatemala City, is one company operating along this route. It runs five buses daily from El Carmen, stopping at Ciudad Tecún Umán, Coatepeque, Retalhuleu, Mazatenango and Escuintla (change for Santa Lucía Cotzumalguapa). Rutas Lima has a daily bus to Quetzaltenango via Retalhuleu and El Zarco junction.

COATEPEQUE

Set on a hill in the midst of lush coffee plantations, Coatepeque is a brash, fairly ugly and chaotic commercial center, noisy and humid at all times. The town is several kilometers north of the Carretera al Pacífico, and there is no reason to stop here.

Of the town's hotels, the 39-room *Hotel Mansión Residencial* (☎ 775-2018), 0 Av 11-49, Zona 2, is about the best, with double rooms with bath for US$8.35 per person.

EL ZARCO JUNCTION

About 40 km east of Coatepeque and nine km east of Retalhuleu on the Carretera al Pacífico is El Zarco, the junction with the toll road north to Quetzaltenango. The road winds up the Pacific Slope, carpeted in tropical jungle, rising more than 2000 meters in the 47 km from El Zarco to Quetzaltenango. The toll is less than US$1. Just after the upper toll booth, the road divides at Zunil: the left fork goes to Quetzaltenango via Los Baños and Almolonga (the shorter route); the right fork goes via Cantel. For information on these places and the beautiful Fuentes Georginas hot springs near Zunil, see Around Quetzaltenango in Guatemala's Highlands chapter.

RETALHULEU

Population 40,000

The Pacific Slope is a rich agricultural region, and Retalhuleu (240 meters) is its clean, attractive capital – and proud of it. Most Guatemalans refer to Retalhuleu simply as Reu (RAY-oo).

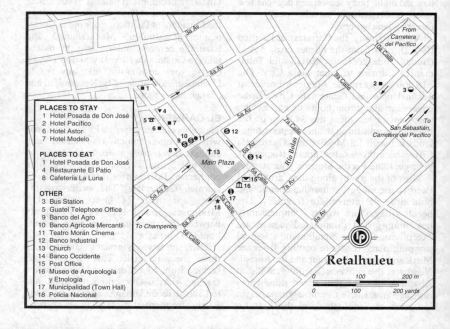

PLACES TO STAY
1 Hotel Posada de Don José
2 Hotel Pacífico
6 Hotel Astor
7 Hotel Modelo

PLACES TO EAT
1 Hotel Posada de Don José
4 Restaurante El Patio
8 Cafetería La Luna

OTHER
3 Bus Station
5 Guatel Telephone Office
9 Banco del Agro
10 Banco Agrícola Mercantil
11 Teatro Morán Cinema
12 Banco Industrial
13 Church
14 Banco Occidente
15 Post Office
16 Museo de Arqueología y Etnología
17 Municipalidad (Town Hall)
18 Policía Nacional

To Champerico

From Carretera del Pacífico

To San Sebastián, Carretera del Pacífico

Main Plaza

Retalhuleu

0   100   200 m
0   100   200 yards

If Coatepeque is where the coffee traders conduct business, Retalhuleu is where they come to relax, splashing in the pool at the Posada de Don José and sipping a cool drink in the bar. You'll see their expensive, big 4WD vehicles parked outside. The rest of the citizens get their kicks strolling through the plaza between the whitewashed colonial church and the wedding-cake government buildings, shaded by royal palms.

The balmy tropical air and laid-back attitude are restful. Tourists are something of a curiosity in Reu and are treated very well.

Orientation & Information

The town center is four km southwest of the Carretera al Pacífico along a grand boulevard lined with towering palm trees. The bus station is on 10a Calle between 7a and 8a Avs, Zona 1, about 400 meters northeast of the plaza. To find the plaza, look for the twin church towers and walk toward them.

Most of the services you may need are within two blocks of the plaza. There is no official tourist office, but people in the Municipalidad, on 6a Av facing the east side of the church, will do their best to help.

The post office is on 6a Av between 5a and 6a Calles. Guatel, at 5a Calle 4-50.

Banco Occidente, 6a Calle at the corner of 6a Av, and Banco Industrial, 6a Calle at the corner of 5a Av, both change US dollars cash or traveler's checks, and give cash advances on Visa cards. Banco del Agro, on 5a Av facing the parque, changes US dollars cash and traveler's checks, and gives cash advances on MasterCard.

Things to See & Do

There's little to see in Retalhuleu proper, but about 30 km to the west is the active archaeological dig at Abaj Takalik (see below).

The Museo de Arqueología y Etnología, 6a Av opposite the church, is a small museum of archaeological relics. Upstairs are historical photos and a mural showing locations of 33 archaeological sites in the department of Retalhuleu. It's open Tuesday to Sunday, 9 am to 1 pm and 2 to 5 pm; admission US$0.15.

You can swim in the pools at the Siboney and La Colonia hotels (see Places to Stay) even if you're not staying there. Cost is US$0.65 at the Siboney, US$1.65 at La Colonia, where there's also a poolside bar and food service.

Places to Stay

There are budget places to stay in Reu and several low-priced, central hotels. Two of the most convenient are just half a block west of the plaza. The better of the two is the *Hotel Astor* (☎ 771-2562, fax 771-2564), 5a Calle 4-60, Zona 1, with a pretty courtyard and 15 well-kept rooms, each with ceiling fan, private bath and color cable TV. Singles/doubles are US$10/20, and there's private parking.

Hotel Modelo (☎ 771-0256), 5a Calle 4-53, Zona 1, opposite the Hotel Astor, is a similar place with seven clean rooms on two floors around a central courtyard. The rooms are of different sizes, with ceiling fans and private bath; singles/doubles are US$8/12 and there's private parking.

For a real cheapie, you could try the very basic *Hotel Pacífico*, 7a Av 9-29, around the corner from the bus station. Rooms are US$2.50 per person, with shared bath.

The nicest place in town is the *Hotel Posada de Don José* (☎ 771-0963, 771-0841, ☎ /fax 771-1179), 5a Calle 3-67, Zona 1, across the street from the former railway station and two blocks northwest of the plaza. On weekends the Don José is often filled with finca owners in town for relaxation; at other times you can get an air-conditioned room with color cable TV, telephone and private bath for about US$23/30/36 a single/double/triple; sometimes reductions are offered. The 23 rooms are on two levels overlooking the swimming pool, and the cafe and restaurant tables are beneath an arcade surrounding the pool.

Out on the Carretera al Pacífico are several other hotels. These tend to be 'tropical motels' by design, with bungalows, swimming pool and restaurant. *Hotel Siboney* (☎ 771-0149, fax 771-0711), Cuatro Caminos, San Sebastian, is four km east of town where Calzada Las Palmas meets the Carretera al Pacífico. The 25 rooms, all with air con, color cable TV, telephone and private bath are all US$34/37/40 for singles/doubles/triples. *Hotel La Colonia* (☎ 771-0038, fax 771-0191), Carretera al Pacífico Km 178, is one km east of the Siboney. It has a fairly luxurious layout, with 42 rooms with the same amenities for US$22/30 for singles/doubles, in bungalows around the swimming pool.

Places to Eat

Several little restaurants facing the plaza provide meals at low prices (under US$3). The *Cafetería La Luna* on the corner of 5a Calle and 5a Av, opposite the west corner of the plaza, is a town favorite; it's open every day. The *Restaurante El Patio* on the corner of 5a Calle and 4a Av is similar. Also around the plaza are several ice cream shops.

For the best meal in town, head for the *Posada de Don José* (see Places to Stay), where the pleasant restaurant offers beef and chicken plates for US$4 to US$6 and a big, full meal can be had for US$7 to US$10. Breakfast is served here as well.

Getting There & Away

Bus As Reu is the most important town on the Carretera al Pacífico, transport is easy. Most buses traveling along the highway stop at the city's bus station, on 10a Calle between 7a and 8a Avs. Long-distance buses include:

Ciudad Tecún Umán (78 km, 1½ hours, US$1.65) Buses every 20 minutes, 5 am to 10 pm.
Guatemala City (186 km, 3½ to four hours, US$4.15) Buses every 15 minutes, 2 am to 8:30 pm.
Quetzaltenango (67 km, one hour, US$0.85) Buses every 15 minutes, 3 am to 7 pm.

Local buses depart for Champerico and El Asintal (for Abaj Takalik).

Car Tabarini Rent A Car (☎ 771-1025) has an office here.

ABAJ TAKALIK

About 30 km to the west of Retal Huleau is the active archaeological dig at Abaj Takalik (ah-BAH tah-kah-LEEK). Large 'Olmecoid' stone heads have been discovered, along with many other objects, which date the site as one of the earliest in all of the Maya realm. The site has yet to be restored and prettified for tourists, so don't expect a Chichén Itzá or Tikal. But if you're truly fascinated with archaeology and want to see it as it's done, make a visit.

It's easiest to reach Abaj Takalik with your own vehicle, but it can be done by private transport. Catch a bus to El Asintal, about 15 km west along the Carretera al Pacífico and then five km down a road heading off to the right. Otherwise, early in the morning take any bus heading west towards Coatepeque, go about 15 km west along the Carretera al Pacífico and get out at the road, on the right, to El Asintal, from here it's five km to El Asintal (you may have some luck hitching). Pickups at El Asintal provide transport to Abaj Takalik, four km away.

CHAMPERICO

Built as a shipping point for coffee during the boom of the late 1800s, Champerico, 38 km southwest of Retalhuleu, is a tawdry, sweltering, dilapidated place that sees few tourists. Nevertheless, it's the only ocean beach easily accessible on a day trip by bus from Quetzaltenango. Most beachgoers come only to spend the day, but there are several cheap hotels and restaurants.

When you get to the beach, walk to the right, go under a pier and keep walking for five more minutes until you get to an estuary. Swimming is pleasant in the warm water at the river mouth, and you'll probably see only a few local families. Swimming can be dangerous in the sea, due to fierce waves and an undertow.

MAZATENANGO

Population 38,000

East of Retalhuleu, about 26 km along the Carretera al Pacífico, is Mazatenango

(370 meters), capital of the department of Suchitepéquez. It's a center for farmers, traders and shippers of the Pacific Slope's agricultural produce. There are a few serviceable hotels if you need to stop in an emergency.

SANTA LUCÍA COTZUMALGUAPA
Population 24,000

Another 71 km eastward from Mazatenango brings you to Santa Lucía Cotzumalguapa (356 meters), an important stop for anyone interested in Mayan art and culture. In the sugar cane fields and fincas near the town stand great stone heads carved with grotesque faces, and fine relief scenes in stone. The mystery is, who carved these ritual objects, and why?

The town itself, though pleasant, is not very exciting. The people in town and in the surrounding countryside are descended from the Pipils, an Indian culture known to have historic, linguistic and cultural links with the Nahuatl-speaking peoples of central Mexico. In Early Classic times, the Pipils who lived here grew cacao, the 'money' of the time. They were obsessed with the Maya/Aztec ball game and with the rites and mysteries of death. Pipil art, unlike the flowery and almost romantic style of the true Maya, is very cold, grotesque and severe, but it's still very finely done.

What were these 'Mexicans' doing in the midst of Maya territory? How did they get here and where did they come from? Archaeologists do not have many answers. There are other concentrations of Pipils, notably in the Motagua Valley of southeastern Guatemala, and in western El Salvador. Today this group of people shares a common lifestyle with Guatemala's other indigenous groups.

A visit to Santa Lucía Cotzumalguapa allows you to examine this unique 'lost culture' by visiting a number of its carved stones. Though the sites are accessible to travelers without their own transport, a car certainly simplifies matters. In your explorations you may get to see a Guatemalan sugar cane finca in full operation.

1 El Baúl Museum
2 Finca Headquarters
3 Guard Post
4 El Baúl Hilltop Site
5 Sign 'Los Tarros'
6 El Calvario Church
7 Finca Las Illusiones
   Headquarters Museum
8 Pensión Reforma
9 Caminotel Santiaguito
10 Hotel El Camino
11 Guatel
12 Esso Fuel Station
13 Lions Club Obelisk
14 Esso Fuel Station

Santa Lucía
Cotzumalguapa

Orientation

Santa Lucía Cotzumalguapa is northwest of the Carretera al Pacífico. In its main square (El Parque), several blocks from the highway, are copies of some of the famous carved stones found in the region.

There are three main archaeological sites to visit: Bilbao, a finca right on the outskirts of Santa Lucía; Finca El Baúl, a large plantation farther from the town, at which there are two sites (a hilltop site and the finca headquarters); and Finca Las Ilusiones, which has collected most of its findings into a museum near the finca headquarters. Of these sites, Bilbao and the hilltop site at El Baúl are by far the most interesting. If time and energy are short, head for these.

If you don't have a car and you want to see the sites in a day, haggle with a taxi driver in Santa Lucía's main square for a visit to the sites. It's hot and muggy and the sites are several kilometers apart, so you will really be glad you rode at least part of the way. If you do it all on foot and by bus, pack a lunch so you won't have to return to town. The perfect place to have a picnic is the hilltop site at El Baúl.

Bilbao

This site was no doubt a large ceremonial center which flourished about 600 AD. Plows have unearthed (and damaged) hundreds of stones during the last few centuries; thieves have carted off many others. In 1880 many of the best stones were removed to museums abroad, including nine stones to the Dahlem Museum in Berlin.

Known locally as simply *las piedras* (the stones), this site actually consists of several separate sites deep within tall stands of sugar cane. The fields come right to the edge of the town. From Santa Lucía's main square, go north uphill on 3a Av to the outskirts of town. Pass El Calvario church on your right, and shortly thereafter turn sharp right. A hundred meters along, the road veers to the right but an unpaved road continues straight on; follow the unpaved road. The cane fields are on your left, and you will soon see a path cut into the high cane.

At times when the cane is high, finding your way around would be very difficult if it weren't for the swarms of local boys that coalesce and follow you as you make your way along the edge of the cane fields. At the first sign of bewilderment or indecision they'll strike: *'Las piedras? Las piedras?'* You answer *'Si!'* and they'll lead you without hesitation into the sea of waving cane along a maze of paths to each site. A tip is expected, of course, but it needn't be large and it needn't be given to every one of the multitude of guides. The boys are in school many days but are dependable on weekends, holidays and during school vacation time.

One stone is flat with three figures carved in low relief; the middle figure's ribs show prominently, as though he were starving. A predatory bird is in the upper left-hand corner. Holes in the middle-right part of the stone show that thieves attempted to cut the stone.

Another is an elaborate relief showing players in a ball game, fruit, birds, animals and cacao bean pods, for which this area was famous and which made it rich.

Although some of the other stones are badly weathered and worn, others bear Mexican-style circular date glyphs and other mysterious patterns which resemble closely those used by people along the Gulf Coast of Mexico near Villahermosa.

To continue on to El Baúl, you can save time by backtracking to the point where you turned sharp right just beyond El Calvario church. Buses heading out to El Baúl pass this point every few hours, or you can hitchhike. If you're driving, you'll have to return to the center along 4a Av and come back out on 3a Av, as these roads are one way.

A reader wrote the following about his experience finding the stones:

I had a hell of a time finding Las Piedras (the Bilbao stones) – the schoolboy guides must have been at school at 9:30 on a Tuesday. Having found them all (with the help of a local), I wrote these instructions:

From the unpaved road in your instructions, continue as far as the blue house (about 100 meters). Opposite this there is a path in the sugar cane (you need to climb through the fence) – the first glyph is just up on the left. From there, continue north, and take the second right – the arch-shaped glyph is on the top of the hill. Continue to the end of the path (about 20 meters), turn left, and left again after 50 meters up a small path to a very large glyph.

Returning to the previous path and following to the end, take a left turn. Eventually you'll come to the road to Finca El Baúl, cutting the corner.

Of course, these may not be the stones you were describing!

Finca El Baúl

Just as interesting as las piedras is the hilltop site at El Baúl, which has the additional fascination of being an active place of pagan worship for local people. This is an excellent place for a picnic. Some distance from the hilltop site on another road, next to the finca headquarters, is the finca's private museum of stones uncovered on the property.

The hilltop site at El Baúl is 4.2 km northeast of El Calvario church. From the church (or the intersection just beyond it), go 2.7 km to a fork in the road just beyond a bridge; the fork is marked by a sign reading 'Los Tarros.' Take the right-hand fork (an unpaved road). From the Los Tarros sign it's 1.5 km to the point where a dirt track crosses the road; on your right is a tree-covered 'hill' in the midst of otherwise flat fields. The 'hill' is actually a great ruined temple platform which has not been restored. Make your way across the field and around the south side of the hill, following the track to the top. If you have a car, you can drive to within 50 meters of the top.

If you visit on a weekend, you may find several worshippers paying their respects to the idols here. They will not mind if you visit as well, and are usually happy to pose with the idols for photographs, in exchange for a small 'contribution.'

Of the two stones here, the great grotesque half-buried head is the most striking. The elaborate headdress, 'blind' eyes with big bags beneath them, beak-like nose and 'have a nice day' grin seem at odds with the blackened face and its position, half-buried in the ancient soil. The

head is stained with wax from candles, with liquor and other drinks, and with the smoke and ashes of incense fires built before it, all part of worship. People have been coming here to pay homage for over 1400 years.

The other stone is a relief carving of a figure surrounded by circular motifs which may be date glyphs. A copy of this stone may be seen in the main square of Santa Lucía Cotzumalguapa.

From the hilltop site, retrace your steps 1.5 km to the fork with the Los Tarros sign. Take the other fork this time (what would be the left fork as you come from Santa Lucía), and follow the paved road three km to the headquarters of Finca El Baúl. (If you're on foot, you can walk from the hilltop site back to the unpaved road and straight across it, continuing on the dirt track. This will eventually bring you to the asphalt road which leads to the finca headquarters. When you reach the road, turn right.) Buses trundle along this road every few hours, shuttling workers between the refinery and the town center.

Approaching the finca headquarters (six km from Santa Lucía's main square), you cross a narrow bridge at a curve; continue uphill and you will see the entrance on the left, marked by a machine-gun pillbox. Beyond this daunting entrance you pass workers' houses, and a sugar refinery on the right, and finally come to the headquarters building, guarded by several men with rifles. The smell of molasses is everywhere. Ask permission to visit the museum and a guard will unlock the gate just past the headquarters building.

Within the gates, sheltered by a palapa, are numerous sculpted figures and reliefs found on the plantation, some of which are very fine. Unfortunately, nothing is labeled.

Finca Las Ilusiones

The third site is very close to Bilbao – indeed, this is the finca which controls the Bilbao cane fields – but, paradoxically, access is more difficult. Your reward is the chance to view hundreds of objects, large and small, which have been collected from the finca's fields over the centuries.

Leave the town center by heading east along Calzada 15 de Septiembre, the boulevard which joins the highway at an Esso fuel station. Go northeast for a short distance, and just past another Esso station on the left is an unpaved road which leads, after a little over one km, to Finca Las Ilusiones and its museum. If the person who holds the museum key is to be found, you can have a look inside. If not, you must be satisfied with the many stones collected around the outside of the museum.

Places to Stay & Eat

Pensión Reforma, Calzada 15 de Septiembre at 4a Av, is certainly not beautiful, but will do for a night. Rooms cost US$4/6 a single/double.

Out on the highway, just a few hundred meters west of the town, is the *Caminotel Santiaguito* (☎ 882-5435/6/7), Km 90.4, Carretera al Pacífico. It's a fairly lavish layout (for Guatemala's Pacific Slope) with spacious tree-shaded grounds, a nice swimming pool and a decent restaurant. The pool is open to nonguests for a small fee. Motel-style air-conditioned rooms with private bath cost US$32/39. They're likely to be full on weekends, as the hotel is something of a resort for local people. In the spacious restaurant cooled by ceiling fans, you can order a cheeseburger, fruit salad and soft drink for US$4, or an even bigger meal for US$6.50 to US$8.

Across the highway from the Caminotel is the *Hotel El Camino* (☎ 882-5316), with rooms that are hot and somewhat noisy because of highway traffic. Singles/doubles are US$10/14.

Getting There & Away

Esmeralda 2nd-class buses shuttle between Santa Lucía Cotzumalguapa and Guatemala City (4a Av and 2a Calle, Zona 9) every half-hour or so between 6 am and 5 pm, charging US$1.50 for the 90-km, two-hour ride. You can also catch any bus traveling along the Carretera al Pacífico between Guatemala City and such points as Mazatenango, Retalhuleu or the Mexican border.

To travel between La Democracia and Santa Lucía, catch a bus running along the Carretera al Pacífico between Santa Lucía and Siquinalá (eight km); change in Siquinalá for a bus to La Democracia.

Between Santa Lucía and Lago de Atitlán you will probably have to change buses at Cocales junction, 23 km west of Santa Lucía and 58 km south of Panajachel.

LA DEMOCRACIA
Population 4200

South of Siquinalá 9.5 km along the road to Puerto San José is La Democracia (165 meters), a nondescript Pacific Slope town that's hot day and night, rainy season and dry. Like Santa Lucía Cotzumalguapa, La Democracia is in the midst of a region populated from early times with – according to some archaeologists – mysterious cultural connections to Mexico's Gulf Coast.

At the archaeological site called Monte Alto, on the outskirts of the town, huge basalt heads have been found. Though cruder, the heads resemble those carved by the Olmecs near Veracruz several thousand years ago.

Today these great 'Olmecoid' heads are arranged around La Democracia's main plaza. As you come into town from the highway, follow signs to the museo, which will cause you to bear left, then turn left, then turn left again.

Facing the plaza, along with the church and the modest Palacio Municipal, is the small, modern Museo Rubén Chevez Van Dorne, with other fascinating archaeological finds. The star of the show is an exquisite jade mask. Smaller figures, 'yokes' used in the ball game, relief carvings and other objects make up the rest of this important small collection. On the walls are overly dramatic paintings of Olmecoid scenes. A rear room has more of the dramatic paintings, and lots of potsherds only an archaeologist could love. The museum is open from 8 am to noon and 2 to 5 pm; admission costs US$0.50.

Places to Stay & Eat

La Democracia has no places to stay and few places to eat. The eateries are very basic and ill-supplied, and it's best to bring your own food and buy drinks at a place facing the plaza. *Café Maritza*, right next to the museum, is a picture-perfect hot-tropics hangout with a *rockola* (jukebox) blasting music, and a small crew of semisomnolent locals sipping and sweltering.

Getting There & Away
Chatia Gomerana, Muelle Central, Terminal de Buses, Zona 4, Guatemala City, has buses every half-hour from 6 am to 4:30 pm on the 92-km, two-hour ride between the capital and La Democracia. Buses stop at Escuintla, Siquinalá (change for Santa Lucía Cotzumalguapa), La Democracia, La Gomera and Sipacate. The fare is US$1.

AROUND LA DEMOCRACIA
The road south from La Democracia continues 42 km to **Sipacate**, a small and very basic beach town. The beach is on the other side of the Canal de Chiquimulilla, an intracoastal waterway. Though there are a few scruffy, very basic places to stay, you'd be better off saving your beach time for Puerto San José, 35 km to the east, reached via the road from Escuintla.

ESCUINTLA
Set amidst lush tropical verdure, Escuintla should be an idyllic place where people swing languidly in hammocks and concoct pungent meals of readily available exotic fruit and vegetables. But it's not.

Escuintla is a hot, dingy, dilapidated commercial and industrial city that's very important to the Pacific Slope's economy, but not at all important to travelers. It is an old town, inhabited by Pipils before the conquest but now solidly ladino. It has some fairly dingy hotels and restaurants.

You might have to change buses in Escuintla. The main bus station is in the southern part of town; this is where you catch buses to Puerto San José. For Guatemala City, you can catch very frequent buses in the main plaza.

Near Escuintla, **Autosafari Chapin** is a drive-through African wild animal park that's a popular outing for families from

Guatemala City. Buses come here; see Buses in Guatemala City.

PUERTO SAN JOSÉ, LIKÍN & IZTAPA
Guatemala's most important seaside resort leaves a lot to be desired, even when it's compared to Mexico's smaller and seedier places. But if you're eager to get into the Pacific surf, head south from Escuintla 50 km to Puerto San José and neighboring settlements.

Puerto San José (population 14,000) was Guatemala's most important Pacific port in the latter half of the 19th century and well into the 20th. Now superseded by the more modern Puerto Quetzal to the east, Puerto San José languishes and slumbers; its inhabitants languish, slumber, play loud music and drink. The beach, inconveniently located across the Canal de Chiquimulilla, is reached by boat.

It's smarter to head west along the coast five km (by taxi or car) to Balneario Chulamar, which has a nicer beach and also a suitable hotel or two.

About five km to the east of Puerto San José is Balneario Likín, Guatemala's only up-market Pacific resort. Likín is much beloved by well-to-do families from Guatemala City who have seaside houses on the tidy streets and canals of this planned development.

About 12 km east of Puerto San José is Iztapa, Guatemala's first Pacific port, first used by none other than Pedro de Alvarado in the 1500s. When Puerto San José was built in 1853, Iztapa's reign as the port of the capital city came to an end, and it relaxed into a tropical torpor from which it has yet to emerge. Having lain fallow for almost a century and a half, it has not suffered the degradation of Puerto San José. Iztapa is comparatively pleasant, with several small, easily affordable hotels and restaurants on the beach. The bonus here is that you can catch a Transportes Pacífico bus from the market in Zona 4 in Guatemala City all the way to Iztapa (four hours), or pick it up at Escuintla or Puerto San José to take you to Iztapa.

MONTERRICO

Similar in many ways to the rest of Guatemala's Pacific Coast, Monterrico is a coastal village with a few small, inexpensive hotels right on the beach, a large wildlife reserve and a center for the hatching and release of sea turtles. The beach here is dramatic, where surf crashes onto black volcanic sand. Behind the beach, on the other side of town, is a large network of mangrove swamps and canals, part of the 190-km Canal de Chiquimulilla.

Monterrico is a good spot for a weekend break at the beach, if you're staying in Antigua or Guatemala City. It's becoming popular with foreigners. On weekdays it's very quiet.

Things to See & Do

Besides the beach, Monterrico's biggest attraction is the Biotopo Monterrico-Hawaii, a 20-km-long nature reserve of coast and coastal mangrove swamps filled with bird and aquatic life. Its most famous denizens are perhaps the endangered leatherback and Ridley turtles, who lay their eggs on the beach in many places along the coast. The mangrove swamps are a network of 25 lagoons, all connected by mangrove canals.

Boat tours of the reserve, going through the mangrove swamps and visiting several lagoons, take around 1½ to two hours and cost US$8.35 for one to three passengers. It's best to go early in the morning, when you can see the most wildlife. Bring binoculars for bird watching, if you have them. To arrange a boat tour of the canal, stop by the Tortugario Monterrico, on the beach. Other villagers also do boat tours, but the guides who work here are particularly concerned with wildlife. Or ask at your hotel.

The Tortugario Monterrico is just a short walk east down the beach from the Monterrico hotels (left, if you're facing the sea). Several endangered species of animals are raised here, including three species of sea turtles.

The Reserva Natural Hawaii is a nature reserve operated by the Asociación de Rescate y Conservación de Vida Silvestre (ARCAS; Association to Rescue and Conserve Wildlife), which has a sea turtle hatchery eight km east along the beach from Monterrico. Volunteers are welcome all year round, but real sea turtle season is from June to November, with August and September being the peak months.

For studying Spanish, the ALM Language School, based in Antigua and Quetzaltenango, has a branch here in Monterrico.

Places to Stay & Eat

Monterrico has four simple beachfront hotels, all with restaurants and all very near one another. From where you alight from the boat that has brought you over from La Avellana, it's about a 15-minute walk through the village to reach the beach and the hotels. If you've brought a vehicle across on a car ferry, you can park it at any of the hotels; all have parking areas.

All the hotels are similar, but the *Hotel Baule Beach* (☎ 473-6196), a cozy 17-room hotel run by former Peace Corps Volunteer Nancy Garver, is probably the best deal. Not only is it the cheapest, but it's also very pleasant; it's friendly and lots of young international travelers stay here. Rooms with private bath, right on the beach, cost US$3.60 to US$7.50 per person, depending on how many people share a room; rooms hold one to six people. Meals are reasonably priced as well. Current schedules for every type of transport serving Monterrico are posted here.

Hotel Pez de Oro (☎ 331-5620) is the most attractive hotel of the four. It has nine clean, pleasant bungalows, each with fan, mosquito nets, private bath and a hammock on the porch. Cost is US$29/40/50 for two/three/four people (singles pay the same as doubles). There's also a swimming pool and the restaurant is operated by Italians.

Kaiman Inn (☎ 202-6513, 369-1258) has eight rooms, each with fan, mosquito nets and private bath, for US$10 per person, with rooms holding two to five people. The restaurant, right on the beach, serves excellent Italian cuisine and seafood.

Johnny's Place (☎ 337-4191, fax 365-8072) has rooms for US$6/12.50 per person on weekdays/weekends. It also has seven bungalows, each with two bedrooms, living room, private bath and fully-equipped kitchen for US$60 for four people (US$30 on weekdays if only two people stay). Two bungalows share a BBQ and small swimming pool. Also here is a swimming pool and restaurant.

Another hotel or two are set back from the beach.

All the beachfront hotels have their own restaurants. Or there's the *Pig Pen Pub*, an open-air beachfront bar a short walk down the beach. It's open from 8 pm 'until you're done drinking.'

Getting There & Away

Getting to Monterrico involves first getting to La Avellana, from where *lanchas* (small passenger boats) and car ferries depart for Monterrico. Direct buses operate between Guatemala City and La Avellana about 10 times daily (124 km, four hours, US$2.10). Or, you can change buses at Taxisco, on CA-2 – buses operate hourly between Guatemala City and Taxisco (106 km, 3½ hours, US$1.65), and hourly between Taxisco and La Avellana (18 km, 20 minutes, US$0.40).

Shuttle buses also serve La Avellana. You can take a shuttle bus roundtrip from Antigua, coming on one day and returning on the next, for US$25, or one-way for US$12. From Antigua it's a 2½ hour trip. The Adventure Travel Center in Antigua (see the Antigua section) comes over every Saturday and returns every Sunday; other shuttle services also make the trip. Shuttle services depart from La Avellana for Antigua at 2 pm on Saturdays and Sundays (US$12), and for Guatemala City on Monday morning at 9 am (US$7). Phone the Hotel Baule Beach in Monterrico to check the current schedule for buses and shuttles, if you need to know in advance.

From Avellana, catch a passenger boat or car ferry to Monterrico. The *colectivo* passenger boats charge US$0.40 per passenger for the half-hour trip along the Canal de Chiquimulilla, a long mangrove canal.

LAGO DE AMATITLÁN

A placid lake backed by a looming volcano, situated a mere 25 km south of Guatemala City – that's Amatitlán. It should be a pretty and peaceful resort, but unfortunately it's not. The hourglass-shaped lake is divided by a railway line, and the lakeshore is lined with industry at some points. On weekends people from Guatemala City come to row boats on the lake (its waters are too polluted for swimming), or to rent a private hot tub for a dip. Many people from the capital own second homes here.

There's little reason for you to spend time here. If you really want to have a look, head for the town of Amatitlán, just off the main Escuintla-Guatemala City highway. Amatitlán has a scruffy public beach area. If you have a car and some spare time, a drive around the lake offers some pretty scenery. Perhaps the lake will one day be restored to its naturally beautiful state.

Central & Eastern Guatemala

North and east of Guatemala City is a land of varied topography, from the misty, pine-covered mountains of Alta Verapaz to the hot, dry-tropic climate of the Río Motagua Valley. The Carretera al Atlántico (Atlantic Highway, CA-9) heads northeast from the capital and soon descends from the relative cool of the mountains to the dry heat of a valley where dinosaurs once roamed.

Along this highway are many interesting destinations, including the beautiful highland scenery around Cobán; the palaeontology museum at Estanzuela; the great at Esquipulas, famous throughout Central America; the first-rate Maya ruins at Copán, just across the border in Honduras; the marvelous Maya stelae and zoomorphs at Quiriguá; and the tropical lake of Izabal and jungle waterway of Río Dulce. The Carretera al Atlántico ends at Puerto Barrios, Guatemala's Caribbean port, from which you can take a boat to Lívingston, a laid-back hideaway peopled by the Garífuna.

In the time before the Spanish conquest, the mountainous highland regions of the departments of Baja Verapaz and Alta Verapaz were peopled by the Rabinal Maya, noted for their warlike habits and merciless victories. They battled the powerful Quiché Maya for a century but were never conquered.

When the conquistadores arrived, they too had trouble defeating the Rabinals. It was Fray Bartolomé de las Casas who convinced the Spanish authorities to try peace where war had failed. Armed with an edict which forbade Spanish soldiers from entering the region for five years, the friar and his brethren pursued their religious mission, and succeeded in pacifying and converting the Rabinals. It was renamed Verapaz (True Peace), and is now divided into Baja Verapaz, with its capital at Salamá, and Alta Verapaz, centered on Cobán.

The two departmental capitals are easily accessible along a smooth, fast, asphalt road which winds up from the hot, dry valley through wonderful scenery into the mountains, through long stretches of coffee-growing country. Along the way to Cobán is one of Guatemala's premier nature reserves, the Biotopo del Quetzal. Beyond Cobán, along rough unpaved roads, are the country's most famous caverns.

SALAMÁ
Population 11,000

Highway 17, also marked CA-14, leaves the Carretera al Atlántico at El Rancho, 84 km from Guatemala City. It heads west through a dry, desert-like lowland area, then turns north and starts climbing up into the forested hills. After 47 km you come to the turnoff for Salamá. Descending the other side of the ridge, the road winds down into the broad valley of the Río Salamá, and enters the capital of the department of Baja Verapaz, 17 km from the Carretera.

Salamá (940 meters) is an attractive town with some reminders of colonial rule. The main plaza boasts an ornate colonial church with many old gold-painted altars. If you arrive on a Sunday, you'll find the market bustling with activity.

Places to Stay & Eat
Should you want to stay the night, *Hospedaje Juárez* (☎ 940-0055), 10a Av 15-55, Zona 1, in the block directly behind the church, is a good, clean, friendly place to stay. All 15 rooms have private hot bath and cost US$6/8.50 a single/double. There's no sign out front.

The *Hotel Tezulutlán* (☎ /fax 940-0141), just off the main square behind the Texaco fuel station, has 15 rooms arranged around a pleasant garden courtyard. All have cable TV and all but two have private bath (four rooms have hot water), and cost US$13/18 a single/double. The two rooms with general bath are US$5/8. Across the street, the *Hotel San Ignacio* (☎ 940-0186) is a clean family-run place where singles/doubles are US$4/5 with shared bath, or US$5/7 with private cold bath; the *Cafetería Apolo XI* is also here.

All of these places have parking.

Near the plaza there are many places to eat. A few doors from the plaza, *Cafe Deli-Donas* is a clean, pleasant coffee shop serving light meals and sweets; it's open every day. At the *Restaurante El Ganadero*, a half-block off the main square on the road out of town, a lunch might cost US$4 to US$6, a sandwich much less. *Restaurante Caña Vieja* on the plaza is also an option.

Getting There & Away
As this is a departmental capital, there are frequent buses to and from Guatemala City, arriving and departing from a small bus station half a block from the central plaza. Buses bound for Guatemala City depart hourly from 2:30 am to 4 pm (151 km, three hours, US$2). Buses coming from Guatemala City continue west from Salamá to Rabinal (19 km, one hour, US$1) and then 15 km further along to Cubulco.

In Guatemala City, buses to Salamá depart hourly, 5 am to 5 pm, from the office of Transporte Dulce María, 9a Av 19-20, Zona 1 (☎ 250-0082).

AROUND SALAMÁ

Ten km along the road to Salamá from the Cobán highway, you come to the turnoff for **San Jerónimo**, which is five km north of Hwy 5. Behind the town's beautiful old church is an old sugar mill now used as a museum. On the plaza are some large stones that were carved in ancient times.

Nine km west of Salamá along Hwy 5 is the village of **San Miguel Chicaj**, known for its weaving. Continue along the same road for another 10 km to reach the colonial town of **Rabinal**, founded in 1537 by Fray Bartolomé de las Casas as a base for his proselytizing. Rabinal has gained fame as a pottery-making center (look especially at the handpainted chocolate cups), and for its citrus fruit harvest (November and December). Market day here is Sunday. Two small hotels, the *Pensión Motagua* and the *Hospedaje Caballeros*, can put you up.

It's possible to continue on from Rabinal another 15 km to the village of **Cabulco**. Or, from Rabinal you can follow Hwy 5 all the way to Guatemala City, a trip of about 100 km on which you pass through several small villages. It's best to traverse this remote route only with a 4WD vehicle. Buses do ply this route, albeit very slowly. Along the way you could visit the **ruins of Mixco Viejo** near **San Juan Sacatepéquez**, about 25 km from Guatemala City.

BIOTOPO DEL QUETZAL

Along the main highway (CA-14) 34 km beyond the turnoff for Salamá you reach the Biotopo Mario Dary Rivera Nature Reserve, commonly called the Biotopo del Quetzal at Km 161, just east of the village of Purulhá (no services).

If you stop here intent on seeing a quetzal, Guatemala's national bird, you may be disappointed, because the birds are rare and elusive. You have the best chance of seeing them from February to September.

Even if you never see a quetzal, though, it's still well worth a visit to explore and enjoy the lush high-altitude cloud forest ecosystem which is preserved here, and which is the quetzals' natural habitat.

Trail guide maps in English and Spanish may be purchased for US$0.50. They contain a checklist of 87 birds commonly seen here. Other animals here include spider monkeys and *tigrillos*, which are similar to ocelots.

Two excellent, well-maintained nature trails wind through the reserve: the 1800-meter Sendero los Helechos (Fern Trail) and the Sendero los Musgos (Moss Trail), which is twice as long. As you wander through the dense growth, treading on the rich, dense, spongy humus and leaf-mold, you'll see many varieties of epiphytes (air plants) which thrive in the humid jungle atmosphere.

Both trails pass by waterfalls, most of which fall into small pools where you can take a dip; innumerable streams have their headwaters here. The Río Colorado cascades through the forest along a geological fault. Deep in the forest is Xiu Ua Li Che (Grandfather Tree), some 450 years old, which was alive when the conquistadors fought the Rabinals in these mountains.

The reserve is open every day from 7 am to 4 pm (you must be in by 4 pm, but you can stay longer); admission costs US$5. There's a visitors' center, and drinks (but no food) are available at the site.

Places to Stay

Camping was once permitted here but no longer.

There are two lodging places within a short distance of the biotopo. Just beyond it, another 200 meters up the hill toward Purulhá and Cobán, is the *Hotel y Comedor Ranchito del Quetzal* (☎ 331-3579 in Guatemala City), a rustic hospedaje. Rustic rooms with shared bath are US$5/8/11 a single/double/triple; rooms with private hot bath are US$8/11/14. Meals are US$1.35 for breakfast, US$2.50 for lunch or dinner (US$1.65 for vegetarian meals).

The more comfortable *Posada Montaña del Quetzal* (☎ 335-1805 in Guatemala

City), Carretera a Cobán Km 156.5, Purulhá, Baja Verapaz, is five km back along the road toward the Carretera al Atlántico. This attractive hostelry has 18 white stucco, tile-roofed bungalow cabins, each with a sitting room and fireplace, a bedroom with three beds and private hot bath, for US$20/26 a single/double; larger two-bedroom bunga-lows are US$28/35. The complex has a restaurant, a large swimming pool and a smaller children's pool. You can usually catch a bus to shuttle you between the Biotopo and the posada, or hitch a ride.

COBÁN
Population 20,000

The asphalt road from the biotopo to Cobán is good, smooth and fast, though curvy, with light traffic. As you ascend into the evergreen forests, tropical flowers are still visible here and there. As you enter Cobán, a sign says 'Bienvenidos a Cobán, Ciudad Imperial,' referring to the charter granted in 1538 by Emperor Charles V. About 126 km from the Carretera al Atlántico, you reach Cobán's main plaza.

The town now called Cobán (1320 meters) was once the center of Tezulutlán (Tierra de Guerra in Spanish, the Land of War), a stronghold of the Rabinal Maya.

In the 19th century when German immi-grants moved in and founded vast coffee fincas, Cobán took on the aspect of a Ger-man mountain town as the finca owners built town residences. The era of German cultural and economic domination ended during WWII, when the USA prevailed upon the Guatemalan government to deport the powerful finca owners, many of whom actively supported the Nazis.

Today Cobán can be a pleasant town to visit, though much depends upon the season. Most of the year it is either rainy or overcast, dank and chill. You can count on sunny days in Cobán for only about three weeks in April. In the midst of the 'dry' season (January to March) it can be misty and sometimes rainy, or bright and sunny with marvelous clear mountain air.

Guatemala's most impressive festival of Indian traditions, the folkloric **Rabin Ajau**

with its traditional dance of the Paabanc, takes place in the latter part of July or the first week of August.

There is not a lot to do in Cobán except enjoy the local color and the mountain scenery, but the town as a good base for visits to the Grutas de Lanquín and Cuevas Semuc-Champey nearby (see Around Cobán below).

Orientation & Information

The main plaza *(el parque)* features a dis-concertingly modern concrete bandstand. Most of the services you'll need are within a few blocks of the plaza and the cathedral. The shopping district is around and behind the cathedral.

The tourist office on the plaza has posted office hours, but you may or may not find it functioning. If you need information, the Hostal de Acuña or the Hostal de Doña Victoria (see Places to Stay) are good places to ask.

The post office is on the corner of 2a Av and 3a Calle. The Guatel telephone office is on the plaza; public coin phones are outside the office.

Banco Occidente, on the plaza, changes US dollars cash and traveler's checks and gives cash advances on Visa cards. Banco G&T, behind the church, also changes money and gives cash advances on Master-Card. Banco Industrial, opposite the police station, changes money and gives cash advances on Visa at its 24-hour ATM.

Laundry service is available from Lavan-dería Providencia on the plaza or from the Hostal de Acuña.

Templo El Calvario

You can get a fine view over the town from the Templo El Calvario, a church atop a long flight of stairs at the north end of 7a Av. Indigenous people leave offerings of natural elements at outdoor shrines and crosses in front of it. You can walk around behind the church to enter the Parque Nacional Las Victorias, though this is not the park's main entrance.

The Ermita de Santo Domingo de Guzmán, a chapel dedicated to Cobán's

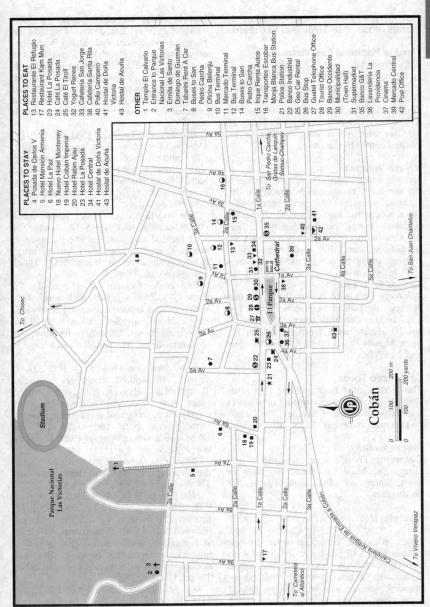

PLACES TO STAY
4   Posada de Carlos V
5   Hotel Mansión Armenia
6   Hotel La Paz
18 Nuevo Hotel Monterrey
19 Hotel Cobán Imperial
20 Hotel Rabin Ajau
23 Hotel La Posada
34 Hotel Central
41 Hostal de Doña Victoria
43 Hostal de Acuña

PLACES TO EAT
13 Restaurante El Refugio
17 Restaurant Kam Mun
23 Hotel La Posada
24 Café La Posada
25 Café El Tiroll
32 Yogurt Renee
33 Cafetería San Jorge
38 Cafetería Santa Rita
40 Pollo Campero
41 Hostal de Doña
    Victoria
43 Hostal de Acuña

OTHER
1   Templo El Calvario
2   Entrance to Parque
    Nacional Las Victorias
3   Ermita de Santo
    Domingo de Guzmán
7   Tabarini Rent A Car
8   Buses to San
    Pedro Carcha
9   Oficina Belenju
10 Bus Terminal
11 Mercado Terminal
12 Bus Terminal
14 Buses to San
    Pedro Carcha
15 Inque Terminal
16 Transportes Escobar
    Monja Blanca Bus Station
21 Police Station
22 Banco Industrial
25 Geo Car Rental
26 Bus Stop
27 Guatel Telephone Office
28 Tourist Office
29 Banco Occidente
30 Municipalidad
    (Town Hall)
31 Supermarket
35 Banco G&T
36 Lavandería La
    Providencia
37 Cinema
39 Mercado Central
42 Post Office

Cobán

Parque Nacional
Las Victorias

Stadium

To Chisec

To San Pedro Carcha,
Grutas de Lanquín,
Semuc-Champey

To San Juan Chamelco

To San Juan Chamelco

To Vivero Verapaz

To Carretera
al Atlántico

Carretera Antigua de Entrada a Cobán

0   100   200 m
0   100   200 yards

patron saint, is 150 meters west of the bottom of the stairs leading to El Calvario.

Parque Nacional Las Victorias

This forested 82-hectare national park, right in town, has several trails, ponds, BBQ and picnic areas, children's play areas, a lookout point and free camping. It's open every day from 8 am to 4:30 pm; admission is free. The entrance is at 9a Av and 3a Calle. Or you can enter by walking around to the rear of the Templo El Calvario.

Vívero Verapaz

Orchid lovers mustn't miss a chance to see the many thousands of species at this famous nursery. The very rare *monja blanca* or white nun orchid, Guatemala's national flower, can be seen here; there are also hundreds of species of miniature orchids, so small that you'll need a magnifying glass to see them. The owners will take you on a tour to see all the species for US$0.85.

Vívero Verapaz is on the Carretera Antigua de Entrada a Cobán, about two km from the center of town. It's a beautiful 20-minute walk from the plaza. It's open Monday to Saturday, 9 am to noon and 2 to 5 pm.

Organized Tours

The Hostal de Acuña and the Hostal de Doña Victoria both operate tour companies with trips to Semuc-Champey, the Grutas de Lanquín, and other places further afield.

Places to Stay

Camping There's free camping at the Parque Nacional Las Victorias, right in town. Water and toilets are available, but no showers.

Hostels *Hostal de Acuña* (☎ /fax 952-1547, fax 952-1268), 4a Calle 3-11, is a clean, pleasant European-style hostel. Cost is US$4.15 per bunk, in rooms with two or four beds. Also here is a good restaurant, a sitting room, gift shop, laundry service and reasonably priced local tours.

Hotels *Hotel Cobán Imperial* (☎ 952-1131), 6a Av 1-12, 250 meters west of the plaza, is administered along with the adjoining *Nuevo Hotel Monterrey*. It's old but clean, popular with Guatemalan families, and has parking in the courtyard. Singles/doubles are US$2.50/5 with shared cold bath, US$3.35/6.65 with private cold bath, or US$7.50/15 with private hot bath and TV.

Hotel La Paz (☎ 952-1358), 6a Av 2-19, 1½ blocks north of the plaza, is cheerful, clean and an excellent deal for the price: singles/doubles are US$4/8 with shared bath, US$5/8 with private bath. It has many flowers, parking in the courtyard, and a cafeteria next door.

The old-fashioned *Hotel Rabin Ajau* (☎ 952-2296), 1a Calle 5-37, Zona 1, is well located and fairly plain; its disco is noisy. There's a restaurant and parking. Rooms with private bath are US$11/14/17 a single/double/triple.

The *Hotel Central* (☎ 951-1442), 1a Calle 1-79, Zona 4, is tidy, with rooms with bath arranged around a flowered courtyard. Singles/doubles/triples are US$8/10/12 for remodeled rooms, US$6/8/10 for those yet to be remodeled. The Cafetería San Jorge is also here.

Hotel Mansión Armenia (☎ 952-2284), 7a Av 2-18, Zona 1, one block from the Templo El Calvario, is a comfortable place, new, clean, quiet and modern, with courtyard parking and a cafeteria. Rooms with private bath and cable TV are US$14/19 a single/double. Even newer is the *Posada de Carlos V* (☎ /fax 952-1780), 1a Av 3-44, Zona 1, with singles/doubles/triples with private bath and cable TV are US$14/24/31.

Hotel Oxib Peck (☎ 952-1039; ☎ /fax 951-3224), 1a Calle 12-11, Zona 1, is 12 blocks (750 meters) west of the plaza on the road out of town. The rooms are clean and pleasant, and there's a dining room, laundry service and parking. Singles/doubles/triples with private bath and cable TV are US$15/22/29.

Hostal de Doña Victoria (☎ 952-2213/4), 3a Calle 2-38, Zona 3, is in a restored mansion over 400 years old. Comfortable rooms with private bath surround a central courtyard with plants and a restaurant/bar. Prices are US$17/26/34/39 for one to four people.

The best hotel in town is the *Hotel La Posada* (☎ /fax 952-1495), 1a Calle 4-12, Zona 2, just off the plaza in the very center of town. Colonial in style, its colonnaded porches are festooned with tropical flowers and furnished with easy chairs and hammocks to enjoy the mountain views. The rooms have nice old furniture, fireplaces and wall hangings of local weaving, and rent for US$26/32/39 a single/double/triple with private bath.

Places to Eat
Most of Cobán's hotels have their own restaurants. The one at the *Hostal de Acuña* is one of the best in town, with good, reasonably priced Italian and other European-style dishes served in an attractive setting. Dinners are around US$5. The restaurant at the *Hostal de Doña Victoria* is also pleasant.

Café El Tirol, near the Hotel La Posada, advertises 'the best coffee' and several types of hot chocolate in four languages. It's a cozy little place in which to enjoy pastries and coffee for US$1 to US$2. Breakfast and light meals are served as well. It's closed on Monday.

Café La Posada on the west end of the plaza has tables on a verandah overlooking the plaza, and a comfortable sitting room inside with couches, coffee tables and a fireplace. All the usual cafe fare is served. In the same building, *Hotel La Posada* has a pleasant dining room with good food but slow service.

Cafetería Santa Rita, also facing the main square, is small, tidy and popular with locals. Good breakfasts, lunches and dinners go for around US$2.

Cafetería San Jorge, 1a Calle between 1a and 2a Avs, near the cathedral, has a varied menu and a dining room with views through large windows. Substantial meat dishes are offered (US$3), along with a variety of sandwiches (US$1 to US$2).

Next door, *Yogurt Renee* makes delicious fruit yogurts and ice cream.

Pollo Campero has an outlet across from the post office on 2a Av at 2a Calle.

Restaurante El Refugio, at the corner of 2a Av and 2a Calle, Zona 4, has rustic wooden decor and a menu with lots of meat dishes (grilled steaks are US$3 to US$8), Mexican dishes and burgers, hot dogs and the like.

Almost 500 meters from the plaza the *Restaurant Kam Mun*, 1a Calle 8-12, Zona 2, is on the road out of town. Its Chinese fare, served in a pleasant, clean place, costs US$5 to US$8 for a full meal.

In the evening, food trucks (kitchens on wheels) park around the plaza and offer some of the cheapest dining in town. Some serve safe food, others don't.

Getting There & Away
Bus The highway connecting Cobán with Guatemala City and the Carretera al Atlántico is the most traveled route connecting Cobán with the outside world, but there are a few other off-the-beaten-track routes, all of which are served by buses. (If you're traveling by private vehicle, cut the bus times in half.)

From Cobán you can bus to Fray Bartolomé de las Casas in about six hours; from there, you can continue another seven hours to Poptún, south of Flores. There's a hospedaje in Fray Bartolomé de las Casas, if you need to spend the night. From Fray Bartolomé de las Casas it's also possible to take a pickup truck to Raxrujá, 20 km away. From Raxrujá you can catch a bus to Sayaxché (four hours), from where there are buses to Flores. (See Sayaxché in the El Petén section.) There's a place to stay overnight in Raxrujá.

Another route is from Cobán to Uspantán, about an eight-hour trip by bus. There are places to stay in Uspantán. You can continue by bus from Uspantán to Huehuetenango in about six hours, or from Uspantán to Santa Cruz del Quiché in about six hours. In Santa Cruz del Quiché there are frequent connections to Chichicastenango and Guatemala City.

Another off-the-beaten-track route is from Cobán to El Estor, on Lago de Izabal, a nine-hour bus trip. From El Estor you can take a boat to Mariscos, from where it's a short bus ride to the Carretera al Atlántico.

Most buses depart from Cobán's bus terminal (☎ 951-3043), a rather large spread-out area on either side of 3a Calle, between 1a and 2a Av. Buses to Guatemala City depart from a different station. From Cobán, buses include:

Biotopo del Quetzal (58 km, one hour, US$1) Any bus heading for Guatemala City will drop you at the entrance to the Biotopo.
Cahabón (85 km, 4½ hours, US$2) Same buses as to Lanquín.
El Estor (168 km, nine hours, US$4) Brenda Mercedes and Valenciana buses depart from the bus terminal several times daily.
Fray Bartolomé de las Casas (110 km, six hours, US$3) Several buses daily.
Guatemala City (219 km, four hours, US$2 to US$3) Transportes Escobar Monja Blanca (☎ 952-1536, 952-1952), 2a Calle 3-77, Zona 4, has buses leaving for Guatemala City every half hour from 2 to 6 am, then hourly from 6 am to 4 pm.
Lanquín (61 km, three hours, US$1.15) Buses depart at 6 am, noon, 1 and 3 pm from Oficina Belenju on 3a Calle. The return buses depart from Lanquín at 5 am, 7 am and 3 pm.
San Pedro Carcha (six km, 20 minutes, US$0.10) Buses every 10 minutes, 6 am to 7 pm.
Uspantán (94 km, eight hours, US$4) Two buses daily.

Car Because it is a good base for exploring the surrounding mountains, Cobán now has several places that rent cars. All of these companies are small, and may not have every type of vehicle available at every moment. It's a good idea to reserve one in advance. If you want to go to the Grutas de Lanquín or Semuc-Champey, you'll need a vehicle with 4WD.

Rental car companies include:

Geo Rental, 1a Calle 3-13, Zona 1, in the same building as the Cafe El Tirol, in the rear right corner of the courtyard (☎ 952-2059)
Inque Renta Autos, 3a Av 1-18, Zona 4 (☎ 952-1994, 952-1172)

Ochoch Pec Renta Autos, opposite La Carrita el Viaje at the entrance to town (☎ 951-3474, 951-3214)
Tabarini Rent A Car, 5a Av 2-43, Zona 1 (☎ /fax 951-3282)

AROUND COBÁN

Cobán is becoming an established base for organized excursions to sites in the surrounding mountains. Several small companies have been founded just for this purpose. For example, Marcio and Ashley Acuña of the Hostal de Acuña run ecotours from Cobán to the Grutas de Lanquín, Semuc-Champey and also to many Maya jungle sites such as La Candelaria, Ceibal, Aguateca, Dos Pilas, Yaxchilán, Yaxhá, Nakun, Tikal, Uaxactún and Río Azul, and rafting tours on the Río Cahabon. The Hostal de Doña Victoria runs similar tours. No doubt other operators will start up by the time you visit Cobán.

San Pedro Carcha

At San Pedro Carcha, six km east of Cobán on the way to Lanquín, is the Balneario Las Islas, with a river coming down past rocks and into a natural pool great for swimming. It's about a five- or 10-minute walk from the bus stop in Carcha; anyone can point the way. Buses operate frequently between Cobán and Carcha; the trip takes 20 minutes.

San Juan Chamelco

About 16 km southeast of Cobán is the village of San Juan Chamelco, with swimming at the Balneario Chio. In Aldea (district) Chajaneb, Jerry Makransky (everyone knows him as 'Don Jeronimo') rents comfortable, simple bungalows for US$15 per person (US$25 per couple) per day, which includes three ample, delicious vegetarian meals fresh from the garden and many activities: tours to caves, to the mountains, inner tubing on the Río Sotzil and more. Jerry dotes on his guests and there's a friendly atmosphere.

To get there, take a bus from Cobán to San Juan Chamelco. From there, take a bus or pickup towards Chamil, and ask the driver to let you off at Don Jeronimo's, in Aldea Chajaneb. Take the footpath to the left for 300 meters, cross the bridge and it's the first house on the right.

Grutas de Lanquín

If you don't mind bumping over bad and/or busy roads, the best excursion to make from Cobán is to the caves near Lanquín, a pretty village 61 km to the east.

The Grutas de Lanquín are a short distance northwest of the town, and extend for several kilometers into the earth. You must first stop at the police station in the Municipalidad (Town Hall) in Lanquín, pay the US$2 admission fee and ask them to open the cave for you; there is no attendant at the cave otherwise. The cave has lights, but bring along a powerful flashlight anyway. You'll also need shoes with good traction, as it's slippery inside.

Though the first few hundred meters of cavern has been equipped with a walkway and is lit by diesel-powered electric lights, most of this subterranean system is untouched. If you are not an experienced spelunker, you should think twice about wandering too far into the caves.

If you have camping equipment you can spend the night near the cave entrance. Otherwise, there are two places to stay at Lanquín. In town, *La Divina Providencia* has simple rooms for about US$2 to US$3 per person. *El Recreo*, between the town and the caves, is more attractive and more expensive; it has singles/doubles for US$14/25. The *Comedor Shalom* is good for a meal.

Semuc-Champey

Ten km south of Lanquín along a rough, bumpy, slow road is Semuc-Champey, famed for a natural wonder: a great limestone bridge 300 meters long, on top of which is a series of pools of cool, flowing river water good for swimming. The water is from the Río Cahabón, and most of it passes beneath the bridge underground. Though this bit of paradise is difficult to reach, the beauty of its setting and the perfection of the pools, ranging from turquoise

to emerald green, make it all worth it. Some people consider this the most beautiful spot in all Guatemala.

It's possible to camp at Semuc-Champey, but be sure to camp only in the upper areas, as flash floods are common down below. It's risky to leave anything unattended, though, as it might get stolen.

Tours to the Grutas de Lanquín and Semuc-Champey, offered in Cobán, are the easiest way to visit these places. On your own, if you're driving, you'll need a 4WD vehicle.

Buses operate several times daily between Cobán and Lanquín, continuing to Cahabón. Buses leave Lanquín to return to Cobán at 5am, 7 am and 3 pm. Since the last return bus departs so early, you should probably plan to stay the night. There are occasional buses and trucks from Lanquín to Semuc-Champey. Otherwise, it's a long, hot walk unless you have your own vehicle, in which case it's a slow, bumpy drive.

RÍO HONDO

Río Hondo lies along CA-9 northeast of Cobán. It's 42 km from El Rancho junction (126 km from Guatemala City) and nine km west of the junction where CA-10 heads south to Chiquimula. Beyond Chiquimula are turnoffs to Copán (Honduras), just across the border; to Esquipulas and on to Nueva Ocotepeque (Honduras); and a remote border crossing between Guatemala and El Salvador at Anguiatú, 12 km north of Metapán (El Salvador).

The town of Río Hondo (Deep River) is northeast of the junction, but lodging places hereabouts list their address as Río Hondo, Santa Cruz Río Hondo or Santa Cruz Teculután – it's all the same place. Nine km west of the junction are several attractive motels right on CA-9, which provide a good base for explorations of this region if you have your own vehicle. By car, it's an hour from here to Quiriguá, half an hour to Chiquimula, or 1½ hours to Esquipulas.

Another big attraction of Río Hondo is the Valle Dorado aquatic park and tourist center (see Places to Stay).

Places to Stay & Eat

Note that the Río Hondo motels are looked upon as weekend resorts by locals and residents of Guatemala City, so they may be heavily booked on weekends. They're popular as bases for visits to the area in general, to the Valle Dorado aquatic park in particular, and also in their own right – all of them are modern, pleasant places, with well-equipped bungalows (all have color cable TV and private bath), spacious grounds, good restaurants, and all except the Hotel Santa Cruz have giant swimming pools. On weekdays they provide lodging for people who work in the area.

The following four motels are all near one another at Km 126 on the Carretera al Atlántico, 126 km from Guatemala City.

Cheapest of the four is the *Hotel Santa Cruz* (☎ 934-7112; ☎ /fax 934-7075), where rooms in duplex bungalows are US$8.35/10 a single/double with fan, US$10/20 with air con. The restaurant here is popular, and cheaper than some of the others. Four new apartments with kitchen are also available.

Hotel El Atlántico (☎ 934-7160, fax 934-7041), Carretera al Atlántico Km 126, is probably the most attractive of the four, with a large swimming pool, beautiful spacious grounds and a good restaurant. Large, well-equipped bungalows are US$20/36/46 a single/double/triple. It's also probably the most popular; reservations are wise.

Across the highway, on the north side, the *Hotel Nuevo Pasabién* (☎ /fax 934-7201, 934-7073, 934-7074) has older, slightly more rustic rooms for US$10/20 a single/double, and newer, larger rooms for US$13/25 with fan, US$15/29 with air con.

Opposite the Hotel Santa Cruz and behind the 24-hour Shell gas station, *Hotel Longarone* (☎ 934-7126, fax 934-7035) is the old standard in this area. Some rooms are in a long row, others are in duplex bungalows. Simple rooms are US$18/24/30 a single/double/triple, or US$24/30/36 with cable TV and fridge; all have air con. It has two large swimming pools, two smaller ones for children, and a tennis court.

The restaurants at all of these hotels are open every day from around 6 am to 10 pm. Along the highway are various other smaller, cheaper eateries.

Nine km east of these places, right at the junction with CA-10, where the road heads south to Chiquimula and Esquipulas, is the *Hotel Río* (☎ 941-1267), Carretera al Atlántico Km 135. It's rather beat-up. Rooms with private bath are US$6/7 with two/three beds.

Valle Dorado (☎ 941-2542, fax 941-2543), on the Carretera al Atlántico at Km 149, 14 km past the Hwy CA-10 junction and 23 km from the other Río Hondo hotels, is an enormous complex including an aquatic park with giant pools, waterslides, toboggans and other entertainment. Rooms are US$46 for one to three people, US$55 for four or US$78 for six. Make reservations on weekends, when it fills up with families.

Many people prefer to stay at one of the other Río Hondo hotels and come to Valle Dorado for the day. Day use costs US$6/5 for adults/children on weekends, US$4/3 during the week. The park is open for day use every day from 8 am to sunset.

ESTANZUELA
Population 10,000

Traveling south from Río Hondo along CA-10 you are in the midst of the Río Motagua Valley, a hot expanse of what is known as 'dry tropic,' which once supported a great number and variety of dinosaurs. Three km south of the Carretera al Atlántico you'll see a small monument on the right-hand (west) side of the road commemorating the terrible earthquake of February 4, 1976.

Less than two km south of the earthquake monument is the small town of Estanzuela, with its **Museo de Paleontología, Arqueología y Geología Ing Roberto Woolfolk Sarvia**, an interesting museum filled with dinosaur bones. The museum is open every day from 8 am to noon and from 1 to 5 pm; admission is free. To find the museum, go west from the highway directly through the town for one km, following the small blue signs pointing to the *museo*; anyone you see can help point the way. Next door to the museum is a small shop selling cold drinks and snacks.

Within the museum are most of the bones of three big dinosaurs, including those of a giant ground sloth some 30,000 years old, and a prehistoric whale. Other exhibits include early Mayan artifacts.

ZACAPA
Population 18,000

Capital of the department of the same name, Zacapa (230 meters) is several kilometers east of the highway. It offers little to travelers, though the locals do make cheese, cigars and superb old rum. The few hotels in town are basic and will do in an emergency; better accommodations are in Río Hondo and Esquipulas.

CHIQUIMULA
Population 24,000

Another departmental capital set in a mining and tobacco-growing region, Chiquimula (370 meters) is on Hwy CA-10, 32 km south of the Carretera al Atlántico. It is a major market town for all of eastern Guatemala, with lots of buying and selling activity every day. It's also a transportation point and overnight stop for those making their way to Copán in Honduras; this is the only reason that most travelers stop here. Among other things, Chiquimula is famous for its hot climate.

Orientation & Information
Chiquimula is easy to get around on foot.

The post office, on 10a Av between 1a and 2a Calle, is in the dirt alley, around to the side of the building opposite the bus station. The Guatel telephone office is on 3a Calle, a few doors downhill from the plaza; coin phones are outside. The Hotel Hernández (not far from the plaza) and the Hotel Victoria (near the bus station) also offer domestic and international telephone services. The busy *mercado* is around the corner from Guatel.

Many banks will change US dollars cash and traveler's checks. Banco G&T, half a block from the plaza at 7a Av 4-75, Zona 1, changes both, and also gives cash advances on Visa and MasterCard; it's open Monday to Friday from 9 am to 8 pm and Saturday from 10 am to 2 pm. These hours are

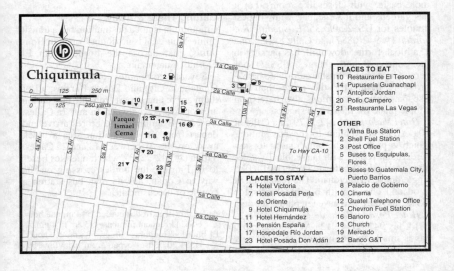

Chiquimula

0   125   250 m
0   125   250 yards

Parque Ismael Cerna

To Hwy CA-10

PLACES TO EAT
10 Restaurante El Tesoro
14 Pupusería Guanachapi
17 Antojitos Jordan
20 Pollo Campero
21 Restaurante Las Vegas

OTHER
1   Vilma Bus Station
2   Shell Fuel Station
3   Post Office
5   Buses to Esquipulas, Flores
6   Buses to Guatemala City, Puerto Barrios
8   Palacio de Gobierno
10 Cinema
12 Guatel Telephone Office
15 Chevron Fuel Station
16 Banoro
18 Church
19 Mercado
22 Banco G&T

PLACES TO STAY
4   Hotel Victoria
7   Hotel Posada Perla de Oriente
9   Hotel Chiquimulja
11 Hotel Hernández
13 Pensión España
17 Hospedaje Río Jordan
23 Hotel Posada Don Adán

typical for most of the banks in town. Banoro at 3a Calle 8-30 has longer Saturday hours, from 9 am to 6 pm.

Places to Stay

Hotel Chiquimulja (☎ 942-0387), 3a Calle 6-51, is on the north side of the plaza. The rooms have fluorescent green walls; other than that, they're about average. All have private bath, and the ones on the street side have wide balconies overlooking the plaza. Rooms with fan are US$4/6 a single/ double, or US$12/16 with air con and cable TV. It has parking, too, as do most of the hotels here.

A block east of the Chiquimulja, downhill on the same street, are several other hotels. *Hotel Hernández* (☎ /fax 942-0708), 3a Calle 7-41, Zona 1, is clean, pleasant and friendly; the owner speaks English, Spanish and a little French. There's a swimming pool, parking, telephone service, and the rooms all have fans and good beds. Singles/doubles with shared bath are US$4/6.65; with private bath and cable TV they are US$8/12, or US$15 with air con.

In the same block, just downhill, the *Pensión España*, 3a Calle 7-81, Zona 1, is more basic, with closet-like rooms, but it has gardens and it's cheaper, with singles/ doubles for US$2.50/3.35. *Hospedaje Río Jordan* (☎ 942-0887), 3a Calle 8-91, Zona 1, a block further downhill, has parking in the courtyard and charges US$2/4 per person in rooms with shared/private bath – probably better for the price than the España. *Antojitos Jordan*, also here, is a simple place for meals and snacks.

Hotel Victoria (☎ 942-2179), 2a Calle at 10a Av, is convenient to the bus station, which is probably the only reason to stay here. Small rooms with fan, cable TV, telephone and private bath are US$6/10/14/19 a single/double/triple/quad. The restaurant is good and cheap, with big breakfasts for US$2, and they also have telephone service.

Hotel Posada Perla de Oriente (☎ 942-0014, fax 942-0534), 12a Av 2-30, Zona 1, has a small swimming pool, a children's play area and a restaurant. Rooms are simple, with private bath, fan and cable TV, and cost US$10/15 a single/double.

Hotel Posada Don Adán (☎ 942-0549), 8a Av 4-30, Zona 1, is new and spotless. It's run by a friendly, efficient señora who charges US$17/23/29 a single/double/triple for rooms with private bath, telephone, cable TV, fan and air con.

Places to Eat

Eating in Chiquimula is easy, as there are plenty of cheap little places. Try the *Pupusería Guanachapi*, opposite the Pensión España. You can fill up for only a few quetzales.

Restaurante El Tesoro, on the main plaza, serves Chinese food at reasonable prices. Near the southeast corner of the plaza, *Pollo Campero*, 7a Av at 4a Calle, serves up fried chicken, burgers and breakfasts. It's open every day, and its air conditioning is a treat.

For a step up in quality, try the *Restaurante Las Vegas*, 7a Av 4-40, half a block from the plaza. It's perhaps Chiquimula's best, with fancy plants, jazzy music, a well-stocked bar, and full meals for around US$6 (sandwiches less). It's open every day from 7 am to midnight.

Getting There & Away

Chiquimula is not a destination but a transit point. Your goal is no doubt Copán in Honduras, just across the border from El Florido, Guatemala.

Several companies operate buses to Guatemala City and Puerto Barrios; all of them arrive and depart from the bus station area on 11a Av, between 1a and 2a Calles. Buses to Esquipulas and Flores arrive and depart from the bus station area a block away, on 10a Av between 1a and 2a Calles. Vilma (☎ 942-2253), which operates buses to El Florido, the border crossing on the way to Copán, has its own bus station a couple of blocks north.

Anguiatú (El Salvador border; 54 km, one hour, US$1) Frequent minibuses, 5 am to 4 pm.
El Florido (Honduras border; 58 km, 2½ hours, US$1.20) Buses depart from the Vilma bus

station at 6, 9, 10:30 and 11:30 am, 12:30, 1:30, 2:30 and 3:30 pm. Coming in the opposite direction, they depart from El Florido at 5:30, 6:15, 7:15, 8:30 and 10:30 am, noon, 1:30 and 3:30 pm.

Esquipulas (52 km, one hour, US$1) Minibuses every 10 minutes, 4 am to 8 pm.

Flores (385 km, 12 hours, US$10) Transportes María Elena buses depart at 6 am and 2:30 pm.

Guatemala City (169 km, three hours, US$2.50) Rutas Orientales, Transportes Guerra and Guatesqui operate buses departing every half hour, 5:30 am to 2 pm.

Puerto Barrios (192 km, 4½ hours, US$2.50) Buses every 15 minutes, 4 am to 3 pm.

Río Hondo (32 km, 35 minutes, US$1) Minibuses every half hour, 5 am to 6 pm. Or take any bus heading for Guatemala City, Flores or Puerto Barrios.

PADRE MIGUEL JUNCTION & ANGUIATÚ

Between Chiquimula and Esquipulas, 35 km from Chiquimula and 14 km from Esquipulas, Padre Miguel Junction is the turnoff for Anguiatú, the border of El Salvador, which is 19 km away. It takes half an hour to reach the border from this junction. Minibuses come by frequently, coming from Chiquimula, Quezaltepeque and Esquipulas. There's nothing much here at the crossroads, only a guard house and a bus stop shelter.

The border at Anguiatú is open every day from 6 am to 6 pm, though you might be able to get through on 'extraordinary service' until 9 pm. Across the border there are hourly buses to San Salvador, passing through Metapán, 12 km from the border, and Santa Ana, 47 km further along.

ESQUIPULAS

From Chiquimula, CA-10 goes south into the mountains, where it's cooler and a bit more comfortable. After an hour's ride through pretty country, the highway descends into a valley ringed by mountains. Halfway down the slope, about a kilometer from the center of town, there is a mirador (lookout) from which to get a good view. The reason for a trip to Esquipulas is evident as soon as you catch sight of the place: the great Basílica de Esquipulas which towers above the town, its whiteness

shining in the sun. The view has changed little in the more than a century and a half since explorer John L Stephens saw it:

Descending, the clouds were lifted, and I looked down upon an almost boundless plain, running from the foot of the Sierra, and afar off saw, standing alone in the wilderness, the great church of Esquipulas, like the Church of the Holy Sepulchre in Jerusalem, and the Caaba in Mecca, the holiest of temples . . . I had a long and magnificent descent to the foot of the Sierra.

History

This town may have been a place of pilgrimage even before the Spaniards' conquest. Legend has it that the town takes its name from a noble Maya lord who ruled this region when the Spanish arrived, and who received them in peace.

With the arrival of the friars, a church was built, and in 1595 an image of Christ carved from black wood was installed in it. The steady flow of pilgrims to Esquipulas became a flood after 1737, when Pedro Pardo de Figueroa, Archbishop of Guatemala, came here on pilgrimage and went away cured of a chronic ailment. Delighted with this development, the prelate commissioned a huge new church to be built on the site. It was finished in 1758, and the pilgrimage trade has been the town's livelihood ever since.

Orientation & Information

The church is the center of everything. Most of the good cheap hotels are within a block or two of it, as are numerous small restaurants. The town's only luxury hotel is on the outskirts, along the road back to Chiquimula. The highway does not enter town; 11a Calle, also sometimes called Doble Vía Quirio Cataño, comes in from the highway and is the town's 'main drag.'

The post office is at 6a Av 2-15, about 10 blocks north of the center. The Guatel telephone office, 5a Av at the corner of 9a Calle, is open every day; coin phones are outside on the sidewalk.

A number of banks change US dollars cash and traveler's checks. Banco del Café, 3a Av 6-68, Zona 1, changes both, gives cash advances on Visa and MasterCard, and is the town's American Express agent.

There's a Honduran consulate (☎ 943-2027, 943-1547, fax 943-1371) in the Hotel Payaquí, facing the park. It's open Monday to Saturday, 8:30 am to noon and 2 to 5 pm.

Basilica

A massive pile of stone which has resisted the power of earthquakes for almost 2½ centuries, the basilica is approached through a pretty park and up a flight of steps. The impressive façade and towers are floodlit at night.

Inside, the devout approach **El Cristo Negro** with great reverence, many on their knees. Incense, the murmur of prayers and the shuffle of sandaled feet fills the air. To get a close view of the famous Black Christ you must enter the church from the side. Shuffling along quickly, you may get a good glimpse or two before being shoved onwards by the press of the crowd behind you. On Sundays, religious holidays and (especially) during the festival around January 15, the press of devotees is intense.

When you leave the church and descend the steps through the park, notice the vendors selling straw hats that are decorated with artificial flowers and stitched with the name 'Esquipulas,' perfect for pilgrims who want everyone to know they've made the trip.

Cueva de las Minas

The Centro Turístico Cueva de las Minas has a 50-meter-deep cave (bring your own light), grassy play and picnic areas, and the Río El Milagro, where people come for a dip and say it's miraculous. The cave and river are half a kilometer from the entrance gate, which is behind the Basilica's cemetery, 300 meters south of the turnoff into town on the road heading towards Honduras. It's open every day, 6:30 am to 4 pm; admission is US$0.35. Refreshments are available.

Places to Stay

Esquipulas has a great abundance of places to stay. On holidays and during the annual festival, every hotel in town is filled, whatever the price; weekends are fairly busy as well, with prices substantially higher. On weekdays when there is no festival, ask for a *descuento* (discount) and you'll probably get it.

Budget The best place to search for a cheap room is in the streets to the north of the basilica.

The family-run *Pensión Santa Rosa* (☎ 943-2908), 10a Calle at 1a Av, Zona 1, is typical of the small back-street places, charging US$5/7 for rooms with shared/private bath. The *Hotel Paris* next door is similar, as is the *Pensión La Favorita*, and there are several others on this street.

Hotel Monte Cristo (☎ 943-1256), 3a Av 9-12, Zona 1, is clean and OK, with parking and a restaurant. Singles/doubles are US$7/9 with shared bath, US$17/21 with private bath.

Hotel El Peregrino (☎ 943-1054, 943-1859), 2a Av 11-94, Zona 1, on the southwest corner of the park, has simple rooms with private bath for US$7/14, plus a new section in the rear where larger, fancier rooms with cable TV are US$13/25. Next door, the *Hotel Los Angeles* (☎ 943-1254), 2a Av 11-94, Zona 1, has 20 rooms arranged around a bright inner courtyard, all with private bath, fan and cable TV, for US$9/17. Both places have restaurants and parking.

In the same block, *Hotel Payaquí* (☎ 943-2025, fax 943-1371) is a large, attractive hotel with 55 rooms, all with private bath, cable TV, telephone and fridge. Rooms are the same price, with or without air con: US$12/24 a single/double. It has two restaurants, one in the rear by the swimming pool and one in front, with a view of the park.

Hotel Villa Zonia (☎ 943-1304), 1a Av at the corner of 10a Calle, Zona 1, is a bright, new hotel with 15 rooms, all with private bath and cable TV. Rooms are US$17/25 with one/two double beds, and there's parking.

Middle *Hotel Internacional* (☎ 943-1131, 943-1530), 10a Calle 0-85, Zona 1, is new, clean and pleasant, with a small swimming pool, sauna, restaurant and parking. The 49 rooms, all with private bath, cable TV and phone, are US$25 with fan, US$37.50 with air conditioning.

Hotel Legendario (☎ 943-1824/5; ☎ /fax 943-1022), at the corner of 3a Av and 8a Calle, Zona 1, is new, modern and quite comfortable. The 40 rooms all have private bath, fan, cable TV and large windows opening onto a pleasant grassy courtyard with a swimming pool; singles/doubles are US$25/42. There's a restaurant and parking.

Hotel Posada del Cristo Negro (☎ 943-1482, fax 943-1829), Carretera Internacional a Honduras Km 224, is two km from the church, out of town on the way to Honduras. Broad green lawns, a pretty swimming pool, a large dining room and other services make it elaborate. In the 1960s, this might have been Guatemala's best country-club resort. Comfortable rooms with private bath, fridge and TV cost US$18/26/34/42 for a single/double/triple/quad. Two or three children (up to age eight) are free in each room.

Places to Eat

Restaurants all are more expensive here than in other parts of Guatemala. Low-budget restaurants are clustered at the north end of the park where hungry pilgrims can find them readily. It is very important to ask in advance the price of each food item you order, and to add up your bill carefully.

3a Avenida, the street running north opposite the church, has many small eateries. *Comedor Rosy No 2* is tidy and cheerful, with meals for around US$2.50 and big bottles of pickled chiles on the tables. *Restaurante y Cafetería Victoria* across the street is a bit fancier, with tablecloths and plants, but prices are higher.

In the same block, the *Comedor y Cafetería Beato Hermano Pedro* advertises '*Coma bien y pague menos!*' ('Eat well and pay less!'). Set prices for full meals are around US$2.

On the west side of the park, *Jimmy's* is a pleasant, bright and clean cafeteria with big windows looking out onto the park. Prices are reasonable and there's a good

selection. Roast chicken is one of the specialties here; you can get a whole chicken 'to go' for US$6, or a quarter chicken with fries, salad and tortillas for US$2.

La Rotonda, on 11a Calle opposite the Rutas Orientales bus station, is a round building with chairs around a round open-air counter under a big awning. It's a pleasant place, clean and fresh. The menu of the day, with soup, a meat main course, rice, vegetables, dessert, tortillas and coffee or lemonade is US$4, and there are plenty of other selections to choose from, including pizza, pasta and burgers.

All of these places are open every day from around 6 or 6:30 am until 9 or 10 pm.

The more expensive *La Hacienda Steak House*, 2a Av at the corner of 10a Calle, is an enjoyable place for grilled steaks, chicken and seafood; it's open every day from 8 am to 10 pm. *Restaurante Los Arcos*, on 11a Calle opposite the park, is another more upscale restaurant, open every day from 7 am to 10 pm.

All of the mid-range and top-end hotels have their own dining rooms.

Getting There & Away

Buses to Guatemala City arrive and depart from the Rutas Orientales bus station (☎ 943-1366) on 11a Calle at 1a Av, near the entrance to town. Minibuses to Agua Caliente arrive and depart across the street; taxis also wait here, charging the same as the minibuses, once they have five passengers.

Minibuses going to Chiquimula and to Anguiatú depart from the east end of 11a Calle; you may see them hawking for passengers along the main street. Transportes María Elena operates buses to Flores.

Anguiatú (El Salvador border; 33 km, one hour, US$1) Minibuses every half hour, 6 am to 4 pm.
Agua Caliente (Honduras border; 10 km, 30 minutes, US$0.70) Minibuses every half hour, 6 am to 5 pm.
Chiquimula (52 km, one hour, US$1) Minibuses every 10 minutes, 5 am to 5 pm.
Flores (437 km, 14 hours, US$12) Transportes María Elena buses depart at 4:30 am and 1 pm.

Guatemala City (222 km, four hours, US$3.50) Rutas Orientales' *servicio especial* buses depart at 6:30 and 7:30 am, 1:30 and 3:30 pm; ordinary buses depart at 3:30, 5, 8:15 and 11:30 am, 1, 3 and 5:30 pm.

EL FLORIDO

If you're crossing the border at El Florido, it's undoubtedly because you are going to or from Copán, 12 km from the border on the Honduras side. The border crossing is open every day from 7 am to 6 pm.

The Guatemalan village of El Florido, which has no services beyond a few soft-drink stands, is 1.2 km west of the border. At the border crossing are a few snack stands and the very basic *Hospedaje Las Rosas*, which can put you up in an emergency.

Moneychangers will approach you on both sides of the border. Sometimes they offer a very poor rate; find out what the current rate of exchange should be, before you arrive at the border. Banks in Copán Ruinas offer a better rate of exchange.

You must present your passport and tourist card to the Guatemalan immigration and customs authorities, pay fees (some of which are unauthorized) of US$6, then cross the border and do the same thing with the Honduran authorities. If you just want a short-term permit to enter Honduras and plan to go only as far as Copán, tell this to the Honduran immigration officer and he will charge you a fee of US$3. With such a permit you cannot go farther than the ruins and you must leave Honduras by the same route. If you want to travel farther in Honduras you may need a tourist card or visa (see the Honduras chapter). If you need a Honduran visa, you can obtain it at the Honduran Consulate in Esquipulas or Guatemala City.

When you return through this border point, you must again pass through both sets of immigration and customs and pay fees (lower this time). The Guatemalan immigration officer should give you your old tourist card back without charging the full fee for a new one.

If you are driving a rented car, you will have to present the Guatemalan customs authorities at the border with a special letter of permission to enter Honduras, written on the rental company's letterhead and signed and sealed by the appropriate company official. If you do not have such a letter, you'll have to leave your rental car at El Florido and continue to Copán by pickup truck.

On the Honduran side of the border are several little cookshacks where you can get simple food and cool drinks while waiting for a pickup truck to leave.

Getting There & Away

It's 280 km (seven hours by bus) from Guatemala City to El Florido. Buses from Guatemala City take you to Chiquimula, where you must change buses and continue on to the border. If you're coming from Esquipulas, you can get off the bus at **Vado Hondo**, the junction of CA-10 and the road to El Florido, and wait for a bus there; but as the bus may fill up before departure, it may be just as well to go the extra eight km into Chiquimula and secure your seat before the bus pulls out.

Coming from the border on the Guatemala side, buses to Chiquimula (58 km, 2½ hours, US$1.20) depart from the border at 5:30, 6:15, 7:15, 8:30 and 10:30 am, noon, 1:30 and 3:30 pm. On the Honduras side, pickup trucks depart from the border every 40 minutes throughout the day. They should charge around US$1.25 for the 14-km, 45-minute ride to Copán Ruinas.

If you travel by organized tour or private car, it's faster. Several Antigua travel agencies offer weekend trips to Copán, which may also include visits to other places including the ruins at Quiriguá.

If you're driving, drive south from Chiquimula 10 km, north from Esquipulas 48 km, and turn eastward at Vado Hondo (Km 178.5 on CA-10). There's a small motel just opposite the turning, which will do if you need a bed. A sign reading 'Vado Hondo Ruinas de Copán' marks the way on the two-hour, 50-km drive from this junction to El Florido.

The road is unpaved but is usually in good condition and fairly fast (an average of 40 km/h). Twenty km north-east of Vado Hondo are the Chorti Maya villages of Jocotán and Camotán, set amidst mountainous tropical countryside dotted with thatched huts in lush green valleys. Jocotán has a small Centro de Salud (medical clinic) and the *Hotel/Pensión Ramirez*, a half-block north of the hilltop church and main square. Rooms with private bath are US$4 per person; rooms with shared bath cost less. There's a small restaurant as well.

Along the road you may have to ford several small streams. This causes no problem unless there has been an unusual amount of rain during previous days.

QUIRIGUÁ

From Copán it is only some 50 km to Quiriguá as the crow flies, but the lay of the land, the international border and the condition of the roads makes it a journey of 175 km. Like Copán, Quiriguá is famed for its intricately carved stelae. Unlike Copán, the gigantic brown sandstone stelae at Quiriguá rise as high as 10.5 meters, like sentinels in a quiet tropical park.

A visit to Quiriguá is easy if you have your own transport; it's more difficult but certainly not impossible if you're traveling by bus. From Río Hondo junction it's 67 km along the Carretera al Atlántico to the village of Los Amates, where there are a couple of hotels and a restaurant. The village of Quiriguá is 1.5 km east of Los Amates, and the turn-off to the ruins is another 1.5 km to the east. Following the access road south from the Carretera al Atlántico, it's 3.4 km through banana groves to the archaeological site.

History

Quiriguás history parallels that of Copán, of which it was a dependency during much of the Classic period. Of the three sites in this area, only the present archaeological park is of interest.

The location lent itself to the carving of giant stelae. Beds of brown sandstone in the nearby Río Motagua had cleavage planes suitable for cutting large pieces. Though soft when first cut, the sandstone

dried hard in the air. With Copán's expert artisans nearby for guidance, Quiriguás stonecarvers were ready for greatness. All they needed was a great leader to inspire them – and to pay for the carving of the huge stelae.

That leader was Cauac Sky (725-784), who decided that Quiriguá should no longer be under the control of Copán. In a war with his former suzerain, Cauac Sky took King 18 Rabbit of Copán prisoner in 737 and later had him beheaded. Independent at last, Cauac Sky commissioned his stonecutters to go to work, and for the next 38 years they turned out giant stelae and zoomorphs dedicated to the glory of King Cauac Sky.

Cauac Sky was followed by his son Sky Xul (784-800), who lost his throne to a usurper, Jade Sky. This last great king of Quiriguá continued the building boom initiated by Cauac Sky, reconstructing Quiriguá's Acropolis on a grander scale.

Quiriguá remained unknown to Europeans until John L Stephens arrived in 1840. Impressed by its great monuments, he lamented the world's lack of interest in them:

Of one thing there is no doubt: a large city once stood there; its name is lost, its history unknown; and . . . no account of its existence has ever before been published. For centuries it has lain as completely buried as if covered with the lava of Vesuvius. Every traveler from Yzabal to Guatimala has passed within three hours of it; we ourselves had done the same; and yet there it lay, like the rock-built city of Edom, unvisited, unsought, and utterly unknown.

Stephens tried to buy the ruined city in order to have its stelae shipped to New York, but the owner, Señor Payes, assumed that Stephens, being a diplomat, was negotiating on behalf of the US government and that the government would pay. Payes quoted an extravagant price, and the deal was never made.

Between 1881 and 1894, excavations were carried out by Alfred P Maudslay. In the early 1900s all the land around Quiriguá was sold to the United Fruit

Company and turned into banana groves. The company is gone, but the bananas and Quiriguá remain. Restoration of the site was carried out by the University of Pennsylvania in the 1930s.

Ruins

The beautiful park-like archaeological zone is open every day from 7:30 am to 5 pm; admission costs US$0.20. A small stand near the entrance sells cold drinks and snacks, but you'd do better to bring your own picnic.

Despite the sticky heat and (sometimes) bothersome mosquitoes, Quiriguá is a wonderful place. The giant stelae on the Great Plaza are all much more worn than those at Copán. To impede their further deterioration, each has been covered by a thatched roof. The roofs cast shadows which make it difficult to examine the carving closely and almost impossible to get a good photograph. But somehow this does little to inhibit one's sense of awe.

Seven of the stelae, designated A, C, D, E, F, H and J, were built during the reign of Cauac Sky and carved with his image. Stela E is the largest Maya stela known, standing some eight meters above ground, with another three meters or so buried in the earth. It weighs almost 60,000 kg. Note the exuberant, elaborate headdresses, the beards on some of the figures (an oddity in Mayan art), the staffs of office held in the kings' hands, and the glyphs on the stelae's sides.

At the far end of the plaza is the Acropolis, far less impressive than the one at Copán. At its base are several zoomorphs, blocks of stone carved to resemble real and mythic creatures. Frogs, tortoises, jaguars and serpents were favorite subjects. The low zoomorphs can't compete with the towering stelae in impressiveness, but as works of art, imagination and mythic significance, the zoomorphs are superb.

Places to Stay & Eat

In the center of the village of Quiriguá, 700 meters south of the Carretera al Atlántico, the *Hotel y Restaurante Royal* is simple,

clean and quiet. Rooms with shared bath are US$4/6 a single/double; larger rooms with private bath and five beds are US$6/9/13/17/20 for one to five people. The restaurant serves meat and vegetarian meals. Most guests here are international visitors who have come to visit the archaeological site.

At Los Amates, on the Carretera al Atlántico three km west of Quiriguá village, is a 24-hour Texaco fuel station. Behind the Texaco station, the *Hotel y Restaurante Santa Mónica* has rooms with private bath for US$6/12/18 a single/double/triple. About 100 meters east of the Texaco station is the *Ranchón Chileño*, the best restaurant in the area, where you can get good, filling meals for about US$6 and light meals for half that much.

The *Comedor y Hospedaje Doña María*, Carretera al Atlántico Km 181, is at the east end of the Doña María Bridge, 20 km west of Los Amates. The 10 rooms here, all with private bath, rent for US$6 per person; they are old but clean, lined up along an open-air walkway beside the river. Across the river there's a large, grassy parklike camping area with coconut palms and fruit trees, covered picnic tables and campsites for US$4 per group, vehicle or tent. Ask at the hotel and they'll open the gate for you. The open-air restaurant, open every day from 6 am to 9 pm, has a great view of the river, and there's good swimming here. You're welcome to go across the footbridge for a picnic, just ask permission first.

Getting There & Away

The turnoff to Quiriguá is 205 km (four hours) northeast of Guatemala City, 70 km northeast of the Río Hondo junction, 43 km southwest of the road to Flores in El Petén, and 90 km southwest of Puerto Barrios.

Buses that run to/from Guatemala City–Puerto Barrios, Guatemala City–Flores, Esquipulas–Flores or Chiquimula–Flores will drop you off or pick you up here. They'll drop you at the turnoff to the archaeological site if you ask.

The transport center in this area is Morales, about 40 km northeast of Quiriguá.

This is where it's easiest to catch a bus for Río Dulce.

Getting Around

From the turnoff on the highway it's 3.4 km to the archaeological site. Buses and pickups provide transport between the turnoff and the site for US$0.15 each way. If you don't see one, don't fret; it's a pleasant walk on a dirt road running through banana plantations to get there.

If you're staying in the village of Quiriguá or Los Amates and walking to and from the archaeological site, you can take a short cut along the railway branch line which goes from the village through the banana fields, crossing the access road very near the entrance to the archaeological site.

LAGO DE IZABAL

This large lake to the northwest of the Carretera al Atlántico is just starting to be developed for tourism. Most visitors who stay here stay at Río Dulce, the village on the north side of the bridge where Highway CA-13, the road heading north to Flores and Tikal, crosses the east end of the lake. East of this bridge are El Golfete and the beautiful Río Dulce, which meets the Caribbean at Lívingston; river trips are a highlight of a visit to eastern Guatemala. Other places to stay around the lake include San Felipe, Mariscos, El Estor and Finca Paraíso.

Other highlights of the lake include the Castillo San Felipe (an old Spanish fortress), the Cerro San Gil wildlife refuge and the Bocas del Polochic river delta.

Río Dulce

Head northwest from Morales and La Ruidosa junction (Carretera al Atlántico Km 245) along the road to Flores in El Petén, and after 34 km you reach the village of Río Dulce, also sometimes called El Relleno or Fronteras. Río Dulce (Fronteras) is the village on the north side of the bridge over the lake, El Relleno is the village on the south side. In addition to the locals, Río Dulce has a sizable population of foreign yachties.

Get off the bus on the north side of the bridge. It stops on the highway, just uphill from the Hollymar Restaurant, which serves as Río Dulce's visitor information center, dining room, lounge, and dock for motorboats making trips down the Río Dulce. You can also rent canoes and kayaks, ask about boat and inner tube trips on the Río Ciénega, and generally hang out. (Hollymar also offers email services; see the Online Resources appendix.) If you need to change money or traveler's checks, there are two banks in town.

The minute you alight from the bus, young men will approach you and try to put you on a motorboat to Lívingston. This may be exactly what you want to do. However, you can spend some relaxing days around the lake if you're so inclined.

For details of the Río Dulce boat trip, see the Lívingston section.

Places to Stay & Eat *Hacienda Tijax* (☎ 902-7825), a 500-acre hacienda a two-minute boat ride across the cove from the Hollymar Restaurant, is a special place to stay. Activities include horseback riding, hiking, bird watching, boat trips and tours around the rubber plantation. Dorm beds in open-air upstairs Thai-style thatch-roofed houses with downstairs kitchens are US$5 per person (US$25 to have the whole house to yourself). Small private rooms over the hacienda's restaurant are US$3.35 per person, or US$1.65 per person in hammocks (yours or theirs). There is also a camping area, where camping costs US$1.65 per tent or US$3.35 per vehicle. Access is by boat from the Hollymar, or by road from the highway about one km north of the village. The owner, Eugene, speaks Spanish, English, French and Italian. There's a restaurant open in high season.

Other places to stay in the village include the *Riverside Motel*, a simple place on the highway, with simple rooms with shared bath and fan for US$4/5 a single/double. *Hotel Don Paco*, a yellow building with no sign, is another simple place; rooms with shared bath are US$4/7. *Hotel Portal del*

Río is the best of the hotels in the village, with rooms with private bath for US$9/13.

For dining you can't beat the *Hollymar*, with an open-air deck over the lake, just on the north side of the bridge. The food here is delicious and cheap, and it has a relaxed international ambiance.

Nearby, *Bruno's*, another open-air place right beside the water, is a restaurant, sports bar with satellite TV and video, and its floating dock makes it popular with yachties. *Cafetería La Carreta*, off the highway on the road towards San Felipe, is often recommended by locals. *Hacienda Tijax* has a restaurant open in high season.

Several more expensive places to stay are on the waterfront farther from town, all with their own restaurants and accessible only by boat. *Hotel Catamaran* (Guatemala City ☎ 361-1937, fax 331-8450) is an upmarket place with rooms for US$36/41, bungalows for US$44/51, and a fancy restaurant and sports bar. Also on the lakeshore, *Mario's Marina* has good food and is a popular hangout for yachties.

Getting There & Away Buses head north along a very bad road to Poptún (95 km, 3½ to four hours, US$2.50) and Flores (208 km, seven hours, US$5). In the other direction, buses go to Guatemala City (488 km, five hours, US$6). To bus to Puerto Barrios, take any bus heading for Guatemala City and change buses at La Ruidosa. The Atitlán Shuttle minibus operates from an office on the highway, near the Hollymar.

Colectivo motorboats go down the Río Dulce to Lívingston whenever there are a minimum of about six or eight people wanting to go. With plenty of stops, the trip takes about three hours and costs around US$12.50 per person (bargain for a fair price). Boats usually leave in the morning, but they may leave throughout the day.

San Felipe & El Castillo de San Felipe

The fortress and castle of San Felipe de Lara, about three km west of the bridge, was built in 1652 to keep pirates from looting the villages and commercial caravans of Izabal. Though it deterred the

buccaneers a bit, a pirate force captured and burned the fortress in 1686. By the end of the next century, pirates had disappeared from the Caribbean and the fort's sturdy walls served as a prison. Eventually, though, the fortress was abandoned and became a ruin. The present fort was reconstructed in 1956.

Today the castle is protected as a park and it's one of the lake's principal tourist attractions. In addition to the fort itself there's a large grassy park grounds, BBQ and picnic areas, and swimming in the lake. It's open every day, 8 am to 5 pm; admission is US$1.

Places to Stay & Eat Near the Castillo, the *Hotel Don Humberto* can put you up for US$6/11/16 for a single/double/triple in simple but clean rooms with private bath. There's also a restaurant here, or you could try the *Cafetería Selva Tropical*. Nearby, the *Viñas del Lago* is a fancier, more expensive hotel.

On the lakeshore about a 10-minute walk from El Castillo, *Rancho Escondido* (Guatemala City ☎ /fax 369-2681) is a pleasant little hotel and restaurant. Downstairs rooms with shared bath are US$5/9 a single/double; more attractive upstairs rooms with private bath are US$7/13, or you can stay in a hammock for US$2.50 per night. There's laundry service, good food, swimming in the lake and other activities. The owners will come to pick you up when you arrive in Río Dulce; ask at the Hollymar and they'll radio for you.

Getting There & Away San Felipe is on the lakeshore, three km west of Río Dulce. It's a beautiful 45-minute walk between the two towns. A colectivo pickup truck provides transport between the two towns for US$0.35, running about every half-hour. In Río Dulce it stops on the corner of the highway and the San Felipe road (see map); in San Felipe it stops in front of the Hotel Don Humberto, at the entrance to El Castillo.

Boats coming from Lívingston will drop you in San Felipe if you ask them to. The Río Dulce boat trips usually come to

El Castillo, allowing you to get out and visit the castle if you like. Or you can come over from Río Dulce by private launch for US$5.

Finca El Paraíso & Río Agua Caliente

On the north side of the lake, between San Felipe and El Estor, the Finca El Paraíso is a popular destination for day trips coming from Río Dulce and other places around the lake. At the finca, which is a working ranch, you can walk to an incredibly beautiful spot in the jungle where a wide hot waterfall drops 30 or 40 feet into a clear, deep pool. You can bathe in the hot water, swim in the cool pool, or duck under an overhanging promontory and enjoy a jungle-style sauna. Also on the finca are a number of interesting caves and good hiking.

El Estor

The major settlement on the northwestern shore is El Estor, once a nickel-mining town but now growing in popularity as a waystation for intrepid travelers on the Cobán-Lago de Izabal route through the beautiful Panzós Valley.

Places to Stay & Eat The *Hotel Vista al Lago* (☎ 949-7205), 6a Av 1-13, Zona 1, is pleasant and clean, and looks out over the lake. The building, built between 1825 and 1830, was once a general store owned by an Englishman and a Dutchman; 'the store' gave the town of El Estor its name. The 21 rooms here, each with private bath and fan, are US$8/10/15 a single/double/triple.

Hotel Santa Clara, 5a Av 2-11, also has clean rooms with private bath. *Hotel Villela*, 6a Av 2-06, is another pleasant place to stay.

Ask at *Hugo's Restaurant* about tours around the lake, and about the cabañas on the Río Sauce.

Getting There & Away Buses operate between El Estor and Cobán, a nine-hour journey. The route, a dirt road in good condition, is slow going but very beautiful. Buses also connect El Estor and Guatemala City.

The link from El Estor to the Carretera al Atlántico is completed by the El Estor–Mariscos ferry, which leaves El Estor every day at 6 am and departs from Mariscos for the return journey at noon. The trip across the lake takes one hour. Buses run from Mariscos down to the highway.

Mariscos

Mariscos is the principal town on the lake's south side.

Denny's Beach, 10 minutes by boat from the town, offers cabañas, tours, hiking and swimming, and a full moon party. It's operated by Dennis Gulck and his wife Lupe. When you arrive in Mariscos, you can radio to them on VHF channel 09 – many people and businesses in Mariscos use radios, so it isn't hard to find one. They'll come to pick you up. *Karlinda's* and *Marinita* are other places to stay in Mariscos; both have restaurants, and offer lake tours.

See El Estor, above, for Getting There & Away.

THE ROAD TO FLORES

North across the bridge is the road into El Petén, Guatemala's vast jungle province. It's 208 km to Santa Elena and Flores, and another 65 km to Tikal.

The road from the Carretera al Atlántico to Modesto Méndez is not bad, but from Méndez to Santa Elena it's in terrible condition. It's a bone-jangling ride of at least six hours to Flores.

The forest here is disappearing at an alarming rate, falling to the machetes of subsistence farmers. Sections of forest are felled and burned off, crops are grown for a few seasons until the fragile jungle soil is exhausted, and then the farmer moves deeper into the forest to slash and burn new fields. Cattle ranchers, slashing and burning the forest to make pasture, have also contributed to the damage.

POPTÚN

Population 8000

The small town of Poptún (540 meters) is about halfway between Río Dulce and Flores. The reason most travelers come here is to visit Finca Ixobel. There are also a couple of other places to stay and eat. Otherwise, there's not much reason to stop in Poptún.

Places to Stay & Eat

The best facilities are at the 400-acre *Finca Ixobel* (☎ /fax 927-7363). For several decades Carole DeVine has offered travelers tent sites, palapas for hanging hammocks, beds and good homemade meals, with or without meat. Finca Ixobel is a special place, famous for its camaraderie – it's friendly and relaxed, a great place for meeting other travelers from around the world. It's also famous for its food and its activities. Horseback riding, camping trips, inner-tubing on the river and a famous cave trip are all organized on a daily basis, for a reasonable charge.

Camping costs US$2 to US$3 per person. Beds are US$4 in dormitories or tree houses, or pay US$6/8 for a single/double private room, or US$12.50 for a bungalow with private bath. Meals offer excellent value, right up to the eat-all-you-like buffet dinner for US$5. Or you can cook in the campground; if you do, you must bring all your own food, as there is no store on the finca.

The turnoff for the finca is marked on the highway, five km south of town. In the daytime, you can ask the bus driver to let you off there; it's a 15-minute walk to the finca. At night, or if you don't feel like making the walk, get off the bus in town and go to the Fonda Ixobel II restaurant, near the bus stop. They will radio for a taxi, which costs US$1.50 per person to the finca. It's important not to walk to the finca at night, as it's an isolated spot and robberies have been known to occur on the way.

There are also a couple of other places to stay in Poptún. *Camping Cocay*, seven km north of town and then 700 meters from the highway, is a very primitive camping ground in the jungle beside the river, good for swimming, inner tubing and fishing. The prices of US$2.50 per person in a tent or hammock, US$3.35 in a dorm, include breakfast; dinner is available for US$2.50.

They, too, offer activities in the area. This place is primitive and remote, and right in the jungle. Bring plenty of mosquito repellent; you'll need it.

The more upmarket *Hotel Ecológico Villa de los Castellanos* (☎ 927-7222, 927-7518, fax 927-7365) is just off the highway, seven km north of Poptún. It, too, is right beside the river, and great for swimming and inner tubing. Thatch-roofed cabins with electricity, private hot bath and two or three double beds are US$20/30/40 a single/double/triple. There's a restaurant here, and acres of gardens with many food and medicinal plants.

Getting There & Away

Bus All the Guatemala City-Flores buses stop in Poptún; see the sections on Flores and Guatemala City for bus details.

Buses also travel the remote route between Poptún and Fray Bartolomé de las Casas (usually called simply Las Casas), on the way to Cobán. From Poptún it's six hours to Las Casas, where there's a pensión where you can spend the night, and then a further five hours to Cobán.

Flores (113 km, 4½ to five hours, US$2.50) Several buses daily.
Fray Bartolomé de las Casas (100 km, six hours, US$4.20) One or two buses daily.
Río Dulce (95 km, 3½ to four hours, US$2.50) Take any bus heading for Guatemala City.
Guatemala City (393 km, seven to nine hours, US$10) Several buses daily.

Car If you're driving, fill your fuel tank before leaving Flores or Río Dulce, take some food and drink and a spare tire, and get an early start. The road is not good in either direction; the excessive ruts mean you'll have to drive slowly. A normal car can make it, though slowly; a 4WD would be fine, but it's not essential.

PUERTO BARRIOS

Population 35,000

Heading eastward from La Ruidosa junction, the country becomes even more lush, tropical and humid until you arrive at Puerto Barrios.

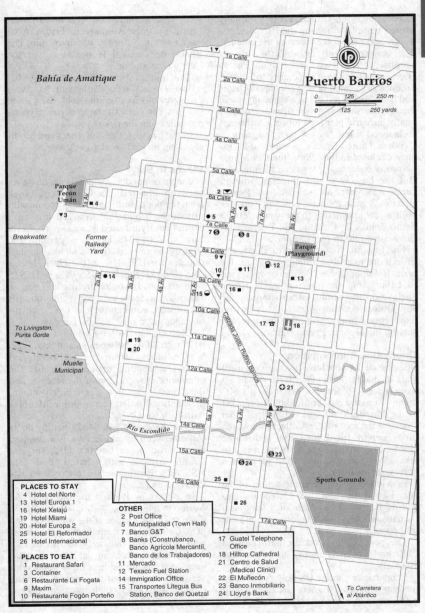

Bahía de Amatique

1a Calle
2a Calle
3a Calle
4a Calle
5a Calle

Puerto Barrios

0   125   250 m
0   125   250 yards

Parque
Tecún
Umán

6a Calle
7a Calle
8a Calle
9a Calle
10a Calle
11a Calle
12a Calle
13a Calle
14a Calle
15a Calle
16a Calle
17a Calle

Breakwater

Former
Railway
Yard

Parque
(Playground)

Calzada Justo Rufino Barrios

To Livingston,
Punta Gorda

Muelle
Municipal

Río Escondido

Sports Grounds

To Carretera
al Atlántico

1a Av
2a Av
3a Av
4a Av
5a Av
6a Av
7a Av
8a Av

PLACES TO STAY
4 Hotel del Norte
13 Hotel Europa 1
16 Hotel Xelajú
19 Hotel Miami
20 Hotel Europa 2
25 Hotel El Reformador
26 Hotel Internacional

PLACES TO EAT
1 Restaurant Safari
3 Container
6 Restaurante La Fogata
9 Maxim
10 Restaurante Fogón Porteño

OTHER
2 Post Office
5 Municipalidad (Town Hall)
7 Banco G&T
8 Banks (Construbanco,
   Banco Agrícola Mercantíl,
   Banco de los Trabajadores)
11 Mercado
12 Texaco Fuel Station
14 Immigration Office
15 Transportes Litegua Bus
   Station, Banco del Quetzal

17 Guatel Telephone
   Office
18 Hilltop Cathedral
21 Centro de Salud
   (Medical Clinic)
22 El Muñecón
23 Banco Inmobiliario
24 Lloyd's Bank

The powerful United Fruit Company owned vast plantations in the Río Motagua Valley and many other parts of the country. The company built railways to ship its produce to the coast, and it built Puerto Barrios early in the 20th century to put that produce onto ships sailing for New Orleans and New York. Laid out as a company town, Puerto Barrios has wide streets arranged neatly on a grid plan, and lots of Caribbean-style wood-frame houses, many on stilts.

When United Fruit's power and influence declined in the 1960s, the Del Monte company became successor to its interests. But the heyday of the imperial foreign firms was past, as was that of Puerto Barrios. A new, modern, efficient port was built a few kilometers to the southwest, at Santo Tomás de Castilla, and Puerto Barrios settled into tropical torpor.

For foreign visitors, Puerto Barrios is little more than the jumping-off point for boats to Punta Gorda (Belize) or for a visit to Lívingston, the fascinating Garífuna enclave on the northwestern shore of the Río Dulce. As the boats for Lívingston leave at odd hours, you may find yourself staying the night in Puerto Barrios.

Orientation & Information
Because of its spacious layout, you must walk or ride farther in Puerto Barrios to get from place to place. For instance, it's 800 meters from the bus terminal by the market to the Muelle Municipal (Municipal Boat Dock) at the foot of 12a Calle, from which boats depart for Lívingston and Punta Gorda. You are liable to be in town just to take a boat, so you may want to select a hotel near the dock.

El Muñecón, at the intersection of 8a Av, 14a Calle and the Calzada Justo Rufino Barrios, is a statue of a *bananero* (banana worker); it's a favorite monument in the town.

The post office is on the corner of 6a Calle and 6a Av. Guatel is on 8a Av near 10a Calle.

Many banks change US dollars cash and traveler's checks. Banco G&T, 7a Calle between 5a and 6a Avs, changes both and gives cash advances on Visa and Master-Card; it's open Monday to Friday from 9 am to 8 pm, Saturday 10 am to 2 pm. The Banco de Quetzal is upstairs over the Litegua bus station.

The immigration office (☎ 948-0802, 948-0327) is at 9a Calle and 2a Av, a couple of blocks from the dock. Be sure to get your entry or exit stamp if you're entering or leaving the country.

In the evening, the noisy bars and brothels along 9a Calle really get going.

Places to Stay
A couple of good, clean hotels are on 3a Av between 11a and 12a Calles, one block from the dock. Both have clean rooms with private bath and fan arranged around a central courtyard used as a car park. *Hotel Europa 2* (☎ 948-1292), is perhaps the slightly more attractive, and has singles/doubles for US$6/10; at the *Hotel Miami* (☎ 948-0537) they are US$9/13, or US$15 with air con. If you're driving and need a safe place to leave your car while you visit Lívingston, you can park in the courtyard of either place for US$2.50 per day.

The original *Hotel Europa 1* (☎ 948-0127), on 8a Av between 8a and 9a Calles, is 1½ blocks from the cathedral and Guatel telephone office (look for the openwork cross on top of the steeple, and the Guatel signal tower). Fairly clean, pleasant and quiet, it has singles/doubles with bath for US$6/12.

Hotel Xelajú (☎ 948-0482), nearby on 9a Calle between 6a and 7a Avs, is a cheaper, more basic place but it's OK; singles/doubles/triples with shared bath are US$4/6/8. Parking in the courtyard costs US$1.65 extra.

In a class by itself is the old *Hotel del Norte* (☎ 948-2116, ☎ /fax 948-0087), 7a Calle at 1a Av, located at the waterfront end of 7a Calle, 1.2 km from the dock (you must walk around the railway yard). In its airy dining room overlooking the Bahía de Amatique, you can almost hear the echoing conversation of turn-of-the-century banana moguls and smell their pungent cigars. Spare, simple and agreeably dilapidated, this is a real museum piece. Rooms with sea view and private bath are US$17/25/31/37 a single/double/triple/quad; interior rooms with shared bath are US$11/17/23/27. Meals are served in the dining room; there's also a bar, and two swimming pools beside the sea. Service is refined, careful and elegantly old-fashioned, but the food can be otherwise.

Southwest of the main road, Calzada Justo Rufino Barrios, are two fancier, more comfortable hotels. The 48-room *Hotel El Reformador* (☎ 948-0533), 16a Calle and 7a Av No 159, is a modern building offering rooms with fan, TV and private bath for US$17/33/44, or US$30/38/48 with air con. It has its own restaurant.

Around the corner, *Hotel Internacional* (☎ /fax 948-0367) on 7a Av between 16a and 17a Calles has a swimming pool, restaurant and parking. Singles/doubles with private bath and TV are US$9/14 with fan, US$14/25 with air con.

Places to Eat

The town's most enjoyable restaurant is *Restaurante Safari*, on a thatch-roofed, open-air dock right over the water at the west end of 5a Av, about a kilometer from the center of town. Locals and visitors alike love to eat here, catching the fresh sea breezes while mariachis stroll from table to table. Seafood meals of all kinds are the specialty, for around US$6 to US$10; burgers, sandwiches and chicken are also served. It's open every day, 10 am to 9 pm.

Restaurante La Fogata, 6a Av between 6a and 7a Calle, is another fancy place, specializing in charcoal-grilled steaks and seafood. There's live music most nights, and a meal of the day for US$3.50 at lunchtime.

Simpler places include the *Restaurante Fogón Porteño*, opposite the bus station, with charcoal-grilled chicken, steak and seafood. *Maxim* is a funky Chinese place at the corner of 6a Av and 8a Calle.

Perhaps the oddest eatery in town is *Container*, a cafe and drinks stand at the foot of 7a Calle, near the Hotel del Norte. It's made of two steel shipping containers, and the chairs and tables set out in the street afford a fine view of the bay.

Getting There & Away

Bus The Transportes Litegua bus station (☎ 948-1172, 948-1002) is near the corner of 6a Av, Calzada Justo Rufino Barrios and 9a Calle. Express buses to Guatemala City (307 km, five hours, US$6) leave at 1, 1:30, 3, 7:30 and 10 am, noon and 4 pm. Regular buses take several hours longer.

You can store your luggage at the terminal for about US$0.20 per day.

Boat Boats depart from the Muelle Municipal at the foot of 12a Calle. Get to the dock at least 30 or 45 minutes prior to departure for a decent seat; otherwise you could end up standing.

A ferry departs for Lívingston every day at 10:30 am and 5 pm; the trip takes 1½ hours and costs US$1.35. On the Lívingston side, it departs for Puerto Barrios every day at 5 am and 2 pm. *Colectivo lanchas* (collective launches) depart from both sides whenever there are 12 people ready to go; they take 45 minutes and cost US$2.50.

Most of the movement is from Lívingston to Puerto Barrios in the morning, returning in the afternoon. From Lívingston, your last chance of the day to come by boat may be on the 2 pm ferry. After that, it might be the next morning before 12 people get together for the colectivo. The ferry arrives in Puerto Barrios at 3:30 pm and the last express bus to Guatemala City leaves at 4 pm, so you'll have to rush from the dock to the bus station.

A 100-passenger boat leaves Puerto Barrios for Punta Gorda (Belize, see that chapter) on Tuesday and Friday at 7 am; it departs Punta Gorda for the return trip at noon. The trip takes 2½ hours and costs US$5.50. Smaller *lanchas* depart from Punta Gorda every day around 8:30 or 9 am, and depart from Puerto Barrios for the return trip at around 1 or 2 pm; these take 50 minutes and charge US$9.

The boats to Punta Gorda used to stop in Lívingston, but no longer do so. If you take one of these boats, you must pass through Guatemalan customs and immigration before boarding the boat. Allow some time, and have your passport and tourist card handy.

Overland Route, Puerto Barrios to Puerto Cortés (Honduras)

Information on this route is based on letters sent to us by Camille Geels and Anja Boye (Denmark), Peter Kügerl (Austria) and Matthew Willson (UK).

This trip takes about six hours, so get an early start. The first thing you need to do is to get your Guatemalan exit stamp from the immigration office in Puerto Barrios. You may want to get it the day before, so you don't have to spend the time on the day of travel.

Take the bus from the mercado in Puerto Barrios to Finca La Inca, which is the last station on the bus line; the buses depart hourly, starting at 7 am. Just before you get to Finca La Inca, get off the bus and walk a few minutes to the Río Motagua, where you take a small boat to El Límite (US$3), at the border. From El Límite, take another boat through marsh and jungle to the small village of Cuyamelito (45 minutes, US$1.50). From Cuyamelito, walk about 30 minutes (or hitch a lift) to the highway, where you can catch a bus or truck going to Puerto Cortés. Be sure to get your Honduran entrance stamp entered into your passport at the first opportunity (Puerto Cortés and Omoa, whichever you come to first, both have immigration offices).

Presumably you could do the same thing in reverse, if you're coming to Guatemala from the Honduras side.

LÍVINGSTON
Population 5500

As you come ashore in Lívingston, you will be surprised to meet black Guatemalans who speak Spanish as well as their traditional Garífuna language; some also speak the musical English of Belize and the islands. The town of Lívingston is an interesting anomaly, with a laid-back, very Belizean way of life, groves of coconut palms, gaily painted wooden buildings, and an economy based on fishing and tourism.

Other people in Lívingston include the indigenous Kekchi Maya, who have their own community a kilometer or so upriver from the main dock, ladinos and a smattering of international travelers.

Beaches in Lívingston are mostly disappointing, as the jungle comes right down to the water's edge in most places. Those beaches which do exist are often clogged with vegetation as well, and they're not good for swimming due to contamination in the water. Safe swimming can be had at Las Siete Altares; see Around Lívingston, below.

Orientation & Information

After being in Lívingston for half an hour, you'll know where everything is. Walk up the hill from the dock along the town's main street. The fancy Hotel Tucán Dugú is on your right, with several small restaurants on your left. The street off to the left at the base of the hill goes to the Casa Rosada and several other hotels, and continues on to a Kekchi Maya community.

There's no tourist information office in Lívingston, but Exotic Travel, based at the Bahía Azul restaurant, hands out free town maps and is a good source of information about the area (see Organized Tours and Getting There & Away).

The post office is half a block off the main road. Guatel is next door.

The Banco de Comercio changes US dollars cash and traveler's checks. Several private businesses do too, including the Restaurante Bahía Azul, which also changes the currencies of Belize and Honduras.

Laundry service is available at the Rigoletto Pizzería & Guest House (more economical) and at the hotel La Casa Rosada.

The immigration office is on the main street coming up from the dock. It's open every day, 7 am to 9 pm.

Use mosquito repellent and other sensible precautions, especially if you go out into the jungle; remember that the mosquitoes here on the coast carry both malaria and dengue fever.

Museo Garífuna

The Museo Garífuna displays arts and implements of Garífuna daily life, with notes in English and Spanish, and has a small variety of Garífuna handicrafts and music cassettes on sale.

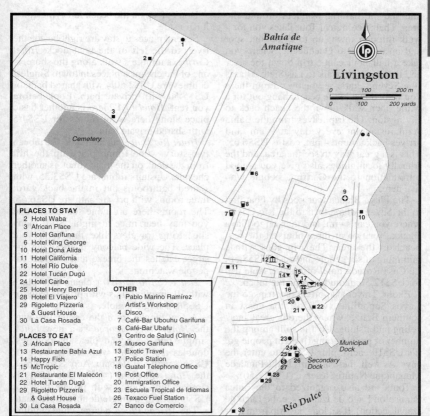

Lívingston

PLACES TO STAY
2 Hotel Waba
3 African Place
5 Hotel Garífuna
6 Hotel King George
10 Hotel Doña Alida
11 Hotel California
16 Hotel Río Dulce
22 Hotel Tucán Dugú
24 Hotel Caribe
25 Hotel Henry Berrisford
28 Hotel El Viajero
29 Rigoletto Pizzería
   & Guest House
30 La Casa Rosada

PLACES TO EAT
3 African Place
13 Restaurante Bahía Azul
14 Happy Fish
15 McTropic
21 Restaurante El Malecón
22 Hotel Tucán Dugú
29 Rigoletto Pizzería
   & Guest House
30 La Casa Rosada

OTHER
1 Pablo Marino Ramírez
   Artist's Workshop
4 Disco
7 Café-Bar Ubouhu Garífuna
8 Café-Bar Ubafu
9 Centro de Salud (Clinic)
12 Museo Garífuna
13 Exotic Travel
17 Police Station
18 Guatel Telephone Office
19 Post Office
20 Immigration Office
23 Escuela Tropical de Idiomas
26 Texaco Fuel Station
27 Banco de Comercio

Pablo Marino Ramírez has a workshop by the sea where he makes Garífuna drums and woodcarvings. You're welcome to visit.

Language Courses
Escuela Tropical de Idiomas (☎ /fax 948-1544) offers Spanish language classes. If you like, they can also arrange homestays with local families for US$50 per week, meals included.

Special Events
Lívingston is packed with holiday-makers during Semana Santa. The day of San Isidro Labrador, who was a cultivator, is celebrated on May 15 with people bringing their agricultural products to a mass in the morning, followed by a procession through the streets with an image of the saint. The national day of the Garífuna is celebrated on November 26 with a variety of Garífuna cultural events. The day of the Virgin of Guadalupe, Mexico's patron saint, is celebrated on December 12.

Organized Tours
Exotic Travel (see Getting There & Away) offers various tours enabling you to get out

and see the natural wonders around the area. Their Ecological Tour takes you for a walk through town, up to a lookout spot and on to the Río Quequeche, where you take a half-hour canoe trip down the river and then a jungle walk to Las Siete Altares (the Seven Altars, see below). From there you walk down to the beach, hang out for a while, then walk down the beach back to Lívingston. The trip leaves from the Bahía Azul restaurant every day at 9 am, and arrives back around 4 pm, cost is US$6.65. This is a great way to see the area, and the friendly local guides also give you a good introduction to the Garífuna people who live here.

The Playa Blanca tour goes by boat first to the Seven Altars, then to the Río Cocolí where you can swim, and then on to Playa Blanca, for two or three hours at the best beach in the area. The trip goes with a minimum of six people and costs US$8.50. La Casa Rosada hotel offers the same trip for US$12.50, including a picnic lunch.

Exotic Travel also offers day trips to the Cayos Sapodillas, well off the coast in southern Belize, where there is great snorkeling and fishing. Cost is split among the number of people going (if eight people go, it's US$19 each), plus US$10 to enter the cays. As well, there are trips to the Punta de Manabique Nature Reserve (US$12.50).

Tours are also organized to the Finca Paraíso on Lago de Izabal (see the Lago de Izabal section). It's a long day trip from Lívingston, leaving at around 6 am and returning by around 7 pm. Hotel La Casa Rosada offers this trip for US$25, lunch included.

All of the above trips are also organized by the Happy Fish restaurant (☎ 902-7143), but not on any fixed schedule.

Places to Stay

When you arrive by boat, you may be met by local boys who will offer take you to a hotel, helping you carry your luggage if you like (there are no taxis in Lívingston). They'll take you to one place after another until you find one you like. They'll expect a small tip from you, and also get a commission from the hotel.

Don't sleep on the beach in Lívingston – it isn't safe.

Several places to stay are right beside the river, to the left of the boat dock. *Hotel Caribe*, a minute's walk along the shore, is one of the cheapest places in town: Singles/doubles are US$2.50/4 with shared bath, or US$5.50 with private bath. Look before you rent. *Hotel El Viajero* is another basic place along here, with rooms for US$4/5 with shared/private bath.

Hotel Río Dulce, an authentic Caribbean two-story wood-frame place up the hill from the dock on the main street, is another cheapie. Upstairs rooms are US$3.35, with shared bathrooms out in the back yard; three rooms with private bath are US$6.65. The rooms here are none too clean, and you may hear mice at night. Still, many shoestring travelers like this funky old place. The wide balcony overlooking the street catches the breeze and is great for people watching.

Hotel California is a clean, fine place with 10 simple rooms with private bath for US$5/8 a single/double.

A few blocks from the center of town, the *Hotel King George* is a new hotel, simple but clean and pleasant. Singles/doubles are US$4/7 with shared bath, or US$6/8 with private bath. Across the street, the *Hotel Garífuna* (☎ /fax 948-1581) is similar, with rooms with private bath for US$6/8/13/15 a single/double/triple/quad.

The *African Place*, a large white building with Moorish arches, is an old favorite in Lívingston. The 25 rooms are clean and pleasant, and there's a big garden in the rear with lots of space and flowers. Rooms with shared bath are US$4/6/8 a single/double/triple; with private bath they are US$8.50 a single, US$12.50 a double or triple, US$20 for four or five people. There's also a good restaurant here. The African Place does have some problems, though. It's a longish walk from town (10 or 15 minutes), the road is unlit and there have been many robberies at night along here. There have also been mixed reports on personal security at the hotel and some travelers have had items stolen from their rooms.

Turn right at the African Place and you come to the *Hotel Waba* (reservations ☎ 948-2065, 948-1367), new in 1996, where clean rooms with private bath are US$7/10 a single/double. The balcony has a sea view, and there's an open-air palapa restaurant in the yard.

For homey, friendly atmosphere, you can't beat the *Rigoletto Pizzería & Guest House*, beside the river 300 meters to the left of the dock. Two clean, pleasant guest rooms sharing a clean bathroom are US$7/11 a single/double. All three meals are served (the owner is a great cook), there's laundry service, and a rear garden with tables and chairs right beside the river. Boats will drop you off here, if you ask.

Hotel Henry Berrisford (☎ /fax 948-1568) beside the river has clean, comfortable rooms with private bath and TV. Beware, though: it often runs out of water, and the swimming pool is not always clean. Rooms with fan are US$7.50 per person, or US$10 per person with breakfast; with air con and breakfast they are US$14 per person.

Hotel Doña Alida (☎ 948-1567), beside the sea a few blocks from the center of town, has a beautiful beach, a restaurant and terraces with a sea view. Singles or doubles are US$14 with shared bath, US$24 with private bath, some with a sea view. A double bungalow is US$29, and extra-large triple rooms are US$49.

La Casa Rosada (fax at Guatel 948-2395) is probably Lívingston's most attractive place to stay. It's right on the river, 800 meters to the left of the dock; boats will drop you here, if you ask. Ample riverside gardens, a dock with a gazebo, and refreshments available anytime all contribute to the relaxed, friendly ambiance. Ten pleasant free-standing thatch-roofed bungalows with fans, screens and mosquito nets sharing three clean bathrooms are US$16 a night. There's laundry service, daily trips and tours, and the restaurant here is one of the best in town.

Places to Eat

Food in Lívingston is a bit more expensive than in the rest of Guatemala because most of it (except fish and coconuts) must be brought across from Puerto Barrios. *Tapado*, a rich stew made from fish, shrimp, crab and other seafood, coconut, plantain, banana and spiced with coriander, is the special local dish.

The main street is lined with little comedores, *tiendas* (shops) and *almacenes* (stores). Your best plan may be to choose the place which is currently the most popular.

On our last visit, the *Restaurante Bahía Azul* was all the rage, a popular gathering spot with pleasant surroundings, good food for good prices and live music some evenings. It's open every day, 7 am to 10 pm.

Other popular places on the main street include the *Restaurante El Malecón*, just up the hill from the dock, on the left. It's airy and rustic, with a loyal local clientele and good views of the water; a full meal of Caribbean-inspired fare can be had for US$4 to US$7. A bit farther up the hill, the *McTropic*, on the right-hand side, is half restaurant and half shop; it's favored by the thriftiest crowd. The *Happy Fish* on the main street is also good.

The *African Place* (see Places to Stay) serves a variety of exotic and local dishes. Full meals, including *tapado*, are available for US$6 or less.

On the road beside the river are a couple of other good restaurants. The *Rigoletto Pizzería* (see Places to Stay), operated by the talented cook María who has lived in several countries, has a menu of Italian, east Indian, Chinese and other dishes, with many meat and vegetarian selections.

Further along, the restaurant at *La Casa Rosada* is another very enjoyable riverside spot. All three meals are served, with good, ample dinners for around US$6 to US$8; dinner reservations are advisable. The coffee here is probably the best in town.

The dining room of the *Hotel Tucán Dugú* is the most expensive spot in town; a good, complete dinner with drinks goes for around US$10 to US$15.

Entertainment

Lívingston is about the only place in Guatemala where Garífuna music and dance are easily accessible for visitors. The

Restaurante Bahía Azul has live Garífuna music on weekends and sometimes on other evenings. The *Café-Bar Ubafu* has live Garífuna music and dancing most evenings; it's liveliest on weekends. Across the street, the *Café-Bar Ubouhu Garífuna* is another popular night spot.

The disco by the sea on the north side of town is open on weekends. Several locals told us that problems had recently occurred there and that it might not be the most recommendable place for travelers.

Some nights of the week, the busiest place in town with the loudest music, is the Templo Evangélico Iglesia del Nazareno (Evangelical Church of the Nazarene), opposite the Restaurant Margoth.

Getting There & Away

The only way to get to Lívingston is by boat. Frequent boats come downriver from Río Dulce and across the bay from Puerto Barrios; see those sections for details. There are also international boats coming from Honduras and Belize.

Exotic Travel (☎ 902-7109; in Guatemala City ☎ 477-4090), based at the Restaurante Bahía Azul, operates a couple of international boat routes, to Omoa (Honduras) and Punta Gorda (Belize). They run on a schedule, but will also go at any other time there are a minimum of six people. Be sure to get your entry and exit stamps entered into your passport at the immigration offices on both ends of the journey.

The boats to Omoa depart from Lívingston at 7:30 am on Tuesdays and Fridays, arriving there 2½ hours later, at about 10 am. In Omoa, the boat docks near the bus stop where you can catch a bus to Puerto Cortés and on to San Pedro Sula. The boat leaves Omoa for the return trip at around noon or 1 pm, arriving back in Lívingston around 3:30 pm. Cost is US$30 from Lívingston to Omoa, US$25 from Omoa to Lívingston. The captain will take you to get your passport exit and entry stamps on both ends of the journey.

The boats to Punta Gorda (Belize) also leave Lívingston at 7:30 am on Tuesdays and Fridays. This is a shorter trip, taking just 45 minutes; cost is US$12 each way. The boats depart Punta Gorda for the return trip at 10:30 am. Get your own exit stamp from the immigration office in Lívingston; the captain will take you to get your entry stamp in Punta Gorda.

Trips to Punta Gorda, Omoa and other places can also be arranged at the Happy Fish restaurant (☎ 902-7143).

The *Osprey* sailboat makes a trip from Utila (one of Honduras' Bay Islands) to Lívingston twice a month or so. Cost to Lívingston is US$96 per person, with a maximum of 12 passengers. Travel agents in Lívingston should have information about it, but they may not. In Utila, information is available from Gunter's Dive Shop (☎ /fax (504) 45-3350).

AROUND LÍVINGSTON
Río Dulce Cruises

Lívingston is the starting point for boat rides on the Río Dulce. Passengers enjoy the tropical jungle scenery, have a swim and a picnic, and explore the **Biotopo Chocón-Machacas**, 12 km west along the river. The 7600-hectare reserve was established to protect the beautiful river landscape, the valuable mangrove swamps and, especially, the manatees which inhabit the waters (both salt and fresh) of the Río Dulce and El Golfete.

There are several ways to make the voyage up the Río Dulce. Almost anyone in Lívingston can tell you who's currently organizing trips up the river. Exotic Travel, based at the Restaurante Bahía Azul, makes trips daily; so does the Hotel La Casa Rosada, and the Happy Fish restaurant. Or you can simply walk down to the dock and arrange a trip – many local boatmen are there, and it's good to support them.

Shortly after you leave Lívingston, the river enters a steep-walled gorge, its walls hung with great tangles of jungle foliage and bromeliads and the humid air noisy with the cries of tropical birds. A hot spring forces sulfurous water out at the base of the cliff, providing a delightful place for a swim.

Emerging from the gorge, the river eventually widens into **El Golfete**, a lake-like body of water that presages the even vaster expanse of Lago de Izabal.

On the northern shore of El Golfete is the Biotopo Chocón-Machacas. The nature reserve's boat dock is good for swimming. A network of 'water trails' (boat routes around several jungle lagoons) provide ways to see the bird, animal and plant life of the reserve. A nature trail begins at the visitors' center and winds its way through forests of mahogany, palms and rich tropical foliage. Jaguars and tapirs live in the reserve, though your chances of seeing one are slight.

From El Golfete and the nature reserve, the boats continue upriver to the village of Río Dulce, where the road into El Petén crosses the river, and to the Castillo de San Felipe on Lago de Izabal (see the Lago de Izabal section).

The trip is also offered from Río Dulce; ask at the Restaurant Hollymar.

From whichever end you begin, you can make it a one-way (US$8) or roundtrip (US$12.50) between Lívingston and Río Dulce. (Trips organized by the Hotel La Casa Rosada, which include a picnic lunch and stop at more places, cost a bit more.)

Las Siete Altares

The Seven Altars is a series of freshwater falls and pools about five km (1½-hour walk) northwest of Lívingston along the shore of the Bahía de Amatique. It's a pleasant goal for a walk along the beach and a good place for a picnic and a swim. Follow the shore northwards to the mouth of a river. Ford the river, and a path into the woods leads to the falls. If you'd rather not do the ford, boats at the mouth of the river will ferry you across for a few quetzals.

Boat trips go to the Seven Altars, but locals say it's better to walk there, because you get to see the pure nature and also the Garífuna people who live along the way. Unfortunately, robberies have been known to happen along the beach here, so don't take valuables with you, or a lot of money. Locals say the walk is still worth doing, as long as you take this precaution.

El Petén

In the dense jungle cover of Guatemala's vast northeastern department of El Petén, you may hear the squawk of parrots, the chatter of monkeys and the rustlings of strange animals moving through the bush. The landscape here is utterly different from that of Guatemala's cool mountainous highlands or its steamy Pacific Slope.

The monumental Maya ceremonial center at Tikal is among the most impressive of the Mayan archaeological sites. The ruins of Uaxactún and Ceibal, though not so easily accessible, are perhaps more exciting to visit for that reason. Several dozen other great cities lie hidden in El Petén's jungles, accessible only to archaeologists with aircraft (or to artifact poachers).

In 1990 the Guatemalan government established the one million-hectare Maya Biosphere Reserve, including most of northern El Petén. The Guatemalan reserve adjoins the vast Calakmul Biosphere Reserve in Mexico and the Río Bravo Conservation Area in Belize, forming a huge multinational reserve of over two million hectares.

There are three reasons travelers would want to penetrate the forests of El Petén: first to visit Tikal, the greatest Maya religious center yet discovered; second to enjoy the great variety of birdlife; and third to see the Guatemala of small farming villages and jungle hamlets, without paved roads or colonial architecture.

Though it is possible to visit Tikal on a one-day excursion by plane from Guatemala City, I encourage you to stay over at least one night, whether in Flores, El Remate or Tikal itself. There is a great deal to see and experience, and a day trip simply cannot do it justice.

Getting Around

The roads leading into El Petén – from the Carretera al Pacífico and from Belize – have been left in a state of disrepair, partly due to lack of funds and partly because better roads would encourage migration of

El Petén

El Petén

farmers and ranchers from other areas of the country. With El Petén's forests already falling to the machete at an alarming rate, good new roads might prove disastrous. Thus road transport in El Petén is slow, bumpy, uncomfortable and sometimes unsafe. There have been several incidents of robbery of buses traveling along the roads between Río Dulce and Flores and the Belizean border at Melchor de Mencos/Benque Viejo del Carmen. For current information on the safety of traveling these roads, call your embassy or consulate in Guatemala City.

The only exception is the road connecting Flores/Santa Elena and Tikal, a good, fast asphalt road built so that tourists arriving by air in Santa Elena can proceed quickly and comfortably to Tikal, 71 km to the northeast. The Guatemalan government long ago decided to develop the adjoining towns of Flores, Santa Elena and San Benito, on the shores of Lago de Petén Itzá, into the region's tourism base. The airport, hotels and other services are here. Though there are a few small hotels and restaurants at Tikal, other services will remain limited.

FLORES & SANTA ELENA
Population 2000 & 17,000

The town of Flores is built on an island on Lago de Petén Itzá. A 500-meter causeway connects Flores to her sister town of Santa Elena (110 meters,) on the lakeshore. Adjoining Santa Elena to the west is the town of San Benito (population 22,000).

Flores, the departmental capital, is more dignified, with its church, small government building and municipal basketball court arranged around the main plaza atop the hill in the center of the island. The narrow streets, paved in cement blocks, hold numerous small hotels and restaurants.

Santa Elena is a disorganized town of dusty unpaved streets, with many small hotels and restaurants. San Benito is even more disorganized but its honky-tonk bars keep it lively.

The three towns actually form one large settlement, usually referred to simply as Flores.

History
Flores was founded on an island (petén) by the Itzaes after their expulsion from Chichén Itzá, and it was named Tayasal.

Cortés dropped in on King Canek of Tayasal in 1524 while on his way to Honduras, but the meeting was peaceable. Only in March of 1697 did the Spaniards finally bring the Maya of Tayasal forcibly under their control.

At the time of its conquest, Flores was perhaps the last major functioning Maya ceremonial center, covered in pyramids and temples, with idols everywhere. The God-fearing Spanish soldiers destroyed these 'pagan' buildings. Today when you visit Flores you will see not a trace of them, although the modern town is doubtless built on the ruins and foundations of Maya Tayasal.

Tayasal's Maya citizens fled into the jungle, giving rise to the myth of a 'lost' Maya city.

Orientation
The airport is on the eastern outskirts of Santa Elena, two km from the causeway connecting Santa Elena and Flores. Each bus company has its own terminal.

4a Calle is Santa Elena's 'main drag.' All the important hotels, restaurants and banks are on this street or just off it.

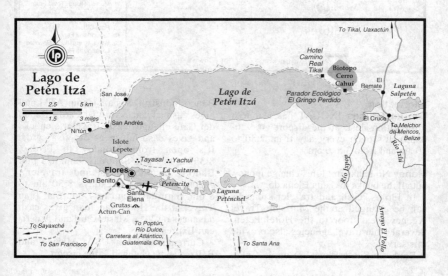

PLACES TO STAY
1 Hotel Sabana
2 Hospedaje Doña Goya
6 Posada Tucán No 2
9 Hotel Casona de la Isla
10 Hotel Isla de Flores
15 Hotel y Restaurante
  La Mesa de los Maya
19 Hotel Petén
21 Hotel Santa Rita
23 Hotelito y Cafe-Bar
  La Casita en Flores
26 Restaurante/Bar
  Posada El Tucán
27 Hotel Villa del Lago
29 Hotel Yum Kax

PLACES TO EAT
14 Restaurante Ranchón
  del Fenix
15 Hotel y Restaurante
  La Mesa de los Maya
16 Restaurante Gran Jaguar
17 Restaurante/Bar Las Puertas
22 Restaurante La Jungla
23 Hotelito y Cafe-Bar
  La Casita en Flores
24 Restaurante La Canoa
26 Restaurante/Bar
  Posada El Tucán
28 Casa Picante
30 Restaurante Chal-tun-ha
31 Restaurante Don Quijote

OTHER
3 Police Station
4 CINCAP
5 Church
7 Gobernación Departamental
  (Departmental Government
  Building)
8 Banco de Guatemala
11 Municipalidad (Town Hall)
12 INGUAT Tourist Office,
  Public Telephones
13 Post Office
18 Lavandería Fenix
20 Cahui International Services
25 Lavandería Petenchel
28 Casa Picante

Lago de
Petén Itzá

Parque
Central

Flores

| 0 | 25 | 50 m |
| 0 | 25 | 50 yards |

To Santa Elena

Information
Tourist Offices INGUAT has a tourist information desk at the airport (☎ 926-0533). It's open every day from 7:30 to 10 am and from 3 to 6 pm.

Money No banks in Flores change money, but all the banks in Santa Elena do.

In Flores, cash and traveler's checks can be changed at the Martsam Travel Agency, next door to the Hotel Petén. Several other travel agencies also provide this service.

Banks in Santa Elena are on 4a Calle.

Banco Industrial has a 24-hour ATM and gives cash advances on Visa cards. Banco del Café changes cash, traveler's checks and gives cash advances on Visa cards. It's open from Monday to Friday, 8:30 am to 7 pm, Saturday 9 am to 1 pm. Banoro changes cash and traveler's checks; it's open weekdays 8:30 am to 8 pm, Saturday 9 am to 4 pm. San Juan Travel at the Hotel San Juan gives cash advances on Visa, MasterCard and American Express.

Currencies of the USA, Mexico and Belize can be changed at the airport.

Post & Communications In Flores, the post office is just off the plaza. The Martsam Travel Agency and Cahuí International Services offer domestic and international telephone and fax services. Casa Picante offers telephone, fax, email and computer services and also has a multi-language book exchange and library.

In Santa Elena, the post office is on the corner of 2a Calle and 7a Av. The Guatel telephone office is open every day. Educomsa Petén (☎ 926-0765), 4a Calle 6-76, Local B, Zona 1, offers email and computer services.

Travel Agencies Several travel agencies in Flores offer a range of services for visitors. Casa Picante, facing the causeway, has information on the area's attractions and affordable tours; it also operates a pizzeria, bookstore/book exchange, and telephone, fax and email services.

Also in Flores, the Martsam Travel Agency (☎ /fax 926-0493) next to the Hotel Petén, and Cahuí International Services (☎ /fax 926-0494) next to the Hotel Santana, offer travel agency and telephone/fax services, tours, money changing and bicycle rental.

Laundry In Flores, try Lavandería Fenix or Lavandería Petenchel, which is open Monday to Saturday 8 am to 8 pm, Sunday 10 am to 6 pm. In Santa Elena, Lavandería Emanuel on 6a Av near the causeway does a good job and the laundry is ready in an hour. It's open Monday to Saturday, 8 am to 7 pm.

Grutas Actun-Can
The caves of Actun-Can, also called La Cueva de la Serpiente (The Cave of the Serpent), are standard limestone. No serpents are in evidence, but the cave-keeper will turn on the lights for you after you've paid the US$1.15 admission fee (8 am to 5 pm daily), and may give you the rundown on the cave formations, which suggest animals, humans and various scenes. Bring a flashlight if you have one, and adequate shoes – it can be slippery. Explorations take about 30 to 45 minutes.

At the cave entrance is a shady picnic area. Actun-Can makes a good goal for a long walk from Santa Elena. To find it, walk south on 6a Av past the Guatel office. About one km from the center of Santa Elena, turn left, go 300 meters and turn right at the electricity generating plant. Go another one km to the site. A taxi from Santa Elena costs US$2.

CINCAP
The Centro de Información sobre la Naturaleza, Cultura y Artesanía del Petén (CINCAP), on the north side of the plaza in Flores, sells handicrafts of the region and has exhibits on the natural resources and forest conservation of the Petén.

ARCAS
ARCAS has a wildlife rescue center about two km from the Hotel Villa Maya, which is about 10 km east of Santa Elena. Animals here include macaws, green and yellow parrots, jaguars, howler and spider monkeys, kinkajous and coatimundis that have been rescued from smugglers and the illegal pet trade. At the center the animals are rehabilitated for release back into the wild. You are welcome to visit, but you should ask permission first (☎ /fax in Guatemala City 591-4731).

Volunteers are welcome to stay here, paying per week for room and board, and volunteering any amount of time. Contact ARCAS for further details (see Work under Facts for the Visitor).

Organized Tours
Land Tours Travel agencies in Flores offer a number of interesting tours around the remote parts of the Petén region. Ask about the Scarlet Macaw Trail, visiting Centro Campesino, El Eprú, Paso Caballos, Buena Vista, El Cruce a Dos Aguadas, San Andrés and Tikal. It takes six days to do the whole tour, but you can also do parts of it.

Monkey Eco Tours (☎ 928-8132, fax 928-8113), based at the Hotel Ni-Tún on the northwest side of the lake, and Epiphyte Adventures (☎ /fax 926-0775), based in Flores, do this along with variety of other adventurous tours. Both are professional operations with bilingual guides.

Lago de Petén Itzá As you stroll around town, particularly in Flores, locals will present themselves and offer boat rides around the lake. Many are freelance agents who get a commission; it's better to talk with the boat owner directly. You should bargain over the price, and inspect the boat. Or ask at the Restaurante/Bar Las Puertas in Flores; Carlos, the owner, offers boat trips around the lake and across to the other side where he has land and a private dock

good for swimming and sunning. The travel agencies may also be able to arrange boat trips.

There's good bird watching on the Río Ixpop, which runs into the east side of the lake. Boat trips start from El Remate, on the east side of the lake.

Places to Stay – budget
Santa Elena *Hotel Posada Santander* (☎ 926-0574) on 4a Calle is a simple but spotless and friendly family-run hostelry in a convenient location. Ample rooms with private bath and two good double beds are

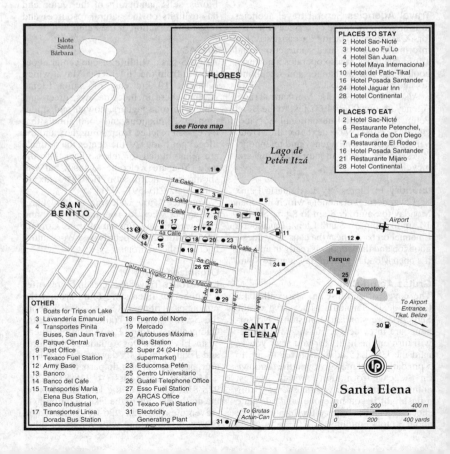

PLACES TO STAY
2 Hotel Sac-Nicté
3 Hotel Leo Fu Lo
4 Hotel San Juan
5 Hotel Maya Internacional
10 Hotel del Patio-Tikal
16 Hotel Posada Santander
24 Hotel Jaguar Inn
28 Hotel Continental

PLACES TO EAT
2 Hotel Sac-Nicté
6 Restaurante Petenchel,
    La Fonda de Don Diego
7 Restaurante El Rodeo
16 Hotel Posada Santander
21 Restaurante Mijaro
28 Hotel Continental

OTHER
1 Boats for Trips on Lake
3 Lavandería Emanuel
4 Transportes Pinita
    Buses, San Jaun Travel
8 Parque Central
9 Post Office
11 Texaco Fuel Station
12 Army Base
13 Banoro
14 Banco del Cafe
15 Transportes María
    Elena Bus Station,
    Banco Industrial
17 Transportes Linea
    Dorada Bus Station
18 Fuente del Norte
19 Mercado
20 Autobuses Máxima
    Bus Station
22 Super 24 (24-hour
    supermarket)
23 Educomsa Petén
25 Centro Universitario
26 Guatel Telephone Office
27 Esso Fuel Station
29 ARCAS Office
30 Texaco Fuel Station
31 Electricity
    Generating Plant

Santa Elena

0   200   400 m
0   200   400 yards

US$6.65/8.35 a single/double. An open-air restaurant upstairs serves all three meals. The family also operates Transportes Inter Petén, with economical minibus service to Tikal and other places.

Nearer the lake, *Hotel Sac-Nicté* (☎ 926-0092) has clean, large upstairs rooms with private bath, balcony and views across the lake to Flores for US$12. Downstairs rooms have no view and are cheaper, at US$8.35. They have a restaurant, parking, a transportation service and are planning to build a swimming pool.

Hotel Continental (☎ 926-0095) on 6a Av at Calle Virgilio Rodríguez Macal is a large hotel built in 1995. Rooms are US$2.50 per person with shared bath, or US$5/8.35 a single/double with private bath. There's a restaurant here, and parking in the courtyard.

Santa Elena has other cheap but less attractive hotels, including the *Hotel Leo Fu Lo* (US$2.50 per person) and the *Hotel San Juan* (US$4/6 with shared bath, US$10/12 with private bath).

Flores The cheerful, family-run *Hotel Villa del Lago* (☎ 926-0629, 926-0508) beside the lake is a clean, pleasant place to stay, much nicer inside than its appearance would suggest. Five rooms sharing three clean bathrooms are US$6.65/8.35 a single/double; rooms with private bath are US$17. Next door, *Restaurante/Bar El Tucán* has forgettable rooms with shared bath for US$7. These are off to one side of the restaurant.

Hotelito y Cafe-Bar La Casita en Flores, near the larger Hotel Yum Kax, is another simple, clean and friendly place, operated by a German-Guatemalan family. Four rooms, each with private bath, are US$6.65/13.35 a single/double. Up on the rooftop is a grill restaurant with a view across the lake to Santa Elena.

Hospedaje Doña Goya is a good economical choice, with rooms with shared/private bath for US$3.35/4.20 per person.

The *Posada Tucán No 2* (☎ 926-1467) is simple but clean and OK. Singles/doubles are US$6/7 with shared bath,

US$8.35/11 with private bath. Some rooms have lake views.

Hotel Santa Rita (☎ 926-0710) is clean and family-run; it's an excellent value at US$9/12 a single/double with private bath.

Hotel Yum Kax (☎ /fax 926-0686) is to the left as you arrive on the island along the causeway. Rooms are US$15/20/25 for a single/double/triple with fan, US$5 more with air con.

Hotel y Restaurante La Mesa de los Mayas (☎ /fax 926-1240) is a lovely place, very clean and well-kept. Rooms with private bath and fan are US$15/22/24 a double/triple/quad, a little more with air con.

Places to Stay – middle
Santa Elena The *Hotel Jaguar Inn* (☎ 926-0002), Calzada Rodríguez Macal 8-79, Zona 1, is comfortable without being fancy, but slightly inconveniently located 150 meters off the main road near the airport. It's good if you have a vehicle. Rooms with private bath are US$18/24 a single/double with fan, US$24/30 with air conditioning. *Hotel Maya Internacional* (☎ 926-1276, fax 926-0087), right beside the water, has singles/doubles/triples for US$30/36/42.

Flores *Hotel Sabana* (☎ /fax 926-1248), on the north side of the island, has a restaurant and sun deck over the water. Rooms with private bath, fan, air con and cable TV are US$20/25/30 a single/double/triple.

Hotel Casona de la Isla (☎ 926-0523, fax 926-0593) is a romantic place with a lakeside swimming pool with a waterfall and an open-air lakeside bar/restaurant. All 27 rooms have private bath, air con and cable TV, and chairs on the balcony outside the room. Singles/doubles/triples are US$25/30/40.

Hotel Petén (☎ 926-0692, fax 926-0593) has a small courtyard with tropical plants, a pleasant lakeside terrace and restaurant, and an indoor swimming pool. The 19 comfy if plain rooms, all with private bath, air con and fan, are US$20/30/40 a single/double/triple. Try to get a room on the top floor with a view of the lake.

Places to Eat

As with hotels, the restaurants in Santa Elena tend to be cheaper than those in Flores. All are fairly simple, and open all the time. Beer, drinks and sometimes even wine are served. Also on the menu at most places are a variety of local game, including tepezcuintle (a rabbit-sized jungle rodent), venado (deer), armadillo, pavo silvestre (wild turkey) and pescado blanco (white fish).

Santa Elena Hotel Posada Santander, Hotel Sac-Nicté and the Hotel Continental have restaurants.

Restaurante El Rodeo at the corner of 2a Calle and 5a Av is often recommended by locals. It's open every day from 11 am to 9 pm. In the same block, *Super 24* is a 24-hour supermarket. In the next block of 2a Calle, *Restaurante Petenchel* and *La Fonda de Don Diego* are also popular. *Restaurante Mijaro*, a simple comedor on the main road, is another place recommended by locals; it's open every day, 7 am to 9 pm.

Flores *Restaurante/Bar Las Puertas* is a popular restaurant/bar with good food, and it's a good spot for friendly conversation as well – this is the hangout for an interesting mixture of people. There's live music on weekends. It's open Monday to Saturday, 8 am to 1 am. *Casa Picante*, a pizzeria and travelers' resource center near the causeway, is another popular place.

Restaurante Chal-tun-ha is small and pleasant, with an open and fresh decor, a terrace right over the water and a fine view across the lake. The menu offers a good selection of inexpensive dishes. It's open daily, 9 am to 7:30 pm. *Restaurante Don Quijote* is another pleasant little place, on a small boat docked near the Hotel Yum Kax.

Restaurante/Bar Posada El Tucán, next to the Villa del Lago, has a thatched roof and a lakeside terrace which catches any breezes. Set breakfasts cost US$2 to US$3, lunches and dinners US$5 to US$8. *Restaurante Ranchón del Fenix*, next to the Hotel Casona de la Isla, is another pleasant restaurant with a lakeside terrace.

Restaurante La Canoa is cheaper and plainer, but its dark, high-ceilinged dining room appeals to budget travelers, as does the decent food at low prices. *Restaurante La Jungla* has a tiny streetside terrace.

Restaurante La Mesa de los Maya is a popular restaurant serving good traditional foods as well as local game. A mixed plate goes for US$9, a vegetarian plate is US$5 and chicken costs even less. It's open every day, 7 am to 11 pm.

The *Restaurante Gran Jaguar* is often recommended by locals. It has a good variety of inexpensive dishes, attractive decor and bar service. It's open Monday to Saturday, 11 am to 10 pm.

Getting There & Away

Air The airport at Santa Elena (usually called 'the airport at Flores') is quite busy these days. International flights include those to/from Belize City with Tropic Air, Island Air and Aerovías; flights to/from Palenque, Chetumal and Cancún with Aerocaribe; and a flight to/from Cancún four times a week with Aviateca.

There's quite a variation in price flights between Flores and Guatemala City, ranging from around US$60 to US$90. Package tours including airfare and accommodations may work out cheaper, and are available at many travel agencies. See the Tikal section for more on this.

More regional airlines will be opening up routes to and from Flores in the near future. Ask at travel agencies in Belize City and Guatemala City. Your travel agent at home may not be able to get up-to-date information on some of these small regional carriers. And travel agents in Flores and Santa Elena may charge more for a ticket than you would pay by buying it at the airport.

When you arrive at the airport in Flores you may be subjected to a cursory customs and immigration check, as this is a special customs and immigration district.

Bus Travel by bus to or from Flores is slow and uncomfortable, with the exception of the road to Tikal. Each bus company has its own bus station. Transportes Pinita buses depart from the Hotel San Juan in Santa Elena (☎ 926-0041/2). Transportes María Elena buses go from the Hotel Santander in Santa Elena (☎ 926-0574). Other bus companies in Santa Elena include Fuente del Norte (☎ 926-0517), Linea Dorada (☎ 926-0070), Autobuses Máxima (☎ 926-0676) and Transportes Rosío.

Belize City (222 km, 5½ hours, US$20) 1st-class buses depart from the Hotel San Juan and Hotel Continental in Santa Elena every day at 5 am, arriving in Belize City around 10:30 am, connecting with the boat to Caye Caulker and San Pedro, Ambergris Caye.

Bethel (Mexico border; 127 km, four hours, US$3) Transportes Pinita buses, 5 am and 1 pm.

Ceibal – see Sayaxché.

El Naranjo – see From El Petén to Chiapas, below.

El Remate/Puente Ixlú (35 km, 45 minutes) Tikal-bound buses and minibuses (see Tikal) will drop you here. Buses to/from Melchor de Mencos will drop you at Puente Ixlú/El Cruce, less than two km south of El Remate.

Guatemala City (506 km, 11 to 12 hours, US$12 to US$15) Fuente del Norte (☎ 926-0517) operates Especial buses at 9:30 and 11:30 am, 1:30 and 3:30 pm, and Pullman buses at 5, 7 and 8 pm. Linea Dorada (☎ 926-0070) luxury buses (US$18.35) depart at 8 pm. Autobuses Máxima (☎ 926-0676) runs Pullman buses at 7 and 8 pm.

La Ruidosa (crossroads to Puerto Barrios; 242 km, eight hours, US$6) Take any bus bound for Guatemala City.

Melchor de Mencos (Belize border; 101 km, three hours, US$2) 2nd-class Transportes Pinita buses at 5, 8 and 10 am. Rosita buses at 5, 7, 9:30 and 11 am, 2, 3 and 6 pm. On the Belize side, buses (US$0.50) and share-taxis (US$2) take you to Benque Viejo and San Ignacio every hour or so.

Palenque (Mexico) – see From El Petén to Chiapas, below.

Poptún (113 km, 4½ to five hours, US$2.50) Take any bus heading for Guatemala City.

Río Dulce (208 km, seven hours, US$5) Take any bus heading for Guatemala City.

San Andrés (around the lake; 20 km, 40 minutes, US$0.65) Transportes Pinita buses, 5:30 am and noon. They depart San Andrés for the return trip at 7 am and 1:30 pm. Boats also make this trip, departing from San Benito, on the west side of Santa Elena.

Sayaxché (61 km, two hours) 2nd-class Transportes Pinita buses (US$2) at 6, 9 and 10 am, 1 and 4 pm. There are also tours from Santa Elena via Sayaxché to the Maya ruins at Ceibal, departing from Hotel San Juan and Hotel Continental at 8:15 am and returning to Santa Elena at 4 pm (US$30).

Tikal (71 km, 2½ hours, US$2.50) Transportes Pinita bus daily at 1 pm, continuing on to Uaxactún. It departs Tikal for the return trip at 6 am. It's quicker and more convenient to take a shuttle minibus to Tikal (see following section).

Uaxactún (96 km, three hours, US$2.50) Transportes Pinita, 1 pm. It departs from Uaxactún for the return trip at 5 am.

Shuttle Minibus Minibuses bound for Tikal depart each morning from various hotels in Santa Elena and Flores (4, 6, 8 and 10 am), and from the airport (meeting all flights). Any hotel can arrange a trip for you. The fare is US$3.35 per person one way, double for roundtrip; the trip takes one to 1½ hours.

Return trips depart from Tikal at 2, 4 and 5 pm. Your driver will anticipate that you'll want to return to Flores that same afternoon; if you know which return trip you plan to be on, they'll hold a seat for you or arrange a seat in a colleague's minibus. If you stay overnight in Tikal and want to take a minibus to Flores, it's a good idea to reserve a seat with one of the minibus drivers when they arrive in the morning. Don't wait until departure time and expect to find a seat.

A taxi (for up to four people) from Flores/Santa Elena or the airport to Tikal costs US$40 roundtrip.

Getting Around

Bus Buses and minibuses bound for the small villages around the lake and in the immediate vicinity depart from the market area in Santa Elena.

Car Several hotels, car rental companies and travel agencies offer rentals, including cars, 4WDs, pickup trucks and minibuses. Rental car companies are located in the arrivals hall at Flores airport.

These rental companies include:

Garrido (24-hour service), ☎ 926-0092
Hertz, ☎ 926-0332, 926-0415
Koka, ☎ 926-0526, 926-1233
Los Compadres, ☎ 926-0444
Los Jades, ☎ 926-0734
Nesa, ☎ 926-0082

A basic car with unlimited km costs a minimum of around US$50 per day. The travel agency at the Hotel San Juan in Santa Elena (☎/fax 926-0041) also has rental cars.

Bicycle Cahuí International Services in Flores (☎/fax 926-0494) rents bicycles for US$0.85 per hour or US$6.65 per day.

Boat Motor launches making cruises and tours on Lago de Petén Itzá depart from the Santa Elena end of the causeway (see map). Colectivo boats to San Andrés and San José, villages across the lake, depart from San Benito, on the west side of Santa Elena; or, bargain for a private boat.

EL REMATE
Once little more than a few thatched huts 35 km northeast of Santa Elena on the Tikal road, the village of El Remate has recently grown into a small town, thanks to the tourist trade. Right on the lakeshore, El Remate is becoming a secondary tourist center between Flores and Tikal. Halfway between the two places, it allows you to be closer to Tikal but still be on the lake.

El Remate is known for its wood carving. Several handicrafts shops on the lakeshore opposite La Mansión del Pájaro Serpiente sell local handicrafts and rent canoes, rafts and kayaks.

From El Remate an unpaved road snakes its way around the northeast shore of the lake to the Biotopo Cerro Cahuí, the luxury Hotel Camino Real, and on to the villages of San José and San Andrés, on the northwest side of the lake. It's possible to go all the way around the lake by road.

With their new prosperity, Rematecos have built a balneario municipal (municipal beach) just off the highway and have opened several cheap pensions.

Biotopo Cerro Cahuí
At the northeast end of Lago de Petén Itzá, about 43 km from Santa Elena and three km from the Flores-Tikal road, the Biotopo Cerro Cahuí covers 651 hectares of hot, humid, subtropical forest. Within the reserve are mahogany, cedar, ramón, broom, sapodilla and cohune palm trees, as well as many species of lianas (climbing plants), bromeliads (air plants), ferns and orchids. The ramón trees yielded fodder to the ancient Maya, and the hard wood of the sapodilla was used in temple door lintels which have survived from the Classic period to our own time.

Animals in the reserve include spider monkeys, howler monkeys, ocelots, white-tailed deer, raccoons, armadillos and some 21 other species. In the water are 24 species of fish, turtles and snakes, and the *Crocodylus moreletti*, the Petén crocodile. The birdlife, of course, is rich and varied. Depending upon the season and migration patterns, you might see kingfishers, ducks, herons, hawks, parrots, toucans, woodpeckers and the famous ocellated (or Petén) turkey, a beautiful big bird resembling a peacock.

A network of loop trails starts at the road and goes up the hill, affording a view of the whole lake and of Laguna Salpetén and Laguna Petenchel. A trail map is at the entrance.

When we visited, the reserve was always open, and admission was free. However, a ranger told us there was a plan to start charging US$5 per person. You may find the gate always open, or it may be open only from 7 am to 4 pm (once in, you can stay as late as you like). If you want to enter earlier and find the gate closed, go to the administration center and they'll let you in.

Places to Stay & Eat
El Remate has several small hotels and pensions, and more are opening all the time.

La Casa de Don David (message ☎ 926-0227), on the lakeshore about 10 meters from the Flores-Tikal road, is operated by American-born David Kuhn (the original 'gringo perdido') along with his friendly

Guatemalan wife. Rooms with shared bath are US$5 per person, or US$7.50 per person for free-standing bungalows with private bath. Economical meals are served on the wide upstairs terrace overlooking the lake. There's horse riding, and in the early evenings they do a two- or three-hour boat ride, crossing the lake and entering the Río Ixpop to see the crocodiles, birds and other wildlife.

Across the Flores-Tikal road from the lake are a couple of other pleasant places with great lake views. At the *Mirador del Duende* (☎ 926-0269, fax 926-0397) you can camp with your own hammock or tent for US$2.50/4.20 a single/double, sleep in an igloo (like a permanent tent) for US$3.35 per person, or stay in a bungalow for US$4.20 per person. Healthy, economical vegetarian food is served. The pleasant owner boasts that this is a 'mosquito-free zone,' due to the breezes blowing off the lake. Forest hiking tours are offered.

A couple of other good places are about three km west of El Remate on the road around the north side of the lake, near the Biotopo Cerro Cahuí. The *Parador Ecológico El Gringo Perdido* (The Lost Gringo Ecological Inn; ☎/fax in Guatemala City 236-3683) is right on the lakeshore. Shady, rustic hillside gardens hold a restaurant, a bucolic camping area, and simple but pleasant bungalows and dormitories. Rates are US$3 per person for a campsite, US$6 per person for a camping bungalow with roof, beds and mosquito netting, US$10 per person for a dorm bunk, and US$14 per person for rooms with private bath. Four-person bungalows, each with its own patio with hammocks and chairs and a small private dock for swimming and sunning on the lake, are US$25 per person, breakfast and dinner included. Two luxury bungalows with air con are US$50. Overall cost is cheaper if you get a room-and-meals package. Activities include swimming, fishing, windsurfing, volleyball, basketball, boat trips on the lake, and bicycling.

Nearby, *Casa Roja* (☎ 926-0269, in Antigua ☎ 832-0162), across the road from the lake, has simple camping bungalows

with outside bathrooms for US$7/12/15 a single/double/triple. It's cheaper if you get meals here: US$13 per person covers accommodations, dinner and breakfast. A swimming dock is in front, and they rent mountain bikes.

Getting There & Away
Any bus or minibus going north from Santa Elena to Tikal can drop you at El Remate. Taxis from Santa Elena or the airport will take you for US$20. Once you are in El Remate, you can hail any passing bus or minibus on the Flores-Tikal road to take you to Tikal or Flores.

AROUND THE LAKE
A small town on the northwest side of the lake, **San Andrés** has the Eco-Escuela de Español (☎ 928-8106, 926-1370; in the USA (202) 973-2264), a Spanish-language school often recommended by those who have studied there. Cost is US$60/70/80/95 per week for four/five/six/seven hours of instruction daily, plus US$50 per week for room and board with a local family.

TIKAL
Towering pyramids rise above the jungle's green canopy to catch the sun. Howler monkeys swing noisily through the branches of ancient trees as brightly colored parrots and toucans dart, squawking, from perch to perch. When the complex warbling song of some mysterious jungle bird tapers off, the buzz of tree frogs provides background noise.

Certainly the most striking feature of Tikal is its steep-sided temples, rising to heights of more than 44 meters. But Tikal is different from Chichén Itzá, Uxmal, Copán and most other great Maya sites because it is deep in the jungle. Its many plazas have been cleared of trees and vines, its temples uncovered and partially restored, but as you walk from one building to another you pass beneath the dense canopy of the rain forest. Rich smells of earth and vegetation, peacefulness and animal noises all contribute to an experience not offered by any other major Maya site.

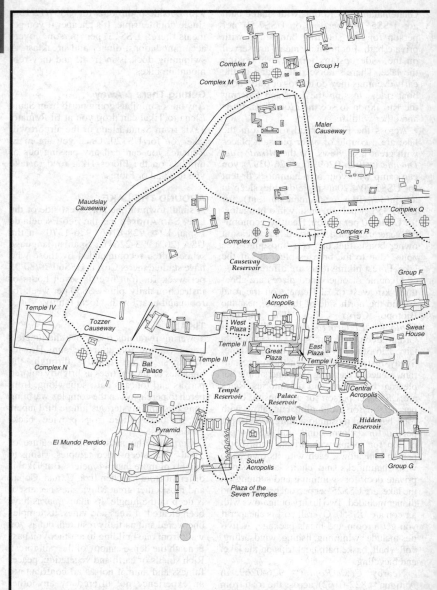

Complex P

Complex M

Group H

Maler
Causeway

Maudslay
Causeway

Complex Q

Complex O

Complex R

Causeway
Reservoir

Group F

Temple IV

North
Acropolis

Sweat
House

Tozzer
Causeway

West
Plaza

Complex N

Temple II

Great
Plaza

East
Plaza

Bat
Palace

Temple III

Temple I

Central
Acropolis

Temple
Reservoir

Palace
Reservoir

Hidden
Reservoir

Temple V

El Mundo Perdido

Pyramid

South
Acropolis

Group G

Plaza of the
Seven Temples

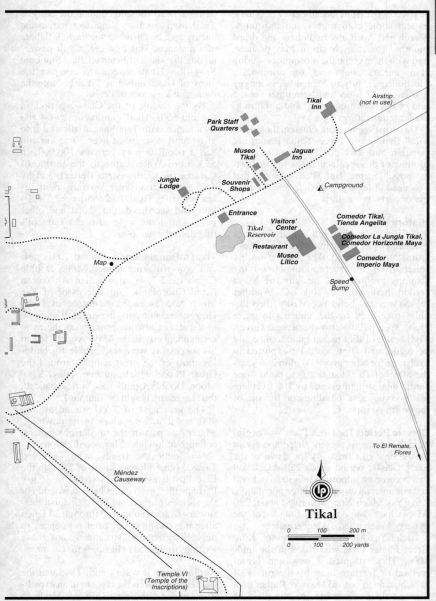

Airstrip
(not in use)

Tikal Inn

Park Staff
Quarters

Museo
Tikal

Jaguar
Inn

Jungle
Lodge

Souvenir
Shops

Campground

Entrance

Visitors'
Center

Comedor Tikal,
Tienda Angelita

Tikal
Reservoir

Comedor La Jungla Tikal,
Comedor Horizonte Maya

Restaurant

Museo
Lítico

Comedor
Imperio Maya

Map

Speed
Bump

To El Remate,
Flores

Méndez
Causeway

Tikal

0   100   200 m
0   100   200 yards

Temple VI
(Temple of the
Inscriptions)

If you visit from December to February, expect some cool nights and mornings. March and April are the hottest and driest months. The rains begin in May or June, and with them come the mosquitoes – bring rain gear, repellent and, for camping, a mosquito net. July to September is muggy and buggy. October and November see the end of the occasional rains and a return to cooler temperatures.

Day trips by air from Guatemala City to Tikal (landing in Flores/Santa Elena) are popular, and they do allow you to get a glimpse of this spectacular site in the shortest possible time. But Tikal is so big that you need at least two days to see even the major parts thoroughly.

History

Tikal is set on a low hill, which becomes evident as you walk up to the Great Plaza from the entry road. The hill, affording relief from the surrounding low-lying swampy ground, may be why the Maya settled here around 700 BC. Another reason was the abundance of flint, the valuable stone used by the ancients to make clubs, spearpoints, arrowheads and knives. The wealth of flint meant good tools could be made, and flint could be exported in exchange for other goods. Within 200 years the Maya of Tikal had begun to build stone ceremonial structures, and by 200 BC there was a complex of buildings on the site of the North Acropolis.

Classic Period The Great Plaza was beginning to assume its present shape and extent by the time of Christ. By the dawn of the Early Classic period about 250 AD, Tikal had become an important religious, cultural and commercial city with a large population. King Yax Moch Xoc, who ruled about 230 AD, is looked upon as the founder of the dynasty which ruled Tikal thereafter.

Under Yax Moch Xoc's successor, King Great Jaguar Paw, who ruled in the mid-300s, Tikal adopted a new and brutal method of warfare used by the rulers of Teotihuacán in central Mexico. Rather than meeting their adversaries on the plain of battle in hand-to-hand combat, the army of Tikal used auxiliary units to encircle the enemy and, by throwing spears, to kill them at a distance. This first use of 'air power' among the Maya of Petén enabled Smoking Frog, the Tikal general, to conquer the army of Uaxactún; thus Tikal became the dominant kingdom in Petén.

By the middle of the Classic period, in the mid-500s, Tikal's military prowess and its alliance with Teotihuacán allowed it to grow until it sprawled over 30 sq km and had a population of perhaps 100,000. In 553, Lord Water came to the throne of Caracol (in southwestern Belize), and by 562, using the same warfare methods learned from Tikal, had conquered Tikal's king and sacrificed him. Tikal and other Petén kingdoms suffered under Caracol's rule until the late 600s.

Tikal's Renaissance Around 700 a new and powerful king named Moon Double Comb (682-734), also called Ah Cacau (Lord Chocolate), 26th successor of Yax Moch Xoc, ascended the throne of Tikal. He restored not only the military strength of Tikal, but also its primacy as the most resplendent city in the Maya world. He and his successors were responsible for building most of the great temples around the Great Plaza, which survive today. King Moon Double Comb was buried beneath the staggering height of Temple 1.

The greatness of Tikal waned around 900, but it was not alone in its downfall, which was part of the mysterious general collapse of lowland Maya civilization.

No doubt the Itzaes, who occupied Tayasal (now Flores), knew of Tikal in the Late Post-Classic period (1200 to 1530). Perhaps they even came here to worship at the shrines of their old gods. Spanish missionary friars who moved through El Petén after the conquest left brief references to these junglebound structures, but these writings moldered in libraries for centuries.

Rediscovery It wasn't until 1848 that the Guatemalan government sent out an expedition, under the leadership of Modesto

Méndez and Ambrosio Tut, to visit the site. This may have been inspired by John L Stephens' bestselling accounts of fabulous Maya ruins, published in 1841 and 1843 (though Stephens never visited Tikal). Like Stephens, Méndez and Tut took an artist, Eusebio Lara, to record their archaeological discoveries. An account of their findings was published by the Berlin Academy of Science, and the world learned about Tikal.

In 1877 the Swiss Dr Gustav Bernoulli visited Tikal. His explorations resulted in the removal of carved wooden lintels from Temples I and IV and their shipment to Basel, where they are still on view in the Museum für Völkerkunde.

Scientific exploration of Tikal began with the arrival of Alfred P Maudslay, the English archaeologist, in 1881; others continued his work: Teobert Maler, Alfred M Tozzer and RE Merwin. Tozzer worked tirelessly at Tikal on and off from the beginning of the century until his death in 1954. The inscriptions at Tikal were studied and deciphered by Sylvanus G Morley.

Since 1956, archaeological research and restoration has been carried out by the University Museum of the University of Pennsylvania and the Guatemalan Instituto de Antropología y Historia. In the mid-1950s an airstrip was built at Tikal to make access easier. In the early 1980s the road between Tikal and Flores was improved and paved, and direct flights to Tikal were abandoned (flights now land in Flores/Santa Elena).

Orientation & Information

Tikal is located in the midst of the vast Tikal National Park, a 575-sq-km preserve containing thousands of separate ruined structures. The central area of the city occupied about 16 sq km, with more than 4000 structures.

The road from Flores enters the national park boundaries about 15 km south of the ruins. When you enter the park you must pay a fee of US$5 for the day; if you enter after about 3 pm, you can have your ticket validated for the following day as well.

The area around the visitors' center includes three hotels, a camping area, three small comedores, a tiny post office, a police post, two museums and a disused airstrip. From the visitors' center it's a 20- to 30-minute walk southwest to the Great Plaza.

The walk from the Great Plaza to the Temple of the Inscriptions is over one km; from the Great Plaza to Complex P, it's one km in the opposite direction. To visit all of the major building complexes you must walk at least 10 km, probably more.

For complete information on the monuments at Tikal, pick up a copy of *Tikal – A Handbook of the Ancient Maya Ruins*, by William R Coe. The guide is widely available and on sale in Flores and at Tikal. *The Birds of Tikal* by Frank B Smithe (Natural History Press, 1966), available at the Tikal museums, is a good resource for bird watchers.

The ruins are open from 5 am to 5 pm. You may be able to get permission to stay until 8 pm by applying to the Inspectorería to the west of the visitors' center. Carry a flashlight if you stay after sunset.

Great Plaza

Follow the signs to reach the Great Plaza. The path comes into the Great Plaza around Temple I, the Temple of the Grand Jaguar. This was built to honor – and to bury – King Moon Double Comb. The king may have worked out the plans for the building himself, but it was erected above his tomb by his son, who succeeded to the throne in 734. The king's rich burial goods included 180 beautiful jade objects, 90 pieces of bone carved with hieroglyphs, pearls and stingray spines which were used for ritual bloodletting. At the top of the 44-meter-high temple is a small enclosure of three rooms covered by a corbelled arch. The zapote-wood lintels over the doors were richly carved; one of them is now in a Basel museum. The lofty roofcomb which crowned the temple was originally adorned with reliefs and bright paint. It may have symbolized the 13 realms of the Maya heaven.

The climb up is dangerous (at least two people have tumbled to their deaths so far), but the view from the top is magnificent.

Temple II, directly across the plaza from Temple I, was once almost as high, but now measures 38 meters without its roofcomb. This one seems a bit easier to climb and the view is just as stupendous.

The North Acropolis, while not as immediately impressive as the twin temples, is of great significance. Archaeologists have uncovered about 100 different structures, the oldest of which dates from before the time of Christ, with evidence of occupation as far back as 400 BC. The Maya built and rebuilt on top of older structures, and the many layers, combined with the elaborate burials, added sanctity and power to their temples. Look for the two huge wall masks, uncovered from an earlier structure and now protected by roofs. The final version of the Acropolis, as it stood around 800 AD, had more than 12 temples atop a vast platform, many of them the work of King Moon Double Comb.

On the plaza side of the North Acropolis are two rows of stelae. Though hardly as impressive as the magnificent stelae at Copán or Quiriguá, these served the same purpose: to record the great deeds of the kings of Tikal, to sanctify their memory and to add 'power' to the temples and plazas which surrounded them.

Central Acropolis
On the south side of the Great Plaza, this maze of courtyards, little rooms and small temples is thought by many to have been a palace where Tikal's nobles lived. Others think the tiny rooms may have been used for sacred rites and ceremonies, as graffiti found within them suggest. Over the centuries the configuration of the rooms was repeatedly changed, suggesting perhaps that this 'palace' was in fact a noble or royal family's residence changed to accommodate different groups of relatives. A hundred years ago, one part of the acropolis, called Maler's Palace, provided lodgings for archaeologist Teobert Maler when he worked at Tikal.

West Plaza
The West Plaza is north of Temple II. On its north side is a large Late Classic temple. To the south, across the Tozzer Causeway, is Temple III, 55 meters high. Yet to be uncovered, it allows you to see a temple the way the last Tikal Maya and first white explorers saw them. The causeway leading to Temple IV was one of several sacred ways built among the temple complexes of Tikal, no doubt for astronomical as well as aesthetic reasons.

South Acropolis & Temple V
Due south of the Great Plaza is the South Acropolis. Excavation has hardly even begun on this huge mass of masonry covering two hectares. The palaces on top are from Late Classic times (the time of King Moon Double Comb), but earlier constructions probably go back 1000 years.

Temple V, just east of the South Acropolis, is 58 meters high and was built around 700 AD. Unlike the other great temples, this one has rounded corners, and one very tiny room at the top. The room is less than a meter deep, but its walls are up to 4½ meters thick. The view (as usual) is wonderful, giving you a 'profile' the temples on the Great Plaza.

Plaza of the Seven Temples
On the other side of the South Acropolis is the Plaza of the Seven Temples. The little temples, all quite close together, were built in Late Classic times, though the structures beneath must go back at least a millennium. Note the skull and crossed bones on the central temple (the one with the stela and altar in front). On the north side of the plaza is an unusual triple ball court; another, larger version in the same design stands just south of Temple I.

El Mundo Perdido
About 400 meters southwest of the Great Plaza is El Mundo Perdido (the Lost World), a large complex of 38 structures with a huge pyramid in its midst. Unlike the rest of Tikal, where Late Classic construction overlays work of earlier periods, El Mundo Perdido exhibits buildings of many different periods: the large pyramid is thought to be essentially Preclassic (with

some later repairs and renovations); the Talud-Tablero Temple (or Temple of the Three Rooms), Early Classic; and the Temple of the Skulls, Late Classic.

The pyramid, 32 meters high and 80 meters along the base, has a stairway on each side, and had huge masks flanking each stairway, but no temple structure at its top. Each side of the pyramid displays a slightly different architectural style. Tunnels dug into the pyramid by archaeologists reveal four similar pyramids beneath the outer face; the earliest (Structure 5C-54 Sub 2B) dates from 700 BC, making the pyramid the oldest Maya structure at Tikal.

Temple IV & Complex N

Complex N, near Temple IV, is an example of the 'twin-temple' complexes popular among Tikal's rulers during the Late Classic period. These complexes are thought to have commemorated the completion of a katun, or 20-year cycle in the Maya calendar. This one was built in 711 by King Moon Double Comb to mark the 14th katun of Baktun 9. The king himself is portrayed on Stela 16, one of the finest stelae at Tikal.

Temple IV, at 64 meters, is the highest building at Tikal and the highest pre-Columbian building known in the Western Hemisphere. It was completed about 741, in the reign of King Moon Double Comb's son. From the base it looks like a steep little hill. Clamber up the path, holding onto trees and roots, to reach the metal ladder which will take you to the top. Another metal ladder, around to the side, lets you climb to the base of the roofcomb. The view is almost as good as from a helicopter – a panorama across the jungle canopy. If you stay up here for the sunset, climb down immediately thereafter, as it gets dark on the path very quickly.

Temple of the Inscriptions (Temple VI)

Compared to Copán or Quiriguá, there are relatively few inscriptions on buildings at Tikal. The exception is this temple, 1.2 km southeast of the Great Plaza. On the rear of the 12-meter-high roofcomb is a long inscription; the sides and cornice of the roofcomb bear glyphs as well. The inscriptions give us the date 766 AD. Stela 21 and Altar 9, standing before the temple, date from 736. The stela had been badly damaged (part of it was converted into a *metate* for grinding corn!) but has now been repaired.

Warning Note that the Temple of the Inscriptions is remote from the other complexes, and there have been incidents of robbery and rape of single travelers and couples. Ask a guard before you make the trek out here, or come in a group.

Northern Complexes

About one km north of the Great Plaza is Complex P. Like Complex N, it's a Late Classic twin-temple complex which probably commemorated the end of a katun. Complex M, next to it, was partially torn down by the Late Classic Maya to provide building materials for a causeway now named after Alfred Maudslay, which runs southwest to Temple IV. Group H had some interesting graffiti within its temples.

Complexes Q and R, about 300 meters due north of the Great Plaza, are very Late Classic twin-pyramid complexes with stelae and altars standing before the temples. Complex Q is perhaps the best example of the twin-temple type, as it has been mostly restored. Stela 22 and Altar 10 are excellent examples of Late Classic Tikal relief carving, dated 771.

Complex O, due west of these complexes on the western side of the Maler Causeway, has an uncarved stela and altar in its north enclosure. An uncarved stela? The whole point of stelae was to record great happenings. Why did this one remain uncarved?

Trails

The Sendero Benilj'a'a, a three-km trail with three sections, begins in front of the Jungle Lodge. Ruta Monte Medio (one hour) and Ruta Monte Medio Alto (two hours) are accessible all year round. Ruta Monte Bajo (35 minutes) is accessible only in summer.

GUATEMALA

Museums

Tikal has two museums. **Museo Lítico**, the larger museum, is in the visitors' center. It houses a number of stelae and carved stones from the ruins. Outside is a large relief map showing how Tikal would have looked during the Late Classic period, around 800 AD. Admission is free.

The **Museo Tikal**, which is smaller, is near the Jungle Lodge. It has some fascinating exhibits, including the burial goods of King Moon Double Comb, carved jade, inscribed bones, shells, stelae, ceramics and other items recovered from the excavations. Admission is US$1.65.

Both museums are open Monday to Friday from 9 am to 5 pm, Saturday and Sunday 9 am to 4 pm.

Organized Tours

All the hotels can arrange guided tours of the ruins, and tours to other places in the region such as Uaxactún, Ceibal, Yaxha, Nakum. The Jungle Lodge is a good place to ask about this.

Places to Stay

Some intrepid visitors sleep atop Temple IV, convincing the guards to overlook this illegal activity for a consideration of US$5 per person, but this is not to be recommended. Safety is a major concern.

Otherwise, there are only four places to stay at Tikal. Most of the places are booked in advance by tour groups, even though most groups (and individuals as well) stay near Lago de Petén Itzá and shuttle up to Tikal for the day. In recent years I have heard numerous complaints of price gouging, unacceptable accommodations and 'lost' reservations at these hotels. It may be best to stay in Flores or El Remate and visit Tikal on day trips.

On the other hand, staying at Tikal enables you to relax and savor the dawn and dusk, when most of the jungle birds and animals can be seen. If you'd like the thrill of staying overnight at Tikal, the easiest way is to forget about making reservations (which can be frustrating) and take a tour. Any travel agency can arrange one

including lodging, a meal or two, a guided tour of the ruins and airfare. The Adventure Travel Center (☎/fax 832-0162, net), 5a Av Norte No 25-B, near the arch in Antigua, is one, and there are plenty of others. There's no need to make reservations if you just want to camp in the camping area.

Camping Cheapest of Tikal's lodgings is the official camping area by the entrance road and the disused airstrip. Set in a large, open lawn of green grass with some trees for shade, it has tent spaces on the grass and also on concrete platforms under palapa roofs. Water for the toilets and showers is more dependable now than it has been in previous years, since it's now brought in. Camping is US$5 per person.

The Jaguar Inn (see below) has a smaller camping area with bathroom and shower facilities. Camping is US$4.20 per person with your own tent or hammock, or you can rent camping gear; cost is US$6.65 for a hammock with mosquito net, US$10/16.65 a single/double for a tent with sheets, pillow and pad.

Hotels Largest and most attractive of the hotels is the *Jungle Lodge* (☎ in Guatemala City 476-8775, 477-0754, fax 476-0294), built originally to house the archaeologists excavating and restoring Tikal. It has 34 pleasant rooms in duplex bungalows, each room with private hot bath and two double beds, for US$48/60/70/80 a single/double/triple/quad. In an older section are 12 much less attractive rooms with shared bath for US$20/25 a single/double. There's a swimming pool, a large garden grounds, and a restaurant/bar with breakfast for US$5, lunch or dinner for US$10.

Tikal Inn (fax 926-0065), past the Jaguar Inn as you walk away from the small museum down towards the old airstrip, is the next more attractive. It has 17 rooms in the main building, as well as bungalows, which are slightly nicer, plus gardens, a swimming pool and restaurant. The rooms are quite simple and clean, all with private hot bath and ceiling fan, but have walls that extend only partway up to the roof and thus afford little conversational privacy. Singles/ doubles are US$25/35 in the main building, US$45/55 in the bungalows. The electricity operates only from 11 am to 10 pm.

The *Jaguar Inn* (☎ 926-0002), to the right of the museum as you approach on the access road, has nine bungalow rooms with private bath and ceiling fan for US$30/48/66/78 a single/double/triple/ quad. The restaurant serves breakfast for US$3, lunch and dinner for US$6.

Places to Eat
As you arrive in Tikal, look on the right-hand side of the road to find the three little comedores: *Comedor Imperio Maya, Comedor La Jungla Tikal, Comedor Tikal* and *Tienda Angelita*. The Comedor Imperio Maya, first on the way into the site, seems to be the favored one. You can buy cold drinks and snacks in the adjoining shop. All three comedores are similar in their lack of comfort and style, all are rustic and pleasant, all are run by local people and all serve huge plates of fairly tasty food at low prices. The meal of the day is almost always a piece of roast chicken, rice, salad, fruit and a soft drink for US$4. All of these places are open every day from around 5 am to 9 pm.

Picnic tables beneath shelters are located just off Tikal's Great Plaza, with itinerant soft-drink peddlers standing by, but no food is sold. If you want to spend all day at the ruins without having to make the 20- to 30-minute walk back to the comedores, carry food with you.

The restaurant in the visitors' center, across the street from the comedores, serves fancier food at fancier prices. Tenderloin of beef (lomito) is featured, as are other steaks, at US$10 a portion. Plates of fruit cost less. All the hotels also have restaurants.

Getting There & Away
For details of transport to and from Flores/ Santa Elena, see that section. Coming from Belize, you can get off the bus at El Cruce/ Puente Ixlú. Wait for a northbound bus or minibus – or hitch a ride with an obliging tourist – to take you the remaining 35 km to

Tikal. Note that there is very little northbound traffic after lunch. If you come to Puente Ixlú in the afternoon, it's probably best to continue to Flores or El Remate for the night rather than risk being stranded at El Cruce.

You don't need a car to get to Tikal, but a 4WD vehicle of your own can be useful for visiting Uaxactún. If you're driving, fill your fuel tank in Flores; there is no fuel available at Tikal or Uaxactún.

UAXACTÚN
Uaxactún (wah-shahk-TOON), 25 km north of Tikal along a poor, unpaved road through the jungle, was Tikal's political and military rival in Late Preclassic times. It was conquered by Tikal's King Great Jaguar Paw in the mid-300s, and was subservient to its great sister to the south for centuries thereafter.

When you arrive at Uaxactún, sign your name in the register at the guard's hut (at the edge of the disused airstrip, which now serves as pasture for cattle). About halfway down the airstrip, roads go off to the left and to the right to the ruins.

Villagers in Uaxactún live in houses lined up on either side of the disused airstrip, making a living by collecting chicle, *pimienta* (allspice) and *xate* in the surrounding forest.

Ruins
The pyramids at Uaxactún were uncovered and put in a stabilized condition so that no further deterioration would result; they were not restored. White mortar is the mark of the repair crews, who patched cracks in the stone to prevent water and roots from entering. Much of the work on the famous Temple E-VII-Sub was done by Earthwatch volunteers in 1974; among them was Jane A Fisher, a Uaxactún-lover who later married Tom Brosnahan, the author of the Belize chapter.

Turn right from the airstrip to reach Group E and Group H, a 10- to 15-minute walk. Perhaps the most significant temple here is E-VII-Sub, among the earliest intact temples excavated, with foundations going back perhaps to 2000 BC. It lay beneath much larger structures, which have been stripped away. On its flat top are holes, or sockets, for the poles which would have supported a wood-and-thatch temple.

About a 20-minute walk to the northwest of the runway are Group A and Group B. At Group A, early excavators sponsored by Andrew Carnegie simply cut into the sides of the temples indiscriminately, looking for graves. Sometimes they used dynamite. This unfortunate work destroyed many of the temples, which are now in the process of being reconstructed.

The ruins are always open and accessible, and no admission is charged. However, the turnoff onto the Uaxactún road is inside the gate to Tikal, so you must pay the US$5 admission fee there.

Organized Tours

Tours to Uaxactún can be arranged at the hotels in Tikal. The Jungle Lodge, for example, offers a trip to Uaxactún departing daily at 8 am and returning at 1 pm, in time to meet the 2 pm buses back to Flores. The trip costs US$60 for one to four people, split among the number of people going, or US$15 per person for over four people.

Places to Stay & Eat

If you have your own camping gear, there are plenty of places to camp. *Eco Camping*, at the entrance to the larger group of ruins, is an organized camping ground with basic cabins.

Posada y Restaurante Campamento El Chiclero, on the left side of the airstrip, is a primitive place with seven musty thatch-roofed rooms with walls going only part way up, and screen the rest of the way. Singles/doubles are US$6.65/9, or you can pitch a tent. Bathrooms are shared, and there's no electricity. It's a 10-minute walk from the ruins. Trips can be arranged here to other places in the area, including Parque Nacional El Mirador-Dos Lagunas-Río Azul, La Muralla, Nakbé and Manantial.

Getting There & Away

During the rainy season (from May to October), you may find it difficult to get to Uaxactún. At other times of the year, ask in Flores or Tikal about the condition of the road. You may be advised to make the hour-long drive only in a 4WD vehicle.

A bus operates daily between Santa Elena and Uaxactún, stopping at Tikal on the way. Cost is US$2.50 for the three-hour ride from Santa Elena, or US$1 for the one-hour ride from Tikal. The bus departs Uaxactún daily at 5 am and departs Santa Elena at 1 pm for the return trip.

If you're driving, fill your fuel tank in Flores; there is no fuel available at Tikal or Uaxactún. You might also want to pack some food and drink, though drinks and a few snacks are available in the village at Uaxactún.

From Uaxactún it's a further 104 km to the Río Azul ruins, or 88 km to San Andrés.

EASTWARD TO BELIZE

It's 101 km from Flores/Santa Elena east to Melchor de Mencos, the Guatemalan town on the border with Belize. You can take a bus from Santa Elena to Melchor de Mencos, where you can transfer to the Belizean side. Alternatively, there's a Transportes Pinita bus at 5 am which goes all the way to Belize City and connects with the boat to Caye Caulker and Ambergris Caye. this bus enables travelers to avoid spending the night in Belize City. See the Flores/Santa Elena section for details on buses.

The road from Flores to El Cruce/Puente Ixlú is good, fast asphalt. If you're coming from Tikal, start early in the morning and get off at El Cruce to catch a bus or hitch a ride eastward. For the fastest, most reliable service, however, it's best to be on that 5 am bus.

East of El Cruce the road reverts to what's usual in El Petén – unpaved mud in bad repair. The trip to Melchor de Mencos takes three or four hours. There has been guerrilla and bandit activity along this road, and there's a remote chance that your bus could be stopped and its passengers relieved of their valuables. (It's been a long time since this has happened.)

At the border you must hand in your Guatemalan tourist card before proceeding to Benque Viejo in Belize, about three km from the border. See the section on Benque Viejo for transportion information to Benque Viejo, San Ignacio, Belmopan and Belize City. If you arrive in Benque Viejo early enough in the day, you may have sufficient time to visit the Maya ruins of Xunantunich on your way to San Ignacio.

FROM EL PETÉN TO CHIAPAS (MEXICO)

There are currently three routes through the jungle from Flores (Guatemala) to Palenque (Mexico). Whichever way you go, make sure you catch customs and get your exit and entry stamps in your passport on both sides of the border.

Via El Naranjo & La Palma

The traditional route is via bus to El Naranjo, then by boat down the Río San Pedro to La Palma, then by colectivo and bus to Tenosique and Palenque.

Transportes Pinita buses to El Naranjo (on the Río San Pedro) depart from the Hotel San Juan in Santa Elena daily at 5, 8 and 11 am, 1 and 2 pm; cost is US$3 for the rough, bumpy, 125-km, five-hour ride. Rosío buses depart for the same trip at 4:45, 8 and 10:30 am and at 1:30 pm.

El Naranjo is a hamlet with a few thatched huts, large military barracks, an immigration post and a few basic lodging places. From El Naranjo you must catch a boat on the river around midday for the four-hour cruise to the border town of La Palma (US$24). From La Palma you can go by colectivo or bus to Tenosique (1½ hours), then by bus or combi to Emiliano Zapata (40 km, one hour), and from there by bus or combi to Palenque.

Going in the reverse direction, travel agencies in Palenque offer to get you from Palenque to La Palma by minibus in time to catch the boat to El Naranjo, which departs between 8 and 9 am. You then catch the bus for the dreadful five-hour ride to Flores, arriving there around 7 pm the same day. The cost is about US$55 per person. However, you can do it yourself by taking the 4:30 am bus from the ADO terminal to

Tenosique, then a taxi (US$10) to La Plama to catch the 8 am-ish boat. If you catch a later bus, there are basic, cheap hotels in Tenosique, or you can find a place to hang your hammock and rough it in La Palma.

Via Bethel & Frontera Corozal

A faster route is by early morning bus from Flores via La Libertad and the El Subín crossroads to the co-op hamlet of Bethel (four hours, US$3), on the Río Usumacinta which forms the border between Guatemala and Mexico.

The early bus should get you to Bethel before noon, but if you're stuck you can spend the night at the *Posada Maya*, beside the river in the tropical forest one km from Bethel. Lodging and meals are available here, and it's not expensive; you can take a cabin, or sleep in a hammock. Food is grown in the organic garden. Activities include swimming in the river and tours to nearby places including Yaxchilán, a natural spring and a lookout point. The owners are friendly and helpful to travelers, and can arrange transport including boats and horses.

Frequent boats make the half-hour trip downriver from Bethel to Frontera Corozal on the Mexico side, charging from US$4 to US$12 for the voyage, depending to some extent on your bargaining power.

At Frontera Corozal (formerly Frontera Echeverría) there's a restaurant and primitive accommodations, but you're better off taking one of the colectivos (shared taxi-minibuses) which wait for passengers to Palenque. The last colectivo tends to leave around 2 or 3 pm.

From Frontera Corozal, a chartered boat to the Yaxchilán archaeological site might cost US$60, but sometimes you can hitch a ride with a group for US$10 or so. Buses from Frontera Corozal take four to 4½ hours to reach Palenque; the fare is US$5.

Coming from Palenque, you can bus to Frontera Corozal (two or three hours, US$4), take a boat upstream (25 minutes to the Posada Maya, 35 minutes to the village of Bethel), and either stay overnight at the Posada Maya or continue on the bus to Flores.

In Palenque, travel agencies may insist that you can't do the trip on your own, that you must sign up for their US$30 trip, and that there is no place to stay overnight at the border. Not so! These organized trips save you some hassle, but you can do the same thing yourself for half the price. Just be sure to hit the road as early as possible in the morning.

Via Sayaxché, Pipiles & Benemérito

From Sayaxché, you can negotiate a ride on one of the cargo boats for the eight-hour trip (US$8) down the Río de la Pasión via Pipiles (the Guatemalan border post) to Benemérito, in Chiapas. From Benemérito, proceed by bus or boat to the ruins at Yaxchilán and Bonampak, and then onward to Palenque. Buses run directly between Benemerito and Palenque (10 hours, US$12) as well.

SAYAXCHÉ & CEIBAL

The town of Sayaxché, 61 km south of Flores through the jungle, is the closest settlement to a half-dozen Mayan archaeological sites, including Aguateca, Altar de Sacrificios, Ceibal, Dos Pilas, El Caribe, Itzán, La Amelia and Tamarindito. Of these, Ceibal is currently the best restored and most interesting, partly because of its Maya monuments and also because of the river voyage and jungle walk necessary to reach it.

Dos Pilas is presently under excavation, but not equipped to receive visitors without their own camping gear. From Dos Pilas, the minor sites of Tamarindito and Aguateca may be reached on foot and by boat, but they are unrestored, covered in jungle and of interest only to the very intrepid.

Sayaxché itself is of little interest, but its few basic services allow you to eat and to stay overnight in this region.

Orientation

The bus from Santa Elena drops you on the north bank of the Río de la Pasión. The main part of the town is on the south bank. Frequent ferries carry you over the river for a minimal fare.

Ceibal

Unimportant during the Classic period, Ceibal grew rapidly thereafter, attaining a population of perhaps 10,000 by 900 AD. Much of the population growth may have been due to immigration from what is now Chiapas, in Mexico, because the art and culture of Ceibal seems to have changed markedly during the same period. The Post-Classic period saw the decline of Ceibal, after which its low ruined temples were quickly covered by a thick carpet of jungle.

Today Ceibal is not one of the most impressive of Maya sites, but the journey to Ceibal is among the most memorable. A two-hour voyage on the jungle-bound Río de la Pasión brings you to a primitive dock. After landing, you clamber up a narrow, rocky path beneath gigantic ceiba trees and ganglions of jungle vines to reach the archaeological zone.

Smallish temples, many of them still (or again) covered with jungle, surround two principal plazas. In front of a few temples, and standing seemingly alone on paths deeply shaded by the jungle canopy, are magnificent stelae, their intricate carvings still in excellent condition.

Places to Stay & Eat

Hotel Guayacan (☎ 926-6111), just up from the dock on the south side of the river in Sayaxché, is basic and serviceable. A double costs around US$8/10 with shared/private bath. The *Hotel Mayapan*, up the street to the left, has cell-like rooms for US$5 a double. The *Hotel Ecológico Posada Caribe* (☎ /fax 928-6114; in Guatemala City ☎ /fax 230-6588) is more expensive.

Restaurant Yaxkin is typical of the few eateries in town: basic, family-run and cheap.

Getting There & Away

Day trips to Ceibal are organized by various agencies and drivers in Santa Elena, Flores and Tikal for about US$30 per person roundtrip. It can be done cheaper on your own, but this is significantly less convenient.

Transportes Pinita buses depart from Santa Elena at 6, 9 and 10 am, 1 and 4 pm for Sayaxché (two hours, US$2.50), where you must strike a deal with a boat owner to ferry you up the river – a two-hour voyage – and back. The boat may cost anywhere from US$30 to US$60, depending upon its size and capacity. From the river, it's less than 30 minutes' walk to the site. You should hire a guide to see the site, as some of the finest stelae are off the plazas in the jungle.

See the previous section for information on crossing into Mexico from Sayaxché, via Pipiles and Benemérito.

Belize

A tiny English-speaking tropical country with a democratic government and a highly unlikely mixture of peoples and cultures – that's Belize.

Belize is tiny. The population of the entire country is less than 200,000, the size of a small city in Mexico, Europe or the USA. The 23,300 sq km of land within its borders is slightly more than that of Massachusetts or Wales.

Belize is English-speaking, officially. But the black Creoles, its largest ethnic group (over half of the population) speak their own dialect as well as standard English. Spanish is a popular second language, and you may also hear Maya, Chinese, Mennonite German, Lebanese Arabic, Hindi and Garífuna, the language of the Garinagu people of the southern townships.

Belize has never had a coup; indeed, it does not have an army, only the tiny Belize Defence Force.

Belize is many other things: friendly, laid-back, beautiful, proud, poor and hopeful for the future.

Belize has been discovered, but it is not prepared to receive lots of visitors. Services are few, far between and basic. Hotels may be full when you arrive. There are only two paved roads in the whole country, so transport is slow. If you expect convenience, comfort and ultra-cheapness, you're in for a surprise. But if you are adaptable and adventurous, you'll love Belize.

Facts about Belize

HISTORY

In the opinion of its Spanish conquerors, Belize was a backwater good only for cutting logwood to be used for dye. It had no obvious riches to exploit and no great population to convert for the glory of God and the profit of the conquerors. Far from

being profitable, it was dangerous because the barrier reef tended to tear the keels from ships attempting to approach the shore. So the Spaniards left Belize alone.

The lack of effective government and the safety afforded by the barrier reef attracted English and Scottish pirates to Belizean waters during the 1600s. In 1670, however, Spain convinced the British government to clamp down on pirate activity. The pirates, now unemployed, mostly went into the logwood business.

During the 1700s, as British interests in Caribbean countries increased, so did British involvement in Belize. By the late 1700s, Belize was already British by tradition and sympathy, and it was with relief and jubilation that Belizeans received the

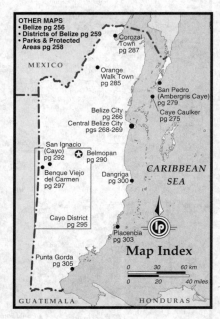

OTHER MAPS
• Belize pg 256
• Districts of Belize pg 259
• Parks & Protected Areas pg 258

MEXICO

Corozal Town pg 287

Orange Walk Town pg 285

San Pedro (Ambergris Caye) pg 279

Belize City pg 266
Central Belize City pgs 268-269

Caye Caulker pg 275

San Ignacio (Cayo) pg 292

Belmopan pg 290

Benque Viejo del Carmen pg 297

Dangriga pg 300

CARIBBEAN SEA

Cayo District pg 295

Placencia pg 303

Punta Gorda pg 305

Map Index

0   30   60 km
0   20   40 miles

GUATEMALA   HONDURAS

255

BELIZE

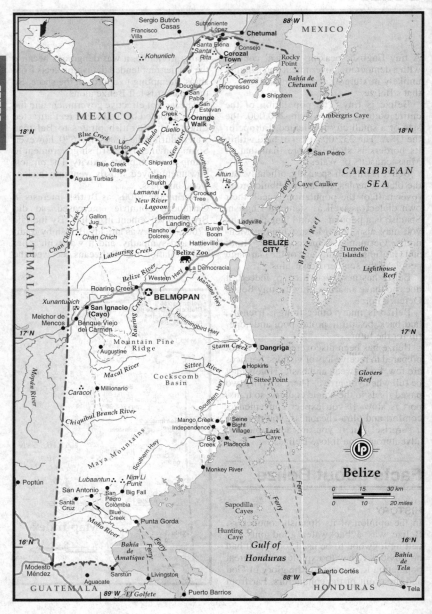

Belize

news, on September 10, 1798, that a British force had defeated the Spanish armada off St George's Caye. Belize had been delivered from Spanish rule, a fact that was ratified by treaty some 60 years later.

In 1862, the USA was embroiled in its Civil War and unable to enforce the Monroe Doctrine, which prohibited 'interference' by European powers in the Western Hemisphere. Great Britain took the opportunity to declare Belize to be the colony of British Honduras, and it encouraged people from numerous parts of the British Empire to settle there, which resulted in the country's present-day ethnic diversity.

After WWII the Belizean economy worsened, which led to agitation for independence from the UK. Democratic institutions and political parties were formed over the years, self-government became a reality, and on September 21, 1981, the colony of British Honduras officially became the independent nation of Belize.

Guatemala, which had claimed Belize as part of its national territory, feared that Belizean independence would kill forever its hopes of reclaiming it. The Guatemalans threatened war, but British troops stationed in Belize kept the dispute to a diplomatic squabble. In 1992 a new Guatemalan government recognized Belize's independence and territorial integrity, and it signed a treaty relinquishing its claim.

GEOGRAPHY

Belize is tropical lowland, though in the western part of the country the Maya Mountains rise to almost a thousand meters. The mountain country is lush and well watered, humid even in the dry season, but more pleasant than the lowlands.

Northern Belize is low tropical country, very swampy along the shore. The southern part of the country is similar, but even more rainy and humid.

Offshore, the water is only about five meters deep all the way out to the islands, called *cayes*. Just east of the cayes in the Caribbean is the barrier reef, a mecca for snorkelers and scuba divers.

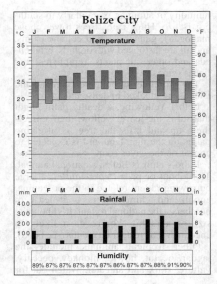

CLIMATE

Though it is comfortably warm during the day in the mountains, cooling off a bit at night, the rest of the country is hot and humid day and night most of the year. In the rain forests of southern Belize the humidity is very high because of the large amount of rainfall (almost four meters per year). Out on the cayes, tropical breezes waft through the shady palm trees constantly, providing natural air conditioning; on the mainland, you swelter. The dry season from October to May is the better time to travel, but prices are lower and lodgings on the cayes easier to find if you avoid the busy winter season from mid-December to April.

Hurricane season in the Caribbean, including all of the Belizean coast and its cayes, is from June to November, with most of the activity from mid-August to mid-September.

FLORA & FAUNA

The lush tropical forests of the Maya Mountains are not quite 'rain forests,' though they certainly seem so in the

BELIZE

humidity of summer, particularly in southern Belize. Huge ceiba trees tower above mahogany, guanacaste and cohune palms, and all are festooned with orchids, bromeliads and other 'air plants' (epiphytes) and lianas (vines).

The shorelines of both the mainland and islands are cloaked in dense mangrove.

Lethal Yellowing, a deadly palm blight that turns the leaves yellow, then shrivels them up and kills the tree, is affecting palms on the mainland and is expected to appear on the cayes soon.

Baird's tapir is Belize's national animal. The gibnut or paca *(tepezcuintle)*, a large burrowing rodent related to the porcupine, agouti and chinchilla is – at least in numbers – the national rodent. It's about the size of a rabbit. You're most likely to encounter it on restaurant menus (see Food).

Other tropical animals include the jaguar, ocelot, howler monkey, peccary, vulture, stork and anteater. Watch out for the occasional deadly boa constrictor or fer-de-lance.

Belize's birdlife is varied and abundant, with hummingbirds, keel-billed toucans, woodpeckers and many kinds of parrots and macaws.

In the seas there are lobsters, manatees, occasional crocodiles and a great variety of fish.

National Parks

Much of the Maya Mountain forest south of San Ignacio is protected as the Pine Ridge Forest Reserve and Chiquibul National Park. There are smaller parks and reserves, including marine reserves, throughout the country.

GOVERNMENT & POLITICS

The British monarch is Belize's head of state, represented on Belizean soil by the governor-general, who is appointed by the monarch with the advice of the Belizean

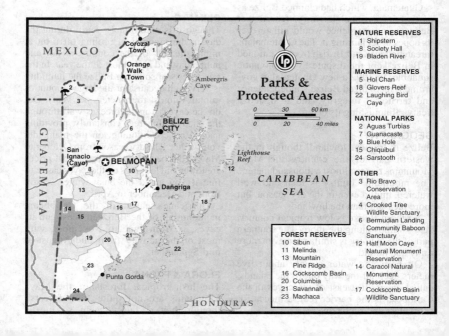

prime minister. The Belizean legislature is bicameral, with a popularly elected House of Representatives and a nominated Senate similar in function to the British House of Lords.

The prime minister is the actual political head of Belize, and for 20 years after independence in 1981 the prime minister was usually George Cadle Price (born 1919), a founder of the People's United Party (PUP). The PUP was born in the 1950s during the early movement for independence from the UK, and it was the leading force for full independence. Despite this success, the party did not fulfill the dreams of Belizeans for a more prosperous economy, a failure due in part to world market conditions beyond its control. The party was also seen as having been in power too long; there were charges of complacency and corruption.

The PUP's main opposition, the multiparty coalition later named the United Democratic Party (UDP), won the elections of 1984, making Manuel Esquivel the prime minister.

PUP squeaked back into power in 1989 by a narrow margin and called early elections in 1993 to solidify their hold on power. PUP adherents were so sure their party would win that they neglected to go to the polls, and the UDP squeaked to victory by the slimmest of margins – a single vote in some districts. Manuel Esquivel became prime minister again, while PUP supporters looked on in disbelief.

In 1996, the venerable George Price announced his retirement as head of PUP, opening the way to a noisy power struggle among his lieutenants.

ECONOMY
Farming and ranching are important in the lands west and south of Belize City. Forestry is important in the Maya Mountains. In the north are large sugar cane plantations and processing plants. The cayes offshore depend on tourism and fishing for their income, but these two pursuits are sometimes in conflict. The spiny lobster and some types of fish have been seriously overexploited.

Districts of Belize

There is an acute shortage of jobs in Belize, and almost no work for visitors looking to earn extra cash.

POPULATION & PEOPLE
Over half of Belize's population is black Creole, descendants of the African slaves and British pirates who first settled here to exploit the country's forest riches. Racially mixed and proud of it, Creoles speak a dialect of English that, though it sounds familiar at first, is utterly unintelligible to a speaker of standard English. Most of the people you meet and deal with in Belize City and Belmopan are Creole.

Pure-blooded Maya make up only about 10% of Belize's population, while fully one-third of Belize's people are mestizos, some of whom immigrated from Yucatán during the 19th century.

Southern Belize is the home of the Garifunas (or Garinagus, also called black Caribs), who account for less than 10% of the population. The Garinagus are of

South American Indian and African descent. They look more African than Indian, but they speak a language that's much more Indian than African, and their unique culture combines aspects of both peoples.

Belize also has small populations of Chinese restaurateurs and merchants, Lebanese traders, German-Swiss Mennonite farmers, Indians from the subcontinent, Europeans and North Americans.

EDUCATION
Crowds of neatly dressed children walk beside country roads each morning and afternoon on their way to school. Public and private (mostly religious) grammar schools are available to most Belizeans, and school is mandatory until age 14. After that, high school is neither mandatory nor free of charge. For education beyond high school, Belizeans go abroad. About 70% of Belizeans can read and write.

SOCIETY & CONDUCT
In Belize's strange and wonderful mixture of cultures, respect for other beliefs and ways of life is congenial. Don't worry about offending the average Belizean by your normal behavior.

RELIGION
Many Belizeans are members of the Church of England, the Roman Catholic Church or any of various Protestant sects that have set up missions here.

Mennonites are the most noticeable religious faction because of their distinctive traditional dress.

Rastafarians pursue enlightenment and *ganja* in Belize City and Dangriga.

LANGUAGE
The Queen's English is Belize's official language, although the people of northern Belize are more likely to speak Spanish as a first language. Many black Belizeans also speak Creole, which is a distinct dialect that is virtually unintelligible to those unfamiliar with it.

Facts for the Visitor

PLANNING
When to Go
The busy winter season, when prices rise and services may need to be reserved in advance, is from mid-December to April. As with the rest of Central America, the dry season (November to May) is the best time to travel, but prices are lower and lodgings on the cayes easier to find in summer. See also Climate, above.

Maps
International Travel Map (ITM) publishes a series of detailed, quite accurate Traveller's Reference Maps, including *Belize* (No 243, 1:350,000).

The various Ordnance Survey maps (1:750,000 to 1:1000) are the most detailed and accurate of all. Contact the OS, Romsey Rd, Southampton, UK SO16 4GU (☎ (170) 379 2000, fax 379 2234). In North America, order them from OMNI Resources (☎ (910) 227-8300, fax 227-8374), PO Box 2096, Burlington, NC 27216. Map Link in California carries ITM and Ordnance Survey maps (for contact information see Facts for the Visitor chapter).

HIGHLIGHTS
Most people come to Belize for the lazy tropical-island ambiance – and the great snorkeling and diving – on the cayes, especially Ambergris and Caulker. Or they come for the homey forest-adventure atmosphere of lodges in the Cayo District around San Ignacio. The Mayan sights are not a highlight when compared to Guatemala.

TOURIST OFFICES
Local Tourist Offices
See the Belize City section and the Online Resources appendix.

Tourist Offices Abroad
In the USA, contact the Belize Tourist Board, 421 7th Ave, New York, NY 10001

(☎ (212) 563-6011, (800) 624-0686). In Europe, contact the Belize Tourist Board, Bopserwaldstrasse 40-G, D-70184 Stuttgart, Germany (☎ /fax (711) 233-947).

VISAS & DOCUMENTS
Visas
British subjects and citizens of Commonwealth countries, citizens of the USA and citizens of Belgium, Denmark, Finland, Germany, Greece, Holland, Mexico, Norway, Panama, Sweden, Switzerland, Tunisia, Turkey and Uruguay who have a valid passport and an onward or return airline ticket from Belize do not need to obtain a Belizean visa in advance. If you look young, grotty or poverty-stricken, the immigration officer may demand to see your return airline ticket and/or a sizable quantity of money or traveler's checks before you're admitted.

Automobile Insurance
Liability insurance is required in Belize, and you must have it for the customs officer to approve the temporary importation of your car. It can be bought at booths just across the border in Belize for about US$1 per day; the booths are closed on Sunday.

EMBASSIES & CONSULATES
Belizean Embassies & Consulates
Because Belize is a small country and far from rich, its diplomatic affairs overseas are usually handled by the British embassies and consulates. Here are a few diplomatic posts:

Canada
    Belize High Commission to Canada, 112 Kent St, Suite 2005, Place de Ville, Tower B, Ottawa, Ontario K1P 5P2 (☎ (613) 232-7389, 232-7453, fax 232-5804)
El Salvador
    See Foreign Embassies in El Salvador.
Germany
    Honorary Consul, Wolf Kahles, Lindenstrasse 46-48, 7120 Beitigheim, Bissingen (☎ (71) 42 39 25, fax 42 32 25)
Honduras
    See Foreign Embassies in Tegucigalpa and San Pedro Sula.

Panama
    See Foreign Embassies & Consulates in Panama City.
USA
    Embassy, 2535 Massachusetts Ave NW, Washington, DC 20008 (☎ (202) 332-9636, fax (202) 332-6741)
    Belize Mission to the United Nations, 820 2nd Ave, New York, NY 10017 (☎ (212) 599-0233, fax (212) 599-3391)

Embassies & Consulates in Belize
See the Belize City and Belmopan sections.

MONEY
Costs
Belize is surprisingly expensive, and recent taxes worsen the damage. The same fried chicken dinner costs US$3 in Mexico but US$5 in Belize and is no better. The same waterless pension room, cheap in Guatemala, costs US$7 to US$10 per person on Caye Caulker. You may find it difficult to live for less than US$15 per day for room and three meals in Belize; US$20 is a more realistic bottom-end figure.

Currency & Exchange
The Belizean dollar (BZ$) is divided into 100 cents. Coins are of one, five, 10, 25 and 50 cents, and one dollar; bills (notes) are of one, two, five, 10, 20, 50 and 100 dollars.

The Belizean dollar's value has been fixed for many years at US$1=BZ$2. You can exchange US and Canadian dollars and pounds sterling at any bank; other currencies are difficult to exchange. Cash US dollars are accepted virtually everywhere, and many establishments will also accept US dollar traveler's checks. Most businesses usually give change in Belizean dollars, though they may return US change if you ask and if they have it. You can exchange them legally on the street, and unlike in a bank, you'll get a full BZ$2 for each US$1.

Often people will quote prices as '20 dollars Belize, 10 dollars US,' just to make it clear. Be sure you know which is being quoted.

Moneychangers at border-crossing points and in downtown business areas will

BELIZE

change your US cash for Belizean dollars legally at the standard rate. If you change money or traveler's checks at a bank, you may get only US$1=BZ$1.97; they may also charge a fee of BZ$5 (US$2.50) to change a traveler's check. Belizean ATMs do not yet accept foreign ATM cards, though you can often get a cash advance against your credit card (Visa and Master-Card are most popular). If you plan to do this, it's wise to dump some money into your credit card account before you travel so you won't have to pay the huge credit-card cash advance interest rates.

Australia	A$1	=	BZ$1.59
Canada	CN$1	=	BZ$1.47
Germany	DM1	=	BZ$1.30
France	FF1	=	BZ$0.35
Italy	L1000	=	BZ$1.31
New Zealand	NZ$1	=	BZ$1.42
United States	US$1	=	BZ$2.00
United Kingdom	UK£1	=	BZ$3.34

Tipping & Bargaining
Tips of 10% are appreciated in the posher restaurants, bars and clubs.

It is possible to haggle over prices for hotel rooms, boat rides and the like if business is slow, but generally prices are set.

Taxes & Refunds
Belize has a value added tax of 15%, which is charged on meals, beverages, tours, transport and many other goods and services. A 7% hotel room tax may soon be increased to 12%.

POST & COMMUNICATIONS
An airmail postcard (BZ$0.30) or letter (BZ$0.60) sent to Canada or the USA may take anywhere from four to 14 days. Airmail postcards (BZ$0.40) or letters (BZ$0.75) to Europe take one to three weeks.

To claim poste-restante mail, present your passport or other identification; there's no charge.

The telephone system is operated by Belize Telecommunications Ltd (BTL), with offices in major towns open Monday to Friday from 8 am to noon and 1 to 4 pm, Saturday 8 am to noon.

Local calls cost BZ$0.25 (US$0.13). You can buy BTL phone debit cards. To call from one part of Belize to another, dial zero (0), then the one or two-digit area code, then the four or five-digit local number.

Calls dialed direct (no operator) from Belize to other Western Hemisphere countries cost BZ$3.20 (US$1.60) per minute; to Europe, BZ$6 (US$3) per minute; to all other countries, BZ$8 (US$4) per minute. Hotels usually add large surcharges. The bill for even a short call can be frighteningly high.

Here are some useful numbers:

Directory assistance	☎ 113
Local & regional operator	☎ 114
Long-distance (trunk) operator	☎ 110
International operator	☎ 115
Fire & ambulance	☎ 90
Police	☎ 911

To reach AT&T's USADirect and World-Connect services, dial 555 from hotels. For Sprint Express, dial 556 from hotels, or 812 from pay phones. For MCI WorldPhone service, dial 557 from hotels, or 815 from pay phones.

At this writing, there is no cheap, easy way for a short-time visitor to access the Internet in Belize. Neither CompuServe nor America Online have nodes in Belize. You must use someone else's BTL Internet account.

MEDIA
The *Miami Herald* and several other US newspapers are available in the shops of expensive hotels.

Local newspapers are mouthpieces for either the PUP or UDP political parties, or factions within them. Sheets like *Amandala, The People's Pulse* and the *Reporter* are filled with purple political diatribe, homey news items, reports of drug busts and traffic accidents. The *San Pedro Sun* of Ambergris Caye reports on local events and tourism.

The best periodical on Belize is Lan Sluder's *Belize First* from Equator Publishing,

280 Beaverdam Rd, Candler, NC 28715, USA (fax (704) 667-1717, net).

Local radio stations play Belizean and world pop music. Belizean TV is US cable with a few hours of local content each evening.

WEIGHTS & MEASURES
Despite its claim to use the metric system, Belize's road signs are marked in miles, and motor fuel is sold in US gallons. Both the US system and the metric system are in use in general commerce.

DISABLED TRAVELERS
Most of Belize is not easy to access. If you travel in a wheelchair, you must arrange every aspect of your trip in detail, in advance.

DANGERS & ANNOYANCES
With a few exceptions, Belize is an admirably friendly, safe and unannoying place. The exception is Belize City, which has beggars, purse-snatchers and a flourishing drug trade. In the city and a few other large Belizean towns, youth gangs with ties to the Los Angeles gangs (Crips, Bloods and so on) cause havoc (rarely) but may control the local rackets in drugs, thievery and other nastiness.

When you get the urge to score some ganja, remember that these are the people you'll be dealing with. In short: don't.

BUSINESS HOURS & PUBLIC HOLIDAYS
Most banks and many businesses and shops are closed on Wednesday afternoon. Banking hours depend upon the individual bank, but most are open Monday to Friday from 8 am to noon or 1 pm; some are also open from 1 to 3 pm, and many have extra hours on Friday until 4:30 pm. Shops are usually open Monday to Saturday from 8 am to noon, Monday, Tuesday, Thursday and Friday from 1 to 4 pm. Some shops have evening hours from 7 to 9 pm on those days as well. Many restaurants – especially in cities – are closed on Sunday.

Here are Belize's legal holidays:

January 1
New Year's Day
March 9
Baron Bliss Day, honoring the English nobleman who dropped anchor in Belizean waters in the 1920s, fell in love with the place, and willed his considerable fortune to the people of Belize.
April 21
Queen's Birthday
May 1
Labor Day
May 24
Commonwealth Day
September 10
Belize National Day, commemorating the Battle of St George's Caye fought in 1798. The British won. Celebrations begin today and continue until Independence Day on the 21st.
September 21
Independence Day, when the colony of British Honduras gained its independence from the UK in 1981.
November 19
Garifuna Settlement Day, commemorating the arrival of the Garinagus (black Caribs) in Belize in 1823.
December 25
Christmas
December 26
Boxing Day

ACTIVITIES
Snorkeling and diving are best on the cayes. Boats depart Ambergris and Caulker on day and overnight voyages to the best spots.

Horseback riding, canoeing and kayaking, hiking, bird watching and archaeology are best in the Cayo District of western Belize. Use San Ignacio as a base.

ACCOMMODATIONS
Lodgings in Belize are generally more expensive and of lower comfort than in neighboring countries. Some have great charm and are well worth the cost; most are just places to stay.

FOOD
The traditional staple of the Belizean diet is certainly rice and beans, often with other

ingredients – chicken, pork, beef, vegetables, even lobster – plus some spices and condiments like coconut milk.

Beef and chicken are the other usual main courses, often served with fried potatoes, often greasy. Grilled or fried fish is always a good bet on the cayes and in coastal towns.

More exotic traditional foods include gibnut or paca, a small brown-spotted rodent similar to a guinea pig. Armadillo and venison are served also, but their value is more as a curiosity than as a staple of the diet.

DRINKS
You should only drink bottled water. In the cayes, local people drink 'catchment' water (rainwater collected in a cistern), which may or may not agree with your digestive system.

Most locals don't drink water; they drink Belikin beer, which has the local market tied up. Belikin Export, the premium version, comes in a larger bottle, is much tastier, costs more and is worth it.

ENTERTAINMENT
There are small discos and nightclubs in Belize City and on Ambergris Caye. Bars with recorded music (usually reggae or punta rock) are found wherever tourists congregate.

Getting There & Away

AIR
American Airlines flies from Miami, Continental from Houston and TACA from Los Angeles. International air routes to Belize City all go through these gateways. Fares are surprisingly high, about US$250 round-trip (return) from Miami, US$500 or more from any other point.

Departure taxes and security fees totaling BZ$30 (US$15) are levied on foreign travelers who are departing by air to foreign destinations.

LAND
For information on reaching Belize by land from the USA, see the Getting There & Away chapter, and the Getting There & Away section in the Guatemala chapter. For information on buses from Flores (and Tikal) in Guatemala, see that section in the Guatemala chapter.

To/From Mexico
It's important to note a one-hour time difference between Belize and Mexico.

Several Belizean bus lines have daily service between Chetumal and Belize City via Corozal and Orange Walk. See the Getting There & Away section in Belize City for details.

There are also buses between Belize City and Benque Viejo del Carmen and Melchor de Mencos on the Guatemalan border, connecting with Guatemalan buses headed for Flores (near Tikal).

SEA
Boats connect Dangriga and Placencia with Puerto Cortés, Honduras; and Punta Gorda with Lívingston and Puerto Barrios, Guatemala. See those towns' sections for details.

Getting Around

AIR
There are two main domestic air routes that small planes follow from Belize City: Belize City-Caye Caulker-San Pedro-Corozal and return; and Belize City-Dangriga-Placencia/Big Creek-Punta Gorda and return.

Tropic Air (☎ (26) 2012, fax (26) 2338), PO Box 20, San Pedro, Ambergris Caye, is the largest and most active of Belize's small airlines.

Maya Airways (☎ (2) 77215, fax (2) 30585; net), 6 Fort St (PO Box 458), Belize City, has a similar schedule of flights to points in Belize.

Island Air (☎ (26) 2435) flies between Belize City and San Pedro via Caye Caulker.

Aerovías (☎ (2) 75445), the Guatemalan regional airline, operates several flights per week between Belize City's Goldson Airport and Flores (near Tikal) in Guatemala (US$70 one way), with onward connections to Guatemala City.

BUS

Belizean buses are usually used American schoolbuses running on marketers' schedules. Major towns are well served, but villages can be difficult to reach. See Getting There & Away in the Belize City section for schedules.

CAR

If you're traveling on a budget, forget car rentals unless you can find three other people to share the cost.

Generally, renters must be at least 25 years of age, have a valid driver's license, and pay by credit card or leave a large cash deposit. Cars may not be driven out of Belize except by special arrangement (best done in advance of rental).

Most car-rental companies have representatives at Goldson International Airport; many will also deliver or take return of cars at Belize City's Municipal Airport.

The best rental rates and service are at Budget Rent-a-Car (☎ (2) 32435, 33986, fax 30237), 771 Bella Vista (PO Box 863), Belize City, opposite the Belize Biltmore Plaza Hotel on the Northern Hwy, 4.5 km north of central Belize City. Most of its Suzuki and Vitara cars are 4WD, and have AM-FM radios and air-conditioning. They are priced from US$78 to US$113 per day (US$469 to US$676 per week), 15% tax included, with unlimited kilometrage. The Loss Damage Waiver costs an additional US$14 per day, tax included; even with the LDW, you're liable for the first US$750 of damage to the vehicle.

National (☎ (2) 31587, 31650, fax 31586), 12 North Front St, Belize City, has offices at the airport and at the Belize Biltmore Plaza Hotel. You might also try Tour Belize Auto Rental (☎ (2) 71271, fax 71421, net), Central American Blvd and Fabers Rd, Belize City.

Driving in Belize Belize has two good asphalt-paved two-lane roads: the Northern Hwy between the Mexican border near Corozal Town and Belize City, and the Western Hwy between Belize City and the Guatemalan border at Benque Viejo del Carmen. The Hummingbird Hwy from Belmopan to Dangriga is unpaved for the first 29 km (18 miles) south and east of Belmopan, then paved for the following 58 km (36 miles) to Dangriga. Most other roads are narrow one or two-lane dirt roads; many are impassable after heavy rains.

Anyone who must drive a lot in Belize has a 4WD vehicle. Sites off the main roads may be accessible only by 4WD, especially between May and November; and sometimes not even by 4WD.

Fuel stations are found in the larger towns and along the major roads. Leaded gasoline/petrol is usually sold by the US gallon (3.79 liters) for about US$2.50; that's US$0.66 per liter. Unleaded fuel is currently unavailable in Belize.

SEA

Fast motor launches connect Belize City, Caye Caulker and Ambergris Caye several times daily. See Getting There & Away in Belize City for details. There is very limited scheduled service to other cayes; most boats are chartered, and thus expensive.

Belize City

Population 80,000

Ramshackle, funky, fascinating, daunting, homely – these are only a few of the words that can be used to describe the country's biggest city and former capital. The tropical storms that periodically razed the town in the 19th and early 20th centuries still arrive to do damage to its aging wooden buildings, but they also flush out the open drainage canals, redolent with pollution, that crisscross the town. When there's no storm, Belize City bustles and swelters.

BELIZE

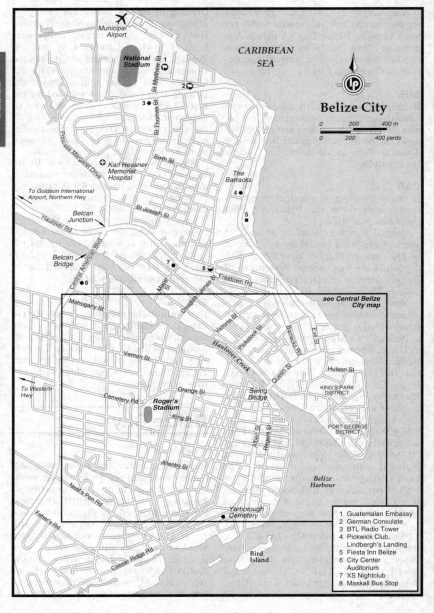

CARIBBEAN
SEA

Belize City

| 0 | 200 | 400 m |
| 0 | 200 | 400 yards |

Municipal
Airport

National
Stadium

St Matthew St

1

2

St Thomas St

3

Princess Margaret Drive

Karl Heusner
Memorial
Hospital

Sixth St

The
Barracks

4

To Goldson International
Airport, Northern Hwy

St Joseph St

5

Belcan
Junction

Haulover Rd

Belcan
Bridge

Central American Blvd

7

8

Freetown Rd

6

Mapp St

Douglas Jones St

see Central Belize
City map

Mahogany St

Victoria St

Pickstock St

Barracks Rd

Eve St

Haulover Creek

Hulson St

To Western
Hwy

Vernon St

Cemetery Rd

Orange St

Roger's
Stadium

King St

Queen St

Swing
Bridge

KING'S PARK
DISTRICT

Albert St

Regent St

FORT GEORGE
DISTRICT

Allenby St

Neal's Pen Rd

Belize
Harbour

Yarborough
Cemetery

Faber's Rd

Caesar Ridge Rd

Bird
Island

1 Guatemalan Embassy
2 German Consulate
3 BTL Radio Tower
4 Pickwick Club,
   Lindbergh's Landing
5 Fiesta Inn Belize
6 City Center
   Auditorium
7 XS Nightclub
8 Maskall Bus Stop

Except for its funky atmosphere, there's little to hold your interest in Belize City.

Orientation

Haulover Creek, a branch of the Belize River, runs through the middle of the city, separating the commercial center (Albert, Regent, King and Orange Sts) from the slightly more genteel residential and hotel district of Fort George to the northeast.

Albert St in the center and Queen St in the Fort George and King's Park neighborhoods are joined by the Swing Bridge across Haulover Creek.

The Belize Maritime Terminal, used by motor launches traveling to Caye Caulker and Ambergris Caye, is at the northern end of the Swing Bridge.

Each of Belize's bus companies has its own terminal. Most are near the Collett Canal, off Cemetery Rd. See Getting There & Away for details.

Information

Tourist Offices The Belize Tourist Board (☎ (2) 77213, 73255, fax (2) 77490, net), 83 N Front St (PO Box 325), just a few steps south of the post office, is open Monday to Thursday from 8 am to noon and 1 to 5 pm and Friday until 4:30 pm; it's closed on weekends.

The Belize Tourism Industry Association (☎ (2) 75717, 78709, fax (2) 78710, net), 10 N Park St (PO Box 62), on the north side of Memorial Park, has an office open Monday to Friday from 8:30 am to noon and 1 to 4:30 pm (Friday till 4 pm).

Embassies & Consulates Some embassies are in Belmopan, Belize's official capital. Embassies and consulates in Belize City tend to be open Monday to Friday from about 9 am to noon.

France
   Honorary Consul, 9 Barracks Rd,
   Belize City (☎ (2) 32708, fax 32416)
Germany
   Honorary Consul, 8 Princess Margaret Dr,
   Belize City (☎ (2) 35940, fax (2) 35413)

Guatemalan Embassy
   6A St Matthews St, Belize City
   (☎ (2) 33150, 33314, fax (2) 35140)
Honduran Consulate
   91 N Front St, Belize City
   (☎ (2) 45-889, fax (2) 30-562)
Italy
   Consular Representative, 18 Albert St,
   Belize City (☎ (2) 78449, fax (2) 73056)
Mexican Embassy
   20 N Park St, Belize City
   (☎ (2) 30193, fax (2) 78742); there is also
   a Mexican embassy building in Belmopan
Nicaragua
   Honorary Consul, 50 Vernon St,
   Belize City (☎ (2) 70621)
Panamanian Consulate
   5481 Princess Margaret Dr,
   Belize City (☎ (2) 34282, fax (2) 30653)
UK
   British High Commission, 34-36
   Half Moon Ave, Roseapple St, Belmopan
   (☎ (8) 22146, fax (8) 22761)
US Embassy
   29 Gabourel Lane, Belize City
   (☎ (2) 77161, fax (2) 30802)

Money The Bank of Nova Scotia (☎ (02) 77027), on Albert St, is open Monday to Friday from 8 am to 1 pm and Friday afternoon from 3 to 6 pm.

The Atlantic Bank Limited (☎ (02) 77124, net), 6 Albert St, is open Monday, Tuesday and Thursday from 8 am to noon and 1 to 3 pm, Wednesday from 8 am to 1 pm and Friday from 8 am to 4:30 pm.

Also on Albert St are the prominent Belize Bank (☎ (02) 77132, net), 60 Market Square (facing the Swing Bridge), and Barclay's Bank (☎ (02) 77211), 21 Albert St.

Post & Communications The main post office is at the northern end of the Swing Bridge, at the intersection of Queen and N Front Sts. It's open daily from 8 am to noon and 1 to 5 pm. If you want to pick up mail at the American Express office, it's at Belize Global Travel Service (☎ (2) 77185, fax (2) 75213), 41 Albert St (PO Box 244).

Belize Telecommunications Limited (BTL; ☎ (2) 77085), 1 Church St, runs all of Belize's telephones. The office has a public

BELIZE

BELIZE

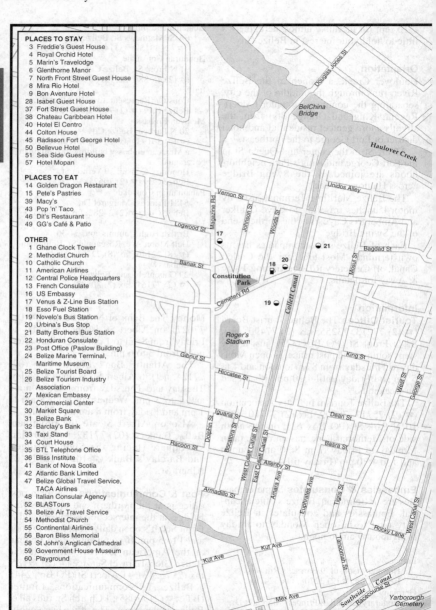

PLACES TO STAY
3 Freddie's Guest House
4 Royal Orchid Hotel
5 Marin's Travelodge
6 Glenthorne Manor
7 North Front Street Guest House
8 Mira Rio Hotel
9 Bon Aventure Hotel
28 Isabel Guest House
37 Fort Street Guest House
38 Chateau Caribbean Hotel
40 Hotel El Centro
44 Colton House
45 Radisson Fort George Hotel
50 Bellevue Hotel
51 Sea Side Guest House
57 Hotel Mopan

PLACES TO EAT
14 Golden Dragon Restaurant
15 Pete's Pastries
39 Macy's
43 Pop 'n' Taco
46 Dit's Restaurant
49 GG's Café & Patio

OTHER
1 Ghane Clock Tower
2 Methodist Church
10 Catholic Church
11 American Airlines
12 Central Police Headquarters
13 French Consulate
16 US Embassy
17 Venus & Z-Line Bus Station
18 Esso Fuel Station
19 Novelo's Bus Station
20 Urbina's Bus Stop
21 Batty Brothers Bus Station
22 Honduran Consulate
23 Post Office (Paslow Building)
24 Belize Marine Terminal,
    Maritime Museum
25 Belize Tourist Board
26 Belize Tourism Industry
    Association
27 Mexican Embassy
29 Commercial Center
30 Market Square
31 Belize Bank
32 Barclay's Bank
33 Taxi Stand
34 Court House
35 BTL Telephone Office
36 Bliss Institute
41 Bank of Nova Scotia
42 Atlantic Bank Limited
47 Belize Global Travel Service,
    TACA Airlines
48 Italian Consular Agency
52 BLASTours
53 Belize Air Travel Service
54 Methodist Church
55 Continental Airlines
56 Baron Bliss Memorial
58 St John's Anglican Cathedral
59 Government House Museum
60 Playground

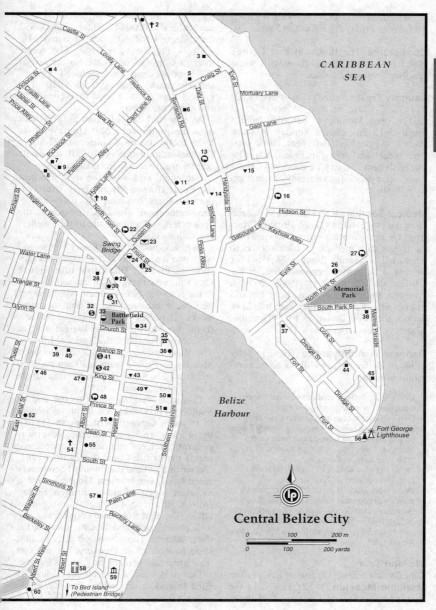

Central Belize City

fax machine (☎ (2) 45211) as well. It's open Monday to Friday from 8 am to 5 pm.

Bookstores The Radisson Fort George Hotel has a small bookshop with some English novels and guides.

Laundry Try the Belize Laundromat (☎ (2) 31117), 7 Craig St near Marin's Travel Lodge, open Monday to Saturday from 8 am to 5:15 pm, closed Sunday. A wash costs US$5 per load, detergent, fabric softener, bleach and drying included. A similar establishment is Carry's Laundry, 41 Hyde Lane, open Monday to Saturday from 8 am to 5:30 pm.

Medical Services Karl Heusner Memorial Hospital (☎ (2) 31548) is on Princess Margaret Dr, in the northern part of town. Many Belizeans with medical problems travel to Chetumal or Mérida (both in Mexico) for treatment. A modern, private clinic is the Clinica de Chetumal (☎ (983) 26508), Avenida Juárez, Chetumal, near the old market and the city's other hospitals. For serious illnesses, Belizeans fly to Houston, Miami or New Orleans.

Dangers & Annoyances There is petty crime in Belize City, so follow some commonsense rules:

* Don't flash wads of cash, expensive camera equipment or other signs of wealth.
* Don't change money on the street, not because it's illegal, but because changing money forces you to expose where you keep your cash.
* Muggers will offer to change money, then just grab your cash and run off.
* Don't leave valuables in your hotel room.
* Don't use or deal in illicit drugs.
* Don't walk alone at night. It's better to walk in pairs or groups and to stick to major streets in the center, Fort George and King's Park. Especially avoid walking along Front St south and east of the Swing Bridge; this is a favorite area for muggers.

Walking Tours
City Center Start at the Swing Bridge. The **Maritime Museum** (☎ (2) 31969) in the Belize Marine Terminal, is open Monday to

Saturday from 8 am to 5 pm (closed Sunday); admission costs US$3 for adults, US$2 for students, US$0.50 for children under 12.

Cross the Swing Bridge. The large, modern Commercial Center to the left at the southwestern end replaced a ramshackle market dating from 1820. The ground floor holds a food market; offices and shops are above.

As you start down Regent St, you can't miss the prominent Court House built in 1926 to be the headquarters of Belize's colonial administrators. It still serves its administrative and judicial functions.

Battlefield Park is on the right just past the Court House. Always busy with vendors, loungers, con men and other slice-of-life segments of Belize City society, the park offers welcome shade in the sweltering midday heat.

Turn left just past the Court House and walk one long block to the Southern Foreshore to find the **Bliss Institute**. Belize City's prime cultural institution, it is home to the National Arts Council, which stages periodic exhibits, concerts and theatrical works. There's a small display of artifacts from the Mayan archaeological site at Caracol and, upstairs, the National Library. The Bliss Institute (☎ (2) 77267) is open Monday to Friday from 8:30 am to noon and from 2 to 8 pm, and on Saturday from 8 am to noon; closed Sunday.

Continue walking south to the end of Southern Foreshore, then south on Regent St to reach **Government House** (1814), the former residence of the governor-general. Belize attained independence within the British Commonwealth in 1981, and since that time the job has been purely ceremonial. Government House is now a museum, open Monday through Friday from 8:30 am to 4:30 pm; admission is US$5. The first floor holds displays of historic photographs and the tableware used at the residence. The admission price is a bit steep to look at old crockery, but you can have a pleasant stroll in the grounds for free.

Down beyond Government House is **Bird Island**, a recreation area accessible only on foot.

Inland from Government House, at the corner of Albert and Regent Sts, is **St John's Cathedral**, the oldest and most important Anglican church in Central America, dating from 1847. A block southwest of the cathedral is **Yarborough Cemetery**, with gravestones outlining the turbulent history of Belize back to 1781.

Walk back to the Swing Bridge northward along Albert St, the main commercial thoroughfare.

Northern Neighborhoods Cross the Swing Bridge heading north and you'll come face-to-face with the wood-frame Paslow Building, which houses the city's main post office. Go straight along Queen St to see the city's quaint wooden police station and, eventually, the American Embassy, in a neighborhood with some pretty Victorian houses.

Make your way to the southern tip of the peninsula. You pass through the luxury hotel district and emerge at the **Baron Bliss Memorial**, next to the Fort George lighthouse. There's a small park here and a good view of the water and the city.

Walk north around the point, pass the Radisson Fort George Hotel on your left and walk up Marine Parade to **Memorial Park**, next to the Chateau Caribbean Hotel and the Mexican Embassy. The park's patch of green lawn is a welcome sight.

Places to Stay

The cheapest hotels in Belize City are often not safe because of break-ins and drug dealing. I've chosen the places below for relative safety as well as price.

North Front Street Guest House (☎ (2) 77595), 124 N Front St, just east of Pickstock St, is very basic but clean and secure, a favorite of low-budget travelers, despite the heavily trafficked street. The eight rooms cost US$8.50/13.50 for a single/double, tax included. Breakfast and dinner are served if you order ahead. Check out the bulletin board.

Next door, the *Bon Aventure Hotel* (☎ (2) 44248, (2) 44134, fax (2) 31134), 122 N Front St, has nine double rooms at US$14

The Legacy of Baron Bliss

Baron Bliss was an Englishman with a happy name and a Portuguese title who came to Belize on his yacht to fish. He seems to have fallen in love with Belize without ever having set foot on shore. When he died – not too long after his arrival – he left the bulk of his wealth in trust to the people of Belize. Income from the trust has paid for roads, market buildings, schools, cultural centers and many other worthwhile projects over the years. ■

(shared bath) and US$24 (private bath). *Mira Rio Hotel* (☎ (2) 44970), 59 N Front St, just across the street, has seven rooms with sink and toilet at similar prices.

Isabel Guest House (☎ (2) 73139), PO Box 362, is above Matus Store overlooking Market Square, but is entered by a rear stairway – walk around the Central Drug Store to the back and follow the signs. Clean and family-run, it offers double rooms with shower for US$24.

Freddie and Tona Griffith keep *Freddie's Guest House* (☎ (2) 44396), 86 Eve St, among the tidiest in Belize. Two double rooms share one bath and cost US$21; the room with private bath costs US$23. The showers gleam and shine.

Sea Side Guest House (☎ (2) 78339), 3 Prince St, between Southern Foreshore and Regent St, is operated by Friends Services International, a Quaker service organization. The six clean, simple rooms share baths; singles/doubles are US$16.50/24. Breakfast is available, as is information on Friends social, educational and environmental projects in Belize.

Marin's Travelodge (☎ (2) 45166), 6 Craig St, is on the upper floor of a fairly well-kept, yellow wooden Caribbean house with a comfy swing on the verandah and seven rooms for rent. Shared showers are clean, and the price for the plain rooms is right – singles/doubles are US$8/12.

Colton House (☎ (2) 44666, fax (2) 30451, net), 9 Cork St, near the Radisson Fort George Hotel, is a gracious 60-year-old wooden colonial house beautifully restored. The large, airy, cheerful rooms with fan and private bath cost US$40/48/56 for a single/double/triple; add US$5 for air conditioning. Morning coffee is served, but no meals.

Places to Eat

Belize City is not noted for its cuisine, but there is some decent food. Unless otherwise noted, all restaurants are closed on Sunday.

GG's Café & Patio (☎ (2) 74378), 2-B King St, has open-air tables for good weather. Burgers cost US$3 or US$4; big plates of rice and beans with beef, chicken or pork the same. GG's is open from 11:30 am to 2:30 pm and 5:30 to 9 pm (to 10 pm on Friday and Saturday).

Macy's (☎ (2) 73419), 18 Bishop St, has consistently good Caribbean Creole cooking, friendly service and decent prices. Fish fillet with rice and beans costs about US$4, armadillo or wild boar a bit more. Hours are 11:30 am to 10 pm.

Dit's Restaurant (☎ (2) 33330), 50 King St, is a homey place with powerful fans and a loyal local clientele who come for huge portions and low prices. Cakes and pies make a good dessert at US$1 per slice. Dit's is open daily from 8 am to 9 pm.

The *Pop 'n' Taco*, at the corner of King and Regent Sts, serves simple Belizean, Chinese and Mexican food at low prices, and it's open daily.

Pete's Pastries (☎ (2) 44974), 41 Queen St near Handyside St, serves good cakes, tarts, and pies of fruit or meat. Pete's is open Monday to Saturday 8:30 am to 7 pm, Sunday 8 am to 6 pm.

Golden Dragon Chinese Restaurant (☎ (2) 72817), in a cul-de-sac off Queen St, is one of the city's several Chinese restaurants. Full meals cost US$6 to US$14.

Entertainment

There's lots of interesting action at night in Belize City, but most of it is violent, illegal or both. Clubs and bars that look like dives probably are. If drugs are in evidence, clear out quick.

The lounges at the upscale hotels – Radisson Fort George, Fiesta Inn Belize – are sedate, respectable and safe. The Belize Biltmore Plaza Hotel, 4.5 km from the center on the Northern Hwy, has karaoke many nights, live music on others. *XS*, Freetown Rd and Mapp St, is the latest hot nightspot. Locals laud it for its lack of violence and its safe parking as well as its music and drinks. Try also *Lindbergh's Landing*, next to the Pickwick Club in the park across from the Fiesta Inn Belize. The longtime local favorite is the *Lumba Yaad*, 300 meters northwest of Belcan Junction, just northwest of a real lumber yard.

Getting There & Away

Air Belize City has two airports. Philip SW Goldson International Airport (BZE), at Ladyville, 16 km northwest of the center, handles all international flights. The Municipal Airport (TZA) is 2.5 km north of the city center, on the shore. Most local flights will stop and pick you up at either airport, but fares are always lower from Municipal, so if you have a choice, use that one.

American Airlines (☎ (2) 32522, fax (2) 31730) is at the corner of New Road and Queen St. Continental (☎ (2) 78309, (2) 78463, fax (2) 78114) is at 32 Albert St between Dean and South. TACA (☎ (2) 77363, 77185, fax (2) 75213), the Costa Rican airline, is at 41 Albert St (Belize Global Travel).

Bus Each major bus company has its own terminal or stop near the Collett Canal. Pilferage of luggage is a problem, particularly on the Punta Gorda route. Give your luggage only to the bus driver or conductor, and watch as it is stored. Be there when the bus is unloaded to retrieve your luggage at once.

Batty Brothers Bus Service (☎ (2) 77146), 54 E Collett Canal, operates buses along the Northern Hwy to Orange Walk, Corozal and Chetumal (Mexico). Escalante's Bus Service runs between Belize City and Chetumal via Orange Walk and

Corozal. Novelo's Bus Service (☎ (2) 77372), 19 W Collett Canal, is the line to take to Belmopan, San Ignacio, Xunantunich, Benque Viejo and the Guatemalan border at Melchor de Mencos. Shaw's Bus Service, based in San Ignacio, runs buses between that town and Belize City via Belmopan. Urbina's Bus Service runs between Belize City and Chetumal via Orange Walk and Corozal. Venus Bus Lines (☎ (2) 73354, (2) 77390), Magazine Rd, operates buses along routes similar to those of Batty Brothers. Z-Line Bus Service (☎ (2) 73937) runs buses south to Dangriga, Big Creek (for Placencia) and Punta Gorda, operating from the Venus Bus Lines terminal on Magazine Rd in Belize City.

Buses from Belize City go to:

Belmopan (84 km, 1¼ hours, US$1.75) See Benque Viejo for details.
Benque Viejo (131 km, three hours, US$3) Novelo's operates buses from Belize City to Belmopan, San Ignacio and Benque Viejo at 11 am, noon, 1, 2, 3, 4, 5 and 7 pm (hourly from noon to 5 pm on Sunday). Batty Brothers operates nine morning buses westward between 5 and 10:15 am. Several of these go all the way to Melchor de Mencos in Guatemala. Returning from Benque/Melchor, buses to San Ignacio, Belmopan and Belize City start at noon; the last bus leaves at 4 pm.
Chetumal, Mexico (160 km, four hours, express 3¼ hours, US$5) Venus Bus Lines has buses departing from Belize City every hour on the hour from noon to 7 pm; departures from Chetumal are hourly from 4 to 10 am. Batty's has buses every two hours on the hour for the same price.
Corozal (155 km, three hours, US$4) Virtually all Batty's and Venus buses to and from Chetumal stop in Corozal, and there are also several additional buses. There are frequent southbound buses in the morning but few in the afternoon; almost all northbound buses depart from Belize City in the afternoon.
Dangriga (170 km, 2½ or four hours, US$3.50 to US$5.50) Z-Line has five buses daily (four on Sunday), at least one of which takes the cheaper, faster Coastal (Manatee) Hwy. Most buses go via Belmopan and the Hummingbird Hwy.

Flores, Guatemala (235 km, five hours, US$20) Take a bus to Melchor de Mencos (see Benque Viejo), and transfer to a Guatemalan bus. Some hotels and tour companies organize minibus trips, which are more expensive but much faster and more comfortable.
Independencia (242 km, seven hours, US$7) Buses bound for Punta Gorda stop at Independencia, from whence you may be able to find a boat over to Placencia (see that section).
Melchor de Mencos, Guatemala (135 km, 3¼ hours, US$3) See Benque Viejo for details.
Orange Walk (94 km, two hours, US$3) Same schedule as for Chetumal.
Placencia (260 km, four hours, US$9) Take a morning Z-Line bus to Dangriga, then another Z-Line bus to Placencia. A bus returns from Placencia to Dangriga at 6 am; there may be others as well, depending upon the number of customers.
Punta Gorda (339 km, eight hours, US$11) Z-Line has three buses daily, at 8 am, noon and 3 pm. Return buses from Punta Gorda via Independencia to Belize City depart at 5 and 9 am, and at noon; on Friday and Sunday there's also a 3:30 pm bus.
San Ignacio (116 km, 2¾ hours, US$2.50) See Benque Viejo for details.

Boat Fast motor launches zoom between Belize City and Caye Caulker and Ambergris Caye several times daily. The Belize Marine Terminal (☎ (2) 31969), on N Front St at the northern end of the Swing Bridge, is the dock for boats to the northern cayes.

Boats depart for Caye Caulker at 9 and 11 am, 1, 3 and 5:15 pm, and charge US$7.50 one way, US$12.50 for a same-day roundtrip. They stop at Caye Chapel on request. The trip against the wind takes 40 minutes to one hour, depending upon the speed of the boat. Departures from Caye Caulker are at 6:45, 8 and 10 am, and 3 pm.

For San Pedro on Ambergris Caye, boats depart Belize City's Marine Terminal at 9 am; for the return trip, the departure from San Pedro is at 2:30 pm. The fare is US$15 one way, US$25 same-day roundtrip for the 1¼- to 1½-hour voyage.

Getting Around
To/From the Airports The taxi fare to or from the international airport is US$15.

You might want to approach other passengers about sharing a cab to the city center.

It takes about half an hour to walk from the air terminal three km out the access road to the Northern Hwy; from here it's easy to catch a bus going either north or south.

Going to Municipal Airport, normal city taxi fares apply.

Taxi Trips by taxi within Belize City (including to and from the Municipal Airport) cost US$2.50 for one person, US$6 for two or three, US$8 for four.

Car See the Getting Around section for all of Belize, above.

The Cayes

Belize's 290-km-long barrier reef, the longest in the Western Hemisphere, is the eastern edge of the limestone shelf that underlies most of Yucatán. West of the reef the water is four or five meters deep, which allows numerous islands called *cayes* (pronounced 'keys') to bask in warm waters.

Of the dozens of cayes, large and small, that dot the blue waters of the Caribbean off the Belizean coast, the two most popular are Caye Caulker and Ambergris Caye. Caulker is commonly thought of as the low-budget island, where hotels and restaurants are considerably less expensive than on resort-conscious Ambergris, though with Caulker's booming popularity this distinction is blurring.

CAYE CAULKER
Population 800

Caye Caulker lies about 33 km north of Belize City and 24 km south of Ambergris Caye. The island is about seven km long north to south and only about 600 meters wide at its widest point. Mangroves cover much of the shore; coconut palms provide shade. The village is on the southern portion of the island. Actually Caulker is

now two islands, ever since 1961, when Hurricane Hattie split the island in two just north of the village. The split is called, simply, The Split (or Cut).

Orientation & Information
The village has two principal streets, Front St to the east and Back St to the west. The distance from The Split in the north to the cabañas at the southern edge of the village is a little more than one km.

The Belize Telecommunications office is open Monday to Friday from 8 am to noon and 1 to 4 pm, on Saturday 8 am to noon, closed Sunday. The BTL office (fax (22) 2239) has the only fax service on the whole island.

Water Sports
The surf breaks on the barrier reef, easily visible from the eastern shore of Caye Caulker. Don't attempt to swim out to it, however – the local boaters speed their powerful craft through these waters and are completely heedless of swimmers. Several foreign visitors have died from boat-propeller injuries. Swim only in protected areas.

A short boat ride takes you out to the reef to enjoy some of the world's most exciting snorkeling, diving and fishing. Boat trips are big business on the island, so you have many to choose from. Ask other island visitors about their boating experiences, and use this information to choose a boat. Virtually all of the island residents are trustworthy boaters, but it's still good to discuss price, duration, areas to be visited and the seaworthiness of the boat. Boat and motor should be in good condition. Even sailboats should have motors in case of emergency (the weather can change quickly here).

There are three standard excursions: a reef trip for US$10 to US$3 per person; Hol Chan Marine Reserve for US$25; and visiting the manatees for US$30. Tours depart midmorning, and return around 5 pm.

Underwater visibility is up to 60 meters. The variety of underwater plants, coral and

BELIZE

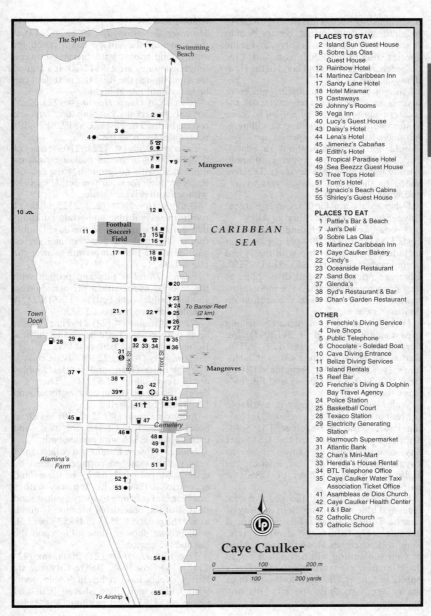

Caye Caulker

PLACES TO STAY
2 Island Sun Guest House
8 Sobre Las Olas
   Guest House
12 Rainbow Hotel
14 Martinez Caribbean Inn
17 Sandy Lane Hotel
18 Hotel Miramar
19 Castaways
26 Johnny's Rooms
36 Vega Inn
40 Lucy's Guest House
43 Daisy's Hotel
44 Lena's Hotel
45 Jimenez's Cabañas
46 Edith's Hotel
48 Tropical Paradise Hotel
49 Sea Beezzz Guest House
50 Tree Tops Hotel
51 Tom's Hotel
54 Ignacio's Beach Cabins
55 Shirley's Guest House

PLACES TO EAT
1 Pattie's Bar & Beach
7 Jan's Deli
9 Sobre Las Olas
16 Martinez Caribbean Inn
21 Caye Caulker Bakery
22 Cindy's
23 Oceanside Restaurant
27 Sand Box
37 Glenda's
38 Syd's Restaurant & Bar
39 Chan's Garden Restaurant

OTHER
3 Frenchie's Diving Service
4 Dive Shops
5 Public Telephone
6 Chocolate - Soledad Boat
10 Cave Diving Entrance
11 Belize Diving Services
13 Island Rentals
15 Reef Bar
20 Frenchie's Diving & Dolphin
   Bay Travel Agency
24 Police Station
25 Basketball Court
28 Texaco Station
29 Electricity Generating
   Station
30 Harmouch Supermarket
31 Atlantic Bank
32 Chan's Mini-Mart
33 Heredia's House Rental
34 BTL Telephone Office
35 Caye Caulker Water Taxi
   Association Ticket Office
41 Asambleas de Dios Church
42 Caye Caulker Health Center
47 I & I Bar
52 Catholic Church
53 Catholic School

The Split
Swimming Beach
Mangroves
CARIBBEAN SEA
Football (Soccer) Field
To Barrier Reef (2 km)
Town Dock
Mangroves
Back St
Front St
Cemetery
Alamina's Farm
To Airstrip

0   100   200 m
0   100   200 yards

BELIZE

tropical fish is wonderful. Be careful not to touch the coral, to prevent damage both to it and to yourself; coral is sharp, and some species sting or burn their assailants. (See the sidebars on diving and coral in the Honduras chapter.)

Among the more interesting places to dive is in the underwater caves off the western shore of the island. The cave system here is elaborate and fascinating, but cave diving is a special art. You should not go down without an experienced guide and the proper equipment (strong lights and other devices). The dive shops on the island can tell you what – and what not – to do.

Other goals are Goff's Caye, Sargent Caye, Shark Alley and Stingray Alley.

A one-day trip including three dives costs US$175 to US$200 per person, gear included. A three-day trip with meals and accommodations costs US$325 to US$350. Compare prices at several dive shops as they can vary significantly. For more information on dive sites, see the section on Ambergris Caye.

Diving, snorkeling and manatee-viewing trips can be arranged at Belize Diving Service (☎ (22) 2143, fax (22) 2217), Carlos Ayala (at Cindy's Café), Chocolate's (☎ (22) 22151), Frenchie's Diving (☎ (22) 2234, fax (22) 2074), and Johnny's Ras Creek.

Water sports equipment is available for rent at several places in town, including Pattie's Bar & Beach at The Split. Snorkeling gear costs around US$5 per day, beach floats the same, sit-on sea kayaks US$20 per half-day, a Hobie cat sailboat US$20 per hour or US$50 a half-day.

Beachgoers will find the water warm, clear and blue, but not much in the way of beach. Though there's lots of sand, it doesn't seem to arrange itself in nice, long, wide stretches along the shore. Most of your sunbathing will be on docks or in deck chairs at your hotel. Caulker's public beach, at The Split to the north of the village, is nothing special – it's tiny and crowded.

Places to Stay

Martinez Caribbean Inn (☎ (22) 2113) at the center of the village has a porch for sitting, and rooms with private showers. Singles/doubles are US$12/20. It's a good location, though the Reef Bar next door can be noisy until late at night.

Island Sun Guest House (☎ (22) 2215) has only two rooms, but both have fans and private baths. The cost is US$17.50/20. It's neat, quiet and near the beach.

Lena's Hotel (☎ (22) 2106) has 11 double rooms in an old building right on the water, with no grounds to speak of. Rates are high for what you get: US$20/30 without/with private shower.

Daisy's Hotel (☎ (22) 2123) has 11 rooms in several blue-and-white buildings that get full sun most of the day. Double rooms with table or floor fan and shared bath cost US$14; with private shower the rate is US$21.

Edith's Hotel is tidy and proper, with tiny rooms, each with a private shower; singles/doubles (one bed) are US$18/21. A double with two beds is US$23.

Hotel Miramar (☎ (22) 2157) has rooms on two floors in a building facing the sea. Rooms with private bath cost US$25.

Castaways (☎ (22) 2294) has six rooms. They're quite clean, and singles/doubles are a reasonable US$12/16. There's a decent restaurant (main courses for around US$8) and bar as well.

Johnny's Rooms (☎ (22) 2149) has clean hotel rooms for US$18 for two, and cabañas for US$26 with private bath.

Ignacio's Beach Cabins is a collection of very simple thatched cottages shaded by dozens of palms. Ignacio is the island eccentric, defending his territory with a machete and refusing to spray against sand fleas. But the beachfront location is good, as are the prices: US$15 to US$25 per hut, with private shower, depending upon the hut and the season.

Tree Tops Hotel (☎ (22) 2008, fax (22) 2115), PO Box 1648, Belize City, run by British expats, has five bright double rooms with fridges and TVs, shared bath and prices of US$22.50 without sea view,

US$25 with sea view; one room with private shower goes for US$30.

Jimenez's Cabañas (☎ (22) 2175) has little thatched huts with walls of sticks, each with a private shower. The place is quaint, quiet, relaxing, atmospheric and family-run, and constitutes very good value. Two/three/four people are US$22 to US$30/32/36.

Lucy's Guest House is not on the shore but it has some trees and gardens, and porches off the bungalows for hanging hammocks. Prices are good: a double with shared bath costs US$15/22 in summer/winter; with private shower, prices are US$25/32 in summer/winter.

Tom's Hotel (☎ (22) 2102) has nice, tidy, white buildings on the beach. The 20 cheapest, very simple waterless rooms cost US$10/12 for a single/double; bigger rooms in the newer building go for US$19/22; and the comfortable cabins cost US$30 with private shower.

Vega Inn (☎ (22) 2142, fax (22) 2269), has several tidy waterless rooms upstairs in a wooden house, with clean showers nearby, for US$20/25. Bigger rooms with private showers cost US$50/60. All rooms have wall fans. A shady camping area has tent spots for US$7.50 per person.

Tropical Paradise Hotel (☎ (22) 2124, fax (22) 2225) has six tidy paneled rooms in a long wooden building (US$28/32 with private shower and ceiling fans), or an equal number of yellow cabins with ceiling fans and private baths (some with tubs) for US$36/42. There's a decent (though pricey) restaurant and bar and a big dock for boats or sunning.

Places to Eat

Prices are not dirt cheap because much food must be brought from the mainland.

Glenda's, on the west side of the island, is favored for breakfast (7 to 10 am): eggs, bacon or ham, bread and coffee for US$3. A big glass of fresh-squeezed orange juice goes for US$1. Lunch is served from noon to 3 pm. Another good place for breakfast and good coffee is *Cindy's*, opposite the basketball court on Front St.

The *Caye Caulker Bakery* on Back St is the place to pick up fresh bread, rolls and similar goodies. Other picnic supplies are available at the *Harmouch Supermarket* and *Chan's Mini-Mart*.

Sobre las Olas (☎/fax (22) 2243), north of the center on the water, is a tidy open-air place with a wooden dock, a bar, umbrella-topped tables and Belgian managers. Belizean and continental fare is served from 7 am to 10 pm every day but Monday. Expect to pay US$8 to US$12 for a full meal.

The *Sand Box* is perhaps the island's most popular place to dine and drink. All three meals (and lots of Belikin) are served. For dinner, try the fish with spicy banana chutney (US$6), or barbecued chicken for less. Pasta plates (including vegetarian lasagna) cost about the same.

Pattie's Bar & Beach at The Split serves a surprisingly extensive menu of burgers, fajitas, vegetable soups and so forth to swimmers and hangers-about. A substantial lunch can be had for US$5 to US$8. The faithful stay here till long after dark.

The *Martinez Caribbean Inn* serves sandwiches, burgers and antojitos (garnaches, tacos, panuchos), as well as rice and beans with chicken or lobster. For breakfast, a coffee and a fruit plate costs less than US$4. Expect lunch and dinner to cost US$4 to US$10. They concoct a tasty rum punch here, which is sold by the bottle or the glass.

Chan's Garden Restaurant has reasonably authentic Chinese food (the owner is from Hong Kong) at moderate prices.

The *Oceanside Restaurant* features daily specials posted on its blackboard menu.

Entertainment

After one evening on the island, you'll know all there is to do at night. The *Reef Bar* has a sand floor and tables holding clusters of bottles (mostly beer) as semi-permanent centerpieces. This is the locals' gathering, sipping and talking place. The *I & I Bar* is a bit classier, with reggae playing constantly, setting the proper island mood.

Getting There & Away

The Caye Caulker Water Taxi Association runs boats from Caulker to Belize City at 6:45, 8 and 10 am, and 3 pm, for US$7.50 one way; children five to 10 pay half fare, those under five ride free. Another water taxi goes from Caulker to San Pedro, Ambergris Caye, at 10 am (US$7.50), returning from San Pedro at 2:30 pm. See also Getting There & Away in the Belize City section.

AMBERGRIS CAYE

Population 2000

The largest of Belize's cayes, Ambergris (pronounced am-BER-griss) lies 58 km north of Belize City. It's over 40 km long and connected to Mexican land on its northern side. Most of the island's population lives in the town of **San Pedro** near the southern tip. Like Caye Caulker, Ambergris has an engaging laid-back atmosphere. (A sign in a local restaurant has it right: 'No shirt, no shoes – *no problem!*')

Orientation

It's about a kilometer from the Paradise Hotel in the northern part of town to the airport in the south, so everything is within easy walking distance.

San Pedro has three main north-south streets, which used to be called Front St (to the east), Middle St and Back St (to the west). Now these streets have tourist-class names: Barrier Reef Dr, Pescador Dr and Angel Coral Dr, but some islanders might still use the old names.

Information

Ambergris has its own Web site; see the appendix.

Post & Communications The post office is on Buccaneer St off Barrier Reef Dr beside the Alijua Suites Hotel. Hours are 8 am to noon and 1 to 5 pm (4:30 pm on Friday), closed Saturday and Sunday.

The Belize Telecommunications office, up north on Pescador St, is open Monday to Friday from 8 am to noon and 1 to 4 pm, and on Saturday from 8 am to noon; it's closed on Sunday.

Money You can change cash US dollars easily on the street in San Pedro, but they're accepted in most establishments.

The Atlantic Bank (☎ (26) 2195), on Barrier Reef Dr, is open Monday, Tuesday and Thursday from 8 am to noon and 1 to 3 pm; Wednesday 8 am to 1 pm; Friday 8 am to 1 pm and 3 to 6 pm; Saturday 8:30 am to noon.

Nearby, the Belize Bank is open Monday to Thursday from 8 am to 3 pm, Friday 8 am to 1 pm and 3 to 6 pm, Saturday 8:30 am to noon.

Laundry There are several laundries at the southern end of Pescador Dr, including J's Laundromat and Belize Laundry & Dry Cleaning.

Medical Services San Carlos Medical Clinic, Pharmacy & Pathology Lab (☎ (26) 2918, 3649; in emergencies (14) 9251), on Pescador just south of Caribeña, treats ailments and does blood tests.

The Lion's Club Medical Clinic is across the street from the Island Air terminal at the airport. Right next door is the island's hyperbaric chamber for diving accidents.

Water Sports

Ambergris is good for all water sports: scuba diving, snorkeling, sailboarding, boating, swimming, deep-sea fishing and sunbathing. Many island hotels have their own dive shops to rent equipment, provide instruction and organize diving excursions. Swimming is best off the pier at the Paradise Hotel. All beaches are public, and you can probably use hotel lounge chairs if it's a slow day.

Among the favorite seafaring destinations for diving and snorkeling are these:

Blue Hole, a deep sinkhole of vivid blue water where you can dive to 40 meters, observing the cave with diving lights

Caye Caulker North Island, the relatively uninhabited northern part of Caulker, with good snorkeling, swimming and places for a beach barbeque

Glover's Reef, about 50 km east of Dangriga, one of only three coral atolls in the Western Hemisphere

BELIZE

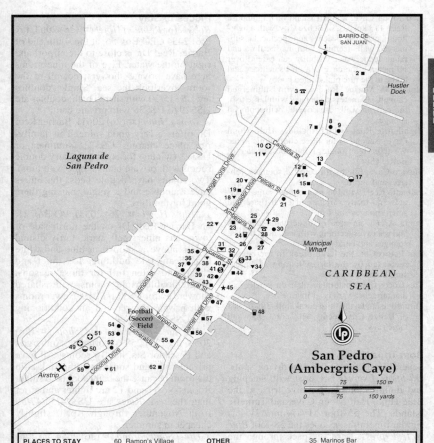

Laguna de San Pedro

BARRIO DE SAN JUAN

Hustler Dock

Caribeña St

Angel Coral Drive

Pelican St

Pescador Drive

Ambergris St

Buccaneer St

Black Coral St

Almond St

Tarpon St

Barrier Reef Drive

Esmeralda St

Coconut Drive

Municipal Wharf

CARIBBEAN SEA

San Pedro (Ambergris Caye)

Football (Soccer) Field

Airstrip

0   75   150 m
0   75   150 yards

PLACES TO STAY
2 Rock's Inn
6 Paradise Hotel
7 Milo's Hotel
12 Hotel San Pedrano
13 Conch Shell Hotel
14 Tomas Hotel
15 Lily's Caribbean Lodge
16 Mayan Princess Resort Hotel
22 Hotel Casablanca
23 Martha's Hotel & Food Shop
25 Barrier Reef Hotel & Restaurant
32 Alijua Suites Hotel
43 Coral Beach Hotel
44 Spindrift Hotel
56 Ruby's (Rubie's) Hotel
57 San Pedro Holiday Hotel
60 Ramon's Village
62 Sun Breeze Beach Hotel

PLACES TO EAT
11 The Reef Restaurant
15 Lily's Restaurant
18 Island Style Food Palace
19 Lagoon Restaurant
20 Ambergris Delight
22 Elvi's Kitchen
25 Barrier Reef Hotel
34 Estel's Dine-by-the-Sea
38 Panadería El Centro
40 Casa de Café
56 Rubie's Caffe
57 Celi's, The Deli
61 Tropical Take-Out

OTHER
1 Statue
3 BTL Telephone Office
4 Electricity Generating Plant
5 Sandals Bar
8 Polo's EZ-Go Rentals
9 Cemetery
10 San Carlos Medical Clinic
17 Andrea & Triple J Boats to Belize City
21 Fido's Courtyard
24 Tarzan Club & Cheetah's Bar
26 Basketball Court
27 Mayan Statue
28 Public Telephone
29 Catholic Church
30 Big Daddy's Disco
31 Post Office
33 Atlantic Bank
35 Marinos Bar
36 J's Laundromat
37 Rock's Store
39 Belize Laundry & Dry Cleaning
41 Belize Bank
42 Amigo Travel
45 Municipality, Police Station
46 Aqua Fresh Drinking Water
47 Adventures in Water Sports
48 Tackle Box Bar
49 Hyperbaric Chamber
50 Island Air
51 Lion's Club Medical Clinic
52 Maya Airways, Ramon's Wheel Rentals
53 Travel & Tour Belize
54 Hustler Tours
55 Catholic Primary School
58 Rental Center
59 Tropic Air Terminal

Half Moon Caye, a small island on Lighthouse Reef, 113 km east of Belize City, with a lighthouse, excellent beaches and spectacular submerged walls teeming with marine flora and fauna (underwater visibility can extend over 60 meters); the caye is a bird sanctuary and home to the rare pink-footed booby

Hol Chan Marine Reserve, with submerged canyons 30 meters deep busy with large fish; the canyon walls are covered with colorful sponges

Lighthouse Reef (which includes Half Moon Caye), second of the three coral atolls in the Western Hemisphere, lying 100 km east of Belize City

Mexico Cave, filled with colorful sponges, lobsters and shrimp

Palmetto Reef, with lots of canyons, surge channels and many varieties of coral (hard and soft), sponges and fish

Punta Arena, an area of underwater canyons and sea caves teeming with fish, rays, turtles, sponges and coral

San Pedro Cut, the large break in the barrier reef used by the larger fishing and pleasure boats

Tres Cocos Cut, a natural break in the barrier reef that attracts a variety of marine life.

Turneffe Islands, the third coral atoll, 30 km east of Belize City, teems with coral, fish and large rays

Boat Trips

Several boats run to the best diving spots. *Off-Shore Express* is a boat with sleeping and dining facilities for dive trips to the Blue Hole, Half Moon Caye and Turneffe Islands. The 55-foot MV *Manta IV* has similar itineraries, as does the 38-foot *Blue Hole Express*. Reserve space through the Blue Hole Dive Center (☎ (26) 2982, net), at the Spindrift Hotel on Barrier Reef Dr, or the Coral Beach Hotel & Dive Club (☎ (26) 2013, fax (26) 2864, net).

The *Winnie Estelle* (☎ (26) 2394, fax (26) 2576), a 66-foot island trader moored at the Paradise Hotel pier, goes out on daily snorkeling trips to Caye Caulker.

The *Reef Seeker* glass-bottom boat, based at the San Pedro Holiday Hotel, makes daily reef trips for US$12.50 per adult, half price for kids. Occasional trips upriver run to Altun Ha ruins (US$60 per person).

Places to Stay

Ruby's (or *Rubie's) Hotel* (☎ (26) 2063, fax (26) 2434), PO Box 56, at the south end of Barrier Reef Dr, is close to the airport and right on the water. Five of the nine rooms here have private showers; not all of the rooms overlook the sea. Singles/doubles are US$15/20 with shared bath; doubles are US$29 to US$38 with private bath.

Tomas Hotel (☎ (26) 2061), Barrier Reef Dr, offers a very good value. This family-run place charges US$21 (summer) or US$28 (winter) for eight light, airy double rooms with private baths (some with tubs). Two rooms have double beds; the others have a double and a single, making them good for families.

Milo's Hotel (☎ (26) 2033), PO Box 21, on Barrier Reef Dr on the north side of town, has nine small, dark, fairly dismal rooms above a shop in a blue-and-white Caribbean-style building. It's quiet and cheap and often full for those reasons. Single/double/triple rooms with shared showers go for US$11/14/19. Newer rooms with private shower and air conditioning cost US$22.

Martha's Hotel & Food Shop (☎ (26) 2053, fax (26) 2589), corner of Ambergris and Pescador Sts, has 16 rooms. All have private bath, and sometimes the sink is in the room because the bathroom is so small. Rooms No 11 and 12 are lighter and airier than the rest. Rates are US$24/35/47/59 from November through April, slightly cheaper in summer.

Hotel San Pedrano (☎ (26) 2054, fax (26) 2093), corner of Barrier Reef Dr and Caribeña St, has one apartment and seven rooms, all with fan and private bath. Though most rooms don't have ocean views, there's a wraparound porch. Single/ double/triple/ quad rooms rent for US$29/35/43/49 in winter; summer prices are about 17% to 20% lower. Add US$10 per room for air conditioning.

Lily's Caribbean Lodge (☎ (26) 2059), off the east end of Caribeña St facing the sea, has 10 clean, pleasant rooms; several (especially those on the top floor) have good sea views. Air conditioned doubles cost US$35 to US$40 in winter. There's a tidy restaurant on the ground floor.

Places to Eat

Several small cafes in the town center serve cheap, simple meals and good java.

Casa de Café, on Barrier Reef Dr just north of the Belize Bank, serves pastries and light meals to go with its high-quality coffee.

Rubie's Caffe, next to Rubie's Hotel on Barrier Reef Dr, is a tiny, little place with good cakes and pastries, but unpredictable opening hours. For simpler take-out pastries and bread, try the *Panadería El Centro* at the corner of Buccaneer and Pescador.

The Deli, on Barrier Reef Dr just north of the San Pedro Holiday Hotel, serves food to go: fried chicken, sandwiches and their own banana bread for US$1.50 to US$5.

Tropical Take-Out, across the street from the Tropic Air terminal at the airport, has daily specials as well as the usual list of sandwiches and light meals.

The menu at *Elvi's Kitchen* (☎ (26) 2176, fax (26) 3056), on Pescador St, includes fish & chips (US$7) and rice and beans with fish (US$5), but the daily specials are unabashed nouvelle cuisine, costing up to US$30 for a full lobster dinner with wine.

Celi's Restaurant (☎ (26) 2014), next to the San Pedro Holiday Hotel, has a long breakfast menu (try the homemade cinnamon rolls or banana bread, US$1.75), and seafood main courses at lunch or dinner are priced from US$10 to US$17.

Estel's Dine by the Sea, on the beach east of the Alijua Hotel, is not particularly cheap, but it has an eclectic menu and a great location. Rice and beans goes for US$7, a Mexican plate for US$14. It's closed on Tuesday.

Jade Garden (☎ (26) 2126), on Coconut Dr a 10-minute walk south of the airport, has a long menu and moderate prices. Fried rice and chow mein dishes cost US$5 to US$9, sweet and sour US$7 to US$10, steaks and fish US$10 to US$18. It's open daily from 11 am to 2 pm and 6 to 10 pm.

Lily's (☎ (26) 2059), on Caribeña St, is a family-run place serving seafood lunches and dinners for US$12 to US$18; breakfasts for US$5.

The *Barrier Reef Hotel & Restaurant*, on Barrier Reef Dr, specializes in pizza: nine, 12 and 16-inch pizzas priced from US$9 to US$22, depending upon ingredients.

Island Style Food Palace, on Pescador north of Ambergris, is a homey eatery with lunch and dinner 'burgers' of beef, chicken, shrimp or lobster for US$2 to US$5, fish & chips for a bit more.

Little Italy Restaurant (☎ (26) 2866), in the Spindrift Hotel, features indoor, patio and beachside dining. Spaghetti plates and Italian main courses cost US$6 to US$20; sandwiches are less. It's closed from 2 to 5:30 pm.

Entertainment

Tackle Box Bar, on a wharf at the eastern end of Black Coral Dr, is a San Pedro institution. Very popular with divers and boat owners, it's a good place to get the latest information on diving trips and conditions, boat rentals and excursions.

Fido's, on Barrier Reef Dr near Pelican St, is the landlubbers' favorite. *Sandals*, near the north end of Barrier Reef Dr, is an alternative.

Big Daddy's, located right next to San Pedro's church, is the town's hot night spot, often featuring live reggae, especially during the winter. Across Barrier Reef Dr, the *Tarzan Club & Cheetah's Bar* is often closed off-season, but rocks in the winter.

To drink with the locals in a real cantina at lower prices, head for *Marinos Bar*, on Pescador St at Buccaneer St. Don't expect a beautiful place; this is a real Mexican-style cantina, and women may not find the atmosphere welcoming or comfortable.

Getting There & Away

By air, a one-way flight between San Pedro and Belize City's Municipal Airport costs US$22, or from Goldson International, it's US$39. See Getting Around earlier in this chapter.

By boat, *Triple J* sails from San Pedro to Caye Caulker daily at 3 pm for US$6 per person, and to Belize City for US$10. The

Banana Boat departs the Wahoo! dock (near the Hustler dock at the northern end of town) Monday through Friday at 8 am for Belize City; it departs Belize City on the return trip to San Pedro at 4 pm. See also Getting There & Away in the Belize City section.

Getting Around
You can rent bicycles, motorcycles and golf carts at several locations, including Polo's EZ-Go Rentals (☎ (26) 2080, (26) 3542), at the north end of Barrier Reef Dr, and the Rental Center and Ramon's Wheel Rentals (☎ (26) 2790, fax (26) 3236), on Coconut Dr just south of the Tropic Air terminal at the airport. Bikes rent for around US$2.50 per hour, US$9 for four hours or US$14 for eight hours.

Northern Belize

Low-lying, often swampy, cut by rivers and lagoons, northern Belize is farming country. Sugar cane is a major crop, but many farmers are branching out to different crops, including marijuana.

The ancient Mayas prospered in northern Belize, scooping up the rich soil and piling it on raised fields while at the same time creating drainage canals. Except for Lamanai, near Orange Walk, northern Belize's Mayan archeological sites are mostly of interest to archaeologists.

BERMUDIAN LANDING COMMUNITY BABOON SANCTUARY
The endangered black howler monkey exists only in Belize, where it's called a baboon. In 1985 a group of local farmers were organized to help preserve the black howler and to protect its habitat by harmonizing its needs with their own. Care is taken to leave the forests undisturbed along the banks of the Belize River, where the black howler feeds, sleeps and – at dawn and dusk – howls loudly and unmistakably. You can learn all about the black howler, and 200 animals and

birds found in the reserve, at the visitors' center (☎ (2) 44405) in the village of Bermudian Landing.

You must tour the sanctuary with a guide, at US$4 per hour, US$12 per half day. For more information about the sanctuary, check with the Belize Audubon Society (☎ (2) 77369, net), 49 Southern Foreshore, Belize City.

Places to Stay & Eat
Camping (US$5 per person) is allowed at the visitors' center and at the *Jungle Drift Lodge* (☎ (2) 32842, fax 78160), PO Box 1442, Belize City, in Bermudian Landing village. The lodge has five cabins priced at US$22 double. Inexpensive meals are served, canoes and kayaks are for rent and tours are offered.

Getting There & Away
Private buses leave Orange St in Belize City (one from the corner of Mussel St, the other the corner of George St) Monday to Saturday after lunch for the hour-long ride to Bermudian Landing. Departures from Bermudian Landing for Belize City are at 5:30 am, meaning that if you take the bus, you must plan to stay the night. The round-trip fare is US$3.50.

ALTUN HA
Northern Belize's most famous Maya ruin is at Altun Ha, 55 km north of Belize City along the Old Northern Hwy near the village of Rockstone Pond, 16 km south of Maskall.

Altun Ha (Maya for Rockstone Pond) was undoubtedly a small Maya community (population about 3000), but it was a rich and important trading town, with agriculture also playing an important role in its economy. Altun Ha had formed as a community by at least 600 BC, perhaps several centuries earlier, and the town flourished until the mysterious collapse of Classic Maya civilization around 900 AD. Most of the temples you see here date from Late Classic times, though burials indicate that Altun Ha's merchants were trading with Teotihuacán in Pre-Classic times.

Of the grass-covered temples arranged around the two plazas here, the largest and most important is the Temple of the Masonry Altars (Structure B-4, 600s AD), in Plaza B.

In Plaza A, Structure A-1 is sometimes called the Temple of the Green Tomb. Deep within it was discovered the tomb of a priest/king dating from around 600 AD.

Altun Ha is open daily from 9 am to 5 pm; admission costs US$5. There are toilets and a drinks shop at the site, but no accommodations.

Buses leave from Douglas Jones St in Belize City (see Belize City map) for Maskall, north of Altun Ha, several times daily.

CROOKED TREE WILDLIFE SANCTUARY

Midway between Belize City and Orange Walk Town, 5.5 km west of the Northern Hwy, lies the fishing and farming village of Crooked Tree. Around it, 12 sq km are a wildlife sanctuary busy with migrating birds during the dry season (November to May). The Belize Audubon Society (☎ (2) 77369, net), 49 Southern Foreshore (PO Box 1001), Belize City, has details.

Places to Stay & Eat

Molly's Rooms has simple waterless single/double rooms for US$10/15. *Sam Tillett's Hotel* (☎ (2) 44333) charges a bit more for its three rooms with private bath.

Paradise Inn (☎ (25) 2535, fax 2534), rents simple cabañas for US$38/50. Rooms at *Bird's Eye View Lodge* (☎ (2) 44101), PO Box 1976, Belize City, are more expensive, but they have campsites.

Getting There & Away

Jex Bus, at 34 Regent St in Belize City, runs three buses daily from Crooked Tree to Belize City early in the morning, returning mid-morning and late afternoon.

If you start early from Belize City, Corozal Town or Orange Walk Town, you can bus to Crooked Tree Junction, walk the 5.5 km to the village (about an hour), learn about the reserve's flora and fauna at the visitors' center, spend some time bird watching, and head out again.

LAMANAI

By far the most impressive site in this part of the country is Lamanai, in its own archaeological reserve on the New River Lagoon near the settlement of Indian Church. Though much of the site remains unexcavated and unrestored, the trip to Lamanai, by motorboat up the New River, is an adventure in itself.

As with most sites in northern Belize, Lamanai (submerged crocodile, the original Maya name of the place) was occupied as early as 1500 BC, with the first stone buildings appearing between 800 and 600 BC. Lamanai flourished in late Pre-Classic times, growing to be a major ceremonial center with immense temples long before most other Maya sites.

Unlike many other sites, Maya lived here until the coming of the Spaniards in the 1500s. The ruined Indian church (actually two of them) to be found nearby attests to the fact that there were Maya here for the Spanish friars to convert. Convert them they did, but by 1640 the Maya had reverted to their ancient forms of worship. British interests later built a sugar mill, now in ruins, at Indian Church. The archaeological site was excavated by David Pendergast in the 1970s and 1980s.

New River Voyage

The roundtrip by boat to Lamanai, including a tour of the ruins, takes most of a day. You motor for 90 minutes up the New River from the Tower Hill toll bridge south of Orange Walk, between river banks crowded with dense jungle vegetation. Along the way, your boatman/guide will point out the many local birds and will almost certainly spot a crocodile or two. You'll also pass the Mennonite community at Shipyard. Finally the river opens out into the New River Lagoon, a broad and very long expanse of water that can be choppy during the frequent rain-showers. See Getting There & Away for tour recommendations

BELIZE

Touring the Ruins

After landing at Lamanai, wander into the dense jungle, past gigantic guanacaste, ceiba and *ramón* (breadnut) trees, strangler figs, allspice, epiphytes and black orchids, Belize's national flower. In the canopy overhead you may see one of the five groups of howler monkeys resident in the archaeological zone.

A tour of the ruins takes a minimum of 90 minutes, and it's more comfortably done in two or three hours.

Of the 60 significant structures identified here, the grandest is Structure N10-43, a huge late Pre-Classic building rising more than 34 meters above the jungle canopy. Other buildings along La Ruta Maya are taller, but this one was built well before the others. It's been partially uncovered and restored.

Not far from N10-43 is Lamanai's ballcourt, a smallish one, partially uncovered.

To the north along a path in the jungle is Structure P9-56, built several centuries later, with a huge stylized mask of a man in a crocodile-mouth headdress four meters high emblazoned on its southwest face. Near this structure is a small temple and a very fine ruined stela.

Lamanai is open daily from 9 am to 5 pm; admission is US$5.

Places to Stay & Eat

In the nearby village of Indian Church, *Doña Blanca* (☎ (3) 23369) rents serviceable double cabins for US$25, breakfast included.

Lamanai Outpost Lodge, a 15-minute walk south of the archaeological zone, has single/double rooms for US$94/115, but lunch can be had for US$10 or so.

Getting There & Away

Lamanai can be reached by road (58 km) from Orange Walk via Yo Creek and San Felipe. The bus service from Orange Walk – departing on Tuesday at 3 pm, and Thursday at 4 pm – is only of use to village people coming to the big city for marketing. The river voyage is much more convenient and enjoyable.

The main base for river departures is the Tower Hill toll bridge seven km south of Orange Walk on the Northern Hwy. The Novelo brothers (Antonio and Herminio) run Jungle River Tours (☎ (3) 22293, fax (3) 23749), 20 Lovers' Lane (PO Box 95), Orange Walk Town, and they have excellent reputations as guides and naturalists. Contact them at the bridge or at their office near the southeast corner of the central park in Orange Walk Town, or make a reservation by phone or fax. Be at their boat dock, on the northwest side of the Tower Hill toll bridge, by 9 am for the day-long trip (back by 4 pm), which includes lunch, beverages and the guided tour along the river and at Lamanai (US$50 per person, with a minimum of four persons).

Reyes & Sons (☎ (3) 23327) run tours from Jim's Cool Pool, just north of the toll bridge (by Novelo's), at 9 am daily (be there by 8:30 am) for the river tour to Lamanai. The boat ride and guided tour costs US$30 per person; a boxed lunch is another US$8.

It's possible to take the 6 am Batty's bus from Belize City to Orange Walk, get out at the Tower Hill toll bridge, and be in time for the 9 am departure of the boats for Lamanai. Boats return to the bridge before 4 pm, allowing you to catch the 4 pm Batty's bus southward back to Belize City.

ORANGE WALK TOWN
Population 10,000

The agricultural and social center of northern Belize is Orange Walk, 94 km north of Belize City. It's important to the farmers (including many Mennonites) who till the soil of the region, raising sugar cane and citrus fruits. Another important crop is said to be marijuana.

Very few travelers will spend any time in Orange Walk. The center of town is the shady central park on the east side of the main road, called Queen Victoria Ave. The town hospital is in the northern outskirts, readily visible on the west side of the highway.

BELIZE

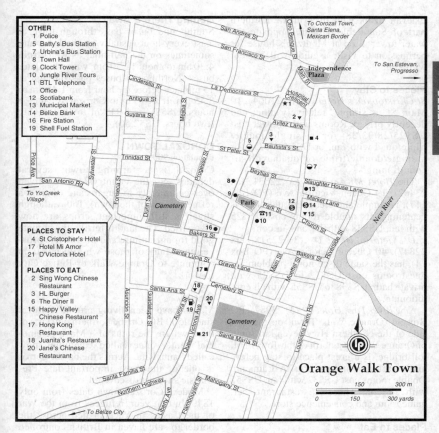

OTHER
1 Police
5 Batty's Bus Station
7 Urbina's Bus Station
8 Town Hall
9 Clock Tower
10 Jungle River Tours
11 BTL Telephone
   Office
12 Scotiabank
13 Municipal Market
14 Belize Bank
16 Fire Station
19 Shell Fuel Station

PLACES TO STAY
4 St Cristopher's Hotel
17 Hotel Mi Amor
21 D'Victoria Hotel

PLACES TO EAT
2 Sing Wong Chinese
   Restaurant
3 HL Burger
6 The Diner II
15 Happy Valley
   Chinese Restaurant
7 Hong Kong
   Restaurant
18 Juanita's Restaurant
20 Jane's Chinese
   Restaurant

Orange Walk Town

0   150   300 m
0   150   300 yards

To Corozal Town,
Santa Elena,
Mexican Border

To San Estevan,
Progresso

To Belize City

To Yo Creek
Village

Cuello & Nohmul Archaeological Sites

Near Orange Walk is Cuello, a Maya site with a 3000 year history but little to show for it. Archaeologists have found plenty here, but only Structure 350, a nine-tiered, stepped pyramid, will draw your interest. This Late Preclassic structure has an even older one beneath it, and was itself covered by a later Early Classic temple. But the Early Classic temple, in ruins, was stripped away when Structure 350 was consolidated.

The site is on private property, that of the Cuello Brothers Distillery (☎ (3) 22141), four km west of Orange Walk along Yo Creek Rd. The distillery, on the left-hand (south) side of the road, is unmarked; the site is through and beyond it. Ask permission at the distillery gate.

Nohmul (Great Mound in Maya), 12 km north of Orange Walk and two km west of the village of San Pablo, was a much more important site. Structure 2, the tallest building at the site, marks a lofty acropolis looming over the surrounding countryside. It's vast, covering more than 18 sq km, and most of it is now overgrown grass and sugar cane. The site is owned by Mr

Estevan Itzab, who lives in the northern part of San Pablo village, opposite the water tower. Stop at Mr Itzab's house for permission to visit; a guide will be sent with you.

Places to Stay

St Christopher's Hotel (☎ (3) 21064), 10 Main St, is simple, relatively quiet and decently priced. Rooms with shower cost US$25/28/33/38 for a single/double/triple/quad with fan, or US$40/45/54 for a single/double/triple or quad with air conditioning.

The *Hotel Mi Amor* (☎ (3) 22031, fax 23462), 19 Queen Victoria Ave (PO Box 117), is simple and clean, but the disco is deafening. Its double rooms cost US$25 with fan, US$38 with TV and air con.

D' Victoria Hotel (☎ (3) 22518, fax 22847), 40 Queen Victoria Ave (PO Box 74), has the same disco noise problem; its guestrooms cost US$22 to US$25 with private bath, US$38 to US$55 with air conditioning.

New River Park Hotel (☎ (3) 23987), PO Box 34, Orange Walk Town, on the east side of the Northern Hwy seven km south of Orange Walk just north of the Tower Hill toll bridge, is a great place to stay before and/or after your boat trip to Lamanai. Double rooms cost US$32 with fan, US$52 with air con. There's a restaurant, bar, game room and convenience store.

Places to Eat

Locals favor *Juanita's*, on Santa Ana St near the Shell fuel station, a simple place with local fare at low prices. Near the square, *The Diner II* is popular.

HL Burger, three blocks north of the park on the main road, has good, cheap burgers (US$2), rice and bean plates and ice cream.

When it comes to Chinese restaurants, Orange Walk has them. *Happy Valley*, at Church and Main Sts, and *Sing Wong*, at Main and Avilez, are about the nicest, along with the *Hong Kong*, right next to the Hotel Mi Amor, and *Jane's Chinese Restaurant*, which is about three blocks farther south.

Getting There & Away

Southbound buses pass through town at least every hour (usually on the hour, and sometimes on the half-hour as well) from 4:30 am to about 12:30 pm, with a few later buses. Northbound buses pass through at 15 minutes before the hour from 1:45 pm to 8:45 pm. It's 61 km to Corozal Town (1½ hours, US$2), and 94 km to Belize City (two hours, US$2.50).

COROZAL TOWN
Population 9000

Corozal is a farming town; several decades ago the countryside was given over completely to sugar cane (there's a refinery south of the town). Today, though sugar is still important, crops are now diversified. The land is fertile, the climate good for agriculture and the town is prosperous. Many of those who do not farm commute to Orange Walk or Belize City to work.

History

Mayas have been living around Corozal since 1500 BC. On the northern outskirts of the town are the ruins of a Maya ceremonial center once called Chetumal, now called Santa Rita. Across the bay at Cerros is one of the most important late Pre-Classic sites yet discovered.

Modern Corozal Town dates from only 1849. In that year, refugees from the War of the Castes in Yucatán fled across the border to safe haven in British-controlled Belize. Hurricane Janet roared through in 1955 and blew away many of the old wooden buildings on stilts. Much of Corozal's cinder-block architecture thus dates from the late '50s.

Orientation & Information

Corozal resembles a Mexican town with its plaza, its Palacio Municipal and its large church. You can walk easily to any place in town.

The Belize Bank on the north side of the plaza is open for currency exchange Monday to Friday from 8 am to 1 pm, and Friday afternoon from 3 to 6 pm.

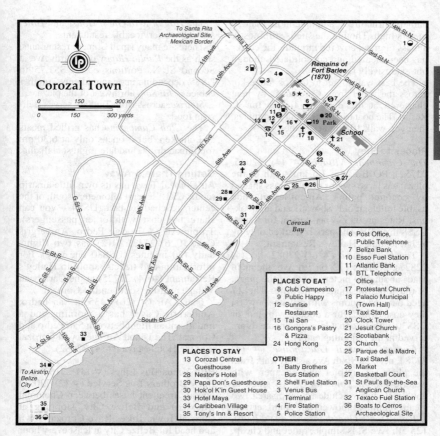

Corozal Town

0   150   300 m
0   150   300 yards

To Santa Rita
Archaeological Site,
Mexican Border

Remains of
Fort Barlee
(1870)

Corozal
Bay

To Airstrip,
Belize
City

BELIZE

Park

School

6   Post Office,
    Public Telephone
7   Belize Bank
10 Esso Fuel Station
11 Atlantic Bank
14 BTL Telephone
    Office
17 Protestant Church
18 Palacio Municipal
    (Town Hall)
19 Taxi Stand
20 Clock Tower
21 Jesuit Church
22 Scotiabank
23 Church
25 Parque de la Madre,
    Taxi Stand
26 Market
27 Basketball Court
31 St Paul's By-the-Sea
    Anglican Church
32 Texaco Fuel Station
36 Boats to Cerros
    Archaeological Site

PLACES TO EAT
8   Club Campesino
9   Public Happy
12 Sunrise
    Restaurant
15 Tai San
16 Gongora's Pastry
    & Pizza
24 Hong Kong

OTHER
1   Batty Brothers
    Bus Station
2   Shell Fuel Station
3   Venus Bus
    Terminal
4   Fire Station
5   Police Station

PLACES TO STAY
13 Corozal Central
    Guesthouse
28 Nestor's Hotel
29 Papa Don's Guesthouse
30 Hok'ol K'in Guest House
33 Hotel Maya
34 Caribbean Village
35 Tony's Inn & Resort

Santa Rita Archaeological Site

A small, nicely kept park with one small restored Maya temple: that's Santa Rita, just over one km northwest of the Venus bus terminal in Corozal. Go north on the main highway; after 700 meters bear right, just before the statue; after another 100 meters turn left at the Restaurant Hennessy and go straight on for 300 meters to the site. The 'hill' on the right is actually a temple. The site is open during daylight hours for free.

Called Chetumal by the Maya, this city sat astride important riverine trade routes,

and it had its share of wealth. The jade and pottery artifacts found here have been dispersed to museums, and the important frescoes destroyed.

Cerros Archaeological Site

Cerros is an oddity in that it flourished in late Pre-Classic times and was not extensively overbuilt during the Classic and Post-Classic periods. The site has thus given archaeologists important insights into Pre-Classic Mayan architecture.

There is more to see at Cerros (also called Cerro Maya) than at Santa Rita:

namely Structure 4, a temple more than 20 meters high. Though the site is still mostly a mass of grass-covered mounds, the center has been cleared and consolidated, though not extensively restored.

The best way to get to Cerros, three km across the water from Corozal, is by boat chartered at the dock of Tony's Inn & Resort. The boat trip takes about 15 minutes, then you walk 10 minutes to the site.

Places to Stay

The Caribbean Village (☎ (4) 22045, 22752), PO Box 55, 1.5 km south of the plaza, has large swaths of lush grass shaded by coconut palms. Amenities include usable toilets, moldy showers and all hook-ups. Rates are US$4 per person for a tent, US$8 in an RV. The park is marked only by a sign reading 'Hailey's Restaurant.'

The *Hotel Maya* (☎ (4) 22082, fax (4) 22827), PO Box 112, on 7th Ave (the main road) about 400 meters south of the plaza, is the longtime budget favorite. The 17 aged but clean rooms with private showers; they cost US$22 for a double with fan, or US$30 with air con. Good, cheap meals are served in the adjoining eatery.

Corozal Central Guesthouse (☎ (4) 22784, net), 22 Sixth Ave a short walk from the plaza, is simpler and cheaper, with waterless rooms going for US$15, single or double. Bonuses include a cooking area, two clean communal showers and email service.

Papa Don's Guesthouse (☎ (4) 22666), 125 5th Ave S, is simple, quiet and cheap. Waterless single/double rooms are US$8/10. The walls are thin here, so beware of noisy or smoky neighbors. *Nestor's Hotel* (☎ (4) 22354), just to the north, is a more expensive second best.

Hok'ol K'in Guest House (☎ (4) 23329, fax (4) 23569), 4th St at 4th Ave (PO Box 145), is a small modern hotel with comfortable rooms, each with two double beds, bathroom and cable TV, for US$32/44.

Places to Eat

For fresh bread and pastries, check out *Gongora's Pastry & Pizza*, off the northwest corner of the plaza.

The *Hok'ol K'in Guest House* and *Hotel Maya* have serviceable restaurants.

There are many small Chinese restaurants, such as the *Public Happy* on Fourth Ave at Second St N. Portions cost US$1.75 to US$5, depending upon ingredients. Another choice is *Tai San*, northwest of the plaza.

Sunrise, across from Tai San, serves Belizean food.

The *Club Campesino* has grilled meats and chicken, but it opens only at 6:30 pm for dinner, drinks and late-night socializing.

Getting There & Away

Air Corozal Town has its own little airstrip (code: CZL) several kilometers south of the center, reached by taxi (US$4 – you can share the cost with other passengers). Tropic Air (☎ in San Pedro, Ambergris Caye (026) 2542, 2012) has two flights daily (20 minutes, US$30 one way). For information and tickets, apply to Hailey's Restaurant (☎ (4) 22725) at the Caribbean Village near the south end of Corozal.

Island Air (☎ (26) 2435 in San Pedro, Ambergris Caye) has a morning and a midafternoon flight between San Pedro and Corozal. The Island Air agency in Corozal is at the Hotel Maya (☎ (4) 22082).

Bus Venus Bus Lines (☎ (4) 22132) and Batty Brothers Bus Service (☎ (2) 72025) operate frequent buses between Chetumal (Mexico) and Belize City, stopping at Corozal Town. Buses leave Corozal Town and head for Belize City at least every hour from 3:30 am to 11:30 am, with extra buses on the half-hour during busy times. From Belize City to Corozal, departures are on the hour between noon and 7 pm.

Belize City (155 km, 2¼ to 2¾ hours, US$4)
Chetumal (30 km, one hour with border
  formalities, US$1)
Orange Walk (61 km, 1¼ hours, US$1.50)

CROSSING THE BORDER TO MEXICO

Corozal Town is 13 km east of the border-crossing point at Santa Elena/Subteniente López. Most of the Venus and Batty Brothers buses traveling between Chetumal and

Belize City stop at Corozal Town. Otherwise, hitch a ride or hire an expensive taxi (US$12) to get you to Santa Elena. From Subteniente López, minibuses shuttle the 12 km to Chetumal frequently all day.

The Santa Elena border station has the requisite government offices and one or two very basic restaurants, nothing more.

Western Belize

Buses depart Belize City heading westward along Cemetery Rd to reach the Western Hwy, a good paved road that penetrates the lush, mountainous western district called Cayo.

BELIZE ZOO
The Belize Zoo and Tropical Education Center (☎ (9) 23310), PO Box 474, Belize City, 46 km west of Belize City and less than one km north of the Western Hwy, is home to a variety of indigenous Belizean cats and other animals kept in natural surroundings.

In 1983, Ms Sharon Matola was in charge of 17 Belizean animals during the shooting of a wildlife film entitled *Path of the Raingods*. By the time filming was over, her animals were partly tame, and thus might not have survived well in the wild. With the movie budget exhausted, there were no funds to support the animals. So Ms Matola founded the Belize Zoo.

The self-guided tour takes from 45 minutes to an hour. You'll see Baird's tapir, Belize's national animal, and the gibnut or paca *(tepezcuintle)*, jaguar, ocelot, howler monkey, peccary, vulture, stork and even a crocodile.

Hours are 9 am to 4:30 pm daily; admission costs US$6.50, and it goes to a worthy cause. The zoo is closed on major Belizean holidays.

See Getting There & Away in the Belize City section for bus information; ask to get out at the Belize Zoo. Look at your watch when you get out; the next bus will come by in about an hour.

GUANACASTE NATIONAL PARK
A few meters north of the junction of the Western and Hummingbird Hwys, right outside Belmopan, is Guanacaste National Park. This small (21 hectare) nature reserve at the confluence of Roaring Creek and the Belize River holds a giant guanacaste tree, which survived the axes of canoe makers and still rises majestically in its forest habitat. The one great tree supports a whole ecosystem of its own, festooned with bromeliads, epiphytes, ferns and dozens of other varieties of plants. Wild orchids flourish in the spongy soil among the ferns and mosses, and several species of 'exotic' animals pass through. Birdlife is abundant and colorful.

Admission is free (donations are accepted). The reserve is open every day from 8 am to 4:30 pm, and seeing the tree takes only about 15 minutes. Stop at the information booth to learn about the short nature trails in the park.

Just west of the highway junction across the bridge is the village of Roaring Creek, with several small restaurants.

BELMOPAN
Population 5000

In 1961, Hurricane Hattie all but destroyed Belize City, and the government resolved to build a new, modern capital city in a more central location, well away from hurricane danger.

Two decades after its founding, Belmopan has begun to come to life. Its population is growing slowly; some embassies have moved here, and when, inevitably, the next killer hurricane arrives, the new capital will no doubt get a population boost.

Unless you need to visit the British High Commission or the US Embassy in Belmopan, you'll probably only stay here long enough to have a snack or a meal at one of the restaurants near the bus stops.

Orientation & Information
Central Belmopan is four km south of the Western Hwy. The bus stops are near the post office, police station, the market and telephone office (see the Belmopan map). The

BELIZE

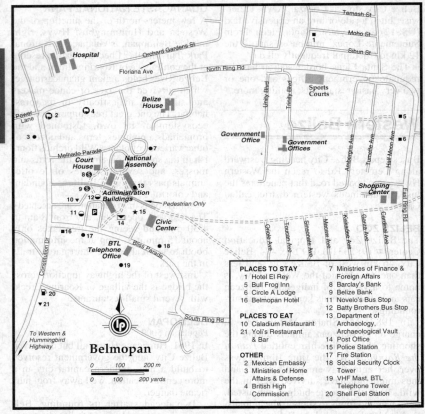

Belmopan

```
0      100      200 m
0      100      200 yards
```

To Western &
Hummingbird
Highway

South Ring Rd

PLACES TO STAY
1 Hotel El Rey
5 Bull Frog Inn
6 Circle A Lodge
16 Belmopan Hotel

PLACES TO EAT
10 Caladium Restaurant
21 Yoli's Restaurant
    & Bar

OTHER
2 Mexican Embassy
3 Ministries of Home
   Affairs & Defense
4 British High
   Commission

7 Ministries of Finance &
   Foreign Affairs
8 Barclay's Bank
9 Belize Bank
11 Novelo's Bus Stop
12 Batty Brothers Bus Stop
13 Department of
    Archaeology,
    Archaeological Vault
14 Post Office
15 Police Station
17 Fire Station
18 Social Security Clock
    Tower
19 VHF Mast, BTL
    Telephone Tower
20 Shell Fuel Station

British High Commission (☎ (8) 22146) is at 34/36 Half Moon Ave; Belmopan also has an office of the US Embassy (☎ (8) 22617).

Things to See

If you're excited about Maya ruins, call and make an appointment for a visit on Monday, Wednesday or Friday afternoon from 1:30 to 4:30 pm, to see the vault at the **state archaeology department** (☎ (8) 22106).

Places to Stay & Eat

Belmopan is a bureaucrats' and diplomats' town, not really one for budget travelers.

The 14-room *Circle A Lodge* (☎ (8) 22296, fax 23616), 35-37 Half Moon Ave, is perhaps the town's oldest hotel, but it still has serviceable doubles for US$25 with fan, US$30 with air conditioning.

A few blocks northwest, the *Hotel El Rey* (☎ (8) 23438), 23 Moho St, is cheapest of all, but cheerless and basic at US$20/25 for a single/double with bath and ceiling fan.

The *Caladium Restaurant* (☎ (8) 22754), opposite Novelo's bus station, offers daily special plates for US$4. *Yoli's*, next to the Shell fuel station on the road into town, is a less convenient alternative.

Getting There & Away

For details on bus transport, see Getting There & Away in the Belize City section.

SAN IGNACIO (CAYO)

Population 8000

San Ignacio, also called Cayo, is a prosperous farming and holiday center in the lovely tropical Macal River valley. In general it's a quiet place whose population includes that of neighboring Santa Elena on the east side of the river. It's a good base from which to explore the natural beauties of Mountain Pine Ridge and to visit the Maya ruins of Xunantunich.

Orientation

The Macal River (also called the Eastern Branch of the Belize River) flows between the twin towns, with San Ignacio to the west of the river and Santa Elena to the east. The towns are joined by the one-lane Hawkesworth Bridge, San Ignacio's landmark suspension bridge. As you come off the western end of the bridge, turn right and you'll be on Burns Ave, the town's main street. Almost everything in town is accessible on foot.

Market day is Saturday, with the marketers setting up behind the Hotel Belmoral at the bus station.

Information

Tourist Offices The town's traditional information exchange is Eva's Restaurant & Bar (see Places to Eat below). The Belize Tourism Industry Association (BTIA) office, in a row of shops off West St, is not always open.

Money Belize Bank, on Burns Ave, is open Monday to Friday from 8 am to 1 pm (also Friday afternoon from 3 to 6 pm) for money exchange. Atlantic Bank is here as well.

Post & Communications The post office is on the upper floor of Government House and is open Monday to Friday from 8 am to noon and 1 to 5 pm, Saturday 8 am to 1 pm.

Belize Telecommunications has an office on Burns Ave north of Eva's in the Cano's Gift Shop building. Opening hours are Monday to Friday from 8 am to noon and 1 to 4 pm, Saturday 8 am to noon. It is closed Sunday. Eva's Restaurant & Bar (☎ /fax (9) 22267, net) has fax and email services.

Medical Services The very simple, basic San Ignacio Hospital (☎ (9) 22066) is up the hill off Waight's Ave, to the west of the center. Across the river in Santa Elena is the Hospital La Loma Luz (☎ (9) 22087, fax (9) 22674), an Adventist hospital and clinic.

Cahal Pech

The best way to visit the hilltop Maya site of Cahal Pech is to take a picnic. It's less than two km uphill from Hawkesworth Bridge. Follow the Buena Vista Rd for a kilometer, uphill and past the San Ignacio and Piache Hotels, until you see a radio antenna and Cahal Pech Village, a hotel with a large thatched main buildings and 14 thatched cabins. Turn left and follow the signs uphill to Cahal Pech.

From the site headquarters building, follow the path down, then up, for 150 meters to the small collection of temples arranged around Plaza B. These have been partially restored, and in some places stuccoed, as they would have been in Classic Maya times. Plaza A is also worth a visit.

The site is open from 9 am to 4:30 pm; admission costs US$5.

Organized Tours

Every hotel and most restaurants in town will want to sign you up for an organized tour. Compare offerings, shop around and talk to other travelers before making your choice. Most of the trips offer a good value, but are not cheap.

Many guides and excursion operators advertise their services at Eva's Restaurant & Bar (see Places to Eat below). Drop by and see what's available.

Boat or canoe trips along the Macal,

BELIZE

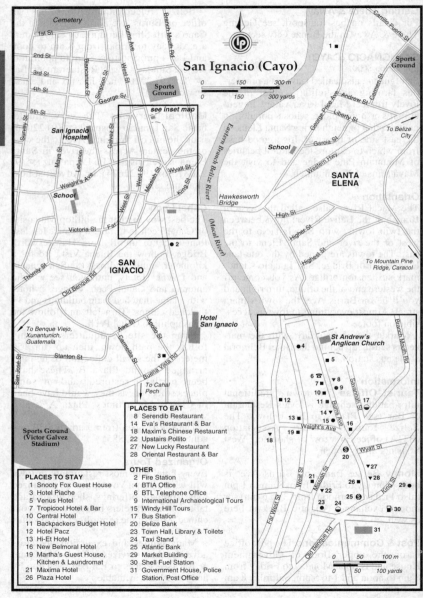

San Ignacio (Cayo)

SANTA ELENA

SAN IGNACIO

To Benque Viejo,
Xunantunich,
Guatemala

To Cahal
Pech

To Belize
City

To Mountain Pine
Ridge, Caracol

Cemetery

San Ignacio
Hospital

School

School

Sports Ground
(Victor Galvez
Stadium)

Hotel
San Ignacio

Sports
Ground

Sports
Ground

Hawkesworth
Bridge

Eastern Branch Belize River

(Macal River)

St Andrew's
Anglican Church

PLACES TO EAT
8 Serendib Restaurant
14 Eva's Restaurant & Bar
18 Maxim's Chinese Restaurant
22 Upstairs Pollito
27 New Lucky Restaurant
28 Oriental Restaurant & Bar

OTHER
2 Fire Station
4 BTIA Office
6 BTL Telephone Office
9 International Archaeological Tours
15 Windy Hill Tours
17 Bus Station
20 Belize Bank
23 Town Hall, Library & Toilets
24 Taxi Stand
25 Atlantic Bank
29 Market Building
30 Shell Fuel Station
31 Government House, Police
   Station, Post Office

PLACES TO STAY
1 Snooty Fox Guest House
3 Hotel Piache
5 Venus Hotel
7 Tropicool Hotel & Bar
10 Central Hotel
11 Backpackers Budget Hotel
12 Hotel Pacz
13 Hi-Et Hotel
16 New Belmoral Hotel
19 Martha's Guest House,
   Kitchen & Laundromat
21 Maxima Hotel
26 Plaza Hotel

Mopan and Belize rivers with a stop at the Rainforest Medicine Trail at Ix Chel Farm on the Macal are popular. Other tours go to a Mennonite community, and the Hershey chocolate company's cacao plantation; the caves at Río Frio; the pools at Río On; the 300-meter waterfall at Hidden Valley (which is less than spectacular in the dry season); the Maya ruins at Caracol; the Tanah Maya Art Museum and Maya slate-carving workshop of the Garcia sisters, just north of San Antonio; and Chechem Ha's Maya ceremonial cave and Vaca Falls. There are also day or overnight excursions to Tikal (Guatemala).

Places to Stay

Martha's Guest House, Kitchen & Laundromat (☎ (9) 23647), 10 West St, is a modern home offering double rooms with shared bath and fan for US$15, good cooking in the ground-floor cafe (see below) and even a laundry, all in a family atmosphere.

Hotel Pacz (☎ (9) 22110), 2 Far West St, is fairly tidy, charging US$15/17/20 for single/double/triple rooms with shared showers.

Hi-Et Hotel (☎ (9) 22828), 12 West St at Waight's Ave, is a simple old house with lots of family atmosphere, clean beds and low rates of US$10/15 for a room with shared bath.

Plaza Hotel (☎ (9) 23332), 4-A Burns Ave, is a good choice, with clean modern rooms with bath for US$20/25, or US$38/45 with air con.

New Belmoral Hotel (☎ (9) 22024), 17 Burns Ave, at Waight's Ave, has 15 serviceable single/double rooms with bath and cable TV for US$15/20 with fan, or US$30/40 with air con.

Maxima Hotel (☎ (9) 23993), on Missiah St, is clean, good and reasonably priced; doubles are US$25 with private bath and fan, US$5 more with air con.

Central Hotel (☎ (9) 22253), 24 Burns Ave, is among the town's cheapest hotels. It charges US$9/12/14 for single/double/triple rooms without running water – it's a bargain. The neighboring *Backpackers*

Budget Hotel competes fiercely for the same clientele.

Venus Hotel (☎ (9) 23203, fax 22186, net), 29 Burns Ave, has 25 rooms with ceiling fans. Most share showers (clean but cramped) and cost US$14/18. Rooms with private shower cost US$20/23. Rooms 10 and 16 have good views of the football field and river.

The *Midas Eco-Resort* (☎ (9) 23172, fax 23845, net), on Branch Mouth Rd, 700 meters from the bus station, has six thatched bungalows all with private bath. The resort's single/double/triple rooms are US$22/25/30. Camping is available at US$3:30/5 for one/ two persons.

At the *Parrot's Nest* (☎ (9) 23702), in Bullet Tree Falls northwest of San Ignacio (US$15 by taxi), guests stay in tree house-like thatched cabins (US$20 double) built high on stilts. Baths are shared; three meals cost US$13 per person. Besides hiking and canoeing, there's horseback riding for only US$18 per day.

Lodges The many lodges in the forests around San Ignacio offer excellent opportunities for hiking, canoeing and kayaking, horseback riding and mountain biking, nature instruction and other outdoor pursuits. They are definitely not budget digs, however, with the typical night's stay costing over US$100 (sometimes well over that), including breakfast and dinner, which you take at the lodge as there is nothing else nearby. For descriptions of lodges, see Lonely Planet's *Guatemala, Belize & Yucatán: La Ruta Maya*.

Places to Eat

Eva's Restaurant & Bar (☎ /fax (9) 22267, net), 22 Burns Ave, is the information and social center. Daily specials at US$4 to US$6 are the best value.

The terrace cafe at *Martha's*, 10 West St, is popular for all three meals, freshly prepared. Breakfasts cost US$4 to US$5, pizzas US$9 to US$11 and sandwiches US$1.50 to US$2.50.

Maxim's Chinese Restaurant, at the corner of Far West St and Bullet Tree Rd, serves fried rice, sweet-and-sour dishes and vegetarian plates, which range in price from US$2.50 to US$5. The restaurant is open from 11:30 am to 2:30 pm and 5 pm until midnight. Other choices for Chinese food are the *New Lucky* and *Oriental* on Burns Ave.

Across Burns Ave and north a few meters from Eva's is the *Serendib Restaurant*, serving Sri Lankan dishes ranging from US$3.50 to US$10. Lunch is served from 9:30 am to 3 pm, dinner from 6:30 to 11 pm.

Several readers have recommended *Upstairs Pollito* on Missiah St.

Getting There & Away
Buses operate to and from Belize City (116 km, 2½ hours, US$2.50), Belmopan (32 km, 45 minutes, US$2) and Benque Viejo (15 km, 20 minutes, US$0.75). For details, see Getting There & Away in the Belize City section.

CAYO DISTRICT
Western Belize has lots of beautiful, unspoiled mountain country dotted with waterfalls and teeming with wild orchids, parrots, keel-billed toucans and other exotic flora and fauna.

Though there is now an unpaved but graded road as far south as the Caracol archaeological site, roads in the Mountain Pine Ridge Forest Reserve are still sometimes impassable from May through October. Relative inaccessibility is one of the reserve's assets, for it keeps this beautiful land in its natural state for visitors willing to see it by 4WD vehicle, on horseback, on foot or along its rivers in canoes. Always check with tour operators in San Ignacio about road conditions, otherwise you may drive deep into the jungle only to be turned back at a forest ranger guardpost. Day tours of Mountain Pine Ridge cost between US$53 and US$79.

Rain Forest Medicine Trail
Formerly called the Pantí Medicine Trail, this herbal-cure research center is at Ix Chel Farm (fax (9) 22267), next to Chaa Creek Cottages, 13 km south of San Ignacio.

Dr Eligio Pantí, who died in 1996, was a healer in San Antonio village who used traditional Maya herb cures.

Dr Rosita Arvigo, an American, studied medicinal plants with Dr Pantí, then began several projects to spread the wisdom of traditional healing methods and to preserve the rain forest habitats that harbor an incredible 4000 species of plants.

One of her projects was the establishment of the Medicine Trail, a self-guiding path among the jungle's natural cures. Admission costs US$5; it's open every day from 8 am to noon and 1 to 5 pm.

Pacbitun
This small Mayan archaeological site 20 km south of San Ignacio near San Antonio seems to have been occupied continuously through most of Maya history from 900 BC to 900 AD.

Today only lofty Plaza A has been uncovered and partially consolidated. Structures 1 and 2, on the east and west sides of the plaza, are worth a look. Within them archaeologists discovered the graves of noble Maya women buried with a variety of musical instruments, perhaps played at their funerals. Most people visit on tours.

Caves
Several caves are open to exploration in the Black Rock Canyon region, including Flour Camp Cave, reached after an uphill hike, and Waterhole Cavern. Barton Creek Cave is best reached by canoe.

Farther south near Vaca Falls, the Chechem Ha (Chumpiate Maya Cave), is a Maya cave complete with ceremonial pots. Members of the Morales family, who discovered the cave, act as guides, leading you up the steep slope to the cave mouth, then down inside, walking and sometimes crouching, to see what the Maya left. A fee of US$25 pays for one to three people. Take water and a flashlight. You can also camp at Chechem Ha,

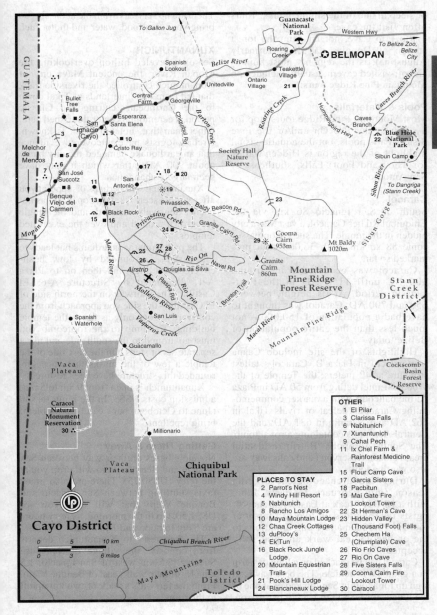

BELIZE

Cayo District

To Gallon Jug

GUATEMALA

Guanacaste National Park
Western Hwy
BELMOPAN
Roaring Creek
To Belize Zoo, Belize City

Belize River
Spanish Lookout
Teakettle Village
Ontario Village
Unitedville
21

Central Farm
Georgeville

Bullet Tree Falls
1

Esperanza
Santa Elena
San Ignacio (Cayo)
9
10
Cristo Ray

3
4
5

Melchor de Mencos

San José Succotz
7
8

Benque Viejo del Carmen

Mopan River

Chiquibul Rd
Barton Creek
Roaring Creek
Society Hall Nature Reserve

Hummingbird Hwy
Caves Branch River
Caves Branch
22
Blue Hole National Park

Sibun River
Sibun Camp
To Dangriga (Stann Creek)

17
18
20
San Antonio
19
11
12
13
14
15
16
Black Rock

23

Privassion Camp
Baldy Beacon Rd
Granite Cairn Rd

Privassion Creek

24

Cooma Cairn 953m
29
Mt Baldy 1020m

Sibun Gorge

Stann Creek District

Macal River

27
28
25
26
Rio On
Navel Rd
Airstrip
Douglas da Silva
Rasna Rd
Rio Frio
Brunton Trail
Granite Cairn 860m

Mountain Pine Ridge Forest Reserve

Mollejon River

San Luis

Vaqueros Creek

Guácamallo
Macal River
Mountain Pine Ridge

Spanish Waterhole

Cockscomb Basin Forest Reserve

Vaca Plateau

Caracol Natural Monument Reservation
30

Millionario

Vaca Plateau

Chiquibul National Park

PLACES TO STAY
2 Parrot's Nest
4 Windy Hill Resort
5 Nabitunich
8 Rancho Los Amigos
10 Maya Mountain Lodge
12 Chaa Creek Cottages
13 duPlooy's
14 Ek'Tun
16 Black Rock Jungle Lodge
20 Mountain Equestrian Trails
21 Pook's Hill Lodge
24 Blancaneaux Lodge

OTHER
1 El Pilar
3 Clarissa Falls
6 Nabitunich
7 Xunantunich
9 Cahal Pech
11 Ix Chel Farm & Rainforest Medicine Trail
15 Flour Camp Cave
17 Garcia Sisters
18 Pacbitun
19 Mai Gate Fire Lookout Tower
22 St Herman's Cave
23 Hidden Valley (Thousand Foot) Falls
25 Chechem Ha (Chumpiate) Cave
26 Rio Frio Caves
27 Rio On Cave
28 Five Sisters Falls
29 Cooma Cairn Fire Lookout Tower
30 Caracol

Chiquibul Branch River

Maya Mountains

Toledo District

0 5 10 km
0 3 6 miles

or sleep in one of the simple bunks. Tours often visit the cave.

Río Frio Cave, not far from the forest station of Douglas da Silva (formerly Augustine), is the region's most famous and oft-visited cavern, usually included on Mountain Pine Ridge tours.

Pools & Waterfalls

Most Mountain Pine Ridge tours stop for a swim at the Río On and/or the Five Sisters Falls pools, but the aquatic visual highlight of the region is Hidden Valley (or Thousand Foot) Falls, southeast of San Antonio.

Caracol

South of San Ignacio 86 km via the Chiquibul Rd lies Caracol, a vast Maya city hidden in the jungle. The site encompasses some 88 sq km, with 36,000 structures marked so far.

Caracol was occupied from around 300 BC until 1150 AD in the Post-Classic period. At its height, between 650 and 700 AD, Caracol was thought to have had a population of 150,000 – not much less than the entire population of Belize today.

Highlights of the site include Caana (sky-palace) in Plaza B, Caracol's tallest structure at 42 meters; the Temple of the Wooden Lintel dating from 50 AD in Plaza A; the ballcourt with a marker commemorating Caracol's defeat of rivals Tikal in 562 AD and Naranjo in 631 AD; and the Central Acropolis containing a royal tomb. The South Acropolis, Barrio residential area, Aguada (reservoir) and causeway are also worth a look.

During the archaeological digging season (mid-February to early June, with a 10-day break at Easter), archaeologists take visitors on two to four-hour tours at 10:30 am and 1 pm; donations to the archaeological work are gratefully accepted.

Caracol can be reached on a long day-trip in a good 4WD vehicle. The best way is to sign up for a tour in San Ignacio or at one of the lodges for US$53 to US$79 per person.

There are no services available at the site, so bring your own food, water and motor fuel.

XUNANTUNICH

Set on a leveled hilltop overlooking the Mopan River, the ancient Maya city of Xunantunich controlled the riverside track that led from the hinterlands of Tikal down to the Caribbean. During the Classic period, a ceremonial center flourished here. Other than that, not too much is known. Archaeologists have uncovered evidence that an earthquake damaged the city badly about 900 AD, after which it may have been largely abandoned.

Xunantunich will perhaps disappoint you after you've seen Tikal or Copán. It has not been extensively restored, and the jungle has grown around and over the excavated temples.

The path from the guardian's hut leads to Plaza A-2, surrounded by low, bush-covered buildings and then on to Plaza A-1, dominated by Structure A-6: El Castillo. The stairway on the north side of El Castillo – the side you approach from the courtyard – goes only as far as the temple building. To climb to the roofcomb you must go around to the south side and use a separate set of steps. On the east side of the temple a few of the masks that once surrounded this structure have been restored.

Xunantunich is open from 9 am to 5 pm; admission costs US$5. In the rainy season (June to October), bugs can be a problem; bring repellent.

Getting There & Away

Novelo's buses on their way between San Ignacio and Benque Viejo will drop you at the ferry (US$0.75). There are also jitney taxis shuttling between San Ignacio and Benque Viejo that will take you for US$1.50. Go in the morning, as ferry hours are 8 am to noon and 1 to 5 pm.

The free ferry to Xunantunich departs from opposite the village of San José Succotz, 8.5 km west of San Ignacio, 1.5 km (15-minute walk) east of Benque Viejo. From the ferry it's a walk of two km uphill to the ruins.

BELIZE

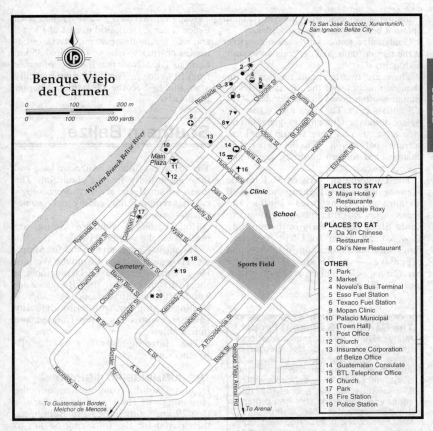

Benque Viejo del Carmen

0   100   200 m
0   100   200 yards

Western Branch Belize River

To San José Succotz, Xunantunich,
San Ignacio, Belize City

Clinic

School

Sports Field

Cemetery

To Guatemalan Border,
Melchor de Mencos

To Arenal

PLACES TO STAY
3 Maya Hotel y
   Restaurante
20 Hospedaje Roxy

PLACES TO EAT
7 Da Xin Chinese
   Restaurant
8 Oki's New Restaurant

OTHER
1 Park
2 Market
4 Novelo's Bus Terminal
5 Esso Fuel Station
6 Texaco Fuel Station
9 Mopan Clinic
10 Palacio Municipal
   (Town Hall)
11 Post Office
12 Church
13 Insurance Corporation
   of Belize Office
14 Guatemalan Consulate
15 BTL Telephone Office
16 Church
17 Park
18 Fire Station
19 Police Station

BENQUE VIEJO DEL CARMEN

Just two km east of the border, Benque
Viejo del Carmen is a foretaste of Guatemala. The name and lingua franca are
Spanish, and the people are Spanish-
speaking Maya or ladinos. The few hotels
and restaurants are very basic. You're
better off staying and eating in San Ignacio
if you can.

Getting There & Away

There are frequent jitney taxis (US$1.50)
and hourly buses (US$0.75) between San
Ignacio and Benque, and a few buses go all

the way to Melchor in Guatemala. From
Benque, taxis shuttle back and forth from
the border charging a high US$4 for the
three-km ride, so you might want to make
the 35-minute walk instead.

CROSSING THE
GUATEMALAN BORDER

Cross early in the morning so as to have the
best chance of catching buses onward. The
border station is supposedly open 24 hours
a day, but officers are usually only on duty
from 6 am to midnight. If you need a
Guatemalan visa, as citizens of most British

Commonwealth countries do, you should obtain it before you reach the border.

Guatemalan tourist cards are obtainable at the border; their cost depends upon your nationality.

There are two banks at the border for changing money, but the itinerant money-changers often give you a better deal – for US dollars cash. The rates for exchanging Belize dollars to Guatemalan quetzals, and vice versa, are very poor. Use up your local currency before you get to the border, then change hard foreign currency, preferably US dollars cash.

The Guatemalan town of Melchor de Mencos has several cheap hotels and restaurants. Transportes Pinita and Transportes Rosalita buses westward to Santa Elena depart early in the morning (3, 4, 5 and 8:30 am) for US$1.50. Sometimes there are more comfortable – and expensive – minibuses (US$10 per person) as well; many travelers feel it is money well spent.

The Garifuna (Garinagu) People

Many of Dangriga's citizens are descendants of the black Caribs, people of mixed South American Indian and African blood, who inhabited the island of St Vincent as a free people in the 17th century. By the end of the 18th century, British colonizers had brought the independent-minded Caribs under their control and transported them from one island to another in an effort to subdue them. In the early 1800s, oppression and wandering finally brought many of the black Caribs to southern Belize. The most memorable migration took place late in 1832, when, in the wake of a failed rebellion against British oppression, a large number of Caribs fled Honduras in dugout canoes, reaching Belizean shores on November 19. The event is celebrated annually in Belize as Garifuna Settlement Day. Dangriga is the place to be on November 19, when the town explodes in a frenzy of dancing, drinking and celebration of the Garifuna heritage. ■

To go on to Tikal, get off the bus at El Cruce (Puente Ixlu), 36 km east of Flores, and wait for another bus, minibus or obliging car or truck to take you the final 35 km north to Tikal. Note that the flow of traffic from El Cruce to Tikal drops dramatically after lunch. See the Guatemala chapter for details.

Southern Belize

The roads to southern Belize are long and they are usually in bad condition. The towns are small, and access to archaeological sites requires time, energy and – sometimes – money.

Both roads to southern Belize are reached via the Western Hwy.

The mostly unpaved Coastal (or Manatee) Hwy goes southeast from the Western Hwy at the village of La Democracia, a short distance past the Belize Zoo. Though the countryside is lush, there's nothing to stop for, and during the rainy summer months it's often flooded and impassable.

The Hummingbird Hwy is the all-weather route.

THE HUMMINGBIRD HIGHWAY

Heading south from Belmopan, the Hummingbird Hwy is unpaved for the first 29 km south and east of Belmopan, then paved for the following 58 km to Dangriga.

St Herman's Cave

About 18 km south of Belmopan, a trail on the right-hand (south) side of the road leads 400 meters south to St Herman's Cave. This large cavern was used by the Maya during the Classic period. The cave entrance is a 60-meter-wide sinkhole. Within the cave it's cool and dark. Don't forget to bring a flashlight.

A rugged nature trail leads 2.5 km east to the Blue Hole. Midway along the trail, a path goes north one mile to the Hummingbird Hwy.

Blue Hole National Park

Just under 20 km south of Belmopan is the visitors' center of the Blue Hole National Park, where underground tributaries of the Sibun River bubble to the surface and fill a deep limestone sinkhole about 33 meters deep and 100 meters in diameter. After running out of the sinkhole and down a short distance, the stream cascades into a domed cavern. Deliciously cool on the hottest days, the cavern makes an excellent swimming hole.

The park is open daily from 8 am to 4 pm. There's another approach trail to the Blue Hole two km southeast of the visitors' center, but parking is not as secure; there have been car break-ins.

DANGRIGA
Population 10,000
Once called Stann Creek Town, this is the largest town in southern Belize. It's much smaller than Belize City but friendlier and quieter.

There's not much to do here except spend the night and head onward – unless it's November 19 (see the sidebar on the Garifuna people).

Orientation & Information

North Stann Creek (also called the Gumaragu River) empties into the Gulf of Honduras at the center of town. Dangriga's main street is called St Vincent St south of the creek and Commerce St to the north. The bus station is at the southern end of St Vincent St just north of the Shell fuel station. The airstrip, two km north of the center, near the Pelican Beach Resort, has Rodney's Place (a cafe) and a small airline building.

The Affordable Corner Store & Laundromat is open from 9 am to noon and 2 to 8 pm (the last wash is at 5 pm). It's closed on Thursday afternoon and on Sunday.

Places to Stay

Pal's Guest House (☎ /fax (5) 22095), 868-A Magoon St, is the best choice, spartan but clean, with a sea breeze and the sound of the surf. Double rooms are US$18 with shared bath, US$24 with private bath and TV.

The tidy, family-run *Bluefield Lodge* (☎ (5) 22742), 6 Bluefield Rd, is recommended; its seven single/double rooms with fan are US$12.50/14.50 with shared bath, or US$17.50 with private bath.

On the south bank of North Stann Creek, at the creek's mouth, are two other cheap choices. The *Río Mar Hotel* (☎ (5) 22201), 977 Southern Foreshore, at the corner of Waight's St, has nine rooms, all with bath and most with TV, for US$18 to US$28, single or double. The upstairs rooms are preferable. The restaurant and bar serve good cheap meals and drinks.

Nearby is *Soffie's Hotel* (☎ (5) 22789), 970 Chatuye St, with 10 serviceable rooms ranging in price from US$22 to US$33, the most expensive having air conditioning; all have private bath. There's a restaurant on the ground floor, and good views of the water from upstairs.

The *Riverside Hotel* (☎ (5) 22168, fax 22296), 5 Commerce St, at the north end of the bridge, has 12 rooms with clean shared showers for US$11 per person.

Bonefish Hotel (☎ (5) 22165, fax 22296), 15 Mahogany St (PO Box 21), is comfortable – the 10 big, clean double rooms have fans, air conditioning, TV and private bath for US$53 to US$75. There's a dining room as well. For reservations in the USA, call ☎ (800) 798-1558.

Places to Eat

Río Mar Hotel and *Soffie's Hotel* both have cheap restaurants. The *Bonefish* is the upmarket place to go.

The *New Riverside Café* on Waight St, 50 meters east of the North Stann Creek Bridge, is run by an expatriate Englishman named Jim, who serves up three tasty meals daily at budget to moderate prices. This is a good place to ask about fishing and snorkeling trips out to the cayes, as well as treks inland.

Otherwise, the locals favor *King Burger*, a tidy lunchroom on Commerce St with a long and varied menu, from burgers to fish fillet and chicken. Their breakfast special of eggs, refried beans, toast and coffee is good at US$2.75.

BELIZE

BELIZE

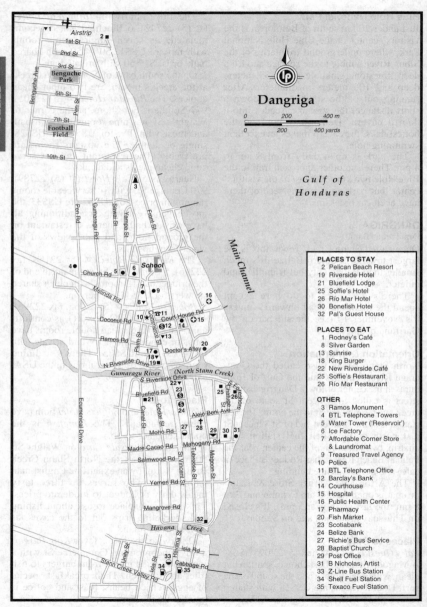

Dangriga

0   200   400 m
0   200   400 yards

Gulf of Honduras

PLACES TO STAY
2   Pelican Beach Resort
19 Riverside Hotel
21 Bluefield Lodge
25 Soffie's Hotel
26 Río Mar Hotel
30 Bonefish Hotel
32 Pal's Guest House

PLACES TO EAT
1   Rodney's Café
8   Silver Garden
13 Sunrise
18 King Burger
22 New Riverside Café
25 Soffie's Restaurant
26 Rio Mar Restaurant

OTHER
3   Ramos Monument
4   BTL Telephone Towers
5   Water Tower ('Reservoir')
6   Ice Factory
7   Affordable Corner Store
    & Laundromat
9   Treasured Travel Agency
10 Police
11 BTL Telephone Office
12 Barclay's Bank
14 Courthouse
15 Hospital
16 Public Health Center
17 Pharmacy
20 Fish Market
23 Scotiabank
24 Belize Bank
27 Richie's Bus Service
28 Baptist Church
29 Post Office
31 B Nicholas, Artist
33 Z-Line Bus Station
34 Shell Fuel Station
35 Texaco Fuel Station

Most of the other restaurants along Commerce St are Chinese: *Sunrise*, *Starlight* and *Silver Garden* serve full meals for about US$6.

Getting There & Away
Air Maya Airways and Tropic Air serve Dangriga. See Getting Around at the beginning of this chapter.

Bus Z-Line has five buses daily from Belize City (via Hummingbird Hwy, 170 km, four hours, US$7; via Coastal Hwy, 79 km, three hours, US$5). Return buses leave Dangriga at 5, 6 and 9 am for Belize City; on Sunday, departures are at 10 am and 3 pm.

Two Z-Line buses (12:15 and 4:30 pm) continue southward to Placencia (85 km, two to 3½ hours, US$4). Richie's Bus Service also has a bus at 5 pm.

Z-Line buses depart Dangriga for Punta Gorda (169 km, six hours, US$5.50), at noon and 7 pm (on Sunday at 2 pm only).

Boat A motor launch departs Puerto Cortés, Honduras, at 8 am on Wednesday and Saturday, arriving in Dangriga at the bridge over North Stann Creek around 12:30 pm, and departing for the return trip

to Puerto Cortés shortly thereafter. The one-way fare is US$35.

SOUTHERN HIGHWAY
The Southern Hwy, south of Dangriga, is unpaved and can be rough going, especially in the rainy months, but along the way are some good opportunities for experiencing untouristy Belize. Some southern reaches of the highway, near Punta Gorda, are being paved.

Hopkins
Population 1100

The farming and fishing village of Hopkins is seven km east of the Southern Hwy, on the coast. Most of its people are Garinagus, living as the coastal inhabitants of Belize have lived for centuries. If you're interested in simple living and Garinagu culture, visit Hopkins and stay at the *Sandy Beach Lodge* (☎ (5) 22023), at the southern end of the village. The lodge, owned and operated by the Sandy Beach Women's Cooperative, has six simple thatched single/double rooms renting for US$13/20 with shared bath, US$20/27 with private bath. Meals cost US$5 for breakfast or dinner, US$7 for lunch. There's also *Jungle Jeanie's* beach

---

Glovers

Glover's Atoll Resort (☎ (1) 48351, (5) 23048), PO Box 563, Belize City, offers an adventurous budget-living experience on the cayes of Glover's Atoll.

Participants help to load and sail their boat, which departs Sittee River Village near Hopkins (south of Dangriga) each Sunday morning at 8 am on the five-km, three- to four-hour voyage to the island. You stay on the island in simple beachfront cabañas – with candles for light, rainwater to drink, an outhouse and so on.

Make a reservation by phone or mail, buy some supplies (food, towels and such), then on Saturday take the 8 am Z-Line bus from Belize City to Sittee River, or the 12:15 pm Z-Line bus from Dangriga to Sittee River, or another bus to the Sittee River junction then hitch to the village and the Glover's Atoll Guesthouse.

You must take some supplies to the island as this is a very simple place, but there's lots of water-sports equipment for rent, excellent diving and very few other people to disturb the tranquillity.

The basic cost is US$102 per person per week for lodging in a beach cabin or tent, US$86 for a camping spot, which includes roundtrip boat transportation between Sittee River and the island (including an average amount of luggage and your small box of supplies) and use of the cooking area. Any other services (drinking water, meals, phone calls, water sports equipment rentals and so on) are at extra cost. ■

huts. The *Swinging Armadillo* has two rooms for rent as well, but they're right next to the bar, and thus noisy.

Sittee River

Another small coastal village where you can get away from it all is Sittee River. *Prospect Cool Spot Guest House and Camp Site* (☎ (5) 22006, 22389; ask for Isaac Kelly, Sr) will put you up in adequate simplicity for US$10/15 for a single/double (US$2.50 in a tent). Simple, inexpensive meals are served.

Cockscomb Basin Wildlife Sanctuary

Almost halfway between Dangriga and Independence is the village of Maya Center, where a track goes 10 km west to the Cockscomb Basin Wildlife Sanctuary, sometimes called the Jaguar Reserve.

Created in 1984, the sanctuary now covers over 40,000 hectares. The varied topography and lush tropical forest make this an excellent place to observe Belizean wildlife.

There's no public transport to the reserve, but the walk through the lush forest is a pretty one. At the reserve is a campsite (US$2 per person), several simple shared cabins available for rent (US$10 per person), a visitors' center and numerous hiking trails.

PLACENCIA

Population 600

Perched at the southern tip of a long, narrow sandy peninsula, Placencia is 'the caye you can drive to.' As on the more popular cayes to the north, activities here include swimming, sunning, lazing, water sports and excursions to other cayes and to points inland.

The village's main north-south 'street' is

Turtle Conservation

Throughout the world there are eight species of sea turtles; all are endangered. Three species inhabit the coasts of Belize.

The green turtle *(Chelonia mydas)*, named for the greenish color of its fat, is prized as food and is the main ingredient in turtle soup. In the wild, it can grow to be more than four feet in length and attain a weight well over 600 pounds. Green turtles have been decimated by hunters and the destruction of their main food source: seagrass.

The loggerhead *(Caretta caretta)* has a large head, short neck, and heart-shaped shell colored red to brown. Females return faithfully to nest on the beach where they themselves were born, usually in June, July or August. They crawl slowly up the beach to a spot above the high tide line, dig a pit and lay up to a hundred white eggs. After covering the eggs with sand, the loggerhead returns to the sea, leaving the eggs to their fate, which may include being eaten by animals, stolen by poachers or stepped on by humans. The eggs that survive these perils hatch after about two months, scratch their way to the surface, wait until nightfall, then crawl down into the sea. Many are eaten by birds, crabs and lizards before reaching the water, or by fish afterward. Only about 5% survive the dangers from egg to reproductive age.

The hawksbill *(Eretmochelys imbricata)* has a narrow bill and a sharp pointed beak. Its shell is not solid but is made up of bony overlapping scales in beautiful colors of orange, brown and gold. Its beauty is the reason it is endangered: sea hunters capture hawksbills to be stuffed and displayed as trophies, or to strip their scales to make into tortoise shell combs, jewelry, eyeglass frames and other items.

What can you do to help turtles survive?

- Don't approach or otherwise disturb or frighten a sea turtle on the beach during nesting season (June through August).
- Don't eat turtle eggs, turtle soup or any other dish made with turtles.
- Don't buy or use any product made from turtle shell.
- Don't litter the beach or seabed with plastic bags.
- Encourage efforts to preserve turtle nesting beaches as natural reserves, staving off resort development. ■

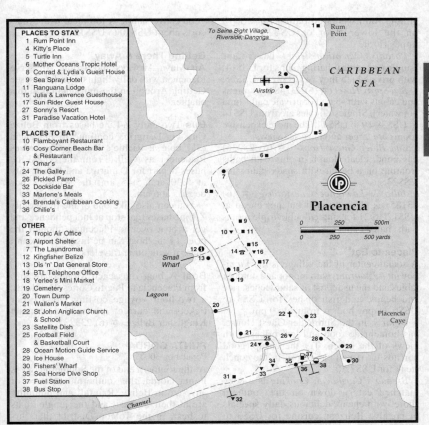

PLACES TO STAY
1 Rum Point Inn
4 Kitty's Place
5 Turtle Inn
6 Mother Oceans Tropic Hotel
8 Conrad & Lydia's Guest House
9 Sea Spray Hotel
11 Ranguana Lodge
15 Julia & Lawrence Guesthouse
17 Sun Rider Guest House
27 Sonny's Resort
31 Paradise Vacation Hotel

PLACES TO EAT
10 Flamboyant Restaurant
16 Cosy Corner Beach Bar
    & Restaurant
17 Omar's
24 The Galley
26 Pickled Parrot
32 Dockside Bar
33 Marlene's Meals
34 Brenda's Caribbean Cooking
36 Chilie's

OTHER
2 Tropic Air Office
3 Airport Shelter
7 The Laundromat
12 Kingfisher Belize
13 Dis 'n' Dat General Store
14 BTL Telephone Office
18 Yerlee's Mini Market
19 Cemetery
20 Town Dump
21 Wallen's Market
22 St John Anglican Church
    & School
23 Satellite Dish
25 Football Field
    & Basketball Court
28 Ocean Motion Guide Service
29 Ice House
30 Fishers' Wharf
35 Sea Horse Dive Shop
37 Fuel Station
38 Bus Stop

To Seine Bight Village,
Riverside; Dangriga

Rum
Point

*CARIBBEAN
SEA*

Airstrip

Placencia

*Small
Wharf*

Lagoon

Placencia
Caye

Channel

BELIZE

actually a narrow concrete footpath less than a meter wide which threads its way 1.5 km among simple wood frame houses (some on stilts) and beachfront lodges.

Information

Placencia has no bank, but you can change travelers checks at Wallen's Market if and when they have enough cash; try in the afternoon.

Laundry service is available at several places, including at The Laundromat (☎ (6) 23123), in the northern part of the village, open from 8 am to 6 pm every day.

Things to See & Do

Unlike most of the cayes, Placencia has good palm-lined beaches on its east side. When you're tired of the beach, contact one of the 16 members of the Placencia Tourist Guide Association and arrange for sailing, snorkeling, scuba diving, fly and sport fishing, bird and manatee watching, overnight camping on remote cayes or excursions to jungle rivers and the Cockscomb Basin Reserve.

Places to Stay

Many houses rent rooms. *Conrad & Lydia's Guest House* (☎ (6) 23117, fax 23354), has simple rooms (shared baths) for US$19 on the lower floor or US$22 on the upper floor.

Paradise Vacation Hotel has rooms (single or double) sharing baths for US$14; with private bath they're US$22 to US$25.

Sea Spray Hotel (☎ (6) 23148) has rooms and cabins with shared or private baths (and hot water). Singles/doubles are from US$14 to US$38/19 to US$44. The more expensive rooms are larger and have sea views.

Sun Rider Guest House (☎ (6) 23236) has good, clean double rooms with baths fronting on a beach with shady palms for US$23.

Julia & Lawrence Guesthouse (☎ (6) 23185) is clean enough but not cheap at US$12/16/21 for single/double/triple rooms with shared baths.

Places to Eat

A social center of the village is the *Flamboyant Restaurant*, with indoor and outdoor tables and the usual list of sandwiches, rice and beans, and fish dishes for US$3 to US$6. Happy hour is from 7 to 9 pm.

Omar's, in the Sun Rider Guest House, has homemade food and low prices, with views of the beach. Try the cheap, good burritos or, if you can afford it, the conch steak for US$7.50.

Brenda's Caribbean Cooking is a cozy thatched eatery down on the southern shore, with cheap, delicious daily specials of creative Belizean cuisine for US$3 to US$5. A few meters to the west is *Marlene's Meals*, run by Brenda's sister, who specializes in snacks and baked goods.

Right by the gas station on the beach is *Chilie's*, a snack stand hangout popular with local boaters. The menu is verbal; a sign boasts 'All you can eat – $5000.'

The *Cosy Corner Beach Bar & Restaurant* is open for lunch and dinner daily, and it goes on with drinks until 2 am. Another good place to hang out late is the *Pickled Parrot*, the restaurant and bar at the Barracuda & Jaguar Inn. Try the enormous pizza for US$15.

The Galley, west of the main part of the village, is a favorite for long dinners with good conversation. A full meal with drinks costs about US$10 to US$15.

Getting There & Away

Air Maya Airways and Tropic Air serve Placencia with daily flights. For details, see Getting Around in the introduction to this chapter.

Bus Two daily Z-Line buses from Belize City via Dangriga continue to Placencia (3½ hours); Richie's Bus Service serves Placencia as well. From there, Z-Line buses depart for Dangriga and Belize City at 5:30 and 5:45 am; the Richie's bus departs at 6 am.

You can also take one of the three daily Z-Line buses that stop at Independence and get a boat over to Placencia, though the price of the boat can be high if you can't share it with other travelers.

Boat A boat runs each Monday (8 am) from Placencia to Puerto Cortés, Honduras, a two-hour voyage costing US$40. For tickets and current information, contact Kingfisher Belize (☎ (6) 23323).

PUNTA GORDA
Population 3000

At the southern end of the Southern Hwy is Punta Gorda, the southernmost town of any size in Belize. Rainfall and humidity are at their highest, and the jungle at its lushest, in the Toledo District that surrounds Punta Gorda. Punta Gordians endure over four meters of rain per year, so be prepared for at least a short downpour almost every day.

Known throughout Belize simply as 'PG,' this sleepy town was founded for the Garinagus who emigrated from Honduras in 1823. Fishing was the major livelihood for almost two centuries, but now farming is important as well.

You will have experienced virtually all of the thrills Punta Gorda offers within a few minutes of your arrival. However, PG is an excellent base for excursions to more exciting places. For ideas, see Around Punta Gorda below.

BELIZE

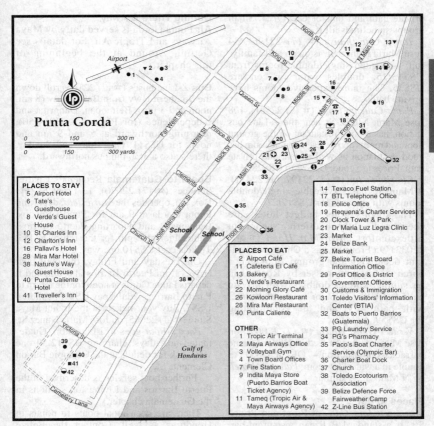

Punta Gorda

PLACES TO STAY
5 Airport Hotel
6 Tate's Guesthouse
8 Verde's Guest House
10 St Charles Inn
12 Charlton's Inn
16 Pallavi's Hotel
28 Mira Mar Hotel
38 Nature's Way Guest House
40 Punta Caliente Hotel
41 Traveller's Inn

PLACES TO EAT
2 Airport Café
11 Cafeteria El Café
13 Bakery
15 Verde's Restaurant
22 Morning Glory Café
26 Kowloon Restaurant
28 Mira Mar Restaurant
40 Punta Caliente

OTHER
1 Tropic Air Terminal
2 Maya Airways Office
3 Volleyball Gym
4 Town Board Offices
7 Fire Station
9 Indita Maya Store (Puerto Barrios Boat Ticket Agency)
11 Tameq (Tropic Air & Maya Airways Agency)
14 Texaco Fuel Station
17 BTL Telephone Office
18 Police Office
19 Requena's Charter Services
20 Clock Tower & Park
21 Dr Maria Luz Legra Clinic
23 Market
24 Belize Bank
25 Market
27 Belize Tourist Board Information Office
29 Post Office & District Government Offices
30 Customs & Immigration
31 Toledo Visitors' Information Center (BTIA)
32 Boats to Puerto Barrios (Guatemala)
33 PG Laundry Service
34 PG's Pharmacy
35 Paco's Boat Charter Service (Olympic Bar)
36 Charter Boat Dock
37 Church
38 Toledo Ecotourism Association
39 Belize Defence Force Fairweather Camp
42 Z-Line Bus Station

Orientation & Information

The town center is the triangular park with a bandstand and the distinctive blue-and-white clock tower. The airstrip is 350 meters to the northwest, and the dock for boats to and from Guatemala is even closer.

The Belize Tourist Board office (☎ (7) 22531) is on Front St and is open every day from 9 am to 5 pm. At the boat dock, the Toledo Visitors' Information Center (☎ (7) 22470), PO Box 73, run by the Belize Tourism Industry Association, is open daily except Thursday and Sunday from 9 am to 1 pm.

Places to Stay

Nature's Way Guest House (☎ (7) 22119) is the intrepid travelers' gathering place. This converted house has waterless rooms with clean, shared, cold showers. It charges US$9/14/18 for singles/doubles/triples. Trips by minibus and boat can be arranged to all points of interest around Punta Gorda.

The sleepy *Airport Hotel*, near the airport, is quiet and identical in price.

St Charles Inn (☎ (7) 22149), 23 King St, offers a good value with clean and well-kept (for PG) single/double rooms with private bath and fan for US$17/23. Small groups sometimes fill it.

Tate's Guesthouse (☎ (7) 22196), 34 José María Nuñez St, is clean and family-run, with good single/double rooms from US$13/15; doubles with air con are US$35. The more expensive rooms have private bath.

Punta Caliente Hotel (☎ (7) 22561), 108 José Maria Nuñez St near the Z-Line bus station, has a good restaurant on the ground floor and rooms above. Each double room has good ventilation as well as fan, and private bath. Prices are good: US$22 to US$28.

Charlton's Inn (☎ (7) 22197, fax 22471), 9 Main St, has serviceable single/double rooms with showers for US$17/23.

The town's other budget hotels are cheap, and rightly so, offering shelter but little comfort. *Mira Mar Hotel* (☎ (7) 22033), 95 Front St, has a Chinese restaurant occupying the ground floor and a porch for watching passersby. Rooms can be simple, singles/doubles with private bath for US$14/26, or more elaborate, with bath, TV and air conditioning for US$59.

Verde's Guest House (☎ (7) 22069), on José Maria Nuñez St, is the standard frame barracks construction – OK at US$11 a double in a waterless room. *Pallavi's Hotel*, on N Main St, is similar.

Places to Eat

Morning Glory Café, at Front and Prince Sts, is a standard Belizean restaurant-bar, more attractive than most. Hours are 7 am to 2 pm and 6:30 to 11 pm (closed on Monday off-season).

Punta Caliente serves stewed pork, fish fillet, beans and rice with chicken and similar dishes for US$3.50 to US$5, and it's all good. *Mira Mar* and *Kowloon* are the places to go for Chinese food for only slightly more.

Cafeteria El Café is a tidy place open for breakfast and lunch.

The *Airport Café* has good, big plates of rice, beans, cabbage and red snapper for US$3.75. It's a good place to meet other travelers.

Getting There & Away

Air Punta Gorda is served daily by Maya Airways and Tropic Air. For details see Getting Around at the beginning of this chapter.

Bus Z-Line buses (☎ (7) 22165) roll down the Southern Hwy from Belize City (8 am, noon and 3 pm), Belmopan, Dangriga and Independence (for Placencia, US$4.50), returning northward at 5 and 9 am and noon, for US$11. On Friday and Sunday, there's also a 3:30 pm bus northward.

Boats to Guatemala Requena's Charter Services (☎ (7) 22070), 12 Front St (PO Box 18), operates the *Mariestela*, departing Punta Gorda at 9 am for Puerto Barrios, Guatemala, and departing Puerto Barrios' Public Pier at 2 pm for the return to PG. Tickets cost US$10 one way.

On Tuesday and Friday, the mail boat arrives from Puerto Barrios at 9 am, and it departs Punta Gorda at noon for the return to Puerto Barrios. Adults pay US$10, children US$7. Buy your tickets at the Indita Maya Store (☎ (7) 22065) on José María Nuñez St.

Paco's Boat goes to Lívingston, Guatemala, most days, charging US$12.50 one way. Ask for details at the Olympic Bar on Clements St.

(Further boat service is described in the Puerto Barrios and Lívingston sections in the Guatemala chapter.)

There are occasional boats to points in Honduras as well. Contact the Belize Tourism Board office for information.

The boats to Punta Gorda (Belize) also leave Lívingston at 7:30 am on Tuesdays and Fridays. This is a shorter trip, taking just 45 minutes; cost is US$12 each way. The boats depart Punta Gorda for the return trip at 10:30 am. Get your own exit stamp from the immigration office in Lívingston; the captain will take you to get your entry stamp in Punta Gorda.

AROUND PUNTA GORDA

Two organizations can help you get a close-up-and-personal look at traditional village life in the Toledo District.

Toledo Ecotourism Association

The Toledo Ecotourism Association (☎ (7) 22119, fax (7) 22199, net), Nature's Way Guesthouse, 65 N Front St (PO Box 75), Punta Gorda, runs a Village Guesthouse and Ecotrail Program that takes participants to any of 13 traditional Mopan Maya, Kekchi, Creole and Garifuna villages.

The basic village guesthouse tour includes overnight lodging in a village home, three meals (each at a different village home), and two nature tours for US$43. The full tour adds music, dancing and storytelling for US$88.

These prices cover your village stay and activities, but not transportation. Local buses run between the villages and Punta Gorda on Wednesday and Saturday for US$5; special charter trips are very expensive – around US$80 – so plan accordingly.

Dem Dats Doin

Dem Dats Doin (☎ (7) 22470), PO Box 73, Punta Gorda, is an innovative ecological farm founded by Antonio and Yvonne Villoria. The farm is a showcase of what a determined, sensitive and knowledgeable couple can do to promote appropriate technology and sustainable farming: photovoltaic cells for electricity, biogas methane for light and refrigeration, natural insect repellents and fertilizers in place of chemicals.

A tour of the farm costs US$5 and takes between one and two hours. Bed and breakfast is sometimes available; check in advance.

The Villorias also supervise a program for home stays with Maya families, called **The Indigenous Experience**. They will put you in touch with a village family, who will welcome you into their home, provide you with a hammock and meals and also let you share in their traditional way of life.

Hammock rental is US$4 per night; meals cost US$1.50 each. The Villorias ask a US$5 fee for putting you in touch with a family. You should inquire in advance by mail if possible, and enclose US$2 to pay for postage and printing.

Lubaantun

The Maya ruins at Lubaantun, two km northwest of San Pedro Columbia village, are aptly named. Lubaantun (Fallen Stones) has been excavated to some extent, but not restored. The many temples are still mostly covered with jungle.

The archaeologists have found evidence that Lubaantun flourished until the late 700s, after which little was built. In its heyday, the merchants of Lubaantun traded with people on the cayes, in Mexico and Guatemala, and perhaps beyond.

Of its 18 plazas, only the three most important (plazas III through V) have been cleared. Plaza IV, the most important, is built along a ridge of hills and is surrounded by the site's most impressive buildings: structures 10, 12 and 33.

Getting There & Away San Pedro Columbia is 41 km northwest of Punta Gorda off the Southern Hwy. A bus can drop you at the fuel station on the highway; from here it's a walk of almost six km to the village. If you catch a San Antonio bus from the main plaza in Punta Gorda, it will get you 2.5 km closer to San Pedro.

Nim Li Punit

About 38 km northwest of Punta Gorda, just north of Big Falls and less than a kilometer west of the Southern Hwy, stand the ruins of Nim Li Punit, a less-impressive site than Lubaantun. Nim Li Punit (big hat), named for the headgear worn by the richly clad figure on Stela 14, may in fact have been a tributary city to larger, more powerful Lubaantun.

The South Group of structures was the city's ceremonial center and is of the most interest. The plaza has been cleared, but the structures surrounding it are largely unrestored. Have a look at the stelae, especially No 14, at almost 10 meters the longest Maya stelae yet discovered, and No 15, dating from 721 AD, the earliest dated work recovered here.

BELIZE

San Antonio & Blue Creek

The Mopan Maya of San Antonio are descended from former inhabitants of the Guatemalan village of San Luis Petén, just across the border. The San Antonians fled oppression in their home country to find freedom in Belize. They brought their ancient customs with them, however, and you can observe a traditional lowland Maya village on a short visit here. If you are here during a festival, your visit will be much more memorable.

About six km west of San Antonio, near the village of Santa Cruz, is the archaeological site of Uxbenka, with numerous carved stelae.

South of San Antonio about 15 km lies the village of Blue Creek, and beyond it the nature reserve of Blue Creek Cave. Hike into the site (less than a kilometer) along the marked trail and enjoy the rain forest around you, as well as the pools, channels, caves and refreshingly cool waters of the creek system.

Places to Stay There is one small hotel in San Antonio: *Bol's Hilltop Hotel*, with beds for US$5. If you'd prefer not to stay the night, arrange a day excursion from Punta Gorda.

Getting There & Away The San Antonio bus departs from the village each morning at 5 am for Punta Gorda and returns from Punta Gorda at 4 pm. The best way to get around this area is on a tour organized by the Toledo Ecotourism Association (see above).

Honduras

The second largest of the Central American countries, Honduras has a cool, mountainous interior and a long, warm Caribbean coastline. Travel is easy, enjoyable and inexpensive.

Among the better known Honduran attractions are the spectacular Maya ruins at Copán near the Guatemalan border, with its pyramids, temples and intricately carved stelae (standing stone monuments). Also popular with travelers are the Bay Islands (Islas de Bahía), the idyllic Caribbean islands just off the north coast. Roatán is the most popular and probably most beautiful of the islands, but the smaller Utila also has many aficionados. The coral reefs here are a continuation of the barrier reef off Belize, which is the second-largest barrier reef in the world. These reefs are excellent for diving and snorkeling.

Several of the Caribbean beach towns, most notably Tela and Trujillo, have fine beaches, plenty of coconut palms, wonderful seafood, lots of opportunities for walking and interesting places to visit nearby. The capital city, Tegucigalpa, in the central highlands is surrounded by piney mountains and has a temperate climate.

Less well known are the national parks and nature reserves. La Tigra, just a few kilometers from the capital, is a lush, cool cloud forest. Several other cloud forests are also protected in national parks – La Muralla, Celaque, Cusuco and Pico Bonito are the most accessible for visitors.

Coastal and marine parks protect coastlands, wetlands and lagoons inhabited by manatees and other wildlife and birdlife. The Río Plátano biosphere reserve, a World Heritage Site, protects a pristine river system flowing through tropical rain forest in the Mosquitia region, one of Central America's large wilderness areas.

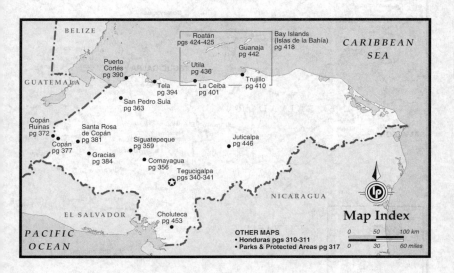

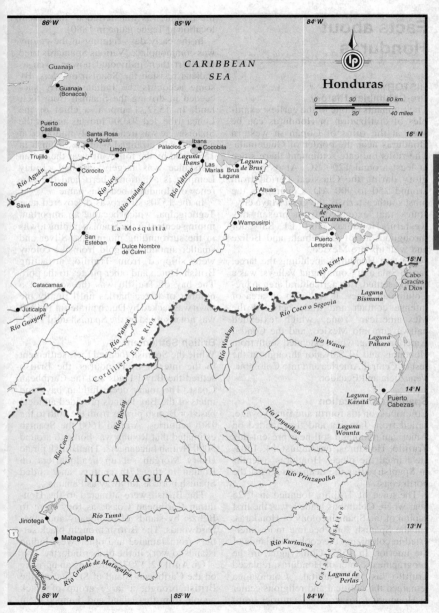

Facts about Honduras

HISTORY
Pre-Columbian History

The remnants of one of the earliest examples of civilization in Honduras can be seen at the ruins of Copán in western Honduras near the border of Guatemala. The ruins indicate settlement there since at least around 1200 BC. At its highest glory during the Classical Period from around 250 to 900 AD, Copán was the most southeasterly of the great Maya city-states that extended from present-day western Honduras and El Salvador throughout all of Guatemala and Belize and well up into Mexico.

Western Honduras, including the large, fertile Sula and Comayagua Valleys, was a heavily settled, rich agricultural area in pre-Columbian times. It was also an area of intense contact and trade between the Mesoamerican zone, which extended halfway up into Mexico, and the Central American zone, which extended south from Honduras and El Salvador throughout the rest of Central America and into Colombia, Venezuela and Ecuador.

Spanish Colonization

Columbus, on his fourth and final voyage, sailed from Jamaica and first landed on American mainland soil near present-day Trujillo, Honduras, on August 14, 1502. He named the place 'Honduras' (depths in Spanish) after the deep waters off the north coast.

The town of Trujillo, founded in 1525 near where Columbus landed, was the first capital of the Spanish colony of Honduras, but the Spanish soon became more interested in colonizing the cooler highlands of the interior. In 1537, Comayagua, in the geographical center of Honduras, replaced Trujillo as the capital. Comayagua remained the political and religious center of Honduras for over three centuries (until the capital was transferred to its present location at Tegucigalpa in 1880).

In the early days fighting in the colony was commonplace. Various Spaniards tried to assert their individual power, even as Indians resisted the Spanish invaders. By some accounts the Indians nearly succeeded in driving the Spanish from their land. In 1537, Lempira, a chief of the Lenca tribe, led 30,000 Indians against the Spanish. He was treacherously murdered at a peace talk arranged with the Spanish in 1538, and by the following year the Indian resistance was largely crushed. Today Lempira is a national hero, and the currency of Honduras bears his name.

In the 1570s silver was discovered near Tegucigalpa, which became an important mining center for the Spanish mining towns in the surrounding mountains. Silver and smaller amounts of gold from the colony were shipped from Trujillo, attracting British, Dutch and other pirates to the port. The bay of Trujillo was the scene of a number of fierce battles until finally the town was sacked by Dutch pirates in 1643. It was not resettled by the Spanish until 1787.

British Settlement

While the Spanish focused their settlement in the interior of Honduras, the British settled the Bay Islands and the Caribbean Coast. The many deep, hidden bays and inlets of the Bay Islands provided an ideal base for British pirates from the 16th to the 18th centuries. Around 1600 the Spanish estimated that Roatán was home to around 5000 British buccaneers. The British pirate Henry Morgan set up headquarters on Roatán in the 17th century and raided Spanish ports as far away as Panama.

The British were attracted to the Honduran Caribbean Coast, as they were to Belize, by stands of mahogany and other hardwoods. The British brought black settlers from Jamaica and other West Indian islands to work in the timber industry.

On April 12, 1797, following an uprising on the Caribbean island of St Vincent, the British brought a large group of black people from that island and dumped them off at Port Royal on the island of Roatán. These people survived, prospered and multiplied; they crossed over to the mainland and eventually fanned out in small fishing settlements all along the Honduran coast. They were the ancestors of Honduras' Garífuna people.

Following an appeal to the British by chiefs of the Miskito Indians, a British protectorate was declared over the entire Mosquitia region, extending from Honduras far into Nicaragua.

Spain was never happy with the British control of the coast, but the British ruled the territory until 1859, when they relinquished the lands to Honduras. The British influence is still evident today, especially on the Bay Islands, where English is the principal language.

Independence

After independence from Spain in 1821, Honduras was briefly part of independent Mexico and then a member of the Central American Federation. The Honduran liberal hero General Francisco Morazán was elected president of the United Provinces in 1830. The union was short-lived, however, largely due to continuing conflicts between liberals and conservatives, and Honduras declared its independence as a separate nation on November 5, 1838.

The liberal and conservative factions continued to wrestle for power in Honduras after independence. Power alternated between the two factions, and Honduras was ruled by a succession of civilian governments and military regimes. (The country's constitution would be rewritten 17 times in the years between 1821 and 1982.) Government has officially been by popular election, but Honduras has experienced literally hundreds of coups, rebellions, power seizures, electoral 'irregularities' and other manipulations of power since achieving independence.

Trujillo gained the spotlight in Central American history once again in 1860 when William Walker, an American who attempted to take over Central America and in fact did gain control of Nicaragua for a time, made his final ill-fated attack on

Central America at Trujillo. His campaign ended in defeat, and he was captured and executed by firing squad.

The 'Banana Republic'

Where William Walker failed to gain control of Honduras for the USA, free enterprise succeeded.

Around the end of the 19th century, US traders took an interest in bananas produced on the fertile north coast of Honduras, just a short sail from the southern USA. With the development of refrigeration the banana industry boomed, and new markets opened up in the USA and Europe.

US entrepreneurs who wanted to buy land for growing bananas were offered generous incentives to do so by a succession of Honduran governments. The three major companies were the Vaccaro brothers (later to become Standard Fruit), which operated around La Ceiba; the Cuyamel Fruit Company near the Río Cuyamel and Tela; and after 1912, United Fruit, to the east, which by 1929 had swallowed up Cuyamel. The three companies owned a large part of northern Honduras, and by 1918, 75% of all Honduran banana lands were held by US companies.

Bananas provided 11% of Honduras' exports in 1892, 42% in 1903 and 66% in 1913. The economic success of the banana industry made the banana companies extremely powerful within Honduras, with policy and politicians controlled by banana company interests. Cuyamel allied itself with the Liberal Party, United Fruit with the National Party, and the rivalries between banana companies shaped Honduran politics.

Honduras failed to develop an indigenous landholding elite, unlike Guatemala, El Salvador and Nicaragua. Instead the economy and politics of the country became controlled by US banana interests.

20th-Century Politics

Along with economic involvement came increasing influence from the USA in various sectors of Honduran affairs, especially in the military. In 1911 and 1912, when it appeared the US banana interests were threatened by political developments, US president William Howard Taft sent US Marines into Honduras to 'protect US investments.'

During the worldwide economic depression of the 1930s, in the midst of civil unrest, General Tiburcio Carías Andino was elected president, establishing a virtual dictatorship that lasted from 1932 until 1949.

In 1954 the USA and Honduras signed a military pact that promised military training and equipment to Honduras in return for unlimited US access to raw materials should the need arise. In 1957 a new constitution put the military officially out of the control of civilian government, and the military then entered politics as an independent power.

Various elections and coups have come and gone, but whether the government has been civilian or military, the military has maintained much control. In 1963 Colonel Osvaldo López Arrellano led a military coup and ruled as president until he was forced to resign because of a scandal involving his acceptance of US$1.25 million in bribes from a US company, United Brands. He was replaced by Colonel Juan Alberto Melgar Castro, but he in turn was ousted by another military coup in 1978, led by General Policarpo Paz García.

The 'Football War'

In 1969, during the rule of Arrellano, Honduras and El Salvador had a brief war known as the Guerra de Fútbol (the Football War or Soccer War).

In the 1950s and 1960s El Salvador's severe overpopulation and economic crisis led to 300,000 Salvadorans illegally crossing the border into Honduras. In 1969, 500 Salvadorans were sent back to El Salvador, and they were followed by a wave of 15,000 Salvadoran refugees alleging mistreatment at the hands of the Hondurans.

In the midst of this, in June 1969, the two countries were competing in World Cup qualifying soccer matches. At the game in San Salvador, visiting Honduran fans were attacked by Salvadorans. Honduras retaliated by evicting thousands more Salvadoran immigrants. El Salvador closed off its

borders, and amid more allegations of abuse against Salvadorans in Honduras, El Salvador invaded Honduran territory on July 14 and bombed Honduran airports.

The war lasted only 100 hours, but the two countries were at odds for over a decade until a peace treaty was signed in 1980. However, relations between the two countries remained strained, especially during the 1980s when El Salvador erupted into civil war, sending fresh waves of refugees across the border into Honduras.

The 1980s

During the 1980s Honduras was surrounded by the turmoil of Central American political developments. In July 1979, the revolutionary Sandinista movement in Nicaragua overthrew the Somoza dictatorship, and Somoza's national guardsmen fled into Honduras. Civil war broke out in El Salvador in 1980 and continued in Guatemala.

Though Honduras experienced some unrest, Honduran politics were far more conservative. This can be attributed largely to the strong US influence, which helped direct the course of Honduran politics and created a strong Honduran military capable of crushing any armed insurrection. Honduran government land reforms between 1962 and 1980 also showed that reform was possible through established channels.

With revolutions erupting on every side, and especially with the success of the Nicaraguan revolution in 1979, Honduras became the focus of US policy and strategic operations in the region.

The USA pressured the government to hold elections after 17 years of military rule. A civilian, Dr Roberto Suazo Córdova, was elected president, but real power rested with the commander-in-chief of the armed forces, General Gustavo Álvarez, who supported an increasingly military US policy in Central America.

With Ronald Reagan's ascendance to the presidency of the USA in January 1981, US military involvement increased dramatically. The USA funneled huge sums of money and thousands of US troops into Honduras as it conducted provocative maneuvers clearly designed to threaten Nicaragua. Nicaraguan refugee camps in Honduras were used as bases for a US-sponsored undeclared covert war against the Nicaraguan government, which became known as the Contra war. At the same time the USA was training the Salvadoran military at Salvadoran refugee camps inside Honduras near the border of El Salvador.

Public alarm and opposition to the US militarization of Honduras increased in the country during 1983, creating problems for the Honduran government. In March 1984, General Álvarez was toppled in a bloodless coup by his fellow officers. General Walter López Reyes was appointed his successor, and before long it was announced that Honduras was planning to reexamine its role as the military base of the USA in the region. In August the Honduran government suspended US training of Salvadoran military within its borders.

The 1985 presidential election, beset by serious irregularities, was won by the Liberal Party candidate José Simeón Azcona del Hoyo, who had obtained only 27% of the votes, while Rafael Leonardo Callejas Romero of the National Party, who had obtained 42% of the votes, lost.

Despite growing disquiet in Washington after the revelations of the Iran-Contra affair in 1986, the Contra war escalated. In 1988 around 12,000 Contras operated from Honduras. Public anger in Honduras increased – anti-US demonstrations drew 60,000 demonstrators in Tegucigalpa and 40,000 in San Pedro Sula – forcing the Honduran government to declare a state of emergency. Finally, in November 1988, the Honduran government refused to sign a new military agreement with the USA, and President Azcona said the Contras would have to leave Honduras. With the election of Violeta Chamorro as president of Nicaragua in 1990, the Contra war ended and the Contras were finally out of Honduras.

The 1990s

Elections in 1989 ushered in Rafael Leonardo Callejas Romero of the National Party, who had lost in 1985, to the presidency in Honduras; he won 51% of the votes and assumed office in January 1990. Early that year, the new administration instituted a severe economic austerity program, which provoked widespread alarm, unrest and protest.

Callejas had promised to keep the lempira stable, but instead, once he was in office, the lempira was devalued. During his four years in office, the lempira went from about 2:1 to the US dollar to 8:1. Prices in lempiras rose dramatically to keep pace with the US dollar, but salaries did not rise, so the Honduran people became continually poorer and poorer – a trend that continues today. Callejas kept assuring the public that the economy had to be tightened temporarily due to the national debt and that soon everything would be better.

Other things happened, however, that started to make the Callejas regime look increasingly suspect. News of a scandal called the 'Chinazo' disclosed the sale of Honduran passports to Hong Kong citizens for astronomical sums, and there were also several other scandals involving Callejas, the armed forces and the judiciary.

In the elections of November 1993 the National Party candidate was convincingly beaten by Carlos Roberto Reina Idiaquez of the center-right Liberal Party, who campaigned on a platform of moral reform, promising to attack government corruption and reform state institutions, including the judicial system and the military. Reina took office in January 1994.

In November 1994, the public prosecutor's office filed formal charges of corruption against former president Callejas and 12 of his former ministers. Apparently Callejas had enriched himself while in office to the tune of several million dollars. Callejas replied that the charges were nothing but political persecution and threatened to take vengeful legal action. In 1996 further intrigues of the Chinazo scam were continuing to surface and make headlines, with more and more officials being implicated.

When Reina became president, he assumed control of an economically suffering country. After he took office, the lempira continued to devalue: By 1996 it had slid past 12:1 to the US dollar and was heading for 13:1. Prices in lempiras kept rising to keep pace with the dollar, while salaries continued to be frozen, and the country as a whole was extremely concerned about where it would all end.

GEOGRAPHY

Honduras is the second-largest country in Central America (after Nicaragua), with an area of 112,492 sq km. This includes 288 sq km of territory formerly disputed with El Salvador and added to Honduras in the September 1992 judgment of the International Court of Justice. Honduras is bordered on the north by the Caribbean Sea, on the west by Guatemala, on the south by El Salvador and the Golfo de Fonseca, and on the east and southeast by Nicaragua. The Caribbean Coast is 644 km long, but the Pacific Coast on the Golfo de Fonseca is only 124 km. Honduras possesses many islands, including the Bay Islands and Swan Islands in the Caribbean and a number of islands in the Golfo de Fonseca.

Honduras is a mountainous country; around 65 to 80% of the total land area is composed of rugged mountains ranging from 300 to 2850 meters high, with many highland valleys. Lowlands are found only along both coasts and in several river valleys.

CLIMATE

The mountainous interior is much cooler than the coastal lowlands. Tegucigalpa, at an elevation of 975 meters, has a temperate climate, with maximum/minimum temperatures varying from 25/14°C in January to 30/18°C in May. The coastal lowlands are much warmer and more humid year round, the Pacific coastal plain near the Golfo de Fonseca being hot indeed. December and January are the coolest months.

The rainfall also varies in different parts of the country. The rainy season runs from around May to October. On the Pacific side and in the interior this means a relatively dry season from around November to April. However, the amount of rain and when it falls varies considerably from year to year.

On the Caribbean Coast it rains year round, but the wettest months are from September to January or February. During this time floods can occur on the north coast, impeding travel and occasionally causing severe damage (400 people died in floods in November 1993).

Hurricane season is June to November.

ECOLOGY & ENVIRONMENT

Deforestation is a problem in Honduras; it proceeds at a rate of 300,000 hectares (3000 sq km) a year. At this rate, the country could become completely deforested within 20 years.

However, here as in other Central American countries, conservationists and a number of ecology-minded organizations are working to halt this trend, set aside protected areas and increase public awareness of conservation. Honduras now has 40 protected areas – mainly national parks and wildlife refuges – and more areas have been proposed for reserves.

Still, conservation is a tense subject, since in many places the wishes of conser-

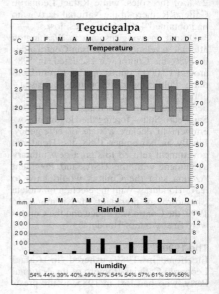

Tegucigalpa

Temperature

Rainfall

Humidity
54% 44% 39% 40% 49% 57% 54% 54% 57% 61% 59% 56%

vationists and government decrees seeking to protect natural areas come into direct conflict with a growing population that wants to settle and agriculturalize virgin lands. Conflicts have also arisen between conservationists and moneyed interests wanting to fund large-scale tourist developments, as happened at Punta Sal near Tela, which resulted in the 1995 murder of conservation activist Jeannette Kawas before the area was finally declared a national park.

FLORA & FAUNA

Honduras is rich in both flora and fauna. The country has a number of different life zones at various elevations, ranging from low-elevation tropical rain forests to high-altitude cloud forests, with each zone comprising its own complex system of flora and fauna. The dominant vegetation of the mountainous interior of the country is pine-and-oak forest.

Some of Honduras' most interesting animals are becoming endangered, primar-ily due to loss of habitat. The national bird, the *guara roja* or scarlet macaw, is on the endangered species list, as are some species of *loras* (parrots), manatees, jaguars and others. Nevertheless, there's still plenty of wildlife to see in Honduras, especially in the national parks, wildlife reserves and other protected areas, where wildlife abounds. As more areas become protected, populations of depleted species may be saved from early extinction.

Honduras is excellent for birding, and bird watching is becoming a popular activity. See the Bird Watching section below for hints on where to see birds.

National Parks

Honduras has 40 protected areas, including 20 national parks and a number of important wildlife refuges, biological reserves, an anthropological reserve and a biosphere reserve. The following is a complete list of the national parks. Some of these areas are easy to reach, while some are very remote;

HONDURAS

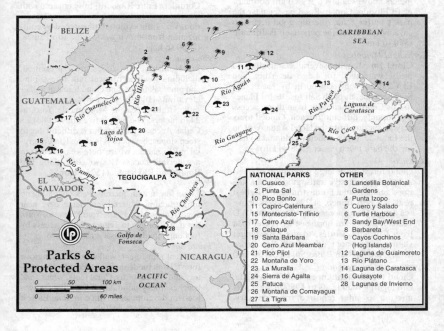

NATIONAL PARKS
1 Cusuco
2 Punta Sal
10 Pico Bonito
11 Capiro-Calentura
16 Montecristo-Trifinio
17 Cerro Azul
18 Celaque
19 Santa Bárbara
20 Cerro Azul Meambar
21 Pico Pijol
22 Montaña de Yoro
23 La Muralla
24 Sierra de Agalta
25 Patuca
26 Montaña de Comayagua
27 La Tigra

OTHER
3 Lancetilla Botanical Gardens
4 Punta Izopo
5 Cuero y Salado
6 Turtle Harbour
7 Sandy Bay/West End
8 Barbareta
9 Cayos Cochinos (Hog Islands)
12 Laguna de Guaimoreto
13 Río Plátano
14 Laguna de Caratasca
16 Guisayote
28 Lagunas de Invierno

Parks & Protected Areas

0   50   100 km
0   30   60 miles

the ones marked with an asterisk are the most accessible (and are discussed at length later in this chapter)

Here's a complete list of the national parks:

Capiro-Calentura
Tropical wet forest, beautiful view of Valle de Aguán and the Caribbean. Radar base on summit of Cerro Calentura, at 1235 meters. Old Spanish cobblestone road leading to cave. Easy access from Trujillo. (50 sq km)

Celaque
Cloud forest; elevated plateau with four peaks over 2800 meters above sea level; including the highest peak in Honduras, at 2827 meters above sea level. Great biodiversity. Access easy, 7.5 km east of Gracias by 4WD vehicle, to the ranger station; other access is through Belén Gualcho, Ocotepeque. (667 sq km)

Cerro Azul
Cloud forest, hot springs, caves with interesting formations, nearby archaeological sites. Highest peak is Cerro Azul, at 2285 meters above sea level. It's 10 km northeast of El Florido, Copán. Road passes near the park's buffer zone, offering good access to cave, but access to the park itself is difficult. (370 sq km)

Cerro Azul Meambar
Cloud forest, with several waterfalls and trails; watershed for Lago de Yojoa and El Cajón. It's 30 km north by road from Siguatepeque, through San José de los Planes to Los Cedros, then walk from there; access by foot only, difficult to reach. Guided tours may be starting from the Hotel Agua Azul on the Lago de Yojoa, which would make visiting the park much easier. (528 sq km)

Cusuco
Cloud forest, with large population of quetzals; has interpretive trails, guides and a visitors' center under construction. Highest peak is Cerro Jilinco, at 2242 meters above sea level. Good access all year with 4WD vehicle; it's 25 km northeast by gravel road from Cofradía, Cortés, to the park ranger station, a two-hour drive from San Pedro Sula. Office in San Pedro Sula. (247 sq km)

Montaña de Comayagua
Cloud forest, eight km east of Comayagua. Old logging road leads to 1980 meters; permission to enter required from military. (445 sq km)

Montaña de Yoro
Cloud forest, with high water production and indigenous population of Tolupan (Jicaque or Xicaque) people. Highest point is Montaña de Yoro, at 2283 meters. Eight km southeast of Yoro. Access difficult. (383 sq km)

Montecristo-Trifinio
Cloud forest, with steep canyons and rugged terrain. At the junction of Honduras, Guatemala and El Salvador, the park contains territory from all three countries. Highest peak is Cerro Montecristo, 2450 meters above sea level. It's 16 km west of Nueva Ocotepeque. From the Honduras side, access is difficult, requiring five hours' hike to reach the park; access is easiest from the El Salvador side, through Metapán, where there are trails, guides and a visitors' center. (133 sq km)

La Muralla
Cloud forest, with visitors' center, marked trails and camping sites. High biodiversity, including large quetzal population. It's 15 km north of La Unión, Olancho; easy access by road, 200 km from Tegucigalpa; or La Ceiba to La Unión. (426 sq km)

Patuca
Proposed park, covers a great portion of the Cordillera Entre Ríos, still fully covered with tropical rain forest and in excellent condition. Very little explored; threatened by colonization front moving down the Río Patuca. (2200 sq km)

Pico Bonito
Six Holdridge life zones are represented, including lowland tropical rain forest, pine and pine/oak forest, and cloud forest at higher elevation. High biodiversity; many waterfalls. Highest peak is Montaña de Yoro, at 2436 meters. The park is five km south of La Ceiba. Access to the interior is difficult due to steep slopes; best access is along Río Cangrejal or Río Zacate, where there's easy access to a waterfall; access is also good along Río Bonito and Río Santo. (1571 sq km)

Pico Pijol
Cloud forest, with quetzals. Park guards but no infrastructure. Waterfall and large cave near Tegucigalpita. It's 32 km from Morazán, Yoro, through Subirana to Tegucigalpita. Access by foot only; guide necessary. (282 sq km)

Punta Sal
Tropical rain forest, wetlands and mangrove forest. High biodiversity, especially of migratory and coastal birds. Coral reefs, white-sand beaches, rocky point, Garífuna villages, ecotourism development. Office in Tela. Easiest access is by tour from Tela. (780 sq km)

Santa Bárbara
Cloud forest; limited surface water, due to extensive cave and sinkhole system. Contains Honduras' second-highest peak, at 2744 meters above sea level. The park is 10 km east of Santa Bárbara, but difficult to access; best access route is from Las Vegas, going through San José de los Andes, on the Lago de Yojoa side. (321 sq km)

Sierra de Agalta
Cloud forest, includes elfin forest, waterfalls; high biodiversity, including quetzals and bell birds. Has 400 sq km of virgin forest; high priority for research and ecotourism. Access by paved road, 2½ hours from Tegucigalpa; access points from Catacamas, Juticalpa, San Esteban, Dulce Nombre de Culmí. (655 sq km)

*La Tigra
Near Tegucigalpa, this park protects a beautiful cloud forest, as well as the city's water supply. It was Honduras' first national park, established in 1980. Interpretive trails; visitors' centers at both entrances; dormitories and houses available, also camping. Access from Tegucigalpa. (330 sq km)

National marine parks include:

*Cayos Cochinos (Hog Islands)
Protected reserve; proposed national marine park. Thirteen cays, two of them large, with beautiful coral reefs, well-preserved forests, fishing villages, a species of pink boa. Access by motorized canoe from town of Nueva Armenia, one hour's drive east of La Ceiba.

Islas del Cisne (Swan Islands)
National marine park; very remote, access difficult and not commercially available. Coral reefs, endemic species, sea turtle breeding, Honduran military base.

*Sandy Bay/West End
Protected reserve; proposed national marine park, on northwestern end of Roatán in the Bay Islands. Coral reefs, easy access, visited frequently by divers.

*Turtle Harbor
Protected reserve; proposed national marine park. On northwestern side of Utila in the Bay Islands. Coral reefs, easy access, visited frequently by divers.

Important wildlife refuges include:

Barbareta
Proposed wildlife refuge (currently privately held but open to visitors). Tropical forest, mangrove forest, off the northeastern tip of Roatán in the Bay Islands.

*Cuero y Salado
Tropical wet and mangrove forest, largest manatee reserve in Central America. Boats available; office in La Ceiba. It's 30 km west of La Ceiba; easy access, arrange a visit in advance with FUCSA office, La Ceiba. (133 sq km)

Laguna de Caratasca
Proposed wildlife refuge. Largest lagoon in the country; high biodiversity, great bird watching. Access by plane from La Ceiba or Tegucigalpa to Puerto Lempira, then by boat into the lagoon. (1200 sq km)

*Laguna de Guaimoreto
Mangrove forest. High coastal biodiversity, especially coastal birds; shrimp breeding grounds, fishing cooperatives. Five km by road east of Trujillo. (54 sq km)

Lagunas de Invierno
Mangrove forest, excellent migratory bird watching. In the Golfo de Fonseca, with various points of access; includes Jicarito, Guameru, La Alemania, Las Iguanas, Monte Cristo, San Bernardo, Teonostal and Quebrachal wildlife refuges.

*Punta Izopo
Tropical wet forest, mangrove forest and wetlands. High biodiversity, many migratory and coastal birds, beautiful rocky point, white-sand beaches, tourism development. It's 16 km by highway and dirt road from Tela to Triunfo de la Cruz, one-hour walk on beach, and one-hour canoe ride. Tours also come from Tela. (115 sq km)

Important biological reserves include:

*Guisayote
Cloud forest. Highly disturbed (roads and other human intrusions), easiest access of any Honduras cloud forest. Highest paved road in Honduras passes through this reserve. It's 16 km north on paved road from Nueva Ocotepeque. (173 sq km)

*Lancetilla Botanical Gardens
Tropical wet forest, botanical garden with over 700 species of plants and 365 species of birds. Largest collection of Asiatic fruit trees in the Western Hemisphere. Interpretive trail, guides, dormitories, visitors' center. Seven km southeast of Tela. (42 sq km)

Honduras has one biosphere reserve:

*Río Plátano
First biosphere reserve in Central America; World Heritage Site. Large and mostly well preserved lowland tropical rain forest, with

HONDURAS

remarkable natural, archaeological and cultural resources. Access to southern zone through Olancho by road beyond Dulce Nombre de Culmí; access to northern zone by plane from La Ceiba to Palacios and then by motorized canoe to other destinations. Central zone is very remote and seeing it requires long expeditions. (5251 sq km)

Honduras also has an anthropological reserve:

Tawahka
Tropical rain forest, last homeland of the Tawahka (Sumo) people, one of the most threatened indigenous groups in Honduras. Beautiful landscape. People live closely with the land. All is threatened by uncontrolled colonization. Access by plane to Wampusirpi, then by boat to Krausirpi and Krautara.

GOVERNMENT & POLITICS

The government of Honduras is a constitutional democracy with three tiers: executive, legislative and judicial. All citizens over 18 can vote.

The president is elected by popular vote to a four-year term that cannot be renewed. The legislature consists of the National Congress with 132 elected legislators. The judiciary consists of a Supreme Court, appointed by the president, which controls all branches of the lower courts, including the appointment of justices.

Honduras is divided into 18 departments, each with a governor appointed by the president. The departments are divided into municipalities, which are further divided into *aldeas* or villages. Rural areas have *caserios*, which are subdivisions of aldeas. Each locality can elect its own council, legal representative and mayor.

Honduras has several political parties, but the two major ones are the Partido Liberal and the Partido Nacional. The president is Carlos Roberto Reina, who took office for a four-year term in January 1994.

ECONOMY

Honduras is a poor country, with one of the lowest GNPs in Latin America; only Haiti and Nicaragua are poorer. It's estimated that 70% of the population lives below the poverty level. Close to 50% of the work force is unemployed or underemployed, the country has a large foreign debt, and it imports more than it exports. Inflation in 1993 was around 12%, double that of 1992 but much lower than in 1991; by 1996 inflation had soared to around 30%.

Agriculture employs 60% of the work force and provides 80% of the country's exports. The main products are corn, bananas, coffee, cattle, dry beans, sugar cane, cotton, sorghum and tobacco. Other main industries, listed here in descending order, are forestry, hunting, fishing, manufacturing, trade, services, transport and communications. Tourism is an increasingly important sector of the economy.

In 1993 coffee provided the largest export income, followed by bananas. The European Union was the biggest purchaser of Honduran products (around 65%, twice as much as the USA), particularly of bananas. The new European banana quota is bound to affect Honduras adversely. Nontraditional Honduran exports such as melon and shrimp are expanding, but the nation remains vulnerable to the volatile prices of bananas and coffee.

The USA was traditionally Honduras' principal trading partner, and economic ties remain very strong. Two giant US companies, United Fruit and Standard Fruit, hold a large part of the country's agricultural land and grow the majority of the banana crop. Aid from the USA also forms a large part of the Honduran economy, though it's much less than in the 1980s. Aid earmarked by the USA in 1993 totaled US$43.5 million, over half going toward development projects and only about 5% going to the military.

POPULATION & PEOPLE

The population of Honduras grew by about 3.4% per annum in the 1980s. Estimates for 1997 put the total population at around 5.75 million, due to reach six million by 1999. Honduras is experiencing the most rapid urbanization in Central America: The urban population was 44% in 1990 and is expected to hit 59% in 2010.

About 90% of the population is mestizo, a mixture of Spanish and Indian. Another 7% or so are pure Indians living in pockets around the country, each group with its own language and culture.

The Tolupanes (also called Jicaque or Xicaque) live in a swath of territory sweeping from San Pedro Sula southeast to Montaña de la Flor. The Lenca live in southwestern Honduras; they hold markets in the towns of La Esperanza, Marcala and Tutule. Chorti live near the Guatemala border, about a quarter of the way up from the border's southern point.

Miskito live in the Mosquitia region in northeastern Honduras, on the coast and along the Río Coco, which forms the border between Honduras and Nicaragua. A dark people, Miskito are believed to be a mixed race of indigenous Indians and black Caribs, themselves a mixture of Africans and Carib Indians.

Pech (also called Paya) live in the interior river regions of the Mosquitia. Tawahka (also called Sumo) live in the interior of the Mosquitia in the area around the Río Patuca.

Garífuna are a mixture of African, Carib and Arawak Indians and make up around 2.5% of the population. They were transported by the British to the island of Roatán from the Caribbean island of St Vincent in 1797. Today there are Garífuna settlements all along the northern coast of Honduras and one on Roatán.

Other black people on the north coast and in the Bay Islands are descendants of Jamaicans and other West Indians who came to Honduras with the British or to work on the banana plantations. They often speak Caribbean-accented English in addition to Spanish and are Protestant rather than Catholic.

EDUCATION
Primary education is free and compulsory, beginning at seven years of age and lasting for six years. Beyond that, education is not compulsory; secondary education, beginning at age 13, lasts for up to five years, with one cycle of three years and a second cycle of two years. Around 93% of children of primary school age are enrolled; the figure drops to only around 30% in the secondary age group. Adult illiteracy is around 27%.

Honduras has six universities, including the Universidad Nacional Autónoma de Honduras (UNAH) in Tegucigalpa.

ARTS
Honduras is not as renowned for its arts as are nearby Guatemala and El Salvador, but it does have some interesting art forms.

Woodcarving is a popular art; many items are made of carved wood, including intricately carved (sometimes also painted) boxes and chests. Other popular arts include basketry, embroidery and textile arts, leather goods and ceramics; the Lencas of western Honduras are especially known for their ceramics.

Honduras' most characteristic style of painting depicts scenes of typical mountain villages, with cobblestone lanes winding among houses with white adobe walls and red tile roofs. This style of painting was made internationally famous by Honduran artist José Antonio Velásquez (1906 – 1983) and is still very popular today.

Theater is popular in the larger cities; plays are presented at the Teatro Nacional in Tegucigalpa and at the Centro Cultural Sampedrano (San Pedro Cultural Center) in San Pedro Sula. The national symphony is based in Tegucigalpa.

Dance is another popular art form. The Garífuna people of the north coast are especially known for their distinctive dance; if you get a chance to see the Ballet Folklórico Garífuna perform, don't miss it. The troupe is based in Tegucigalpa. The Garífuna's style of popular dance, the punta, is easy to see if you travel on the north coast.

The Garífuna also have their own distinctive music, musical instruments and handicrafts. Their traditional band is a combination of three large drums, a turtle shell (hit with a stick) and a large conch shell (blown into). The band usually plays accompanied by song.

SOCIETY & CONDUCT
Honduras is becoming a modern society; you won't see Indians dressed in traditional

costume, as in Guatemala or Panama. Also see Society & Conduct in the Facts about Central America chapter.

RELIGION

Roman Catholicism is the predominant religion of Honduras, and the vast majority (around 90%) of Hondurans are Catholics. The country has freedom of religion, however, and there are many other Christian sects, including Mormons, Jehovah's Witnesses, Seventh-Day Adventists, Baptists, Pentecostals, Assemblies of God, Evangelicals and so on. The Baha'i faith is also growing in Honduras, especially along the north coast.

The indigenous groups have their own religions, often existing alongside Christianity; these include elements of African and Indian animism and ancestor worship.

LANGUAGE

Spanish is the principal language and is spoken throughout the country. The various ethnic groups also have their own languages, which they speak among themselves.

In the Bay Islands the language of choice is English, spoken with a broad Caribbean accent. The locals can also speak Spanish, since it is taught in the schools, though some of the older people cannot speak it. On these islands the accent is reminiscent of the English and Scots who settled the islands centuries ago. Nowadays, with more people from the Honduran mainland settling in the islands, more Spanish is being spoken there.

Facts for the Visitor

PLANNING
When to Go

The most popular time to visit Honduras, especially the beach areas on the Caribbean Coast and the Bay Islands, is from around February to April during the North American winter but after the rainy season. This is an excellent time to visit, but outside this time you will find fewer tourists and prices may be lower.

As elsewhere in Central America, the rainy season brings extra humidity to the lowlands, making it feel especially hot.

Maps

The Instituto Geográfico Nacional in Tegucigalpa publishes a tourist map with the country of Honduras on one side and city maps of Tegucigalpa, San Pedro Sula, La Ceiba and the Bay Islands on the other side. In Tegucigalpa it's sold at the post office, at the tourist office and at the institute itself. Tourist maps are also available from some petrol stations for about the same price.

The Instituto Geográfico Nacional also publishes excellent color topographical and regional maps, which are available at their office (see Maps under Tegucigalpa).

ITM publishes an excellent color map of Honduras, showing the geographical features (mountains, lowlands, rivers), cities, towns and national parks and reserves. It also publishes an excellent 1:1,800,000 color map of Central America as a whole. See Maps in the Facts for the Visitor chapter for information on where to obtain ITM publications.

What to Bring

On the north coast, the Bay Islands and in the Mosquitia, be sure to bring insect repellent against the mosquitoes and sandflies. A mosquito net is also a good idea. Be sure to bring antimalaria pills as malaria is endemic to the region (chloroquine is easily available in most Honduran cities).

Since tap water is not safe to drink, carry your own means of purifying water. Bottled water is usually easy to find, but you don't want to be caught short.

HIGHLIGHTS
Copán

The magnificent Maya ruins at Copán are definitely a highlight of a visit to Honduras. The town of Copán Ruinas is a pleasant little place, and there are other enjoyable things to see and do in the area as well.

National Parks & Nature Reserves
Twenty national parks and a number of nature reserves protect cloud forests, coastal wetlands and lagoons and other beautiful natural features (see the list of national parks above).

Diving & Snorkeling
Diving and snorkeling are excellent in the Bay Islands, which are a continuation of the barrier reef off the coast of Belize. The Bay Islands, in particular Utila, offer the world's cheapest diving certification courses. More advanced divers will enjoy a variety of specialized diving opportunities.

Museums
Museum buffs will enjoy the institutions in Tegucigalpa, San Pedro Sula and Copán (both the museum in the town and the newer sculpture museum at the ruins). The small but engaging little Garífuna Museum in Tela is also a fun place to visit and to sample some traditional Garífuna food.

TOURIST OFFICES
Local Tourist Offices
The office of the Instituto Hondureño de Turismo is in Tegucigalpa. It also has electronic information kiosks with general information at the Toncontín (Tegucigalpa), San Pedro Sula, La Ceiba and Roatán airports.

They used to have more offices in other parts of the country; since those were closed, various other businesses connected with tourism are filling the gap. We've mentioned these places in the various towns under 'Information.'

Tourist Offices Abroad
The Instituto Hondureño de Turismo has an office in the USA at 299 Alhambra Circle, Suite 510, Coral Gables, FL 33134 (☎ (305) 461-0600, (305) 461-0601, fax (305) 461-0602, net).

VISAS & DOCUMENTS
Citizens of most Western European countries, Australia, Canada, Japan, New Zealand, the UK and the USA can stay for up to 30 days without a visa if they are visiting as tourists.

Once inside Honduras, you can apply for an extension every 30 days, for a total stay of up to six months. After that you may have to leave the country for three days and reenter. To extend your stay, take your passport to any immigration office and ask for a *prorroga*; you'll have to fill out a form and pay around US$1 to US$2, depending on your nationality. Practically every city and town in Honduras has an immigration office *(migración)* where you can do this. Most are open Monday to Friday from 8:30 am to 4:30 pm; some may have additional hours on Saturday mornings.

The regulations seem to change quite frequently, so check the current situation at a Honduran embassy or consulate before you arrive at the border.

EMBASSIES
Honduran Embassies & Consulates Abroad
Honduran embassies are listed below. Visas to visit Honduras can be obtained at these embassies and at Honduran consulates. Sometimes there are many consulates in a single country; in the USA, Honduras maintains consulates in Atlanta, Baltimore, Boston, Chicago, Dallas, Denver, Honolulu, Houston, Los Angeles, Miami, Minneapolis, New Orleans, New York, St Louis, San Diego, San Francisco, Tampa and elsewhere, in addition to the embassy in Washington, DC.

Honduran embassies and consulates in other countries include:

Australia (consulate only)
   19/31 Pitt St, Sydney (☎ 02-9252-3779)
Belize
   See Embassies & Consulates in Belize City.
Canada
   151 Slater St, Suite 908A, Ottawa, Ontario K1P 5H3 (☎ (613) 233-8900,
   ☎ /fax (613) 232-0193)
Colombia
   Carretera 16, No 85-15, Apto 302, Santa Fe de Bogotá (☎ 236-0357, 616-0856, fax 616-0774)

HONDURAS

Costa Rica
  See Foreign Embassies in Costa Rica.
El Salvador
  See Foreign Embassies in El Salvador.
France
  8 rue Crevaux, 75116 Paris
  (☎ (1) 4755-8645, fax (1) 4755-8648)
Germany
  Ubierestrasse-15300 Bonn 2
  (☎ 0228-356394, ☎ /fax 0228-351981)
Guatemala
  See Embassies in Guatemala City.
Mexico
  Alfonso Reyes No 220, Colonia Condesa,
  México DF 06140 (☎ (5) 211-5747, (5)
  211-5250, (5) 211-6689, fax (5) 211-5425)
Nicaragua
  See Foreign Embassies in Managua.
Panama
  See Foreign Embassies & Consulates
  in Panama City.
UK
  115 Gloucester Place, London W1H 3PJ
  (☎ 171-486-4550, fax 171-486-4880)
USA
  3007 Tilden St NW, Washington DC 20008
  (☎ (202) 966-7702, (202) 966-4596,
  fax (202) 966-9571)

Foreign Embassies in Honduras

Foreign embassies and consulates in Honduras are in Tegucigalpa and San Pedro Sula; see those cities for particulars. There's also a Nicaraguan consulate in Choluteca.

CUSTOMS

Customs regulations are the usual 200 cigarettes, 100 cigars or half a kilogram of tobacco, and two liters of alcohol.

MONEY
Currency & Exchange

The unit of currency is the *lempira*. Notes are of one, two, five, 10, 20, 50 and 100 lempiras.

There are 100 centavos in a lempira; coins are of one, two, five, 10, 20 and 50 centavos.

These were the currency exchange rates at the time of writing:

Australia	A$1	=	L10.35
Canada	C$1	=	L8.25
Germany	DM1	=	L8.65
New Zealand	NZ$1	=	L9.35
Great Britain	UK£1	=	L18.40
United States	US$1	=	L12.50

The US dollar is the only foreign currency that is easily exchanged in Honduras; away from the borders it's even difficult to change the currencies of Guatemala, El Salvador or Nicaragua. Lloyd's Bank in Tegucigalpa also changes the Canadian dollar, the British pound sterling and the Deutchmark.

Cash usually receives the same rate as traveler's checks. The black-market rate for

---

Costs & Inflation

In recent years, inflation in Honduras has been running at about 30% a year, with prices in lempiras rising accordingly. This has been a disaster for local people: While prices in lempiras have soared, salaries have remained the same, and many people have slid further into poverty. The minimum wage in Honduras, which many people earn, is about US$50 per month.

Prices given in US dollars are somewhat more stable. A few places, hotels for example, are starting to calculate their prices in terms of US dollars and translate them into lempiras at the daily rate, keeping the US dollar price steady. Each day this price translates into a few more lempiras.

In this guide we're giving all prices in US dollars, but don't be too surprised if you find prices considerably changed by the time you reach Honduras. For example, just in the weeks we were in Honduras doing our research, the lempira was falling in value daily and there was also a hike in fuel prices. Overnight all the domestic airfares rose by about 30%, doubling what they had been a couple of years before. A favorite hotel also suddenly hiked its rate by 30%. If inflation continues at its current rate – as is likely – more and more places will have to start raising their prices. ■

cash and traveler's checks is only slightly higher or even the same as the official rate. Travelers' checks can be changed in all of the major towns.

Cash advances on Visa and MasterCard are available at Credomatic offices and at Futuro and Ficenza banks. Some other banks will take Visa, which is more widely accepted than MasterCard. Check the credit-card exchange rate, as it can be unfavorable compared to the rate for cash or traveler's checks. There's no transaction charge on the Honduran end for Visa or MasterCard cash advances.

Tipping & Bargaining
Most Hondurans do not tip. In places with a lot of tourist and foreign influence, tipping is more common, from a little loose change up to 10% of the bill.

As for bargaining, watch to see what the local people are doing. Bargaining is not as common in Honduras as in some other places in Central America. Usually you should bargain at open markets and on the streets; prices at indoor stores are fixed. Even taxis often have a fixed rate, which you can sometimes bargain down a lempira or two.

Taxes
A 7% sales tax will be added to the price of just about every transaction you make in Honduras, including hotels and restaurants.

POST & COMMUNICATIONS
Post offices in most Honduran towns are open Monday to Friday from 8 am to 5 pm (often with a couple of hours off for lunch between noon and 2 pm) and on Saturday from 8 am to noon. In large cities they may be open longer hours.

Postal Rates
The postal service in Honduras is not the best, but these are the rates and theoretical delivery times :

To the USA	US$0.45	seven to eight days
To Europe	US$0.45	14 days
To Australia	US$0.45	16 to 17 days

Sending & Receiving Mail
You can receive poste-restante mail at any post office; have it directed to you at '(Name), Lista de Correos, (town and department), República de Honduras, Central America.'

Honduras is notorious for problems with receiving incoming mail from the USA; since Hondurans working in the USA send money to their families back home, and a certain amount of the mail arriving from that country never reaches its destination. Other times there can be inexplicable delays. Most mail, however, does manage to get through. It seems to have a better chance if there is no way it could even *appear* to have money in it; aerograms (which can't contain enclosures) or postcards are two such options. Outgoing post is more reliable.

Express Mail Service (EMS) courier service offers a faster and safer alternative to the regular mail system for both incoming and outgoing mail, though it's more expensive. EMS has offices in every city and major town in Honduras, usually beside or near the post office. In Tegucigalpa, Aerocasillas offers a direct connection to the US mail system.

Several courier services also operate in Honduras, including Urgente Express and DHL.

Telephone & Fax
International telephone, telegraph, telex and fax services are offered at Hondutel offices in every city and town. (There are still some small towns that don't have fax service, but most of them do, and it's on the way to the rest.)

Hondutel offices are open 24 hours every day in Tegucigalpa, San Pedro Sula and La Ceiba. In smaller towns they're open every day from 7 am until around 9 or 10 pm. Fax services are available during more limited hours, usually Monday to Friday from 8 am to 4 pm.

International calls are expensive: At press time, a minimum three-minute call costs US$19.30 to the UK or Australia, US$16.10 to Germany, US$8 to the USA

HONDURAS

and US$3 to Costa Rica, and prices are rising. International calls are about 30% cheaper between 10 pm and 6:30 am every day.

An interesting quirk in the system is that you can send a fax much cheaper than you can phone; sending a one-page fax costs US$2 to the UK and Europe, US$2.50 to Australia and US$1.45 to the USA or Canada. You can also receive faxes at Hondutel offices; the cost is US$0.08 per page.

There are public telephones outside Hondutel offices and often in public places such as parks and on busy corners. You need a 20 centavo coin for a three-minute local call or a 50 centavo coin for a six-minute local call; keep putting in coins, or you'll get cut off when your time is up. These are the only two coins the public phones will accept. Domestic long-distance calls cost L2 (US$0.15). If you still have time remaining when your call is finished, you can push the 'A' button on the phone, receive a dial tone and make another call: Two local calls can be made with a 20 centavo coin or five local calls with a 50 centavo coin. If you hang up, the phone takes your coin and your time is up.

Most public phones now accept phone cards as well as coins. Phone cards valued at L50 (US$4.15) and L100 (US$8.30) are sold at Hondutel offices.

To reach a local operator, dial 192; for a domestic long-distance operator, dial 191; for an international operator, dial 197. A direct connection to an operator in the USA is available by dialing 121 for Sprint, 122 for MCI and 123 for AT&T.

The country code when calling Honduras from abroad is 504.

Online Services

Honduras has email connections; however, it may be a challenge to find a place to hook up to it while you're on the road.

In Tegucigalpa there are a few places you can connect: Telemática has an email service, and the Granada Hotel and Shakespeare & Co bookstore also offer Internet and email connections for travelers. Another email service is available in West End Village on Roatán. In other places, you may just have to ask around to find someone with a connection. The Telemática office in Tegucigalpa might be able to provide more information about connecting to email.

BOOKS
Guidebooks

Honduras Travel Guide by Brad Martin contains up-to-date 'travelers tips' for Honduras. The author continually updates the book by computer and sends you periodic updates; he also has a computer database on Honduras and he is available (by email or regular mail) to answer any questions or explore special interests. The book is available for US$15 from the author at PO Box 531, Mountain View, CA 94042 USA (24-hour message ☎ (415) 965-2441, net). Or you can get it from Equator Travel Publications, 280 Beaverdam Rd, Candler, NC 28715 USA (☎ (704) 667-1717).

La Mosquitia: A Guide to the Savannas, Rain Forest, and Turtle Hunters is an informative book providing the adventurous with detailed maps and travel information about the sparsely populated Mosquitia region, one of Central America's largest and least explored natural territories. The book can be ordered from the author: Derek Parent, 134 St George, Chateauguay, Quebec, Canada J6K 256 (net). Or you can get it from the Adventurous Traveler Bookstore, PO Box 1468, Williston, VT 05495 (☎ (802) 860-6776, (800) 282-3963).

Honduras Handbuch is a German-language guidebook to Honduras in the Reise Know-How series.

Politics & Economics

Some good books for understanding social, political and economic developments in Honduras include:

Honduras: The Making of a Banana Republic by Alison Acker (South End Press)
Honduras: State for Sale by Richard Lapper (Latin America Bureau, London)
Honduras: Portrait of a Captive Nation edited by Nancy Peckenham & Annie Street (Praeger Publishers)

Inside Honduras by Tom Barry & Kent
  Norsworthy (Inter-Hemispheric Education
  Resource Center, Albuquerque)
Prisión Verde by Ramón Amaya Amador
  (in Spanish). A famous book about the
  Honduran banana industry.
Reinterpreting the Banana Republic by Darío A
  Euraque. A history of Honduras exploring
  the relations of the various regions, agricul-
  ture, and the development of the Honduran
  government from 1870 to 1972.

Fiction

On a lighter note, Guillermo Yuscarán
(William Lewis, in his former incarnation
as a professor of Hispanic studies in Santa
Barbara, California), who writes mostly in
English and now lives near Tegucigalpa, is
one of Honduras' most wonderful painters
and writers. His books, all in paperback,
include (in chronological order) *Blue
Pariah*, *Points of Light: Honduran Short
Stories*, *Conociendo a la Gente Garífuna*
(The Garífuna Story), *Beyond Honduras:
Tales of Tela, Trujillo and Other Places*, *El
Gran Hotel*, *Northcoast Honduras: Tropi-
cal Karma and Other Stories* and *Gringos
in Honduras: The Good, the Bad, and the
Ugly*. Yuscarán's biography, *Velasquez:
The Man and His Art*, is the first and only
biography to be published on the life of
Honduras' most acclaimed primitivist
painter. All of Yuscarán's books are avail-
able in Tegucigalpa at Shakespeare & Co,
Metromedia, and the gift shop of the Hotel
Honduras Maya; at the Luces del Norte
restaurant and the Hotel Tela in Tela; and at
the Casi Todo bookshops on Roatán.

Photography Books

Vicente Murphy is an amazing photographer, probably the best photographer in
Honduras. If you're in Honduras for long,
you'll start to notice his photographs everywhere.

Honduras Al Natural, an annual weekly
agenda/datebook, is published every year,
with a Vicente Murphy photograph for
each week. The photos are exquisite color
prints, mostly of Honduran wildlife and
outdoor scenes. You can find the datebooks
for sale in many places, including Metro-

media in Tegucigalpa. Or you could order
one from Ecoarte, Apdo Postal 163, Tela,
Atlántida, Honduras.

Honduras (Transamérica, in Tegucigalpa) is a coffee-table-size book of brilliant photos and text, with photos by
Vicente Murphy and David W Beyl.

MEDIA

Honduras has six daily newspapers. *El
Heraldo, La Tribuna* and *El Periódico* are
published in Tegucigalpa, *La Prensa, El
Tiempo* and *El Nuevo Día* in San Pedro Sula.
El Tiempo and *La Prensa* are on the Web.

Honduras This Week is a weekly
English-language newspaper published in
Tegucigalpa. It comes out every Saturday
and can be found in major hotels and
English-language bookshops in Tegucigalpa, San Pedro Sula, La Ceiba, Roatán
and Utila. You can subscribe by contacting
them at Apdo Postal 1312, Tegucigalpa,
MDC, Honduras (☎ (504) 31-5821, 32-
0832, fax (504) 32-2300, net). *Honduras
aktuell* is a more recent German-language
weekly.

Honduras Tips is a bilingual (English/
Spanish) quarterly magazine excellent for
anyone traveling in Honduras. It gives lots
of information on things to see and do and
places to stay and eat, with maps and
photos. It's available free in Honduras and
can be found in many places frequented by
travelers. Or contact the publisher at Apdo
Postal 2699, San Pedro Sula (☎ 56-8567,
fax 56-7762, net).

The *Coconut Telegraph*, 'the Bay
Islands' magazine,' is produced on Roatán
and carries stories about all the Bay
Islands. The office (☎ 45-1833/4, fax 45-
1826, net) is in the center of Coxen Hole,
the largest town on Roatán. The magazine
is published every two months. A one-year
subscription (six issues) costs US$35 in
Central America and the USA (Canada
US$5 more, elsewhere US$10 more). On
Utila, check out the *Utila Times*.

Over 150 radio stations and six television
stations broadcast in Honduras. Movies and
news in English come from the USA by
cable TV.

PHOTOGRAPHY & VIDEO

Color film costs around US$2.80/3.50 for 24/36 exposures; color slide film is US$4.20/5.85 for 24/36 exposures. Kodak, Fuji and Agfa film are available, as is video film. Larger cities have one-hour photo processing shops. In general, it's better to wait for processing until you get to a more developed country.

ELECTRICITY

Honduras has both 110 and 220 volt electricity supplies; find out which it is in your hotel before you plug in any appliance. Most places use 110 volts, as in the USA and the rest of Central America.

LAUNDRY

Most hotels have somewhere you can wash your clothes; ask to use the *lavadero*. Expensive hotels usually have an expensive laundry service, but in cheaper places you can offer chamber staff a few lempiras to wash your clothes for you. Laundries in most towns offer wash, dry and fold for around US$1.85 for 10 lbs of laundry.

HEALTH

No vaccinations are required to enter Honduras, but you should be vaccinated against typhoid and tetanus.

Tap water is not safe to drink in Honduras. Most restaurants and hotels provide purified drinking water, but be sure it really is purified before you drink it, and of course, watch out for ice cubes. Bottled purified water is available almost everywhere, but it's a good idea to carry your own method of purifying water, just in case. Raw salads (lettuce, cabbage) are suspect if they have been washed with unpurified water.

Digestive problems such as stomach ache and diarrhea are likely, especially if you eat from street stands; pharmacies are well equipped with medicines and can often cure whatever ails you. In larger towns there is usually a *farmacia de turno* open at all hours.

Malaria-carrying mosquitoes are a problem on the north coast, the Bay Islands and in the aptly named Mosquitia; be sure to follow a regimen of antimalarial medication. Dengue fever is also present. Since both are carried by mosquitoes, it's best to avoid being bitten (see the Health section in the Facts for the Visitor chapter).

Over 1000 cases of cholera (resulting in 49 deaths) have been diagnosed in Honduras since an epidemic broke out in October 1991. The most recent cases were reported in Tegucigalpa and in the departments of Choluteca, Cortés, Santa Bárbara, Valle and El Paraíso. Be vigilant about the hygiene standards of what you eat and drink everywhere in Honduras. Don't rely on a cholera vaccination to protect you, as it is ineffective.

In early 1997, Honduran health officials announced that 65,000 people in the country were in the late stages of Chagas' disease and would die from the parasitic illness during the next few years. They estimated that around 300,000 people (around 5% of the population) were infected with some stage of the disease (see Chagas' Disease in the Health section in the Regional Facts for the Visitor chapter).

Over 3000 cases of AIDS have been diagnosed in Honduras since 1985, and the World Health Organization estimates that one in 25 Hondurans has the HIV virus. Don't have sex with a local without using a condom. The north coast and San Pedro Sula have the highest concentration of AIDS cases.

WOMEN TRAVELERS

Honduras is basically a good country for women travelers. As elsewhere, you'll probably attract less attention if you dress modestly. On the Bay Islands, where there are lots of beach-going foreign tourists, standards of modesty in dress are much more relaxed. (The suggestions in the Women Travelers section of Facts for the Visitor apply throughout Honduras.)

Cases of rape against foreign tourists have been reported in a few places along the north coast. As peaceful and idyllic as the coast looks – and usually is – be wary of going to isolated stretches of beach alone, and don't walk on the beach at night. The issue of rape takes on an added dimension here, when you consider the high rate of AIDS.

GAY & LESBIAN TRAVELERS

Honduras is very much 'in the closet.' So it's a joy to find Prisma, a gay and lesbian group in Tegucigalpa that holds BBQs, parties, camping trips and other gay and lesbian get-togethers. They also hold discussion/consciousness-raising meetings for women (Wednesday evenings) and men (Thursday evenings), in which many different topics are discussed.

At the time we were in Honduras, Prisma did not have an office or phone, but they told us they'd welcome meeting travelers. They check their PO Box every day; if you drop them a note at PO Box 4590 in Tegucigalpa, they'll get it the next day and will contact you.

The only specifically gay and lesbian gathering place we found in Honduras is a small, comfortable bar/disco in Tegucigalpa, appropriately named *El Closet*, open Thursday, Friday and Saturday nights from around 8 pm on. There's no sign; it's near the stadium, but there's no street name or address so it's not easy to explain how to get there. Not many taxi drivers know, either. The folks at Prisma can give you directions.

DANGERS & ANNOYANCES
Crime

Crime is on the increase in Honduras. Tegucigalpa and San Pedro Sula are the worst places for street crime; walking downtown in the daytime and early evening is fine, but locals will tell you it's dangerous to walk in the downtown streets past around 9 pm or so. The 'better' districts are much safer. Comayagüela is worse than the rest of Tegucigalpa: Don't *ever* walk through the market area of Comayagüela after dark.

In general, small towns are much safer than the big cities. Watch yourself on the north coast, though, as we have received several reports from travelers of muggings, thefts and rapes there. One American traveler who wrote to us was even shot in broad daylight on a beach in La Ceiba; luckily, he was only wounded. It's not safe to walk on the north-coast beaches after dark, and you should use caution even in daytime, especially in isolated places.

Nevertheless, there's no need to be overly paranoid about visiting Honduras. Using normal caution, most travelers travel in Honduras easily with no problems. See the Facts for the Visitor chapter for helpful hints on safe traveling. You can avoid most problems before they occur just by the way you conduct yourself.

Critters

Malaria-carrying mosquitoes and biting sandflies on the north coast, the Bay Islands and the Mosquitia are definitely an annoyance, and along with unpurified water can be the greatest threat to your well-being. Also watch out for jellyfish and stingrays, which are present on both the Caribbean and Pacific Coasts.

If you go hiking through wild places, beware of poisonous snakes, especially the *barba amarilla* or fer-de-lance *(Bothrops asper)*; the coral snake is also present. There are crocodiles and caymans in the waterways of the Mosquitia, in addition to the peaceful manatee and much other wildlife. Honduras also has scorpions (not lethal), black widow spiders, wasps and other stinging insects. You probably will never see a dangerous animal, but do be aware that they exist, and know what to do if you encounter them.

BUSINESS HOURS & PUBLIC HOLIDAYS

Business hours are normally Monday to Friday from 9 am to noon and 2 to 4:30 or 5 pm, and often also on Saturday from 9 am to noon. Bank hours are generally Monday to Friday from 9 am to 3 pm, usually with additional Saturday morning hours. Most government offices are open Monday to Friday from 8:30 am to 4:30 pm, sometimes with a lunch break that may last from noon to 1 or 2 pm.

HONDURAS

For post office and Hondutel hours, see Post & Communications above.

Honduran public holidays include:

January 1
  New Year's Day
April 14
  Day of the Americas
March/April
  Holy Week: Thursday, Friday and Saturday before Easter Sunday
May 1
  Labor Day
September 15
  Independence Day
October 3
  Francisco Morazán Day
October 12
  Columbus Day
October 21
  Army Day
December 25
  Christmas Day

SPECIAL EVENTS

As elsewhere in Central America, just about every city, town and village in Honduras has a patron saint and celebrates an annual festival or fair in the days around their saint's day. Some are big events, attracting crowds from far and wide.

One such fair is the Carnaval at La Ceiba, celebrated during the third week in May; the third Saturday is the biggest day, with parades, costumes, music and celebrations in the streets. The fair at San Pedro Sula, held in the last week of June, is another popular one. The fairs at Tela (June 13), Trujillo (June 24), Danlí (last weekend in August) and Copán Ruinas (March 15 to 20) are also good, and there are many others.

The fair for the Virgen de Suyapa, patron saint of Honduras, is celebrated in Suyapa, near Tegucigalpa, from around February 2 to 11; February 3 is actually the saint's day. The services and festivities bring pilgrims and celebrants from all over Central America.

The Feria Centroamericana de Turismo y Artesanía (FECATAI), an all-Central-American international tourism and crafts fair, is held every year from December 6 to 16 in Tegucigalpa. Another annual all-Honduras artisans' and cultural fair is held in the town of Copán Ruinas from December 15 to 21.

If you get a chance to attend a fair or presentation of any of Honduras' indigenous groups, do so. Several Garífuna music and dance troupes give presentations throughout the country, including the excellent Ballet Folklórico Garífuna. April 12, the anniversary of the arrival of the Garífuna people in Honduras in 1797, is a joyful occasion celebrated in all the Garífuna communities.

ACTIVITIES
Walking & Hiking

National parks are great places for hiking. Several of the parks offer well-maintained trails, visitors' centers for information and orientation, and even guides. Going with a guide is a good idea, as you will learn more about the environment (cloud forest, tropical rain forest or whatever) and see more wildlife than if you go on your own. The park trails usually range in lengths and levels of difficulty.

Along the north coast are unlimited opportunities for beach walks along white sandy beaches fringed by coconut palms and other tropical vegetation – it's said you could walk along the beach just about all the way along the entire coast, with just a few detours for rocky outcrops and points. Or you can have some fine times just walking in local areas, wherever you happen to be.

Diving & Snorkeling

The Bay Islands are great for diving and snorkeling. The reef is magnificent, and many diving operators offer diving and snorkeling tours, as well as diving certification courses. Utila is said to be the cheapest place in the world to get diving certification. Snorkeling gear can be rented, or bring your own – there are many excellent places where you can just jump off the beach into the water and enjoy great snorkeling, and it doesn't cost a cent if you have your own gear.

Kayaking, Canoeing & Small-Boat Tours

Small-boat tours are a good way to visit a number of national parks, wildlife refuges and nature reserves along the north coast, including Punta Sal and the Laguna de los Micos near Tela, Cuero y Salado near La Ceiba and the Laguna de Guaimoreto near Trujillo. Kayaking tours of the Refugio Punta Izopo near Tela let you slip silently among the canals of the mangrove forests, where you'll see plenty of wildlife.

The Mosquitia region, though more remote, is easily accessible by airplane and offers many more possibilities for canoe and boat trips on rivers and lagoons. The Mosquitia is a pristine, unspoiled area with plenty of wildlife.

Canoeing and 'soft rafting' is available on the Río Copán from the Hotel Hacienda de Jaral, an ecotourism resort near Copán Ruinas.

White-Water Rafting

White-water rafting is popular on the Río Cangrejal near La Ceiba; several companies in La Ceiba offer rafting tours on this river. One of these, Ríos Honduras, also offers rafting trips farther afield on the Río Sico in Olancho.

Bird Watching

Birding is becoming a popular activity in Honduras, where there are hundreds of species. It's difficult to name the most impressive birds, as there are so many; quetzals, toucans, scarlet macaws (Honduras' national bird) and brilliant green and green-and-yellow parrots are all contenders. National parks and wildlife refuges have been established to protect many environments good for seeing birds – for example, cloud forests, tropical rain forests and coastal wetlands. Quetzals are seen in many of the cloud-forest national parks, including Cusuco, Celaque, La Muralla and La Tigra.

Migratory birds are present along the north coast during the North American winter months from November to February. Good places to see them are in the lagoons,

national parks and wildlife refuges, and at Lancetilla Botanical Gardens near Tela. Each December 14 and 15 the Audubon Society does a 24-hour bird count at Lancetilla and other places nearby; the record for Lancetilla so far is 365 species counted in a 24-hour period. You can participate in the bird count if you like; further information is available at the PROLANSATE office in Tela. Even at other times of year when the migratory birds are not around, Lancetilla is still an excellent spot for birding.

The Lago de Yojoa is another excellent place for birding – 375 species have been counted here so far.

In some places you can go on bird-watching tours. A couple of companies in Copán Ruinas offer birding tours in the local area and farther afield, such as to the Lago de Yojoa. Also near Copán Ruinas at the Hacienda de Jaral is a lagoon visited by thousands of migratory herons from November to May.

Horseback Riding

Horseback riding is a popular activity at Copán Ruinas. Horseback tours are also conducted into Parque Nacional Pico Bonito near La Ceiba.

LANGUAGE COURSES

Honduras is not as famous for language courses as Guatemala, but there are a couple of schools where you can study Spanish; see the Copán Ruinas and Trujillo sections. One of the schools in Trujillo also offers instruction in the Garífuna language, folklore and dance.

ACCOMMODATIONS
Camping

Camping is allowed in several national parks and reserves; where it is, we've mentioned it in the text. Water and toilets or latrines are usually available, and sometimes even kitchens, but generally you should bring your own gear. In Gracias, the Restaurante Guancascos rents camping gear for camping in the Parque Nacional Celaque.

HONDURAS

Hotels

Economical accommodations are available just about everywhere in Honduras. The cheapest places have a shared cold bath; these can range from truly awful to fine places that would pass the white glove test. If you're traveling on a shoestring and going to the cheapest places, it's a good idea to get into the habit of asking to see a room and its facilities before you pay for it.

When you ask the price for a room, low-priced hotels will usually give you the price *including* the tax, while higher-priced hotels will usually give the price *without* the tax, meaning you'll have to pay 7% more. We've calculated the 7% into the hotel prices we've given in this chapter.

A step up is private cold bath. Hot showers are considered a luxury by Central American standards, and you will pay more for them. You'll also often pay more for two beds than for one – you can save money by sleeping with a friend.

The same goes for air conditioning, only more so. Air conditioners are expensive to operate, and electricity costs have gone sky high, so it's an expensive luxury – but available almost everywhere. In general, you can get whatever level of comfort you're willing to pay for almost everywhere in Honduras.

Many hotels have restaurants, which are pleasant and handy for that first cup of coffee or early morning breakfast before you head out into the world. Many of the more expensive hotels also have bars or restaurant/bar combinations.

'Theme hotels' are relatively new to Honduras. They include diving resorts in the Bay Islands and a couple of 'eco-tourism ranches' on the mainland, notably the Eco Rancho and Río Coto at Omoa and the Hotel Hacienda El Jaral near Copán Ruinas. As ecotourism increases in popularity, there will probably be more of these kinds of places.

FOOD

The typical meal *(plato típico)* in Honduras usually includes beans, rice, tortillas, chicken or meat (on the coast often fried fish), fried bananas, potatoes or yucca, cream, cheese, and a cabbage and tomato salad, or some combination of these. Most restaurants have the plato típico on the menu, and it's usually the cheapest and most filling meal, whether for breakfast, lunch or dinner.

Most places also offer a *comida corrida* or *plato del día* at lunchtime – usually a good, large, cheap meal.

Baleadas – white flour tortillas folded over a filling of refried beans, cream and crumbled cheese – are a good, filling snack. They usually cost around US$0.25; a couple of them with a soft drink for another US$0.25 will fill you up for a while. Another good snack is *tortillas con quesillo*, two crisp fried corn tortillas with melted white cheese between them. *Enchiladas* in Honduras are not what they are in Mexico – here they are what a *tostada* is in Mexico: a crisp fried tortilla topped with spicy meat, which is then topped with salad and crumbled cheese. Fried chicken is another common favorite in Honduras.

On the coasts and around the Lago de Yojoa, the fish is fresh and cheap. Commonly it's fried, though you can find it prepared in other ways, too. On the Caribbean Coast, fish and seafood soups, including *sopa de caracol* (conch soup made with coconut), are delicious, as is fish cooked in coconut sauce. Another specialty of the Caribbean Coast, *pan de coco* (coconut bread), is also very tasty.

On Sundays, *sopa de mondongo* (tripe soup) is eaten everywhere in Honduras. As in some other parts of the world, it's said to be the best medicine for a hangover!

Tajaditas, crispy fried banana chips, are sold in little bags on the streets, as are sliced green mangos sprinkled with a mixture of salt and cumin. But be cautious about the cleanliness of preparation of any type of food on the street, especially hot foods, or you could end up with amoebas!

DRINKS

Soft drinks are everywhere, with all the regulars in evidence plus a few local flavors, including banana. *Licuados* (milk blended with fruit) are always good; watch out for added ice, which might not have been purified. *Frescos*, fruit drinks blended with water and sugar, are a favorite everywhere, but remember they could have been made with unpurified water, and the ice could be suspect, too. Many places do use purified water to make frescos and ice; ask before you drink.

Five brands of beer are made in Honduras: Salva Vida, Port Royal Export, Nacional, Imperial and Holsten. Various kinds of wines are also made here, each in its own region. *Vino de naranja* (orange wine) is made in Siguatepeque, under the Siguata brand name; vino de naranja is also made in Güinope in the El Paraíso department. *Vino de mora* (raspberry wine) is made in Marcala in the La Paz department, and it can be found under the Malcallí brand name in some supermarkets in Tegucigalpa, as well as locally. *Vino de papa* (potato wine) is an interesting concoction made in La Esperanza in the Intibucá department.

Various brands of *aguardiente* are also made in Honduras, including Ron Flor de Caña, Ron Plata and the national favorite, Yuscarán. Yuscarán, fondly called the 'aguardiente nacional de Honduras,' is used as the base for drinks typical of various parts of the country. In the Copán department, *timochenko* is Yuscarán mixed with aromatic plants of the region. On the north coast, the Garífuna people mix Yuscarán with various aromatic and marine plants, resulting in *guífiti*. In the town of Yuscarán, where the aguardiente is made, it is mixed with fermented mamey juice to make *mameyazo*.

Cave, a coffee liqueur, is made in San Juancito, a small village near Tegucigalpa. You can find it in markets and even at the airport in bottles decorated with woven fibers.

ENTERTAINMENT

There's plenty of nightlife in Honduras – more in Tegucigalpa and San Pedro Sula, of course. La Ceiba also has plenty to do in the evening, with a number of discos and a couple of places with traditional Garífuna music groups and dancing. Trujillo also has pleasant nightlife – dances on the beach at Cocopando on weekends and a children's dance on Sunday afternoons. In Tela the Garífuna museum hosts a fun Saturday night party.

There are cinemas not only in the big cities but also in smaller towns. Even tiny Copán Ruinas has a couple of places showing video movies.

Most towns have somewhere pleasant to go for a drink in the evening. Often they are sociable places where you can meet both locals and other travelers. Places that come to mind are the Tunkul Bar in Copán Ruinas, the Expatriates Bar & Grill in La Ceiba and a whole bunch of places in Trujillo.

SPECTATOR SPORTS

As elsewhere in Latin America, *fútbol* (soccer) is the national passion. The professional soccer season runs from around September to March; the National Stadium in Tegucigalpa and the large stadium in San Pedro Sula are the venues for the biggest professional games. But soccer is much more than a professional sport – it's played in every city, town and village in the country, all year round. You can always see a soccer game, especially on Sunday afternoons.

Basketbol (basketball) and *beisbol* (baseball) are up-and-coming spectator sports; boxing is also popular. Cockfights have been banned in Tegucigalpa, but they are still held in San Pedro Sula and Choluteca.

THINGS TO BUY

Honduras produces a number of typical handicrafts, including woodcarving and wooden musical instruments, woven *junco* basketry, embroidery and textile arts, leather goods and ceramics. Colorful woven baskets and hats are the specialty at Santa Bárbara. Brightly painted ceramics (especially depicting roosters) are for sale along the road from El Amatillo to Nacaome. Ceramics are also a specialty of the Lenca people of western Honduras.

Paintings of typical mountain villages, with cobblestone lanes winding among houses with white adobe walls and red tile roofs, can be found in many places, including Tegucigalpa, Valle de Angeles and San Pedro Sula. For more details about this style of painting, see Arts above.

All of these things can be found not only in the places they're made, but also in Tegucigalpa and San Pedro Sula.

Tobacco is grown in Honduras, and Honduran cigars are said to be some of the finest. Danlí has several cigar factories where you can buy good hand-rolled cigars. In Santa Rosa de Copán, the La Flor de Copán cigar factory also makes excellent hand-rolled cigars. Ask for a free tour to see the cigars being made.

Getting There & Away

AIR

Frequent direct flights connect Honduras with all the other Central American capitals and many destinations in North America, the Caribbean, South America and Europe. Most international flights arrive and depart from the airports at Tegucigalpa and San Pedro Sula; there are also direct flights between the USA and Roatán, coming from Houston, New Orleans and Miami.

All the Central American airlines, as well as American, Continental, Iberia and KLM, have regular flights serving Honduras. American Airlines' flights connect through Miami; Continental's flights connect through Houston. TACA and Lacsa offer flights connecting Honduras with Houston, Los Angeles, Miami, New Orleans, New York, San Francisco and Washington, DC, in addition to all the other Central American capitals. KLM connects Honduras with all of Europe; these flights connect through San José, Guatemala City and Houston. Iberia has a flight between Madrid and San Pedro Sula, with a stopover in Miami.

If you fly out of Honduras, you must pay a US$9 departure tax at the airport.

LAND

Most Honduran border crossings are open daily from around 7 am to 5 pm. Everyone leaving or entering is usually charged around US$2. In theory this is an overtime payment only applicable between noon and 2 pm and on the weekends after noon on Saturday; in practice it's charged almost any time. It's best to pay up unless the amount demanded is excessive.

To Guatemala, the main crossings are at El Florido (Guatemala) and Agua Caliente. To El Salvador, the main crossings are El Poy and El Amatillo; there is also a crossing at Sabanetas, southwest of Comayagua. The crossings to Nicaragua are at El Espino (Nicaragua), Las Manos and Guasaule (Nicaragua).

Bus

Frequent buses serve all of these border crossings. Most buses do not cross the border, meaning you have to cross on foot and pick up another bus on the other side.

The exceptions are international buses. Tica Bus (☎ 38-7040), on 16a Calle between 5a and 6a Avs in Comayagüela, just across the river from Tegucigalpa, has buses leaving the capital every morning at 9 am, heading to Guatemala City via San Salvador, and to Panama City via Managua and San José. The 9 am buses reach San Salvador (US$15) that afternoon at 5 pm, and continue on to Guatemala City (US$23 from Tegucigalpa) the following morning, arriving there at noon. Heading south, they arrive at Managua (US$20) at 5 pm that afternoon, continuing on the following day to San José (US$35 from Tegucigalpa) and the day after that to Panama City (US$60 from Tegucigalpa).

Another international bus is the Crucero del Golfo (☎ 33-7415), which operates two buses daily between Tegucigalpa and San Salvador; see the Tegucigalpa section for details. If you're traveling between Tegucigalpa and Guatemala City by bus, the Crucero del Golfo makes it possible to make the trip all in one day (you change buses at the station in San Salvador). On Tica Bus, this trip takes two days: one day from Tegucigalpa or Guatemala City to San Salvador, an overnight there, and continuing on the following day.

Car

If you're driving, there is a lot of paperwork, fees and red tape involved in bringing a car into Honduras; you will be issued a special permit for your vehicle that must be renewed at regular intervals.

Trekking

The Jungle Trail is the name given to the route between Puerto Cortés in Honduras and Puerto Barrios in Guatemala. Allow two days for the trip, and get your exit stamp from one of those towns before you leave.

Corinto is the last place to stay and eat on the Honduran side and marks the end of the road. From there the trail bordering the jungle leads to Sujade Frontera (two hours), where you cross the river. From here the trail gets muddy and less defined. After two hours turn right beyond the gate (you're now in Guatemala) and continue for an hour to the next gate and a small settlement. Here you can either walk to the immigration office at El Cinchado (two hours) or hire a dugout to Finca Chinook (on the west side of the Río Motagua), where you can pick up a half-hourly bus to Puerto Barrios. You should be able to get from Corinto to Puerto Barrios on the same day. (The above itinerary is based on information supplied by John Peluso of the USA.)

Don't embark on this crossing without adequate preparation; if you lose your way, you may have to spend the night in the open. Hiring a guide would avoid this scenario, and should also provide some measure of protection against bandits, who have been known to operate in the area. One traveler warned of quicksand. Take water, food, good hiking boots and a compass.

See the Getting There & Away section of the Guatemala chapter for information on a simpler overland route, going from Puerto Barrios to Puerto Cortés. Presumably you could do the same thing in reverse, if you're coming from the Honduras side.

Another off-the-beaten-track crossing is through the Mosquitia to Nicaragua, but it's not without its own problems (see the Mosquitia section for details).

SEA

The only regularly scheduled passenger boat services between Honduras and other countries are the small boats that go twice weekly between Puerto Cortés and Dangriga (Belize), and the small boats that go twice weekly between Omoa and Lívingston (Guatemala). There's also a sailboat going approximately twice a month between Utila and Lívingston; see the Utila section for details.

Otherwise, it is often possible to arrange passage with cargo or fishing vessels if you pay your way. Don't waste time negotiating with an ordinary crew member: Speak to the captain. On the Caribbean Coast you can try to find a boat around Puerto Cortés, Tela, La Ceiba, Trujillo or the Bay Islands. The most common international destinations for these boats are Puerto Barrios (Guatemala), Belize, Puerto Cabezas (Nicaragua), Caribbean islands including Grand Cayman and Jamaica, and New Orleans and Miami in the USA.

On the Pacific side, the Golfo de Fonseca is shared by Nicaragua, Honduras and El Salvador, so you may be able to get a ride on boats sailing between the three countries. San Lorenzo is the main Honduran port town in the gulf.

If you arrive or depart from Honduras by sea, be sure to clear your paperwork (entry and exit stamps, and so on) immediately with the nearest immigration office.

Getting Around

AIR

Domestic air routes have proliferated in Honduras recently; it's now easy to fly to any of the Bay Islands from La Ceiba, Tegucigalpa and San Pedro Sula, and to fly among these three major cities. (Flights to the Bay Islands from Tegucigalpa and San

Pedro Sula may connect through La Ceiba.) More air routes into the Mosquitia region are also making that remote area more accessible.

TACA offers flights twice daily between Tegucigalpa and San Pedro Sula. Isleña, Sosa and Caribbean Air domestic airlines all offer flights connecting the north coast and the Bay Islands for the same rates. Isleña operates flights connecting Teguci-

Flight Route	Fare	Frequency
La Ceiba-Ahuas	US$52	2 weekly
La Ceiba-Brus	US$52	2 weekly
Laguna La Ceiba-Guanaja	US$26	2 daily
La Ceiba-Palacios	US$36	1 daily (except Sunday)
La Ceiba-Puerto Lempira	US$52	4 weekly
La Ceiba-Roatán	US$21	12 daily
La Ceiba-Trujillo	US$21	1 daily (except Sunday)
La Ceiba-Utila	US$18	3 daily (except Sunday)
La Ceiba-Puerto Lempira	US$52	3 weekly
San Pedro Sula-Guanaja	US$52	(via La Ceiba)
San Pedro Sula-La Ceiba	US$26	2 daily
San Pedro Sula-Roatán	US$47	(via La Ceiba)
San Pedro Sula-Tegucigalpa	US$32	2 daily
San Pedro Sula-Utila	US$44	(via La Ceiba)
Tegucigalpa-Guanaja	US$62	(via La Ceiba)
Tegucigalpa-La Ceiba	US$36	2 daily
Trujillo-Palacios	US$24	1 daily (except Sunday)
Tegucigalpa-Roatán	US$57	(via La Ceiba)
Tegucigalpa-Utila	US$54	(via La Ceiba)
Roatán-Guanaja	US$21	1 daily (except Sunday)

galpa with the north coast and the Bay Islands. Isleña, Sosa and Rollins Air operate flights connecting La Ceiba with the Mosquitia region. Travel agents have information on all flights, or you can phone the airline offices. Local telephone numbers for all the domestic airlines are given in the individual city sections. (Rollins Air has only one office, and it's in La Ceiba.)

Airfares are especially subject to change, so check current prices; it's quite likely they'll be higher than the fares listed here. When fuel prices fluctuate, so do airfares. Prices in the adjacent table are for one-way fares (double for return).

BUS
Buses are an easy and cheap way to get around in Honduras, as buses run frequently to most places in the country. The first buses of the day often start very early in the morning; the last bus often departs in the late afternoon. Buses between Tegucigalpa and San Pedro Sula run later.

On major bus routes you'll often have a choice between taking a *directo* or a regular bus. When this is the case, the regular bus will make stops all along the way, wherever someone wants to get on or off. On a long trip, eventually it can start to feel like it will take you forever to get where you're going. The 'directo' buses cost a few cents more, but only make very brief stops at the major towns.

Relatively new services of *ejecutivo* (executive) or express buses offer faster deluxe service between Tegucigalpa and San Pedro Sula in modern airconditioned buses with video movies and soft drinks. Most other buses are not air conditioned.

In addition to long-distance buses operating between cities and towns, buses also operate on shorter routes connecting major towns with the small villages nearby. Often these are old school buses from the USA.

Shuttle Buses
Adventure Shuttle operates a shuttle bus between Copán Ruinas and San Pedro Sula, making stops both in downtown San

Pedro and at the San Pedro Sula airport. It's considerably more expensive than the regular bus but goes a lot faster. Details are given in the San Pedro Sula section.

TRAIN
The only passenger train in Honduras is the one that runs twice a week between Puerto Cortés and Tela. See the Puerto Cortés section for details.

CAR & MOTORCYCLE
The main highways are for the most part excellent paved roads. Away from the highways the roads may be paved or unpaved, with their condition ranging from excellent to disastrous.

Rental cars are available in Tegucigalpa, San Pedro Sula, La Ceiba and on Roatán, but they are not cheap.

Motorcycles can be rented in Trujillo and on Roatán.

HITCHHIKING
While we don't officially recommended it, hitching is generally easy in Honduras, especially in the rural areas where not many people have private vehicles and buses may be few and far between. It is normal in rural areas for pickup trucks to stop to take on passengers. It's polite to offer to pay for your ride; likely the driver will refuse your offer, but as elsewhere in Central America, gasoline is expensive for the locals and it's normal for someone who gets a ride to offer to chip in for gas.

BOAT
A comfortable air-conditioned passenger ferry, the MV *Tropical* (☎ 42-0780 in La Ceiba, ☎ 45-1795 in Roatán), operates between La Ceiba, Roatán and Utila. The service is convenient, and since airfares have recently risen, it's also quite a bit cheaper than flying. The trip takes about two hours between La Ceiba and Roatán and about an hour between La Ceiba and Utila.

The schedule seems to change regularly, so check before you plan to travel.

Route	One-Way	Roundtrip
La Ceiba–Roatán	US$9.20	US$17.50
La Ceiba–Utila	US$7.50	US$14.20
Roatán–Utila	US$12.50	US$24.20

Monday
    La Ceiba – Roatán, 5 am
    Roatán – La Ceiba, 7:30 am
    La Ceiba – Utila, 10:30 am
    Utila – La Ceiba, Noon
    La Ceiba – Roatán, 3:30 pm
Tuesday to Friday
    Roatán – La Ceiba, 7 am
    La Ceiba – Utila, 10 am
    Utila – La Ceiba, 11:30 am
    La Ceiba – Roatán, 3:30 pm
Saturday
    Roatán – La Ceiba, 7 am
    La Ceiba – Roatán, 11 am
    Roatán – La Ceiba, 2 pm
Sunday
    La Ceiba – Roatán, 7 am
    Roatán – La Ceiba, 3:30 pm

The MV *Starfish* (☎ 45-3197), based on Utila, carries passengers and cargo to and from La Ceiba (see Boat under Utila). There's always a chance of catching a ride on less regular cargo boats or even fishing boats. Cargo boats operate frequently between the Caribbean Coast and the Bay Islands. To try your luck catching a ride, just go down to the docks and ask around to see what boats are going and when. Cargo boats leave Trujillo for Guanaja and the Mosquitia every couple of days or so; you can also find cargo and fishing boats at the docks in Puerto Cortés, La Ceiba and Tela, as well as on all the Bay Islands.

Boats are also a good way to see some of the natural wonders of the Caribbean Coast. Small boat trips are popular for visiting Parque Nacional Punta Sal, the Laguna de los Micos and the Refugio Punta Izopo, all near Tela; the Cuero y Salado Wildlife Refuge near La Ceiba; and the Laguna de Guaimorteo Wildlife Refuge near Trujillo. Tour companies organize trips to all of these places, or you could probably arrange a boat trip on your own.

In the Mosquitia, where there is just one road, almost all transport is along the waterways. Boat trips on the Río Plátano,

HONDURAS

in the Río Plátano Biosphere Reserve, allow you to see a lot of wildlife; boat trips can also be made on other rivers and lagoons in the Mosquitia, and in this remote area, you'll see plenty of wildlife just about everywhere. See the Mosquitia section for more details on boat trips in this area.

Boat trips on the Lago de Yojoa are also a pleasant pastime; it's only a short hop by boat from the hotels on the north shore of the lake to the Los Naranjos archaeological site. Bird watching is also excellent on and around the lake.

LOCAL TRANSPORT
Bus
Buses service major towns and cities along a network of local and suburban routes. These are often on old school buses from the USA. On most routes, buses run every day very frequently – every five minutes or so – and cost about US$0.05.

Taxi
There are numerous taxis in most towns in Honduras. Fares can start as low as US$0.40, charged either as a flat rate for the destination or per person; this would be the normal fare for an average ride in a small or medium-size town. You can expect longer journeys in a major city to cost around US$1.50.

In the major cities, *colectivos* (shared taxis) ply a number of prescribed routes, costing around US$0.25 per passenger.

Taxis are not metered in Honduras, so be sure to negotiate the fare before you take off.

Bicycle
Bicycles are the main way that people get around in some of the medium-size towns; Tela, in particular, is full of people riding bikes.

Rental bicycles are available in only a few places in Honduras. On our last visit we found them in Tela at Garífuna Tours and (more expensive) at the Hotel Villas Telamar. The Hotel Hacienda El Jaral, 11 km from Copán Ruinas, also rents bicycles.

ORGANIZED TOURS
Organized tours are a good way to visit some of the more out-of-the-way areas. In this chapter we've mentioned local tour operators in the Tegucigalpa, San Pedro Sula, Copán Ruinas, Tela, La Ceiba, Trujillo and Mosquitia sections. Most of the operators offer tours not only in their own local areas, but also to places farther afield.

Tegucigalpa

Population 785,000

Tegucigalpa, the capital of Honduras, is a busy, noisy city nestled in a bowl-shaped valley and surrounded by a ring of mountains. At an altitude of 975 meters, it has a fresh and pleasant climate, much cooler than the coasts. The surrounding mountainous region is covered in pine trees.

The name Tegucigalpa is a bit of a mouthful; Hondurans often call the city 'Tegus' (TEH-goos) for short. The name, meaning 'silver hill' in the original local dialect, was bestowed when the Spanish founded the city as a silver and gold mining center in 1578, on the slopes of Picacho. Tegucigalpa became the capital of Honduras in 1880, when the government seat was moved from Comayagua, 82 km to the northwest.

In 1938 Comayagüela, on the opposite side of the river from Tegucigalpa, became part of the city.

Orientation
The city is divided by the Río Choluteca. On the east side is Tegucigalpa, with the city center and the more affluent districts. With its beautiful cathedral, Plaza Morazán, usually called Parque Central, is at the heart of the city. Most local bus lines stop there or nearby.

On the west side of Parque Central, Av Miguel Paz Barahona has been turned into a pedestrian shopping street, extending four blocks from the plaza on Calle El Telégrafo; this section has been renamed Calle Peatonal, and it's a busy thoroughfare with many shops, restaurants and banks.

Across the river from Tegucigalpa is Comayagüela, generally poorer and dirtier, with a sprawling market area, lots of long-distance bus stations, cheap hotels and comedores. The two are connected by a number of bridges.

Maps The tourist map published by the Instituto Geográfico Nacional is for sale for US$1.65 at the tourist office or for US$2.10 at the post office. Unfortunately the city map has only a few street names on it. At the Instituto itself, you can buy excellent color topographical and regional maps. The office (☎ 33-7166) is in the SECOPT building, Barrio La Bolsa, in Comayagüela, just across the river from Tegucigalpa. It's open Monday to Friday, from 8 am to 4 pm.

Information
Tourist Offices The Instituto Hondureño de Turismo (☎ 22-2124, 38-3974, fax 38-2102) which is on the 5th floor of the Edificio Europa, at the corner of Av Ramon Ernesto Cruz and Calle República de México, in Colonia San Carlos. It's between Blvd Morazán and Av La Paz; Lloyd's Bank is on the ground floor. The office is open Monday to Friday from 8:30 am to 4:30 pm. From the downtown area, take any Lomas, Tiloarque Sosa or Hospital San Felipe bus, or take a San Felipe colectivo.

The staff can sell you a city map (see Maps above). Also available are several free tourist publications. A special office has information on ecotourism in Honduras, including national parks and wildlife refuges.

The tourist office also operates an automatic information kiosk at Tegucigalpa's Toncontín Airport, with general tourist information.

The national office of the Corporación Hondureña de Desarrollo Forestal (COHDEFOR) in Colonia El Carrizal has information on all of Honduras' national parks, wildlife refuges and other protected areas. Ask for the Departamento de Areas Protegidas (☎ /fax 23-4346); it's open Monday to Friday, 8 am to 4 pm.

Foreign Embassies There are various foreign embassies and a number of consulates in Tegucigalpa. Several countries also have consulates in San Pedro Sula. Those in Tegucigalpa include:

Belize (consulate only)
  Hotel Honduras Maya, Centro de Convenciones (☎ 39-4019, 39-4021, fax 39-0134)
Canada (consulate only)
  Edificio El Castaño, 6th floor, Blvd Morazán (☎ 31-4538, 31-4545, fax 31-5793)
Colombia
  Colonia Palmira, Edificio Palmira, 4th floor, opposite Hotel Honduras Maya (☎ 32-9709, 32-5131, fax 32-8133)
Costa Rica
  Colonia El Triángulo, subida a Lomas del Guijarro (☎ 32-1054, 32-1768, fax 32-1876)
El Salvador
  Colonia San Carlos, 2a Av, No 205, 1½ blocks from Blvd Morazán (☎ 36-8045, 36-7344, fax 36-9403)
France
  Colonia Palmira, Av Juan Lindo, frente a Escuela Liceo Español (☎ 36-5583, 36-6432, fax 36-8051)
Germany
  Blvd Morazán, Edificio Paysen, 3rd floor (☎ 32-3161/2, fax 32-9518)
Guatemala
  Colonia Las Minitas, 4a Calle and Av Juan Lindo, No 2421 (☎ 32-9704, 32-1543, fax 31-5655)
Japan
  Colonia San Carlos, Calzada República de Paraguay, between 4a and 5a Calles (☎ 36-5511, fax 36-6100)
Mexico
  Colonia Palmira, Av República de México, No 2402 (☎ 32-6471, 32-0138, fax 31-4719)
Nicaragua
  Colonia Lomas del Tepeyac, Bloque M-1, Calle 11 (☎ 32-7218, 32-7224, fax 31-1412)
Panama
  Colonia Palmira, Edificio Palmira, 2nd floor, No 200, opposite Hotel Honduras Maya (☎ /fax 31-5441)
UK
  Colonia Palmira, Edificio Palmira, 3rd floor, opposite Hotel Honduras Maya (☎ 32-0612, 32-0618, fax 32-5480)
USA
  Edificio Embajada Americana, Av La Paz (☎ 36-9320, fax 36-9037)

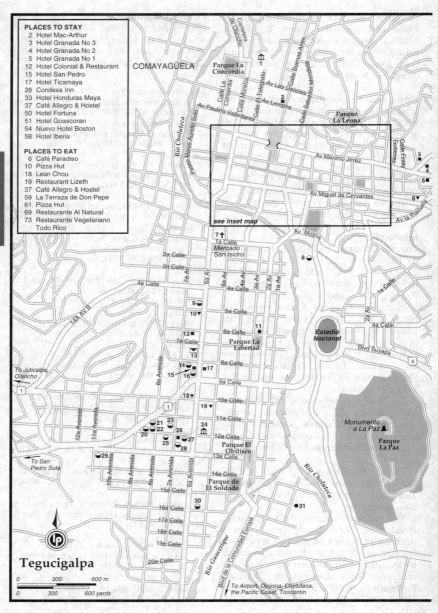

PLACES TO STAY
2 Hotel Mac-Arthur
3 Hotel Granada No 3
4 Hotel Granada No 2
5 Hotel Granada No 1
12 Hotel Colonial & Restaurant
15 Hotel San Pedro
17 Hotel Ticamaya
26 Condesa Inn
33 Hotel Honduras Maya
37 Café Allegro & Hostel
50 Hotel Fortuna
51 Hotel Goascoran
54 Nuevo Hotel Boston
58 Hotel Iberia

PLACES TO EAT
6 Café Paradiso
10 Pizza Hut
18 Lean Chou
19 Restaurant Lizeth
37 Café Allegro & Hostel
59 La Terraza de Don Pepe
61 Pizza Hut
69 Restaurante Al Natural
73 Restaurante Vegetariano
   Todo Rico

COMAYAGÜELA

Tegucigalpa

0   300   600 m
0   300   600 yards

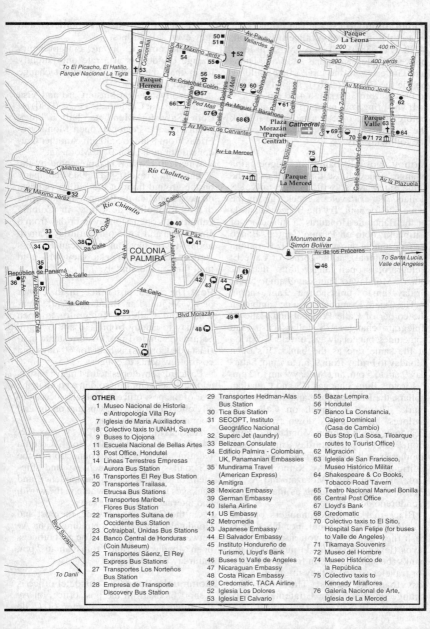

OTHER

1 Museo Nacional de Historia e Antropología Villa Roy
7 Iglesia de María Auxiliadora
8 Colectivo taxis to UNAH, Suyapa
9 Buses to Ojojona
11 Escuela Nacional de Bellas Artes
13 Post Office, Hondutel
14 Lineas Terrestres Empresas Aurora Bus Station
16 Transportes El Rey Bus Station
20 Transportes Trailasa, Etrucsa Bus Stations
21 Transportes Maribel, Flores Bus Station
22 Transportes Sultana de Occidente Bus Station
23 Cotraipbal, Unidas Bus Stations
24 Banco Central de Honduras (Coin Museum)
25 Transportes Sáenz, El Rey Express Bus Stations
27 Transportes Los Norteños Bus Station
28 Empresa de Transporte Discovery Bus Station

29 Transportes Hedman-Alas Bus Station
30 Tica Bus Station
31 SECOPT, Instituto Geográfico Nacional
32 Superc Jet (laundry)
33 Belizean Consulate
34 Edificio Palmira - Colombian, UK, Panamanian Embassies
35 Mundirama Travel (American Express)
36 Amitigra
38 Mexican Embassy
39 German Embassy
40 Isleña Airline
41 US Embassy
42 Metromedia
43 Japanese Embassy
44 El Salvador Embassy
45 Instituto Hondureño de Turismo, Lloyd's Bank
46 Buses to Valle de Angeles
47 Nicaraguan Embassy
48 Costa Rican Embassy
49 Credomatic, TACA Airline
52 Iglesia Los Dolores
53 Iglesia El Calvario

55 Bazar Lempira
56 Hondutel
57 Banco La Constancia, Cajero Dominical (Casa de Cambio)
60 Bus Stop (La Sosa, Tiloarque routes to Tourist Office)
62 Migración
63 Iglesia de San Francisco, Museo Histórico Militar
64 Shakespeare & Co Books, Tobacco Road Tavern
65 Teatro Nacional Manuel Bonilla
66 Central Post Office
67 Lloyd's Bank
68 Credomatic
70 Colectivo taxis to El Sitio, Hospital San Felipe (for buses to Valle de Angeles)
71 Tikamaya Souvenirs
72 Museo del Hombre
74 Museo Histórico de la República
75 Colectivo taxis to Kennedy Miraflores
76 Galería Nacional de Arte, Iglesia de La Merced

Immigration Office You can extend your visa at the immigration office (Migración; ☎ 22-7711, 38-1957) on Av Máximo Jeréz between Calle Las Damas and Calle Dionicio Gutierrez, in the large office building beside the Hotel Rondo. It's open Monday to Friday from 8:30 am to 4:30 pm.

If you bring your passport in the morning before 10 am, you can usually get it back the same afternoon; otherwise, pick it up the following day.

Money Not all banks in Tegucigalpa change money; those that do all offer the same rates. Most will change only US dollars cash or traveler's checks, giving the same rate for both. Try the Banco Atlántida or the Banco de Honduras (a subsidiary of Citibank), both on Parque Central. Banco La Constancia on Av Miguel Paz Barahona (Calle Peatonal), at the corner of Calle El Telégrafo, is open longer hours than the others: Monday to Thursday 9 am to 5 pm, Friday 9 am to 6 pm, Saturday 9 am to noon.

The Cajero Dominical casa de cambio on the corner of Calle Peatonal and Calle El Telégrafo changes US dollars cash (and sometimes, but not always, traveler's checks) at the same rate as the banks. It's open Monday to Friday from 9 am to 7 pm, Saturday 9 am to 5 pm, and Sunday 9 am to 2 pm.

Lloyd's Bank changes US and Canadian dollars, the British pound and the Deutschmark. There's a branch on Calle Los Dolores, half a block down from Calle Peatonal, which is open Monday to Friday from 9 am to 4 pm, Saturday 9 am to noon; another branch is on the ground floor of the Edificio Europa on Av Ramon Ernesto Cruz, between Blvd Morazán and Av La Paz, in the same building as the Instituto Hondureño de Turismo.

Black-market moneychangers operate all along Calle Peatonal. For US dollars cash they might give you about 10 centavos (less than US$0.01) more than the banks (be sure to bargain for a good rate); for traveler's checks they might give you less than the banks! They will also change money from Guatemala, Nicaragua and El Salvador (but you'll get a better rate at the respective borders), and they even sell dollars.

At the airport, private entrepreneurs change US dollars at a rate only slightly lower than the banks; they won't change any other currency.

Cash advances on MasterCard and Visa are available at Credomatic (☎ 22-0380) on Calle Salvador Mendieta, half a block south of Calle Peatonal, open Monday to Friday from 8 am to 5:30 pm. Another Credomatic branch is on Blvd Morazán.

American Express is represented by the Mundirama Travel (☎ 32-3943) company on the ground floor of the Edificio Ciicsa, on Av República de Panamá at the corner of Av República de Chile, in Colonia Palmira. It's open Monday to Friday from 8 am to noon and 1 to 5 pm, Saturday 8 am to noon. If you have an American Express card or traveler's checks, they will hold mail for you indefinitely.

Post The central post office, on the corner of Av Miguel Paz Barahona (Calle Peatonal) and Calle El Telégrafo, is open Monday to Friday from 7:30 am to 7 pm, Saturday 8 am to 1 pm. Poste-restante mail (Lista de Correos) is held for 60 days and costs a few cents to collect.

Postcards, envelopes, tourist maps, posters and other souvenirs are sold in a booth in the rear of the post office, which also occasionally offers a fax service. Upstairs on the 2nd floor is a philatelic bureau.

Aerocasillas (☎ 36-7420, ☎ /fax 32-7420) at Av Juan Lindo, No 4, Colonia Palmira, offers a direct connection to the US mail system, with delivery and shipment of documents, correspondence and packages to or from anywhere in the world, and international courier services.

On the Comayagüela side, the post and Hondutel offices share a building on 6a Av between 7a and 8a Calles. The post office is open Monday to Friday from 8 am to 7 pm, Saturday 8 am to 1 pm.

Communications The Hondutel office is a short block from the post office, on Av Cristobal Colón at the corner of Calle

El Telégrafo. The office for international telephone calls is open 24 hours daily; in the same office are several public phones, where you can use coins or phone cards for local and domestic calls. Phone cards for L50 (US$4.15) and L100 (US$8.35) are sold in the Tesorería office down the hall, which is open Monday to Friday from 8 am to 4 pm.

In the same building, Hondutel has a separate office with fax, telex and cablegram services, open Monday to Friday from 8 am to 4 pm. You can send and receive faxes here (fax 37-9715); a list of faxes received is posted on the window.

In Comayagüela, the Hondutel office is in the same building as the post office; it's open Monday to Friday from 8 am to 8 pm. Another branch of Hondutel at the Toncontín Airport is open every day.

Domestic and international email services are available from Telemática (☎ 32-9963, net) on Blvd Centroamérica, opposite the Cámera de Comercio, in Colonia Miraflores. It's open Monday to Friday 7 am to 4 pm. The Hotel Granada (see Places to Stay) and Shakespeare & Co Books (see Bookstores) offer Internet and email connections for travelers.

Travel Agencies Mundirama Travel (see Money), the agent for American Express, offers card services as well as travel agency services. Check in the telephone directory yellow pages under 'Agencias de Viajes' for other travel agencies; there are dozens scattered around the city.

Bookstores Shakespeare & Co Books (☎ 37-3909, net), on Av Miguel Paz Barahona in the block east of Iglesia de San Francisco, carries a wide selection of new and used books in English, German, French and other languages. It sells used books at half the cover price and will trade used books. Email services are also available here. The store also offers trips to nearby sights (see Organized Tours). The Tobacco Road Tavern is also here at the bookstore.

Metromedia (☎ /fax 32-7108) in the Edificio Casa Real, Av San Carlos, Colonia San Carlos, is the new incarnation of the old Book Village, which has sold English-language books, newspapers and magazines for many years. The new store, four times bigger than the old one, offers books, magazines, videos and music, and it runs a cafe. It's open Monday to Saturday from 10 am to 8 pm, Sunday noon to 5 pm.

Lonely Planet books are available at both Shakespeare & Co and Metromedia.

The gift shop of the Hotel Honduras Maya carries a small selection of paperback books in English.

The weekly English-language newspaper, *This Week in Honduras*, is available at the English-language bookshops and in many hotels; you can pick it up for free at the Hotel Plaza, on Calle Peatonal near the corner of Calle El Telégrafo.

Cultural Centers The Instituto Hondureño de Cultura Interamericana (IHCI; ☎ 37-7539) on Calle Real de Comayagüela offers cultural events relating to all the Americas, and they have a small English-language library.

Alianza Francesa (Alliance Française; ☎ 39-1529) in Colonia Las Lomas del Guijarro offers cultural events, French classes and weekly French films. Centro Cultural Alemán (The German Institute; ☎ 37-1555), at Calle La Fuente, No 1465, offers German cultural events and literature, courses in Spanish (for foreigners) and German languages and a German-Honduran cultural exchange.

Laundry At Superc Jet (☎ 37-4154, 37-4155) on Av Juan Gutemberg, Barrio Guanacaste, you can have laundry washed, dried and folded for US$0.15 per pound. Drop it off in the morning, and it will be ready that afternoon; dry-cleaning service is also available. It's open Monday to Saturday, 8 am to 6:30 pm.

Medical Services Tegucigalpa has several hospitals and clinics; look in the yellow pages of the telephone directory under 'Hospitales.' You might want to ask your hotel or embassy for a recommendation.

HONDURAS

Pharmacies are numerous around the city. There's always a 'farmacia de turno' on duty – the pharmacies take turns staying open 24 hours. A schedule for the farmacias de turno is published in the major daily newspapers. For simple ailments, it's often unnecessary to go to a doctor – pharmacists can often give you the medicine you need to fix you up.

Emergencies

Police (FUSEP) ☎ 199, 52-3128, 52-3171
Policía Femenina ☎ 37-2184
Ambulance (Red Cross) ☎ 37-8654
Paramedics ☎ 39-9999
Hospital ☎ 32-2322, 32-3021
Fire ☎ 198, 56-8790, 56-6180

Walking Tour – Tegucigalpa

At the center of the city is the fine **cathedral** and, in front of it, the **Plaza Morazán**, often called Parque Central. The domed 18th-century cathedral (built between 1765 and 1782) has an intricate baroque altar of gold and silver, and lots of other fine art. Parque Central, with its statue of Morazán on horseback, is the hub of the city. Most local buses stop here or nearby. Opposite the south side of the cathedral is the *Alcaldía* (City Hall).

Three blocks east of the cathedral on Av Miguel Paz Barahona is the **Parque Valle**, with the old **Iglesia de San Francisco**, the first church in Tegucigalpa, founded in 1592 by the Franciscans. The building beside it was first a convent, then the Spanish Mint; it now houses the **Museo Histórico Militar**, with exhibits on Honduras' military history (open Monday to Friday from 7:30 am to 4 pm).

Across the street on the south side of the church, the **Museo del Hombre** occupies the former Supreme Court building, the Antiguo Edificio Corte Suprema de Justicia. Cultural events and exhibitions are held here; the museum is only open when there's something going on. (The entrance is on Av Miguel de Cervantes, around the block.)

From Parque Central, head two blocks south to another major plaza, Parque La Merced. The unusual modern building on stilts is the **Palacio Legislativo**, where Congress meets. Next to it in striking contrast is the Antiguo Paraninfo Universitario building, which now houses the **Galería Nacional de Arte** (☎ 37-9884), the impressive national art gallery (open Tuesday to Sunday from 8 am to 5 pm). In the same building is the 18th-century **Iglesia La Merced**. In 1847 the convent of La Merced was converted to house Honduras' first university; the national gallery was established there in 1996. The well-restored building is just as interesting as the paintings in the gallery – the building, too, is a work of art.

One block west of Parque La Merced is the **Museo Histórico de la República** (☎ 37-0268), on the corner of Paseo Marco Aurelio Soto and Calle Salvador Mendieta. This museum holds exhibits on the history of Honduras from the winning of independence to the present. Just as interesting as the exhibits is the building itself, which was the Casa Presidencial (the Presidential Palace) from 1920 until 1992. It's open Wednesday to Sunday from 8:30 am to noon and from 1 to 4 pm; admission is US$1.65 for foreigners, free for children under seven, and free for everyone on the last Thursday of each month.

Head west from Parque Central along Av Miguel Paz Barahona. This lively pedestrian-only section, which is also called Calle Peatonal, has many street vendors. It stretches four blocks west from the plaza to Calle El Telégrafo.

Three blocks west along Calle Peatonal from Parque Central, turn right on Calle Los Dolores and head to another fine colonial church, **Los Dolores** (1732), with a plaza out front and religious art inside. On the front of Los Dolores are figures representing the Passion of Christ – his unseamed cloak, the cock that crowed three times – all crowned by the more indigenous symbol of the sun.

On Av Miguel Paz Barahona, two blocks west of Calle Telegráfo is Parque Herrera, another pleasant plaza. There stands the national theater, **Teatro Nacional Manuel Bonilla**, dating from 1912; its interior was inspired by the Athens Theatre of Paris.

Performances are still given in the theater; during the daytime you're welcome to go in and have a look. Also on this park is a peaceful 18th-century church, **El Calvario**.

Walking north for four long blocks from El Calvario on Calle La Concordia, you reach **Parque La Concordia**, an interesting park full of reproductions of the Maya ruins at Copán, including a pyramid and many stone carvings.

A couple of blocks northeast, way up on a hill, is the **Museo Nacional de Historia e Antropología Villa Roy** (☎ 22-3470, 22-1468), the national museum of anthropology and history. The grand building was the personal home of Julio Lozano, one of Honduras' former presidents. It now contains salons with displays on anthropology, archaeology and the pre-Hispanic history of Honduras, the 'moment of contact' when the Spanish arrived, the colonial period and an interesting section on ethnography, with displays on Honduras' eight indigenous groups showing where and how they live. The museum is normally open Wednesday to Sunday from 8:30 am to 3:30 pm, but recently it was closed for remodeling; phone to see if it has reopened.

About five blocks east is **Parque La Leona**, an attractive park with a fine view over the city. From there you can make your way down the steep streets to the city center.

Walking Tour – Comayagüela
Just across the Río Choluteca (also called Río Grande) is Comayagüela, about a five-minute walk from central Tegucigalpa.

If you cross the bridge leading to 6a Av in Comayagüela, you immediately come to Comayagüela's famous market, **Mercado San Isidro**, which sprawls for many blocks. The leather shops have some good handcrafted leatherwork and saddles, and also sell handwoven hats.

From the copper-domed church of **María Auxiliadora**, on the corner of 1a Calle and 5a Av, a statue of the Virgin and Child (on the church's tower) oversees the market area.

Comayagüela is more a commercial center and has fewer old buildings and plazas than Tegucigalpa. On Parque La Libertad is the

Escuela Nacional de Bellas Artes, the national school of fine arts.

Five blocks south on 2a Av is the **Parque El Obelisco**, with an obelisk commemorating the centennial of Central American independence. Nearby on 12a Calle is the towering Banco Central de Honduras; inside is the **Museo Numismático Rigoberto Borjas** (☎ 37-7686, ext 108), a numismatic museum displaying historic coins and notes of Honduras and other countries. Aside from valuable notes and coins (one 1888 Honduran gold coin is worth US$12,000), there's an interesting exhibit on the idealized Indian face chosen to represent Lempira on the one lempira note. Also look for the 1993 banknote issued by Kuwait to thank nations that provided military assistance in the Gulf War; Honduras' name appears on the note, despite the denials of the Honduran government that they sent any soldiers! The museum is open Monday to Friday from 9 am to noon and 1 to 4 pm.

Parque y Monumento a la Paz
Near the river and opposite the Parque El Obelisco is Parque a la Paz, a wooded hill with a large monument to peace at its summit, which commands a sweeping view of the entire city; you can walk or drive up here for a magnificent view. Nearby is the giant **Estadio Nacional**, the national stadium, where soccer matches are played.

Sala Bancatlán
The headquarters of Bancatlán on Blvd Miraflores, southeast of the center in Miraflores, has the Sala Bancatlán, with a coin collection and an archaeological collection of Maya statues, vessels and artifacts from Copán and other sites, plus explanatory maps and photos. It's open Monday to Friday from 9 am to 3 pm; admission free. Take bus No 5 (Carrizal-Miraflores) from the center.

Centro de Ecoturismo Rehabilitación Diseño
This center (☎ /fax 30-6346) at Calle Principal, No 2285, in the Colonia La Joya,

propagates hundreds of iguanas for eventual release into the wild. You can visit the center to see iguanas at all stages of development and learn about their life cycle. Also here are a cactus garden, local handicrafts and a cafe. From the center of town, any Kennedy bus or colectivo will drop you there.

El Picacho

On this peak on the north side of Tegucigalpa is the **Parque de las Naciones Unidas** (United Nations Park), established to commemorate the UN's 40th anniversary. There's also a soccer field where games are held on Sunday, several lookout points for excellent views over the city and a zoo. Food and drink are available.

The zoo is not extravagant but it does have some interesting local wildlife. It's open weekdays from 9 am to 3 pm, weekends 9 am to 4 pm; admission is US$0.15.

Buses to Picacho run only on Sunday; take bus No 9 from the bus stop outside the Farmacia Santa Bárbara behind Iglesia Los Dolores. Be sure you get on the right bus; several other No 9 buses also stop here. The last bus leaves at 5 pm for the return trip to town. A taxi from the center costs US$2.10.

Organized Tours

Shakespeare & Co Books (see the Bookstores section) offers trips to nearby attractions, including Parque Nacional La Tigra, Valle de Angeles and Santa Lucía, Ojojona and Yuscarán.

La Moskitia Ecoaventuras (☎ /fax 37-9398), Apdo Postal 3577, and Adventure Expeditions (☎ 37-4793, fax 37-9953), 1020 Altos de la Hoya, offer trips to the Mosquitia region and other destinations.

Some of the travel agencies also offer tours of the local area; ask the tourist office for details.

Special Events

The Feria de Suyapa (February 2 to 11) is held every year in Suyapa, seven km southeast of Tegucigalpa, to honor the Virgen de Suyapa, Honduras' patron saint. Her day is February 3, but the fair lasts for an entire week, attracting pilgrims and celebrants from all over Central America.

Good Friday is commemorated with processions through the streets. Participants bear religious figures over pathways carpeted with intricate designs of colored sawdust. A similar procession takes place in Comayagua (see below) on the morning of Good Friday; in Tegucigalpa it starts at around noon and continues until around 1 am. As in Comayagua, people work through the night to create the fragile, colored sawdust carpets, and you're welcome to join them.

The Feria Centroamericana de Turismo y Artesanía (FECATAI) is an all-Central American international artisans' and tourist fair. It's held from December 6 to 16; the location changes, so check with the tourist office.

Places to Stay

There are many places to stay on the Tegucigalpa side or across the river in Comayagüela. Comayagüela has the central market area and lots of bus stations; the Tegucigalpa side is cleaner, safer and more pleasant. Everyone says it is cheaper to stay in Comayagüela, but it all depends which hotel you pick. Neither side has to be expensive.

If you do stay in Comayagüela, remember that it is *definitely not safe* to walk through the market area at night. The hotels mentioned here are away from the market. If you have to pass through the market area after dark, take a bus or taxi.

Tegucigalpa The *Café Allegro* (☎ 32-8122; see Places to Eat) offers hostel rooms upstairs over the coffeehouse, with four beds in each room, for US$5 per person. Rooms are separated by sex, but if a couple shows up and there's a spare room available, they're welcome to share it. There's a terrace and a sitting room with cable TV. It's in Colonia Palmira, one of Tegucigalpa's more upmarket districts.

All three Granada hotels have hot water and are large (48 rooms), clean, modern and a bit impersonal, but they're a good deal. They are in a district with restaurants, movies and stores, not far from the city center. Parking in their enclosed garage is available for US$0.85 per day, and they will soon have an Internet connection for guests to use.

A good deal for the price is *Hotel Granada No 1* (☎ 37-2381) at Av Juan Gutemberg, No 1401, Barrio Guanacaste. Lots of Peace Corps workers and other volunteers stay here. Singles/doubles go for US$3.75/4.60 with shared bath, US$5.85/7.50 with private bath, and there are some larger rooms with two or three beds; color cable TV is US$3.35 extra, and a fan is an extra US$1.25.

A block away, at *Hotel Granada No 2* (☎ 37-4004, fax 38-4438), Subida Casamata, No 1326, all the rooms have telephone and private bath, and there's a hotel restaurant, free wake-up service and free coffee. The rates are US$6.65/8.35 for singles/doubles or US$10/13.35 for two/three beds. Color cable TV is optional and costs another US$4.15. Across the street, *Hotel Granada No 3* (☎ 22-0597, 37-7079) is the newest of the three Granadas, with singles/doubles for US$5.85/7.50 or two/three beds for US$9.15/12.50.

A row of basic hospedajes beside Iglesia Los Dolores provide some of the most inexpensive accommodations in town. On the rear corner is the *Hotel Fortuna,* which has singles/doubles with general bath for US$2.10/3.35; rooms with private bath are US$4.15/5. A couple of doors down, *Hotel Goascoran* (☎ 38-1903) has rooms for US$2.50 with general bath or US$4.15 with private bath. Both of these places are very basic, and the showers are cold, but they're relatively clean and shoestring travelers often stay at them.

The *Hotel Iberia* (☎ 37-9267), upstairs on Calle Los Dolores in front of Iglesia Los Dolores, has singles/doubles for US$5/5.40 with general bath or US$5.85/6.25 with private bath. Windows open onto an inside sitting area.

Much more pleasant, the *Nuevo Hotel Boston* (☎ 37-9411, fax 37-0186) at Av Máximo Jeréz, No 321, Barrio Abajo, is an excellent place to stay, very clean and well kept, with a comfortable sitting room. Free coffee and purified water are always available. Street-facing rooms, though noisy, are especially large and have doors opening onto a small balcony; these are US$15/16 for singles/doubles. Quieter, smaller interior rooms are US$13/15. All have private hot baths.

A still more upmarket choice is *Hotel Mac-Arthur* (☎ 37-9839, 37-5906), Av Lempira, No 454, where large, attractive, clean singles/doubles with telephone and private hot bath are US$19/23 with fan or US$26/30 with air con and color cable TV.

Comayagüela The 90-room *Hotel San Pedro* (☎ 22-8987), on 6a Av between 8a and 9a Calles, is popular with shoestring travelers on the Comayagüela side; it's clean and there are a couple of parking spaces out front. Rooms with one bed are US$2.10 with general bath, US$4.15 with private bath; with two beds they're US$2.90/5.85. It's handy to the El Rey and Aurora bus stations for buses to San Pedro Sula or Juticalpa, and it has an inexpensive cafe.

Opposite this is the *Hotel Ticamaya* (☎ 37-0084, 37-5232), which charges US$2.90/4.60/5.85 for singles/doubles/triples with general bath, and US$4.60/6.25/8.75/10 for one to four people with private bath.

Hotel Colonial (☎ 37-5785), on 6a Calle between 6a and 7a Avs, is more cheerful, clean and modern; 15 singles/doubles with private hot bath go for US$4.15/5. The clean and inexpensive Cafe Colonial is on the ground floor.

On 12a Calle at the corner of 7a Av, the *Condesa Inn* (☎ 37-7857) has a variety of rooms starting at US$6 with one bed, US$7 with two beds; all rooms have private hot bath, fan and TV, and the Cafetería Condesa is downstairs. Many of the rooms have little ventilation; some are better than others. The Condesa is near the Transportes Norteños and Sáenz bus stations, where you can get buses to San Pedro Sula.

If you're at the end of your economic rope, there are plenty of other hotels that are a few cents cheaper, but most are a lot less pleasant.

Places to Eat

Tegucigalpa Most of the good restaurants are on the Tegucigalpa side of the river.

La Terraza de Don Pepe (☎ 37-1084), an upstairs restaurant on Av Cristobal Colón, two blocks west of Parque Central, is 'a tradition in Honduras,' the sign announces. It's a popular place, open daily from 10 am to 10 pm, with good prices, a family atmosphere and live music in the evenings. While you're here, take a look at the unusual shrine to the Virgin of Suyapa, who was once abducted from the Basilica de Suyapa and later turned up here, in the men's restroom. The restroom is now a shrine, with newspaper clippings and photos of the event.

Directly behind the cathedral, *Restaurante Al Natural* is lovely and relaxing, removed from the hubbub of the city, with tables set around a lush covered garden. The food is good and fresh, with a large menu to select from, and it's not expensive. It's open Monday to Friday from 8 am to 7 pm, Saturday 8 am to 3 pm, closed Sunday.

At lunchtime vegetarians should try the simple little *Restaurante Vegetariano Todo Rico* on Av Miguel de Cervantes, between Calle El Telégrafo and Calle Morelos. The plato del día lunchtime meal is just US$0.85, or US$1.50 if you also get soup, dessert and a fresh fruit *fresco*; fruit salad, vegetable salad and enchiladas are also available. It's open Monday to Saturday, 11:30 am to 2:30 pm.

A popular air-conditioned *Pizza Hut* is on the corner of Av Cristobal Colón and Calle La Leona, half a block west of Parque Central. You can fill up at the salad bar as many times as you like for US$2.50; lunchtime specials featuring pizza or pasta, with one trip to the salad bar and unlimited soda, are served Monday to Friday, 11 am to 4 pm, for US$2.50 to US$3.30. Phone for free delivery (☎ 37-5717). It's open every day from 9 am to 10 pm, and there are other branches around town.

Opposite this is a *Dunkin' Donuts*. There are many branches of Dunkin' Donuts and Burger King all around Tegucigalpa; *Burger King* has a branch on the south side of Parque Central.

Many other simple places for a bite are on Calle Peatonal in the blocks west of Parque Central. Just a few doors from the plaza, *Super Donuts* is a large place offering not only donuts but also a cafeteria buffet; it's open every day from 6 am to 8 pm. *Wendy's* is in the same block. Additional inexpensive places to eat are in the blocks behind the cathedral on the other side of Parque Central.

There are fancier, more expensive restaurants in Colonia Palmira, the area around the Hotel Honduras Maya and along Blvd Morazán. In Colonia Alameda, southeast of the center, *Restaurante Debarro* at Av Juan Manuel Galvez, No 719, has good, traditional Honduran dishes; it also has art, literature and music of Honduras. It's open Monday to Thursday from 9:30 am to 8 pm, Friday and Saturday 9:30 am to midnight, Sunday 11:30 am to 9 pm, closed on Tuesday.

Coffeehouse lingerers will like the *Café Paradiso* coffeehouse/gallery at Av Miguel Paz Barahona, No 1351, near El Arbolito; it's open weekdays from 9 am to 8 pm, Saturday 9 am to 6 pm. The *Café Allegro* at Av República de Chile, No 360, half a block south of Av República de Panamá in Colonia Palmira, is another fine coffeehouse, open every day from 10 am to 10 pm.

Comayagüela Comayagüela has plenty of Chinese restaurants where you can eat for US$2 or less; *Lean Chou* on the corner of 6a Av and 10a Calle has huge portions. At *Restaurant Lizeth* on 5a Av between 10a and 11a Calles, smaller portions are offset by very low prices; breakfasts are around US$0.60 to US$1.25. *Pizza Hut* has a branch on 6a Av between 4a and 5a Calles.

Entertainment

It's especially pleasant to sit in Parque Central at sunset, when the loud cacophony of birds *(zanates)* in the trees practically drowns out the sounds of the city and traffic. You can buy some *tajaditas* (fried banana chips) or sliced mangoes on the plaza and spend an enjoyable hour sitting and listening to the zanates in the trees and watching the pigeons on the ancient façade of the cathedral and the people lounging in the plaza or scurrying to catch buses. The exuberant zanates are quiet at night, sleeping in the trees, but they crank up again at dawn.

Tegucigalpa has a couple of districts with lots of choice in nightlife. Blvd Morazán-Av República de Chile is the 'night on the town' zone, with discos including *Sueños, Confetis, Paladium* and *Chico Lara*, where there's live music.

A newer nightlife zone is on Av Juan Pablo II-Av República de Uruguay, in the area around the Sheraton. Dancing is good at the *Tropical Port* disco, which has a Caribbean-Coast flavor; it's opposite *Las Gemelas* drive-in. *Backstreet* is another nightspot in the same area.

Gays and lesbians will enjoy *El Closet*; see the Gay & Lesbian Travelers section for more on this friendly little bar/disco and how to find it.

The *Teatro Nacional Manuel Bonilla* (☎ 22-4366) on Parque Herrera hosts a variety of performing arts, and it's a very enjoyable place to attend a performance.

There are cinemas everywhere you turn in Tegucigalpa, and several on the Comayagüela side, too. Most of the hotels mentioned under Places to Stay have at least one cinema nearby; entry is around US$1. You can often find films in English, with Spanish subtitles, in the theaters. Check the daily newspapers for movie listings.

The expensive *Hotel Honduras Maya* has a gambling casino (no dress code), restaurants and a bar. The area around the hotel (Colonia Palmira) is the upper-class district of Tegucigalpa, the area for fancy, expensive, excellent restaurants. Other casinos include *Monte Carlo* near Blvd Morazán, *Palacios* on Calle Principal in Colonia Loma de Guijarro and *Video* near the Toncontín Airport in the south part of town. Bingo is played at *Metro Bingo*, also near Blvd Morazán.

Things to Buy

Honduran handicrafts are sold at many places around town.

On the west side of Iglesia Los Dolores plaza, on the corner of Av Máximo Jeréz, Bazar Lempira (☎ 37-9436) is a handicrafts shop with a good selection of leatherwork, woodcarvings, paintings and souvenirs. Best of all is their collection of handmade wooden musical instruments of all shapes and sizes. Most of the instruments are not expensive; you could purchase a resonant guitar, violin or mandolin for as little as US$22. Tikamaya Souvenirs on the corner of Av Miguel de Cervantes and Calle Salvador Corletto also has handicrafts and souvenirs.

In Comayagüela you can find just about anything in the sprawling blocks of the market, from vegetables to second-hand clothing to some excellent leatherwork.

For higher quality handicrafts, it's worth making a trip to Valle de Angeles (see Around Tegucigalpa).

Getting There & Away

Air Domestic and international flights arrive and depart from Toncontín International Airport on the southern outskirts of Tegucigalpa.

TACA (☎ 39-1841, 39-0614) offers two flights daily between Tegucigalpa and San Pedro Sula. The main office is on Blvd Morazán not far from the main tourist office. Isleña (☎ 37-3370), Edificio Galería La Paz, on Av La Paz half a block west of the US embassy, connects Tegucigalpa with La Ceiba, Roatán, Guanaja and Utila. See the Honduras Getting Around section for details on domestic fares, and see the Honduras Getting There & Away section for information on international flights.

Bus Excellent bus services connect Tegucigalpa with other parts of Honduras. However, the buses do not depart from a central bus station; each bus line has its own station, all of them in Comayagüela. The tourist office can give you a complete list showing bus lines, departure times and prices. See the Honduras Getting There & Away section for further information on Tica Bus international services. Long-distance buses depart from Tegucigalpa for the following Honduran destinations:

San Pedro Sula (241 km)
Transportes El Rey (☎ 37-1462), corner 9a Calle and 6a Av, Comayagüela – buses hourly from 2:30 to 4:30 am, then every half-hour until the last bus at 7 pm (four hours, US$2.10).
Transportes Sáenz (☎ 37-6521), 12a Calle between 7a and 8a Avs, Comayagüela – buses hourly from 2 am to 5 pm (four hours, US$2.10).
Transportes Los Norteños (☎ 37-0706), 12a Calle between 6a and 7a Avs, Comayagüela – buses hourly from 6:15 am to 5 pm (four hours, US$2.10).
San Pedro Sula Express Service (241 km)
Transportes El Rey Servicios Express (☎ 37-8584, 37-8561), 12a Calle between 7a and 8a Avs, Comayagüela – hourly express buses, 5:30 am to 6:30 pm (3¼ hours, US$2.90)
Transportes Sáenz Servicio Ejecutivo (☎ 33-4429, 33-4249), Centro Comercial Perisur, Blvd Comunidad Económica Europea on the way to the airport – executive buses leaving at 6, 8 and 10 am, 2, 4 and 6 pm (3¼ hours, US$6.65).
Transportes Hedman-Alas (☎ 37-7143), at the west end of 13a Calle, Comayagüela – first-class (primera clase) buses 12 times daily, 6:30 am to 5:30 pm (four hours, US$2.90); servicio ejecutivo buses at 5:45 am, 11:30 am and 4:45 pm Monday to Saturday (4 pm Saturday), and once on Sunday at 3:30 pm (3¼ hours, US$5.40 with food included, or US$4.60 without food).
Comayagua (84 km, 1½ to two hours, US$0.90) Empresas Unidas (☎ 22-2071), 7a Av between 11a and 12a Calles, Comayagüela – buses every two hours, 5:45 am to 5:45 pm. Or take any bus heading for San Pedro Sula and get off at the crossroads.
Siguatepeque (117 km, 2¾ hours, US$1) Empresas Unidas (☎ 22-2071), 7a Av between 11a and 12a Calles, Comayagüela – buses every two hours, 5:45 am to 5:45 pm. Transportes Maribel (☎ 37-3032), 8a Av between 11a and 12a Calles, Comayagüela – seven buses daily from 6:10 am to 4:45 pm. Or take any bus heading for San Pedro Sula and get off at the crossroads.

La Paz (85 km, 1¾ hours, US$1) Transportes Flores (☎ 37-3032), 8a Av between 11a and 12a Calles, Comayagüela – hourly buses from 7:30 am to 5 pm.
Tela (293 km, five hours, US$4.60) Transportes Traliasa (☎ 37-7538), 12a Calle at 8a Av, Comayagüela – buses at 6 and 9 am. Etrucsa (☎ 20-0137), 12a Calle between 8a and 9a Avs, Comayagüela – buses at 8 am, 10 am and 4 pm.
La Ceiba (397 km, 6½ hours, US$4.60) All the buses to Tela continue on to La Ceiba.
Trujillo (567 km, eight hours, US$5) Transportes Cotraipbal (☎ 37-1666), 7a Av between 11a and 12a Calles, Comayagüela – buses at 5 am, 9 am and noon, via Limones, Savá and Tocoa.
Juticalpa (170 km, three hours, US$1.60) and Catacamas (210 km, four hours, US$1.70) Empresas Aurora (☎ 37-3647), 8a Calle between 6a and 7a Avs, Comayagüela – buses to Juticalpa hourly from 4:30 am to 5 pm; every second bus continues on to Catacamas.
Empresa Discovery (☎ 22-4256), 7a Av between 12a and 13a Calles, Comayagüela – buses every two hours from 6:45 am to 4:30 pm. Direct buses to Juticalpa leave at 6:15 am, 9:15 am and 2:15 pm (two hours, US$2.25).
Choluteca (133 km, three hours, US$1.55) Mi Esperanza (☎ 38-2863), 6a Av, southern end, between 23a and 24a Calles, Comayagüela – 12 buses daily from 4 am to 6:30 pm.
San Marcos de Colón (191 km, four hours, US$1.65) Every other bus heading for Choluteca continues on to San Marcos de Colón.
Santa Rosa de Copán (393 km, seven hours, US$3.35) Sultana de Occidente (☎ 37-8101), 12a Calle at 8a Av, Comayagüela – buses at 6 and 10 am.
La Entrada (365 km, six hours, US$3.35) Buses to Santa Rosa de Copán stop at La Entrada.
Danlí (92 km, two hours, US$1) Transportes Discua Litena (☎ 32-7939), Mercado Jacaleapa, in Colonia John F Kennedy, southern Tegucigalpa (take bus No 26 from Av Molina, or a colectivo for US$0.25 at Calle Adolfo Zuniga). Buses leave every 40 minutes from 6 am to 6:30 pm.

Buses to the Honduran borders with other countries include:

- El Paraíso (Nicaraguan border; 111 km, 2½ hours, US$1.10) The buses leaving for Danlí at 8 am, 10 am and 1 pm continue on to El Paraíso. Take another bus (US$0.30) for the half-hour trip from El Paraíso to the border station.
- El Amatillo (El Salvador border; 130 km, 2½ hours, US$1.25) Various companies do this route. Take a bus from Mercado Zonal Belén, 6a Av between 10a and 13a Calles, Comayagüela. Buses depart about every half-hour, 4 am to 5:30 pm.
- San Salvador, El Salvador (seven hours, US$15) Crucero del Golfo (☎ 33-7415), Barrio La Granja, next to Cruz Lorena tire shop; buses twice daily, departing at 6 am and 1 pm.
- San Salvador, Guatemala City, Managua, San José & Panama City Tica Bus (☎ 38-7040), 16a Calle between 5a and 6a Avs, Comayagüela; bus departs every day at 9 am. See the Honduras Getting There & Away section for details on Tica bus.

Getting Around
To/From the Airport Toncontín International Airport is 6.5 km south of the center of Tegucigalpa. Local 'Loarque' buses Nos 1 and 11 stop frequently right outside the entrance to the airport; these run every day from 5:30 am to 9 pm. The cost is the usual city bus fare (US$0.05). To go to the airport from the city center, catch the Loarque buses on Av Jeréz.

A taxi to the airport costs about US$5; from the airport to town, colectivo taxis are cheaper.

Bus An excellent system of city buses operates every day from 5:30 am to 9 pm. Buses are frequent and cost US$0.05. Many buses heading east stop on the north side of Parque Central or a couple of blocks away at the corner of Av Cristobal Colón and Calle Salvador Mendieta. Many other buses run westward along Av Máximo Jeréz and turn south to Comayagüela by Parque Herrera.

Rental Car At all the rental-car companies you have the best chance of getting one of the cheapest cars if you reserve it about

three days (or more) in advance. As always, prices vary considerably so it pays to shop around. Rental car companies include:

Avis (☎ 32-0088, 32-3191, airport 33-9548)
Budget (☎ 33-5161, 33-5171)
Hertz (☎ 39-0772, airport 34-3784)
Maya (☎ 32-0682, 32-0992)
Molinari (☎ 32-8691, airport 33-1307)
Toyota (☎ 25-5790, airport 34-3183)

Taxi Taxis cruise all over town, giving a little honk to advertise they're available. A ride in town costs around US$1.65. You can also phone for a taxi (☎ 22-3304, 22-0533, 22-3748, 22-0418).

AROUND TEGUCIGALPA
Suyapa
La Virgen de Suyapa is the patron saint of Honduras; in 1982 a papal decree made her the patron of all Central America. On the Suyapa hillside, about seven km southeast of the center of Tegucigalpa, the huge Gothic **Basílica de Suyapa** dominates the landscape. The construction of the basilica, famous for its large, brilliant stained-glass windows, was begun in 1954, and finishing touches are still added.

La Virgen de Suyapa herself is a tiny painted wooden statue, only six cm tall. Many believe she has performed hundreds of miracles. She is brought to the large basilica on holidays, especially for the annual Feria de Suyapa beginning on the saint's day (February 3) and continuing for a week; the celebrations attract pilgrims from all over Central America. Most of the time, however, the little statue is kept on the altar of the very simple old church of Suyapa, built in the late 18th and early 19th centuries. It's on the plaza a few hundred meters behind the newer basilica.

The basilica of Suyapa is just up the hill from **UNAH**, the Universidad Nacional Autónoma de Honduras. The campus is called Ciudad Universitaria and houses several museums (history, anthropology, biology, fauna, entomology and herbs), all open Monday to Friday from 9 am to 4 pm.

HONDURAS

Getting There & Away You can get from Tegucigalpa to Suyapa by catching either a bus (US$0.05) or a colectivo taxi (US$0.25) from a colectivo stop near the river (see Tegucigalpa map), taking it to the university and walking the short distance from there. The No 31 Suyapa-Mercado San Isidro bus, departing from the San Isidro market in Comayagüela, also goes to Suyapa.

Santa Lucía
Population 5200

Santa Lucía is a charming old Spanish mining town on a hill. Lots of lanes and walkways wind around the hillside. The town has great views of the piney hills and Tegucigalpa away in the valley. The 18th-century church perched on a hillside is especially beautiful; inside are many old Spanish paintings and the Christ of Las Mercedes, given to Santa Lucía by King Felipe II in 1572. If the doors of the church are closed, walk around to the office at the rear and ask to have them opened for you.

Santa Lucía is an attractive and peaceful town for walking around in the fresh mountain air. Many possible walks lead out of town and into the hills, where there are many farms. An old mule trail leads down to the capital, a hike of several hours; unfortunately we've recently heard this mule trail has gotten dangerous due to young thugs. Ask locals for current advice.

There are no hotels in Santa Lucía.

Places to Eat The *Restaurante Miluska* (☎ 31-3905) is a favorite, with tables indoors and outdoors on a pleasant covered patio. A 'European corner in the heart of Honduras,' it serves German and Czech dishes in addition to typical Honduran fare; it's open Tuesday to Sunday, 10 am to 8 pm. It's well signed from the highway. On the road coming into town from the highway, *Restaurant Donde El Francés* is another little European corner.

Getting There & Away Santa Lucía is 14 km east of Tegucigalpa, 2½ km off the road leading to Valle de Angeles and San Juancito.

A direct bus to Santa Lucía departs every 45 minutes, 7 am to 6 pm, from Mercado San Pablo in Colonia Reparto (US$0.15). Bus route No 6, 'Carrizal-El Sitio,' departing from the Parque Central, goes to Mercado San Pablo (US$0.05); colectivo taxis also go there, departing from the corner of Calle Miguel Paz Barahona and Calle Adolfo Zuniga, two blocks behind the cathedral (US$0.16).

Or you can take the Valle de Angeles bus from the stop on Av La Paz, get off at the crossroads and walk or hitch the 2½ km into town.

Valle de Angeles
Population 8400

Eight km past Santa Lucía, Valle de Angeles is another beautiful, historic Spanish mining town. It's been declared a tourist zone, and much of the town has been restored to its original 16th-century appearance. In front of the old church is an attractive shady plaza. The annual fair takes place on October 4.

There are many artisans' shops and souvenir emporiums in Valle de Angeles where you can find excellent Honduran artesanías that are marginally cheaper and of better quality than in Tegucigalpa. Woodcarving, basketry, ceramics, leatherwork, paintings, dolls, wicker and wood furniture and other items are featured. Avoid the weekend crowds.

Places to Stay & Eat Most people come to Valle de Angeles as a day trip from Tegucigalpa, but it would be a quiet, relaxing place to stay over. The only time it gets busy is on weekends and holidays; otherwise, the town is quiet.

About three blocks from the church, the *Posada del Angel* (☎ 76-2233) is a beautiful place with a restaurant and clean single/double rooms with private hot bath for US$7.50 per person, all facing onto a large grassy courtyard.

For a cheaper and much more basic alternative, try the rooms over the little grocery shop in the two-story wooden building on the road to the right of the church; the building is behind the church a couple of blocks uphill. The rooms are primitive, but the price is right: singles/doubles are US$1.25/1.65, or US$2.50 with two beds, all with shared bath.

Valle de Angeles has a great number of small, simple restaurants serving typical Honduran fare.

Getting There & Away A bus bound for Valle de Angeles departs every 45 minutes, 7 am to 5 pm, from a stop just off Av La Paz in Tegucigalpa, half a block south of the Hospital San Felipe (US$0.25). The Lomas and San Felipe buses departing from the corner of Av Cristobal Colón and Calle Salvador Mendieta will drop you at Hospital San Felipe.

San Juancito

About 11 km past Valle de Angeles, San Juancito is a small village nestled into a crevasse beside an even smaller river, at the foot of a steep mountain. It's a historic 19th-century mining town, but there's not much to it now; people mostly just pass through on their way to or from Parque Nacional La Tigra, at the top of the mountain.

Nonetheless, the town has been declared a historic place, and there are plans to establish museums, build *balnearios* by the river, restore hotels and buildings to their colonial appearance and build a funicular cable car from the town right up to El Rosario, the ghost town at the top of the mountain at the entrance to La Tigra. Nobody has put the money up yet, but it may happen one day.

Getting There & Away A direct bus service between Tegucigalpa and San Juancito does exist, but it's inconvenient; a bus departs from Mercado San Pablo in Tegucigalpa at 3 pm, and from San Juancito for the return trip at 6 am (33 km, two hours, US$0.40). On weekends the buses depart Tegucigalpa at 8 am and 3 pm, leaving San Juancito for the return trip at 6 am and 1 pm. Alternatively, from the same place, you can take a bus (infrequent) heading for Cantarranas or San Juan de

Flores and get off at the turnoff for San Juancito; the town is a two-km walk. Or you can take the bus to Valle de Angeles and hitch from there, continuing along the same road; just about any vehicle passing by will give you a lift.

Parque Nacional La Tigra & El Rosario

La Tigra is one of the most beautiful places in Honduras, preserving a lush cloud forest. Only a short distance from Tegucigalpa, at an altitude of 2270 meters, this pristine 330 sq km reserve was Honduras' first national park.

The forest is home to a great abundance of wildlife – ocelots, pumas, peccaries, white-tailed deer, armadillos, opossums, agoutis, pacas, toucans, quetzals and other bird life and much more. It is also a botanist's delight, with lush trees, vines, lichens and large ferns, colorful mushrooms, bromeliads, orchids and other flowering plants. Even when it's not cloudy in a cloud forest, the sun rarely shines on the ground because of the canopy of trees, so it's always damp.

Six trails, all well maintained and easy to follow, have been cut through the forest, and you should stay on them. It is a very rugged, mountainous area, and the damp ground can give way unexpectedly off the trails; people have also been lost for days in the dense forest when they wandered off the trails. Most of the trails are on the Juticalpa side of the park, but one, the three-hour La Cascada Trail, goes all the way from one park entrance to the other, passing a waterfall on the way. It's easiest to do this trail from Juticalpa to El Rosario, as that way it's mostly downhill. The trails vary in length and difficulty, taking half an hour to six hours to traverse. On the El Rosario side of the park there are many old mineshafts.

On weekends, guides are available to take you along the trails, pointing out features of the forest and its wildlife. Though not required, a guide doesn't cost much, maybe around US$3 for one of the longer trails, and you'll learn a lot more about the forest if you go with one. On weekdays, the park rangers will guide you along the trails. You can walk from one entrance to the other in a couple of hours by the old disused road (no vehicles allowed), but you see more if you take La Cascada Trail.

The climate at La Tigra is fresh and brisk; in fact it's often quite cold – bring plenty of warm clothes with you. At night the temperature can drop to around 5°C. Long pants and long sleeves are best, as the forest has many mosquitoes. It's also advisable to bring sturdy tennis shoes or hiking boots, mosquito repellent, and your own drinking water and food.

The park is open Tuesday to Sunday, 8 am to 5 pm, closed Monday. A new entrance fee, inaugurated in 1996, requires foreigners to pay US$10 to visit the park (US$3 for children under 12, seniors and disabled people); Central American nationals pay US$0.85. There have been many complaints about the new fees, and visits to the park have dropped off considerably, so perhaps the policy will be changed. Amitigra in Tegucigalpa will have current details.

Information Amitigra (☎ /fax 35-8494), in the Edificio Italia, 4th Floor, Office No 6, Colonia Palmira, Tegucigalpa, has information and manages overnight visits to the park. It's open Monday to Friday, 8:30 am to 5:30 pm.

Places to Stay To stay overnight in the park, you must first get written permission from Amitigra.

At the park entrance at El Rosario, there's a visitors' center with displays on the wildlife and plants in the park, as well as dormitories, houses, camping spots and a cafeteria. A ranger is always there. You can stay in dormitories for US$5 per person; there are 10 rooms, each with six beds. Bring your own bedding and warm clothes. There's no place for you to cook, but there is a cafeteria. Or you can buy simple meals at the white house at the bend, 300 meters down from the visitors' center, but only up to about 6 pm.

Also at El Rosario are several houses, each holding three to five persons, which

come complete with kitchen and cost US$50 per night; you still must provide your own bedding. There are also two camping sites, with water and latrine, available for US$5 per person. Children up to 12 years old pay half price for all accommodations.

On the Jutiapa side, the visitors' center does not have overnight facilities, but you can camp there. Bring everything you'll need.

Getting There & Away There are two entrances to La Tigra.

The western entrance to the park, above Jutiapa, is the closest to Tegucigalpa, 22 km away. There's a visitors' center where rangers are always on duty. This entrance is reached by taking a turnoff from the top of El Picacho and passing through the villages of El Hatillo, Los Limones and Jutiapa.

Buses depart from Parque Herrera in Tegucigalpa and go as far as Los Limones; from there it's five km, about a 1½-hour uphill walk, to the park gate. If you don't fancy the walk, it's easy to hitch on weekends – if you go on a weekday, you may be the only person on the road. If there are enough passengers, the bus may continue on two km to Jutiapa, still leaving you three km from the park gate, but you can't count on this bus. The bus leaves Parque Herrera four times daily, around 6:30 am, 9 am, 2 pm and 5 pm, and takes about an hour to reach Los Limones (US$0.35). Buses returning to town leave Los Limones at approximately 8 am, noon and 3 pm.

The eastern park entrance is at El Rosario, a 'ghost town' mining settlement of old wooden houses about four km up the hill from San Juancito (see above for details on how to get there). It's a very steep climb up a dirt road from San Juancito to El Rosario; any passing vehicle would probably give you a lift up, but unless you go on a weekend, you may be the only person on the road. A 4WD vehicle is needed.

With your own vehicle you can easily see the park on a day trip from Tegucigalpa. By public transport it's very tricky to try to visit the park in one day; you're better off planning an overnight stay. If you don't have your own transport but want to visit the park in one day, taxis will bring you from Tegucigalpa to the Juticalpa side of the park, but these aren't cheap. The taxi driver will probably end up spending the whole day up there, rather than making the long drive back to town and then back again to retrieve you, so the taxi will cost around US$30 for up to four people. If you just want the taxi to drop you off, it will still cost around US$25; it's about an hour's drive from the city. Shakespeare & Co Books (see Bookstores) offers day trips to La Tigra for US$20 per person.

Ojojona
Population 8500

Yet another attractive 16th-century Spanish mining town in the hills near Tegucigalpa, Ojojona has a couple of simple old churches with religious art; the main church has a painting long said to be a Murillo, though this claim has now been disproven. Ojojona is historically important as the home of General Francisco Morazán. It is also the birthplace of the contemporary artist Pablo Zelaya Sierra, whose paintings can be seen at the Galería Nacional de Arte in Tegucigalpa.

The bus to Ojojona leaves every half-hour from 6 am to 6:15 pm, departing from a bus stop on 4a Calle at the corner of 6a Av, between 6a and 7a Avs, in Comayagüela (32 km, 1¼ hours, US$0.25).

Western Honduras

Western Honduras is the most settled part of the country and holds some of Honduras' principal attractions, most notably the Maya ruins of Copán.

Other attractions include Honduras' principal lake, the Lago de Yojoa, a couple of national parks, and Comayagua, Honduras' historic first capital.

Also here is San Pedro Sula, second-largest city in the country. The road between San Pedro Sula and the capital is probably the most traveled in Honduras, connecting as it does the country's two major cities as well as the southern, western and northern regions.

TEGUCIGALPA TO SAN PEDRO SULA

It's 241 km along Honduras' Highway 1 from Tegucigalpa to San Pedro Sula, about a four-hour trip. The route passes Comayagua, Siguatepeque, the Lago de Yojoa and several archaeological sites. The beautiful Pulhapanzak waterfall is about an hour's drive west of the highway.

This region, called the Valle de Comayagua, was well settled in pre-Columbian times; the Valle de Comayagua formed a cultural 'corridor' between the Valle de Sula (the valley where San Pedro Sula is today) and the peoples living on the Pacific Coast of El Salvador and Nicaragua. Agriculture has been practiced in the Valle de Comayagua for at least 3000 years.

Fourteen archaeological sites have been identified in the department of Comayagua; apparently one or another of the sites was the primary center of settlement at various times in history. Pottery, jewelry and stone carvings of various styles have been unearthed from the sites.

Based on styles of pottery, archaeologists have identified three major periods in the history of the region. During the preclassic period (600 BC to 300 AD), figures of animals and humans formed much of the basis of design, and the agricultural society became increasingly highly organized. During the classic period (300 to 1000 AD) the style of pottery changed, with geometric figures predominating. Apparently, around 1000 AD fighting or warfare occurred, and the organized social structure became more disintegrated until the time of the Spanish conquest in the 16th century.

Between Tegucigalpa and the Lago de Yojoa are three archaeological sites: **Yarumela** (near Comayagua), **Tenampua** (near Siguatepeque) and **Los Naranjos** (near Lago de Yojoa). None of them are developed archaeological parks like Copán Ruinas, though there are plans to develop Los Naranjos as an archaeological park open to the public by sometime in 1997. Still, all of the sites are easy to visit.

COMAYAGUA
Population 82,000

Comayagua, 84 km northwest of Tegucigalpa, is the historic first capital of Honduras. The town's colonial past is evident in several fine old churches (including the famous cathedral), three plazas and two interesting museums.

A few kilometers from town is the Honduran military base Sotocano. During the 1980s, when the US was waging the Contra war in Nicaragua, up to 10,000 US soldiers were stationed here, and the base was called Palmerola; since then, it's been converted to a Honduran base, but about a thousand American soldiers are still stationed there. You'll see plenty of signs around town written in both English and Spanish.

History
Comayagua was founded as the capital of the colonial province of Honduras in 1537 by Spanish Captain Alonso de Cáceres, fulfilling the orders of the Spanish governor of Honduras to establish a new settlement in

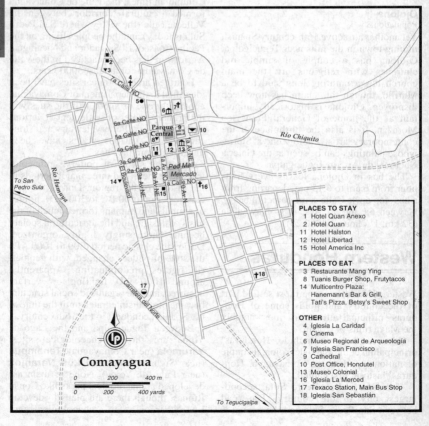

Comayagua

0   200   400 m
0   200   400 yards

PLACES TO STAY
1 Hotel Quan Anexo
2 Hotel Quan
11 Hotel Halston
12 Hotel Libertad
15 Hotel America Inc

PLACES TO EAT
3 Restaurante Mang Ying
8 Tuanis Burger Shop, Frutytacos
14 Multicentro Plaza:
   Hanemann's Bar & Grill,
   Tati's Pizza, Betsy's Sweet Shop

OTHER
4 Iglesia La Caridad
5 Cinema
6 Museo Regional de Arqueología
7 Iglesia San Francisco
9 Cathedral
10 Post Office, Hondutel
13 Museo Colonial
16 Iglesia La Merced
17 Texaco Station, Main Bus Stop
18 Iglesia San Sebastián

the geographic center of the territory. The town was initially called Villa de Santa María de Comayagua; in 1543 the name was changed to Villa de la Nueva Valladolid de Comayagua.

Comayagua was declared a city in 1557, and in 1561 the seat of the diocese of Honduras was moved from Trujillo to Comayagua for the more favorable conditions, central position and closer proximity to the silver- and gold-mining regions that Comayagua afforded.

Comayagua was the center for the political and religious administration of Honduras; for over three centuries, it was the capital city until the capital was shifted to Tegucigalpa in 1880.

Churches

The **cathedral** in the center of town is a gem of colonial style. It was built from 1685 to 1715 and is abundantly decorated. It contains much fine art, both inside and out. The altar is similar to that of the Tegucigalpa cathedral; both were made by the same artist.

The clock in the church tower is one of the oldest in the world, and is probably the oldest in the Americas. It was made over 800 years ago by the Moors for the palace of Alhambra in Granada.

Comayagua's first church was **La Merced**, built from 1550 to 1558. Other fine churches are **San Francisco** (1584) and **La Caridad** (1730). **San Sebastián** (1585) is farther from the center on the south end of town. All are worth seeing. Another colonial church, San Juan de Dios (1590), was destroyed by an earthquake in 1750, but samples of its artwork, along with artwork from all the other churches, are on display in the Museo Colonial (see below).

If you can read Spanish, look for a small book entitled *Las Iglesias Coloniales de la Ciudad de Comayagua*, which contains an interesting history of Comayagua and its churches. It's available at both museums.

Museums

The first university in Central America was founded in 1632 in the Casa Cural, the building to the right of the cathedral that now houses the **Museo Colonial**; priests have occupied this building since 1558. The university operated there for almost 200 years.

The museum is small but remarkable. Totally renovated in 1990, it contains artwork and religious paraphernalia culled from all the five churches of Comayagua, spanning the 15th to the 18th centuries. In one salon is a display of jewels and ornaments that people gave to the statues in the churches, including pearls and emeralds the size of a thumbnail.

This museum, opened in 1962, was the first in Honduras. The well-informed curator can give you an interesting tour, explaining (in Spanish) the history of each piece. The museum is open every day from 9:30 am to noon and 2 to 4:30 pm (admission US$0.45).

A block north of the cathedral, the **Museo Regional de Arqueología** (☎ 72-0386) has displays of Honduran archaeological discoveries, including pottery, metates (stone tools used to grind grain), stone carvings, petroglyphs and mastodon bones. It's open Wednesday to Friday from 8 am to 4 pm, Saturday and Sunday 9 am to 4 pm; closed Monday and Tuesday. Admission is US$0.85.

Special Events

On the morning of Good Friday, religious images are carried through the streets in a procession over intricate carpets of colored sawdust. Watching the sawdust designs being made the night before the procession is as interesting as the procession itself; you may even be able to join in.

Places to Stay

On the north side of town, *Hotel Quan* (☎ /fax 72-0070) is in a quiet residential area. It has a variety of rooms both in the main building and in the newer annex across the street. Single/double rooms with private cold bath and fan are US$3.35/5.85; with hot water they're US$5/8.35. Rooms including air con and cable TV are US$14.15/16.70 with one/two double beds.

HONDURAS

Hotel America Inc (☎ 72-0360, ☎ /fax 72-0009), at the corner of 1a Calle NO (Noroeste, northwest of the town center) and 1a Av NO, has rooms with fan for US$5.40/6.25, or US$6.25/7.10 with cable TV; rooms with air con are US$10.85.

The *Hotel Halston* (☎ 72-0557) on 3a Calle NO, between 1a and 2a Avs NO, is an upstairs hotel where rooms with private bath and fan are US$5 for one or two people.

All these three places are pleasant, clean and a good value.

If you're challenging yourself to see how cheaply you can travel, *Hotel Libertad* (☎ 72-0091) on the main plaza is your spot; rooms with one/two/three/four beds are US$1.65/2.50/2.90/3.35. The rooms share a common cold bath and they have no windows; they encircle a quiet courtyard containing hammocks and plants.

Places to Eat
Tuanis Burger Shop on the southwest corner of the main plaza serves all meals and snacks. Try the excellent burgers. It's open every day from 8 am to 11 pm. Just around the corner, *Frutytacos* also serves all three meals (US$1) plus a variety of fruit juices, fruit licuados de leche and snacks; it's open till 8 pm.

Several good places to eat are in the Multicentro Plaza on El Blvd; if you've been traveling in Central America for a while and want to eat something different, this is your spot. Upstairs toward the rear, *Hanemann's Bar & Grill* is popular with travelers and the local American soldiers. Sean (from the US) serves up delicious Cajun-style food, with dishes for carnivores and vegetarians alike. Customers rave about the good, safe salads; the big, sloppy BBQ sandwiches; and the twice-baked potatoes with cheese. It's open Monday to Saturday from 5 pm on, Sunday 11:30 am to 2:30 pm and 5:30 to 10 pm; closed Tuesday.

Tati's Pizza is also upstairs in the Multicentro Plaza.

Downstairs in the Multicentro Plaza, *Betsy's Sweet Shop* serves American baked goods, coffee, cappuccino, deli sandwiches and breakfast on weekends; also here is a

collection of high-quality Honduran handicrafts. It's open every day from 9 am to 7 pm.

For Chinese food, you can't beat the beautiful *Restaurante Mang Ying*, farther north on El Blvd near Hotel Quan. It's a large, attractive Chinese restaurant open every day from 9 am to 10 pm. Good food is served in huge portions, with most dishes costing around US$2.50 to US$4.

Getting There & Away
Comayagua is about one kilometer east of the highway. Any Tegucigalpa-San Pedro Sula bus will drop or pick you up at the crossroads; you can walk the one km into town or take a taxi for US$0.40. To Tegucigalpa, express buses cost US$0.90 and take about 1½ to two hours. Catch them at the Texaco gas station.

AROUND COMAYAGUA
Yarumela
This site on the Río Humuya, between Comayagua and La Paz, consists of two major archaeological mounds. The larger one is about 60 feet high; from the top of it you can get a view of the whole Valle de Comayagua.

To the untrained eye, both of the mounds could look simply like hills covered with brush. However, the smaller mound, right beside the river, has been reconstructed on one side, revealing a step pyramid with several platforms and a stairway going up the middle. The other half of the mound has been left in its original state.

To get there, take a bus to La Paz – buses come from Tegucigalpa, or you could pick the bus up from the Tegucigalpa-San Pedro Sula highway at the turnoff for La Paz. In La Paz, you can ask any taxi driver to take you to the Zona Arqueológica Yarumela and to come pick you up in a couple of hours; the ride takes about 15 or 20 minutes and costs about US$8.50 roundtrip.

If you have a private vehicle, you can get there from Comayagua in about 15 minutes. From the highway, take the turnoff for La Paz and go over the Río Humuya. Just before you come to a traffic roundabout, there's a dirt road taking off to the right; following this, you will come to the large mound on the right side of the road. The smaller, half-excavated mound is nearby beside the river.

Marcala

At this town 36 km southeast of La Esperanza is the Comarca coffee cooperative, which you can visit. There's somewhere to stay overnight. Several buses per day run from Comayagua.

SIGUATEPEQUE

Population 53,000

Siguatepeque is halfway between Tegucigalpa (117 km) and San Pedro Sula (124 km), about a two-hour drive from either. There's no real reason to stop in Siguatepeque, though it's not a bad place to break up a journey

Orientation

At the heart of town is the shady Parque Central, with lots of trees, a dry fountain and the church and city hall. Three blocks to the west is Plaza San Pablo, with basketball courts, the market and the Empresas Unidas bus station. This is the park you'll see first if you're coming in from the highway, which is two km from the center of town. Around and between the two plazas are several good places to stay and eat. South of the town is the turnoff for La Esperanza and Marcala.

Special Events

The annual festival days are January 25 and April 18 to 27.

Places to Stay

Hospedaje Elena (☎ 73-2210), a block west of Plaza San Pablo, is a simple but clean little place with 12 rooms with shared cold bath for US$1.65 per person.

Hotel Gomez (☎ 73-2868) on Calle 21 de Junio is a clean, modern motel with courtyard parking, a cafeteria, cable TV and fan in the rooms, and hot water. Singles/doubles are US$3.35/4.15 with shared bath; rooms with private bath are US$5.85, or US$5 without TV.

On Parque Central, the *Boarding House Central* (☎ 73-2108) has single/double rooms with private hot bath and cable TV for US$3.75/6.65, plus a restaurant and a parking garage in the rear. On another

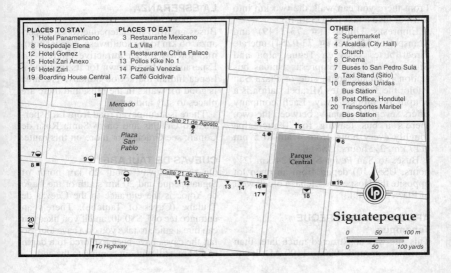

PLACES TO STAY
1 Hotel Panamericano
8 Hospedaje Elena
12 Hotel Gomez
15 Hotel Zari Anexo
16 Hotel Zari
19 Boarding House Central

PLACES TO EAT
3 Restaurante Mexicano La Villa
11 Restaurante China Palace
13 Pollos Kike No 1
14 Pizzería Venezia
17 Caffé Goldivar

OTHER
2 Supermarket
4 Alcaldía (City Hall)
5 Church
6 Cinema
7 Buses to San Pedro Sula
9 Taxi Stand (Sitio)
10 Empresas Unidas Bus Station
18 Post Office, Hondutel
20 Transportes Maribel Bus Station

Mercado

Calle 21 de Agosto

Plaza San Pablo

Calle 21 de Junio

Parque Central

To Highway

Siguatepeque

0   50   100 m
0   50   100 yards

corner of Parque Central, the newer *Hotel Zari* (☎ 73-2015, 73-2198) has clean, pleasant rooms with private hot bath, cable TV and ample parking for US$4.45/7.10. The new *Hotel Zari Anexo* is being built across the street.

Hotel Panamericano (☎ 73-2202), just off Plaza San Pablo, is another new place with clean singles/doubles, all with cable TV and private hot bath, for US$4.60/9.15 with fan, US$8.35/12.50 with air con and phone.

Places to Eat

Between and around the two plazas, and also in the market, are several comedores where you can get basic meals. Between the two plazas, *Restaurante China Palace* serves Chinese and international food, with dishes for around US$2.75 to US$4.15. Just off Parque Central are the *Pizzería Venezia* for pizza, *Pollos Kike No 1* for chicken, and the *La Villa* Mexican restaurant. *Caffé Goldivar*, beside the entrance to the Hotel Zari, is another good spot.

Getting There & Away

Any bus going between Tegucigalpa and San Pedro Sula will drop you at the crossroads at the entrance to Siguatepeque. From there you can walk the two km into town or take a taxi for US$0.40.

Empresas Unidas (☎ 73-2149) and Transportes Maribel (☎ 73-0254) operate direct buses between Tegucigalpa and Siguatepeque. The Empresas Unidas bus station is on the south side of Plaza San Pablo; the Transportes Mirabel station is a couple of blocks away. Each company offers seven buses daily; between the two, there's a bus leaving for Tegucigalpa roughly every hour, from 4 am to 5 pm (117 km, 2½ hours, US$1).

Buses to San Pedro Sula (124 km, 2¾ hours, US$1.10) depart from an open lot opposite the Hospedaje Elena, a block west of Plaza San Pablo.

AROUND SIGUATEPEQUE
Tenampua

This site was constructed much later than Yarumela, around 1000 to 1100 AD. It sits on top of a large hill with a sweeping view overlooking the entire valley. Features include a ball court, walls and archaeological mounds; though ball courts are typical of the Maya, whose area was farther to the west, by this period the ball court had filtered over to this region.

Apparently Tenampua was constructed when warfare was occurring in the valley. The site is well protected and would have been easy to defend; from up here you could easily see anyone approaching the site. The ascent is very steep on three sides; on the fourth the people constructed a high, massive wall about two meters thick.

The site is near Siguatepeque, just off the Tegucigalpa-San Pedro Sula highway. Any bus will drop you off at the Restaurante Tenampua, on the east side of the highway at the foot of the Tenampua hill. The people at the restaurant will show you how to hike up the hill to the site; it's a steep climb and takes about one or 1½ hours, but it's rewarding.

When you're ready to leave, you can flag down a bus on the highway. If you have a private vehicle, you could get here from Comayagua in about half an hour.

LA ESPERANZA
Population 6900

Buses go from Siguatepeque to La Esperanza, 66 km to the southwest. A quiet colonial town with an attractive church, La Esperanza is best known for its traditional Lenca Indian market on Sunday. The area is good for walks in the hills, and there are places to stay and eat.

There is an unpaved road from La Esperanza to Gracias and on to Santa Rosa de Copán; see Gracias for more on this route.

CUEVAS DE TAULABÉ

On the highway about 25 km north of Siguatepeque and 20 km south of the Lago de Yojoa is the entrance to the Cuevas de Taulabé (Caves of Taulabé). There's an entrance fee of US$0.40, and if you like, you can hire a guide to take you on a cave tour. So far, the caves have been explored to a depth of 12 km, still without coming to the end.

The first 400 meters of the cave have been made easier with the addition of lights and a pathway with steps; the pathway can be slippery, so wear adequate shoes. If you want to explore farther into the cave, you must bring your own gear and let the guards at the entrance know of your intentions. Serious explorations into the cave require a permit from the mayor of Taulabé town.

LAGO DE YOJOA

The Lago de Yojoa, about three hours (157 km) north of Tegucigalpa and one hour (84 km) south of San Pedro Sula, is a popular recreation area and highway stopover.

This is a large and beautiful lake, attracting abundant bird life. Bird watchers like to make expeditions here in the early morning; over 375 species of birds have been counted. One morning while sitting on the terrace at the hotel Agua Azul, a birder was surprised to count 37 different species in a single tree.

Fishing on the lake is also good, especially for black bass. Bring your own tackle, as it may not be available locally. All the hotels around the lake can arrange boat and fishing trips.

On the northwest corner of the lake, **Los Naranjos** archaeological site was first occupied around 600 or 700 BC. Features include a moat and several archaeological mounds. Plans include opening the site as an archaeological park, with a nature trail and interpretive trail. You can get there by taking a small boat from the hotel Agua Azul or one of the other hotels on the north side of the lake.

Two national parks are near the lake: **Santa Bárbara** on the north side and **Cerro Azul Meambar** on the south. Both are cloud forest parks but somewhat difficult to access. Guided tours may be available; ask at the hotel Agua Azul.

Places to Stay & Eat

The highway passes by the lake, but there are only a few places with direct lake access. Right on the highway, on the south side of the lake, *Hotel Los Remos* has rooms for US$8.35 per person and has a restaurant overlooking the lake. When we visited it looked quite dilapidated, but new owners were trying to fix it up. Any regular bus between Tegucigalpa and San Pedro Sula will drop you there.

About one kilometer north of the Hotel Los Remos, a row of about thirty restaurants and small comedores serving fried fish fresh from the lake stretches along the highway. The lake is famous for its tasty black bass. A meal of fried fish, salad and tortillas will cost from US$1.50 to US$3, depending on the size and kind of fish.

On the north side of the lake, a road taking off to the west toward La Guama and Peña Blanca provides access to several good hotel/resorts on the north shore. The turnoff is marked with a large sign advertising the Hotel Brisas del Lago. This is also the turnoff for the Pulhapanzak waterfall (see below).

The first resort you come to is the *Agua Azul* (☎ 52-7125, 57-3982, fax 57-2763), a beautiful, peaceful resort 4½ km in from the highway. It's right on the lake and has a dock for small boats, plus a swimming pool, restaurant and bar. Rooms in duplex cabins with private hot bath are US$17.85 for one, two or three people. Boat trips on the lake, horse riding and trips to Parque Nacional Azul Meambar can be arranged.

About half a kilometer along the lake, the restaurant *Only Bass* is often recommended. Farther along the lake is the larger and more expensive *Hotel Brisas del Lago* (☎ 52-7030), with 72 rooms for US$30 per night. Still farther along, the *Finca Las Glorias* (☎ 56-0736) is a luxurious, private and peaceful resort on a large coffee plantation right on the lake, with rooms for US$26.70.

PULHAPANZAK

Pulhapanzak, a magnificent 43-meter waterfall on the Río Lindo, can be visited as a stop along the route from Tegucigalpa to San Pedro Sula, or as a day trip from San Pedro or the Lago de Yojoa – it's about 40 km from the lake. Near the waterfall is a very pleasant park and places to swim in the river. It's a popular spot that can be crowded on weekends and holidays. You can camp here if you have your own gear.

From San Pedro, Pulhapanzak is 60 km (about one hour) south on the highway to Tegucigalpa, then another hour on an unpaved road heading west from the highway; take the La Guama/Peña Blanca turnoff from the highway. Buses reach the waterfall from San Pedro Sula every 40 minutes (see the San Pedro bus section).

BALNEARIO BAHR
Off the highway between San Pedro Sula and the Lago de Yojoa, Balneario Bahr is a pleasant balneario. It's marked by a sign from the highway.

SANTA BÁRBARA
Population 29,000
About 53 km west of the Lago de Yojoa, Santa Bárbara, capital of the department of the same name, is a small town known for its woven *junco* handicrafts. There are places to stay and eat in Santa Bárbara.

Roads connect Santa Bárbara with the Tegucigalpa-San Pedro Sula highway, and also with the San Pedro Sula-Nueva Ocotepeque highway running along the western side of Honduras. If you're driving between Tegucigalpa and western Honduras, you can cut about 1½ hours off your driving time by making a short cut through Santa Bárbara, rather than going all the way north to San Pedro Sula.

You can get a bus directly from Tegucigalpa to Santa Bárbara (202 km), though the buses run infrequently. Buses run every half-hour between Santa Bárbara and San Pedro Sula (94 km, 1½ to two hours, US$1 to US$1.25).

SAN PEDRO SULA
Population 415,000
The second largest city in Honduras, San Pedro Sula (often called simply San Pedro) is the major industrial, commercial and business center of the country. It is also the major center for the agricultural products of the fertile lowlands surrounding the city.

San Pedro is the transportation hub for the western half of Honduras and for travel to the north coast. The city doesn't have many sights or attractions for visitors, but there are always travelers passing through.

San Pedro is extremely hot and humid for much of the year; the town lies in a valley just 76 meters above sea level, with little movement of air. January and February are the coolest months, and October to March may be bearable, but from around April to September, San Pedro sizzles. The rainy season runs from May to November.

In the last week of June, San Pedro celebrates a large festival and fair in honor of its founding and the day of San Pedro.

History
The Valle de Sula, hot, rich and fertile, has been heavily settled for thousands of years by various groups. Many archaeological sites have been found in the area, dating from various periods. You can learn all about the area's history at the Museo de Arqueología e Historia (see Things to See & Do, below).

San Pedro Sula was founded by Pedro de Alvarado in June 1536. The original name of the town was San Pedro de Puerto Caballos, and it was founded in the nearby Valle de Chooloma (Valle de los Pájaros, or Valley of the Birds). The Spaniards later moved the town to its present location, which was the site of Azula, an Indian village beside the Río Las Piedras. The name San Pedro Sula is a mixture of the names of the two towns.

From 1525 to 1575 the population of the valley declined dramatically, from an estimated 50,000 people at the time of the first Spanish contact to an estimated 5000. After that, they quit counting the indigenous people, because they were so few. The population was reduced by war, massive exportation of slaves, epidemics of European and African diseases to which the indigenous people had no resistance, the fleeing of survivors into the mountains, exploitation in Spanish gold mines established in the area and by the social disorganization following the Spanish conquest.

African slaves were imported by the Spanish to work in the Sula gold mines, but

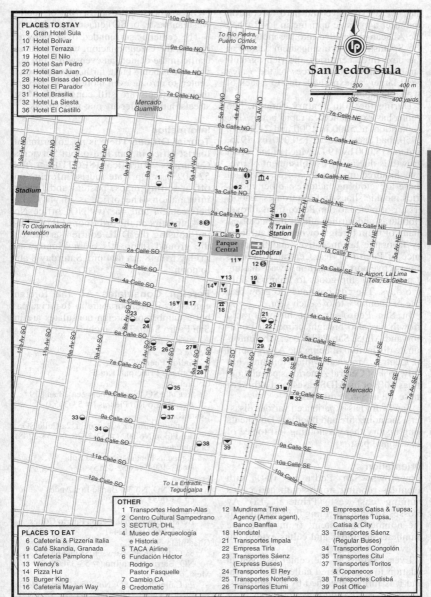

PLACES TO STAY
9 Gran Hotel Sula
10 Hotel Bolívar
17 Hotel Terraza
19 Hotel El Nilo
20 Hotel San Pedro
27 Hotel San Juan
28 Hotel Brisas del Occidente
30 Hotel El Parador
31 Hotel Brasilia
32 Hotel La Siesta
36 Hotel El Castillo

San Pedro Sula

Stadium

Mercado
Guamilito

To Río Piedra,
Puerto Cortés,
Omoa

To Circunvalación,
Merendón

Train
Station

Parque
Central

Cathedral

To Airport, La Lima
Tela, La Ceiba

Mercado

To La Entrada,
Tegucigalpa

PLACES TO EAT
6 Cafetería & Pizzería Italia
9 Café Skandia, Granada
11 Cafetería Pamplona
13 Wendy's
14 Pizza Hut
15 Burger King
16 Cafetería Mayan Way

OTHER
1 Transportes Hedman-Alas
2 Centro Cultural Sampedrano
3 SECTUR, DHL
4 Museo de Arqueología
  e Historia
5 TACA Airline
6 Fundación Héctor
  Rodrigo
  Pastor Fasquelle
7 Cambio CA
8 Credomatic

12 Mundirama Travel
   Agency (Amex agent),
   Banco Banffaa
18 Hondutel
21 Transportes Impala
22 Empresa Tirla
23 Transportes Sáenz
   (Express Buses)
24 Transportes El Rey
25 Transportes Norteños
26 Transportes Etumi

29 Empresas Catisa & Tupsa;
   Transportes Tupsa,
   Catisa & City
33 Transportes Sáenz
   (Regular Buses)
34 Transportes Congolón
35 Transportes Citul
37 Transportes Toritos
   & Copanecos
38 Transportes Cotisbá
39 Post Office

they were expensive and hard to control, and after a massive uprising in 1542 when the African slaves fled into the mountains, the Spanish quit bringing them here. For the next three centuries, the rich agricultural and mineral resources of the valley went largely unexploited, due to a lack of available laborers.

During the 20th century, though, San Pedro has experienced a rapid boom. The population, at 5000 in 1900 and 21,000 in 1950, had increased to 150,000 by 1975, and to 415,000 by 1997. Much of the recent growth is due to the establishment of over two hundred modern factories. Most of these are clothing factories; other industries include shoes and electronics. Laborers are attracted to San Pedro from all over Honduras and farther afield; the factories, many of them foreign-owned, are attracted by favorable tax incentives and the presence of Puerto Cortés, Central America's most active port, just an hour away, making it possible to ship goods to Miami in only two days. The city continues to grow at a rate of about 5% to 6% each year.

In San Pedro's recent history, rapid growth has also brought crime, air pollution and AIDS. San Pedro bears the unfortunate distinction of being the AIDS capital of Central America; while Honduras has only 16% of Central America's population, it has 60% of its AIDS cases, and a third of these are in San Pedro Sula.

San Pedro has experienced various disasters, including fire and flooding. Despite its long history there is nothing left to see of its colonial past.

Orientation

Downtown San Pedro is flat, with avenidas running north-south and calles running east-west. Primera (1a) Av crosses 1a Calle, forming the beginning of the numbering system; from there, the numbered avenidas and calles extend out in every direction.

Every address in the center is given in relation to a numbered calle and avenida, and it is further specified by the northeast (noreste, or NE), northwest (noroeste, or NO), southeast (sureste, or SE) or southwest (suroeste, or SO) quadrant of the city.

The center is surrounded by a highway bypass, the Circunvalación, which reduces traffic in the center; an even wider circunvalación is being built, farther from the city center, to reroute even more traffic. Nevertheless, streets are still congested. Most streets in the center are one-way streets.

Information

Tourist Offices There is no government tourist office in San Pedro, but Servicios Culturales y Turísticos (SECTUR; ☎ /fax 52-3023) is a private tourist information office selling maps, posters and tourist information. The office is on 4a Calle between 3a and 4a Avs NO, office No 304, upstairs on the 3rd floor of the building housing the DHL courier service on the ground floor. It's open Monday to Friday from 8 am to 4 pm, Saturday 8 am to noon.

Foreign Consulates All the foreign embassies in Honduras are in Tegucigalpa, but a number of foreign consulates are in San Pedro Sula. They include:

Belize
    Salida Puerto Cortés,
    Entrada Principal, Km 5
Colombia
    6a Calle SO, No 139, between 18 and 19
    Avs, Barrio Río Piedras (☎ 53-2052)
Costa Rica
    Edificio Martinez Valenzuela, 2a Calle SO,
    3rd Floor, No 307 (☎ 52-2326, fax 53-3208)
El Salvador
    Agencias Panamericana de Sula
    (☎ 53-4604, fax 52-8215)
France
    12 Av NO, No 30, Barrio Los Andes
    (☎ 53-0953, 58-0732)
Germany
    Berkling Industrial, Salida Puerto Cortés
    (☎ 53-1868, 53-1244)
Guatemala
    8a Calle, No 38, between 5a and 6a Avs
    NO, Barrio Guamilito (☎ 53-3560)
Mexico
    2a Calle, 20 Av SO, No 205, Colonia Río de
    Piedras (☎ 53-2604, 53-2605, fax 52-3293)

HONDURAS

Nicaragua
      6a Calle, No 36, at 16a Av, Barrio
      Los Andes (☎ 52-9069, fax 53-1739)
UK
      Terminales Cortés, Edificio Bonilla Castell,
      2nd Floor, 4a Calle at 4a Av NO
      (☎ 57-3939, fax 57-7000)

Money Banco Banffaa by the cathedral
changes traveler's checks. Cash advances
on Visa and MasterCard are available at
Credomatic (☎ 57-4350) on 5a Av between
1a and 2a Calles NO. It's open Monday to
Friday from 8 am to 7 pm, Saturday 8 am
to 2 pm.

The Mundirama travel agency (☎ 52-
3400) in the Edificio Martinez Valenzuela
(just south of the cathedral) is the agent for
American Express; they will hold mail for
six months for Amex card and check users.

Post & Communications The post office
is on 9a Calle at 3a Av SO. It's open
Monday to Friday from 7:30 am to 8 pm,
Saturday 7:30 am to 12:30 pm. Maps,
posters, cards and postcards are sold here
but only until 2:30 pm.

The Hondutel office on the corner of 4a
Calle and 4a Av SO is open for domestic
and international telephone calls 24 hours,
every day. Fax service is available Monday
to Friday, 8 am to 4 pm.

Media There's a small selection of books
and magazines in English, as well as the
Miami Herald newspaper, at the tobacco
shop of the Gran Hotel Sula on the north
side of the plaza.

Things to See & Do
The large **cathedral**, facing onto a large
shady plaza, is the central feature of San
Pedro Sula. It was built during the 1950s.

The **Museo de Arqueología e Historia**
(☎ 57-1496) on the corner of 3a Av and 4a
Calle NO is a large and excellent museum
exhibiting hundreds of archaeological artifacts in excellent condition from the Valle
de Sula. It illustrates the changes over time
of civilization in the valley and the connections between this region and others in

pre-Columbian times. Another section features large paintings illustrating the
Spanish conquest, life, and events of the
colonial era, with exhibits on into modern
times. It's open Tuesday to Sunday from 10
am to 4:15 pm; admission is US$0.40.

The **Mercado Guamilito** is on the
northwest side of town in the block
between 8a and 9a Avs, 6a and 7a Calles
NO. In addition to the usual fruits, vegetables, household goods and comedores, it
houses the **Mercado de Artesanías
Guamilito**, a section with a large number
of stalls displaying a wide selection of arts
and handicrafts from all over Honduras,
Guatemala and El Salvador. The market is
open Monday to Saturday from 7 am to
5 pm, Sunday 7 am to noon.

The main **mercado** is in the southeast
section of town, in the block between 6a and
7a Calles, 4a and 5a Avs. There are stalls in
the streets spreading out for blocks around
the market. This is a distribution center, and
you can sometimes see meters-high piles of
green bananas and other produce.

The **Centro Cultural Sampedrano**
(☎ 53-3911), three blocks north of the
plaza at the corner of 3a Calle and 4a Av
NO, has an art gallery, a library with books,
magazines and newspapers in English and
Spanish, and a theater where plays are presented. **Alliance Française** (☎ 53-1178),
on 4a Calle at 23a Av SO, has a lending
library of books and magazines in French
and runs classes in French and occasional
cultural events.

Beside the Río Las Piedras on the northern outskirts of town, the **Parque Pre-
sentación Centeno** is an attractive
natural forest reserve and park. Also on the
outskirts of town, up on the mountain near
the Coca-Cola sign, the **Mirador Bella
Vista** offers a sweeping view of San Pedro
and the surrounding region. There are no
buses going up there, but you could take a
taxi for around US$8 roundtrip.

Pulhapanzak waterfall, Balneario Bahr,
the Cuevas de Taulabé, the Lago de Yojoa,
Puerto Cortés and Omoa are all easy excursions from San Pedro Sula. **La Lima**,
which is 14 km east of San Pedro, is a

HONDURAS

banana 'company town' established by United Brands, where you can see the banana plantation and packing operations.

Organized Tours
Cambio Centroamérica (Cambio CA; ☎ 52-7274, fax 52-0523, net) offers ecological tours to Parque Nacional Cusuco and to places farther afield, including the Mosquitia region. The office is on 1a Calle between 5a and 6a Avs SO.

Places to Stay
San Pedro has many good, clean, cheap places to stay. The *Hotel San Pedro* (☎ 53-1513, 53-4014, ☎ /fax 53-2655), on 3a Calle between 1a and 2a Avs SO, is large and offers several types of rooms with hot water in the showers. With shared bath and fan, single rooms are US$2.90 or US$4.15, doubles US$5.85. With private bath and fan, singles/doubles are US$6.25/8.75 or US$7.90/10.85. Fancier rooms with private bath, air con, TV and telephone cost US$13.35/15.85.

In the next block, on 3a Calle between 2a and 3a Avs SO, *Hotel El Nilo* (☎ 53-4689) has spacious rooms with private cold bath and fan for US$5 with one bed, US$8.35 with two beds.

The *Hotel Brisas del Occidente* (☎ 52-2309), on 5a Av between 6a and 7a Calles SO, is popular with Peace Corps volunteers. The building is old but clean; all the rooms have fan and shared bath and cost US$3.35 per room, with one or two beds.

A block away, *Hotel San Juan* (☎ 53-1488), on the corner of 5a Av and 6a Calle SO, has rooms with shared bath for US$3.50, or with private cold bath for US$5. Rooms with three beds and shared bath are US$4.30; with two beds and private bath they cost US$5.40.

Hotel El Castillo (☎ 53-1490), on the corner of 6a Av and 8a Calle SO, has rooms with shared bath for US$3.10/3.50, often with a sink in the room, or US$4.35/5.20 with private bath.

The *Hotel El Parador* (☎ 57-6687), on the corner of 2a Av and 6a Calle SE, is in a loud location, but the rooms are clean; singles/doubles with private cold bath and fan are US$3.35/5.

Hotel Brasilia (☎ 52-6765), nearby at the corner of 2a Av and 7a Calle SE, offers rooms with private cold bath and color cable TV for US$6.65 with fan, US$11.65 with air con. Diagonally opposite, *Hotel La Siesta* (☎ 52-2650) is another reasonable place. Singles/doubles go for US$4.15/5 with shared bath, or US$5/6.65 with private cold bath. Other cheap hotels are nearby.

A bit more upmarket, *Hotel Terraza* (☎ 53-3108), 6a Av between 4a and 5a Calles SO, has rooms with private hot bath, telephone, cable TV and one or two beds for US$11.25 with fan, or US$13.35 with air con.

More upmarket again is *Hotel Bolívar* (☎ 53-3224, 53-3218, fax 53-4823) at the corner of 2a Av and 2a Calle NO, with a swimming pool, bar/restaurant and private parking. All the rooms have air con, private hot bath, cable TV and phone and cost US$27.50 per night. If you really want to live it up, the *Gran Hotel Sula* (☎ 52-9999) on the central plaza is one of the most luxurious places in town, with 120 rooms priced at over US$100.

Javier Pinel (☎ /fax 57-4056, net) offers B&B accommodations in a room in the family home at 239D Calle 9, between 23a and 24a Avs SO in the residential Barrio Río Piedras district. It's a bit overpriced at US$40/45 for one/two people, but the price includes breakfast, free transport to/from the airport or bus station, and all the helpful orientation you need. Javier speaks fluent English and Spanish.

Places to Eat
There are a couple of supermarkets on 5a Av near 5a Calle.

One of the most enjoyable places to eat or just hang out in San Pedro is the *Café Skandia*, the cafeteria of the Gran Hotel Sula on the north side of the plaza. It's air-conditioned, open 24 hours and not expensive; you can get breakfast, sandwiches or burgers for around US$2. It also has lots of foods you don't normally see in Central America, such as waffles, onion rings and apple pie. There are tables beside the swimming pool, and it's an easy place to meet foreigners or locals. Upstairs is a fancier restaurant, the *Granada*, with buffets at breakfast and lunch, a la carte service at dinner.

On the opposite side of the plaza, *Cafetería Pamplona* is another popular, air-conditioned restaurant, open every day from 7 am to 8 pm.

Pizza Hut, Wendy's and *Burger King* all have air-conditioned branches at the corner of 3a Calle and 4a Av SO, a block south of the plaza. All are open every day from 7 am to 10 pm. Pizza Hut and Wendy's both have safe salad bars; Pizza Hut's weekday lunchtime special, served from noon to 4 pm, is a good deal, with an individual pizza, a trip to the salad bar and unlimited soft drinks for US$2.75.

The *Cafetería & Pizzería Italia*, two blocks west of the plaza on the corner of 1a Calle and 7a Av NO, serves good, inexpensive pizza and pasta. It's open Tuesday to Sunday, 10 am to 10 pm.

For typical Honduran dishes there's the *Cafetería Mayan Way*, on 6a Av SO near 5a Calle SO, where a choice of three lunch specials (including soup) is just US$1.

Also good for typical Honduran fare are the comedores at the two markets, especially those on the south side (inside) of the general market, on 7a Calle between 4a and 5a Avs SE. Prices are low and there are long tables seating lots of customers; as markets go, this one is quite clean and well set up for dining. The even cleaner Mercado Guamilito also has dining.

San Pedro also has several popular more upmarket restaurants. A few blocks west of the stadium, the *Cafe des Artes* on 1a Calle is an artsy cafe/bar with light food and good music. *TGIF* (also called *Fridays)* on Blvd Los Próceres is another popular spot.

Several other good restaurants are on the southwest side of the Circunvalación, called the 'Zona Viva' for its restaurants and nightspots. *Las Tejas* and *Restaurante La Tejana*, both on Calle 9 SO at the Circunvalación in the Zona Viva, are often recommended for their seafood and beef.

Restaurante Mexiquense at 14a Av and 10 Calle SO is good for Mexican food. *Chef Mariano* at 16a Av between 9a and 10a Calles SO serves typical Garífuna, Honduran and international dishes.

On the outskirts of town on the Blvd del Sur, the highway heading toward Tegucigalpa, *Shauky's Place* is a pleasant open-air family restaurant/bar where mariachis wander from table to table in the balmy evening air. Come for a meal (they specialize in beef dishes) or just for a drink and a snack. It's open Monday to Saturday from 4 pm on.

Entertainment
Shauky's Place and the *Cafe des Artes* (see Places to Eat) are pleasant bars with good music; they're nice places to go in the evening. *Frog's Sports Bar* on Blvd Los Próceres between 19a and 20a Calles SO has three different bars, beach volleyball, mini soccer, pool tables, giant TV screens and a snack bar. It's open every day from 5 pm on.

Discos popular with young people include *Confetis, Henry's* and *La Terraza*, all on the Circunvalación. *El Quijote*, on 11a Calle between 3a and 4a Av SO, attracts a bit older crowd.

San Pedro has no specifically gay places, but gay people will feel comfortable at *Confetis* and *La Terraza*. The *Cafetería Mayan Way* (see Places to Eat), also gay-friendly, is an unassuming, low-key spot for a drink in the evening.

A variety of cultural events are presented at the *Museo de Arqueología e Historia*; ask about the current schedule. The *Centro Cultural Sampedrano* usually has a play going on. There are plenty of cinemas; check the local newspapers for current schedules.

Getting There & Away
Air San Pedro Sula is an air transport hub. It is served by daily direct flights to all major cities in Central America; to Houston, Los Angeles, Miami, New Orleans, New York and San Francisco in the USA; to Mexico City and Cancún in Mexico;

and, within Honduras, to Tegucigalpa, La Ceiba and all the Bay Islands.

International airlines serving San Pedro include:

American Airlines
(☎ 58-0518/9, airport 68-2165)
Continental (☎ 57-4141, airport 59-0577)
COPA (☎ 53-2640, airport 68-2518)
Iberia (☎ 53-1530, airport 68-1091)
Lacsa (☎ 53-2646, airport 56-2391)
TACA (☎ 53-2640, 53-2626)

Isleña (☎ 52-8322, airport 68-2218) and Sosa (airport ☎ 68-1742) are the two domestic airlines; TACA also offers a domestic flight between San Pedro and Tegucigalpa. See the Honduras Getting Around section for fares.

Bus San Pedro is also a hub of land transport, with many bus lines and routes departing in all directions. As in Tegucigalpa, there is no central bus station; each bus company operates from its own terminal.

Buses of different categories travel to most places. The 'direct' or 'express' buses cost slightly more but will get you there faster, without dozens of stops along the way. Going to Copán Ruinas, the shuttle bus service is much faster than the bus.

Tegucigalpa, regular buses (241 km, four hours) Transportes Hedman-Alas (☎ 53-1361), 3a Calle between 7a and 8a Avs NO – 12 buses daily, 6:30 am to 5:30 pm, US$2.90. Transportes El Rey (☎ 53-4969, 53-4264), 7a Av between 5a and 6a Calles SO – hourly buses, 4:30 am to 7 pm, US$2.10. Transportes Sáenz (☎ 53-1829), 9a Av between 9a and 10a Calles SO – buses at 2, 5 and 7 am, then hourly until 5:30 pm, US$2.10. Transportes Los Norteños (☎ 52-2145), 6a Calle between 6a and 7a Avs SO – hourly buses, 6 am to 5 pm, US$2.10.

Tegucigalpa, direct or express buses (3½ hours) Transportes Hedman-Alas (see above) – servicio ejecutivo buses, super deluxe, every day at 5:45 am, 11:30 am and 4:45 pm, plus on Sunday at 3:30 pm, US$5.40. Transportes El Rey Servicios Express (☎ 57-

8355), 10a Av, between 9a and 10a Calles SO – hourly buses, 5:30 am to 6:30 pm, US$2.90.
Transportes Sáenz Servicio Ejecutivo (☎ 53-4969), 8a Av between 5a and 6a Calles SO – buses at 6, 8 and 10 am, 2, 4 and 6 pm, US$8.35.

Puerto Cortés (64 km, direct buses 1½ hours, US$0.65; regular buses two hours, US$0.50) Transportes Citul (☎ 58-1594), 6a Av between 7a and 8a Calles SO – direct buses every half-hour, 5 am to 7:30 pm; regular buses every 15 minutes, 4:30 am to 9:30 pm. Transportes Impala (☎ 53-3111), 2a Av between 4a and 5a Calles SO – direct buses every 45 minutes, 6 am to 7 pm; regular buses every 10 or 15 minutes, 4:30 am to 10 pm.

La Lima & El Progreso (14 km to La Lima, 30 minutes, US$0.15; to El Progreso, one hour, 28 km, US$0.30) Empresas Tupsa, Catisa & City (☎ 53-1023, 52-6199), 2a Av between 5a and 6a Calles SO – buses every five minutes, 4:30 am to 10 pm.

Trujillo (373 km, five to six hours) Take a bus to La Ceiba and change buses there.

La Ceiba (202 km, three hours, US$1.90) Empresas Tupsa, Catisa & City (☎ 53-1023, 52 6199), 2a Av between 5a and 6a Calles SO – hourly buses, 5:30 am to 5:30 pm.

Tela (99 km, 1½ hours, US$1.90) Same buses as to La Ceiba. Or take a bus to El Progreso and change buses there.

Copán Ruinas, regular buses (169 km, five hours, US$2.10) Transportes Etumi, buses depart from the corner of 6a Av and 6a Calle SO – twice daily, 11 am and 1 pm.

Copán Ruinas, express buses (169 km, three hours, US$5) GAMA, in front of Hotel Palmira, 6a Calle between 6a and 7a Avs SO – express bus departs daily at 3 pm. Or take the shuttle bus (see below).

Santa Rosa de Copán (152 km, direct buses 2½ hours, US$1.85; regular buses 3½ hours, US$1.35) Transportes Torito & Copanecos (☎ 53-1954), 6a Av between 8a and 9a Calles SO, beside Hotel El Castillo – direct buses 8 am, 9:30 am, 2 pm and 3 pm; regular buses every half-hour, 3:45 am to 5:30 pm. Also, same buses as to Agua Caliente.

Agua Caliente, Guatemala border (241 km, express bus five hours, US$4.15; regular buses six hours, US$2.90) Transportes Congolón (☎ 53-1174), 8a Av between 9a and 10a Calles SO – one express bus at midnight;

regular buses at 6:30 am, 10:30 am, 1 pm and 3 pm.

Nueva Ocotepeque (247 km, six hours, US$2.90) Same buses as to Agua Caliente.

La Entrada (124 km, direct buses 1½ hours, US$1.50; regular buses 2½ hours, US$1.15) Same buses as to Santa Rosa de Copán, Agua Caliente and Copán Ruinas.

Santa Bárbara (94 km, direct buses 1½ hours, US$1.25; regular buses two hours, US$1) Transportes Cotisbá (☎ 52-8889), 4a Av between 9a and 10a Calles SO – direct buses at 8 am and 4 pm; regular buses every half-hour, 5:20 am to 6 pm.

Pulhapanzak (60 km, 1½ to two hours, US$0.65) Empresa Tirla, buses depart from a stop on 1a Av between 4a and 5a Calles SE – buses every 40 minutes, 6:50 am to 5 pm. Return buses depart every 40 minutes, 5 am to 5:30 pm.

Adventure Shuttle offers fast, air conditioned shuttle service between San Pedro Sula and Copán Ruinas. The schedule has changes occasionally, so check the current schedule before you plan your trip.

The shuttle departs from Copán Ruinas at 8 am, arriving at the San Pedro Sula Airport at 11 am and at downtown San Pedro Sula at 11:30 am. From downtown San Pedro Sula it departs at 3:30 pm for the return trip, arriving back in Copán Ruinas at 6:15 pm. There's no service to Copán on Wednesday afternoon, and no service from Copán on Thursday morning.

Prices are US$20 between Copán and San Pedro Sula, US$25 between Copán and the San Pedro Sula Airport.

In San Pedro Sula, buy tickets and catch the shuttle at Aventuras Centroamericanas (☎ 57-2380) in the Edificio Nina on 1a Calle between 16a and 17a Avs NO. In Copán, buy tickets and catch the shuttle at the Hotel Yaragua (☎ 98-3464) on Parque Central.

Train The train station (☎ 53-4080) is in the center of town, on the corner of 1a Calle and 1a Av. Passenger trains no longer operate from San Pedro; there's only one passenger train route in the whole country, operating between Puerto Cortés and Tela.

However, the office here in San Pedro is the national train office (the Ferrocarril Nacional de Honduras); you can get current information about this one train route.

Getting Around

To/From the Airport The Villeda Morales Airport is about 15 km east of town. There is no direct bus, but you can get on any El Progreso bus, alight at the airport turnoff, and walk for 10 minutes. Taxis cost about US$2.80 from the airport to town but double that going the other way.

Bus There are local buses to the suburbs that cost US$0.05.

Car Rental Agencies in San Pedro Sula include:

American Car Rental
  (☎ 52-7626, airport 68-2337)
Avis (☎ 53-0888, airport 68-1088)
Blitz (☎ 53-2405)
Budget (☎ 53-4311)
Dollar (☎ 52-7626)
Martha Elena (☎ 53-4672)
Maya (☎ 52-2670)
Molinari (☎ 53-2639, airport 68-2580)
National (☎ 57-2644)
Toyota (☎ 57-2644)

Taxi The average taxi ride in town costs around US$1.25. There are always lots of taxis cruising.

PARQUE NACIONAL CUSUCO

Parque Nacional Cusuco, 20 km west of San Pedro in the impressive Merendón mountain range, is a cloud forest park. Its highest peak (Cerro Jilinco) is 2242 meters. Abundant wildlife includes a large population of quetzals and many other tropical birds, among them toucans and parrots. Quetzals are spotted most frequently from April to June.

At the park there is a waterfall, swimming hole, interpretive forest trails of various lengths, visitors' center with exhibits and an audiovisual center. A guide will take you along the trails for around US$4; you'll see more wildlife with a guide. The best time of day to spot wildlife is early in the morning. The park is open every day from 8 am to 4:30 pm; admission costs US$10 for foreigners, US$0.85 for Hondurans.

Accommodations are available in the park at a small two-bedroom house for US$5.85 per person; each bedroom has two beds, complete with bedding, and there's a kitchen. Camping may also be possible; ask at the Fundación Héctor Rodrigo Pastor Fasquelle (☎ 52-1014, 57-6598, fax 57-6620, net), in San Pedro upstairs over the Pizzería Italia and the corner of 1a Calle and 7a Av NO. It's open Monday to Friday from 8 am to noon and 1 to 5 pm. The staff also has general park information, including maps and a bird checklist.

Getting There & Away
Access is easiest with a 4WD vehicle, especially during the rainy season. To get there, take the highway out of San Pedro as if going to Tegucigalpa; at the Chamelecón intersection, take the western highway (marked 'Occidente'). After 30 km (about 30 minutes), take the turnoff toward Cofradía; from Cofradía it's about 25 km to the park by a gravel road. Go through Cofradía and after about an hour you'll come to Buenos Aires, the last place where food and drink are available. When the road divides, take the left fork and ascend for about 20 more minutes to reach the park visitors' center.

Getting there by public transport is more of a challenge, but it can be done. Buses to Cofradía are operated by Empresa Etica, opposite the cemetery on Av Los Leones in San Pedro Sula; they depart every 20 minutes and take about an hour to reach Cofradía. From Cofradía you can take a pickup to Buenos Aires; they provide public transport between the two towns, but they don't go every day. You could probably hitch a ride to Buenos Aires if no pickups are going.

Cambio Centroamérica (Cambio CA; see Organized Tours under San Pedro Sula) offers overnight camping trips into the park.

CARRETERA DE OCCIDENTE
From San Pedro Sula, the Carretera de Occidente runs southwest, roughly parallel with the Guatemalan border, though rather far into the Honduran side. At La Entrada, 124 km southwest of San Pedro Sula, the road forks. One fork heads west to Copán Ruinas and the Guatemalan border, the other south to Santa Rosa de Copán, Nueva Ocotepeque and the two borders of Agua Caliente (Guatemala) and El Poy (El Salvador).

LA ENTRADA
La Entrada is a crossroads town with several places to stay and eat; lots of buses and traffic pass through on the way northeast to San Pedro Sula, south to Santa Rosa de Copán and Nueva Ocotepeque, and southwest to Copán Ruinas. You never have to wait long for a bus in La Entrada.

Parque Arqueológico El Puente
The town's major attraction is this archaeological park with 210 archaeological structures, a museum and cafeteria. It is estimated that around a thousand Maya people lived on this site from around 650 to 900 AD, when it was a town pertaining to Copán, which was the regional capital. The turnoff for the park is five km from the crossroads at La Entrada on the road heading to Copán; the archaeological park is another 6 km from the turnoff. It's open every day from 8 am to 4 pm; admission costs US$2.50.

Places to Stay & Eat
Right at the crossroads, *Hotel y Restaurant El San Carlos* (☎ 98-5187, 98-5228) is an attractive place to stay. All the rooms have private hot bath, color cable TV, telephone and fan; rooms are US$8.35 with one double bed, US$10 with two single beds, or US$16.65 with a double and single bed. The hotel has a restaurant/bar open every day from 7 am to 10 pm.

Two blocks north of the crossroads, *Hotel Tegucigalpa* (☎ 98-5046) is a clean hotel with a relaxed, homey feel.

All the rooms have private cold bath and color cable TV. Rooms with fan are US$8.35/10.85 with one/two beds or US$12.50/16.65 with air con. There's parking in the central courtyard, where there's also a simple cafeteria open every day from 6 am to 8 pm.

Half a block north of the crossroads, *Hotel Central* (☎ 98-5084) has single/double rooms for US$2.50/5 with shared bath, or US$4.15/8.35 with private cold bath. There's parking in the central courtyard. It's not as spiffy as the other two places, but it's not bad.

Several small comedores are near the bus stop at the crossroads. For more upmarket dining, the *La Terraza Steak House* is often recommended; it's two blocks north of the crossroads, upstairs beside the Hotel Tegucigalpa.

Getting There & Away

Buses pass through La Entrada frequently in all directions, stopping at the crossroads. These include:

San Pedro Sula (124 km) Direct buses at 9 am and 3 pm (two hours, US$1.65); regular buses (with stops) every 20 minutes from 5 am to 7:30 pm (2½ hours, US$1.10).

Copán Ruinas (61 km, 2¼ hours, US$1.25) Buses every 45 minutes from 5 am to 4:30 pm.

Santa Rosa de Copán (28 km, 1¼ hours, US$0.60) Same buses as to Nueva Ocotepeque.

Nueva Ocotepeque (123 km, 3½ hours, US$1.75) Buses every 20 minutes from 6 am to 8:30 pm.

COPÁN RUINAS

Population 6000

The town of Copán Ruinas, also sometimes simply called Copán, is about two km from the famous Maya ruins of the same name. It is a beautiful little village with cobblestone streets, white adobe buildings with red-tile roofs and a lovely colonial church on the plaza. This valley was inhabited by the Maya for around two thousand years, and an aura of timeless peace fills the air. Copán has recently become a primary tourist destination, but this hasn't disrupted the peace to the extent one might expect.

The town's annual festival is from March 15 to 20. The annual Artisans' Fair with handicrafts and cultural presentations runs from December 15 to 21.

Orientation

Parque Central, with the church on one side, is the heart of town. The town is very small, and everything is within a few blocks of the plaza. The ruins are two km outside of town, on the road to La Entrada – a pleasant 15-minute stroll along a footpath to one side of the highway. The Las Sepulturas archaeological site is a couple of kilometers farther along.

Information

Banco de Occidente on the plaza changes US dollars and traveler's checks, Guatemalan quetzales and Salvador colones, and it gives cash advances on Visa and MasterCard. Banco Atlántida, also on the plaza, changes US dollars and traveler's checks and gives cash advances on Visa cards. For US dollars, both banks give a better rate than the moneychangers at the border, but slightly less than banks elsewhere in Honduras. Both banks are open Monday to Friday from 8 am to noon and 2 to 4:30 pm, Saturday 8 am to 11:30 am.

The post office and Hondutel are side by side, a few doors from the plaza.

The Justo A Tiempo laundry offers an expensive laundry service and English-language book exchange. The family at Hotel Los Gemelos operates a less expensive laundry service.

Things to See & Do

Of course, the No 1 attraction is the Copán archaeological site, two km outside of town on the road to La Entrada (see Copán Archaeological Site below). Other fine places to visit in the area are covered in the Around Copán Ruinas section.

In town, the **Museo de Arqueología Maya** (☎ 98-3437) on the town plaza is well worth a visit. It contains the original Stela B, portraying King 18 Rabbit; he was

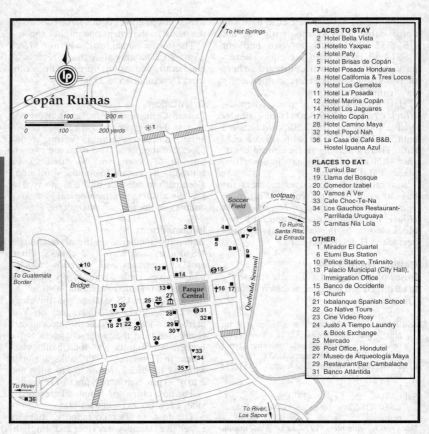

Copán Ruinas

| 0 | 100 | 200 m |
| 0 | 100 | 200 yards |

To Hot Springs

Soccer Field

footpath

To Ruins, Santa Rita, La Entrada

To Guatemala Border

Bridge

To River

Parque Central

Quebrada Sesesmil

To River, Los Sapos

PLACES TO STAY
2　Hotel Bella Vista
3　Hotelito Yaxpac
4　Hotel Paty
5　Hotel Brisas de Copán
7　Hotel Posada Honduras
8　Hotel California & Tres Locos
9　Hotel Los Gemelos
11　Hotel La Posada
12　Hotel Marina Copán
14　Hotel Los Jaguares
17　Hotelito Copán
28　Hotel Camino Maya
32　Hotel Popol Nah
36　La Casa de Café B&B,
　　Hostel Iguana Azul

PLACES TO EAT
18　Tunkul Bar
19　Llama del Bosque
20　Comedor Izabel
30　Vamos A Ver
33　Cafe Choc-Te-Na
34　Los Gauchos Restaurant-
　　Parrillada Uruguaya
35　Carnitas Nia Lola

OTHER
1　Mirador El Cuartel
6　Etumi Bus Station
10　Police Station, Tránsito
13　Palacio Municipal (City Hall),
　　Immigration Office
15　Banco de Occidente
16　Church
21　Ixbalanque Spanish School
22　Go Native Tours
23　Cine Video Rosy
24　Justo A Tiempo Laundry
　　& Book Exchange
25　Mercado
26　Post Office, Hondutel
27　Museo de Arqueología Maya
29　Restaurant/Bar Cambalache
31　Banco Atlántida

the great builder-king who unfortunately lost his head to the king of Quiriguá. Other exhibits of painted pottery, carved jade, Maya glyphs and a calendar round are also interesting and informative, as is the 'Tumba del Brujo,' the tomb of a shaman or priest who died around 700 AD and was buried with many items under the east corner of the Plaza de los Jaguares. The museum is open every day from 8 am to 4 pm; admission is US$2.

About four blocks north of the plaza is the **Mirador El Cuartel**, the old jail, with a magnificent view over town. The building is now used as a school; you can still go up there to enjoy the view.

A pleasant, easy walk on the road on the south side of town provides a fine view over the corn and tobacco fields surrounding Copán. It's also a pleasant walk to the river, also on the south side of town.

Horseback Riding & Los Sapos

You can rent a horse in Copán Ruinas to go out to the ruins or make other excursions. Horses can be arranged by either of the town's tour companies or by most hotels. There's also a horse operation just outside town on the way to the ruins. Or you could probably find a horse if you just ask around town and do some bargaining; many of the locals have horses. The Hotel Hacienda El Jaral (see Places to Stay) also has horseback riding.

A popular horseback riding excursion is to **Los Sapos**, five km from town in the Aldea de San Lucas. The *sapos* (toads) are old Maya stone carvings in a spot with a beautiful view over town; you can get there by horseback in about half an hour or walk in about 45 minutes, all uphill. From Los Sapos you can walk to a stela.

Language Courses
The Ixbalanque Spanish School (☎ 98-3432, fax 98-0004, 57-6215) in the same block as the Tunkul Bar offers 20 hours weekly of one-on-one instruction in Spanish for US$150 per week, including homestay with a local family that provides three meals a day. Instruction only, for 20 hours a week, costs US$95. Ixbalanque also operates another school in Trujillo.

Organized Tours
Go Native Tours (☎ 98-3432, fax 57-6215), with an office in the same block as the Tunkul Bar, offers both local tours and ecological tours farther afield, including to the Mosquitia region, Celaque, Cusuco and Punta Sal. It also organizes bird-watching tours to the Lago de Yojoa.

Xukpi Tours (☎ 98-3435, evening 98-3503), operated by Jorge Barraza, also offers a number of ecological tours both locally and farther afield. His ruins and **bird-watching tours** are justly famous; some of the locals call him the *hombre pájaro* for his enthusiasm and knowledge about birds. He offers ecological tours to all parts of Honduras (including the Mosquitia region and all the national parks) and to Quiriguá in Guatemala. He is quite an ebullient, knowledgeable, capable and wonderful guide.

Places to Stay – budget
Camping Attractive campsites are available at the *Hotel Hacienda El Jaral*, an ecotourism resort 11 km from town (see the Around Copán Ruinas section below).

Hostel *Hostel Iguana Azul* (☎ 52-7274, fax 52-0523) is next door to La Casa de Café B&B (see below) and operated by the same friendly people. New in 1997, it has 24 dorm-style bunk beds (US$4 per person) in four rooms with shared hot bath in a colonial-style ranch home. There's a pleasant garden and the common area has books, magazines, travel guides and lots of travel information.

Hotels The *Hotel Los Gemelos* (☎ 98-3077), a block behind the plaza, is a long-time favorite with budget travelers. Operated by a very friendly family, it has a garden patio, a place to wash your clothes (or a laundry service if you prefer) and enclosed parking; coffee is always available. Singles/doubles with shared cold bath are US$4.15/5.

Across the street, *Hotel California & Tres Locos* (☎ 98-3515), new in 1996, has four attractive rooms decorated with lots of bamboo and woven mats, all sharing a hot bath, for US$8.35 per room.

In the same block, *Hotel Posada Honduras* (☎ 98-3082) has 13 simple rooms encircling a courtyard full of mango, mamey, lemon and coconut trees, with enclosed parking out back. Singles/doubles with shared cold bath are US$2.50/5; with private cold bath they are US$5/5.85. Also on the same street, the simple *Hotelito Copán* (☎ 98-3411) has single/double/triple rooms with shared bath for US$3.35/5/6.25, or with private cold bath for US$5/6.65/8.35.

Other simple places include *Hotelito Yaxpac* (☎ 98-3025) with just four plain rooms, all with private hot bath, for US$6/5.85. The *Hotel La Posada* (☎ 98-3070, 98-3072), half a block from the plaza, has rooms with shared cold bath for US$3.35/5.

The *Hotel Popol Nah* (☎ 98-3095) is a clean, new place with seven rooms for US$15, all with private hot bath; it will soon have 12 rooms, some with air con. The

HONDURAS

Hotel Paty (☎ 98-3021) near the entrance to town has rooms around a courtyard, all with private hot bath, for US$11.65.

Places to Stay – middle

Copán also has a number of more upmarket places. One of the most attractive is *Hotel Brisas de Copán* (☎ 98-3018), near the entrance to town. Attractive upper rooms with cable TV, shared terraces and plenty of light are US$20.85; larger rooms with two double beds but no TV are US$16.65. They also have lower rooms for US$10 each, but these are darker and not as good. All the rooms come with private hot bath.

Also new in 1996, *Hotel Bella Vista* (☎ 98-3502) is up on a hill overlooking town, four blocks from the plaza. It has a beautiful view; large, comfortable rooms for US$13.35 with private hot bath, cable TV and phone; and parking in the courtyard.

For B&B accommodations there's the *La Casa de Café* (☎ 52-7274, fax 52-0523), four blocks from the plaza, operated by a friendly Honduran-American couple. It's a beautiful place in a beautiful setting; an outdoor area with tables and hammocks has a view over cornfields to the mountains of Guatemala. Five rooms with private hot bath are US$38 for one or two people; three rooms with shared hot bath are US$20/28. All prices include a hearty breakfast.

Other more expensive places in town include *Hotel Los Jaguares* (☎ 98-3451) with singles/doubles for US$30/34; *Hotel Camino Maya* (☎ 98-3446, 98-3517, fax 39-3056) with singles/doubles for US$35/44; and the large *Hotel Marina Copán* (☎ 98-3070, 98-3071) with a swimming pool, restaurant/bar and singles/doubles for US$70/81. All of these places are beautiful, luxurious and right on the plaza.

The *Hotel Hacienda El Jaral* is a beautiful ecotourism resort with many activities, 11 km from town on the way to La Entrada (see Around Copán Ruinas).

Places to Eat

The *Tunkul Bar*, two blocks from the plaza, is the main gathering spot in town. It's an attractive covered-patio bar/restaurant with good food, good music, good company and a book exchange. A variety of meat and vegetarian meals all cost around US$2.50. The Tunkul is open every day from 7 am to 11 pm or midnight; happy hour runs from 7 to 8 pm for beer, 8 to 9 pm for mixed drinks.

Across the street, the *Llama del Bosque* is another popular place to eat, offering a good selection of meals and snacks; their *anafre* (fondue) is especially tasty. In the same block, *Comedor Izabel* is a cheap, typical comedor with decent food. Both are open every day from 6:30 am to 9 pm.

Another pleasant spot is the *Vamos A Ver* cafeteria/restaurant/cinema, half a block from the plaza. Owned by a friendly Dutch couple, it's a pleasant little covered-patio place with good, inexpensive foods that you don't always see while traveling in Central America: good homemade breads, a variety of international cheeses, good soups, fruit or vegetable salads, good coffee, fruit licuados, a wide variety of teas and always something for vegetarians. It's open every day from 7 am to 10 pm; movies are shown every night at 7 pm.

In the next block, the *Cafe Choc-Te-Na* is another simple little cafe with a pleasant ambiance.

Farther along, *Carnitas Nia Lola* is an open-air restaurant with a beautiful view over corn and tobacco fields toward the mountains. It's a relaxing place with simple and economical food; the specialties are charcoal-grilled chicken and beef. It's open every day from 7 am to 10 pm.

Los Gauchos Restaurant-Parrillada Uruguaya is the fancy restaurant in town – come here for a splurge. It's great for meat-eaters; meat and seafood main courses are around US$6.25 to US$11, or you can get the giant Parrillada Especial for four people for US$20. There's a fine view from the tables outside on the verandah and beautiful decor inside.

Entertainment

The *Tunkul Bar* is the happening spot in the evening. Video movies (often in English) are shown at the *Vamos a Ver* cafe every night at 7 pm. *Cine Video Rosy*, a block from the plaza, also shows video movies. Next door to Vamos a Ver, the *Cambalache* restaurant/bar is another popular spot.

Getting There & Away

All the buses and pickups serving Copán Ruinas depart from the tiny Etumi bus station at the entrance to town, except for the GAMA express bus, which departs from Hotel Paty.

To/From San Pedro Sula & La Entrada

Direct buses to San Pedro Sula depart at 4 and 5 am (169 km, 4½ hours, US$2.10). If you don't want to get up so early, you can easily take a bus to La Entrada (61 km, 2¼ hours, US$1) and transfer there to a bus heading to San Pedro. Buses to La Entrada depart every 40 minutes from 4 am to 5 pm.

The GAMA express bus departs from Hotel Paty every morning at 6 am, arriving in San Pedro Sula at 9 am (US$5). It departs San Pedro Sula for the return trip at 3 pm from in front of Hotel Palmira, 6a Calle between 6a and 7a Avs SO.

The Adventure Shuttle bus offers faster but more expensive transport between Copán and San Pedro Sula (see Bus in San Pedro Sula). Go Native Tours (see Organized Tours) offers shuttle service to San Pedro Sula for US$12 but not every day; check to see when they're going.

To/From Guatemala Copán Ruinas is about 14 km (45 minutes) from the Guatemalan border at El Florido (see the Guatemala chapter). The border crossing is open daily from 7 am to 6 pm.

Pickups depart for the border from the Etumi bus station every 40 minutes from 6 am to 6 pm and charge US$1.25. Make sure you are charged the correct price – ask around beforehand to find out what the price should be.

At the time we were in Copán, pickup drivers had been overcharging tourists for many months on the ride from the border to Copán. Bus service had been suspended when the road between Copán and the border fell into disrepair, and though the road had been improved (still not paved but

in excellent shape), the bus service had still not resumed. If there is still no bus service, stand your ground with the pickup drivers and demand to pay a fair price. Often the pickup drivers begin by asking for a ridiculous sum but will eventually relent if they see you won't pay more than a reasonable price.

The moneychangers at the border sometimes offer a very unfavorable rate. Before you arrive at the border find out what the rate of exchange should be.

From the border, regular buses leave for Chiquimula on the Guatemala side (58 km, 2½ hours, US$2).

If you are entering Honduras from Guatemala only to visit the ruins at Copán, read the section on El Florido in the Guatemala chapter.

AROUND COPÁN RUINAS
Santa Rita de Copán & El Rubí Waterfall

A few kilometers from town (20 minutes by bus) on the road toward La Entrada, Santa Rita de Copán is a lovely village built at the confluence of two rivers. Here, too, cobblestone streets wind among adobe houses with mud ovens standing alongside. The town has a beautiful little plaza and a simple, peaceful colonial church. Santa Rita is pleasant to walk around, and it makes an enjoyable excursion from Copán Ruinas.

Just outside Santa Rita is the El Rubí waterfall, with a pleasant swimming hole. It's about a half-hour uphill walk on a trail departing from opposite the Esso gas station beside the bridge on the highway; ask people along the way how to get there. Another waterfall is farther on past the first one, another half-hour uphill climb through the jungle. To reach this one you must go with a guide or someone who knows the way.

Hacienda El Jaral

The *Hotel Hacienda El Jaral* (☎ 52-4457, ☎ /fax 52-4891), on the highway 11 km from town heading toward La Entrada, is an ecotourism resort that offers many activities, including bird watching in a bird sanctuary-lagoon (thousands of herons are here from November to May), horseback riding, bicycling, hiking, river swimming, inner tubing, canoeing and 'soft rafting' on the Río Copán. Also on the grounds are a swimming pool, a childrens' play area and two restaurants.

Guests and nonguests alike are welcome to use all the facilities (the exception is the swimming pool, which is for hotel guests only). If you want to stay over, luxurious rooms with air con, private hot bath, cable TV and fridge, all in duplex cabins with outdoor terraces, are US$55/60 for singles/doubles, with larger rooms available. Or there are campsites with access to the river, champas (thatched-roof shelters) and bathrooms for US$6.25 per site.

Hot Springs & Caves

There are some hot springs 24 km north of town, about an hour's drive or hitchhike along a beautiful mountain dirt road going through lush, fertile mountains with many coffee plantations. Take the road heading out of town (see Copán Ruinas map) and just keep going for 24 km. A small white sign at the entrance says 'Agua Caliente'; it's on the right-hand side, but it's a small sign so watch out for it. Admission is US$0.85. There are a couple of artificial pools, or you can sit in the river, where the boiling hot spring water mixes with the cool river water. Bring warm clothes if you come in the evening. There are also caves in the area.

COPÁN ARCHAEOLOGICAL SITE

Designated by UNESCO as a World Heritage Site, the Copán archaeological site is two km outside of town on the road to La Entrada – a pleasant 15-minute stroll along a footpath to one side of the highway. Las Sepulturas archaeological site is a couple of kilometers farther along.

The archaeological site is open every day from 8 am to 5 pm. The Museum of Sculpture also at the site closes an hour earlier. Admission to the ruins costs US$10 for foreigners (US$1.65 for Central Americans) and includes entry to Las Sepulturas site.

Admission to the museum costs US$5 (US$1.25 for Central Americans).

At the entrance to the ruins, the visitors' center (centro de visitantes) houses the ticket seller and a small exhibition about the site and its excavation. Nearby are a cafeteria and souvenir and handicrafts shops. Cheaper food is available across the road at the Comedor Mayapán. There's a picnic area along the path to the Principal Group of ruins. A nature trail (sendero natural) entering the forest several hundred meters from the visitors' center passes by a small ball court.

Pick up a copy of the booklet History Carved in Stone: A Guide to the Archaeological Park of the Ruins of Copán by William L Fash and Ricardo Agurcia Fasquelle, available at the visitors' center for US$1.65. It will help you understand and appreciate the ruins. It's also a good idea to go with a guide, who can help to explain the ruins and bring them to life.

History

Pre-Columbian People have been living in the Copán valley since at least around 1200 BC and probably before that; ceramic evidence has been found from around that date. Copán must have had significant commercial activity since early times; graves showing significant Olmec influence have been dated to around 900 to 600 BC.

Around 426 AD one royal family came to rule Copán, led by a mysterious king named Mah K'ina Yax K'uk' Mo' (Great Sun Lord Quetzal Macaw), who ruled from 426 to 435 AD. Archaeological evidence indicates that he was a great shaman; later kings revered him as the semidivine founder of the city. The dynasty ruled throughout Copán's florescence during the Classic period (250 to 900 AD).

Of the early kings who ruled from about 435 to 628 we know little. Only some of their names have been deciphered: Mat Head, the second king; Cu Ix, the fourth king; Waterlily Jaguar, the seventh; Moon Jaguar, the 10th; and Butz' Chan, the 11th.

Among the greatest of Copán's kings was Smoke Imix (Smoke Jaguar), the 12th

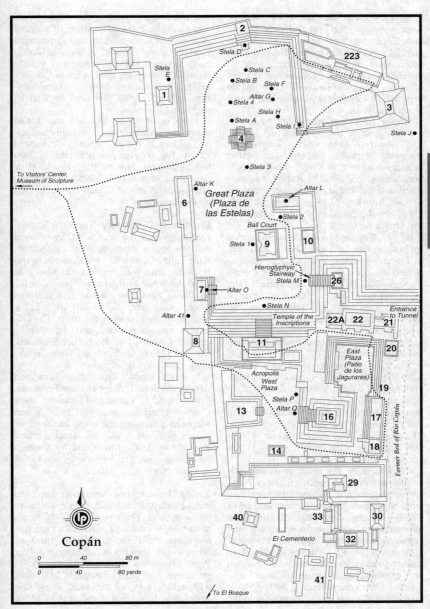

HONDURAS

2

Stela D

223

Stela E

1

Stela C

Stela B

Stela F

Altar G

Stela 4

Stela H

Stela A

Stela I

3

Stela J

To Visitors' Center,
Museum of Sculpture

Stela 3

Altar K

Great Plaza
(Plaza de
las Estelas)

Altar L

6

Stela 2

Ball Court

Stela 1

9

10

Hieroglyphic
Stairway
Stela M

26

7

Altar O

Entrance
to Tunnel

Altar 41

Stela N

Temple of the
Inscriptions

22A

22

21

8

11

20

Acropolis
West
Plaza

East
Plaza
(Patio
de los
Jaguares)

19

Stela P

13

Altar Q

16

17

18

14

29

Copán

40

33

30

0   40   80 m

0   40   80 yards

El Cementerio

32

41

To El Bosque

king, who ruled from 628 to 695. Smoke Imix was wise, forceful and rich, and he built Copán into a major military and commercial power in the region. He may have taken over the nearby princedom of Quiriguá, as one of the famous stelae there bears his name and image. By the time he died in 695, Copán's population had grown significantly.

Smoke Imix was succeeded by Uaxaclahun Ubak K'awil (18 Rabbit) (695 – 738), the 13th king, who willingly took the reins of power and pursued further military conquest. In a war with his neighbor, King Cauac Sky, 18 Rabbit was captured and beheaded, to be succeeded by Smoke Monkey (738 – 749), the 14th king. Smoke Monkey's short reign left little mark on Copán.

In 749, Smoke Monkey was succeeded by his son Smoke Shell (749 – 763), one of Copán's greatest builders. He commissioned the construction of the city's most famous and important monument, the great Hieroglyphic Stairway, which immortalizes the achievements of the dynasty from its establishment until 755, when the stairway was dedicated. It is the longest such inscription ever discovered in the Maya lands.

Yax Pac (Sunrise or First Dawn) (763 – 820), Smoke Shell's successor and the 16th king of Copán, continued the beautification of Copán even though it seems that the dynasty's power was declining and its subjects had fallen on hard times. The final aspirant to the throne, U Cit Tok', became ruler in 822, but it is not known when he died.

Until recently, the collapse of the civilization at Copán has been a mystery. Now, archaeologists are starting to understand what happened. Apparently near the end of Copán's heyday, the population grew at an unprecedented rate, straining agricultural resources; in the end, Copán was no longer agriculturally self-sufficient and had to import food from other areas. The urban core expanded in the fertile lowlands in the center of the valley, forcing both agriculture and residential areas to spread onto the steep slopes surrounding the valley. Wide areas were deforested, resulting in massive erosion that further decimated agricultural production and resulted in flooding during rainy seasons. Skeletal remains of people who died during the final years of Copán's heyday show marked evidence of malnutrition and infectious diseases, as well as decreased lifespans.

The Copán valley was not abandoned overnight – agriculturists probably continued to live in the ecologically devastated valley for maybe another one or two hundred years. But by the year 1200 or thereabouts even the farmers had departed, and the royal city of Copán was reclaimed by the jungle.

European Discovery The first known European to see the ruins was Diego García de Palacios, a representative of Spanish King Felipe II, who lived in Guatemala and traveled through the region. On March 8, 1576, he wrote to the king about the ruins he found here. Only about five families were living here then, and they knew nothing of the history of the ruins. The discovery was not pursued, and almost three centuries went by until another Spaniard, Coronel Juan Galindo, visited the ruins and made the first map of them.

It was Galindo's report that stimulated Americans John L Stephens and Frederick Catherwood to come to Copán on their Central American journey in 1839. When Stephens published the book *Incidents of Travel in Central America, Chiapas, and Yucatán* in 1841, illustrated by Catherwood, the ruins first became known to the world at large.

Today The history of the ruins continues to unfold today, as archaeologists continue to probe the site. The remains of 3450 structures have been found in the 24 sq km surrounding the Principal Group, most of them within about half a kilometer of the Principal Group. In a wider zone, 4509 structures have been detected in 1420 sites within 135 sq km of the ruins. These discoveries indicate that at the peak of Maya civilization here, around the end of the 8th century AD, the valley of Copán had over 20,000 inhabitants – a population not reached again until the 1980s.

In addition to examining the area around the Principal Group, archaeologists are continuing to explore the Principal Group itself and making new discoveries. Five separate phases of building on this site have been identified; the final phase, dating from 650 to 820 AD, is what we see today. But buried underneath the visible ruins are layers of other ruins, which archaeologists are exploring by means of underground tunnels. This is how the Rosalila temple was found, a replica of which is now in the Museum of Sculpture; below Rosalila is yet another, earlier temple, Margarita.

Archaeologists are currently working on opening one such underground tunnel to the public. It will begin at the Archaeological Court and go right under Temple 22, emerging in the Patio de los Jaguares. Archaeologists also continue to decipher more of the hieroglyphs and to get greater understanding of the early Maya.

Sculpture Museum
The newest addition to the ruins at Copán is this magnificent museum, opened in August 1996. Entering the museum is an impressive experience by itself: You enter through the mouth of a serpent and wind through the entrails of the beast before suddenly emerging into a fantastic world of sculpture and light. While Tikal is celebrated for its tall temple pyramids, and Palenque is renowned for its limestone relief panels, Copán is unique in the Maya world for its sculpture.

The highlight of the museum is a true-scale replica of the Rosalila temple, discovered in nearly perfect condition by archaeologists in 1989 by means of a tunnel dug into Structure 16, the central building of the Acropolis. Rosalila, dedicated in 571 AD by Copán's 10th ruler, Moon Jaguar, was apparently so sacred that when Structure 16 was built over it, Rosalila was not destroyed but was left completely intact.

The original Rosalila temple is still in the core of Structure 16. Under it is a still earlier temple, Margarita, built 150 years before, as well as other earlier platforms and tombs.

The other displays in the museum are stone carvings, brought here for protection from the elements. Archaeological conservation specialists from around the world have concluded that the best way to preserve the sculptures is to remove them from ground moisture and fluctuations in temperature and secure them in a more stable environment. Eventually, all the important stelae may be housed here, with detailed reproductions placed outdoors to show where the stelae originally stood. So far, Altar Q and Stelae A, N, P and 2 have been brought into the museum, and the ones you see outdoors are accurate reproductions.

The Principal Group
The Principal Group of ruins is about 400 meters beyond the visitors' center across well-kept lawns, through a gate in a strong fence and down shady avenues of trees.

Stelae of the Great Plaza The path leads to the Great Plaza and the huge, intricately carved stelae portraying the rulers of Copán. Most of Copán's best stelae date from 613 to 738 AD, during the reigns of Smoke Imix (628 – 695) and 18 Rabbit (695 – 738). All seem to have originally been painted; a few traces of red paint survive on Stela C. Many stelae had vaults beneath or beside them in which sacrifices and offerings could be placed.

Many of the stelae on the Great Plaza portray King 18 Rabbit, including Stelae A, B, C, D, F, H and 4. Perhaps the most beautiful stela in the Great Plaza is Stela A (731 AD); the original has been moved inside the Museum of Sculpture, and the one outdoors is a reproduction. Nearby and almost equal in beauty are Stela 4 (731); Stela B (731), depicting 18 Rabbit upon his accession to the throne; and Stela C (782) with a turtle-shaped altar in front. This last stela has figures on both sides. Stela E (614), erected on top of Structure 1 on the west side of the Great Plaza, is among the oldest stela.

At the northern end of the Great Plaza at the base of Structure 2, Stela D (736) also portrays King 18 Rabbit. On its back are two columns of hieroglyphs; at its base is an altar with fearsome representations of Chac, the rain god. In front of the altar is the burial place of Dr John Owen, an archaeologist with the expedition from Harvard's Peabody Museum who died during the work in 1893.

On the east side of the plaza is Stela F (721), which has a more lyrical design, with the robes of the main figure flowing around to the other side of the stone, where there are glyphs. Altar G (800), showing twin serpent heads, is among the last monuments carved at Copán. Stela H (730) may depict a queen or princess rather than a king. Stela 1 (692), on the structure that runs along the east side of the plaza, is of a person wearing a mask. Stela J, farther off to the east, resembles the stelae of Quiriguá in that it is covered in glyphs, not human figures.

Ball Court & Hieroglyphic Stairway

South of the Great Plaza, across what is known as the Central Plaza, is the ball court (Juego de Pelota, 731), the second-largest in Central America. The one you see is the third one on this site; the other two smaller ones were buried by this construction. Note the macaw heads carved at the top of the sloping walls. The central marker in the court was the work of King 18 Rabbit.

South of the ball court is Copán's most famous monument, the Hieroglyphic Stairway (743), the work of King Smoke Shell. Today it's protected from the elements by a roof. This lessens the impact of its beauty, but you can still get an idea of how it looked. The flight of 63 steps bears a history – in several thousand glyphs – of the royal house of Copán; the steps are bordered by ramps inscribed with more reliefs and glyphs. The story inscribed on the steps is still not completely understood because the stairway was partially ruined and the stones jumbled.

At the base of the Hieroglyphic Stairway is Stela M (756), bearing a figure (probably King Smoke Shell) in a feathered cloak; glyphs tell of the solar eclipse in that year. The altar in front shows a plumed serpent with a human head emerging from its jaws.

Beside the stairway, a tunnel leads to the tomb of a nobleman, a royal scribe who may have been the son of King Smoke Imix. The tomb, discovered in June 1989, held a treasure trove of painted pottery and beautiful carved jade objects that are now in Honduran museums.

Acropolis The lofty flight of steps to the south of the Hieroglyphic Stairway is called the Temple of the Inscriptions. On top of the stairway, the walls are carved with groups of hieroglyphs. On the south side of the Temple of the Inscriptions are the East Plaza and West Plaza. In the West Plaza, be sure to see Altar Q (776), among the most famous sculptures here; the original is inside the Museum of Sculpture. Around its sides, carved in superb relief, are the 16 great kings of Copán, ending with its creator, Yax Pac. Behind the altar was a sacrificial vault in which archaeologists discovered the bones of 15 jaguars and several macaws that were probably sacrificed to the glory of Yax Pac and his ancestors.

The East Plaza also contains evidence of Yax Pac – his tomb, beneath Structure 18. Unfortunately, the tomb was discovered and looted long before archaeologists arrived. Both the East and West Plazas hold a variety of fascinating stelae and sculptured heads of humans and animals. To see the most elaborate relief carving, climb Structure 22 on the northern side of the East Plaza. Excavation and restoration is still under way.

El Bosque & Las Sepulturas

Excavations at El Bosque and Las Sepulturas have shed light on the daily life of the Maya of Copán during its golden age.

Las Sepulturas, once connected to the Great Plaza by a causeway, may have been the residential area where rich, powerful nobles lived. One huge, luxurious residential compound seems to have housed some 250 people in 40 or 50 buildings arranged around 11 courtyards. The principal structure, called the House of the Bacabs (officials), had outer walls carved with the full-size figures of 10 males in fancy feathered headdresses; inside was a huge hieroglyphic bench.

To get to the site, you have to go back to the main road, turn right, then right again at the sign (two km).

Other Stelae
There are a few stelae, standing isolated and alone, around the Copán valley. **Stela 13** is just off the highway toward La Entrada, seven km from town on the right, roughly opposite the Hotel Los Gobernantes.

Stela 10 is about a 15-minute ride from town on the road toward Guatemala; it's up on a mountain, from which there's a good view over town. From the road there's an easy 10- to 15-minute trail to get up to it; there's no sign, but you can take a pickup heading for Guatemala and ask the driver to let you off at the trailhead. It's easy to hitch a ride back to town.

Stela 12 can be seen with binoculars from Templo 18 at the ruins, if you know where to look for it; it's on the mountainside across the river valley. On the spring equinox, the sun rises directly behind Stela 10 if you're standing at Stela 12, and it sets directly behind Stela 12 if you're standing at Stela 10. To the agricultural Maya people, spring equinox was an important point in the year.

SANTA ROSA DE COPÁN
Population 37,000

Santa Rosa de Copán is a small, cool, very Spanish mountain town, with cobbled streets and a lovely colonial church beside the plaza. It doesn't have any world-class tourist sights like Copán Ruinas, a few hours away; consequently, it doesn't have as many tourists. It's just a quiet, beautiful little town with a fresh climate and friendly people. The annual festival day is August 30.

Orientation & Information
The town is up on a hill, about one kilometer from the bus station on the highway.

There's no tourist information office, but

HONDURAS

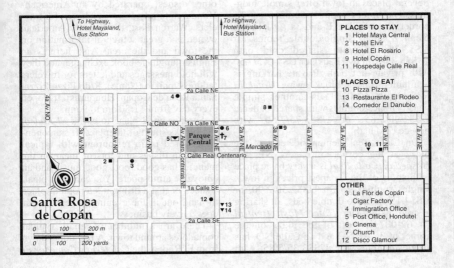

Map legend:

To Highway, Hotel Mayaland, Bus Station

To Highway, Hotel Mayaland, Bus Station

3a Calle NE

2a Calle NE

1a Calle NO — 1a Calle NE

Parque Central

Mercado

Calle Real Centenario

1a Calle SE

2a Calle SE

Santa Rosa de Copán

0   100   200 m
0   100   200 yards

PLACES TO STAY
1   Hotel Maya Central
2   Hotel Elvir
8   Hotel El Rosario
9   Hotel Copán
11 Hospedaje Calle Real

PLACES TO EAT
10 Pizza Pizza
13 Restaurante El Rodeo
14 Comedor El Danubio

OTHER
3   La Flor de Copán
    Cigar Factory
4   Immigration Office
5   Post Office, Hondutel
6   Cinema
7   Church
12 Disco Glamour

Warren Post at Pizza Pizza (see Places to Eat) is happy to help with information about the town and the area. Max Elvir at the Hotel Elvir, operator of both the hotel and Lenca Land Tours, is another helpful source of information.

The post office and Hondutel are side by side on the west side of the plaza.

Santa Rosa has banks where you can change traveler's checks or get cash advances on credit cards. There's an immigration office a block from the plaza.

Things to See & Do

La Flor de Copán cigar factory (☎ 62-0185), 1½ blocks west of the plaza, is an interesting place to visit. Ask for a free tour – you'll learn how the hand-rolled cigars are made. The factory is open Monday to Friday from 7 am to noon and 1 to 5 pm, Saturday 7 am to noon.

Organized Tours

Lenca Land Tours at the Hotel Elvir offers tours to places in the area, such as Parque Nacional Celaque, the hot springs and fort at Gracias and Belén Gualcho.

Places to Stay

Several places in town offer simple lodgings. The *Hotel Copán* (☎ 62-0265), at the corner of 1a Calle NE and 3a Av NE, has clean if small single/double rooms for US$3.35/5.85 with shared cold bath (US$8.35 with two beds), or US$4.15/7.50 with private hot bath. Private parking is available. Half a block away, *Hotel El Rosario* (☎ 62-0211) is another simple place; singles/doubles with shared bath are US$2.90/5.85, or US$3.75/7.50 with private cold bath.

On Calle Real Centenario, east of the plaza at the corner of 6a Av NE, the *Hospedaje Calle Real* is a very basic place with some of the cheapest prices in town: singles/doubles go for US$2.50/2.90, or US$4.15 with two double beds, all sharing a cold bath. The *Hotel Maya Central* (☎ 62-0073), west of the plaza on the corner of 3a Av NO and 1a Calle NO, has singles/doubles for US$3.35/5.85 with

private cold bath, or US$5/5.85 with private hot bath and TV.

Down on the highway, one kilometer from town, are a couple of places offering more comfortable accommodations. The *Hotel Mayaland* (☎ 62-0233) on the highway opposite the bus station is a clean and modern motel with single/double/triple rooms for US$8.90/14.25/19.60, all with private hot bath and set around a grassy courtyard; most of the rooms have TV. Nearby, *Hotel El Rey* (☎ 62-0620) has attractive rooms in a new section of the hotel for US$7.90/15.85, all with private hot bath and TV. Both of these hotels have restaurants, and there are also many cheap comedores along this stretch of the highway near the bus station.

The fancy place to stay in Santa Rosa is *Hotel Elvir* (☎ 62-0805, ☎ /fax 62-0103) on Calle Real Centenario, two blocks west of the plaza. Singles/doubles are US$13.35/19.60, all with private hot bath, TV and phone. The hotel has both a restaurant and cafeteria.

Places to Eat

Pizza Pizza, on Calle Real Centenario 4½ blocks east of the plaza, offers pizza and other dishes; operated by an American-Honduran family, it's also a haven for travelers. Warren Post, the friendly American owner, is a great source of information on the town and the area. Also here is an English-language book exchange, and they will hold messages and letters for travelers (address mail to (Name), R/do Pizza Pizza, Santa Rosa de Copán, Honduras). It's open every day from 11:30 am to 9 pm.

Another good place to eat is *El Rodeo*, 1½ blocks south of the plaza. It's an open-air covered patio restaurant with typical Honduran dishes and lots of meat on the menu; it has good food, good music and an enjoyable atmosphere. You can get a meal, a snack or just a drink; it's a popular place to hang out in the evening, when the bar does a lively business.

There are a number of small, typical comedores around town. A few doors down from El Rodeo, the *Cafetería y Comedor El*

Danubio is a very unassuming little place, but it's popular with the locals; it's open every day from 6 am to 10 pm.

The *Hotel Elvir* (see Places to Stay) has both a restaurant and cafeteria. Both are pleasant, clean and inexpensive.

Entertainment
The *El Rodeo* restaurant/bar is a good place to go for a drink in the evening, with a jovial, relaxed atmosphere and good music. In the same block, *Disco Glamour* attracts mostly a young crowd; discos are held on Friday and Saturday nights and on Sunday afternoons. There's a *cinema* on the plaza, next to the church. Otherwise, you can sit in the plaza and count the stars.

Getting There & Away
Buses from Santa Rosa de Copán come and go from the Terminal de Transporte (☎ 62-0076) on the main highway opposite the Hotel Mayaland, about one kilometer from the center of town. Sultana (☎ 62-0940) buses to Tegucigalpa depart from a house marked with a sign saying 'Torito,' on the highway two blocks south of the bus station. Taxis wait at the bus station and charge US$0.40 for a ride up the hill into town.

If you're going to San Pedro Sula, it's much better to catch one of the direct buses, which makes only one stop (at La Entrada). The regular buses go more frequently, but they make hundreds of stops.

Buses serving Santa Rosa include:

San Pedro Sula (152 km, regular buses 4½ hours, US$1.25; direct buses three hours, US$1.85) Regular buses every 25 minutes from 4:20 am to 5:15 pm; direct buses at 8:10 am and 2:10 pm.
La Entrada (28 km, 1¼ hours, US$0.60) Same buses as to San Pedro Sula.
Copán Ruinas (107 km, three hours, US$1.25) Buses at 11:30 am, 12:30 and 2 pm. Or take any bus heading to San Pedro Sula, get off at La Entrada and take another bus from there.
Nueva Ocotepeque (95 km, 2½ hours, US$1.20) Buses at 6, 9 and 11:30 am; 1, 3 and 4:45 pm.
Gracias (47 km, 1½ hours, US$1) Buses at 7:15, 8:30, 10 and 11:45 am; 1:15, 2:15, 4 and 5:30 pm.

Tegucigalpa (393 km, seven hours, US$3.35) Buses at 4 and 9:45 am, departing from a house marked 'Torito' on the highway two blocks south of the bus station.

AROUND SANTA ROSA DE COPÁN
La Montañita is a quiet country park with a pond and picnic tables, about 15 minutes from Santa Rosa on the road to Gracias; any bus heading for Gracias will drop you at the entrance. Farther away, **Gracias** and the **Parque Nacional Celaque** also make popular outings from Santa Rosa.

The **Reserva del Guisayote** is a biological reserve in a cloud forest that can be visited from Santa Rosa; see the Nueva Ocotepeque section.

GRACIAS
Population 24,000
Gracias is a small, attractive mountain town 47 km southeast of Santa Rosa de Copán. A colonial Spanish town, it still retains its Spanish character, with cobblestone streets and colonial churches and buildings. Gracias is quiet, slow and peaceful, and it feels like it hasn't changed in centuries.

Gracias has a long history. It was founded in 1526 by Spanish Captain Juan de Chavez; its original name was Gracias a Dios. The Audiencia de los Confines, the governing council for all Central America, was established here on April 16, 1544; the buildings that the council occupied are still here. The town was important and grew for several years, but it was eventually eclipsed in importance by Antigua Guatemala and Comayagua.

The area around Gracias is mountainous and beautiful. Much of it is forested. The town makes a good base for exploring Parque Nacional Celaque. While you're here, don't miss a trip to the hot springs.

Orientation & Information
Gracias is a small town, and everything is within walking distance.

For information about the area, go to the Restaurante Guancascos on the southwest corner of the plaza. Frony, who speaks English, Dutch and Spanish, and

HONDURAS

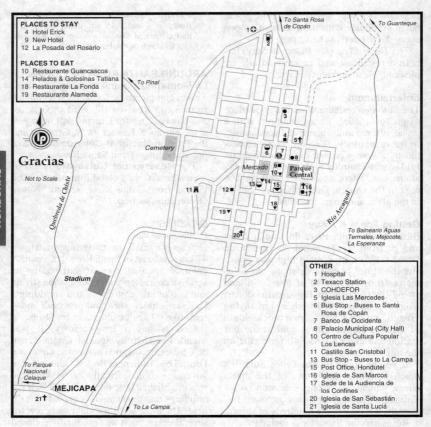

PLACES TO STAY
4 Hotel Erick
9 New Hotel
12 La Posada del Rosario

PLACES TO EAT
10 Restaurante Guancascos
14 Helados & Golosinas Tatiana
18 Restaurante La Fonda
19 Restaurante Alameda

Gracias

Not to Scale

To Santa Rosa de Copán

To Guanteque

To Pinal

Cemetery

Quebrada de Chiste

Stadium

To Parque Nacional Celaque

MEJICAPA

To La Campa

Mercado

Parque Central

Río Arcagual

To Balneario Aguas Termales, Mejocote, La Esperanza

OTHER
1 Hospital
2 Texaco Station
3 COHDEFOR
5 Iglesia Las Mercedes
6 Bus Stop - Buses to Santa Rosa de Copán
7 Banco de Occidente
8 Palacio Municipal (City Hall)
10 Centro de Cultura Popular Los Lencas
11 Castillo San Cristobal
13 Bus Stop - Buses to La Campa
15 Post Office, Hondutel
16 Iglesia de San Marcos
17 Sede de la Audiencia de los Confines
20 Iglesia de San Sebastián
21 Iglesia de Santa Luciá

HONDURAS

her Honduran partner, Suyapa, have lots of information about the town and the surrounding area. Information about the Parque Nacional Celaque is available here and at the COHDEFOR office.

The post office and Hondutel are side by side, a block south of the plaza.

Things to See & Do
Castillo San Cristobal, on a hill about five blocks west of the plaza, is worth the walk for its fine view over the town. It's open every day from 7 am to 5 pm.

Gracias has several **colonial churches**:

San Marcos, Las Mercedes and San Sebastián. Next door to the Iglesia de San Marcos, the **Sede de la Audiencia de los Confines**, important in the town's history, is now the *casa parroquial.*

Most of the town's other attractions, including a fine hot springs and the Parque Nacional Celaque, are a few kilometers out of town (see below).

Places to Stay
A block north of the plaza, *Hotel Erick* (☎ 98-4066) is a good place to stay; it's clean, friendly, family-run and inexpensive.

All the rooms have private bath; singles/doubles with cold bath are US$2.30/3.60. With hot bath they are US$6.25 for up to three people, or with hot bath and TV they are US$8.90. Enclosed parking is available. You can leave your luggage here if you stay overnight in the park.

La Posada del Rosario (☎ 98-4516), four blocks west of the plaza, is another good place to stay. Built in 1996, it has just three comfortable rooms, all with private hot bath; there's a garden and it's very private. Singles/doubles are US$6/8. It's owned and operated by Frony of the Restaurante Guancascos.

The owners of the much more basic Hotel y Disco Iris are building a *new hotel* (☎ 98-4086) with 26 rooms half a block west of the plaza. All have private bath; some will have hot water and TV. We met them during construction, and they say the rooms won't be too expensive.

Right at the boundary of Parque Nacional Celaque is *Cabaña Guancascos*, a house with two bedrooms, four beds and a fully equipped kitchen, available for US$10 per night. Bungalow tents are also here, and there are campsites; you can camp with your own gear, or the Restaurante Guancascos has camping gear available for rent. Information about all of these is available from the Restaurante Guancascos.

Places to Eat

Restaurante Guancascos on the southwest corner of the plaza is the place to go for good food, good company and good information about the area. Operated by Frony, a Dutchwoman who came to Gracias and stayed, and her Honduran partner, Suyapa, the restaurant also doubles as the *Centro de Cultura Popular Los Lencas*, the local Lenca Indian cultural center, with Lenca handicrafts, herbal medicines and plenty of good books for sale. The restaurant has tables inside and out in the garden; it has a fine selection of Honduran and international dishes, vegetarian selections and fresh fruit juices. It's open every day from 7 am to 10 pm.

Other good restaurants in town, serving typical Honduran fare, are *Restaurante La Fonda*, two blocks south of the plaza, and *Restaurante Alameda*, five blocks from the plaza. *Helados y Golosinas Tatiana* is good for ice cream and snacks.

Getting There & Away

The winding mountain road between Santa Rosa de Copán and Gracias is very scenic. The turnoff for Gracias is on the highway two km north of Santa Rosa de Copán; from the turnoff, it's 45 km to Gracias.

Buses to Santa Rosa de Copán (47 km, 1½ hours, US$1) leave from a bus stop two blocks from the plaza in Gracias at 5:30, 6:30, 7:30, 8:30 and 10:15 am; noon, 2 and 4 pm. See the Santa Rosa de Copán section for details on buses coming from Santa Rosa to Gracias.

Buses to La Campa (16 km, 1¼ hours, US$0.90) depart once a day, around noon, when the road is OK; they depart from another stop, two blocks from the plaza in Gracias. The same buses continue on to San Nauel Colohete, which is 16 km beyond La Campa.

An unpaved road continues southeast from Gracias to La Esperanza (83 km), and from there northeast to Siguatepeque on the San Pedro Sula-Tegucigalpa Hwy. On the map this looks like a shortcut from Santa Rosa de Copán to Tegucigalpa; however, it's a very winding (though also very beautiful) mountain road, and it takes a long time, maybe four hours or so, to get from Gracias to La Esperanza. The road is being improved, one section at a time; when (and if) it is finally finished, travel time will be much shorter. Check for current information locally if you're thinking of taking this route.

Last time we were in Gracias, bus service between Gracias and La Esperanza, which was never very frequent, had been suspended altogether. Perhaps it will be started up again, when and if the road improvement project is completed. From La Esperanza to the highway the road is better and you can traverse it in about an hour; buses make the trip between La Esperanza and Siguatepeque.

AROUND GRACIAS

The hot springs at **Balneario Aguas Termales**, 6½ km out of town, are one of Gracias' main attractions. The hot springs have several pools at various temperatures, including a big, cold pool for swimming; also here is a restaurant, and inner tubes and towels are available for rent. The springs are open every day from 6 am to 8 pm; admission is US$0.85.

Several small towns near Gracias are also worth a visit, if you have time. The people in this area, mostly Lencas, produce distinctive handicrafts, especially pottery. **La Campa**, a scenic little town 16 km south of Gracias, is known for its pottery; it also has a fine colonial church. **San Manuel Colohete**, 16 km further past La Campa, is another attractive little mountain town with a beautiful colonial church.

Belén Gualcho is another beautiful little town in the area; it's a colonial town clinging to the side of a mountain. At 1600 meters above sea level, it's cool and fresh. Attractions include an interesting church and a Lenca Indian market on Sunday. There's an entrance to Parque Nacional Celaque here, and although access to the park is easier from the Gracias side, people sometimes walk all the way through the park from Gracias to Belén Gualcho. Buses connect Belén Gualcho and Santa Rosa de Copán.

A bus runs from Gracias once a day to La Campa and on to San Manuel Colohete; you might also be able to catch a lift with a pickup truck. Or the route from Gracias out to the villages could make a fine walk. You could walk from Gracias to La Campa, on to San Manuel, then on to **San Sebastián** and on to Belén Gualcho, from where you could catch a bus to Santa Rosa de Copán.

Each of the villages is about a four- to five-hour walk from the previous one; there are no hotels, but if you wanted to stay overnight, you could arrange to stay with a local family.

PARQUE NACIONAL CELAQUE

Seven km uphill from Gracias is an entrance to Parque Nacional Celaque. Another entrance is at Belén Gualcho on the park's western side, with accommodations available in the town, but access is better from the Gracias side, which has more facilities and more pristine forest.

Celaque (which means 'box of water' in the local Lenca dialect) is one of Honduras' most impressive national parks. In the park, the Montaña de Celaque, at 2827 meters above sea level, is the highest peak in Honduras and is covered by a lush cloud forest. The park contains the headwaters of 11 rivers, a majestic waterfall visible from the entire valley and very steep slopes including some vertical cliffs that are a challenge to expert mountain climbers.

The park is rich in plant and animal life, including several rare or endangered species; jaguars, pumas, ocelots, quetzals and much other wildlife can be seen. A number of endemic species are also found here, due to the geographical isolation. Most wildlife can be seen very early in the morning. Temperatures in the park are much chillier than down below in Gracias, so bring some warm clothes and adequate hiking boots. Also be prepared for dampness and rain – the park gets around 2000 to 4000 mm of annual precipitation, and remember, it's always damp in a cloud forest.

It's a steep walk from Gracias along the Río Arcagual up into the park; it takes around 1½ hours to walk from town to the entrance and another half-hour to reach the park visitors' center. You can drive to the visitors' center if you have a 4WD vehicle; if not, rather than walking, you might want to arrange a lift up the hill to the park entrance, saving your time and energy for hiking in the park itself. The folks at the Restaurante Guancascos in Gracias will take you up there; cost is US$10 per load, for as many people as can fit in the 4WD. (Their cabin, Cabaña Guancascos, is just outside the boundary of the park; see Gracias Places to Stay.)

At the visitors' center there are bunks for 15 people (bring your own bedding), a kitchen, water, a shower and latrines. Entrance to the park costs US$1; it's another US$1 to stay overnight. The warden's mother will cook you a simple meal for another US$1 if you ask. Near the visitors' center is a river great for swimming.

From the visitors' center, the next cabin, called Campamento Don Tomás, at 2050 meters above sea level, is about a two- to three-hour uphill walk along a well-marked forest trail. This cabin is smaller and much more basic, but it does have a few bunks, running water and a latrine (no kitchen).

From here, it's about another two hours of steep uphill climbing along a well-marked trail to reach the Naranjo campsite, at 2560 meters. There's no cabin here, so you'll need camping gear; there are three tent sites, a latrine and the Quebrada Naranjo for water. You're right in the cloud forest here; it's a beautiful spot, and quetzals have been seen right in camp. Be prepared for cold temperatures, even in daytime; at night it can be quite cold indeed, maybe even near freezing.

From the Naranjo campsite it's about a 1½-hour climb to the top of the peak. The trail may or may not be well marked; bring trail markers, just in case. Be sure to stay on the trail; this is very thick forest and if you don't stay on the trail, you will get lost.

It's possible to hike through the park all the way to Belén Gualcho on the other side, spending two nights in the park, but you need a guide to do it. The Restaurante Guancascos can recommend guides.

More information on the park is available from the Restaurante Guancascos on the plaza in Gracias; the owners also rent camping gear. The COHDEFOR office in Gracias also has information; it's open Monday to Friday, 8 am to 4:30 pm.

NUEVA OCOTEPEQUE
Population 15,000

In the southwest corner of Honduras, Nueva Ocotepeque is a crossroads town, with a lot of traffic to and from the nearby borders at Agua Caliente (Guatemala) and El Poy (El Salvador). There's not much to the town, but it's a convenient place to stay overnight before or after crossing the border.

There's not much to do in Nueva Ocotepeque. A reader wrote to recommend going for a swim in the river; he said you can get any of the local children to show you the way. The **Reserva del Guisayote** is a biological reserve in a cloud forest that is the easiest to access of any cloud forest in Honduras. Sixteen km north on a paved road from Nueva Ocotepeque, it is a good place to see wildlife, including the quetzal.

Places to Stay & Eat

All the places to stay and eat in Nueva Ocotepeque are on or near the main highway through town, within about five blocks of one another.

Basic, cheap places to stay include the *Hospedaje San Antonio* (☎ 63-3072), a few doors west of the highway; it's basic but good value, with single/double rooms for US$1.65/2.10 with shared bath, or US$3.35/6.65 with private cold bath. There's enclosed parking in the courtyard. Across the highway, a block from where the buses to El Poy and Agua Caliente are parked, the *Mini Hotel Turista* is another basic place; singles/doubles with shared bath are US$2.10/4.15, or US$2.90/5.85 with private bath.

The *Hotel y Comedor Congolón* is on the highway half a block south of the plaza, 3½ blocks south of most of the bus stations. It's a basic, family-run place that includes the hotel, a tiny restaurant and the bus station for the Congolón buses. All the activity can make it a little loud, but the rooms are clean, and all have windows opening onto a central courtyard; they share a common cold bath and the price is right at US$2.90 per room.

Much more upmarket, *Hotel Maya Chortis* (☎ 63-3377) is east of the highway, three blocks behind the bus stop for the buses to El Poy and Agua Caliente. Built in 1996, it's an excellent place to stay; the rooms are clean and attractive, and all have private hot bath, color cable TV, telephone and two double beds. Single/double rooms are US$7.50/15 with ceiling fan, or US$10.85/21.65 with air con. Two larger suites, each with three double beds, one single bed and a fridge, are US$10.85 per person. The *Restaurante Don Chepe* in the lobby is open every day from 6 am to 10 pm. There's also enclosed parking.

There are many simple restaurants on the highway in the blocks near the bus station. For more upmarket dining, try *Restaurante Don Chepe* at the Hotel Maya Chortis, or *Restaurante Sandoval* at the expensive Hotel Sandoval, one block east of the highway and one block south of the buses to El Poy and Agua Caliente.

Getting There & Away

Nueva Ocotepeque is served by frequent buses. They include:

El Poy, Salvadoran border (nine km, 15 minutes, US$0.25) Buses every half-hour, 6 am to 8 pm, departing from a bus stop on the highway. Colectivo taxis also go to El Poy for US$0.35.

Agua Caliente, Guatemalan border (22 km, 30 minutes, US$0.50) Buses every half-hour from 6 am to 6 pm, leaving from the same bus stop on the highway as for El Rey.

San Pedro Sula (247 km, five to six hours, US$2.50; midnight express bus US$4.15) Toritos & Copanecos buses to San Pedro Sula depart from Agua Caliente at 7:30, 9:30 and 11:30 am, 1:30 and 3:30 pm; the same buses depart half an hour later from Nueva Ocotepeque. They also have one express bus, departing Nueva Ocotepeque at midnight and making no stops along the way. Their bus station is a few doors from the highway in Nueva Ocotepeque.

Congolón buses depart from the Hotel Congolón, on the highway half a block south of the plaza and 3½ blocks south of the other bus stops. Buses depart at 1, 7:30 and 10 am, noon, 2 and 4 pm.

Santa Rosa de Copán (95 km, 2½ hours, US$1.20) Transporte San José buses depart Nueva Ocotepeque at 6, 8, 9:30 and 10:45 am, 1 and 3 pm. Or take any bus heading toward San Pedro Sula.

La Entrada (123 km, 3½ hours, US$1.75) Same buses as to San Pedro Sula.

EL POY & AGUA CALIENTE

Near Nueva Ocotepeque are the border crossings of El Poy (to El Salvador) and Agua Caliente (to Guatemala). The El Poy crossing is open every day from around 6 am to 6 pm. The Agua Caliente crossing is open a little later, until around 8 pm. The nearest place to stay is at Nueva Ocotepeque.

Northern Honduras

The Caribbean Coast of Honduras is for the most part a narrow coastal plain backed by mountains; another large plain in the area is the Río Ulua valley, also called the Valle de Sula, with Honduras' second-largest city, San Pedro Sula (see the Western Honduras section). These plains are among Honduras' most fertile and productive agricultural areas: It is here that Standard and United Fruit grow bananas and pineapples for export to the USA. The two companies own a large part of northern Honduras, and several of the towns, ports, railways, roads and banks in the area were established by the banana companies.

The Caribbean Coast has an interesting mixture of races. In addition to the mestizos found everywhere in Honduras, there are many black people descended from Jamaicans and other West Indians who came during the years when the British occupied the Caribbean Coast.

A very interesting north-coast people are the Garífuna, a mixture of African and Carib Indian peoples, brought by the British from the island of St Vincent to the island of Roatán in the late 18th century. From Roatán they spread out along the coast and now have small coastal fishing villages all the way from Belize to Nicaragua. Their language has a strong West African sound and is a mixture of several languages – Arawak, French, Yoruba and perhaps others as well. The Garífuna have their own religion, music, dance, foods and other cultural patterns.

The principal towns of the north coast are Puerto Cortés (Honduras' major port), Tela, La Ceiba and Trujillo. All of them have their attractions, but probably the two most enjoyable for travelers are Tela and

Trujillo. La Ceiba is a popular jumping-off point for travel to the Bay Islands.

The attractions of the Caribbean beach towns are about what you'd expect: lovely beaches lined by coconut palms and delicious fresh seafood (try the coconut bread and the seafood soups made with coconut). All of these towns have interesting places to visit nearby and many kilometers of beaches good for walking and exploring.

The coast fills up with tourists during Semana Santa, when Hondurans have their one week of holiday, beach-going and merry-making. If you're on the coast at this time, make sure you've secured a place to stay in advance. Hotels fill up for this week and prices double. The rest of the time, you probably won't see too many tourists.

Safety on the North Coast
Though we have never had any problems on the north coast, a number of travelers have, and many have written to urge us to warn travelers about crime. James Renn (USA) was shot one morning on a beach in La Ceiba, the city that seems to have the most crime and drug problems. Other travelers have been accosted at several other places along the coast, including Tela and Triunfo de la Cruz, sometimes in broad daylight.

James had assumed the attack was a freak accident, as could occur anywhere in the world. However, while waiting in La Ceiba for his health to stabilize, he met many European travelers and every one of them had a story to relate. Within a three-week period, tourists had been robbed, beaten, raped and shot – alarming news, indeed.

After reading these letters, we felt a little nervous about traveling on the coast, but when we went there, we had no problems and met many other travelers who were also enjoying great trips with no problems. It seems the thing to do is to exercise all your traveling safety skills: Don't do anything to make yourself a target; don't walk in isolated places (including on the beaches) at night, and stay alert even in daytime; carry with you only the money you'll need that day, and carry it underneath your clothing;

and don't leave valuables on the beach while you go swimming.

Another nerve-wracking aspect on the subject of safety is that the north coast has a very high rate of HIV. Keep this in mind in your relations with others – be vigilant against exposing yourself to it. We haven't heard that rape is any more common here than elsewhere, but it might happen and the consequences could be even more serious than usual. We heard of one foreign tourist being raped in La Ceiba, and she spent a very tense six months waiting to be tested for HIV.

PUERTO CORTÉS
Population 79,000

Puerto Cortés, 64 km north of San Pedro Sula, is the westernmost of Honduras' major Caribbean towns. It is also the country's most important port, as it's the only port in the country that can handle big cargo containers. Puerto Cortés handles over half of Honduras' export shipping trade. It's just a two-day sail from the USA, with frequent cargo ships sailing to New Orleans and Miami laden with bananas, pineapples and other produce. The docks, right in the town, are the town's focal point and raison d'être.

The best beaches in Puerto Cortés are outside of town. Playa de Cieneguita, a good stretch of beach a few kilometers from town on the road to Omoa, is a white sandy beach with a couple of beachside hotel/restaurants where you can get meals and snacks. Other good beaches at Omoa, Travesía and Baja Mar are within a short distance and are easy to access by bus. It takes only an hour by bus to reach Puerto Cortés from San Pedro Sula, so the beaches around the area are popular day trips for visitors from that city. The Spanish fortress at Omoa is a half-hour bus ride from town.

Another attraction of Puerto Cortés is its twice-weekly boat service to Belize – it's the only regularly scheduled boat transport between the two countries. The only passenger train in Honduras also departs from Puerto Cortés, operating twice a week between here and Tela.

HONDURAS

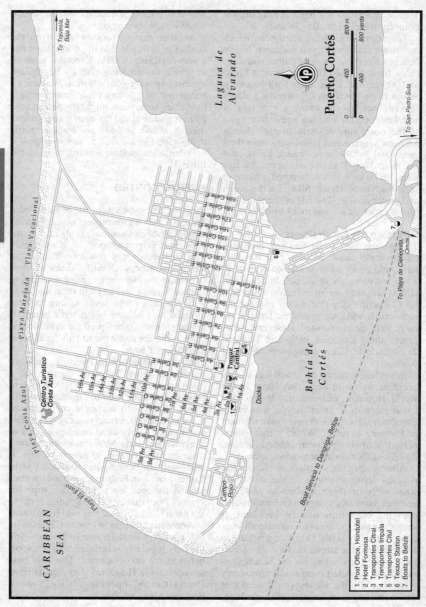

Puerto Cortés

CARIBBEAN SEA

Laguna de Alvarado

Bahía de Cortés

To Travesía, Baja Mar

To San Pedro Sula

To Playa de Cieneguita, Omoa

Boat Service to Dangriga, Belize

Playa Costa Azul

Playa Marejada

Playa Vacacional

Playa El Faro

Centro Turístico Costa Azul

Parque Central

Docks

Campo Rojo

0   400   800 m
0   400   800 yards

1 Post Office, Hondutel
2 Hotel Formosa
3 Transportes Citral
4 Transportes Impala
5 Transportes Citul
6 Texaco Station
7 Boats to Belize

Puerto Cortés' annual fair is held on August 15.

Places to Stay & Eat

Most people visit Puerto Cortés as a day trip from San Pedro Sula, but there are some cheap lodgings if you want to stay over. The *Hotel Formosa* (☎ 55-0853) on 3a Av, three blocks west of the plaza, has 68 rooms, all with private cold bath, for US$3.60 with fan, US$10 with air con. The owner speaks English and Spanish; you can find him in the store next door to the hotel. The Formosa is dreary, but it's about the best you can do in downtown Puerto Cortés. The other cheap places to stay in town are even less appealing.

On Playa de Cieneguita, a good stretch of beach a few kilometers from town on the road to Omoa, there are some good beach-front hotels, but they're more expensive. The cheapest of the lot is *Hotel Los Arcos* (☎ 55-1889), opposite the beach, with rooms for US$21 per night. *Hotel Playa* (☎ 55-0453), a fancier place right on the beach, is more expensive, with singles/doubles starting at US$45/55.

A much more pleasant alternative is to stay not in Puerto Cortés itself but nearby in the charming Travesía, or a bit farther away in Omoa (see these sections below).

There are lots of restaurants around the plaza, and on 2a and 3a Avs, the town's two main streets.

Getting There & Away

Bus Buses operate frequently between Puerto Cortés and San Pedro Sula (64 km, 1½ hours, US$0.65).

Two companies operate along this route. Transportes Citul (☎ 55-0456), 5a Calle Este near 2a Av, has direct buses every half-hour from 6 am to 6:30 pm. Transportes Impala (☎ 55-0606), 3a Av near 4a Calle Este, has direct buses every half-hour from 4:30 am to 9 pm.

See the sections below for information on buses to Travesía, Baja Mar and Omoa.

Train A passenger train operates between Puerto Cortés and Tela twice a week on Friday and Sunday. On both days it departs from Puerto Cortés at 7 am, arriving in Tela at 10:30 am. It leaves Tela for the return trip at 2 pm, arriving back in Puerto Cortés around 6 pm. The cost is US$0.85. In Puerto Cortés you can catch the train from a stop a couple of blocks behind the Hotel Formosa; in Tela it departs from the train station.

You might want to check the schedule before making travel plans. If you can't get information locally (which is quite possible), stop by or phone the office of the Ferrocarril Nacional de Honduras (☎ 53-4080) at the train station in San Pedro Sula.

Boat Twice a week, a small 20-passenger lancha makes a trip between Puerto Cortés and Dangriga, Belize. It departs Puerto Cortés on Wednesday and Saturday at 8 am, arriving in Dangriga around 12:30 pm. The cost for the trip is around US$35. You must come with your passport the day before travel to sign up for the trip. The office is beside the bridge, just after the turnoff to Omoa (see map). They told us their office might be moving, but that if it does, it will probably only move to the other side of the bridge.

A boat to Lívingston, Guatemala, departs from Omoa; see the Omoa section.

Otherwise, there are no regularly scheduled passenger boats from Puerto Cortés, but it's possible to come and go by cargo or fishing boat if you're prepared to wait a few days. Ask around at the docks for information. The *Utila Express* (☎ 45-3183) operates boat service once a week between Puerto Cortés, Utila and Roatán, but not on any set schedule; it's a cargo boat, but it sometimes will take on passengers.

If you are entering or leaving the country by boat, be sure to stop at the immigration office to get your entrance or exit stamp; there is an office in Puerto Cortés on the northeast side of the plaza, or you can do it in San Pedro Sula or Omoa.

TRAVESÍA & BAJA MAR

Just to the east of Puerto Cortés, Travesía and Baja Mar are two seaside Garífuna villages with good beaches and lots of palm trees. The road from Puerto Cortés runs along the sea, first through Travesía and on into Baja Mar; the two villages form a continuous row of wooden houses beside the sea, with small fishing boats lining the shore. The beach is lovely along the whole stretch. There are one or two restaurants in each village for beachgoers.

Places to Stay & Eat Right on the beach in Travesía, *Hotel Frontera del Caribe* (☎ 55-1914) is the most pleasant place to stay near Puerto Cortés if you're on a budget. Six upstairs rooms, all with private cold bath and ceiling fan, are US$8.35 per room (sleeping up to three people); the rooms are simple but clean and pleasant. Downstairs is an inexpensive beachside restaurant where all three meals are served. The bus coming from Puerto Cortés stops just outside the door.

Getting There & Away The bus from Puerto Cortés to Travesía and Baja Mar departs from 5a Calle Este, in the block southeast of the plaza. From Puerto Cortés it departs at 6, 8 and 11 am, 1 and 3 pm; for the return trip, it departs from the end of the line at Baja Mar at 9 am, 12:30, 3 and 5 pm. Cost is US$0.10 to Travesía (about 20 minutes from Puerto Cortés) or US$0.25 to the end of the bus line at Baja Mar (a 45-minute ride). The bus runs less frequently on Sunday. Otherwise you can take local bus Ruta 2, get off where it swings round for the return leg (at Comaguey), and walk along the coast road for 20 minutes.

A taxi will take you between Puerto Cortés and Travesía in about five minutes for US$2.50.

OMOA
Population 28,000
At Omoa, by the sea 13 km west of Puerto Cortés, stands an old Spanish fortress, the **Fortaleza de San Fernando de Omoa**. It was built between 1759 and 1777 under orders from King Fernando VII of Spain to protect the coast from rampant piracy, but

in 1779 the fortress was captured by the British after only a four-day battle.

Still in good shape, the fort is maintained by the Instituto Hondureño de Antropología e Historia. It is open Tuesday to Sunday from 8 am to 5 pm; admission is US$2.

Omoa also has a decent beach, popular on weekends. Along the waterfront are many little seafood restaurants. The beach is at the end of the paved road, a few blocks' walk from the fortress. Omoa's annual festival is held on May 30.

Places to Stay & Eat
Outside of Omoa, *Eco Rancho* (☎ 56-9410, ☎ /fax 56-6156) is a delightful place on a big dairy and horse ranch with coffee and spice plantations. The ranch land stretches from the beach up into the mountains, where there's a magnificent view of Honduras, Guatemala and Belize. The emphasis is on nature – there's hiking, butterfly and bird watching, horse riding, swimming, sea fishing, diving or just relaxing. There's a restaurant and bar and a variety of accommodations. Cabins with private bath are US$38/42 for singles/doubles; five guest rooms in the ranch house are US$54/60 and have air con. There's also camping in already-set-up camping tents with good air mattresses; these cost US$12 to US$30 per night, plus US$6 per person, depending on the size of the tent – some of the tents are large family models.

Another great place to stay in Omoa is *Río Coto*, with six cabins and an excellent restaurant right on the beach, plus a farm in the mountains, a swimming hole on the river, and camping. The cabins are not expensive, around US$12.50 per night, and the camping is even cheaper.

The *Fisherman Restaurant* and the *Botín Suizo Restaurant* are near the dock.

Getting There & Away
Bus Buses to Omoa depart from Puerto Cortés every half-hour from 6:20 am to 8 pm from the Transportes Citral depot (☎ 55-0888) on 3a Calle Este, one block west of the plaza (13 km, one hour,

US$0.20). They let you off on the highway, a short walk from the fort.

From Omoa back to Puerto Cortés, the buses depart every half-hour from 4:30 am to 6:30 pm.

Boat A 10-passenger lancha goes from Omoa to Lívingston, Guatemala, on Tuesday and Friday, departing from the dock near the Fisherman Restaurant. The boat leaves at around noon or 1 pm; get there by 10 am to sign up. The cost is around US$25 for the one-way trip. Be sure to get your exit and entry stamps when entering or leaving the country; there's an immigration office in the Omoa city hall. Other immigration offices in the area are in Puerto Cortés and San Pedro Sula.

Current information about the boat service is available from the Botín Suizo Restaurant, just west of the dock (ask for Ulrich), or in Puerto Cortés from the Ocean Travel travel agency (☎ 55-2445) on 2a Calle Este near 3a Av, around the corner from the Hotel Formosa.

TELA
Population 86,000

Tela is many travelers' favorite Honduran Caribbean beach town; it's small and quiet with superb seafood, several good places to stay and some fine white-sand beaches. This is a great place for relaxing on the beach and enjoying the simple life. Pleasant excursions can also be made to several places nearby (see Around Tela).

Tela is somnolent most of the year, but it's quite another story during Semana Santa, when the town fills up with holidaymakers. At this time hotel rates double and advance bookings are essential if you want to get a room; it's a riotous weeklong party. Tela's annual fiesta day is June 13.

Standard Fruit once had quite a 'company town' here, but it is now converted to a luxury resort, the Hotel Villas Telamar.

Orientation
Tela is divided into two sections: Tela Vieja, the 'old town,' on the east bank where the Río Tela meets the sea, and Tela Nueva, on the west side of the river, where the Hotel Villas Telamar hugs some of the best stretch of beach.

Information
There's no tourist information office in Tela. Filling the gap, Garífuna Tours (see Organized Tours) is the place to come for information about the town and the area. Prolansate (☎ 48-2042), on 9a Calle NE (Calle del Comercio) between 2a and 3a Avs NE, has information on Lancetilla Botanical Garden and Punta Sal.

Many banks in Tela won't change traveler's checks. The Casa de Cambio La Teleña on 4a Av NE changes US dollars in traveler's checks and cash, giving a slightly better rate for cash. It's open Monday to Friday, 8 am to 11:45 am and 1 to 4:30 pm, Saturday 8 am to noon. Cash advances on Visa and MasterCard are available from the Banco de Occidente on 6a Av NE, which also is the Western Union agent in Tela.

The post office and Hondutel are beside one another on 4a Av NE.

The Lavandería El Centro on 4a Av NE charges US$1.65 to wash, dry and fold 12 lbs of clothes.

Things to See & Do
Tela's main attraction is its **beaches**, which stretch around the bay for several kilometers on either side of the town. The beach right in front of the town is not the best, but the one just over the bridge in Tela Nueva, in front of the Hotel Villas Telamar, is much better; its pale, powdery sand and shady grove of coconut trees and lawn just behind it are kept clean.

The **Garífuna Museum**, at the river end of 8a Calle NE, is an interesting cultural museum with exhibits on many aspects of daily life in the Garífuna villages along the north coast of Honduras. The charming Garífuna women who run the museum will take you on a tour of the exhibits, explaining things and answering questions in English or Spanish. Garífuna paintings and handicrafts are for sale; you can also eat a traditional Garífuna meal here (see Places

HONDURAS

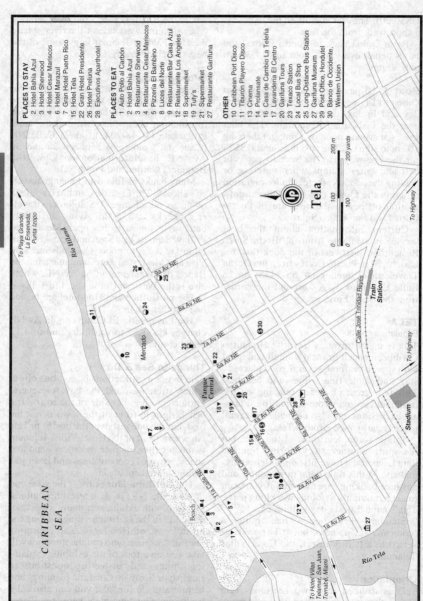

PLACES TO STAY
2 Hotel Bahía Azul
3 Hotel Sherwood
4 Hotel César Mariscos
6 Hotel Marazul
7 Gran Hotel Puerto Rico
15 Hotel Tela
22 Gran Hotel Presidente
26 Hotel Preluna
28 Ejecutivos Aparthotel

PLACES TO EAT
1 Auto Pollo al Carbón
2 Hotel Bahía Azul
3 Restaurante Sherwood
4 Restaurante César Mariscos
5 Pizzería El Bambino
8 Luces del Norte
9 Restaurante/Bar Casa Azul
12 Restaurante Los Angeles
18 Supermarket
19 Tuty's
21 Supermarket
27 Restaurante Garífuna

OTHER
10 Caribbean Port Disco
11 Tiburón Playero Disco
13 Cinema
14 Prolansate
16 Casa de Cambio La Telería
17 Lavandería El Centro
20 Garífuna Tours
23 Texaco Station
25 Local Bus Stop
25 Long-Distance Bus Station
27 Garífuna Museum
29 Post Office, Hondutel
30 Banco de Occidente, Western Union

Tela

CARIBBEAN SEA

to Eat) and come to a Garífuna party on Saturday night (see Entertainment). The museum is open Monday to Saturday, 8 am to 5:30 pm; admission is US$0.40.

The **Hotel Villas Telamar** is expensive to stay in, but you can pay US$2 per day for the use of its large swimming pool, sauna and Jacuzzi. The cafe by the pool is not too expensive. The Club Telamar, east of the pool, has a bar and various indoor games such as billiards. The hotel rents horses for US$2.50 per hour and bicycles for US$1.25 per hour or US$5.85 per day.

Garífuna Tours (see below), near the southwest corner of the plaza, rents 18-gear mountain bikes for US$3.75 per half day or US$5 per day. They also rent canoes, kayaks, windsurf boards and launches, and they offer tours to natural reserves in the area.

Organized Tours

Garífuna Tours (☎ /fax 48-2904), on 9a Calle NE near the south corner of the plaza, offers all-day boat excursions to Parque Nacional Marino Punta Sal (US$15); morning bird-watching excursions to Los Micos Lagoon (US$14); and afternoon kayak excursions to the Refugio Punta Izopo (US$11.50). All tours are given in English and Spanish. Their office is open every day from 7:30 am to 7 pm.

The Hotel Bahía Azul (see Places to Stay) also offers trips around the local area and to Punta Sal. They also organize fishing, diving and snorkeling trips. Prolansate also offers occasional trips to Punta Sal (see Around Tela).

Places to Stay

The best of the cheapies is *Hotel Marazul* (☎ 48-2313) at the corner of 11a Calle NE and 4a Av NE, half a block from the beach. It's a simple but clean little place with 13 rooms around a sandy courtyard. It has a *lavadero* where you can wash your clothes (there's also laundry service if you prefer), and you can use the kitchen if you ask nicely. One single room with outdoor bath is US$2.90; the other 12 rooms, all with private cold bath, are US$6.65.

The *Hotel Preluna* (☎ 48-2435) on 9a Calle NE near the bus station is cheaper, with singles/doubles for US$2.10/2.50, but it's a very basic place.

The *Hotel Tela* (☎ 48-2150) on 9a Calle NE has a large rooftop terrace and clean, spacious rooms with private cold bath for US$7.10/13.35, plus a restaurant and parking.

The *Gran Hotel Presidente* (☎ 48-2821, fax 48-2992) on the central plaza is an upstairs hotel with a cafeteria and small but very clean rooms with private hot bath. Rooms are US$14 with fan, US$18 with air con; most come with cable TV, telephone and fridge.

Several hotels are right on the beach. The cheapest of these is *Hotel Bahía Azul* (☎ 48-2381). It has a good beachfront restaurant/bar, but the rooms themselves don't face the beach. All rooms have private bath and cost US$12.50 with fan (some with cable TV), US$20.85 with air con and TV.

The *Gran Hotel Puerto Rico* (☎ 48-2413), also right on the beach, has pleasant upstairs beachfront rooms with balcony and chairs overlooking the beach, air con, cable TV and fridge; the price of US$21/29 with one/two beds includes breakfast at their beachfront restaurant.

The *Hotel y Restaurant Cesar Mariscos* (☎ /fax 48-2083), also on the beach, has six newish rooms, all with air con, private hot bath and cable TV; rates are US$23/25 with one/two double beds. Next door, *Hotel y Restaurante Sherwood* (☎ 48-2416, fax 48-2294) has a beachfront swimming pool and attractive beachfront rooms with all the amenities for US$38/43 for downstairs/upstairs rooms. The restaurants at both of these hotels serve some of the best seafood in Tela.

The *Ejecutivos Aparthotel* (☎ /fax 48-2047), at the corner of 8a Calle NE and 4a Av NE near Hondutel, offers luxurious studio apartments with fully equipped kitchen, air con, two double beds, color cable TV, hot bath and other amenities (including enclosed parking and 24-hour vigilance) for US$25 for one or two people, US$29.15 for three or US$33.35 for four.

Hotel Villas Telamar (☎ 48-2196, fax 48-2984, in USA (800) 742-4276) on the west side of town is a beachfront resort created from the village built for the officials of the Standard Fruit Company. Amenities include tennis, golf, swimming pool, sauna, Jacuzzi, restaurant and bar, and a beautiful stretch of beach. It's an expensive place: single/double rooms start at US$65/71, higher for one-bedroom suite apartments and villas with two to five bedrooms.

Places to Eat

Seafood is plentiful, delicious and inexpensive around Tela. Seafood soups are a particular delicacy of the town; fish, shrimp, lobster and conch *(caracol)* are all found in many restaurants. Another specialty of the town is coconut bread *(pan de coco)*; you'll see Garífuna women or their children walking around town selling it. Try it – it's delicious!

Half a block from the beach, *Luces del Norte* is popular with foreign backpackers and has a casual atmosphere. Breakfasts are good, but it serves any meal anytime (plus alcohol). It's open every day from 7 am to 10 pm. Near the plaza, *Tuty's* is a pleasant, clean, inexpensive little place for pastries, simple meals and a variety of fruit cocktails, fruit drinks and ice cream. The lunchtime buffet for US$1.65 is a great deal. It's open every day from 6 am to 10 pm, but meals are served only from 6 am to 2 pm.

Along the beach there are several cheap comedores and some reasonably priced better restaurants. *Hotel Sherwood* is an attractive bar/restaurant with wood decor and a deck with palm trees, right on the beach. *Cesar Mariscos* is another attractive open-air bar/restaurant with great fresh seafood, including seafood soups for around US$3. These are two of the town's best seafood restaurants; both are open every day from 7 am to 11 pm.

Also on the beach, the open-air bar/restaurant at the *Gran Hotel Puerto Rico* has good seafood and a nice breeze but very slow service. The bar/restaurant at *Hotel Bahía Azul* is another good beachfront place, and there are several others. *Auto Pollo Al Carbón* is a simple open-air chicken shack with good roast chicken.

For authentic Italian fare, head for *Casa Azul*, a pleasant little bar/restaurant with good food, good atmosphere and good music, half a block from the beach. *Pizzería El Bambino* is a simple open-air place serving decent pizza, plus sandwiches and spaghetti. The air-conditioned *Restaurante Los Angeles* on 9a Calle NE serves good Chinese food in huge portions.

Traditional Garífuna food is offered at *Restaurante Garífuna* behind the Garífuna Museum at the west end of 8a Calle NE. It's not expensive, and different foods are featured each day; try the *casave* – it's great! If you tour the museum, they'll explain how casave is made – there's more to it than meets the eye. It's a relaxing place to eat, with tables on covered decks overlooking the river.

Across the river, the luxurious *Hotel Villas Telamar* has two pleasant restaurants: the main restaurant/bar beside the beach, with some tables out by the swimming pool; and another thatch-roofed bar right on the beach, where more basic meals are served. Their specialty is a delicious conch soup (US$3.35), but there are plenty of other choices, and it's not outrageously expensive.

Entertainment

When we were in town, the most fun entertainment was the Saturday night party at the *Garífuna Museum*, held in the open-air restaurant behind the museum. A traditional Garífuna band of drums, turtle shells and conch shells plays, while costumed dancers perform the punta; after you see how it's done, don't be surprised if they pull you up to have a go. It's all in good fun, and the price is right – free. Food is served afterward, and it's a good time for all.

Tela has many discos, but some of them can get rough. Ask around for current advice if you want to go dancing. The

Tiburón Playero and the *Caribbean Port* have been recommended.

The bar-on-the-beach at the *Villas Telamar Hotel* is pleasant in the evening, with a fine view of the sunset. Basic meals are served, and they sometimes have dance parties.

There's a *cinema* on 9a Calle NE, three blocks west of the plaza.

Getting There & Away

Bus The long-distance bus station is on the corner of 9a Calle NE and 9a Av NE, three blocks northeast of the plaza. Buses depart from Tela bound for La Ceiba every half-hour from 4 am to 6 pm (103 km, 2½ hours, US$0.85).

There are no direct buses between Tela and San Pedro Sula; the only way to get a direct bus to San Pedro is to catch one on the highway, as it comes through from La Ceiba. From the bus station in town, you have to catch a bus to El Progreso and change buses there. Regular buses to El Progreso leave half-hourly from 4:30 am until 6 pm (63 km, two hours, US$0.65); direct buses leave for El Progreso twice daily, in the morning on weekdays and in the afternoon on weekends (one hour, US$0.85). From El Progreso to San Pedro Sula it's another hour's ride; the buses leave about every five minutes, with the last bus at 9 pm.

Local buses to the Garífuna villages near Tela depart from the east side of the market; see the Around Tela section for details.

Train A passenger train operates between Puerto Cortés and Tela on Friday and Sunday. See the Puerto Cortés section for details.

Boat Boats depart from Tela for Puerto Cortés and other destinations but not on any fixed schedule. If you have a group, Garífuna Tours might make a special trip to Utila or other places.

Getting Around

Tela has many taxis; a ride in town costs US$0.40. A taxi to Lancetilla or San Juan is about US$2.50; to Triunfo de la Cruz, La Ensenada or Tornabé it's about US$3.50.

AROUND TELA
Lancetilla Jardín Botánico

The Lancetilla Botanical Garden and Research Center is famous throughout Honduras. The United Fruit Company founded Lancetilla in 1926 with the purpose of experimenting with the cultivation of various tropical plants in Central America; some of the plants that were first planted here are now important crops in Central America. Of its 1680 hectares, some protecting natural forest forming the watershed for Tela, 78 hectares contain the arboretum, with open public access; 321 hectares are planted with experimental plants and endangered species, mainly of interest to scientists; and 1281 hectares are a biological reserve, which you can tour with a guide if you reserve in advance.

The garden features fruit trees from every continent, cacao, fine timber plantings, nuts and palms, and a long tunnel formed by an arch of bamboo. There is a swimming hole on the Río Lancetilla at the far end of the park, about 1½ km from the visitors' center.

Another attraction of Lancetilla is its bird life. The various plantings have created habitats for over 365 recorded species of birds. A bird checklist is available at the visitors' center. Birders frequently come here, and each year on December 14 and 15 the Audubon Society conducts a 24-hour bird count; you can participate if you're here at that time. Migratory species are present from November to February. Bird watching is best in the early morning or late afternoon; though the entrance gate closes at 2:30 pm, you can stay later to see the birds at dusk.

The park has six dormitories of various sizes with four to 16 beds in each room. Bedding, towels, soap and so on are all provided; the cost is US$4.15 per bed. They are also putting up free-standing cabins, with all the comforts. The dorms are often full when a group of students arrives to study in the park, but sometimes there is space available; contact Esnacifor in Siguatepeque (☎ 73-2011, fax 73-2300) or Prolansate in Tela (☎ 48-2042) to check on availability. Large groups must reserve in advance, but individuals don't need to, and you're welcome to stay if there's room. The dorms don't have kitchens, but food and refreshments are sold in the park.

Lancetilla is about five km southwest of the center of Tela. There's a ticket kiosk on the highway about two km from Tela, and the park is another 3.5 km inland. You can usually hitch a lift with any passing vehicle past the ticket booth entrance. There's a visitors' information center where the park begins, and an explanatory map in English is available.

Lancetilla is open every day from 7:30 am to 2:30 pm; admission is US$5. Free guided tours of the garden are given every half-hour and take about an hour; four-hour tours of the biological reserve are also given but must be arranged in advance (usually the day before is fine). Or you can do a self-guided tour; a map and self-guided tour brochure are available in English or Spanish for US$0.40. Further information is available from Prolansate in Tela.

Parque Nacional Marino Punta Sal

Standing on the beach at Tela, you can look out and see a long arc of land curving out to the west to a point almost in front of you. This point, Punta Sal, is the site of the Parque Nacional Marino Punta Sal.

Within this national marine park are various habitats, including mangrove forests and swamps, a small tropical forest, offshore reefs, several coves and the rocky point itself. On the east side of the park, the Laguna de los Micos (Lagoon of the Monkeys) contains extensive mangrove forests. It's a habitat for hundreds of species of birds (especially from November to February, when migratory species are here), as well as for the monkeys that the lagoon is named for.

Completely unspoiled and undeveloped, this park makes a fine outing from Tela. All-day tours including hiking, snorkeling, swimming and lunch are given by Garífuna

Tours and the Hotel Bahía Azul (see Tela above), or there are morning bird-watching trips to the Laguna de los Micos. Prolansate (☎ 48-2042), the foundation managing the park, also sometimes offers trips out here, usually for students and those interested in conservation. Information about the park is available at the Prolansate office and at Garífuna Tours.

There's a movement afoot to rename the park after Jeanette Kawas, the director of Prolansate who was murdered in 1995 during a bitter struggle with big-money interests who wanted to develop the area.

Refugio de Vida Silvestre Punta Izopo

Standing on the beach at Tela and looking to the east, you can see another point: Punta Izopo, with the Punta Izopo Wildlife Refuge. The Ríos Plátano and Xicaque flowing through the wildlife refuge spread out into a network of canals passing through mangrove forests. These are home to abundant wildlife including monkeys, crocodiles, turtles and many species of birds, including toucans and parrots.

Garífuna Tours in Tela offers kayak trips to the refuge. Gliding silently through the mangrove canals in a kayak, you can get close to the wildlife without disturbing it.

Garífuna Villages

Several Garífuna villages are within easy reach of Tela. All of them are right on the coast, with splendid beaches, simple houses shaded by coconut trees, fishing canoes resting on the sand and tiny restaurants serving delicious Garífuna food; the specialities are seafood soups and fish cooked in coconut. You can spend some idyllic days walking along the beaches from Tela and visiting the coastal villages (see Dangers & Annoyances below).

The larger villages may hold dances on the weekends, and attending a Garífuna dance is a great experience. San Juan and El Triunfo de la Cruz have cultural dance troupes that have performed in many places.

The closest village is **La Ensenada**, a three-km, half-hour walk east along the arc of the beach from Tela, just before you reach the point, Punta Triunfo, crowned by the Cerro El Triunfo de la Cruz. Along the way you need to ford a river up to one meter deep. La Ensenada is a lovely little village with seafood restaurants (although most are only open on the weekend), places for a drink and a great beach.

Rocks prevent you walking around the point, but you can keep walking on the inland road for another 1½ to two km and reach the larger village of **El Triunfo de la Cruz**; buses also come here from Tela, departing from the corner on the east side of the market. Another beautiful spot, this village was the site of the first Spanish settlement in Honduras.

Other Garífuna villages are west of Tela. **San Juan** is five km west of Tela; it's a beautiful place worth visiting. **Tornabé**, three km farther on, is a larger village and equally lovely. So far, these villages have not been plagued with the problems of rowdy youths that Triunfo de la Cruz has experienced, and the people here are peaceful and friendly.

Past Tornabé, the beach road becomes rougher and can only be negotiated by 4WD vehicles. It continues for several more kilometers to **Miami**, a beautiful Garífuna village on a narrow sand bar between the Caribbean Sea and the Laguna de los Micos. Miami is more primitive than the other villages; the houses are all made of traditional materials, and there's no electricity. In Miami you can arrange for a boat trip on the Laguna de los Micos, or you can take a tour coming from Tela.

Río Tinto, another Garífuna village west of Tela, is more remote, and it can only be reached by boat. It takes about an hour to get there from Tela.

Dangers & Annoyances Take care along the beach from Tela to La Ensenada, and on the inland road to Triunfo de la Cruz: A traveler wrote about a violent assault and cited other unpleasant incidents. Be sure not to walk along here at night. Also avoid swimming at the rocks by Triunfo de la Cruz, as youths have attacked people there.

HONDURAS

Garífuna Dancing

While you're on the north coast, try to catch some live Garífuna music and dancing. The traditional Garífuna band is composed of three large drums, a turtle shell, some maracas and a big conch shell, producing throbbing, haunting rhythms and melodies. The chanted words are like a litany, to which the audience often responds. The dance is the *punta*, a Garífuna dance with a lot of hip movement. Often the dancers are in costume, with the women in long, loose, colorful skirts.

You can attend a Garífuna dance at a number of places along the north coast; Garífuna people live all along here, and they like to have a good time, especially on weekends. In Tela, the Garífuna Museum has a Saturday night party with traditional music and dance at which visitors will feel very comfortable. In La Ceiba, a couple of places in Barrio La Isla have Garífuna dances on weekends.

In Trujillo, the Los Menudos group used to play in Cocopando, but since they became world famous and began tour in places like Europe and Japan, they perform less often locally. Still, if you go to a dance in Cocopando, you'll see plenty of punta dancing. Los Menudos sometimes play in Trujillo at special events.

The smaller Garífuna villages along the coast also often have music and dancing on weekends. Another good option is attending a Garífuna cultural event, if one happens to be held while you're visiting. All the towns and villages have annual fiestas, and cultural events and gatherings of one kind or another take place throughout the year. Garífuna Day (April 12), a big holiday for all the Garífuna communities, commemorates the day in 1797 when the Garífunas arrived in Honduras.

The national Ballet Folklórico Garífuna, based in Tegucigalpa, is a first-rate dance troupe that has performed around the world; if you get a chance to attend a performance, don't miss it. ■

La Ensenada, much smaller than Triunfo de la Cruz, is more peaceful and low-key.

Places to Stay & Eat With the possible exception of Miami, all the villages have places to stay and at least a couple of restaurants beside the beach, specializing in seafood (of course).

In San Juan, at the west end of the village beside the Laguna de los Micos, a group of five cabins has a small sign out front announcing 'Rooms for Rent.' Each cabin is a studio house with two beds, private bath and a hammock on the porch. With fan they are US$10 for one or two people; with air con they're US$10 per person. Boats are available for trips on the lagoon or to places around the area.

In Tornabé, the *Restaurante y Cabañas Afulurijani* (call Prolansate in Tela, ☎ 48-2042), operated by the community of Tornabé, has two beachside cabins built of native materials. Each cabin has two bedrooms, living room and private bath, and can sleep five people; each costs US$21 per night, whatever the number of people. The restaurant here is not expensive. Also in Tornabé, *The Last Resort* (☎ /fax 48-2545) is a more upmarket place with nine cabins, each US$55 a night (US$110 for larger family cabins); they also have a restaurant and a beachfront deck, and can arrange local boat trips.

In La Ensenada, *Budari* is run by a friendly Italian-Garífuna family. It has four rooms with private bath for US$8 per room, plus several other cabins made of traditional Garífuna materials. Guests can get a ride into Tela with the owner. Also here is the *Comedor Budari*, serving traditional Garífuna and Italian foods. Also in La Ensenada, *Hotelito Mirtha* has simple rooms for US$3.35/4.15 with shared/private bath, plus some newer, larger cabins. Both places are on the road just behind the beach road; many places to eat are nearby on the beach.

Triunfo de la Cruz is the largest of the Garífuna villages. It's more developed, it has problems of crime and drugs among the young people, and all in all it doesn't have

as much of the peaceful, somnolent feeling of the other villages. Still, there are places to stay here, if you want to. Profesor Margarito Colón has three rooms with private bath, plus another room made of traditional materials, all right on the beach and costing US$6.65. Next door are a number of small free-standing rooms, all made of traditional materials but not as well cared for, for US$3.35. You can find more places to stay in Triunfo if you ask around.

Getting There & Away You can walk along the beach from Tela to any of the villages. It takes about half an hour to walk to La Ensenada, longer to reach the others (see Dangers & Annoyances above).

Local buses to the Garífuna villages depart from the east side of the market in Tela. There are two routes: one heading west through San Juan and on to Tornabé, another heading east to Triunfo de la Cruz. Buses on both routes depart hourly from around 6 am to 5 pm; cost is about US$0.25 and it takes about half an hour to 45 minutes to reach the villages.

If you're driving or cycling, you can get to San Juan on the beach road heading west from Tela and continue on to Tornabé. Be careful where you cross the sandbar at the Laguna de los Micos between San Juan and Tornabé; vehicles regularly get stuck in the sand here. You need a 4WD vehicle to get past Tornabé to Miami. Or you can get to Tornabé from the highway; the turnoff, five km west of Tela, is marked by a sign directing you to The Last Resort. To drive to La Ensenada or Triunfo de la Cruz, take the highway to the turnoff for Triunfo de la Cruz, five km east of Tela. About one kilometer down this road, the road forks and goes left to La Ensenada, right to Triunfo de la Cruz.

LA CEIBA
Population 109,000

La Ceiba is the largest of Honduras' Caribbean port towns, though Puerto Cortés actually takes the lead as the busiest port. Situated on the narrow coastal plain between the towering Cordillera Nombre

HONDURAS

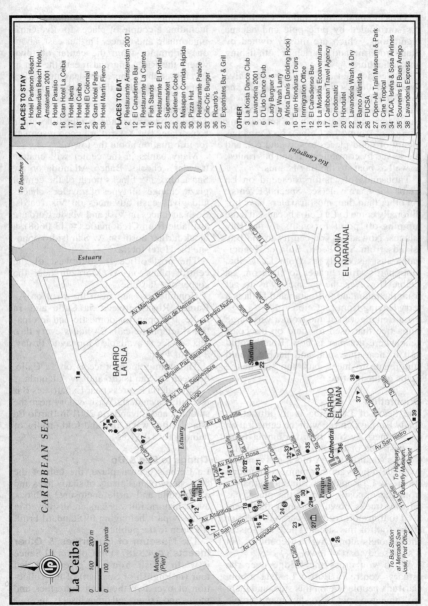

La Ceiba

0   100   200 m
0   100   200 yards

To Beaches

CARIBBEAN SEA

Muelle
(Pier)

Estuary

Estuary

Río Cangrejal

BARRIO
LA ISLA

COLONIA
EL NARANJAL

BARRIO
EL IMAN

Av Manuel Bonilla
Av Dionisio de Herrera
Av Pedro Nuño
Av Miguel Paz Barahona
Av 15 de Septiembre
Av Víctor Hugo
Av La Bastilla
Av Ramón Rosa
Av 14 de Julio
Av La República
Av San Isidro
Av Atlántida
Av La República
Av San Isidro

Parque
Bonilla

Parque
Central

Mercado

Cathedral

Stadium

To Bus Station
at Mercado San
José, Post Office

To Highway,
Butterfly Museum,
Airport

PLACES TO STAY
1   Hotel Partenon Beach
4   Rotterdam Beach Hotel,
     Amsterdam 2001
9   Hotel Paraíso
16 Gran Hotel La Ceiba
17 Hotel Iberia
18 Hotel Caribe
21 Hotel El Colonial
29 Gran Hotel París
39 Hotel Martín Fierro

PLACES TO EAT
2   Restaurante Amsterdam 2001
12 El Canadiense Bar
14 Restaurante La Carreta
15 Fish Stands
21 Restaurante El Portal
23 Supermarket
25 Cafetería Cobel
28 Masapan Comida Rápida
30 Pizza Hut
32 Restaurante Palace
33 Cric-Cric Burger
36 Ricardo's
37 Expatriates Bar & Grill

OTHER
3   La Kosta Dance Club
5   Lavandería 2001
6   D'Lido Dance Club
7   Lady Burguer &
     Car Wash Larry
8   Africa Danis (Golding Rock)
10 Euro Honduras Tours
11 Immigration Office
12 El Canadiense Bar
13 La Moskitia Ecoaventuras
14 Caribbean Travel Agency
19 Credomatic
20 Hondutel
22 Lavandería Wash & Dry
24 Banco Atlántida
26 FUCSA
27 Open-Air Train Museum & Park
31 Cine Tropical
34 TACA, Isleña & Sosa Airlines
35 Souvenirs El Buen Amigo
38 Lavandería Express

de Dios mountain range and the Caribbean, it's surrounded by pineapple and banana plantations, which are mostly owned by Standard Fruit, and it's rich in both fishing and agriculture.

La Ceiba is not a particularly attractive town and there's not much to see in the town itself, but the butterfly museum is worth a visit, and a number of enjoyable excursions can be made in the surrounding area (see Around La Ceiba). La Ceiba has plenty of good places to stay and eat, and it's served by convenient air and bus routes, as well as boats to the Bay Islands.

Thousands of visitors descend on La Ceiba for Carnaval (see Special Events), but other than that, most travelers have traditionally come to La Ceiba because it's the jumping-off point for visits to the Bay Islands. Nowadays you can fly to the Bay Islands from San Pedro Sula or Tegucigalpa just as easily as from La Ceiba, though it's still cheaper to fly from La Ceiba. However, the cheapest way to get from the mainland to Roatán and Utila is a ferry leaving from La Ceiba.

La Ceiba got its name from a very large ceiba tree that used to stand on the coast near where the pier is now. Boats would pull in near this spot, and people would congregate to meet, buy and sell in the shade of the big tree.

Orientation
The heart of La Ceiba is its attractive, shady Parque Central, with the cathedral on one corner. Av San Isidro, running from the east side of the plaza to the sea, is La Ceiba's 'main drag.' A block or two over, Av 14 de Julio is another major commercial street. Av La República, running to the sea from the opposite side of the plaza, has railway tracks down its center that were used to transport fruit and cargo to the pier at the foot of this street. There are lots of cheap hotels along Av La República, but it's the seedy part of town.

When you cross the bridge over the estuary, you're in Barrio La Isla. Many Garífuna people live on this side, and there are some good places to stay, many simple

restaurants and several popular discos, including a couple of places for live Garífuna music and dance. Farther east, about one kilometer from the center of town where the Río Cangrejal meets the sea at several sandbars, there are pleasant beaches that are cleaner than those in the center.

Information
There's no tourist office, but the folks at the Expatriates Bar & Grill are good resources for information about the town.

Many banks in the center will change traveler's checks. Banco Atlántida on Av San Isidro, 1½ blocks north of the central plaza, changes all types of traveler's checks and gives cash advances on Visa cards. Cash advances on Visa and MasterCard are available from Credomatic (☎ 43-0668), a block farther north on Av San Isidro opposite the Hotel Iberia.

The post office is southwest of the central plaza on Av Morazán near the corner of 13a Calle.

Hondutel is back from the road on Av Ramón Rosa between 5a Calle and 7a Calle. It's open for domestic and international telephone calls 24 hours every day. Fax service is available Monday to Friday, 8 am to 4 pm.

The immigration office is on 1a Calle, between Av San Isidro and Av Atlántida.

Lavandería Express near Expatriates Bar & Grill, Lavandería Wash & Dry near the stadium, and Lavandería 2001 in Barrio La Isla all offer wash, dry and fold (10 lbs of laundry for US$1.85).

Things to See & Do
La Ceiba's central plaza, the hub of the city's activity, has plenty of shady trees and a crocodile and turtle enclosure. A block away, historic railway cars are displayed in a grassy park belonging to Standard Fruit. It's open to the public.

The **Museum of Butterflies & Other Insects** (☎ 42-2874) in Colonia El Sauce is worth a visit. You'll be given a guided tour (in English or Spanish) of the collection of over five thousand butterflies and moths and a thousand other insects, most of them collected in Honduras by school-teacher Robert Lehman, all with notes telling where they were found. The largest moth in the world, with a 30-cm (one-foot) wingspan, and the most iridescent butterfly in the world, are highlights of the collection (both were found in Honduras). There's a 25-minute video about insects. The museum is open Monday to Saturday from 8 am to noon and 2 to 5 pm, evenings by appointment (closed Wednesday afternoons); entrance is US$1.25 (students US$0.85). It's on Calle Escuela Internacional in Colonia El Sauce, Segunda Etapa, Casa G-12, about a 20-minute walk from the center of town.

The sea water is not too clean at La Ceiba, but you can find better beaches on either side of the center. **Playa La Barra** is the most popular, near the sandbars where the Río Cangrejal meets the sea, and there's also **Playa Miramar**, about one kilometer in the opposite direction, west of the center of town. There are plenty of good, cleaner beaches a few kilometers from town. All of the beaches are dangerous at night.

The public can swim at the pool at the Gran Hotel Paris for US$1.50 per day.

There's a view of La Ceiba, the coastline and the Bay Islands from Colonia La Merced (go up the road that ascends the hill behind the golf course; it's about an hour's walk). Alternatively, take 'La Merced' bus from near the southwest corner of the central plaza. A taxi from town costs US$0.40. Bring binoculars if you have them.

Organized Tours

Several tour companies operate in La Ceiba, offering trips to sights near La Ceiba and farther afield. They include:

La Moskitia Ecoaventuras, Av 14 de Julio near the corner of 1a Calle (La Ceiba ☎ 42-0104, Tegucigalpa ☎ /fax 37-9398). Local trips to Pico Bonito, Cuero y Salado, white-water rafting on Río Cangrejal, and trips into the Mosquitia region.

Euro Honduras Tours, beach end of Av Atlántida (☎ 43-3893, ☎ /fax 43-0933, net). Local tours include a Scenic Overview tour (to Río Cangrejal, Río María and Sambo Creek), a Forest Waterfall & City Tour, Cuero y Salado, Pico Bonito, white-water rafting on Río Cangrejal, and tours farther afield. German, French, English and Spanish are spoken.

Ríos Honduras, in rear of Caribbean Travel Agency, Av San Isidro near Hotel San Carlos (☎ /fax 43-0780, 43-1360, in USA (800) 255-5784, net). Tours to Cuero y Salado; also white-water rafting trips on the Río Cangrejal and rivers farther afield.

Tropical Jungle Tours (☎ /fax 43-2055) White-water rafting trips on Río Cangrejal and other ecological tours.

Harry's Horseback Riding, contact at El Canadiense bar, Av 14 de Julio near the corner of 1a Calle. All-day horseback riding trips into Pico Bonito.

Special Events

Visitors from far and wide descend on La Ceiba for its annual Carnaval, held during the week of May 15, which is the day of San Isidro, the town's patron saint. People dress up in costumes and masks and dance themselves silly; it's a great time.

Places to Stay

Town Center *Hotel Caribe* (☎ 43-1857) on 5a Calle between Av San Isidro and Av Atlántida has some quite spacious and sunny rooms up on the 3rd floor that share a wide balcony. All have private cold bath and are US$5/8 with one/two double beds.

Hotel Martín Fierro (☎ /fax 42-2812) on the corner of Av San Isidro and 13a Calle is not right downtown, but it's just a short walk away. A clean, pleasant upstairs hotel that feels more like a guesthouse, its 10 rooms have air con, cable TV and hot showers. Rooms with shared or private bath cost about the same (US$8.35/11.25 for singles/doubles).

In downtown, *Hotel Iberia* (☎ 43-0401, fax 43-0100) on Av San Isidro has a nice inner courtyard and large, clean, comfortable rooms with private hot bath and cable TV, plus enclosed parking. Rooms cost US$12.50/16.70 with one/two double beds. Next door, the *Gran Hotel La Ceiba* (☎ 43-2747, ☎ /fax 43-2737) has singles/doubles with all the same amenities, plus air con, for US$15/18.70.

If you want to spend up, La Ceiba has some fancier places. *Hotel El Colonial* (☎ 43-1953, 43-1954, fax 43-1955) on Av 14 de Julio between 6a and 7a Calles has a rooftop bar with Jacuzzis and saunas and a good air-conditioned restaurant/bar. The 50 rooms, all with air con and cable TV, are US$21/23 with one/two double beds; you can get a 20% discount if you ask for it.

On the north side of the central plaza, the *Gran Hotel Paris* (☎ 43-2391, 43-1659, fax 43-1614) has a swimming pool, air con, color cable TV and a breakfast cafeteria; singles/doubles are US$30/33.

The *Euro Honduras Guest House* (☎ 43-3893, fax 43-0933) is an attractive, luxurious five-room guesthouse operated by the same Honduran-German-French family that runs Euro Honduras Tours. It's in Colonia El Naranjal, a residential area 10 minutes' walk from downtown. There's a swimming pool, BBQ area, tropical garden, laundry and self-service mini bar, and all the rooms have air con and private bath. Rooms are US$43 for one or two people, with a good homemade breakfast for another US$5. Another B&B is next door to the Expatriates Bar & Grill.

Barrio La Isla *Amsterdam 2001* (☎ 43-2311), beside the beach in Barrio La Isla, has been a haven for backpackers for many years. Upstairs is a dorm room with a wide sea-view porch; downstairs around the garden are five rooms, each sleeping three people. All have private cold bath and good beds and cost around US$3 per person. Owner Jan van Halderen, an old Dutch sailor who speaks several languages, and his charming wife, María, are like a 'mom and pop' to travelers. A popular restaurant/-bar, the Restaurante 2001, is next door, right on the beach.

Next door the other way, the *Rotterdam Beach Hotel* (☎ 43-2859, 42-2292) is newer and more upmarket, with eight clean, comfortable rooms with private cold bath and fan opening onto a grassy garden. It's a great deal for US$7.50 per room.

Hotel Paraíso (☎ 43-3535, fax 43-3536) on 4a Calle, three blocks from the beach, is another newer place. All the rooms have air con, private hot bath, phone and color cable TV; also here is a cafeteria and enclosed parking. Singles/doubles are US$10.85/15.40.

A bit more pricy but right on the beach in Barrio La Isla, *Hotel Partenon Beach* (☎ 43-0404, ☎ /fax 43-0434) is a luxurious place with a swimming pool, restaurant, nightclub, casino and Jacuzzi; all rooms have air con, cable TV and phone. Rooms are US$18 with one bed, or US$24 with two beds.

Places to Eat
Town Center *Masapan Comida Rápida* on 7a Calle between Av San Isidro and Av La República, a block from the central plaza, is popular and inexpensive. It's air-conditioned and has a long cafeteria buffet; it's open from 6:30 am to 10 pm every day. *Cafetería Cobel*, on 7a Calle between Av Atlántida and Av 14 de Julio, is another popular place that's always packed with locals.

Pizza Hut on the northeast corner of the central plaza has air con and a good, safe salad bar. Weekday lunch specials, served from noon until 4 pm, include an individual pizza or pasta, a trip to the salad bar and unlimited soft drink refills for US$2.75. It's open every day from 10 am to 10 pm.

Restaurante Palace on Av 14 de Julio at the corner of 8a Calle is a large air-conditioned restaurant with good Chinese food. *Cric-Cric Burger*, around the corner on 8a Calle, serves basic snacks like burgers, chicken and sandwiches.

The *Expatriates Bar & Grill & Travelers Exchange*, on the east end of 12a Calle in Barrio El Imán, is upstairs on the roof of the Refricon refrigeration shop. The bar and some tables under a high thatched palapa roof, and others out under the stars, all catch any breeze that comes by. It's great for vegetarians and meat-eaters alike, with delicious food in large portions. It's a friendly gathering place that has books and TV in English. It's open every day but Wednesday from 4 pm to midnight. During the USA football season it opens at 11 am on weekends so patrons can catch the game on TV.

Food is also served at the *El Canadiense* bar which is on Av 14 de Julio near the corner of 1a Calle.

Restaurante La Carreta on 4a Calle is a pleasant open-air restaurant specializing in meats *al carbón*.

Ricardo's on the corner of Av 14 de Julio and 10a Calle is more expensive, but it's reputed to be one of the finest restaurants in northern Honduras. Seating is inside in an air-conditioned section or outdoors in the garden patio. It's open Monday to Saturday from 11 am to 1:30 pm and again from 5:30 to 10 pm.

El Portal upstairs in the Hotel El Colonial (see Places to Stay) is another fine restaurant/bar, with plush decor, air con and good service; the excellent and extensive menu includes Thai cuisine. Prices are not as high as you'd expect, with main dishes from US$2.50 to US$11.50 – well worth splashing out for. It's open every day from 6 am to 10 pm.

If you have a place to prepare it, you can buy fresh fish every morning from a row of fish stands on Av Ramón Rosa near the corner of 5a Calle.

Barrio La Isla Many inexpensive open-air seafood restaurants line the beach, all the way from the estuary on the west side to the estuary and Playa La Barra on the east side.

Right on the beach, beside the Rotterdam Beach Hotel and Amsterdam 2001, *Restaurante Amsterdam 2001* is a pleasant palapa-covered restaurant/bar with good food at reasonable prices. It's open every day from around 10 am to midnight.

Entertainment

La Ceiba has several popular dance clubs, most of them in Barrio La Isla – 1a Calle in Barrio La Isla is known as the 'Zona Viva' for its nightlife. Popular clubs include *D'Lido* and *La Kosta*, which are both on 1a Calle beside the beach, and there are plenty of others. Also here on 1a Calle, *Lady Burguer & Car Wash Larry*

and *Africa Dani's*, also known as *Golding Rock*, are popular for Garífuna music and dancing.

The *Cine Tropical* cinema is on 8a Calle between Av San Isidro and Av 14 de Julio.

The *Expatriates Bar & Grill* and the *El Canadiense* bar (see Places to Eat) are popular gathering spots in the evening.

Things to Buy

Souvenirs El Buen Amigo, a souvenir shop on Av 14 de Julio between 8a and 9a Calles, has a good selection of souvenirs and postcards.

Getting There & Away

Air TACA (☎ 43-1915), Isleña (☎ 43-0179, airport 43-2683) and Sosa (☎ 43-1399, airport 43-0884) all have offices on the east side of the central plaza. Rollins Air (☎ 41-0641, 43-4181) has an office at the airport.

Frequent flights connect La Ceiba with San Pedro Sula, Tegucigalpa, the Bay Islands, Trujillo and various places in the Mosquitia region. See the Getting Around section earlier in this chapter for details on domestic flights.

The TACA office represents all five of the Central American airlines (TACA, Lacsa, COPA, Nica and Aviateca). It offers direct international flights to Miami daily and to New Orleans and New York five days a week. International flights to many other places connect through San Pedro Sula. Isleña offers two flights weekly from La Ceiba to Grand Cayman Island for US$200 one-way, US$350 roundtrip.

Bus The bus station is at Mercado San José, about two km west of the center of La Ceiba. A local bus runs between the bus station and the central plaza (US$0.05), or you can take a taxi (US$0.40).

Buses go from La Ceiba to:

Trujillo (171 km, four hours, US$1.90) Eight buses daily from 4 am to 3:50 pm.
Tela (103 km, 1½ hours, US$1.90) Same buses as to San Pedro Sula for same price.
San Pedro Sula (202 km, three hours, US$1.90) Catisa (☎ 43-4091) operates direct buses,

HONDURAS

with one stop at Tela, 10 times daily from 5:30 am to 6 pm.

Tegucigalpa (397 km, 6½ hours, US$4.60) Trailasa (☎ 41-0875) has direct buses at 6 and 9 am; Etrucsa (☎ 41-0340) has direct buses at 3, 10 and 11:30 am.

Corozal (15 km, 40 minutes, US$0.15) Same buses as to Sambo Creek.

Sambo Creek (20 km, one hour, US$0.25) Buses every 45 minutes from 6:30 am to 6 pm.

Nueva Armenia (40 km, 2½ hours, US$0.70) One bus daily leaves Nueva Armenia at 5 am, arriving in La Ceiba at 8 am then leaves La Ceiba at 11:30 am for the return trip, arriving at Nueva Armenia at 2 pm.

El Porvenir (15 km, 45 minutes, US$0.25) Same buses as to La Unión.

La Unión (20 km, 1½ hours, US$0.35) Monday to Saturday, hourly buses from 8:30 am to 5:30 pm; Sunday, hourly buses from 9 am to 5 pm.

Boat Boats operate from the Muelle de Cabotaje, which is about a 20-minute drive east of town. Taxis will take you there for US$2.50 per person. Be there an hour before departure to buy your ticket.

The MV *Tropical* (☎ 42-0780 in La Ceiba, ☎ 45-1795 in Roatán) is a comfortable, air-conditioned ferry sailing between La Ceiba and Roatán every day, and between La Ceiba and Utila on weekdays. From La Ceiba it takes about two hours to reach Roatán and about an hour to reach Utila. (See the Getting Around section earlier in this chapter for schedule and fares.)

The MV *Starfish* (☎ 45-3197), based on Utila, carries passengers and cargo. It sails from Utila to La Ceiba on Monday at 5:30 am, returning from La Ceiba the following day at noon. The crossing takes two or three hours and costs US$4.20. In rough weather the boat doesn't sail.

You could ask around the Muelle de Cabotaje for boats to other destinations. Captains of cargo and fishing boats might be persuaded to take along a passenger.

Getting Around

To/From the Airport La Ceiba's airport, the Aeropuerto Internacional Golosón, is seven km west of La Ceiba on the highway

to Tela. Any bus heading west could drop you there. A slow local bus goes from the central plaza to near the airport; taking a colectivo from the southwest corner of the plaza is a more reliable option (US$0.40). A normal taxi costs about US$2.50.

Coming from the airport, don't take one of the taxis right at the airport door, which charge about US$2.50 per person for the ride into town; walk out to the main road and flag down a taxi there, which will take you into town for around US$0.50 per person.

Car Rental Agencies include Dino's (☎ 43-0434) at the Partenon Beach Hotel; Maya (☎ 43-3079) at the Hotel La Quinta; Molinari (☎ 43-0055) at the Gran Hotel Paris; and Toyota (☎ 43-1976) on Av San Isidro.

Taxi There are lots of taxis in La Ceiba. A taxi ride in town costs US$0.40.

Bicycle Harry's Horseback Riding may have mountain bikes for rent; check at the El Canadiense bar.

AROUND LA CEIBA

Parque Nacional Pico Bonito (see below) lures many visitors just outside the city, but there are plenty of other nearby attractions as well.

Beaches

A number of good beaches are only a few kilometers from La Ceiba. East toward Trujillo there's **Boca Vieja**, five km from La Ceiba and two km from the highway; the popular **Playa Peru**, six km from La Ceiba and one km from the highway; and **Villa Nuria**, 16 km from La Ceiba and one km from the highway. At **Cuyamel**, 17 km from La Ceiba and 1½ km from the highway, there's a small admission fee and you can purchase barbecued fish by the beach and the river, especially on Sunday. *Las Sirenas* at Cuyamel offers camping on the beach for US$8 per tent. See also the Garífuna Villages below.

Dantio is six km west toward Tela from La Ceiba; it has a beach, estuary and fresh fish for sale. **El Porvenir** is 15 km from La Ceiba; it boasts a beach, river and typical Garífuna food.

Garífuna Villages

Corozal, 15 km east of La Ceiba, and **Sambo Creek**, six km farther east, are two seaside Garífuna fishing villages that are easy to reach from La Ceiba. They are enjoyable places, offering good beaches and fresh seafood. Both villages have Garífuna musical groups; dances are held on weekend nights.

The annual fair at Corozal, held from around January 6 to 18, is a big event that attracts people from far and wide, especially on the weekends of the fair when you'll find dancing, partying, games and competitions, lots of fun on the beach and good seafood. The annual fair at Sambo Creek is held in June.

Local buses connect both villages with La Ceiba; see the La Ceiba section.

At Sambo Creek, *Hotel Hermanos Avila* is opposite the beach and beside the Río Sambo, at the end of the beach road and the end of the bus line. It has 12 clean rooms with fan and shared bath for US$2.50 per room, plus four newer rooms with private bath for US$5 per room. They also have a small restaurant where meals cost around US$1.25 to US$2.50, and there are other restaurants nearby. You can hire a dugout canoe for exploring on the river. You can also arrange a motorboat ride out to Cayos Cochinos from Sambo Creek; the crossing takes about an hour.

At Corozal, *Hospedaje David* is in a quiet spot several blocks from the beach. It has eight simple rooms, with fan and shared bath, for US$2.50 per room.

River Balnearios

On the **Río Maria**, seven km east of La Ceiba on the highway to Trujillo, about eight blocks from the highway, is a delightful freshwater balneario with pools in the tropical forest, a waterfall and a viewpoint from which you can see the Bay Islands. Any eastbound bus from La Ceiba or any taxi can drop you on the highway here, and

you can walk the 15 minutes up to the balneario; local children can show you the way. Euro Honduras Tours (see Organized Tours in La Ceiba) also comes here.

Los Chorros, 10 km east of La Ceiba, is another pleasant balneario.

Villa Rhina (☎ 43-1222), 14 km east of La Ceiba, right on the highway, is another pleasant riverside balneario. There's no charge to swim in the refreshing, cool pools, but you're expected to spend a minimum of US$2 at the restaurant/bar. Also here are some rather expensive *hotel rooms* (US$30).

Several other balnearios and riverside beaches are along the Río Cangrejal.

Río Cangrejal

You can take an attractive scenic drive along the Río Cangrejal, starting about three km east of La Ceiba on the highway to Trujillo. The riverside road is the Old Highway to Olanchito (Antigua Carretera a Olanchito), also called La Culebra because it is such a snakelike, winding road.

The road passes waterfalls, rapids and several balnearios, including **Playa de Venado**, eight km from La Ceiba; **Playa de los Lobos**, two km farther on; and **Balneario Las Mangas**, 16 km from La Ceiba, with its iron bridge. The route passes through a lovely forest of precious woods and has some good views.

Several companies now operate **whitewater rafting trips** on this river, classified Class III and IV. They include Ríos Honduras, Euro Honduras, La Moskitia Ecoaventuras and Tropical Jungle Tours (see Organized Tours in La Ceiba).

If you come on a rafting tour, the company will provide transport to/from La Ceiba. Otherwise, buses depart hourly from La Ceiba bus terminal (US$0.40) and go as far as Balneario Las Mangas. Bring your lunch along, as there's nowhere to buy food here; fishing is also good.

There's an important archaeological site in this area, at **La Colorada**. It is unexcavated as yet, but there are around 60 mounds. Experts speculate that the site may one day rank among the important

Honduran ruins. Unlike at Copán, the people who built this site were not Maya, but Macrochibcha people.

Refugio de Vida Silvestre

On the coast about 30 km west of La Ceiba, the Cuero y Salado Wildlife Refuge takes its name from two rivers, the Cuero and Salado, that meet at the coast in a large estuary. This estuary, now a reserve, protects varied and abundant wildlife, including howler and white-faced monkeys, jaguars, ocelots, anteaters, sloths, agoutis, peccaries, iguanas, boa constrictors, otters, manatees, river and sea turtles, crocodiles, caymans, fish and 196 species of birds, including toucans, parrots, herons, pelicans, kingfishers and eagles. Migratory birds are here from around August/September to April/May.

To see the most wildlife, it's best to visit the reserve early in the morning or late in the afternoon. During the heat of the day, the animals are hiding from the sun. Bring food, water, sunscreen and insect repellent.

You can visit the reserve on a one-day tour from La Ceiba; La Moskitia Ecoaventuras, Ríos Honduras and Euro Honduras Tours all offer tours (see La Ceiba's Organized Tours section). Fundación Cuero y Salado (FUCSA), the organization running the reserve, arranges group tours.

Or you can come on your own; FUCSA or Ríos Honduras will help you organize your trip.

To get to the reserve, take a bus (1½ hours) or drive (30 minutes) from La Ceiba to La Unión, past El Porvenir; a taxi to get out there from La Ceiba could cost around US$8. At La Unión the road meets some old railway tracks. From this point, you take a *burra*, a small rail car propelled by poles, half an hour out to the reserve; the cost for the burra is around US$6.65 to US$10, depending on the number of people in the group (up to eight). Alternatively, if you reserve in advance with FUCSA, you can hire a *motocarro* train for US$5 to take you in. If you walk along the railway tracks, it takes 1½ hours to reach the reserve at a brisk pace (it's about eight km).

When you reach the reserve, there is an entry fee of US$10. Inside are houses and offices belonging to FUCSA and to Standard Fruit. You can tour the reserve by canoe or motorboat. A two-hour boat trip with guide costs about US$11; make a reservation in advance with FUCSA, to ensure that a boat will be available.

You can visit the park all in one day (the last bus leaves La Unión to return to La Ceiba at around 4 pm), or you can allow a couple of days for a leisurely visit. FUCSA is building overnight accommodations in the park; ask them for details. Or you can camp in the park if you have all your own gear. It doesn't cost anything, but you must first obtain permission from FUCSA.

You can get more information from the FUCSA office (☎ /fax 43-0329) in the Edificio Ferrocarril Nacional, Zona Mazapan, La Ceiba (see La Ceiba map). It's open Monday to Friday from 8 am to 11:30 am and 1:30 to 4:30 pm, Saturday 8 am to 11:30 am. They have a large wall map that will make all the above directions crystal clear.

Cayos Cochinos

Cayos Cochinos (the Hog Islands), 29 km from La Ceiba and just 17 km from the shore, can be visited as a day trip or camping trip from La Ceiba. See the Bay Islands section later in this chapter.

PARQUE NACIONAL PICO BONITO

Pico Bonito, a few kilometers behind La Ceiba, is one of Honduras' best-known national parks, with an unexplored core area of 500 sq km. It was already the largest national park in Honduras when additional forest territory was included in July 1992. It has magnificent and varied types of forests at different elevations, rivers, waterfalls and abundant wildlife, including jaguars, armadillos, wild pigs, tepescuintes, squirrels, monkeys, doves, toucans, insects and more.

The peak itself, at 2436 meters, is very difficult to ascend; climbers need ropes and mountain-climbing experience. Few groups have succeeded in climbing it, and the ascent and descent would take several days.

However, easier walks around the fringes of the park are possible. From the hacienda at the Río Bonito entrance to the park, an easy one-km trail leads to a good swimming hole, where the Río Bonito and Río Quebrada meet. From here there's also a three-hour loop trail, La Guatusa, which goes up to a lookout point.

To get to the park, take a local bus (Colonia 1 de Mayo – Parque Bonilla route; catch it in La Ceiba at Parque Bonilla), which will bring you to the Aldea Armenia Bonita; from there it's about a 20-minute walk to the park entrance. Anyone can point you in the right direction. If you're driving, take the highway west from La Ceiba for about eight km, and then turn toward the mountains on the road just beyond the Honduras Armed Forces camp, which is immediately after the airport. To reach the park entrance, follow this road for 4.5 km through the village, taking a right just after the soccer field. You'll cross the Río Bonito just before you reach the entrance.

Alternatively, you could leave the highway and walk up the Río Bonito for 4.5 km to the park entrance. About 10 km west of La Ceiba on the highway to Tela, opposite the Posta de Tránsito, you can walk through La Piñera, the Standard Fruit pineapple plantation, to the river.

About 300 meters past the park entrance is the hacienda, where a visitors' center is being built. There's usually a ranger on duty. There are plans for upgrading interpretive trails and providing guides. When all this is in place, it will cost US$6 to enter the park; until then, the entrance fee is US$2.50.

At the hacienda is a house where you can sleep overnight. There's no kitchen or bedding, so bring along everything you'll need. You can also camp there if you have your own gear.

You can easily visit the park in one day if you stay on the trails near the hacienda. You could see more of the forest, however, if you allowed two days or more, one for the ascent and one for the descent.

This is the most accessible entrance to the park, but it's a large park and there are other entrances, including one beside the Río Cangrejal.

For more information on the park, contact the park office in La Ceiba, which shares office space with FUCSA (see Cuero y Salado, above). They will be offering tours into the park. Several of the tour companies in La Ceiba also offer trips into the park (see Organized Tours in La Ceiba).

AMARAS

In 1991 a law was passed in Honduras forbidding the capture and sale of wild birds, mammals and reptiles. Several of Honduras' wild species are in danger of extinction, including Honduras' national bird, the *guara roja* (red macaw) and various species of *lora* (parrot). In the case of the birds, the threat largely derives from the destruction and fragmentation of their natural forest habitat and also from the practice of routinely capturing and selling the birds in other countries as pets.

The Asociación del Medio Ambiente y Rehabilitación de Aves Silvestres (AMARAS) was created by FUCSA in 1991 when the law was passed. It takes in macaws, parrots and other wild birds that have been illegally captured. Many birds arrive in deplorable condition; when they have regained their health, they are released back into the wild in protected areas of Honduras.

In addition to seeing the birds here, you can go for a swim at a river swimming hole about a half-hour's walk from the aviaries; a guide will show you the way.

AMARAS is on the highway 12 km west of La Ceiba in the Aldea El Pino. Any bus heading west from La Ceiba can drop you at the entrance, or you could come by taxi. It's open Tuesday to Sunday, 8 am to 5 pm. Admission is US$3 – a donation to a worthy cause. You can even 'adopt a bird' and receive its photo as well as information about the bird and where it is eventually released. Information is available in La Ceiba at the FUCSA office (see Cuero y Salado, above).

TRUJILLO
Population 36,000

Capital of the department of Colón, Trujillo sits on the wide arc of the Bahía de Trujillo. It is famous for its lovely beaches with coconut palms and gentle seas. Though it's known as one of Honduras' most attractive Caribbean coastal towns, it is not usually full of tourists, except during the celebration of Semana Santa and the annual fair of the town's patron saint, San Juan Bautista, in the last week of June (June 24 is the exact day, but the festival goes on for a week).

History
Trujillo is not a large town, but it has played an important part in the history of Central America. It was near Trujillo, on August 14, 1502, that Columbus first set foot on the American mainland, having sailed from Jamaica on his fourth (and final) voyage. The first mass on American mainland soil was said on the spot where he and his crew landed.

Founded on May 18, 1525, Trujillo was one of the earliest Spanish settlements in Central America. The first Spanish town in the colonial province of Honduras, it was the

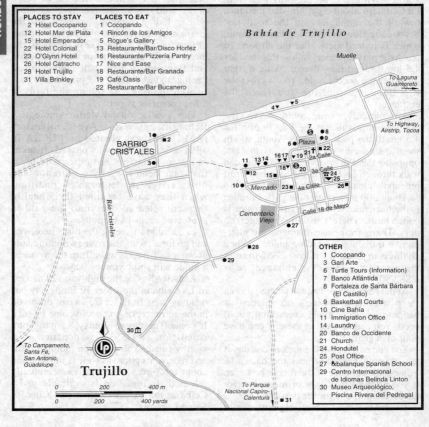

PLACES TO STAY
2 Hotel Cocopando
12 Hotel Mar de Plata
15 Hotel Emperador
22 Hotel Colonial
23 O'Glynn Hotel
26 Hotel Catracho
28 Hotel Trujillo
31 Villa Brinkley

PLACES TO EAT
1 Cocopando
4 Rincón de los Amigos
5 Rogue's Gallery
13 Restaurante/Bar/Disco Horfez
16 Restaurante/Pizzería Pantry
17 Nice and Ease
18 Restaurante/Bar Granada
19 Café Oasis
22 Restaurante/Bar Bucanero

OTHER
1 Cocopando
3 Gari Arte
6 Turtle Tours (Information)
7 Banco Atlántida
8 Fortaleza de Santa Bárbara (El Castillo)
9 Basketball Courts
10 Cine Bahía
11 Immigration Office
14 Laundry
20 Banco de Occidente
21 Church
24 Hondutel
25 Post Office
27 Xbalanque Spanish School
29 Centro Internacional de Idiomas Belinda Linton
30 Museo Arqueológico, Piscina Rivera del Pedregal

Bahía de Trujillo

Muelle

To Laguna Guaimoreto

To Highway, Airstrip, Tocoa

BARRIO CRISTALES

Plaza
2a Calle
3a Calle
Mercado
4a Calle
Calle 18 de Mayo

Río Cristales

Cementerio Viejo

To Campamento, Santa Fe, San Antonio, Guadalupe

Trujillo

0   200   400 m
0   200   400 yards

To Parque Nacional Capiro-Calentura

HONDURAS

provincial capital until the seat was shifted to Comayagua in 1537. The Catholic bishop's see remained in Trujillo until 1561, when it too was moved to Comayagua.

The Spanish used the port at Trujillo to ship out gold and silver from the interior of Honduras, an activity that attracted pirates to the bay. The Bahía de Trujillo was the scene of several great battles when the town was attacked by pirates, including van Horn, Aury and Morgan.

The Spanish built several fortresses, the ruins of which are still visible; the ruins of the fort of Santa Bárbara lie near the plaza in town. Despite the fortifications, the buccaneers prevailed, and after a sacking by Dutch pirates in 1643, the town lay in ruins for over a century until it was resettled in 1787.

William Walker (see his story in the Nicaragua chapter) made his final attack on Central America at Trujillo; he was captured and executed here on September 12, 1860. His grave can be seen in the old cemetery in town.

The American short-story writer William Sidney Porter (better known by his pen name O Henry) came to Trujillo around 1896. He wrote about Trujillo in his book *Cabbages and Kings*.

Orientation
Trujillo is a small town and you can easily walk everywhere you need to go; there are also taxis. Several good restaurants, a couple of hotels and the best beaches are near the airstrip, which is a few kilometers east of town; you can get there by walking about 20 minutes east along the beach.

Information
Tourist Offices There's no tourist information office in Trujillo, but the folks at Café Oasis are very helpful with information about the town.

Immigration The immigration office is on the west end of 2a Calle.

Money The Banco de Occidente changes traveler's checks, gives cash advances on both Visa and MasterCard and represents Western Union. It's open Monday to Friday from 8 am to noon and 2 to 5 pm, Saturday 8 to 11:30 am. Right on the plaza, Banco Atlántida changes traveler's checks and gives cash advances on Visa cards.

Post & Communications The post office and Hondutel are side by side, three blocks inland from the plaza. Hondutel is open for domestic and international phone calls Monday to Friday from 7 am to 9 pm, Saturday and Sunday 8 am to 4 pm. Fax service is available Monday to Friday from 7 am to 5 pm, Saturday 7 to 11 am.

Laundry Laundry service is available next door to the Restaurant, Bar & Disco Horfez. The shop is open Monday to Friday from 7 am to 5:30 pm, Saturday 7 am to noon.

Things to See & Do
Trujillo is best known for its attractive white-sand beaches. Some of the best are near the airstrip, a 20-minute walk east along the beach from town; several beachside open-air thatched-roof restaurant/bars provide shade, food and a cool drink for beachgoers, and keep the beaches clean. This isn't the only good beach, however. White-sand beaches stretch for several kilometers around the bay – you can walk along the beach in either direction from town and pick your spot.

The ruins of the 17th-century Spanish fortress, properly named the Fortaleza Santa Bárbara de Trujillo but usually called **El Castillo**, are in the center of town near the plaza, behind the basketball courts and overlooking the sea. The fort contains several old cannons and other relics, a plaque marking the place where Walker was executed and an excellent view along the coast. Operated by the Instituto Hondureño de Antropología e Historia, the ruins are open every day from 8 am to noon and from 1 to 4 pm; admission is US$0.10.

William Walker's grave is in the Cementerio Viejo (Old Cemetery), a few blocks from the plaza. On the plaza itself is a historic church, built in 1832.

Near the Río Cristales, the **Museo Arqueológico** has a fascinating collection: interesting archaeological relics and historical objects are arrayed alongside household junk (seemingly selected on the basis of 'if it's old and rusty, display it'!). Exhibits range from Maya carvings to mangled typewriters; there's even the remains of an aircraft wrecked in the bay in 1985. It is open every day from 7 am to 5 pm. The US$0.85 admission includes entry to the **Piscina Rivera del Pedregal** at the rear, with a couple of open-air swimming pools, children's play areas and picnic areas. Food and drink are not always available.

Just west of town, where the Río Cristales flows into the sea, you can find **Cocopando**, in the Garífuna barrio of Cristales. Several open-air restaurants right on the beach offer meals and snacks; in the evening, this is the best spot in Trujillo for dancing and music.

Other good places to visit (including Parque Nacional Capiro-Calentura) are a short distance from town; see Around Trujillo.

Language Courses
Trujillo has two language schools, both of which charge US$150 for one week (20 hours) of one-on-one language instruction, plus a home stay with a local family including three meals daily; instruction alone is US$95.

The Centro Internacional de Idiomas Belinda Linton (☎ /fax 44-4777) offers courses in Spanish, English and Garífuna languages and in Garífuna folklore and dance. The Ixbalanque Spanish School (☎ 44-4461, fax 57-6215) offers Spanish courses; it is affiliated with the school of the same name in Copán Ruinas, making it possible to do part of your course at the ruins and part at the beach.

Organized Tours
Turtle Tours (☎ 44-4444, fax 44-4431) offers tours to places in the area including Capiro y Calentura, Laguna Guaimoreto, the crocodile reserve and Garífuna villages. It also organizes snorkeling at Cayos Blancos and a Trujillo city tour, and it conducts tours farther afield into the Mosquitia region. German, English and Spanish are spoken. The office is at the hotel Villa Brinkley; information about tours is also available in the restaurant on the west side of the central plaza.

Trujillo Ecotours (☎ 44-4101) offers tours to all the same places, plus a few more. Information about their tours is available at Chino's Bar on the beach near the airstrip.

Now that flights are available from Trujillo to Palacios, Trujillo is becoming a jumping-off point for tours to the Mosquitia region. Turtle Tours can give you information about the Mosquitia. Alternatively, stop by the Rincón de los Amigos bar/restaurant on the beach in front of town; these guys have been there many times, and they can tell you all about it.

Places to Stay
Trujillo has a number of good places to stay. During Semana Santa you should book ahead.

Hotel Catracho (☎ 44-4438) on 4a Calle has a row of nine simple wooden rooms built in the garden, each with private cold bath, plus a bar and restaurant. Singles/doubles are US$3.35/4.15.

A couple of blocks up the hill from the plaza is *Hotel Mar de Plata* (☎ /fax 44-4458), a friendly, family-run place. Singles/doubles with shared bath are US$3.35/5, or US$5/5.85 with private bath.

Closer to the plaza is *Hotel Emperador* (☎ 44-4446), which offers small but well-equipped rooms with private bath and fan for US$5.85; a larger, better room with cable TV is US$8.35.

Hotel Trujillo (☎ 44-4202) on Calle 18 de Mayo is also good, with very clean rooms with private bath, fan, and TV; singles/doubles are US$7.10/10.85, or US$10/15 with air con.

Beside the plaza, the recently renovated *Hotel Colonial* (☎ /fax 44-4011) has rooms with air con, cable TV and private cold bath for US$17.85; you'll also find a good restaurant/bar.

Three blocks from the plaza, the *O'Glynn Hotel* (☎ /fax 44-4592) has comfortable rooms with air con, cable TV and private hot bath for US$15 for one person, US$25 for two or three.

Villa Brinkley (☎ /fax 44-4444), perched on the hill about one kilometer from the center of town, enjoys a magnificent view of the bay. Rooms start at US$15 with fan, or US$23.35 with air con; large rooms with four beds and fan are US$20.85. All have private hot bath; children 17 and under are free. The hotel constantly has a construction project under way. Amenities include a bar, two restaurants, a swimming pool, a recreation room and the office of Turtle Tours. Peggy Brinkley is a charming host.

Near the airstrip, a couple of kilometers from town, the *Trujillo Bay Hotel* (☎ /fax 44-4732) has large, comfortable singles/doubles with air con, cable TV and private hot bath for US$20.85/29.15. It's on the land side of the airstrip; just across the airstrip are several good beachside restaurant/bars on one of the finest stretches of beach in the area.

One of these, *Chino's Bar* (☎ 44-4101), has some cabañas right on the beach, each with air con, two bedrooms (each with one double bed and two bunk beds), sitting room and private bath (no kitchen). The cost is US$25 per bedroom or US$50 for the whole house. Also by the airport is the large and expensive *Christopher Columbus Hotel* (☎ 44-4966, fax 44-4971), which does much of its business in package tours.

At Cocopando, in the Barrio Cristales right by the beach, *Hotel Cocopando* (☎ 44-4748) is a three-story hotel run by a friendly Garífuna family; backpackers will love this place. Simple rooms, all with two beds, fan and private cold bath, are US$4.15/5 for singles/doubles. Many open-air restaurants are here on the beach in front of the hotel. The dances from Thursday to Sunday nights are held right in front of the hotel, too. This is a blessing or a curse, depending on your point of view; it's fun if you like music and partying, not so fun if you wanted a quiet night's sleep.

Other beachside accommodations are available at Campamento, Santa Fe and Guadalupe, all a few kilometers west of Trujillo (see Around Trujillo).

Places to Eat

There are several good inexpensive restaurants in town. *Café Oasis* is a pleasant little place with an outdoor patio and good vegetarian or meat meals and snacks. The foods are different from what you see at most other places, and they also make a variety of fruit drinks. There's an international book exchange and a message board for travelers. Natalie and Daniel, the Canadian-Honduran proprietors, are friendly and helpful with information about the town. It's open Monday to Saturday from 9 am, Sunday from 4 pm, and stays open until around 11 pm or midnight.

Other good restaurants in town include the *Granada*, the *Pantry* and the *Bucanero*, the latter at the Hotel Colonial near the plaza. All have air con and bars, and all serve much the same selection of seafood, meats, soups, sandwiches and burgers, breakfasts and so on at much the same prices; the Pantry also serves pizza. Try *Nice and Ease* for fruit drinks, ice cream and pastries.

Restaurante, Bar & Disco Horfez is an open-air spot with lots of plants; it's open Tuesday to Sunday from 4 pm on. Discos are held here on Friday, Saturday and Sunday nights.

The restaurants at the *Villa Brinkley* up on the hill have an excellent view. They serve a pleasant breakfast for US$2, dinners for around US$5 to US$7. The menu is varied and includes seafood prepared in many styles.

On the beach just below the plaza there's a row of thatch-roof open-air seafood restaurant/bars. The *Rincón de los Amigos* has excellent seafood, Cajun food and Spanish paella; it's a pleasant, friendly place, with tables, hammocks and the bar. Once or twice a week there's live Garífuna music and dancing. It's open every day from around 9:30 am to 11 pm. Also along here, *Rogue's Gallery* has seafood, bar, cable TV, an English-language book exchange, catamaran and boat rentals and 'the best bathrooms on the beach,' owner Jerry from California proudly proclaims.

Several other pleasant open-air beach-front restaurant/bars are on a fine stretch of beach near the airport, a couple of kilometers east of town (coming from town, walk east along the beach for about 20 minutes). They include the *Bahía Bar, Chino's Bar* and the *Gringos Bar*; walk along and take your pick. Each has its own special features (hammocks, a volleyball net, boats or water sports for rent). All are open every day from around 7 am until 10 pm or later. *Chino's Bar* (☎ 44-4101) operates a tour agency, Trujillo Ecotours, and has cabins for rent.

A number of simpler open-air beachfront restaurants are at Cocopando in Barrio Cristales.

Other good restaurants are at Campamento, four km west of Trujillo, and in Santa Fe, the Garífuna village 10 km west of Trujillo (see Around Trujillo).

Entertainment

At Cocopando, on the beach in Barrio Cristales where the Garífuna residents live, dances are held on Thursday to Sunday nights. Weekend nights are very lively. On Sunday afternoons, local children have a children's dance; children that barely reach up to your waist are already quite skillful at dancing the punta, and it's a happy time for all.

Once or twice a week, the *Rincón de los Amigos* on the beach below the plaza has a dance with a traditional Garífuna band.

In town, *Restaurant, Bar & Disco Horfez* is a popular open-air night spot with disco dancing on Friday, Saturday and Sunday evenings.

Things to Buy

In Barrio Cristales, Gari Arte (☎ 44-4207) offers a selection of Garífuna handicrafts, music and souvenirs.

Getting There & Away

Air Trujillo has a small airstrip, a few kilometers west of town. Isleña (☎ 44-4965) has a daily (except Sunday) flight between La Ceiba and Palacios that stops at Trujillo; from Trujillo it's US$21 to La Ceiba, US$24 to Palacios.

Bus Buses arrive and depart from the central plaza. Direct buses to San Pedro Sula (373 km, five to six hours, US$4.60), operated by the Cotuc and Cotraipbal companies, depart at 2, 3, 5, 6:30 and 8 am. These buses are the quickest and most painless way to get to La Ceiba (2½ hours) and Tela (3½ hours).

Otherwise, buses making plenty of stops depart from Trujillo every day for La Ceiba at 2, 3, 4, 5, 6:30, 7:30, 8:30 and 10 am and at noon, 1 and 2 pm (171 km, four to 4½ hours, US$2). Minibuses to Tocoa, along the way to La Ceiba, also depart frequently.

There are two inland routes to Tegucigalpa. A direct bus departs daily at 4 am and goes over the mountains via La Unión; it's about a nine-hour trip. Another bus departs at 9 am for the same route, though you have to change buses in the mountains. The longer route is via Juticalpa: A bus departs for Juticalpa every other day at 4 am from a house up the hill behind the Hotel Catracho (278 km, eight hours, US$4.20). From Juticalpa you can continue on to Tegucigalpa.

Local buses go from Trujillo to the Garífuna villages of Santa Fe, San Antonio and Guadalupe to the west, and to Puerto Castilla across the bay. Buses to Santa Fe, San Antonio and Guadalupe depart four times a day. Ask when they're leaving, and be careful not to miss the bus; they don't always run on schedule, but may depart whenever they're full.

Catching a Ride The folks at the Rincón de los Amigos restaurant, on the beach below the plaza, often give people a lift when they go to Santa Rosa de Aguán or to Puerto Castilla to buy fish.

Motorcycle Rental Turtle Tours (see Organized Tours) rents Suzuki 350 motorcycles for US$35 per day.

Boat Boats depart from the *muelle* (pier) at Trujillo for various destinatioins including the Bay Islands, the Mosquitia region, the Nicaraguan coast, some Caribbean islands (including the Cayman Islands and Jamaica) and the USA (usually New Orleans, four days away by boat). None of these are scheduled departures; you just have to walk down to the pier, see what boats are there and try your luck. They are usually fishing or cargo boats, but you can often pay passage.

Cargo boats usually depart from this pier for Guanaja every couple of days; the passage takes about five hours and should cost you around US$6 or US$7 – much cheaper than flying. Cargo boats also depart every couple of days for the Mosquitia region.

Also check for boats at Puerto Castilla, round the bay.

AROUND TRUJILLO
Parque Nacional Capiro-Calentura
The mountain behind Trujillo, called Cerro Calentura, 1235 meters above sea level at the summit, is part of the Parque Nacional Capiro-Calentura. It can be most easily accessed by heading straight up the hill from town; take the road going up past the Villa Brinkley hotel and just keep on going. The gravel road goes all the way up to the summit, which is 10 km from town. Though a 4WD vehicle would be best, we made it in a regular car (you could also walk it). Turtle Tours and Trujillo Ecotours (see Organized Tours in Trujillo) also make trips up there.

On the way up the hill you pass through a couple of distinct vegetation zones. At around 600 to 700 meters the vegetation changes from tropical rain forest to subtropical low-mountain rain forest, and you find yourself in a zone of giant tree ferns, with lush forest, large trees, vines and flowering plants. There's plenty of wildlife in the park, too, including many species of tropical birds and butterflies, reptiles, monkeys and more. About a third of the way up, a couple of trails take off from the road, to the left, leading to a waterfall and a tiny reservoir; they're not marked, but you can see them distinctly from the road.

It can be sunny, clear and warm in Trujillo, and cloudy and much cooler at the top of the hill. If it isn't cloudy, you can·get a great view from the summit over the beautiful Valle de Aguán, along the coast as far as Limón, and across to Roatán, Guanaja and the Cayos Cochinos (Hog Islands). A radar station is at the summit.

When we were in Trujillo, this road was open and freely accessible, and there was no fee to enter the park. However, a visitors' center is being built and interpretive trails are being laid out; once all this is in place, there will be guides to take you along the trails, and you'll pay an entrance fee of US$10. The park and visitors' center will be open every day from 6 am to 6 pm.

There are also a few other entrances to the park. La Culebrina, a stone road from the Spanish colonial days, takes off from the road between Trujillo and Santa Fe and goes all the way to the Cuevas de Cuyamel, some caves in the southwest part of the park; the Spanish used to transport gold along this road, bringing it from Olancho and the Valle de Aguán to the coast. The Cuevas de Cuyamel are in the community of Cuyamel; anyone in that town can show you the way to the caves.

It's possible to enter the park on a trail which goes up the Río Negro. It starts near the stadium, which is several km from town, heading towards the airport. Up here there's a lovely waterfall, where you can swim. Be sure not to swim in the reservoir that's above the waterfall, as this is Trujillo's water supply.

Still another entrance to the park is from the community of Silín, seven km from Trujillo on the road to Tocoa.

Information about the park is available from the visitors' center, which is just beyond the entrance to the park on the road that passes the Villa Brinkley, or from the office of the Fundación Capiro-Calentura Guaimoreto (FUCAGUA; ☎ /fax 44-4294) on the second floor of the kiosk building in the middle of the central plaza; it's open Monday to Friday, 8 am to noon and 2 to 4:30 pm.

Laguna Guaimoreto

Five km east of Trujillo, past the airstrip and the Río Negro, Laguna Guaimoreto is a large lagoon with a natural passageway onto the bay. About six km by nine km, the lagoon is a protected wildlife refuge; its complex system of canals and mangrove forests is home to abundant animal, bird and plant life, including thousands of migratory birds from around November to February.

Information about the lagoon is available from the FUCAGUA office in the central plaza (see Capiro-Calentura, above). Turtle Tours and Trujillo Ecotours (see Organized Tours in Trujillo) both offer tours on the lagoon. A less expensive option is to walk out here along the beach from Trujillo to the old bridge between Trujillo and Puerto Castilla. Sometimes you can hire a boat from here to take you to the lagoon.

Hot Springs

Agua Caliente (☎ 44-4249, fax 44-4248), a spa with a number of outdoor mineral hot springs, is seven km from Trujillo on the road to Tocoa. The hot springs are a popular outing from Trujillo. They are open every day from 7 am to 9 pm, and admission is US$2.50. Massage and a Jacuzzi are also available. There is also a restaurant (on the road is a sign for the Restaurante Praga) and a hotel with luxurious cabins for US$40 per night.

Any bus heading to Tocoa could drop you here. The spa is right on the highway about 10 minutes from Trujillo.

Hacienda Tumbador

About 10 km from Trujillo, there's a crocodile reserve at the Hacienda Tumbador, a cattle ranch on the Río Chapagua. The crocodiles living in the river there are an endangered species; they are protected, and the folks at the ranch give them food, so the crocs are numerous. You can get right up close to them if you want to.

The turnoff to the ranch is signed from the road to Tocoa, eight km from Trujillo, but past this point it's unmarked – without more signs or someone with you who knows the way, it's impossible to find on your own. Turtle Tours and Trujillo Ecotours (see Organized Tours in Trujillo) conduct trips here.

Puerto Castilla

East of Trujillo around the bay is Puerto Castilla, the port on the inward arm of the Cabo de Honduras, which forms the bay. This is one of Honduras' major ports, from which fruit and other products are shipped to the Caribbean ports of the USA. Buses come here from Trujillo.

Campamento

On a beautiful stretch of beach four km west of Trujillo, Cabañas y Restaurante Campamento (☎ 44-4244, fax 44-4200) has an excellent open-air restaurant/bar; large, grassy grounds with many coconut trees; a fine beach; and several types of accommodations. The cabañas here (and the place as a whole) are really something special. They are widely spaced around the grounds; all have private bath and are very comfortable. Simple thatch-roof cabañas are US$16.65 per night for one or two people; larger, more sophisticated cabañas are US$25 per night, and there's a large, luxurious two-bedroom house with kitchen for US$70 or US$80 per night, depending on the length of stay. They also have plans to build a small 12-room hotel.

This is a beautiful, tranquil, peaceful place to stay or just to come for the day or to eat at the restaurant. They have horses for rent and soon will have a boat available for trips to Cayos Blancos.

Any bus heading for Santa Fe can drop you at the turnoff, from which it's a 350-meter walk out to the beach. A taxi will bring you from town for around US$2.50 or US$3. If you're staying overnight here, they'll give you a ride into town.

Garífuna Villages

Several Garífuna villages, all with houses stretching along the beach, are west of Trujillo. **Santa Fe**, the largest village, is 10 km west of Trujillo. A couple of kilometers farther are the smaller Garífuna villages of **San Antonio** and then **Guadalupe**.

Santa Fe's annual fair is on July 16.

Places to Stay & Eat A simple *hospedaje* is in Santa Fe about a block past the Comedor Caballero. Rooms are around US$5 per night. There's no sign, but anyone can tell you where it is.

In Guadalupe, *Hotel Franklin* is a simple little place near the beach with just five clean rooms, each with fan and private bath. Singles/doubles are US$4.15/5.85 per night, with cheaper weekly rates. Nikolasa, the friendly owner, will cook meals for you, and there's also a little shop and other places to eat nearby.

If you go to Santa Fe, eat at *Comedor Caballero*. Meals start at US$1.70, but as Sr Caballero is thought by many to be the best cook in northern Honduras, it's worth splashing out on his *especial carte*, with dishes starting at US$4.20. It's open every day from around 8 am to 6 pm.

Getting There & Away A dirt road runs out to these villages from Trujillo, and buses connect with Trujillo four times a day (see Getting Around in Trujillo). You can walk along the beach to reach any of the villages; as everywhere on the north coast, though, don't walk on the beach at night.

Cayos Blancos

A few kilometers west of Trujillo, the Cayos Blancos have a reef good for snorkeling. Turtle Tours and Trujillo Ecotours run trips out there (see Organized Tours in Trujillo), or you could hire a boat from Campamento on the way to Santa Fe to take you out here. You could probably also hire a boat from Santa Fe, San Antonio or Guadalupe; most of the families there have small boats.

SANTA ROSA DE AGUÁN
Population 7000

About an hour east of Trujillo, Santa Rosa de Aguán is a Garífuna village straddling the Río Aguán near the Barra del Aguán, where the river meets the sea. The village is quiet and peaceful, the people friendly. Canoes can provide passage across the river for US$0.10.

You can take a boat trip upriver here, seeing wildlife in the early morning and late afternoon; if you won't be able to take a boat trip on any of the big rivers in the Mosquitia region, this is the next best thing. Ask for Marcos, a popular boatman; he speaks English, Spanish, Garífuna and Miskito. Or you can walk down to the river mouth, where there are many kilometers of unpopulated beach. You can walk to Limón along the beach in about three hours or get there by horseback in about 1½ hours.

Special Events

Santa Rosa's annual festival day is August 29. Celebrations start a week beforehand on August 22, with the old people's dance and escalate throughout the week; the 28th is the biggest day. People come from all over the north coast for this celebration.

Places to Stay & Eat

There are two simple *hospedajes* in Santa Rosa, one on either side of the river. Rooms are not luxurious, but they're also not expensive, about US$2.50 to US$3.50 per night. Anyone can tell you where they are.

One of the attractions of Santa Rosa is the giant crayfish (*langostinos*) caught in the river here. You can buy some crayfish to prepare yourself, or you can find someone to cook them for you. You can get a soda or beer beside the canoe dock and the little store when you first get to town; the comedor across the river is the place locals recommend for a meal.

Getting There & Away

Buses come to Santa Rosa from Trujillo, Tocoa and La Ceiba. The one coming from Trujillo takes about an hour; it departs from Trujillo's plaza at 10 am and leaves Santa Rosa for the return trip at 1 pm. Two buses a day come from Tocoa, one in the early and one in the late morning, and one bus a day comes from La Ceiba, four hours away.

If you're driving, take the Barra del Aguán turnoff from the highway between

Trujillo and Corocito, about 20 km from Trujillo. From this turnoff it's 21 km to Santa Rosa de Aguán.

LIMÓN
Population 7300

A couple of hours east of Trujillo is Limón, a Garífuna village by the sea at the mouth of the Río Limón. From the village you can go upriver by canoe and see plenty of wildlife. Many birds, including toucans and parrots, and monkeys go to the river early in the morning. There are also good beaches around Limón.

Limón has a basic hospedaje where you can stay and places to eat.

Getting There & Away

Buses depart for Limón from Trujillo and Tocoa; you can catch them at the crossroads at Corocito if you like. Travelers have recently told us that the road, which is unpaved, now extends east past Limón to Punta Piedra; from here, it's about half an hour by boat to Palacios. They say the bus goes all the way to Punta Piedra, taking about seven hours from Tocoa, but that the road is pretty bad beyond Limón. East of

Limón is the beginning of the sparsely inhabited Mosquitia region.

Bay Islands

About 50 km off the north coast of Honduras, the three Bay Islands (Islas de la Bahía) – Roatán, Utila and Guanaja – are prime attractions for visitors, who come from around the world to dive and snorkel on the extensive reefs teeming with colorful fishes, corals, sponges, lobsters and much other marine life. These reefs, a continuation of the Belize reefs, are the second-largest barrier reef in the world after Australia's Great Barrier Reef.

Utila is known as the cheapest place in the world to take a scuba-diving certification course. Several dive schools on Roatán offer diving courses for not too much more; this island is larger and more varied. Both islands offer great diving, and both have many aficionados. Diving is also good on Guanaja, though this island is not a tourist destination on the same scale as the others.

The Bay Islands Conservation Association

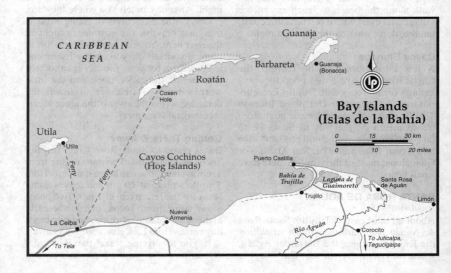

Bay Islands (Islas de la Bahía)

(BICA) works to protect and preserve the reef. Reefs in several parts of the islands are now protected areas awaiting designation as national marine parks.

The island economy is based mostly on fishing and shrimp and lobster catching. Many islanders also work as merchant seafarers. All the island settlements hug the sea, and the culture is as much oriented toward the sea as toward land. Nowadays, tourism is becoming an ever more important facet of the island economy.

History

Ruins on all three of the Bay Islands indicate that they were inhabited well before the Europeans arrived. Apparently human habitation began around 600 AD, though evidence is slim until after around 1000 AD. The early settlers might have been Maya; there are also caves that may have provided shelter for groups of Pech (Paya) Indians. There also seems to have been a Nahuatl-speaking people here (Nahuatl was the language of the Aztecs in Mexico).

Christopher Columbus, on his fourth and final voyage to the New World, landed on the island of Guanaja on July 30, 1502. He encountered a fairly large population of Indians, whom he believed to be cannibals. The Spanish enslaved the islanders and sent them to work on the plantations of Cuba and in the gold and silver mines of Mexico. By 1528 the islands were completely depopulated.

They didn't stay empty for long, however. English, French and Dutch pirates established settlements on the islands and raided the cumbersome Spanish cargo vessels laden with gold and other treasures from the New World. The English buccaneer Henry Morgan established his base at Port Royal on Roatán in the mid-17th century; at that time as many as 5000 pirates were ensconced on the island.

In March 1782, after many vain attempts, the Spanish waged a successful land attack against Port Royal, killing most of the pirates and selling the rest off as slaves. Then once again, the islands were left uninhabited – once again not for long.

In 1795 a Garífuna uprising on the Caribbean island of St Vincent was quickly quelled by British troops. The survivors were rounded up, and those that didn't die of fever were shipped by the British to Roatán; some 3000 were dumped at Port Royal on April 12, 1797. From Roatán the Garífuna migrated to the mainland, eventually setting up small fishing and agricultural villages along the coast all the way from Belize to Nicaragua but mostly along the north coast of Honduras. There is still one settlement of Garífuna people at Punta Gorda on Roatán.

The Bay Islands, along with the large Mosquitia territory in northeastern Honduras, remained in the hands of the British until 1859, when Great Britain signed a treaty ceding the Bay Islands and the Mosquitia to Honduras. Only in the last few decades, however, when the Honduran school system decided that Spanish must be spoken in all the country's schools, did the islanders begin to speak Spanish. English, spoken with a broad Caribbean accent, remains the preferred language of the islanders.

The orientation of the islands is still, in many ways, more toward England and the USA than toward the Honduran mainland just 50 km away; many islanders are more likely to have visited the USA than their own capital, Tegucigalpa, and many have relatives in the USA.

Climate

The rainy season on the islands runs roughly from October or November to February. March and August are the hottest months; at other times the sea breezes temper the heat. Tropical storms are possible in September.

Population

The population of the Bay Islands is very diverse. The Isleñas are blacks whose heritage is African and Carib Indian, European and other groups. English is the dominant spoken language, and Spanish is a second language. On Roatán there is a Garífuna settlement at Punta Gorda,

HONDURAS

where Garífuna, English and Spanish are all spoken.

There are still some white descendants of early British settlers. You may meet people who look like they just got off the boat from England, Scotland or Ireland, though actually their ancestors came here over a century ago.

More recently, there has been a large influx of Latinos from the mainland, especially to Roatán, which attracts Hondurans looking for work because it is economically better off than the mainland. The Latino migration is changing the language on the island; you will hear much more Spanish spoken here now than even just a few years ago.

There is also a small population of foreign whites, mostly from Europe and the USA. Many of them work for the dive shops and other tourist-oriented businesses; in most dive shops you can be instructed in a variety of languages including English, Spanish, German, Italian, French and Hebrew, to name a few.

Costs

The Bay Islands are more expensive than the mainland. Guanaja tends to be the most expensive of the three islands, followed by Roatán. Food is more expensive than on the mainland, and the average accommodations are more expensive, too. Still, you can find a few cheap places to stay on Roatán, especially in West End, the most popular part of the island for tourism. Prices are cheaper in Utila, where costs are about the same as on the mainland.

Still, visiting the islands doesn't have to send you to the poorhouse. Hiking, swimming and sunning cost nothing, and if you bring your own snorkeling gear, you can enjoy the reefs just offshore without paying a cent.

Dangers & Annoyances

The islands are generally safer than the mainland, but the mosquitoes and sandflies are voracious, especially during the rainy season. You'll need plenty of repellent, which you can bring along or buy on the islands. Off, the most popular repellent on the islands, is effective against both sandflies and mosquitoes. Or you can use a mixture of coconut oil or baby oil and repellent; it must be applied copiously, so that the sandflies will get stuck in the oil and drown. The sandflies are only about the size and color of a grain of sand, but their bite is even itchier than that of the mosquitoes. If you go hiking through the jungle on the islands, you must also protect yourself against the numerous ticks.

It's very important that you take anti-malarial medication, as malaria is endemic on the islands along with the mosquitoes. Dengue fever is also carried by mosquitoes.

In the water, keep an eye out for spiny sea urchins and beware of unseen stinging critters in the marine grass. If something stings you, douse yourself with vinegar and the sting will go away. Don't touch, walk or stand on coral: It damages the reef and will probably cut or sting you, too.

When swimming or snorkeling, don't leave unattended valuables on the beach. There have been reports of thefts from West Bay in Roatán and from the airport beach in Utila.

Diving

Diving is by far the most popular tourist activity on the Bay Islands, and dive shops have proliferated in the last few years. Prices have come down, and it's now one of the cheapest places in the world to get a diving qualification. Most dive shops offer a range of options, from an introductory resort course (basic instruction plus a couple of dives) to a full PADI certification course qualifying you to dive worldwide. Though most dive shops are affiliated with PADI, SSI courses are also available and are preferred by some divers. An open-water diving certification course lasts 3½ to four days and includes two confined water and four open-water dives. Advanced courses are also available. Despite the low cost, safety and equipment standards are reasonable.

Utila is the cheapest island for diving certification courses and scuba diving in general. Though the dive shops on both Roatán and Utila have gotten together to standardize a reasonable price for their courses and dives, competition is fierce and prices can fluctuate – when one shop drops its prices, the other shops may respond in kind, igniting a price war. When comparing diving prices, check whether tax and the certificate are included. Prices listed for Roatán usually include the diving certificate; in Utila you might have to add from US$14 to US$20.

But don't make the mistake of selecting a course purely on the basis of price. Assess the experiences of other travelers, talk to the instructors and inquire about the structure of the course, the size of the class (the smaller the better) and the standard of the equipment (see sidebar on next page).

Qualified divers also have plenty of options, including fun dives, 10-dive packages, night dives, deep dives, wreck diving and customized dive charters, as well as dives to coral walls and caves. There is a great variety of fish and marine life present, and the visibility is great. The waters between Roatán and Utila are among the best places in the world to view whale sharks, which are here from approximately May to September.

Equipment for dives is provided by the dive shops. If you have your own gear, you might be able to negotiate a small discount.

Getting There & Away

Air Planes fly to all the islands from La Ceiba (most flights are less than 25 minutes); see the Getting Around section earlier in this chapter for details on domestic flights and fares. There are also daily flights connecting Roatán with San Pedro Sula and Tegucigalpa. Through these two cities, flights connect with all the other major Central American airports, the USA and other international destinations. It's quite easy to come from the USA and be in the Bay Islands in a few hours.

TACA (☎ 45-1387 on Roatán) offers direct flights between Roatán and New Orleans (Friday), Houston (Saturday) and Miami (Sunday). It also offers flights to Guatemala City, Los Angeles, Managua, Panama City and San José, all connecting through San Salvador.

Isleña (☎ 45-1833/4 on Roatán, ☎ 45-4208 on Guanaja) offers eight flights daily between Roatán and La Ceiba, and flights several times a week connect Roatán with Tegucigalpa and San Pedro Sula.

Sosa (☎ 45-1154 on Roatán, ☎ 45-3161 on Utila, ☎ 45-4359 on Guanaja) offers four flights daily between Roatán and La Ceiba. It offers three flights between La Ceiba and Utila (US$18) every day except Sunday.

Isleña and Sosa offer daily flights between La Ceiba and Guanaja (Sosa does not fly on Sunday). Sosa's flights, and some of Isleña's, go via Roatán, making it possible to fly directly between Roatán and Guanaja. Fares are US$21 between Guanaja and Roatán, US$26 between Guanaja and La Ceiba.

Caribbean Air (☎ 45-1466, 45-1933 on Roatán; ☎ 45-3260 on Utila) offers daily flights between Roatán and La Ceiba. On Saturday it has a direct flight from Roatán to Utila (US$23), returning from Utila to Roatán on Sunday. They also offer a Saturday flight between Roatán and Belize City (US$78).

Boat The MV *Tropical* offers fast, comfortable ferry service every day between Roatán and La Ceiba, and on weekdays between La Ceiba and Roatán, and La Ceiba and Utila. The trip between La Ceiba and Utila takes about an hour. See the Getting Around section at the beginning of this chapter for schedule and fares.

The MV *Starfish* (☎ 45-3197) based on Utila operates once a week between La Ceiba and Utila, carrying passengers and cargo. It sails from Utila to La Ceiba on Monday at 5:30 am, returning from La Ceiba the following day at noon. The crossing takes two or three hours and costs US$4.20. You can sleep on board on Sunday night for no additional charge. In rough weather the boat doesn't sail.

The *Utila Express* (☎ 45-3183) operates once a week between Puerto Cortés, Utila and Roatán, but not on any set schedule; you just have to walk down to the pier and

HONDURAS

How to Choose a Dive Shop & Guidelines for Safe Diving

Diving has become a big industry in the Bay Islands. On Utila it's the main activity for visitors – there's only one small town on the island but about 15 dive shops. Roatán and Guanaja also have a variety of diving businesses, ranging from small, simple outfits to luxurious dive resorts.

Because Utila is known as the cheapest place in the world to be certified as a diver, it attracts many visitors looking for a bargain. But simply finding the cheapest dive school or shop doesn't necessarily get you the best school or diving experience. In the competition to offer the cheapest prices, some dive schools may skimp in undesirable ways, such as having too high a ratio of students to instructors or divers to dive masters, or not having or properly maintaining some important equipment.

A magnificent sport, diving enables you to enter another world. But diving safety is a prime consideration that must be taken seriously. Needless deaths have resulted when safety measures were skimped on or when underwater supervision was inadequate. The majority of diving accidents involve beginners with fewer than 25 dives, and these types of accidents can often be fatal or cause permanent injury.

On our last visit to the Bay Islands, we asked several diving operators to suggest criteria for inexperienced persons choosing a dive school or diving operator. Here's what they said to look for:

- Small groups – no more than about four to six students per instructor. The more individualized the instruction, the better.
- Experienced diving instructors. Ask to see the instructor's card, and make sure it has a validation sticker for the current year. Ask how long the instructor has been teaching diving and how much experience he or she has as a dive guide or dive master. Ask how many students the instructor has personally certified. Generally, the more you know about the instructor and the more experience he or she has, the better your experience will be. You can also ask to see the instructor's dive log book – someone with 100 dives or less is still relatively new at diving, someone with 500 dives has been around for a while.

Someone with no diving experience is unlikely to know what to check for in diving equipment. Here are some tips:

- Regulators must have two mouthpieces, a depth gauge, a pressure (air supply) gauge and a hose to put air into the life jacket. A timer is also desirable.
- Buoyancy compression devices (BCDs, which resemble life jackets) should look clean and not be patched or glued.
- The tanks should have clean air. Take the black dust cover out of the silver 'yoke' on the regulator and look inside. There should be a silver or dark gray filter. If it looks oily, rusty or has white powder, do not trust the shop to have clean air. Also ask to taste and smell the air in the tanks – any oily smell or odor like car exhaust means bad air. Leave immediately – do not dive with a shop with bad air.

ask when it's going. It's a cargo boat, but it sometimes takes on passengers.

No scheduled passenger boats serve Guanaja. Cargo and fishing boats sail between Guanaja and Roatán (three hours), and between Guanaja and Puerto Castilla or Trujillo (four hours), but there is no set schedule and you might spend days waiting for a boat. You could always try to hitch with private yacht owners.

The *Osprey* sailboat based on Utila

makes a trip to Lívingston, Guatemala, twice a month or so (see Getting There & Away under Utila).

Getting Around

Both Isleña and Sosa airlines offer direct flights between Roatán and Guanaja. Caribbean Air offers direct flights between Roatán and Utila on weekends.

Rudy at Rudy's Coffee Stop in West End village on Roatán (☎ 45-1794, fax 45-

Whether looking for a dive school, or, after you're certified, a diving operator to take you on a dive, look for:
- Small groups in the water – no more than about six divers per group.
- Good, well-maintained equipment.
- Commitment to safety. Every boat should have someone on board while the divers are underwater; each boat should also have oxygen, a medical first-aid kit and a two-way radio.
- Dive sites appropriate to the level of experience of the divers. Accidents happen when inexperienced divers go too deep – the first couple dives should not exceed 40 feet, and the second couple dives should not exceed 60 feet. Inexperienced divers should not be diving on a deep wall – buoyancy is a problem for beginners, and it may take an instructor or dive master 20 to 30 feet to catch up with a sinking diver. On wall dives a dive master should be watching from behind, as well as the guide in front.

Actively monitor your own safety:
- Accept responsibility for your own safety on every dive. Always dive within the limits of your ability and training.
- Evaluate the conditions before every dive. Be sure the conditions fit your personal capabilities.
- Be familiar with and check your equipment both before and during every dive. Don't ever dive with suspicious equipment.
- Use and respect the buddy system – it saves lives.
- Do not surface if you hear a boat motor unless you are pulling yourself slowly up by the dive-boat mooring line. Many accidents have occurred when boats collided with divers who were on the surface or just underwater.
- Do not go into caves. Go through tunnels and 'swim-throughs' only with qualified personnel.
- If you feel unsure of a diving operator, don't dive with that company. Your life and health are at risk. 'When in doubt, turn about.'
- Don't ever drink or do drugs and dive. This seems like a very obvious point, but we've heard that some operators permit these activities. Don't go with one of these operators, and don't risk your life by doing this.
- If you haven't dived for a while, consider taking a refresher course before you jump into deep water. It takes about an hour and only costs around US$15. It's much better to discover that you remember all your diving skills in four feet of water than that you don't in 40.

(Thanks to Tyll Sass & Helen Sykes of West End, Roatán; JL 'Doc' Radawski of Otley Cay, French Harbour, Roatán; Bernd Birnbach on Utila, and several other Bay Islands diving operators who gave us helpful suggestions for this section.) ■

1205) offers charter boat trips to Utila whenever there are eight to 10 people wanting to go. The trip takes two hours and costs US$20 per person.

ROATÁN
Population 14,000

Roatán is the largest and most popular of the Bay Islands. It is about 50 km off the coast of Honduras from La Ceiba. About 50 km long and just two to four km wide, it is surrounded by over 100 km of living reef, making it a paradise for diving and snorkeling. Parts of Roatán, especially the West End and West Bay beaches, are as idyllic as the most tempting tourist brochure, with clear turquoise water, colorful tropical fish, powdery white sand and coconut palms.

Orientation
Coxen Hole is Roatán's main town; the airport is about a 10-minute drive east of

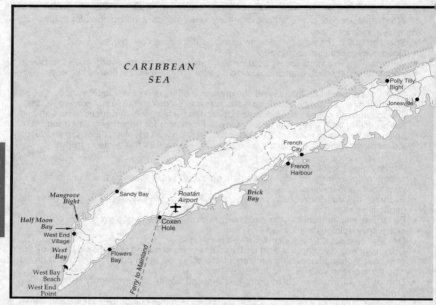

here. The best place to stay on the island is West End village, with nearby Sandy Bay a good second option.

Information

There's no tourist office on Roatán, but Coxen Hole's Casi Todo Bookstore and the office of the *Coconut Telegraph* magazine provide information about the island.

Waterloo Design & Communications (☎ 45-0017, fax 45-1289, net) in West End is another good source of information about the island.

Dangers & Annoyances

Sandflies and mosquitoes are the most annoying thing on the island. Take measures to keep yourself from being bitten and take antimalarial medication. Five types of malaria have been identified on the island, and dengue fever is present as well.

When swimming, beware of rip tides that can pull you out to sea (see Swimming

Safety in the Facts for the Visitor chapter), especially at West End.

A traveler wrote to warn that taxi drivers in Roatán can be a bit shifty: They have been known to drive off with people's gear on board or they may claim they have no change. When taking you from the airport to Coxen Hole, they may tell you the bus no longer runs to West End.

Things to See & Do

Diving, snorkeling, swimming, boating, kayaking, fishing, hiking, meeting the locals and other travelers and just lazing around on the beach are all popular activities on Roatán.

In Sandy Bay, the Institute for Marine Sciences and the Roatán Museum, both at the Anthony's Key Resort, are worth a visit, as is the Carambola Botanical Gardens.

The Sandy Bay/West End marine reserve, extending offshore from Sandy Bay all the way to the western tip of the island, is a protected reserve awaiting

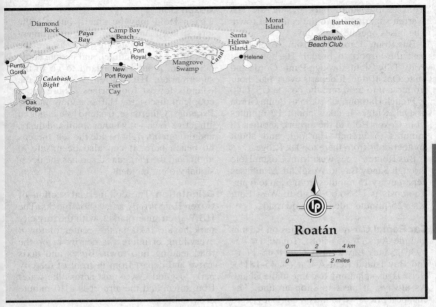

formal status as a national marine park. Diving and snorkeling are excellent here – you can snorkel just offshore from any beach along here and see some magnificent coral, sponges and marine life.

The eastern end of the island, from Punta Gorda in the north around to Port Royal in the south, including the islands of Morat, Barbareta, Santa Helena and the mangrove swamps, has been declared a national marine park. It's also good for diving and snorkeling, but it doesn't attract as many divers because it's more remote.

There are a number of very expensive resorts you can visit. Fantasy Island resort, three km beyond French Harbour, is about the most luxurious; it has a superb location, and you can partake of all kinds of water sports. Anthony's Key Resort in Sandy Bay specializes in diving, and there are others.

Averyl Muller of the Casi Todo Bookshop (☎/fax 45-1961 in Coxen Hole, ☎ 45-1255 in West End) offers island tours to out-of-the-way places not reachable by public transport. The tours take about five hours and cost US$25.

Getting There & Away
It takes only 10 minutes to fly between La Ceiba and Roatán. La Ceiba is the cheapest and fastest place from which to fly to Roatán, but there are other possibilities. Arriving by boat is also a possibility. See Getting There & Away above.

Getting Around
To/From the Airport Bus Route 1 stops at the airport. The cost is US$0.40 from the airport to Coxen Hole; a taxi costs about twice that. If you're arriving at the airport and going to the west end of the island, go to Coxen Hole (10 minutes from the airport) and catch a bus from there; a taxi from the airport to West End is much more expensive.

Bus Roatán has two bus routes, both originating in Coxen Hole. The bus stop is in front of the small park beside the HB Warren supermarket in the center of town. The buses operate every day.

Bus Route 1 goes east from Coxen Hole past the airport to French Harbour, past Polly Tilly Bight, through Punta Gorda and on to Oak Ridge. It departs every half-hour from 6 am to 5:30 pm; the cost is US$0.40 to French Harbour, US$0.85 to Punta Gorda or Oak Ridge. It takes about 10 minutes from Coxen Hole to the airport, another 20 minutes to French Harbour, and about another hour from there to Oak Ridge.

Bus Route 2 goes west from Coxen Hole through Sandy Bay to West End. Minibuses depart every 15 minutes from 6 am to 6 pm. The costs is US$0.60 to go to West End; it's a 25-minute ride on a good road.

Car Rental Car-rental agencies on Roatán include Avis (☎ 45-1568), Toyota (☎ 45-1936), Sandy Bay Rent-A-Car (☎ 45-1710) and Bay Island Rent-A-Car (☎ 45-1815). Hertz is also planning to come to the island. As always, it pays to shop around. The cheapest prices we found on our last visit to the island were US$42 per day, or US$75 for two days, with unlimited mileage.

Taxi There are plenty of taxis operating around the island. Most taxis operate as colectivos during the day and don't charge much more than buses; from Coxen Hole a colectivo to West End is US$1.65 or to French Harbour it's US$0.85. If you are the first passenger, let them know you want to go colectivo, as this is cheaper than a private ride. As everywhere in Honduras, always clarify the price of the ride before you start.

Boat The settlements on Roatán all hug the seashore, and the islanders are very much a sea-oriented people. Anywhere there are people, someone will have a boat. You can easily hire someone to take you in a motorboat almost anywhere you could want to go.

Hitchhiking Hitchhiking is easy on Roatán in the daytime. It's much more difficult to get a ride at night.

Coxen Hole

Coxen Hole may be small, but it's the largest town on Roatán. The government and shipping offices are here, as are the post office and Hondutel, and people come here from around the island to go to the supermarket, HB Warren, which has the island's lowest food prices. There are a couple of discos, the Harbour View and the Paraguas. Otherwise, Coxen Hole is not an attractive town – it's rather small and dusty, and though it's right beside the sea, there is no beach here. It can also be unsafe at night, and the Paraguas disco has the occasional violent incident.

Orientation The commercial section of Coxen Hole is only a few short blocks. The HB Warren supermarket, with the tiny city park beside it, is at the center of town; everything of interest is nearby or on the road leading into town. Buses and taxis arrive and depart from in front of the city park. Osgood Cay is just across the water from town, and the airport is a 10-minute drive to the east.

Information The post office is open Monday to Friday from 8 am to noon and 2 to 5 pm, Saturday 8 am to noon.

Hondutel is up the narrow passageway opposite the post office; it's open for domestic and international phone calls every day from 7 am to 9 pm. Fax service is available Monday to Friday, 8 am to 4 pm.

Banffaa, Banco Sogerin and Bancahsa all have offices in Coxen Hole. All change US cash dollars and traveler's checks, and Bancahsa gives cash advances on Visa cards. Credomatic, also in the center of town, gives cash advances on both Visa and MasterCard.

The Casi Todo Bookstore (☎ /fax 45-1961), on the road leading into town, carries new and used books in English (buy or trade). It's a good place to come for information about the island, or just to hang out at the ¿Qué Tal? Café, which shares the same space.

The *Coconut Telegraph* office (☎ 45-1833/4, fax 45-1826, net) is another good source of information about the island; you can also pick up a copy of the magazine. It's on the top floor of the three-story building opposite the HB Warren supermarket and Credomatic. Isleña Airlines has an office in the same building.

Places to Stay Most visitors don't stay in Coxen Hole but rather in more attractive places around the island. Still, the town does have a couple of decent hotels.

Hotel Mom (☎ 45-1139), new in 1996, has six rooms with shared bath and fan for US$8.35/12.90 for singles/doubles. Another room with air con and shared bath is US$12.50/16.65, and a room with air con and private bath is US$16.65/20.85. It's on the road leading into town, a couple of blocks from the town center. The *Hotel Cay View* (☎ 45-1202) is more expensive, with singles/doubles/triples for US$28/31/40; its restaurant/bar looks across the water to Osgood Cay.

Places to Eat The cafeteria in the *HB Warren supermarket* has low prices, a selection of meals and snacks, great ice cream and some of the best fried chicken on the island. The cafeteria and the supermarket are open Monday to Saturday from 7 am to 6 pm.

The *¿Qué Tal? Café* at the Casi Todo Bookstore, on the road leading into town a couple of blocks from the town center, has good coffee, salads, sandwiches and baked goods. Food is served Monday to Friday from around 9 am to 3:30 pm, Saturday 9 am to 2 pm.

The bar/restaurant at *Hotel El Paso* has a pleasant patio looking over the water to the palm-covered Osgood Cay nearby. The specialty of the house is the *super sopa marinera* (super seafood soup), with lobster, shrimp, crab, conch, fish and squid, for US$12.50. Other seafood dishes are around US$7 to US$12. It's open every day from around 8 am to 9:30 pm.

Several other cheap eateries are dotted around Coxen Hole. *Rolando's*, a tiny comedor located in the center of town, is recommended by locals for good, cheap typical meals.

French Harbour

French Harbour is the second-largest town on Roatán. An important port town, it's home to a large fishing, shrimp and lobster fleet.

At the entrance to the town is the *French Harbour Yacht Club* (☎ 45-1478, fax 45-1459) with a good restaurant/bar, very comfortable rooms (singles/doubles from US$38/48) and a fine view of the marina. It's a good place to ask around if you want to hitch a ride on a boat.

Other places to stay in French Harbour include the clean and comfy *Hotel Harbour View* (☎ 45-1390), which has single/double rooms for US$14.60/17.35 with fan, or US$17.85/22.25 with air con; and the simpler *Hotel & Restaurant Joee* beside the water, with rooms for US$8.35 with shared bath, or US$13.35 with private bath.

French Harbour also has several places to eat, including the *French Harbour Yacht Club, Romeo's* and *Gio's*.

Near French Harbour, *Fantasy Island* (☎ 45-1222, fax 45-1268, in USA (800) 676-2826) is probably Roatán's most luxurious resort, with diving and every amenity.

Just past French Harbour at French Cay, Sherman Arch operates an **iguana farm** that you're welcome to visit. The best time to visit is at noon during the dry season, when he feeds the iguanas; iguanas of all shapes and sizes emerge from the greenery and come running for their feeding when he calls them. Baby iguanas up to about two years old are nursed in cages until they are large enough to be released into the wild without danger.

Oak Ridge

On Roatán's eastern side is another port town, Oak Ridge, a more attractive town than French Harbour or Coxen Hole. With old-fashioned wooden houses nestled around the sea, it looks like it could be on Cape Cod as easily as on the Caribbean. The tiny town consists of the port facilities and lots of colorful boats, a long row of wooden houses stretching in an arc around a point of land and a town on a small cay just a two-minute motorboat ride from shore.

Water Taxi Tours Water taxis take passengers across to the cay for about US$0.40; they dock in front of the bus stop. Oak Ridge is the end of the line for buses coming east from Coxen Hole.

In Oak Ridge you can hire a water taxi to take you on a pleasant tour through mangrove canals to Jonesville, a small town on a nearby bight. There's no public transport serving Jonesville, so don't get off there – just return to Oak Ridge. A one-hour boat tour will cost around US$10 for up to four people, or US$15 for up to eight people.

Places to Stay & Eat There are several small, simple places to stay in Oak Ridge, both on land and on the cay. From the bus stop, walk a couple of blocks toward the sea and you'll come to a small sign saying 'Hotel.' This is the home of Joy Gough and Sally Kirkconnell (☎ 45-2291), who have two clean and pleasant *rooms* right over the water, each with private bath, for US$7.50/10.40 for one/two people. A bit farther along, Miss Alice has *rooms* usually full with long-term renters, but she would probably rent short-term if there was a vacancy.

Keep walking a little farther along toward the sea to *BJ's Backyard*, a pleasant restaurant/bar where you can eat, hang out and ask information about the town and the area. Several other places to eat are also along this footpath.

Across the water from town, *Hotel Blue Bayou* (☎ 45-2161) is another simple place, but it's more expensive; rooms with shared/private bath go for US$17/21.

On the cay, the *Reef House Resort* (☎ 45-2142, 45-2297) is an expensive place to stay, but you can spend the day at the restaurant/bar on a terrace right over the water and snorkel just offshore – there's a shallow reef here and the Reef House Wall, a good spot for diving. You can rent snorkeling gear from the resort's dive shop or bring your own; ask them about diving.

Near the Reef House, *Hotel San José* (☎ /fax 45-2328) is a simple hotel with six rooms for US$15/20 with shared/private bath. Also nearby, Redell Foutz (☎ 45-

2271) rents out a *two-bedroom house* for US$20 per night, but the price is probably going to rise. Teresa Cooper also rents a *house* on the cay, as does Romelia Dilbert.

West End

On the west end of the island, on a turquoise bay laced with coconut palms, West End is a small but exceptionally lovely village. It's probably the most beautiful part of the island.

West End is the area to which most backpacking travelers flock. Unfortunately, cheap accommodations are very limited, and most places are now geared to tourists with more money to spend.

If you're in West End, be sure to also check out Sandy Bay, a long walk but only a short bus ride away.

Information The Casi Todo Bookshop (☎ /fax 45-1255) is a good spot to come for a book or for information about the island. It's on the main road in West End near the turnoff for the road going to Coxen Hole.

Waterloo Design & Communications (☎ 45-0017, fax 45-1289, net) is another good source of information about the island. Their Web page offers information about all of the Bay Islands. They also have a public email service where you can send or receive messages for US$2 each.

In the same building, Southern Exposure offers underwater camera rentals, underwater and on-land photography, film sales and developing.

Telephone and fax service is available at Rudy's Coffee Stop (see Places to Eat) and at the Super Tienda Chris, next to the Baptist church. Cheaper fax service is available at Hondutel in Coxen Hole.

Beaches & Hikes The beach at West Bay, about four km south of West End village, is reputed to be the most beautiful on Roatán. It's a lovely 40-minute stroll down the beach from West End (bring repellent for the sandflies), or you can take a motorboat from Foster's Inn restaurant for US$0.85 each way – it operates every 15 minutes or so, 9 am to 9 pm, and the trip takes about

10 minutes. The beach is fringed by palm trees, houses and cabins, and there are a couple of restaurants. There's good snorkeling and diving at West Bay; the reef here is protected.

You can hike across the island from West End to Flowers Bay; it's about a three-km walk. When you reach the ridge, you can look out over both sides of the island. A loop from West End to Flowers Bay, then south almost to the tip of the island, over the ridge to West Bay and back up the beach to West End makes a good five- or six-hour hike. The Flowers Bay side of the island on this walk looks quite different from the West Bay side. Be sure to bring fresh water and adequate repellent against the numerous ticks.

There are other trails to some Maya ruins on this end of the island. Jimmy Miller (see Jimmy's Lodge under Places to Stay) sometimes takes people on trips into the jungle. Carambola Botanic Gardens, nearby in Sandy Bay, is another place with hiking and nature trails.

Snorkeling There's good snorkeling just offshore at West End. Stop by Ocean Divers for a map of the reef. It's protected all the way from Sandy Bay to the western tip of the island. The Blue Channel, directly off the small pier in front of Jimmy's Lodge, is an especially beautiful spot, and there are many others. Half Moon Bay is another beautiful spot. Snorkeling gear can be rented from the dive shops for around US$5 per day.

Diving West End has several dive shops offering a variety of dives and courses. The

HONDURAS

Don't Touch the Coral!

Coral comes in many shapes, sizes and colors, especially here in the Bay Islands. Some coral, such as fan coral, resembles a plant. Other coral, such as brain coral, looks more like a rock.

Coral is neither a plant nor a rock, however. It is an animal.

'Don't touch the coral' is a refrain you will often hear in the Bay Islands, where thousands of inexperienced divers and snorkelers come every year to explore the magnificent reefs just a few yards offshore.

Coral is so fascinating and beautiful that it tempts you to touch it, especially if you're seeing it for the first time. If you resist the temptation, you might accidentally bump against it with a fin as you swim past. If you're learning to dive, you might accidentally rub up against it as you struggle to maintain neutral buoyancy.

But avoiding such contact is really extremely important. You can kill the coral just by touching it. A huge mass of coral can be killed by only one diver touching it in one spot.

Coral has an invisible covering of slime that protects it, much the same way that our outer layer of skin protects us. If you touch the coral, you make a lesion in the animal's protective covering, exposing it to infection and disease. Humans can die as result of only one cut; the same is true of the coral.

The coral ecosystem is very fragile. Coral grows at only about one centimeter (less than half an inch) per year under ideal conditions; the fastest growing sponges grow at about one inch per year. The coral and sponge formations you see here in the Bay Islands are the result of centuries of growth.

Only recently have the islands been inundated with divers and snorkelers, many of them first-timers. If every diver and snorkeler touched the coral only once, the delicate reef and the abundance of life it supports could soon be destroyed.

Another good reason not to touch the coral is that it will sting you. Fire coral is the most famous for this – you'll feel like you're on fire if you touch this coral. But many types of coral sting – especially corals that are a rich mustard color.

If you are stung by coral, use vinegar on it and the stinging will stop. The coral, however, has nothing it can apply for the injury you've inflicted.

So enjoy the reef – but be sure that you don't touch the coral! ∎

dive shops usually stick to small groups and offer friendly, relaxed, personalized instruction in several languages (see Diving sidebar above). Prices are pretty standard among the shops. A four-day PADI Open Water diver certification course costs around US$175 to US$195; one-day resort courses are US$50 to US$60; and a one-hour diving refresher course is US$15. A variety of more advanced courses are also available. Fun dives for those already certified cost US$25 or US$100 for a five-dive package.

Among the dive shops in the center of West End village is Ocean Divers (☎ /fax 45-1005, net), which offers diving and accommodations packages at their hotel, the Sunset Inn. Tyll's Dive Shop (☎ /fax 45-0020) is a long-established shop that can also help you arrange accommodations. West End Divers (☎ /fax 45-1531) is another centrally located shop. The Seagrape Plantation Dive Center (☎ /fax 45-1717, 45-1428) is on the far end of West End village beyond the road to Coxen Hole; diving and accommodations packages are available at the Seagrape Plantation.

Sea Kayaking Sea Blades, based at the Casi Todo Bookshop (☎ /fax 45-1255), offers guided sea-kayak trips for a minimum of two people for US$30/45 for a half/full-day trip. Or you can rent a kayak, including instruction and all gear, for US$12/20 for a half/full day. They also run longer guided trips to the east side of the island.

Ocean Divers (see Diving) offers kayak and snorkeling packages, which include all equipment. The price for one person is US$4/11/20 per hour/half day/full day; for two people in a double kayak it costs US$7/18/30.

Kayaks can also be rented from the Foster's Inn restaurant for US$3/7/10 per hour/half day/full day.

Other Activities Far Tortuga Charters, also based at the Casi Todo Bookshop (☎ /fax 45-1255), is a trimaran sailboat operating from Half Moon Bay. It offers half- and full-day snorkeling/sailing trips for US$25/45, with all gear included. Extended trips to the Cayos Cochinos, Barbareta, Santa Helena and other islands can be arranged.

Belvedere's Water Sports Lodge (see Places to Stay; ☎ 45-1171) offers a one-hour glass-bottom-boat tour every day at 10 am and noon. Snorkeling gear is provided. Their sailing yacht, the *Surfbird*, does sunset sails and cocktail cruises by reservation. The *Maid'en Desert* (☎ /fax 45-1620) also offers sailing trips and diving.

Jimmy's Lodge and Keiffito's Plantation Retreat (see Places to Stay) rent horses for beach rides or inland tours of the island. Talk to Jimmy's brother Forest Miller (☎ 45-1335) about deep-sea fishing trips.

The Jungle Gym at the Bamboo Hut has a weights room open to the public.

Places to Stay – West End Whatever type or standard of accommodations you're looking for, you can find it in West End. This is the part of the island to which most tourists flock. Even though there are so many places to stay, they can still fill up, especially during the busy tourist seasons during July-August and from mid-December to Easter. At these times, it might be wise to book ahead to get the place you want.

The cheapest place to stay in West End is *Jimmy's Lodge*, right on the beach on the far (south) end of town. Upstairs is a dormitory with mattresses on the floor, covered by mosquito netting, for US$2 each; downstairs are rooms for US$7. It's friendly and sociable but extremely basic, with just one outside shower and no electricity. It's operated by Jimmy Miller, who has been a friend to budget travelers for many years.

Sam's Lodge, operated by Jimmy's older brother, is a few houses inland from Jimmy's Lodge at the corner of the footpath. It's another very basic place. The Millers's sister Zoey (☎ 45-1335) rents out two simple rooms with shared bath behind the Church of God for US$10 each; Zoey is in the house just behind.

Valerie's beside Tyll's Dive Shop has two six-bed dorm rooms for US$5 a bunk, plus three rooms at US$15 for one or two people (they can sleep three or four); you can do your own cooking here in the outdoor kitchens.

Inland from Yoly's restaurant, the *Kenny Inn* has three rooms sharing one bathroom, in the downstairs part of the family home, for US$10; they also allow camping on the lawn for US$2 per tent.

The *Bamboo Hut* has three rooms out in the garden behind the Bamboo Hut restaurant/bar, all sharing one bathroom, for US$10/15 single/double.

The *Hotel Suárez*, in the green house behind Southwind Properties, has four rooms with shared bath for US$15.

Robert's Hill Hotel (☎ 45-1176), opposite the Foster's Inn restaurant, has pleasant, simple rooms, each with private bath and fan, for US$20.

Anderson's Place (☎ 45-1171) has several small oceanside cabins. Each has two rooms sharing one bathroom and a pleasant porch. These are some of the coolest rooms in West End, built with good insulation – you'll appreciate this if you're here in hot weather. They cost US$20 per room. One cabin with private bath is US$30.

Behind Anderson's Place, *Belvedere's Water Sports Lodge* (☎ 45-1171) is tucked away on the slip of land between West End and Half Moon Bay, with water on both sides. There's a BBQ, picnic tables and coolers, and an Italian restaurant in the evening. The rooms each have two double beds, private hot bath (solar heating), fan and a porch with hammock; they cost US$35 per night in high season, with discounts in low season or for weekly stays.

The *Sunset Inn* (☎ /fax 45-1005) has 19 rooms, ranging from US$21.40 for rooms with fan and shared cold bath up to US$48.15 for an apartment with kitchen for up to six people. Ocean Divers is in the same building; dive and accommodations packages come out cheaper than getting them both separately.

Ask at Tyll's Dive Shop (☎ /fax 45-0020) about some attractive *apartments* a short walk uphill; each has a kitchen and hot water, and costs around US$25 or US$30 per night. Also ask them about backpacker accommodations.

Up on a hill, the *Hillside Garden Cabins* (☎ /fax 45-0505), a two-minute walk from the beach road, has seven cabins for US$30/40/50 for singles/doubles/triples. It's quiet and peaceful up there, and it catches any breezes that come by; it also has a secluded area with trees and many hammocks.

Georphi's Tropical Hideaway (☎ 45-1794, fax 45-1205) behind Rudy's Coffee Stop has a variety of attractive cabins stretching up the hill. The simplest accommodations are US$5 per bunk in a cabin holding six or seven people, or US$10 each for a minimum of three people in a cabin holding six people. They also have a two-bedroom cabin for US$45 (US$60 with air con) and a bungalow with kitchen for US$50 sleeping up to four people. These are low-season prices; in high season the prices go up.

Foster's Inn (☎ 45-1008, 45-1124) has bungalows opposite its restaurant for US$43 and US$53, each with two double beds, fan, private bath, a small fridge and a porch.

About a 10-minute walk south along the beach past Jimmy's Lodge, *Keiffito's Plantation Retreat* (☎ 45-1252) is in a quiet location, away from town. Cabins here are US$20, or US$30 with a stove and two beds; also here are a restaurant/bar, hiking trails, and horses for rent.

Places to Stay – Half Moon Bay & Mangrove Bight

Just a short walk from West End village, beyond the road leading to Coxen Hole, Half Moon Bay is a beautiful little bay with fewer tourists. Just past Half Moon Bay is Mangrove Bight. There are places to stay on Half Moon Bay, and on the land jutting out between Half Moon Bay and Mangrove Bight.

In Half Moon Bay, the *Half Moon Bay Cabins* (☎ /fax 45-1075) has duplex cabins for US$30/45/55/65 for one/two/three/four people with fan, or US$45/60/75/90 with air con. They provide free snorkeling gear, kayaks and paddle boats; offer snorkeling classes for children; and have an excellent waterside restaurant/bar. Dive/accommodations packages are also available.

Also on Half Moon Bay, at the junction between the West End village road and the road to Coxen Hole, the *Coconut Tree Restaurant & Cabins* (☎ 45-1648) has cabins, most with kitchen, for US$35 to US$40 for singles, US$50 to US$60 for doubles. The cabins have one, two or three bedrooms.

Walk a little farther beyond Half Moon Bay to Mangrove Bight and you'll find three more places to stay, all with ample grounds. This is a peaceful, quiet, family area – just a short walk from the tourist-oriented businesses at West End but without as many people around.

On Mangrove Bight, *Burke's Place* (☎ 45-1252) has a variety of duplex cabins with private bath and kitchen for US$20 to US$25. One larger cabin sleeping four people is US$35, and a small one for one person is US$15. Nearby, *Casa Calico* (fax 45-1171) has three ample, attractive upstairs rooms with kitchen, front and back porch, and private bath for US$50 for one or two people; each one can sleep four. They also have two rooms with shared bath for US$25 each.

The *Seagrape Plantation Resort* (☎ /fax 45-1717, 45-1428) on Mangrove Bight is more expensive. Dive/accommodations packages are US$344 for four nights, US$599 for a week, including three meals and three boat dives every day, a night dive and unlimited shore diving.

Places to Stay – West Bay Beach Cabins on West Bay Beach tend to be more expensive than those in West End village. *Foster's Inn* (☎ 45-1008, 45-1124) in West End village has cabins here for US$85, each with three double beds, private bath, kitchen and a big porch. The *Coconut Tree* (☎ 45-1648) in West End also has cabins here for US$75. *Cabana Roatana* (☎ /fax 45-1271) has well-equipped cabins with kitchen, right on the beach, priced from US$60 to US$80 most of the year, US$75 to US$95 during high season from mid-December to Easter.

Places to Eat Food in West End tends to be expensive – count on spending a minimum of around US$2 for breakfast, and US$4 to US$8 each for lunch and dinner, possibly more. If you stay at a place where you can do your own cooking, you'll save money on food, especially if you go into Coxen Hole to shop at the supermarket or bring your own food from the mainland.

Rudy's Coffee Stop is the place to come for breakfast. Good banana pancakes ('the best in the world,' Rudy exclaims modestly) cost US$1.25; the coffee is decent here, too. Lunch and dinner are also served, and it's a pleasant place to hang out, with tables spaced around a shady garden.

Cindy's Place makes typical island food, and it's not expensive. Up the hill, *Stanley's* also serves island food. The *Sea View Restaurant* serves the usual selection of local foods including chicken, fish and lobster; it's especially popular in the evening, when they set up a TV on the terrace and show movies in English. The *Bamboo Hut* serves food in the evening and shows nightly movies; the bar here is popular, too.

The *Blue Mango* serves a variety of seafood, meat and vegetarian foods, and it has a bar with live music and dance parties several nights a week. Check the blackboard out front for the entertainment schedule.

Pinocchio, a short walk up the hill from the village road, serves delicious Italian and other European foods prepared by a European chef. It's a little more elegant than most of the places in town, though the prices are the same. The *Lo Sfizio* pizzeria/restaurant also serves Italian food. Another Italian restaurant is at *Belvedere's Water Sports Lodge* behind Anderson's Place and the Super Tienda Chris.

Foster's Inn, built on stilts out over the water, is pleasant in the evening, with a magnificent view of the sunset and the starry sky.

HONDURAS

In Half Moon Bay, check out the waterfront restaurant/bar of the *Half Moon Bay Cabins*.

The restaurant at *Keiffito's Plantation Resort*, about a 10-minute walk along the beach from West End (see Places to Stay) is also worth investigating. Along the way, the *Cool Lizard*, on the beach just a short walk south of town, is operated by Germans. A couple more restaurants are down the beach at West Bay.

Entertainment You'll find live music and dancing at the *Blue Mango* and *Foster's Inn* (see Places to Eat); the bars at both of these places are popular hangouts in the evening even when there is no music on. The *Bamboo Hut* shows movies in English on a big screen nightly at 7:30 pm; their bar is also a popular hangout. The *Sea View Restaurant* shows TV movies on the terrace in the evening.

Sandy Bay
About four km before you reach West End is Sandy Bay, another lovely little town on the sea. It's not as developed as West End, and it doesn't have a town center – it's just a long settlement along several kilometers of beach and between the beach and the main road. The beach here is not as good as the one at West End or West Bay, and it's a little shallow for swimming.

However, the Sandy Bay community passed an ordinance many years ago protecting its reef as a nature reserve, so it's an excellent place to snorkel, offering lots of marine life. In more recent years, the reserve has been extended all the way past West End village and West Bay beach to the western tip of the island.

There's a nature trail on Bailey's Cay, opposite Anthony's Key Resort, which has good snorkeling. Across the road from Anthony's Key Resort, the Carambola Botanical Gardens has nature trails, orchids, spices and an 'iguana wall.'

At Anthony's Key Resort, the **Institute for Marine Sciences** (☎ 45-1327, fax 45-1329) is a research and educational facility working with dolphins. There are several dolphin-training demonstrations every day, which you are welcome to attend; you can also go for a swim with the dolphins, but this is expensive. A classroom has videos and educational material about dolphins, coral reefs and other sea life. Also here is the small but interesting **Roatán Museum**, with displays on the archaeology, history, geology and wildlife of the islands and the sea. The museum is open every day except Wednesday, from 8:30 am to 5 pm; admission is US$2.

Places to Stay *Beth's Hostel* (☎ 45-1266) is on a hill overlooking Sandy Bay not far from the sea. Two single and two double rooms face onto a comfortable kitchen-dining-sitting room. Beds are US$12 per person, US$75 per week or US$250 per month from mid-November to April; from May to mid-November it's US$10 per night, or US$60 per week. Reduced rates are offered for Peace Corps or other volunteers, and snorkeling gear is available for US$5 per day. Nonsmokers only. The Baha'i Library of Roatán is also at the hostel.

The *Caribbean Seashore B&B* (☎/fax 45-1123), on the beach half a mile west of Anthony's Key Resort, offers five rooms in a two-story house for US$30/35 for singles/doubles. There's good swimming here, it's peaceful and quiet, and they serve all three meals.

Also on the beach west of Anthony's Key Resort, *Judy's Fantasea* (☎ 45-1349, 45-1209) has four rooms upstairs, sharing two bathrooms, and one room downstairs. Rooms are US$20 per day, US$100 per week or US$300 per month. There's a bar and store, and they'll prepare food if you like. On the beach but in a different part of Sandy Bay, Miss Effie (☎ 45-1233) has two *rooms* without kitchen for US$25 each, and one room with kitchen for US$30.

Near the dolphin enclosure at Anthony's Key Resort, the *Oceanside Inn* (☎ 45-1552) is beside the water, though there is no beach here. It has eight rooms, each with ceiling fan and lots of windows; the cost is US$30/45 for singles/doubles for room only, or you can arrange for room plus meals – a restaurant is also here.

Anthony's Key Resort (☎ 45-1274, fax 45-1140, in USA (800) 227-3483) is one of the major diving resorts on the island, with facilities for diving, underwater photography and so on, but it's expensive.

Places to Eat *Rick's American Cafe*, up the hill from the main road, has a fine view, good steaks and hamburgers and an international menu. Food is served every day from noon to 9:30 pm, with a happy hour from 5 to 6 pm; the bar stays open until 11:30 pm.

You can see the dolphins from the deck restaurant at *Anthony's Key Resort*, open every day except Wednesday. Nearby, the *Oceanside Inn* (see Places to Stay) also has a deck restaurant, overlooking Anthony's Key and Bailey's Key.

Other Towns & Sites
There are various other towns around Roatán, including Punta Gorda, a Garífuna village on the north shore of the island, and Polly Tilly Bight, a small settlement also on the north shore. You pass both of these on the bus runs from French Harbour to Oak Ridge, and there are a few other villages around the island's coast. At most of them you could probably ask around among the locals and come up with some accommodations.

Ben's Dive Resort (☎ /fax 45-1916) in Punta Gorda offers diving, accommodations and meals. Ben's is a good place to eat, or you might try the *Chicken Shack*. If you want to find a place to stay in Punta Gorda, you could ask Ben, or Robbie at the Chicken Shack, or Marcelino Álvarez at the store near Ben's. Near Punta Gorda, *Henry's Cove Resort* (☎ 45-2180, fax 45-2193) is another dive resort, with 14 rooms, 10 bungalows and an Olympic-size swimming pool, all up on a hill with a great view.

At Diamond Rock, Marble Hill Farms is a pleasant place to visit; there's no public transport, but if you have a rental car, you could stop here, or come on Averyl Muller's island tour (see Things to See &

Do above). At the farm they make jams and jellies from exotic ingredients, batik T-shirts and wall hangings, and there's a beautiful tropical garden with labeled plants and many hummingbirds.

At Paya Bay there's a restaurant up on a hill, with a great view of Barbareta Island and Guanaja off in the distance. Alligator Nose Beach is also here. The *Paya Bay Resort* (☎ /fax 45-2139) is the place to find accommodations.

Just past Paya Bay, Camp Bay Beach is a beautiful white-sand beach. There are no businesses here, so bring your own food and drink.

The small island of Santa Helena, on the east end of Roatán, is a beautiful place with good diving. You can eat well and cheaply in Santa Helena town, and there are almost always some houses for rent.

Barbareta Island
Off the eastern tip of Roatán, Barbareta Island is a privately owned 1200-acre island that has been a wildlife refuge for many years. It has plenty of wildlife, beautiful white-sand beaches, rain-forest hiking trails, a Pech (Paya) archaeological site and pristine reefs. Diving, snorkeling, fishing, sailing, windsurfing, kayaking, mountain biking, horseback riding and hiking are all popular activities on the island.

The *Barbareta Beach Club* (fax 42-2629) is the only place to stay on the island. Contact the club through the Casi Todo Bookshop in Coxen Hole (☎ /fax 45-1961). It has a variety of accommodations, including lodge rooms for US$35/40, beach bungalows for US$40/45 and efficiency units with kitchen for US$45/50. Food is good but expensive on the island (US$50 for three meals per day), so you can save by bringing your own food. You must make a reservation prior to arrival.

There's no regularly scheduled transport to the island. You can hire a boat from Oak Ridge, a two-hour trip; from Punta Gorda the trip takes about 45 minutes; it's even less from Camp Bay, which is closer. A boat from Oak Ridge costs around US$60 for the trip – expensive for just a couple of people but not so bad for a group, as the boats can hold around eight. The folks at the Casi Todo Bookshop can probably help you get a group together to share the boat trip.

Another option for visiting Barbareta is to come with a sea-kayak tour. Sea Blades, based in West End village, organizes trips to the island.

UTILA
Population 2000

Utila is a welcoming place where the locals always have time to shout a friendly greeting. The pace of life on the island is very slow. Most visitors come here to dive. It's the cheapest of the three Bay Islands to visit; the big spenders go to Roatán or Guanaja.

Utila is a small island, about 13 km long and five km wide, with several tiny cays on the south side. The closest island to La Ceiba, just 32 km away, Utila is practically flat, with only one small hill. The population lives almost entirely in one settlement on a curving bay; another small settlement is on a cay about a 20-minute boat ride away.

Be sure to bring plenty of insect repellent, especially if you come during the rainy season. The mosquitoes and sandflies on the island are voracious.

Orientation
There's only one town on Utila, and it has only one main road. At one end of the main road is the airport, just a few hundred meters from the 'center' of town. Along this road are houses, places to stay, restaurants, bars, small food shops, a disco and two banks.

The public dock, where the MV *Tropical* ferry arrives and departs, meets the main road at the intersection of Cola de Mico Rd, which heads inland. A couple of blocks up this road are the Bucket of Blood Bar and several other places to stay and eat.

At the foot of the dock, Captain Morgan's Dive Centre passes out free town maps, and they'll let you leave your pack or luggage there while you go to look for a place to stay.

The main road leads along the shore all the way to Oyster Bed Lagoon, also called Lower Lagoon, about a 20-minute walk west of the dock. This part of the road, called Sandy Bay Rd, has several more places to stay and eat along it. Henderson's Supermarket, the island's main supermarket, and Hondutel are also along here. The post office is at the foot of the public dock.

The Bay Islands Conservation Association (BICA), on the main road, sells a good map of the island, showing the surrounding reefs and dive spots, for US$0.65. Also pick up a copy of their free brochure, *Utila's Reef and You*. This organization works hard to protect the island's reefs, and it's good to give them your support.

Information
Immigration There's an immigration office on Sandy Bay Rd.

Money Banco Atlántida and Bancahsa are the two banks on Utila. Bancahsa changes traveler's checks and gives cash advances on Visa cards. Banco Atlántida does not change traveler's checks, but they, too, give cash advances on Visa cards. Henderson's Supermarket changes traveler's checks, usually for a better rate than the bank.

Post & Communications The post office is at the foot of the public dock. Hondutel, on Sandy Bay Rd, is open for domestic and international telephone and fax service Monday to Friday from 7 am to 5 pm, Saturday 7 to 11 am. Electricity on the island shuts off between midnight and 5 am, so you cannot receive a fax at this time.

Media The *Utila Times* comes out every two months with news and interesting features about the island. You can buy it at the Green House Book Exchange in Utila or at Hotel Colonial in La Ceiba.

Bookstore The Green House Book Exchange has a fine selection of books in English and other languages and runs a good cafe.

HONDURAS

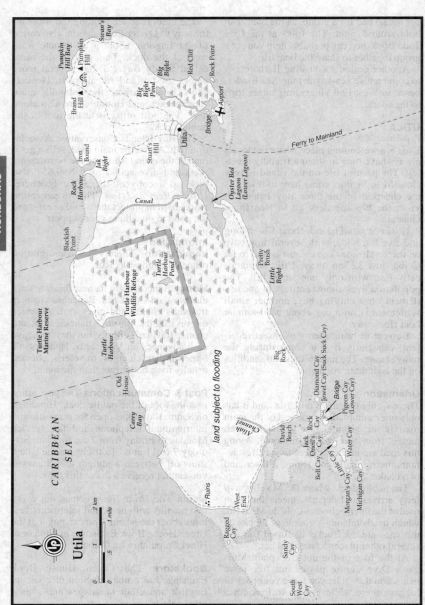

CARIBBEAN
SEA

Utila

Turtle Harbour
Marine Reserve

Turtle Harbour
Wildlife Refuge

Turtle Harbour
Pond

Blackish
Point

Rock
Harbour

Jak
Bight

Iron
Bound

Brand
Hill

Cave

Pumpkin
Hill Bay

Stuart's
Bay

Pumpkin
Hill

Big
Bight
Pond

Big
Bight

Red Cliff

Rock Point

Airport

Bridge

Utila

Ferry to Mainland

Stuart's
Hill

Canal

Oyster Bed
Lagoon
(Lower Lagoon)

Pretty
Brush

Little
Bight

Big
Rock

Diamond Cay

Jewel Cay (Suck Suck Cay)

Bridge

Pigeon Cay
(Lower Cay)

Water Cay

Bell Cay

Jack
Rock

Onel's
Cay

Little Cay

Morgan's Little Cay

Michigan Cay

Ahh
Channel

David
Beach

Carrey Bay

Old
House

land subject to flooding

Ruins

West
End

Ragged
Cay

Sandy
Cay

South
West
Cay

0   1   2 km
0   .5   1 mile

Medical Services The Utila Community Clinic on Sandy Bay Rd is a good clinic run by an American doctor; travelers have written us letters to praise and recommend the clinic. It's open Monday to Friday, 8 am to noon.

Dangers & Annoyances Electricity shuts off in Utila from midnight to 5 am.

Utila's sandflies and mosquitoes are a force to be reckoned with. They are worse during the rainy season than at other times of year. Off, a repellent sold at Henderson's Supermarket, keeps away both sandflies and mosquitoes; mosquito coils are also sold there. You might want to bring some repellent of your own, so you don't get bitten before you can reach the supermarket. Be sure to take a regimen of antimalarial medication.

The Cays
A visit to Utila is incomplete without making a trip to the cays on the southwest side of the island. Attractions of the cays include beautiful beaches, sunsets, fantastic snorkeling, and on Diamond Cay, diving, a daily seafood BBQ and economical accommodations. Another attraction is that the cays have no mosquitoes or sandflies!

Water Cay is a beautiful little island with great snorkeling. The island is uninhabited, but there's a caretaker who keeps it clean and charges US$1.25 per visitor for the upkeep of the island.

Pigeon Cay is completely covered by a village; it's actually two tiny cays, connected by a bridge, with an even smaller little cay off to one side. There's a bungalow where you can stay for US$5 per person or US$4.20 per room; the village also has shops and small restaurants.

On Sandy Cay, a very small cay, you can rent a house that holds five or six people for US$75 per day. Ask about it on Pigeon Cay – the owner lives there.

On Diamond Cay, the Utila Cays Dive Shop offers accommodations, diving, snorkeling gear (US$2.50 per day) and water-taxi service to other cays; contact them through the Green House Book Exchange.

Bungalows with shared bath are US$5 per person, or you can stay in tents or hammocks for US$2.50 per person. (If you bring along your own tent or hammock, it's US$1.25 per person.) Breakfast (US$1.70) and a seafood BBQ dinner (US$2.50) are available. They also offer various special events such as full-moon parties, night diving and other events.

There are several ways of getting to the cays. A snorkeling trip departs every morning from the Green House Book Exchange when at least four people want to go; it costs US$2.50 each way for transport only or US$6.25 with snorkeling gear included.

The Utila Cays Dive Shop makes one roundtrip each day from Diamond Cay to Utila; you can catch a ride with them to Diamond Cay at 1 pm from the Green House Book Exchange. However, since they only make one trip a day, you'll have to stay overnight if you go with them. They charge US$2.50 each way for transport to/from the cays (if you go diving with them, the ride is free).

The Red Diamond water taxi goes from Gunter's Dive Shop to Water Cay; a ride costs US$10 per boatload for one to four people, or US$2.50 per person if there are more people.

Tropical Travel offers trips to Water Cay for US$25 for one to six people, US$4.20 each for more than six people. Cap't Roy's Bahía del Mar Restaurant also does trips to the cays. Or you can ask around and hire a dory to take you out there.

Other Attractions
Most of Utila's coast is rocky, but there's a sandy beach on Pumpkin Hill Bay about a three-km walk across the island from town. Nearby, Pumpkin Hill has some caves; one is supposed to have been a hideout for the pirate Henry Morgan.

Gunter's Driftwood Gallery (☎ 45-3113) is a couple of blocks inland, off Cola de Mico Rd; turn left after you pass the Monkey Tail Inn and walk past Tony's Place; you'll see the sign on your right. Gunter displays his artwork here, and there's a small museum. He also offers tours to remote places around the island, including a stalactite cave and Indian sites.

Shelby McNab (☎ 45-3223) is a good source of stories and history of Utila; he sometimes offers guided tours of historical places.

Durell Cooper offers dory trips to Rock Harbour via the mangrove canal and to other places. He also offers guided hikes on the nature trail leading to Turtle Harbour Marine Reserve & Wildlife Refuge. He stops at mangrove lagoons, caves, Indian burial grounds, tropical vegetation and birds. Contact him at the Seven Seas restaurant.

Ask at Cap't Roy's Bahía del Mar Restaurant about glass-bottom-boat trips and fishing trips. Windsurfing equipment may also be available on the island; just ask around.

Diving

Diving is Utila's biggest industry. The island is said to be the cheapest place in the world to learn to dive, and it attracts backpackers and budget travelers from everywhere. The warm Caribbean waters are crystal clear, and the tropical fishes, corals, sponges and other marine life are abundant and colorful.

There are many excellent diving spots around Utila and many diving operators to help you explore them – at last count there were 15 dive shops on the island. Most start a course just about every day of the week, and all offer instruction in a number of languages.

PADI open-water dive courses take 3½ days and cost around US$129 to US$149. A complete spectrum of more advanced courses is also available. Fun dives cost around US$25 for two dives or US$100 for a 10-dive package; special trips such as night dives and deep dives are also offered. Many operators offer discounts on accommodations when you dive with them or throw in a couple of extra dives. Always ask if the certificate costs extra.

However, don't let your desire to find the cheapest price outweigh your need for safety, especially if you are a beginner.

Because the diving situation on Utila is so competitive, some dive shops skimp in undesirable ways – whether by not having or properly maintaining all their safety equipment or by having too many divers per instructor. Take this seriously: Any accident or mishap while diving is potentially fatal, and deaths occur every year. You will do better to choose a dive shop on the basis of safety rather than price, and see the sidebar How to Choose a Dive Shop above for more information on this.

Dive shops in Utila include Gunter's Dive Shop (☎ /fax 45-3350), the Utila Watersports Center (☎ /fax 45-3239), the Utila Dive Center (☎ 45-3326, fax 45-3327), Captain Morgan's Dive Centre (☎ /fax 45-3161), the Cross Creek Dive Center (☎ 45-3134, fax 45-3334), Paradise Divers (☎ 45-3148, fax 45-3348), Underwater Vision (☎ 45-3195, fax 45-3103), and Reef Adventures (☎ 45-3254), and there are plenty of others. The Utila Cays Dive Shop is on Diamond Cay; contact them at the Green House Book Exchange.

Snorkeling

There's excellent snorkeling on the reef by the airport. The easiest approach to the coral is from the east end of the runway. There's also great snorkeling on the south side of Water Cay, about a half-hour boat ride from town.

Another fine snorkeling spot is at the point of land beside Oyster Bed Lagoon, in front of the Hotel & Restaurant Blue Bayou, a pleasant 20-minute walk west of town on a dirt road running beside the sea. The Blue Bayou charges US$1 for use of its hammocks, beach and dock and rents snorkeling gear for US$1.35 per hour.

The dive shops are cheaper, however. They rent snorkeling gear for about US$2.50 per day.

Kayaking & Canoeing

You can kayak to Rock Harbour by going into Oyster Bed Lagoon, and then into Lower Lagoon and along the mangrove canal. There's a good beach at Rock Harbour, and it's very private, since the only way to get there is by boat or hiking across the island. A roundtrip from town, with time at the beach, takes about four hours.

Another option is to kayak under the bridge separating town from the airport, into the lagoon and then up the channel to Big Bight Pond.

Kayaks can be rented from Gunter's Dive Shop for US$2.50 per hour, US$5.85 for four hours or US$8.35 for a day; double kayaks are double the price. Or you can rent a wooden cayuco from the Blue Bayou Restaurant at the entrance to Oyster Bed Lagoon for US$4.20 per day.

Kayaks also allow you to reach some out-of-the-way snorkeling spots.

Places to Stay

Utila has some great deals on cheap accommodations. It doesn't take long to walk around and find something that suits you. Many of the dive shops offer discounted accommodations if you take a diving course with them.

Remember that the electricity on the island goes off between midnight and 5 am. This means that if you're using a fan to keep away the mosquitoes, you're a sitting duck as soon as the power goes off. Many hotels operate their own power systems to provide 24-hour power; ask about this when you choose a place to stay. Also look for good screens on the windows.

Though there are so many places to stay, it can still be hard to get a good room during the busy tourist seasons (July to August and mid-December to Easter). Reservations are advisable at these times.

Main Road Several good places to stay are along the main road between the public dock and the airport.

Trudy's (☎ 45-3195, fax 45-3103) is a longtime favorite; it has power and water 24 hours, screens on the windows, a waterside terrace and friendly management. Singles/doubles are US$5/8 with shared bath, or US$10/15 with private bath. Across the street, *Hotel Laguna del Mar* is run by the same people. The Underwater Vision Dive Shop is also here.

Rubi's Hotel (☎ 45-3240) is a clean, simple little place that has a kitchen where you can cook your own meals; singles/doubles are US$3.75/6.25, all with shared bath. *Hotel Celena* (☎ 45-3228) is a clean, pleasant place with rooms with private bath for US$5/7. *Cooper's Inn* (☎ 45-3184) has rooms for US$4.60; under the house, Delany's Island Kitchen specializes in pizza and lasagne.

The *Utila Reef House* (☎ 45-3254) has rooms with screens, 24-hour power and shared bath for US$6.25; the Reef Bar & Grill on the back deck overlooking the sea is a popular hangout in the evening, and the Reef Adventures Diving School is also here.

Sandy Bay Rd More good places to stay are on Sandy Bay Rd, the main route heading west from the public dock.

The *Bayview Hotel* (☎ 45-3114) is an attractive place right on the water with a private dock and swimming area, hammocks, pleasant porches and 24-hour power and water. The rooms have good screens and good ventilation; windows are on both sides to catch the sea breezes. Rooms cost US$10 with shared bath (two rooms to one bath), US$12 with private bath, or US$15 for larger rooms with two double beds and private bath.

The *Hotel & Restaurant Sea Side Inn* (☎ 45-3150) also has everything you need. Downstairs rooms with shared bath are US$5, upstairs rooms with private bath are US$8. *Hotel Tropical* (☎ 45-3216), on Mamey Lane Rd one door inland from Sandy Bay Rd, is a simple place; rooms with shared bath go for US$6.25. The *Hotel Utila* (☎ 45-3340, fax 45-3140) is more luxurious and more expensive, with singles/doubles/triples for US$15/20/25 downstairs, US$5 more upstairs.

About a five-minute walk along Sandy Bay Rd from town, the *Margaritaville Beach Hotel* (☎ 45-3266), new in 1996, is an attractive hotel where spacious, clean rooms with private bath and two double beds cost US$8. Prices will probably rise, as the rooms are worth more.

HONDURAS

Inland A couple of blocks inland from the main road are several more good places to stay.

The *Country Side Inn* (☎ 45-3216) on Mamey Lane Rd has a quiet, country location, three blocks from Sandy Bay Rd and removed from the hubbub of town. New in 1996, it offers a variety of well-equipped rooms with 24-hour power and good screens. Simple rooms with shared bath and kitchen are US$6.25; larger, newer rooms in the building out back are US$12 downstairs, US$15 upstairs, and there's also a two-bedroom furnished apartment. The owners, Woody & Annie, are friendly and helpful.

The cheapest places to stay on the island are on Cola de Mico Rd, which runs inland from the public dock. *Blueberry Hill* (☎ 45-3141) is run by a friendly older couple, Norma and Will. Rooms with screen, fan and shared bath are US$4.20; older rooms without screen or fan are US$2.10. Some of the rooms share a kitchen where you can cook your own meals.

Also up here is the *Loma Vista* (☎ 45-3243), with 10 rooms sharing bath and kitchen; all have screens, and there's laundry service and 24-hour power. Singles/doubles are US$4.20/5. Other cheap hotels up this way include *Selly's Hotel, Tony's Place* and the *Monkey Tail Inn*.

Places to Eat

There's a good selection of eating places for such a small settlement. In addition, several of the places to stay provide kitchens where you can cook. Fruits and vegetables are scarcer and more expensive on the island than on the mainland, so you might want to bring some over when you come. The *Starfish* supply boat comes from the mainland on Tuesday, so Wednesday is your best chance to find fresh produce in the markets.

Thompson's Bakery, inland on Cola de Mico Rd, is popular for breakfast and baked goods. The *Jade Seahorse Restaurant*, also on Cola de Mico Rd, is popular for all meals, offering both seafood and vegetarian dishes, good fresh fruit licuados and shakes.

The air-conditioned *Cap't Roy's Bahía del Mar Restaurant/Bar* near the airport is good for all meals. Some people say the breakfasts here are the best on the island; there's also a good selection of other dishes, such as pizza, lasagna, steaks, seafood, BBQ, salads and vegetarian meals. Also near the airport is *Sharky's Reef*, with Caribbean, California-style and Asian food, vegetarian selections and nightly specials.

The *Reef Bar & Grill*, overlooking the sea on the back deck of the Utila Reef House, serves delicious food, with nightly specials. It's a popular gathering place.

Delany's Island Kitchen on the main road specializes in pizza and pasta. *Mermaid's Corner* also makes pizza, pasta and salads. For typical foods, try the *Island Cafe* on Sandy Bay Rd, the *Seven Seas* or *Las Delicias*.

The *Bundu Café* at the Green House Book Exchange is a good place to relax with a book or to socialize in the daytime. Food is served from around 9 am to 2 pm; try to get here early for lunch, as it's a popular place and they may run out of food.

Entertainment

The *07* disco on the main road is popular for dancing on weekends; the music blares out long after the rest of the island has lost its electricity. The *Bucket of Blood Bar* on Cola de Mico Rd also has its aficionados, as does the *Reef Bar & Grill*.

Getting There & Away

Air The flights between Utila and La Ceiba or Roatán take about 15 minutes (see the Getting Around section earlier in this chapter for schedule and fares).

Mermaid's Travel Agency (☎ 45-3260) on the main road can give you current details about flights serving the island.

Boat Getting to the island by boat is also a possibility (see the Getting Around section earlier in this chapter for schedule and fares).

The *Osprey* sailboat makes a trip to Lívingston, Guatemala, twice a month or so; it may also stop off at Puerto Cortés and/or Omoa. The cost to Lívingston is US$96 per person, with a maximum of 12 passengers. Ask about it at Gunter's Dive Shop (see Diving above).

Getting Around
Bicycles can be rented at several places in town for US$1.70 per day.

GUANAJA
Population 5500

Easternmost of the three Bay Islands, Guanaja is a small island, roughly 18 km long and six km wide at its widest point. The highest of the three Bay Islands, Guanaja is covered in a forest of Caribbean pine; when Christopher Columbus came to the island in 1502, he named it the 'Isla de Pinos' (Isle of Pines). About 90% of the island has been declared a national forest reserve and marine park.

Many kilometers of coral reefs encircle the island and the 15 or so cays around it; the reefs and some sunken ships make Guanaja attractive for snorkeling and diving. Several dive resorts have appeared on the island. Still, the diving and tourist boom that has hit Roatán and Utila has yet to arrive on Guanaja.

There are a few tiny settlements on the main island, including one on Savannah Bight and another on Mangrove Bight. But the island's principal town, Guanaja, called 'Bonacca' by the locals, is on a small cay just off the island's east coast. Every inch of the cay has been built on; wooden houses with sloping roofs stand on stilts at all different heights. There are no cars on the cay and no roads; walkways wind around among the houses, and narrow canals allow the residents to pull their boats right up to the house. Guanaja town is known as the 'Venice of Honduras.'

You can find everything you need in town: accommodations, restaurants, a post office and Hondutel office, two banks (Bancahsa and Banco Atlántida) and even a disco. As on the other Bay Islands, the residents here can speak Spanish if they have to, but their preferred language is English.

The sandflies on the main island are amazing, especially during the rainy season; you can be eaten alive in 15 minutes. Be sure to bring plenty of repellent. In town, out on the cay, there are few, if any, sandflies or mosquitoes.

Money
Bancahsa changes traveler's checks and gives cash advances on Visa cards.

Things to See & Do
Snorkeling, diving and visits to the cays and beaches are the activities on Guanaja (see How to Choose a Dive Shop sidebar). You can snorkel right off the town cay; the Hotel Alexander beside the water is a good place to start. There's good snorkeling around South West Cay and several other cays, at Michael Rock Beach on the main island and at many other places. Surprisingly, though, snorkeling gear is not readily available on the island; you should bring your own.

On the main island are a number of hiking trails and a waterfall. You can hire a boat to take you across if you're staying in town. Diving trips can be arranged through the dive resorts on the main island.

Places to Stay & Eat
There are places to stay both in Guanaja town and on the main island.

In town, *Hotel Miller* (☎ 45-4327, ☎ /fax 45-4202) has singles/doubles with ceiling fan and shared bath for US$12.50/15; rooms with private bath are US$15/19, or US$24/29 with air con and cable TV. The hotel also has a restaurant, where meals cost US$3. The Millers own half of South West Cay, and you can make trips there to snorkel, BBQ and swim.

Nearby, *Hotel Rosario* (☎ /fax 45-4240) has five clean, modern rooms with private bath and cable TV for US$16 with fan, US$22 with air con. You can arrange boat trips and other activities.

The *Hotel Alexander* (☎ 45-4326, fax 45-4369), looking across the water toward

HONDURAS

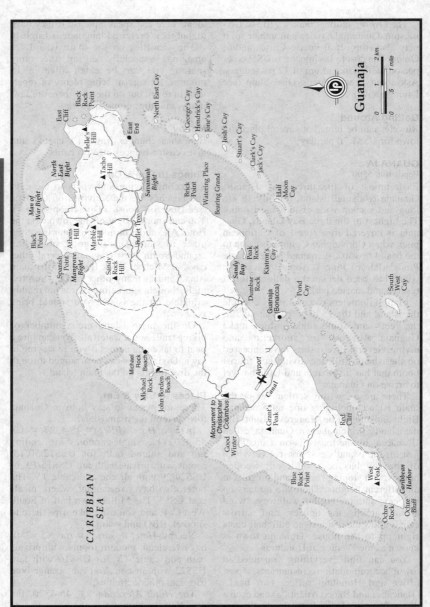

Guanaja

0   1   2 km
0   .5   1 mile

CARIBBEAN SEA

Black Rock Point
East Cliff
Helle's Hill
North East Bight
Man of War Bight
East End
North East Cay
George's Cay
Hendrick's Cay
Jone's Cay
Josh's Cay
Stuart's Cay
Clark's Cay
Jack's Cay
Tacho Hill
Savannah Bight
Brick Point
Watering Place
Bearing Grand
Half Moon Cay
Black Point
Athens Hill
Marble Hill
Bullet Tree
Spanish Point
Mangrove Bight
Sandy Rock Hill
Sandy Bay
Dumbar Rock
Peak Rock
Kiatron's Cay
Guanaja (Bonacca)
Pond Cay
South West Cay
Michael Rock Beach
Michael Rock
John Borden Beach
Monument to Christopher Columbus
Grant's Peak
Airport
Canal
Good Winter
Red Cliff
Blue Rock Point
West Peak
Caribbean Harbor
Ochre Rock
Ochre Bluff

Pond Cay and South West Cay, is very comfortable with lots of amenities. Singles/doubles are US$35/40; a larger penthouse apartment is available. Children under 12 stay for free. You can snorkel right off the dock here, and they can make arrangements for diving. On our last visit they were building a restaurant overlooking the water.

Places to eat in town include *Restaurante El Portal* on the town's main walkway and *Little Pino's Palace Restaurant* opposite the Baptist church.

More places to stay are on the main island. If you stay over here, bring plenty of repellent.

On the waterside beside the airport, the *Airport Hillton* has three rooms for US$17 per person for overnight only, or US$50 per person including accommodations, three meals, laundry service, fishing, snorkeling and 'honky-tonking' around the island. All the rooms have private bath, two beds, fan and satellite TV. It's run by the famous Captain Al, who can make arrangements for anything you could want to do on the island.

The dive resorts around the island tend to be expensive. All offer diving, accommodations and meals; some also offer activities such as hiking, horseback riding and various water sports.

On Sandy Bay are three small dive resorts: the *Nautilus* (☎ 45-4389, 58-0514), the *Manatee* (☎ 45-8182) and the *Stress Free* (☎ 45-4368). The *Bahía Resort* (☎ 45-4212), across the channel from Guanaja town, is more expensive, but it's one of the most pleasant resorts on the island. The *Bayman Bay* (☎ 45-4179) on the west side of the island and *Posada del Sol* (☎ /fax 45-4186, 52-7862) on the east side are more upscale resorts.

The *West Peak Inn* on the southwest side of the island near West Peak is 'an island getaway for the not so rich and famous.' Situated on three miles of pristine, secluded beach, it has a restaurant/bar and a hiking trail to the top of West Peak, with a view of Barbareta and Roatán. Accommodations are in tents, with all camping gear and facilities provided; the cost of US$28 per day

includes all meals. Sea kayaking, diving, snorkeling and fishing can all be arranged.

The *Casa Sobre el Mar* (☎ 45-4269), on a small cay not far from Guanaja town, is just what the name says: a house built right over the sea.

Getting There & Away
Air Flights from La Ceiba take 25 minutes (see Getting There & Away in the introduction to the Bay Islands).

There's a dock near the airport where a motorboat meets incoming flights and charges US$1.65 for the five-minute ride to town. For departing flights, the boat meets the passengers at the dock by the airline office in town to take them back to the airport. If you're staying at one of the resorts around the island and they know you are coming, they will be at the airport to meet you.

Boat No scheduled passenger boats serve Guanaja. Cargo and fishing boats sail between Guanaja and Roatán (three hours) and between Guanaja and Puerto Castilla or Trujillo (four hours), but there is no set schedule and you might spend days waiting for a boat. You could always try to hitch with private yacht owners.

Getting Around
If you stay in town, you can take boat rides to the main island and to the cays; almost everyone on the island has a motorboat. The standard price for any boat trip is not low, however, at around US$20 per trip out and back. Economically it works out better if you get a group together; the boats hold up to 10 people, and the price is charged by the trip, not by the number of passengers. You may be able to find a boatman to take you for as little as US$8 if you're lucky.

CAYOS COCHINOS (HOG ISLANDS)
The Cayos Cochinos, or Hog Islands, are a group of small privately owned islands, 17 km off the coast near La Ceiba. Two of the islands, though small, are forested and of some size, and can properly be called islands; the others are tiny cays. The Hog

HONDURAS

Islands are visible from the beaches at both La Ceiba and Trujillo.

The islands were once inhabited by the Maya; ancient Maya pottery, ornaments and statues have been found. The islands got their name from the conquistador Cortés, who tried farming on them. In addition to Spanish conquerors, the islands were visited by pirates, including the infamous Henry Morgan. Today the islands are inhabited by only a few private owners.

The Hog Islands and the waters and reefs around them are designated a biological marine reserve – it is illegal to anchor on the reef, and commercial fishing is prohibited. Consequently, the reefs are pristine and fish abundant. Diving and snorkeling are excellent around the islands, with black coral reefs, wall diving, cave diving, seamounts and a plane wreck.

You can hire a boat to go out to the small cays, and there are some interesting nature walks. The islands are also known for their unique pink boas.

Places to Stay & Eat

The only official lodgings on the islands are at the *Plantation Beach Resort* (☎ /fax 42-0974, in USA (800) 628-3723, net) on the smaller island. It's expensive at US$795 a week, although this does include three meals a day, three dives a day, unlimited shore and night diving, sea kayaking, nature trails and boat transport to/from La Ceiba.

Otherwise, you should be able to camp on the small cays, but ask permission of the owners first. Bring your own food and water.

Getting There & Away

To get to the Hog Islands, take a bus from La Ceiba to Nueva Armenia (40 km, 2½ hours, US$0.70). From there you can hire a motorboat to take you to the islands (17 km, one hour, around US$10 to US$20 for a boat carrying up to 15 people – negotiate the price). You could also hire a boat at Sambo Creek if you happen to be there, but Nueva Armenia is the usual landing for boats to the islands.

With an early start, you could visit the islands in a day trip from La Ceiba, but you'll have a more leisurely visit if you plan to stay overnight on the islands or in Nueva Armenia. It's good to make the sea crossing early in the morning, when the sea is calm, as the boats may not make the trip if the sea is too rough.

Eastern Honduras

The eastern part of Honduras, including the entire department of Gracias a Dios and the eastern sides of Olancho and Colón, is a vast, sparsely inhabited area of rivers and forests. The easternmost part of Honduras is known as the Mosquitia, through which there is just one minor road.

Only two major roads traverse the area northeast of Tegucigalpa. Both run between Tegucigalpa and Trujillo, and both are traversed by bus routes. One goes between Tegucigalpa and Trujillo (via Limones, La Unión, Olanchito, Savá and Tocoa); it climbs the mountains west of Juticalpa and can be driven in about eight hours. The other, longer route goes via Juticalpa (three hours), where you have to change buses; it's another seven hours to Trujillo.

La Unión and Juticalpa are both pleasant towns for an overnight stop. La Unión is the gateway for the Parque Nacional La Muralla, which is beautiful, with its cool cloud forest.

LA UNIÓN

La Unión is a small, typical Honduran mountain town, nestled into a valley surrounded by pine-covered mountains. It's the gateway to beautiful Parque Nacional La Muralla and a convenient stopover on the way between Tegucigalpa and Trujillo. It's about three to four hours by car from either place.

Places to Stay & Eat

Hotel La Muralla and *Hotel Karol* are both clean little places, each with 10 rooms and shared toilet and showers. Singles/doubles at Hotel La Muralla are US$1.65/2.50; at Hotel Karol they're US$1.25/2.50.

La Unión has several comedores where you can get simple meals. *Cafetería La Muralla* is a good place to eat and also to get information about the national park – one of the park guides lives here. *Auto Pollos*, on the outskirts of town, makes rotisserie chicken (eat there or take out), as does the *Cafetería El Oasis*. Other comedores in town include *Comedor Cindy* and *Café y Naranja*.

Getting There & Away
All the buses between Tegucigalpa and Trujillo stop at La Unión; by bus it's about 4½ to five hours from either place. If you're coming from La Ceiba, you can catch one of these buses at Savá or Olanchito. In La Unión the bus stop is in front of Auto Pollos on the outskirts of town. By private vehicle it takes about three to four hours to drive to La Unión from Tegucigalpa (200 km), La Ceiba (200 km) or San Pedro Sula (175 km).

AROUND LA UNIÓN
Of course the number one attraction is the Parque Nacional La Muralla, but there are also a couple of other enjoyable places to visit near La Unión.

Near town, the road heading toward La Muralla crosses a small river, the Río Camote. Following the river toward town from this crossing, in less than 150 meters you come to **El Chorrón**, a pleasant and refreshing waterfall about six meters high with a fine swimming hole at the bottom.

You can make a pleasant four-km hike from La Unión to the nearby village of **Los Encuentros**, where many of the houses are decorated with interesting hand-painted designs. The old wooden *trapiches* (ox-driven sugar mills) are used only during sugar-cane harvest, which is around the month of March, but they are interesting to see anytime.

PARQUE NACIONAL LA MURALLA
This national park protects a beautiful virgin cloud forest. Since it's rather remote, it isn't overrun with tourists, yet it's easily accessible through La Unión.

A visitors' center at the park entrance provides plenty of information. Starting near the visitors' center are several well-maintained trails, including an easy one-km loop trail and several longer trails. Toucanettes and quetzals can be seen from certain spots on the trails; two of the trails have camping sites. To camp in the park, bring all your own gear. Otherwise it's easy to stay in La Unión.

The visitors' center has a map and information on all of the trails. Guides are available and charge about US$2.50 per trail. It's highly recommended you go with a guide, as you will see more wildlife and learn more about the forest. Be sure to bring along a sweater or jacket, good hiking boots and rain gear; it's quite cool in the park. You'll see the most wildlife if you come early in the morning.

Information
The COHDEFOR office in La Unión, three blocks south of the church on the central plaza, has information on the park; it's open Monday to Friday, 8 am to 5 pm. You must stop here to register before going up to the park. If you arrive on a weekend, go to the information office across the plaza to get information and to register.

The COHDEFOR office in Tegucigalpa (☎ 23-4346) also has information on the park; ask for the Departamento de Areas Protegidas.

Sr Hubert Argueta at the Cafetería La Muralla in La Unión also has information on the park; he is one of the park guides.

Getting There & Away
A good dirt road leads from La Unión into the park, 14 km uphill from town. There's no public transport into the park, but you can probably arrange a ride in La Unión or hitch. An ordinary vehicle can make the trip; it's not necessary to have 4WD.

JUTICALPA
Population 93,000
The only major town in northeastern Honduras is Juticalpa, capital of the department of Olancho. There's nothing much to see,

PLACES TO STAY
1 Hotel Antunez Anexo
2 Hotel Antunez
10 Hotel El Paso

PLACES TO EAT
7 Restaurante El Rancho
9 Restaurante El Tablado

OTHER
3 Hondutel
4 Post Office
5 Church
6 Texaco Station
8 Cinema

but it's a pleasant, friendly town in which to spend a night. The annual festival is held on December 8.

Information
The post office is right on the plaza. Hondutel is one block north of the plaza.

Places to Stay
On the corner of 1a Av NE and 6a Calle SO, between the bus station and the central plaza, *Hotel El Paso* (☎ 85-2311) is quiet, spacious and clean, with enclosed parking and rooms around a grassy courtyard. It has a small shop, and there are restaurants in the same block. Singles/doubles, all with private bath, overhead fan and wood decor, are US$4.15/7.10.

Hotel Antunez (☎ 85-2250), a block from the plaza, is a large hotel with various types of rooms priced according to the amenities you choose (TV, fan, fridge and so on). Singles/doubles with shared bath are US$2.25/3.45 or US$4.50/6.85; with private bath they are US$6.75/11.25 or US$8.30/15.85. *Hotel Antunez Anexo* (☎ 85-2034), half a block away, is simple but clean and has rooms for US$2.25 per person with shared bath, or US$5.40 per person with TV and private bath.

Places to Eat
There are several simple comedores around the plaza. Behind the church, *Restaurante El Rancho* is a covered outdoor patio with wooden picnic tables and a good selection of food; it's open daily from 9 am to 11:30 pm. Four blocks from the plaza, on the entrance road into town, *Restaurant El Tablado* is a fancier restaurant with a bar.

Getting There & Away
The bus station is about one km from town on the entrance road from the highway. Plenty of taxis run between town and the station (US$0.40).

Transportes Aurora (☎ 85-2237) operates several bus routes:

Tegucigalpa (170 km, three hours, US$1.50) Hourly buses from 5 am to 6 pm.
Catacamas (40 km, one hour, US$0.50) Buses at 9:15 am and then hourly from 12:30 to 6:30 pm.
Trujillo (278 km, seven hours, US$4.20) One bus daily at 4 am.
La Ceiba (345 km, eight hours, US$5). One bus daily at 3 am.
Tocoa (235 km, seven hours, US$4.20) One bus daily at 5 am.
San Esteban (125 km, three hours, US$2.50) Two buses daily at 8 am and noon.

The road from Juticalpa to Trujillo passes from pine-forested mountains down to the coastal lowlands covered in jungle and coconut palms. Along the way are cattle ranches and lots of cowboys.

One direct bus a day runs from Juticalpa to Trujillo, departing at 4 am. If you don't want to get up so early, it's possible to do this journey via bus and minibus with changes at San Esteban and Tocoa. Ask about connections, or you may have to overnight in San Esteban.

CATACAMAS
Population 75,000

Catacamas, 40 km northeast of Juticalpa (about 45 minutes by bus), is a more attractive town than Juticalpa, and it's the end of the line for buses coming from Tegucigalpa; many of the Tegucigalpa-Juticalpa buses continue to Catacamas, and additional buses go just between these two towns. There are places to stay in Catacamas. From Catacamas, other buses traverse the dirt road to the small town of Dulce Nombre de Culmí.

THE MOSQUITIA
The Mosquitia region, comprising the entire northeast portion of the country, is very different from the rest of Honduras. There are no roads going through the vast area, and most of the region is uninhabited. Those people who do live there – mostly Miskito Indians, with isolated groups of Pech (Paya) and Tawahka (Sumo) Indians in the interior – have their own distinct cultures.

The settlements of the Mosquitia are remote and a little backward; if you go there, don't expect city life. The Mosquitia is mainly worth visiting for its pristine natural beauty. Manatees and much other wildlife live in the eastern lagoons. Monkeys visit the forested areas along the rivers early in the morning, and there is abundant bird life, including toucans, macaws, parrots, egrets, herons and many others. Crocodiles can be seen in many of the waters, especially at night and especially in the mangrove-lined rivers; if you're traveling by water, keep your hands inside the boat!

Most travelers who make it to the region are highly enthusiastic about what they find. All the towns mentioned have inexpensive accommodations for visitors (and somewhere to eat), whether in formal hospedajes or with families who rent rooms; some provision will always be made. You can also camp out.

Fish dishes are magnificent in the Mosquitia; other food has to be imported into the region and can be scarce or expensive. If you intend to get really off the beaten track, bring as much food with you as you can, as you'll end up sharing meals with families. Be sure to bring along a method of water purification.

Mosquitoes and sandflies are a major irritation; bring insect repellent, a mosquito net and antimalaria pills. It can rain anytime, so rain gear is a good idea, as is a flashlight, since many places have no electricity. Bringing toilet paper is a good idea, too.

As the place is so remote, and accommodations and transport are relatively unstructured, a working knowledge of Spanish is more important here than elsewhere in Honduras. Such mandatory interaction with the locals makes a visit all the more of an adventure.

It may seem tempting to get into Nicaragua through the Mosquitia and avoid backtracking to Tegucigalpa. However, Paul Roos (Netherlands) reported the following experience taking the crossing used by locals called 'Lemuch,' 40 km south of Puerto Lempira:

After acquiring his exit stamp at the Puerto Lempira immigration office he took the thrice-weekly pickup (US$4) to the small village at the border crossing. The police officer on the Nicaraguan side had no entry stamp. The trip to Puerto Cabezas was straightforward, but at the immigration office there he was told he had entered illegally and a payment of US$200 was demanded. This was eventually reduced to US$80 (all the money he had) for the entry stamp – but only after hours of negotiation and threats.

Río Plátano Biosphere Reserve
The Río Plátano Biosphere Reserve is probably the most magnificent nature reserve in Honduras. A World Heritage Site

HONDURAS

established jointly in 1980 by Honduras and the United Nations, it is home to abundant bird, mammal and aquatic life, including a number of exotic and endangered species in the river and surrounding jungle.

A good trip on the Río Plátano might start in Palacios at the northwestern edge of the reserve (see below), where there are flights to La Ceiba and Trujillo, and places to stay and eat. The best time of year to do this trip is from November to July, and the best time for seeing birds is during February and March, when many migratory birds are here.

From Palacios, take a cayuco down the Río Negro and across the Laguna Ibans to Belén, near Cocobila. The trip takes about 1½ hours and costs around US$2 per person.

On the way to Belén you'll pass Plaplaya, a lovely Garífuna village about half an hour's boat ride from Palacios. Giant leatherback sea turtles nest here; volunteers are needed to help during the turtles' nesting season, which is usually from around April to June (talk to Bonnie Larsen).

Nearer to Belén is Cocobila, and between Cocobila and Belén, Raista. Be sure to check out the butterfly farm at Raista, where 12 different kinds are raised, each in their own type of tree. Cocobila, Raista and Belén are all small villages on a narrow strip of land between Laguna Ibans and the sea. From Belén it's about a 2½-hour walk along the beach to Barra Plátano.

At Barra Plátano, where the Río Plátano meets the sea, there's an *hospedaje* operated by Morgan, where beds are US$2.50 per person. At Barra Plátano you can arrange for a cayuco to take you up the Río Plátano to Las Marías, which is about eight hours upriver. Morgan has a cayuco, as do many others; most of these cayucos are large cargo and passenger boats that can hold about eight to 10 people and all their gear.

As you head upriver from Barra Plátano you'll see much wildlife, including crocodiles, howler and white-faced monkeys, tapirs, macaws, parrots, toucans, herons

and about 250 other kinds of birds, especially early in the morning – you'll want to get an early start.

At Las Marías, a village of about 200 or 300 people right in the center of the biosphere reserve, there are two places where you can spend the night: the *Hospedaje Ovidio* and *Hospedaje Mariano*, both of which charge around US$2.50 per bed, and another US$2.50 per meal. The village is bicultural, with Pech people living at one end and Miskitos at the other; a Peace Corps volunteer is also stationed here.

Starting out again from Las Marías the next day, you can take a boat trip about five hours farther upriver to view some ancient petroglyphs. You can camp overnight at the petroglyphs (bring all your own gear) or return to Las Marías – from the petroglyphs it takes about two hours to get back downriver to Las Marías. From Las Marías it takes about another five hours to get back downriver to Cocobila.

If you stay in Barra Plátano on the way up, you might like to stay in Cocobila on the way back – Rubén Balladares has a *hospedaje* there with rooms for US$2.50. Rubén has two boats and he'll take you back to Palacios the next day in time to catch the flight back to Trujillo or La Ceiba; the flight leaves at around 11 am, and the boat trip from Cocobila to Palacios only takes an hour (around US$2). Rubén is the Isleña agent in Cocobila; when you arrive, have him radio to Palacios to reserve you a seat on the airplane if you haven't already done so, as the flight often fills up.

Everything about this trip is very affordable, except for one leg: the boat trip upriver from Barra Plátano. This will cost between US$85 and US$125; you can bargain the price down to a point, but don't count on getting it for much less than this. If you can get a few people together to split the cost, it's much more affordable. Several tour companies also make this trip.

A more affordable option than taking the boat trip upriver from Barra Plátano is hiking through the jungle to Las Marías. From the south (inland) side of Laguna

Ibans, the hike takes about six hours. It's worth paying a local guide to take you; one might do so for about US$5. Once you reach Las Marías, you can organize a boat trip upriver from there to see the petroglyphs; it would cost about US$25 to US$50.

Information on this trip is based on interviews with René Hernandez of Go Native Tours (Copán Ruinas), John & Peter at the Rincón de los Amigos (Trujillo), and on letters from Ingrid Robeyns (Belgium), Brenda Nims & Rob Ajlun (USA) and Thieran Haurahan (country unknown).

Palacios
A small town with only about a hundred houses, Palacios is the most accessible place from which to visit the Río Plátano, with regular flights coming in from La Ceiba and Trujillo. From Palacios you can easily arrange boat trips on the river or across the lagoon to the Garífuna village of Batalla.

The best place to stay is the new 12-room hotel operated by Don Felix, next door to the Isleña office. It has a view of the river, and the rooms, all with private bath, cost around US$7. *Trek* is a cheaper and more basic place, with rooms for around US$4. Don Felix operates a restaurant serving inexpensive meals. He is also the agent for Isleña airline. Reserve in advance with him for your flight leaving Palacios to go back to Trujillo or La Ceiba. These flights often fill up, and if you just show up at the airport, you may not get a seat.

Brus Laguna
Population 14,000
Beside the lagoon of the same name at the mouth of the Río Patuca, Brus Laguna is a small Mosquitia town. There is a friendly *hospedaje* for accommodations and where you can cook if you have your own food. Boat trips can be taken on the lagoon and upriver on the Río Patuca, where there's much wildlife.

Ahuas
Ahuas, a small town with a population of under a thousand, is inland from the coast about two hour's walk from the Río Patuca.

From here you can take boat trips upriver to the village of Wampusirpi or downriver to Brus Laguna. At certain times of year, however, the river may not be navigable due to too much water (rainy season) or too little (dry season). Check current conditions before you go.

Puerto Lempira
Population 34,000
Puerto Lempira, the largest town in the Mosquitia, is situated on the inland side of the Laguna de Caratasca. Connecting with several sublagoons, the lagoon is very large but not deep; its average depth is about three meters, with deeper pockets in a few places.

Because the depth clearance over the sandbar forming the entrance to the lagoon is only about two meters, large vessels cannot enter the lagoon, and only small boats ply the waters. There is a lot of small boat traffic, especially between Puerto Lempira and Cauquira, a village on the lagoon's north side, from which you can easily walk to the sea.

Manatees, birds, fish and other wildlife are found in the lagoon. Mopawi, a tiny place outside of town, has a water buffalo farm which you can ask permission to visit.

Organized Tours
Several travel companies undertake organized tours into the Mosquitia region, providing an easy if more expensive way to get a taste of the Mosquitia. All of the following ones have been recommended. Information on each company is given under the town where its office is located.

Tegucigalpa
    La Moskitia Ecoaventuras, Adventure
    Expeditions
San Pedro Sula
    Cambio Centroamérica
La Ceiba
    La Moskitia Ecoaventuras,
    Euro Honduras Tours
Trujillo
    Turtle Tours
Copán Ruinas
    Go Native Tours, Xukpi Tours

HONDURAS

Getting There & Away

Air La Ceiba is the hub for flights to the Mosquitia, with services to Palacios, Puerto Lempira, Ahuas and Brus Laguna. Isleña, Sosa and Rollins Air all have flights from La Ceiba to the Mosquitia. Isleña's La Ceiba-Palacios flight stops in Trujillo on the way, making Trujillo another viable starting point. See the Getting Around section at the beginning of the Honduras chapter for details on domestic flights.

Bus We've heard that there's a bus going past Limón to Punta Piedra, from which it's a half-hour boat ride to Palacios. See the Limón section.

Boat There are no regularly scheduled boats to the Mosquitia, but cargo and fishing boats go frequently from La Ceiba, Trujillo and Guanaja, and may take passengers. Just go down to the docks in any of these places and ask around for a boat.

We've heard that cargo boats go every couple of days or so from the pier at Trujillo, making stops along the way at Palacios, Plaplaya, Cocobila and Brus Laguna, which is at the end of the line.

Getting Around

Air Most of the flights from La Ceiba to the Mosquitia return directly, so there's not much of a network of flights within the region. An exception is Sosa's twice-weekly flight (La Ceiba-Brus Laguna-Ahuas-La Ceiba).

Alas airline, a small enterprise in the Mosquitia for missionaries and hospitals, will take passengers, but space is not always available. They serve the mission hospital in Ahuas and several other places; fares are around US$25.

Pickup A thrice-weekly pickup truck runs along the road heading southwest from Puerto Lempira. The only other land transport is by foot or mule.

Boat Ground-level transport is almost entirely by boat, on the lagoons and rivers as well as the sea, though prices can be high. Flat-bottomed *pipante* boats, propelled by poles or paddles, are the main transport used on rivers and in the lagoons. Cayucos, with more angular hulls, are the principal transport in the sea, and they also enter the lagoons. Cayucos are propelled by poles, paddles, or small engines; the motorized canoes are called 'tuk-tuks,' taking their name from their sound. Cayucos are more stable in the sea, but pipantes are more stable in the lagoons and rivers.

The rainy season in the Mosquitia is normally from June to December. At this time too much water (sometimes to the point of flooding) and flotsam in the water can occasionally impede navigation of rivers; during the dry season, some waterways can become too shallow to navigate. The riskiest times for boat travel are during the driest time of year (April) and the wettest (October). Most of the time, though, there is no problem getting around by boat. Locals say that here as elsewhere in the world, patterns of rainfall have been less predictable in recent years.

Southern Honduras

Honduras touches the Pacific with a 124-km coastline on the Golfo de Fonseca. Bordered by the gulf on the seaward side and by hills on the land side, the strip of lowland here is part of the hot coastal plain that extends down the Pacific side of Central America through several countries. It's a fertile agricultural and fishing region; much of Tegucigalpa's fish, shrimp, rice, sugar cane and hot-weather fruits (like watermelon) come from this area. Honduras' Pacific port is at San Lorenzo.

Southern Honduras is a much-traveled region; it is where the Interamericana crosses Honduras, carrying all the north and southbound traffic of Central America, and also where the highway branches north from the Interamericana toward the rest of Honduras.

TEGUCIGALPA TO NICARAGUA

The most direct route from Tegucigalpa to Managua is via **El Paraíso**. It's only 122 km from Tegucigalpa to the border going this way (2½ hours by bus, US$1.10). You can make it from Tegucigalpa to Managua in a day if you get an early start.

The border crossing is at **Las Manos** near El Paraíso. Coming from Tegucigalpa, take a bus to El Paraíso and then change buses to continue on the half-hour journey to the border station (US$0.30), which is open every day from 7 am to 5 pm.

There are several interesting stopovers along this route. About 40 km east of the capital at Zamorano, there's a turnoff for **San Antonio de Oriente**, an attractive Spanish colonial mining village about five km north of the highway. This is the village immortalized by Honduran primitivist painter José Antonio Velásquez.

Farther east is a turnoff south to **Yuscarán**, 66 km from Tegucigalpa. Capital of the department of El Paraíso, it is another pleasant Spanish colonial mining village. Its annual fair is held on December 8.

Danlí (population 126,000), 92 km east of Tegucigalpa and 19 km from El Paraíso, is the largest town along this route. An attractive town, Danlí is the center of an agricultural area producing sugar cane and tobacco; the town has several cigar factories where you can buy good hand-rolled cigars. The annual festival at Danlí, the Festival del Maíz in the last weekend in August, is a big event and attracts people from far and wide. The Laguna de San Julian, 18 km north of Danlí, is a manmade lake popular for outings.

There are several places to stay and eat at Danlí. El Paraíso also has accommodations. The *Quinta Av Hotel-Restaurante* (☎ 93-4298) in El Paraíso on 5a Av is recommended; single/double rooms with private hot bath are around US$5/6, and it also offers Mexican food and secure parking.

TEGUCIGALPA TO THE PACIFIC

Highway CA 5 heads south about 95 km from Tegucigalpa until it meets the Interamericana at Jícaro Galán, winding down from the pine-covered hills around the capital to the hot coastal plain. From the crossroads at Jícaro Galán, it's 40 km west to the border with El Salvador at **El Amatillo**, passing through the town of Nacaome six km west of Jícaro Galán, or it's 115 km east to the Nicaraguan border at **El Espino**, passing through Choluteca 50 km from Jícaro Galán.

If you are traveling along the Interamericana, crossing only this part of Honduras in transit between El Salvador and Nicaragua, you can easily make the entire crossing in a day; from border to border it's only 150 km (three hours by bus).

If, however, you want to stop off, there are a few possibilities. The border stations close at 5 pm, so if you can't make it by that time you'll have to spend the night.

GOLFO DE FONSECA

The shores of Honduras, El Salvador and Nicaragua all touch the Golfo de Fonseca; Honduras has the middle and largest share, with 124 km of coastline and jurisdiction over nearly all of the 30-plus islands in the gulf. A ruling of the International Court of Justice in September 1992 eased previous tensions by ruling that sovereignty in the gulf must be shared by the three nations, barring a three-mile maritime belt around the coast. Of the islands in the gulf, sovereignty was disputed by Honduras and El Salvador in three cases. The court found in favor of Honduras regarding the island of El Tigre, while El Salvador prevailed on Meanguera and Meanguerita.

The European discovery of the Golfo de Fonseca was made in 1522 by Andrés Niño, who named the gulf in honor of his benefactor, Bishop Juan Rodríguez de Fonseca. In 1578 the buccaneer Sir Francis Drake occupied the gulf, using El Tigre as a base as he made raids as far afield as Peru and Baja California. There is still speculation that Drake may have left a hidden treasure, but it has never been found.

El Salvador has a major town on the gulf (La Unión), but Honduras doesn't; on the Honduras part of the coastline there are only small settlements, and the highway never meets the sea except on the outskirts of San Lorenzo. The Golfo de Fonseca is an extremely hot region.

San Lorenzo
Population 28,000

The Interamericana touches the Golfo de Fonseca only on the outskirts of San Lorenzo. San Lorenzo is the Pacific port town of Honduras, but there's not much to the town, which is small, sleepy and hot. San Lorenzo is in a deep inlet, the Bahía de San Lorenzo, so although you can get to the water and jump in for a swim, there's no view out into the gulf.

From the bus stop on the highway, it's about 10 blocks to the water on a road that passes the market, church and plaza. At the end, beside the shrimp packing plant, *Hotel Miramar* (☎ 81-2138) has a restaurant and bar, with a large deck hanging over the water. Meals, mostly seafood, are about US$6. Canoes and small boats pass by in the channel and there's a small beach beside the hotel. Buses plying the Interamericana all stop at San Lorenzo, some at the bus stop on the highway, some coming the few blocks into town to the market.

Cedeño & Punta Ratón
These are the two principal swimming beaches on the Golfo de Fonseca. Cedeño is the more popular; it has very basic places to stay and eat. The turnoff from the Interamericana is about halfway between Choluteca and San Lorenzo. Buses come from both towns but only a few times a day; it takes about one to 1½ hours to get to the beaches from either town. There are also buses that run directly between Cedeño and Tegucigalpa.

Amapala
Population 10,000

Amapala is a quiet fishing village on the island of El Tigre, an inactive volcanic island 783 meters high. Founded in 1833, Amapala was once Honduras' Pacific port town before the port was moved to the mainland at San Lorenzo. Visitors come here for holidays during Semana Santa, but otherwise the place is very quiet. A view of Amapala is on the back of the L2 note.

There are a few places to stay and eat in Amapala, and some good hikes around the island; from El Vijía, about 100 meters up, there's a good view of the gulf and its islands. El Tigre also has several good beaches: Playa Grande, with the Cueva de la Sirena (Mermaid Cave), and Playa Negra, with tranquil shores. Other beaches are Caracolito and El Caracol. The island's seafood is very good.

Places to Stay & Eat The *Hotel Internacional* has been recommended; you can see it on the L2 note, right at the foot of the pier. The downstairs rooms are hot and dark, but the upstairs rooms are large and airy, facing the sea. From the upstairs rooms doors open onto a large balcony with plenty of room for hammocks. This is an old, cheap hotel; rooms might cost around US$3 or US$4 per night. The *Villas Playa Negra* (☎ in Tegucigalpa 37-8822, 37-8301, fax 38-2457), around the island on Playa Negra, is more luxurious and expensive.

Getting There & Away Small boats and a car ferry depart from Coyolito, 30 km from the Interamericana; the boat trip takes about 20 minutes. Buses go to Coyolito infrequently from San Lorenzo; you could also hitch. There are no overnight facilities at Coyolito.

CHOLUTECA
Population 114,000

Choluteca, capital of the department of the same name, is the largest town in southern Honduras. It's built near the Río Choluteca, the same river that runs through Tegucigalpa.

There's not much to do in Choluteca; it's principally a commercial center for the agricultural region and a stopping-off point between the borders. It is a pleasant, though very hot, town. The annual festival day is December 8.

Orientation
The streets in Choluteca are laid out in a straightforward grid, with calles running

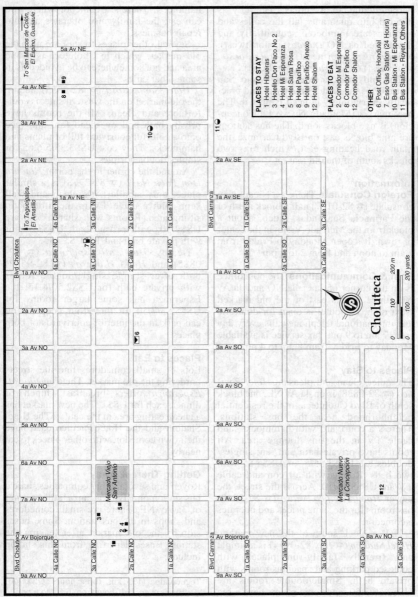

PLACES TO STAY
1 Hotel Hibueras
3 Hotelito Don Paco No 2
4 Hotel Mi Esperanza
5 Hotel Santa Rosa
8 Hotel Pacifico
9 Hotel Pacifico Anexo
12 Hotel Shalom

PLACES TO EAT
2 Comedor Mi Esperanza
8 Comedor Pacifico
12 Comedor Shalom

OTHER
6 Post Office, Hondutel
7 Esso Gas Station (24 Hours)
10 Bus Station - Mi Esperanza
11 Bus Station - Royeri, Others

To San Marcos de Colón,
El Espino, Guasaule

To Tegucigalpa,
El Amatillo

Choluteca

0   100   200 m
0   100   200 yards

Blvd Choluteca
Blvd Carranza
Av Bojorque

5a Av NE
4a Av NE
3a Av NE
2a Av NE
1a Av NE
1a Av NO
2a Av NO
3a Av NO
4a Av NO
5a Av NO
6a Av NO
7a Av NO
9a Av NO

2a Av SE
1a Av SO
2a Av SO
3a Av SO
4a Av SO
5a Av SO
6a Av SO
7a Av SO
8a Av NO
9a Av SO

4a Calle NE
3a Calle NE
2a Calle NE
1a Calle NE
1a Calle SE
2a Calle SE
3a Calle SE
4a Calle NO
3a Calle NO
2a Calle NO
1a Calle NO
1a Calle SO
2a Calle SO
3a Calle SO
4a Calle SO
5a Calle SO

Mercado Viejo
San Antonio

Mercado Nuevo
La Concepción

perpendicular to avenidas. The city is divided into quadrants; all the calles and avenidas are numbered sequentially and designated as NO *(noroeste,* northwest), NE *(noreste,* northeast), SO *(suroeste,* southwest) or SE *(sureste,* southeast).

The old market (Mercado Viejo San Antonio) is the center of activity and practically everything you need is near it. The new market (Mercado Nuevo La Concepción) is five blocks south. The bus stations are nine blocks east on Blvd Carranza, the main road heading east, which runs two blocks south of the old market.

Information

Foreign Consulate There's a Nicaraguan consulate (☎ 82-0127) half a block north of the Farmacia San Judas Tadeo, about a block from the Mercado Viejo, in the center of town. It's open Monday to Friday from 7 am to noon and from 2 to 4 pm.

Post & Communications The post office is on the corner of 2a Calle NO and 3a Av NO, three blocks east of the old market. Next door, Hondutel is open for domestic and international telephone calls every day from 7 am to 9 pm; fax service is available Monday to Friday from 8 am to 4 pm.

Places to Stay

The quiet, clean and pleasant *Hotel Pacífico* (☎ 82-0838) is on 4a Av NE, one block south of Blvd Choluteca, in the residential neighborhood near the bus stations. There's a courtyard with hammocks, and cable TV in the tiny lounge area. All rooms have private bath and fan; singles/doubles are US$3.35/5, or US$5.85 with two beds. Rooms with air con and cable TV are US$8.35/10. Across the street, the newer *Hotel Pacífico Anexo* (☎ 82-3249) has rooms for the same prices and operates a comedor.

Half a block south of the new market, *Hotel Shalom* (☎/fax 82-0914) is a simple and friendly family-run place, with enclosed parking and spacious rooms with private bath. Single/double rooms are US$2.50/3.50, and some rooms have a big hammock. There's a comedor where you can eat; the family also operates an auto repair business.

Several other places to stay are near the old market, which in Choluteca is a fine area and not somewhere to be avoided as in some other cities.

Hotel Santa Rosa (☎ 82-0355), facing the old market on the western side, is comfortable and clean. All the rooms have private bath and overhead fan, and face onto a colorful courtyard full of plants and hammocks. They cost US$3.35/5/6.65 for singles/doubles/triples.

Around the corner to the north, *Hotelito Don Paco No 2* (☎ 82-2778) is a similar place, only smaller; it's clean and well kept, with a cable TV in the little patio sitting area. Rooms with shared bath are US$2.50, with private bath US$3.35, or with private bath and TV US$5.85.

Nearby, *Hotel Mi Esperanza* (☎ 82-0885) and *Hotel Hibueras* (☎ 82-0512) both offer simple single/double rooms with private bath for US$2.50/4.15; the Esperanza has some larger rooms for US$5.85/7.50 for three/four people. You can park in the interior courtyards of both places.

Places to Eat

Lots of small comedores line the streets bordering the old market. The *Comedor Mi Esperanza* offers breakfast, lunch or dinner, each for US$1. The new market has a cheap eating area in the center. The Hotel Shalom and the Hotel Pacífico each have their own comedor, with other places to eat nearby.

Getting There & Away

Royeri and several other companies share a bus station on Blvd Carranza, at the corner of 3a Av NE. There are small comedores and shops in the bus station. Some buses stop by the old market after leaving the station. Buses departing from this station include:

Tegucigalpa (133 km, three hours, US$1.40)
 Buses every half-hour from 6 am to 6 pm.

San Marcos de Colón (Nicaraguan border; 58 km, one to 1½ hours, US$0.50) Buses every 45 minutes from 6 am to 6 pm.

Guasaule (Nicaraguan border; 44 km, one hour, US$0.60) Buses every half-hour from 5 am to 6 pm.

El Amatillo (Salvadoran border; 85 km, two to 2½ hours, US$0.90) Buses every half-hour, 4 am to 5:30 pm.

Mi Esperanza has its own bus station (☎ 82-0841) on 3a Av NE, 1½ blocks north of the other station. Mi Esperanza is one of the main companies doing the Tegucigalpa-Choluteca-San Marcos de Colón route, and their buses are both more direct and more comfortable than some of the others; people at the Royeri terminal will advise you to take a Mi Esperanza bus if you're going to Tegucigalpa. Mi Esperanza's buses include:

Tegucigalpa (133 km) Regular bus (three hours, US$1.40); 12 buses daily from 4 am to 6 pm. Saturday and Sunday buses are more frequent, leaving about every 15 or 20 minutes. 'Especial' bus (two hours, US$4.15) departs at 6 and 10 am, 2 and 6 pm.

San Marcos de Colón (Nicaraguan border; 58 km, one to 1½ hours, US$0.50) Five buses daily from 6:30 or 7 am to 7 pm.

Local buses connect Choluteca with other places in the south around the Golfo de Fonseca.

SAN MARCOS DE COLÓN
Population 23,000

San Marcos de Colón is the closest town to the Nicaraguan border at El Espino. It is a small, pleasant mountain town, cool at night, with several places to stay and eat. Some families here offer comfortable accommodations in private homes; you may be approached by their children at the bus station. It's easy to change money in San Marcos.

Honduran buses to the border go only as far as San Marcos. From San Marcos, colectivo taxis will take you the seven km to the border station at **El Espino** (open

daily from 7 am to 5 pm) for US$0.40. If you need a visa for either country, be sure you already have it before you reach the border.

If it's getting late in the day, you may want to stay over in Choluteca or San Marcos and make the crossing the following day. The choice of accommodations is better here than on the Nicaraguan side near the border. There is no place to stay at El Espino.

Crossing the border in the other direction, you can catch direct buses from San Marcos to Tegucigalpa (191 km, 4½ hours, US$1.65) and Choluteca (58 km, one to 1½ hours, US$0.50); the last bus of the day leaves San Marcos at around 4:45 pm. Choluteca has connecting buses to El Amatillo on the Salvadoran border.

BORDER CROSSING TO NICARAGUA
The border crossing at **Guasaule** reopened in 1992 after the European Community repaired the bridge there. It's open from 7 am to 5 pm daily.

Buses operate every half-hour between Guasaule and Choluteca (44 km, one hour, US$0.60). On the Nicaraguan side, buses go to both Chinandega and León.

BORDER CROSSING TO EL SALVADOR
El Amatillo, the border crossing between Honduras and El Salvador, is open daily from 7 am to 5 pm. It is a relaxed border post; Honduran *campesinos* cross the border here every day to go to market in Santa Rosa de Lima, 18 km from the border on the El Salvador side. There are places to stay at Santa Rosa de Lima, or you could press on to San Miguel or La Unión, each a two-hour bus ride from El Amatillo. There's also a basic hospedaje at El Amatillo on the Honduran side.

From El Amatillo, buses leave frequently for Tegucigalpa (130 km, three hours, US$1.25) and Choluteca (85 km, two to 2½ hours, US$0.90). At Choluteca you can continue to the Nicaraguan border.

HONDURAS

El Salvador

El Salvador's name alone evokes images of the chaotic civil war fought from 1980 to 1992 in the tangle of mountains and quilts of farmland. But the war is now long past, and this small but varied country is doing its best to pull itself beyond its sordid past.

The landscape remains the most turbulent aspect of El Salvador. Volcanoes rise out of flat valleys, and lakes fill in the spaces where once there were craters. The Pacific Ocean slams into its side and mixes with the sweet waters of the many rivers that slither through the country.

El Salvador is not as geared to backpack tourism as neighboring countries, but a trip through El Salvador affords a whole new experience of watching a country redefine itself. Nongovernmental organizations (NGOs) from the US, Australia and Europe are helping to put the country's pieces back together, be it through education, agricultural reform, reforestation, human rights or health care. Observing or participating in these developments and talking to the locals about their experiences and hopes can be the most fulfilling part of a trip.

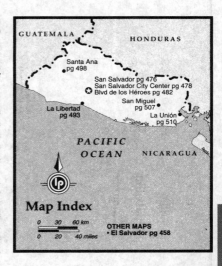

EL SALVADOR

Facts about El Salvador

HISTORY

The Olmec people lived in El Salvador at least as early as 2000 BC. The Olmec Boulder, a stone sculpture of a giant head found near Chalchuapa in western El Salvador, testifies to an early Olmec presence or influence.

The step pyramid ruins at Tazumal and San Andrés show that the Maya lived in western El Salvador for over 1000 years. Groups that inhabited the eastern part of the country included the Lenca and Pokoman – the former being the most influential.

When the Spanish arrived in the 16th century, the country was dominated by the Pipil, descendants of Nahuatl-speaking Toltecs and Aztecs, both Mexican tribes. The Pipil probably came to central El Salvador in the 11th century just after the Maya dynasty collapsed. They called the land Cuscatlán, which means Land of Happiness, and made what is now Antiguo Cuscatlán, outside San Salvador, the capital. Their culture was similar to that of the Aztec, with heavy Maya influences and a maize-based agricultural economy that supported several cities and a complex culture including hieroglyphic writing, astronomy and mathematics. They spoke Nahua, a dialect related to Nahuatl. Tazumal, San Andrés and Joya de Cerén all show signs of Pipil life.

Spanish Conquest & Independence
See History in Facts about the Region for details on the role of the Spanish Conquest and independence of Central American

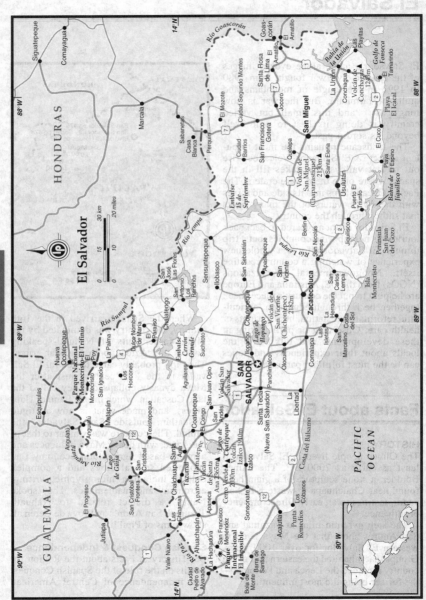

Evidence of a Better Past

The Laguna Caldera Volcano erupted some 1400 years ago, sending ash spewing in all directions. Between four and six meters of that ash settled on a farming village. The intense heat from the eruption (between 100 and 500°C) preserved not only the structures, but pottery, plants, seeds and animal remains.

The village was accidentally discovered in 1976. While no human remains were found (it is believed residents fled prior to the explosion), archaeologists dug up tools, seeds and polychrome pots. They discerned what crops were planted – corn, beans, squash, cacao and chiles – and what meat the people ate. Medicinal plants and maguey (still used to make twine) were growing in the gardens. Houses had thick walls and firm structures, with separate rooms for the kitchen and sleeping areas. This site, now called Joya de Cerén (Jewel of Cerén, named after the Spanish family that owned the land) is right outside San Salvador where thousands of descendants of this community now live in leaking corrugated iron shacks and subsist on little more than rice and beans. ■

states. In El Salvador, the Spanish developed plantations of cotton, balsam and indigo. Throughout the 1700s agriculture soared, with indigo leading as the No 1 export. The elite Europeans (namely 14 families) maintained control of most of the land. As elsewhere, they enslaved the indigenous peoples in return for their 'conversion' to Christianity. Slaves from Africa were also used; according to one report at least 2000 were brought in, but after an uprising in 1625, blacks were restricted access into the country.

El Salvador gained independence from Spain on September 15, 1821. The same wealthy families held tight to their land and continued to push locals off it. Anastasio Aquino led an unsuccessful Indian rebellion in 1833, with the motto 'Land for those who work it'; he is still a national hero. In 1841, following the dissolution of the Central American Federation, El Salvador adopted a constitution as a sovereign independent nation.

In Comes Coffee

Synthetic dyes undermined the indigo market, and coffee took main stage. A handful of wealthy landowners expanded their properties, encroaching into the mountainous areas and displacing more indigenous people. Coffee became the most important cash crop and 'cafetaleros' earned purses full of money that was not taxed nor distributed at reasonable wages to the workers. By the 20th century, 95% of El Salvador's income derived from coffee exports, but only 2% controlled that wealth.

The 20th Century

Intermittent efforts by the poor majority to redress El Salvador's social and economic injustices were met with severe repression, and the government vigorously eradicated any union activity in the coffee industry during the 1920s.

In January 1932, Augustín Farabundo Martí, a founder of the Central American Socialist party, led an uprising of peasants and Indians. The military responded by systematically killing anyone who looked 'Indian' or who supported the uprising. In all, 30,000 people were killed in what became known as La Matanza (the Massacre). Martí was arrested and killed by firing squad. His name is preserved by the FMLN (Frente Martí Liberación Nacional).

During the 1970s the population suffered from landlessness, poverty, unemployment and overpopulation. In government the polarized left and right tangled with each other for power through coups and electoral fraud. In 1972, José Napoleon Duarte, cofounder of the Christian Democrat Party (PDC), was elected president. He was immediately arrested and exiled by the military, who put their own people in power. Guerrilla activity increased and the right-wing responded with the creation of 'death squads.' Thousands of Salvadorans were kidnapped, tortured and murdered.

In 1979 a junta of military and civilians overthrew President Romero and promised reforms. When these promises were not met, opposition parties banded together under the party name Federación Democrático Revolucionario, of which the FMLN was the largest group. The successful revolution in Nicaragua in 1979 encouraged many Salvadorans to seek reforms and consider armed struggle the only way to create change.

On March 24, 1980, Archbishop Romero was assassinated while saying Mass in the chapel of the San Salvador Divine Providence Cancer Hospital. The murder of the beloved archbishop ignited an armed insurrection that same year.

Cold War Hype
The Reagan administration, unnerved by the success of Nicaragua's socialist revolution, pumped huge amounts of money into the Salvadoran government, then under the control of Duarte (PDC). The guerrillas gained control of areas in the north and east, and the military retaliated by decimating villages. In 1981 in the town of El Mozote, Morazán, some 900 men, women and children were brutally massacred. As many as 300,000 citizens fled the country.

In 1982, Major Roberto D'Aubisson, the leader of the extreme right ARENA party became president of the Assemby, and quickly initiated a law that the Assembly had power over the president. D'Aubisson created death squads that sought out trade unionists and others who supported the PDC-proposed agrarian reform. The FMLN continued its offensive by blowing up bridges, cutting down power lines, destroying coffee plantations and killing livestock – anything to stifle the country's economy. Death squads raped and killed four US churchworkers. The FMLN proposed peace negotiations that were ignored by the government. The FMLN thus refused to participate in the 1984 presidential elections, in which Duarte was elected over D'Aubisson. For the next few years the PDC and FMLN engaged in

peace talks unsuccessfully. Death squads continued their pillaging and the guerrillas engaged in offensives to undermine the military powers and jeopardize municipal elections.

Nearing the End of the War
In March 1989 Alfredo Cristiani, a wealthy businessman in the ARENA party, was elected president. In September, neighboring countries urged the two sides to begin peace talks. On November 11, the FMLN launched an offensive. Five days later, the military murdered six Jesuit priests, their housekeeper and her daughter. In a counteroffensive by the military an estimated 4000 people were killed.

In April 1990 negotiations began between the government and the FMLN, mediated by the United Nations. One of the first agreements was a human-rights accord signed by both parties in July 1990, but violations occurred practically as soon as the ink was dry. Violent deaths actually increased in 1991, the year that a UN mission arrived in the country to monitor human rights.

Finally, on January 16, 1992, the agreement, or rather compromise, was signed. The ceasefire took effect on February 1. The FMLN became an opposition party, and the government agreed to various reforms, including dismantling paramilitary groups and death squads, and replacing them with a national civil police force. Land was to be distributed to citizens and human-rights violations to be investigated, but the government gave amnesty to those responsible for human-rights abuses. Land distribution has been a bureaucratic process involving loans to the government and USAID (which forgave the unpaid loans in 1997) and land that is uncultivable.

During the course of the 12-year war, an estimated 75,000 people were killed, and the US government gave a staggering US$6 billion to the Salvadoran government's war effort, despite knowledge of government members involved in the operation of the death squads and atrocities carried out by the military, such the massacre of El Mozote in 1981. In March 1994, Calderón Sol (ARENA) was voted president, amidst allegations of electoral fraud.

Current Events
While many of the agreements outlined in the peace accords have been addressed, most notably the land-transfer program, many are still outstanding. Ex-combatants, from both the FMLN and military, still await a 'severance package' to help them deal with reorientation to society. The amount of homicides has increased as unemployment and poverty (see Economy) combine with the proliferation of arms in the country. Gang warfare is an increasing problem. The government has proposed legislation to 're-educate' gang members in prisons. Salvadorans deported from the US on felony charges also face this 're-education' program. Many consider the situation in the country to be no better than it was at the beginning of the civil war.

In March 1997 elections for the municipalities and national assembly were held. The FMLN won in the cities of six of the 14 departments; it now governs a greater percentage of the population than ARENA. Within the National Assembly both ARENA and FMLN won a third of the seats. The presidential elections are scheduled for 1999.

GEOGRAPHY
El Salvador is the smallest country in Central America, with a total area of 20,688 sq km (about the size of the US state of Massachusetts). It is bordered by Guatemala to the west, Honduras to the north and east, and the Pacific Ocean to the south. The coastline is about 320 km long.

More than 25 extinct volcanoes dot the country, the largest being San Salvador, San Vicente, Santa Ana and San Miguel. Volcanic and natural lakes plus a web of rivers add to the landscape.

CLIMATE
The wet season (*invierno* or winter) is from May to October and the dry season (*verano* or summer) from November to April.

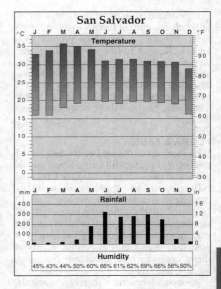

In San Salvador, the maximum temperature varies from 30°C in November to 34°C in March and April; the minimum nighttime temperatures range from 16°C to 19°C all year round. The coastal lowlands are much hotter than the rest of the country. San Salvador, at a medium elevation (680 meters above sea level), has a 'moderate' climate compared to the other parts of the country, but you'll sweat all the same.

ECOLOGY & ENVIRONMENT
With the highest level of environmental damage in the Americas, El Salvador runs the risk of losing its beauty. Unfortunately it is also the only country in Latin America without environmental protection laws. Six percent of the country is forest or woodland, and a mere 2% of that is original growth. The highlands are cultivated for coffee, the coastal plain for cotton, and the lowlands for sugar.

The Río Lempa, an important watershed, suffers from pollution, as are many other rivers and lakes. Some fear that at the current rate of destruction the country will run out of drinking water in 10 to 15 years.

EL SALVADOR

Industrial development and construction of hotels are current threats to the environment. Private organizations protect such areas as Bosque El Imposible and Cerro el Aguila, establish reforestation campaigns, and sponsor clean drinking-water projects. The most visible problem is trash. A circle of soaring vultures usually indicates where a new load has been dumped by the side of the road.

FLORA & FAUNA

With so much of the land cultivated, few of the original plants still exist. Small stands of balsam trees survive along the Costa del Bálsamo, and mangroves line the many estuaries. Bosque Montecristo and El Imposible harbor the greatest variety of indigenous plants in their small areas. The park in Cerro Verde has a good variety of plants, as does Cerro el Aguila. Plants in these areas include mountain pine, fig, mezcal, and ferns.

Around Montecristo there are quetzals, toucans, white-tailed deer and a couple of species of monkeys. Plenty of birds live in the coastal areas. Herons, kingfishers, brown pelicans, egrets, parakeets and sandpipers can all be spotted. Around 400 species of birds exist throughout the country. Butterflies of all colors and sizes frolic everywhere at all elevations.

Endangered animals include marine turtles and armadillos. In all about 90 species are in danger of extinction – three fish, three amphibians, 16 reptiles, 50 birds and 18 mammals.

National Parks

El Salvador's main national park is Bosque Montecristo-El Trifinio. It is only open half the year to humans to leave the animals in peace during their breeding season. Bosque El Imposible is just about impossible to get to, which means wildlife stays protected. Cerro Verde, just a bus ride from the capital, is a beautiful expanse of forest with easy access to volcanoes. Nancuchiname, along the eastern side of the Río Lempa near its convergence with the ocean, ensures that important riverbank areas aren't deforested.

GOVERNMENT & POLITICS

El Salvador's government has three divisions. Executive power is held by a president, elected by popular vote to a five-year term. Legislative power is vested in the National Assembly, with 84 members elected to a three-year term. The 13-member Supreme Court is elected by the National Assembly. The country is divided into 14 departments.

Calderón Sol, of the right-wing Alianza Republicana Nacionalista (ARENA) party, was elected president in 1994. Other main political parties are the Frente Farabundo Martí para la Liberación Nacional (FMLN), the Partido Demócrata Cristiano (PDC), the Convergencia Democratia and the Partido de Conciliación Nacional (PCN).

ECONOMY

El Salvador has one of the stronger economies in Central America and has maintained a 5 to 7% growth rate since 1990. Inflation is at 10%, and the 1995 GDP was US$9.6 billion. However, it is estimated that only 2% of the population could be described as upper class, with the relatively new middle class (mostly in the towns) accounting for another 8%. Everyone else is poor. Unemployment is around 50%.

In 1995 exports grew by 35% to US$1.7 billion and have increased by 4000% in the last 10 years. Leading exports include coffee, sugar, cotton, textiles and people. Over one million Salvadorans living in the US sent close to US$1 billion in dollar transfers to relatives in El Salvador in 1995, making them the main source of the country's revenue. In 1995 the maquila industry, 90% of which is apparel assembly, grew by 53%, surpassing coffee as the top export earner. Textile exports from El Salvador to the US are virtually quota-free. While such industry creates jobs, wages do not reflect inflation and real wages are half what they were 10 years ago.

Privatization of telecommunications, electricity distribution, and seaports and airport services is under way. The governments of El Salvador and Honduras are considering the development of a 'dry canal' – a 362-km container rail system – from the Golfo de Fonseca to the Honduran Puerto Cortés. The Japanese government has plans to invest in developing the main port at the Golfo de Fonseca. Japan is also funding the reconstruction of two bridges that the FMLN blew up during the war (Cuscatlán and Puente de Oro); these span the Río Lempa, connecting the western and eastern parts of the country.

POPULATION & PEOPLE

The population, as of 1997, is 5.9 million. Of that 94% are mestizo (a mixture of Spanish and Indian), 5% Indian and 1% of European ancestry. One report estimates that the population could double by 2020.

Over one million Salvadorans left the country during the civil war, emigrating to either the US or neighboring countries. The one million who continue to live in the US are El Salvador's greatest source of revenue (see Economy).

Women fought alongside guerrillas during the course of the war, and when it ended, many refused to reintegrate into the old ways. Women have made inroads into politics and business. Unwanted pregnancy is a growing problem, made worse by the lack of sex education and the Church's condom condemnation. In fact, half of the population is between the ages of 0 and 15, and malnourishment affects half of that population. Around 75,000 children work to bring money to the family – that's nearly a third of children ages 0 to 14. The elderly are in no better shape: one human-rights organization estimates that a third of the country's senior citizens live in extreme poverty.

EDUCATION

1995 estimates of the illiteracy rates range from 28.5% to 35% of people over the age of 15. In 1995 a presidential commission was established to study educational policy. The report proposed increasing teacher salaries, modernizing classrooms and making education a main governmental priority.

There are two main universities in San Salvador: Universidad de El Salvador and the Jesuit Universidad de CentroAmerica (UCA). There is an abundance of private and church-affiliated universities.

ARTS

Most of the music on the radio comes from the USA, Mexico or other parts of Latin America, and it's standard pop. However, there is a small underground movement of *canción popular* (folk music), focusing on the life and current events among the people of El Salvador.

The village of La Palma, in the Chalatenango Department, has become famous for a school of art started by Fernando Llort, who also maintains his own gallery, El Arbol de Dios, in San Salvador. Ilobasco is known for its ceramics, and San Sebastián for textile arts.

Poetry is very popular in El Salvador. The poetry movement in El Salvador was first inspired by Rubén Darío, the Nicaraguan poet. Roque Dalton is a revolutionary poet whose many works include *Poemas Clandestinas* (Clandestine Poems).

Salvador Salazar Arrué, writing under the pen name of Salarué, is one of El Salvador's famous older writers. His *Cuentos de Barro* (Tales of Mud), published in 1934, is said to mark the beginning of the modern Central American short-story genre.

Other well-known writers from El Salvador include Manlio Argueta *(Un Día en la Vida*, translated as One Day of Life in 1983) and Francisco Rodriguez *(Life for Those Who Come After).*

SOCIETY & CONDUCT

It can come as quite a shock to visitors traveling around Central America that El Salvador does not have the amount of indigenous populations as neighboring countries. You will rarely find villages full of colorful crafts markets, and most of the tourist artesanías in El Salvador are brought in from Guatemala. Pockets of indigenous peoples do survive in isolated villages. Don't expect friendly locals dressed in colorful robes posing for photos. They are more cautious and private here.

Given the country's delicate political

situation, it is wise not to speak of politics to someone you don't know that well unless they instigate the conversation. Don't assume that you won't be understood if you speak in English – many will understand but may not let you in on that secret. While a few cultural centers sell left-leaning T-shirts of Che or like heroes, it's wise not to wear them while in the country. Stay gracious and relaxed, and the charms of the people will win you over. The pace is slower and you'll be expected to follow that rhythm.

As a foreigner you'll be associated with the upper class. Walking around in rags or dirty clothing will make you appear a freak – even the poorest wash their clothes and look as presentable as possible.

RELIGION
El Salvador is predominantly Roman Catholic. However, during the war the government assumed that the Catholic Church supported communism through its sympathizing with the poor, and it targeted the Catholic Church for violence. Many fled the religion either fearing for their lives or unhappy with the Church's affiliation with the opposition. Protestantism, especially Evangelism, offered a welcome alternative, and between 1976 and 1985 individuals registered in Assemblies of God increased from 65,000 to 200,000 (150%). By 1992 one-fifth of the population claimed Evangelism as their chosen affiliation.

Other churches include the Baptist Church, Church of the Latter-Day Saints, Seventh-Day Adventists, Jehovah's Witnesses, and Evangelical and Pentecostal groups. The Lutheran Church continues the philosophies of liberation theology. The current archbishop is conservative and much more traditional than his predecessors.

LANGUAGE
Spanish is the national language. Many men, mainly between the ages of 20 and 40, learned some English in the US during the war. Indigenous languages have died out in daily use, but there is some academic interest in preserving the Nahua language of the Pipils. Only in a few Indian villages do people still speak Nahua.

Facts for the Visitor

PLANNING
You may want to do some preliminary research and planning to make your trip more enjoyable. Refer to Useful Organizations for places that can line up volunteer work or stay with families; Language Courses in San Salvador to sign up for classes and stay in a family's home; Centros Obreros under Accommodations for a free bed; Cordes under Isla Montecristo for contact numbers to explore that island; and Important Offices in San Salvador for SalvaNatura (and information on Bosque El Imposible).

When to Go
The dry season is an easier to time to go: roads are in better condition, Bosque Montecristo is open, you won't get drenched every evening and more cultural festivals take place. In the rainy season, however, prices are lower, beaches less crowded and the evenings slightly cooler after the rainstorms.

Maps
Finding good maps in the country poses a challenge, so buy some maps in your home country. International Travel Map Productions (ITM; see Maps in the Facts for the Visitor chapter). Corsatur (see Tourist Offices below) has maps that aren't very easy to read, but they are free. Otherwise, you can pick up a map (US$2) from Bargain Rent-a-Car or Budget Rent-a-Car either at the airport or at their offices in San Salvador. Even these maps need updating. See the San Salvador section for more details on where you can obtain maps in the city.

What to Bring

Bring along, or buy while traveling, a rice sack to put your pack in when on the bus. This protects it from getting scratched up and makes it less conspicuous. Take clothes that dry fast (rayon, woven cotton, polyester) and allow your skin to breathe.

A mosquito net (make your own using bridal veil material) and a bedsheet are musts if you plan on staying at Centros Obreros or along the coast. Acidopholus tablets are a good idea for avoiding minor stomach upsets. During the rainy season take along a poncho for the rain and sandals that dry fast. Some travelers like to take some incense to cover up the smelly bathroom fumes. A water bottle comes in handy not only for water but also for sodas (you won't have to wonder what to do with the plastic bag and straw).

THE BEST & THE WORST

Hands down, the best part of El Salvador is the people. Most locals you meet will be friendly and willing to help. Drivers let you cut them off if you're nice about it and bus drivers tell you when to get off. Many people, after they know you better, will tell of their experiences during the war and their opinions about the country's state of affairs. Children are polite, curious and quick with a smile. Other highlights are the volcanoes (climbing them or just admiring them on the horizon), the sobering memorial in El Mozote, misty mornings in La Palma, the mangroves and beaches around Isla Montecristo, and an ice-cold Pilsner wrapped in a napkin.

Things that could make you weary fast are the trash dumps and the circles of buzzards overhead; trying to drive on roads with more potholes than pavement; thick exhaust from buses careening through city streets; the notion that the louder the TV or radio the more enjoyable it must be; starving, inbred mongrels; and crime and the lack of control the police have over it.

TOURIST OFFICES

In 1997 the Corporación Salvadoreña de Turismo (Corsatur) was established. This is now the main tourist office, replacing the former Instituto Salvadoreño de Turismo (ISTU). Corsatur (☎ 243-0427) Blvd Hípodromo 508 in Colonia San Benito, San Salvador, is open weekdays from 8 am to 12:20 pm and 1 to 5:30 pm. You can find basic, not-so-up-to-date information (car rental, museum descriptions in English, etc) and maps of the city. Corsatur also has an office at the international airport that is open from 10 am to 5:30 pm.

The former ISTU will be renamed Instituto Recreación Popular (IRP) and will be responsible for the development and maintenance of the Turicentros (see Activities) and the national parks. The office (☎ 222-8000, 222-3241), is in the the center of San Salvador at 619 Calle Rubén Darío between 9a and 11a Avs Sur. It is open Monday to Friday from 8 am to 4 pm and Saturday from 8 am to noon (but these hours may change). The staff may still have handouts and maps.

VISAS & DOCUMENTS

US and Canadian citizens don't need a visa but must buy a US$10 tourist card upon entering the country, be it at the airport or at border crossings. The card is valid for 90 days. Each time you enter the country you must buy another card, even if your reentry is within those 90 days. Citizens of Australia and New Zealand need a visa. The visa stamp is good for a single entry to the country within 90 days of issue. Visas can be extended twice, for a total stay of three months. After that, if you want to stay longer you must apply for a temporary resident's permit. Visas can be extended in San Salvador at the Oficina de Migración (☎ 221-2111) on the 2nd floor of the federal building in the Centro de Gobierno. The office is open Monday to Friday from 8 am to noon and 1:30 to 4 pm.

No vaccinations are required unless you are coming from an area infected by yellow fever (some are recommended, however; see Health below).

Immigration officials can decide whether to admit you or not, and have the right to determine your length of stay.

EL SALVADOR

EMBASSIES
El Salvadoran Embassies
If you need a visa, get it from a Salvadoran embassy or consulate before you arrive.

Belize
  See Embassies & Consulates in Belize City.
Canada
  209 Kent St, Ottawa, Ontario K2P 1Z8
  (☎ (613) 238-2939)
Colombia
  Carrera 9, No 8015, Oficina 503, Bogotá
  (☎ 1-212-5952, 211-00012)
Costa Rica
  See Foreign Embassies in Costa Rica.
France
  12 rue Galilee, Paris 75116
  (☎ 01-47.23.98.23, fax 01-40.70.01.95)
Guatemala
  See Embassies in Guatemala City.
Honduras
  See Foreign Embassies in Tegucigalpa and
  Foreign Consulates in San Pedro Sula.
Italy
  Via Carlo Botta 19, Milano 20135
  (☎ 2-550-17890)
Mexico
  Monte Altai No 320, Lomas de
  Chapultepec, Deleg. Manuel Hidalgo,
  Mexico DF 11000
  (☎ 520-0856, 202-8280)
New Zealand
  Ross, France, Barristers, Union Law Center,
  PO Box 22-544, Otahuhu
Nicaragua
  See Foreign Embassies in Managua.
Panama
  See Foreign Embassies & Consulates
  in Panama City.
UK
  Tennyson House 159, Great Portland St,
  London W1N 5FP (☎ 0171-436-8282)
USA
  2308 California NW, Washington
  DC 20008 (☎ (202) 265-9671)

Foreign Embassies in El Salvador
The tourist office keeps a current listing of all embassies and consulates in San Salvador. Most offices are open 8 am to noon or 2 pm. Others are also open in the afternoon, but it's best to go in the morning.

Belize
  Condominio Médico B, Local 5, 2nd Floor,
  Blvd Tutunichapa, Urbanización
  La Esperanza (☎ 226-3588)
Colombia
  Calle El Mirador, No 5120, Colonia Escalón
  (☎ 279-3290, 279-3204)
Costa Rica
  Alameda Roosevelt, No 3107, Edificio
  Centroamericana, 3rd Floor (☎ 279-0303)
Guatemala
  15a Av Norte, No 135, between Calle Arce
  and 1 Calle Poniente (☎ 271-2225)
Honduras
  3a Calle Poniente, No 3697, between 69
  and 71 Av Norte, Colonia Escalón, two
  blocks right of Simón Cosa building
  (☎ 223-4975)
Mexico
  Pasaje 12 and Av Circunvalación, Colonia
  San Benito, behind Hotel Presidente
  (☎ 298-1079, 278-1084)
Nicaragua
  71a Av Norte & 1a Calle Poniente,
  No 164 (☎ 223-7729, fax 223-7201)
Panama
  Alameda Roosevelt & 55a Av Norte, No
  2838, Altos de la Compañía Panameña de
  Aviación, San Salvador (☎ 298-0884)
UK
  Paseo General Escalón, No 4828
  (☎ 298-1763)
USA
  Near the end of Blvd Santa Elena, Antiguo
  Cuscatlán; take bus or micro No 44
  (☎ 278- 4444)

CUSTOMS
It is always best to present yourself as a clean, financially solvent, respectable tourist when going through customs. As in most Central American countries, you can expect less investigation at the airport than if you arrive overland, since people arriving by plane are presumed to have money.

Importation of fruit, vegetables and plant and animal products is restricted, and questionable articles may be confiscated or fumigated. You can bring in three cartons of cigarettes or one kg of tobacco, and two bottles of liquor.

MONEY
Costs
Accommodations and food are more expensive than neighboring countries. Bus transportation is cheap, both in cities and

EL SALVADOR

long distance. Be prepared to pay entrance to archaeological sites and national parks.

Currency & Exchange

There are 100 centavos in a colón. Coins are of one, five, 10, 25 and 50 centavos value and come in two different series of sizes, which can get confusing. Notes are in denominations of ¢5, ¢10, ¢25, ¢50 and ¢100.

US dollars are the only currency that you can be sure of always exchanging. Exchange rates for other currencies are based on US dollar value. At press time the exchange rate was US$1=¢8.72.

Change any extra colones before you leave El Salvador for neighboring countries, or you may have to resort to the black market to change Salvadoran currency.

Traveler's Checks

Few banks change traveler's checks readily and easily, and the practice seems to be determined by each branch rather than the bank; for example, in San Salvador, Banco Hipotecario changes checks, but the one in Santa Ana doesn't. Some casas de cambio will ask to see the receipts for the traveler's checks in order to compare signatures (which, of course, you are supposed to keep *separate* from the checks). Try showing a photocopy, or explain to the checker that you don't have them and would be willing to show other forms of ID (you'll need your passport to make the transaction in any case).

Taxes

Value-added tax (IVA) of 10% should apply on all goods and services in El Salvador; make sure you know whether this is already included in prices or will be added on later. You will mainly find that it is already included, or not charged, except in more expensive hotels, where it is added to your final bill. At higher-end restaurants, tips are also already added to the final charge.

POST & COMMUNICATIONS

There are three rates for sending mail: surface, air mail and express mail. Rates and transit time for mail sent from El Salvador to the US are air mail (US$0.25, eight days) and express mail (US$0.55, five days). To Europe and Australia rates for air mail are US$0.35 (12 days) and express US$0.35/0.55 (10 days).

General delivery mail should be addressed to Lista de Correos. Be sure to conclude the address with 'República de El Salvador, Central America.'

Telephone boxes are found in many public places, including gas stations. Local calls require a 10-centavo coin for three minutes. Put in more coins if you want to talk longer, or you'll be cut off.

Make long-distance phone calls and send telegraphs and faxes from Antel offices – every city and town has one. Most hotels can also place local or national calls for you and make collect calls, but they charge excessively for the service. If you are willing to wait out the bureaucracy of Antel, that is your better choice. New phones are popping up all over the country and work well enough to place international calls. Dial the following numbers to reach long-distance companies directly:

AT&T	☎ 800-1785
MCI	☎ 800-1767
Sprint	☎ 800-1776

The country code when calling El Salvador from abroad is 503. There are no internal area codes.

BOOKS & FILMS

If you plan on staying any length of time in El Salvador, find a copy of *On Your Own in El Salvador* by Jeff Brauer, Julian Smith & Veronica Wiles (On Your Own Publications), a very informative, entertaining travel guide to the country. Another good read and easy to tote around is *Salvador* by Joan Didion. *El Salvador: The Face of Revolution* by Robert Armstrong & Janet Shenk is a very readable history of the country, focusing on the roots, reasons and development of the civil war. It also comments on Honduras, Nicaragua, Guatemala, and the role of the USA in the region.

EL SALVADOR

Witness to War: An American Doctor in El Salvador by Charles Clements, MD, is the personal story of a Quaker American doctor who worked in the war zone of Chalatenango in 1982 and 1983. It has become a classic, and a film was made from the book. *The Massacre in El Mozote* by Mark Danner is a moving account of one of the worst massacres in Latin American history.

Watch videos of the movies *Romero*, produced by Ellwood Kieser in 1988 and *Salvador*, in true Oliver Stone style. Both offer insights into events of the civil war.

MEDIA

San Salvador's main newspapers, both distributed in the morning, are *La Prensa Gráfica* and *El Diario de Hoy*; check them for entertainment listings. *El Mundo* and *Diario Latino* are afternoon papers but are not as comprehensive as the other two.

Eight commercial TV stations broadcast throughout the country. Many hotels have cable TV. Currently there are over 100 radio stations.

LAUNDRY

While you'll see laundry hanging from bushes and barbed wire fences, finding a place to have some done can be a chore. Most hotels will do your laundry, but it can get expensive as they charge by the item, not the weight. You may be able to wash clothes by hand and hang them up in the hotel; ask what the rules are. In the rainy season it takes clothes forever to dry; electric dryers come in handy.

HEALTH

Recommended immunizations include hepatitis A. It's also wise to take a course of malaria pills if you'll be heading off the beaten track. Take along mosquito *(zancudos)* repellent and a mosquito net.

Your safest bet for staying healthy is watching what you eat. While cheaper, eating off the streets is a lot riskier. Hep A and cholera outbreaks spread like wildfire in the cities. In better restaurants, watch out for meat, both chicken and

steak, and avoid the chicharrón offered at pupuserías. Make sure the seafood is same-day fresh.

Don't drink the tap water, and always make sure ice or any juices are made with purified water *(agua purificada)* or *agua cristal* – a brand of bottled water.

If (or maybe better stated, when) you get diarrhea, be sure to replenish body fluids. Buy Gatorade or similar electrolyte-replacing drinks. If you don't have that, coconut water is reputed to also help. Another natural remedy is papaya; both the 'meat' and the seeds of this fruit are known to help ease stomach upsets. Should you end up in a hospital, you'll have to pay for your medical treatment.

TOILETS

In hotels with shared bath facilities, the toilets are separated from the showers (luckily). Private baths in cheap hotels mean you get to sit on the toilet and shower at the same time. And in those way-off-the-beaten-track places where there are no latrines, follow the local instructions and head out of the village in the suggested direction. While in transit, it's OK to go into a restaurant and ask to use the toilet.

USEFUL ORGANIZATIONS

Centro Internacional de Solidaridad (CIS; 226-2623, net), Blvd Universitario, Casa No 4, San Salvador, manages logistics for large educational and political groups that come through, but they can also arrange or help individuals organize meetings with politicians and NGOs. If you want to do some volunteer work, they require a three-month stay. They also run a Spanish-language school and an English school (English teachers are volunteers but scholarships to study Spanish may be available). Dozens of political and cultural groups flourish in San Salvador; the CIS can provide information on particular aspects of the country and may even help you organize trips to the repopulated communities. Contact these groups for information about the following subjects:

EL SALVADOR

Christian communities
CEBES   ☎ 226-0888
Development
ASDI   ☎ 271-2465
FUNDE   ☎ 226-6887
Environment
CESTA   ☎ 225-6746
Human rights
PDH   ☎ 222-1604
Repopulation
CRIPDES   ☎ 226-3717
Women's rights
DIGNAS   ☎ 298-6002

Centro Cultural La Mazorca ASTAC (☎ 226-5219) on Calle San Antonio Abad near the university hosts seminars, sponsors lectures on politics and women's issues and has art shows from time to time.

WOMEN TRAVELERS
Traveling alone here presents quite a challenge. Crime is a problem, and being a woman in a macho culture makes you an easier target. Women here make the effort to look nice. Follow their example, and dress moderately and conservatively. Also note that they wear a T-shirt over their bathing suits at beaches and swimming holes. Just wearing a bathing suit, especially a bikini, will get you a lot more attention. Avoid showing cleavage, or you'll never have an eye-to-eye conversation with any gentleman. Pack skirts and T-shirts rather than dresses to allow access to your money pouch. Ignore the hissing sounds – to acknowledge them is to ask for more unwanted attention.

Even if you like a cold beer as much as the guys you are hanging out with, be aware of groups of men drinking together, especially in *chupaderos* (see Entertainment). This is usually a sign of their bonding time, and your attendance may make some think you are fair game. Soft drinks are more a 'woman's drink.' Women don't go out at night unless escorted or in large groups, and then only to safe, well-lit areas. Keep that in mind when looking for entertainment.

GAY & LESBIAN TRAVELERS
Little tolerance is given to the openly gay man or woman. Two women traveling together will not be as scrutinized as two men, but in either case avoid making public displays of affection. In San Salvador, the area around Blvd de los Héroes has cultural centers and clubs that, being more 'bohemian,' are also more tolerant. You can also dance it up at such clubs as Olimpo (mainly gay men) and K'OZ. CIS (see Useful Organizations above) has information about Centro Cultural Girasol, which offers a support network for gay men.

DANGERS & ANNOYANCES
El Salvador has the unfortunate reputation of being a violent country. It has suffered not only a chaotic civil war, but all the problems that plague post-war countries. The military presence has been replaced by a civilian police force that is too small and too young to deal with the complexity and immediacy of the problems now plaguing the country. Crime is a growing problem, aggravated by unemployment, severe poverty and US gang culture. Guns are the strongest muscle for many people, and while the government did start a program to trade guns for food coupons in 1996, many citizens remain armed with a variety of weapons (see the sidebar on gangs).

The main problem for travelers is petty thievery. Tourists are an easy target, so carry as little as possible during day trips. Using a shoulder-strap woven bag (the kind you can pick up in Guatemala or Mexico) is better than a cloth day pack. Some locals will advise against taking public buses, but as long as you do so during daylight and keep one eye open, all should be OK. Should you be mugged, don't argue – give all you have without hesitation.

Women are subject to annoying hissing and remarks, and the occasional perturbed male reaching for a breast. Seek local advice about when and where it's safe to walk around, and take a taxi if in doubt.

BUSINESS HOURS & PUBLIC HOLIDAYS
Normal business hours are Monday to Friday from 8 am to noon and from 2 pm until 4 or 5 pm. From noon to 2 pm is *almuerzo*, the largest meal of the day.

EL SALVADOR

Banks are open Monday to Friday from 9 am to 4 pm. Shopping hours are longer, usually from 8 am to 6 pm, and Saturday mornings until noon. Restaurants serve dinner early, and 4 pm is the pupusa hour (see Food below).

The festival day of El Salvador del Mundo, patron of El Salvador, is August 6. Celebrations, including a fair and a big parade, are held in San Salvador on this day and during the week preceding it. Other celebrations are held during Semana Santa (Holy Week) and on December 12, the day of the Virgen de Guadalupe. Each city, village and town has a festival for its patron saint sometime during the year.

The year's public holidays are as follows:

January 1
    New Year's Day
March-April
    Holy Thursday, Good Friday,
    Easter Saturday and *Easter Sunday*
    (Semana Santa)
May 1
    Labor Day
1st week in June
    Corpus Christi
August 3 to 6
    Festival of El Salvador del Mundo
September 15
    Independence Day (1821)
October 12
    Columbus Day
November 2
    All Souls' Day
November 5
    Anniversary of First Call for Independence
    (1811)
December 25 to 31
    Christmas

ACTIVITIES
Rafting & Kayaking
Ríos Tropicales (☎ 223-9480) in San Salvador runs rafting trips down the Lempa, Torola and Paz Rivers between May and October (and down the Guajoyo from October to March). Rapids range from Class II to IV. A one-day tour costs US$70, and trips of up to four days run up to US$625. The rest of the year you can go sea kayaking in the bays and estuaries,

which is a good way to explore some inaccessible areas. Prices for the kayaking are about the same as for rafting. If interested, contact them a good two weeks in advance.

For longer trips you have to make a reservation 30 days in advance and pay half the price early. Write to Ríos Tropicales at Apartado Postal 3258, San Salvador, or in the US at PO Box 997402, Miami, FL 33299. Once in San Salvador you can visit the office on Calle Mirador, No 4620, in Colonia Escalón. SET Tours (see Organized Tours in Getting Around below) can also make arrangements for you.

Turicentros
In an attempt to develop national tourism, ISTU created 14 'Turicentros' from the late 1950s to the 1970s. The majority of these are near lakes and natural springs or in the forest. Most have swimming pools. Cabins hold little more than a picnic table, and tables and chairs are often painted in bright prime colors that clash with the natural emerald green that engulfs the spot. As they are all located close to a main town, locals use them a lot on weekends. Some are well kept, others are hardly maintained. The price is the same for all: US$0.80 to get in, US$0.70 to park, US$4 to use a cabin (not for overnighting); open 8 am to 5 pm. Only Los Chorros and Cerro Verde are worth a trip in themselves; the rest are good for chilling out away from the crowds of the cities but only on weekdays.

Volunteering & Courses
See Useful Organizations for information on places that can arrange work in cooperatives, schools and environmental projects. Also see Spanish Courses in San Salvador.

ACCOMMODATIONS
You get what you pay for. If you want to spend only US$5 a night, your lodging will be near a bus terminal, and the rooms may be rented out more often by the hour than by the night. Women traveling alone should exercise caution in areas where these hotels are located. You pay more for security and the ability to leave after dark – such places

are mainly *casas de húespedes*, someone's home turned into a guesthouse.

A single room may only have a single bed in it, but some have a double bed. If you're traveling as a couple or as friends, getting a room with a double bed will cut down on cost. Double rooms have two beds, usually a double and single, which means three people could stay, so when traveling with friends, ask to see the room and then decide how many rooms you need.

The best deal is at government workers' centers (*centros de obreros*), where you can stay free of charge, but there are only three – at Lago de Coatepeque, El Tamarindo, and just outside La Libertad (see country map). These are large compounds developed for government workers to catch up on their R&R. They must be getting it somewhere else these days, as the compounds are virtually empty during the week and house school groups on the weekends. The one at Coatepeque is the better maintained. You can stay at any as long as you like, subject to availability, but to do so you must get written permission from the Ministerio de Trabajo (open 8 am to 4 pm), near the back of the Centro Gobierno (see San Salvador). Take along your passport to get permission. You can only apply to stay at one place at a time, but since you can apply for more than one person, you can get around this by getting permission for two to stay at one place and having a travel buddy do the same for another place. If you have it, take extra bedding as the mattresses in the dorms can be really grotty.

FOOD
Eating a big cheap breakfast and lunch, as locals do, is the cheapest way to get through the day, as dinner in restaurants can be overpriced. Eggs, *casamiento* (rice and beans mixed together), fried plantain, a couple of tortillas and coffee get the day going. If you don't like big breakfasts, head for a *panadería* for a decent selection of morning cakes, but few have anything to drink but sodas and weak coffee with powdered milk. *Almuerzo* or lunch is the largest meal of the day. All cities and towns have restaurants

---

Con Queso, Frijoles, Revueltas . . .
Ask anyone where to get the best pupusas and a heated discussion will no doubt ensue. Pupusas are simple and filling – a corn meal mass stuffed with farmer's cheese, refried beans (or a mixture of both), chicharrón (fried pork fat), or all three (*revuelta*). Ordering just one or two will elicit a look of shock from the woman making the pupusas. Surely you would need more than that, and more often than not, even if you order two, a couple more will appear on your plate. The big jar of salad on the table is called *curtido* – a mixture of pickled cabbage, beets and carrots. Drop some of that on the pupusas with a bit of hot sauce, and you've got a meal. While most are made of corn, pupusas made with rice flour (*arroz*) are highly acclaimed and stalls advertising such are worth checking out. The texture is lighter and a bit crispier.

Restaurants in San Salvador are starting to make gourmet pupusas with such fillings as broccoli and chicken curry, but the basic pupusa *con queso y frijoles* is always the best bet. ■

EL SALVADOR

with *comida a la vista* – a cafeteria/buffet setup. This is a saving grace for those who don't know much Spanish or are picky eaters since you get to see the items before choosing them. Usually available are a meat, chicken and vegetable dish, rice and tortillas. Around 4 pm is *pupusa* time (see the sidebar above). While some places do have pupusas throughout the day, pupuserías open at 4 pm and stay open until about 9 or 10 pm.

Another passion is *pavo* (turkey) also referred to as *chumpipe*. Turkey sandwich chain restaurants (Panes con Pavo is one) are common and are a better bet than places catering to *pollo* passion, such as Pollo Campero. Pizza is another fair go for a decent meal.

DRINKS
Licuados (fruit drinks), coffee and *gaseosas* (soft drinks) are easily had. See the Facts for the Visitor chapter for details. A great

refresher is *agua de jamaica,* which tastes like a sweet fruity iced tea. A common beverage to wash down the pupusas is *horchata*, made from rice water, sugar and cinnamon. And, of course, there are coconuts.

Popular local beers include Pilsner and Suprema, the former being the most popular and lighter. In some towns, you get free *bocas* (little appetizers) with your Pilsner. *Aguardiente*, firewater made from sugar cane, is very strong but low quality; Tic-Tack and Torito are some of the brand names.

THINGS TO BUY

El Salvador doesn't have the variety of arts and crafts that Guatemala or Honduras has. Hammocks are cheap here; the cotton ones are better quality and cost around US$35. The most popular art form is inspired by Fernando Llort (see La Palma). You can find napkin holders, key rings, necklaces and tin cups, all with the colorful, simple drawings. Organic mountain-grown coffee is sold at the crafts markets; Pipil is a good brand.

Sorpresas are the most typical form of ceramics and can be a fun purchase (see Ilobasco).

Getting There & Away

AIR

The three largest carriers to El Salvador are TACA (the national airline), United and American. Continental also flies here. Both United and American have deals with TACA to keep prices stabilized. Flights leave from major points in Central and North America (Dallas, Houston, Miami, New York, San Francisco, Los Angeles, Mexico City). Flights from New York, Los Angeles or San Francisco range from US$450 to US$600 depending on the season. Flights from Miami cost US$350 to US$550.

Central American airlines that fly into San Salvador's Comalapa Airport include COPA (Panamanian) and Lacsa (Costa Rican). These are owned by Central America Corporation, which has a Visit Central America program (see Air Passes in the Getting Around chapter). For information, call TACA (☎ (800) 535-8780 within the USA). An example of individual (not on the program) fares within Central America are a roundtrip to Panama US$550; to San José, Costa Rica US$360.

There's a US$23 departure tax to fly out of the airport payable in colones or US dollars.

LAND
Border Crossings

Border crossings to Guatemala are La Hachadura, Las Chinamas, San Cristóbal and Anguiatú. The main border crossings to Honduras are El Amatillo and El Poy. There is a crossing at Sabanetas, north of Perquín, but no buses go up there because the roads are so bad.

Avoid arriving late in the afternoon, especially if crossing on national buses. If you aren't required to have a visa (see Visas & Documents above), you must buy a tourist card, which costs US$10. As soon as you leave the country the tourist card expires. Should you want to reenter, you will have to buy another one. No one is charged a customs or immigration fee; however, small payments to those who offer to help you through the crossing, with your luggage, will make for a more expedient crossing. Closing hours for the borders are as follows:

Chinamas (Guatemalan border)	10 pm
San Cristóbal (Guatemalan border)	9 pm
La Hachadura (Guatemalan border)	9 pm
Anguiatú (Guatemalan border)	9 pm
El Poy (Honduras border)	8 pm
Amatillo (Honduras border)	10 pm

Buses to/from Guatemala

In San Salvador, buses to and from Guatemala operate from two terminals and various hotels. International bus services can also be picked up in Santa Ana; see that section for details.

Terminal Puerto Bus Bus lines TACA, Galvos, Vencedora, Melva, Galgos and Pezzarossi share the route to Guatemala City. The trip takes five hours. Buses depart each hour from 3:30 am to 4:30 pm Monday to Saturday, and 5:30 am to 4:30 pm Sunday. One-way costs US$6.30. King Quality buses also use this terminal (make reservations at Hotel International above the station). This bus departs at 5:30 am and 2:30 pm; the trip takes 4½ hours and costs US$18.30/30.40 one-way/roundtrip with a steward, air con and movies. Terminal Puerto Bus (☎ 222-2158) is on Alameda Juan Pablo II at 19a Av Norte. Take city buses 29, 101D, 7C or 52.

Terminal de Occidente National bus route No 498 goes to La Hachadura, and No 406 goes to Las Chinamas (both on the Guatemalan border). Both cost around US$1 one-way and take about three hours.

Take bus No 201 to Santa Ana (1½ hours) and from there take bus No 235A to Anguiatú or No 236 to San Cristóbal (both on the Guatemalan border). Either route costs about $US0.80 and takes about 1½ hours, but only three buses a day go to San Cristóbal, so plan ahead.

Hotel San Carlos Tica buses leave from the hotel for Guatemala City at 6 am. They take five hours and cost $US1/2 one-way/ roundtrip. The hotel (☎ 222-4808) is on Calle Concepción between 10 and 12 Avs Norte.

Hotel El Presidente Pullmantur buses for Guatemala City leave at 7 am and 3 pm *exactly*, cost US$45 roundtrip and take three hours. You can buy tickets at the hotel. King Quality (see Puerto Bus above) buses leave from here for Guatemala City at 6:30 am and 3:30 pm and cost US$30 roundtrip.

Hotel El Salvador (Sheraton) Comfort Lines leaves for Guatemala City at 8 am and 2 pm, takes three hours and costs

US$25 roundtrip. You can buy tickets on the bus. Make sure to be there on time, if not earlier.

Buses to/from Honduras
In San Salvador, buses to and from Honduras operate from two terminals and one hotel. International buses can also be picked up in San Miguel; see that section for details.

Terminal Puerto Bus Crucero de Golfo buses leave every day for Tegucigalpa at 6 am and 1 pm. The direct trip takes seven hours and costs US$16; for that price you get air con and a toilet.

Terminal de Oriente Bus No 119 goes to El Poy (Honduras border). The very slow, bumpy trip takes at least three hours, passes through some gorgeous mountain regions and costs US$1. At the border, you can pick up a colectivo to Nueva Ocotepeque and continue by bus from there.

To go to El Amatillo (Honduras border), you have to transfer in San Miguel. From San Salvador take bus No 301 to San Miguel (three hours, US$2) and then take No 330 to the border (two more hours, US$0.50). After crossing the border, you can transfer directly onto a bus to Tegucigalpa or Choluteca.

Hotel San Carlos Tica buses leave for Tegucigalpa at 5:30 am, take eight hours and cost US$1.70/3.40 colones one-way/ roundtrip.

Buses to/from Nicaragua, Costa Rica & Panama
Ticabus leaves the Hotel San Carlos at 5:30 am and arrives in Managua, Nicaragua, at 6 pm. If continuing farther, spend the night (US$7) and leave the following morning at 7 am. The bus arrives in San José, Costa Rica, at 4:30 pm. It then leaves at 10 pm for Panama, where you arrive at 3 pm the following day, making for a grand total of three days of bus travel.

Car

If you drive into El Salvador, you must show a driver's license (an International Driving Permit is accepted) and proof that you own the car. You must also fill out extensive forms. Car insurance is available and advisable but not required. Vehicles may remain in El Salvador for 30 days. To stay any longer, get permission from the Ministerio de Transporte Terrestre (☎ 226-6440) in Colonia El Refugio.

SEA

Ask around at the Golfo de Fonseca for boat rides to Honduras and even Nicaragua. Owners will be happy to comply for the right price. See La Unión for details.

Getting Around

AIR

Transportes Aéreos de El Salvador (TAES; ☎ 227-0314, 227-2046) has daily flights from the Ilopango Airport, 13 km east of San Salvador, to points around the country, but it is absurd to spend money on such a puddle-jump of a trip.

BUS

Buses run frequently to points throughout the country and are very cheap (fares range between US$0.40 and US$3). Note, however, that rates have increased over the last year and will probably increase again. Weekend fares increase up to 50%. Still, they are a great deal for a traveler. Some routes have different categories: regular, directo, preferencial. The last two options cost more, but they get you where you want to go that bit faster. The last bus of the day usually departs in time to reach its destination at or soon after dark. As much as possible take buses early in the morning to make sure you arrive at your destination before dark. Remember, these buses don't drop you off at some secure guesthouse but rather into the chaos of a bus terminal.

Riding buses around the country is a lesson in appreciating the journey as much as the destination. Trips take patience and a tolerance for having your spine realigned. Anyone over 1.6 meters in height (five feet, four inches) will wish for kneepads to soften the blows from the seat in front. If traveling with a backpack that takes up a place someone could sit, you'll be charged twice. This, however, is preferable to putting your pack on the roof.

Locals may caution against taking buses at all, but just take precautions. Sit close to the front, and befriend the guys working on the bus; they are very helpful and will watch out for you.

CAR & MOTORCYCLE

Driving around the country does allow you to see more of it in less time and offers opportunities to see small villages not serviced by buses. However, navigating through areas where roads and turnoffs are not marked can be frustrating. Gas is not cheap either – a gallon of regular unleaded is about US$1.70.

Road Safety

Many roads, even the most traveled, have potholes everywhere. The constant downpours during the rainy season further damage the road and repairs aren't made until the weather clears. Occasionally you'll come across roads that are well paved and marked. In fact, of the 12,250 km of highway in the country, only 1740 km are paved. Get in the habit of lightly honking frequently, especially when passing a car or before turning a curve. Watch out for cows, dogs, chickens, children, oncoming traffic. Also watch for signals from other cars, usually a hand waving for you to pass them or for them to cut you off. Stay alert always and you'll be OK.

Police set up checkpoints, especially on roads to border crossings. Carjacking is a problem, as is stealing parts off parked cars. Use common sense, don't drive alone in areas of ill-repute and park in safe places (find hotels either in safe neighborhoods or with a guarded parking lot). Car insurance is, of course, a good idea, but it is not required. Motorcycle helmets are also not required but likewise recommended.

In the capital city, traffic moves very fast and erratically. Again, stay alert and wave out the window to cut in front of someone when your lane suddenly stops.

Rental

If you decide to drive around, rent a car in San Salvador. Avis, Budget and Hertz all have offices at the international airport as well as in town, but their prices are high (US$35 to US$50 a day). The price usually reflects unlimited mileage *(kilometraje)*.

Cheaper companies include Sure Rent A Car (☎ 225-1488) on Blvd de los Héroes at 23a Calle Poniente, with cars at US$23 per day for one to three days or cheaper if renting for longer periods (US$128 per week). Superior (☎ 222-9111), on the corner of 3a Calle Poniente and 15a Av Norte, has similar rates.

Keep in mind, however, that the cheapest rates are for cars that will be unfit for some of the roads you may want to drive on. Four-wheel drive (4WD) costs quite a bit more, up to US$60 a day. Tropic (☎ 223-7947) at 3579 Av Olímpica (in the same building as SET Tours) rents out 4WD vehicles at competitive rates, especially when renting for longer periods. Corsatur in San Salvador may have a list of other rental-car companies.

HITCHHIKING

See the Getting Around chapter for details.

LOCAL TRANSPORT

Most towns in El Salvador have taxis, all of them painted a bright yellow. You will see them cruising around everywhere in San Salvador and most other large towns, or you can phone for one. A typical fare in any town is about US$2, but negotiate the fare before you get into the cab.

ORGANIZED TOURS

SET Tour (☎ 279-3235), Av Olímpica, No 3597, in San Salvador's Colonia Escalón, offers tours around the city, the country and elsewhere in Central America. Their Adven-Tours series includes 4WD trips around El Salvador, Honduras and Guatemala for two weeks for US$1000. Trips around El Salvador range from two to five days and cost US$130 to US$510. In the US write to PO Box 52-5364, Vip No 1514, Miami, FL 33152-5364.

San Salvador

Population 493,194

San Salvador is the largest city in El Salvador and the principal center for the entire country. It takes only a few hours to get from the capital to any point in the country, so the city makes a convenient base.

The declining economy during the war set off an internal migration of people from the countryside to the city, which expanded with new urban poor. Unemployment is high and people do whatever they can to get by. Everywhere people are trying to sell things, be it lottery tickets, armloads of T-shirts, pieces of fruit (from Washington state in the US at that) to Velcro gun holsters. Some districts, such as San Benito and Colonia Escalón are as luxurious as any well-to-do neighborhoods in wealthier countries, while other areas of the city are large colonies of shacks made of corrugated tin and mud, balancing precariously on the edges of polluted rivers.

Despite its long history, there are no old buildings to see. The city has been destroyed several times – by earthquakes in 1854 and 1873, by the most recent eruption of the San Salvador Volcano in 1917, and yet again by floods in 1934. The earthquake of October 10, 1986, caused considerable damage in San Salvador. Reconstruction is still going on; the elegant Palacio Nacional, for example, is still being repaired, and the national museum is still closed.

History

San Salvador was founded in 1525 by the Spanish conqueror Pedro de Alvarado about 30 km to the northeast of where it now stands, near Suchitoto. Three years

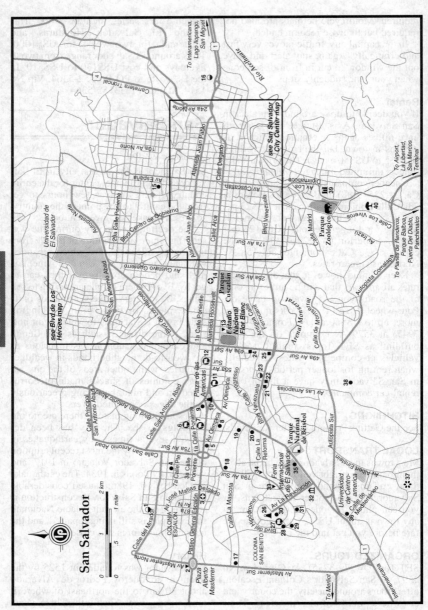

San Salvador

PLACES TO STAY	7	Nicaragua Embassy	23	Terminal de Occidente
21 Hotel Roma	8	SET Tours/Tropic	26	Monumento a la
22 Hotel Pasadena		Car Rental		Revolución
24 Hotel Occidental	9	Taca Airlines	27	Mexico Embassy
25 Hotel Valencia	10	Monumento a El Salvador	28	Corsatur
		del Mundo	29	Zone Disco
PLACES TO EAT	11	Costa Rica	30	Hotel El Presidente
2 Kalapataru		Embassy/American		(Pullmantur)
13 Palace Cafe		Airlines, Edificio Centro	31	Mario's
33 Pizza Hut		Americana: United Airlines	32	Museo Nacional
34 L'Opera	12	Panama Embassy,		Davíd J Gúzman
		Copa Airlines	35	Mercado Nacional
OTHER	14	Hospital Rosales		de Artesanías
1 Hotel El Salvador	15	Cuscatlán Escuela	36	La Ceiba de Guadalupe
(Comfort Lines)		de Idiomas	37	Jardín Botánico La Laguna
3 Hospital de la Mujer	16	Terminal de Oriente	38	Estadio Cuscatlán
4 SalvaNatura Office	17	El Arbol de Dios	39	Casa Presidencial
5 Ríos Tropicales	18	Bargain Rent-a-Car	40	Parque Saburo Hirao,
6 Honduras Embassy	19	American Express/El		Museo de Historia Natural
		Salvador Travel Service		
	20	K'OZ		

later it was moved to its present site; it was declared a city in 1546.

San Salvador was the capital of the colonial province of Cuscatlán. It was here, in 1811, that Father José Matías Delgado made the first call for the independence of Central America. From 1834 to 1839 San Salvador was the capital of the United Provinces of Central America. It has been the capital of El Salvador since 1839.

Orientation

San Salvador's central area follows the same grid as most Central American cities. Unfortunately, someone forgot to put up signs or repaint the names on the curbs. Refer to the San Salvador map to see the main roads around the city.

From the '0' point where the cathedral is (see Central San Salvador map), Av España goes north and Av Cuscatlán south; Calle Arce runs to the west and Calle Delgado to the east.

Av España leads up to 29a Calle Poniente, which leads to Blvd de los Héroes, Autopista Norte and Calle San Antonio Abad (to the west). Av Cuscatlán crosses Blvd Venezuela, which leads to Terminal de Occidente (west) and to Terminal de Oriente (east). Av Cuscatlán continues south, crossing Autopista Comalapa, which goes to the airport, and to Parque Balboa and Puerto del Diablo.

From the city center, 1 Calle Poniente and 2 Calle Poniente (Calle Rubén Darío) are the main roads heading west and they cross 49a Av Norte, which in turn becomes Blvd de los Héroes. 2a Calle Poniente turns into Alameda Roosevelt, passes Plaza de las Americas and turns into Paseo General Escalón. From Plaza de las Americas, the Interamericana leads southwest towards the Zona Rosa and out of the city. Universidad de El Salvador is near the intersection of Blvd de los Héroes and Calle San Antonio Abad. Universidad de CentroAmerica is near the intersection of Interamericana and Autopista Sur.

Maps You can get maps at the tourist office (see below) or Bargain Rent-a-Car (☎ 223-1668), 79a Av Sur, No 6, near the corner of Calle La Mascota or at the airport for US$2. Larger stationery stores, such as Papelería Ibérica on Calle San Antonio Abad, sell an excessively detailed map of San Salvador made by Instituto Nacional de Geographía (ING). Go straight to ING (☎ 276-5900, ext 231 or 232) in Ciudad Delgado for the same map, and photocopies of maps of other towns and topographic maps. It's open 8 am to 12:20 pm

EL SALVADOR

EL SALVADOR

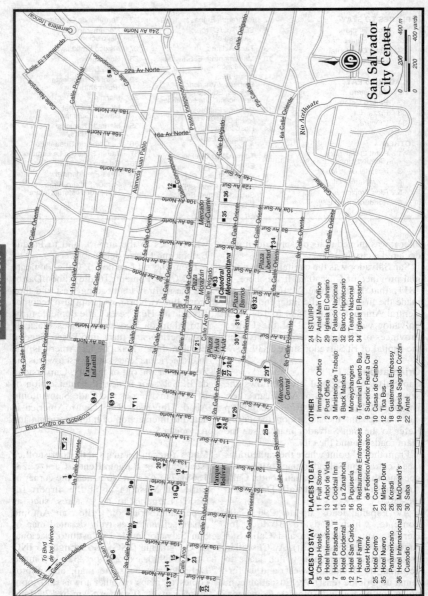

San Salvador
City Center

0   200   400 m
0   200   400 yards

PLACES TO STAY
5   Cheap Hotels
6   Hotel International
7   Hotel Pasadena II
8   Hotel Occidental
12 Hotel San Carlos
17 Hotel Family
    Guest Home
25 Hotel Centro
35 Hotel Nuevo
    Panamericano
36 Hotel Internacional
    Custodio

PLACES TO EAT
11 Fruit Store
13 Arbol de Vida
14 Cocktail Inn
15 La Zanahoria
16 Pupusería
20 Restaurante Entremeses
    de Federico/Actoteatro
21 Corona
23 Mister Donut
26 Koradi
28 McDonald's
30 Saba

OTHER
1   Immigration Office
2   Post Office
3   Ministerio de Trabajo
4   Black Market
    Moneychangers
6   Terminal Puerto Bus
10 Casas de Cambio
12 Tica Bus
19 Guatemala Embassy
19 Iglesia Sagrado Corzán
22 Antel
24 ISTU/IRP
27 Antel Main Office
29 Iglesia El Calvario
31 Palacio Nacional
32 Banco Hipotecario
33 Teatro Nacional
34 Iglesia El Rosario

and 2:10 to 5 pm. Take bus No 443B from downtown; a taxi costs about US$3.50.

Information

Tourist Offices See Tourist Offices under Facts for the Visitor for details.

Important Offices Visa renewal and other immigration matters are handled at the Oficina de Immigración (☎ 221-2111) in the federal building in the Centro Gobierno. The office is open Monday to Friday from 8 am to noon and 1:30 to 4 pm.

To get permission to stay at the three government-run centers go to the Ministerio del Trabajo (☎ 222-8151) in Edificio Urrutia Abrego in the Centro Gobierno.

For permission to visit Parque El Imposible, head to SalvaNatura (☎ 223-3620, 298-4001, fax 223-3620), Pasaje Istmania 315 between 77a and 79a Avs Norte in Colonia Escalón.

El Salvador Travel Service (☎ 279-3844), Centro Comercial Mascota, Calle La Mascota, is an American Express agent and will hold mail for card and check holders.

Foreign Embassies See the Facts for the Visitor section at the start of this chapter for a listing of foreign embassies.

Money Banco Hipotecario across the street from Plaza Barrios in the center changes traveler's checks without a problem. Most other banks require long waits and unnecessary paper work. A string of casas de cambio are along Alameda Juan Pablo II by Parque Infantíl. You'll find black-market moneychangers in this area as well, but their rates are worse than the casas or bank and you must trade cash. Terminal Puerto Bus has a couple of casas de cambio. There's a bank in the same building as American Express (see above) that changes at decent rates.

Post & Communications The central post office is in the Centro Gobierno complex. It's open Monday to Saturday from 8 am to 4 pm but closes from noon to 1 pm. There are smaller branches in the Mercado Central at Local No 3; on Plaza Morazán, fronting the Teatro Nacional on 2a Av Norte, on the 1st floor over the PHL stationery shop; and on the first level of Metrocentro on the Blvd de los Héroes.

Also at the main post office is an EMS international courier office. You can find dozens of other courier services throughout the country, but we can't vouch that one is any more reliable than the others.

Antel's main office is in the center, on the corner of Calle Rubén Darío and 5a Av Sur. The office is open daily from 6 am to 10 pm. Another branch is in the large white Torre Roble by Metrocentro on Blvd de los Héroes, open Monday to Saturday, 7 am to 6 pm, closed Sunday. Yet another is at the corner of 23 Calle Poniente and Calle Rubén Darío. From these offices you can also send faxes and telegraphs. Antel's large building in the Centro Gobierno is a business office only.

Bookstores You can find *librerías* along 4a Av Norte and on Calle Arce, but none are particularly inspiring and few have any books in English. Shaw's, a coffee shop in Metrocentro, has some English books, along with decent coffee. The most interesting books can be found in cultural cafes and centers like La Ventana and La Luna (see Places to Eat and Entertainment as well as the Blvd de los Héroes map).

Laundry There is a laundry next to Hotel Happy House (see Places to Stay) behind Camino Real.

Medical Services Hospital Rosales on the corner of Alameda Roosevelt and 25a Av Sur is a basic hospital, but by all accounts avoid landing there. The US Embassy recommends Hospital de la Mujer (☎ 223-8955) between 81a and 83a Avs Sur and Calle Juan José Cañas.

Emergency For emergencies dial ☎ 123 or 121. However, check with Corsatur whether these codes still exist or have changed.

EL SALVADOR

Dangers & Annoyances Crime is a growing problem, especially crime involving gangs and firearms. The central area, in particular, is considered unsafe for walking after 8 pm. Other more well-to-do districts are safer, but it's still wise to get a taxi if you're out late at night (the buses stop running at 9 pm). See Facts for the Visitor for more information.

The biggest annoyance is pollution. The smoke emitted from buses is like oily air that gets into your eyes, nose, mouth. Sunglasses provide good protection not only from the bright sun but from all those nasty particles. A scarf comes in handy, too, for either wiping off the sweat or breathing into when you see the smoke arising.

Things to See

City Center Look for the large, tall dome of the **Catedral Metropolitana**. This marks the '0' intersection of the city – Av Cuscatlán/Av España and Calle Arce/Calle Delgado. The cathedral is in a constant state of repair, and the pink concrete mass is not as inspiring as some other churches around the city. Archbishop Romero's tomb is here. Across the street is **Plaza Barrios**, the city's large principal plaza, now with cracked cement, graffiti-marred statues and hammock vendors. The **Palacio Nacional** is better off than the cathedral, but it's still surrounded by twisted wire fences and sheets of corrugated iron. This is where the government met before the devastation of the 1986 earthquake. Photo exhibits are sometimes shown in the lobby of the palace.

Behind the cathedral and one street over, on the corner of Calle Delgado and 2a Av Sur, is the gem of the city, **Teatro Nacional**. It was built in 1917 in an opulent style, with ornate golden boxes and trimmings, lots of lush red velvet and a sensuous ceiling mural. If you can't go to see a show, ask if you can take a look around. The theater faces onto the small **Plaza Morazán**, which is best avoided.

Two blocks east of Plaza Barrios is the equally large **Plaza Libertad**, with a winged statue of Liberty facing **El Rosario**, an unusual 'modern' style church built on the site of a demolished older one. It looks like a gymnasium with stained glass. The father of Central American independence, Father Delgado, is buried here.

Mercado Ex-Cuartel has a mixture of handicrafts, ceramics and artesanías, as well as clothing and towels. Vendors here can be pushy, but prices for handicrafts are cheaper than in other markets, especially when you bargain. It covers one city block, bordered by Calle Delgado and 1a Calle Oriente and 8a and 10a Avs Norte, three blocks east of the Teatro Nacional along Calle Delgado.

The most interesting part of the center is the huge **Mercado Central**, in the area of 8a and 10a Calles Poniente, Calle Gerardo Barrios, and 5a Av Sur. Stacks of shoes and moldy plantains, large blocks of cheese and every possible household good are crammed together along the streets. The stalls wind around the decaying **Iglesia El Calvario** on Gerardo Barrios and 3a Av Sur. To the south of the church are stalls of natural medicines, including magic potions to splash on yourself for good luck to armadillo skins to cure the flu.

West of the Center Calle Rubén Darío heads west out of the center, changing names a couple of times along the way and passing by the following parks and monuments. Bus No 52 rumbles down the entire length of this road. When the street is Alameda Roosevelt, it goes by **Parque Cuscatlán**, a spot of green but not one that is well kept. Farther along, it passes Estadio Nacional Flor Blanc, the national stadium where soccer games and an occasional rock concert are held. At 65a Av you come to the **Plaza de las Américas**, with the statue **El Salvador del Mundo**. This symbol of the country depicts Jesus standing on top of the world.

West beyond this plaza the road changes to Paseo General Escalón. It passes Parque Escalón and goes through the upper-class **Colonia Escalón**, one of San Salvador's better nightlife and residential districts, with cinemas, *galerías* (shopping centers) and pricey restaurants. Roads from here lead to Hotel El Salvador to the north, and Colonia San Benito and the Zona Rosa to the south. Farther west you hit Plaza Masferrer.

At Plaza Masferrer, turn south onto Av Masferrer and walk about four long blocks to **El Arbol de Dios**, the gallery and restaurant of famous La Palma artist Fernando Llort. This gallery houses an extensive collection of his work, with excellent sculptures and canvas paintings that are very different from his simpler and better-known wood paintings. The gallery is open Monday to Saturday from 9 am to 6 or 6:30 pm.

Southwest of the Center From Plaza de las Américas, head southwest on the Interamericana as if you were leaving the city. Bus No 34 comes this way from the center; you can catch it at the corner of 4a Calle Poniente and 7a Av Sur.

As you head out of the city you'll pass the grounds of the Feria Internacional de El Salvador, where you'll find the **Mercado Nacional de Artesanías**. Prices and quality for handicrafts are higher here than at Mercado Ex-Cuartel.

A bit north of the fairground is the **Cuartel**, where the military is trained. Beside it is the **Parque Nacional de Béisbol**, the national baseball stadium.

Opposite the Feria Internacional on Av la Revolución, almost at the corner of the Interamericana, is the **Museo Nacional Davíd J Guzmán**, which has been closed for restoration for a number of years. Check with Corsatur about its status. If and when it does open, it holds most of the country's notable archaeological finds.

Venture up Av la Revolución to **Zona Rosa**, San Salvador's ritzy and exclusive restaurant and nightlife district in Colonia San Benito. You'll recognize it by the plush Blvd del Hipódromo lined with manicured lawns and street lamps indiscreetly advertising Coca-Cola, MasterCard and Levi's. Up Av la Revolución from Blvd del Hipódromo is the larger-than-life stone mosaic **Monumento a la Revolución** juxtaposed next to swanky hotels – Hotel El Presidente,

and (by the time you read this), one of the 'most technologically advanced hotels in the world,' Hotel Princesa.

At Universided de CentroAmerica (UCA) on Autopista Sur, **Centro Monseñor Romero** is a well-organized museum that pays homage to Romero, the Jesuits and massacres in the northern reaches of the country. In another room are photo albums with very graphic and equally disturbing photos of the six Jesuits, their housekeeper and her daughter as they were found after the brutal massacre. The Jesuits are buried in the chapel just a few meters away.

To reach the center, take the road to the left and up after passing the guard. It's open weekdays 8 am to noon, 2 to 5 pm. There is no admission fee.

Farther southwest on the Interamericana is the elegant white **La Ceiba de Guadalupe**, an attractive church and a welcome refuge from the heat and smoke of the road. Round stained-glass windows rotate to let air circulate.

If it's time to breath some oxygen, head to the **Jardín Botánico La Laguna**, also called Plan de La Laguna, an attractive botanical garden in an area that was once a swamp at the bottom of a volcanic crater. The park is shady and cool even on a hot day and has a pleasant cafeteria next to a pond.

The garden is open every day 9 am to 5:30 pm, except Monday; admission is US$0.50. It is near Antiguo Cuscatlán on the outskirts of San Salvador. Take bus No 44 from the center; the bus driver will let you off at the right spot, from which it's a one-km downhill walk to the garden.

Blvd de los Héroes From the center, take bus No 29 or 30 to this wide US-influenced boulevard, replete with fast-food chains, gas stations, video stores and lots of neon signs. North of the boulevard is a residential area where quite a few 'internationals' live and where the majority of casas de húespedes are. You'll find some interesting cultural centers (see Entertainment), a good variety of restaurants and decent nightspots. **Universidad de El Salvador** is near the corner of Blvd de los Héroes and

EL SALVADOR

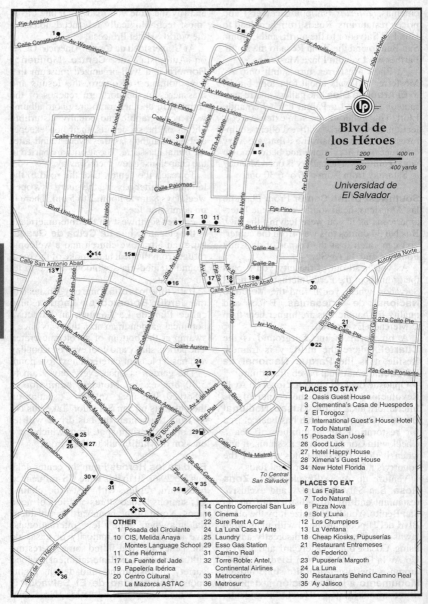

Blvd de los Héroes

0   200   400 m
0   200   400 yards

Universidad de El Salvador

PLACES TO STAY
2   Oasis Guest House
3   Clementina's Casa de Huespedes
4   El Torogoz
5   International Guest's House Hotel
7   Todo Natural
15 Posada San José
26 Good Luck
27 Hotel Happy House
28 Ximena's Guest House
34 New Hotel Florida

PLACES TO EAT
6   Las Fajitas
7   Todo Natural
8   Pizza Nova
9   Sol y Luna
12 Los Chumpipes
13 La Ventana
18 Cheap Kiosks, Pupuserías
21 Restaurant Entremeses de Federico
23 Pupusería Margoth
24 La Luna
30 Restaurants Behind Camino Real
35 Ay Jalisco

OTHER
1   Posada del Circulante
10 CIS, Melida Anaya Montes Language School
11 Cine Reforma
17 La Fuente del Jade
19 Papelería Ibérica
20 Centro Cultural La Mazorca ASTAC

14 Centro Comercial San Luis
16 Cinema
22 Sure Rent A Car
24 La Luna Casa y Arte
25 Laundry
29 Esso Gas Station
31 Camino Real
32 Torre Roble: Antel, Continental Airlines
33 Metrocentro
36 Metrosur

To Central San Salvador

EL SALVADOR

Calle Abad. Bus 44 also runs from the city center and along Blvd Universitario.

Opposite Hotel Camino Real is **Metrocentro** and **Metrosur**, two shopping malls. Prices are higher than elsewhere, but it offers one-stop shopping with a supermarket, Antel office (inside Torre Roble), casa de cambio, post office and a food court all in close proximity.

South of the Center Sites of interest south are quite far away, but worth the trip. The **Teleférico de San Jacinto** is an amusement park that reopened in August 1996 after a few years' hiatus caused by lack of funds. The gondola ride up to the top of the hill is a must; the 10-minute ride takes you to the sky and exposes the volcanoes and lakes surrounding the city. Green parakeets circle the park below and the city's immensity spreads out before you. The amusement park at the top of the hill is uncommonly clean and full of rides, video arcades and restaurants serving overpriced food and drinks. The park is open Wednesday to Sunday 10 am to 9 pm, but on weekend nights it stays open until later as long as there are crowds. (Last ride to the top is at 9 pm though.) US$3 gets you in and a ride to the top (roundtrip, of course). Rides cost US$1.20 to US$1.60. Plan to go around sunset for a real thrill. Bus No 9 takes you to the entrance.

South on Av Cuscatlán a few sites hold some partial interest: **Parque Zoológico** is open Wednesday to Sunday from 9 am to 5 pm. About 350 meters farther south, **Parque Saburo Hirao**, open Wednesday to Sunday from 9 am to 4 pm, has the **Museo de Historia Natural**, with so-so exhibits. Bus No 2 goes to the zoo, leaving from Av Cuscatlán between Calle Arce and Calle Rubén Darío.

If you head straight south on Av Cuscatlán without turning off for the zoo, you pass the **Casa Presidencial**, the presidential palace. Continue south on Calle Principal to go to the **Planes de Renderos**, **Parque Balboa**, **Puerta del Diablo** and **Panchimalco** (see South of San Salvador).

Language Courses

Both of the following schools have structured programs and hours and are recommended by travelers and NGOers alike. Melida Anaya Montes Language School operates out of the Centro Internacional de Solidaridad (CIS, ☎ 225-0076, net; see Useful Organizations). Intensive all-day classes cost US$95 per week. Should you wish to be placed with a family, room and board is US$50 a week including two meals per day. There is an additional administration fee of US$12.50 tacked on per week.

Cuscatlán Escuela de Idiomas (☎ /fax 226-0800), 1a Av Norte and 19 Calle Poniente, offers 20 hours of lessons a week for US$100 and can arrange lodging with a family for US$75. Three-day cultural/political trips cost US$40. Take bus No 2 from the center, get off at Mercado San Miguelito and walk two blocks.

Organized Tours

See Organized Tours in the Getting Around section.

Places to Stay

While there is no shortage of hotels around San Salvador, you may need to do some thinking about what you are willing to pay for. Many cheap hotels can be found around the two main bus terminals, but the neighborhoods are not safe, especially at night, and necessitate caution, especially for women traveling alone. You can find better service and safety in a few places near the center and a whole slew of guesthouses above Blvd de los Héroes. These cost about US$10 a night but offer safety, clean sheets and more freedom to go out at night.

City Center If braving the *centro* is for you, one of the best deals is the large, clean *Hotel Internacional Custodio* at 10a Av Sur, No 109, right near Mercado Ex-Cuartel. Single/double rooms here are US$4.50/7, with private bath US$9. A triple with private bath runs around US$17. Checkout time is at noon, and you can ask to do laundry.

Hotel Nuevo Panamericano (☎ 222-2959) at 8a Av Sur, No 113, is a smaller place, with 18 rooms arranged around a central courtyard/parking area. Rates are US$8.60/10 for rooms with a private bath behind a wall reaching only halfway to the ceiling.

Hotel San Carlos (☎ 222-4808, 222-8975) at 121 Calle Concepción, between 10a and 12a Avs Norte, is a good deal if taking Tica buses early in the morning – they leave from here. Rates for clean, small rooms with private bath are US$6.50 per person. They also have a locked parking lot.

Close to the Mercado Central and in an area full of machismo, *Hotel Centro* (☎ 271-5045) at 9a Av Sur, No 410, is a clean and attractive hotel catering mainly to couples. All the rooms have TV, telephone and private bath and cost US$10/17 for 12/24 hours. You can climb up a ladder to get to the 'roof garden.'

The following are about a 10-minute walk from the center in a residential area to the west. They are convenient to the Puerto Bus terminal and the Centro Gobierno. *Hotel Family Guest Home* (☎ 222-1902, 221-2349) at 1a Calle Poniente Bis, No 925, is half a block north of 1a Calle Poniente between 15a and 17a Avs Norte. Single rooms with double bed and private bath are US$16. The couple of rooms with shared bath cost US$9/10.30 for two/three people. Upstairs there is a host of beds for US$7.50 each, but la señora will only rent them out to groups of four or more. The workers here are delightful, and the food is good and cheap. If you have special requests, the cook can accommodate you.

On 3a Calle Poniente, No 1037, is *Hotel Pasadena II* (☎ 221-4786) with single/double/triple rooms for US$8/11.50/17 with private bath. A block away on the other side of the street is the rundown *Hotel Occidental* (☎ 221-0605) with similar prices.

Near the Terminal de Oriente About a 10-minute walk from the Terminal de Oriente you'll find a cluster of cheap hotels on Calle Concepción near the traffic circle

at 24a Av Norte. The area is a little seedy, so be careful, especially at night. No one hotel outshines the others, so check out a few and decide which you feel better about. Bus No 4 runs to the city center from Calle Concepción.

Hotel Imperial (☎ 222-4920) at No 659 charges US$4 – 6/8 for singles/doubles with shared bath, with private bath US$7/14. *Hospedaje Emperador* (☎ 222-7572) at No 665 has only doubles for US$5.70/8.60 with shared/private bath.

Hotel Yucatán (☎ 221-2585), No 673, charges US$2.80/4.60, with private bath US$4/7. *Hotel Cuscatlán* (☎ 222-3298), No 675, has the most selection with single or double/triple rooms costing US$6.80/10.30, all with private bath and TV. *Hospedaje Figueroa* (☎ 222-1541), No 653, charges US$3.40/4, with private bath US$8.

Near the Terminal de Occidente Turn right (west) on Blvd Venezuela from the terminal to find *Hotel Pasadena* (☎ 223-1905) at No 3093; single/double/triple rooms cost US$6.80/11.50/17, all with private baths that are rather grotty. Another few doors west at No 3145 is the poorly maintained *Hotel Roma* (☎ 224-0256) with rooms with shared bath at US$4.60/5.70. Both of these hotels look over a shanty town and balance precariously on the 'Aguas Negras' (Black Waters, as in sewage runoff).

Turn left (west) out of the terminal and at the corner of 49a Av there is *Hotel Valencia* (☎ 223-1521). Singles/doubles with tiny bathrooms are US$6.80/11.50. Going north on 49a Av Norte you'll find *Hotel Occidental* (☎ 223-7715) at 49a Av Sur, No 171. Singles/doubles/triples cost US$11.50/17/23 for large rooms with large bathrooms, air con and TV. If you stay, ask for a room away from the street. Bus No 44 passes by the hotel.

Near Blvd de los Héroes During the war a few FMLN-supporters who lived around Universidad de El Salvador began opening their houses to people who wanted to learn more about the leftists' ideologies. Some of these guesthouses are run by ex-FMLN combatants. Most of them charge around US$10 a person, more for a private bath. All offer breakfast – sometimes it's complimentary, but most of the time you pay about US$2. Many of these places house large groups, so call to make sure there is space available. Buses No 29 and No 30 run frequently between here and the center.

The following are north of Blvd de los Héroes along 39a Av Norte (also referred to as Gabriela Mistral or Morazán). *Ximena's Guest House* (☎ 226-9268) at 202A Calle San Salvador charges US$6/6.50 for dorm-style rooms with shared bath. Otherwise, you pay US$13.80/27 for a private bath. A few steps north from the corner of 39a Av Norte and Blvd Universitario is a restaurant called *Todo Natural*. Inquire here about lodging in the guesthouse in the same building (US$15 a person, including breakfast) or at *Posada San José* (☎ 226-2100), with rooms for US$10 to 15. Both places are run by a nice, energetic group of people.

Turn right at Blvd Universitario and turn left at 35a Av Norte to get to *International Guest's House Hotel* at No 35. Rooms cost US$11.50 single, US$20 a couple, US$23 double, all with private bath and including a free continental breakfast. This place is very pleasant, and the managers try to make sure it stays that way. Next door is *El Torogoz* (☎ 225-1656) with similar prices but without the breakfast; however, there are some cheaper shared rooms.

Clementina's Casa de Huéspedes (☎ 225-5962), Av Morazán (39a Av Norte), No 34, has doubles for US$17 and singles for US$11.50. There's a quiet garden area with hammocks, and meals are available. Follow Av Morazán north to *Oasis Guest House* (☎ 226-5983, net) at the corner of Pasaje Santa Marta. The price per person is US$10. The lodging isn't *lujoso*, but the owners, Carolina and Damián, are friendly and helpful, and can answer all your questions about the war (from their perspective at least), and they have email!

Farther north is *Casa Maya* (☎ 274-5267) on Av Cuchumatanes, Polígono 'C,'

No 12. It's far away but comes highly recommended by NGOers. Rooms cost around US$12. Bus No 30 passes nearby on Av Bernal.

South of Blvd de los Héroes is *New Hotel Florida* (☎ 226-1858) at 115 Pasaje Los Almendros. From Héroes, go down Pasaje Las Palmeras (where there's a Pops restaurant) for two short blocks and turn right into a tiny cul-de-sac. The rooms and bathrooms are small and cost too much: single/double/triple rooms go for US$20/25/30. The best deal is to be with someone else and ask for rooms 14 or 15, which have excellent views.

Behind Camino Real are other and rather overpriced hotels. *Hotel Happy House* (☎ 226-6866) at Av Sisimiles, No 2951, charges single/double/triple US$22/26/30 and *Good Luck* (☎ 226-8287) at No 2943 charges US$25/28 single/double and that's without air con.

Places to Eat

City Center One good breakfast place is *Palace Cafe* (☎ 222-2562) at the corner of 43a Av Sur and 4a Calle Poniente. A plate of eggs, casamiento, bananas and coffee costs about US$2.

Another good choice is *Mister Donut*; there's one on Calle Arce near 21a Av Norte. The food is consistently decent and if you are fed up with eggs, you can get donuts instead.

Koradi, on 9a Av Sur near 4a Calle Poniente, is a vegetarian restaurant serving tamales and pupusas for breakfast from 7:30 am, and vegetarian comida a la vista for lunch. It's also a store, so it stays open until 6 pm on weekdays, 3 pm on Saturday.

Arbol de Vida on 21a Av Norte near Calle Arce (look for the sign at the Plaza Real complex) serves up a great variety of vegetarian dishes from noon to 3 pm, closed Sunday. A block away, *La Zanahoria*, at 1144 Calle Arce between 19a and 21a Avs Norte, is also vegetarian. It doesn't have the same variety but does have a good juice bar, and it stays open weekdays from 8 am to 7 pm (lunch is only served until 2 pm), Saturday 8 am to 2 pm.

EL SALVADOR

On 1a Calle Poniente between 13a and 15a Avs Norte, *Restaurante Entremeses de Federico* serves up an ample buffet in the old Actoteatro building; a full plate runs about US$2.50. It is open only from noon to 2 pm, Monday to Saturday.

On 9a Av Norte between 3a and 5a Calles Poniente there's a fruit store that excels in quality and variety. Behind the Palacio Nacional on 1a Av Sur you'll find *Saba*; supposedly it's Chinese, but there's no soy sauce on the tables. Skimpy platos del día cost US$1.50, larger ones US$3. Or go to the pastelería next door.

Around 4 pm, the pupusa hour, kiosks open up at Plaza Hula Hula. On the west side are hot dog and torta vendors, and on the north side are the pupusa vendors. A block from Plaza Hula Hula is *Corona*, open 7 am to 8 pm with buffet breakfasts and lunch.

Food stalls and pupusa vendors are around the markets.

For dinner there isn't much choice around the center – not surprising since everything shuts down early. However, *chupaderos* (see Entertainment) serve basic sandwiches and fries until later. One such, *Cocktail Inn*, is on 21a Av Norte between Calle Arce and 1a Calle Poniente.

Blvd de los Héroes Welcome to fast-food heaven. If you've got a hankering for a burger but can't decide what style, you have your choice along this strip. Remember, however, that US fast-food restaurants maintain US prices, and you could get a more filling, cheaper meal at a local restaurant.

In Metrosur, south of Av Los Andes, is *El Ranchón*, a large open-air food court with food stalls for Mexican, Chinese, fish & chips, baked potatoes and other varieties. On Pasaje Las Palmeras, near New Hotel Florida, *Ay Jalisco* serves over-salted Tex-Mex food for around US$4 to US$8.

Take Calle Los Sisimiles up behind Camino Real, where you'll find cheap Chinese restaurants mixed in with fancier

steak and seafood places. Better yet, go up 39a Av Norte (also called Gabriela Mistral). On nearby Calle Berlin there is *La Luna*, where you can order good grilled sandwiches along with cheese plates and salads. (See also Entertainment.)

For anyone missing good coffee, *La Ventana* (☎ 226-5129) across from Comercial San Luis on Calle Abad, serves espresso drinks. For breakfast, large omelets come with potatoes, bread and coffee, and cost about US$3.50. Sweet crepes cost US$2.50. You can read the local paper or the *New York Times* while you wait. It is also open for lunch and dinner (closed Monday). The neighborhood around Comercial San Luis is currently growing fast, so there will be plenty of other good places to check out.

At the corner of 39a Av Norte and Blvd Universitario is a cluster of restaurants. *Las Fajitas* serves Mexican; quesadillas cost around US$2.50. Up 39a a bit is *Todo Natural* (for lunch only). The well-prepared and filling vegetarian lunches are offered on a fixed-price menu and cost US$2. At *Pizza Nova* you can get a slice and a soda or beer for US$1.20.

Going down Blvd Universitario you come to *Sol y Luna*, another vegetarian restaurant with a fixed-price menu (US$2). It stays open until 9 pm and serves pupusas and fruit salad in the evening. Across the road is *Los Chumpipes*, specializing in messy turkey sandwiches costing around US$1.50. Monday is their two-for-one day. Other than that you'll find makeshift pupusa stands in the neighborhood.

Up Blvd de los Héroes toward the university, *Restaurant Entremeses de Federico* at 25a Calle Poniente, No 1144, behind the Bloom Hospital, has a lunchtime buffet. It's open from 11 am to 2 pm Monday to Saturday. If you venture up this way from Metrocentro, you can't miss *Pupusería Margoth*, a large thatch-covered lot with women slapping out pupusas con queso, frijoles, and chicharrón by the bucket loads. It's open late, too.

Other Areas Experience wealth without blowing your budget at the French restaurant *L'Opera* (☎ 223-7289) on Calle La Reforma near 79a Av Sur in Zona Rosa. A lunchtime 'menu ejecutivo' costs about US$8 and includes an appetizer, entree and dessert. From 3 to 7 pm order crepes – a ham-and-cheese crepe costs US$3.20 or a chocolate one US$2.50. The food here is delicious and filling, and the service impeccable. Also in Zona Rosa is a *Pizza Hut* popular with teenagers.

Kalapataru (☎ 279-2306) on Av Masferrer, right off the plaza of the same name is open for lunch and dinner with vegetarian specials, either a la carte or buffet-style. And they serve gourmet pupusas with such stuffings as spinach, broccoli and garlic.

Entertainment

Performances *Teatro Nacional* hosts dance, theater and musical performances including folkloric music and the national symphony. Tickets cost about US$3 and can be purchased at the box office before the show.

Other theatrical performances and poetry readings take place at *Posada del Circulante*, on the bus No 26 route on Av Washington one block up from the gasoline station and two blocks east of Av Bernal, in front of the Parque Satilite (see Blvd de los Héroes map). You can't miss it. Of course, the mariachis that stroll along Blvd de los Héroes and entertain patrons in bars and people walking along the street are one of the best forms of entertainment.

Dance Clubs The city comes alive on weekends. In fact dance clubs start promotional deals on Wednesday – ladies' night, student night, two-for-one night and so on. Colonia San Benito and Colonia Escalón is where all the action is. *K'OZ* on the 3rd floor of the Plaza Suiza on the Interamericana is a good, fun venue open to a mixed crowd. The cover Wednesday to Saturday is US$6.

Another relaxed place is *Zone Disco* on Blvd Hipódromo. There's no cover Wednesday or Thursday, but you're obliged to order a drink; the cover on Friday and Saturday is US$6, including a drink. It stays open until around 3 am.

The *Olimpo*, Condominio Juan Pablo Segundo in Colonia Miramontes, is gay friendly; open Saturday only. *Lapsus*, in Colonia Escalón, and *Mario's*, on Blvd del Hipódromo, are private 'in' clubs, but the cover is outrageous (around US$12) and the dress code will challenge backpackers.

Cinemas *Cine Reforma* on Blvd Universitario is a decent movie house with overzealous air con. La Luna and La Fuente de Jade both screen videos at their venues (see Bars & Clubs below).

Bars & Clubs The NGO-hood north of Blvd de los Héroes has a cluster of artistic venues. The trendsetter is *La Luna Casa y Arte* (☎ 225-4987), 228 Calle Berlin, the coolest club in the city, offering live jazz and rock, movies, and guest chefs. Cover ranges from free to US$3.50. The food is good, sangria fresh, and you can order from a whole range of mixed drinks.

La Ventana (see Places to Eat) is also a popular hangout and a place to down German beers. Check out some of the other nearby places that have opened recently.

La Fuente del Jade (☎ 225-8226), Av C, No 116, near Calle Abad in Colonia el Roble, presents movies on Saturday afternoons (US$1.15) and has live music on Friday and Saturday (US$1.70). During the week they may also host poetry readings, tarot card readings, guitar workshops and cultural events.

When in the mood to hammer down a few Pilsners, head to the *chupaderos* around the city. You can identify these beer gardens by large advertisements for either Pilsner or 'Mi Barrilito.' Some will have live music and most offer mediocre food. This is definitely a guy's place to drink; if a woman shows up unescorted, she'll likely be the focus of excessive male attention.

EL SALVADOR

Spectator Sports
In San Salvador, soccer games are held in the Estadio Nacional (on 49a Av Sur) and Estadio Cuscatlán (just off Autopista Sur). Entry is around US$1.70.

Baseball is another favorite. San Salvador's Parque Nacional de Béisbol is southwest of the center on the Interamericana. Basketball is becoming more popular, especially in schools. Check newspapers for game schedules.

Things to Buy
See Things to Buy in Facts for the Visitor for a rundown on what to buy. Mercado Ex-Cuartel, (see Things to See, above) has various stalls selling handicrafts. Prices are lower here than at other markets, but the vendors are more pushy. Bargain for a good price.

The Mercado Nacional de Artesanías is in the grounds of the Feria Internacional. Prices are higher here, but so is the quality. The last stall to the west in the first row has a good selection of La Palma-influenced tin boxes. Cultural centers like La Luna and galleries like El Arbol de Dios also have stores, but the prices will be higher than in the markets.

Getting There & Away
Air See the Getting There & Away section for information on flights. Airline offices in San Salvador include: American Airlines (☎ 298-0777) and United Airlines (☎ 279-3900), both in Edificio Centro America on Alameda Roosevelt; Continental (☎ 279-2233) in Torre Roble on Blvd de los Héroes; and Taca (☎ 298-5577) in the Altos Edificio Caribe on Paseo Escalón.

Bus San Salvador has three main terminals for national long-distance buses. See the chapter introduction for information on international buses leaving from the hotels and Puerto Bus.

Buses serving all points east, including Honduras and the CA-4 highway, arrive and depart from the Terminal de Oriente, on the eastern side of the city, where Alameda Juan Pablo II becomes Blvd Ejército Nacional. Buses serving all points west, including the border to Guatemala, arrive and depart from the Terminal de Occidente, on the corner of Blvd Venezuela and 49a Av Sur. Most buses headed for these stations go along Calle Arce or 1a Calle Poniente.

Bus Terminal San Marcos, in the south of the city, serves destinations towards the Pacific, such as Costa del Sol and Zacatecoluca. Buses also depart from there for La Libertad, but it's easier to pick one up at Parque Bolívar in the city center. To get to San Marcos take either bus A or 11B from Calle Rubén Darío.

From Terminal de Oriente (take bus No 7, 29, 33 or 34 from city center):

Destination	Bus Number
Aguilares	117
Chalatenango	125
El Poy (Honduran border)	119*
Ilobasco	111
La Palma	119
La Unión	304
San Miguel	301
San Sebastián	110
San Vicente	116
Suchitoto	129
Usulután	302

* (for Guatemalan borders, transfer in La Unión or San Miguel)

From Terminal de Occidente (take bus No 4, 27 or 34 from center, or No 44 from Blvd de los Héroes):

Destination	Bus Number
Acajutla	207
Ahuachapán	202
Cerro Verde	201 to El Congo, then 209A
Guatemalan borders	transfer from Santa Ana to 236, 238
Izalco	205
Joya de Cerén	108
La Hachadura (Guatemalan border)	498
Lago Coatepeque	201 to El Congo, then 220

Las Chinamas (Guatemalan border)	
	406
Los Cóbanos	207A from
	Sonsonate
Metapán	201A
Ruinas de San Andrés	201
Santa Ana	201
Santa Tecla	any bus leaving
	from this
	terminal, but
	101 is best
Sonsonate	205

From San Marcos (take bus No 26A or No 11B from city center):

Destination	Bus Number	Duration
Costa del Sol	495	2½ hours
La Herradura	134	2 hours
La Libertad	166	1 hour
Puerto El Triunfo	185	2¼ hours
Usulután	132	2 hours
Zacatecoluca	133	1 hour

Getting Around

To/From the Airport
The international airport is near the coast about 44 km from San Salvador at Comalapa. It is about a 45-minute drive on a well-maintained highway.

Taxis Acacya (☎ 271-4937/8), on the corner of 19a Av Norte and 3a Calle Poniente, runs colectivo vans between the airport and the capital. They depart from San Salvador daily at 6, 7, 10 am and 2 pm near the Hospital de Maternidad/Hospital Rosales on 25a Av Norte and Calle Arce (call to find out exact departure times and whether location has changed), and from the airport whenever they fill up with passengers. It costs US$3 for the one-way trip. A taxi to or from the airport costs about US$15.

Bus
Most people in San Salvador get around on buses. The extensive network can get you to just about anywhere. City buses are red and white and cost 1.50 colones. There are a few cheaper blue buses, but most of this service has been phased out. If the bus you want looks too crowded, just wait for the next one to smoke by. The guys working the buses will expect you to board quickly, and in return will let you know when you need to get off to make a connection or arrive at your destination. Stay close to the front when you can. Microbuses (vans) run roughly the same routes but go into more residential areas where the large buses don't fit. The fare is the same.

Buses run daily from 5 am to 7:30 pm with frequent service; on Sunday they run during the same hours but less frequently (50% service). Between around 7:30 and 8:30 pm the buses become less frequent and finally stop; the microbuses run later until around 9 pm. After 9 pm you'll have to take a taxi. Bus fares increase from time to time, so don't be surprised if prices quoted here have changed.

Car
You may have to navigate by landmarks, since roads are rarely marked, especially in the center. You may be able to decipher the name from the eroded paint on the gutter. Once you get the system of even/odd, north/south, avenida/calle down you'll fare better, but let me know if you figure out how to predict which road is one way in which direction. Around town the best bet is to leave the car in a safe lot and take the bus. Carjackings are a business on the rise, so stay cautious. Nice cars could get stripped quickly. Locals can tell you where to go to buy the parts back though. The map distributed by the tourist office shows the main roads to use to get between the main points in the city. Traffic jams are common.

Taxi
Taxis are plentiful in San Salvador. A ride in town costs about US$2.30 (20 colones) during the day; late at night the rates are higher, about half again as much. Taxis are not metered, so negotiate an acceptable price before you climb in.

If you don't spot a taxi passing by at the moment you want one, which would be unusual, you can always phone for one.

Acontaxis	☎ 222-3361, 222-3268
Acosat	☎ 225-4015, 225-4140
Taxis Acacya	☎ 271-4937/8
Taxis Dos Pinos	☎ 221-1285/6

EL SALVADOR

EAST OF SAN SALVADOR
Lago de Ilopango

In about the second century AD, a volcano exploded 15 km east of San Salvador, just beyond what is now San Salvador's Ilopango Airport. El Salvador's largest lake, 15 km long, eight km wide and 248 meters deep, formed in the volcanic crater. Another eruption in early 1880 formed the Cerros Quemados (Burnt Hills) Islands in the middle of the lake, which you can visit by boat.

At the village of Apulo, there's a Turicentro (admission US$0.80). A half-hour boat ride around the lake or to the Cerros Quemados will run about US$4. Restaurants serve fresh fish and crayfish, but the lake is said to be polluted by heavy metals discharged from the enterprise zone on the shore. To reach the lake from the city, take bus No 15 from 3a Av Sur at Plaza Hula Hula.

Suchitoto

Well worth a trip out of San Salvador, Suchitoto is a sleepy village, 47 km north of San Salvador and 380 meters above sea level, overlooking Lago Suchitlán, a reservoir made by damming the Río Lempa. It is presumed that Yaquis and Pipils settled the area some thousand years ago.

The town has old buildings, a blinding white church and cobblestone streets that turn green with grass in the rainy season. Keep your eyes open for information on jazz concerts held here. Down the road from the church, *El Obraje* serves up comida a la vista for lunch and dinner. Around the plaza are two bars that serve Guiness. Ask for directions to (or look for signs to) *La Posada de Suchitlán* (☎ 335-1064), at the end of 4a Calle Poniente. The view from the posh restaurant is incredible and may just be worth the US$2.30 for a large fruit drink.

Take bus No 129 from Terminal Oriente. If in a car, go towards Cojutepeque on the Interamericana. When you get to San Martín, turn left at the Texaco sign.

WEST OF SAN SALVADOR
Santa Tecla

Santa Tecla, or Nueva San Salvador, was actually the capital for four years in the 1950s. Today there is little of interest in the town itself. From here you can catch buses to the San Salvador Volcano, Quetzaltepec. After hiking around the volcano, a good place for lunch in Santa Tecla is *Pizzería Italia* on 3a Calle Poniente between 2a and 4a Avs Sur. A thin crust pizza served with salsa costs around US$5.

Boquerón

Quetzaltepec (the San Salvador Volcano) has two peaks. The higher peak, at 1960 meters, is called Picacho. The other, Boquerón (Big Mouth), is 1893 meters high and has a second crater – 45 meters high and perfectly symmetrical – inside, formed in 1917. The beauty of this place lies not only in the panoramic views as far as the eye can see, but also in the immensity of the crater and all its lush foliage. Television stations have their satellites up on the peak, so parts of it are fenced off, but you can still hike around the rim; it takes about two or three hours. From the parking lot there's a small path to your left that leads to the trail. The road itself leads to the gate of Canal 12. You can skirt around the fence to get to two nice viewing areas. Once on the trail you can follow another one down 543 meters into the crater itself. The paths can be steep and narrow in places.

Get an early start if you want to hike as getting there by bus from San Salvador takes a couple of hours. Take bus No 101 to Santa Tecla; it departs every few minutes from the stop on 1a Calle Poniente at 3a Av Norte. From Santa Tecla, bus No 103 departs from 6a Av Sur. The bus is sporadic, but pickups depart from the same place. It's an 11-km trip uphill to the village of Boquerón, from which it's a one-km walk up a plastic-bag paved road to the crater. Some buses only go as far as the crossroads, a 30-minute walk below the village. Be sure to find out when the last bus returns to San Salvador.

Los Chorros

Cool, clear water springs forth from fern-covered volcanic cliffs and cascades into three large swimming pools at different levels at this Turicentro. A shady and relaxing escape from San Salvador, the park is within easy reach. The pools near the top are the best and cleanest. It's best not to stray out of the main area, as thefts along hidden trails have been reported. Don't leave belongings unguarded either. As with any Turicentro, go on a weekday to avoid the throngs of people. Entrance is US$0.80 and it's open daily, 7 am to 5 pm. The *comedores* serve a BBQ chicken or beef lunch for about US$3, or bring a picnic.

Los Chorros is 18 km west of San Salvador, beyond Santa Tecla right on the Interamericana. Bus No 79 leaves frequently from the stop at 11a Av Sur and Calle Rubén Darío.

Ruinas de San Andrés

In 1977 a step pyramid and a large courtyard with a subterranean section were unearthed in this site inhabited by Maya, Aztec and Pipil groups. It is also known as 'Ruinas de la Campana' for the bell-shaped pyramids still unexcavated. In the courtyard are squares for performing speeches or offering sacrifices. The area near the pyramid 'campana' may have been used as a playing field or market area. The pyramids mark the entrance to this site. Past them is the Río Sucio and on the other side the village now known as Joya de Cerén. Another 15 mounds are yet to be unearthed.

A tiny museum has photographs, but other than that there is little information about the place. The spaciousness and quiet are the best part. The site is open Tuesday to Sunday, 9 am to 5 pm, and costs US$3.

The ruins are about 300 meters north of the highway, 33 km west of San Salvador in the Valle Zapotitan. You can take any bus heading west from San Salvador's Terminal de Occidente and get off at Km 33 where there's a small black sign for the ruins, near a ceiba tree. Turn right (north) down this road to get to the ruins.

Joya de Cerén

When the Laguna Caldera Volcano erupted in 600 AD, a small Maya settlement was buried under four to six meters of volcanic ash. The intense heat from the eruption (between 100°C and 500°C) preserved not only the structures, but pottery, plants, seeds and animal remains (see the sidebar in History).

So far 10 of the 18 identified buildings in three separate compounds have been uncovered. The compounds are closed off, but you can overlook two of them from viewing areas. This is the only site that gives clues on how people lived back then: their intricate farming techniques, gardens of flowers and vegetables, bodegas and kitchens. The on-site museum has a good collection of artifacts and models of the villages, but the information is in Spanish. Before you head to the site, drop by Corsatur in San Salvador to pick up information in English. It is open Tuesday through Sunday from 9 am to 5 pm; admission is US$3 (25 colones).

The site is 36 km west of San Salvador; take bus No 108 from Terminal de Occidente and get off after crossing the bridge over the Río Sucio.

SOUTH OF SAN SALVADOR
Los Planes de Renderos

Within this district you will find **Parque Balboa**, one of the most popular parks around San Salvador. Close to 28 hectares are preserved for family fun; you'll find a few trails to take some quick walks, a skating rink, playgrounds and some pre-Columbian-style sculptures. The best time to come here is on a Saturday or Sunday afternoon, when you can really see how people enjoy their time here, and then kick back at one of the many pupuserías. Admission is US$0.80. The park is 12 km from the center.

A couple of kilometers past Parque Balboa is **Puerta del Diablo** (the Devil's Door). Two huge, towering boulders, reputedly once a single stone split in two, form this ominous lookout. During the war this place was an execution point, the cliffs offering easy disposal of the bodies. When it's clear, the view is fantastic, and when the fog starts up in the afternoon and rolls through like smoke, the sun casting your shadow on the thick mist, well, it's positively surreal. No wonder so many couples hide away in the secret crevices of the rocks. Meander along the trails that wind up and around the boulders, but forewarn any lovebirds of your presence.

Take the No 12 'Mil Cumbres' bus from the east side of the Mercado Central, at 12a Calle Poniente. If you're driving, head down Av Cuscatlán until you see the signs.

Panchimalco

Toltec immigrants founded this pre-Columbian town. Today, the road winds down the lush valley to arrive in this quiet, culturally proud town. The baroque church was built between 1543 and 1730 by the indigenous population and has some interesting woodwork inside. The town has two cultural centers along 1a Av that display ceramics and dance costumes and have some literature. The one by Calle Arce has a great mural. Try to come during one of their festivals, May 1 to 3, September 12 to 14, or around Christmas. Near the church are some kiosks selling tortas, pupusas and the like. Closer to Antel you'll find some clean public toilets.

Microbus and bus No 17 depart for Panchimalco from 12a Calle Poniente, which is behind the Mercado Central in San Salvador.

Costa del Sol

This long strip of clean, white beach has been taken over by high-class resorts, some holdovers from the tourist boom of the 1970s, others under construction in preparation for a wishful resurgence. On the other side of the peninsula is the Estero de Jaltepeque with mangroves and plenty of birds, including herons, sandpipers and kingfishers. While Playa Costa del Sol is more expensive than other beach areas, it is close to San Salvador (67 km) and easy to get to.

Because of the area's high-end status, shoestring travelers are almost out of luck around here. You are allowed to camp out at the Turicentro if the guards agree. Entrance is US$0.80, a *cabaña* US$4 with a US$1.70 deposit, and hammock rental US$1.15. Note that you can't sleep in the cabañas unless you find picnic tables comfortable; you have to string up a hammock outside. The water is turned off at night. Use discretion; there are no security gates, lights or guards at night. The alternative is to head out to the other side of the Bocana (see below) and pitch a mosquito net in the shrubs along the deserted beach. Just arrange with the guy who runs the boat to pick you up in the morning.

If you want to spend some cash though, *Izalco Cabaña Club* (☎ 334-0616) charges a hefty US$60 for a double room that can fit three. The owner's son wants to start some ecotoury lodging on the other side of the street. If he hasn't started yet, keep encouraging him to do so. They also offer beach access and use of facilities for a fee. *Haydee-Mar*, a bit east of Izalco, charges US$29 for a room they say can fit four people (if you sleep sardine-style). The beach access is through a shacky beachtown. *Hotel Pacific Paradise* (☎ 271-2606) charges US$14 a day for use of their facilities but does throw in lunch.

At the end of the peninsula, about 11 km from the Turicentro, is **La Puntita**, where the estuary meets the ocean. A small, relaxed community runs ranchos selling shrimp cocktails. Until 1998 La Puntita will stay public, but after that, hotel companies could win a bid, which would displace the community with another five-star vacancy lot.

Boat rides from La Puntita to the other side of La Bocana are US$3.50, to the coconut palm with three trunks US$5.70, around the estuary US$11.50, to Río Lempa US$23 to US$34, to La Pita US$20 one-way (see Isla Montecristo below) or to La Herradura US$17/23 one-way/roundtrip. These prices are for the boat, not by the person.

Bus No 495 goes to Costa del Sol from

Terminal San Marcos. The trip takes 2½ hours each way, so leave early if you're just going for a day. The last bus back to the city leaves at 3 pm. Bus No 193 originates in Zacatecoluca and goes all the way to La Puntita.

Western El Salvador

LA LIBERTAD
Population 40,623

If you surf, you've probably already heard of this place and would prefer that fewer people knew about it. This is a 'been-there-done-that' surfer destination. If you don't surf nor care to partake in the culture of it, there isn't much to do in this small seaside fishing town, 37 km south of San Salvador. The pier is interesting, full of fish – dried and diced, alive and dead – all emitting a pungent, salty smell. Also note the shark oil ointments, seahorses and turtle eggs.

The closest beach to the capital, it fills up with city dwellers on weekends. In the winter (March to October), the beach is rocky with large black boulders, and the riptide, along with sewage, makes the water uninviting. In the summer the rocks get covered in sand, but the boulders are still whipped up by the waves. If you want to frolic in the waves, head over to the Costa del Bálsamo or Playa San Diego, or go to the waterslide at Manny's Restaurant or the pools at some of the hotels (see below). Buses to Costa del Bálsamo (No 102) and Playa San Diego leave from the bus stop on 2a Calle Oriente.

Information
Banco de Fomento Agropecuario on 2a Calle Oriente changes traveler's checks and is open Monday to Friday 9 am to 4 pm, weekends 9 am to 1 pm. If the bank is closed, head a couple of storefronts down from the post office and you'll find money-changers who will take your cash at a cut

EL SALVADOR

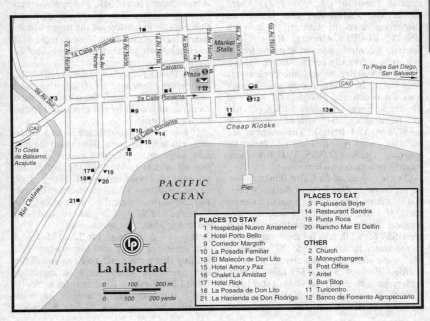

La Libertad

PACIFIC OCEAN

Río Chilama

To Costa de Bálsamo, Acajutla

To Playa San Diego, San Salvador

Market Stalls

Calvario

Plaza

Cheap Kiosks

Pier

0   100   200 m
0   100   200 yards

PLACES TO STAY
1 Hospedaje Nuevo Amanecer
4 Hotel Porto Bello
9 Comedor Margoth
10 La Posada Familiar
13 El Malecón de Don Lito
15 Hotel Amor y Paz
16 Chalet La Amistad
17 Hotel Rick
18 La Posada de Don Lito
21 La Hacienda de Don Rodrigo

PLACES TO EAT
3 Pupusería Boyte
14 Restaurant Sandra
19 Punta Roca
20 Rancho Mar El Delfín

OTHER
2 Church
5 Moneychangers
6 Post Office
7 Antel
8 Bus Stop
11 Turicentro
12 Banco de Fomento Agropecuario

rate. Crime is a growing problem, so be cautious, especially at night. More drunks are around here, too, feeling the heat of aguardiente.

Places to Stay

Some hotels in La Libertad charge for 12 hours at a time, so 24 hours is double the rate. Be sure you clarify what you're paying for when you check in. For a free night head to the government workers' center (see La Costa del Bálsamo). The cheapest rooms are dark damp stables with bare bulbs, dusty fans, a hammock and limp mattresses.

Three blocks from the beach, *Hospedaje Nuevo Amanecer*, 1a Calle Poniente, charges US$5.70 for double rooms. Another cheapie is *Comedor Margoth* on 3a Av Sur. It's a little rundown but charges US$4.50 for one bed or US$7 for two (24 hours). Take the more ventilated one-bed rooms upstairs, but don't come back drunk; the stairs are precarious. Next door is *La Posada Familiar* (☎ 335-3252), where rooms with shared bath cost US$9 and single/double rooms with private bath are US$11.50/14.30 (24 hours). Rooms look out onto a central courtyard/parking lot.

Run by a friendly couple, *Hotel Amor y Paz* (☎ 335-3187), on 4a Calle Poniente, is very basic, but some rooms are directly over the beach and afford good views of the break. Singles/doubles with a cot, use of hammock and shared bath are US$5/6.90 (24 hours). The owners are building more rooms. Nearby *Chalet La Amistad* charges US$5.70/4 for basic rooms upstairs/downstairs.

On the corner of 2a Calle Poniente and 1a Av Norte is *Hotel Porto Bello* (☎ 335-3013), a dark, labyrinthine hotel that can be eerie if traveling alone, especially for women. Rooms with shared/private bath are US$4.60/9.20. Ask for the room on top of the water tank; for US$5.70 you get a 360° view and some fresh air.

Hotel Rick (☎ 335-3033) fills up with surfers, so call first if you want to stay here. Rooms are simple but clean, all with private bath. Rooms with one/two beds cost US$11.50/17.20. The staff is friendly; they'll watch your luggage if you take off for a few days.

Down the street are the swankier *La Posada de Don Lito* and *La Hacienda de Don Rodrigo* (☎ 335-3166). A double room with fan/air con is US$46/50.50 for 24 hours (half that for 12). *El Malecón de Don Lito* (☎ 335-3201), on the east side of town, is under the same management and charges the same rates. Nonguests can use the pool at any of these places for US$2.80.

Places to Eat

The best place for breakfast is at *Hotel Rick*, where you can get coffee, a large orange juice and pancakes for around US$2. Lunch and early dinners are equally good.

Open-air, over-priced restaurants line the beach and all offer fresh fish and *mariscada* (cream-based soup overflowing with seafood) for lunch or dinner. Restaurants shut down early, so plan on early dinners. A meal with drinks will cost close to US$10. Across from Hotel Rick, *Punta Roca*, run by ex-pat surfer Bob, has a varied menu that isn't as expensive as the other beach-front places. *Restaurant Sandra*, right next to Hotel Amor y Paz, and *Rancho Mar El Delfín* are also recommended.

You'll see plenty of kiosks around the Turicentro serving up fried fish and seafood, but the smell from the polluted river running right by the pier can infringe on your appetite.

If you can coerce someone to let you use their kitchen, buy some fish out on the pier and some fresh veggies at the outdoor market in town. Most of the hotels are willing to cook up meals for guests. *Comedor Margoth* is a decent, cheap option. *Pupusería Boyte* near the corner of 2a Calle Poniente and 9a Av Sur gets crowded with surfers and locals in the evening.

Manny's Restaurant (☎ 223-1754) is a fancy restaurant with a 70-meter waterslide spilling down the cliff. You can spend the day here, but you'll have to consume US$11.50 worth of food or drinks. You'll find it right beyond the intersection with the road heading back to San Salvador.

Also en route to Playa San Diego is a waterfall and swimming hole. Ask around for directions.

Getting There & Away

Bus No 102 goes to/from San Salvador (1¼ hours); it costs US$0.45. In San Salvador, catch it on 4a Calle Poniente at 13a Av Sur beside the Parque Bolívar. If you're driving from San Salvador, go in the direction of Santa Tecla; the turnoff will be to your right, just after passing under the overpass. When you get to the end of the road (about a 45-minute drive), turn right into the town center.

From La Libertad take bus No 192 to beaches along Costa del Bálsamo. Surfers note: You can take boards on the buses. From La Perla you could take bus No 261 to Sonsonate (you may have to change again in Mizata). Allow four hours for the 76-km trip. Bus No 287 runs direct from La Libertad to Sonsonate at 6 am. From La Libertad to Playa San Diego, take bus No 80-B. All buses leave from near the intersection of 4a Av Norte and 2a Calle Poniente.

LA COSTA DEL BÁLSAMO

The coastal area between La Libertad and Acajutla, 72 km to the west, is called La Costa del Bálsamo (the Balsam Coast) after all the balsam trees from which dyes were once extracted. Today only a handful of trees still remain, and the main industry is cotton.

While the road along the coast is windy and areas are not well maintained, it can be a pleasant trip. Hills drop down to a rocky coast with many sheltered coves and sandy beaches (most are private). El Zunzal is the site of international surfing competitions, but surfers usually go to La Libertad. Even here, the beach becomes rocky and deserted in the rainy season.

Beaches that make good day trips from La Libertad include Conchalío (five km west), El Zunzal (eight km), El Zonte (16 km), Mizata (40 km) and Sihuapilapa (43 km). Buses No 192, 107 and 80 run along the coast. Just tell the driver where you want to get off. Beaches farther west than these are better accessed from Sonsonate.

Places to Stay

About half a kilometer west of La Libertad, *Hotel Los Arcos* (☎ 335-3490) is a fancy hotel with a fountain and swimming pool in the courtyard. All the rooms have air con, TV, telephone and private bath; MasterCard and Visa are accepted. The rates are US$26 a night with one double bed, US$42 with two (the latter could sleep up to four people).

A little farther west on Playa Conchalío is the free government workers' center, *Centro Obrero Dr Humberto Romero Alvergue*. The setting is very pretty, right on a long expanse of sandy beach. Cabins are dorm-style with rusty mattresses. You can use the pool during the day, but it closes at night, and the restaurant serves food if there are enough people around. Gates lock up at 7 pm, so if you plan on hanging out in La Libertad, make arrangements with the guard to let you back in. To stay here, you need prior written permission from the Ministerio de Trabajo in San Salvador (see Accommodations in Facts for the Visitor).

Three km west of La Libertad, *La Cabaña de Don Chepe* (☎ 335-3333) is set back from the highway. Dingy double rooms cost US$15.50, US$17.20 with air con and US$16 for the top floor (with a view). Pay US$3 more for an additional bed. There's a nice, clean swimming pool in the new courtyard and hammocks you can take to the beach; meals are served for US$2.90.

Fifteen km from La Libertad is *Atami Beach Club* (☎ 223-9000), a lovely, private beach club. Take along your passport to show them that you are a tourist and they'll let you use the facilities for US$5.70 a day. Staying overnight costs US$17 a person. It's closed on Monday and gets crowded on weekends, so come during the week. Buses No 192 and 107 pass by.

LAGO DE COATEPEQUE

On the eastern slope of the Santa Ana Volcano, Lago de Coatepeque is a clean, sparkling blue volcanic crater lake, six km wide and 120 meters deep, surrounded by green crater slopes rising above it. Cerro Verde, Izalco and Santa Ana volcanoes loom above the lake. It's a popular weekend retreat for San Salvador's well-to-do, many of whom have private homes that obstruct public access to most of the lake. The rest stay at the hotels, so there are few cheap hotels here. During the week it is a peaceful, quiet oasis. The bus takes you along the northeast side of the lake to an area with hotels and public access. For a small fee, usually around US$2.30 or the price of a meal, you can hang out for the day at one of the hotels listed below.

Places to Stay & Eat

The following are around the northeast section of the lake. The best deal on the lake is the deserted *Balneario Los Obreros*, where you can stay for free with written permission in advance from the Ministerio de Trabajo in San Salvador. Readers also report that if you want to camp, they may let you stay without permission. This government workers' center has lake access, but the water here is murky, as is the swimming pool. You can get food when the restaurant is open. Cabins have four beds, a table, and private bathroom. Bring mosquito nets, as windows don't have screens. It is on the right, shortly after the bus loops round to circle the lake.

A couple of kilometers farther is *Amacuilco Guest House* (☎ 441-0608). This communal-feeling place is run by friendly people who offer private Spanish lessons. They also run an art gallery, workshops and a trip up to Santa Ana for some nightlife. The food is reasonably priced and fresh, and served on a relaxing dock over the lake. Rooms with shared bath are US$10.30/15 or US$12.60/16 depending on room size and US$15/19 with private bath. It's overpriced, but it's still the cheapest hotel. The lake is clean enough for swimming here.

Another 500 meters brings you to *Hotel Torremolinos* (☎ 446-9437). It has ample, clean singles or doubles with private bath for US$25.80, and a three-bed room is

US$34.40. There's a swimming pool and an expensive restaurant over the water.

Hotel del Lago (☎ 446-9511) is another 1.5 km round the lake near where the bus stops. Old Spanish-style double rooms with high ceilings and wooden shutters are US$29, newer rooms US$46. An elegant terrace overlooks the lake, a sandy beach and a swimming pool. Meals are available but expensive.

Small kiosks line the road near the hotels and sell lake crabs *(cangrejo del lago)* and fish dishes.

Getting There & Away

From San Salvador take bus No 210 heading to Santa Ana. Get off at El Congo (five km from the lake), walk up the hill to the road crossing the highway and from there take bus No 220 from Santa Ana. The last bus back to the city leaves the lake at 4:30 pm. From Santa Ana (16 km away), take the 'El Lago' No 220 bus, which leaves hourly.

CERRO VERDE & VOLCÁN IZALCO

One of the gems of the country, Cerro Verde lies high above Lago de Coatepeque. It's a national park on top of an old volcano and affords incredible views of the lake below and the still steaming and impressive Volcán Izalco. Be sure to get there early in the morning and on a clear day; otherwise, a thick fog bank tends to envelop the area. Bring a sweater or rain gear, as it can get chilly and wet here.

Volcán Izalco has a famous history. Before February 1770, there was nothing where Izalco now stands but a hole in the earth from which columns of black sulfuric smoke would rise. Then a cone began to form where the smoke fumed. Within a short time the cone had grown to a prodigious size – today it stands 1910 meters high. Izalco continued to erupt into this century, sending out smoke, boulders and flames: an impressive sight by night or day, earning it a reputation as 'the lighthouse of the Pacific.'

In 1957, after erupting continuously for

187 years, Izalco stopped. The only time it's been heard from since was a small burp in 1966, but it's still classified as active. Today, the perfect cone, black and bare, stands devoid of life in an otherwise incredibly fertile land.

The entrance fee for Cerro Verde is US$0.80; parking costs another US$0.80; and on weekends it's an additional US$0.80 to get into the hotel area.

Hiking

This is the place to climb a couple of volcanoes. To ascend Izalco (1910 meters), take the marked path on the road before the Cerro Verde parking lot. The rocky three-hour hike to the top takes you past graffitied rocks on a not-so-ecotouristy trail. If you prefer to just admire Izalco from a distance, the best viewpoint is from the picnic areas at Cerro Verde, which at 2030 meters above sea level allows you to look down on the volcano.

A short, 40-minute circular trail near the hotel gives views of the lake and Santa Ana Volcano (2365 meters). From there a well-used path branches off to the top of the volcano (three hours roundtrip).

Places to Stay & Eat

You can camp out near the picnic areas in Cerro Verde at no charge apart from the entrance fee.

The *Hotel de Montaña* (☎ 271-2434) is a government-run hotel, which doesn't mean much other than that you have to pay US$0.80 to even go close on a weekend, and the furniture and architecture are decidedly '70s and not well kept. Twenty large rooms (10 with forest view, 10 with volcano view) with private bath (sporadic hot water) cost US$30 for one or two people from Monday to Thursday, US$9 for an additional person. On weekends it's US$64/71 for forest/volcano view, including breakfast and dinner. Make advance reservations (especially for weekends) either at the Corsatur or IRP office in San Salvador.

There's a cafeteria – cheaper than the restaurant – in the hotel complex. On the hill above the parking lot you'll find a pupusería.

Getting There & Away

Cerro Verde is 37 km from Santa Ana and 44 km from Sonsonate. From San Salvador, take buses going to Santa Ana and get off at El Congo on the Interamericana, walk up the hill to the overpass and catch bus No 248 or No 215 from Santa Ana for Cerro Verde. The trip just from El Congo to Cerro Verde is incredibly scenic but driven at a snail's pace. If coming by bus, start early.

From Santa Ana bus No 248 leaves five times a day. The last bus back is at 5:30 pm. The Santa Ana-Sonsonate No 209 buses (they're marked 'Cerro Verde') skirt the lake, so you can get off at the Cerro Verde turnoff and hop on a pickup to get up the 14 km hill.

If you're driving, Cerro Verde is 67 km from San Salvador along CA-8 route (the road to Sonsonate) or 77 km by the more scenic Interamericana towards Santa Ana.

SANTA ANA

Population 237,587

Santa Ana is the second largest city in El Salvador and capital of the department of the same name. It's a pleasant town, and the people are relaxed and friendly, making it a good base from which to explore areas in the west and northwest corners of the country. The city is wealthier than most, probably because it is a commercial base for the coffee plantations nearby. Be aware, however, that petty thievery is as much a problem here as in other cities.

The original name of Santa Ana is Cihuatehuacán, which means Place of Holy Women in Nahua.

Information

Banco Salvadoreño is open Monday to Friday 9 am to 4 pm and changes traveler's checks. Or go to the moneychangers, across the street from the bank. Antel is on the corner of 5a Av Norte and Libertad Oriente.

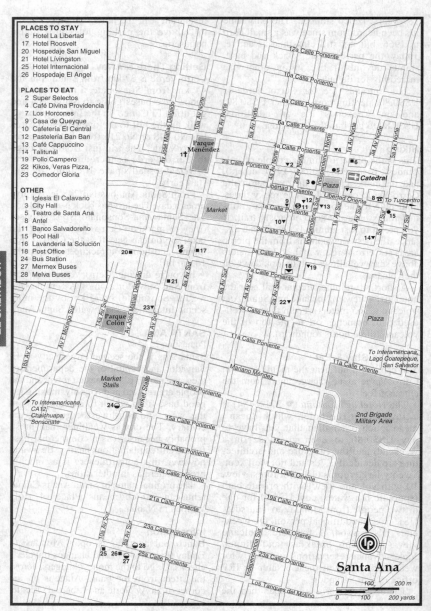

PLACES TO STAY
6 Hotel La Libertad
17 Hotel Roosvelt
20 Hospedaje San Miguel
21 Hotel Lívingston
25 Hotel Internacional
26 Hospedaje El Angel

PLACES TO EAT
2 Super Selectos
4 Café Divina Providencia
7 Los Horcones
9 Casa de Queyque
10 Cafetería El Central
12 Pastelería Ban Ban
13 Café Cappuccino
14 Talitunál
22 Kikos, Veras Pizza,
23 Comedor Gloria

OTHER
1 Iglesia El Calvario
3 City Hall
5 Teatro de Santa Ana
8 Antel
11 Banco Salvadoreño
15 Pool Hall
16 Lavandería la Solución
18 Post Office
24 Bus Station
27 Mermex Buses
28 Melva Buses

EL SALVADOR

Santa Ana

Lavandería la Solución is on 7a Calle Poniente between 8 and 10 Avs Sur. A wash-and-dry cycle here costs about US$2.50.

Things to See & Do

The most notable sight in Santa Ana is its large neo-Gothic **cathedral**. Ornate moldings cover the entire front of the church, and the inside has that characteristic sense of high-arched spaciousness and peace.

On the square in front of the cathedral is another notable edifice, the **Teatro de Santa Ana**, which has been undergoing restoration since 1979. Inquire at the box office about taking a peek inside.

On the outskirts of town is a typical Turicentro, **Sihuatehuacán**, which is much used by the locals. Admission is US$0.80, and cabañas cost US$4. It's open 8 am to 4 pm daily. Take local bus No 51A from the plaza in front of the cathedral.

Places to Stay

Most basic and cheap hotels charge by the hour. And since the clients don't stay for long, there's not much emphasis on aesthetics – rooms are dark and basic (bed and sheets only).

Hospedaje San Miguel (☎ 441-3465) at 7a Calle Poniente and Delgado has thin mattresses but at least the rooms are clean. Singles/doubles with smelly shared toilets are US$3.50/4; a double bed with private bath is US$5.70. Often recommended by readers, *Hotel Lívingston* (☎ 441-1801) at 10a Av Sur, No 17-A, has more comfortable rooms and a friendlier staff. Singles/doubles with private bath cost US$8/9.80, while doubles/triples with shared bath cost US$5/7.50.

Hotel La Libertad (☎ 441-2358), one block around the corner from the cathedral at 4a Calle Oriente, No 2, on the corner of 1a Av Norte, is clean and pleasant. Single/double/triple rooms all with double beds are US$9/13.80/17.20 with private bath and fan. Rooms on the top floor are nicer and have a partial view of the cathedral. The hotel has safe parking too.

Hotel Roosvelt (☎ 441-1702) charges US$11.50 for rooms with private bath and

US$6.70 for shared bath. Close to the buses going to Guatemala is *Hotel Internacional* (☎ 440-0804/10), on the corner of 25a Calle Poniente and 10a Av Sur. It's modern, clean and comfortable, but it is on a loud and busy corner; ask for a room away from the street. All the rooms have private bath, TV and fan; rooms are US$14.30 with one double bed, US$17.20 with two beds. *Hospedaje El Angel* (☎ 440-1598), less than 50 meters away, has clean rooms with shared bath and a double bed for US$4 and US$6.90 for two beds.

Places to Eat

Café Cappuccino, open 7 am to 8:30 pm everyday, serves up espresso drinks and good, cheap breakfasts, made to your liking. An omelet costs about US$1.70. The lunch and dinner selections aren't as good. Across the street in the Ahorromet bank parking lot is *Pastelería Ban Ban* with air con and a good choice of pastries. Along 8a and 10a Avs Norte are more pastelerías to get you going.

If you want to test your stomach, try the market in the block between 1a and 3a Calles Poniente, and 6a and 8a Avs Sur. You can pick up snacks at the bus station.

Comedor Gloria on 10a Av Sur serves up decent food and is open for all three meals (closing at 8 pm). *Café Divina Providencia* on 4a Calle Oriente and 1a Av Norte specializes in typical food such as pupusas and tamales. *Los Horcones* is next to the cathedral. Lunch is pretty good, and the view from the 2nd floor quite nice.

Along Av Independencia you'll find a cluster of places to eat, including *Kikos* near 7a Calle Oriente (readers claim it has the best roast chicken and pizza in town) and *Veras Pizza*, which has a salad bar. *Talitunál* on 5a Av Sur between 1a and 3a Calles serves up very good vegetarian food buffet-style. A full plate plus hearty whole-wheat rolls costs about US$2. It is open for lunch and dinner from noon to 7:30 pm. If you wish to buy your own foodstuffs, head to Super Selectos across the road from the Alcaldea. It has a deli and a selection of plastic-wrapped produce.

Getting There & Away

Because of its location, Santa Ana is a good place from which to explore this area. At the bus station and on the buses, remember to watch your bags carefully. Buses from Santa Ana's bus station include:

Destination	Distance	Bus #	Duration
Ahuachapán	34 km	202, 210	1 hour
Cerro Verde	37 km	248	1½ hours
Lago de Coatepeque	16 km	220, 209	1 hour
Las Chinamas (Guatemalan border)	57 km	210	1½ hours
Metapán	45 km	201A, 235	2 hours
San Cristóbal (Guatemalan border)		236	
San Salvador	63 km	201	1½ hours
Sonsonate	40 km	209, 216	1½ hours
Tazumal, Chalchuapa	13 km	218, 236	45 min

Mermex (☎ 440-1598) leaves from Hospedaje El Angel (see Places to Stay) at 5 am and 10 am to Guatemala City. The cost is US$6 one-way. Melva (☎ 440-1608, 440-3606), across the street from Mermex, runs buses to Guatemala City at 4:30 and 6:30 am and every hour after that until 3:30 pm. Both services take four hours and cost US$6 one-way.

LAGO DE GÜIJA

This large lake lies 15 km south of Metapán and about 30 km north of Santa Ana along CA-12. It's shared with Guatemala and considered the most beautiful in El Salvador. Come here to see archeological sites that line the shores. In the rainy season the lake floods, so you need to rent a boat to access the ruins and rock carvings; in the summer, you can walk to them. Locals can take you around by boat for the right price. Turn off the road at El Desagüe, across the road from the sign for the Lempa hydroelectricity project. A gravel road leads two km to the lake and the tiny community on its shores.

METAPÁN

Most people just zoom right through this sleepy village on the way to much loftier destinations like the Honduran border or Montecristo Cloud Forest. Granted, the town doesn't have a lot to offer. But the friendly people and a couple of lovely 200-year-old whitewashed churches make Metapán a nice place to rest the hiking boots. The area around here was heavily mined for silver by the Spaniards. Now the only excavating is for rock; the nearby cement factory is the largest business in the area.

On the road leading to the border about one kilometer from Hotel San José is *Hotel California* (☎ 442-0561) with six rooms costing US$5.70 with double beds. Right across the street is the lively *Pupusería Alonzo*. Spend some colones on the jukebox and eat up some delicious pupusas. About six km south of town on CA-12 is *Los Remos*, a fancier outdoor restaurant overlooking Laguna de Metapán. Take insect repellent if you go.

From Santa Ana (45 km, 1½ hours) take bus No 201A or No 235. To continue to the border at Anguiatú, take bus No 211A.

PARQUE NACIONAL MONTECRISTO-EL TRIFINIO

Surrounding the area where the borders of El Salvador, Honduras and Guatemala converge is the Parque Nacional Montecristo. At the highest point in the park (2418 meters), the borders meet at an area referred to as El Trifinio. The cloud forest starts at 2100 meters and is home to a variety of wildlife. This is the most humid region in the country, with 2000 mm annual precipitation and 100% average relative humidity. Oak and laurel trees grow to 30 meters, and their leaves intertwine at the top to make a canopy impenetrable to sunlight. The forest floor provides a habitat for abundant exotic plant life including orchids, mushrooms, lichens and mosses, and the numerous ferns include tree ferns growing up to eight meters high. The temperature averages between 10°C and 15°C.

Animals seen (albeit rarely) include spider monkeys, two-fingered anteaters, porcupines, spotted and hooded skunks, pumas, red and gray squirrels, wild pigs, opossums, coyotes and agoutis. The forest is also home to at least 87 species of bird, including quetzals, green toucans, woodpeckers, hummingbirds, nightingales, white-faced quail and striped owls.

For anyone interested in botany or animals the park is a great place to visit, but it's a challenge to get there. While the park may be protected by the Salvadoran government, its sheer inaccessibility, especially from the bordering two countries, is its best protection.

Ideally come in a 4WD, but if you can't land that, first get to Metapán (see above). From there you'll have to hitch a ride in one of the pickups that goes to/from the community of Majadita in the park. The road to the main gate (five km) branches off the highway at Hotel San José. You could walk to the gate if you wanted, but you can't walk into the park – that's the rule.

Three km past the gate is a turnoff to Casco Colonial, a restored foundry built in 1783 during the Spanish-mining heyday. Clean whitewashed walls, red-tile roofs, musty brick floors and warm patios lined with hanging plants make this a pleasant place to stop. Climbing up the road you'll pass the community of Majaditas and after another 12 km you'll arrive at Los Planes. A soccer field lies in the cup of the lush hill rising up to El Trifinio. A few landscaped gardens and a small store take away from the wildness of the place, but there are plenty of hiking trails that lead to vistas of the multihued lands below or to the tangle of jungle above. To access the cloud forest, hike up the road right by the entrance to Los Planes. It's seven km to El Trifinio.

Information

The area of the park from Los Planes and higher is closed from May to November, the breeding season of the local fauna. And while the remaining part of the park is open the rest of the year, you can only venture a few kilometers up the road.

To take full advantage of being here when the park is open, you will need to spend the night. Los Planes has camping sites and firepits; Casco Colonial (very close to the main gate) has a couple of ill-kept rooms with cots in them. To stay at either place you need permission in advance from the Department of National Parks at the Ministerio de Agricultura in San Salvador (☎ 279-1579); the office is in Calle Al Matazano in Colonia Santa Lucia (bus No 33A from the city center). Getting permission is usually no problem, except for weekends.

Take your own food, warm clothes and waterproof gear. The guards at the front gate can sell you firewood. Make sure to arrive before 3 pm if you want to camp. Admission to the park is US$1.15 for locals, US$2.90 for foreigners. Depending on the size of car, entrance costs US$0.35 to US$1.15.

RUINAS DE TAZUMAL

The Maya ruins of Tazumal, considered the most important in El Salvador, are in the town of **Chalchuapa**, 13 km west of Santa Ana and on the way to Ahuachapán. In the Quiché language the name Tazumal means Pyramid Where the Victims Were Burned.

The excavated ruins on display here are only one part of a zone covering about 10 sq km, much of it buried under the town. Archeologists estimate that the first settlements in the area were around 5000 BC. The excavated structures date from a period spanning over 1000 years. The artifacts found at Tazumal gave evidence of ancient and active trade between Tazumal and other places as far away as Panama and Mexico. Even though these are some of the most important ruins in El Salvador, they pale in comparison to ruins in neighboring countries. Restoring the ruins in drab concrete didn't help either, but at least there's a good view from the top.

The museum has artifacts with some explanations in English. Other artifacts, including Estela de Tazumal, a basalt monolith 2.65 meters high and 1.16 meters wide, with hieroglyphics inscribed in the sides, are at the Museo Nacional Davíd G Guzmán in San Salvador, which as of press time is still closed.

Tazumal is open Tuesday to Saturday from 9 am to 5 pm; admission is US$2.90 for foreigners. Buses No 218, 202 and 210 come from Santa Ana, 13 km (20 minutes) away; a sign on the main road through Chalchuapa points towards the ruins, about a five-minute walk from the highway. If driving from Santa Ana, stay to the right at the fork in the road, continuing toward Ahuachápan, and turn left at the Texaco station in Chalchuapa. The ruins are at the end of the road.

AHUACHAPÁN
Population 87,000

The small town of Ahuachápan is capital of the department of the same name. It's the closest town to the Las Chinamas border 16 km away. If you have just crossed the border from Guatemala, you might want to spend the night here; otherwise, you could forge on to Santa Ana, 34 km to the east.

The most notable sight in the area of Ahuachápan is **Los Ausoles** (the Cauldrons), a geothermal area of boiling mud pools, hot springs, geysers and steaming earth. It is possible to walk among the 'cauldrons' even though the area is tapped for geothermal power. There is no public transport, but the 'El Barro' bus from Ahuachápan will take you to within five km of Los Ausoles.

On the way to/from Chalachuapa is **Atiquizaya**, where Alfredo Melara Farfán has a gallery at the junction with the main road. He makes interesting sculptures using old bits of metal. Don Quixote is a favorite theme, but the simple crosses are nicer. You can also buy his artwork at the Mercado de Artesenías in San Salvador.

Places to Stay & Eat
The best place in town is *Hotel Casa Blanca* (☎ 443-1505) at the corner of 2a Av Norte and Calle Barrios. The central courtyard has a garden, bar and restaurant area.

The eight rooms are clean and large. Singles/doubles are US$16/26 with private bath with hot water.

Hospedaje Granada, on 8a Calle Poniente between 4a and 6a Avs Norte, has rather dark rooms with a shared bath, but it's clean and costs from US$4.60 to US$7 for one or two beds. *Hotel San José* (☎ 443-1820), across the street from Plaza Menéndez, charges US$6.90/13.80/17.20 for single/double/triple rooms.

La Estancia, on 1a Av Sur between Calle Barrios and 1a Calle Oriente, is in an old colonial house built in 1910. It's a charming place to come eat breakfast for US$1.50. Other meals are more expensive and heavy; they specialize in meats and seafood. You could come for afternoon tea though. *Hotel Casa Blanca* also serves all meals. There is cheap eating in the large indoor market, completed in 1990, beside the Plaza Menéndez a block from the bus station. Around Plaza Concordia you'll find a choice of places to eat, including pupuserías. Or you can try one of the kiosks around the park and bus stop.

Getting There & Away
Bus transport from Ahuachápan includes:

Destination	Distance	Bus #	Duration
Las Chinamas (Guatemalan border)	16 km	265	30 min
San Salvador	100 km	202	3 hours
Santa Ana	34 km	210	1 hour
Sonsonate	36 km	285	2 hours

APANECA
Situated in the Sierra Apaneca Ilamatepec, Apaneca enjoys clean mountain air surrounded by the dark green fields of coffee plantations. You won't find much to do other than soak up the tranquillity and take a few walks around the town. There's a bit more money around here, and the prices of accommodations reflect the kind of clientele that come here. Since it's only about a half-hour away from Ahauchápán or 1½ hours from Sonsonate, this is a good place to go to experience some of the country's mountainous beauty. Bus No 249 runs between Ahuachápán and Sonsonate.

SANTA ANA TO SONSONATE

Hwy CA-12 between Sonsonate and Santa Ana is one of the prettier drives in the country. The road is paved and well maintained (probably due to the many wealthy coffee-plantation owners). On both sides of the road, the slopes of the Sierra Apaneca Ilamatepec fold out in quilt-like patterns of dark green coffee plants, woven with lighter green rompevientos, trees planted to protect the coffee plants from strong winds. Random acres of fruit trees pop into view, and Santa Ana and Izalco Volcanoes and the valleys below round it all out. Between the distanced gates to the plantations are villages clinging to the sides of the road, clothes hung to dry on the barbed wire fences and children running around every which way. Make sure to make the trip in broad daylight.

SONSONATE

Population 90,318

There is no reason to come to Sonsonate other than to check out some of the villages nearby or to transfer to a bus to go to the coast or Apaneca. The town has a seedy, truck stop tension that can be unnerving. The villages around here have the highest concentrations of indigenous populations, but most are only accessible by horseback. If you're interested in visiting them, make prior arrangements with organizations like CIS in San Salvador.

Nahuizalco, about 10 km to the north, is a Pipil Indian village specializing in wicker baskets and furniture. Occasionally you will see a woman in traditional Pipil clothing, a colorful wraparound skirt.

Near the village of **Izalco**, eight km to the northeast at the foot of the Izalco Volcano, is **Atecozol**, a Turicentro with the usual swimming holes, kiosks and gardens. Around the grounds are stone sculptures by Agustín Estrada. One is of Atonatl, the Indian who shot an arrow through the leg of the conquistador Pedro de Alvarado here in 1524. Another is Tlaloc, the god of rain, and another is of a frog, which led to the discovery of the spring here. Entrance is US$0.80, cabañas US$4.

Places to Stay & Eat

Hotels around the bus station and market are grotty and not very safe, but the best in that area is *Hotel Florida* (☎ 451-0967). Rooms with one double bed are US$4 with shared bath, US$5.70 with private bath; two beds cost US$6.70 or US$10.30. It's on 18 Av Sur: Turn right as you leave the bus station, then take the first right. *Hospedaje Blue River* on 10 Av Sur and Marraquín charges US$4 for a double bed, US$5.20 for two beds, and US$6.30 for a room with a private bathroom.

In a nicer area of town you'll find *Hotel Centroamericana* (☎ 451-4606) on the corner of Calle Alberto Masferrer and 6a Av Norte. The proprietors usually take in long-term tenants, so call to see if a room is available for a night. Rates for double rooms are US$11.50/17.20 with/without private bath for 24 hours. For less time, try to negotiate a lower price. The safest place is motel-style *Hotel Orbe* (☎ 451-1416, 451-1517) on the corner of 4a Calle Oriente and 2a Av Sur. Clean single/double rooms, all with private bath, are US$8/13.80 or US$16/20 with air con.

Down 6a Av Norte from Hotel Centroamericana is *Santa Cecilia*, a comedor serving up 'comida corriente.'

Getting There & Away

Bus No 53D goes to Nahuizalco, bus No 53A to Izalco, and buses No 209 and 216 to Santa Ana (40 km, 1½ hours). Bus No 261 goes east along La Costa del Bálsamo to La Perla, from which No 192 continues to La Libertad. Bus No 259 goes to La Hachadura (Guatemalan border; 59 km). Bus No 257 goes to Los Cóbanos, and buses No 252 and 207 to Acajutla (20 km). Direct buses leave from the terminal. Ordinary routes leave from the street right outside the terminal.

ACAJUTLA

Unless you want to glance over a cliff at the country's largest port, there's no reason to come all the way down here. Beach access is restricted because of the port, and the downtown is forlorn and dirty. Should you end up here and need a place to cool your heels, *Motel Miramar* (☎ 452-3183) has a pool and eating area overlooking the ocean. You could spend the night here too if you get stuck. Rooms are about US$6.

Buses No 252 and 207 run between here and Sonsonate, which is a better town from which to access beaches farther east.

PARQUE NACIONAL EL IMPOSIBLE

Decreed a national park in 1989, El Imposible is a tropical mountain forest between 300 and 1450 meters above sea level in the mountains around Apaneca. The majority of the park has original forest, all that remains of a threatened ecosystem. Nearly 400 varieties of trees grow in the area, and endangered animals such as puma, tigrillo, wild boar, king hawk and black crested eagle are protected here.

While the park is not open to the public, all you need to do is get prior written permission from SalvaNatura in San Salvador. In order to visit the park, go to the office or write for permission (see Important Offices in San Salvador).

The best time to visit is from October to February, as the rainy season hinders travel. Hiking trails meander throughout the park and camping is possible with prior permission, but no fires are allowed.

To get to the park by bus, take No 201 from Terminal de Occidente in San Salvador. At Sonsonate transfer to a bus going to San Francisco Menéndez (you'll be right by the park) or to Cara Sucia (take a pickup to San Benito). By car go straight to San Benito. Presently there is no entrance fee, but a US$10 entrance fee may soon be instituted.

Eastern El Salvador

The eastern corners, especially the northeast, have always been poor, the peasants doing what they can to live off what little land they have. The FMLN gained control in this region by rallying many of those peasants to fight for land reform. Many

towns remained ambivalent but were affected nonetheless. The department of Morazán was one of the most heavily impacted during the war. A war museum in Perquín and a memorial in El Mozote are sobering reminders of what atrocities befell fighters and families alike.

Two bridges crossing the Río Lempa still bear the scars of the war. The FMLN blew both of them up, successfully cutting the eastern part of the country off from commerce during the war. Years later, the FMLN graffiti is still on the bridge towers and cars cross on the old railway lines. The Japanese government has invested money into the reconstruction of the bridges and is throwing money into rejuvenating the port at La Unión.

There are two ways to access the eastern portions – along the Interamericana or along the Carretera del Litoral (CA-2), the latter accessing the beaches and the former the northern reaches. You can reach San Miguel and the Honduran border by taking either route. Taking buses along the Interamericana makes for a faster trip. For full coverage of the area, you could make a roundtrip from San Salvador using both roads.

THE INTERAMERICANA

The Interamericana goes east from San Salvador to San Miguel, on to La Unión and up again to the border at El Amatillo (Honduras). Despite the importance of the road, you'll still be playing roulette with the potholes if you're driving and it's a bumpy ride in a bus. Highway CA-7 is a shorter, more direct connection between San Miguel and El Amatillo.

A few towns of interest lie between San Salvador and San Vicente on the Interamericana. **Cojutepeque**, 32 km east of San Salvador, is a small town best known for the Cerro de las Pavas (Hill of the Turkeys), which offers good views and has an outdoor shrine to the Virgen de Fátima, who appeared to three shepherd children on May 13, 1917, near Fátima, Portugal. The statue was brought here from Fátima in 1949. The shrine attracts religious pilgrims, especially on Sunday and on May 13, El

Día de la Virgen. Bus No 113 comes from the Terminal de Oriente in San Salvador; it's about an hour's ride.

Farther along the highway (54 km from San Salvador or 22 km from Cojutepeque) is the turnoff to **Ilobasco**, a town known for ceramics, especially sorpresas (see the sidebar). The name Ilobasco is Nahua for Place of Much Milpas (corn fields). Today the area certainly has much of something: The road to Ilobasco is smooth, well marked, and with plenty of road signs pointing out mileage, telephones, lodgings.

Right after the entrance to the town is a string of artesanía shops along Av Carolo Bonilla. Taller y Escuela de Cerámicas Kiko (to the right) sells ceramics and also gives tours. A couple blocks farther down is Centro Artesana de Cerámica Ilobasco (☎ 332-2116), a store and school. Both stores are open 8 am to noon and 1 to 5 pm Monday through Friday. Across the road at No 20 (look for the 'Venta de Juguete Fina' sign) is another shop, full of ceramics, sorpresas and miniatures. In the back, order some delicious banana fritters (nuégados) in a molasses sauce (one colón each).

Take bus No 111 or No 142 from the Terminal de Oriente or from Cojutepeque. If you are driving from San Vicente, the turnoff is not marked; watch out for a fork in the road about 8.5 km after the turnoff for San Sebastián. The annual Feria Artesanal runs September 22 to 29.

Another 8.5 km heading east along the Interamericana is the road to **San Sebastián**, known for woven hammocks and textiles. Unless you want to seek out someone making that one hammock you

just have to buy, there's not much of interest here. January 20 is the annual fair. Bus No 110 goes there, or catch a bus in Cojutepeque.

Cruising farther down the Interamericana you'll spot **San Vicente**, a town of about 73,000, sitting in the Valle Jiboa by the Río Alchuapa at the foot of the tall, twin-peaked San Vicente Volcano, also called Chinchontepec. You can recognize the town by the unusual white clocktower in the main plaza. Climb up to the top for a view. Also of note is El Pilar, the colonial church built in the 1760s. The town festival is held on November 1. Near San Vicente are two swimming holes. Amapulapa is an overused Turicentro. Take bus No 177 from San Vicente's plaza. The better option is Laguna Apastapeque. It is cleaner and cheaper at US$0.35. Take bus No 156 from the plaza.

Bus No 116 runs to San Vicente from Terminal de Oriente in San Salvador.

CARRETERA DEL LITORAL

The Carretera del Litoral (Hwy CA-2) runs from San Salvador southeast through Zacatecoluca and Usulután, eventually coming to a crossroads with routes heading north to San Miguel and south to the Pacific Coast. This road varies between stretches of one-lane gravel nightmare to slick four-lane highway with shoulders.

The first town of any size you come to heading southeast from San Salvdor is **Zacatecoluca** (57 km). The largest Turicentro in El Salvador, Ichanmichen, is to the south. Admission is US$0.80, and cabañas cost US$4.

EL SALVADOR

Típica or Pícara?

Sorpresas (surprises) are tiny, detailed scenes and figures in little egg-shaped shells about the size of a walnut. The outside may be designed as a walnut, egg, apple, orange or basically anything round. Open one up to view the 'típica' (typical) delightful little scene of daily life around a village. An artist in Ilobasco got smart and added a new dimension to the surprise: a naked couple in the throes of sexual passion (or at least in that position). Even though the priest in town condemns the making of these and at one point made the stores confiscate their sinful goods, the 'pícara' (sinful) sorpresas still sell, albeit tightly wrapped in paper. ■

Bus No 133 runs to Zacatecoluca from Terminal San Marcos in San Salvador; there are also buses from San Vicente. From the center of Zacatecoluca you can take the local bus No 92 to Ichanmichen or walk the one km from town.

As you leave Zacatecoluca, the road is suddenly paved and well marked until you get to Río Lempa. From here it's a straight shot through Usulután to La Unión. Interesting sites along the way are detailed below.

ISLA MONTECRISTO

Where the Río Lempa meets the Pacific Ocean, mangroves flourish, brown pelicans challenge the tree bows, egrets pose gracefully and fish skip over the river's surface. This area is still undeveloped and more pristine than the accessible beaches around it. Getting to this natural spot takes some planning, but you will be rewarded by the nature and the people who live in the area. Isla Montecristo is inhabited by a community of about 17 families. Besides subsistence agriculture, they also grow cashews as an export crop.

Families can provide food and lodging in their homes and take you on boat tours of the river and mangroves, and also to the ocean. Lodging is very rudimentary; you rent out cots and mosquito nets, and it's a good idea to bring some food to share with the family you will be staying with. Pigs, chickens, roosters, dogs and tons of kids add to the atmosphere. Or you could stay at the beach, but do so only if accompanied by a local.

To visit the island, first call Cordes, an NGO in San Salvador (☎ 225-2547, net). Explain that you want to go to the island and they will fill you in on details. Basically you will need to go to San Carlos Lempa. By car from San Salvador take the Carretera del Litoral toward Usulután. At the town of San Nicolas Lempa is a turnoff to your right. Follow it down about nine km to the first sign of a town. By bus take No 302 from San Salvador. At Zacatecoluca transfer onto a No 155 or No 158 (you could also switch at the turnoff before the bridge). These buses go all the way down the road to El Porvenir.

The road down to La Pita, from which you take dugout canoes or lanchas, challenges any 4WD expert in the rainy season. Allow yourself time to stop in **La Sabana** to see a humble war memorial.

You can also visit Taura, on the banks of the river, from which **Parque Nacional Nancuchiname**, on the other side of the river, can be accessed. It's also worth spending some time talking to the locals of these towns, many of whom are ex-FMLN fighters or people displaced during the war. San Carlos Lempa is a well-organized community with programs in education, self-sufficient agriculture and livestock raising. Expect to pay about US$10 per day for transportation, food and lodging on Isla Montecristo.

USULUTÁN

Use Usulután as a jump-off point to visit other places. The turnoff for **Playa El Espino** is just past El Tránsito, 10 km east of Usulután on CA-2. You'll need a 4WD to drive the bumpy, windy road. It takes close to two hours to get there, but you are rewarded with your very own beach. Explore some of the small towns in the area, like Santa Elena. **Laguna El Jocotál**, farther east, is a protected reserve for migratory birds.

SAN MIGUEL
Population 222,100

San Miguel is the country's third-largest city and the main hub for the eastern half of the country. Founded in 1530, it still shows the signs of Spanish influence. The town has quite a few park areas, and its cathedral and theater are in better shape than those in many towns. The market burgeons out of its central area onto many streets. Truck loads of bananas, crates of coconuts and women precariously balancing racks of eggs on their heads add some excitement to the active town – active, that is, until the sun sets bright orange and then it's downright dead. When the center shuts down, make sure you are somewhere you want to be.

PLACES TO STAY
14 Hotel La Terminal
16 Hotel San Rafael
17 El Motelito
18 Hotel Migueleño
23 Hospedaje Modelo
24 Hotel Diana

PLACES TO EAT
2   Pupusería San Rafael
3   Pastelería Francesa
4   Bati Carnitas
5   Pizza Hut
10 Comedor Chilita
11 Comedor Esmeralda
12 Comedor Jazmín
15 Pupusería/Comedor
20 MultiMart
21 Comedor Carolina
24 Restaurant
    El Gran Tejano

OTHER
1   Crucero del Golfo Bus Stop
    (Hotel & Drive-Inn Milian's)
6   Banco Cuscatlán
7   Palacio Nacional
8   Antel
9   Antiguo Teatro Nacional
13 Bus Terminal
19 Military Barracks
22 Post Office

San Miguel

| 0 | 200 | 400 m |
| 0 | 200 | 400 yards |

EL SALVADOR

Hovering over the town is 2130-meter San Miguel Volcano, also called Chaparrastique. The volcano is still active: It has erupted at least 10 times in this century, most recently in 1976.

Information

Change traveler's checks at Banco Cuscatlán on the corner of 4a Calle Oriente and Av Gerardo Barrios. The post office is on 4a Av Sur between 3a and 5a Calles Oriente. Antel is on 2a Calle Oriente right by the Palacio Nacional.

Things to See & Do

The **cathedral** in San Miguel dates from the 18th century. Around the corner behind it is the **Antiguo Teatro Nacional**, an elegant edifice in which art shows are sometimes held.

Turicentros abound around here. The largest, and therefore the one in worst condition, is **Altos de la Cueva** – same price and deal as all the other Turicentros. A better option is to go to the private Turicentros. **Club Aramuaca** is on the road to La Unión (take bus No 324). You pay US$1.15 to get in to a club bordering a gravel quarry and with a clear view of the volcano in front. You can bathe in either the sulfuric waters of the lagoon or the fresh water in a series of swimming pools. Two large cages are home to a variety of tropical birds and a couple of friendly monkeys. On the road to San Salvador the small town of **Moncagua** sports El Capulín. Pay US$0.60 to get in and swim in shallow waters that come out of caves. The water is cleaner than other Turicentros, and as an added bonus there are tiny fish in the water.

The **Ruinas de Quelepa** are just a bit farther down the Interamericana from Moncagua; take local bus No 90 to get to either (a half-hour ride to the ruins).

Places to Stay

As usual the cheapest places are by the bus station, which is fine if you don't mind being in your room by 7 pm and out early in the morning. Plenty of bus drivers and brawly men socialize around these areas, so women need to be particularly careful. *Hotel Migueleño* (☎ 660-2737) on 4a Calle Oriente, No 610, charges US$4.60 for a good room with one double bed, US$5.70 for same room with a cot; all rooms have private bath and overhead fan. *Hotel San Rafael* (☎ 661-4113), at 6a Calle Oriente in the block east of the bus station, is run by friendly people. The rates are US$4.45/6.30 for singles/doubles, with private bath US$7.80/10.30. Air-conditioned rooms cost US$14.30.

Southeast of the bus station, *El Motelito* (☎ 660-2703) at 10a Av Norte, No 104, charges US$4/5.70 for one/two beds and private bath. More upscale, and safer, is *Hotel La Terminal* (☎ 661-1086), right across from the terminal on 6a Calle Oriente. Rooms with one/two double beds with air con and TV cost US$14/20, or US$11.50 for one double bed with a fan. The rooms are cramped but clean, and there's a restaurant below.

In a quiet residential district south of the center you'll find *Hospedaje Modelo* (☎ 661-3122) on 17a Calle Poniente, No 208. Large, clean rooms, some with high ceilings and all with private bath, overhead fan, a double bed and a big hammock, cost US$8 from 6 pm to 8 am. A triple costs US$11.50. Note that the windows don't have screens, so bring nets and spray. They say they fumigate every evening, but bring your own protection. Stay any earlier or later, and you'll pay US$2.30 an hour! Rooms are set around spacious grounds with ample parking.

A couple of blocks farther south, *Hotel Diana* (☎ 667-0429) at the corner of 21a Calle Poniente and 3a Av Sur, No 1202, is another pleasant place, quiet and clean. A large single/double room with air con costs US$11.50/14.30, with a fan a more reasonable US$6.30/8.60. All rooms have clean private baths. Microbuses drive along 3a Av to the center. Otherwise, a taxi to or from the bus station is about US$1.70.

Places to Eat

Bati Carnitas on 4a Calle Poniente between 1a Av Norte and Av Gerardo Barrios serves filling breakfasts for less than US$3. The lunch and dinner menu is a bit pricey (US$6 to US$8) and meat-based, but come here anyway for an exotic fruit or vegetable juice (US$2 to US$3). Across the street is a *Pizza Hut*. Just around the corner on 1a Av Norte is *Pastelería Francesa* with a wide selection of sweet and savory pastries and some decent coffee.

You have a wide selection of comedores to choose from. All have comida a la vista for lunch but keep the food out until later in the day. Come for lunch when the food is fresh and try other places for dinner. *Comedor Jazmín* is on 4a Calle Oriente and *Comedor Esmeralda* is on 8a Av Norte. *Comedor Carolina* on Av José Simeón Cañas is bigger and more popular but closes earlier. A local favorite is *Comedor Chilita* on 6a Calle Oriente between 4a Av Norte and 6a Av Norte. You can get a full plate of food from these places for close to US$2.50.

Round the corner from Hotel Diana (see above) is *Restaurant El Gran Tejano*, serving steak dishes for lunch and dinner. Vegetarians note: You can order a baked potato and veggies instead.

Later in the day try *Pupusería San Rafael* at the corner of 10a Calle Poniente and Av Monseñor Romero. There's a *MultiMart* on Calle Sirama between 4a and 6a Av Norte. It stays open till about 9 pm.

At MetroCentro, a flashy mall to the south of town, you'll find all sorts of overpriced US restaurants. The *Pizza Hut* here has a salad bar; a large plate costs US$3.60.

La Pema is well known throughout the country for its mariscada. One large bowl of this seafood soup with two thick cheese tortillas costs US$9. A *licuado de fruta* costs about US$1 and is more like a dessert than a drink. La Pema is open 10 am to 5 pm everyday. It's about one kilometer down the road to El Cuco.

Getting There & Away

The following buses travel to/from San Miguel:

Destination	Distance	Bus #	Duration
El Amatillo (Honduras border)			
	58 km	330	2 hours
El Cuco	37 km	32	1½ hours
El Icacal*		385	
El Tamarindo		85	2 hours
La Unión	47 km	324	1¼ hours
Puerto El Triunfo		377	
San Salvador	136 km	301	2½ to 3 hrs
Usulután		373	1½ hours

*Take No 385, get off at the fork in the road and walk down.

To go to Turicentro Altos de la Cueva, take No 94 Servicio Urbano from the plaza near the cathedral. To go to the volcano, take buses marked 'Las Placitas'; they also leave from the plaza.

Crucero del Golfo leaves from Hotel y Drive-Inn Milian's (☎ 669-5053) for Tegucigalpa at 8:30 am and 3:30 pm. The trip takes five hours and costs US$10. Buses arrive from Honduras at the same spot at 11:30 am and 5:30 pm. To get to Milian's from the bus terminal, take buses going towards Chaparristique. A taxi costs about US$1.40.

EL CUCO

Because **Playa El Cuco** is the more developed beach to the east, you won't find a pristine, secluded beach right by San Miguel or anywhere close by for that matter. The town is a sad strip of seafood comedores, aguardiente shops and shacks. A few surfers scope out the waves. Three decrepit hospedajes with less-than-adequate sanitary facilities are crunched together at the eastern corner of the town. A room will cost about US$3 single. Buy fresh-water showers along the beachfront.

For better beach access, take the road heading east near the beginning of town. *Palmeras*, next door to Leones Marinos, charges US$12 to US$17, and they'll let you cram as many people into one room as you can bear. The bathrooms are shared. *Tropico Inn* (☎ 661-0774) has cabañas that could fit up to five people for US$40. The beach here is very nice and away from town. To use their facilities for a day, without staying, you can pay US$5. You'll find other places along this road if these don't work out. Expect similar rates. Take bus No 320 from San Miguel (37 km, two-hour ride).

Farther along this road you can access Playa El Icacal (you'll have to walk part of the trip). You can also get to this area by going through the town of Intipucá from CA-2. Taking a 4WD is highly recommended.

LA UNIÓN
Population 39,648

La Unión, on the Golfo de Fonseca, was once El Salvador's most important port town, but it is largely neglected these days. Less than a boat a month now uses the harbor, leaving the town in a state of unemployment and government neglect. The Japanese government, however, has proposed renovation of the port, elevating some hopes. For some respite from the heat and views of the gulf, head to **Conchagua**, a town at the base of the volcano of the same name. Because of the economic problems, La Unión suffers from high levels of crime and closes down early.

Information

There's an Office of Immigration on 3a Calle Poniente between 2a and 4a Avs Norte. Banco AgroComercial on 1a Calle Poniente between 1a and 3a Avs Norte changes traveler's checks; check your guns, machetes and cameras at the door. It's open 9 am to 5 pm weekdays. The post office is at the end of Av General Cabanes.

Islands in Golfo de Fonseca

You can take a launch out to the islands either from La Unión or Las Playitas. On a good day you may spot dolphins and sea

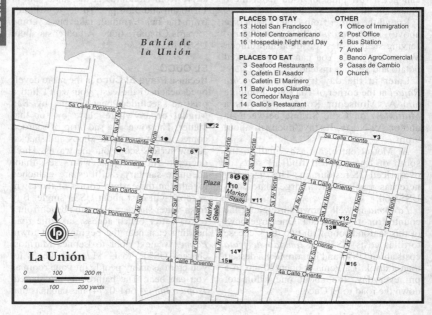

PLACES TO STAY
13 Hotel San Francisco
15 Hotel Centroamericano
16 Hospedaje Night and Day

PLACES TO EAT
3 Seafood Restaurants
5 Cafetín El Asador
6 Cafetín El Marinero
11 Baty Jugos Claudita
12 Comedor Mayra
14 Gallo's Restaurant

OTHER
1 Office of Immigration
2 Post Office
4 Bus Station
7 Antel
8 Banco AgroComercial
9 Casas de Cambio
10 Church

Bahía de la Unión

La Unión

0   100   200 m
0   100   200 yards

turtles. Prices below reflect trips from La Unión and will vary depending on distance from Las Playitas. Agree on a price before the adventure commences, and pay in halves to ensure that someone will pick you up. Some of the islands have rudimentary lodging, but safety is not assured. The islands are pretty close, so day trips are feasible. Take along food and water.

Isla Conchagüita
Fewer people, more mountainous and clean black-sand beaches. Go to Isla Zacatillo first, and take another launch for US$1.15 roundtrip (10 minutes).

Isla El Tigre, Honduras
Boats go to Amapala, from which you can get to Coyolito on the mainland. It costs about US$17 for the ride; split among a group, it's a good deal. Make sure your papers are in order before doing this.

Isla Martín Pérez
This one has the nicest beaches and the fewest people. Take a launch from Isla Zacatillo (they only leave every few days though). On weekends you could stay on the naval base; otherwise, camp. Ríos Tropicales (see Activities in Facts for the Visitor) takes sea kayaks to their base camp here.

Isla Meanguera
There's a small town here; ask around for places to sleep. From here you could go to Puerto de Potosí, Nicaragua (1½ hours, US$50). Launches take two hours depending on conditions.

Isla Zacatillo
Locals say there is a hospedaje called Miguel Guevarra on the island where you can spend the night. Launches leave around 11 am and cost US$1.15 roundtrip (20 minutes).

Places to Stay

Hotel San Francisco (☎ 664-4159) on Calle General Menéndez, between 9a and 11a Avs Sur is the best option in town, with large, clean and sunny rooms at US$8 with single bed and hammock, or US$14.30 with air con and double bed.

Hotel Centroamericano (☎ 664-4029) is a large, fenced-in hotel on 4a Calle Oriente between 1a and 3a Avs Sur. Single/double rates are US$8/17.

On 11a Av Sur between 2a and 4a Calles Oriente, *Hospedaje Night and Day*

(☎ 664-4109) is small and family-run. The 14 rooms have reasonably clean bathrooms (added plus – the toilets have seats). Rooms with one/two/three beds cost US$4.60/5.70/6.90.

Places to Eat

Comedor Mayra, opposite the Hotel San Francisco, is cheap and not bad. *Cafetín El Marinero*, on the corner of Av General Cabañes and 3a Calle Poniente, one block from the plaza, charges US$7.50 for a mariscada and US$5.70 for a full plate of fish or shrimp. Or there's *Cafetín El Asador* on the corner of 1a Calle Poniente and 4a Av Norte, which has similar prices. If you can find a place to cook, you can buy a dozen lobsters for US$11 at the fish market across from the post office.

On the corner of Calle General Menéndez and 3a Av Norte, *Baty Jugos Claudita* has an OK assortment of pastries, a variety of fruit shakes and licuados and decent breakfasts for around US$2.50. *Gallo's* on 3a Av Sur has fairly decent Mexican food, swimming in grease. This place also sees some life on weekends. The restaurant's owner spent many years in Washington, DC. Many locals have family living in the DC area or have lived there and returned.

Getting There & Away

The bus station is on 6a Av Sur between 1a and 3a Calles Poniente. Buses to destinations listed below leave throughout the day. Ask one of the drivers or company agents in the outdoor offices. Bus service to nearby destinations include:

Destination	Distance	Bus #	Duration
Conchagua	5 km	382	1/2 hour
El Amatillo (Honduras border)			
	41 km	353, 342	2 hours
El Tamarindo	45 km	383	1½ hours
Las Playitas	8 km	418	1 hour
San Miguel	47 km	324	1¼ hours

EL TAMARINDO

This small fishing village has a Centro Obrero where you can stay for free. The main beach is cluttered with fishing boats and can become kind of messy when the villagers clean the catch. If you prefer clean beach to local color, a fine sandy beach to the east curves round the bay.

Centro Obrero Dr Miguel Felix Charlaix is about 800 meters before you get to the main village. It's more basic than other government workers' centers in that you have to draw water from the well, the cabins are musty and the closest place to eat is *Comedor Viajero* halfway towards the center. Or try *Comedor y Pupusería Janeth*, in the main village. Bus No 383 runs frequently to/from La Unión (1½ hours) and to/from San Miguel (three hours).

SANTA ROSA DE LIMA

Santa Rosa de Lima is the closest town to the border at El Amatillo. If you need to stay the night, *Hospedaje Gomez* on 2a Av Sur south of 6a Calle Oriente, has clean rooms with bed, hammock and fan for US$5 a double. Bus No 330 passes through Santa Rosa de Lima every half-hour on its way between El Amatillo and San Miguel. Buses stop in the bus station, east of the market between 4a and 6a Calles Oriente. From Santa Rosa it is 18 km (30 minutes) to El Amatillo, 40 km (1¼ hours) to San Miguel and five long hours to San Salvador.

CIUDAD SEGUNDO MONTES

Named after one of the six Jesuit priests murdered by the military in 1989, this is one of the best organized cooperatives in the country, with several local communities and programs covering health, culture, education and conservation. In the first community of San Luis, turn left off the main road up to Centro Cultural. If you're interested in getting involved in the communities, the woman who works here can put you in touch with the right people in each discipline. Take a look through the guest book to see the variety of groups who venture through here.

Get information from the Centro Cultural in the main settlement of San Luis. There are good views and hikes close to the

village. Also there are four-bed dorms for US$2.90 per person, usually full of NGOers, and up the hill a comedor is open for all meals. The office is open weekdays and Saturday morning. On the main road is the intriguingly named comedor, *La Guacamaya Subversiva*.

Buses going to/from Perquín stop here. Make sure to tell the driver you need to stop at San Luis. You could also hop on a pickup in either direction.

PERQUÍN

Perquín, in the district of Morazán, was the headquarters of the FMLN guerrillas during the war, so it is fitting that the village now has the **Museo de la Revolución**. It charts the causes and progress of the armed struggle with photos, posters, weapons and histories of those who died in action. Weapons range from hi-tech hardware to homemade bombs and mines. The museum is open Tuesday to Sunday from 9 am to 5 pm and entry costs US$1.15.

Places to Stay & Eat

The only place to stay is *Casa de Huéspedes El Gigante*, down the turnoff road to the left before you reach the village sign (when heading north). It's a converted lumber mill and the rooms are separated into cubicles by two-meter-high boards, with space for little else except the bed. Cost for singles/doubles is US$2.30/2.85 overnight or US$2.85/3.45 for 24 hours.

Next to the basketball court and near the church is the PADECOMSM cafeteria. A plateful of food costs about US$1.50. To the west of the government offices is *Flor de Pino*; more expensive but recommended by locals, it serves daily specials.

Getting There & Away

Bus No 332 runs from San Miguel and takes three hours (US$1.30); departures are only every one to two hours. The last bus back to San Miguel is at 1:30 pm, so get a very early start. There are no buses from Perquín to Sabanetas on the Honduran border.

EL MOZOTE

Once a town hidden in the lap of the northern hills, El Mozote is now a destination for people who pay homage to one of the worst massacres in Latin American history, which occurred in 1981 (see the History section). The town remains eerily quiet, with a somber air surrounding the houses and the new residents. This is not a 'welcoming' little village and is recommended primarily for those who have read of the town's history. A simple iron silhouette of a family is backed by a brick wall on which wooden boards hang with the names of those killed in the massacres of El Mozote and neighboring villages. On the road up to Perquín turn right at the fork in the road to Arambala. This town is still in the process of rebuilding – it was bombed and the village decimated by massacres. Take the road to the left and follow it for four km to El Mozote.

Locals may be used to internationals passing through but are more apprehensive about talking or posing for photos.

Northern El Salvador

The districts of Chalatenango and Morazán were the principal areas of warfare between the government army and the FMLN guerrillas. One of the tactics used by the military was called 'tierra arrasada' (scorched land), in which they would burn the land and kill the cattle. Villages around Chalatenango were heavily affected by this practice. The people who fled the villages have now returned, and such places provide a fascinating opportunity to witness the process of reconstruction and to talk to the people about their war experiences. There's rarely anywhere to stay in the smaller places, though you may be able to stay overnight in a family home if you ask around. If there are any Western volunteers around, they're normally happy to help. Food is basic, too, and public transport fairly infrequent.

The north has some of the best scenery in the country: attractive rivers, valleys and hills that seem to roll on forever.

CHALATENANGO

Population 29,720

While the town of 'Chalate,' capital of the Chalatenango Department, has little of interest, it is a good base from which to explore the surrounding areas. The reward of coming this far is seeing how villages are coping after the war.

Orientation

The main street running east-west is Calle José María San Martín to the west and Calle Morazán to the east. Where Av Libertad crosses this street is where the name changes and the roads form the '0' point. The market is right at this point and attenuates out. The church and military garrison are within a stone's throw of each other on Calle San Martín and 3a Av.

Things to See & Do

Follow Calle Morazán 400 meters to the east and you reach a sign pointing 500 meters north for the Turicentro, **Agua Fría**. It's like all the others but has cleaner swimming pools and access to a waterfall. Entrance is US$0.80.

Venturing into the nearby small communities can be interesting. **San Antonio Los Ranchos** to the southeast, **San José Las Flores** to the east, and **Las Vueltas** are good places to go. Don't expect much when you get there, though. Unless you make some sort of an arrangement, perhaps through Cordes, it's hard to find places to stay. In Las Vueltas, ask at the physical therapy hospital for Alex; he may allow you to crash on the floor for a nominal fee.

Places to Stay & Eat

Hotel California (☎ 335-2170) on Calle Morazán between 2a and 4a Avs charges US$8.60 for a double bed and private bath. You're supposed to leave before 7 am though. The place is clean and has parking. West of the church and just opposite Antel

EL SALVADOR

is a nameless place, identified by a small 'Pilsner' sign outside. For US$2.90 per person you can sleep on some scary thin mattresses. Most rooms also have cots, which could be more hygienic.

Comedor y Cafetín El Portalito on 4a Calle Poniente and Av Libertad has comida a la vista. A plate of chicken and rice with a gaseosa costs about US$1.70. *Comedor Karlita* and *Comedor Campesino*, both on 1a Calle Poniente, serve comida a la vista as well.

Getting There & Away
Bus No 125 runs regularly from San Salvador (a 2¼-hour trip) and terminates near the church. Just beyond the Agua Fría sign is the stop for the bus going to San Antonio Los Ranchos and then to San José Las Flores, the end of the route. It departs at 11 am and returns the next day at 6 am. In between bus times, cars and trucks on these dirt roads usually stop to pick up passengers. Either way expect to pay about US$0.30 for the ride. To get back, try hitching a ride; ask around for the place to wait for the pickups. Bus No 124 goes to Dulce Nombre de María.

DULCE NOMBRE DE MARIA
The road up here may be strenuous, but it takes you through the beauty of fields of corn, through small villages painted in warm pastels, past cobbled roads and pigs getting chased by stray yet territorial dogs. This small town of low red-tile roofs and white walls rests peacefully in the rolling hills. People are subdued but friendly, and many hang out at the plaza during the hot afternoons, waiting for the bus to come by around 3 pm.

Farther north of this town is a cooperative of ex-FMLN combatants, called **El Manzano**. The 10-km road up hugs the hills and leads you to incredible views of the flat valleys dotted with volcanoes below and the mountains leading into Honduras. When you get to the bombed plane, take the road down to your right. If you don't have 4WD, ask around at the plaza for any pickups that might be going that way. The

accommodations are very basic. You can either camp up the hill or stay in a rudimentary dorm or in wooden cabins, depending on availability. Families will soon be offering lodging as well. Bring your own bedding. It's a co-op, so you eat with the families and you bathe by the waterfall, a good 15-minute walk through the coffee fields. To stay one night and eat three meals costs about US$10. Call ☎ 294-0105 for details and to arrange transportation if you don't have any.

LA PALMA
Surrounded by verdant mountains dotted with bright flowering plants and storming rivers and bathed in fresh mountain air, La Palma may be a long 84 km north of San Salvador, but it is well worth the climb and a must if heading into Honduras via El Poy.

Fernando Llort moved to La Palma in 1972 and soon developed an art trend that still represents El Salvador around the world. Llort's childlike, almost cartoony images of mountain villages, campesinos or images of Christ are painted in bright colors on anything from seeds to walls of churches. He taught some residents in La Palma how to create the same images and soon began a cooperative that churned out dozens of painted artifacts, from letters to crosses to keyrings to napkin holders. Today 75% of the village makes a living by mass-producing this art, none deviating too far from the traditional drawings or colors. As part of the regular school curriculum children learn to draw the images and to color them in. Llort, on the other hand, allowed his artistic whims to flow. His skillful and moving paintings are on display at Arbol de Dios in San Salvador.

Things to See & Do
As you walk around town you can peek into workshops and see families painting away. They will let you in to observe, and of course, to buy their works. Most are right at the entrance to town on the road to the right.

If hiking is of more interest, you'll stay busy. From San Ignacio you can access El

Pital (a Honduran biological reserve), the highest point in the area. Camping is possible, but it gets very cold. Ask locals at San Ignacio for directions. To go to Río Nunuapa (in the Nahua language, the name means 'silent river'), take the road leading to Los Horcones, past the Casa de Cultura and post office on 1a Calle Poniente. It's about a one-hour hike.

Places to Stay & Eat

Hotel y Restaurante de Montaña 'La Palma' (☎ 335-9202) is a perfect mountain getaway. You'll find good service, friendly staff, relaxing sounds of a river, swimming pools, beautiful scenery, hot showers (when the electricity is on) and a diverse menu. You pay for the luxury, though: Rooms cost US$23/28/34 for single/double/triple rooms all with double beds,

bath and TV. If it looks slow you could bargain for a deal. They also have an art store and school. Down the road from the hotel, *Restaurante El Pueblo* serves a variety of omelets and a good *plato típico* (bananas, beans, cheese, cream) for US$2.50. On the other road, Calle Gerardo Barrios, is *Cafetería La Estancia* with burgers, snacks, and meals for around US$2. Pupuserías line the plaza.

Getting There & Away

Bus No 119 runs hourly from San Salvador to the El Poy border with Honduras (four hours) and stops at La Palma. The northern section of the road is paved but in poor condition; La Palma is only about 12 km south of the border yet it's a 50-minute bus trip. The last bus south from El Poy leaves around 3 pm.

EL SALVADOR

Nicaragua

The largest of the Central American countries, Nicaragua has been the scene of dynamic events in recent decades, making headlines all over the world. But no matter what you might have heard about Nicaragua, being there yourself is guaranteed to lead to revelations. A visit to Nicaragua is an illuminating and memorable experience.

The country has many noteworthy features, including islands, volcanoes, navigable rivers, colonial cities and deserted beaches. The most interesting aspect, though, may be seeing how this post-revolutionary society is operating and talking to people who have seen it all.

Facts about Nicaragua

HISTORY
Early History
The earliest traces of human habitation in Nicaragua are the Footprints of Acahualinca, a 6000-year-old archaeological site within the city of Managua (see the description under Museums).

Pre-Columbian Nicaragua was inhabited by many different indigenous groups, including the ancestors of today's Ramas and Sumos on the Caribbean Coast and the Chorotegas and Nicaraos, who lived between the lakes and the Pacific. The Nicaraos, who are thought to have been descendants of groups who migrated from Mexico, spoke a form of Nahuatl, the language of the Aztecs. Many Nicaraguan places have Nahuatl names.

European Arrival
The first contact with Europeans was in 1502, when Columbus sailed down Nicaragua's Caribbean Coast.

The first Spanish exploratory mission, led by Gil González de Avila, came north

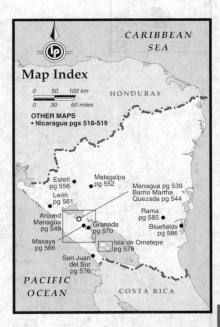

from the Spanish settlement at Panama and reached Nicaragua in 1522. It found the southern shores of Lago de Nicaragua heavily populated by the Nicarao tribe. The Spanish derived the name Nicaragua from their chief, also named Nicarao. The population under Nicarao interacted peacefully with the Spanish and were among the first indigenous Americans to voluntarily convert to Christianity.

Two years later the Spanish were back to colonize the region, led this time by Francisco Hernández de Córdoba, who founded the city of Granada, and then the city of León, in 1524. Both were established near indigenous settlements whose inhabitants were subjugated by the Spanish. The land around Managua was also densely populated by an agricultural, hunting and fishing

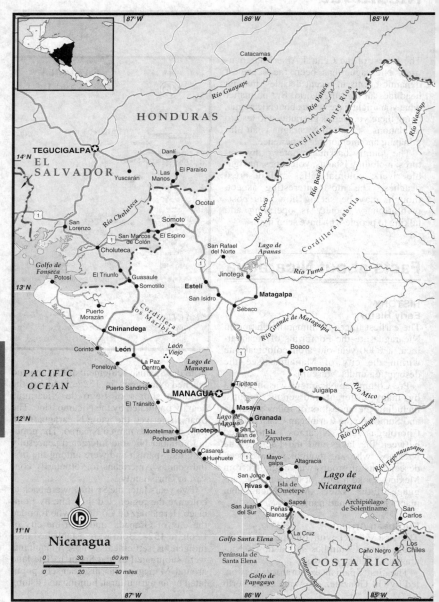

Nicaragua

people. They put up fierce resistance to the Spanish and their city was destroyed. For the next three centuries, Managua was but a village.

Colonial Settlement

The gold that had initially attracted the Spanish settlers to Nicaragua soon gave out, but Granada and León remained. Granada, on the north shore of Lago de Nicaragua, became a comparatively rich colonial city, its wealth due not only to surrounding agriculture but also to its importance as a trading center. The navigable Río San Juan, flowing out of Lago de Nicaragua, gave Granada a direct shipping connection to the Caribbean, and thence to Europe. With its wealthy business class, Granada became the center for the Conservative Party, favoring traditional Spanish values of monarchy and Catholic authority.

León was originally founded on the shore of Lago de Managua. The city was destroyed by earthquake in 1610, and a new city was established near the Indian village of Subtiava. It was poorer than Granada, but the Spanish made it the capital of the colonial province. León became the center for radical clerics and intellectuals, which formed the Liberal Party, and supported the unification of Central America and reforms based on those of the French and American revolutions.

The difference in wealth between the two cities, and the political supremacy of the poorer one, led to conflicts that raged into the 1850s, at times erupting into outright civil war. The continual fighting between them only stopped when the capital was moved to the neutral location of Managua.

While the Spanish were settling the Pacific lowlands, the English, who were becoming a major power in the Caribbean, were the dominant influence on the Caribbean side of Nicaragua. English, French and Dutch pirates plied the Caribbean waters and attacked the Caribbean Coast as well as Granada repeatedly in the 17th century.

NICARAGUA

Early Independence

Along with the rest of Central America, Nicaragua gained independence from Spain in 1821, was part of Mexico for a brief time, then part of the Central American Federation, and finally achieved complete independence in 1838. León and Granada continued to feud.

After independence, not only the liberals and conservatives were vying for power. With the Spanish out of the picture, Britain and the USA both became interested in Nicaragua and its strategically important passage from Lago de Nicaragua to the Caribbean. Both powers wanted to put a canal somewhere in Central America to connect the Atlantic and Pacific Oceans, and Nicaragua looked like the spot.

In 1848 the British seized the Caribbean port of San Juan del Norte, at the mouth of the Río San Juan, and renamed it Greytown. Meanwhile, the California gold rush had added fire to the quest for an interoceanic passage. Spurred by the sudden flood of passengers wanting to reach California by the quickest means possible, Cornelius Vanderbilt established the Accessory Transit Company to take passengers from Greytown, up the Río San Juan, across Lago de Nicaragua to the port at San Jorge (near Rivas), then 20 km by stagecoach to the Pacific port at San Juan del Sur, where they boarded ships bound for California.

William Walker

The growing US interest in Nicaragua took a new twist in the person of William Walker. Born in Nashville, Tennessee (USA), in 1824, Walker graduated from university in 1838, received his medical degree in 1843 and then became a lawyer. The early 1850s found him working as a journalist in the California gold rush boom town of San Francisco.

An opportunistic fellow, Walker became a filibuster, intent on taking over Latin American territory. In 1853 he led a small party to attack Mexico, where he declared himself president of 'independent' Baja California and the state of Sonora before he was ignominiously driven out.

In 1855, the liberals of León asked Walker to come and help them seize power from Granada's conservatives. Walker entered Nicaragua with 56 followers, attacked Granada and prevailed.

Walker soon had himself elected president of Nicaragua, and the US recognized his government. Three months after gaining the presidency he instituted slavery in order to gain favor with the southern states of the US. He declared English the official language, seized Cornelius Vanderbilt's transport company and took out a large loan, putting the territory of Nicaragua up as collateral.

Walker then adopted the slogan 'five or none,' and announced his intention to take over the remaining Central American countries. These countries united to drive him out, supported by Vanderbilt. In May 1857, Walker was defeated at Rivas and surrendered to the US navy, to avoid capture by the Central American forces. They evacuated him back to the USA.

Walker did not give up, however. Six months later, he landed at Greytown with another invading party, only to be arrested and deported again by the US navy. In 1860, he embarked on yet another attempt to conquer Central America. Landing near Trujillo, on the coast of Honduras, he was captured by the British navy, who turned him over to the Honduran authorities. He was tried and executed by firing squad on September 12, 1860; his grave is in Trujillo's Old Cemetery.

Late 19th Century

When Walker was defeated in 1857, the liberals, who had invited him into the country, lost power to the conservatives. In the same year the capital was transferred from León to Managua, in an attempt to quell the rivalry between Granada and León. Managua was chosen largely because it lay between the two cities; it was then little more than a village.

In 1860 the British signed a treaty ceding the Caribbean region, called the Mosquito Coast, to the now independent governments of Honduras and Nicaragua. The

Nicaraguan section remained an autonomous region until the 1890s.

The conservatives ruled Nicaragua from Managua in relative peace from 1857 until 1893.

Zelaya & the Marines

In 1893 a liberal general, José Santos Zelaya, deposed the conservative president and became dictator. A nationalist, Zelaya soon antagonized the US. The conservatives rebelled in 1909, and after Zelaya ordered the execution of two US mercenaries who were assisting the conservatives, the US government forced his resignation. In 1912, the US responded to another rebellion by sending 2500 marines to Nicaragua.

For most of the next two decades the USA dominated politics in Nicaragua, installing presidents it favored and ousting ones it didn't like, using the leverage of its force of marines. In 1914 the Bryan-Chamorro Treaty was signed, giving the US exclusive rights to build a canal in Nicaragua and to establish US naval bases there.

In 1925, a new cycle of violence began with a conservative coup. The marines were withdrawn but more political turmoil ensued, and in 1926 the marines returned.

Augusto C Sandino & the Somoza Era

The conservative regime was opposed by a group of liberal rebels including Juan Bautista Sacasa, General José María Moncada and, most importantly in the long run, Augusto C Sandino, 'General of Free Men.' Moncada and Sacasa attained power with US support.

Sandino, however, fought on, inspiring rebels throughout the Hispanic world. Moncada was president from 1928 to 1933, Sacasa from 1933 to 1936. In 1933 the marines withdrew from Nicaragua, but left behind a new Nicaraguan Guardia Nacional (National Guard), which they had set up and trained. It was led by Anastasio Somoza García.

In February 1934, Somoza engineered the assassination of Sandino. A couple of years later he overthrew Sacasa. Fraudulent elections were held and Somoza became president himself in 1937. Somoza created a new constitution to give himself more power, and he ruled Nicaragua as an internationally notorious dictator for the next 20 years, sometimes as president and at other times from behind a puppet president.

Somoza amassed huge personal wealth by corrupt means. The Somoza land holdings grew to the size of El Salvador. Nicaragua was virtually the personal possession of the Somozas and their friends.

Somoza supported the US (the CIA used Nicaragua as a staging area for both the 1954 overthrow of Guatemala's leader Arbenz and the 1961 'Bay of Pigs' invasion of Cuba) and was in turn supported by the US government. US President Franklin Roosevelt reportedly said of him, 'He may be a son of a bitch, but at least he's our son of a bitch.'

On September 21, 1956, the day after Somoza had been nominated for another presidential term by his party, a celebration was held by dignitaries in León. Rigoberto López Pérez, a radical young poet and journalist, arrived dressed as a waiter and shot Somoza. López Pérez was killed on the spot, becoming a national hero. Somoza died eight days later in Panama.

Somoza was succeeded by his elder son, Luis Somoza Debayle, and the Somoza family, with the help of the Guardia Nacional, continued to rule Nicaragua. In 1967 Luis died, and his younger brother, Anastasio Somoza Debayle, assumed the presidency.

Rising Opposition

In 1961, Carlos Fonseca Amador, a prominent figure in the student movement that had opposed the Somoza regime in the 1950s, joined forces with an old fighting partner of Sandino, Colonel Santos López, and other activists to found the Frente Sandinista de Liberación Nacional (Sandinista National Liberation Front), or FSLN.

On December 23, 1972, at around midnight, an earthquake devastated Managua, leveling over 250 city blocks, killing over 6000 people and leaving 300,000 homeless. As international aid poured in it was

NICARAGUA

diverted to Anastasio Somoza and his associates, while the people who needed it suffered and died. This obvious abuse increased opposition to Somoza among all classes of society. Over time, more and more moderate business leaders turned against Somoza as they saw their own companies being eclipsed by the Somoza family's corrupt business empire.

By 1974, opposition was widespread. Two groups were widely recognized – the FSLN (also called Sandinistas), led by Carlos Fonseca, and the Unión Democrática de Liberación, led by Pedro Joaquín Chamorro, popular owner and editor of the Managua newspaper *La Prensa*, which had long printed articles critical of the Somoza regime.

In December 1974, the FSLN kidnapped several leading members of the Somoza regime, and they gained ransoms and the release of political prisoners in exchange for the release of the hostages. The Somoza government responded with a campaign of systematic killings over the following 2½ years. Carlos Fonseca was assassinated in 1976.

Revolution & the FSLN

In January 1978, Pedro Joaquín Chamorro was assassinated. This was the last straw for the Nicaraguan public. The people erupted in violence and declared a general strike, and the former moderates joined with the FSLN in their efforts to oust the Somoza dictatorship by whatever means necessary.

In August 1978, the FSLN occupied the Palacio Nacional, took a thousand hostages and held them for two days. The government acceded to the FSLN's demands and the hostages were released. The revolt spread, and another general strike was called.

The FSLN launched its final offensive in June 1979. The FSLN forces won city after city, with the support of thousands of civilians fighting on their side. On July 17, as the revolutionary forces had won everywhere and were preparing to march on Managua, Somoza resigned the presidency

and fled the country. (He was assassinated by Sandinista agents a year later in Asunción, Paraguay.) The Sandinistas marched victorious into Managua on July 19, 1979.

The Sandinistas inherited a country in a shambles of poverty, homelessness, illiteracy, insufficient health care and many other problems. An estimated 30,000 people had been killed in the revolutionary struggle and perhaps 150,000 more left homeless.

The FSLN and prominent anti-Somoza moderates (including Violeta Barrios de Chamorro, widow of the martyred Pedro Joaquín Chamorro) set up a five-member junta to administer the country. The constitution was suspended, the national congress dissolved and the Somoza Guardia Nacional was replaced by the Sandinista People's Army.

However, the alliance between anti-Somoza moderates and the FSLN did not last long. In April 1980, Mrs Chamorro and the one other moderate resigned from the ruling junta when it became clear that the FSLN intended to dominate the Council of State, which was being set up to serve as the nation's interim legislature. In 1981, the junta was reduced from five members to three, with revolutionary commander Daniel Ortega Saavedra appointed coordinator.

The first reaction of Nicaragua's big neighbor to the north was to try to salvage what it could of its influence over the country. The US under President Jimmy Carter authorized US$75 million in emergency aid to the Sandinista-led government, but by late 1980 it was becoming very concerned about the increasing numbers of Soviet and Cuban advisors in Nicaragua and indications that the Sandinistas were beginning to provide arms to the rebels in El Salvador.

The Contra War

After Ronald Reagan became US president in January 1981, relations between Nicaragua and the US took a turn for the worse. Reagan suspended all aid to Nicaragua, but secretly offered to accept the irreversibility of the Sandinista revolution if the FSLN would promise not to aid the Salvadoran guerrillas. The FSLN rejected the deal, and the US quickly began funding the counterrevolutionary military groups known as Contras, operating out of Honduras and, eventually, out of Costa Rica as well. Most of the original Contras were ex-soldiers of Somoza's Guardia Nacional, but as time passed, its ranks filled with disaffected local people.

The Contra war escalated throughout the 1980s. As US money flowed to the Contras, their numbers grew from a few thousand to over 12,000 fighters. Honduras was heavily militarized, with large-scale US-Honduran maneuvers giving the impression of preparations for a military invasion of Nicaragua. The Sandinistas responded by instituting conscription and building an army that eventually numbered 95,000. Soviet and Cuban military and economic aid poured in, reaching US$700 million a year in 1987. A CIA scheme to mine Nicaragua's harbors was revealed in 1984 and eventually resulted in a judgment against the US by the International Court of Justice.

Nicaraguan elections in November 1984 were boycotted by leading non-Sandinistas who complained of the FSLN control of most of the nation's media. (The Chamorro family's newspaper *La Prensa* was independent, but even it was frequently censored and occasionally closed by the Sandinistas.) Daniel Ortega was elected president with 63% of the vote, and the FSLN won 61 of the 96 seats in the new National Assembly.

In May 1985, the US implemented an embargo on trade with Nicaragua, and it pressured other countries under its influence to do the same. The economic embargo lasted for the next five years and helped to strangle Nicaragua's economy.

After the US congress rejected new military aid for the Contras in 1985, the Reagan administration secretly continued the funding through a scheme in which the CIA illegally sold weapons to Iran at inflated prices and used the money to fund the Contras. When the details leaked out, the infamous 'Iran-Contra Affair' blew up.

Various peace plans were proposed by other countries throughout the years of conflict, but no agreement could be reached. The Costa Rican president, Oscar Arias Sánchez, finally came up with a peace plan that was signed in August 1988 by the presidents of Costa Rica, El Salvador, Nicaragua, Guatemala and Honduras. It was hailed as a great stride forward, but it was never fully implemented.

The 1990 Election

By the late 1980s the Nicaraguan economy was in a shambles. Civil war, the US trade embargo, falling world prices for leading Nicaraguan export commodities and the inefficiencies of a Soviet-style centralized economy had produced hyperinflation, falling production and rising unemployment. As it became clear that the US congress was readying to reinvigorate the Contras with new aid, Daniel Ortega called elections that he fully expected would give the Sandinistas a popular mandate to govern.

The FSLN, however, underestimated the disillusionment and fatigue of the Nicaraguan people, who were tired of shortages, food rationing, buses that could not be fixed for lack of spare parts, press censorship, political repression and having their sons conscripted to fight and die far from home. These problems came to eclipse the dramatic accomplishments of the Sandinista's early years: redistributing Somoza lands to small farming cooperatives, reducing illiteracy from 50% to 13%, eliminating polio through a massive immunization program and reducing the rate of infant mortality by one-third.

The Unión Nacional Opositora (UNO), a broad coalition of 14 parties opposing the Sandinista government, was formed in 1989. UNO presidential candidate Violeta Barrios de Chamorro had the backing and financing of the US. The US and leaders of the former Soviet Union began joint efforts to end the Central American conflict. The US also promised to lift the trade embargo and give hundreds of millions of dollars in economic aid to Nicaragua if UNO won.

Under the watchful eyes of almost two thousand international observers, election day on February 25, 1990, shocked the world (and certainly the Sandinistas) when Chamorro won 55% of the vote for president, to Daniel Ortega's 41%. In the National Assembly, UNO won 51 seats and the FSLN 39 seats.

The 1990s

Chamorro took office in April 1990. The Contras stopped fighting at the end of June with a symbolic and heavily publicized turning-in of their weapons. The US trade embargo was lifted, and US and other foreign aid began to pour in.

Chamorro faced a tricky balancing act in trying to reunify the country and satisfy all interests. General Humberto Ortega, Daniel's brother, remained as head of the army until early 1995. The FSLN split that same year into hard-line and moderate factions; the radical wing, mainly based on the Sandinista unions, remained a potent political and social force.

The promised economic recovery was slow in coming. Growth began in earnest only in 1994 and by 1996 had not nearly restored the economy to the level it enjoyed on the eve of the Sandinista revolution. Unemployment remained stubbornly high.

Against this background Nicaragua went to the polls again on October 20, 1996. The race quickly boiled down to a contest between the FSLN's Daniel Ortega and former Managua Mayor Arnoldo Alemán of the center-right Liberal Alliance. The Nicaraguan people, fearful of a return to the hardships of the 1980s, once again rejected the Sandinistas. In a massive voter turnout closely monitored by international observers, Alemán won 51 percent to Ortega's 38 percent (21 minor parties split the remaining votes). The Liberal Alliance won 42 National Assembly seats, the FSLN 36 seats and minor parties 15 seats. President Alemán was sworn in on January 10, 1997.

GEOGRAPHY

Nicaragua, with 118,360 sq km, is the largest country in Central America. It is bordered on the north by Honduras, south by Costa Rica, east by the Caribbean Sea and west by the Pacific Ocean.

The country has three distinct geographical regions: the Pacific lowlands, the north-central mountains and the Caribbean lowlands, also called the Mosquito Coast or Mosquitia.

Pacific Lowlands

The Pacific coastal region is a broad, hot, fertile lowland plain, broken by 11 major volcanoes. Some of the largest are San Cristóbal (1745 meters), northeast of Chinandega; Concepción (1610 meters), on Isla de Ometepe in Lago de Nicaragua; Momotombo (1280 meters) on the north shore of Lago de Managua; and Masaya, also known as Santiago (635 meters).

The fertile volcanic soil, and the hot climate with its distinct rainy and dry seasons (191 cm annual rainfall), make these Pacific lowlands the most productive agricultural area in the country. This region holds three major cities, Managua, León and Granada, and most of Nicaragua's population. The Pacific lowlands are also notable for their lakes. Lago de Nicaragua, also known by its indigenous name Cocibolca, or 'the sweet sea,' is the largest lake in Central America and the 10th largest freshwater lake in the world. In it live the earth's only freshwater sharks and other unusual life forms; scientists say this is because the lake was part of the Pacific Ocean until up-lifting land isolated it from the sea. The lake has over 400 islands. Lago de Nicaragua is linked to the Caribbean by the Río San Juan.

Lago de Managua, or Xolotlán, while smaller than Lago de Nicaragua, is nevertheless a large lake. There are also a number of beautiful crater lakes beside, and even inside, some of the volcanoes.

North-Central Mountains

The north-central region, with its high mountains and valleys, is cooler than the Pacific lowlands and also very fertile. About 25% of the country's agriculture takes place here. The region is not as heavily populated as the lowlands, but there are several major towns, including Estelí and Matagalpa. The highest point in the country, Pico Mogotón (2103 meters) is near the Honduran border, in the region around Ocotal. Lago de Apanás, an artificial reservoir on the Río Tuma near Jinotega, provides much of Nicaragua's electricity. North of Matagalpa, the Selva Negra (Black Forest), a combination resort, coffee plantation and private nature preserve, is one of Nicaragua's best walking areas.

Mosquito Coast

The Caribbean region, or Mosquito Coast, occupies about half of Nicaragua's area. It is the widest lowland plain in Central America, averaging around 100 km in width. The 541-km coastline is broken by many large lagoons, river mouths and deltas; 23 rivers, some of them big, flow from the central mountains into the Caribbean. Some of the most notable are the Río Coco (685 km long), Nicaragua's longest river, which forms much of the border between Nicaragua and Honduras; the Río Grande Matagalpa (430 km), the second longest river, with its source near Matagalpa; and the Río San Juan (200 km), which flows from Lago de Nicaragua and defines much of the border between Nicaragua and Costa Rica.

The Caribbean region is not quite as hot as the Pacific side and gets an immense rainfall. The region is very sparsely populated, and is covered by tropical rain forest and pine savanna. The largest towns are Bluefields and Puerto Cabezas, both coastal ports.

There are a number of small islands off the Caribbean Coast, surrounded by coral reefs. The largest islands, though even they are small, are the Corn Islands (Islas del Maíz) about 70 km off the coast.

CLIMATE

Two factors dominate Nicaragua's climate: altitude and season. The entire Pacific lowland zone, including Managua, is hot year round. The mountainous northern regions, around Matagalpa and Estelí, are

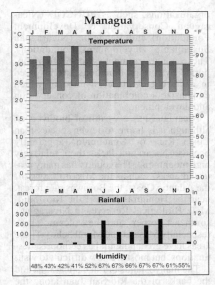

much cooler. The rainy season in these two regions runs from May to November. It can rain quite hard, but rarely for more than a few hours at a time. The rain makes the countryside green and the air fresh, though humid. The dry season runs from December to April. By mid-January, the plains are parched and brown. March and April are the hottest, driest months and, in the Pacific lowlands, the time when the wind blows and clouds of dust turn the air brown.

The Caribbean Coastal lowlands are hot and much wetter than the rest of the country, with an annual rainfall anywhere between 330 and 635 cm. The dry season here only lasts from March to May, and it can rain heavily even during those months.

ECOLOGY & ENVIRONMENT

Ecological awareness is growing at all levels of Nicaraguan society, though the environmental movement is still in its infancy. While the government's Ministry of Environment & Natural Resources (Marena) plays a policy-setting and regulatory role, the workhorses of the movement are the many nongovernmental

NICARAGUA

organizations, such as FUNCOD (Nicaraguan Conservation & Development Foundation) and Fundenic (Nicaraguan Sustainable Development Foundation). These nongovernment offices, often supported by foreign donations, are involved in a myriad of projects, most of which emphasize a combination of conservation and development.

Nicaragua has a wealth of biodiversity, although it is home to fewer species than Costa Rica or Guatemala (apparently because Nicaragua lacks their relatively high mountains). The country has many protected areas, such as the Miskito Cays, off the Atlantic Coast; the Bosawas rain forest, near the Honduras border; the Río Indio-Maíz Biological Reserve, in Nicaragua's southeast corner; and the volcanic chain (especially Masaya and Mombacho). These areas have great potential as ecotourist destinations, but most are now difficult to visit.

The many islands of Lake Nicaragua and the banks of the Río San Juan along the Costa Rican border are other fine places to observe nature.

GOVERNMENT & POLITICS
The government is divided into four branches: executive, legislative, judicial and a Supreme Electoral Council, which runs voter registration and elections. The executive is headed by a president, elected by popular vote to a five-year term, assisted by a vice-president and an appointed cabinet. Arnoldo Alemán was elected president in the election of 1996. The legislative branch consists of a 90-member National Assembly, elected by popular vote on a proportional representation basis.

Nicaragua is divided into 15 'departments' and two autonomous regions on the Caribbean Coast.

Since independence from Spain, Nicaragua has had 12 constitutions. The current one came into effect in 1995.

ECONOMY
Agriculture and livestock form the basis of the Nicaraguan economy, accounting for 26% of national income and employing

31% of the labor force. Important crops include maize, beans, sorghum, bananas, coffee, sugar cane, rice, sesame and tobacco. Manufacturing represents 22% of national income and employs 10% of the work force. Services and commerce constitute the third largest sector of the economy. The principal exports are coffee, beef, shrimp, lobster and apparel. Unemployment rates are high, with 1996 estimates of 18% unemployed and 33% underemployed.

POPULATION & PEOPLE
The 1995 census placed the population of Nicaragua at 4,139,486. As a result of the turbulent 1980s, perhaps another 500,000 Nicaraguans are living and working in the US, Costa Rica and elsewhere. Since the change of government, some of these people are starting to return home.

The great majority of the population lives in the Pacific lowland belt. The Caribbean region is sparsely populated; it makes up half the country's land area but has only 9% of its population.

There are six ethnic groups in the Caribbean region. Indigenous groups include the Miskitos, Sumos and Ramas. The Sumos and Ramas speak their individual languages to this day. The Nahuatl-speaking Nicaraos have essentially been assimilated. There are two groups of blacks: those of West Indian (often Jamaican) descent, who are often English-speaking, and a small number of Garífunas (see the Honduras chapter for more on Garífuna people). And then there are mestizos of mixed Spanish and native Indian ancestry. There has been a lot of mixing, so population grouping estimates are rather fuzzy.

Mestizos form the majority with 77% of the population. Spanish and other Europeans constitute 10%, blacks 9% and native Indians 4%.

The drift of people within Nicaragua from rural to urban areas has swollen the cities; although agriculture is important to the economy, 55% of the population is urban. Nicaragua is a nation of young people: 74% of the population is under 30 years old, and 46% of the population is under 15.

EDUCATION

Literacy increased under the Sandinistas, but it has declined in recent years due to a burgeoning population and scarce funds for basic education. According to government statistics, only 28% of primary school children complete the sixth grade.

ARTS

Poetry is one of Nicaragua's most important and beloved arts. Hispanic scholars count the country with Spain, Mexico, Argentina and Cuba as a leader in the development of literary models and achievements, and no other Central American nation can match Nicaragua's literary output. Rubén Darío (1867-1916), a poet who lived in León, was known as the 'Prince of Spanish-American literature.' His writings inspired poetry movements and literary currents throughout the Latin world.

Three outstanding writers emerged soon after Darío, and their works are still popular: Azarías Pallais (1884-1954), Salomón de la Selva, and Alfonso Cortés. In the 1930s an experimental group, the 'Vanguardia' movement, came on the scene, led by José Coronel Urtecho, Pablo Antonio Cuadra, Joaquín Pasos and Manolo Cuadra. The latter two, each brilliant in his own way, died early, but Pablo Antonio Cuadra remains a national intellectual figure as editor of *La Prensa*. The work of these poets is widely read and quoted. You can walk into bookstores in Nicaragua and find the work of current Nicaraguan poets, fiction writers and essayists. A number of leading personalities in the Sandinista leadership, including Sergio Ramírez, Rosario Murillo and Ernesto Cardenal, were literary as well as political intellectuals.

The Caribbean Coast, with its distinct culture, has its own art forms, too. In Bluefields, a largely English-speaking Caribbean town, reggae is the popular music.

In visual arts, probably the most distinctive painting comes from a collective of artists in the Archipiélago de Solentiname, in the south of Lago de Nicaragua. Ernesto Cardenal established a commune of artists, poets, craftspeople and other creative types. The area has since become well known for its colorful, primitivist style of painting.

Many *artesanías* (handicrafts) are produced in Nicaragua, some of them traditional arts, some of more modern origin. See the Things to Buy section later in this chapter for more details on handicrafts and where to find them.

RELIGION

Roman Catholicism is the dominant religion in Nicaragua, claiming almost 90% of the population. There is freedom of religion, however, and a number of Protestant denominations also exist; notable among these are Pentecostals and Baptists.

The Moravian church, a Protestant denomination that was introduced by missionaries in the days of the British, is important on the Caribbean Coast.

LANGUAGE

Spanish is the language of Nicaragua. On the Caribbean Coast, which was under British influence for over a century, English is also spoken, as are various indigenous languages. English is the language of the Corn Islands.

Facts for the Visitor

PLANNING
When to Go

As detailed in Climate above, Nicaragua has two distinct seasons, the timing of which varies from coast to coast. The most pleasant time to visit the Pacific or central regions is early in the dry season (December and January), when temperatures are cooler and the foliage is still lush. With the possible exception of the last month of the dry season (usually mid-April to mid-May) when the land is parched and the air full of dust, there is really no bad time to visit. Nicaraguans spend Semana Santa at the beach; all available rooms will be sold out weeks or even months in advance.

Maps

The *Guía Mananic*, which includes maps of Nicaragua and Managua, is sold for US$6 at the Mintur office in Managua. The Guía is available at bookstores for a higher price.

What to Bring

Most of Nicaragua is hot, especially the western lowlands around Managua; you probably won't need warm clothes unless you go to places in the mountains, like Matagalpa. Take rain gear if you are traveling during the rainy season or planning to visit the Caribbean Coast at any time.

Bring a flashlight for power failures. Carry your own toilet paper, as you normally won't find it in public facilities including bus stations.

Pharmacies can be found all over, and most standard medical supplies and medicines are widely available, including the antimalarial medication chloroquine, which is necessary since malaria is endemic to Nicaragua.

You can find almost anything that is available in Nicaragua at the large Mercado Central/Roberto Huembes in Managua.

HIGHLIGHTS
Regions

If you just rush through the country on the Interamericana, you'll be missing an opportunity. Take the time to see and feel something of the variety of regions in Nicaragua.

The mountainous, rural region to the north of the western lowlands is cool and fresh. Then there's the Caribbean region, most of it impenetrable tropical rain forest, where English is still spoken by a mixture of Indian and West Indian ethnic groups. The Corn Islands, just 70 km offshore, are small, idyllic Caribbean islands with white sandy beaches and palm trees, surrounded by coral reefs.

You can make some interesting journeys while exploring Nicaragua's different regions: by boat down the Río Escondido from Rama to Bluefields on the Caribbean Coast, by boat down the Río San Juan from San Carlos to El Castillo, or by bus through some beautiful mountains and valleys between Matagalpa and Jinotega.

Colonial Cities

León and Granada were Nicaragua's two principal colonial cities. Both were founded in the 1520s and retain their Spanish colonial character.

The highlights of the university city of León include the magnificent cathedral, the largest in Central America, the cathedral plaza, with its lion statues, and the Museo Rubén Darío, which is in the famous poet's boyhood home.

Highlights in Granada include similarly distinctive churches and other buildings, a ride through the old city to the lake in one of the horse-drawn carriages still used as taxis, and a day trip to Las Isletas and Isla Zapatera just offshore. In both towns, simply walking through the streets is interesting.

Masaya, another old city, has the most famous handicrafts market in the country. The town sits beside a volcanic crater lake, the Laguna de Masaya, over which rises the Volcán Masaya. The volcano is a national park, with a road going all the way to the top of the smoldering crater.

Managua, the capital, is much more recent, and most of its few old buildings have been destroyed by earthquake. However, there's one old building in Managua that's hauntingly memorable: the ruins of the cathedral, standing eerily silent beside the lake.

Matagalpa, Jinotega and Estelí are interesting cities in the mountainous north of the country.

Islands

There are over 400 islands in Lago de Nicaragua; some are especially worth seeing.

Ometepe, the largest island, has two volcanoes (one with a remote volcanic lake), good beaches, plenty of walks and places to stay. Las Isletas, a group of 356 small islands, are just offshore from Granada and can be visited as a day trip. So can Isla Zapatera, known for its archaeological finds. The Archipiélago de Solentiname in the south of the lake is a haven for artists, poets and artisans.

Petroglyphs, ancient Indian rock carvings, as well as statuary and pottery, are found on Zapatera, Ometepe and the Solentiname islands.

The Corn Islands, off the country's eastern coast, are as idyllic as Caribbean islands are supposed to be.

Conversation

Nicaragua has been the scene of some of the most profound political developments in the world in the last 20 years. The people of Nicaragua have a lot to say. If you express interest, ask questions and listen to their stories of living through the years of dictatorship, the revolution and all that's happened since, you'll hear many points of view and many remarkable things. A few weeks spent doing this can teach you more than years of reading newspapers.

TOURIST OFFICES

Mintur, the Ministry of Tourism, has an office in Managua (☎ 222-2498), a block west of the Intercontinental Hotel, and an office in the Augusto C Sandino international airport. See the Managua section for details. There is also a Mintur office in León.

VISAS & DOCUMENTS

To enter Nicaragua every visitor must have a passport that is valid for at least the next six months.

As of 1996, citizens of Argentina, Belgium, Bolivia, Chile, El Salvador, Greece, Guatemala, Honduras, Hungary, Liechtenstein, Luxembourg, Netherlands, Scandinavian countries, Spain, Switzerland, the UK and the USA do not need visas; they are issued a tourist card (US$5) for 30 days' stay in the country upon arrival. Citizens of Australia, Canada, New Zealand and other European countries do need visas, and these are good for 30 days from the date of issue for entry, and for 30 days after actual entry into the country.

Visa requirements may change, so check at a Nicaraguan embassy before you go.

Visa Extensions

Visas can be extended twice, for 30 days each time, for a total stay of three months. Visas can be extended at the Migración (immigration) office in Managua, which is near Km 7, Carretera Sur (☎ 265-0014). If you want to stay after the second extension runs out, you must leave and re-enter.

EMBASSIES
Nicaraguan Embassies

Visitors should obtain visas from a Nicaraguan embassy or consulate before entering the country. In the USA, Nicaragua has consulates in Houston, Los Angeles, Miami, New York and San Francisco, and an embassy in Washington, DC. Other embassies include the following:

Belize
　　See Embassies & Consulates in Belize City.
Canada
　　130 Albert St. Suite 407, Ottawa, Ontario KIP 5G4 (☎ (613) 234-9361/2, fax (613) 238-7666)
Costa Rica
　　See Foreign Embassies in Costa Rica.
El Salvador
　　See Foreign Embassies in El Salvador.
Guatemala
　　See Foreign Embassies in Guatemala City.
Honduras
　　See Foreign Embassies in Tegucigalpa; and Foreign Consulates in San Pedro Sula and in David.
Mexico
　　Payo de Rivera 120, Lomas de Chapultepec, CP 11000, Delegación Miguel Hidalgo, México DF (☎ 540-5625, fax 520-6960)
Netherlands
　　Zoutmanstraat 53-E, 2518 GM Den Haag (☎ 363-0967, fax 310-6869)
Panama
　　See Foreign Embassies & Consulates in Panama City.
Sweden (also Denmark, Finland and Norway)
　　Sandhamnsgatan 40, 6TR, 11528 Stockholm (☎ 667-1857, fax 662-4160)
UK
　　84 Gloucester Rd, London SW 4PP (☎ 0171-938-2373)
USA
　　1627 New Hampshire Ave NW, Washington, DC 20009 (☎ (202) 939-6570, fax (202) 939-6542)

NICARAGUA

Foreign Embassies in Nicaragua
See the Managua section for details.

CUSTOMS
Customs regulations are the usual 200 cigarettes or half-kg of tobacco and three liters of alcohol.

MONEY
The 33,000%-a-year inflation of the late 1980s has long since been conquered. The national currency, the *córdoba*, has been stable since 1993. You may still hear some prices quoted in US dollars, but payment in dollars is no longer demanded.

While the last few years have witnessed the rapid expansion of the private banking system, traveler's checks remain difficult to cash, except at border crossings and in Managua. *Casas de cambio* such as Pinolero and Multicambios provide this service, but it's not easy to find a bank that will do so. (See the Managua section for details.)

All over Nicaragua, many moderately priced hotels and restaurants accept Visa and MasterCard, and in Ometepe, even most of the cheapest places accept them. One company in Managua, Credomatic, gives cash advances on Visa and MasterCard.

Nicaragua's local affiliate of American Express is located in Managua one block east of Plaza España in the Viajes Atlantida office (☎ 266-4050); unfortunately, it does not cash traveler's checks. If all else fails, you can have money sent to you in most major Nicaraguan cities via Western Union (☎ 266-8126 in Managua).

Note that Nicaraguan córdobas cannot readily be changed in any other country. Once you cross the border, they are only good for souvenirs.

Costs
You can usually find a cheap hotel room for around US$3 to US$5 per person and an inexpensive meal for around US$2 to US$4; it costs around US$1.50 for a 100-km bus ride. But these prices can vary quite a bit, depending on where you are. The Carib-

bean Coast is a bit more expensive than elsewhere in the country.

Currency & Exchange
The córdoba is divided into 100 centavos. Bank notes come in denominations of one, five, 10, 20, 50 and 100 córdobas. There are smaller notes for one, 10 and 25 centavos. Coins come in five, 10, 25 and 50 centavos. You may hear prices given in *pesos*, another name for the córdoba.

It is often difficult to get change for 100 córdoba notes, so break them when you can.

Since 1993, the Nicaraguan government has devalued the córdoba by one percent a month against the US dollar in order to maintain stable relative prices despite local inflation. The rate is expected to reach 10 córdobas to the dollar in 1997. The rates below are as of mid-1997.

Australia	A$1	=	7.2 córdobas
Canada	C$1	=	6.6 córdobas
Gemany	DM1	=	5.5 córdobas
France	FF1	=	1.6 córdobas
New Zealand	NZ$	=	6.4 córdobas
Great Britain	UK£1	=	15.1 córdobas
Unitied States	US$1	=	9.2 córdobas

Tipping & Bargaining
Most Nicaraguans do not leave tips in cheap restaurants. In good restaurants you could leave up to 10% of the bill. Some restaurants include a service charge with the bill, and this is usually clearly shown. Do not confuse a tip with the nationwide 15% value added tax that is shown on each bill.

As usual, be certain to bargain in large outdoor markets, especially when buying *artesanías*. In small indoor grocery stores, known as *pulperías*, you don't bargain.

Taxes
A 15% value added tax is supposed to be applied to all business transactions, but this is not always the case, especially at very inexpensive places. As a general rule, places that provide a receipt will collect this tax. There is no refund procedure for foreign visitors.

Travelers departing by air must pay a US$18 airport tax.

POST & COMMUNICATIONS
Post, telephone and telecommunications services are provided at Enitel (formerly Telcor) offices in every city and town in Nicaragua.

Sending Mail
The basic mailing charge for a postcard from Nicaragua to the US (air mail) is 7½ córdobas or US$0.90, and delivery time can be anywhere between seven to 21 days. Rates to Europe and Australia are about 30% to 50% higher, with much longer delays. Travelers are strongly urged to register any important mail.

Receiving Mail
You can receive poste restante mail at any Enitel office by having it addressed to: (name); Poste Restante; Correo Central; (town name); (department name); Nicaragua. It will usually be held for one month, though sometimes only for a week or two.

Telephone
Long-distance domestic or international telephone calls can be made from Enitel offices. It may not be possible to make collect (reverse-charge) calls from every office or to every country. A number of foreign telephone companies (including the USA's Sprint, MCI and AT&T) have access numbers that holders of their company's calling cards may use to call home. In Managua, fax services are available in dozens of photocopying/camera shops as well as in many Enitel offices.

Nicaragua recently adopted a nationwide seven-digit system, eliminating the need for city codes. When calling between cities in Nicaragua, dial 0 before the seven-digit number.

To call Nicaragua from another country, the country code is 505.

Online Services
IBW Communications (☎ 278-6328) can provide tourists with temporary access to the Internet. IBW is two blocks north of the Villa Fontana Enitel Office in Managua.

BOOKS
Political events and developments in Nicaragua have inspired a flood of books about the country. Some informative or insightful ones include:

History & Politics
A Twilight Power: American Power and Nicaragua, 1977-1900, by Robert Kagan. An insider's view of the debate that raged within various branches of the US government on how to respond to the Nicaraguan revolution.

Comandos: The CIA & Nicaragua's Contra Rebels, by Sam Dillon. A detailed analysis of the Contra war by a leading US newspaper correspondent.

Culture & Politics in Nicaragua, by Steven White. Fascinating interviews and related material on the link between literature and revolution in Nicaragua.

Fire from the Mountain: The Making of a Sandinista, by Omar Cabezas. The classic account of the Sandinista guerrilla experience.

Nicaragua: Revolution in the Family, by Shirley Christian. A historical narrative of the 1979 revolution by the leading US journalist on the ground at that time.

Sandino, by Gregorio Selser. An authoritative biography of Nicaragua's outstanding revolutionary.

The War in Nicaragua (University of Arizona Press). William Walker's own account of his actions in Nicaragua. It was first published in 1860, the year he was shot by firing squad in Honduras.

Una Tragedia Campesina (UCA, Managua), by Alejandro Bendaña (a prominent Sandinista). An insightful account of the impact of the Contra war on Nicaraguan society.

Poetry
Useful collections of Nicaraguan poetry, which will offer the traveler many insights into the national culture, include:

Poets of Nicaragua, 1918-1979 (Unicorn Press, Greensboro, NC), by Steven White. A useful bilingual anthology.

The Birth of the Sun: Selected Poems (Unicorn Press), by Pablo Antonio Cuadra. A judicious selection from the work of Nicaragua's outstanding contemporary writer.

NICARAGUA

Antología General de la Poesía Nicaragüense
(Ediciones Distribuidora Cultural, Managua), by Jorge Eduardo Arellano. An excellent anthology of Nicaraguan poetry.

Riverbed of Memory (City Lights Books), by Daisy Zamora and translated by Barbara Paschke. An anthology of poems by a Nicaraguan poet.

MEDIA

Four daily newspapers are published in Managua. *La Prensa*, long established as the leading national daily, is owned by the Chamorro family. *Barricada* is run by the Sandinistas and *El Nuevo Diario* by the break-away Reformed Sandinistas. *La Tribuna* emphasizes business and foreign reporting. Generally, *La Prensa* and *Barricada* are available throughout the country. There are also several weeklies, as well as numerous radio and TV stations.

Barricada also created an international monthly magazine, *Barricada Internacional*, with Spanish and English editions. It costs US$35 per year for a regular subscription, US$25 per year for low-income earners, or US$18 for six months. For information or subscriptions, contact its offices at the following addresses:

Nicaragua
    Apartado 4461, Managua
USA
    PO Box 410150, San Francisco,
    CA 94141 (☎ (415) 621-8981)

PHOTOGRAPHY & FILM

Film is available everywhere, including office supply stores called *librerías* or bookstores (although they often do not sell books), as well as pharmacies and *pulperías* (grocery stores). A roll of 36 color-print film costs US$6.

One-hour processing is available at Kodak Express stores located throughout Managua and in major cities.

TIME

Nicaragua is six hours behind Greenwich Mean Time (GMT), the same as Honduras and Costa Rica. There is no daylight savings time; thus Nicaragua is one hour behind Eastern Standard Time in the USA from October to April and two hours behind the rest of the year.

WEIGHTS & MEASURES

The metric system is standard for weights and measures. Various other measures are also used, including the US gallon for gasoline and the *vara* (0.825 meters, or 33 inches) for distance.

HEALTH

Tap water is safe to drink in Managua, but outside the capital it's best to use bottled or boiled water. You should still exercise the usual care about eating unpeeled raw foods, salads, meats and food from unsanitary street stalls.

Be sure to take precautions against malaria. Malaria-carrying mosquitoes are a problem, especially during the rainy season. Chloroquine is available in pharmacies, but it's always a good idea to bring anything you think you might need with you.

WOMEN TRAVELERS

AMNLAE (☎ 277-1661), which started as the Sandinista women's organization but now is autonomous, has *casas de la mujer* in Managua and many cities of Nicaragua. AMNLAE provides health, legal and counseling services for women, especially those with limited resources. IXCHEN (☎ 268-0266) is a nongovernmental organization that offers similar services for women; it, too, has centers in many cities. Visiting women are welcome to drop in at any AMNLAE or IXCHEN women's center.

There are no special dangers for women traveling in Nicaragua, but the same advice applies as for the rest of Central America about dress and so on. (See the Women Travelers section in the Facts about the Region chapter.)

GAY & LESBIAN TRAVELERS

A Nicaraguan statute forbids homosexual activity, but this law is usually enforced only in cases that involve a minor. To be safe, gay tourists should avoid public displays of affection (there is no problem with activity in private or in gay clubs).

For more information, contact *Fundación Xochiquetzal* (☎ 249-0585), an organization that promotes freedom of expression and the prevention of sexually transmitted diseases (including AIDS).

DANGERS & ANNOYANCES

While the Contra war is long over, kidnappings and other bandit-like activities by rearmed former Contras (known as *recontras)* and former Sandinista soldiers (similarly dubbed *recompas)* continue to take place, primarily in the remote mountainous region northeast of Jinotega and Matagalpa.

Crime in Nicaragua has not reached the high levels of other Central American countries, but it is worsening. Most of it is sneak theft like pickpocketing and bag-slashing in crowded places (especially on buses), but armed robbery is increasing as well. Occasionally an entire busload of people is held up.

Expect at least one attempt during your visit, and protect yourself in advance. Wear a day pack on your chest rather than your back, don't wear jewelry, and do not allow yourself to be distracted in public places. You don't need to be paranoid, but do be alert and aware, especially in Managua.

Remember that some of Nicaragua's freshwater lakes, including Lago de Managua and Laguna de Masaya, are seriously polluted.

BUSINESS HOURS
& PUBLIC HOLIDAYS

Business and government office hours are Monday to Friday from 8 am to noon and 2 to 4 or 5 pm. Some businesses are also open on Saturday from 8 am to noon. Banks are open slightly shorter hours, but most include Saturday morning.

Public holidays include:

January 1
    New Year's Day
March/April
    Semana Santa (Holy Week) – Thursday,

Friday and Saturday before Easter Sunday
May 1
    Labor Day
July 19
    Liberation Day (anniversary of 1979 revolution) – no longer an official holiday, but still observed with large commemorative events by the Sandinistas
August 1-10
    Festival of Santo Domingo (Managua only)
September 14
    Battle of San Jacinto
September 15
    Independence Day
November 2
    Día de los Muertos (All Souls' Day)
December 8
    La Purisima (Immaculate Conception)
December 25
    Navidad (Christmas)

SPECIAL EVENTS

Each town and city in Nicaragua has annual celebrations for its patron saint. Two of the most famous of these celebrations occur in January and July, when the towns of Diriamba, Jinotepe and San Marcos, in the department of Carazo south of Managua, celebrate St Sebastian's and St James' (Santiago) Days. These celebrations, known as Toro Guaco, include distinctive masked processions and mock battles involving folkloric figures satirizing the Spanish conquistadors. Another Toro Guaco festival – the term covers a number of Nicaraguan folkloric celebrations – is held in honor of St Jerome (San Jerónimo) in the city of León.

ACTIVITIES
Hiking

Hiking is good in the Selva Negra, north of Matagalpa. On the islands in Lago de Nicaragua – Ometepe, the Solentiname archipelago and Zapatera – there are ancient petroglyphs (rock carvings), left by the Nicaraos, which make good destinations for hikes. Volcanoes are another good excuse for hiking; the Volcán Masaya National Park and the two volcanoes on Isla de Ometepe (Concepción and Madera) are the best.

NICARAGUA

Water Sports

Nicaragua has various possibilities for water sports. The Corn Islands offer excellent swimming and snorkeling (unfortunately, good diving equipment is not available on the islands). Off the coast of the big Corn Island, there's an old Spanish galleon in shallow enough water to be seen by snorkelers, and there are reefs full of marine life for exploring.

Fishing is good on Lago de Nicaragua, in other lakes and rivers, and in the sea. Surfing is popular at Poneloya beach near León (but watch out for the undertow), as well as at Playa Popoyo in the department of Rivas. The Montelimar resort offers sea kayaking and windsurfing.

There is good swimming at any number of Pacific beaches (Pochomil and San Juan del Sur are very popular), in various lagunas (volcanic crater lakes), including the Laguna de Xiloá, just 20 km from Managua, and in Lago de Nicaragua.

LANGUAGE COURSES

The following schools run intensive Spanish-language programs:

CENAC (☎ 713-2025), Apartado 10, Estelí; US contact: Rodolfo Celis, ☎ (312) 677-9276. US$120/week for four hours a day of one-on-one instruction; room and board with a family. Includes field trips, work on community projects and meetings with local leaders.

Escuela Horizonte (fax 713-2240), Apartado 72, Estelí. Program similar to CENAC's for US$120/week. The school is run by Sandinistas and linked to the Unemployed Women's Movement.

Casa Xalteva (telefax 552-2436), Calle Real Xalteva, Casa 103, Granada. From US$80 a week for four hours a day of instruction in classes of one to four students. Room and board with a family is an additional US$60/week; lodging at the Casa itself is US$40 a week (meals not included). Seminars, field trips and other special events are offered. Internships in many fields are available.

Escuela de Español en La Laguna de Apoyo (☎ 088-25413), Apdo Postal 60, Masaya. US$175/week for one-on-one instruction; includes meals and rustic accommodations on Apoyo Lagoon.

WORK

The FSLN no longer runs volunteer programs as it did in the 1980s when *internacionalistas* from around the world came to help the Sandinista effort. Many Sandinistas are now involved with the Movimiento Comunal Nicaragüense (☎ 265-1348), an independent organization that runs community projects all over the country and which welcomes foreign volunteers. A few international volunteer organizations operate in Nicaragua; one of the better known ones, Habitat for Humanity (☎ 266-1435), constructs houses.

Due to a combined unemployment and underemployment rate of over 50 percent, it is difficult for foreigners to find any paid work. Teaching English is an option, but it pays very poorly.

ACCOMMODATIONS

Most budget accommodations in Nicaragua are in small, family-operated *hospedajes* or hotels. Usual costs are around US$3 to US$5 per person for a room with shared bath, which will almost certainly have cold water only. Better quality accommodations are widely available for US$7 to US$15 per person per night.

FOOD

Since the early 1990s the restaurant sector has exploded in Nicaragua, though the majority of restaurants seem to offer the same standard beef, chicken and seafood dishes. The limited international cuisine available in Managua includes Italian, Chinese and French; foreign food is rare outside the capital. Hamburgers, sandwiches, fried chicken and pizza are popular; vegetarian food has begun to catch on.

The most typical (and inexpensive) Nicaraguan food is usually found in street stands and market stalls. Typical favorites include *gallo pinto*, a blend of rice and beans, often served with eggs for breakfast; *nacatamales*, leaf-wrapped tamales made of ground corn; *quesillos*, soft cheese and onions folded in a tortilla; and *vigorón*, *yuca* (a root vegetable) with pork rind and shredded cabbage.

Comida corriente usually consists of meat or chicken, beans, rice, salad (cabbage and tomatoes) and plantain. Available in comedores and even in many pricier restaurants, it's usually US$2 or less.

DRINKS
Bottled water and soft drinks such as Coca-Cola and Pepsi are found everywhere in Nicaragua. You run the risk of contracting parasites if you drink fresh fruit drinks mixed with water and ice (except in Managua, where the tap water is considered safe). Nicaraguan beers include Toña and Victoria. Rum is also produced in Nicaragua; the two major brands are Flor de Caña and Ron Plata. Many connoisseurs of rum consider Flor de Caña superior to Cuban and other expensive brands.

ENTERTAINMENT
Managua has many night clubs, with music ranging from Latin American to rock and reggae. All major cities have discos. Most of the nation's cinemas have been converted to evangelical churches, but there are a few left, including Cinemas 1 & 2 in Managua's Zona Rosa, which play first-run movies.

THINGS TO BUY
A wide variety of handicrafts are produced in Nicaragua. Some are particular to certain towns or villages. Distinctive Nicaraguan artesanías include quality cotton hammocks, basketry, ceramics, *junco* and other woven mats, ropes, threads, twines, weavings and textile arts, woodcarving, jewelry, paintings, carved and painted gourds and leatherwork.

Two large markets specialize in artesanías, selling arts & crafts from all over Nicaragua. The most famous handicrafts market in the country is at Masaya, 26 km from Managua. It's well worth visiting, and there are other places around Masaya where you can see crafts made and displayed. The Centro de Artesanías in Masaya has a large map which outlines these regions.

Nicaragua's other well-known artesanías market is in one section of Mercado Central/Roberto Huembes in Managua, but the selection is not quite as wide as at Masaya.

You can also go to other towns where handicrafts are produced, see how they're made, and buy them there. Some of the towns known for ceramics are San Juan de Oriente (near Masaya), La Paz Centro (between Managua and León) and Somoto (near the Honduran border).

The islands of the Archipiélago de Solentiname, in the south of the Lago de Nicaragua, are known for a unique primitivist style of painting.

Other handicrafts are more widespread within regions. Large baskets of bamboo or cane, for example, are made in the Masaya department as a whole, as are *petate* mats (made of *tule*, a species of junco).

Be advised that it is illegal to remove pre-Columbian pottery from Nicaragua.

Getting There & Away

AIR
Nicaragua's international airport, the Augusto C Sandino airport, is 12 km east of Managua's downtown. There's a US$18 airport tax on departing flights.

Nica, the national airline, has daily flights that connect to/from Miami. Also serving Miami are American, Aviateca, Iberia and LACSA. Houston, Texas, is serviced by Continental. Los Angeles is served by Aviateca.

Other international flights to/from Nicaragua include Guatemala (Aviateca, Copa), Mexico City (Aviateca, Copa, TACA), Panamá (Aviateca, Copa), San José (Aviateca, Copa, LACSA), San Salvador (Aviateca, Copa, TACA), Tegucigalpa (Nica, TACA), Havana (Aeroflot, Aerosegovia) and Madrid (Iberia). Note that these are not all direct flights. Each airline has a local office, which is listed in the telephone book.

NICARAGUA

LAND

Nicaragua has four overland border stations: three at the Honduran border and one at the Costa Rican border. The stations at Guasaule (Honduras) and Sapoá/Peñas Blancas (Costa Rica) are open daily from 8 am to 7 pm; El Espino and Las Manos (both Honduras) are open from 8 am to 5:30 pm. There's a US$2 exit tax at the borders.

Extensive international bus services are available to, from and through Nicaragua. Tica Bus operates from Managua to Guatemala City, San Salvador, Tegucigalpa, San José and Panama City.

In Managua, the Tica Bus station (☎ 222-3031) is seven blocks west of the Intercontinental Hotel, in the Barrio Martha Quezada where the budget hotels are found. Non-Nicaraguans are required to pay fares in US dollars. Riders are advised to purchase tickets at least a couple of days in advance. The station is open Monday to Friday from 8 am to 5 pm, Saturday from 8 am to noon and 3 to 5 pm, and Sunday from 3 to 5 pm.

The Sirca Express bus company has service only to San José. Sirca bus tickets are slightly cheaper, but their buses are somewhat older and in worse repair than the Tica buses. The Sirca bus office (☎ 277-3833) is located in the south central part of Managua, on Avenida Eduardo Delgado in the Altamira district, behind the Plaza de Compras. The station is open Monday to Friday from 8 am to 5 pm, and Saturday from 8 am to 1 pm; it would be wise to purchase tickets a few days in advance.

To/From Honduras

The three border crossings between Nicaragua and Honduras are at Las Manos (near Ocotal), El Espino (near Somoto) and Guasaule between El Triunfo (Honduras) and Somotillo (Nicaragua). Buses go to all three border crossings.

Tica Bus services to Tegucigalpa cost US$20 one way and US$40 roundtrip, leaving Managua at 5 am and arriving around 1 pm.

To/From Costa Rica

The Nicaraguan side of the main border crossing with Costa Rica is at Sapoá (Peñas Blancas). The Costa Rican border station at Los Chiles is reachable by boat from San Carlos on the Río Frío (see that section later in the chapter for details).

Remember that Costa Rica has an onward ticket requirement, although it seems not to be rigorously enforced for non-Central American residents. Two bus companies, Tica Bus and Sirca Express, operate international buses between Managua and San José. Tica Bus advises that Nicaraguans, at least, may not be allowed across the border into Costa Rica unless in possession of an outward-bound ticket. This can be either an air or bus ticket. However, Tica Bus also advises that its bus drivers will sell passengers a return ticket if one is demanded by zealous border personnel. To be completely secure, you could buy a one-way ticket out of San José, either back to Managua (available from both companies) or on to Panama City (available from Tica Bus) to satisfy the requirement. (If you are driving your own vehicle into Costa Rica, of course, no onward ticket will be required, but you will be required to buy Costa Rican car insurance for around US$15.)

A cheaper option is to take a regular Nicaraguan bus up to the border, go across, and continue on the other side on a Costa Rican bus. You may still need your onward ticket from Costa Rica to cross the border, but you could buy a one-way ticket out of San José from one of the international operators in Nicaragua. Local buses to the border depart frequently from Rivas.

Tica buses leave Managua daily at 6 am and 7 am, arriving in San José at around 5 pm and cost US$15 one way or US$30 roundtrip.

Sirca buses, which leave Managua on Monday, Wednesday, Friday and Saturday at 6 am, cost US$13 one way or US$26 roundtrip. They stop at Rivas around 8:45 am before reaching the border, so you can board Sirca buses at Rivas (paying the same ticket price as in Managua).

To/From Other Central American Countries

The Tica buses that leave Managua daily at 6 am and 7 am (arriving in San José at around 5 pm) continue on to Panama the next day at 10 am, arriving there at 5 pm. The fare is US$40 one way or US$80 roundtrip.

The Tica service to San Salvador costs US$35 one way (US$70 roundtrip). Buses leave Managua at 5 am and reach the Salvadoran capital by 5 pm. The same bus continues on to Guatemala City, arriving noon the next day. The fare from Managua is US$43 one way and US$86 roundtrip.

SEA & RIVER

Nicaragua's major Caribbean ports are Bluefields and, less importantly, Puerto Cabezas. On the Pacific Coast, the main ports are Corinto, Puerto Sandino and San Juan del Sur, in that order of importance.

There are no organized passenger boat services to these places. Although local fishing and cargo boats come and go, you are unlikely to be able to hitch a ride to another Central American or Caribbean country.

The Río Coco, also called Río Segovia, defines much of the border between Nicaragua and Honduras, while the Río San Juan forms part of the border with Costa Rica. It's unlikely you'll be crossing into or out of Nicaragua by either of these rivers. There is a Costa Rican border station at Los Chiles on the Río Frío, just south of San Carlos. If you do enter Costa Rica this way, have your passport stamped at the San Carlos immigration office.

Getting Around

AIR

La Costeña (☎ 263-2142) has four daily flights between Managua and Bluefields (US$43 one way, US$86 roundtrip); two of these flights continue on to big Corn Island (US$54 one way, US$108 roundtrip from Managua; US$34 roundtrip from Blue-fields). There are two flights a day between Managua and Puerto Cabezas (US$50 one way, US$100 roundtrip). La Costeña also flies to San Carlos (near the Costa Rican border) on Monday, Wednesday and Friday (US$74 roundtrip) and has service to Waspán, between Bluefields and Puerto Cabezas, and to three mining villages.

BUS

There are buses to most cities, towns and villages in Nicaragua. Intercity buses – most of which are former US school buses – are regular and frequent, albeit often crowded. Bus services usually start very early in the morning and finish in the late afternoon.

Nicaraguan buses are famous for their pickpockets. Expect someone to try to pickpocket you on every journey, and take appropriate precautions. If you have luggage that must be put into the storage compartment or on the roof, watch it whenever there would be any possibility of someone either taking off with it or going through it.

Nicaraguan buses often charge an extra fare for your baggage: In fact, you may have to pay the same fare for your pack to ride the bus as for yourself – or sometimes even more. You can haggle over this, but usually you will have to pay. Many travelers stash their baggage somewhere safe and use only a day pack to carry essentials while traveling within the country, avoiding the extra fare and the problem of guarding belongings every minute. Just about any hotel will store baggage for you while you travel.

TRAIN

Nicaragua's railway no longer operates.

CAR

Nicaragua has no unusual traffic regulations. Drivers are urged to comply with speed limits, especially in towns, where there are many 'police traps.' Any driver involved in an accident producing a serious injury is likely to spend at least one night in jail.

There are several car rental agencies in Managua; see Managua's Getting Around section for details. Throughout Nicaragua, unleaded gasoline is widely available.

BICYCLE
There's no reason why you couldn't bicycle through Nicaragua, except that it is hot, the roads are narrow and many drivers are careless. Bring any spare parts you might need with you.

HITCHHIKING
Hitching is a common and accepted practice in Nicaragua. As elsewhere in Central America, it's polite to offer a little money when you're given a ride. See also the Hitchhiking section in the Getting Around chapter at the front of the book.

BOAT
Boats are the only way to get to some places in Nicaragua. On the Caribbean Coast, boats go down the Río Escondido from Rama to Bluefields, from Bluefields to the Corn Islands, and from Bluefields to other places along the coast, including Laguna de Perlas.

Regularly scheduled boat services on Lago de Nicaragua include three routes from Granada: to Ometepe, to San Carlos (on the Costa Rican border) via Ometepe, and to San Carlos via a couple of villages on the eastern lakeshore. A quicker service goes several times daily between Ometepe and San Jorge, near Rivas. Boats also depart from Granada for shorter day trips to explore Las Isletas and Isla Zapatera. The Archipiélago de Solentiname in the south of the lake can be reached from San Carlos.

A speedy hydrofoil service runs six times a week from Granada to the Solentiname archipelago and San Carlos.

Public boats regularly travel down the Río San Juan from San Carlos to El Castillo, an old Spanish fortress. There is no public boat service to San Juan del Norte (Greytown), and private boats to this region are prohibitively expensive. (See the relevant sections.)

LOCAL TRANSPORT
Taxis operate in all the major towns and cities of Nicaragua. They're not metered; be sure to negotiate the fare before getting in.

ORGANIZED TOURS
Numerous Managua-based tour companies offer a wide selection of tours all over the country. You could also contact the Ministry of Tourism (Mintur). See the Managua section for details.

Managua

Population 819,731

The capital of Nicaragua, Managua is a large city spread across the southern shore of the lake of the same name. The lake itself, which indigenous people called Xolotlán, is 58 km long and 25 km wide, and there are a number of other lakes in the craters of old volcanoes within and near the city.

More than a fifth of Nicaragua's people live in Managua, and more are migrating all the time from the countryside. The city is the commercial center for the surrounding agricultural land as well as the national center for business, commerce, manufacturing, higher education and government. It is always hot, being only 50 meters above sea level: Daytime temperatures hover around 30°C to 32°C (86°F to 90°F) throughout the year.

History
The site of Managua has been inhabited for a very long time. See the Huellas de Acahualinca archaeological site, under Museums below, for details.

At the time of the Spanish conquest, Managua was an Indian city. The settlement stretched along the south shore of the lake as far as Tipitapa, and the Indians who lived here practiced agriculture, hunting and fishing. They put up a vigorous resistance to the Spanish, who consequently destroyed their city and established principal cities at León and Granada. Managua

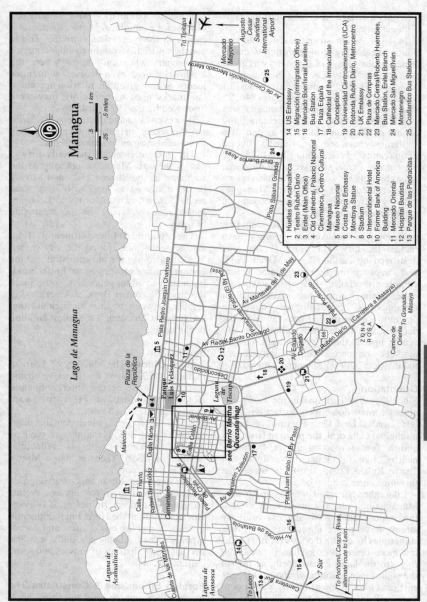

Managua

Lago de Managua

0   .25   .5   1 km
0   .5   1 miles

To Tipitapa

Augusto
Cesar
Sandino
International
Airport

Mercado Mayoreo

Mercado Maruy

1   Huellas de Acahualinca
2   Teatro Rubén Darío
3   Entel (Main Office)
4   Old Cathedral, Palacio Nacional
    Cinemateca, Centro Cultural
    Managua
5   Museo Nacional
6   Costa Rica Embassy
7   Montoya Statue
8   Stadium
9   Intercontinental Hotel
10 Former Bank of America
    Building
11 Mercado Oriental
12 Hospital Bautista
13 Parque de las Piedracitas
14 US Embassy
15 Migración (Immigration Office)
16 Mercado Boer/Israel Lewites,
    Bus Station
17 Plaza España
18 Cathedral of the Immaculate
    Conception
19 Universidad Centroamericana (UCA)
20 Rotonda Rubén Darío, Metrocentro
21 UK Embassy
22 Plaza de Compras
23 Mercado Central/Roberto Huembes,
    Bus Station, Entel Branch
24 Mercado San Miguel/Iván
    Montenegro
25 Coatlántico Bus Station

NICARAGUA

was only a village from then until the mid-19th century.

In 1811, when struggles for independence were spreading through Central America, the village of Managua was given the title of Villa Leal de Santiago de Managua (loyal town of St James of Managua) by the Spanish king. In 1846, 25 years after independence, Managua was proclaimed a city. It was declared the capital of Nicaragua in 1857, as part of a settlement between the fiercely liberal León (capital of Nicaragua since 1524) and the equally fiercely conservative Granada, after conflicts between the two had repeatedly erupted into civil war. Managua, midway between the two, was chosen as a compromise capital.

A number of natural disasters, including two major earthquakes this century, have racked the city. The colonial city was destroyed by earthquake in March 1931, and swept by fire five years later. It was completely rebuilt, only to be destroyed once again by another earthquake in December 1972. Geologists found the downtown to be riddled with faults, so the decision was made not to rebuild the city center. Instead the city decentralized, with markets, commercial centers and residential districts built on Managua's outskirts.

Orientation

Since the 1972 earthquake, most of Managua's former downtown district has been left as vacant land. Only the ruins of the old municipal cathedral, the plaza in front of it and a few important intact buildings nearby, like the Palacio Nacional and Teatro Rubén Darío, testify to where the thriving center used to be.

Like other Nicaraguan cities and towns, Managua has very few street names. Only the major roads have names; ordinary streets have none. Directions are given sometimes by cardinal points (north, south) but more often by a system in which *al lago* (to the lake) means north, *al sur* (to the south) means south, *arriba* (up) means east, and *abajo* (down) means west. Locations will be given in these directions, in relation to landmarks, and usually by blocks; for example, *del Cine Dorado, una cuadra al sur y dos cuadras arriba*. This is a rather difficult system to negotiate for newcomers who don't know where the landmarks are; even worse, sometimes locations are given in relation to where landmarks used to be before they were destroyed by the 1972 earthquake.

However, signage is improving, with most markets, neighborhoods and public monuments somewhat easier to find.

The Interamericana (Panamerican Hwy) passes through Managua; entering in the southeast as the Masaya Hwy and leaving in the northeast as the North Hwy. Carretera Sur and two highways to Leon are major roads entering on the west side of town.

The pyramidal Intercontinental Hotel can be seen from around the city center. You can also use the old cathedral and the communications towers of the Enitel building nearby to orient yourself as you explore the city. The former Bank of America skyscraper, between the Intercontinental Hotel and the old Cathedral, is the tallest building in Nicaragua.

Information

Tourist Offices The Ministry of Tourism (Mintur; ☎ 222-2498), one block south and one block west of the Intercontinental Hotel, is open Monday to Friday from 8 am to noon and 1:30 to 5 pm.

The *Guía Mananic*, which contains maps of Nicaragua and Managua, as well as maps of other major cities, is available at Mintur for US$6. There is also a Mintur office at the airport.

The excellent bimonthly tourist guide *Guía Fácil* has listings for services, events, art galleries and entertainment. It is available at Mintur, in the Hotel Intercontinental gift shop and at bookstores and larger grocery stores. Managua's daily newspapers also print listings of movies and some cultural events.

Foreign Embassies & Consulates The tourist office and the local telephone book have complete lists of Managua's many embassies and consulates. They include:

Costa Rica
From Montoya statue, 2 blocks north and one block east (☎ 266-5719, fax 266-3955)

Denmark
From the Hospital de Especialidades, three blocks north, Bolonia (☎ 266-8095)

El Salvador
Pasaje Los Cerros, Avenida del Campo, Las Colinas, No 142 (☎ 276-0712, 277-1734)

France
Reparto El Carmen, 1½ blocks west of the church (☎ 222-6210)

Germany
Two blocks north of Plaza España, Bolonia (☎ 266-3917)

Guatemala
Km 11½, Carretera a Masaya (☎ 279-9609)

Honduras
Km 12½, Carretera a Masaya (☎ 279-8233, 279-8241)

Mexico
Km 4½, Carretera a Masaya, beside Optica Matamoros (☎ 277-5886)

Netherlands
From Canal 2, a half block north, one block west, Bolonia (☎ 266-2890)

Panama
Pancasán No 61; from Hotel Colón, one block south and half a block east (☎ 278-1619)

UK
Entrada Principal de la Primera Etapa, Los Robles (☎ 278-0014, 278-0887)

USA
Km 4½, Carretera Sur (☎ 266-6010, 266-6038 after hours)

Immigration The Migración office (☎ 265-0014, 265-0020) is near Km 7, Carretera Sur. It's open Monday to Friday from 8 am to noon and 2 to 4 pm. You must come here to extend your visa.

Money Finding a bank in Managua to change US dollars is no problem. Street-corner 'coyotes' will also be glad to change dollars on the black market, but pay close attention to the transaction. Many merchants gladly accept dollars.

Traveler's checks, however, are difficult to cash in most of Nicaragua, and travelers are advised to change them in Managua or at border crossings. In Managua, the *casa de cambio* Pinolero (☎ 222-5933), two blocks north and two blocks west of the former Cine Dorado, changes all brands of dollar-denominated traveler's checks into dollars (at a 2% commission) or córdobas. It is open Monday to Friday from 8 am to 5:30 pm, and Saturday from 8 am to noon. Multicambios (☎ 266-8407), just south of Plaza España, also changes all brands of dollar-denominated traveler's checks, but their commission is 3%, and they only pay in córdobas. Neither Pinolero nor Multicambios will change foreign currencies besides the dollar. The private bank Bancentro will change traveler's checks; most other banks do not.

One company, Credomatic, located in the Zona Rosa on Camino de Oriente, gives cash advances on Visa and MasterCard for a 2.5% commission. It is open Monday to Friday from 8:30 am to 5 pm, and Saturday from 8:30 am to noon.

The local affiliate of American Express is located one block east of Plaza España in the Viajes Atlantida office (☎ 266-4050), which is open Monday to Friday from 8:30 am to 5 pm, and Saturday from 8:30 am to noon. The affiliate does not change traveler's checks.

If all else fails, you can have money sent to you via Western Union (☎ 266-8126), whose main office is opposite El Retiro Hospital, Bolonia, in Managua.

Post & Communications Enitel (formerly Telcor) is the combined post and telecommunications office. The main office is in the large building with a rooftop satellite antenna tower, two blocks west of the Plaza de la República near the lake. Enitel has branch offices in various parts of the city, including one at the Mercado Central/ Roberto Huembes.

The post office in the main Enitel office is open Monday to Saturday from 8 am to 5 pm. It will hold poste restante mail for a month.

International calls can be made from the main Enitel office from 7 am to 10:30 pm. It is possible to make collect (reverse-charge) international phone calls. Domestic telephone calls can be made from the main office as well.

Fax services are available in the main Enitel office Monday to Friday from 8 am to 7 pm. The fax number is ☎ 228-4004.

IBW Communications (☎ 278-6328), two blocks north of the Villa Fontana Enitel office, can provide tourists with temporary access to the Internet.

Travel Agencies Travel agencies in and near Plaza España include Viajes América (☎ 266-1130), Agencia de Viajes Fronteras (☎ 266-4134) and Aeromundo (☎ 266-3408).

Bookstores Librería Vanguardia (☎ 222-5944) is half a block east of the José Martí monument at Paseo Tiscapa. A good selection of Spanish-language books can be found at Hispamer (☎ 278-3216), located on the east side of Universidad Centroamericana (UCA).

Medical Services Hospital Bautista (☎ 249-7333, 249-7118), about one km southeast of the Intercontinental Hotel, is the country's best.

Pharmacies are found all over Managua, with some operating 24 hours.

Emergency Emergency phone numbers in Managua are:

Police	☎ 118
Fire	☎ 265-0162
Ambulance (Red Cross/Cruz Roja)	☎ 265-1761

Things to See & Do

Several of Managua's most notable buildings stand around the **Plaza de la República** near Lago de Managua.

The **old cathedral**, once a richly impressive edifice, was heavily damaged by the 1972 earthquake. But the ruin, still standing beside the lake, is one of Managua's most famous sights. Next to the ruined cathedral is the **Palacio Nacional**, one of the few colonial-style buildings not demolished by earthquake. Once renovation is completed, it will house the Museo Nacional and the national library.

On the plaza itself is the **tomb of Carlos Fonseca** and a monument to Rubén Darío, Nicaragua's best known and beloved poet. Behind the monument, near the lake, is the large, white, modern **Teatro Rubén Darío**.

On the other side of the plaza, behind the former Cine Gonzalez on the corner of Avenida Bolívar, is the **Cinemateca** theater, which sometimes hosts excellent international films. Next door is the old Grand Hotel, now reopened as the **Centro Cultural Managua**, which hosts occasional art and historical exhibits, as well as an arts-and-crafts fair the first Saturday morning of every month. It also has a small artsy snack bar.

On the west side of the plaza, the communications antennae towering over the Enitel building make it visible from all over the city center.

A large *malecón*, or walkway, has been built at the lakeside, but unfortunately the lake is too polluted for swimming.

The best view of the city is from the **Loma de Tiscapa**, the hill that rises behind the Hotel Intercontinental. Once the site of Somoza's Presidential Palace, it is now a national historical park. To get there, take the road immediately behind the Hotel Intercontinental and ask the soldiers at the military checkpoint to let you go to the top. It is open weekdays from 2 to 6 pm and weekends from 8 am to 6 pm.

Several kilometers away from the city center is the new **Cathedral of the Immaculate Conception**. Most of the money for its construction was provided by Tom Monaghan, owner of a chain of pizza restaurants. It is a modern but curious concrete structure; some say its many small domes make it resemble a mosque, others see a nuclear reactor. Cardinal Miguel Obando y Bravo, who formerly celebrated mass at a small colonial church at Santo Domingo de las Sierritas, now officiates at the new cathedral. It is located south of Tiscapa.

Several lagunas, or volcanic crater lakes, lie within and just outside the city limits. Behind the Intercontinental Hotel is the **Laguna de Tiscapa**. On the city's western outskirts is the **Laguna de Asososca**, with the **Parque de las Piedrecitas** on its south rim. On the northwestern outskirts of the city, near Lago de Managua, is the **Laguna de Acahualinca**.

There are several popular swimming spots a short distance from Managua. The **Laguna de Xiloá** is a beautiful crater lake about 20 km northwest of Managua off the road to León. It has clean water, picnic areas and restaurants around the shore. It is crowded on weekends, but quite peaceful the rest of the week.

At **El Trapiche**, a balneario 17 km from Managua in the other direction, east off the old road to Tipitapa, water from natural springs has been channeled into large outdoor pools surrounded by gardens and restaurants. Nearby, in Tipitapa, medicinal hot sulfur pools were once open to the public but are now ruined. Buses to Tipitapa (which pass by El Trapiche) depart from Mercado Central/Roberto Huembes; to Tipitapa it's about a 45-minute trip.

Museums The **Huellas de Acahualinca** museum preserves some of the most ancient evidence of human habitation in Central America: a long line of footprints of men, women, children and animals running toward Lago de Managua. The footprints are believed to be around 6000 years old and to have been made during a volcanic eruption, possibly of the Masaya volcano, that buried them under a layer of ash and mud. This preserved the prints until their discovery in 1874. The museum (☎ 266-5774) is open Monday to Friday from 8 am to 4 pm; admission is US$1.20. It is located in the northwest corner of town, six blocks west and one block north of El Arbolito. To get there, take a taxi or catch bus No 112 in front of the former Cine González, near the Plaza de la República, and head 2½ km west.

The **Museo Nacional** (☎ 222-5291), six blocks east of the ruined cathedral just off of Pista Pedro Joaquín Chamorro, has a modest collection of pre-Columbian artifacts and zoological specimens and interesting displays on earthquakes and

volcanology. The museum's collection is to be relocated to the Palacio Nacional when restoration of that structure is finished. It is open Monday to Friday from 8 am to 4 pm; admission is US$1.20.

The **Museo de la Revolución** and **Museo de Alfabetización**, victims of budget cuts (or politics), are now closed.

Markets The most interesting of Managua's large outdoor markets is **Mercado Central**, also known as Mercado Roberto Huembes, which has a large section devoted to artesanías from all over the country. This is a huge market and almost anything available in Nicaragua can be found in it. The Eduardo Contreras complex beside the market includes a major bus station and a branch office of Enitel. Bus Nos 109 and 119 come to Mercado Central; No 109 departs from in front of the Intercontinental Hotel or from the Plaza de la República, while No 119 departs from Plaza España.

Other major outdoor markets include the Mercado Oriental, Mercado Bóer (formerly Israel Lewites), Mercado San Miguel (formerly Ivan Montenegro) and Mercado Mayoreo.

Organized Tours

There are many private tour companies in Managua, most of which are pricey (US$25 to US$75 per person for day trips). Most arrange excursions around Managua as well as packages to Ometepe, Solentiname and the San Juan River. Among these companies are:

Careli Tours	☎ 269-6752
Continental Tours	☎ 278-1233
Eco-Tropic Tours	☎ 278-6647
ICN Tours	☎ 277-1694
Tropical Tours	☎ 266-1387

Two companies that provide more off-the-beaten-track tours are Aventurismo (☎ 265-2063) and Munditur Tours (☎ 267-0047). Tours Nicaragua (☎ 266-8689) is run by an American-Nicaraguan couple.

CEPAD Nicaventures (☎ 266-4628, fax 266-4236) is a nonprofit development organization offering ecotourism packages to the remote Bosawas Reserve (along the Honduran border) for US$60 per person per day. This educational tour includes swimming, canoeing, hiking, camping and lodging with local families in the Bosawas rain forest.

Special Events

The **festival of Santo Domingo**, Managua's patron saint, is held from August 1 to 10, and it features a carnival, a horse parade, cockfights and other sports. A procession with music and dancers takes the statue of the saint to its shrine at Sierritas de Managua, culminating in fireworks. Local holidays are observed on August 1 and 10.

May Day (May 1), the anniversary of the 1979 Sandinista Revolution (July 19), and Independence Day (September 15) are also celebrated in Managua.

Places to Stay

Barrio Martha Quezada, an eight-by-five-block residential district to the west of the Intercontinental Hotel, has many simple, cheap guesthouses and places to eat. International travelers have always tended to congregate here. There are few street

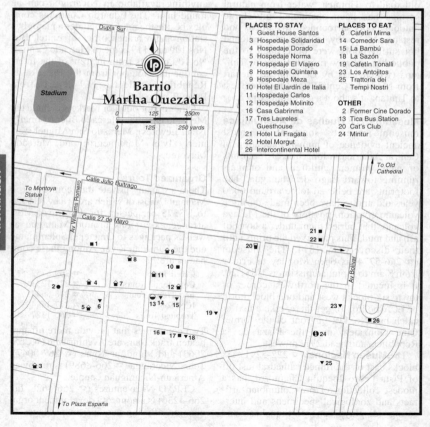

Barrio Martha Quezada

PLACES TO STAY
1 Guest House Santos
3 Hospedaje Solidaridad
4 Hospedaje Dorado
5 Hospedaje Norma
7 Hospedaje El Viajero
8 Hospedaje Quintana
9 Hospedaje Meza
10 Hotel El Jardín de Italia
11 Hospedaje Carlos
12 Hospedaje Molinito
16 Casa Gabrinma
17 Tres Laureles Guesthouse
21 Hotel La Fragata
22 Hotel Morgut
26 Intercontinental Hotel

PLACES TO EAT
6 Cafetín Mirna
14 Comedor Sara
15 La Bambú
18 La Sazón
19 Cafetín Tonalli
23 Los Antojitos
25 Trattoría dei Tempi Nostri

OTHER
2 Former Cine Dorado
13 Tica Bus Station
20 Cat's Club
24 Mintur

names in this district; directions are usually given in relation to the Tica Bus station or the former Cine Dorado.

Hospedaje Norma (☎ 222-3498), one block south and 1½ blocks west of the Tica Bus station, is about the cheapest lodging in the district, charging US$2.40 per person for rundown, basic rooms.

Guest House Santos (☎ 222-3713), a block north and 1½ blocks west of the Tica Bus station, is not very clean or well-maintained, but nevertheless popular with backpackers, who gather in its large covered patio every evening. Its cafeteria is open daily until 11 pm. Rooms with private bath and fan cost US$3 per person.

A block east on the same street, *Hospedaje Quintana* has very clean, well-kept rooms at US$4 per person, with fan and shared bath. Another block farther east, still on the same street, *Hospedaje Meza* (☎ 222-2046) has rooms at US$3 per person, with or without private bath; meals are available. It's a very basic wood and concrete structure, but colorful murals brighten its appearance.

Half a block north of the Tica Bus station, the family-run *Hospedaje Carlos* (☎ 222-7946, fax 222-2554) has clean, decent rooms, all with private bath and fan, for US$7 per person; air con is available. There's no patio, but guests may relax in the family's TV room.

On the road that runs east-west in front of the Tica Bus station are three more hospedajes. *Hospedaje Dorado* (☎ 222-6012) has basic rooms from US$4 per person. There is secure parking and laundry service, and guests receive a passkey. *Hospedaje El Viajero* has clean basic rooms for US$4 per person, and nicer rooms with private bath for US$6 per person. Two blocks east of the station, at the end of the block, *Hospedaje Molinito* (☎ 266-4431) has no sign, but it has rooms at US$2.50 per person. It's basic, but safe and friendly. The Tica Bus station itself offers decent rooms for US$6 a person.

There are also a few more expensive (and better quality) places to stay in this area. *El Jardín de Italia* (☎ 222-7967) charges US$7.50/15 for singles/doubles. The clean rooms have comfortable beds, private bath and fan (air con costs extra), and there's a TV and a large airy porch.

Two blocks south on the same street, the *Tres Laureles* (☎ 222-4440) is an excellent small guesthouse with singles/doubles for US$16/24. Two doors down is the homey *Casa Gabrinma*, run by a friendly, helpful young couple. Rooms with private bath are US$7 to US$15 per person. It's secure, and meals are available. On the same street, very nice, modern rooms with private bath are available in the unnamed B&B behind the La Sazón restaurant (☎ 222-2243); doubles go for US$30, with breakfast and laundry service included.

Two upscale hotels are the *Hotel Morgut* (☎ 222-3340) and the adjacent *Hotel La Fragata* (☎ 222-4179, fax 222-4133), one block north and one block west of the Intercontinental. Both hotels have singles starting at US$34.50, with private bath, air con, TV and phone. The newer La Fragata is wheelchair accessible and has a restaurant.

Lodging is also available in nearby Barrio Bolonia. *El Portal* (☎ 266-2558), across from the San Francisco church, has five rooms with private baths for US$10 per person. *Hospedaje Solidaridad* (☎ 222-6453), two blocks south and half a block west of the former Cine Dorado, has hostel-like accommodations for US$3 per person. It's run by a cooperative of handicaped people.

Places to Eat

Travelers will have no trouble finding cheap places to eat anywhere in Managua. Barrio Martha Quezada is no exception. Its inexpensive restaurants are also good places to meet other travelers.

Cafetín Mirna, next to Hospedaje Norma, is an excellent place for breakfast or lunch; both cost US$2 or less. The food is well-prepared and the service is fast and friendly. It's open every day from 6:30 am to 3 pm.

A good place for inexpensive vegetarian meals is *La Bambú*. It's open Monday to Saturday from 7 to 10:30 am and 5 to 9 pm.

It also has two rooms for rent (US$5 per person). The *Comedor Sara*, next to the Tica Bus station, is popular with foreigners. Open from 11 am to 10 pm, it serves a variety of dishes, including curries, omelets, pasta and vegetarian tacos.

La Sazón, two blocks east of Cafetín Mirna, has a big buffet lunch for around US$2. It's open Monday to Saturday from 11 am to 3 pm. Two blocks east and half a block north of La Sazón is *Cafetín Tonalli*, open from 8 am to 6 pm, which serves excellent whole-grain breads and cereals, sandwiches and quiche.

Los Antojitos, a fancy patio restaurant on the eastern edge of Barrio Martha Quezada opposite the Intercontinental Hotel, is a good place to sample typical Nicaraguan food, but it's expensive: most meals are around US$8. Two blocks south and half a block west, *Trattoría dei Tempi Nostri* is one of many moderate-to-expensive Italian restaurants that have appeared in Managua. Its fresh, delicious dishes of pasta start at US$4.

Ananda (☎ 228-4140), which is across from the Montoya statue, is a popular vegetarian restaurant.

Entertainment

El Quelite, five blocks west of the Villa Fontana Enitel office, features Latin music (live bands on weekends) and cheap beer. It's popular with locals. *Cat's Club*, one block north and a few blocks west of the Intercontinental Hotel, is a dance club popular with couples and groups.

On the eastern rim of the Tiscapa Laguna, the *Tiscapa* offers dancing to Latin music (live bands on weekends) in a patio setting. *El Cartel*, a block south of the Rotonda on the Masaya Hwy, has food, drinks and dancing.

La Buena Nota, on Km 3½ of the South Hwy, is a popular club that features live music by noted local bands. The nearby *Ruta Maya*, 150 meters east of the Montoya statue, offers live music in a patio setting.

Conchas Negras, located in the Zona Rosa on Camino de Oriente, is a quiet place to relax on an outside patio with live music. It is popular with the post-20s crowd. The nearby disco, *Lobo Jack*, is much larger and noisier.

Nicaraguans from the Caribbean Coast patronize the *Reggae Mansion* nightclub on Km 6 of the Carretera Norte.

Midnight (☎ 266-3443), two blocks north and one block west of Restaurante Munich, is a gay club.

Concerts, dance, theater and other performances are presented at the *Teatro Rubén Darío* (☎ 222-3630), on the Plaza de la República. On the ground floor is a separate theater, the *Teatro Experimental*.

Among Managua's few movie houses are *Cinemas 1 & 2*, located in the Zona Rosa, which feature newly released Hollywood fare. The *Cinemateca*, on the south side of the Plaza de la República, frequently presents international films.

Managua's daily newspapers are good sources of information on the city's diversions, as is the bimonthly tourist guide *Guía Fácil*.

Spectator Sports

A legacy of the US Marine presence during the 1910s and 20s, baseball is Nicaragua's national sport. Games are held several times weekly during the baseball season (October to April) at the large stadium on Avenida Williams Romero near the Barrio Martha Quezada.

Things to Buy

The best place in the city for Nicaraguan and other Central American artesanías is Mercado Central/Roberto Huembes (see Markets, above).

Getting There & Away

Air For information on international and domestic air services, see the introductory Getting Around section earlier in this chapter.

Bus The major bus stations for long-distance routes are at large outdoor markets. Only the major routes are mentioned here; there are many other bus services to smaller towns. Intercity bus fares in Nicaragua are generally US$1 to US$2 one way, and only rarely higher. You can phone ENABIN (☎ 265-2138) for information on intercity bus routes.

The principal bus stations are: Mercado Central/Roberto Huembes, Mercado Bóer/Israel Lewites and the Coatlantico station near Mercado Mayoreo.

Mercado Central/Roberto Huembes – COTRAN Cooperative (☎ 289-7820)

Estelí – 149 km, 3¼ hours, US$1.75; buses leave every 30 minutes, 4 am to 5:30 pm.

Granada – 44 km, one hour, US$0.60; buses leave every 15-30 minutes, 5:20 am to 9 pm.

Masaya (Express) – 26 km, 45 minutes, US$0.40; buses leave every 30 minutes, 7:25 am to 7:30 pm.

Matagalpa – 129 km, three hours, US$1.65; buses leave every 30 minutes, 4:15 am to 5:45 pm.

Ocotal (Express) – 227 km, four hours, US$3.30; buses leave at 5 and 8:45 am, 2:15 and 4:15 pm.

Rivas – 109 km, 2½ hours, US$1.30; buses leave every 30 minutes, 4:30 am to 6 pm.

San Juan del Sur – 138 km, 3½ hours; take bus to Rivas and transfer there.

Somoto (Express) – 217 km, four hours, US$3.20; bus leaves at 7:15 am, or take bus to Estelí and transfer there.

Mercado Bóer/Israel Lewites – Bus Station Office (☎ 265-2152). Buses also leave here for Chinandega, the Carazo pueblos, and areas close to Managua.

León (Express) – 90 km, 1½ hours, US$1.20; buses leave every 30 minutes, 5 am to 7 pm.

Pochomil and Masachapa – 65 km, 1½ hours, US$0.85; buses leave every 30 minutes, 4 am to 5:30 pm.

Coatlantico Bus Station – about one km south of Mercado Mayoreo (☎ 263-1559).

Rama (via Juigalpa) – 292 km, seven hours, US$4.75; buses leave at 4, 5, 6, 7:30, 8:45 and 11:30 am.

Rama (Express) – buses leave daily at 10:30 am to connect with boats to Bluefields.

If you miss the through bus to Rama, take one of the frequent buses to Juigalpa (137 km, three hours, US$1.75), and hitch-hike or transfer there to another bus for Rama. The last bus from Juigalpa to Rama leaves at 1 pm. Buses also leave here for Nueva Guinea and Boaco.

The Tica and Sirca bus companies run direct buses between Managua and San José, Costa Rica. Tica also services Guatemala, Panama City, Tegucigalpa and San Salvador. The Tica Bus station (☎ 222-3031) is in Managua's Barrio Martha Quezada, two blocks east of the former Cine Dorado. The Sirca station (☎ 277-3833, 277-5726) is in the Altamira district in south-central Managua, on Avenida Eduardo Delgado behind the Plaza de Compras. For information on international buses, see the introductory Getting There & Away section of this chapter.

Hitchhiking As always, it's best to take a local bus to the outskirts of Managua before you start hitching along the major routes heading out of town. To hitch to León, take bus No 118 to Parque Las Piedrecitas. To hitch to Masaya and Granada, take bus No 119 to the Camino de Oriente.

To hitch to Rivas, take bus No 118 or 114 to Km 7, Carretera Sur. To hitch to Estelí or Matagalpa, take bus No 112 along the Carretera Norte; get off when it turns off the main road and take bus No 105 to the outskirts.

Getting Around
To/From the Airport The Augusto C Sandino international airport is 12 km east of the city, near the lake. To get there, take bus No 116 or 118 from the Intercontinental Hotel to Mercado San Miguel/Iván Montenegro, change there to a bus heading for Tipitapa, and get off at the airport.

Mundi tur Tours (☎ 267-0047) provides shuttle service to the airport for US$10 per person.

Taxis at the airport charge around US$20 for the ride into town. If you want to bargain down this outrageous price, the best bet is to walk the short distance out of the airport and hail a passing taxi on the highway; these drivers are not part of the airport taxi clique. A taxi from town to the airport should cost US$8.

Bus Most people get around by bus in Managua. Buses are frequent, very crowded and justly famous for their professional pickpockets, so be alert. On all the city bus routes, the buses run every 10 minutes from 4:45 am to 6 pm, and then every 15 minutes from 6 pm until 10:15 pm. The fare is US$0.12.

Camionetas or pickup trucks, which you will see loaded with passengers, are a cheap but adventurous way to travel around the city. Standing and waving is the normal method for getting aboard; the fare is US$0.12.

Some of the bus routes you might have occasion to use are:

No 109 – Plaza de la República to Mercado Central/Roberto Huembes, stopping en route at the Intercontinental Hotel
No 118 – Intercontinental Hotel to Mercado Bóer/Israel Lewites
No 116, 118 & 109 – Intercontinental Hotel to Mercado San Miguel/Iván Montenegro
No 119 – Plaza España to Mercado Central/ Roberto Huembes; Plaza España to Linda Vista
No 112 – runs along Carretera Norte, by the lake, past the Plaza de la República (catch it at the former Cine González on the corner of Avenida Bolívar), the Museo Nacional, and on toward the airport
No 101 & 106 – Mercado San Miguel to Mercado Mayoreo/Coatlantico Station

Car Rental Car rental agencies in Managua include:

Auto Express
From the Intercontinental Hotel, two blocks north (☎ 228-4144); it's one of the least expensive companies, with models such as Lada, Hyundai and Daewoo, starting at US$29/day
Budget
Intercontinental Hotel (☎ 222-3520, ext 148); Montoya, one block west (☎ 266-6226)
Hertz
Intercontinental Hotel (☎ 222-2320); airport (☎ 233-1237); Km 4, Carretera Sur, Edificio Caribe Motor (☎ 266-8400)
Lugo
Airport (☎ 263-2368); from Canal 2, two blocks north, one block west (☎ 266-5240)

Reysi
From Intercontinental Hotel, one block north, two blocks west (☎ 222-6331)
Targa
Intercontinental Hotel (☎ 222-4875); airport (☎ 233-1176); from the Simón Bolívar Statue, one block east, 1½ blocks north (☎ 222-4881)
Toyota
Hotel Intercontinental (☎ 222-2269); airport (☎ 233-2192); Casa Pellas (☎ 266-1010 ext 210)

Taxi The average taxi ride in town costs around US$1. Taxi drivers' cooperatives decide fares, so rates are usually pretty standard, but it still never hurts to bargain, especially on medium to long trips.

You can phone for a taxi: ☎ 249-4669 for the Nicaragua Libre Cooperative; ☎ 222-7937 for the Carlos Fonseca Cooperative; or ☎ 222-5700 for the Renée Chavez cooperative (located in the Martha Quezada barrio).

Around Managua

There are several places worth visiting within a short distance of Managua. The most notable is the Volcán Masaya National Park, but even Nicaragua's other principal cities are close enough to be comfortably visited in day trips from the capital. Masaya is only 45 minutes away by bus, Granada an hour away and León 1½ hours.

In Managua's hot climate, it's natural to seek out places to swim and cool off. The most popular are crater lakes such as the Laguna de Xiloá, mentioned above, and Pacific beaches such as Pochomil.

PARQUE NACIONAL VOLCÁN MASAYA
Volcán Masaya national park is one of Nicaragua's most interesting features. Also known as Volcán Santiago (after the name of its principal crater), this 635-meter-high volcano is still quite active. You will likely find it smoking and steaming; the flanks of the volcano feature several tiny smoking

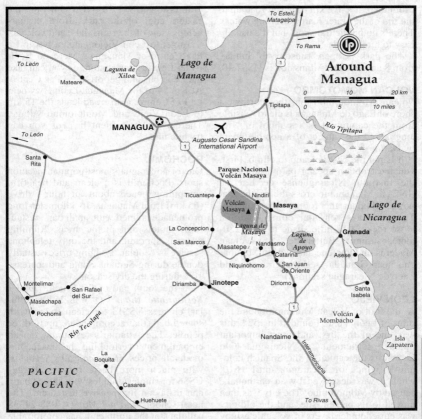

vents and places where there are thermal waters and hot earth.

This volcano has had an important role in the history of both the Indians and the Spanish. Legends say that the Indians would throw young women into the boiling lava at the bottom of the crater to appease Chaciutique, the goddess of fire, and skeletons of these human sacrifices have been found in lava tunnels near the volcano. You can walk up to the summit, where there now stands a cross; it is said the Spanish first placed a cross because they believed the volcano was an entrance to Hell, inhabited by devils.

From the top you get a wide view of the surrounding countryside, including the Laguna de Masaya and the town of Masaya beside it. For the best view of the glowing-red floor vent, take the paved road past the large parking lot to the far side of the crater. The park has several marked hiking trails and impressive lava tunnels that can be explored by flashlight (obtain a brochure at the park entrance).

The park entrance is just 23 km from Managua, on the road to Masaya. You can get there on any bus heading for Masaya or Granada. Two km from the entrance is a visitors' center and an excellent museum.

From there it's five km of paved road up to the rim of the crater (carry drinking water). There's no public transport, but it's usually easy to hitch a ride.

The park is open Tuesday to Sunday from 8 am to 5 pm. Admission is US$2.40.

VOLCÁN MOMOTOMBO

Volcán Momotombo on the northwest shore of Lago de Managua is clearly visible from the capital. It is a symbol of Nicaragua and the subject of a notable poem by Darío.

It is not the best volcano to climb. First, you must obtain special permission from the Instituto Nicaragüense de Energía (INE) in Managua to cross the geothermal power plant at the foot of the volcano. Then, it's a seven-hour climb on often loose rocks with little shade to the 1280-meter summit. Better bets are Volcán Maderas on Ometepe and Volcán Mombacho near Granada (see the Granada and Lago de Nicaragua sections).

LEÓN VIEJO

At the foot of Volcán Momotombo are the ruins of León Viejo. Founded in 1524, this was one of the first and most important Spanish settlements in Nicaragua. Old León was the capital of the Spanish colonial province of Nicaragua until 1610, when it was destroyed by an earthquake caused by Momotombo. The city was then moved to its present site, and the old city was buried under layers of volcanic ash by subsequent eruptions.

The foundations of several notable buildings have been unearthed by archaeologists, including the cathedral and the main plaza. It was here that the city's founder, Hernández de Córdoba, was beheaded. Later, 18 Indians were dismembered here after a rebellion against the Spanish. Along the main street are the remains of private homes and the church and convent of La Merced, where the tomb of Pedrarias stands. Father Bartolomé de las Casas, Protector of the Indians, resided for a time in León Viejo in the 1530s. A small archaeological museum is adjacent to the park

(admission US$1.20). The hill on the eastern edge of the park affords a marvelous view of the ruins, lake and volcano.

To get to León Viejo, catch a bus to La Paz Centro at Managua's Mercado Bóer/ Israel Lewites bus station, or you can take the León bus and get off at La Paz Centro. At Km 54 of the Managua-León Hwy near La Paz Centro, a dirt road leads the 15 km to León Viejo and Momotombo village. There is an infrequent bus, or you can try hitching.

POCHOMIL

One of Nicaragua's most popular vacation spots, Pochomil is a clean and beautiful swimming beach about an hour's drive (65 km) from Managua. Its kilometer-long promenade is lined with small bars, restaurants, hotels and picnic areas. Running water is sporadic and the only telephone service is cellular. Lodging prices usually double during Semana Santa and increase 10% during the dry season.

At the south end of the beach, *Hotel y Restaurante Altamar* (☎ 088-26406 cellular) charges US$13 for clean rooms with shared bath that accommodate up to three people. The Altamar's restaurant, on an embankment overlooking the beach, has moderate prices. *Hospedaje Las Segovias*, with much more basic rooms, charges US$6 for singles/doubles with shared bath, and it has an inexpensive restaurant. The hotel school *Villa del Mar* (☎ 088-24338 cellular), at the north end, has comfortable bungalows with private bath and air con; the charge is US$35 for up to three people. Its restaurant serves good, relatively inexpensive food.

The bus to Pochomil departs every half hour from Managua's Mercado Bóer/Israel Lewites bus station. The trip takes 1½ hours and costs US$0.85.

Watch your belongings while luxuriating on the beach.

OTHER BEACHES

Several other pleasant Pacific beaches are popular on weekends.

A small fishing village with basic places

to stay, **Masachapa** is located two km north of Pochomil. Its beach is not quite as clean as Pochomil. The *Hotel Summer* has worn, basic but spacious rooms, all with private bath and fan, for US$8 for up to four people. Its beach-front restaurant serves meals from US$3 to US$6. The same Managua bus that goes to Pochomil also stops in Masachapa.

About five km up the coast from Pochomil, **Montelimar** is the former beach house of dictator Somoza. It was expanded during the Sandinista period and is now a world-class resort managed by the Spanish firm Barceló (☎ 269-6762). If you can afford to splurge, this is the place to do it. Its daily rates of US$50 per person (higher during the dry season) include a bungalow, unlimited food and drink, plus windsurfing and kayaking on a two-km wide private beach.

Heading south on the coast, **La Boquita** beach is 72 km from Managua. To get there take a bus from the Mercado Bóer to the town of Diriamba, then change for La Boquita. *Hotel Palmas Del Mar* (☎ 412-3351) has comfortable doubles with view, fan and shared bath for US$25; the friendly owners can be persuaded to lower the price for shoestring travelers. French and English are spoken. Two basic hospedajes, *El Pelicano* and *El Sardinerio*, charge about US$12 for doubles with shared bath.

The same bus to La Boquita continues a little farther south to **Casares**, whose beach is often covered with fishing boats. Another 10 km south is the pretty beach at **Huehuete**, which is not reachable on public transit.

Up the coast northward, off the old road to León, are two more good beaches: **El Velero** and **El Tránsito**. Buses to El Tránsito depart from the Mercado Bóer/Israel Lewites bus station in Managua, but only infrequently. Facilities at these beaches are very limited.

All of these beaches are popular on weekends during the dry season (from December to April) and are packed during Semana Santa, when all Central America goes on holiday. At other times, you'll have the beaches almost to yourself.

North of Managua

From Managua, the Interamericana runs north to the departments of Matagalpa, Estelí and Madriz, highland regions with mountains and fertile valleys rich with crops and livestock. The climate here is cooler and fresher than in the lowlands, and this part of Nicaragua has its own distinct character. Many people like this part best.

Estelí is the principal town between Managua and the Honduran border. South of Estelí, at Sébaco, there's a turnoff for Matagalpa and Jinotega; both are pleasant towns and worth visiting. North of Estelí the road forks to different points on the border. The Interamericana route goes through Somoto, crosses the border at El Espino into the southern lowlands of Honduras and goes on to El Salvador. The other road leads through Ocotal to the border crossing at Las Manos and continues through the mountains to Tegucigalpa, the capital of Honduras.

Another route between this highland region and the Nicaraguan lowlands runs between León, Nicaragua's second largest city, and San Isidro, a tiny town at a crossroads on the Interamericana.

MATAGALPA
Population 49,148

The capital of the department of the same name, Matagalpa is a quiet, pleasant mountain town beside a river. Its climate is refreshingly cool. The Spanish conquistadores found three indigenous communities here: Matagalpa itself, which was Nahuatl-speaking; Molaguina or Laborio; and Guanuca, made up of Sumo Indians brought to the area. One tradition traces the name to the Nahuatl, as Matlatlcallipan (house of nets). Coffee is grown and cattle raised in the surrounding area. The nearby Selva Negra is one of Nicaragua's best walking areas.

The Río Grande Matagalpa is only small here, but by the time it reaches the Caribbean it is one of Nicaragua's largest

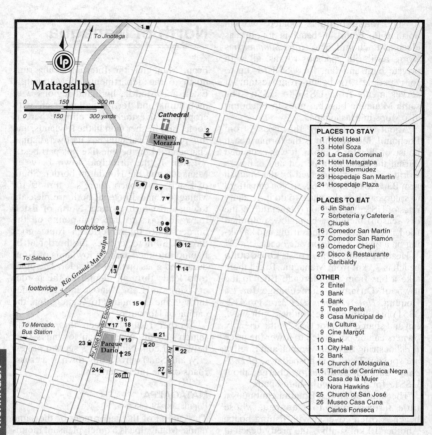

Matagalpa

PLACES TO STAY
1 Hotel Ideal
13 Hotel Soza
20 La Casa Comunal
21 Hotel Matagalpa
22 Hotel Bermudez
23 Hospedaje San Martín
24 Hospedaje Plaza

PLACES TO EAT
6 Jin Shan
7 Sorbetería y Cafetería Chupis
16 Comedor San Martín
17 Comedor San Ramón
19 Comedor Chepi
27 Disco & Restaurante Garibaldy

OTHER
2 Enitel
3 Bank
4 Bank
5 Teatro Perla
8 Casa Municipal de la Cultura
9 Cine Margót
10 Bank
11 City Hall
12 Bank
14 Church of Molaguina
15 Tienda de Cerámica Negra
18 Casa de la Mujer Nora Hawkins
25 Church of San José
26 Museo Casa Cuna Carlos Fonseca

rivers, and the second longest after the Río Coco.

Matagalpa is famous as the birthplace of Carlos Fonseca, father of the Sandinista revolution; the house where he was born, one block off the Parque Darío plaza, is now a museum.

For nightlife, there's a cinema and several discos.

Orientation & Information
Matagalpa has two plazas at opposite ends of the town. Parque Morazán, at the northern end of town beside the big cathedral, is the larger. Parque Darío is at the southern

end, beside the church of San José. Near this plaza are various places to stay and eat. The market and bus station are together, about a 10-block walk west of this plaza and beside the river.

Enitel, the combined telecommunications and post office, is one block east of the cathedral.

Things to See & Do
Matagalpa is a pleasant place to walk around. The **Museo Casa Cuna Carlos Fonseca**, birthplace of the revolutionary, is open Monday to Friday from 9 am to noon and 2 to 5 pm.

The **Casa Municipal de la Cultura**, 2½ blocks south and one block west of Parque Morazán, offers music and art classes for young people. Matagalpa also has a women's center, the **Casa de la Mujer Nora Hawkins**, half a block east of Parque Darío.

The famous **Selva Negra Hotel** (☎ 612-3883), 12 km north of town, is owned by Eddy and Mausi Kühl, descendants of German immigrants who settled here in 1889. The hotel, which gets its name from Schwarzwald or Black Forest, features a restaurant, a small artificial lake and many kilometers of (often muddy) hiking and horse trails through the Selva Negra. The primary forest here is full of wildlife, including Congo (howler) monkeys, spider monkeys, ocelots and sloths. It is also known for its bird life. Bird watching is best early in the morning or late in the afternoon; among the many you might see are quetzals, toucans, woodpeckers, hummingbirds, wrens and hawks. The Kühls also own the adjacent coffee farm and take pride in their ecologically sound farming methods.

To get to the Selva Negra Hotel, take any bus heading north from Matagalpa and get off where an old military tank marks the turnoff to the hotel; from there it's a pleasant two-km walk. The US$2.50 admission fee is good toward a meal at the restaurant. The hotel is pricey, with rooms/cabins starting at US$30/50, but on weekdays backpackers can get a room for US$10 per person. A youth hostel is available to groups of 15 or more for US$10 per person.

A visit to Jinotega, 34 km north of Matagalpa, makes a very enjoyable day trip from Matagalpa (see Jinotega for details). The ride there takes you through one of the most scenic parts of Nicaragua, and Jinotega itself is a pleasant town with a beautiful church.

The town of **Sébaco**, southwest of Matagalpa, in a valley of the same name, has an interesting history. Sébaco was an important ceremonial center for the Chorotega, a powerful indigenous community. Its name is traced to Cihuacuatl (ser-

pent mother), the Chorotega goddess of the earth and reproduction. In the nearby lagoon of Tecomapa are the ruins of a temple to the goddess.

Special Events
Matagalpa's annual festival is September 24, the Día de la Virgen de las Mercedes.

Organized Tours
Douglas Smith (☎ 612-3379, 612-2974) leads inexpensive excursions to beautiful sites in the Matagalpa region, where you can hike, swim and camp.

Places to Stay
There are various inexpensive places to stay around the Parque Darío. The best deal in town is *La Casa Comunal* (☎ 612-2695), a round, brick building a block east of Parque Darío. It's just US$1.20 per person for hostel-like rooms with shared bath; you may have to share your room with others. Some may be put off by the rickety metal beds and skimpy mattresses, but the rooms are spacious with large windows. There is a 10 pm curfew. The hospedaje is run by the Indigenous Community of Matagalpa, and profits go toward helping indigenous people get land titles.

Hospedaje Plaza (☎ 612-2380), on the south side of the park, is not bad for the price. Upstairs rooms with shared bath are US$2.75; downstairs rooms with private bath are US$4; try to get a room with a window. It has a nice breezy sitting room.

Also on the park, the *Hospedaje San Martín* (☎ 612-3737) is another decent place for the price: Rooms with shared bath are US$3.60/6 for singles/doubles. Two blocks east of the park, the *Hotel Bermudez* (no phone) is a cut below the San Martín; it charges US$3.60 for singles with shared bath, US$7 for doubles with private bath.

Half a block west of Avenida Central is the *Hotel Matagalpa*, a clean, friendly place that charges US$4.80/$8.25 for singles/doubles with shared bath; rooms with private bath are available also. Inexpensive meals are served.

Near the cathedral, the *Hotel Ideal* (☎ 612-2483) is the best in town, charging US$15 for singles/doubles with private bath; the Ideal has two restaurants and a disco. Beside the river, the *Hotel Soza* (☎ 612-3030) charges US$4.80/7 for simple but comfortable single/double rooms with private bath.

Places to Eat

Comedor San Martín and *Comedor San Ramón*, both located on the block directly north of the Parque Darío, are good, basic restaurants that are open every day from around 6:30 am to 10 pm. On the northeast corner of Parque Darío, a few doors from the church, *Comedor Chepi* serves full meals for US$1.75. It's open daily from noon to 11 pm.

Jin-Shan, a block south of Parque Morazán, is a popular restaurant that serves standard fare plus some Chinese-style dishes. Prices range from US$4 to US$9.50, but you can order smaller portions for half price. Around the corner, the *Sorbetería y Cafetería Chupis* serves burgers, hot dogs and sandwiches as well as ice cream. *Disco and Restaurante Garibaldy*, two blocks east of Parque Darío, has more upscale dining.

Things to Buy

Matagalpa is famous for its unique black pottery; many of the pieces are small enough to tuck easily into a backpack. The pottery is sold in a kiosk in Parque Darío and at Tienda de Ceramica Negra, located one block east and 1½ blocks north of Parque Darío.

Getting There & Away

Buses arrive and depart from the bus station beside the market, near the river, southwest of Parque Darío. Buses from Matagalpa include:

Estelí – 70 km, two hours, US$1.10; buses leave every 30 minutes, 6 am to 5:45 pm.

Jinotega – 34 km, 1½ hours, US$1; buses leave every 40 minutes, 5 am to 6:20 pm.

León (Express) – 143 km, three hours, US$2.20; buses leave at 6 am and 3 pm, or take the Estelí bus to San Isidro and change (146 km, four hours).

Managua – 129 km, three hours, US$1.65; buses leave every 30 minutes, 4 am to 5:10 pm.

JINOTEGA
Population 41,053

Jinotega is a quiet town 34 km north of Matagalpa, set in a valley amid a mountainous coffee-growing region. It is nicknamed the 'city of mists' because of its agreeable climate. Though it's peaceful today, there was heavy fighting in town and in the surrounding mountains during and after the revolution; murals on the plaza are a testimony to these years.

Jinotega is the capital of the very large department of the same name that extends northeast to the Honduran border. The security situation in the remote areas of this department is still unstable, with armed bands of criminals operating beyond the reach of the police and army.

The drive from Matagalpa to Jinotega is one of the most beautiful in Nicaragua. Even during the dry season, when the rest of the country is parched and brown, these mountains, some of them 1500 meters above sea level, are green and cool.

Roadside stands along the highway sell carrots, beets, cabbages, lettuce, tomatoes, bananas, flowers and more – a colorful sight that refreshes the spirit, especially if you've been in Managua a while. It's worth coming to Jinotega for the day from Matagalpa, just to ride on this road, visit the little town and see Jinotega's beautiful church.

Things to See & Do

The church doesn't look so remarkable from the outside. When you get inside, though, there is much magnificent religious art and statuary; the architecture, too, is notable, with excellent natural lighting and acoustics. Among the most famous statues is the Black Christ of Esquipulas, but there are many that are equally fine.

On the plaza in front of the church are some reminders of the revolutionary years in Jinotega. A large, colorful mural showing coffee pickers with rifles on their backs has been painted on the old Somoza jail, now a youth center, on the south side of the plaza. Another depicts young people at war. On the plaza itself there is a monument to Carlos Fonseca.

Places to Stay

Hotel Sollentuna Hem (☎ 632-2334), a favorite of budget travelers, is two blocks east and three blocks north of the central plaza. Its name comes from Sollentuna, a suburb of Stockholm, where the owner lived for 15 years. English, Spanish and Swedish are spoken. The hotel is clean and pleasant, with unusual touches like Chinese hand-embroidered bedclothes. Room prices range from US$4 for spartan singles with shared bath to US$14 for homey doubles with private bath. Some rooms have hot water. There's an enclosed garage for cars, and meals are served on request.

Hotel Tito (☎ 632-2049), 1½ blocks north of the church, offers nice, clean rooms with shared bath for US$4 per person; light meals and drinks are available. *Hospedaje El Tico* (☎ 632-2530) is a pleasant, clean place with a restaurant and secure parking. Located across from the Colegio La Salle, it charges US$5/7 for singles/doubles with private bath. If you don't mind basic, windowless rooms, a cheap alternative is the *Hospedaje Primavera* (☎ 632-2400), four blocks north of Esso, which charges US$2.25 per person. *Hotel La Colmena* (☎ 632-2017), located half a block behind the church, has three exceptionally nice rooms; those with semi-private bath with hot water start at US$18.

Places to Eat

Restaurante Jin-Shan, 1½ blocks north of the plaza, serves meat and seafood dishes as well as chop suey and chow mein. Open from Friday to Sunday, it's one of Jinotega's better restaurants, with meals from US$4 to US$7. You can get half portions for US$2.50. *La Colmena*, the nicest restaurant in town, is expensive, with standard meals costing US$5 to US$8, but it also offers a few 'budget' meals for US$3. The restaurant at the *Hotel Tico* serves meals starting at US$4 and sandwiches starting at US$1.25. *Soda Tico*, one block east and half a block south of the plaza, offers inexpensive light meals.

Getting There & Away

The bus station is near the town's southern entrance. Buses to Matagalpa depart every 40 minutes from 5:00 am until 6:20 pm (34 km, 1½ hours, US$1). Express buses to Managua (162 km, 3½ hours, US$3) depart five times a day, from 4 am to 3 pm.

LAGO DE APANÁS

The Lago de Apanás is a beautiful site about 10 km north of Jinotega. Its popularity as a swimming and fishing spot has declined in recent years, due to increasing levels of pollution. Buses to the lake leave from beside the market.

ESTELÍ

Population 65,036

Estelí, the main center between Managua and the Honduran border, is a quiet, pleasant, friendly town in a valley between the mountains, and it's a good stopover on the way to or from the border.

Capital of the department of the same name, Estelí is the center for the surrounding agricultural area, where tobacco, grains, sesame, potatoes, many other vegetables and fruits and also livestock and cheese are produced. During the Sandinista years many farming collectives were established in the region around Estelí, and many *internacionalistas* came here. The popular Sandinista-era Spanish-language school has been replaced by two newer schools, CENAC and Escuela Horizonte. See Nicaragua's Facts for the Visitor section for more information on these schools.

There was heavy fighting in Estelí during the revolution, and the town continued to be one of strongest support bases for the Sandinistas. Estelí, along with León, was one of only two important cities where the FSLN won a majority in the 1990 and 1996 elections.

As the major city between Managua and the Honduran border, and the capital of a large department, Estelí has a large number of places to stay and eat.

Orientation & Information

Avenida Bolívar, the main street in Estelí,

NICARAGUA

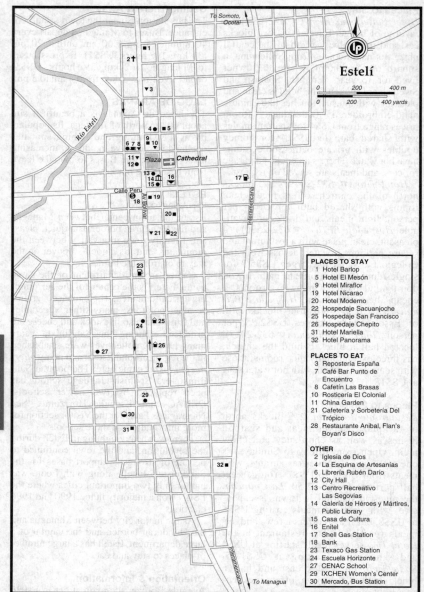

Estelí

0   200   400 m
0   200   400 yards

Río Estelí

Plaza   Cathedral

Calle Peru

Av Bolívar

Interamericana

To Somoto,
Ocotal

To Managua

Interamericana

PLACES TO STAY
1   Hotel Barlop
5   Hotel El Mesón
9   Hotel Miraflor
19 Hotel Nicarao
20 Hotel Moderno
22 Hospedaje Sacuanjoche
25 Hospedaje San Francisco
26 Hospedaje Chepito
31 Hotel Mariella
32 Hotel Panorama

PLACES TO EAT
3   Repostería España
7   Café Bar Punto de
    Encuentro
8   Cafetín Las Brasas
10 Rosticería El Colonial
11 China Garden
21 Cafetería y Sorbetería Del
    Trópico
28 Restaurante Anibal, Flan's
    Boyan's Disco

OTHER
2   Iglesia de Dios
4   La Esquina de Artesanías
6   Librería Rubén Darío
12 City Hall
13 Centro Recreativo
    Las Segovias
14 Galería de Héroes y Mártires,
    Public Library
15 Casa de Cultura
16 Enitel
17 Shell Gas Station
18 Bank
23 Texaco Gas Station
24 Escuela Horizonte
27 CENAC School
29 IXCHEN Women's Center
30 Mercado, Bus Station

NICARAGUA

runs south to north for about 25 blocks. Most of the town's commerce, and many hospedajes and restaurants, are found along it. Avenida Bolívar crosses the river at the northern end of town; at the southern end, it curves east to join the Interamericana. There are many gas stations and restaurants along the highway to serve the traffic heading north to Honduras and south to Managua. The bus station and market are together, a block west of Avenida Bolívar at the southern end of town.

The Enitel post and telephone office is about a block from the plaza. There are several banks. A good bookshop, Librería Rubén Darío, is half a block west from the northwest corner of the plaza.

The women's center, IXCHEN, is half a block east of the bus station.

Things to See & Do
On the main plaza, Estelí has a big, modern cathedral.

The city-run **Centro Recreativo Las Segovias**, on the south side of the plaza, does not run as many youth activities as it used to. It is now closed during the day, opening weekday evenings for youth basketball; a disco party is held every Saturday and Sunday beginning at 7:30 pm. The adjoining restaurant is also city-run. On the footpath in front of the Centro Recreativo Las Segovias are several boulders with prehistoric carvings of human, animal and bird movement. They come from Las Pintadas, an archaeological site about eight km to the west.

Around the corner, half a block south of the cathedral, is the **Galería de Héroes y Mártires**, a museum and gallery devoted to the memory of the town's fallen revolutionaries. It has murals around the outside and is riddled with bullet holes, further testimony to Estelí's bloody past. It is open Monday to Saturday.

Around the corner again there is the **Casa de Cultura**, which sponsors many interesting activities. The center has art exhibits and an artesanía shop, and it offers classes in art, music, theater, dance and crafts. About once a month, the Casa hosts

a *peña cultural*, an evening of music and dance performed by students. The center's swimming pool has long been empty and unused due to lack of funds, but you might check to see if by chance it's been opened again.

Salto Estanzuela is a waterfall about five km south of town. This waterfall is about 25 meters high and falls into a deep pool good for swimming; it isn't so great in the dry season. To get there, turn off the Interamericana onto the dirt road half a kilometer south of town and go about five km, through San Nicolás. The road may be a rough go for cars, but it makes a fine walk from town.

Puente La Sirena, on the river north of town, is another good swimming spot.

Places to Stay
Estelí has a good selection of places to stay in various price ranges.

The best of the budget lodgings, *Hotel Mariella* (☎ 713-2166), near the bus station, is simple but clean, with rooms with shared bath at US$5/7 for singles/doubles. Along Avenida Bolívar are several other inexpensive hospedajes. The *Chepito* (☎ 713-3784), 3½ blocks north of the bus station, has plain clean rooms with shared bath at US$3/4 for singles/doubles; there is no patio. In the next block north, the *Hospedaje San Francisco* (☎ 713-3787) charges US$3/6 for small, dark singles/doubles with shared bath. The *Hotel Miraflor* (☎ 713-2003), half a block north of the plaza's northwest corner, is simple but clean enough; rooms with shared bath are US$3.60 per person; rooms with private bath are available, as are inexpensive meals.

There are several good medium-priced hotels. One of them, the *Hotel El Mesón* (☎ 713-2655), a block north of the cathedral, changes traveler's checks and operates a travel agency, restaurant and artesanía shop (located across the street). Its comfortable singles/doubles, all with private bath and hot water, run US$11.50/13.50. On Avenida Bolívar, 1½ blocks south of the plaza, the friendly *Hotel Nicarao* (☎ 713-2490) has nice, clean singles/doubles with

NICARAGUA

private bath for US$11. There's a pleasant central patio with tables where meals are served for US$3 to US$4. Found 3½ blocks south of the cathedral, *Hotel Sacuanjoche* (☎ 713-2482) charges US$6/9.50 for comfortable, well-kept singles/doubles with private bath. It has a homey guest sitting area. The adequate *Hotel Barlop* (☎ 713-2486), six blocks north of the plaza on Avenida Bolívar, charges US$9.50 to US$14 for doubles with private bath. It also has a couple of singles with shared bath for US$5.30. Secure parking is available.

Hotel Moderno (☎ 713-2278, fax 713-4315), one block east and 2½ blocks south of the cathedral, is unquestionably the best in town. It charges US$23/28.50 for very comfortable singles/doubles with private bath and hot water. On the main highway, *Hotel Panorama* (☎ 713-3147) has nice rooms (facing a noisy parking lot); doubles with private bath and hot water run US$23. Both hotels have a restaurant.

Places to Eat

Estelí has an equally ample selection of places to eat. Right on the plaza, on the north side, the *Rosticería El Colonial* serves roast meat meals for around US$4; it's open daily. Meat and chicken meals at the *Cafetín Las Brasas*, a block west, cost around US$3.50; it's open every day except Tuesday. Next door, *Café Bar Punto de Encuentro* has an inexpensive if limited menu, including so-so pizza. The popular *China Garden*, in a Quonset hut on the plaza's west side, serves the usual Nicaraguan fare, as well as a few 'Chinese' dishes (such as chow mein garnished with ketchup). Meals start at US$3.50. The city-run restaurant at the Centro Recreativo Las Segovias, on the south side of the plaza, serves comida corriente for US$2; standard meals start at US$4. It's open 11 am to 9 pm.

There is a good bakery four blocks north of the plaza on Avenida Bolívar, the *Repostería España*. Four blocks south of the plaza, *Cafetería y Sorbetería Del Trópico* is an ice cream parlor that also serves fresh tropical fruit drinks and snacks.

Three blocks north and 1½ blocks east

of the market, *Restaurante Anibal* offers a varied menu that includes tacos and *tostones* (fried plantain slices). Most meals cost US$4. The restaurant operates a disco, *Flan's Boyan's*, on Friday, Saturday and Sunday.

As always, the market offers the cheapest fare in town. In Estelí, the bus station and market are together; there's a double row of little restaurant stalls on the east side.

Getting There & Away

The airport here does not have regular service. Long-distance buses depart frequently from Estelí, heading in every direction. They include:

Jinotega – 104 km, five hours, US$1.75; two direct buses daily, at 8:30 am and 1:30 pm.

León – 141 km, three hours, US$2.50; two direct buses daily, at 6:45 am and 3:10 pm, or take the Managua or Matagalpa bus and change at San Isidro.

Managua – 149 km, 3¼ hours, US$1.75; buses leave every 30 minutes, 3:30 am to 5:00 pm.

Matagalpa – 70 km, two hours, US$1; buses leave every 30 minutes, 5:20 am to 5:30 pm.

Ocotal – 78 km, 2¼ hours, US$1; buses leave hourly, 6 am to 5:30 pm.

Somoto – 67 km, two hours, US$0.85; buses leave every 30 minutes, 5:30 am to 6 pm.

NORTH TO HONDURAS

There are two ways north to Honduras. The shortest way to Tegucigalpa in Honduras is through Ocotal and on to the border crossing at Las Manos. On the Honduran side, you will go through Danlí on your way to Tegucigalpa; it's 132 km (2½ hours by bus) from the border to Tegucigalpa.

If, on the other hand, you want to continue on the Interamericana into southern Honduras, take the highway to the town of Somoto, then to the El Espino border crossing, and on into Honduras, passing through the village of San Marcos de Colón on your way to Choluteca, the principal city in the southern Honduran lowlands. San Marcos is just a few kilometers from the border; to Choluteca it's 60 km (one hour by bus). If you're continuing through to El Salvador on the Interamericana, you can cross the southern part of Honduras and be at the Salvadoran border in three hours (plus waiting time for a connecting bus at Choluteca).

Whichever way you go to Honduras, if you're going by bus, you will have to take one bus to the border, go through, and take another bus on the other side. The border stations are open daily from around 8 am to 5:30 pm.

Ocotal
Population 22,631

The closest town to the Honduran border at Las Manos, Ocotal is about two hours north of Estelí. The capital of the department of Nueva Segovia, Ocotal is a small town, with a typical church and a plaza with a few blocks around it.

Orientation & Information The bus station is on the highway half a kilometer from the southern entrance of town. Enitel, the post and telephone office, is 1½ blocks north of the northwest corner of the main plaza. The market is around the corner from Enitel.

Places to Stay & Eat The best place to stay is the friendly *Hotelito Mirador* (☎ 732-2369), on the highway opposite the bus station. Nice, clean rooms with shared bath are US$6. The hotel restaurant serves inexpensive meals. The Mirador has an annex, two blocks east, which has even nicer rooms with private bath for US$10.

About one km north of the bus station, half a block west of the highway and opposite the Shell station, is the *Hospedaje Centroamericana* (☎ 732-2627). It's a good deal, with simple, clean rooms with shared bath at US$2 per person. Doubles with private bath and a small sitting room are US$6. The much less inviting *Pensión Segovia*, half a block south of Enitel, has tiny dark rooms starting at US$1.20 per person.

As for places to eat, the *Centro Recreativo Cafetín*, on the southwest corner of the plaza, serves light meals and snacks. The popular, open-air *Restaurante La Merienda*, about a half kilometer north and

two blocks east of the bus station, serves good meals for US$5 to US$6. Its menu includes comida corriente (US$1.75) and inexpensive snacks.

Getting There & Away Buses to Estelí depart hourly from 4 am to 4:45 pm (78 km, 2¼ hours, US$1). Direct express buses to Managua leave at 5 and 9 am, 12:30 and 3:15 pm (227 km, 3¾ hours, US$3.30). There are also hourly buses to Somoto from 5:45 am to 3:30 pm (33 km, one hour, US$0.50) and to Las Manos (Honduras border) between 5 am and 5:15 pm (25 km, one hour, US$0.35).

Somoto
Population 13,160

Somoto, 20 km from the Honduran border at El Espino, is a small, quiet mountain town and capital of the department of Madriz. The colonial church on the plaza is one of the oldest in Nicaragua.

If you're crossing the border and it's late in the day, you might want to spend the night in Somoto. The *Panamericano* (☎ 722-2355), right on the plaza, is a good, clean hotel; its singles with shared bath are US$5.

The bus station at Somoto is on the main highway, a short walk from the center of town. Buses depart hourly for the border (20 km, 30 minutes, US$0.50) and for Estelí (67 km, two hours, US$0.85). Direct buses bound for Managua (217 km, six hours, US$2.60) depart at 4:00, 4:40 and 7:20 am. An express bus to Managua departs at 2 pm (3½ hours, US$3.30).

Northwest of Managua

The area northwest of Managua, extending along the southwest shore of Lago de Managua all the way to the Golfo de Fonseca, is rich agricultural country. Principal products include maize, sugar cane, rice, cotton and livestock. These are lowlands and, like Managua, get very hot.

The major city in this region, and the only one much visited by travelers, is historic León. It was the capital of Nicaragua for about three centuries and today is Nicaragua's second largest city. The other towns in the region are Chinandega, an agricultural center, and Corinto, Nicaragua's principal Pacific port.

LEÓN
Population 124,117

One of Nicaragua's oldest cities, León was founded in 1524 by Hernández de Córdoba at the site of an indigenous village, Imbita. The location at the foot of the Momotombo volcano, on the shore of Lago de Managua, is 32 km from where León stands today. In 1610 the volcano's activity triggered an earthquake that destroyed the city. León's present site, at the indigenous community of Yococayoguas, was chosen for the reconstruction because it was close to the existing Indian capital, Subtiava.

León was the capital of Nicaragua from the colonial period until Managua became the capital in 1857. It was also the ecclesiastical capital for the bishop of Nicaragua and Costa Rica. It has many fine colonial buildings, including its impressive cathedral. As befits a city named León, there are a number of lion statues around the cathedral and in the plaza. The Universidad Autónoma de Nicaragua, the country's first university, was founded here in 1812; the city streets are lined with old Spanish-style houses, with white adobe walls, red-tiled roofs, big thick wooden doors and cool interior garden patios.

León is traditionally the most liberal of Nicaraguan cities and today remains the radical and intellectual center of the country. During the revolution, virtually the entire town fought against Somoza; in the 1990 and 1996 elections, the only major cities where the Sandinistas won were León and Estelí.

Orientation & Information
León has three open markets: one behind the cathedral, the Mercado San Juan near the old railway station and another on the outskirts of town, next to the bus station.

The Mintur tourist office (☎ 311-3682) is located four blocks north and 1½ blocks east of Enitel. The Enitel telecommunications and post office is on the northwest corner of the plaza (Parque Jerez).

Things to See & Do
Churches & Plazas León's **cathedral** is the largest in Central America. Its construction began in 1747 and took more than a hundred years to complete. Local legend holds that the original plans for the structure were so sumptuous that the city's leaders feared they would be turned down by the Spanish imperial authorities, and they therefore sent a more modest but phony set of plans to Spain. The cathedral's magnificent artworks include huge paintings of the *Stations of the Cross* by Antonio Sarria that have been called masterpieces of Spanish colonial religious art. The cathedral was restored with help from Spain in the early 1990s.

The cathedral is a kind of Pantheon of Nicaraguan culture: the tomb of poet Rubén Darío, León's favorite son, is on one side of the altar, guarded by a life-size statue of a sorrowful lion. Darío's tomb bears an inscription: 'Nicaragua is created of vigor and glory, Nicaragua is made for freedom.'

Nearby in the cathedral are also buried Alfonso Cortés (1893-1969) and Salomón de la Selva (1893-1959), two lesser-known but important figures in Nicaraguan literature. Cortés remains one of Nicaragua's most popular poets. 'Don Sal,' as the latter was universally known, also wrote stinging verse in English during the various US interventions that is worth reading today. Other illustrious personalities buried here include governors, bishops, and chroniclers, including Miguel Larreynaga, the pioneer of the independence movement throughout Central America.

On the south side of the cathedral are **La Asunción**, a theological college that was the first college in Nicaragua; the rather pretty **Palacio Episcopal** (Bishop's Palace); and the **Colegio San Ramón**. The latter is a famous institution that educated,

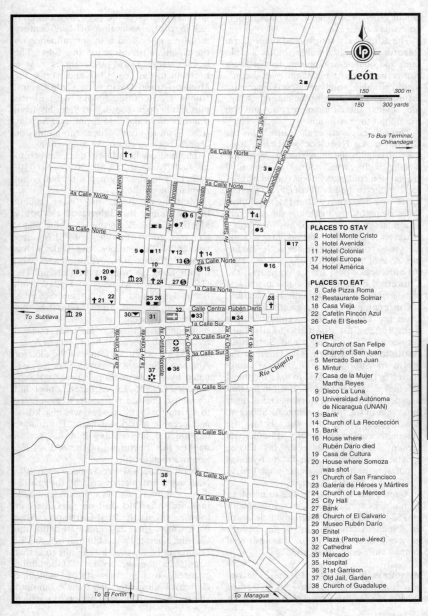

León

To Bus Terminal, Chinandega

To Subtiava

To El Fortín

To Managua

Río Chiquito

PLACES TO STAY
2 Hotel Monte Cristo
3 Hotel Avenida
11 Hotel Colonial
17 Hotel Europa
34 Hotel América

PLACES TO EAT
8 Café Pizza Roma
12 Restaurante Solmar
18 Casa Vieja
22 Cafetín Rincón Azul
26 Café El Sesteo

OTHER
1 Church of San Felipe
4 Church of San Juan
5 Mercado San Juan
6 Mintur
7 Casa de la Mujer
  Martha Reyes
9 Disco La Luna
10 Universidad Autónoma
  de Nicaragua (UNAN)
13 Bank
14 Church of La Recolección
15 Bank
16 House where
  Rubén Darío died
19 Casa de Cultura
20 House where Somoza
  was shot
21 Church of San Francisco
23 Galería de Héroes y Mártires
24 Church of La Merced
25 City Hall
27 Bank
28 Church of El Calvario
29 Museo Rubén Darío
30 Enitel
31 Plaza (Parque Jérez)
32 Cathedral
33 Mercado
35 Hospital
36 21st Garrison
37 Old Jail, Garden
38 Church of Guadalupe

NICARAGUA

among others, Larreynaga, whose portrait is on display.

The attractively refurbished main plaza, **Parque Jérez**, is notable for its simple lines and openness. Opposite its northeast corner is the most outstanding of León's many murals, which in starkly dramatic fashion tells the story of the nation's struggle against the Somoza regime and the triumph of the revolution.

Three blocks north of the cathedral is the **Church of La Recolección**. Dating from the 18th century, the church has an interesting facade, with carved stone vines wound around stone pillars. Symbols carved in relief recall events in the Passion of Christ: There is the rooster that crowed after Peter had three times denied knowing Jesus; the shirt and dice refers to the casting of lots for Christ's cloak; and a spike, hammer and tongs for the nails used on the cross are below the crowning scene of the Resurrection.

Four blocks east of the cathedral, the **Church of El Calvario** also has an unusual facade and ceiling, built in the 18th century.

Other colonial churches worth visiting in León are **La Merced**, originally dating from 1662; **San Juan**, originally built between 1625 and 1650; and **San Juan Bautista de Subtiava**. The latter, in the barrio of Subtiava, is the oldest intact church in León and is said to have the finest colonial altar in Nicaragua. Built in the first decade of the 18th century, it stands near the center of the Indian village of Subtiava, which occupied the area long before the Spaniards transferred the city of León to its present site. Bartolomé de las Casas, apostle and benefactor to the indigenous population of the Americas, preached in Subtiava on several occasions.

A few blocks away are the ruins of an even older church, **Vera Cruz**. It was built in 1524-1600 as the original nucleus for the 'Spanish city' within the indigenous town of Subtiava. Vera Cruz was destroyed in a volcanic eruption in 1835.

Museums & Monuments Rubén Darío, born on January 18, 1867, is esteemed worldwide as one of Latin America's greatest poets. As the poet most committed to the introduction of 19th-century modernism, he had a major influence on the Spanish literature of his time. The house where Darío grew up is now a museum to the poet's life and works: the **Museo Rubén Darío** is on Calle Central Rubén Darío, three blocks west of the plaza. It is open Tuesday to Saturday from 9 am to noon and 2 to 5 pm, and Sunday from 9 am to noon. There's no admission charge, but you can make a donation.

The house where Darío died, on February 6, 1916, is at 2a Calle Norte, No 410-412. It is marked by a plaque but is not open to the public.

Monuments to León's more recent history include the **Galería de Héroes y Mártires**, a block northwest of the plaza. Run by a group of mothers of FSLN veterans and fallen heroes, the Galería has photos of over 300 revolutionaries who died fighting the Somoza dictatorship. The Galería is open Monday to Friday, from 8 am to noon and 2 to 5 pm, and Saturday from 9 am to noon. Admission is free, but donations are welcome.

Around the corner to the west, marked by a large plaque, is the house where Anastasio Somoza García, father of the dictator Anastasio Somoza Debayle, was assassinated by Rigoberto López Pérez on September 21, 1956. López Pérez, a poet and journalist, dressed as a waiter to gain entry to a party for dignitaries; he was also killed and became a national hero. The plaque outside the house says that his action marked the 'beginning of the end' of the Somoza dictatorship.

Several places where Somoza's Guardia Nacional were overpowered by the revolutionary fighters are now commemorated, including the **Old Jail** on 4a Calle Sur (now a garden), the **21st Garrison** around the corner to the east and **El Fortín**, the Guardia Nacional's last holdout in León. El Fortín can be reached by the dirt road that begins on the west side of Guadalupe cemetery (two blocks south of Guadalupe church). Follow this road for 2½ km until you reach the abandoned hilltop fort, which affords a panoramic view of León and the range of volcanoes in the distance.

The small **Museo de Tradiciones y Leyendas** (☎ 311-2886), 4½ blocks west of the plaza on 2a Calle Sur, has a quirky collection of life-size papier-mâché figures from Leonese history and legend. The museum is in the home of founder Señora Toruño, who will gladly share the story behind each figure. There are no fixed hours of operation.

One block north of San Juan Bautista de Subtiava is a small museum, the **Museo Adiact**, with archaeological finds from the area. It's open Monday to Friday.

Special Events

Festival days in León include September 24, November 1 and June 20, the anniversary of the date the Sandinistas defeated Somoza's soldiers in León.

Places to Stay

Half a block north of the old railway station, on Avenida Pedro Aráuz, *Hotel Avenida* (☎ 311-2068) is probably the best deal in town. Each of its clean rooms has a window facing the inner garden. Singles with fan and shared bath are US$4.50.

Two blocks farther north on the same street, *Hotel Monte Cristo* (☎ 311-6516) offers clean accommodations in a middle-class home; singles with fan and shared bath are US$6. The friendly owner speaks English.

Two blocks behind the cathedral on 2a Avenida Oriente near the corner of 1a Calle Sur, the *Hotel América* (☎ 311-5533) is a bit worn but still pleasant, with plants and hammocks around the interior patio. All rooms have fan and private bath; the rate is US$6 per person.

A comfortable place to stay is the *Hotel Europa* (☎ 311-6040, fax 311-2577) on 3a Calle Norte, near the old railway track bed, where rooms start at US$12. Each room has a fan and private bath, and air con is available. The hotel is clean and well kept, with a restaurant serving breakfast and snacks, a house bar, and sitting areas among the plants on the patio.

Hotel Colonial (☎ 311-2279, fax 311-3125), about 2 blocks north of Enitel, is a stately old converted villa. The rooms are clean and comfortable, though small, and the spacious front sitting room and inner courtyard are delightful. Rooms with shared bath and fan are US$14. There is a cafeteria on the premises.

Places to Eat

There are several comedores on the edges of the market behind the cathedral. On the southwestern corner of the market, the *Comedor Popular Raul Cabezas L* is nothing fancy but you can get a good, big breakfast or lunch for under US$1.50. It's open every day from around 7 am to 6 pm.

On the plaza, the *El Sesteo* is a pleasant cafe with tables outside; it's open every day from 7 am to 10 pm. *Cafetín Rincon Azul*, a block west of Enitel, is a cool young people's hangout with colorful, multilingual graffiti on the walls. It serves sandwiches (US$1) and beer (US$0.60), as well as other items, and is open daily from 3 pm 'until the last customer leaves.'

Café Pizza Roma, a block north of Hotel Colonia, serves good pasta (starting at US$2.75) and pizzas (US$5.50 for a medium), as well as other meals. Two blocks west and 1½ blocks north of the main plaza, *Casa Vieja*, a small place with a bohemian atmosphere, serves inexpensive sandwiches, hamburgers and juices. It's open every evening except Wednesday.

Restaurante Solmar, three blocks north of the cathedral on Avenida Central Noreste, is a fancier restaurant, with original art on display. Meals cost around US$4 to US$6; it's open every day, except Wednesday, from noon to 10 pm.

In Subtiava, one block south and 1½ blocks west of San Juan Bautista, *Los Pescaditos* is a popular, moderately priced seafood restaurant. Two blocks farther west, the open-air *Las Caperas* serves very good food at reasonable prices.

Entertainment

The *Casa de Cultura*, one block north and 1½ blocks west of Enitel, hosts art exhibits and offers classes in art, folklore, dance and music. It sponsors several cultural events each month. León also has a couple of discos: *La Luna*, across from the Hotel Colonial, and *El Tunel*, on the highway heading toward Chinandega (take a taxi).

Getting There & Away
Bus The bus station is located about one km from the center of town, on 6a Calle Norte. Local buses run frequently between the station and the center of León (see also Getting Around).

Buses to Managua depart every 20 minutes from 4:30 am to 6:20 pm (90 km, 2½ hours). Express buses to Managua (1½ hours, US$1.20) depart hourly from 5 am to noon and at 2 and 4 pm.

The bus to Chinandega and Corinto departs every 15 minutes, from 4:30 am and 6 pm; it's one hour to Chinandega (39 km) and two hours to Corinto (58 km).

An express bus to Matagalpa departs at 4:30 am and 2:45 pm (four hours, 146 km, US$2.20). Alternatively, you could take a bus to San Isidro (three hours) and change buses there to continue to Matagalpa. You can also change there to go to Estelí and on to the Honduran border.

See the Around León section for information on getting to Poneloya.

Hitchhiking Take a local bus to the outskirts to hitch from León to Managua, just as many university students do.

Getting Around
León has plenty of taxis; the fare within town is about US$1. There are also local buses.

PONELOYA
The beach town of Poneloya, 20 km west of León, has two sides: Las Peñitas and Poneloya (the rock formation separating them offers a fine vantage point). The beach is practically deserted on weekdays, but lots of people come here on weekends and holidays. Use extreme caution when swimming here. People drown each year in Poneloya's strong currents.

The *Hotel Posada* (☎ 311-4612, 317-2377) offers nice singles/doubles/triples with private bath and air con for US$12. The only other option is the run-down *Hotel Lacayo*, which charges US$4 per person for a dingy room with bats in the ceiling.

Poneloya's seafood restaurants include *Pariente Salinas*, which has meals from US$3.50, and the beachfront *Bar Caceras* on the Peñitas side, open from 7 am to 10 pm with meals from US$5.

Buses to Poneloya depart every half-hour from early morning to evening from El Mercadito in Subtiava, one block north and one block west of San Juan Bautista; the trip is about 40 minutes. It's easy to hitch between León and Poneloya on weekends.

NORTHWEST FROM LEÓN
About 10 km north of León, near Telica, a road turns off the main highway for San Isidro. It's 104 km (about three hours) from León to San Isidro, where you can catch buses to Matagalpa, or to Estelí and on to the Honduran border.

Another 10 km north of Telica is the small town of San Jacinto, home to hot springs where the bubbling pools of water and mud provide an impressive glimpse of the forces that created the nearby Telica volcano. Local kids will gladly show you around for a few córdobas. (Buses pass San Jacinto coming and going to León.)

This region is hot, heavily agricultural, and gets little tourist traffic. **El Viejo** is the focus of several annual religious pilgrimages. **Chichigalpa**, further south, is the home of the Ingenio San Antonio, the largest sugar mill in Central America, and of the Flor de Caña rum factory.

The road from León continues 39 km northwest to **Chinandega**, the center of an agricultural region where sugar cane and bananas are the principal crops. In Chinandega, the *Hotel/Restaurant Glomar* (☎ 341-2562), a block south of the market, has adequate rooms with fan and shared bath for US$13. Four blocks east and 1½ blocks south of the main square, *Hotel Chinandega* charges US$4.75 for decent, simple rooms with fan and shared bath.

From Chinandega roads branch out in several directions: to Puerto Morazán and Potosí on the Golfo de Fonseca; to Corinto, Nicaragua's principal Pacific port, 19 km away; and to the Honduran border crossing at Guasaule, just a few kilometers past Somotillo.

South of Managua

The area south of Managua includes some of Nicaragua's most productive agricultural land and most important towns and cities, including Masaya, famous for its traditional handicrafts, and Granada, the beautiful colonial city. Both cities can easily be visited as day trips from Managua, but both also have places to stay. Near Masaya is the Parque Nacional Volcán Masaya, which is one of Nicaragua's top attractions. (See the Around Managua section for more details.)

There are many small farming villages around Masaya and Granada. Due south of Managua are the towns of Jinotepe, Diriamba, and San Marcos, site of the religious and folkloric celebration known as Toro Guaco. Continuing south toward the Costa Rican border, the only significant town is Rivas. San Jorge, the port for ferries to Isla de Ometepe in Lago de Nicaragua, is near Rivas, as is the turnoff to San Juan del Sur, a fishing village and one of Nicaragua's favorite small, inexpensive beach towns. The trip from Managua to the Costa Rican border takes about four hours.

MASAYA
Population 80,051

Masaya is said to have received its nickname, 'the city of flowers,' from Rubén Darío, who was impressed by the abundant flowers in the city's gardens. The gardens have since largely disappeared, but Masaya remains attractive to visitors as the heart of Nicaraguan handicrafts and folklore. Masaya's artesanías are some of the best produced in Nicaragua. As a handicrafts center, its markets also sell work from all over the country.

Orientation & Information
Masaya is located just 26 km southeast of Managua, with Granada another 18 km down the road. The city sits at the edge of the crater lake, Laguna de Masaya. On the lake's opposite side, Vulcán Masaya rises over the town.

Enitel, the combined telecommunications and post office, is just west of the main plaza (Parque 17 de Octubre).

Things to See & Do
Artesanías There are several places around town where you can see Masaya's famous artesanías. By far the most extensive selection is at the **Mercado de Artesanías**, at the eastern end of town. It includes excellent-quality cotton hammocks, colorful basketry and woven mats, carved and painted gourds, woodcarvings, paintings, ceramics and pottery, marimbas, coral jewelry, leatherwork and (if looking at them, let alone buying them, doesn't disgust you) goods made of reptile skins (crocodile, snake, iguana and frog). It's a busy, colorful market, and well worth visiting. Be sure to bargain.

The Mercado de Artesanías will eventually be moved to Masaya's original market, the **Mercado Viejo**, two blocks east of the main plaza, which was destroyed during the revolution and is now being restored.

The **Centro de Artesanías** (Cecapi) is at the other end of town, on the malecón overlooking the lake. The crafts are of very good quality but more expensive than at the mercado, and there is not nearly as much coming. It's worth coming, though, if for no other reason than to see the wall-sized country map that shows where all the various artesanías of Nicaragua are produced. The center is open weekdays from 8:30 am to 5 pm, and weekends from 8:30 am to 4 pm.

Near the malecón is Barrio San Juan, famous for its hammocks and tapestries. About a block from Cecapi is Los Tapices de Luis, where Luis will gladly show you his traditional and contemporary tapestries. Two blocks to the west are a number of hammock workshops.

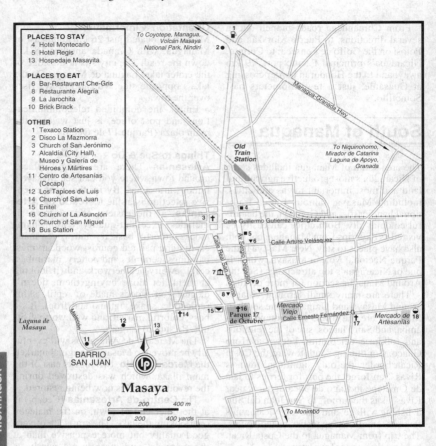

PLACES TO STAY
4   Hotel Montecarlo
5   Hotel Regis
13 Hospedaje Masayita

PLACES TO EAT
6   Bar-Restaurant Che-Gris
8   Restaurante Alegría
9   La Jarochita
10 Brick Brack

OTHER
1   Texaco Station
2   Disco La Mazmorra
3   Church of San Jerónimo
7   Alcaldía (City Hall),
    Museo y Galería de
    Héroes y Mártires
11 Centro de Artesanías
    (Cecapi)
12 Los Tapices de Luis
14 Church of San Juan
15 Enitel
16 Church of La Asunción
17 Church of San Miguel
18 Bus Station

To Coyotepe, Managua,
Volcán Masaya
National Park, Nindirí

Managua-Granada Hwy

Old
Train
Station

To Niquinohomo,
Mirador de Catarina
Laguna de Apoyo,
Granada

Calle Guillermo Gutierrez Rodríguez

Calle Arturo Velásquez

Av. Sergio Delgadillo

Calle Real San Jerónimo

Mercado
Viejo
Calle Ernesto Fernández G.

Parque 17
de Octubre

Mercado de
Artesanías

Laguna de
Masaya

Malecón

BARRIO
SAN JUAN

Masaya

0   200   400 m
0   200   400 yards

To Monimbó

Some of the best artesanías in Nicaragua are produced in **Monimbó**, an Indian suburb, the heart of which is around San Sebastian Church, about one km south of the main plaza. You can visit the many workshops scattered throughout this barrio and see how the shoes, saddles, baskets, woodcarvings and so on are made.

Churches & Plazas Masaya has several old churches, including the **Church of San Jerónimo**, on the northern side of town between two plazas, and the **Church of La Asunción**, on the main plaza (Parque 17 de Octubre), built in 1833. These are the two largest, but there are also the **Church of San Miguel**, the **Church of San Juan**, and the **Church of San Sebastian**, which is in the Monimbó section of town.

Museo y Galería de Héroes y Mártires Two blocks north of the main plaza is the Alcaldía (city hall), which houses this museum. The collection contains photographs of revolutionaries killed in Masaya's struggle against Somoza and personal articles and arms used by them. It is open Monday to Friday from 8 am to 5 pm.

NICARAGUA

Coyotepe On a hill just outside of town, overlooking the Managua-Granada Hwy, Coyotepe is a century-old fortress. It was the last stand of Benjamín Zeledón, the 1912 hero of resistance to US intervention. During the revolution, Somoza's National Guard fired mortars on Masaya from here. Now being restored by the Scouts of Nicaragua, it will eventually house a human rights museum. It's a one-km hike to the top; admission is US$0.60. Those not fond of exploring old forts will enjoy the panoramic view of the entire region.

Laguna de Masaya & Volcán Masaya
On the western side of town, the malecón, or lakeside walk, offers an excellent view of the Laguna de Masaya and the Volcán Masaya beyond it. From up here the lake appears crystalline blue, but it is too polluted for swimming.

A steep staircase that follows an ancient Indian path descending to the laguna begins just beside the Muebles Lisseth furniture store at Km 26 of the Managua-Masaya Hwy.

The entrance to Vulcán Masaya national park is three km down the road toward Managua (see the Around Managua section).

Special Events
Masaya celebrates an extraordinary number of feast days. The city's patron saint is St Jerónimo, and on his day, September 30, a large procession of people carrying flowers escorts a statue of the saint through the streets. The festival continues on each Sunday through November, with folklore dances at San Jerónimo Church and in the streets. Another important festival day is March 16, when statues of the Virgen de Masaya and Cristo de Milagros of Nindirí are taken by a procession to the lake for a blessing of the waters. Of the many remaining festivals, the most unique is that of San Lazaro, celebrated a week before Palm Sunday with a procession of costumed dogs.

Places to Stay
The *Hotel Regis* (☎ 522-2300), on Avenida Sergio Delgadillo, has small dark rooms, but it's clean and well cared for, with singles with fan and shared bath at US$5. The owner is especially friendly and helpful and can tell you many interesting things about the town. A generous breakfast is available for US$1.75. There is a 10 pm curfew.

The brighter and airier *Hotel Montecarlo* (☎ 522-2166), two blocks north of the Regis, is open 24 hours and has a small restaurant. Singles with fan and shared bath are US$7. *Hotel Cailagua* (☎ 522-4435), at Km 29½ on the highway to Granada, is attractive and friendly, with its own restaurant. It has singles with fan for US$18; air con is available. A cheap alternative is *Hospedaje Masayita*, two blocks west of the main plaza, with basic but clean accommodations; singles with shared bath are US$2.50.

Places to Eat
If you're just in Masaya to go to the Mercado de Artesanías, you can eat there; the market has several stalls serving inexpensive food.

Around the corner from Hotel Regis, the *Bar-Restaurant Che-Gris*, a good, popular restaurant, has a selection of meats and seafood and vegetarian meals. Comida corriente is US$2.50, with other meals starting at US$3.50. Che-Gris is open every day from 11 am to midnight.

For a change of pace, *La Jarochita*, on Avenida Sergio Delgadillo one block north of the main plaza, serves very good Mexican food. Prices range from US$2 to US$5; it's open daily. Around the corner, *Brick Brack* is both a cafeteria and ice cream shop. Open daily, it serves comida corriente for US$1.75.

A block north of the main plaza, the *Restaurante Alegría* is a good, basic restaurant. It's open daily from 11 am to 9 pm, with the usual meat and seafood meals, as well as pizza.

Entertainment
Masaya's popular and inexpensive dance place, *La Mazmorra*, is across from Texaco near the entrance to town on the Managua-Granada Hwy.

NICARAGUA

Getting There & Away

Buses arrive and depart from the eastern side of the Mercado de Artesanías. There are buses to Managua (26 km, 45 minutes, US$0.35) as well as to Granada (18 km, 20 minutes, US$0.35) about every 20 minutes starting around 5 am. The last bus to Granada leaves at 6:30 pm, the last bus to Managua at 9 pm. Between 5 am and 6 pm, buses leave frequently for the Carazo pueblos. The route is Catarina/San Juan de Oriente, Niquinohomo, Masatepe, San Marcos, Diriamba and, finally, Jinotepe.

Getting Around

Taxis charge around US$0.75 for a ride in town; horse-drawn carriages are around US$0.50.

AROUND MASAYA
Nindirí

The village of Nindirí (unique for its many wheelchair ramps) is just a few kilometers northwest of Masaya (15 minutes by bus); the turnoff is at the 26 Km marker on the Managua-Granada Hwy, between Masaya and the entrance to the volcano.

Nindirí has a small but interesting museum, the **Museo Tenderí**, which contains ancient Indian artifacts found around this region, such as stone carvings, large burial jars and musical instruments. The museum is one block north of the Rubén Darío library on the main plaza, and is open Monday to Friday, and Saturday mornings.

San Juan de Oriente & Catarina

San Juan de Oriente, not far from Masaya on the Interamericana, is a village famous for its pottery. You can shop at the **Cooperativa Quetzalcóatl** and at a number of pottery workshops on the main road.

The nearby village of Catarina has a lookout, known as the **Mirador de Catarina**, that offers a spectacular view of the Laguna de Apoyo, Lago de Nicaragua and the city of Granada. It is said to have been a favorite spot for youthful meditation by Sandino, who was born nearby. This is appropriate since Catarina is also the site of the grave of Benjamín Zeledón, whose burial Sandino witnessed. To reach the Mirador from the Interamericana, keep heading uphill for one km through the center of town. The Mirador has several small restaurants.

Laguna de Apoyo

The swimming is nice at the picturesque Laguna de Apoyo, once you get past the rocky shoreline. From the Km 38 turnoff on the Managua-Granada Hwy, it's about a 1½-hour walk down. Where the road forks at the bottom of the hill, go left about half a kilometer until you reach the Spanish language school; next to the school is a favorite swimming spot. There is no public transport to the lake, but you might have luck hitching on weekends.

Niquinohomo

Augusto C Sandino was born and grew up in the village of Niquinohomo. His boyhood home, in the house opposite the northwest corner of the main plaza, is now a library. The name of the town, interestingly enough, means 'valley of the warriors.'

Jinotepe, Diriamba & San Marcos

Southwest of Masaya, in the Carazo department, are the towns of Jinotepe and Diriamba, known as 'twin cities,' and San Marcos. These three towns, set in an area known for coffee, citrus and other fruit-tree cultivation, are the site of a distinctive Nicaraguan religious and folklore celebration, Toro Guaco.

Toro Guaco is a complex of festivals in which the Nicarao town of Jinotepe and the Chorotega town of Diriamba, traditional rivals before the arrival of Europeans, commemorate their relationship. Jinotepe's patron is St James (Santiago), whose day is July 25; Diriamba's is St Sebastian (January 20). The two towns and San Marcos carry out ceremonial visits to each other, involving dances, mock battles and plays that also satirize the Spanish invaders. The pantomime figure of 'El Güegüense' is a symbol of Nicaraguan identity. The costumes, masks and processions are striking.

The area does not get much tourist traffic. San Marcos is home to the Nicaragua campus of the University of Mobile, a US institution. In nearby Jinotepe, Mobile students staff the *Hotel Jinotepe* (☎ 412-2514), a hotel school offering comfortable rooms starting at US$30.

GRANADA
Population 74,396

Granada, nicknamed 'La Gran Sultana' in reference to its Moorish namesake in Spain, is Nicaragua's oldest Spanish city. Founded in 1524 by Francisco Hernández de Córdoba, it stands at the foot of Volcán Mombacho on the northwestern shore of Lake Nicaragua. With its access to the Caribbean Sea via the lake and the San Juan River, Granada soon became a rich and important trade center and remained so throughout the 1800s. This same passage to the Caribbean also made Granada an easy target for English and French buccaneers and pirates, who sacked the city three times between its founding and 1685.

From early on, conservative Granada was locked in bitter rivalry with liberal León, with which it vied for political supremacy. Their rivalry intensified after independence from Spain in 1821, and it erupted into full-blown civil war in the 1850s. In 1855, to gain the upper hand, the Leonese contracted the services of the American filibuster William Walker, who conquered Granada and ruled Nicaragua from there. When Walker was forced to flee in 1856, he had the city put to the torch, with his retreating troops leaving only the infamous placard, 'Here was Granada.' In more recent times, Granada was the scene of brief street fighting between Sandinista and pro-Somoza forces, but it was spared the shelling suffered by other Nicaraguan cities.

Today's Granada is a quiet town that retains its colonial character, although many of its buildings reflect the economic hard times Nicaragua has endured during the past two decades. Like León, its streets are lined with Spanish-style houses, with white adobe walls and large wooden doors opening onto cool interior patios. Granada is a wonderful walking city, with most of its attractions within a six-block radius and the lake a 15-minute walk from the central plaza. At night, families can be seen through open doors and windows relaxing in wicker rocking chairs. Many visitors will prefer Granada's lived-in authenticity to the tourist-trap trendiness that characterizes historic towns elsewhere.

As the home of Nicaragua's 'Vanguardia' poets, including Joaquín Pasos and Pablo Antonio Cuadra, Granada is also a major literary city.

Orientation
The cathedral and the plaza (Parque Colón) in front of it form the center of the city, and there are several buildings of interest on or near the plaza. The neoclassic market, built in 1890, is three blocks to the south. The main bus station is about six blocks to the west; other intercity buses can be caught at stations near the market.

La Calzada, one of Granada's principal streets, runs eastward from the plaza for one km to the city dock on Lake Nicaragua. Just south of the dock is the lakefront park and beach. Boats depart from the southern end of the beach for day trips.

Information
Granada has no tourist office, but the Hotel Alhambra front desk is happy to provide information. The hotel's energetic, English-speaking guide Marcos Menocal (☎ 552-4562) is excellent. He will lead groups through the city or even up Volcán Mombacho for around US$4 per person.

Enitel, the telephone and post office, is near the cathedral plaza's northeastern corner.

Casa Xalteva, located next to the colonial Xalteva church, is a new Spanish language school and cultural center. See Nicaragua's Facts for the Visitor section for more information.

City Center
The nicely restored main plaza, **Parque Colón**, with its mango and malinche trees, is a pleasant shady spot. The **cathedral**, on

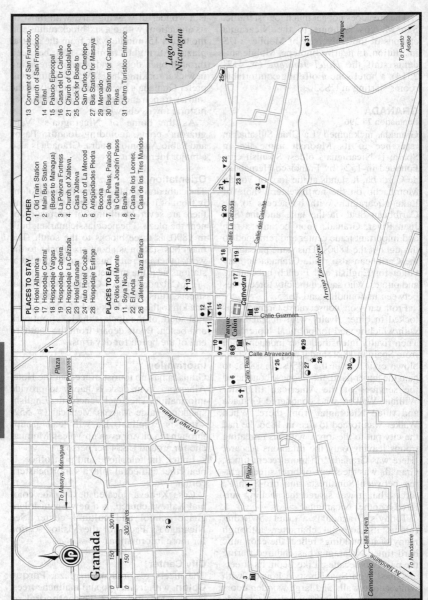

Granada

PLACES TO STAY
10 Hotel Alhambra
17 Hospedaje Central
18 Hospedaje Vargas
19 Hospedaje Cabrera
20 Hospedaje La Calzada
23 Hotel Granada
24 Auto Hotel Cocibal
28 Hospedaje Esfinge

PLACES TO EAT
9 Pollos del Monte
11 Soya Nica
22 El Ancla
26 Cafetería Taza Blanca

OTHER
1 Old Train Station
2 Main Bus Station
    (Buses to Managua)
3 La Pólvora Fortress
4 Church of Xalteva,
    Casa Xalteva
5 Church of La Merced
6 Antigüedades Piedra
    Bocona
7 Casa Pellas, Palacio de
    la Cultura Joachin Pasos
8 Banks
12 Casa de los Leones,
     Casa de los Tres Mundos
13 Convent of San Francisco,
     Church of San Francisco
14 Entitel
15 Palacio Episcopal
16 Casa del Dr Carballo
21 Church of Guadalupe
25 Dock for Boats to
     San Carlos, Ometepe
27 Bus Station for Masaya
29 Mercado
30 Bus Station for Carazo,
     Rivas
31 Centro Turístico Entrance

Lago de
Nicaragua

the east side of the plaza, has a simple, well-kept interior. Just north is the neoclassical **Palacio Episcopal** (bishop's palace). A half block farther north is the **Casa de los Leones**, which gets its name from the carved lions on the stone portal, the only part remaining from the original structure that was destroyed by William Walker. Rebuilt as a stately private home in 1920 and recently renovated, it now houses the **Casa de los Tres Mundos** (House of the Three Worlds), a foundation that sponsors cultural events (see Entertainment for details). The casa, open daily from 8 am to 6 pm, has a small coffee bar and sells a good selection of books on Nicaraguan history and literature.

On the plaza's southeast corner is one of the few private buildings dating from colonial times, the **Casa del Dr Carballo**. An impressive building on the southwest corner is the neoclassical **Casa Pellas**, a private home. You can get a glimpse of its Moorish-style courtyard through its south window. Also worth seeing is the **Palacio de Cultura Joaquin Pasos**, named for a Granadino poet who wrote *Canto de Guerra de las Cosas* (War Song of Things), a surrealist masterpiece and one of the glories of 20th-century Spanish verse. The Palacio, originally a social club, is now used for music and language classes. Farther down the colonnade is the Hotel Alhambra. Its portico restaurant is a relaxing place to hang out.

The **Convent and Church of San Francisco**, two blocks northeast of the plaza, was founded in 1529 as the city's first church. Bartolomé de las Casas, benefactor and apostle to the Indians, preached here and, on October 15, 1535, penned a letter of protest to the Spanish court denouncing the conversion of the indigenous people to Christianity by violent means. The structure was partially burned by pirates in 1665 and 1685, completely burned by Walker in 1856 and rebuilt for a third time in 1867-68. The convent once served as a university (shut down by Somoza in 1951), was Walker's headquarters and prison and is now the city's must-see museum. Artwork, usually paintings by Nicaraguan artists, is exhibited in the front section. The back courtyard houses the notable Squier-Zapatera collection of 28 pre-Columbian stone figures carved by the Chorotega Indians between 800 and 1200 AD. The collection is named after Ephraim George Squier, the US diplomat who discovered the impressive statues on the island of Zapatera in 1849. Restoration work on the convent, funded by the Swedish government, is ongoing. Entrance is US$1.20.

The **Church of La Merced**, three blocks west of the plaza, is the most beautiful of Granada's churches. Completed in early 1783, it was damaged by Leonese forces in 1854, then restored and remodeled in 1862. It has a baroque facade and a more elaborate interior than the city's other churches. Ask permission from the caretaker to climb the bell tower for a panoramic view of Granada's tile roofs and church towers. Antigüedades Piedra Bocona, just north of La Merced, is an antique store that is, in effect, a museum of 19th-century furnishings. Another notable colonial structure is the **Church of Guadalupe** on Calle La Calzada, which was used as a stronghold by William Walker.

Eight blocks west of the plaza, **La Polvora Fortress**, a military garrison built in 1749, was used by Somoza forces to interrogate and execute opponents. The recently restored fort, which now houses an arms museum, is open daily except Monday. A contribution is requested.

Lago de Nicaragua

The **Centro Turístico** is a two-km stretch of lakefront eateries and picnic areas shaded by mango trees; though people do swim at the beach here, the water is polluted. Boats depart for day trips to the nearby islands from restaurants at the southern end of the beach, or from the Puerto Asese dock. See the Around Granada section for more on these islands close to Granada, and see the Lago de Nicaragua section for more on the islands farther away: Isla de Ometepe and the Archipiélago de Solentiname.

An attractive swimming beach with clean water, **Malacatoya** is about 25 km north of Granada. Colectivo trucks headed for this beach leave from the Masaya bus stop around 10 am, returning to Granada in the afternoon.

Special Events
The Assumption of Mary (August 15) is a big holiday in Granada; festivities include a horse parade through town. Other festivals include La Purisima (Conception of Mary), celebrated November 27 to December 8, and Semana Santa.

Places to Stay
Granada has a disappointing selection of budget lodgings, most found on Calle La Calzada. *Hospedaje La Calzada*, located five blocks east of the plaza, charges US$2.50 per person for a basic room with shared bath; breakfast, lunch and dinner are available. *Hospedaje Cabrera* (☎ 552-2781), three blocks from the plaza, with a pleasant sitting room and nice proprietor, charges US$3.75 for adequate singles with fan and shared bath; no meals are provided. Across the street, *Hospedaje Vargas* (☎ 552-2897) is open 24 hours and has cable TV; guests have kitchen privileges. Windowless rooms with fan and shared bath are US$3 per person. The more basic *Hospedaje Central* (☎ 552-5900), one block west of Cabrera, charges US$2.50 per person; breakfast is US$1.25. Directly across from the main market is *Hospedaje Esfinge* (☎ 552-4826); it charges US$3.75 per person for dark rooms with fan and shared bath. The Esfinge has cable TV and will order in food from a nearby eatery for guests.

A more comfortable option is the *Auto Hotel Cocibal* (☎ 552-2204), 3½ blocks southeast of the plaza. Like Nicaragua's other auto hotels (motels), it is designed for 'romance,' but its rooms are clean, comfortable and have private bath at US$12 for a double.

Hotel Alhambra (☎ 552-4486, fax 552-2035), on the main plaza, is Granada's classy hotel. A single room with private bath is US$26; all rooms have air con, and the hotel has a small swimming pool. *Hotel Granada* (☎ 552-2974), located on La Calzada five blocks east of the plaza, has singles with private bath and air con for US$23. It has a coffee shop and bar.

If you want to splurge and sleep on a beautiful island in Las Isletas, the company Nicarao Lake Resort offers a package including a cabin, three meals, drinks, water sports and roundtrip boat ride from Puerto Asese for US$49 per person (☎ 228-1316, fax 222-2706).

Places to Eat
El Ancla, opposite Hotel Granada, serves good, reasonably priced food (most dinners US$4.25; breakfast from US$1.25). The restaurant at *Hotel Alhambra* is pricier (dinners start at US$5) but it's pleasant dining under the portico, facing the park. *Soya Nica*, on the northwest corner of the plaza, serves cheap, basic vegetarian meals. *Pollos del Monte*, popular with locals, one block west of Hotel Alhambra, offers inexpensive fried chicken. *Cafetería Taza Blanca* (from La Merced, one block south and one block east), a local favorite, serves meals for US$2. Cheap meals are available at the market, which is open Monday to Saturday from 6 am to 4 pm, and Sunday from 6 am to 2 pm.

There are many nice restaurants along the Centro Turistico. One of the least expensive of these is *Rancho Colomer*, with prices similar to *El Ancla*. Farther on down the beach are cheaper comedores.

Entertainment
The Casa de los Tres Mundos sponsors cultural events such as concerts, art exhibits and poetry readings; Latin American folklore performances are held Thursday evenings at the *Casa's* coffee bar. *Rancho Colomer* and some of the other lakeside restaurants are popular on Saturday and Sunday, when they are open long past midnight for dancing.

Getting There & Away
Bus Buses to Managua (44 km, one hour, US$0.60) depart from the main bus station,

six blocks west and 1½ blocks north of the plaza, every 20 to 30 minutes between 4:30 am and 7 pm. These buses will also drop passengers off at the entrance of Masaya.

Buses to Masaya (18 km, 20 minutes, US$0.35) depart from a stop a block west of the market. Colectivos to Malacatoya beach depart from here around 10 am.

Buses to Rivas depart from another bus stop, a block south of the market, at 5:45 and 11:25 am (65 km, 1½ hours, US$1). However, if you miss the direct bus, you can take a bus from the same stop to the crossroads at Nandaime and catch any bus heading south to Rivas. Buses to the Carazo pueblos (Diriamba, Jinotepe and San Marcos) also leave from this stop.

Boat The ticket office (☎ 552-4313) at the dock, at the foot of La Calzada, opens at 9 am. Tickets are usually sold the day of the trip. Buy tickets early and watch out for pickpockets on the dock. It is wise to verify departure times a day in advance.

Large boats leave for Altagracia on Isla de Ometepe on Monday and Thursday at 4 pm, and Saturday at noon, arriving about 4½ hours later. Tickets are US$1.50. The boat continues on to San Carlos at the south end of Lake Nicaragua, arriving eight hours later (fare is US$2). These boats return to Granada by the same routes on Tuesday and Friday, leaving Altagracia around 11 pm, and Sunday, leaving Altagracia around 10 am. Also on Monday and Thursday, another boat leaves Granada at 3 pm for Morrito, San Miguelito and San Carlos. From about October to April, banana boats depart for Ometepe daily at 11 am. This uncomfortable five-hour trip costs US$1.50.

Many Ometepe-bound travelers catch a bus to Rivas, board another bus to San Jorge, and then take the 45-minute boat trip to Moyogalpa.

Travelers to San Carlos can also take the comfortable, speedy hydrofoil (four hours, US$16 one way), which operates daily except Wednesday. The hydrofoil departs Granada at 8:30 am, stops in Solentiname

at 11 am, arrives in San Carlos at 12:30 pm and heads back to Granada at 1:30 pm. Tickets can be purchased at the Granada port or at the Bielonica, SA, office in Managua near the Montoya statue (☎ 266-4137), which is open Monday to Friday.

Getting Around
Granada's horse-drawn carriages, used routinely by locals, are a pleasant way to get around. A ride from the plaza to the lakefront costs US$0.40. An hour-long guided tour costs US$12. Inexpensive taxis are also available.

AROUND GRANADA
Las Isletas & Isla Zapatera
Just offshore from Granada, Las Isletas is a group of 356 small islands formed thousands of years ago by volcanic activity. The islands can be reached by motorboat and are well worth visiting. Many of them are inhabited, usually by one family; some have restaurants. Waterbirds such as herons, egrets and cranes are commonly seen, especially in early mornings and late afternoons.

Boats may be rented from Cabaña Amarilla and other restaurants located at the southern end of the Centro Turístico, or from postcard-pretty **Puerto Asese**, located at the end of a dirt road two km past Cabaña Amarilla. A covered boat holding 15 people costs US$10 for a half hour, or US$15 for an hour. You can arrange to be dropped off at an island restaurant and picked up later. A nice package deal at **Isla El Morro** includes lunch, water sports and roundtrip transportation from Puerto Asese for US$20 per person (☎ 228-1316, fax 222-2706). The swimming here is fine.

On **San Pablo Island** you can visit El Castillo, a small fort built in 1784 to guard against British incursions. Its rooftop observation deck affords great views of both Granada and the Mombacho volcano. The island is a 15-minute boat ride from Cabaña Amarilla.

Beyond Las Isletas is the much larger **Isla Zapatera**. Two hours away by motorboat from Granada, this island is one of Nicaragua's most important archaeological

NICARAGUA

areas. Giant stone statues erected by Indians in pre-Columbian times have been moved elsewhere (most notably to Granada's Convent and Church of San Francisco), but you can see where the statues stood and visit other ancient constructions and tombs. There are more tombs and some good rock carvings on nearby **Isla del Muerto**.

The lake's more distant islands, Ometepe and the Archipiélago de Solentiname, are covered in the Lago de Nicaragua section.

Volcán Mombacho

Mombacho's jagged peaks (the highest is 1363 meters) stand guard over Granada. Several dirt roads head up its slopes through coffee plantations; the best begins just south of where the road from San Marcos/Catarina intersects the Granada to Nandaime Hwy. It is a steep seven-km hike up (bear left at the fork in the road 3/4 km from the highway). Halfway is a gate where you may have to tip a coffee picker to let you continue through the plantation. On a clear day, the view from here is spectacular. Because lush vegetation obscures some of the most interesting features, it pays to have a guide. Granada's Hotel Alhambra has an excellent English-speaking guide who will lead a group of five for US$20.

RIVAS

Population 22,255

Rivas is a small crossroads town that has had its moments of importance since its establishment in 1736. Some significant battles have been fought here, and during the California gold rush Rivas was an important stop on Cornelius Vanderbilt's overland stagecoach route taking fortune-seekers across Nicaragua to San Juan del Sur.

Today Rivas is a departmental capital and the center of an agricultural region where maize, beans, rice, sugarcane, coffee and tobacco are grown and livestock is raised. Buses go from here to the Costa Rican border at Peñas Blancas, to the Pacific town of San Juan del Sur, to Granada and Managua, and to San Jorge on

the Lago de Nicaragua, where boats depart for Isla de Ometepe. (From Rivas, you can see Ometepe's Concepción volcano towering in the east.) Most of the places to stay in Rivas are on or near the highway.

Things to See

From the highway, it's worth walking the six blocks into town to see the old colonial church on the plaza. Among its curious artworks is a fresco in the cupola showing a battle at sea, with Communism, Protestantism and Secularism as burning hulks, and Catholicism as a victorious ship entering the harbor.

Also worth visiting is the **Museo de Antropología**, four blocks northwest of the main plaza, with its collection of pre-Columbian artifacts found in the region. It is open Monday to Friday from 8:30 am to noon and 2 to 5 pm, and on Saturday from 8:30 am to noon; admission is US$1.

Places to Stay

The nicest budget place is the *Hospedaje & Comedor Lidia* (☎ 453-3477), half a block behind the Texaco station on the main highway. It's a well-maintained, family-run place where rooms with fan and shared bath are US$6 per person, and meals are about US$2.50.

On the highway, the *Hospedaje Internacional* (☎ 453-3652) is basic and rundown, but the proprietor is helpful. It charges US$2.50 per person for a room with shared bath. A few doors down, the slightly nicer *Coco* (☎ 453-3298) charges US$3.50 per person. Both hospedajes serve inexpensive meals.

The best hotel within 50 km is the *Cacique Nicarao*, 1½ blocks from the northwest corner of the main plaza. Very nice singles with private bath and fan run US$12; singles with air con are US$19.

Places to Eat

The city's small market is several blocks west of the highway, beside the open lot where the buses pull in. The comedores there are the cheapest places in town to eat. There are a few inexpensive open-air comedores on the main plaza, such as *Rinconcito Salvadoreño*. Also on the plaza, the *Restaurante Chop Suey* serves both 'Chinese' and regular Nicaraguan food for moderate prices. The restaurant in the *Hotel Cacique Nicarao* offers very good meals from US$5. Out on the highway are a few simple comedores.

Getting There & Away
Buses from Rivas, with the exception of those to San Jorge, depart from the market, about 10 blocks west of the highway. They also stop at the Texaco station on the highway before leaving town, but it's best to walk the extra distance to the market if you want to get a seat.

The buses to San Jorge leave from the stop near the Shell station on the highway. A taxi for the four-km trip to San Jorge costs US$1.

If you miss the direct bus to Granada, you can take a bus heading for Managua, get off at the crossroads at Nandaime (45 km from Rivas), and take another bus the next 20 km to Granada. Buses from Rivas include:

Granada – 65 km, two hours, US$1; buses leave every one to two hours, 6 am to 4:25 pm.
Managua – 109 km, 2½ hours, US$1.30; buses leave every 30 minutes, 4 am to 6 pm.
San Jorge – four km, 30 minutes, US$0.50; buses leave every 30 minutes, 6:30 am to 5 pm.
San Juan del Sur – 29 km, one hour, US$0.60; buses leave every 45-60 minutes, 6:45 am to 5 pm.
Sapoá/Peñas Blancas (Costa Rica) – 35 km, one hour, US$0.60; buses leave every 30-60 minutes, 6:30 am to 3:30 pm.

RIVAS TO COSTA RICA
Getting to Sapoá (Peñas Blancas), the border crossing between Nicaragua and Costa Rica, is a one-hour bus ride. Alternatively, it's an easy hitch.

Remember that you may have to show a ticket out of Costa Rica when you arrive at the border crossing. See the introductory Getting There & Away section for information on satisfying this requirement.

If you are in Rivas and still do not have your onward ticket from Costa Rica, you can buy one from the Sirca bus company, based at the Hospedaje Internacional on the main highway through town. You can only buy a ticket between Managua and San José, and it costs the same price here as in Managua: US$13 one way, US$26 roundtrip.

The Sirca buses leave Managua on Monday, Wednesday, Friday and Saturday at 6 am and pass through Rivas at about 8:45 am. Another bus company, Tica Bus, also runs buses between Managua and San José (US$15 one way, US$30 return.) The Tica buses do not stop in Rivas on their way to the border, though they will stop there to let you off if you are coming into Nicaragua from Costa Rica.

The border station at Sapoá (Peñas Blancas) is open daily from 8 am to 7 pm. Arrive well before closing time and expect delays.

SAN JUAN DEL SUR
Population 4985
San Juan del Sur is a fishing village on a pretty horseshoe-shaped cove with low mountains rising around it.

The town was once important as the terminus of Cornelius Vanderbilt's transport company, established in 1848. Steamboats brought passengers from east coast US ports up the Río San Juan to Lago de Nicaragua; they then traveled 20 km by coach to the port at San Juan del Sur. From here, boats took them on to California.

During the Sandinista years, San Juan was a favorite refuge for internacionalistas taking a break by the sea. Today it remains a leading beach town and is typically quiet except for the holidays at Semana Santa. The town's own beach is nice enough, but for real untamed beauty you must go up or down the coast. The best beaches are to the south starting with El Romanso (a six-km walk down the dirt road that begins at the eastern outskirts of town) and ending near the Costa Rican border at the protected turtle nesting beach of La Flor (another 13 km down that same road). The closest

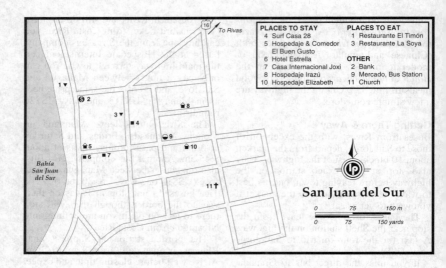

PLACES TO STAY
4 Surf Casa 28
5 Hospedaje & Comedor
   El Buen Gusto
6 Hotel Estrella
7 Casa Internacional Joxi
8 Hospedaje Irazú
10 Hospedaje Elizabeth

PLACES TO EAT
1 Restaurante El Timón
3 Restaurante La Soya

OTHER
2 Bank
9 Mercado, Bus Station
11 Church

San Juan del Sur

Bahía
San Juan
del Sur

0   75   150 m
0   75   150 yards

beach to the north is Marsella (eight km down the dirt road that begins behind the Lago Azul restaurant). These beaches are undeveloped, so bring food and water and ask directions along the way to make sure you are headed right. Infrequent buses pass near many of these beaches; inquire about schedules at your hospedaje. The Joxi (see below) arranges sailboat charters, rents bicycles and windsurf boards and provides transportation to the area's beaches, such as La Flor (US$14 for two people).

San Juan del Sur is also known for its annual procession to La Virgen del Carmen, patron of the port's mariners, on July 16.

Because many of San Juan's hospedajes do not have screens, visitors should bring protection against mosquitoes, such as insect repellent, coils or netting.

Places to Stay

San Juan del Sur has quite a selection of places to stay.

Surf Casa 28 (☎ 458-2441) offers rustic but adequate accommodations one block from the beach. The friendly caretaker will provide mosquito coils or netting if you wish. Rooms with shared bath cost US$3 per person.

Three blocks from the beach, the *Hospedaje Irazú* (no sign) (☎ 458-2371) has good, clean rooms, all with private bath and fan. At US$3.50 per person, it's nicer than what you usually get at that price.

On the town's sea front there is the *Hotel Estrella* and, opposite it, the *Hospedaje & Comedor El Buen Gusto*. The *El Buen Gusto* (☎ 458-2304) asks US$8 per person, breakfast included. The rooms are basic, but the hotel has a large pleasant terrace facing the ocean, and the restaurant is very nice. The *Estrella* (☎ 458-2210), a weathered wood building with high ceilings, has spartan rooms for US$4 per person.

Casa Internacional Joxi (☎ 458-2348), half a block from the beach, is a good, clean hotel operated by a friendly Norwegian-Nicaraguan couple; English is spoken. The most economical rooms have four bunks, fan and shared bath and cost US$7 per person. Other rooms, with private bath and air con, are US$15 per person. Meals and international drinks are available. The owners are especially hospitable and offer activities (see above).

NICARAGUA

Two blocks east of the Joxi is *Hospedaje Elizabeth* (☎ 458-2270), a clean, friendly place with a wall map of the area's beaches. A single with shared bath and fan is $3.50. Guests may order meals (a vegetarian plate is available) or use the kitchen.

Hotel Barlovento (☎ 458-2450), on a hill overlooking the town, has comfortable rooms with good views and private bath and air con for US$24. It has no restaurant.

Places to Eat
Fresh fish and seafood are, of course, the specialties of San Juan del Sur, and they are delicious.

There are a number of restaurants along the beach that, though not cheap, are good for their fine views of the cove. *El Buen Gusto* and *El Timón* offer seafood from US$4 to US$7. On the north end of the beach is *Lago Azul*, one of the best restaurants in town, with meals from US$5. It has a small hospedaje upstairs (☎ 458-2325).

A cheap place to eat is *La Soya*, a small comedor that is operated by the women's organization AMNLAE. Located a block from the beach, the comedor serves comida corriente for US$1.25. La Soya has a basic room for rent, and plans to build several more (☎ 458-2132). The cost is US$2.50 per person.

As everywhere in Nicaragua, you can also eat economically in the market.

Getting There & Away
Buses come and go from beside the market, three blocks from the beach. Buses to Rivas (29 km, one hour, US$0.60) depart every 45 to 60 minutes, from 5 am to 3:30 pm. From Rivas you can transfer onto buses for many other places.

Lago de Nicaragua

Lago de Nicaragua, also known by its indigenous name Cocibolca and as La Mar Dulce (the sweet sea), is the 10th largest freshwater lake in the world: it is 177 km long by an average 58 km wide, covers 8157 sq km and is around 60 meters deep at its deepest point.

Forty-five rivers flow into it, including the Río Tipitapa flowing from Lago de Managua. One large river, the Río San Juan, flows from Lago de Nicaragua to the Caribbean.

The world's only freshwater sharks live in Lago de Nicaragua. Although they are big – about three meters long – they are very rarely seen. The lake is home to many other unusual fish, including freshwater swordfish, sawfish and tarpon.

This strange aquatic life reflects the way the lake was formed. It is believed that both Lago de Nicaragua and Lago de Managua were originally part of a large Pacific bay that was cut off from the ocean by the uplifting of the Earth's crust. Isolated from the sea, the marine creatures trapped in the new lakes adapted as the salt water gradually became fresh.

An ancient Indian story relates how the Chorotega and Nahuatl peoples were overpowered by the Olmecs in Mexico, and thus forced to embark upon a massive migration south. Consulting their oracles, they were told that they would find a place to settle near a freshwater sea, where they would see an island with two high mountains.

There is ample evidence of ancient human habitation on the lake's 400 islands. Over 350 of these are in the group called Las Isletas, just offshore from Granada. Zapatera, the second largest island in the lake, is just to the south of this group. The Archipiélago de Solentiname, near the south end of the lake, has 36 islands. The largest of all the islands, Ometepe, is formed by two massive volcanoes. Lago de Nicaragua is, indeed, just as the oracle described it.

Ancient Indian artifacts found on the islands, particularly on Zapatera, Ometepe and the Solentiname group, include statues of people and animals, and petroglyphs with images of people, mammals, birds and geometric shapes. Many tombs have been found, too, notably on Zapatera and the Isla del Muerto beside it.

The link created by the lake and the Río San Juan between Granada and the

Caribbean was exploited for centuries by British and other pirates bent on attacking Granada and León. The possibility of using this link as part of a trans-isthmian sea crossing also lent the lake strategic importance, firing imperial imaginations from the early 16th century. Lago de Nicaragua, its islands, and the people who inhabit them are memorialized in Pablo Antonio Cuadra's *Cantos de Cífar*, one of the most famous works of contemporary Nicaraguan literature.

ISLA DE OMETEPE

Ometepe is an ecotouristic jewel, but infrastructure there is still largely undeveloped. This makes the island all the more attractive for those who like unspoiled nature and who don't mind expending extra effort to see it.

Ometepe ('between two hills' in Nahuatl) is the largest island in the world that is located in a freshwater lake. It is formed by two large volcanoes: Volcán Concepción, which rises 1610 meters above the lake in an almost perfect cone, and Volcán Madera, which is 1340 meters high. Lava flowing from the two volcanoes created an isthmus between them to make a single island. Concepción is still active: Its last major eruption was in 1957.

Ometepe is dotted by small settlements around the island's edges where people live by fishing and growing bananas, citrus fruits, maize, sesame, beans and other crops; Ometepe's volcanic soil is very fertile. Parts of the island are still covered in primary forest, which harbor abundant wildlife including white-faced monkeys, Congo (howler) monkeys, green parrots and many other animals and birds.

Ometepe is famous for its ancient stone statues and petroglyphs made by the Chorotega people depicting humans, animals, birds and geometric shapes, especially spirals. They have been found all over the island, but there are many on Volcán Madera, between Santa Cruz and

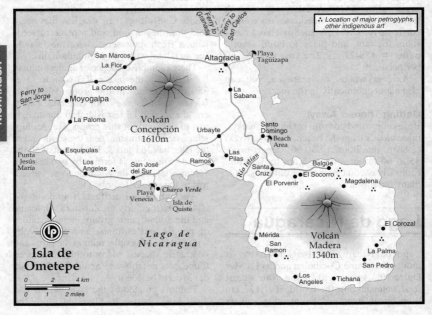

La Palma. Others are displayed in Altagracia in front of the church and in the town museum.

A gravel road goes all round the part of the island formed by Volcán Concepción; at the isthmus it connects to a road that goes around the Volcán Madera side as far as Balgue on the north coast and Mérida on the south. The rest of Madera is only accessible by foot, horseback or boat.

The island's two major towns are Altagracia and Moyogalpa; both are connected to the mainland by ferries. Both have Enitel (combined post and telephone office) stations, and Moyogalpa has a small hospital.

Unless Moyogalpa's only bank, Banco Nacional de Desarrollo, has reopened, there are no banking services on the island. Credit cards are accepted at many hotels, traveler's checks at some.

Books
Ometepe: Isla de Círculos y Espirales (1973, Hildeberto María), by Joaquín Matilló Vila, is an excellent illustrated book about the petroglyphs and other ancient evidence of civilization found on the island. It is out of print, but Señor Ramón Castillo, owner of the Hospedaje Castillo in Altagracia, gladly shares his copy with visitors.

Things to See & Do
Ometepe is great for walking, exploring and swimming. However, the terrain is rough, signage nonexistent and trails hard to follow. Even independent travelers are well advised to hire an inexpensive local guide (see Getting Around for details).

On the Volcán Concepción side of the island, excellent half-day hikes partially up the volcano begin at La Flor, La Sabana and San José del Sur. They offer breathtaking views and take you deep into the forest. If you really want a challenge, La Sabana is the recommended place to start the 10-hour hike to and from the summit crater. Lakeside destinations include Punta Jesús María, a nice swimming and picnic spot 5½ km south of Moyogalpa; Playa Venecia and Charco Verde Lagoon, 12 km southeast of

Moyogalpa; the Isla de Quiste, a beautiful island not far from Charco Verde; and Playa Tagüizapa, four km east of Altagracia.

The coast south of Altagracia has nice wide beaches. The most popular is Santo Domingo, accessible via a rough three-km road that begins six km south of Altagracia.

The road through Santo Domingo leads to the Madera side of the island. There are some fine walks through forests full of wildlife and several hikes to see petroglyphs. The petroglyphs near the village of El Porvenir are a 30-minute walk from Santo Domingo; ask hotel staffers for directions. Others are found at El Socorro and Magdalena. If you are up to it, an eighthour roundtrip climb starting at Balgue leads to Volcán Madera's exquisitely beautiful crater lake. It is highly recommended to hire a local guide, who will provide the rope required for the final descent to the laguna. On the south side of Madera, a 35-meter-high waterfall is located a couple hours' hike above San Ramon.

A less strenuous way to see the island is simply to ride a bus around Volcán Concepción, across the isthmus and down to Balgue on the Madera side, passing through many small villages and varied farming country. The gorgeous blue-tailed birds seen everywhere on the island are called *urracas*.

Organized Tours
Ecotur (telefax 459-4118), three blocks east and 1½ blocks south of Moyogalpa's dock, provides a wide range of inexpensive tours, led by guides specially trained in the island's flora, fauna and ecology. They charge US$3 per person to lead a group of five to the summit of either volcano (excluding transportation). Daylong tours to Charco Verde or the Madera petroglyphs cost even less.

Most hotels in Moyogalpa and Altagracia will be happy to arrange tours, guides or horses. Inexpensive local guides, called *baqueanos*, are available to lead groups on volcano or petroglyph hikes. Fundación Entre Volcanes (next door to Ecotur) can provide a list of such guides.

NICARAGUA

Getting Around the Island

Buses go all the way around the side of the island formed by Volcán Concepción, and from Altagracia across the isthmus and down to Balgue on the Madera side. Ask your hotel for a schedule. The trip from Moyogalpa to Altagracia takes 45 minutes (US$0.70) and from Altagracia to Balgue takes another hour.

You can make a very enjoyable day trip from Moyogalpa by taking the 6 or 7:30 am bus to Altagracia, passing around Volcán Concepción on the way; the 9:30 am bus from Altagracia across the isthmus to Balgue; the return bus from Balgue back to Altagracia at 3:30 pm; and another bus from Altagracia at 4:30 pm to return to Moyogalpa.

A taxi service called ATTO (☎ 459-4272) located near the dock in Moyogalpa provides service to most of the island; for example, the roundtrip fare from Moyogalpa to Venecia beach is US$19.50. ATTO handles groups large and small.

Finally, if you want to explore on your own, you can rent 4WD vehicles in Moyogalpa at the Hotel Ometepetl (US$29 for 12 hours) and also the Cari Hotel (US$49 for 6 hours). Both also rent bicycles and motorcycles. Moyogalpa's Hospedaje Aly has the cheapest bike rentals at US$6.50 a day.

Moyogalpa

Population 2470

Moyogalpa is the principal village on the west side of the island; ferries run several times daily to and from the mainland at San Jorge, near Rivas. The fastest boat takes only 45 minutes and is the easiest crossing to Ometepe. Though Altagracia is the larger town, Moyogalpa has more hotels and restaurants. You will spot its only real attraction before you even reach the dock: a traffic circle containing an enormous model of the island with fountains jetting out of the two peaks.

Places to Stay & Eat Right next to the dock, *Hotel El Puerto* (☎ 459-4194), a simple hospedaje with comfortable beds, charges US$3 per person for rooms with shared bath; rooms with air con are US$6. One block uphill from the dock, *Hotel Ometepetl* (☎ 459-4276, fax 459-4132) is the best in town. It offers small but well-kept rooms, all with private bath, starting at US$7 per person; singles/doubles with air con are US$20. The hotel has a good restaurant and a pleasant porch with hammocks and rocking chairs. The Ometepetl has a cheaper annex next door, the *Hospedaje Moyogalpa*, which has simple rooms with shared bath for US$3 with fan, US$2.50 without.

One block up the same road, the *Hospedaje y Restaurante Aly* (☎ 459-4196) has modest rooms around a peaceful, attractive central patio with tables, hammocks and lots of plants. Rooms with shared bath start at US$3 per person; meals are US$3.50. Across the street, the *Hotel Bahia* (☎ 459-4116) has nice enough rooms with private bath starting at US$4. A less attractive place is *Pensión Jade*, with basic rooms with shared bath for US$1.75 per person.

A block south of the main road, right on the beach, the *Cari Hotel y Marina* (☎ 459-4263) offers lakeside eating and rents horses and canoes. Its rooms are comfortable enough; doubles with private bath are US$12, US$25 with air con. Prices are higher during the dry season. *El Pirata* (☎ 459-4262), three blocks uphill from the Cari, has rather large rooms, all with private bath, beginning at US$12; air con is available. Ecotur (telefax 459-4118), three blocks east and 1½ blocks south of Moyogalpa's dock, can arrange lodging with local families for US$2 per day with meals an additional US$2.

Most lodging places in Moyogalpa have restaurants. There are other places to eat as well, such as *Comedor Los Ranchitos*, two blocks east and half a block south of dock, which offers inexpensive open-air dining.

Getting There & Away The *El Diamante* ferry operates seven days a week, departing from Moyogalpa Monday through Saturday at 8:15 am and 5 pm and reaching San Jorge 45 minutes later. From San Jorge, it departs at 10 am and 6 pm. The Sunday schedule from Moyogalpa is 8:15 am and 5 pm, with only one departure from San Jorge at 6 pm. The trip costs US$2.50.

A slower and cheaper boat (US$1) departs from Moyogalpa Monday through Saturday at 6, 6:30 and 7 am and 1:30 pm. It departs San Jorge at 11 am, noon, 3 and 5 pm. The Sunday schedule from Moyogalpa is 7 am and 1:30 pm, with departures from San Jorge at noon and 5 pm.

It's best to buy tickets as soon as the dockside offices in Moyogalpa and San Jorge open, an hour before departure times. If the ferries fill up, they will depart ahead of schedule.

Altagracia
Population 2719

Altagracia is the largest town on Isla de Ometepe. The dock is five km from town; from here, the ferry runs several times weekly to Granada (4½ hours) and to San Carlos (eight hours). There is not much to see in Altagracia besides the ancient stone statues in front of the church, which are quite fine, and the **Museo de Ometepe**, which has a modest display of archaeological, geological and cultural artifacts. The museum is open weekdays from 9 am to 5 pm (closed for an hour at noon) and weekends 9 am to 5 pm; admission is US$1.25.

Places to Stay & Eat The most popular place to stay is the *Hospedaje Castillo* (telefax 552-6045), one block south and half a block west from the church. The owner, Señor Ramón Castillo, and his son are exceptionally accommodating and very knowledgeable about Ometepe. The hospedaje is simple; rooms with shared bath start at US$2.50 per person. There is a nice little restaurant and covered patio; meals are good and inexpensive. You can come here to eat and to talk to Señor Castillo whether or not you're a guest at the hospedaje.

Two blocks south of the main plaza, *Hotel Central* (☎ 552-6072) offers simple rooms with shared or private bath starting at US$2.50 per person. There are also very nice little cabins with private bath, set amid

a pretty garden, for US$12 per person. The hotel has a pleasant porch, a sundries store and a bar and restaurant that serves meals starting at US$4 (comida corriente is US$2.25). The *Hotel Astagalpa* has more basic lodging for US$2.50 per person. Ecotur (telefax 459-4118) in Moyogalpa can arrange lodging with local families for US$2 per day with meals an additional US$2.

Getting There & Away The boat from Granada to San Carlos (on the Costa Rican border) departs on Monday and Thursday at 4 pm. It arrives in Altagracia about 4½ hours later and takes off for the eight-hour trip to San Carlos, on the south end of the lake. It costs US$1.50 from Granada to Altagracia and US$2 to San Carlos. The boat returns to Granada from Altagracia on Tuesday and Friday at 11 pm.

On Saturday, another boat leaves from Granada at noon bound for Altagracia and begins the return trip at 10 am on Sunday. Travelers are urged to purchase tickets ahead of departure time at the dockside ticket offices.

Santo Domingo Beach
The Santo Domingo beach area has two small hotels. *Finca Hotel Santo Domingo* is a converted farmhouse; its clean rooms with shared bath are US$3.60 per person. Though aged, the building retains an old farmhouse charm, with a breezy porch facing the beach. Nearby is the newer *Villa Paraíso* (☎ 453-4675), whose pleasantly rustic rooms with shared bath start at US$3 per person; cabins with private bath go for US$6 per person. Both hotels have restaurants with meals starting at US$3.50; the Paraíso's menu includes vegetarian dishes. Reservations are recommended for weekend stays. Call the Paraíso to reserve at either hotel.

ARCHIPIÉLAGO DE SOLENTINAME
The Archipiélago de Solentiname, in the southern part of the Lago de Nicaragua, is composed of 36 islands; the largest are Mancarrón, San Fernando and La Venada.

The Solentiname islands are a sort of

NICARAGUA

haven for artists. The Nicaraguan poet Ernesto Cardenal established a communal society here for artists, poets and crafts-people, and the islands are now known for their distinctive school of colorful primitivist painting, with a characteristic style of charming simplicity.

The islands are great for hiking, fishing and taking it easy. The vegetation is lush and there are a number of ancient petroglyphs and stone carvings.

The *Albergue Mancarrón* (☎ 552-2059, 260-3345 in Managua), on Mancarrón island, has comfortable rooms with bath for US$35 per person (meals included). The staff can arrange for a roundtrip boat from San Carlos for US$75 for a group of eight. The *Hotel Isla Solentiname* on San Fernando island is a little less expensive.

A public boat departs San Carlos for Solentiname on Tuesday and Friday at 2 pm (two hours, US$3), and travels back to San Carlos at 5 am on the same two days. Pangas are also available; a roundtrip to Solentiname runs about US$70.

Hydrofoils depart Granada daily (except Wednesday) at 8:30 am for Solentiname (three hours, US$14 one way) and continue on to San Carlos. Contact Bielonica, SA (☎ 266-4137 in Managua) for more information.

SAN CARLOS
Population 6746

San Carlos is a small town on the south-eastern corner of Lago de Nicaragua, beside the Río San Juan. Boats go from here down the river as well as to Archipiélago de Solentiname and the border with Costa Rica.

While people usually visit San Carlos on the way to other places, the town does have the ruins of an old fortress, which was built by the Spanish to fight off pirates coming up the river. There are numerous places to eat. Decent lodging can be found at the *Cabinas Lekyo* (☎ 283-0354), with clean (if musty) rooms with shared bath starting at US$7 per person; doubles with private bath are US$16. *Hotel Azul* (☎ 283-0282), near

the market, and *Hospedaje Peña*, both charge about US$2.50 for basic rooms with shared bath.

Getting There & Away

Boats leave from Granada for San Carlos on Monday, Thursday and Saturday, with return trips on Tuesday, Friday and Sunday. The trip takes 12½ hours and costs US$2. See the Granada section for details.

Hydrofoils depart Granada daily (except Wednesday) at 8:30 am, arrive in San Carlos at 12:30 pm and head back to Granada at 1:30 pm. The one-way fare is US$16. Contact Bielonica, SA (☎ 266-4137 in Managua) for more information.

The commuter airline La Costeña has flights from Managua for US$74 round-trip on Monday, Wednesday and Friday. There is also a gravel road to Juigalpa that is traveled by buses.

Small boats head to the Costa Rican border station at Los Chiles (20 minutes, US$3; be sure to get your exit stamp at the San Carlos immigration office) and down the Río San Juan (see below).

RÍO SAN JUAN & EL CASTILLO

The Río San Juan flows 180 km from Lago de Nicaragua to the Caribbean, where it meets the coast at the port of San Juan del Norte (formerly called Greytown). For much of its length, the river serves as the border between Nicaragua and Costa Rica. The original rain forest still lines the banks in some places, although you will also see ranches and farms.

Boat trips on the Río San Juan are once again popular among visitors to Nicaragua after being suspended during the war years. About 15 minutes downriver from San Carlos is the *San Pancho Lodge* (☎ 283-0250, 266-5173 in Managua), with comfortable rooms with bath and three meals for US$35 per person. People come here to fish, hike or simply relax on the porch watching the river flow by. Guided boat tours and horseback rides run US$5 to US$10 per person. The lodge will pick you up in San Carlos.

About one-third of the way from the lake to the ocean is El Castillo, a fortress built by the Spanish in 1675 at a strategic point on the river to try to block English, French and other pirates from coming up the river to attack Granada and León. It was one of several fortifications designed for this purpose, including those at San Carlos, and on San Pablo Island, near Granada.

Bitter battles were fought at El Castillo against flotillas of assailants. In 1762 there was a fierce battle to repel a force 2000-strong on 50 British ships, led by the legendary captain Henry Morgan. The fort was subsequently captured and briefly held by the British in 1780 (the young Horatio Nelson took part). The British sought to annex the strategic trans-isthmian route, seize rich Granada and León and divide the Spanish territory in two. There is a small museum that details the fort's turbulent history.

Public boats depart San Carlos for El Castillo daily at 2 pm. It's a five-hour trip (US$2). The boat returns to San Carlos daily at 5 am. You can charter a faster eight-person motorboat (two hours to El Castillo), but it is not cheap. The fare from San Carlos to El Castillo is US$200 and to San Juan del Norte at least US$400.

In Castillo, the *Albergue El Castillo* (☎ 552-6127 ext 3, 267-8276 in Managua) has capacity for 25 people at US$15 per person, or US$30 with meals. *Hotel Richardson* has simpler accommodations for about US$10 per person, with meal service available. Some 20 km further downriver, the *Refugio Bartola* (☎ 289-4167 in Managua) offers eight rustic rooms at US$15, or US$30 with meals. A new ecotouristic lodge in San Juan del Norte, *Albergue Greytown* (☎ 265-3415 in Managua), funded by a British aid project, charges US$10 per person for simple but comfortable accommodations.

The Nicaraguan government has set aside a large area between El Castillo and San Juan del Norte (Greytown), as the Río Indio/Río Maíz Biological Reserve.

The Caribbean Coast

The Caribbean Coast of Nicaragua is a long (541 km), wide, flat plain covered in tropical rain forest. In many places the virgin jungle is so thick that it is practically impenetrable, and it provides a home to abundant wildlife. The coast is hot and gets much more rain than the Pacific and inland regions: anywhere between 3300 and 6350 mm annually. Even during the March to May 'dry' season rain is possible at any time.

Nicaragua's Caribbean Coast is part of the larger Mosquitia region that extends well into Honduras. The Río Coco, which forms the border between present-day Honduras and Nicaragua, runs right through the traditional Mosquitia region, and the Miskito Indians, today numbering around 70,000, live on both sides of it.

Other ethnic groups in the region include the Sumo and Rama Indian tribes, the black Creoles originally brought from other parts of the Caribbean by the British, a small number of other blacks known as Garífunas (see the Honduras chapter) and mestizos from other parts of Nicaragua. The races have mingled a good deal over the centuries.

Unlike the rest of Nicaragua, the Mosquitia was never colonized by Spain. In the 18th century, leaders of the Mosquitia requested that it be made a British protectorate, as a defense against the Spanish. It remained British for over a century, with a capital at Bluefields, where the Miskito kings were crowned in the Protestant church.

The British signed treaties handing the Mosquitia over to the governments of Honduras and Nicaragua in 1859 and 1860. In Nicaragua, the region retained its autonomy until 1894, when it was brought under direct Nicaraguan government control.

The English language, and the Protestant religion brought by British missionaries, persist as important aspects of the regional culture. Timber, shrimp and lobster are important exports.

NICARAGUA

The only part of the coast much visited by international travelers is the city of Bluefields. From Bluefields, boats depart for the Corn Islands off the coast.

MANAGUA TO THE CARIBBEAN

The trip from Managua to Bluefields has long been a favorite with travelers. The easiest way to make the trip is to fly, but the journey overland is what many people like best about visiting the coast.

To go overland from Managua involves traveling 292 km to Rama at the end of the highway, a journey of about seven hours, then taking a boat down the Río Escondido to Bluefields on the coast, a further five hours (or two hours if you take a speed boat). Most people find it a tiring but very enjoyable journey. You could make the trip in one big push, departing Managua on the 10:30 pm bus and arriving in Rama in time to transfer to a boat, but it's more relaxing to break up the journey by spending the night in either Juigalpa or Rama, and then taking a boat the following day.

JUIGALPA
Population 41,792

Juigalpa, the capital of the department of Chontales, has an archaeological museum with a large collection of pre-Columbian idols excavated in the area. The museum, named after the local scholar Gregorio Aguilar Barea, is 1½ blocks behind the town's modern concrete church. A beautifully landscaped park is opposite the church. Juigalpa is also interesting as a center of Catholic *comunidades de base* (popular communities).

Hospedaje El Viajero (☎ 812-0291), a block southeast of the church, offers decent rooms (with outhouses) for US$2.50 per person. The *Hotel Imperial* (☎ 812-2294), behind the church, has clean, simple singles with shared bath for $5.50; meals are served every day except Saturday. The fancier *La Quinta* (☎ 812-2485), across from the hospital on the main highway, has doubles with private bath, air con and individual cable TV for US$14. It also has a restaurant and disco.

Buses leave for the three- to four-hour trip to Rama from Juigalpa's market, one block behind the church, at regular intervals from 4 am to 1 pm.

RAMA
Population 7782

Rama is at the end of the highway heading east from Managua. There's not much to it – the town is just a few blocks square – and there's nothing in particular to do, but it's a peaceful place to spend the night while waiting for the boat to the coast. The simple, tropical-style church, with its stained glass and patterned decorations, is worth a visit. Rama is at the confluence of two rivers, the Río Síquia and the Río Rama. From here to the coast, the river is called the Río Escondido.

Places to Stay & Eat

Most of the places to stay in Rama are old wooden buildings offering basic rooms with fan and shared bath. The riverside *Hotel Amy* (☎ 817-0034), which appears on the verge of collapse, charges US$2.50 per person; its restaurant is pleasant enough. *Hotel Johanna*, a few blocks away, has rooms starting at US$3. The *Ramada Inn* is nothing like the well-known chain bearing its name, but a rough wood and bamboo structure with rooms at US$2.50 per person; English is spoken. *Hospedaje Jiménez El Viajero* and *Hospedaje Central* are in better repair than the others, with rooms costing US$3 per person; both have outhouse facilities. The *Restaurante Expresso* is a pleasant open-air restaurant with good, inexpensive food.

Getting There & Away

Bus Buses take seven to eight hours to travel between Managua and Rama (292 km, US$4.75); though still rough in spots, this road has improved in recent years. In Managua, there are six departures, between 4 am and 11:30 am every day, from the Coatlantico station (☎ 263-1559), one km south of the Mercado Mayoreo. Express buses to Rama (seven hours, US$6) depart from the same station at 10:30 pm; these

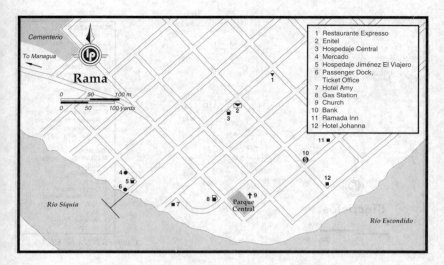

1 Restaurante Expresso
2 Enitel
3 Hospedaje Central
4 Mercado
5 Hospedaje Jiménez El Viajero
6 Passenger Dock,
   Ticket Office
7 Hotel Amy
8 Gas Station
9 Church
10 Bank
11 Ramada Inn
12 Hotel Johanna

buses wait at the dock in Rama to meet boats coming back from Bluefields, then leave immediately for the return trip to Managua.

If you miss the direct bus from Managua to Rama, you could take a bus to Juigalpa (137 km, three hours) and take a second bus or hitch the rest of the way to Rama. The last bus leaves Juigalpa for Rama at 1 pm.

Boat The slow boat from Rama to Bluefields departs at noon on Tuesday, Thursday, Saturday and Sunday. Tickets go on sale at 9 am, but get there earlier if you want a good spot on the often-crowded boat. Tickets cost US$4.50 and the trip takes five hours. Smaller motorboats called *pangas* leave every day around 8 am and make the trip in 2 hours; the fare is US$12. Pangas sometimes are available later in the day as well. It's a good idea to go to the dock well in advance to verify departure times.

Food and drinks are sold at the dock; take some with you as there is nothing available on the journey.

BLUEFIELDS
Population 30,208

Bluefields is Nicaragua's principal Caribbean port, but the port itself is actually across the bay at Bluff. The town was destroyed by Hurricane Joan in 1988, but has been rebuilt (including its beautiful bayside Moravian church). Bluefields' economy is based on shrimp, lobster and deep-water fish; other food and merchandise is brought in from Managua and is consequently more expensive than in the capital.

Bluefields has no swimming beaches – the water here is murky, anyway – and it's not a particularly attractive town, but it's a fascinating place. There's a mix of ethnic groups including Indians (Miskitos, Ramas and Sumos), blacks (including Creoles and a small number of Garífunas) and mestizos from the rest of Nicaragua. Walking down the street you are just as likely to hear English as Spanish; music ranges from reggae to country and western. The people of Bluefields like to have a good time, and there is plenty of nightlife. In May there's a week-long festival, with a maypole, music and dance.

Bluefields gets its English-sounding name not from any nearby blue fields (guess again) but from the Dutch pirate, Blewfeldt, who made a base here in the mid-17th century.

NICARAGUA

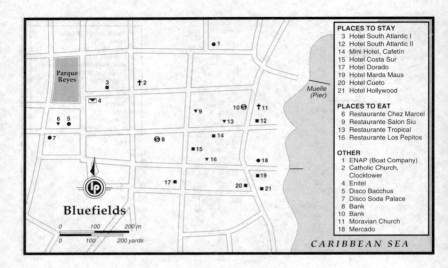

PLACES TO STAY
3 Hotel South Atlantic I
12 Hotel South Atlantic II
14 Mini Hotel, Cafetín
15 Hotel Costa Sur
17 Hotel Dorado
19 Hotel Marda Maus
20 Hotel Cueto
21 Hotel Hollywood

PLACES TO EAT
6 Restaurante Chez Marcel
9 Restaurante Salon Siu
13 Restaurante Tropical
16 Restaurante Los Pepitos

OTHER
1 ENAP (Boat Company)
2 Catholic Church,
   Clocktower
4 Enitel
5 Disco Bacchus
7 Disco Soda Palace
8 Bank
10 Bank
11 Moravian Church
18 Mercado

Parque Reyes

Muelle (Pier)

Bluefields

0   100   200 m
0   100   200 yards

CARIBBEAN SEA

Orientation & Information

Most of Bluefields' commerce, hospedajes and restaurants are found in a nine-sq-block area between Parque Reyes and the Caribbean. The dock is four blocks east of the park. The Enitel post and telephone office is on the southeast corner of the park. There are several banks. The airport is about three km south of downtown.

Places to Stay

Try to find a place to stay as soon as you get off the boat: arriving tourists make a mad dash from the dock to the hotels, and whoever gets there first grabs the available rooms. Prices below are for single/doubles with fan and shared bath unless otherwise stated.

The *Hotel Hollywood* (☎ 822-2282), two blocks south of the Moravian church, is the best budget hotel, although walls between rooms have gaps near the ceiling. It has a view of the bay from its back balcony. Rooms go for US$5/8. Around the corner by the Mercado, the *Hotel Marda Maus* (☎ 822-2429) charges US$6/9. It has a nice balcony and serves meals for just US$2. The nearby *Hotel Costa Sur* (☎ 822-2452)

has small but modern rooms for US$6/9; it also has a nice balcony but serves meals to guests only. The *Mini-Hotel y Cafetín* (☎ 822-2362) is very popular and somewhat noisy, with rooms from US$6/12.

The *Hotel Dorado* (☎ 822-2365), on a quiet street, is a step up from the budget places, with small rooms with private bath and air con for US$15. The *Hotel South Atlantic I* (☎ 822-2242), near Enitel, and *Hotel South Atlantic II* (☎ 822-2265), next to the Moravian church, are Bluefields' best. Both have comfortable, modern rooms with private bath, air con and cable TV for US$26/37.

If the others are full, try the *Hotel Cueto* (no sign) with dark, unventilated rooms for US$5/8 or the *Hotel Claudia* with very basic rooms for US$4/6.

Places to Eat

In Bluefields, you can eat shrimp and lobster that were caught a few hours earlier for prices lower than elsewhere in Nicaragua. The *Restaurante El Flotante*, four blocks south of the Moravian Church where the bayside street meets the water, has dining on a covered patio with a marvelous view of the bay. Meals start at US$4. One block north is the *Restaurante Bella Vista*, less breezy with much louder music. Other restaurants you might try include the *Restaurante Los Pepitos*, *Restaurante Tropical* and *Salon Siu*. For air con and cloth napkins go to *Restaurante Chez Marcel*, one block south of Parque Reyes, with meals from US$6. Hotels South Atlantic I & II and Hotel Hollywood have very good restaurants.

Entertainment
Bluefields has an active nightlife, especially on weekends. The popular dancing spots are the *Disco Bacchus*, just south of Parque Reyes, and the *Disco Soda Palace*, across from Chez Marcel restaurant. Other night spots include *Lego Lego*, the *Caimito* and *Restaurante El Flotante*. You need go no farther than the Parque Reyes to find a crowd enjoying good music.

Getting There & Away
Air La Costeña flies between Managua and Bluefields four times a day. Tickets cost US$43 one way and US$86 roundtrip. There is one La Costeña flight a day between Bluefields and Puerto Cabezas. Ticket offices are at the airport, about three km south of town. A taxi to the airport costs US$1.20. For information on flights to Corn Island, see that section.

Boat Brooks Hamilton (☎ 249-6953 in Managua) offers bus/boat service all the way from Managua to Bluefields for US$14. Buses depart from Managua (Km 3 on Carretera Norte, 2 blocks north) on Monday, Wednesday and Friday at 1 am; after arriving in Rama, passengers continue by motorboat to Bluefields, arriving there around 11 am.

Passenger boats from Bluefields to Rama depart at 5 am on Tuesday, Thursday, Saturday and Sunday; the five-hour trip costs US$4.50. Tuesday and Saturday tickets are sold at the dockside office of Motonave Lynx. Thursday and Sunday tickets are sold at the ENAP office one block from the dock. Buy tickets one day in advance. Buses wait at the dock in Rama to meet the arriving boats to take passengers directly to Managua. If you want to take one, try to be first off the boat and make a flying run for a seat.

Small pangas make a two-hour trip to Rama seven days a week departing Bluefields at 5 am. The US$12 tickets are sold at the dockside office of Vargas Peña.

Cargo boats depart Bluefields for Puerto Cabezas via Laguna de Perlas from time to time; inquire at the dock. You are unlikely to find a ride to Costa Rica or Colombia's San Andres island.

See the Laguna de Perlas and Corn Island sections for details on getting to and from these destinations.

LAGUNA DE PERLAS
The Laguna de Perlas (Pearl Lagoon), formed where the Río Kurinwas meets the sea about 80 km north of Bluefields, is large – about 50 km long and very wide in places. Miskitos living in the villages around the lagoon make a living from the abundant fish, shrimp and lobster.

Places to Stay & Eat
At Laguna de Perlas village, travelers can find inexpensive lodging at *Miss Ingrid's*. The hospedaje, which is just a few rooms added onto the family home, also serves meals. Another option is *Aire Libre*, which also has its own restaurant. You might have luck reaching either of these hospedajes by calling the local Enitel office at ☎ 822-2762. There is also a restaurant in the village called *Relax*.

Getting There & Away
Pangas leave Bluefields every morning around 7 am for Laguna de Perlas; the fare is US$12. Slow cargo boats stop at Laguna de Perlas on their way to Puerto Cabezas. These boats have no fixed departure times, so inquire at the dock.

PUERTO CABEZAS
Population 19,713
Puerto Cabezas, on the northeast coast of Nicaragua, is the country's second most important Caribbean port. It's mainly a

NICARAGUA

fishing town, and there's nothing there of much interest to travelers except its inhabitants, who reflect an interesting mixture of indigenous and Hispanic cultures. The closest decent beach is two km north of town. The *Hotel Cayos Miskitos* is quite comfortable and has a nice patio; it charges US$8 for a single with shared bath. *Hotel El Viajante* charges about the same and *Hotel Rivera* a little less. There are two movie theaters and various places to eat.

Getting There & Away

Air La Costeña flies between Managua and Puerto Cabezas twice a day. Tickets cost US$50 one way and US$100 roundtrip. There is one La Costeña flight a day between Puerto Cabezas and Bluefields. Tickets are sold at the airport, two km outside of town. A taxi to the airport costs US$1.

Boat Cargo boats coming north from Bluefields via Laguna de Perlas stop at Puerto Cabezas. Check at the dock for details.

CORN ISLANDS
Population 4868

The Corn Islands (Islas del Maíz), about 70 km off the coast from Bluefields, are made up of two islands. The larger island is only about six sq km, and the other island, 18 km away, is only about 1½ sq km.

Like other islands near the Caribbean Coast, the Corn Islands were once a haven for buccaneers. Now, the islands (especially the larger one) are popular holiday spots, with clear turquoise water, white sandy beaches fringed with coconut palms, excellent fishing, coral reefs good for snorkeling and an unhurried, peaceful pace of life.

People on the islands are of British West Indian descent and speak English. Most live on the larger island, making a living from fishing, particularly lobster fishing. The islands were hit hard by hurricanes in 1988 and 1996, but have bounced back.

Places to Stay & Eat

On the larger island, *Hotel Morgan* and the *Playa Coco* have rooms starting at US$7 and US$10, respectively. The oceanside *Beach View*, with flush toilets and balconies, charges US$12 for doubles. *La Rotonda*, near the airport, has the best food for the best price. There are several little restaurants and two discos.

On little Corn Island, *Hotel Iguana* (fax in Bluefields: 822-2688; allow 10 days for delivery of the fax) has comfortable accommodations (flush toilets, solar power); cabins start at US$12, and campsites are also available. The hotel arranges boat excursions and rents snorkeling gear. Cheaper, more basic accommodations are available at *Brigid's*. The island has several comedores.

Except for seafood, meals are more expensive on the islands than on the mainland.

Getting There & Away

La Costeña flies between Managua and big Corn Island three times a day. Tickets cost US$55 one way and US$110 roundtrip. Those same flights stop first in Bluefields, where a roundtrip ticket to Corn Island runs US$34.

The only scheduled boat service to Corn Island is operated by Motonave Lynx leaving the Bluefields dock at 8:30 am on Wednesday and returning the next day (four hours, US$4.60). To get from the big to the little island, take an early morning water taxi (US$3 to US$6 per person) from Doña Coco's Wharf.

Costa Rica

Costa Rica is famous for its enlightened approach to conservation. About 27% of the country is protected in one form or another, and over 11% is found in the national park system. The variety and density of wildlife in the preserved areas attracts people whose dream is to see monkeys, sloths, caymans, sea turtles and exotic birds in their natural habitat. Some national parks have volcanoes, including Volcán Arenal, which erupts several times a day and is a spectacular sight.

Costa Rica has had democratic elections since the 19th century and is now one of the most peaceful nations in the world. Armed forces were abolished after the 1948 civil war, and Costa Rica has avoided the despotic dictatorships, frequent military coups, terrorism and internal strife that have torn apart other countries in the region. Costa Rica is the safest country to visit in Latin America.

But it is not only safe – it is friendly. Costa Ricans delight in showing off their lovely country to visitors, and wherever you go you will find the locals to be a constant source of help, smiles and information.

Facts about Costa Rica

HISTORY
Costa Rica has been strongly influenced by the Spanish conquest. The pre-Columbian cultures put up little and insufficient resistance to the Spanish. Few archaeological monuments remain, so our knowledge of

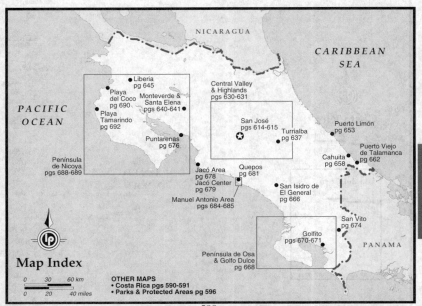

Map Index

0   30   60 km
0   20   40 miles

OTHER MAPS
• Costa Rica pgs 590-591
• Parks & Protected Areas pg 596

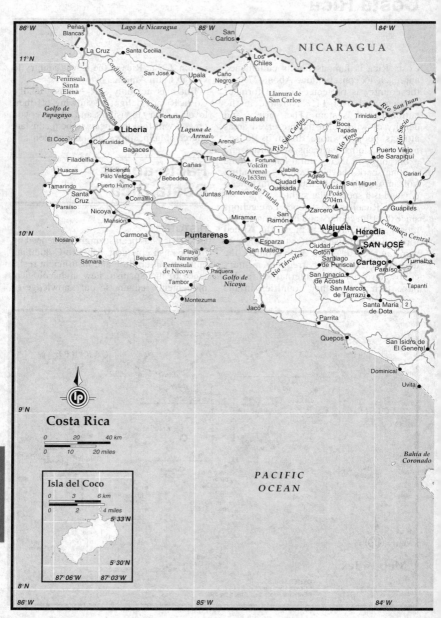

Costa Rica

Costa Rica's pre-Columbian history is scanty. Despite this, a visit to see artifacts at San José's Museo de Jade or Museo del Oro Precolombino is worthwhile.

The Spanish Conquest

The first European arrival was Christopher Columbus, who landed near present-day Puerto Limón on September 18, 1502, on his fourth (and last) voyage to the Americas. During his 17-day stay, he noted that some of the natives wore gold decorations. Because of this, the area was dubbed *costa rica* (the rich coast) by the Europeans, who imagined that there must be a rich empire lying farther inland.

The Spanish king, Ferdinand, appointed Diego de Nicuesa as governor of the region, and sent him to colonize it in 1506. The colonizers were hampered by the jungle, by tropical diseases and by small bands of indigenous peoples who used guerrilla tactics to fight off the invaders. About half the colonizers died and the rest returned home, unsuccessful.

Further expeditions followed, but they were unable to form a permanent colony, and many Spaniards died of hunger and disease. Meanwhile, the indigenous population was decimated by European diseases to which the natives had no resistance. In 1562, Juan Vásquez de Coronado arrived as governor and founded a colony in the central highlands. Cartago was founded in 1563, and the healthy climate and fertile volcanic soil enabled the colony to survive.

For the next 150 years the colony remained a forgotten backwater, isolated from the coast and the major trading routes and surviving only by dint of hard work and the generosity and friendliness that were to become the hallmarks of the Costa Rican character.

Eventually, in the early 18th century, the colony began to spread and change. Settlements were established throughout the fertile central highlands, including San José in 1737 and Alajuela in 1782. Much of Cartago was destroyed in an eruption of Irazú in 1723, but the survivors rebuilt the town. This expansion reflected slow growth

COSTA RICA

from within Costa Rica, but the colony remained one of the poorest in the Spanish Empire.

Independence

Central America became independent from Spain on September 15, 1821. Costa Rica was briefly a part of Iturbide's Mexican Empire, and then it became a state within the United Provinces of Central America. The first elected head of state, from 1824 to 1833, was Juan Mora Fernández.

Coffee was introduced from Cuba in 1808, and it was first exported during Juan Mora's term in office. The rest of the 19th century saw a steady increase in coffee exports, which improved Costa Rica's economy. Some of the coffee growers became rich and a class structure began to emerge. In 1849, a coffee grower, Juan Rafael Mora, became president and governed for 10 years.

Mora's presidency is remembered both for economic and cultural growth, and for a somewhat bizarre military incident that has earned a place in every Costa Rican child's history books. In June 1855, the American filibuster, William Walker, arrived in Nicaragua to conquer Central America, convert it into slaving territory and then use slaves to build a Nicaraguan canal to join the Atlantic and Pacific. Walker defeated the Nicaraguans and marched south.

Costa Rica had no army, so Mora organized 9000 civilians to gather what arms they could, and in February 1856, they marched north. In a short but determined battle at Santa Rosa, the Costa Ricans defeated Walker, who retreated to Rivas in Nicaragua, followed by the victorious Costa Ricans. Walker made a stand in a wood fort, and Juan Santamaría, a drummer boy from Alajuela, volunteered to torch the building, thus forcing Walker to flee. Santamaría was killed in this action, and he is now remembered as one of Costa Rica's favorite national heroes.

Despite his defeat, Walker returned to Central America several more times, unsuccessfully, before finally being captured and shot in Honduras in 1860. In the meantime, Mora lost favor in his country (he and his army were thought to have brought back cholera, which caused a massive epidemic in Costa Rica) and was deposed in 1859. In 1860 he led a coup against the government. The coup failed, and Mora was executed.

Democracy

The next three decades were characterized by power struggles among members of the coffee-growing elite. In 1889, the first democratic elections were held, although women and blacks were not allowed to vote. Democracy has been a hallmark of Costa Rican politics since then, with few lapses. One was between 1917 and 1919 when the Minister of War, Frederico Tinoco, overthrew the democratically elected president and formed a dictatorship. After opposition from the rest of Costa Rica and the US government, the dictatorship was ended and Tinoco was exiled.

In 1940, Rafael Angel Calderón Guardia became president. His presidency was marked by reforms supported by the poor but criticized by the rich. These included a recognition of workers' rights to organization, the introduction of minimum wages and a social security system. To further widen his power base, Calderón allied himself, strangely, with both the Catholic Church and the communist party to form the United Christian Socialist Party. This further alienated him from conservatives, intellectuals and the upper classes.

Calderón was succeeded in 1944 by Teodoro Picado, a United Christian Socialist who was a supporter of Calderón's policies, but the conservative opposition claimed the elections were a fraud. In 1948, Calderón again ran for the presidency, this time against Otilio Ulate. The election was won by Ulate but Calderón claimed fraud because some of the ballots had been destroyed. Picado's government did not recognize Ulate's victory, and the tense situation escalated into civil war.

Calderón and Picado were opposed by José (Pepe) Figueres Ferrer. After several weeks of civil warfare, over 2000 people had been killed, and Figueres emerged victorious. He took over an interim government, and in 1949 he handed over the presidency to Otilio Ulate of the Partido Liberación Nacional (PLN; National Liberation Party). The year marked the formation of the Costa Rican constitution, which is still in effect. Women and blacks received the vote, the army was abolished, presidents were not allowed to run for successive terms and a neutral electoral tribunal was established to guarantee free and fair elections.

Although there are over a dozen political parties, since 1949 the PLN has dominated, usually winning elections every other four years. Figueres continued to be popular and was returned to two more terms of office (in 1954 and 1970). Another famous PLN president was Oscar Arias, who governed from 1986 to 1990. For his work in attempting to spread peace through Central America, Arias received the 1987 Nobel Peace Prize.

The Christian Socialists have continued to be the favored party of the poor and working classes, and Calderón's son, Rafael Angel Calderón Fournier, has played a large role in that party, running for president three times. After two losses, he was finally elected president, succeeding Oscar Arias in 1990.

The 1994 presidential elections were narrowly won by PLN candidate José María Figueres (son of Don Pepe Figueres), who defeated Miguel Angel Rodriguez of the Partido Unidad Social Cristiana (PUSC; Social Christian Unity Party). He became the 51st president and, at 39, was Costa Rica's youngest president ever. Figueres had campaigned on a populist platform, promising improved healthcare and education, but his presidency has thus far proved unpopular. It has been marked by price hikes, tax increases and strikes.

A May 1996 poll showed that 50.2% of Costa Ricans felt that the president had been doing a bad or very bad job, while only 12.7% rated his work as good or very good. The government's economic policies were especially unpopular, with 76% of

people polled saying the economy was not well run and only 10% approving economic policies.

GEOGRAPHY

Costa Rica is bordered to the north by Nicaragua, to the northeast by the Caribbean Sea, to the southeast by Panama, and to the west and southwest by the Pacific Ocean. Costa Rica is an extremely varied country despite its tiny size of 50,100 sq km.

A series of volcanic mountain chains runs from the Nicaraguan border in the northwest to the Panamanian border in the southeast, thus splitting the country in two. The highlands reach 3820 meters, and changing altitudes play an important part in determining geographical and ecological variation. In the center of the highlands lies a plain called the *Meseta Central*, between about 1000 and 1500 meters. It contains Costa Rica's three largest cities, including the capital, San José. Over half of the population lives on this plain, which has fertile volcanic soils. Most of the mountains are volcanoes; some are active.

On either side of the volcanic central highlands lie coastal lowlands that differ greatly in character. The smooth Caribbean coastline is 212 km long and is characterized by year-round rainfall, mangroves, swamps, rain forests, an intracoastal waterway and sandy beaches. Tidal variations are small. The Pacific Coast is much more rugged and rocky, and the 1016-km-long tortuous coastline has numerous gulfs and peninsulas. The northwest coast is bordered by tropical dry forests that receive almost no rain for several months each year, as well as by mangroves, swamps, rain forests and beaches. The tidal variation is quite large, and there are many offshore islands.

CLIMATE

The dry season is from late December to April and is called *verano* (summer) by Costa Ricans – contrary to most Northern Hemisphere terminology. The rest of the year is rainy and is called *invierno* (winter)

COSTA RICA

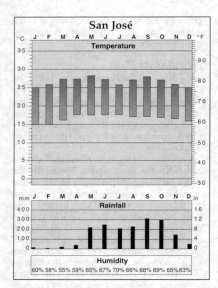

San José

°C J F M A M J J A S O N D °F

Temperature

mm J F M A M J J A S O N D in

Rainfall

Humidity
60% 58% 55% 59% 65% 67% 70% 66% 68% 69% 65% 63%

by the locals, although the tourist industry dubs it the 'green season' to attract tourists.

The Caribbean region is wetter than the rest of the country and the dry season has rainy days mixed with spells of fine weather. In the highlands the dry season really is dry, with only one or two rainy days per month. The north and central Pacific coastal regions have a similar rain pattern to the highlands, while the southern Pacific Coast can experience rain year-round, but with less falling in the dry season.

Temperature is mainly influenced by altitude. San José has average lows of 15°C and average highs of 26°C. The coasts are much hotter, with the Caribbean averaging 21°C at night and 30°C during the day, and the Pacific Coast averaging about 3°C higher than that.

ECOLOGY & ENVIRONMENT
The major problem facing the nation's environment is deforestation. Most of Costa Rica's natural forest has been cleared, mainly for pasture or agriculture. The UN Food and Agriculture Organization esti-

mates that between 1973 and 1989 Costa Rica's forests were lost at an average annual rate of 2.3%. Over the last decade, tree plantations have appeared and the availability of commercially grown timber means there is less pressure to log the forests. Nevertheless, deforestation continues at a high rate, and there is now very little natural forest outside of the protected areas. Even within national parks, some of the more remote areas have been logged illegally.

Deforestation has led to soil erosion. The topsoil is washed away, thus lowering land productivity and silting up watersheds. Some deforested lands become banana plantations, which use pesticides and blue plastic bags to protect the fruit. Both pesticides and bags end up polluting the environment.

From 1988 to 1993, the annual number of foreign visitors doubled. This tourism boom has led to controversy over how this rapidly growing industry should develop. There are those who want to bring in mass tourism and build huge hotels. Critics say that Costa Rica is simply not capable of handling any more tourists and that mass tourism would lead to severe environmental and cultural degradation, spoiling the country that people flock to see. Haphazard building and development, without adequate controls and a national master plan for the development of environmentally sensitive tourism, threatens Costa Rica today. The debate continues to rage at all levels.

FLORA & FAUNA
Costa Rica is a small country, yet its diverse habitats harbor some of the richest flora and fauna in the world. This biodiversity attracts nature-loving visitors from all over the world.

Flora
About 10,000 species of vascular plants have been described and more are added every year. Orchids alone account for some 1200 species, and about 1400 tree species have been recorded.

Three-quarters of Costa Rica was forested in the late 1940s; by the early

1990s under a quarter of the country remained covered by forest. To try to control this deforestation and protect its wildlife, Costa Rica has instigated the most progressive national park system in Latin America.

Mammals

Costa Rica has over 200 species of mammals. Visitors are likely to see some of the four monkey species found here. Other tropical specialties include sloths, armadillos, coatis, agoutis (large rodents), peccaries (wild pigs), kinkajous, raccoons, skunks, otters, foxes, squirrels and bats. Mammals such as ocelots, jaguars and tapirs are extremely rare to glimpse.

Birds

The primary attraction for many naturalists is the birds, of which some 850 species have been recorded – more than in any one of the continents of North America, Australia or Europe. Many birders want to see the resplendent quetzal – Monteverde is a good place to see them in season.

Over 50 species of hummingbirds have been recorded from Costa Rica. Other tropical birds include scarlet macaws and 15 other parrot species; six different toucans with their incredibly large and hollow bills; the huge and very rare harpy eagle, which is capable of snatching monkeys and sloths off branches as it flies past; and a large array of other tropical birds such as flycatchers (78 species), tanagers (50 species), antbirds (30 species) and many others.

Insects

At least 35,000 species of insects from Costa Rica have been described, and many thousands remain unnamed. There are thousands of butterflies, including the dazzling morphos with 15-cm wingspans and electric-blue upper wings. There are many ant species – a favorite is the leafcutter ants (genus Atta), seen marching in columns along the forest floor, carrying pieces of leaves into their underground colony. The leaves rot and support a fungus that the ants eat.

Amphibians

The approximately 160 species of amphibians include red, black, blue and yellow poison-arrow frogs. They have skin glands that can exude a toxin capable of causing paralysis and death in many animals if it is introduced into the bloodstream.

Reptiles

Some 220 species of reptiles are found in Costa Rica. About half are snakes, which are much talked about but seldom seen. Bright green basilisk lizards live near water – the males have huge crests along their head, body and tail, and reach almost a meter in length. The young are nicknamed Jesus Christ lizards for their ability to run across water. There are 14 species of marine and freshwater turtles. Marine turtles nest in large numbers on sandy beaches – a spectacular sight. The largest marine turtles are the leatherbacks, whose carapace (shell) can reach 160 cm in length and average a stunning 360 kg in weight. The smaller olive ridley turtles practice synchronous nesting, when thousands of females emerge from the sea on a single night.

National Parks

The national park system began in the 1960s. There are now about three dozen national parks and other protected areas in Costa Rica – about 13% of the land area. In addition, various buffer zones and forest reserves boost the total area of protected land to about 27%, but these buffer zones allow farming, logging and other exploitation, and are not fully protected. Also, there are dozens of privately owned lodges, reserves and haciendas that are set up to protect the land.

Not all of the protected areas are accessible to travelers. Some reserves are closed to everyone except researchers with permits. Indigenous reserves are for the few remaining tribes in Costa Rica and have almost no infrastructure for tourism. Most visitors stick to the main national parks and a few reserves that have trails and other facilities. Only these are mentioned in the text.

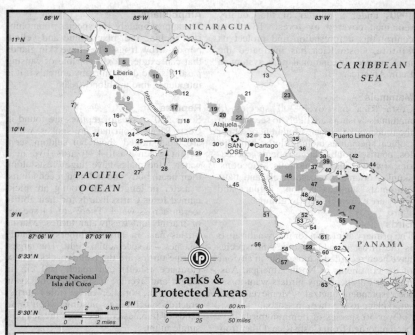

Parks & Protected Areas

COSTA RICA

1 Refugio Nacional de Fauna Silvestre Isla Bolaños
2 Parque Nacional Santa Rosa
3 Parque Nacional Guanacaste
4 Estación Experimental Horizontes
5 Parque Nacional Rincón de la Vieja
6 Refugio Nacional de Vida Silvestre Caño Negro
7 Parque Nacional Marino Las Baulas de Guanacaste
8 Reserva Biológica Lomas Barbudal
9 Parque Nacional Palo Verde
10 Parque Nacional Volcán Tenorio
11 Reserva Indígena Guatuso
12 Parque Nacional Volcán Arenal
13 Refugio Nacional de Fauna Silvestre Barra del Colorado
14 Refugio Nacional de Fauna Silvestre Ostional
15 Reserva Indígena Matambú
16 Parque Nacional Barra Honda
17 Reserva Biológica Bosque Nuboso Monteverde
18 Refugio Silvestre Peñas Blancas
19 Parque Nacional Juan Castro Blanco
20 Parque Nacional Volcán Poás
21 Estación Biológica La Selva
22 Parque Nacional Braulio Carrillo
23 Parque Nacional Tortuguero
24 Reserva Biológica de los Pájaros
25 Reserva Biológica Isla Guayabo
26 Refugio Nacional de Vida Silvestre Curú
27 Reserva Natural Absoluta Cabo Blanco
28 Reserva Biológica Islas Negritos
29 Reserva Biológica Carara
30 Reserva Indígena Quitirrisí
31 Reserva Indígena Zapatón
32 Parque Nacional Volcán Irazú

33 Monumento Nacional Guayabo
34 Parque Nacional Tapantí
35 Reserva Indígena Barbilla
36 Reserva Indígena Alto y Bajo Chirripó
37 Reserva Indígena Telire
38 Reserva Indígena Tayní
39 Reserva Biológica Hitoy-Cerere
40 Reserva Indígena Talamanca-Cabécar
41 Reserva Indígena Talamanca-Bribrí
42 Parque Nacional Cahuita
43 Reserva Indígena Cocles/KéköLdi
44 Refugio Nacional de Vida Silvestre
   Gandoca-Manzanillo
45 Parque Nacional Manuel Antonio
46 Parque Nacional Chirripó
47 Parque Internacional La Amistad
48 Reserva Indígena Ujarrás
49 Reserva Indígena Salitre
50 Reserva Indígena Cabagra
51 Parque Nacional Marino Ballena
52 Reserva Indígena Térraba
53 Reserva Indígena Boruca
54 Reserva Indígena Curré
55 Zona Protectora Las Tablas
56 Reserva Biológica Isla del Caño
57 Parque Nacional Corcovado
58 Parque Nacional Osa
59 Parque Nacional Corcovado (Piedras Blancas Sector)
60 Refugio Nacional de Fauna Silvestre Golfito
61 Reserva Indígena Coto Brus
62 Reserva Indígena Abrojo-Montezuma
63 Reserva Indígena Conte Burica

National parks information is provided by the public information office of the Servicio de Parques Nacionales (SPN; ☎ 257-0922), Calle 25, Avs 8 and 10, San José; it's open Monday to Friday from 8 am to 4 pm. SPN headquarters (☎ 233-4118, 233-4246, fax 223-6963), Apdo 10104-1000, San José, is also here. The SPN has a toll-free number (☎ 192) that provides up-to-date admission and other information Monday to Friday from 7 am to 5 pm. Recently, national park information was best obtained from the Fundación de Parques Nacionales (☎ 257-2239, 222-4732, 220-1744), Av 15 east of Calle 23, (300 meters north and 175 meters east of Santa Teresita church) in San José. Office hours are Monday to Friday from 8 am to 4 pm. Park information availability may change in the future, so call first.

National parks charge an entrance fee of US$6 per day plus US$2 for overnight camping per person. A few parks and refuges provide basic camping facilities or food and accommodations in ranger stations. Those most often visited by campers are Santa Rosa in northwestern Costa Rica (tropical dry forest, wildlife, beaches) and Corcovado in the Península de Osa (rain forest, wildlife). Cahuita and Tortuguero, on the Caribbean, and Volcán Rincón de la Vieja in northwestern Costa Rica are parks that allow camping but have very basic campsites. Others either have no campground or prohibit camping.

You can volunteer to work in the national parks – jobs vary from office work in cities to helping in remote areas. Volunteers pay US$5 to US$10 per day toward costs and make a two-month commitment. For an application, write to the Asociación Voluntarias de Parques Nacionales (☎ 222-5085), Apdo 10104-1000, San José.

GOVERNMENT

Government is based on the constitution of November 9, 1949. The president wields executive power, assisted by two vice presidents and a cabinet of 18 ministers. Elections are held every four years and an incumbent cannot be reelected.

There are seven provinces, each with a governor appointed by the president. Provinces are divided into 81 *cantóns* (counties) and subdivided into 429 districts. For every 30,000 people in each province, a congressional representative is elected to the Legislative Assembly every four years. This is where much of the power of Costa Rica's government lies.

The Legislative Assembly appoints 22 Supreme Court judges for eight-year terms. The Supreme Court selects judges for the lower courts.

Although there are about a dozen political parties, only two groups have been in power since 1949; the National Liberation Party or one of the Christian Socialist parties.

The vote is mandatory for all citizens over 18.

There is no army in Costa Rica. Instead, there are Rural and Civil Guards, which are a form of an armed police force totaling about 7500 members.

ECONOMY

Until the mid-19th century, Costa Rica was a very poor country with an economy based on subsistence agriculture. Then the introduction of coffee provided a product suitable for export. This was followed by bananas, and today these two crops generate the most export income for the country. Beef and sugar are also traditional agricultural exports, and in recent years, nontraditional products such as ornamental plants, pharmaceuticals, textiles, tires, furniture and others have become increasingly important. In 1993, exports were worth US$1.95 billion (over half went to the USA) and imports cost US$2.9 billion.

In Costa Rica, tourism has had an unprecedented boom. The number of foreign visitors rose from 376,000 in 1989 to 710,000 in 1993, when the value of tourism revenues was US$577 million, making tourism the single most important earner of foreign currency for the first time. Since then, the increase in tourism has begun to level off, but it still remains the country's biggest industry.

COSTA RICA

Inflation dropped steadily in the early 1990s, (27.3% in '90, 25.3% in '91, 16.9% in '92, 9.2% in '93). This is now changing, and inflation soared to 19.9% in '94, and preliminary figures for '95 (the only figure available at press time) indicate a further increase.

The standard of living is the second highest in Central America (after Panama). The economic growth of the country in 1992 was 7.3%, the highest total in almost a decade. In '93, growth was 6.5%, second only to Peru in Latin America. In '94, growth receded to 4.7%, which indicates a mid-'90s recession. In mid-'96, the minimum wage was US$146 a month, and average income was a little over US$200 a month. Unemployment is between 5% and 6%, but there is much underemployment.

POPULATION & PEOPLE

In 1997, the estimated population of Costa Rica is expected to reach 3.5 million. About 60% of the population lives in the highlands, and the annual growth rate is 2.3%. The country's population density is almost 70 people per sq km.

Most people are of Spanish descent. Less than 2% of the population is black, living mostly in the Caribbean region and often tracing their ancestry to immigrants from Jamaica, who built the railroads and worked the banana plantations in the late 19th century. Many blacks speak a dated form of English. They were actively discriminated against in the early 20th century, but since the 1949 constitution they have legally won equal rights.

Indians make up about 1% of the population. Small tribes include the Bribri from the Talamanca area in the southeast and the Borucas in the southern Pacific coastal areas.

Costa Ricans call themselves *ticos* (males) or *ticas* (females). Visitors are constantly surprised at the warmth and friendliness of the people.

EDUCATION

Literacy is over 90% – among the best in Latin America. About 20% of the national budget goes toward education. In 1993,

there were about 54,000 students in preschool, 485,000 in primary school, 160,000 in secondary school and 80,000 in higher education. There are six universities.

With compulsory education through ninth grade (age 14), the education system appears to be in good shape. However, there are problems that don't show up in the official picture. A recent Ministry of Public Education study reported in the Costa Rican press in mid-1996 indicates that there are six times more dropouts from secondary school than there are students in the final year of legally mandated study. This is blamed on various factors, including the need for a convenient secondary school, lack of interest by the students, lack of encouragement and a desire to enter the work force.

ARTS

There is very little indigenous cultural influence. Cultural activities have blossomed only in the last hundred years. Ticos consider San José to be the cultural center of the country, and it is here that the most important museums are found.

There are many theaters, and acting is one of the favorite cultural activities. The Teatro Nacional (National Theater) in the heart of San José is the venue for plays, performances by the National Symphony, ballet, opera, poetry readings and other cultural events. The Teatro Nacional building is also an architectural attraction in its own right and a highlight of any city tour of San José.

SOCIETY & CONDUCT

Costa Rican society is the least diverse of any Central American nation. The majority are of Latin descent and practice Roman Catholicism. Traditionally, Costa Ricans have prided themselves on being a classless society.

Despite the apparent homogeneity, societal differences exist. Historically, a small noble class led the colony's affairs, and since Costa Rica became independent, the descendants of three hidalgo families have provided the country with most of its presidents and congressional representatives.

COSTA RICA

Nevertheless, the politicians from the president down take pride in mingling with the public and maintaining some semblance of a classless society. The distribution of land and wealth is uneven, but less so than in other Central American countries.

Until 1949, the small black minority was actively discriminated against; blacks were not allowed to vote nor to travel into the highlands away from their Caribbean coastal homes. Now, racism is officially a thing of the past, and black travelers are unlikely to encounter problems in the main cities and on the Caribbean Coast, although some racist attitudes might still be encountered off the beaten path.

Indians, with very few exceptions, remain a marginal element of Costa Rican society, and little is being done to change this.

Appearances are important to Costa Ricans. They dress conservatively and act in an agreeable and friendly manner, which has become a hallmark of tico culture. A well-dressed appearance is strived for as much as possible. Despite their conservatism, they loosen up in certain settings. Flirtation and public displays of affection are often seen (but see Women Travelers in Facts for the Visitor). Neither Costa Rican men nor women wear shorts in the highlands; once you get down to the coast, beachwear can become quite skimpy, though nudity or toplessness is inappropriate (yet a few foreigners ignore this).

Prostitution is legal for women over 18. Professionals carry a card showing how recently they have had a medical checkup, though some women don't bother with these cards. Some sexually transmitted diseases can take weeks before they can be detected, so even an up-to-date health card doesn't guarantee that a prostitute is disease-free.

RELIGION

Over 80% of the population is Roman Catholic, at least in principle. Still, religious processions on holy days are less fervent and less colorful than in other Latin American countries. Semana Santa (Holy Week) is a national holiday in Costa Rica, and everything, including the bus system, stops from mid-Thursday until mid-Saturday. Buses run again on Saturday afternoon and Easter Sunday, but banks and many other businesses stay closed till Monday.

The blacks on the Caribbean tend to be Protestants, and most other Christian denominations have a church in or around San José. There is a small Jewish community.

LANGUAGE

Spanish is the official language, but English is understood in many hotels, airline offices, tourist agencies and along much of the Caribbean. Spanish courses are available in San José.

The following colloquialisms and slang are used in Costa Rica:

¡Adiós!
  Hi! (used when passing a friend in the street, or anyone in remote rural areas; also means 'Farewell' but only when leaving for a long time)
bomba
  petrol (gas) station
buena nota
  OK, excellent (literally 'good note')
chapulines
  a gang, usually of young thieves
chunche
  thing (can refer to almost anything)
¿Hay campo?
  Is there space? (on a bus)
cien metros
  one city block (literally 100 meters)
macho/a
  blonde person (male/female)
mae
  buddy (pronounced MAH-eh; mainly used by boys and young men)
mi amor
  my love (used by both sexes as a friendly form of address)
pulpería
  corner grocery store
pura vida
  super, far out (literally 'pure life,' can be used as an expression of approval or even as a greeting)
sabanero
  Costa Rican cowboy, especially from Guanacaste Province
salado
  too bad, tough luck

soda
cafe or lunch counter
tuanis
cool!
¡Upe!
Is anybody home? (used mainly in the countryside at people's houses, instead of knocking)
vos
you (informal, equivalent to 'tu')

Facts for the Visitor

PLANNING
When to Go
The dry season is considered the best time to visit Costa Rica. During this time beach resorts are busy; they are often full on the weekends and holidays, especially Easter week, which is booked months ahead. School vacations are from December to February.

Travel in the wet season may be difficult on the poorer roads, but there are fewer visitors and hotel prices may be lower, especially at the better ones.

Maps
An excellent map is the 1:500,000 sheet by International Travel Map Productions available around the world. Many more are available in Costa Rica.

What to Bring
Clothes of all sizes are available in San José, but shoes in sizes larger than 43 (10½ US) are hard to find. Tampons are available in Costa Rica but imported items are heavily taxed, so women should bring their favorite brand from home. The same applies to contraceptives. Bring insect repellent and strong sunblock, as only moderate blocking lotions (SPF 4 or 8) are easily found. For wildlife viewing, binoculars are recommended.

HIGHLIGHTS
Monteverde Cloud forests and the elusive quetzal, plus a chance to escape from the tropical heat!

Montezuma Beautiful beaches, nearby wildlife reserves and reasonably priced accommodations attract budget travelers from all over the world.

Parque Nacional Chirripó A sleeping bag, warm clothes and strong legs are all you need to climb Cerro Chirripó, the country's highest peak at 3820 meters.

Parque Nacional Corcovado Backpack and camp in pristine rain forest with Costa Rica's largest colonies of scarlet macaws.

Parque Nacional Santa Rosa The largest remaining tropical dry forest in Central America offers good camping and wildlife watching.

Parque Nacional Volcán Poás A short walk from the summit parking area takes you to the rim of the steaming crater.

Puerto Viejo de Talamanca This laid-back destination has an intriguing mix of Bribri Indian and black Caribbean culture.

Tortuguero A Caribbean village reached by inland waterways through a monkey-filled rain forest.

Volcán Arenal The most active volcano in Central America has spectacular lava flows and erupts every few hours.

Wilson Botanical Gardens The country's best botanical garden, in the south near San Vito, has comfortable, though pricey, lodge accommodations.

TOURIST OFFICES
For local tourist offices, see Tourist Offices under San José.

The Costa Rican Tourist Board (☎ (305) 358-2150, (800) 343-6332) maintains a US office: 1101 Brickel Ave, BIV Tower, Suite 801, Miami, FL 33131.

Citizens of other countries can ask their Costa Rican consulate for tourist information, or write to ICT in San José.

There are many web sites with travel

COSTA RICA

information on Costa Rica; see the Online Resources appendix.

VISAS & DOCUMENTS
Visas
Passport-carrying nationals of the following countries are allowed 90 days' stay with no visa: most western European countries, Argentina, Canada, Israel, Japan, Panama, Romania, South Korea, UK, USA and Uruguay.

Passport-carrying nationals of the following countries are allowed 30 days' stay with no visa: most eastern European countries, Australia, Belgium, Bolivia, Brazil, Colombia, Ecuador, Ireland, El Salvador, France, Guatemala, Honduras, Iceland, Liechtenstein, Mexico, Monaco, New Zealand, Sweden, Switzerland, Vatican City and Venezuela.

Others require a US$20 visa from a Costa Rican consulate. These lists are subject to change.

Visa Extensions Extending your stay beyond the authorized 90 or 30 days is a time-consuming hassle. It is easier to leave the country for 72 hours or more and then reenter. Otherwise go to the migración office in San José. Many travel agents in San José will take care of the red tape for you for a small fee. Tikal Tours in San José has been recommended.

Requirements for stay extensions include three passport photos, a ticket out of the country, sufficient funds to support yourself and maybe even a blood test to prove you don't have AIDS. Requirements change – allow several working days. It really is easier to cross the border to Panama or Nicaragua for a couple of days and then return.

If you overstay your 30 or 90 days, you need an exit visa from migración to leave the country. They require a form from the Tribunales de Justicia on Calle 17, Avs 6 and 8, San José, stating that you aren't leaving dependents in the country. You pay a fine of US$6 per month of overstay, plus a departure tax of US$50. The exit visa is valid for 30 days.

Children's Permits Children (under 18) are not allowed to stay over 30 days unless *both* parents request permission from the Patronato Nacional de la Infancia (National Child Protection Agency) on Calle 19 at Av 6 in San José. If a child is planning a stay of more than 30 days and will not be traveling with both parents, then obtain a notarized permit from the Costa Rican consulate of the child's home country.

Onward Ticket
Travelers officially need a ticket out of Costa Rica before they are allowed to enter. Most airlines will not let you board unless you have a return or onward ticket, or an MCO. In recent years, overland travelers have rarely been asked for onward tickets.

Passport
The law requires that you have your passport at all times. A photocopy of the pages bearing your photo, passport number and entry stamp will suffice for most purposes, but the passport should be in the hotel you are staying at, not in San José.

EMBASSIES
Costa Rican Embassies & Consulates
Australia
    30 Clarence St, 11th Floor, Sydney, NSW 2000 (☎ (2) 9261-1177, fax (2) 9261-2953)
Canada
    135 York St No 208, Ottawa K1N 5T4 (☎ (613) 562-2855, fax (613) 562-2582)
El Salvador
    See Foreign Embassies in El Salvador.
France
    35 avenue de Versailles, 75016 Paris (☎ (01) 40501274, fax (01) 40500961)
Germany
    Langenbachstrasse 19, 53113 Bonn (☎ (0228) 540040, fax (0228) 549053)
Guatemala
    See Embassies in Guatemala City.
Honduras
    See Foreign Embassies in Tegucigalpa and Foreign Consulates in San Pedro Sula.
Israel
    13 Diskin St No 1, Jerusalem 91012 (☎ (02) 666197, fax (02) 630777)
Italy
    Vía Bartolomeo, Eustacho 22, Interno 6,

Rome 00161 (☎ (6) 44251046,
(6) 44251042, fax (6) 44251048)

Nicaragua
See Foreign Embassies in Managua.

Panama
See Foreign Embassies & Consulates
in Panama City.

South Africa
PO Box 68140, Bryanston 2021, Johannes-
burg (☎ (11) 705-3434, fax (11) 705-1222)

Spain
Paseo de la Castellana 166, No 5, 28046
Madrid (☎ 345-9622, 345-9521,
fax 345-6807)

UK
Flat 1, 14 Lancaster Gate, London W2 3LH
(☎ (0171) 706-8844, fax (0171) 706-8655)

USA
2112 S St NW, Washington, DC 20008
(☎ (202) 234-2945, (202) 234-2946,
fax (202) 265-4795)

Other countries with Costa Rican embassies or consulates include Austria, Belgium, Colombia, Denmark, Finland, Japan,
Mexico, Netherlands, Sweden, Switzerland
and many others.

Foreign Embassies in Costa Rica

Most European countries and many non-
European countries have embassies in San
José. The smaller embassies seem to
change address quite often, so phone first.

The nearest Australian and New Zealand
consulates are in Mexico.

Canada
Oficentro Ejecutivo La Sabana, Edificio 5,
3rd Floor, behind La Contraloría,
Sabana Sur (☎ 296-4149, fax 296-4270)

Colombia
175 meters west of Taco Bell San Pedro,
Barrio Dent (☎ 283-6871, 283-6861,
fax 283-6818)

El Salvador
Av 10, Calles 33 and 35, Los Yoses
(☎ 225-3861, fax 253-5067)

France
200 meters south, 25 meters west of the
Indoor Club, Carretera a Curridabat (☎ 225-
0733, 225-0933, 225-0058, fax 253-7027)

Germany
200 meters north, 75 meters east of the
Oscar Arias residence, Rohrmoser
(☎ 232-5533, 232-5450, fax 231-6403)

Guatemala
100 meters north, 50 meters east of Pizza
Hut de Plaza del Sol, Curridabat
(☎ 224-5721, 283-2555, fax 283-2556)

Honduras
300 meters east, 200 meters north of ITAN,
Los Yoses Sur
(☎ 234-9502, 234-9504, fax 253-2209)

Israel
Calle 2, Av 2 and 4
(☎ 221-6011, 221-6444, fax 257-0867)

Italy
Calle 33, Avs 8 and 10, Quinta entrada de
Los Yoses (☎ 224-6574, 224-9415,
234-2326, fax 225-8200)

Nicaragua
Av Central, no 2540, Calles 25 and 27,
Barrio La California
(☎ 222-2373, 233-3479, fax 221-5481)

Panama
Calle 38, Av 5 and 7
(☎ 257-3241, 256-5169, fax 257-4864)

UK
Paseo Colón, Calles 38 and 40, Edificio
Centro Colón (☎ 221-5566, 221-5816,
221-5716, 255-2937, fax 233-9938)

USA
Carretera Pavas frente de Centro Commercial (☎ 220-3939, fax 220-2305)

CUSTOMS

Three liters of wine or spirits and 500 cigarettes or 500 grams of tobacco are allowed
duty free. Officially, you are limited to six
rolls of film, but this is rarely checked or
enforced. There's rarely a problem in
bringing in items for personal use.

MONEY
Costs

Travel costs are higher here than in most
Central American countries, but less than
in the USA or Europe. San José and the
most popular tourist areas are more expensive than the rest of the country, and the
dry season (December to April) is more
expensive.

Budget travelers will find the cheapest
hotels start at about US$3 or US$4 per
person for a box with a bed. Fairly decent
hotels with private bathrooms, hot water
and maybe air conditioning are US$10 per
person and up. Meals cost from about
US$2 and up. The cheaper set lunches

offered in many restaurants cost around US$2. The counter-lunch places, called *sodas*, have cheap meals. A beer will cost US$0.70 to US$3. Movie theaters charge up to US$2.50.

Transport is also cheap, with the longest bus journeys, from San José to the Panamanian border for example, costing about US$7. A taxi, particularly when you're in a group, isn't expensive and costs US$1 to US$2 for short but convenient rides.

A budget traveler economizing hard can get by on US$12 to US$20 per day. If you want rooms with private baths, meals other than set meals, expect to spend about twice that amount.

Currency

The Costa Rican currency is the *colón*, plural *colones*, normally written as ¢.

Bills come in 10, 20, 50, 100, 500, 1000 and 5000 colones, though the 10 and 20 colones bills are being phased out, and the 50 colones bill will follow. A 10,000 colones bill is planned. Coins come in 1, 2, 5, 10, 20, 25, 50 and 100 colones. The 2 colones coins will be phased out in the late 1990s.

Currency Exchange

For years the exchange rate has dropped steadily against the US dollar, although occasionally the value of the colón may rise sharply against the dollar. Prices are therefore given in US dollars throughout this chapter. A few major currencies can be changed in San José, but rates are poor, so bring your money in US currency. It's difficult to change currencies other than US dollars outside the capital. Therefore I don't give exchange rates for other currencies, as they are not practical.

Traveler's checks are usually exchanged at one or two colones lower than the rate for cash, so plan accordingly. The US dollar was worth 222¢ in February 1997, and it's increasing by almost 2¢ each month on average.

Banks can be slow in changing money. You stand in one line to have your transaction approved, then in a second line to actually get your money. Some banks will take only certain kinds of traveler's checks. American Express is usually good.

Banking hours are Monday to Friday from 9 am to 3 pm, or till 4 pm in San José. You'll need your passport when changing money. Travelers have reported that, when changing traveler's checks, they have been asked to show proof of purchase, so carry a copy of the receipt with you. Private banks (such as Banco Lyon, Banco Popular, Banex or Banco Mercantil) are often faster than national banks (such as Banco Nacional, Banco de Costa Rica) though the latter may have branches open later. In San José the Banco Nacional, Av 3, Calles 2 and 4, or the Banco de Costa Rica, Av Central, Calles 4 and 6, may be open longer still. The bank at the international airport is open weekdays from 8 am to 4 pm, and weekends and holidays from 8 am to 1 pm. Banks are closed on national holidays.

I found a few *casas de cambio* in San José that gave the same rates as the banks and provided faster service. Some hotels change money for their guests but rates vary.

Street changers are found in San José and at the land borders. They are mainly interested in US cash dollars, though traveler's checks can be negotiated. Street changing is technically illegal, but the authorities turn a blind eye. Count your money carefully before handing over your dollars. Rip-offs are common, so many travelers prefer to change money legally. Street rates are as good as the best bank rates.

If visiting small towns, change enough money beforehand. Changing large colones bills can be difficult in rural areas.

You can change excess colones back into dollars at the banks and the airport, but you may need to show your exit ticket and an exchange receipt before you can buy back dollars. A maximum of US$50 can be bought back.

Credit-card holders can buy colones and sometimes US dollars in some banks. Visa and MasterCard are both widely accepted, though not in budget places. Some places add a 7% surcharge if you pay a bill with a credit card. Visa cards can be used in a few ATMs, especially at Bancos Popular, but these are new and problems have been reported. Cards linked to currencies other than US dollars get abysmal rates, so don't use them.

If you need money sent from home, you'll find the main branches of San José banks will accept cash transfers but charge a commission. Shop around for the best deal.

Tipping

Better restaurants add 13% tax as well as a 10% tip to the bill. Cheaper restaurants might not do this. Taxi drivers are not normally tipped. If you take a guided tour, a tip of about US$2 per person per day is about right – if the guide does a good job!

POST & COMMUNICATIONS
Sending Mail

Airmail letters to the USA are about US$0.30 for the first 20 grams and US$0.40 to Europe or Australia. Parcels can be mailed from the post office, but are expensive and theft has been reported, so I don't recommend mailing valuables.

Receiving Mail

Have post restante mail sent to you 'c/o Lista de Correos, Correos Central, San José, Costa Rica.' Letters usually arrive within a week from North America; it's a little longer from more distant places. There is a US$0.25 fee per letter received. Avoid having parcels sent to you, as they are held in customs and cannot be retrieved until you have paid a duty equivalent to the value of the gift plus the value of the mailing cost.

Telephones

Public phones are found all over Costa Rica, marked with a telephone symbol. They accept coins of 5, 10 and 20 colones. Telephone numbers have seven digits, and you can call anywhere in the country from a public booth for under US$0.50 per three minutes. There are no area codes. In remote areas, operator-assisted radio telephones are used.

To call internationally, dial 116 on any phone for an English-speaking international

operator and ask for a collect (reverse charges) call. Some countries (for example the USA) with reciprocal agreements will accept collect calls, some won't. The party you call can call you back at the telephone you are calling from.

To pay for an international call, go to a Radiográfica or ICE office or to an operator-assisted telephone facility, such as a hotel telephone. Costs of calls per minute from Costa Rica are approximately US$2 to US$3 to North America, US$3 to US$4 to Europe and US$5 to Australia. Cheaper rates are from 8 pm to 7 am and during weekends.

About 30 countries have direct lines to an operator in that country, after which you can call collect or use your credit card. Consult a telephone directory.

If you are calling Costa Rica from abroad, use the international code (506) before the seven-digit Costa Rican telephone number.

Fax & Telex

Radiográfica and ICE offices also have telex and fax machines for use by the public. They will hold incoming faxes for 30 days.

BOOKS

There are several guidebooks to Costa Rica; look for Lonely Planet's guide to Costa Rica.

Birders will need the excellent and thorough *A Guide to the Birds of Costa Rica* by F Gary Stiles and Alexander F Skutch. Louise H Emmons' *Neotropical Rainforest Mammals – A Field Guide* describes and illustrates rain forest mammals throughout Latin America. *The Butterflies of Costa Rica and Their Natural History* by Philip J DeVries is recommended for lepidopterists. *The Quetzal and the Macaw* by David Rains Wallace describes the formation and development of the parks system; it's written for the general reader.

A book with a historical perspective on politics and social change in Costa Rica is *The Costa Ricans* by Richard Biesanz.

Look for the following books in Costa Rica. Two books written by former Peace

Corps volunteer Paula Palmer about the people of the south Caribbean Coast of Costa Rica are *What Happen: A Folk History of Costa Rica's Talamanca Coast* (Publicaciones en Inglés, San José) and *Wa'apin Man* (Editorial Costa Rica). *Taking Care of Sibö's Gifts* by Paula Palmer, Juanita Sánchez and Gloria Mayorga (Asociación de Desarrollo Integral de la Reserva Indígena Cocles/KéköLdi, San José) is subtitled 'An Environmental Treatise from Costa Rica's KéköLdi Indigenous Reserve.' This excellent booklet discusses the traditional Bribri lifestyle from the point of view of their natural surroundings. Book profits go to indigenous conservation and educational programs.

La Loca de Gandoca by Anacristina Rossi (EDUCA, San José) describes the struggle of a local conservationist trying to halt the development of a hotel in a protected area of the Caribbean Coast, as well as problems with corruption at various levels of government. Although the characters are imaginary and any similarity to reality is coincidental, local cognoscenti will tell you that remarkably similar events happened here recently. It's available locally and only in Spanish, but it's short and simply written, so it makes a good choice for someone who is interested in local conservation issues, even if their Spanish is limited.

Costa Rica – A Traveler's Literary Companion, edited by Barbara Ras (Whereabouts Press), is a fine collection of 26 short stories by modern Costa Rican writers. *There Never Was a Once Upon a Time* by Carmen Naranjo, translated by Linda Britt (Latin American Literary Review Press) contains short stories by a major Costa Rican writer.

Pura Vida: Gay & Lesbian Costa Rica by Joseph Itiel (Orchid House) is a source for gay and lesbian travelers.

NEWSPAPERS & MAGAZINES

The best local daily newspapers are *La Nación* and *La República*; both are fairly conservative. *La Prensa Libre* is an afternoon paper with a left-wing slant. The recommended English-language newspaper, *The Tico Times*, is published every Friday. *Esta Semana* is the best local weekly news magazine. Major bookstores in San José carry some US and other newspapers (two or three days late) and magazines such as *Time* or *Newsweek*.

RADIO & TV

There are six local TV stations (programming is poor), but many of the better hotels/bars also receive US cable TV.

Some of the over one hundred local radio stations broadcast in English. Radio 2 (99.5 FM) has news, rock favorites and a morning show from 6 to 9 am. For classical music, there's Radio Universidad (96.7 FM). Radio Paladin (107.5 FM) has bilingual coverage of world news and music.

FILM & PHOTOGRAPHY

Camera gear is expensive in Costa Rica and film choice is limited, so your favorite type of film may be unavailable. Film processing is not very good – although it's OK for simple snapshots.

In the rain forest you will need high-speed film, flash or a tripod. The light penetrating the layers of vegetation is surprisingly dim.

If you're making an international flight through San José airport, carry your films by hand, or use a lead bag. The X-ray machine there is vicious.

TIME

Costa Rica is six hours behind Greenwich Mean Time (GMT), the same as Central Standard Time in the USA. There is no daylight saving time.

ELECTRICITY

Electricity is 110V AC at 60Hz (similar to the USA). You will need a voltage converter if you want to use 240/250V AC-powered items. This definitely applies to Europeans.

LAUNDRY

There are a few self-service laundry machines in San José, charging about US$4 a load for washing and drying. Many cheap hotels will do your laundry for about US$1 for a change of clothes. Allow two or three days if it's raining and they can't be dried. If you want to wash clothes yourself, ask the hotel staff where to do it.

HEALTH

Costa Rica has one of the highest standards of health care and hygiene in Latin America. The authorities do not, at present, require anyone to have a current international vaccination card to enter the country, though you should make sure that your vaccinations are up to date.

You can drink tap water in San José and the major towns. In out-of-the-way places, especially in the lowlands, purify it or drink bottled drinks. Uncooked fruits and vegetables are best avoided unless they are peeled.

The social security hospitals in the major cities provide free emergency services to everyone, including foreigners. Private clinics are also available. For emergencies in San José, call the Red Cross (Cruz Roja, ☎ 128, no coin needed) for ambulances in the San José area. Outside the capital, the Cruz Roja has a different number in each province:

Alajuela	☎ 441-3939
Cartago	☎ 551-0421
Heredia	☎ 237-1115
Guanacaste	☎ 666-0994
Limón	☎ 758-0125
Puntarenas	☎ 661-0184

Also see Health in the front of this book, and see Dangers & Annoyances below for other emergency numbers.

WOMEN TRAVELERS

Women are traditionally respected in Costa Rica (Mother's Day is a national holiday!) but only recently have women made gains in the workplace. A female vice president (Victoria Garrón) was elected in 1986; Margarita Penon ran as presidential candidate in 1993. Women routinely occupy roles in the political, legal, scientific and medical professions, which used to be overwhelmingly dominated by men.

Despite this, Costa Rican men generally consider *gringas* to have looser morals and to be easier 'conquests' than ticas. They will often make flirtatious comments to single women, both local and foreign. Women traveling together are not exempt from this; women traveling with men are less likely to receive attention. Comments are rarely blatantly rude; the usual thing is a smiling 'mi amor' or an appreciative hiss. The best way to deal with this is to do what the ticas do – ignore the comments completely and don't look at the man making them.

Neither men nor women wear shorts in the highlands (unless actively jogging).

GAY & LESBIAN TRAVELERS

The situation for gay and lesbian travelers is poor, though better than in most Central American countries. Legally, homosexuality is not a criminal offense, and most Costa Ricans are tolerant at a 'Don't ask; don't tell' level. Despite legal protection and theoretical equality, police harassment in gay clubs and other locales has resulted in a string of human rights violations. People who come out publicly are discriminated against by employers and even their own families.

In 1992, Triángulo Rosa (☎ /fax 234-2411, net), the first legally recognized gay group in Central America, was founded to support human rights and promote education and information for the gay community, despite opposition from the political and religious establishment. They are helpful with local gay community information.

DANGERS & ANNOYANCES

There has been an increase in tourist-oriented crime recently, probably because there are many more visitors. However, you'll find Costa Rica is still less prone to crime and thievery than many countries. You should, nevertheless, take simple precautions, as recommended in the introductory chapters.

If you are robbed, police reports (for insurance claims) should be filed with the Organismo de Investigación Judicial (OIJ; ☎ 255-0122) in the Corte Suprema de Justicia (Supreme Court) complex at Av 6, Calle 17 and 19, in San José.

If you are caught in an earthquake, the best shelter in a building is in a door frame or under a sturdy table. In the open, don't stand near anything that could collapse on you.

Be aware of the dangers of rip tides on both coasts.

The general emergency number (☎ 911) is available in the central provinces and is expanding. Police (☎ 117) and fire (☎ 118) are, theoretically, reachable throughout the country.

BUSINESS HOURS & PUBLIC HOLIDAYS

Government offices are open Monday to Friday from 8 am to 4 pm, but they often close between about 11:30 am and 1 pm. Stores are open Monday to Saturday from 8 am to 6 or 7 pm, but a two-hour lunch break is normal.

There are no buses at all on the Thursday afternoon and Friday before Easter, and many businesses are closed during the week before Easter. From Thursday to Easter Sunday all bars are closed and alcohol sales are prohibited. The week between Christmas and New Year's Day tends to be an unofficial holiday, especially in San José, celebrated with bullfights, equestrian events and a dance on New Year's Eve.

The dates below are official national holidays when banks and businesses are closed throughout the country.

January 1
    New Year's Day
April 11
    Día de Juan Santamaría – honors the national hero at the Battle of Rivas against William Walker in 1856. Major events are in Alajuela, his home town.
May 1
    Labor Day – especially colorful around Puerto Limón

March or April
    Semana Santa (Holy Week) – Thursday and Friday before Easter
July 25
    Día de Guanacaste – annexation of Guanacaste Province, formerly part of Nicaragua
August 2
    Virgen de Los Angeles – patron saint of Costa Rica; a walking pilgrimage from San José to Cartago
August 15
    Día del Madre – Mother's Day; coincides with Catholic Feast of the Assumption
September 15
    Independence Day – children march in evening lantern-lit parades
October 12
    Día de la Raza – Columbus Day (discovery of the Americas), carnival in Puerto Limón
December 25
    Día de Navidad – Christmas

SPECIAL EVENTS
Additionally, various towns have celebrations for their own particular day.

March
    Día del Boyero – on the second Sunday ox cart drivers parade in Escazú
March 19
    Día de San José – St Joseph's day, patron saint of the capital
June 29
    Día de San Pedro & San Pablo (St Peter & St Paul)
Mid-July
    Fiesta de La Virgen del Mar (Fiesta of the Virgin of the Sea) – colorful regattas in Puntarenas and Playa del Coco
November 2
    Día de los Muertos (All Soul's Day)
December 8
    Immaculate Conception – a former national holiday

ACTIVITIES
The parks and preserves and their attendant wildlife and scenery draw travelers from all over the world. Outdoor enthusiasts will find many adventurous activities.

Hiking & Backpacking Parque Nacional Corcovado for rain forest backpacking, Santa Rosa for tropical dry forest camping

COSTA RICA

and Chirripó for highland hiking are some of the best trips.

Horseback Riding Wherever you go, you are sure to find someone giving riding tours or renting horses. Rates vary from about US$30 to US$90 a day and shorter (two hours), and overnight trips can be arranged.

Rafting *The Rivers of Costa Rica: A Canoeing, Kayaking, and Rafting Guide* by Michael W Mayfield and Rafael E Gallo might be useful. One-day trips on the popular Río Reventazón and the Río Pacuare including roundtrip bus transportation from San José and lunch start around US$69 per person.

Rain Forest Canopy Tours Canopy tours using ropes, cables and treetop platforms to tour the rainforest are US$45, US$35 for students with ID. Monteverde is the most popular place.

Scuba Diving & Snorkeling The water is warm and there is plenty of marine life, though visibility is often low. Good places for diving are at Playa del Coco, Playa Ocotal and Playa Hermosa, where you can do a couple of boat dives for US$60 per person. Beginners can learn to dive here. Snorkeling is popular in Manuel Antonio, Montezuma and Cahuita.

Sea Kayaking Several places along the coast rent sea kayaks. It's fun and easy to learn.

Surfing There are about three dozen recognized surfing areas, most of which have good waves and are uncrowded. Places in Jacó, Quepos, Tamarindo and Puerto Viejo de Talamanca rent boards.

Wildlife Watching Birding in Costa Rica is considered world-class. Most visitors also see monkeys, sloths, leafcutter ants, blue morpho butterflies, poison arrow frogs, crocodiles and iguanas, to name a few. The national parks are good places for observation, but private areas such as gardens around rural hotels can also yield a good number of birds, insects, reptiles and even monkeys. Early morning and late afternoon are the best times to watch for wildlife. Carry binoculars. An inexpensive pair from home will improve wildlife observation tremendously.

Have realistic expectations. It's hard to see wildlife in the rain forest because the vegetation is so thick. You could be 50 feet from a jaguar and not even know it is there. Walk slowly and quietly; listen as well as look.

Windsurfing Complete windsurfing equipment is available for rent in several hotels at the west end of Laguna Arenal, the best windsurfing area in the country. The pricey Hotel Tilawa has the best selection and location. The Rock River Lodge is also a good place.

LANGUAGE COURSES

Many schools in San José offer Spanish courses, and there are also schools in Heredia, Monteverde, Dominical and Manuel Antonio. Tuition is usually intensive, with class sizes from two to five per teacher and individual tuition available. Classes are given for several hours every weekday. Students are encouraged to stay with a Costa Rican family to immerse themselves in the language. Family homestays are arranged by the schools, and so are the necessary visa extensions.

Costs average US$300 a week with homestays or half that without. Many schools advertise in the *Tico Times* every week; see also the Online Resources appendix for online addresses of some schools.

ACCOMMODATIONS

There is a small youth hostel system that charges US$9 per night at the main hostel in San José and more elsewhere. It's cheaper to stay in a budget hotel. Cheap camping facilities are available in some national parks.

Beach hotel choice may be limited

during dry season weekends. Sometimes it's difficult to find single rooms. Rooms, often in hotels called *cabinas*, may have four to six beds and are a cheap per-person choice if you are traveling with a small group. In the text, I give high (dry) season (Christmas to Easter) rates. Expect discounts in the wet season.

Cheap hotels often lack hot water. Many hotels have electric showers that are not as dangerous as they appear! Hotels will advertise hot water – but if supplied by an electric shower, it's usually tepid.

Used toilet paper should be placed in the receptacle provided – the plumbing cannot handle the paper.

FOOD

The *casado* (see below) offered in most restaurants at lunchtime is cheap. Also try the cheap luncheon counters called sodas. There are reasonably priced Chinese and Italian restaurants in most towns. Better restaurants add a 13% tax plus 10% service to the bill – the cheapest don't.

Costa Rican specialties include:

gallo pinto – a mixture of rice and black beans that is traditionally served for breakfast, sometimes with *natilla* (a form of sour cream) or fried eggs. This dish is lightly spiced with herbs and is filling and tasty.
tortillas – either Mexican-style corn pancakes or omelets, depending on what kind of meal you're having
casado – a filling and economical set meal of rice, black beans, fried plantain, beef (or other meat or fish), chopped cabbage and maybe an egg or an avocado
palmitos – hearts of palm, usually served in a salad with vinegar dressing
pejibaye – a rather starchy-tasting palm fruit also eaten as a salad
arroz con pollo – a basic dish of rice and chicken
elote – corn on the cob

Traditional desserts include:

mazamorra – a pudding made from corn starch
queque seco – pound cake
dulce de leche – milk and sugar boiled to make a thick syrup which may be used in a layered cake called *torta chilena*

cajeta – similar to dulce de leche, but thicker, like fudge
flan – a cold caramel custard

The following are snacks, often obtained in sodas:

arreglados – little puff pastries stuffed with beef, chicken or cheese
empanadas – Chilean-style turnovers stuffed with meat or cheese and raisins
pupusas – El Salvadoran-style fried cornmeal and cheese cakes
gallos – tortilla sandwiches containing meat, beans or cheese
ceviche – seafood marinated with lemon, onion, garlic, sweet red peppers and coriander. It can be made with *corvina* (a white sea bass), *langostinos* (shrimps) or even *conchas* (shellfish).
patacones – a Caribbean specialty consisting of slices of plantain deep-fried like French-fried potatoes
tamales – boiled or steamed cornmeal which is stuffed with filling, usually wrapped in a banana leaf (you don't eat the leaf). At Christmas they traditionally come stuffed with chicken or pork, at other times of year they may be stuffed with corn and wrapped in a corn leaf. *Tamales asado* are sweet cornmeal cakes.

DRINKS
Nonalcoholic

Coffee, tea and herbal tea are easily found. The usual soft drinks are available. *Refrescos* are drinks made with local fruits. *Pipas* are green coconuts with a straw stuck in to drink the coconut 'milk' – a slightly bitter but refreshing and filling drink. *Agua dulce* is boiled water mixed with brown sugar, and *horchata* is a corn meal drink flavored with cinnamon.

Alcoholic

Costa Ricans like to drink, though they don't like drunks. Most restaurants serve a variety of alcoholic drinks. Imported drinks are expensive, but local ones are quite cheap. There are five local beers, which are all good. The local wines are cheap, taste cheap and provide a memorable hangover.

COSTA RICA

Distilled liquor is made from Costa Rican-grown sugar cane. The cheapest is *guaro* – the local firewater, drunk by the shot. Also inexpensive and good is local rum, usually drunk as a *cuba libre* (rum and Coke). A locally made coffee liqueur is Café Rica.

Many bars traditionally serve *bocas*. These are little savory side dishes designed to make your drink more pleasurable – maybe you'll have another one! If you had several rounds, you'd eat enough bocas to make a very light meal. Some bars charge a small amount extra for them and a few don't have them at all.

ENTERTAINMENT
San José has the expected cinemas, theaters, nightclubs and bars, but things are relatively quiet outside the capital.

SPECTATOR SPORTS
Fútbol (soccer) is the national sport, and Sunday games have a strong following of (mostly male) fans. No other sports, including baseball, compare to the popularity of soccer.

THINGS TO BUY
Coffee is excellent; many visitors take some freshly roasted coffee beans home.

Wood and leather crafts are well made and inexpensive. Wood items include salad bowls, plates, carving boards and other kitchen utensils, jewelry boxes and a variety of carvings and ornaments. Leatherwork includes the usual wallets and purses, handbags and briefcases.

Ceramics and jewelry are popular souvenirs. Some ceramics are replicas of pre-Columbian artifacts. Colorful posters and T-shirts with wildlife, national park and ecological themes are also popular.

Getting There & Away

AIR
Juan Santamaría international airport is 17 km outside San José and is the main international airport. There is a US$17 departure tax (depending on the exchange rate) on international flights from San José. This is payable in US dollars cash, or in colones.

The national Costa Rican airlines are LACSA and Aero Costa Rica. They fly from the USA to Costa Rica and other Central American countries. Because Houston, New Orleans and Miami are roughly north of Central America, they make the best gateway cities to Costa Rica.

A local agency specializing in student and youth fares is OTEC (☎ 256-0633, fax 233-8678), Calle 3, Av 3, San José.

LAND
Costa Rica shares land borders with Nicaragua and Panama. There are no problems crossing these borders, provided your papers are in order.

To/From Nicaragua
Via Peñas Blancas The main border post is on the Interamericana at Peñas Blancas in northwestern Costa Rica. The Costa Rican Oficina de Migraciones (☎ 679-9025) is next to the Restaurant La Frontera (☎ 679-9156, 679-9175). There are tourist information and bus ticket offices in this building. Opening hours are daily from 8 am to 5 pm on the Costa Rican side, till 4 pm on the Nicaraguan side. Lunch is from noon to 1 pm. It is four km between the Costa Rican and Nicaraguan immigration offices – minibuses charge about US$1 and there are taxis. Exit fees are reportedly US$0.75 to US$2 to enter or leave Nicaragua. It's US$0.75 for Costa Rica. There are no other fees to enter Costa Rica. (See the Nicaragua chapter for details of entering that country.)

Moneychangers at the Costa Rican post give good rates for US cash dollars, but traveler's checks receive worse rates in the border bank. Both colones and córdobas are freely available. Excess córdobas or colones can be sold, but at a small loss.

There are four or five buses a day to the first Nicaraguan city, Rivas (37 km). Get to the border by early afternoon to get on a bus, and watch your luggage – many cases of pilfering on Nicaraguan buses have been reported. Many nationals require a visa to enter Nicaragua – see that chapter or check with the Nicaraguan Embassy in San José.

Buses to Liberia and San José leave five times a day – the last in early afternoon. There are later buses to the first Costa Rican town, La Cruz, 20 km away.

Via Los Chiles This border crossing is rarely used by foreign travelers. It's reportedly hassle-free if your papers are in order.

Heading north from Los Chiles, a 14-km 4WD road goes to San Carlos, Nicaragua, a town on the southeastern corner of Lago Nicaragua. Boats on the Río Frío go from Los Chiles to San Carlos every day. Boats from here go on to Granada, Nicaragua.

To/From Panama
Panama's time zone is one hour ahead of Costa Rica.

Via Paso Canoas This crossing on the Interamericana is the major border point with Panama. Hours (subject to change) are 6 to 11 am, 1 to 5 pm and 6 to 9 pm daily, but there are no buses after dark. See Paso Canoas for more details.

US, Canadian, New Zealand, Australian and some European citizens require Panamanian visas (up to US$20). Visas are not available at the border. Check with the Panamanian consul in San José about current requirements. In Panama, a bus stop near the border has buses to David, about 1½ hours away. The last bus is at 7 pm. There is a Costa Rican consul in David.

Via Sixaola/Guabito This crossing is on the Caribbean Coast. See Sixaola for details of how to get there and basic hotels. The border is open 7 to 11 am and 1 to 5 pm daily, and frequent buses from Guabito go to Changuinola, Panama, where there is a hotel and onward connections.

SEA
Expensive cruises dock at Costa Rica, but there are no budget options for travel by sea.

Getting Around

AIR
Costa Rica's domestic airlines are SANSA and Travelair.

SANSA flies from the domestic terminal of Juan Santamaría airport. Services are with small aircraft (up to 32 passengers), and passenger demand is high, so book ahead. Baggage allowance is 12 kg. SANSA flies between San José and Quepos, Golfito, Puerto Jímenez, Palmar, Coto 47, Liberia, Tamarindo, Nosara, Carrillo, Tortuguero and Barra del Colorado.

Travelair flies from Tobías Bolaños airport in the San José suburb of Pavas, about five km from the city center. It uses smaller aircraft for flights between San José and the places above (except Coto 47) plus Jacó, Tambor and (starting in 1997) Fortuna.

SANSA demands full payment at one of its offices before a reservation can be confirmed. It's cheaper but has a reputation for delays and canceled flights. Travelair can be booked through any travel agent and has a better record for on-time flights, but it's a little more expensive. More details are given under the appropriate towns.

Tobías Bolaños airport also has light planes (three to five passengers) for charter to anywhere in Costa Rica for about US$300 per hour.

BUS
San José is the transportation center for the whole country. There is no central bus terminal in the capital, though some smaller towns have one. Larger companies with terminals sell tickets in advance. Smaller companies with just a bus stop expect you to queue for the next bus, but normally there is room for everyone. The exception is the days before and after a major holiday, especially Easter, when buses are ridiculously full. I have resorted to hitching in these cases. Friday nights and Saturday mornings out of San José can be very

crowded, as can Sunday afternoons and evenings coming back.

Buses are of two types: *directo* and *normal*, or *corriente*. The direct buses are faster and about a quarter more expensive. Luggage space is limited, so leave what you don't need in San José. If you have to check luggage, watch that it gets loaded on the bus and that it isn't 'accidentally' given to the wrong passenger at intermediate stops. Trips over four hours have a rest stop – there are no toilets on buses.

The ICT tourist office in San José has a current listing of many bus departures.

Local buses serve urban and suburban areas and a few other towns. There are no bus maps, so ask locals for information. Many towns are small enough that it's easier to walk where you want to go.

TAXI

Taxis serve remote parts of the country as well as city streets. Most small towns have 4WD taxis to surrounding areas. Public buses do not go to all national parks – a taxi for a day trip may cost about US$50 to US$70.

CAR & MOTORCYCLE

Most car rental agencies are in San José. Car rental is expensive, about US$300 per week during the high season for the smallest car without air conditioning, over US$400 for a small air-conditioned jeep. This includes mandatory insurance and unlimited mileage. The insurance usually requires you to pay for the first US$750 of any damage. Rental agencies insist you rent a 4WD vehicle to drive on dirt roads in the wet season. Cheaper rates are offered privately in newspaper ads – but there is no back-up if things go wrong.

To rent a car you need a valid driver's license, a major credit card and your passport. Your driver's license from home is acceptable for up to 90 days. Most companies won't rent to drivers under 25. (Ada Rent-a-Car claims to have a minimum of 18 years; American, Pilot and U-Haul claim 21 years and Adobe 23 years.) Some companies take a $700 deposit instead of a credit card.

Carefully inspect rented cars for minor damage and ensure it is noted on the rental agreement. Never leave valuables in sight even when you briefly leave the car, and always use a guarded parking lot at night and remove all your luggage.

Motorcycles can be rented in San José and along the coast – they cost about US$200 a week.

Fuel costs about US$0.45 per liter (US$1.70 per US gallon) and costs the same at all fuel stations.

Driving in San José is not recommended because of the crowded one-way system on narrow streets. Outside the capital, roads are narrow, steep and winding – drive very carefully. Speed limits are 80 km/h on primary roads and 60 km/h on others. Traffic police use radar and enforce speed limits. It is illegal to drive without using seat belts.

BICYCLE

There are no bike lanes and traffic can be hazardous on the narrow, steep and winding roads. However, touring cyclists report that locals are very friendly. There are bike shops in San José.

HITCHHIKING

Hitchhiking is not common, especially on main roads that have frequent buses. On minor rural roads, hitching is possible. Vehicles pass infrequently and you should wave them down in a friendly fashion and ask for a ride. (Watch how the locals do it.) If you get a ride, offer to pay for it when you arrive: *Cuanto le debo?* (How much do I owe you?) Your offer may be waved aside or you may be asked to help with money for *gasolina* (gasoline, petrol).

I haven't heard a negative story about single women hitching, but nevertheless, discretion is urged. Talk to the occupants of the car to get an idea of their disposition; hitch from somewhere (a gas station, store, restaurant, police post) that you can retreat to if you don't like the look of your prospective ride. Hitch with a friend.

BOAT

Ferries from Puntarenas cross the Golfo de Nicoya several times daily for Playa Naranjo (cars and passengers) and Paquera (passengers) with bus connections to Montezuma.

A daily passenger ferry links Golfito with Puerto Jiménez on the Osa Peninsula.

Boats ply the inland waterway from Moín (near Limón) to Tortuguero. Motorized dugout canoes go from Puerto Viejo de Sarapiquí down the Río Sarapiquí toward the Nicaraguan border and from Los Chiles up the Río Frío to the Refugio Caño Negro.

ORGANIZED TOURS

See Organized Tours under San José.

San José

Population 330,000; metropolitan area 900,000

Compared with other Central American capitals, San José is more cosmopolitan, even North American in character. There are department stores and shopping malls, fast-food restaurants and blue jeans. It takes a day or two to get the real tico feel of the city. Perhaps the first sign of being in Costa Rica is the friendliness of the people. Asking someone the way will often result in a smile and a genuine attempt to help you out.

The city was founded in 1737, but little remains of the colonial era. Until the Teatro Nacional was built in the 1890s, San José was not a notable city. Today the capital boasts several excellent museums, good restaurants and a fine climate, which are San José's main attractions. Costa Rica's road system radiates from San José, and the capital is a good base from which to visit the rest of the country.

The city stands at 1150 meters in a wide and fertile valley called the Meseta Central. Inhabitants of San José are called joséfinos.

Orientation

The city center is arranged in a grid. The streets are numbered in a logical fashion, and you should learn the system because all street addresses rely on it. *Avenidas* (Av, or Avs) run east to west and *calles* run north to south. Avenidas south of Av Central have even numbers (Av 2, Av 4), while avenidas north of Av Central have odd numbers. Calles west of Calle Central have even numbers while calles east of Calle Central have odd numbers.

Street addresses are given by the nearest street intersection. Thus the address of the ICT tourist office is Calle 5, (between) Avs Central and 2. This is often abbreviated to C5, A Ctl/2, or C5, A 0/2. This system is used in many other Costa Rican towns.

Avenida Central becomes Paseo Colón west of Calle 14. The building on the north side of Paseo Colón, Calles 38 and 40, is known as Centro Colón and is a local landmark. Ticos use local landmarks to give directions or even addresses – an address may be 200 meters south and 150 meters east of a church, pulpería or radio station. Sometimes the landmark no longer exists, but because it has been used for so long it's known by all the locals. A good example is the Coca-Cola bus terminal – it used to be a Coke bottling plant. A city block is called *cien metros*, literally 100 meters, so if someone says '250 metros al sur' they mean 2½ blocks south regardless of the actual distance.

Information

Tourist Offices The ICT, or Instituto Costarricense de Turismo (☎ 222-1090, 222-1733 ext 277, fax 223-5452, net), Apdo 777-1000, San José, answers questions (in English!) and sometimes provides maps. Their office on the Plaza de la Cultura at Calle 5 and Av Central was recently closed for remodeling but should be open by the time you go. Meanwhile, their administration building on Av 4, Calles 5 and 7, provides information. For national park information, see that section in Facts for the Visitor.

Immigration The Oficina de Migraciones for visa extensions or exit visas is opposite the Hospital Mexico, about four km north

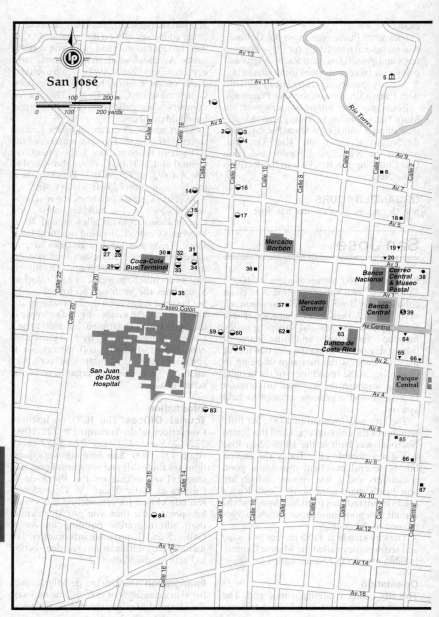

San José

0   100   200 m

0   100   200 yards

Av 13

Av 11

Río Torres

Av 9

Calle 18

Calle 16

Av 9

1

Calle 14

2

3

4

Av 7

Calle 12

Calle 10

Calle 8

Calle 6

Calle 4

Calle 2

6

14

16

18

Av 5

15

17

19

20

Mercado Borbón

Av 3

27 28

30 32 31

Correo Central & Museo Postal

38

29

Coca-Cola Bus Terminal

33 34

Banco Nacional

Calle 22

Calle 20

36

Av 1

35

Paseo Colón

37

Mercado Central

Banco Central

39

59 60

62

63

Av Central

61

Banco de Costa Rica

64

65 66

San Juan de Dios Hospital

Av 2

Parque Central

Av 4

83

Av 6

85

Av 8

86

Calle 16

Calle 14

Av 10

87

Calle 12

Calle 10

Calle 4

84

Calle Central

Av 12

Av 12

Av 14

Calle 16

Av 16

COSTA RICA

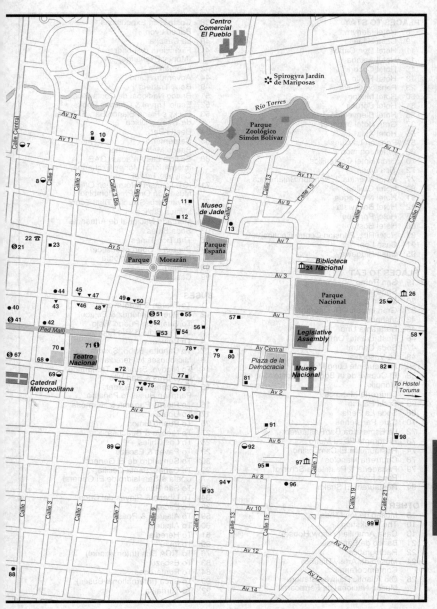

PLACES TO STAY
6	Hotel Marlyn
9	Casa Hilda
11	Hotel Don Carlos
12	Hotel Astoria
15	Hotel Cocorí
18	Hotel Rialto
23	Pensión Otoya
30	Hotel Musoc
31	Hotel Boruca
36	Hotel Bienvenido
37	Gran Hotel Imperial
56	Hotel Asia
57	Pensión La Cuesta
62	Hotel Johnson
70	Gran Hotel Costa Rica
72	Tica Linda
77	Hotel Avenida 2, Pensión Salamanca
80	Hotel Galilea
81	Hotel Nicaragua
82	Hotel Bellavista
85	Hotel Príncipe
86	Hotel Boston
87	Hotel Ritz, Pensión Centro Continental
91	Casa Leo
95	Casa Ridgeway

PLACES TO EAT
19	San Remo
20	Soda Nini
36	Meylin 2
37	Gran Imperial Restaurant
43	Vishnu
45	Naturama Uno
46	Restaurante Omni
47	Soda Central
48	La Vasconia
50	Restaurante Lung Mung
58	El Cuartel de la Boca del Monte
63	Mönpik
64	Churrería Manolos
65	Soda Palace
66	Soda La Perla
70	Café Parisienne
72	La Esmeralda Bar/Restaurant
73	Ristorante Pizza Metro
74	Restaurante El Campesino
78	Churrería Manolos
79	Panadería & Pastelería Schmidt, Pops Ice Cream
94	Restaurant El Shakti

OTHER
5	Museo de los Niños
10	The Bookshop
13	Casa Amarilla (Yellow House)
21	Banco de San José
22	Radiográfica
24	Museo de Arte y Diseño Contemporaneo
26	Old Atlantic Railway Station, Museo Nacional de Ferrocarril
38	Costa Rica Expeditions
39	Banco Lyon
40	La Casona
41	Financiera de Londres (Money Exchange)
42	Lehmann's
44	Adventure Land
49	Book Traders
51	Banco Nacional de Costa Rica
52	Ecole Travel & Chispas Books
53	Lucky's Piano Blanco Bar, El Túnel de Tiempo Disco
54	Beatle Bar
55	Serpentario
67	Banco Metropolitano
68	Edificio Las Arcadas (GAB International Money Exchange, Calypso Tours)
71	ICT Tourism Information Office, Museo de Oro Precolombino
75	Lavandería Sixaola, Tikal Tours
88	Clínica Bíblica
90	Mercado Nacional de Artesanía
93	Soda Blues
96	The Tico Times
97	Supreme Court of Justice, Museo de Criminología
98	Akelare
99	Casa Matute

BUSES
1	To Tilarán & Monteverde
2	To Puerto Jiménez & Bejuco
3	To Guápiles, Puerto Viejo de Sarapiquí & Río Frio
4	To Bejuco
7	To Cahuita, Bribri, Sixaola
8	Microbuses to Heredia
14	To Nicoya, Sámana, Tamarindo, Coto Brus & San Vito
15	To Nicaraguan Border, Panaline Buses to Panama
16	To Playas Panamá & Hermosa
17	To Upala
25	To Puerto Limón
27	To Nicoya & Beaches
28	To Los Chiles
29	To Pavas & Escazú
30	To San Isidro de El General
32	To Cañas, Santa Cecilia, Upala & San Isidro de El General
33	To San Ramón
34	To Liberia & Playas del Coco
35	To Escazú
59	To Alajuela & Poás
60	To Alajuela
61	To Heredia
69	To Irazú
76	To TICA Bus (International)
83	To Escazú
84	To Puntarenas
89	To Sirca (International Buses)
92	To Turrialba

COSTA RICA

of Parque La Sabana. Any Alajuela bus will drop you nearby. Hours are Monday to Friday 8 am to 4 pm, and lines can be long. Some travel agencies will do the paperwork for you and charge a small processing fee; Tikal Tours is recommended (see Organized Tours below).

Money Any bank will change US dollars into colones. Commissions, when charged, should be small (1% or less); otherwise, go elsewhere. Banco Nacional de Costa Rica and Banco de Costa Rica are very slow. The non-national banks give faster service.

Some recommended non-national banks include:

Banco Banex
    Calle Central, Av 1 (☎ 257-0522)
Banco de San José
    Calle Central, Avs 3 and 5 (☎ 256-9911)
Banco Lyon
    Calle 2, Avs Central and 1 (☎ 257-9511)
Banco Mercantil
    Calle 2, Av 3 (☎ 257-6868)
Banco Metropolitano
    Calle Central and Av 2 (☎ 257-3030)
Banco Popular
    Calle 1, Avs 2 and 4 (☎ 257-5797)

Each has many branches and there are many other banks.

Most banks are open Monday to Friday from 9 am to 3 pm. The Banco Nacional de Costa Rica at Av 1, Calle 7, is open Monday to Friday from 10 am to 5 pm.

There are a few exchange houses that give good rates, fast service and claim to accept foreign currency other than US dollars.

Companía Financiera de Londres
    Calle Central and Av Central
    (☎ 222-8155, fax 221-2003)
Especialides Electricas
    Av Central, Calles 5 and 7
GAB International Money Exchange
    in the Edificio Las Arcadas on Av 2,
    Calles 1 and 3; open Monday to Friday
    from 8:15 am to 4 pm.

After hours, moneychangers are a choice – they hang out around Av Central and Calle 2. Go with a friend and be careful of scams.

Post & Communications The Correo Central (central post office) is on Calle 2, Avs 1 and 3. Hours are Monday to Friday 8 am to 5 pm, and there is a stamp vending machine available 24 hours. This is the best post office at which to receive mail.

There are many public phones from which you can make international calls, either collect or with a telephone credit card. To make international calls for cash, go to Radiográfica (☎ 287-0087), Calle 1, Av 5. Hours are daily 7 am to 10 pm. Radiográfica also provides telex and fax services. ICE at Av 2, Calle 1, provides the same services. Telephone directories are available in hotels and at Radiográfica.

Travel Agencies There are over 200 tour operators recognized by the Costa Rica Tourist Board, with the majority in San José. Most tours are beyond the budget of most readers of this book, but a few reasonably priced options exist. Check Organized Tours below for agencies that can help with budget travel.

TAM (☎ 222-2642, fax 221-6465), Calle 1, Avs Central and 1, has been recommended for airline ticketing and general sightseeing.

Cosmos Tours (☎ 234-0607, fax 253-4707, net), Av 7, Calles 37 and 39, is good for airline reservations and hotel and tour bookings. Other agencies that readers have recommended for general travel and tours include Camino Travel (☎ 257-0107, 234-2530, fax 257-0243, 225-6143), Calle 1, Avs Central and 1, and Central American Tours (☎ 255-4111, 239-0291, fax 255-4216), with an office in the Cariari Hotel and friendly staff. Note that hotels and tours booked through these are not the cheapest ones.

Bookstores The Bookshop, Av 11, Calles 3 and Calle 3 bis, is in an attractive early-20th-century house and has a coffee shop and art gallery as well as guidebooks and books in English and Spanish. Chispas Books (☎ 223-2240), Calle 7, Avs Central and 1, has books in English and other languages and houses the budget travel agency

COSTA RICA

Ecole Travel. Lehmann's (☎ 223-1212), Av Central, Calles 1 and 3, has some books, magazines and newspapers in English and a selection of Costa Rican maps. Book Traders (☎ /fax 255-0508), Av 1, Calles 5 and 7, sells and exchanges new and used English books and magazines. Librería Francesa (☎ 223-7979), Calle 3, Avs Central and 1, sells French books.

Laundry There are few laundries in Costa Rica (though plenty of dry cleaners). Lavamás (☎ 225-1645), Av 8, Calle 45, is about US$4 per load for self-service wash and dry. Burbujas (☎ 224-9822), 50 meters west and 25 meters south of the Más x Menos Supermercado in San Pedro, has coin-operated machines. Nearby is Lava y Seca (☎ 224-5908), 10 meters north of the Más x Menos, which has drop-off laundry or dry-cleaning service.

Downtown, the Sixaola (☎ 221-2111), Av 2, Calles 7 and 9, charges US$4 a load (wash and dry) and has same-day laundry service. They claim to have been scrubbing since 1912.

Medical Services The free Hospital San Juan de Dios (☎ 257-6282) is centrally located at Paseo Colón, Calle 14. The best private clinic is the Clínica Bíblica (☎ 257-5252, 257-0466 for emergencies), on Av 14, Calles Central and 1. It has some English-speaking staff and is open 24 hours for emergencies. It carries out laboratory tests.

Emergency Call ☎ 911 for all emergencies. Call ☎ 128 for Red Cross ambulance, ☎ 118 for the fire department and ☎ 222-9330 or 222-9245 for the Policía de Transito (traffic police).

Dangers & Annoyances Take all the normal precautions you would in any large city – there are thieves and pickpockets. The area around Av 2 and the Parque Central has been the scene of many pickpocketing attempts, particularly later at night, so be careful (though I go there at night). A few readers have reported being mugged in the Coca-Cola area, and it's worth taking a taxi to and from bus terminals there at night.

Museo de Jade

This is Costa Rica's most famous museum, housing the world's largest collection of American jade. Many pieces are mounted with a backlight so that the exquisite translucent quality of the gemstone can be fully appreciated. There are also archaeological exhibits of ceramics, stonework and gold, arranged by cultural regions.

The museum (☎ 287-6034, 223-5800 ext 2584) is on the 11th floor of the Instituto Nacional de Seguros at Av 7, Calles 9 and 11. Hours are Monday to Friday from 9 am to 3 pm, and admission is US$2.

There is a good city view from here – bring your camera.

Museo Nacional

Housed in the Bellavista Fortress, the old army headquarters on Calle 17, Avs Central and 2, this museum (☎ 257-1433) shows Costa Rican archaeology, some jade and gold, colonial furniture and costumes, colonial and religious art, historical exhibits and natural history displays. Some pieces are labeled in English as well as Spanish. There is a garden with cannons; some of the walls are pockmarked with bullet holes from the 1948 civil war. There's a gift shop. Hours are Tuesday to Saturday 8:30 am to 4:30 pm, and Sunday and holidays 9 am to 4:30 pm. Admission is US$1; students with ID and children under 10 free.

Museo de Oro Precolombino

This houses a dazzling collection of pre-Columbian gold, a small numismatic museum and a display of Costa Rican art. The museum (☎ 223-0528) is next to the ICT on Calle 5, Avs Central and 2. Hours are Tuesday to Saturday 10 am to 4:30 pm, and admission is US$5, for students with ID US$1.50. Security is tight: You must leave your bags at the door.

Museo de Arte Costarricense

This small museum houses a collection of local paintings and sculpture from the 19th and 20th centuries. The sculptures are especially worth a look. There are also changing shows of work by local artists.

The museum (☎ 222-7155) is in Sabana Park, which used to be San José's airport. The collection is housed in the old airport terminal just off Calle 42, Paseo Colón and Av 2. Hours are Tuesday to Sunday 10 am to 5 pm. Admission is US$2, free to children and students with ID. Everyone gets in free on Sunday.

Museo de Arte y Diseño Contemporaneo
This museum (☎ 257-7202) houses changing exhibits of work by contemporary Costa Rican artists. The museum is next to the National Library on Av 3, Calles 15 and 17. Hours are Tuesday to Sunday 10 am to 5 pm; free admission.

Serpentario
Live snakes and other reptiles, many native to Costa Rica, are on exhibit here with a bilingual biologist sometimes available to explain the collection. There is a small gift shop. The serpentarium (☎ 255-4210) is on Av 1, Calles 9 and 11. Hours are weekdays 9 am to 6 pm and weekends 10 am to 6 pm; admission is US$3.

Museo de los Niños
This children's museum (☎ 233-2734, 223-7003) is housed in the old *penitenciario* (penitentiary) at Calle 4, north of Av 9. The hands-on displays allow children to learn and experience science, music, geography and other things. Part of the old jail can be visited. There are exhibits about children's rights and lives in Costa Rica. Hours are Tuesday to Sunday 9 am to noon and 2 to 5 pm. Adult admission is US$5, with substantial discounts for children depending on age.

Parque Zoológico Simón Bolívar
This small national zoo (☎ 233-6701) is in the park of the same name. Many of Costa Rica's animals can be seen, along with a few exotics. Some visitors have not been impressed with the conditions in which the animals are kept (though it's better than in some zoos). The gate is at Av 11, Calles 7 and 9 (go north on Calle 7 to get there). Hours are weekdays 8 am to 3:30 pm and weekends 9 am to 5 pm. Admission is US$1.

Museo de Ciencias Naturales
The natural history museum (☎ 232-1306) is in the old Colegio La Salle (high school) near the southwest corner of Sabana Park. This collection of stuffed animals and mounted butterflies is a resource to those wishing to identify species they may see in the wild. There are also paleontology and archaeology exhibits. Hours are daily 7 am to 3 pm (subject to frequent change); admission is US$1 (half price for students).

Museo de Insectos
This fine collection of insects is curated by the Facultad de Agronomía at the Universidad de Costa Rica. The museum (☎ 207-5318, 207-5647) is in the basement of the Artes Musicales building on campus. There are signs, or ask. Hours are weekdays 1 to 5 pm. Ring the bell to gain admission (US$1.50).

Spirogyra Jardín de Mariposas
This butterfly garden (not to be confused with a large, and much more expensive, butterfly farm in La Guacima) offers a close-up look at Costa Rican butterflies in a garden setting close to the city center. The garden is 100 meters east and 150 meters south of Centro Comercial El Pueblo. Spirogyra (☎ 222-2937) is open daily from 8 am to 3 pm. Admission is US$4.

Museo Postal, Telegráfico y Filatélico de Costa Rica
This philatelic museum (☎ 223-9766 ext 269) is upstairs in the central post office, Calle 2, Avs 1 and 3. Hours are weekdays 9 am to 2 pm; free.

Museo de Criminología
The stated objective of the criminological museum (☎ 223-0666 ext 2378) is the prevention of crime through the presentation of exhibits of criminal acts. The display

reportedly includes such niceties as limbs that have been separated from their rightful owners by machete-wielding criminals. The museum is in the Supreme Court of Justice, Calle 17, Av 6; it's open Monday, Wednesday and Thursday from 1 to 4 pm.

Museo Nacional de Ferrocarril

See the first locomotive serving the San José-Limón run, as well as a model railway, old photographs and railroad paraphernalia. The museum is in the old Atlantic railway station at Av 3, Calle 19, and is open erratically.

Teatro Nacional

This is considered San José's most impressive public building. Built in the 1890s, it is the center of Costa Rican culture. The outside is not particularly impressive: a columned facade and statues of Beethoven and Calderón de la Barca (a 17th-century Spanish dramatist) flanking the entrance. Inside there are some paintings of Costa Rica, of which the most famous is a huge canvas showing coffee harvesting and export. (This painting is on the old five colón note, which street vendors outside will sell you for US$1 or US$2.) The marble staircases, gilded ceilings and parquet floors of local hardwoods are worth seeing.

Performances are held frequently and this is the best way to see the inside of the building. The cheapest seats are just a few dollars. Otherwise, it is open Monday to Saturday from 9 am to 5 pm, and it costs US$3 to visit.

Mercado Central

This is interesting to visit, although a little tame compared to the markets of other Central American countries. It is at Avs Central and 1, Calles 6 and 8. A block away is the similar **Mercado Borbón**, at Av 3 and Calle 8. Beware of pickpockets in these areas.

Parks & Plazas

The pleasant and shady **Parque Nacional** is between Avs 1 and 3 and Calles 15 and 19. In the park center is the Monumento Nacional showing the Central American nations driving out William Walker. Opposite the southwest corner is a statue of national hero Juan Santamaría. Important buildings surrounding the park include the Asemblea Legislativa (Congress Building) to the south, the Biblioteca Nacional to the north and the Fábrica Nacional de Licores (founded in 1856 and now housing an art gallery) to the northwest.

The small **Parque de España** has the tallest trees in San José and is a riot of birdsong just before sunset. On Sunday, there is an outdoor art market. The park is between Avs 3 and 7 and Calles 9 and 11. To the north is the Museo de Jade in the INS building fronted by a huge statue of 'The Family.' To the northeast is the Casa Amarilla, which houses the Ministry of Foreign Affairs.

Parque Morazán covers four city blocks and is graced in the center by the dome-roofed Templo de Música. The northeast quarter of the park has a small Japanese garden and a playground.

The **Plaza de la Cultura** is the site of the Teatro Nacional, Museo de Oro and ICT office. The west side of the plaza is an open-air market of arts and crafts – it's very busy just before Christmas. Young people hang out here and check out what everyone else is doing.

Parque Central is between busy Avs 2 and 4 and Calles Central and 2. This is the place to catch many of the local city buses. To the east is the fairly modern and not very interesting Catedral Metropolitana.

Parque La Sabana has tennis, volleyball and basketball courts, baseball areas and jogging paths. There's an Olympicsized swimming pool, but it's only open from noon to 2 pm, and it costs US$3 to swim there.

Organized Tours

See also Travel Agencies, above.

Ecole Travel (☎ 223-2240, fax 223-4128), Calle 7, Avs Central and 1, specializes in budget travel, especially to Tortuguero, but also to other destinations. 'Budget' means that you might stay in rock bottom-priced hotels and meals aren't included, but they get you there. Others running cheaper Caribbean canal cruises include Cotur (☎ 233-0155, fax 233-0778, net), Calle 36, Paseo Colón and Av 1 and Mitur (☎ 255-2031, fax 255-1946, net), Paseo Colón, Calles 20 and 22.

Companies specializing in river rafting include Ríos Tropicales (☎ 233-6455, fax 255-4354, net), Calle 32, Av 2; Aventuras Naturales (☎ 225-3939, 224-0505, fax 253-6934, net), Av Central, Calles 33 and 35; and Costa Rica Expeditions (☎ 257-0766, 222-0333, fax 257-1665, net), Calle Central, Av 3. Rafting tours start around US$65 a day and other (expensive) tours are offered.

Tikal (☎ 223-2811, 257-1494, fax 223-1916) Av 2, Calles 7 and 9, has a wide variety of tours ranging from day trips to week-long tours. I've heard that they are helpful with visa extensions.

Ecotreks (☎ 228-4029, fax 289-8191), in Escazú, specializes in adventure travel and equipment rental: mountain biking, scuba diving, snorkeling, kayaking. Canopy Tour (☎ /fax 257-5149, 256-7626, net), San José, has pioneered rain forest canopy tours near Monteverde and at Iguana Park near Orotina.

Adventure Land (☎ 222-3866, fax 222-3724), Av 1, Calles 1 and 3, is an agent representing several companies and can set you up with a wide variety of adventure tours.

Places to Stay – budget
Hostels The *Hostel Toruma* (☎ 234-8186, ☎ /fax 224-4085), Av Central, Calles 29 and 31, is associated with Hostelling International. Bunks in segregated dormitories are US$9 for HI members, US$12 for non-members. Hot showers are sometimes available and inexpensive meals are served in the cafeteria. There are laundry facilities, a message board, and information and reservations for other Costa Rican hostels can be made here. (Note that the San José hostel is by far the cheapest.)

The *Casa Ridgeway* (☎ 221-8299, ☎ / fax 233-6168), Calle 15, Av 6 bis, No 1336, is operated by Quakers. There is a small library and the center is staffed mainly by volunteers. Accommodations are US$8 per person in clean small rooms with four beds and individual lockers, or US$10/20 for a few singles/doubles. There are basic kitchen and laundry facilities, communal hot showers and quiet hours from 10 pm to 7 am.

Hotels Many budget hotels are found west of Calle Central. The area around the Coca-Cola bus terminal, Mercado Central and Parque Central has had reports of occasional thefts and a mugging. I've stayed in this area and haven't had any problems, but travelers should keep their eyes open and use taxis if arriving at night.

The basic *Gran Hotel Imperial* (☎ 222-7899), Calle 8, Avs Central and 1, is currently popular with shoestringers and international backpackers. This cavernous hotel provides security, reasonably clean beds, communal showers that have hot water once in a while and one of the best-value cheap restaurants in town. Rooms are US$4 per person (few singles), and they'll hold a room until the afternoon if you call ahead.

Another popular place is the (poorly signed) *Tica Linda* (☎ 233-0528), Av 2, Calles 5 and 7, next door to La Esmeralda Bar (where mariachis play late into the night). Ring the bell to get in. Cramped rooms sleeping four are US$4 per person; a private little box is US$5 per person. The place is noisy but friendly and secure, and it has laundry facilities.

Other basic places include the *Hotel Nicaragua* (☎ 223-0292), Av 2, No 1167, Calle 13. It is family-run, reasonably clean and secure. There are only cold water showers, and rooms are US$5/7 for singles/ doubles. The place is popular with travelers from other Central American countries. Nearby is the basic but clean and OK *Hotel Avenida 2* (☎ 222-0260), Av 2, Calles 9 and 11, which has communal hot showers and charges US$7.50/12. Nearby, the super-basic *Pensión Salamanca* charges US$3 per person in boxlike rooms and has cold showers only – perhaps the cheapest in town.

COSTA RICA

The *Hotel Rialto* (☎ 221-7456), Calle 2, Av 5, is decent, has hot water in the mornings and charges US$5/9 for a single/double, or US$13 for a double with a private washbasin and toilet. The very secure *Hotel Marlyn* (☎ 233-3212), Calle 4, Avs 7 and 9, charges US$6 for a small single with communal cold showers, or US$12 with private bath and hot water. The basic but secure *Hotel Asia* (☎ 223-3893), Calle 11, Avs Central and 1, charges US$6.50/10 for a single/double in small but clean rooms and has hot water in the communal showers.

The *Hotel Boruca* (☎ 223-0016), Calle 14, Avs 1 and 3, is convenient for buses but some rooms are noisy because of them. It is family-run, friendly, secure, clean and has hot water some of the time. Small rooms are US$6/11. The *Hotel Astoria* (☎ 221-2174), Av 7, Calles 7 and 9, is often full. Rates are US$8.50 for a double with communal hot showers and US$14 for a double with a private bath. A few cheaper rooms at the back are very basic and grim. The *Pensión Otoya* (☎ 221-3925), Calle 1, Avs 3 and 5, is clean, friendly, popular with foreigners and often full. Decent rooms are US$7/10 or US$10/13 with private bath and hot water.

The *Hotel Boston* (☎ 221-0563, fax 257-5063), Av 8, Calles Central and 2, has large rooms with private baths and tepid water for US$10/16 a single/double. The management is friendly. Ask for an inside room to avoid street noise. Note that nearby Calle 2 has a seedy red-light district, though the hotel is decent. Nearby, the *Hotel Príncipe* (☎ 222-7983, fax 223-1589), Av 6, Calles Central and 2, is secure and has good rooms with tepid showers for US$14/18.

The *Pensión Centro Continental* (☎ 222-4103), Calle Central, Avs 8 and 10, has kitchen facilities and tepid electric communal showers. Rooms are US$8/15 and US$4 per extra person, up to five people. One reader writes 'Beware of extra taxes on the bill.' Next door, under the same ownership, the midrange *Hotel Ritz* (☎ 222-4103, fax 222-8849) charges US$18/24 or US$21/29 with private bath-

rooms and hot water. Both are clean, friendly and popular.

The *Hotel Musoc* (☎ 222-9437, fax 255-0031), Calle 16, Avs 1 and 3, is convenient for the Coca-Cola bus terminal. The hotel is clean, has English-speaking staff and accepts credit cards. Rates are US$9.50/16, or US$12/18 in rooms with private hot showers. Be careful at night around the bus terminal area.

The *Hotel Johnson* (☎ 223-7633/827, fax 222-3683), Calle 8, Avs Central and 2, accepts credit cards and reservations, has hot water in the private showers and has reasonably sized rooms with telephone and use of the fax. Rates are US$16/18. Some rooms with TV will take up to six people for about US$30.

Places to Stay – middle

The friendly *Casa Leo* (☎ 222-9725), Av 6 bis, Calles 13 and 15, is US$8 per person in clean dormitories, US$12/22 in singles/doubles or US$15/25 with private bath. Hot showers, kitchen privileges and tourist information are available. The *Hotel Bienvenido* (☎ 233-2161, 223-0500, fax 221-1872), Calle 10, Avs 1 and 3, is secure, has helpful staff and good clean rooms with hot water sometimes. Rates are US$19/23. The *Hotel Bellavista* (☎ 223-0095; US reservations (800) 637-0899), Av Central, Calle 19 and 21, is friendly and clean, and has pleasant rooms with private baths and hot water for US$19/25. Their restaurant is good and cheap.

The *Hotel Galilea* (☎ 233-6925, fax 223-1689), Av Central, Calles 11 and 13, is clean, pleasant, helpful and near several museums. Students can get a discount. Rooms with private bath and hot water are US$25/30 – inside rooms are quiet. *Casa Hilda* (☎ 221-0037, fax 255-4028), Av 11, Calles 3 and 3 bis, is in a recently renovated house. Nice rooms with private bathroom and hot water are a good value for US$23/29. The owners are friendly, serve free coffee in the morning, and professional massage and tour services are available.

Pensión La Cuesta (☎ /fax 255-2896) Av 1, Calles 11 and 15, is an attractive house with plenty of artwork and a pleasant living room for hanging out. Eight simple but clean and pleasant bedrooms sharing communal baths rent for US$25/35 for a single/double including breakfast. The place has 24-hour security, is safe and friendly, has kitchen and laundry facilities and has received several readers' recommendations. The *Hotel Aranjuez* (☎ 223-3559, fax 223-3528), Calle 19, Avs 11 and 13, has rooms with private hot showers and TV for US$35 for a single or double. Rooms with shared bath start around US$15 a single. All rooms have phones with free local calls. The place is run by a friendly Costa Rican family who enjoy international guests and allow them to use the kitchen. There is plenty of parking.

Places to Eat

Budget The *Mercado Central* has several cheap eateries inside. It's a great place to eat elbow to elbow with ticos – plenty of atmosphere. Nearby on Av 1 are a variety of other cheap places. The area around the market is not dangerous, but it is a little rough and women may prefer not to go there alone.

The *Restaurant El Campesino* (☎ 255-1438, 222-1356), Calle 7, Av 2, is a pleasant place with a homey atmosphere. It serves roasted (not fried) chicken, at about US$2 for a quarter, as well as Chinese dishes.

La Vasconia, Av 1, Calle 5, is a cheap but decent place – I like it. A *pinto con huevo* (rice with beans topped with an egg) breakfast is about US$1 and a casado is under US$2. The clean *Restaurante Omni*, Av 1, Calles 3 and 5, serves a good set lunch from 11:30 am to 1:30 pm for about US$2.

The *Meylin 2*, attached to the Hotel Bienvenido, the *Gran Imperial Restaurant*, in the hotel of that name, and the *Toruma* in the Hostel Toruma are all inexpensive and open to the public. The Meylin 2 is surprisingly good for the price.

There are also plenty of US-style fast-food places.

Sodas These inexpensive snack bars are rather featureless, but they're popular with ticos looking for a cheap meal. They cater to students and working people, and some close on weekends.

A popular one is the *Soda Central*, Av 1, Calles 3 and 5, where the empanadas are good and you can have gallo pinto with egg for US$1.50 or casado for US$2. The cheap *Soda Nini*, Av 3, Calles 2 and 4, has both tico and Chinese food. The *Soda Magaly*, Av Central, Calle 23, has a good variety of meals under US$2. The *Soda Pulpería La Luz*, Av Central, Calle 33, is an old local landmark near the youth hostel and serves cheap but tasty snacks and small meals.

The *Soda Palace*, Av 2, Calle 2, and the *Soda La Perla*, Av 2, Calle Central, are open 24 hours. The Palace is a classic tico joint, particularly at night, and the Perla serves good food – these last two are a little pricier than the others.

Cafes & Coffee Shops These are good places for journal or letter writing. Prices are not necessarily cheap, but you don't have to buy much and can sit for hours. A favorite place is the *Café Parisienne*, the pavement cafe of the upmarket Gran Hotel Costa Rica, Calle 3, Av 2, where you get a good view of the comings and goings in the Plaza de la Cultura. Nearby, the Teatro Nacional has an elegant but simple little coffee shop, *Café Ruisenor*.

Churrería Manolos at Av Central, Calle Central and 2, and Av Central, Calle 9 and 11, is famous for its cream-filled churros (hollow doughnut tubes) as well as a variety of other desserts and light meals. The first location is especially popular, with a 2nd floor from which you can watch the people on the pedestrian-only street below. It's a popular breakfast spot. Nearby, *Panadería Schmidt* has two locations: on Av 2, Calle 4, and on Av Central, Calle 11. It's locally popular for cakes, pastries and breads for carry-out (though there are small eat-in areas).

Ice cream eaters should look for *Pops* and *Mönpik* for the best ice creams; each chain has several locations in San José and can be found outside the capital.

COSTA RICA

Vegetarian This isn't big in Costa Rica, but there are a few decent vegetarian restaurants. One is the *Vishnu* chain, of which the one at Av 1, Calles 1 and 3, serves a set lunch for about US$2.50 and is currently popular. You have to ask the waiter for prices. Other *Vishnus* are at Calle 14, Avs Central and 2, and at Av 4, Calle 1. *Restaurant El Shakti*, Av 8, Calle 13, has also been recommended. The newer *Naturama Uno*, Av 1, Calles 3 and 5, has a good three-course vegetarian lunch plus fruit drink for under US$3, as well as a good variety of other plates for US$1.50 and up.

For lunches only, but a good value, try *Don Sol*, Av 7 bis, Calles 13 and 15. A more upmarket macrobiotic restaurant is *La Mazorca*, 100 meters north and 25 meters west of the Banco Anglo in San Pedro.

Italian *San Remo*, Calle 2, Avs 3 and 5, serves pizza, Italian and tico food. It's popular for lunch. Also locally popular, the *Ristorante Pizza Metro*, Av 2, Calles 5 and 7, has pizzas and pastas in the US$5 range. Students eat at the lively *Pizzería Il Pomodoro*, 100 meters north of the San Pedro church and near the Universidad de Costa Rica. Two *Pizza Huts* are at Calle 4, Avs Central and 2, and at Paseo Colón, Calle 28. They have a salad bar.

Chinese The *Restaurante Lung Mun*, Av 1, Calles 5 and 7, has large Chinese lunches for not much over US$2. It's popular and there is sometimes a line to enter when they open at noon.

Entertainment

The free weekly leaflet *Info-Spectacles*, available at many of the places mentioned here and at the ICT office, has information on live music. *La Nación* has the best listing (in Spanish) of clubs, theaters, cinemas and more in its Viva section. The *Tico Times* has a weekend section that tends more to theater, music and cultural events.

Bars & Discos *El Cuartel de la Boca del Monte* (☎ 221-0327), Av 1, Calles 21 and 23, is a restaurant by day and a popular nightspot for young people. The music is sometimes recorded, sometimes live (on Wednesday especially), but always loud. The packed back room has a small dance floor – a good place to meet young ticos.

Casa Matute (☎ 222-6808), Av 10, Calle 21, became one of the city's trendiest nightclubs in 1995 and 1996. Live and recorded music, dancing, lounging, drinking, seeing and being seen occupy most nights in this three-story mansion. Friday nights, especially, have live acts, when a US$5 cover may be charged. Nights without live music are often free. The *Akelare* (☎ 223-0345), Calle 21, Avs 2 and 6, is in a huge mansion with a variety of bands playing usually on weekends.

Contravía (☎ 253-6989), 100 meters south of the Banco Popular in San Pedro, is popular with politically aware students for it's Nueva Trova music (folk music with a social theme) and *peñas* as well as rock and blues. *La Maga* (☎ 283-5040), Av Central, Calle 1 (100 meters east of the San Pedro church), is more avant-garde, with occasional theatrical, dance or musical performances, as well as foreign movie showings, a coffee bar/reading area and an art gallery. A block north is *Copas*, a lively student bar for talking, not dancing. *Club Cocodrilo*, Calle Central about 200 meters east of the San Pedro church, is a large bar with dance floor and videos, popular with university students. *La Villa*, 125 meters north of Cocodrilo, is a favored university-area bar in a great old house.

Well-known *La Esmeralda* (☎ 221-0530), Av 2, Calles 5 and 7, is open all day and night (except Sunday), and is the center of the city's mariachi tradition. At night there are dozens of strolling musicians around.

El Pueblo shopping center has a variety of pricey restaurants and nightspots – wander around on Friday or Saturday night and take your pick; some spots are cheaper than others. Several discos charge US$4 to get in. The best known is *Infinito* (☎ 221-9134) with three dance floors – one with salsa and reggae, another with rock and pop and a third with romantic music.

Discos downtown include *El Tunel de Tiempo*, Av Central, Calles 7 and 9, with flashing lights and music. *Dynasty* and *Partenón*, in the Centro Comercial del Sur near the Puntarenas railway station, have soul, reggae, calypso and rap. These have US$2 to US$4 covers. Cheaper is the *Salsa 54*, Calle 3, Avs 1 and 3, with Latin music and expert local salseros.

Popular bars include the *Beatle Bar* (☎ 257-7230), Calle 9, Avs Central and 1, with inexpensive beers and lots of ex-pats. Ticos like *Las Risas* (☎ 223-2803), Calle 1, Avs Central and 1, on two floors in an attractive older building. Upstairs there's a disco and in the bar there are rock videos. *Soda Blues* (☎ 221-8368), Calle 11, Avs 8 and 10, has occasional live blues or jazz. Also popular is *Río Bar & Restaurant* (☎ 225-8371), Av Central, Calle 39 in Los Yoses, with an outdoor verandah and occasional live bands. The *Sand Bar*, on Av Central in Los Yoses, in the shopping center just west of the fountain, is the loudest and most-dancing place for the latest rock and heavy metal.

Theater Theaters advertise in the local newspapers, including the *Tico Times*. Many performances are in Spanish, but prices are moderate.

The most important theater is the Teatro Nacional (☎ 221-5341) – the season is March to November, when there are National Symphony Orchestra concerts and other events every few days. There are fewer performances out of season. Tickets are cheap by US/European standards. There are several other theaters featuring music, dance and drama. Buy tickets as early as possible. Theaters rarely have performances on Monday.

Cinemas Cinemas advertise in the *Tico Times* and local newspapers. Recent Hollywood films with Spanish subtitles and English sound are about US$3.

Spectator Sports
International and national soccer games (the national sport) are played in the Estadio Nacional in Parque La Sabana.

Things to Buy
A recommended souvenir shop is in the Hotel Don Carlos, Calle 9, Av 9. The prices are good and the selection is wide. Other reasonably priced stores with good selections include the government-organized crafts cooperatives, such as CANAPI, Calle 11, Av 1, and Mercado Nacional de Artesanía, Calle 11, Avs 2 and 4. Also reasonably priced are Arte Rica, Av 2, Calles Central and 2, specializing in folk art, and ANDA, Av Central, Calles 5 and 7, specializing in pottery and gourd crafts produced by the few local Indians.

La Casona, Calle Central, Avs Central and 1, is a complex with a wide selection of items, including imports from other Central American countries. Malety, Av 1, Calles 1 and 3, specializes in leather goods, especially cases, handbags and wallets.

Mercado Central, Avs Central and 1, Calles 6 and 8, has a small selection of handicrafts, and it's also the best place to buy fresh coffee beans at a fraction of the price you'd pay at home.

Getting There & Away
Air Juan Santamaría international airport is between San José and Alajuela; for information call ☎ 441-0744.

Tobías Bolaños airport is in Pavas; for information call ☎ 232-8049 or 232-2820.

SANSA (☎ 221-9414, 233-3258, fax 255-2176) flies from Juan Santamaría airport to Quepos (US$30/60 one way/roundtrip), Barra del Colorado and Tambor (US$40/80), Nosara, Carrillo, Tamarindo, Coto 47, Golfito, Palmar Sur, Puerto Jiménez and Liberia (US$50/100). There are one to three flights a day to each of these.

SANSA can check you in at its city office (Calle 24, Paseo de Colón and Av 1) and provide transportation to the airport's domestic terminal, a few hundred meters to the right of the international terminal. SANSA reservations must be paid before they will confirm the booking. You should reconfirm several times – delayed, canceled or oversold flights are common.

Travelair (☎ 232-7883, 220-3054, fax 220-0413) is a newer, more expensive domestic airline. It has a better service record and flies from Tobías Bolaños airport. You can buy a Travelair ticket from any travel agent or from the Travelair desk at the Tobías Bolaños airport. A taxi is about US$3 from the city center – no buses.

Travelair charges roughly 60% more for a one-way flight than SANSA, though roundtrips are less than 50% more.

Charter flights are available on request from Tobías Bolaños airport.

The following international airlines have flights to/from San José (Juan Santamaría airport). Other airlines are listed in the telephone directory.

Aero Costa Rica
San Pedro (☎ 253-4753)
American Airlines (USA)
Av 5 bis, Calle 40 and 42 (☎ 257-1266)
Aviateca (Guatemala)
Calle 40, Av 3 (☎ 255-4949)
Continental Airlines (USA)
(☎ 296-4911, 296-5554, fax 296-4920)
COPA (Panama)
Calle 1, Av 5 (☎ 223-7033, 221-5596)
Iberia (Spain)
Paseo Colón, Calle 40
(☎ 257-8266, fax 223-1055)
KLM (Holland)
Sabana Sur (☎ 220-4111, fax 220-3092)
LACSA (Costa Rica)
Calle 1, Av 5 (☎ 296-0909, fax 232-3622)
LTU (Germany)
(☎ 234-9292)
Mexicana
Calle 5, Avs 7 and 9
(☎ 257-6334, fax 233-3667)
SAM (Avianca, Colombia)
Centro Colón (☎ 233-3066)
TACA (El Salvador)
Calle 40, Av 3
(☎ 222-1790, 222-1744, fax 223-4238)
United (USA)
Sabana Sur (☎ 220-4844, fax 220-4855)
Varig (Brazil)
Av 5, Calles 3 and 5
(☎ 257-0094, fax 257-0096)

Bus The Coca-Cola, Av 1, Calles 16 and 18, is a well-known landmark in San José. Many companies have buses leaving from within three or four blocks of the Coca-Cola, so this is an area to know. It is not in

the best part of town; watch for pickpockets. The area is reasonably safe, although late at night you might take a taxi.

ICT (see Information, above) has detailed bus information. Buses are very crowded on Friday evenings and Saturday mornings.

To/From Nicaragua & Panama International bus companies are used to dealing with border procedures and will wait for passengers taking care of formalities. They are a bit more expensive than taking a bus to the border and changing there, but they're convenient and worthwhile. For more on border crossings, see the Getting There & Away section above.

To Managua, TICA bus (☎ 221-8954), Calle 9, Avs 2 and 4, has daily buses at 6 am (11 hours, US$9). Buses continue to San Salvador, Tegucigalpa or Guatemala City. Cheaper but less reliable service to Managua is provided by Sirca buses (☎ 222-5541, 223-1464), Calle 7, Avs 6 and 8, on Wednesday, Friday and Sunday at 5 am.

To Panama City, TICA has a daily service at 6 am and 10 pm (20 hours, US$18). Panaline (☎ 255-1205), in the Hotel Cocorí at Calle 16, Av 3, has express bus service to Panama City daily at 2 pm (15 hours, US$21).

Service to Changuinola, Panama (Caribbean Coast), was planned by Panaline departing at 10 am. This has not yet been confirmed.

From Managua and Panama City to San José, the same companies have buses, but those fares are different because of currency regulations.

To David, in Panama, TRACOPA (☎ 221-4214, 223-7685), Av 18, Calle 4, has daily direct buses at 7:30 am (nine hours, US$7.50). TICA also has service to David.

To/From Southern Costa Rica To Ciudad Neily, TRACOPA (see earlier) has five daily buses (seven hours, US$5.50). These go on to the Panamanian border at Paso Canoas.

To Palmar Norte, TRACOPA has seven daily buses; to Golfito there are three daily buses (eight hours, US$4.75); and one bus to San Vito (direct, five hours, US$6.50; normal, six hours, US$5.50).

To Coto Brus, buses en route to San Vito leave four times a day from Empresa Alfaro (☎ 222-2750, 223-8361), Calle 14, Avs 3 and 5.

To San Isidro de El General, there are many buses (three hours, US$3) with Transportes Musoc (☎ 223-0686, 222-2422), Calle 16, Avs 1 and 3, next to the Coca-Cola terminal. Opposite, TUASUR (☎ 222-9763) also serves San Isidro.

To Puerto Jiménez, Autotransportes Blanco (☎ 771-2550), Calle 12, Av 9, has buses at 6 am and noon (eight hours, US$6.75).

To/From Meseta Central

Buses to Cartago (US$0.40) leave several times an hour from SACSA (☎ 233-5350), Calle 5, Av 18.

Some buses continue to Turrialba (two hours, about US$1), but more Turrialba buses leave from TRANSTUSA (☎ 556-0073), Av 6, Calle 13.

Buses to Heredia (☎ 233-8392) leave several times an hour from Calle 1, Avs 7 and 9 (30 minutes, US$0.30).

Buses for Alajuela leave every few minutes from TUASA (☎ 222-5325), Av 2, Calle 12 – many stop at the international airport. Across the street, buses leave for Heredia.

Buses to Grecia (one hour, US$0.40), and on to Sarchí (US$0.50) leave about once an hour from the Coca-Cola terminal.

Buses to San Ramón, halfway to Puntarenas, leave several times an hour from Calle 16, Avs 1 and 3, across the street from the Hotel Musoc.

To/From the Pacific Coast

Buses for Quepos and Manuel Antonio leave from the Coca-Cola terminal with Transportes Morales (☎ 223-5567). Direct buses to Manuel Antonio, with reserved seats, leave at 6 am, noon and 6 pm (3½ hours, US$5). Slower, cheaper buses to Quepos leave five times a day.

To Jacó, buses (☎ 232-1829, 223-1109) leave from the Coca-Cola terminal at 7:30, 10:30 am and 3:30 pm.

Service to Puntarenas is by Empresarios Unidos de Puntarenas (☎ 222-0064, 233-2610, 221-5749), Calle 16, Avs 10 and 12. Buses leave two or three times an hour from 6 am to 7 pm (two hours, US$2.40).

To/From the Península de Nicoya

The following are dry season schedules – during the wet season services may be curtailed.

Buses for the Península de Nicoya either use the Río Tempisque ferry or take the longer route through Liberia. Thus bus times can vary. Empresa Alfaro (see To/From Southern Costa Rica above) has seven daily buses to Nicoya (six hours, US$4), also going to Santa Cruz and Filadelfia. They have daily buses for beaches at Sámara (noon) and Tamarindo (3:30 pm), as well as a bus to Quebrada Honda, Mansión and Hojancha (2:30 pm).

To Jicaral and the beaches at Bejuco and Islita, a small office on Calle 12, Avs 7 and 9, has afternoon buses (five hours, US$5.50).

TRALAPA (☎ 221-7202), Calle 20, Av 3, has daily buses to Playa Flamingo (8 and 11 am), Junquillal (2 pm) and Santa Cruz (six daily, US$4.50).

To Playas del Coco, the Pulmitan bus station (☎ 222-1650), Calle 14, Avs 1 and 3, has buses at 8 am and 2 pm (US$3.50).

Buses for Playas Panamá and Hermosa leave daily at 3:20 pm from the stop in front of Los Rodriguez store, Calle 12, Avs 5 and 7.

To/From Northwestern Costa Rica

Buses to Monteverde leave from the Tilarán terminal (☎ 222-3854), Calle 14, Avs 9 and 11, at 6:30 am and at 2:30 pm (four hours, US$5). Advance purchase is recommended. Buses for Tilarán leave at 7:30 am, 12:45, 3:45 and 6:30 pm. The ticket office is closed from 12:30 to 2 pm.

Buses for Cañas with Transportes La Cañera (☎ 222-3006) leave five times a day from Calle 16, Avs 1 and 3. La Cañera has buses serving La Cruz and Santa Cecilia at 2:45 am and Upala at 6:30 am (6 am on Saturday). Upala buses also leave from Calle 12, Avs 3 and 5, at 3 and 3:45 pm daily.

Buses for Liberia leave eight times a day from Pulmitan (see above, 4½ hours, US$3).

To the Nicaraguan border at Peñas Blancas, there are three buses daily (six hours, US$4), with stops at the entrance to Santa Rosa national park and La Cruz. The office (☎ 224-1968) is next to the Hotel Cocorí, Calle 16, Avs 3 and 5.

To/From Northern Costa Rica Buses to Ciudad Quesada (☎ 255-4318; three hours, US$2) via Zarcero (one hour) leave every hour from the Coca-Cola terminal.

Direct buses to Puerto Viejo de Sarapiquí (3½ hours, US$3) leave from Calle 12, Av 9, six times a day. Some go via Río Frío and Horquetas (for Rara Avis) and return to San José via Varablanca and Heredia; some do the route in reverse. Buses for Puerto Viejo via Heredia leave at 6 am and noon from the Coca-Cola terminal.

Buses for Los Chiles (five hours, US$3.75) leave from Av 3, Calles 18, at 5:30 am and 3:30 pm.

To/From the Caribbean Coast Coopelimon (☎ 223-7811), Av 3, Calles 19 and 21, has hourly departures to Puerto Limón (2½ hours, US$3) via Guápiles.

For buses direct to Cahuita, Bribri and Sixaola, Autotransportes MEPE (☎ 221-0524, 257-0129), Calle Central, Avs 9 and 11, has departures at 6 am and 1:30 and 3:30 pm. The fare is US$5.75 to Sixaola and US$4.75 to Cahuita (four hours).

Some MEPE buses will detour to Puerto Viejo de Talamanca en route to Sixaola; there is a direct bus to Puerto Viejo at 10 am.

To Guápiles, Coopetragua (☎ 223-1276) or Empresarios Guapileños, both at Calle 12, Avs 7 and 9, have frequent departures with a few buses continuing to Río Frío. These buses pass the Parque Nacional Braulio Carrillo ranger station.

Getting Around
To/From the Airport Taxis from the international airport to San José cost US$10. Buses from Alajuela to San José pass the airport several times an hour from 5 am to 9 pm, and often have room for passengers. Fares are US$0.40.

Bus Local buses are useful to get into the suburbs and surrounding villages, or to the airport. They have set routes and leave regularly from particular bus stops downtown. Buses run from 5 am to 10 pm and cost from US$0.05 to US$0.30. There are too many to list here – ask at ICT.

Tram A new tram service is planned to begin operation in 1998 or 1999.

Taxi Taxi cabs are red and have a small 'TAXI' sticker in the windshield. In San José, taxis have meters (*marías*), which should be used; drivers may try to overcharge tourists by saying the meter is broken. (Outside of the city, fares are agreed in advance and taxi drivers are less likely to overcharge you.) Within San José fares are US$0.60 for the first kilometer and US$0.30 for each additional kilometer. The shortest ride costs about US$1. A ride across town is about US$2 or US$3. There is a 20% surcharge after 10 pm.

Central Valley & Highlands

The local name for this area is La Meseta Central. Historically and geographically it is the heart of Costa Rica. To the north, east and south the region is bounded by mountain ranges containing several volcanoes, including the famous Poás and Irazú. To the west, the Central Valley drops to the Pacific. Four of Costa Rica's seven provinces have fingers of land within the Central Valley, and all four have their political capitals there. About 60% of Costa Rica's population lives in the region.

Many visitors use San José as a base for day trips to the other cities and attractions of the area. Travelers pass through attractive, rolling agricultural countryside that is covered with the shiny-leafed green plants bearing the berries that made Costa Rica famous – coffee.

ALAJUELA
Population 172,000

This provincial capital is 18 km northwest of San José; it is 200 meters lower in elevation and has a slightly warmer climate. The international airport is 2.5 km southeast of Alajuela.

Things to See
Alajuela is the birthplace of the national hero, Juan Santamaría, for whom the international airport is named. He is commemorated by a museum and park in Alajuela. The small **Museo Juan Santamaría** (☎ 441-4775) is in a former jail northwest of the pleasant and shady Parque Central. Hours (subject to change) are daily except Monday 10 am to 6 pm; it's free. Two blocks south of the Parque Central is the **Parque Juan Santamaría** where there is a statue of the hero in action flanked by cannons.

Places to Stay
The *Hotel El Real* by the bus terminal is US$8 for a double, but not well recommended – 'much street life' as a local told me. The *Hospedaje La Posada* (☎ 442-7014, 442-9738), one block north and two blocks east of the Parque Central, charges US$8 per person with shared hot showers. Weekly rates are available.

The *Villa Real Hostel* (☎ 441-4022) is clean and friendly (English spoken) but has only cold water in the shared bathrooms. Rates are US$11 per person or US$13 with breakfast. Kitchen privileges are available and the place is popular with budget travelers.

The *Tuetal Lodge* (☎ 442-1804), four km north of the center, has camping (US$5 for one person and US$2 for each extra person). Solar showers, lockers, laundry and tent rental are available, and there is a restaurant. They have tree houses (US$9/12 for singles/doubles) and six cabins (US$30 single plus US$6 for each extra person).

Places to Eat & Drink
Most restaurants are near the Parque Central. The *Marisquería La Sirenita* has seafood dinners starting at US$3.50. The *Bar Restaurant La Jarra*, upstairs at the corner of Calle 2, Av 2, serves good typical food from about US$5 and has some tables on little balconies with views of the Parque Juan Santamaría.

For good inexpensive breakfasts, there's *Mi Choza*, Calle 1, Avs 1 and 3. Coffee and a variety of yummy desserts are the standby at the *Café Almíbar* (☎ 441-8434) on Av Central, Calles 1 and 3. *Mönpik* on the corner of the Parque Central has good ice cream and snacks.

Joey's, on the Parque Central, is a popular bar and restaurant serving burgers, beer and tico food. They have US sports on TV and live music on the weekends. By Joey's, *Kalahari Discotheque* has salsa and merengue. *La Troja*, Av 3, Calle Central, is a favorite of young people for live music.

Getting There & Away
To get to the airport, take a San José bus (US$0.40) and get off at the airport, or take a taxi (US$2) from the Parque Central.

Buses to San José leave from Calle 8, Avs Central and 1. Behind this stop is the Alajuela bus terminal, from where buses to other towns leave.

SARCHÍ
Sarchí is Costa Rica's most famous craft center. It is commercial and touristy, but there is no pressure to buy anything and there is the opportunity to see wooden handicrafts being made – ask around. The shopping area in the south part of town is modern but the north part of town is more attractive.

A few decades ago, the usual form of transport in the countryside was by *carretas*, gaily painted wooden carts drawn by oxen. The carreta is now a traditional craft and a symbol of agricultural Costa Rica. Nowadays, they are used to decorate people's gardens, scaled-down versions are made for use as indoor tables, sideboards and bars, and miniature models are used as

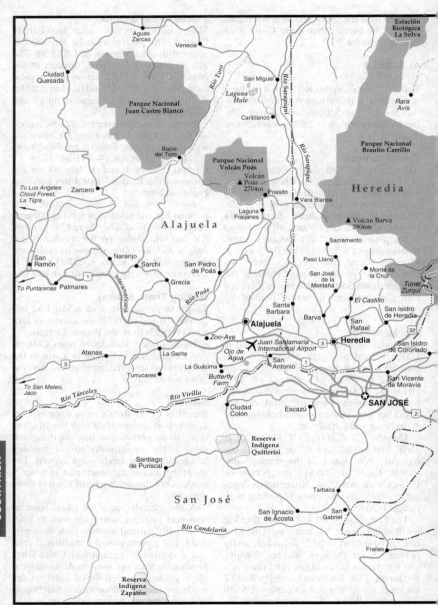

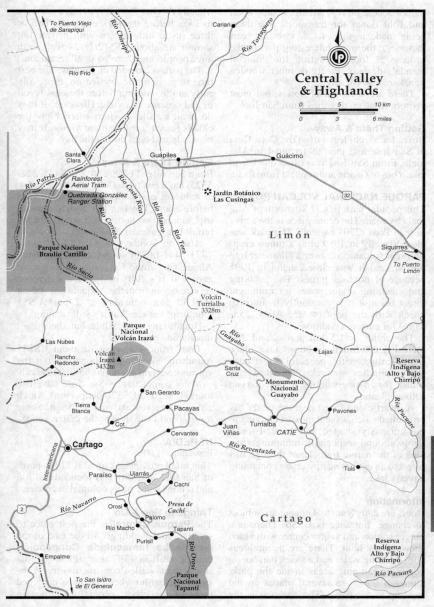

indoor accent pieces. All sizes come apart and fold down for transport. See them being made in *fábricas de carretas* (cart factories); the most interesting part of the process is locals painting the colorful mandala designs. Plenty of other wooden items are also for sale.

There are a couple of hotels, but most visitors come on day trips from San José.

Getting There & Away
Buses for Sarchí leave from the Coca-Cola in San José and the bus terminal in Alajuela. From San José it is often quicker to take a bus to Grecia and connect from there.

PARQUE NACIONAL VOLCÁN POÁS
This popular park lies 37 km north of Alajuela by road. The centerpiece is the active Volcán Poás (2704 meters). The park was closed briefly in 1989 after a minor eruption sent volcanic ash over a kilometer into the air, and it was closed again in 1995 because of noxious fumes. The bubbling and steaming crater poses no imminent threat because it is constantly monitored; check with the park (☎ 255-4104, 255-4116) for current conditions.

The crater is 1.5 km across and 300 meters deep. Small eruptions take place periodically, with peaceful interludes lasting minutes or weeks. This park is a 'must' for anyone wanting to peer into an active volcano.

A dwarf cloud forest near the crater has bromeliads, lichens and mosses clinging to the curiously shaped and twisted trees. Birds abound, especially hummingbirds. One of the nature trails leads through this forest to an extinct nearby crater containing a pretty lake.

Information
Hours are daily 8 am to 4 pm but are subject to change. Entrance is US$6. There is a ranger station and visitor center with video shows every hour. There are picnic areas with drinking water and a snack bar, but no hotels or camping areas inside the park, although there are several places on the road up to the park. (The cheapest is the friendly *Lo Que Tu Quieres Lodge* just over five km before the park entrance. Two or three rustic little cabins with private hot shower are about US$12/18/24 for one to three people, and there's a small restaurant.)

The park is crowded on Sunday. The best time to go is in the dry season, especially early in the morning before the clouds roll in and obscure the view. However, if they do, wait awhile – winds often blow the clouds back for intermittent views. It may be windy and cold during the day.

Getting There & Away
From San José, TUASA (☎ 233-7477, 222-5325) has a bus from Calle 12, Avs 2 and 4, at 8:30 am every Sunday. Get there well before 8 am. The fare is US$4.50 (round-trip, almost two hours each way), and the return bus leaves at 2:30 pm.

Also on Sundays, a TUASA (☎ 441-1431, 441-0631) microbus leaves from Alajuela's Parque Central at 8:30 am, or earlier if it's full. In 1996, a daily bus service began from the Alajuela bus station at 8:30 am, returning at 2 pm (US$5 roundtrip) but check if it's still running.

Hitchhiking is possible but there isn't much midweek traffic.

Taxis from Alajuela cost about US$35 roundtrip, allowing an hour to visit the volcano. Several people could share the cab.

Many companies in San José advertise tours (US$20 to US$70 per person), which arrive at the volcano about 10 am. Some tours spend little time at the crater, so ask.

HEREDIA
Population 74,000
This small provincial capital is 11 km north of San José. The city was founded in 1706 and retains some of its colonial character.

Things to See & Do
The **Parque Central** is the best place to see the older buildings. To the east of the park is **La Inmaculada Concepción** church, built in 1797 and still in use. Its squat, thick-walled construction has withstood the earthquakes that have damaged most of the other colonial buildings in

Costa Rica. To the north of the park is a colonial tower called simply **El Fortín**, which is a national historic site. At the park's northeast corner is the **Casa de la Cultura** with art and historical exhibits.

Universidad Nacional on the east side of town contains the **Museo Zoo Marino** (☎ 277-3240), open weekdays 8 am to noon and 1 to 4 pm; it's free.

Language Courses
These give the opportunity to stay near San José without being in the capital. Try the Centro Panamericano de Idiomas (☎ 265-6866, ☎ /fax 265-6213, net), in a suburb about a 10-minute bus ride from Heredia, or the Instituto de Lenguaje Pura Vida (☎ / fax 237-0387), Av 3, Calles 8 and 10.

Places to Stay
The basic *Hotel El Parqueo* (☎ 238-2882), Calle 4, Avs 6 and 8, at US$4.50 per person is friendly and clean enough but lacks hot water. The *Hotel Verano* (☎ 237-1616), Calle 4, Av 6, is similar at US$5 per person. The *Hotel Colonial* (☎ 237-5258), Av 4, Calles 4 and 6, is clean and family-run and charges US$7.50/12.50 for singles/doubles with fans. There are communal hot showers.

The clean *Hotel Heredia* (☎ 238-0880), Calle 6, Avs 3 and 5, changes US dollars and charges US$17.50/25 for singles/ doubles with private bath and hot water. Meals are available. The pleasant and attractive *Casa de Huespedes Ramble* (☎ 238-3829), Av 8, Calles 10 and 12, is US$30 for a single or double with private hot bath.

Places to Eat & Entertainment
Student bars and cafes near the university include the *El Bulevar* (☎ 237-1832) and *Restaurant La Choza* (☎ 237-4166). Nearby, *Restaurant Fresas* (☎ 260-4074) serves fairly typical meals in the US$4 to US$7 range and has an outdoor dining area. There are clean sodas in the market for inexpensive meals. *Restaurant Nueva Floresta* (☎ 237-0336) serves reasonably priced Chinese food on the south side of Parque Central.

For good ice cream and coffee, try *Azzura Heladería y Cafeterá Italiana* on the west side of the park.

Entertainment possibilities include the *Oceano Bar*, Calle 4, Avs Central and 2, with loud music and popular with students. *Miraflores Disco* reportedly has dancing to salsa and rock until 7 am (!) on weekends.

Getting There & Away
Buses to San José leave from bus stops near the Parque Central and market areas. The half-hour ride costs US$0.30.

Buses north for Barva leave from in front of the Cruz Roja on Calle Central, Avs 1 and 3. Buses to San José de la Montaña leave every hour from Av 8, Calles 2 and 4. At 6:30 and 11 am and 4 pm. These buses continue past San Pedro toward Sacramento for access to the Volcán Barva in the Parque Nacional Braulio Carrillo. Ask around the market for other destinations.

BARVA
This colonial village, 2.5 km north of Heredia, is a historic monument. It has a pleasant old-world ambiance and is fun to stroll around in. To the southwest is **Café Britt** (☎ 260-2748, net) which has 'coffeetours' for US$15 per person, including a visit to a finca, a bilingual multimedia presentation using actors to describe the historical importance of coffee, and a tasting session. Tours are at 9 am and 11 am.

PARQUE NACIONAL BRAULIO CARRILLO
This national park protects the virgin rain forest that was threatened by the new highway between San José and Puerto Limón. The pristine areas on either side of the highway support many plants and animals and no development is allowed. One reason there is such a huge variety of plant and animal life in Braulio Carrillo is the large range of elevations within the park, from 2906 meters at the top of Volcán Barva to less than 50 meters in the Caribbean lowlands.

Most people see the park by driving through on one of the frequent buses between San José and Limón. The difference between this highway and other roads in the Central Valley is marked: Instead of small villages and large coffee plantations, the panorama is one of rolling hills clothed with thick mountain rain forest. This is the way much of Costa Rica looked in the 1940s. Although there are a couple of ranger stations along this road, trails are very short, facilities are minimal and there is nowhere to park safely except at the ranger stations.

Hiking

Visiting the park from the Sacramento entrance near San José de la Montaña is the best way to go, especially if you want to climb Volcán Barva. Buses leave from Heredia. Ask the driver where to get off for Volcán Barva. There is a ranger station near Sacramento, which is open erratically. Rangers have been known to accompany hikers on the trail to the summit.

The trail up Barva from Sacramento is fairly obvious and there is a sign. From the road the signed track climbs to the summit, about four or five hours roundtrip at a leisurely pace. Near the summit there are several lakes. Camping is allowed anywhere you can pitch a tent, but no facilities are provided so you must be self-sufficient. The best time to go is supposedly the 'dry' season (December to April), but it is liable to rain then, too. Night temperatures can be below freezing.

RAIN FOREST AERIAL TRAM

This is on the right of the San José-Limón road, just after leaving the national park. The 2.6 km aerial tram has 22 cars, which each take five passengers and a naturalist guide. The tram is designed to go silently through the canopy and provide a unique view of the rain forest. It takes 90 minutes roundtrip, costs US$47.50 (five to 18-year-olds half price) and includes transport to the tram (over two km from the road), an orientation talk and use of trails before and after the tram ride. There is a small visitor center, restaurant and snack bar. This is an expensive but unique attraction. Call

☎ 257-5961 for information, or see their site on the Internet (see Online Resources appendix).

CORONADO

This is the general name for several villages centered on San Isidro de Coronado, about 15 km northeast of San José. It is a popular destination during the dry season for josefinos looking for an escape from the city. There are some simple restaurants but no accommodations. The village has an annual fiesta on May 15.

Instituto Clodomiro Picado

This snake 'farm' is at Dulce Nombre, about one km from San Isidro de Coronado. The university-run institute (☎ 229-0344, 239-3135, fax 292-0485) has a selection of local poisonous snakes on display. On Friday at 2 pm visitors can see the snakes being 'milked' for their poison, which is then used to make antivenin. Hours are Monday to Friday 9 am noon and 1 to 4 pm; it's free.

Getting There & Away

Buses for Coronado leave San José from Av 3, Calles 3 and 5. From San Isidro it's about a kilometer back to the institute – ask the bus driver.

CARTAGO

Population 120,000

Cartago was founded in 1563 and was the colonial capital until 1823. Major earthquakes in 1841 and 1910 ruined almost all the old buildings. The city is the capital of Cartago Province, and it lies at 1435 meters, between the Cordillera Central and the Cordillera de Talamanca. Volcán Irazú looms nearby. The city is 22 km southeast of San José; they're connected by a good road.

Churches & La Nigrita

The church, at Av 2, Calle 2, was destroyed by the 1910 earthquake, and **Las Ruinas** are now home to a pretty garden.

East of the town center, at Av 2, Calle 16, is the most famous church of the Central

Valley – **La Basílica de Nuestra Señora de los Angeles**. The story goes that a statue of the virgin was discovered on the site on August 2, 1635, and it miraculously reappeared after being removed. A shrine was built on the spot, and today the statue, La Negrita, represents the patron saint of Costa Rica. La Negrita has miraculous healing powers attributed to her, and every year on August 2 pilgrims arrive on foot from San José, 22 km away. Inside the Basilica is a chapel dedicated to La Negrita, where gifts from cured pilgrims can be seen. Most are metal models of parts of the human body that have been miraculously healed. The Basilica was destroyed in the 1926 earthquake and rebuilt in Byzantine style.

Lankester Gardens

Six km east of Cartago, the university-run Lankester Gardens (☎ 551-9877, 552-3247) feature an extensive orchid collection, an arboretum and many plants. Catch a Paraíso bus and ask for the turnoff for the gardens. From the turnoff, walk 0.75 km to the entrance. Hours are daily 8:30 am to 3:30 pm; admission is about US$2.50. All year is good, but February, March and April are best for viewing orchids. Free guided tours are sometimes given.

Río Orosi Valley

This extends southeast of Cartago and is a popular day trip from Cartago, though there are places to stay. There are pretty views, colonial buildings, hot springs, a lake and a wildlife refuge. Many San José companies offer day tours to the valley, but you can visit cheaply by public bus from Cartago. The first village is **Paraíso**, eight km east of Cartago, with decent restaurants. Seven km east of Paraíso is **Ujarrás**, flooded and abandoned in 1833. The ruined 17th-century church and other buildings are interesting to see. La Virgen de Ujarrás is celebrated on April 16 with a procession, mass, music and local food. A short distance above Ujarrás is a lookout point for the artificial **Lago de Cachí**, formed by a hydroelectric dam.

Six km south of Paraíso is the village of **Orosi** (population 8000) named after a 16th-century Huetar Indian chief and now the center of an important coffee-growing region. Orosi boasts an early-18th-century church – one of the oldest still in use in Costa Rica. Orosi Turismo (☎ /fax 533-3333) provides local information and rents bikes and horses. There are hot springs on the outskirts of town. *Montaña Linda* (☎ 533-3640), charges US$5.50 per person and has a hostel environment. Hot showers, kitchen privileges and inexpensive meals are offered, and local information is available.

Near **Purisil** village, about eight km southeast of Orosi, is the private **Monte Sky** cloud forest reserve, which features good birding. Ask at Orosi Turismo about guided walks (US$8), camping and overnight stays (US$25 per person including meals). Almost three km further east is the **Parque Nacional Tapantí** (formerly a wildlife refuge). It has trails and is open at 6 am for birding, which it is known for. There is a ranger station and admission is US$6, but there are few facilities. It is possible to camp with a permit from the ranger. The area is very wet, and dry-season visits are recommended.

Parque Nacional Volcán Irazú

This is the highest active volcano in Costa Rica (3432 meters). A major eruption on March 19, 1963, covered San José and most of the Central Valley with several centimeters of volcanic ash – over 50 cm deep in places. Since then Irazú's activity has been limited to gently smoking fumaroles in a bare landscape of volcanic ash and craters.

A paved road leads to the summit, where the main crater is 1050 meters across and 300 meters deep. There are several smaller craters. There's a parking area and a small information center, open from 9 am to 4 pm daily. There are no overnight accommodations, camping facilities or food. The entrance fee is US$6. From the summit it is possible to see both coasts, but it is rarely clear enough to do so. The best chance is in the early morning during the dry season (January to April). It tends to be

COSTA RICA

cold and cloudy on the summit, so bring warm clothes.

Places to Stay & Eat

Cartago lacks good budget accommodations. A couple of cheap flophouses (not recommended) are found by the old railway station. A couple of other hotels charge in the US$30s for a double. Your best bet is to stay at the Montaña Linda in Orosi (see above). There are restaurants in town along Avs 2 and 4.

Getting There & Away

Buses arrive from San José on Av 2, go as far as the Basilica, then return along Av 4. Buses returning to San José leave from Av 4, Calles 2 and 4, several times an hour between 5 am and 11 pm (¾ hour, US$0.50).

Buses for Turrialba leave every hour from in front of the Tribunales de Justicia on Av 3, Calles 8 and 10 (1½ hours, US$0.90).

Volcán Irazú cannot be reached from Cartago by bus. From San José, Buses Metropolí (☎ 272-0651, 591-1138) leaves from across the Gran Hotel Costa Rica, Av 2, Calles 1 and 3, on Saturday and Sunday (possibly Thursday in high season) at 8 am, returning at 12:15 pm. The fare is US$4.50, and the schedule allows about two hours on the summit.

Getting Around

For Paraíso and the Lankester Gardens, the bus leaves from Av 1, Calles 2 and 4. For Orosi, the bus leaves from Calle 4 near Av 1. These buses leave at least once every hour. A few buses continue past Orosi, but none go beyond Purisil, so for Tapantí park you have to walk a few kilometers or take a cab from Orosi.

The taxi rank is on the plaza west of the ruined church. A taxi to Irazú is about US$25.

TURRIALBA

Population 70,000

This pleasant, friendly and laid-back little town, near the headwaters of the Río Reventazón, is popular with river runners and kayakers. It is a good base for visiting the nearby archaeological monument and agricultural station (see CATIE and Monumento Nacional Guayabo, below).

CATIE

The acronym CATIE stands for Centro Agronómico Tropical de Investigatión y Enseñanza (Center for Tropical Agronomy Research & Education). It's the most important center of its kind in Central America, with an extensive library and research facility. Guided tours (US$10) can be arranged in advance by calling ☎ 556-6431, 556-1149. Visitors not on a tour can walk around the grounds, which have pleasant paths and a pond that is a good place to see water birds. The center is four km east of Turrialba on the road to Limón.

Places to Stay & Eat

Three cheap hotels by the old railway station are the *Hotel Interamericano* (☎ 556-0142), *Hotel Central* and *Hospedaje Chamango*. The best is the Interamericano, which charges US$6/10 for singles/doubles or US$12 for doubles with private cold showers. The other two are cheaper.

The *Hotel Turrialba* (☎ 556-6654) or the *Hotel La Roche* (☎ 556-1624) look basic but clean at rates similar to the Interamericano. Other cheapies to try are *Whittingham's Hotel* (☎ 556-0214) with large dark rooms with private bath and hot water – about US$12.50 for a double. The basic *Hospedaje Hotel Primavera* is about US$4 per person.

The *Restaurant Nuevo Hong Kong* has reasonably priced Chinese food. The *Pizzería Julian* is popular with young locals. The *Bar/Restaurant La Garza* sell a variety of meals for US$2 to US$5. All three are by the Parque Central.

Getting There & Away

Buses to San José leave every hour from Av 4 near Calle 2. Buses for Siquirres leave every two hours from the same place.

The terminal at Av 2 and Calle 2 has buses for nearby villages, including Santa

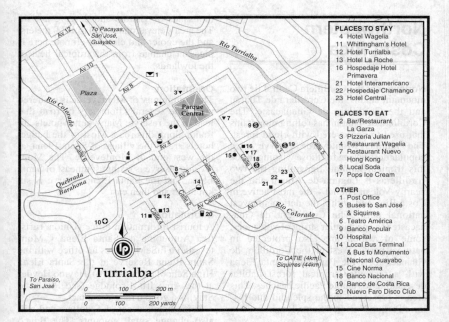

PLACES TO STAY
4 Hotel Wagelia
11 Whittingham's Hotel
12 Hotel Turrialba
13 Hotel La Roche
16 Hospedaje Hotel
    Primavera
21 Hotel Interamericano
22 Hospedaje Chamango
23 Hotel Central

PLACES TO EAT
2 Bar/Restaurant
    La Garza
3 Pizzería Julian
4 Restaurant Wagelia
7 Restaurant Nuevo
    Hong Kong
8 Local Soda
17 Pops Ice Cream

OTHER
1 Post Office
5 Buses to San José
    & Siquirres
6 Teatro América
9 Banco Popular
10 Hospital
14 Local Bus Terminal
    & Bus to Monumento
    Nacional Guayabo
15 Cine Norma
18 Banco Nacional
19 Banco de Costa Rica
20 Nuevo Faro Disco Club

Turrialba

Teresita (close to Guayabo) at 10:30 am and 1:30 pm. There are also buses direct to Guayabo on the weekends and possibly midweek, but the schedule keeps changing, so ask locally.

MONUMENTO NACIONAL GUAYABO

This is the most important archaeological site in Costa Rica, although it is not as impressive as the Maya sites of northern Central America. The area was occupied from about 1000 BC to 1400 AD and supported 10,000 inhabitants at its height. Archaeologists do not know the exact significance of the site nor why it was abandoned. The excavated area comprises about 10% of the monument.

Visitors to Monumento Nacional Guayabo can see stone-lined canals, mounds and carved stones. The remaining area is rain forest, and there are short trails for bird watching and wildlife observation.

Hours are daily from 8 am to 3 pm. Excavation work done during the week may cause the ruins to be closed. Rangers are available on the weekends to show you around. Entrance is US$6.

Places to Stay & Eat

Camping is permitted next to the information center. There are latrines, drinking water and a picnic area.

About one km from the monument is the friendly *Albergue La Calzada* (☎ 556-0465, fax 556-0427), which charges US$16 for singles or doubles (with shared bath) or US$24 (with private bath). There is a restaurant here selling local food. Be sure to call in advance.

Getting There & Away

The monument is 19 km north of Turrialba. There is a bus from Turrialba's main bus station on weekends, but schedules keep changing, so ask locally. Buses for Santa Teresita (also called Lajas) pass within four km of the monument. Taxis charge about US$15 one way.

COSTA RICA

Northwestern Costa Rica

Northwest of the Cordillera Central lie two mountain chains, the Cordillera de Tilarán and the Cordillera de Guanacaste. The Cordillera de Tilarán has rolling mountains that used to be covered with cloud forest. The famous Monteverde reserve is a popular destination for those wishing to see this tropical habitat. Separating the two cordilleras is Laguna de Arenal and the nearby Volcán Arenal – the most active in Costa Rica and within the nation's newest national park. The Cordillera de Guanacaste is a spectacular string of volcanoes, some of which are also protected in national parks. West of the Cordillera de Guanacaste is the Peninsula Santa Elena with a rare, dry tropical forest habitat descending to remote Pacific beaches. This area is preserved in the splendid and historic Parque Nacional Santa Rosa.

MONTEVERDE & SANTA ELENA

Monteverde is a small community founded by North American Quakers in 1951. The Quakers bought about 1500 hectares and began dairy farming and cheese production.

When the settlers arrived, they preserved a third of their property to protect the watershed above Monteverde. In 1972 about 2000 hectares were added – this became the **Reserva Biológica Bosque Nuboso Monteverde** (Monteverde Cloud Forest Biological Reserve). This famous cloud forest reserve is just to the east of the community. The Monteverde Conservation League (MCL; net), formed in 1985, continues to expand the protected area. In 1988 the MCL launched the International Children's Rainforest project, whereby school groups from all over the world raise money to save tropical rain forest adjacent to the reserve.

The Reserva Santa Elena was created in 1989 and relieves some of the heavy visitor pressure from Monteverde. Each year these two cloud forest reserves attract many thousands of visitors and deserve a visit. The area's elevation is 1200 to 1600 meters, and the cooler and cloudier climate here is pleasant change from the tropical heat of the lowlands.

Orientation

The community of Monteverde is scattered along the several kilometers of road that lead to the reserve. Many better hotels are found along this road. Most of the budget hotels are in the village of Santa Elena, at the west end of Monteverde. The Monteverde reserve is six km southeast of Santa Elena, and the Santa Elena reserve is six km north and then east.

Information

A tourist information office (Unión Turística Autónoma de Santa Elena y Monteverde; uTaSeM) shares an office with the Santa Elena Reserve at the Santa Elena High School (☎ 645-5014). Haymo Heyder at the Arco Iris Ecolodge (see Places to Stay) is a good uTaSeM contact.

Some hotels accept US dollars and will also change small amounts. The Banco Nacional (☎ 645-5027) and the Coop-Supermarket (☎ 645-5006) in Santa Elena both change money.

Chunches (☎ /fax 645-5147) in Santa Elena is a bookstore/coffee shop with books in English and US newspapers. Fax, laundry and information are available here.

Monteverde Cloud Forest Reserve

No matter what time of year, trails in the reserve are muddy (though the main ones have recently been stabilized with blocks to prevent erosion) and the cloud forest is dripping. Bring rainwear and suitable boots. During the wet season some trails turn into quagmires, but there are fewer visitors. Because of the fragile environment, a maximum of 120 people are allowed in at any one time, although the limit is reached only occasionally on mornings in the high season.

You'll stand a better chance of seeing wildlife if you hire a guide. Half-day guided visits are arranged at the information office for US$15 per person (plus entrance fee). These start at 8 am and include a half-hour slide show and a 2½- to three-hour walk limited to groups of about 10 people. Night tours (US$13, 2½ hours) are given at 7:30 pm. Some hotels and the reserve can arrange for a local to guide you within the reserve or in the nearby surrounding areas.

There are marked and maintained trails but no camping. Bird watching is good both in and around the reserve. Over 400 species have been recorded but most visitors want to see the resplendent quetzal, most easily seen when it is nesting in March and April. The reserve can arrange half-day birding tours (US$17 per person, three to six people). Remember that the cloud forest, a misty and mystical habitat, is hard to see wildlife in – don't go with unreasonable expectations.

The information office (☎ 645-5112) at the reserve entrance is open daily from 7 am to 4 pm. Entrance is US$8 per day, US$4 for students with ID, and children over 11, and free for younger children. The adjoining shop sells trail guides, bird and mammal lists, maps and souvenirs.

Reserva Santa Elena
The reserve has an office (☎ /fax 645-5014) in the Santa Elena High School, though its entrance is almost six km northeast of there. Santa Elena has a good trail system, you can see quetzals and other birds, and one trail leads to views (weather permitting) of Volcán Arenal. This is an excellent alternative to the Monteverde reserve with similar habitat and wildlife.

The reserve is open daily from 7 am to 4 pm, and entry is US$5, or US$2.50 for students with ID. Guided tours can be arranged for US$20. There's a small information center and gift shop.

Other Things to See & Do
Several places in Monteverde and Santa Elena advertise **horseback riding tours** for US$6 to US$10 per hour.

The interesting **Butterfly Garden** is open daily from 9:30 am to 4 pm. Admission is US$5 (US$4 for students) and includes an informative tour (in Spanish, English or German) of the butterfly-raising greenhouses, guided by a biologist – you can then stay all day and get good photos of butterflies.

The **Hummingbird Gallery**, near the Monteverde reserve entrance, has feeders attracting several species of humming-birds – great photo opportunities!

The **Serpentarium** (☎ 645-5238) has about 20 snakes and lizards well displayed with informative signs in English and Spanish. Hours are 8 am to 5 pm and admission is US$3.

Totiqui Mau (☎ /fax 645-5323) is a new ethnohistorical museum due to open in mid-1997 in the Cerro Plano area.

The local women's arts & crafts cooperative, CASEM, sells embroidered and hand-painted blouses, handmade clothing and other souvenirs. Profits benefit the local community.

Hiking & Nature Trails
Outside the reserves there are several other trails. The 3.5 km **Sendero Bajo del Tigre** operated by the MCL (☎ 645-5003) is open from 7:30 am to 5:30 pm, and day-use is US$5 (US$2 for students with ID). The trail is more open than in the cloud forest and hence spotting birds tends to be easier.

The **Finca Ecológica** (☎ 645-5222) is a private property with four loop trails (longest takes 2½ hours walking slowly) through forest and coffee and banana plantations. Coatis, agoutis and sloths are often seen, and monkeys, porcupines and other animals are occasionally sighted. Some of these are at feeders, but they are still wild animals. Birding is good. Hours are 7 am to 5 pm, and admission is US$5, or US$3 for children and students with ID.

The **Reserva Sendero Tranquilo** (☎ 645-5010 for information) offers 3½-hour guided hikes for US$12.50 per person – group size is two to six people, and no more than two groups are allowed on the trail at any time. The **Hidden Valley Trail** is behind the Pensión Monteverde Inn (see Places to Stay). This is free to inn guests

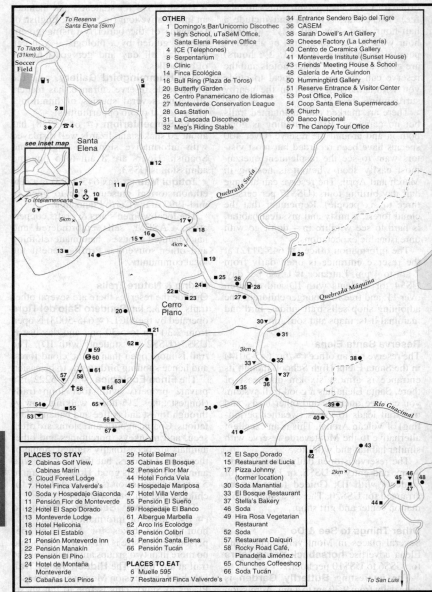

OTHER
1   Domingo's Bar/Unicornio Discothec
3   High School, uTaSeM Office,
    Santa Elena Reserve Office
4   ICE (Telephones)
5   Serpentarium
9   Clinic
14 Finca Ecológica
16 Bull Ring (Plaza de Toros)
20 Butterfly Garden
26 Centro Panamericano de Idiomas
27 Monteverde Conservation League
28 Gas Station
31 La Cascada Discotheque
32 Meg's Riding Stable

34 Entrance Sendero Bajo del Tigre
36 CASEM
38 Sarah Dowell's Art Gallery
39 Cheese Factory (La Lechería)
40 Centro de Ceramica Gallery
41 Monteverde Institute (Sunset House)
43 Friends' Meeting House & School
49 Galería de Arte Guindon
50 Hummingbird Gallery
51 Reserve Entrance & Visitor Center
53 Post Office, Police
55 Coop Santa Elena Supermercado
56 Church
60 Banco Nacional
67 The Canopy Tour Office

To Reserva
Santa Elena (5km)

To Tilarán
(31km)

Soccer
Field

Santa
Elena

see inset map

To Interamericana

Quebrada Sucia

Quebrada Máquina

Cerro
Plano

Río Guacimal

To San Luis

PLACES TO STAY
2   Cabinas Golf View,
    Cabinas Marín
5   Cloud Forest Lodge
7   Hotel Finca Valverde's
9   Soda y Hospedaje Giaconda
11 Pensión Flor de Monteverde
12 Hotel El Sapo Dorado
13 Monteverde Lodge
18 Hotel Heliconia
19 Hotel El Establo
21 Pensión Monteverde Inn
22 Pensión Manakín
23 Pensión El Pino
24 Hotel de Montaña
    Monteverde
25 Cabañas Los Pinos

29 Hotel Belmar
35 Cabinas El Bosque
42 Pensión Flor Mar
44 Hotel Fonda Vela
45 Hospedaje Mariposa
47 Hotel Villa Verde
55 Pensión El Sueño
59 Hospedaje El Banco
61 Albergue Marbella
62 Arco Iris Ecolodge
63 Pensión Colibrí
64 Pensión Santa Elena
66 Pensión Tucán

PLACES TO EAT
6   Muelle 595
7   Restaurant Finca Valverde's

12 El Sapo Dorado
15 Restaurant de Lucia
17 Pizza Johnny
    (former location)
30 Soda Manantial
33 El Bosque Restaurant
37 Stella's Bakery
46 Soda
49 Hira Rosa Vegetarian
    Restaurant
52 Soda
57 Restaurant Daiquiri
58 Rocky Road Café,
    Panadería Jiménez
65 Chunches Coffeeshop
66 Soda Tucán

COSTA RICA

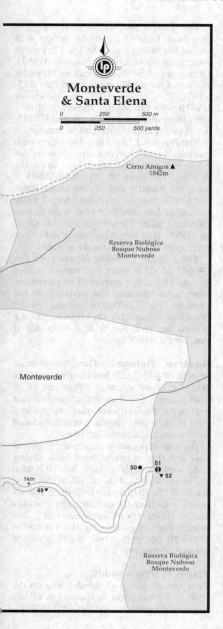

Monteverde
& Santa Elena

0   250   500 m
0   250   500 yards

Cerro Amigos ▲
1842m

Reserva Biológica
Bosque Nuboso
Monteverde

Monteverde

51
50 ● ❶
▼ 52

1km
49 ▼

Reserva Biológica
Bosque Nuboso
Monteverde

and US$1.50 to others. A free hiking option
is the track leaving from behind the Hotel
Belmar and climbing up to **Cerro Amigos**
(1842 meters) about three km away.

Courses

The Monteverde Institute (☎ 645-5053, fax
645-5219, net), Apdo 69-5655, Monteverde, Puntarenas, is a nonprofit educational institute offering interdisciplinary
courses in tropical biology, agroecology,
conservation, sustainable development,
local culture, Spanish and women's
studies. They also have a volunteer place-
ment program for individuals who wish to
teach in local schools or work in reforestation programs.

Ten- to 14-day courses for high school
and college students and adults are US$700
to US$1500, all inclusive from San José.
Eight to 10-week courses are university-
accredited programs for undergraduates
and emphasize tropical community ecology.
Costs are about US$4000.

The Centro Panamericano de Idiomas
(☎ /fax 645-5026) has recently opened a
Spanish language program in Monteverde
with homestays available.

Canopy Tour

The Canopy Tour (☎ 645-5243, see also
San José) is in the grounds of the Cloud
Forest Lodge and has an information office
in Santa Elena.

Their tour begins with a short hike
through the forest to a series of three platforms between 20 and 33 meters up in the
trees. The first platform is reached by a
rope ladder up the inside of a giant hollow
fig tree, then you traverse across fixed
ropes to the 2nd and 3rd platforms, culminating with a rappel descent to the ground.
All participants are harnessed to safety
equipment throughout the tour, which lasts
about 2½ hours. Costs are US$45 for
adults, US$35 for students with ID and
US$30 for children.

The company has a daily bus from San
José for US$15. Reservations are needed in
the high season. Tours leave daily at 7:30
and 10:30 am and at 2:30 pm.

COSTA RICA

Monteverde Music Festival

Held annually throughout January and February, this is one of the top music festivals in Central America. Music is mainly classical, jazz and Latin with an occasional experimental group to spice things up. Concerts are held daily at the Hotel Fonda Vela at 5 pm to take advantage of a scenic sunset. Tickets are US$9. Children, locals and penniless travelers have been allowed to listen for free, standing in the balcony, on a space-available basis.

Places to Stay – budget

Camping *Pensión Flor Mar* (☎ 645-5009, 645-5088) and the *Cabinas El Bosque* allow camping for about US$2.50 per person and allow you to use a shower. Ask around about other places.

Hotels Most budget hotels are in Santa Elena. The family-run *Pensión El Sueño* (☎ 645-5021) cooks meals on request. Basic quads are US$5 per person, and rooms with private hot shower are US$10 per person. The *Pensión Santa Elena* (☎ 645-5051, fax 645-5147) is associated with HI. It is clean, friendly and has warm showers. Small rooms are US$5 per person, or US$10 with private bath. Breakfasts (US$3) and casados (US$4.50) are served. Nearby, the small, clean and friendly *Pensión Colibrí* charges US$5 per person with warm communal showers. Cheap casados as well as horse rental are available.

The *Hospedaje El Banco* (☎ 645-5204) is basic but friendly for US$7 per person with shared warm showers. Laundry service and meals are available on request. Nearby, the clean, friendly and recommended *Albergue Marbella* (☎ 645-5153) is US$10 per person or US$15 per person with private bath. The helpful *Pensión Tucán* (☎ 645-5017) is also clean and has hot water. Rooms are US$7 per person or US$10 with private bath. Good meals are available. About half a kilometer north of Santa Elena is the quiet *Cabinas Marlin*, which has clean rooms with communal bath and hot showers for US$7 per person. Nearby is the similarly priced *Cabinas Golf View* with bunk beds.

The *Soda y Hospedaje Giaconda* has four basic little single/double rooms with shared hot showers for US$5/8. They serve good meat or vegetarian casados (US$3). Farther out is the small, clean and friendly *Pensión Flor de Monteverde* (☎ /fax 645-5236). They charge US$7 per person or US$10 with private hot shower, and they offer three meals a day for another US$15. Tours and transportation can be arranged.

The *Pensión El Pino* has five rooms with bunkbeds and shared warm showers for US$6 per person. Almost next door, the *Pensión Manakín* (☎ /fax 645-5080) is basic but friendly and has hot water. Rates are US$8 per person with shared bathrooms. A few double rooms with private bath are US$26. Good breakfasts are US$2 to US$5. Box lunches, laundry, kitchen privileges and local tours are offered.

The friendly *Pensión Monteverde Inn* (☎ 645-5156) is quiet and remote with a private 11 hectare reserve. The rooms are spartan but adequate and have private hot showers for US$10/18 single/double; breakfast is available on request, and the owners can pick you up at the bus stop if you have a reservation.

Reserve Refuges The Monteverde reserve (☎ 645-5122) has a dormitory-style refuge near the entrance where one of 35 bunks costs US$3. Researchers and student groups have priority but travelers can stay here if space is available. There are shared bathrooms and kitchen facilities.

Backpackers carrying sleeping bags and food can stay in one of three basic shelter cabins on the reserve. Each has 10 bunks, drinking water, shower, electricity and kitchen. The shelters are two, three and six hours' hike from the entrance along muddy trails. Reservations are necessary, but usually you can go the next day. The cost is US$3.50 per person per night, plus the reserve admission.

Places to Stay – middle

Four km northwest of Santa Elena on the road to Tilarán there is *Monte Los Olivos Ecotourist Lodge* (reservations ☎ 283-8975, fax 283-9116 in English or ☎/fax 283-8305 in Spanish), developed by the Canadian WWF and other agencies. This grassroots ecotourism project protects forest and directly benefits small communities. Cabins with shared bathrooms are US$10/15 for singles/doubles, and with private bathrooms they are US$17/24/29/35 for one to four people. Breakfasts for US$2 and other meals for US$5 are served. Guided hikes and horseback rides are available.

The small *Arco Iris Ecolodge* (☎ 645-5067, fax 645-5022, net) is helpful and well run. Two small double rooms with private hot showers are US$25, and four larger doubles are US$40.

The *Cabinas El Bosque* (☎ 645-5221, ☎/fax 645-5129) has 22 simple but clean, bright and spacious rooms with hot showers for US$24/32/38/42 for one to four people – good for the money.

Places to Eat
Budget travelers eat in Santa Elena, where a casado can be had for US$3. Try the *Restaurant Daiquiri* and the restaurants associated with the hotels above. *Chunches* (see Information) has espresso and homemade snacks. The *Rocky Road Café* has barbecued chicken, hamburgers, sandwiches and ice cream, and a balcony overlooking 'downtown' Santa Elena. Below is *Panadería Jiménez* for baked goods.

For picnics, *Stella's Bakery* has homemade bread and rolls and *La Lechería* has fresh cheese. Or try the *Coope Santa Elena* grocery store next to CASEM.

In Cerro Plano *Pizza Johnny* (☎ 645-5066) is liked by both travelers and locals. The *Soda Manantial* is an inexpensive choice in Monteverde. There are also sodas by the Monteverde reserve entrance and another is about 1.5 km away. Between the two is the inexpensive little *Hira Rosa Vegetarian Restaurant*. The *El Bosque Restaurant* is a popular place serving good lunches and dinners for about US$5 to US$9.

Entertainment
La Cascada is a popular dance club open Thursday to Sunday 9 pm to 1 am. There may be a cover charge. Locals like *Domingo's Bar/Unicornio Discotec* at the north end of Santa Elena. Popular bars are *Bar Amigo* in Santa Elena and the *Valverde Bar* in the Hotel Finca Valverde's.

Getting There & Away
In Monteverde, the last bus stop from San José is by La Lechería – ask to get off near your hotel. Buses return to San José (four hours, US$5) from La Lechería at 6:30 am and 2:30 pm daily, stopping at the bus office (☎ 645-5032) opposite the Banco Nacional in Santa Elena en route.

There is a bus from Puntarenas to Santa Elena at 2:15 pm daily, arriving in Santa Elena (by the bank) about 5:30 pm and returning the next day at 6 am.

A bus leaves Tilarán at 1 pm for Santa Elena; it returns from a stop in front of the church at 7 am daily.

CAÑAS
This small, hot, lowland town is an agricultural center that travelers use as a base for visits to the nearby Parque Nacional Palo Verde and for Corobicí river trips. Cañas is also the beginning/end of the Arenal back roads described later.

Float Trips
Safaris Corobicí (☎/fax 669-1091) are five km north of Cañas on the Interamericana. Daily two-hour float trips on the Río Corobicí are US$35 per person, a three-hour bird watching float is US$43 per person, and a half-day saltwater estuary trip along the Bebedero and Tempisque rivers, bordering the Parque Nacional Palo Verde, costs US$60 per person, lunch included.

Places to Stay & Eat
The *Hotel Guillén* (☎ 669-0070) and *Hotel Parque* on the southeast side of the Parque Central charge US$3.50 per person. The *Gran Hotel* on the northwest side is similarly priced and has a few basic doubles with bath for US$10. The *Cabinas Corobicí* (☎ 669-0241), Av 2 and Calle 5, are a little more pleasant and charge US$7 per person with private bath. None of these has hot showers.

The best place downtown is the *Hotel Cañas* (☎ 669-0039, 669-1319), Calle 2, Av 3. Singles/doubles with private cold baths and fan are US$13/19; with air conditioning, it's US$26 for a double. This hotel has a good, reasonably priced restaurant and is very popular.

There are a couple of unremarkable inexpensive Chinese restaurants to be found in the park.

Getting There & Away

The main Cañas bus terminal and market is at Calle 1 and Av 11 – most buses leave from here. Some San José buses still leave from La Cañera bus stop at Av Central and Calle 5. Check both terminals or ask Transportes La Cañera (☎ 669-0145) for departure times and locations. It's probable that all buses will eventually leave from the main terminal.

The new terminal has seven daily buses to Liberia, seven to Tilarán, six to Bebedero (near Parque Nacional Palo Verde), five to Upala, seven to Puntarenas and others to local destinations. Not all buses originate in Cañas – many just stop here, such as the Liberia-Cañas-Puntarenas bus.

PARQUE NACIONAL PALO VERDE

This park on the northeastern banks of the mouth of Río Tempisque, 30 km west of Cañas, is a major bird sanctuary. Several different habitats are found: swamps, marshes, mangroves, lagoons and a variety of seasonal grasslands and forests. Low limestone hills provide lookouts over the park.

The December through March dry season is marked and much of the forest dries out. During other months, large areas are flooded. September to March has a huge influx of migratory and endemic birds – one of the greatest concentrations of waterfowl and shorebirds in Central America. When the dry season begins, birds congregate in the lakes and marshes, trees lose their leaves and the massed flocks become easier to observe. December to February are the best months – bring binoculars.

Park admission is US$6 per day. Camping (US$2 per person) is permitted near the Palo Verde ranger station, where there are toilets and shower facilities.

Limited information is available from the Area de Conservación Tempisque office (ACT; ☎ 671-1062, fax 671-1290) in Bagaces, 22 km north of Cañas on the Interamericana.

The park is reached by a 28-km road leaving the Interamericana from in front of the ACT office. There are no buses.

RESERVA BIOLÓGICA LOMAS BARBUDAL

This reserve is just north of Palo Verde and is a tropical dry forest with riparian areas. Lomas Barbudal is locally famous for its abundance and variety of insects, including some 250 different species of bees – about a quarter of the world's bee species. A devastating brushfire burnt 85% of the reserve in 1994. The plant life is beginning to recover.

The reserve is administered by the SPN – information can be obtained from their ACT office in Bagaces. The group Amigos de Lomas Barbudal (☎ 667-1203, fax 667-1069) also has a Bagaces office and sells bird checklists and trail guides and provides information.

Entrance is US$1, US$6 or free, depending on whom you ask. Camping is allowed. At the entrance is a small local museum and information center run by the nearby community of San Rafael de Bagaces. The reserve is on the other side of the Río Cabuyo behind the museum.

The turnoff to Lomas Barbudal from the Interamericana is at Pijije, 12 km northwest of Bagaces. The seven-km road to the reserve is signed and is in poor shape. Walk or use 4WD.

LIBERIA

Population 40,000

Liberia, the capital of Guanacaste Province and Costa Rica's most important northerly town, is a ranching center and transport hub. It is a good base for visiting the nearby national parks.

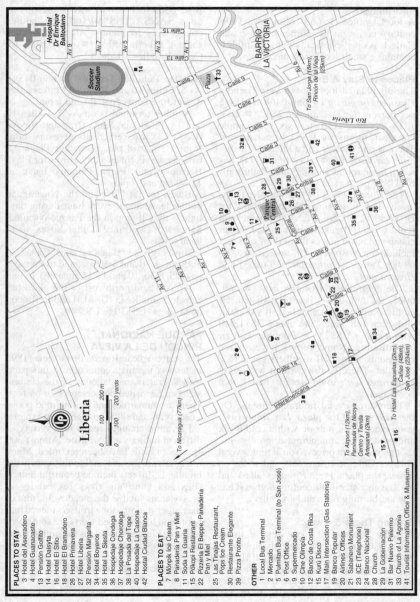

Liberia

0   100   200 m
0   100   200 yards

To Nicaragua (77km)

Hospital Dr Enrique Baltodano

Soccer Stadium

BARRIO LA VICTORIA

Río Libería

Parque Central

Plaza

To San Jorge (18km), Rincón de la Vieja (25km)

To Airport (12km), Península de Nicoya Center y Tienda Artesanal (2km)

To Hotel Las Esquelas (2km), Cañas (48km), San José (234km)

PLACES TO STAY
3   Hotel del Aserradero
4   Hotel Guanacaste
13   Pensión Golfito
14   Hotel Daisyta
16   Hotel El Sitio
18   Hotel El Bramadero
26   Hotel Primavera
27   Hotel Libería
32   Pensión Margarita
34   Hotel Boyeros
35   Hotel La Siesta
36   Hospedaje Condega
37   Hospedaje Chorotega
38   La Posada del Tope
40   Hospedaje La Casona
42   Hostal Ciudad Blanca

PLACES TO EAT
7   Mönpik Ice Cream
8   Panadería Pan y Miel
11   Soda La Guaria
15   Pökopi Restaurant
22   Pizzería El Beppe, Panadería Pan y Miel
25   Las Tinajas Restaurant, Pops Ice Cream
30   Restaurante Elegante
39   Pizza Pronto

OTHER
1   Local Bus Terminal
2   Mercado
5   Pulmitan Bus Terminal (to San José)
6   Post Office
9   Supermercado
10   Cine Olimpia
12   Banco de Costa Rica
15   Kurú Disco
17   Main Intersection (Gas Stations)
19   Banco Popular
20   Airlines Offices
21   Sabanero Monument
23   ICE (Telephone)
24   Banco Nacional
28   Church
29   La Gobernación
31   Bar Nuevo Palermo
33   Church of La Agonía
41   Tourist Information Office & Museum

COSTA RICA

Information

A tourist office (☎ 666-1606), in a 19th-century house on the corner of Av 6 and Calle 1, is open erratically but is helpful. It contains a small local museum.

Places to Stay & Eat

The dilapidated-looking but very friendly *Pensión Margarita* (☎ 666-0468) is US$5 per person. *La Posada del Tope* (☎ 666-1313, fax 666-2136) has six very simple but clean rooms for US$5.50 per person. There is one shower and a kitchen. *Hospedaje La Casona* (☎ /fax 666-2971) has seven basic rooms sharing three bathrooms for US$5 per person.

The *Hotel Liberia* (☎ /fax 666-0161) has basic, dark little single/double rooms for US$7.50/12 or US$12/22 with private bath (cold water). Breakfast is included. Other cheap and basic places that I didn't inspect include the *Hospedaje Chorotega* (☎ 666-0898), *Pensión Golfito* (☎ 666-0963) and *Hospedaje Condega*.

The helpful *Hotel Guanacaste* (☎ 666-0085, fax 666-2287) is affiliated with HI and has a restaurant attached. It's popular and often full. Rates are about US$13/19 with a fan or US$24 for a double with air conditioning. Some rooms have shared bathrooms. Youth HI members get a 15% discount. There is also a room with eight *camarotes colectivos* (bunk beds) that is cheaper.

There are several midrange hotels. On the west side of the plaza, *Las Tinajas* is a good place to sit outside with a cold drink and watch the unenergetic goings on, though meals are pricey. You'll find several cheaper Chinese restaurants and sodas on or near the plaza. *Pizza Pronto*, Calle 1 and Av 4, is in a nice 19th-century house; it has a wood-burning oven and art gallery.

Getting There & Away

Air The airport is 12 km west of town, about 1.6 km off the main highway to Nicoya. LACSA has international flights to/from Miami that are usually through San José, though there are a few direct ones. Travelair has daily flights to San José (US$88/148 one way/roundtrip) as does SANSA (US$50/100). Schedules change very frequently. All three airlines share a Liberia office (☎ 666-0303), Av Central, Calles 10 and 12.

Bus The Pulmitan Terminal (☎ 666-0458), Av 5, Calles 10 and 12, has 11 buses a day to San José between 4 am and 6 pm.

Another terminal is on Av 7, Calles 12 and 14. Filadelfia, Santa Cruz and Nicoya (US$1.25) are served about every hour from 5 am to 8 pm. Buses for Playa del Coco leave six times a day. Buses for Playa Hermosa and Playa Panamá leave at 11:30 am and 7 pm.

Buses for La Cruz and the Nicaraguan border leave about every hour during daylight – they'll stop at the Parque Nacional Santa Rosa entrance. Other buses go to local towns.

Buses go to Bagaces and Cañas at 5:45 am, 1:30 and 4:30 pm, and to Puntarenas at 5, 8:30, 10 and 11:15 am and 3:15 pm.

A taxi stand northwest of the plaza has cabs to Santa Rosa (US$15) and to Rincón de la Vieja (US$30 to US$40).

PARQUE NACIONAL RINCÓN DE LA VIEJA

The active Volcán Rincón de la Vieja (1895 meters) is the main attraction to this park. Cones, craters and lagoons in the summit area can be visited on horseback or on foot. There are fumaroles and boiling mud pools, steam vents and sulfurous springs to explore.

Elevation changes result in a variety of different habitats and wildlife. Almost 300 species of birds have been recorded. Many mammals are present, including tapirs in the highlands. Insects include beautiful butterflies and annoying ticks (especially in grassy areas such as the meadow in front of the ranger station – long trousers tucked into boots and long-sleeved shirts are some protection). Plant life includes the orchid *Cattleya skinneri*, Costa Rica's national flower.

Information & Walking Tour

The park is 25 km northeast of Liberia by a poor road and is not heavily visited. It's in the Area de Conservación Guanacaste (ACG) administered by the SPN – information is available from the ACG headquarters at Santa Rosa (☎ 695-5598). Entrance is US$6 and camping is US$2 per person. Insect repellent is recommended.

The Santa María Ranger Station in the southeast corner of the park is the main station. From the station, a trail leads three km west to sulfurous hot springs with supposed therapeutic properties. A farther three km takes you to the boiling mud pools of Las Pailas. Watch your step because the edges are sometimes weak. From Las Pailas a trail leads north. After about two km, a fork to the left leads to Las Hornillas – sulfurous fumaroles about four km from the mud pools. There are waterfalls nearby. Continuing north from the fork takes you to the summit area. The highest point is about eight km beyond the mud pools. Two km west of Las Pailas is the Las Pailas Ranger Station in the southwest corner (also called Las Espuelas and not always open).

Places to Stay

In the Park You can camp in most places if you are self-sufficient and prepared for cold and foggy weather. A compass is useful. The wet season is very wet, and there are lots of mosquitoes. The dry season is better. Camping at Santa María Ranger Station is US$2, and there are latrines, water and picnic sites. You can sleep at the ranger station if you make arrangements with the park service in advance. There are a couple of old beds, or you can sleep on the wooden floor – bring your sleeping bag. Meals can be arranged for about US$3 each, and horses can be hired.

Outside the Park Near the village of San Jorge, in the Santa María area, is the friendly *Rinconcito Lodge*, which lacks electricity and phone. Rates are US$10/16 for single/double cabins sharing cold showers. Breakfasts are US$4, other meals are US$6. Guides and horses can be hired. Make reservations and get directions from the Badillas (☎ 666-0267, 666-2764,

666-0636) who live in Liberia. They offer transport to the lodge for about US$40 roundtrip and will take up to six people for that price. Reportedly, there are some budget rooms available in the village of San Jorge itself.

Both of the following lodges offer meals (pricey!), tours, guides and horse rentals:

The private *Hacienda Lodge Guachipelín* (☎ 442-2828, 442-2864, fax 442-1910) is near the Las Pailas sector. A basic bunkhouse is US$10 per person, a dormitory is US$16 per person and more expensive accommodations are available. Five km further is the *Rincón de la Vieja Mountain Lodge* (☎ /fax 695-5553, in San José ☎ 225-1073, 234-8835) affiliated with HI. Dormitory rooms start at US$20 and more expensive private rooms are available. This lodge is two km from the mud pools and five km from the hot springs. There is a canopy platform tour here.

Getting There & Away

To/From Santa María Hike 25 km or take a taxi (US$30 to US$40) on the road that heads northeast out of Liberia through the Barrio La Victoria suburb. After 18 km the road passes San Jorge village and continues as far as the station. Call the ACG in Santa Rosa to ask if any SPN vehicles are going up – occasionally a ride can be arranged.

To/From Las Pailas The Rincón de la Vieja Lodge is an eight-km hike from Santa María station. Alternatively, go five km north of Liberia on the Interamericana, turn right onto a gravel road (very small signs) 10 km to the village of Curubandé, then follow the blue arrows to Hacienda Lodge Guachipelín (six km) and on to the Rincón de la Vieja Lodge (five more km). The lodges can provide transport – otherwise you're on your own.

PARQUE NACIONAL SANTA ROSA

The park is named after Hacienda Santa Rosa, where a battle was fought in 1856 between Costa Rica and the invading forces of William Walker. The park protects the largest remaining stand of tropical dry forest in Central America, as well as important sea turtle nesting sites.

It's a good place to see wildlife, especially in the dry season, though the wet season (especially September and October) is best for turtle watching.

Information

The park entrance is on the west side of the Interamericana, 35 km north of Liberia. Hours are daily 7:30 am to 5:30 pm. Admission is US$6, and camping costs US$2 per person.

It is seven km (no transport) to the park (and ACG) headquarters (☎ 695-5598). Here are administrative offices, scientists' quarters, an information center, campground, museum and nature trail. A 4WD trail leads down to the coast, 12 km away. The campground (one of the best-developed in the SPN) has drinking water, picnic benches, flush toilets and cold showers. Large fig trees provide shade. Campsites on the coast have drinking water and latrines, but no showers. Meals can be arranged in advance with the SPN, or bring your own food. Horses are available for hire, and rangers may allow travelers to accompany them on their patrols.

Things to See & Do

The **museum** is in the historic Santa Rosa Hacienda. Exhibits explain the 1856 war and show Costa Rican life in the 19th century. There are antique firearms, furniture and tools. A display interpreting the ecological significance and wildlife of the park is also here.

Near the museum is a one-km **nature trail**, with signs interpreting the ecological relationships between the plants, animals and weather patterns of Santa Rosa. You will see a variety of plants and birds and probably, if you move slowly and keep your eyes and ears open, monkeys, snakes, iguanas and other animals.

The best turtle beach is **Nancite**, and during September and October you may see as many as 8000 olive ridley turtles on the beach at once! Nancite beach is strictly protected and restricted, but permission can be

obtained from the park service to see this spectacle. Flashlights and flash photography are prohibited. Avoid nights near the full moon as it is too bright for the turtles.

Playa Naranjo, south of Nancite, has good surfing but no drinking water or facilities.

Getting There & Away

Buses between Liberia and Peñas Blancas will stop at the entrance. The ranger has a timetable for buses passing the park.

PARQUE NACIONAL GUANACASTE

This park is separated from Santa Rosa by the Interamericana and is an extension of Santa Rosa's habitats, but the terrain soon begins to climb toward Volcán Orosí (1487 meters) and Cacao (1659 meters). The park enables animals to range from the coast to the highlands, just as many of them have always done.

Places to Stay

Three biological stations in the park have dormitories for 30 to 40 people and bathrooms with cold water. A bed and three meals cost about US$20 a day, if you can get in (researchers get preference and there's no transport). Camping near the stations costs US$2 per night. Horses are available for hire. Make arrangements at Santa Rosa headquarters (☎ 669-5598) or in San José to camp or stay.

PEÑAS BLANCAS

This is the border with Nicaragua, but there's nowhere to stay. See Costa Rica's Getting There & Away section earlier. The nearest town is **La Cruz** (20 km), with the best budget hotel: *Cabinas Santa Rita* (☎ 679-9062) with clean doubles with private cold showers for US$15. There are three cheaper places and a couple of pricier ones.

CIUDAD QUESADA

Population 31,000

Locals call this town San Carlos. It's not a major destination but is convenient for hotels en route to Arenal. Almost everything of importance is on the Parque

Central, or close to it. It's known as a cowboy town, and there are several memorably aromatic saddle shops.

Places to Stay & Eat

The cheapest is the very basic and noisy *Hotel Terminal* (☎ 460-2158), in the bus terminal half a block from the parque. West of the terminal, the clean *Hotel del Norte* (☎ 460-1959) is better at US$4 per person with shared hot showers. North of the parque, the first two blocks of Calle 2 have several basic but adequate hotels for US$3 to US$5 per person, including the *Ugalde* (☎ 460-0260), *Axel Alberto* (☎ 460-1423), *Hotel Diana* (☎ 460-3319) and *Hotel Los Helechos*.

The *Hotel El Retiro* (☎ 460-0463, 460-1900) on the parque charges US$7/12 for basic, clean rooms with electric showers. The *Hotel Don Goyo* (☎ 460-1780, ☎ /fax 460-6383), a block south of the parque, has small, clean, pleasant rooms with fans and private hot showers. Rates are US$12/17. Both have parking lots.

Half a dozen restaurants around the parque offer plenty of choice.

Getting There & Away

The Quesada terminal is half a block from the Parque Central. San José buses (two hours, US$1.80) leave hourly during the day – an attractive ride over the western flanks of the Cordillera Central. Buses to Fortuna (1½ hours) leave five times a day. Buses to Tilarán (4½ hours) leave at 6 am and 3 pm. There are five buses daily east to Venecia (one hour) and on to Puerto Viejo de Sarapiquí. Buses go to other nearby villages throughout the day.

FORTUNA & VOLCÁN ARENAL
Population 7000

Fortuna is the nearest village to the spectacular Volcán Arenal (1633 meters), which looms six km to the west. The volcano was dormant until 1968; in that year huge explosions triggered lava flows that killed several dozen people. Despite this massive eruption, the volcano retains its almost perfect conical shape, and with its continuing activity, Arenal is everyone's image of a typical volcano. The best night-time views are from the north and west side of the volcano. The degree of activity varies from week to week; sometimes there is red-hot lava flowing and incandescent rocks flying through the air.

The Parque Nacional Volcán Arenal was created in 1995 but visitor services are minimal. You can see the eruptions from outside the park just as well and save the US$6 entrance.

Many local hotels and tour operators will arrange night tours to view the phenomenon – prices are US$5 to US$20 per person. This is a very popular trip. Many of these tours include a dip in the Tabacón hot springs after the volcano visit. Other tours include horseback rides to local waterfalls (La Catarata de Fortuna) or all-day rides to Monteverde (US$65, more interesting than taking the bus) and visits to Caño Negro (US$25 to US$45). All of these are worthwhile tours. You can walk to La Catarata – it's about six km and is signed (see map). Admission for the path to the base is US$1.50. Hotels change US dollars. This is a small town – ask around for what you need.

Places to Stay

Camping A campground with basic shower and toilet facilities is 1.5 km west of town, opposite the Restaurante La Fiesta del Mar. Six km west of Fortuna is *Senderos Los Lagos* (☎ /fax 479-9126), also known as El Mirador. Swimming pools and cabins (US$40) are by the entrance, and a three-km road leads to a lake with volcano views where you can camp for US$4. There are toilets, showers and hiking trails. Horses can be hired, and it's the best campsite near the volcano.

Hotels The friendly, basic but clean *Cabinas Charlie* (☎ 479-9454) is popular with backpackers. Rates are US$4 or US$5 per person. *Cabinas Jerry* (☎ 479-9063) has doubles with shared hot baths from US$6, but it receives mixed reports. For US$3 per person, the basic little *Cabinas Andrea* is popular with shoestringers.

Cabinas Elsy (☎ 479-9123) is friendly and clean for US$5 per person. Family-run *Cabinas Manuel* (☎ 479-9069) does laundry and charges US$7.50/10 for singles/doubles with private hot bath. *Cabinas Sissy* is US$10 for a small double with hot bath.

Several clean and adequate hotels charge around US$15 for a double with hot bath, including *Cabinas Grijalba* (☎ 479-9129), *Cabinas La Amistad* (☎ 479-9035), *Cabinas El Bosque*, *Cabinas y Soda El Río* and *Cabinas Karen*.

Clean *Cabinas Carmela* (☎ 479-9010) has fairly large doubles with private hot-water bath and fan for US$20. *Cabinas Rolopz* (☎ 479-8058) is similar. There are several pricier options. Discounts are possible in the low season.

Places to Eat

The popular *El Jardín* has casados for about US$2, but these are not mentioned on the 'menu,' which is otherwise overpriced. Other inexpensive eateries include the good *Restaurante Vegetariano*, the simple *Soda El Río*, the Italian *Pizzería Luigi's* and the ubiquitous *Mönpik* for ice cream. The attractive *Rancho La Cascada* and *Restaurant Nene* are more upmarket but fair value.

Getting There & Away

Buses from San José's Coca-Cola terminal leave for Fortuna at 6:15, 8:40 and 11:30 am – otherwise go to Quesada and change.

Fortuna has two bus stops – one in front of the gas station with buses for Tilarán at 7 am and 4 pm; one down the block with buses for San José at 2:45 pm (direct, four hours, US$2.50) or with connections through Ciudad Quesada. Buses for Ciudad Quesada leave from both stops several times a day.

There are also buses *de paso* that come through town on their way to somewhere else – ask about times.

TILARÁN

This small town, near the southwest end of Laguna de Arenal, is a ranching center. There's a rodeo here the last weekend in April, when the hotels are often full. There's another fiesta on June 13. It is also the main windsurfing center in Costa Rica – the nearby lake (five or six km away) has consistently high winds that attract experienced windsurfers. It's not cheap.

Places to Stay & Eat

Cabinas Mary (☎ 695-5479), on the south side of the parque, is good, clean, pleasant and has a recommended reasonably priced restaurant. Rooms with private hot shower are US$16 double or US$6 per person with communal shower. The *Hotel Central* (☎ 695-5363), southeast of the church, has basic but clean rooms at US$4 per person, or cabins with private bath for US$20 (up to four people). *Cabinas Lago Lindo* (☎ 695-5555) is a block from the parque and has clean rooms for US$6 per person. The similarly priced but more basic *Hotel Grecia* is on the west side of the parque. The friendly *Cabinas El Sueño* (☎ 695-5347), next to Cabinas Lago Lindo, is very clean and has a restaurant. Singles/doubles with private warm shower are US$14/20.

Getting There & Away

Buses from Tilarán leave from the bus terminal, half a block from the parque. Buses to San José on Sunday afternoon may be sold out by Saturday. The route between Tilarán and San José goes via Cañas and the Interamericana, not the Arenal-Fortuna-Ciudad Quesada route.

As of this writing, the timetable for departures from Tilarán is:

Buses To	Duration	Departures
San José	3½ hours	5, 7, 7:45 am, 2, 4:45 pm
Cañas	45 minutes	5, 7:30, 10 am, 12:30, 3:30 pm
Ciudad Quesada (via Fortuna)	4 hours	7 am, 12:30 pm
Arenal	1¼ hours	10 am, 4, 10 pm
Puntarenas	2 hours	6 am, 1 pm
Santa Elena	2½ hours	12:30 pm

Buses may take longer than advertised. A few other local villages are also served.

Northern Lowlands

The original vegetation of the northern lowlands was mixed tropical forest, becoming increasingly evergreen toward the Caribbean. Now, much of this has been replaced by cattle pasture. The climate is wet and hot, and toward the Caribbean the dry season is shorter and not entirely dry. The population density is low, with a few small towns, a skeleton of roads, and limited tourist facilities.

LOS CHILES
Population 8000
This small town is on the Río Frío*, three km from the Nicaraguan border (see Getting There & Away). There is a migraciones office (☎ 471-1153), open Monday to Friday 8 am to 4 pm. Servitur (☎ 471-1055, fax 471-1211) is a tour operator and information center.

Refugio Nacional de Vida Silvestre Caño Negro
Boat tours go from the Río Frío dock into the refuge. This is one of the country's best places for bird and wildlife observation. Boats cost US$45 to US$80 to hire for half a day, so get a group together.

Servitur charges US$33 per person (four minimum) for a half-day tour, including lunch, or hook up with a group in Fortuna.

Places to Stay & Eat
The *Hotel Onassis* on the corner of the parque and the *Hotel Río Frío* (☎ 471-1127), a block away from the parque, have rooms with shared cold bath for US$5 per person.

Cabinas Jabirú is close to Servitur, which takes reservations. Rates are US$15/20/25/30 for one to four people in simple, large units with two bedrooms, sitting area and hot shower. There is parking.

Restaurant El Parque serves tico food and is open 6 am to 9 pm.

Getting There & Away
There are 10 buses daily between Ciudad Quesada and Los Chiles.

A boat leaves every morning for San Carlos, Nicaragua (1½ hours, US$2.50).

PUERTO VIEJO DE SARAPIQUÍ
Locally called Puerto Viejo, this shouldn't be confused with Puerto Viejo de Talamanca on the Caribbean. The town is at the confluence of the Río Puerto Viejo and the Río Sarapiquí, and it used to be an important port on the trade route to the Caribbean. Today the region is known for its nearby undisturbed premontane tropical wet forest, which extends out from the northern arm of Parque Nacional Braulio Carrillo. The easiest access to the rain forest is from the local lodges and research station – all expensive but good.

La Selva
This biological station is five km southeast of Puerto Viejo and is run by the Organization of Tropical Studies (OTS; ☎ 240-6696, fax 240-6783, net). The place teems with researchers and grad students of tropical ecology. Educational, guided 3½-hour walks are offered at 8 am and 1:30 pm (US$20 or US$30 for both). Reservations are required.

Places to Stay & Eat
Budget travelers stay on the main street. The *Cabinas Restaurant Monteverde* (☎ 766-6236) charges US$6.50/9 for singles/doubles with private cold bath. The restaurant is popular and reasonable. The very basic *Hotel Santa Marta* charges US$3 per person, as does the spartan *Hotel Gonar* (☎ 766-6196) above the Ferretería Gonar (hardware shop).

The nicest budget hotel is *Mi Lindo Sarapiquí* (☎ 766-6281), south of the soccer field. Rates are US$10/14/20 for one/two/three people with private hot shower. They have a decent restaurant open from 9 am to 10 pm.

Getting There & Away
Bus Buses leave from two bus stops on the

main street. Schedules change regularly; a recent one was:

Buses To	Departures
San José	
(via Braulio Carrillo)	7, 8 am, 3 pm
San José	
(via Vara Blanca)	7:45 am, 4:15 pm
San Carlos	5:45, 8:45 am,
	12:15, 2, 3:30 pm
Guápiles	6:30, 9 am,
	1:15, 4, 6 pm

Boat Motorized dugouts can be rented (at expensive rates) from the small port. A daily 11 am boat goes down the Río Sarapiquí to **Trinidad** on the Río San Juan (US$3). Trinidad has basic cabins charging about US$10 per person.

Caribbean Lowlands

The Caribbean Coast is very different from the Pacific. Half of the Caribbean Coast is protected, with two national parks and two national wildlife refuges. There is rain year round, though February to March and September to October are less wet. The Caribbean is part of Limón Province, which has 250,000 inhabitants, 30% of which are blacks. Most live near the coast and speak some form of English, providing a cultural diversity that is missing in the rest of Costa Rica. Also, several thousand indigenous Bribri and Cabecar people survive in the south. The Caribbean Coast has fewer roads and has been developed more slowly than the Pacific.

PUERTO LIMÓN
Population 76,000

Puerto Limón is the capital of Limón Province, and locals simply call the city Limón. This seedy but lively port has a mainly black population and is not a tourist town. People spend a night here en route to somewhere else. Note that the locals don't use street names, but only local landmarks like the Municipalidad on Parque Vargas, or Radio Casino.

Information
Helennik Souvenirs Shop, Calle 3, Avs 4 and 5, is helpful with local information.

The Banco de Costa Rica (☎ 758-3166) and other banks change money. Exchange facilities are poor elsewhere along the coast.

The Hospital Tony Facio (☎ 758-2222), at the north end of the malecón, serves the entire province.

Stick to the main, well-lit streets at night. Watch for pickpockets during the day.

Things to See & Do
The main attraction is **Parque Vargas**, on the southeastern corner of town by the waterfront. The park has tropical trees, flowers, birds and sloths hanging out (literally) in the trees. From the park, walk north along the sea wall for views of the rocky headland upon which the city is built. Another focal point is the colorful **public market**. Also check out the **Ethnography Museum** (☎ 758-2130, 758-3903), open erratically. The nearest beach is **Playa Bonita**, four km northwest of town, which is OK for bathing though nothing special.

Columbus landed at Uvita Island, one km east of Limón, and *Día de la Raza* (Columbus Day) is celebrated enthusiastically in October most years. Thousands of ticos stream into town for street parades: dancing, music, singing and drinking go on for days. Hotels are booked in advance.

Places to Stay
Single women should avoid the cheapest hotels, which are a poor value and used by prostitutes. I'm not listing the worst ones.

The *Cariari Hotel* (☎ 758-1395) has small, basic rooms for US$4.50 per person and has singles. The *Hotel Oriental* (☎ 758-0117) is US$7 a double with shared cold showers but is OK. The *Hotel Ng* (☎ 758-2134) is filled with workers during the week and has very basic single/double rooms for US$6.50/10 or US$8/12.50 with private cold shower.

The *Hotel Fung* (☎ 758-3309) is fair and charges US$5.50/9 with communal cold

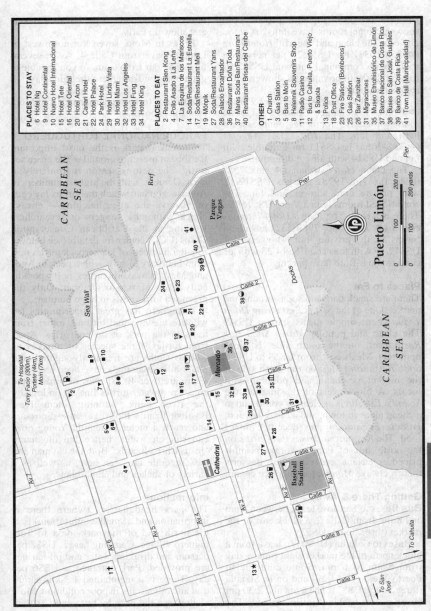

PLACES TO STAY
6 Hotel Ng
9 Hotel Continental
10 Nuevo Hotel Internacional
15 Hotel Tete
16 Hotel Oriental
20 Hotel Acon
21 Cariari Hotel
22 Hotel Palace
24 Park Hotel
29 Hotel Linda Vista
30 Hotel Miami
32 Hotel Los Angeles
33 Hotel Fung
34 Hotel King

PLACES TO EAT
2 Restaurant Sien Kong
4 Pollo Asado a La Leña
7 La Esquina de los Mariscos
14 Soda/Restaurant La Estrella
17 Soda/Restaurant Meli
19 Mönpik
27 Soda/Restaurant Yans
28 Palacio Encantador
36 Restaurant Doña Toda
37 Mares Soda Bar/Restaurant
40 Restaurant Brisas del Caribe

OTHER
1 Church
3 Gas Station
5 Bus to Moín
8 Helenik Souvenirs Shop
11 Radio Casino
12 Bus to Cahuita, Puerto Viejo
    & Sixaola
13 Police
18 Post Office
23 Fire Station (Bomberos)
25 Gas Station
26 Bar Zanzbar
31 Migraciones
35 Museo Etnohistórico de Limón
37 Banco Nacional de Costa Rica
38 Buses to San José, Guápiles
39 Banco de Costa Rica
41 Town Hall (Municipalidad)

Puerto Limón

COSTA RICA

showers or US$8/11 with private cold shower. Some rooms have fans! A good choice is the clean and cheerful *Hotel King* (☎ 758-1033) for US$5.25 per person in rooms with communal bath and US$13.50 for doubles with private cold shower. Most rooms have fans.

The old but interesting *Hotel Palace* (☎ 758-0419) charges US$6/11 for basic rooms or US$15 for better doubles with bath and fan. The *Hotel Los Angeles* (☎ 758-2068) is US$11 for a double with fan and US$14 with air conditioning.

The clean *Hotel Miami* (☎ /fax 758-0490, fax 758-1978) charges US$12/18 with private cold shower and fan; air-conditioned rooms with TV are US$15/23. There is a cafe. The *Nuevo Hotel Internacional* (☎ 758-0662, 798-0532) has clean rooms with private hot showers for US$12/15 with fans and US$14/23 with air conditioning. Both have parking.

Places to Eat

There are snack bars and sodas around the market. One of the best is *Restaurant Doña Toda*, where simple meals start at US$2. The clean and popular *Mares Soda Bar Restaurant*, on the south side, is more upmarket. Meals cost from US$3 to US$7. *Soda Restaurant Meli* on the north side of the market is cheap and popular with locals. A block west of the market, the *Soda La Estrella* is as clean as you'll find in a cheap place in town, and a block beyond, *Palacio Encantador* has decent Chinese food. The *Restaurant Brisas del Caribe* on the north side of Parque Vargas is mid-priced, pleasant and airy. For desserts there's always *Mönpik* for good ice cream.

Getting There & Away

Bus Buses to San José leave between 5 am and 8 pm from Calle 2, a block east of the market (three hours, US$3).

Buses to Cahuita (US$0.80) leave from a block north of the market eight times a day from 5 am to 6 pm. Some continue to Puerto Viejo (US$1.20) and on to Sixaola (three hours, US$2). The 6 am and 2:30 pm buses go on to Manzanillo instead. The

buses are crowded, so get advance tickets and show up early.

Buses to Moín, seven km northwest of Limón, leave from Calle 4, Av 5, several times an hour from 6 am, so you are able to get a boat for Tortuguero the same day.

Boat Boats to Tortuguero leave from Moín (see Bus, above).

PARQUE NACIONAL TORTUGUERO

This coastal park is the most important Caribbean breeding ground of the green sea turtle. The nesting season is from July to early October, with the highest numbers in August. You can watch the turtles lay eggs or observe the eggs hatching – always check with park rangers or researchers working at the Caribbean Conservation Corps (CCC) center for details (see below). Smaller numbers of leatherback turtles nest from February to July, with a peak in April and May. Hawksbill turtles nest sporadically from March to October. Only the green sea turtle nests in large numbers.

Tortuguero has great opportunities for wildlife viewing and birding, either from trails in the park or on boat trips. Apart from turtles, three species of monkey as well as sloths are frequently sighted, and many other mammals have been recorded. There are over 400 species of birds in the area. Freshwater turtles line up on logs by the river bank, sunning themselves. Basilisk lizards look like little dinosaurs and reach a meter in length. Young ones can run on water, hence the nickname 'Jesus Christ lizards.' Both the cayman and the crocodile are seen here, as well as a variety of snakes and amphibians.

Information

The park headquarters (where there is information and a small exhibit room) is at the north end of the park, next to Tortuguero village. Camping here is US$2 per person, and drinking water and pit latrines are provided. Park entrance is US$6 per day. There is a maintained 1.3-km nature trail and other trails in poor condition. Most visitors see the park by boat, both as they arrive from the south and by hiring a boat in Tortuguero village.

The beaches are not suitable for swimming. The surf is very rough, the currents are strong and sharks regularly patrol the waters. Rain gear and insect repellent are recommended.

Observing the Turtles

Watching hundreds of huge marine turtles nesting on the best nights of the season is a spectacular sight. So much so that the huge numbers of tourists admiring the spectacle have caused many of the turtles to leave and not lay their eggs – this is a serious problem. It is important to avoid harassing the turtles; the best way to do this (apart from not going) is to go with trained rangers or researchers and follow their instructions. I discourage trying to watch turtles without a guide because visitors can unwittingly scare off the animals. Flash photos are particularly disturbing to the egg-laying. This applies to all beach areas, inside and outside the park. Guided night walks are offered during laying periods for US$5 per person.

TORTUGUERO
Population 600

This little village is at the north end of the national park. Several places have boats for hire. You can paddle your own dugout canoe for about US$1.50 per person per hour, or go with a guide for twice that. It is worth hiring a guide, at least for a few hours, because you are able to see so much more.

In the center of the village is an informative kiosk explaining the natural history, cultural history, geography and climate of the region. The community appears to take some pride in 'its' turtles and national park. Instead of harvesting the turtles, the people exploit them and the accompanying park in nondestructive yet economically satisfactory ways, especially tourism.

Caribbean Conservation Corporation

The CCC, about one km north of Tortuguero, has a worthwhile visitor's center explaining turtle conservation and research

work; hours are daily 9 am to noon and 2 to 5 pm. An 18-minute video is shown on request. Admission is free but donations are welcomed. The CCC also has a US office; both offices can be reached by email (see the Online Resources appendix).

Cerro de Tortuguero

This 119-meter-high hill, about six km north of the village, is the highest point on the coast north of Limón. You need to hire a boat to get there. The path is very steep and usually muddy but has good views of the forest, canals, sea and birds. I saw several howler monkeys hanging out in the trees below the trail.

Boating

Several places north of the park entrance have boats for rent. You can paddle a dugout canoe for US$1.25 to US$1.50 per hour, or go with a guide for twice that (per person). Local guides include Damma, Bananero and Jim.

Motorboat tours are substantially more expensive. These tours cover more ground, and boatmen normally switch the motor off and paddle for a while.

Organized Tours

The cheapest tours are with Ecole Travel (☎ 223-2240, ☎ /fax 223-4128) in San José. They charge from US$55 for roundtrip transportation from San José (bus and boat), but you have to pay for hotels and meals in Tortuguero, and the 'guides' don't always speak English. They also have more expensive options including lodging.

Cotur (☎ 233-0155, fax 233-0778, net), Calle 36, Paseo Colón and Av 1, or Mitur (☎ 255-2031, fax 255-1846, net), on Paseo Colón, Calles 20 and 22, run three-day/two-night tours to Tortuguero for US$215 to US$240 per person, double occupancy (singles US$30 extra). All transport, guides, meals and accommodations are included. Day one includes a drive from San José to Moín, a five-hour boat ride to Tortuguero, and an overnight stay in one of their lodges (rooms have private bath). The boat slows for photographs, and a bilingual guide is aboard. Day two has guided walks and boat tours of the area, and a night visit to the beach is added during the turtle nesting season. On day three you return by boat and bus. Their lodges are across the river from Tortuguero village, and boat visits can be arranged.

More expensive tours with other companies are available.

Places to Stay & Eat

The friendly, family-run *Cabinas Mariscar* (reservations in San José ☎ 296-2626) has basic, clean rooms with fans and shared bath for US$6 per person. Two rooms with private bath and three beds are US$30. The basic, clean *Cabinas Sabina* has 31 rooms at US$10/15 for doubles/triples, but they lack fans. They have a few cheaper and even more basic boxes. Food is available at both these places. The unsigned *Tropical Lodge* has a few basic rooms at US$5 per person. *Miss Junie's* (☎ 710-0523) has new clean single/double rooms with fan and private bath for US$25/30. (Miss Junie is Tortuguero's best-known cook and she serves good meals for about US$5.) If these hotels are full, ask around; you may be able to stay in someone's house.

The *Cabinas Tatani* (also called 'Jardín Tropical') is a five-minute boat ride away – ask in the village for a boat. Basic rooms with four to six beds are US$7.50 per person and bathrooms are in a separate building. There are several mid and top end-priced places.

Restaurants charge about US$3 to US$4 per meal, and it is fairly basic food. Slightly cheaper and better meals are available by asking around and eating in private houses. One of the cheapest places is *Soda La Liliana* with basic casados for US$3.

Getting There & Away

Most people go to Tortuguero on a tour – getting there independently is difficult. In addition to air and bus travel, you may be able to reach Tortuga (and beyond to Barra del Colorado) by a combination of asking around, hitching, luck, bus, boat, patience and time.

Air Travelair has daily flights to and from San José that cost US$77/118 one way/roundtrip. There is a Travelair office in Tortuguero village; the airport is four km north. SANSA recently began flights on this route four days a week (US$40/80). Some flights with both airlines provide connections with Barra del Colorado.

Boat Boats to Tortuguero leave from the dock in Moín, a village north of Punto Limón. In Tortuguero, the boat dock is about 300 meters to the left of the main port, through a guarded gate. Cargo boats leave most days. A few travelers have been able to persuade captains to allow them aboard – it's cheaper but not easy to do.

Most travelers take a private boat for US$50 per person roundtrip with a three-person minimum (less with large groups). Boatmen hang around the dock in the early morning and boats normally leave between 7 am and 8 am. The trips take about five hours to Tortuguero (allowing for photography and wildlife viewing). After lunch and a brief time in Tortuguero, the return trip is done in 2½ hours. Overnights and returning the next day can be arranged.

You can make arrangements in Limón. Helennik Souvenirs, Calle 3, Avs 4 and 5, and Laura's Tours (☎ 758-2410) have both been recommended. Alfred Brown Robinson (☎ 758-1940, 758-0824) of Tortuguero Odysseys Tours was recently offering US$35 roundtrips on Tuesday, Thursday and Saturday, returning the following day, if there were enough people interested. He also offered US$75 tours including a cheap hotel and meals. Other boatmen include Willis Rankin (☎ 798-1556), Modesto Watson (☎ in San José 226-0986) and Mario Rivas.

BARRA DEL COLORADO

This is a village and also the biggest national wildlife refuge in Costa Rica. It is virtually an extension of Tortuguero national park. The area is expensive and known particularly for sportfishing (tarpon and snook), but excellent birding and wildlife watching opportunities are beginning to draw nature tours.

Orientation

The village lies near the mouth of the Río Colorado and is reached by air or boat. The airstrip is on the south side of the river (Barra del Sur) but more people live on the north bank (Barra del Norte). There are no roads, though a very rough one reaches the hamlet of Puerto Lindo, almost an hour away up the Río Colorado.

Places to Stay

Hotels, mostly sportfishing lodges, are expensive and reached by boat. The cheapest hotel is *Tarponland Lodge* (☎ pager 297-1010) next to the airport. Basic, clean rooms with bath and fan start at US$45 per person including meals. You may stay more cheaply with a local family if you ask around.

The German-run *Samay Lagoon Lodge* (☎ in San José 284-7047, fax 234-0646) is eight km south of the airport, with a beach a quarter kilometer away (swimming unsafe). Most visitors come on a three-day/two-night package beginning at Puerto Viejo de Sarapiquí with a five-hour boat ride down the Sarapiquí, San Juan and Colorado rivers to the lodge. The second day includes a guided canoe trip and hike into the rain forest, and the third day you return the way you came. This costs US$204 per person, double occupancy, from Puerto Viejo and includes meals, two nights' lodging in clean rooms with private hot showers, transportation and tour. Extra days are US$45 a day including meals and canoe use. Guided horseback riding (US$15 an hour), fishing or other tours can be arranged.

Getting There & Away

Air Services are similar to Tortuguero.

Bus Ulysses and his boat *Mamita* leave Barra del Norte at 4:30 am to connect with a daily 6 am bus from Puerto Lindo to Cariari (two to six hours, depending on road conditions). In Cariari there are buses

to Guápiles. The road is sometimes closed after heavy rains; it's also the subject of much contention between developers and conservationists.

Boat There is no regular service. Boats from Tortuguero charge about US$50; they'll take three to five passengers. If you have time, wait for a group of locals going there and ride more cheaply with them.

The tour with the Samay Lagoon Lodge is a good way of getting here.

CAHUITA

This village, 43 km southeast of Limón, is known for the attractive beaches that can be found in Parque Nacional Cahuita, a small peninsula immediately to the south. Although only three hours by car from San José, the area has a provincial and unhurried ambiance.

Many of the 3500 inhabitants of the Cahuita district speak a Creole dialect. Much of the Creole culture remains for those who look for it, particularly in cooking, music and medicinal plants. Cahuita is expanding as a tourist destination.

Information

Cash US dollars are readily exchanged. Cahuita Tours and the better hotels sometimes change traveler's checks. The public telephone office is at the Soda Uvita.

Warning Don't leave your gear on the beach when swimming, don't walk the beaches alone at night, and be prudent if you enter some of the local bars. (I hear occasional complaints about local men who accuse tourists of being racist for not buying them drinks.) Some locals do take advantage of tourists, but this is not generally a major problem. Beware of drug sellers who may be in cahoots with the police.

Some single women travelers have been hassled by a few of the local men. Traveling with a friend may be a safer alternative to traveling alone. (I have also met single women travelers who have had a great time, but you can't always avoid unpleasant situations.)

COSTA RICA

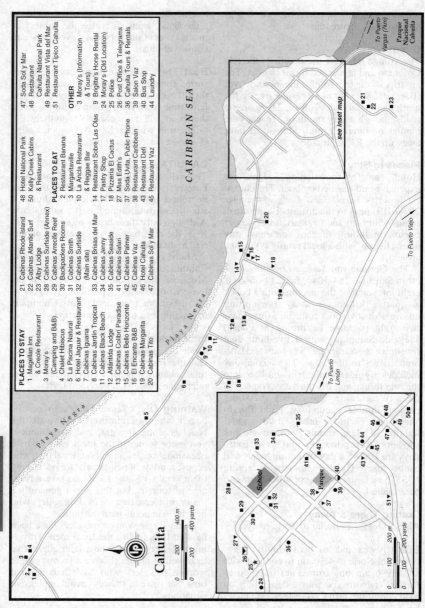

Cahuita

PLACES TO STAY
1   Magellan Inn
    & Creole Restaurant
3   Moray's
    (Camping and B&B)
4   Chalet Hibiscus
5   La Piscina Natural
6   Hotel Jaguar & Restaurant
7   Cabinas Iguana
8   Cabinas Jardin Tropical
11 Cabinas Black Beach
12 Atlantida Lodge
13 Cabinas Colibri Paradise
15 Cabinas Bello Horizonte
16 El Encanto B&B
19 Cabinas Margarita
20 Cabinas Tito
21 Cabinas Rhode Island
22 Cabinas Atlantic Surf
23 Alby Lodge
28 Cabinas Surfside (Annex)
29 Cabinas Arrecife Reef
30 Backpackers Rooms
31 Cabinas Smith
32 Cabinas Surfside
    (Main site)
33 Cabinas Brisas del Mar
34 Cabinas Jenny
35 Cabinas Seaside
41 Cabinas Safari
42 Cabinas Palmer
45 Cabinas Vaz
46 Hotel Cahuita
47 Cabinas Sol y Mar
48 Hotel National Park
50 Kelly Creek Cabins
    & Restaurant

PLACES TO EAT
2   Restaurant Banana
3   Margaritaville
10 La Ancla Restaurant
    & Reggae Bar
14 Restaurant Sobre Las Olas
17 Pastry Shop
18 Pizzeria El Cactus
27 Miss Edith's
37 Soda Uvita, Public Phone
38 Restaurant Caribbean
43 Restaurant Defi
45 Restaurant Vaz

47 Soda Sol y Mar
48 Restaurant
49 Restaurant Vista del Mar
51 Restaurant Tipico Cahuita

OTHER
3   Moray's (Information
    & Tours)
9   Brigitte's Horse Rental
24 Moray's (Old Location)
25 Police
26 Post Office & Telegrams
36 Cahuita Tours & Rentals
39 Salon Vaz
40 Bus Stop
44 Laundry

'Safe sex' is rarely practiced here, but AIDS and other STDs are on the increase. If you are tempted by local sexual liaisons, bring your own condoms.

Nude bathing is not accepted. Wearing skimpy swimsuits in the villages is frowned upon. Wear a T-shirt and shorts.

Beaches
At the northwest end of Cahuita is a long black-sand beach with good swimming. The white-sand beach at the eastern end of town is in the national park, and a trail in the jungle behind it leads to a third beach about six km away. These last two beaches are separated by a rocky headland with a small coral reef.

Organized Tours & Rentals
The following places provide tourist information and offer tours and rentals. They include Moray's (☎ 755-0038), Cahuita Tours (☎ 755-0082, 755-0083) and others. Sample day rentals are mask, snorkel and fins for US$7.50; bicycles for US$7.50 to US$10; binoculars or surfboards for US$7.50. Boat trips to the reef in a glass-bottomed boat, with snorkeling opportunities, are US$15 per person for three or four hours. Day trips to Tortuguero are about US$65.

Local hiking and horseback riding trips are offered. Brigitte (☎ 755-0053), a Swiss woman, offers half-day guided horseback tours for US$25 to US$35 and horse rental at US$10 per hour. Recommended local guides include Walter Cunningham (who specializes in birding), Carlos Mairena and José McCloud. Ask in your hotel about these men.

Places to Stay
Budget travelers can economize by renting rooms for two or more people – singles are at a premium. Hotels in the center are cheaper than those in quieter locations.

Cabinas Bello Horizonte (☎ 755-0206) has basic but clean rooms with communal hot showers for US$5/7.50 for singles/doubles and cabins with private shower for US$20. Another cheapie is Backpackers Rooms with four basic rooms for US$5 per person.

Cabinas Surfside (☎ 755-0246) has clean concrete-block rooms with fan and private bath. There's a guarded parking area. Rates are US$12 for a double, and they have a couple of better cabins a block away for US$18. The clean and friendly Cabinas Smith (☎ 755-0068) has good rooms with warm showers and fans for US$15.

Cabinas Vaz (☎ 755-0218) has clean concrete-block rooms with bath and fan for US$11/14, though some rooms above the restaurant suffer from noise. The similarly priced Cabinas Rhode Island (☎ 755-0086) has clean rooms with bath and fan. Pleasant Cabinas Atlantic Surf (☎ 755-0086) has wood rooms with fans, cold showers and porches, for US$11/16.

Cabinas Brisas del Mar (☎ 755-0011) charges US$15 to US$20 for clean double rooms with cold showers and good beds. The Cabinas Sol y Mar (☎ 755-0237) has decent rooms with fan and hot shower for US$17. Friendly Cabinas Seaside (☎ 755-0210) is on the beach and has hammocks and coconut palms outside. Clean doubles with private cold showers are US$16. Tour information is available.

Hotel Cahuita (☎ 755-0233) is US$9/18 with fans and private bath; OK for a single but overpriced for a double. Cabinas Palmer (☎ 755-0243) is owned by friendly locals. Clean rooms with hot showers are US$12/17. (Avoid the old rooms at the front.) Cabinas Safari (☎ 755-0078) has decent rooms with hot showers for US$16/20. Cabinas Arrecife Reef (☎ 755-0081) has plain rooms with hot showers for US$15/20 and a breezy porch with good sea views.

Out on Playa Negra, La Piscina Natural has simple but adequate cabins with hot showers for US$18 double. Cabinas Margarita (☎ 755-0205) has clean rooms with electric showers for US$14/20. Cabinas Black Beach (☎ 755-0251) has four pleasant double rooms with balcony and private bath for US$25.

The friendly Cabinas Tito (☎ 755-0286) has six pleasant rooms with cold showers and fans, some with kitchenette, for US$25/30. The friendly, multilingual *Cabinas Colibrí Paradise* (☎ 755-0055) in a quiet, wooded location has a handful of cabins with fans, kitchenette, refrigerator and hot showers for US$32.

Near the park entrance, the *Hotel National Park* (☎ 755-0244) has decent clean rooms with hot showers for US$25 or US$30 with views. A popular restaurant is attached.

Places to Eat & Drink
Most eateries are geared toward travelers and are not very cheap. *Miss Edith's* is traditionally popular and has recently expanded. Meals are US$4 and up and service is very laid-back (sloooow!). Alcohol isn't served. *Restaurant Defi* is currently in vogue and features Caribbean music (occasionally live), and it serves anything from Creole cooking to Italian food (rasta pasta?). They open from early breakfast till late. Near the parque, the *Restaurant Caribbean* serves a whole fresh fish for US$4.

On a side road northwest of the center, *Pizzería El Cactus* has pizzas and pastas in the US$3 to US$6 range. They are open for dinner only. Out toward the black-sand beach, *Restaurant Sobre Las Olas* is a popular but slightly pricey beachfront restaurant. Nearby is the *Pastry Shop* – delicious bread, cakes and pies. *La Ancla Restaurant and Reggae Bar* has a limited menu, but it's a popular place for a beer with the rastas. *Restaurant Banana* sells good local food. Nearby, the Canadian-run *Margaritaville* serves home-cooked dinners daily.

Restaurant Cahuita National Park by the entrance to the park is a little pricey but popular for all meals. *Restaurant Vista Del Mar* across the street serves seafood (US$3 and up) all day long. Nearby *Soda Sol y Mar* and *Restaurant Vaz*, attached to the cabinas of the same names, are both good. *Restaurant Típico Cahuita* has a variety of local food – budget travelers should order the casado for US$3.

Local ladies may set up shop on the street and sell homemade stews and snacks direct from the pot.

Entertainment
This can be summed up in one word: bars. The 'safest' bets are any of the restaurants mentioned above. For local color, the *Salon Vaz* is open all day and into the night and is known for its cracking loud games of dominoes. At night, the back room pounds to the sounds of a Caribbean disco.

Getting There & Away
Buses from San José to Sixaola stop at Cahuita. The fare is US$7 or US$4.50 depending on whether you get a directo or not. Buses may drop you on the main road (10 minute walk) or at the crossroads stop in the town center (see map).

Alternately, take a bus from San José to Puerto Limón and change there for buses to central Cahuita.

Buses return to San José from the crossroads. These buses leave from Sixaola and may be late by the time they pass through Cahuita. Schedules are liable to change so ask locally. For Sixaola, catch the bus at the main road, southwest of the bus crossroads. For other places, wait at the crossroads in town. Recently, the timetable was:

Buses To	Cost	Departures
San José	US$4.50 or US$7	7, 9:45, 11:30 am, 4:30 pm
Limón	US$0.80	6:30, 10 am, noon, 1:30, 3, 4:30, 5:30, 6:30 pm
Puerto Viejo	US$0.50	6, 9, 11 am, 2, 5, 7 pm
Manzanillo	US$1.50	7 am, 3:30 pm
Sixaola	US$2 or US$2.50	10 am, 5:30, 7:30 pm

PARQUE NACIONAL CAHUITA
This small park is one of the more frequently visited in Costa Rica. It has easy access, nearby hotels, attractive beaches, a coral reef and a coastal rain forest.

The main entrance is east of Cahuita village, through the Kelly Creek station. A two-km white-sand beach stretches to the east. The first 500 meters have warning

COSTA RICA

signs about unsafe swimming, but beyond that the waves are gentle. The rocky Punta Cahuita (Point Cahuita) separates this beach from Vargas Beach, at the end of which is the Puerto Vargas ranger station, seven km from Kelly Creek. The two stations are linked by a trail through the coastal jungle behind the beach. A river near the end of the first beach can be thigh-deep at high tide. Many animals and birds can be seen by an observant hiker.

Information

The park stations are open daily from 8 am to 4 pm; entrance is US$6, though at the Kelly Creek entrance, the locals have set up a 'donate what you want' station because the US$6 fee was driving away travelers (and business). You can get in and out after hours, though cars can't get into Puerto Vargas after hours.

Camping (US$2 per person) is at Vargas Beach, about one km from the Puerto Vargas ranger station. There are outdoor showers and pit latrines at the administration center near the middle of the camping area. There is drinking water, and some sites have picnic tables. The area is rarely crowded. Camp close to the administration center for greater security; it is safe if you don't leave your gear unattended.

A good day hike is to take the 6 am Cahuita-Puerto Viejo bus to the Puerto Vargas entrance road, walk one km to the coast, then seven km more back to Cahuita. Carry water, insect repellent and sunscreen.

PUERTO VIEJO DE TALAMANCA

Locally known as Puerto Viejo (don't confuse it with Puerto Viejo de Sarapiquí), this village is more tranquil than Cahuita. There is more influence from the local Bribri indigenous culture and less development. The surfing is good.

The village is 18 km southeast of Cahuita. The inhabitants traditionally lived by small-scale agriculture and fishing, although tourism is now becoming a minor industry. The mixture of black and indigenous cultures is interesting: you can buy Bribri handicrafts or listen to reggae; take

horseback riding trips or go fishing with the locals; and surf, swim or hang out with the old-timers and talk. There's plenty to do, but things are very relaxed – take your time.

Note There is no bank and few places accept dollars, so change before you arrive.

Asociación Talamanqueña de Ecoturismo y Conservación

ATEC (☎ /fax 750-0191, 750-0188) is a nonprofit grassroots organization promoting local tourism in ways that enhance nearby communities and provide a learning experience for visitors. Hours are daily 7 am to noon and 1 to 9 pm.

ATEC is an information center about local issues, and they can arrange homestays with locals and a variety of tours with an emphasis on native cultures, natural history and environmental issues. Tours are about US$12.50 for half a day and US$25 for a full day and involve a fair amount of hiking. Overnight trips are possible.

Indigenous Reserves

There are several reserves in the area but entrance is by permits, which can be difficult to obtain for some reserves. Mauricio Salazar from the Cabinas Chimuri (see below) can guide you on day tours to the small KéköLdi reserve. Tours run twice a week, US$25 per person including lunch, two-person minimum, six maximum; 10% of tour cost goes directly to the reserve.

Surfing

The waves are best from December to early March, with another season in June and July. The people at the Hotel Puerto Viejo are local surfing experts.

Horse & Bicycle Rental

Several places rent horses and bikes – ask around.

Places to Stay

Puerto Viejo is currently more popular and more expensive than Cahuita. High season weekend rates are given; discounts are available at other times. Most hotels

COSTA RICA

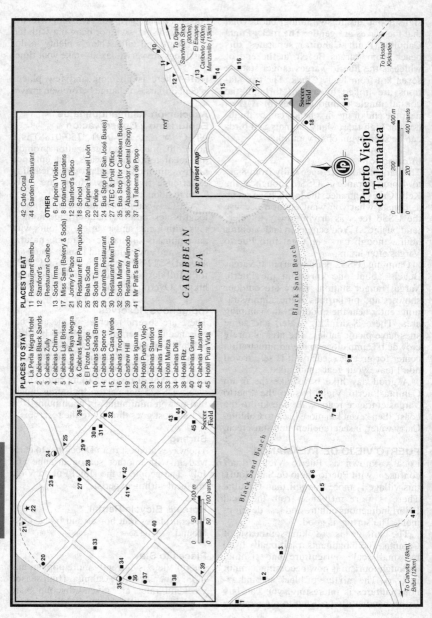

PLACES TO STAY
1 La Perla Negra Hotel
2 Cabinas Black Sands
3 Cabinas Zully
4 Cabinas Chimuri
5 Cabinas Las Brisas
7 Cabinas Playa Negra
   & Cabinas Maribe
9 El Pizote Lodge
10 Cabinas Salsa Brava
14 Cabinas Spence
15 Cabinas Casa Verde
16 Cabinas Tropical
19 Cashew Hill
23 Cabinas Iguana
30 Hotel Puerto Viejo
31 Cabinas Stanford
32 Cabinas Tamara
33 Cabinas Diti
34 Hotel Maritza
38 Hotel Ritz
40 Cabinas Grant
43 Cabinas Jacaranda
45 Hotel Pura Vida

PLACES TO EAT
11 Restaurant Bambu
12 Stanford's
   Restaurant Caribe
13 Soda Irma
17 Miss Sam (Bakery & Soda)
21 Jonny's Place
25 Restaurant El Parquecito
26 Bela Soda
28 Soda Tamara
29 Caramba Restaurant
30 Restaurant MexiTico
32 Soda Marley
39 Restaurante Alimodo
41 Mr Patt's Bakery
42 Café Coral
44 Garden Restaurant

OTHER
6 Puperia Violeta
8 Botanical Gardens
12 Stanford's Disco
18 School
20 Puperia Manuel León
22 Police
24 Bus Stop (for San José Buses)
27 ATEC & Post Office
35 Bus Stop (for Caribbean Buses)
36 Abastecedor Central (Shop)
37 La Taberna de Popo

To Digalo
Sandwich Shop (300m);
El Escape,
Caribeño (400m);
Manzanillo (13km)

To Hostal
Kiskadee

CARIBBEAN
SEA

reef

Black Sand Beach

Black Sand Beach

Black Sand Beach

Soccer
Field

Puerto Viejo
de Talamanca

see inset map

0   200   400 m
0   200   400 yards

Soccer
Field

0   50   100 m
0   50   100 yards

To Cahuita (18km),
Bribri (12km)

provide mosquito netting or fans (a breeze helps keep mosquitoes away). Cold water showers are the norm and may work intermittently in the cheapest places.

A reader reports that a campground charging US$2 a night has opened on the beach west of Stanford's restaurant. They have kitchen facilities, lockers for backpacks and so on. I haven't checked this out.

The friendly *Hostal Kiskadee* (☎ 750-0075), a six- or seven-minute walk southeast of the soccer field on a steep, unlit path, has dormitory-style accommodations for US$5 per person. The friendly *Cashew Hill* has two basic rooms for US$10/12. They have kitchen privileges and a hot shared shower. A larger room with private bath is US$15/20. The *Hotel Puerto Viejo* is the biggest place in town and is popular with surfers. Basic but clean upstairs rooms are US$5 per person; poorer downstairs rooms are a little cheaper. Doubles with private cold showers are US$16.

Also popular with surfers is the basic *Cabinas Iguana*, which is US$14 for doubles with private bath, but the water supply is poor. Another cheapie is the basic *Hotel Ritz* at US$10 for a single cubicle with shared bath or US$15/18 with private cold bath.

Cabinas Jacaranda (☎ 750-0069) has nice rooms with fans and mosquito nets at US$13/16 with shared showers or US$22 for a double with private hot shower. They have a restaurant. *Cabinas Spence* has decent rooms with private bath for US$15.50, single or double.

Cabinas Diti is OK and has four doubles with private baths for US$16 – ask at Taberna de Popo for information. *Cabinas Stanford* is also OK and has private cold baths and fans – ask at Stanford's Restaurant for information. They charge US$13 for a double. *Cabinas Salsa Brava* has basic doubles with private bath and good sea views for US$20; you pay for the view. The attractive, clean *Hotel Pura Vida* (☎ / fax 750-0002) charges US$13/17 in decent rooms with shared hot showers. Two rooms with private bath are US$23/27. The helpful *Cabinas Grant* (☎ 758-2845) has decent rooms with private cold bath and

fan for US$15/20. *Cabinas Tamara* (☎ 750-0157) has good doubles with private baths and fans for US$16.

Cabinas Las Brisas (also called 'Mr O'Conner's,' over a kilometer west of town) has four basic but decent double rooms for US$13 and two larger ones for US$23. *Cabinas Maribe* (☎ 750-0182, 758-3884), has decent doubles with cold bath and fan for under US$20. Still farther west, the popular (and often full) *Cabinas Black Sands* is thatched in the local Bribri style and set in a pleasant garden. Three basic rooms with mosquito nets are US$8 per person (less if you book all six beds) with communal kitchen and bathroom facilities.

The *Hotel Maritza* (☎ /fax 750-0199) is US$22 for a double in nice cabins with fan, private bath and electric shower. They have a few basic older rooms for US$13. The clean, friendly, multilingual *Cabinas Casa Verde* (☎ 750-0047, fax 750-0015) has pleasant rooms with warm communal showers for US$15/20 or US$25/30 with private bath.

Cabinas Chimuri (☎ 750-0119), run by Mauricio Salazar, who knows about Bribri culture as well as anyone in town, has a few Bribri-style A-frame cabins for US$17/25 and one quadruple cabin for US$35. Students get discounts. The communal kitchen and bathroom are simple. The cabins are set in a 20-hectare private reserve with trails and good birding possibilities.

Places to Eat & Drink

Several small locally owned places serve typical meals and snacks – ask at ATEC for recommendations about these or about eating with a family. The bakery and soda at *Miss Sam* and *Soda Irma* are run by women who are long-term residents. *Doña Juanita* and *Doña Guillerma* cook out of their houses near the entrance to town; ask locally for information.

Bela Soda has cheap but good breakfasts. The *Restaurant Bambu* is inexpensive if you avoid the tourist menu, and it has a popular bar. *Jonny's Place* has cheap, large Chinese meals. The *Café Coral* has yogurt, granola, homemade wholewheat pancakes and such for breakfast from Tuesday to

Sunday 7 am to noon. For breakfasts and snacks throughout the day, try the friendly *Soda Tamara*.

Stanford's Restaurant Caribe is good for seafood (most at US$5 to US$8) and has a disco on the weekends. *Restaurant Parquecito* has quite good meals around US$4. The *Soda Marley* is popular with ticos and has local food. The *Restaurant MexiTico* in the Hotel Puerto Viejo serves Mexican snacks and meals, while *Caramba Restaurant* has Italian. *Digalo* serves tasty and healthy sandwiches. The best in town is the recommended *Garden Restaurant*, serving vegetarian, Caribbean and Asian food. Vegetarian entrees begin around US$5.50, others are pricier.

Entertainment

La Taberna de Popo is a locally popular bar with Caribbean and rock music and live entertainment on occasion. *Jonny's Place* is the most happening dance club on the weekends. There's quieter weekend dancing at *Stanford's Disco*. *Restaurant Bambu* has a popular bar and good reggae nights (with DJ) from Monday to Friday.

Getting There & Away

Autotransportes MEPE in San José has a 3:30 pm bus to Puerto Viejo; other buses drop you off at the intersection *(cruce)* almost six km from Puerto Viejo. Check with the bus company to confirm this. Alternatively, go from Puerto Limón, where more buses go into Puerto Viejo. It's cheaper to change in Limón than go direct.

Buses from Puerto Viejo leave from the bus stops shown on the map. Buses usually start elsewhere and may be late going through Puerto Viejo. The following recent schedule from Puerto Viejo will change; check with ATEC for the latest. Other buses can be caught from the *cruce*.

Buses To	Cost	Departures
San José	US$5	6:30, 9 am, 4 pm
Cahuita/Limón	US$0.50/1.20	6, 8:30 am, 1, 4, 5, 5:15 pm
Manzanillo	US$1.20	7.20 am, 3:30 pm

Bribri/Sixaola	US$0.50/2.50	6:20, 9:20 am, 5:20, 7:15 pm
Bribri only	US$0.50	11:20 am

EAST OF PUERTO VIEJO

A 13-km dirt road heads east from Puerto Viejo along the coast, past sandy beaches and rocky points, through the small communities of Punta Uva and Manzanillo and sections of the Reserva Indigena Cocles/KéköLdi, and ends up in Refugio Nacional de Vida Silvestre Gandoca-Manzanillo. There has been much discussion about the pros and cons of tourism in this remote area – talk to ATEC or read *La Loca de Gandoca* for some interesting perspectives. New hotels have opened, but few are cheap.

Playa Cocles, two km east, has good surfing – surfers stay at *Cabinas & Soda Garibaldi*. Rooms with private bath and sea views are US$12. There are several houses with 'Rooms for Rent.' *Kapalapa* has music and videos and a few budget rooms.

Near **Playa Chiquita**, five km east, is *Picasso Hotel* (in San José ☎ 233-3652) with spacious rooms and cabins with private baths for US$20 to US$40 a double. Nearby, *Hotel Lapa Lapa* (in San José ☎ 221-9592, fax 255-3941) has basic double rooms with private hot shower for US$30. They have a restaurant, bar and dance club next door. Also near here is the *Sloth Club* with a few rustic doubles from US$10 to US$25 and the clean *Ranchita Blanca* with a few doubles with private bath for US$30 and bicycles for rent. Here, too, several houses advertise rooms for rent. *Elena Brown's Soda & Restaurant* is a nice local place to eat, and the *Soda Acuarius* bakes homemade bread and has a couple of basic rooms for rent.

Punta Uva is seven km east. A sign advertises *Caminata Guiada al Bosque* (guided hikes in the forest). Beyond are *Selvin's Cabins* with basic double rooms for US$16 and a cabin with private bath for US$30 for four people. There is a restaurant (closed Monday and Tuesday). About 200 meters farther is *Walaba Cabinas* with basic rooms and dormitories from US$10 per person.

Manzanillo village is 12.5 km east and within the Gandoca-Manzanillo wildlife refuge(it already existed when the refuge was established). The schoolmaster, Don German, is a fountain of local information. The road continues for about a kilometer and then peters out. Footpaths continue around the coast through Gandoca-Manzanillo.

Near the bus stop in Manzanillo, the basic *Cabinas Maxi* are about US$15 per room. There is a restaurant/bar, with dancing on weekends. Local women prepare traditional meals in their homes – ask around.

The **Gandoca-Manzanillo** refuge continues southeast as far as Panama. A coral reef is about 200 meters offshore and snorkeling is possible. There is some rain forest and some of the most beautiful beaches on the Caribbean. A coastal trail leads 5.5 km from Manzanillo to Punta Mona.

Florentino Grenald lives in Manzanillo and acts as the reserve's administrator. He can recommend guides and provide information. Camping is permitted, but there are no organized facilities.

Getting There & Away

Buses leave Limón for Manzanillo (2½ hours, US$1.90) at 6 am and 2:30 pm, passing through Cahuita and Puerto Viejo. Return buses leave Manzanillo at 8:30 am and 4:30 pm.

SIXAOLA

Sixaola is an unattractive border town with Panama. Most overlanders go via Paso Canoas on the Interamericana.

There are a few cheap and basic places to stay and eat. *Cabinas Sanchez* at US$9 for a double is one of the best.

There are three buses a day with Autotransportes MEPE from San José to Sixaola – the first one arrives by late morning. Buses return to San José at 5 and 8 am, and 2:30 pm (six hours, US$5.75). There are three buses a day to and from Limón.

Crossing the Border to Panama

The Panamanian town across the border from Sixaola is **Guabito**. There are no banks in Guabito, but stores accept colones, balboas and US dollars. Border hours are 7 to 11 am and 1 to 5 pm. Frequent minibuses go from Guabito to Changuinola (16 km), which has a bank, an airport with daily flights to David, and buses to Almirante (30 km), where there are cheaper hotels. From Almirante continue into Panama by boat. Panamanian time is one hour ahead of Costa Rican time.

Southern Costa Rica

The Interamericana reaches its highest point near the 3491-meter mist-shrouded peak of Cerro de la Muerte, about 100 km south of San José. From there the road drops steeply to the town of San Isidro de El General (702 meters), the entry point to the nearby Parque Nacional Chirripó, which includes Costa Rica's highest mountains.

From San Isidro, the Interamericana continues southeast, through mainly agricultural lowlands, to Panama just over 200 km away. Towns are small but of interest to those wanting to see Costa Rica off the main tourist trail. These towns provide access to some of the more remote protected areas in the country.

Two places along the Interamericana between San José and San Isidro are of interest to budget travelers. The **Finca del Eddie Serrano** (☎ 534-4415, 454-4746) is one km off the highway near Km marker 70 (south of San José). The finca has quetzals nesting from November to early April. You can stay in bunk-rooms for US$30 per person, including three meals and a guided hike to see quetzals.

Avalon Reserve (☎ 380-2107, ☎ /fax 771-7226) is 3.5 km west of the Interamericana from División at Km 107. It's a new cloud forest reserve with hiking trails. Day use is US$3, camping is US$6, dorm beds are US$9 and doubles with shared bath are US$22. There is hot water and a restaurant.

SAN ISIDRO DE EL GENERAL
Population 40,000

San Isidro is the main town on the Interamericana Sur. The Río General valley is important for agriculture. A bustling, pleasant and fairly modern town, San Isidro is a transport hub and the commercial center of the coffee fincas, cattle ranches and plant nurseries that dot the mountain slopes. There's a small Museo Regional del Sur at Calle 2 and Av 1.

Information
The tourism office (☎ 771-6096) is on Calle 4, Avs 1 and 3. The Parque Nacional Chirripó office (☎ 771-3155, fax 771-4836) is open Monday to Friday 8 am to noon and 1 to 4 pm. Several banks change money.

Special Events
The annual agricultural fair is held at the beginning of February. San Isidro is the patron saint of farmers, who bring animals into town to be blessed on May 15.

Places to Stay
Shoestringers use *Hotel El Jardín* (☎ 771-0349), which has clean, basic rooms

San Isidro de El General

0   100   200 m
0   100   200 yards

PLACES TO STAY
6 Hotel Balboa
7 Hotel Amaneli
11 Hotel Jerusalen
13 Hotel El Jardín
15 Hotel Iguazú
16 Hotel Lala
17 Hotel Astoria
20 Hotel Chirripó Cafe
    & Restaurant
30 Pensión Eiffel

PLACES TO EAT
9 Soda El Bingo
10 Pizzería/Bar Paramó
13 Restaurant El Jardín
14 Restaurant El Tenedor
18 Restaurant Hong Kong
20 Café & Restaurant Chirripó
27 Marisquería Marea Baja

OTHER
1 Gas Station
2 TUASUR Buses to
    San José
3 Musoc Buses to San José
4 ICE (Telephone Office)
5 Tourist Information Office
8 Banco Nacional de
    Costa Rica
12 Museo Regional del Sur,
    Centro Cultural
19 24-hour Gas Station, Buses
    to Puerto Jiménez
21 TRACOPA Bus Terminal
22 National Park
    Regional Office
23 Banco de Costa Rica
24 Mercado Municipal
25 New Bus Terminal
26 Post Office
28 Banco de San José
29 Buses to Dominical,
    Uvita & Quepos
31 Selvamar (Travel Agency)

To San José (136km)
To Dominical (34km)
Río San Isidro
Interamericana
Parque Central
Cathedral
Estadio de Fútbol (Soccer Stadium)
To Hotel del Sur (6km), Panama (220km)

(US$3.75 per person) and a cheap restaurant. The very basic *Hotel Lala* (☎ 771-0291) charges US$2.20 per person or US$6.50 a double with private cold shower. The OK *Hotel Balboa* is US$4/6 for singles/doubles. The *Hotel Astoria* (☎ 771-0914) has very basic boxes for US$5/9, or slightly better boxes for US$6/10 with private cold shower. The usually full *Pensión Eiffel* (☎ 771-0230) is US$4.50 per person.

The modern *Hotel Chirripó* (☎ 771-0529) costs US$5.50/9.50 or US$9/15 in rooms with private electric shower. It has a decent restaurant. The clean and secure *Hotel Iguazu* (☎ 771-2571) is US$14/21 with private electric shower, TV and fan. The *Hotel Amaneli* (☎ 771-0352) is US$9 per person in clean rooms with private hot shower and fans.

Places to Eat
There are good sodas in the center of town and in the market/bus terminal area. The *Hotel Restaurant El Jardín* is cheap and good. The *Hotel Chirripó Café* opens at 6:30 am and is cheap and popular. The *Restaurant El Tenedor* has a balcony overlooking a busy street – snacks and meals (including pizza) range from US$1 to US$5. *Soda El Bingo* serves casados for under US$2. The *Restaurant Hong Kong* is OK for Chinese food.

Getting There & Away
Frequent buses to San José (three hours, US$3.30) leave from Musoc (☎ 771-0414) or TUASUR (☎ 771-0419) at Calle 2 and the Interamericana.

Buses for San Gerardo de Rivas (for Chirripó) leave at 5 am from the Parque Central and 2 pm from the new bus terminal. This terminal serves local destinations.

Buses to Puerto Jiménez leave at 5:30 am and noon from a fruit stand on the Interamericana (six hours, US$4). Southbound buses stop here to pick up passengers. Buses for Quepos (via Dominical) leave at 7 am, 1:30, 3 pm; to Uvita (via Dominical) at 6 am and 3 pm.

TRACOPA buses pass through San Isidro for Golfito, Paso Canoas, Ciudad Cortés (near Palmar Norte), Coto 47 (near Neily), San Vito and David, Panama. Tickets are sold on a space-available basis. If they are full, take a bus originating in San Isidro and go to Palmar Norte for better connections to Sierpe and Ciudad Cortés, to Río Claro for connections to Golfito, and to Neily for Paso Canoas.

SAN GERARDO DE RIVAS
This village is the base for climbing Chirripó. Buses from San Isidro stop outside the ranger station at the entrance to the village. A couple of kilometers north are thermal springs where you can soak all day for US$1.

The most popular hotel is *Hotel y Restaurant Roca Dura* at US$3 per person with shared hot showers. The friendly *Cabinas & Soda El Descanso* is also good at US$4 per person. There are others.

Return buses to San Isidro leave for the two-hour trip from near the ranger station at 7 am and 4 pm.

PARQUE NACIONAL CHIRRIPÓ
This mountainous park is named for Cerro Chirripó (3820 meters), the highest peak in the country. The ranger station at San Gerardo is at 1350 meters, but most of the park is over 2000 meters above sea level. There are hiking trails and mountain huts near Chirripó's summit. Camping is prohibited throughout the park.

Information
During the busy dry season weekends (especially Easter), the two mountain huts (40 bunks total) may be full. The wet season is uncrowded, and it rarely rains before 1 pm. Another hut with solar-heated water and 20 more beds may open in 1997. It can freeze at night. Bring a warm sleeping bag and a camping stove.

Pay fees (US$6 per day and US$2.50 per night at the huts) and obtain information at the San Gerardo ranger station (daily 5 am to 5 pm) or at the San Isidro office. Usually, you can climb the same day if you arrive in the morning, but you may have to wait a day or two if the huts are full. It is a steep

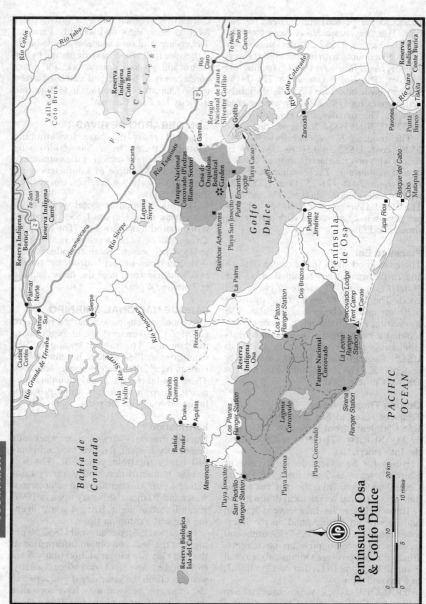

Península de Osa & Golfo Dulce

16-km climb on a good trail to the Chirripó summit area where the huts are; there are signs. Allow seven to 16 hours for the climb and carry water. In the dry season only one place has water before the huts. In emergencies, a small cave and a dilapidated hut are along the way. From the huts it is an additional two-hour hike to the summit.

PALMAR NORTE & PALMAR SUR
This small town is a northern gateway to Parque Nacional Corcovado (described below). Palmar Norte has a bank, buses and hotels; Palmar Sur has the airport.

Places to Stay & Eat
On the Interamericana, *Cabinas Tico Aleman* (☎ 786-6232) have clean rooms with private bath and fan for US$9 per person, and *Cabinas & Restaurant Wah Lok* (☎ 786-6777) charge US$7/11 with shower. In town, *Hotel Xenia* (☎ 786-6129) is slightly cheaper, and *Cabinas Amarillas* (☎ 786-6251) is the best at US$17 for a double.

Bar/Restaurante El Puente serves tico food and is locally popular. There are several Chinese restaurants.

Getting There & Away
Air Travelair (US$78/127) and SANSA (US$50/100) both have daily flights from San José.

Bus TRACOPA has seven buses a day to and from San José, four buses to San Isidro, and southbound buses on a space-available basis. Buses leave from the Supermercado Terraba four times a day to Sierpe.

SIERPE
This village on the Río Sierpe has boats to Bahía Drake from about US$15 per person (if there is a group). Ask at the dock next to the Las Vegas Bar/Restaurant. The *Hotel Margarita* has basic clean rooms for US$3 per person or US$11 for a double with private bath.

BAHÍA DRAKE
This community has several expensive lodges. The cheapest are the basic *Cabinas Cecilia* (☎ 382-3299 evenings only) for US$25 per person including meals. *El Mirador Cabinas* is reportedly the same price. The laid-back *Cocalito Lodge* (☎ / fax 786-6150) has tents for US$10 per person, or sites for US$7 with your own tent, and rooms from US$24 and up per person. There is a restaurant. Wilderness camping is possible.

From Bahía Drake it's about a five-hour hike to the San Pedrillo ranger station at the north end of Parque Nacional Corcovado (described below) or a US$15 boat ride to Sierpe and buses.

GOLFITO
Golfito is a former banana port now struggling to survive by tourism. It is strung out along a coastal road backed by the steep forested hills of the **Refugio Nacional de Fauna Silvestre Golfito**. Boats cross the Golfo Dulce to Puerto Jiménez, which is the point of entry to the southern and eastern sides of Parque Nacional Corcovado.

Two km south of the town center, a gravel road goes past a soccer field and up to some radio towers, seven km away and 486 meters above sea level. This is a good access road to the refuge. Another possibility is to continue north along the road past the airstrip – there are trails. Camping is permitted, but there are no facilities.

Places to Stay
The *Hotel Uno* (☎ 775-0061) has basic boxes without fans for US$3 per person. A better choice is the friendly *Cabinas Mazuren* (☎ 775-0058) with two rooms (shared bath) for US$4 per person and three rooms with private bath and fan for US$4.75 per person. The *Hotel Delfina* (☎ 775-0043) has basic rooms for US$5 per person or doubles with private bath and fan for US$15. The *Hotel Golfito* (☎ 775-0047) has doubles with private bath and fan for US$10. The *Hotel Costa Rica Surf* (☎ 775-0034) has doubles with fan and shared bath for US$13, or with private bath for US$18. Many rooms lack windows.

In the quieter north end several families take guests. The friendly *Cabinas El Vivero*

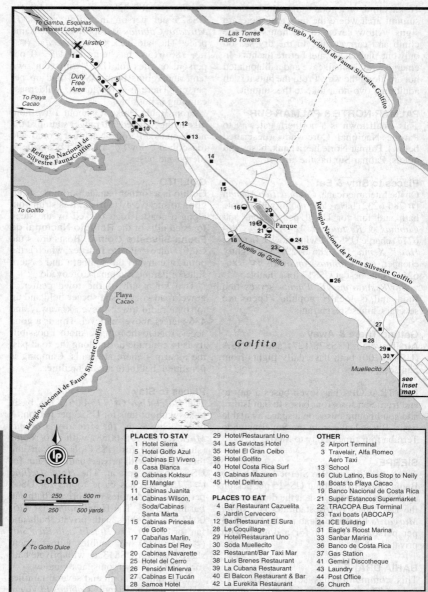

COSTA RICA

Golfito

0   250   500 m
0   250   500 yards

To Golfo Dulce

PLACES TO STAY
1   Hotel Sierra
5   Hotel Golfo Azul
7   Cabinas El Vivero
8   Casa Blanca
9   Cabinas Koktsur
10 El Manglar
11 Cabinas Juanita
14 Cabinas Wilson,
    Soda/Cabinas
    Santa Marta
15 Cabinas Princesa
    de Golfo
17 Cabañas Marlin,
    Cabinas Del Rey
20 Cabinas Navarette
25 Hotel del Cerro
26 Pensión Minerva
27 Cabinas El Tucán
28 Samoa Hotel

29 Hotel/Restaurant Uno
34 Las Gaviotas Hotel
35 Hotel El Gran Ceibo
36 Hotel Golfito
40 Hotel Costa Rica Surf
43 Cabinas Mazuren
45 Hotel Delfina

PLACES TO EAT
4   Bar Restaurant Cazuelita
6   Jardín Cervecero
12 Bar/Restaurant El Sura
28 Le Coquillage
29 Hotel/Restaurant Uno
30 Soda Muellecito
32 Restaurant/Bar Taxi Mar
38 Luis Brenes Restaurant
39 La Cubana Restaurant
40 El Balcon Restaurant & Bar
42 La Eurekita Restaurant

OTHER
2   Airport Terminal
3   Travelair, Alfa Romeo
    Aero Taxi
13 School
16 Club Latino, Bus Stop to Neily
18 Boats to Playa Cacao
19 Banco Nacional de Costa Rica
21 Super Estancos Supermarket
22 TRACOPA Bus Terminal
23 Taxi boats (ABOCAP)
24 ICE Building
31 Eagle's Roost Marina
33 Sanbar Marina
36 Banco de Costa Rica
37 Gas Station
41 Gemini Discotheque
43 Laundry
44 Post Office
46 Church

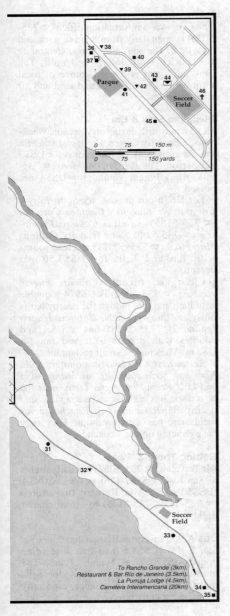

To Rancho Grande (3km),
Restaurant & Bar Río de Janeiro (3.5km),
La Purruja Lodge (4.5km),
Carretera Interamericana (20km)

(☎ 775-0217) charges US$4.50 per person in airy rooms with fans and shared baths. The *Casa Blanca* (☎ 775-0124) has doubles with fan and private bath for US$9. The *El Manglar* (☎ 775-0510), *Cabinas Wilson* (☎ 775-0795) and others are similarly priced. Also try around the parque by the TRACOPA bus.

The friendly *Hotel del Cerro* (☎ 775-0006, fax 775-0551) has dormitories for US$5 per person ('backpacker rates') as well as rooms with fan and private bath for US$10/15.

Places to Eat

Inexpensive *Restaurant Uno* serves decent Chinese food and fish dinners. Luis Brenes' *Pequeño Restaurant* is popular and a good place for swapping information. The *Soda Muellecito* is good for early breakfasts. In the north zone, *Bar Restaurant Cazuelita* has decent Chinese meals.

Getting There & Away

Air Two airlines have daily flights to and from San José: Travelair (☎ 775-0210) charges US$81 one way, US$138 roundtrip; SANSA (☎ 775-0303) charges US$50/100. Some flights stop at Palmar Sur or Puerto Jiménez.

Alfa Romeo Aero Taxi (☎ 775-1515) has light aircraft for charters to Corcovado and other areas.

The airport is four km north of the town center.

Bus TRACOPA (☎ 775-0365) has buses to San Isidro (US$4) and San José (US$5.50) at 5 am and 1 pm.

Buses for Neily leave hourly from the north end of town. Buses for Pavones and Playa Zancudo leave from the *muellecito* boat dock in the early afternoon in the dry season.

Boat The daily passenger boat to Puerto Jiménez (1½ hours, US$3) leaves at 11 am from the muellecito. Boats for Playa Zancudo (US$2) leave at 4:30 am and 12 noon. More expensive taxi boats serve other places.

COSTA RICA

Getting Around
There are buses (US$0.15) and shared taxis (US$0.75) that travel up and down the main road of Golfito.

SOUTH OF GOLFITO
Playa Zancudo
This good swimming beach, 15 km south of Golfito, is popular with locals, especially in the dry season. There are several places to stay from about US$10 per person. One of the best is *Bar/Cabinas Suzy* (☎ 776-0107), which also serves decent casados and has a popular bar. Also good are *Cabinas Tranquilo* (tasty food), *Cabinas Petier* and *El Coquito*. Single rooms are hard to find in the dry season. The bus back to Golfito (three hours) leaves from El Coquito at 5 am in the dry season; boats leave at 6 am and 1:15 pm.

Pavones
Ten km south of Playa Zancudo, Pavones has good surfing, especially from April to October. The nicest hotel is *Cabinas La Ponderosa* (☎ 775-0131, 771-9166, fax 775-0631), with four clean rooms with fan and private bath for US$17 per person or US$35 with three meals. The owners are helpful surfers. Nearby is the *Impact Surf Lodge*, which also provides decent rooms and meals in this price range. The popular *Esquina del Mar Cantina* is a bar with basic noisy rooms for US$5 per person. There are a few other basic places. There is a daily bus serving Golfito if the road is open: It leaves Golfito at 2 pm and returns at 5 am.

PUERTO JIMÉNEZ
Population 6000
This is the main town on the Peninsula de Osa. It is 76 km (32 unpaved) from the Interamericana at Chacarita, or 20 km away from Golfito by boat. Gold mining and logging have made Puerto Jiménez fairly important, and with improved access, there is a burgeoning tourist industry. This is the main entry town to Parque Nacional Corcovado. The town of Puerto Jiménez is pleasant and friendly.

Information
The Corcovado information office (☎ 735-5036) is open daily from 8 am to noon and 1 to 4 pm. The adjoining Banco Central de Costa Rica buys dollars and gold. The Travelair agent is a good source of local information about lodges and land and air transportation.

Places to Stay & Eat
Hotels may fill during dry-season weekends, especially Easter. The *Hotel Valentin* has clean but tiny, airless rooms for US$3 per person. The *Pensión Quintero* (☎ 735-5087) has bigger rooms for US$4 per person.

For US$6 per person, try *Soda Katy y Cabinas, Restaurant y Cabinas Carolina* (☎ 735-5185) as well as *Cabinas Thompson* (☎ 735-5140). The friendly *Cabinas Marcelina* (☎ 735-5007) has clean rooms with fan and bath for US$7.50 per person.

Clean and friendly *Cabinas Puerto Jiménez* (☎ 735-5090) is US$14 a double with bath and fan, though the nearby bar is noisy on the weekends. *Cabinas Iguana Iguana* (☎ 735-5158) has a pool and doubles with private bath and fan for US$18. They have a small restaurant.

Restaurant Carolina is popular. *Soda Katy* and *Soda Ranchito* are inexpensive and OK. *Restaurant Agua Luna*, near the boat dock, has seafood and a sea view, and nearby *Bar/Restaurant El Rancho* serves meals and has a happy hour. They may have dancing on the weekends.

Getting There & Away
Air Travelair (☎ 735-5062) has daily flights to San José (US$87/146) as does SANSA (US$50/100). Alfa Romeo Taxi Aereo (☎ 735-5112, 735-5178) has local charter flights.

Bus Autotransportes Blanco, has buses via San Isidro (US$4.50) to San José (nine hours, US$7.50) at 5 and 11 am. The unnamed soda next to the bus stop sells tickets. Buy tickets in advance, especially for the 5 am departure.

Buses to Neily (US$3) leave at 5:30 am and 2 pm, passing La Palma (23 km away) for the eastern entry into Corcovado.

Truck A truck leaves the main street daily, except Sunday, at 6 am for Carate, at the south end of Corcovado (US$5).

Boat The passenger ferry (☎ 735-5017) to Golfito leaves at 6 am.

PARQUE NACIONAL CORCOVADO

This park has great biological diversity and has long attracted the attention of tropical ecologists. The park covers the southwestern corner of the Península de Osa and protects the best remaining Pacific coastal rain forest in Central America. Corcovado is home to Costa Rica's largest population of scarlet macaws and many other animals and plant species.

Trails lead to five ranger stations (see peninsula map). The trails are primitive, and the hiking is hot, humid and insect-ridden, but it's a good way to see the rain forest. It's more pleasant in the dry season (January to April).

Information

Park fees are US$6 per day. Four ranger stations are at the park boundaries, and a fifth is the headquarters at Sirena, in the middle of the park. Sirena has basic bunkhouse accommodations (US$5) if booked in advance. Camping is US$2 at any station, and meals may be arranged (US$11 per day for three meals) in advance at the park office in Puerto Jiménez. Most people bring their own food.

Hiking

It is safest to hike in a small group. From Carate it is a 90-minute hike to La Leona ranger station; from there it is six to seven hours to Sirena. From Sirena, hike inland for seven to eight hours to Los Patos ranger station; from there it is four hours to La Palma. There are over 20 river crossings.

Buses go from La Palma to Puerto Jiménez. The last bus is at 2 pm. Alternatively, continue along the coast from Sirena to San Pedrillo ranger station (eight to 10 hours), then hike out to Bahía Drake (five hours).

The coastal trails often involve wading and may have loose sand and no shade; be prepared. Ask about tide tables and don't get cut off. The rangers are helpful.

NEILY

This hot but friendly agricultural center, 17 km from Panama, is called 'Villa' locally. It is an important transport hub but of no interest otherwise. Several banks change money.

Places to Stay & Eat

The basic but friendly *Pensión Elvira* (☎ 783-3057) is US$3 to US$4 per person with shared cold showers. Other cheap and basic places are the *Pensión Bulufer* (☎ 783-3216) and *Hotel El Viajero* (☎ 783-5120).

Cabinas El Rancho (☎ 783-3201) is OK for US$5 per person with simple rooms with bath and fans. They have a decent restaurant. The clean and secure *Hotel Musuco* (☎ 783-3048) offers small, basic rooms for US$4.50 per person, or US$5.50 with bath and fan. *Cabinas Andrea* (☎ /fax 783-3784) has the best rooms with bath and fans for US$8 per person.

The good *Restaurant La Moderna* has meals in the US$2 to US$6 range. *La Cuchara de Margot* serves ice cream and snacks.

Getting There & Away

Air SANSA (☎ 783-3275) has daily flights from San José to Coto 47, seven km southwest of Neily. Local buses pass the airport.

Bus TRACOPA (☎ 783-3227) has six daily buses to San José (seven hours, US$5.50); four daily to San Isidro; 19 daily to Paso Canoas; 18 daily to Golfito; five daily to San Vito (2½ hours, US$1.50); two daily to Puerto Jiménez.

SAN VITO

Population 10,000

This pleasant town, 980 meters above sea level, offers respite from the heat of the

COSTA RICA

nearby lowlands. It was founded by immigrants from Italy in the early 1950s. You can still hear Italian spoken and eat Italian food. The steep and winding drive up from Neily is scenic, as is the route from San José.

Information

The Centro Cultural Dante Alighieri has tourist information. Two banks will change money.

Wilson Botanical Gardens

These attractive and well laid out gardens are six km south (uphill) from San Vito and are well worth a visit. There are thousands of plants displayed in this world-class collection. Short educational trails are named after the plants found along them, such as the Heliconia Loop Trail or the Bromeliad Walk. Birding is excellent.

The gardens (☎ /fax 773-3278, net) are open daily (except December 24 and 25) from 7 am to 5 pm. Admission is US$8 for

the day or US$4 a half day. A trail map is provided. The money goes to maintaining the gardens and research facilities. Students with ID can stay in dorms for US$32 including meals. Others pay US$80/130 for private rooms.

Some buses to Neily pass the gardens. Otherwise walk or take a taxi (US$2.50).

Places to Stay & Eat

The *Hotel Tropical* is friendly and secure, though noisy. Basic rooms are US$3 per person. The *Hotel Colono* is another cheap and basic choice.

Clean and quiet *Cabinas Las Mirlas* (☎ 773-3054) charges US$5 per person and has private electric showers. The *Hotel Collina* (☎ 773-3173) is US$6/10 for basic dark rooms with private cold shower. *Cabinas Las Huacas* (☎ 773-3115) has decent rooms for US$6.25/10.50 with private electric showers. The *Albergue Firenze* (☎ 773-3206) is similar.

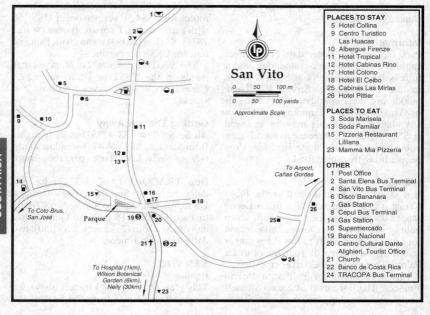

San Vito

| 0 | 50 | 100 m |
| 0 | 50 | 100 yards |

Approximate Scale

To Coto Brus, San José

Parque

To Airport, Cañas Gordas

To Hospital (1km), Wilson Botanical Garden (6km), Neily (30km)

PLACES TO STAY
5 Hotel Collina
9 Centro Turistico Las Huacas
10 Albergue Firenze
11 Hotel Tropical
12 Hotel Cabinas Rino
17 Hotel Colono
18 Hotel El Ceibo
25 Cabinas Las Mirlas
26 Hotel Pittier

PLACES TO EAT
3 Soda Marisela
13 Soda Familiar
15 Pizzería Restaurant Lilliana
23 Mamma Mia Pizzería

OTHER
1 Post Office
2 Santa Elena Bus Terminal
4 San Vito Bus Terminal
6 Disco Bananara
7 Gas Station
8 Cepul Bus Terminal
14 Gas Station
16 Supermercado
19 Banco Nacional
20 Centro Cultural Dante Alighieri, Tourist Office
21 Church
22 Banco de Costa Rica
24 TRACOPA Bus Terminal

COSTA RICA

The *Hotel El Ceibo* (☎ 773-3025) is the best at US$15/24 with private hot shower. There is a reasonable restaurant.

Pizzería Restaurant Lilliana has Italian and local food for US$3 to US$4. The fancier *Mamma Mia Pizzería* is good. The *Soda Familiar* and *Soda Marisela* have good cheap food.

Getting There & Away
TRACOPA (☎ 773-3410) has four daily buses to San José (six hours, US$6.50) and two buses to San Isidro.

Other bus terminals in the center have local buses to Neily and other nearby villages.

PASO CANOAS
This small town on the Interamericana is the main port of entry between Costa Rica and Panama. Hotels are often full with tico bargain hunters during weekends and holidays. Most of the shops and hotels are on the Costa Rican side.

Money
Moneychangers near the border give better rates than banks for cash US dollars. You can change colones to dollars, but you will find that other currencies are harder to deal with. Traveler's checks can be negotiated with persistence.

Places to Stay & Eat
The hotel selection is poor. The best is *Cabinas Interamericano* at US$12 for a double with bath. One of the better restaurants is attached. *Cabinas Los Arcos* is US$10 for a double with bath. There are several cheaper places and some cheap sodas.

Getting There & Away
TRACOPA buses leave San José several times a day. The Friday night bus is full of weekend shoppers who return to San José on Sunday afternoon. Five daily buses leave Paso Canoas (☎ 732-2119) for San José (eight hours, US$6.50).

Buses for Neily (more buses here) leave the border every hour during the day.

Central Pacific Coast

The Pacific Coast is more developed for tourism than the Caribbean Coast, though you can still find deserted beaches, wildlife and small coastal villages.

There are marked wet and dry seasons along this coast. The dry season is the high season, and hotel reservations are advised for Easter week. During the wet season, ask about low-season discounts. High-season rates are given here.

PUNTARENAS
Population 101,000

This is the capital of the coastal province of Puntarenas. During the 19th century, Puntarenas was Costa Rica's major port. Now, Puerto Limón and the new port at Caldera, 18 km southeast of Puntarenas, take much of the shipping. Puntarenas remains a bustling place during the dry season, when tourists arrive. During the wet months it's much quieter.

The city is on the end of a sandy peninsula almost eight km long but only 100 to 600 meters wide – arriving here is intriguing. You are always close to the ocean, but the beaches are too polluted for swimming. Puntarenas has traditionally been popular with ticos, but foreigners prefer destinations where they can swim. Many people come to Puntarenas to catch the ferry to the Península de Nicoya. It's a friendly port.

Information
A helpful tourist information office (☎ 661-1985) is in the Casa de Cultura. Banks on the map change money.

Things to See & Do
The **Museo Histórico Marino** describes the city's history through audio-visual presentations, old photos and other artifacts. Hours are daily, except Monday, 9 am to noon and 1 to 5 pm; admission is US$1.

The **Casa de Cultura** has an art gallery. The main **church** is one of the most attractive buildings. A walk along the **Paseo de**

COSTA RICA

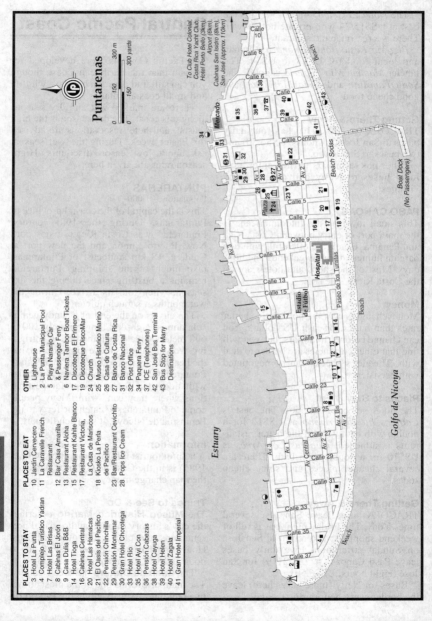

Puntarenas

0   150   300 m
0   150   300 yards

To Club Hotel Colonial,
Costa Rica Yacht Club,
Hotel Porto Bello (3km),
Cabinas San Isidro (6km),
Airport (6km),
San José (approx. 110km)

Estuary

Golfo de Nicoya

Beach

Beach Sodas

Paseo de los Turistas

Boat Dock
(No Passengers)

Mercado

Plaza

Hospital

Estadio
de Fútbol

PLACES TO STAY
3   Hotel La Punta
4   Complejo Turístico Yadran
7   Hotel Las Brisas
8   Cabinas El Jorón
9   Casa Dulia B&B
14 Hotel Tioga
16 Cabinas Central
20 Hotel Las Hamacas
21 El Oasis del Pacífico
22 Pensión Chinchilla
29 Pensión Montemar
30 Gran Hotel Chorotega
33 Hotel Río
35 Hotel Ayi Con
36 Pensión Cabezas
38 Hotel Cayuga
39 Hotel Helen
40 Hotel Zagala
41 Gran Hotel Imperial

PLACES TO EAT
10 Jardín Cervecero
11 La Caravelle French
    Restaurant
12 Bar Casa Amarilla
13 Restaurant Aloha
15 Restaurant Kahite Blanco
17 Restaurant Victoria,
    La Casa de Mariscos
18 Kiosko La Perla
    de Pacífico
23 Bar/Restaurant Cevichito
28 Pops Ice Cream

OTHER
1   Lighthouse
2   La Punta Municipal Pool
5   Playa Naranjo Car
    & Passenger Ferry
6   Naviera Tambor Boat Tickets
17 Discoteque El Primero
19 Discoteque DiscoMar
24 Church
25 Museo Histórico Marino
26 Casa de Cultura
27 Banco de Costa Rica
31 Banco Nacional
32 Post Office
34 ICE (Telephones)
42 San José Bus Terminal
43 Bus Stop for Many
    Destinations

Turistas is pleasant. A new area of stores, restaurants and an aquarium is planned.

Special Events
The Fiesta del Virgen del Mar on the Saturday closest to July 16 has a parade of boats bedecked with lights and flags. There is a carnival, boat races, and food, drink and dancing.

Places to Stay
The basic but clean *Hotel Helen* (☎ 661-2159) charges US$8 for a double with shared bath, or US$8/13 with private cold shower.

The basic, friendly *Hotel Río* (☎ 661-0938), Calle Central, Av 3, has rooms with fans for US$4 per person or with private shower for US$7 per person. The area, by a dock and the market, is a little rough but not very dangerous.

For US$4 per person, *Pensión Chinchilla* (☎ 661-0638), Calle 1, Avs Central and 2, and *Pensión Montemar* (☎ 661-2771), Av 3, Calles 1 and 3, are clean and secure. The basic but clean and friendly *Pensión Cabezas* (☎ 661-1045), Av 1, Calles 2 and 4, is worth US$5 per person.

The *Hotel Ayi Con* (☎ 661-0164, 661-1477), Calle 2, Avs 1 and 3, has basic clean rooms with fan for US$6 per person, or US$8 with cold shower, or US$10 with air conditioning. The *Hotel Zagala* (☎ 661-1319) has somewhat nicer rooms with fans for US$8/13 for singles/doubles, but the showers are shared.

The Toruma Youth Hostel in San José makes reservations (which are strongly advised) for HI members at *Cabinas San Isidro* (☎ 221-1225, 663-0031, fax 221-6822) for US$10 per person (more for non-members). San Isidro is eight km east of the town center and there are buses that head there. The cabinas are near a beach, and there are cooking facilities, a restaurant and a swimming pool.

The *Hotel Cayuga* (☎ 661-0344), Calle 4, Avs Central and 1, has basic but clean air-conditioned rooms with private cold showers for US$13/19. They have a parking lot and restaurant.

Places to Eat
Restaurants along the Paseo de los Turistas are tourist oriented and slightly pricey – but not outrageously so.

Cheapish sodas along here are between Calles Central and 3. About 300 meters east are two reasonably priced places: *La Casa de Mariscos*, with meals for US$5, and the *Restaurant Victoria*, serving Chinese food and seafood. Other good places for a fish meal under US$5 are *Kiosko La Perla de Pacífico* and *Bar/Restaurant Cevichito*. The cheapest food is in the sodas near the market. Several inexpensive Chinese restaurants are within 200 meters of Calle Central and Av Central.

Restaurant Kahite Blanco (☎ 661-2093), Av 1, Calles 15 and 17, is locally popular and serves good seafood in the US$4 to US$9 range and generous bocas. They have music and dancing on the weekends. There are several good but pricey international restaurants west of the Hotel Tioga.

Getting There & Away
Bus Frequent buses to San José (two hours, US$2.50) leave from Calle 2, near Paseo de los Turistas, from 5:30 am to 7 pm. Across the Paseo is a bus stop where buses leave for the following towns:

Liberia	five times a day
Esparza	every hour or so
Tilarán	11:30 am and 4:15 pm
Santa Elena	2:15 pm
Quepos (passing Jacó)	5 am and 2:30 pm

Boat The Conatramar car/passenger ferry (☎ 661-1069) sails from the northwest end of town to Playa Naranjo on the Península de Nicoya (1½ hours). There are three to five daily departures. Fares are US$1.50 for passengers and US$10.50 for cars (with driver). Foot passengers continue by bus to Nicoya. Naviera Tambor (☎ 661-2084) also has a new car/passenger ferry from this dock to Paquera four times a day. Fare is US$2/4 for second/first class and US$12.50 for cars.

The Paquera passenger ferry (☎ 661-2830) sails from the dock behind the market at 6:15 and 11 am and 3 pm (1½ hours, US$1.50). Passengers continue to Montezuma by bus.

Getting Around
Buses marked 'Ferry' run up Av Central to the Playa Naranjo terminal, 1.5 km from downtown.

RESERVA BIOLÓGICA CARARA
This is in the transition zone between rain forest and tropical dry forest, which creates both an abundance and variety of wildlife. Scarlet macaws live here but it can be difficult to see anything without an experienced guide. Going on a tour is expensive, but guides who visit several

times a week know where the wildlife is. Day tours to Carara from San José are US$75 per person; those offered by Geotur are good. The dry season from December to April is the best time to go.

You can get off at Carara from any bus bound for Jacó or Quepos, though avoid weekends when getting back on may be difficult if buses are full. This budget option has pleased some travelers, though others complain they 'didn't see anything' in the reserve, which is why it's worth going on a guided trip from San José.

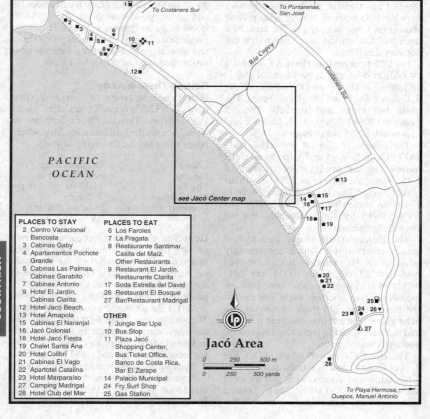

PLACES TO STAY
2   Centro Vacacional Bancosta
3   Cabinas Gaby
4   Apartamentos Pochote Grande
5   Cabinas Las Palmas, Cabinas Garabito
7   Cabinas Antonio
9   Hotel El Jardín, Cabinas Clarita
12 Hotel Jacó Beach
13 Hotel Amapola
15 Cabinas El Naranjal
16 Jacó Colonial
18 Hotel Jacó Fiesta
19 Chalet Santa Ana
20 Hotel Colibrí
21 Cabinas El Vago
22 Apartotel Catalina
23 Hotel Marparaíso
27 Camping Madrigal
28 Hotel Club del Mar

PLACES TO EAT
6   Los Faroles
7   La Fragata
8   Restaurante Santimar, Casita del Maíz, Other Restaurants
9   Restaurant El Jardín, Restaurante Clarita
17 Soda Estrella del David
26 Restaurant El Bosque
27 Bar/Restaurant Madrigal

OTHER
1   Jungle Bar Upe
10 Bus Stop
11 Plaza Jacó Shopping Center, Bus Ticket Office, Banco de Costa Rica, Bar El Zarape
14 Palacio Municipal
24 Fry Surf Shop
25 Gas Station

Jacó Area

PACIFIC OCEAN

To Costanera Sur
To Puntarenas, San José
Río Copey
Costanera Sur
see Jacó Center map
To Playa Hermosa, Quepos, Manuel Antonio

JACÓ

Jacó is the closest developed beach resort to San José and is popular and crowded by Costa Rican standards. It is 2.5 km off the coastal highway. Hotels and restaurants are scattered along the road, which parallels the three-km-long beach. Jacó has a reputation as a 'party beach,' but it is pretty sedate compared to North American party beaches like Daytona. The beaches are reasonably clean and swimming is possible, though be careful of rip currents.

Jacó is a popular surf spot with consistent waves and an annual tournament in August at **Playa Hermosa**, five km south of Jacó.

Information

Two banks change money, though GAB exchange house is faster. Several places rent bikes for US$9 a day. Surfboards and mopeds can also be rented.

Places to Stay

Camping Friendly *Camping El Hicaco* (☎ 643-3004) is US$2.50 per person and

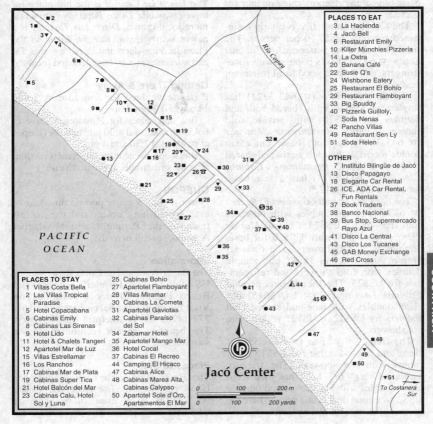

PLACES TO EAT
3   La Hacienda
4   Jacó Bell
6   Restaurant Emily
10 Killer Munchies Pizzería
14 La Ostra
20 Banana Café
22 Susie Q's
24 Wishbone Eatery
25 Restaurant El Bohío
29 Restaurant Flamboyant
33 Big Spuddy
40 Pizzería Guilloly,
    Soda Nenas
42 Pancho Villas
49 Restaurant Sen Ly
51 Soda Helen

OTHER
7   Instituto Bilingüe de Jacó
13 Disco Papagayo
18 Elegante Car Rental
26 ICE, ADA Car Rental,
    Fun Rentals
37 Book Traders
38 Banco Nacional
39 Bus Stop, Supermercado
    Rayo Azul
41 Disco La Central
43 Disco Los Tucanes
45 GAB Money Exchange
46 Red Cross

PACIFIC OCEAN

Jacó Center

To Costanera Sur

COSTA RICA

PLACES TO STAY
1   Villas Costa Bella
2   Las Villas Tropical
    Paradise
5   Hotel Copacabana
6   Cabinas Emily
8   Cabinas Las Sirenas
9   Hotel Lido
11 Hotel & Chalets Tangerí
12 Apartotel Mar de Luz
15 Villas Estrellamar
16 Los Ranchos
17 Cabinas Mar de Plata
19 Cabinas Super Tica
21 Hotel Balcón del Mar
23 Cabinas Calu, Hotel
    Sol y Luna
25 Cabinas Bohío
27 Apartotel Flamboyant
28 Villas Miramar
30 Cabinas La Cometa
31 Apartotel Gaviotas
32 Cabinas Paraíso
    del Sol
34 Zabamar Hotel
35 Apartotel Mango Mar
36 Hotel Cocal
37 Cabinas El Recreo
44 Camping El Hicaco
47 Cabinas Alice
48 Cabinas Marea Alta,
    Cabinas Calypso
50 Apartotel Sole d'Oro,
    Apartamentos El Mar

0   100   200 m
0   100   200 yards

has a lock-up for your gear, picnic tables and bathrooms. Don't leave valuables in your tent. The sandy campsites cut down on chiggers. For US$2 per person, there's the grassier *Camping Madrigal* (☎ 643-3230).

Hotels Reservations are recommended during dry season weekends. There are few single rooms and shoestringers won't find many bargains. Camping is an option. Low season and surfer discounts are available.

Cabinas Calypso (☎ 643-3208) are US$15 for very basic doubles with shared bath. *Cabinas Bohío* (☎ 643-3017) has basic old cabins sleeping three or four for US$22.

The *Cabinas Super Tica* is poorly maintained but only US$7.50 per person. The similarly priced but better quality *Cabinas Emily* (☎ 643-3513) is popular with shoestringers, and it has a good local restaurant next door.

Cabinas Garabito (☎ 643-3321) has singles for US$10 with shared bath and doubles for US$18 with private cold shower. Nearby, *Restaurante Santimar* (☎ 643-3605) has four basic but clean double rooms with beach views and shared cold bath at US$15. *Restaurante y Cabinas Clarita* (☎ 643-3013) has a few basic rooms for US$7.50/12.50.

The basic but friendly *Cabinas El Recreo* (☎ 643-3012) has doubles with fans and cold showers for US$23. *Cabinas Mar de Plata* (☎ 643-3580) are US$20 for basic doubles with hot showers. The *Cabinas Marea Alta* (☎ 643-3554) has simple doubles with cold showers and refrigerators for US$23. The friendly and popular *Cabinas La Cometa* (☎ 643-3615) has clean doubles with fans and shared cold showers for US$22 or US$32 with private hot showers.

The *Hotel Sol y Luna* (☎ 643-3558) is clean and a good value for US$15/20 in rooms with hot showers. The friendly *Cabinas Calu* (☎ 643-1107) has good-sized clean doubles with hot shower and fans for US$25 – a good deal at this price. There are dozens of more expensive places.

Places to Eat
At the north end, the *Restaurant Casita del Maíz* charges US$3.50 for a casado, and there are several other cheapish local places near here, including *Restaurante Santimar*.

In the center, *Soda Nenas* has good casados. Also try the *Soda Helen*, open from 7 am to 10 pm during the high season, and the soda *Estrella del David* at the south end.

Pizzería Guilloly has small individual pizzas for US$3 to US$6 depending on the toppings. They show surfing videos. There are many pricier restaurants.

Entertainment
The *Disco La Central* is the hip place for travelers, while *Disco Papagayo* attracts a more local crowd. *Disco Los Tucanes* is a newer nearby spot. *Bar El Zarpe* in the Plaza Jacó has darts and satellite sports TV and attracts a mix of travelers and locals.

Getting There & Away
Buses leave Jacó for San José at 5 and 11 am and 3 pm daily.

Bus departures for Puntarenas leave at 6:45 am, noon and 4:30 pm; and for Quepos at 6:30 am, 12:30 and 4 pm.

Bus stops are near the supermercado and near the crossroads at the north end.

QUEPOS
Quepos, once a major port, is now known as a sportfishing center and the nearest town to the Parque Nacional Manuel Antonio, seven km away.

Information
The Banco Nacional de Costa Rica changes US dollars and traveler's checks and Banco Popular allows withdrawals on Visa. Lynch Tourist Service (☎ 777-0161, 777-1170, net) is a helpful travel agency. The beaches are not recommended for swimming.

Places to Stay
The *Hotel Majestic* has basic boxes for US$4 per person. The *Hotel La Unica* (☎ 777-0012) is even more basic at US$4.50 per person. The *Hospedaje La*

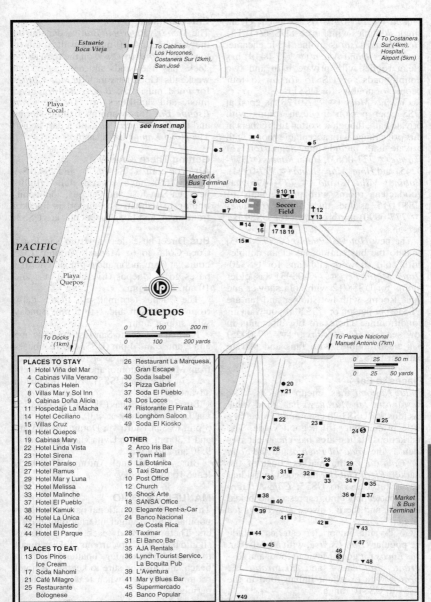

Quepos

| 0 | 100 | 200 m |
| 0 | 100 | 200 yards |

PLACES TO STAY
1 Hotel Viña del Mar
4 Cabinas Villa Verano
7 Cabinas Helen
8 Villas Mar y Sol Inn
9 Cabinas Doña Alicia
11 Hospedaje La Macha
14 Hotel Ceciliano
15 Villas Cruz
18 Hotel Quepos
19 Cabinas Mary
22 Hotel Linda Vista
23 Hotel Sirena
25 Hotel Paraíso
27 Hotel Ramus
29 Hotel Mar y Luna
32 Hotel Melissa
33 Hotel Malinche
37 Hotel El Pueblo
38 Hotel Kamuk
40 Hotel La Única
42 Hotel Majestic
44 Hotel El Parque

PLACES TO EAT
13 Dos Pinos
Ice Cream
17 Soda Nahomi
21 Café Milagro
25 Restaurante
Bolognese

26 Restaurant La Marquesa,
Gran Escape
30 Soda Isabel
34 Pizza Gabriel
37 Soda El Pueblo
43 Dos Locos
47 Ristorante El Pirata
48 Longhorn Saloon
49 Soda El Kiosko

OTHER
2 Arco Iris Bar
3 Town Hall
5 La Botánica
6 Taxi Stand
10 Post Office
12 Church
16 Shock Arte
18 SANSA Office
20 Elegante Rent-a-Car
24 Banco Nacional
de Costa Rica
28 Taximar
31 El Banco Bar
35 AJA Rentals
36 Lynch Tourist Service,
La Boquita Pub
39 L'Aventura
41 Mar y Blues Bar
45 Supermercado
46 Banco Popular

| 0 | 25 | 50 m |
| 0 | 25 | 50 yards |

COSTA RICA

Macha (☎ 777-0216) is basic but clean; singles/doubles with fan cost US$6/11. The *Hotel Linda Vista* is another basic cheapie.

Cabinas Doña Alicia (☎ 777-0419) has clean rooms with private bath and two double beds for US$15 for up to four people, or doubles for US$11.

Cabinas Mary (☎ 777-0128) is good at US$7 per person in clean rooms with private bath, though it's often full. Others in this price range with acceptable rooms with private bath include the clean *Hotel El Parque* (☎ 777-0063), *Hotel Ramus* (☎ 777-0245) and *Hotel Mar y Luna* (☎ 777-0394). *Cabinas Villa Verano* (☎ 777-1495) has good clean rooms with private bath for US$11/15, as does the *Cabinas Horcones* (☎ 777-0090) north of town for US$9 per person.

The new *Hotel El Pueblo* (☎ 777-1003) next to the bus station has clean doubles with cold showers and fans for US$20. *Hotel Malinche* (☎ 777-0093) has older rooms for US$8/12 with cold shower and fans. Rooms with hot shower and fan are US$12 per person or US$20 if you want air conditioning. There are big discounts in low season. *Hotel Melissa* (☎ 777-0025) has clean doubles with fans and private bath for US$20.

Places to Eat

Soda Nahomi has cheap snacks. The *Restaurant La Marquesa* has good-value casados for US$2.20. The *Soda Isabel* is a little pricier but still a good value. The market/bus station area has cheap eateries such as the *Soda El Pueblo* and the *Soda La Coquita* in the market. East of the market, *Pizza Gabriel* has good individual pizzas for US$3 to US$5. *Café Milagro* has great cappuccino, espresso and baked desserts, and there's also a *Dos Pinos Ice Cream*.

Good-value but pricier eateries include the popular *Gran Escape*, with a lively bar, *Dos Locos* for good Mexican food, and *Ristorante Bolognese* and *Ristorante El Piratea* with excellent Italian food in the US$4 to US$10 range.

Entertainment

The *Arco Iris Riverboat Bar* has dancing on the weekends. A 20-minute walk south of town, the *Maracas Disco* on the road to the docks has live bands and dancing on the weekends. Good bars include *Mar y Blues* for good music, *El Banco Bar* for good music and satellite sports TV, the *Gran Escape Bar* for swapping fishing stories and the *La Boquita Pub* with a dart board. The *Hotel Kamuk* has a casino.

Getting There & Away

Air Travelair (US$48/77) and SANSA (US$30/60) have several daily flights between San José and Quepos, some continuing to Palmar. The airport is five km from town, and taxis to Quepos are US$3.

Bus Direct buses leaving from San José's Coca-Cola go to Manuel Antonio (3½ hours) at 6 am, noon and 6 pm, and normal buses go to Quepos (five hours) at 7 and 10 am, 2 and 4 pm.

The Quepos terminal sells tickets daily from 6 to 11 am and 1 to 5 pm; Sunday sales stop at 2 pm.

Normal services to San José are daily at 5 and 8 am, 2 and 4 pm (US$3). Direct buses to San José leave three or four times a day from Manuel Antonio, and pick up passengers in Quepos (US$5). Buy tickets in advance.

Buses to Puntarenas (3½ hours, US$2.75) via Jacó leave daily at 4:30, 10:30 am and 3 pm; to San Isidro via Dominical at 5 am and 1:30 pm; and to Uvita via Dominical at 9:30 am and 4 pm.

Buses for Manuel Antonio (US$0.25) leave 16 times a day.

MANUEL ANTONIO

This village at the national park entrance is popular with younger international travelers. There is a good beach, but swimmers should beware of rip currents. Take care not to leave your belongings unattended on any beach, and also be sure to keep your hotel room locked even when leaving for brief periods.

Information

La Buena Nota (☎ 777-1002, net) is an informal information center that sells maps, guide books, US newspapers, beach supplies and souvenirs and also rents boogie boards.

Places to Stay & Eat

There are dozens of hotels between Quepos and Manuel Antonio but none are cheap.

In Manuel Antonio itself, *Costa Linda* (☎ 777-0304; affiliated with the Tica Linda in San José) is reasonably clean. Basic stuffy rooms with shared showers are US$7 per person. *Cabinas Anep* (☎ 777-0565) have cheaper rooms but may be full of government employees on vacation.

Cabinas Irarosa have simple, clean rooms with fan and private cold bath for US$14/20. *Hotel Manuel Antonio* (☎ 777-0212) has six simple rooms with cold showers that sleep up to four for US$25 to US$30. People camp outside for US$2.50 per person – watch your possessions at ALL times.

Cabinas Ramírez (☎ 777-0003) is US$25/30 for a double/triple with private cold shower. Rooms on the ocean side are better than the road side. *Cabinas Piscis* (☎ 777-0046) are US$25 for a clean double sharing a shower and US$35 for a double with private shower.

The pleasant *Hotel Vela Bar* (☎ 777-0413, fax 777-1071) is US$26 to US$45 for a double with bath, depending on the size. The *Hotel Del Mar* (☎ 777-0543) has simple but clean, spacious rooms with fans and private cold showers for US$35/40.

The *Restaurant Mar y Sombra* has casados and chicken and pasta plates for about US$3 and fish dinners for twice that. There are good sunset views and a loud disco on the weekends. The *Restaurant y Soda Marlin* is often crowded and has meals for around US$3 to US$5. They serve breakfast. There are a number of other cheap sodas and roadside stands in the beach area.

Getting There & Away

See the earlier Quepos entry for details on air and bus travel. Buses leave from the end of the road leading to the national park. Buy your San José tickets in advance if possible, particularly on the weekends. Call ☎ 777-0263 for bus reservations in Manuel Antonio.

PARQUE NACIONAL MANUEL ANTONIO

Manuel Antonio is the smallest national park but also one of the most popular ones. There are beautiful forest-backed tropical beaches, rocky headlands with ocean and island views, prolific wildlife and a maintained trail system. This has led to intense pressure on both the park and the area: too many visitors, too many hotels and too much impact on the wildlife and environment. Therefore the park is closed on Monday and limited to 600 visitors on other days. To avoid the crowds, go early in the morning, midweek during the rainy season.

Cars are prohibited, and arriving on foot is a minor adventure – the estuary at the park entrance must be waded. The water is thigh deep at high tide. Trails lead to three beaches within an hour's walk. Another trail climbs a cliff with good views.

Most visitors who spend a day walking around will see monkeys. Sloths, agoutis, armadillos, coatis and raccoons are also sometimes seen. Over 350 bird species are reported for the park, and a variety of lizards, snakes, iguanas and other animals may be observed. There is a small coral reef off Manuel Antonio beach, but the water is rather cloudy and the visibility limited.

Information

The visitor information center (☎ 777-0644) is near Playa Manuel Antonio. Drinking water is available, and there are toilets nearby. Park hours are Tuesday to Sunday 7 am to 5 pm, and guards come round in the evening to make sure that nobody is camping, which is prohibited.

COSTA RICA

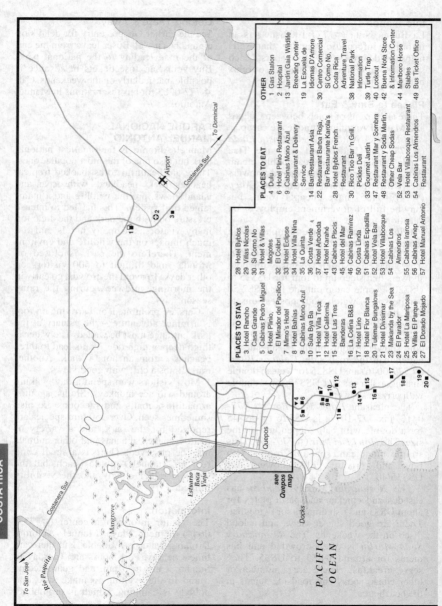

PLACES TO STAY
3　Hotel Rancho
　　Casa Grande
5　Cabinas Pedro Miguel
6　Hotel Plinio,
7　El Mirador del Pacifico
7　Mimo's Hotel
8　Hotel Bahias
9　Cabinas Mono Azul
10　Sula Bya Ba
11　Hotel Villa Teca
12　Hotel California
15　Hotel Las Tres
　　Banderas
16　La Colina B&B
17　Hotel Lirio
18　Hotel Flor Blanca
20　Tulemar Bungalows
21　Hotel Divisimar
23　Makanda by the Sea
24　El Parador
25　Hotel La Mariposa
26　Villas El Parque
27　El Dorado Mojado

28　Hotel Byblos
29　Villas Nicolas
30　Si Como No
31　Hotel & Villas
　　Mogotes
32　El Colibri
33　Hotel Eclipse
34　Hotel Villa Nina
35　La Quinta
36　Costa Verde
37　Hotel Arboleda
41　Hotel Karahé
43　Cabinas Piscis
45　Hotel del Mar
46　Cabinas Ramirez
50　Costa Linda
51　Cabinas Espadilla
52　Hotel Vela Bar
53　Hotel Villabosque
54　Cabinas Los
　　Almendros
55　Cabinas Irarosa
56　Cabinas Anep
57　Hotel Manuel Antonio

PLACES TO EAT
4　Dulu
6　Hotel Plinio Restaurant
9　Cabinas Mono Azul
　　Restaurant & Delivery
　　Service
14　Bar/Restaurant Asia
22　Restaurant Barba Roja,
　　Bar Restaurante Karola's
28　Hotel Byblos French
　　Restaurant
30　Rico Tico Bar 'n Grill,
　　Pickles Deli
33　Gourmet Jardin
47　Restaurant Mar y Sombra
48　Restaurant y Soda Marlin,
　　Other Cheap Sodas
52　Vela Bar
53　Hotel Villabosque Restaurant
54　Cabinas Los Almendros
　　Restaurant

OTHER
1　Gas Station
2　Hospital
13　Jardin Gaia Wildlife
　　Breeding Center
19　La Escuela de
　　Idiomas D'Amore
30　Centro Comercial
　　Si Como No,
　　Costa Rica
　　Adventure Travel
38　National Park
　　Information
39　Turtle Trap
40　Lookout
42　Buena Nota Store
　　& Information Center
44　Marlboro Horse
　　Stables
49　Bus Ticket Office

To San José

Río Paquita

Costanera Sur

COSTA RICA

Mangrove

*Estuario
Boca
Vieja*

Docks

Quepos

**see
Quepos
map**

*PACIFIC
OCEAN*

Costanera Sur

Airport

To Dominical

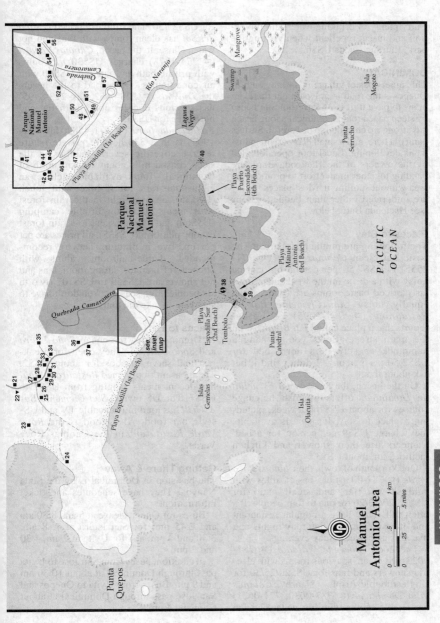

Manuel Antonio Area

COSTA RICA

Carry plenty of drinking water, sun protection and insect repellent when visiting the park. Entrance costs US$6.

DOMINICAL

This quiet coastal village is 44 km south of Quepos – the road is graveled but there are plans to pave it. It is 34 km from San Isidro by steep paved road. Dominical's long beach has strong rip currents, so be careful. Surfers hang out here, and a small ecotourism industry is developing. Local tour operators, led by the owners of the Hacienda Barú, are banding together in an effort to promote the area without spoiling it. Most places to stay are midpriced rather than budget options (see Hacienda Barú, below).

Places to Stay

The following are on the main street. The basic but clean *Cabinas Coco* (☎ 771-2555) is US$7.50 per person but can be noisy with a disco on the weekends. Similarly priced basic rooms are found at the equally noisy *San Clemente Bar & Restaurant* (☎ 771-2095). A reader reports that a place called *Fat Breakfast* on the main street allows you to hang a hammock or stay in a dorm bed for US$2.50 per person – I didn't find it but ask about this.

On the beach, the low-key *La Escuelita de Dominical* offers Spanish language courses for about US$200 a week, including a place to stay. If space is available, they charge US$9 per person for a bed. Campers use their shower and kitchen facilities for about US$3.

One km south of town, the *Cabinas Roca Verde* (☎ 787-0036) has basic cabins with cold shower, fan and small patio for US$15/20/23/26 for one to four people. It's often full. They have a popular restaurant and often a dance on Saturday nights and live music on Wednesday evenings.

The good *Albergue Willdale* (☎ 787-0023) has clean, spacious rooms with electric showers and fans for US$20/25/30 for singles/doubles/triples. Nearby, *Cabinas Villa Dominical* (☎ 787-0030, 771-0621) has simple rooms with hot water and fan

for US$25/30. The similarly priced *Posada del Sol* has clean rooms with fans and hot water. Closer to the beach, *Cabinas Nayarit* (☎ 771-1878) charges US$30 for rooms with private bath and fan and US$40 with air conditioning. On a road to the beach, the *DiuWak* (☎ 223-0853, fax 223-8195) has spacious double rooms with fan and hot water for US$35.

Hacienda Barú (☎ 771-4582, fax 771-1903) is in a 330-hectare private nature reserve covering several habitats in the steep coastal hills about 1.5 km north of Dominical. Tours available include an eight-hour rain forest hike with lunch (US$35), an overnight in the rain forest with meals and comfortable camping (US$60) and a rope ascent to a rain forest canopy platform (US$35); all prices are per person, two minimum. They're recommended. Three-bedroom cabins with kitchen, refrigerator, sitting room, fans and hot shower are US$59 to US$107 (two to six people, high season). You don't have to stay here to take the tours.

Places to Eat

In Dominical, try the cheap *Soda Laura* and *Soda Nanyoa*. They open for breakfast and serve casados for about US$2. The pleasant tico-owned *Restaurant Maui* has decent meals ranging from US$2 to US$7. The US-owned *San Clemente Bar & Grill* has loud music, cable TV and US-style bar food. Also good is the *Roca Verde Restaurant* in the Cabinas Roca Verde.

Getting There & Away

The bus stop in Dominical is by the Soda Nanyoa. They have schedules and ticket information.

Buses for Quepos leave at 5 and 8:30 am and 2:45 pm; for San Isidro at 7, 8 am, 3:30 and 4 pm; and for Uvita at 7 am, 4:30 and 7 pm.

In addition, buses from San José to Uvita pass through Dominical at about 10:30 am and 9 pm. Buses from Uvita to Quepos and San José pass through Dominical at about 6 am and 4 pm.

UVITA

This hamlet, 17 km south of Dominical, is a loose straggle of farms and houses and the entry point for the new Parque Nacional Marino Ballena. In 1996, the road beyond Uvita was opened to the Interamericana via Ciudad Cortés, and buses and hotel development can be expected.

Reserva Biológica Oro Verde

This private reserve on the Duarte family farm is two-thirds rain forest. Their tours visit the forest, show you waterfalls and wildlife and give you a look at traditional rural Costa Rican life. Horse rental is US$5 per hour and hikes with a local guide are US$15 per person for three to four hours. A simple cabin sleeps seven (one room with a double bed and another with five bunk beds) for US$10 per person. There is a kitchen, shower and patio. They provide homecooked meals in their house, about 400 meters away, for another US$10 per day. This recommended local sustainable tourism venture is three or four km inland from Uvita along a signed rough road.

Rancho La Merced

Opposite the Oro Verde turnoff is Rancho La Merced, a working cattle ranch of which half is still forest. Horseback tours include 'Cowboy for a Day,' where you ride with local cowboys and help on the ranch. They'll demonstrate what to do if this is your first time, dude. A three- to five-hour tour is US$20 (three minimum) or US$30 (one person). Other horseback and hiking tours are offered. They have simple rooms for US$45/55 for a double/triple.

Places to Stay & Eat

Expect more hotels since the road through to the Interamericana opened.

Cabinas Los Laureles, a few hundred meters to the left of the *abastecedor* (general store), has three cabins with bathrooms for US$12/20/25 for one to three people. They arrange horseback tours. *Cabinas El Cocotico* has six simple, clean double rooms with private bath for US$20.

A soda is attached. A reader raves about *Cabinas Hegalva* run by Doña Cecilia, who cooks great food and charges about the same as El Cocotico. Several more expensive options are available.

Getting There & Away

Since the road improved, the bus situation is changing all the time. Ask locally.

PARQUE NACIONAL MARINO BALLENA

This park protects coral and rock reefs in 4500 hectares of ocean around Isla Ballena, south of Uvita. The island has nesting seabird colonies and many green iguanas and basilisk lizards. Humpback whales migrate through the area from December to March. Southeast of Punta Uvita the park includes 13 km of sandy and rocky beaches, mangrove swamps, river mouths and rocky headlands. Turtles nest on sandy beaches from May to November, with a peak in September and October.

Information

The ranger station is in Bahía, on the sea three km from Uvita. Boats from Bahía to Isla Ballena can be hired for about US$15 to US$20 per hour; landing on the island and snorkeling is permitted. From the ranger station you can walk onto Punta Uvita and snorkel (best on a dropping/low tide). The park remains undeveloped and there is no fee or facilities at this writing, though this may change.

Península de Nicoya

This peninsula has few paved roads, but some of Costa Rica's major beach resorts are here, which are sometimes difficult to get to. There are several small wildlife reserves and parks, but for the most part people come here looking for relaxing beaches. Because of poor roads, public transport is not very convenient and travelers should allow plenty of time to get around. Hitching is a definite possibility. If you want to cook for yourself, bring food from inland. Stores are few and far between on the coast. Hotels tend to be expensive.

PLAYA DEL COCO

This beach area is 35 km west of Liberia and is the most easily accessible of the Península de Nicoya beaches, connected by good roads to San José. It is attractively set between two rocky headlands, with a small village and some nightlife. It's a popular resort for ticos in particular, and foreign travelers to a lesser extent, and it's less expensive than most other beach towns.

The beach has strong rip currents. This is the best place to scuba dive on the mainland, and there are several competitively priced outfitters. Two tank dives from a boat are typically US$65 (all gear provided), and beginners' classes are available.

A bank opened in 1996 and will change cash US dollars and traveler's checks.

Places to Stay

Camping A campground just off the main road and another one a few minutes west of the soccer field (look for signs) have basic bathrooms and showers for US$3 per person.

Hotels I've read that *Cabinas Catarino* (☎ 670-0156) is US$6 per person but I couldn't find them. Otherwise, budget hotels are pricier than most of Costa Rica.

Cabinas El Coco (☎ 670-0110, 670-0276, fax 670-0167) is to the right as you arrive at the beach. Fairly basic rooms, all with private bath, are US$12 per person with fans or US$23/28 with air conditioning. There is a midpriced restaurant on the premises and a disco next door. *Cabinas Luna Tica* (☎ 670-0127, or annex 670-0279) has rooms with private bath and a double bed for US$21, or US$26 with air conditioning. All rooms have a fan. The hotel is near the beach, but the annex is set back from the beach and has nicer rooms. A restaurant is attached.

Other cheapies include the *Cabinas Las Brisas* (☎ 670-0155) for US$18 for a double with shower and fan. The *Cabinas Chale*

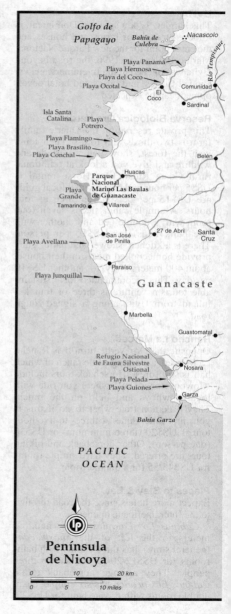

Península de Nicoya

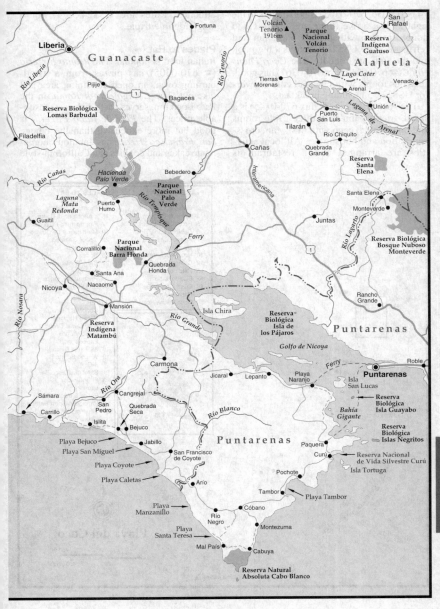

(☎ 670-0036, 670-0303) is 600 meters to the right as you arrive (there are signs). Good double rooms with private bath, fan and refrigerator are US$25. There is a big pool, and the staff are friendly. The *Coco Palms Hotel* (☎ 670-0117, fax 670-0367) has good, spacious rooms with fans and cold showers for US$23/35 including breakfast.

The *Pato Loco Inn* (☎ /fax 670-0145) is a small, friendly inn with three triple rooms and one double, each with desk, fan, cross-ventilation and hot shower. All local activities are arranged and a restaurant is

attached. Rates are US$24/35/47 for a single/double/triple.

Places to Eat

Italian food is popular. The *Pronto Pizzería* (☎ 670-0305) has pizzas from a wood-burning oven, an open-air dining area and take-out. The *L'Angoletto di Roma*, in the Pato Loco Inn, serves pasta dishes at reasonable prices. The *Flor de Itabo Pizzería* is good but more expensive than the others. *San Francisco Treats* has fabulous home-made cakes and cookies and California-style

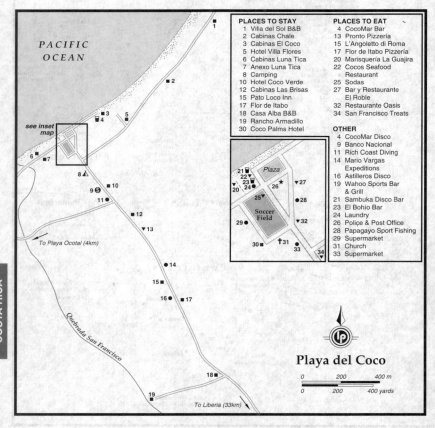

PLACES TO STAY
1 Villa del Sol B&B
2 Cabinas Chale
3 Cabinas El Coco
5 Hotel Villa Flores
6 Cabinas Luna Tica
7 Anexo Luna Tica
8 Camping
10 Hotel Coco Verde
12 Cabinas Las Brisas
15 Pato Loco Inn
17 Flor de Itabo
18 Casa Alba B&B
19 Rancho Armadillo
30 Coco Palms Hotel

PLACES TO EAT
4 CocoMar Bar
13 Pronto Pizzería
15 L'Angoletto di Roma
17 Flor de Itabo Pizzería
20 Marisquería La Guajira
22 Cocos Seafood Restaurant
25 Sodas
27 Bar y Restaurante El Roble
32 Restaurante Oasis
34 San Francisco Treats

OTHER
4 CocoMar Disco
9 Banco Nacional
11 Rich Coast Diving
14 Mario Vargas Expeditions
16 Astilleros Disco
19 Wahoo Sports Bar & Grill
21 Sambuka Disco Bar
23 El Bohío Bar
24 Laundry
26 Police & Post Office
28 Papagayo Sport Fishing
29 Supermarket
31 Church
33 Supermarket

PACIFIC OCEAN

see inset map

To Playa Ocotal (4km)

Plaza

Soccer Field

To Liberia (33km)

Playa del Coco

0   200   400 m
0   200   400 yards

COSTA RICA

cuisine ranging from huge sandwiches to vegetarian lasagna.

There are several inexpensive *sodas* at the northeast corner of the soccer field. Almost opposite, *Bar y Restaurante El Roble* and *Restaurante Oasis* serve tico food. Around the small plaza, you can eat seafood at *Cocos Seafood Restaurant* (which serves pizza as well). Just off the plaza, *Marisquería La Guajira* is a local seafood place and *CocoMar Bar* is popular with ticos on vacation.

Entertainment
The *CocoMar Disco* adjacent to the CocoMar Bar and the *Sambuka Disco Bar* on the west corner of the plaza have loud music and dancing. The restaurants around the plaza double as bars, with *El Bohío Bar* currently being a favorite.

Getting There & Away
The Pulmitan bus stop on the plaza by the police station has buses to San José (US$3.50) at 8 am and 2 pm. Buses to Liberia leave six times a day during the dry season, less frequently in the wet.

PLAYA TAMARINDO
There is a small community and a large and attractive beach here. Both surfing and windsurfing are good, and there is a wildlife refuge nearby. Parts of the beach have rip currents.

Information
Tourist information is available from Tienda Tamarindo (☎ 653-0078) near the center. The Banco Nacional changes US dollars cash and traveler's checks.

Organized Tours & Rentals
Papagayo Excursions (☎ 653-0254) near the entrance of town arranges boat tours, snorkeling, diving, horse rentals, visits to turtle nesting areas and other activities. Tienda Tamarindo rents surfboards, kayaks, snorkels and bikes and sells international newspapers. The friendly Iguana Surf Aquatic Outfitters (☎ /fax 653-0148) rents kayaks, surfboards, boogie boards,

snorkeling gear and Hobie cats and gives lessons and tours.

Places to Stay & Eat
Tito's Camping on the beach at the south end of town offers basic facilities for US$2 per person. They have a soda serving inexpensive local food.

Cheap single rooms are at a premium during the high season, so budget travelers need to find a buddy. The popular *Hotel Dolly* has small doubles with fans and private bath that are quickly snapped up at US$18. Opposite, *Cabinas Marielos* (☎ 653-0141) provides slightly larger doubles with fans and bath for US$30.

Cabinas Pozo Azul (☎ 653-0280) has spartan rooms with bath in the US$20s with fan and the US$30s with air conditioning. Some have a kitchenette and refrigerator, and there is a pool. *Cabinas Zullymar* (☎ 653-0140) is popular. Basic rooms with private bath and fan are in the US$20s; the best rooms (in the US$40s) are air conditioned and have a refrigerator and warm shower. The *Restaurant Zully Mar* is opposite with good sea views and meals in the US$5 to US$10 range.

Arco Iris is a vegetarian restaurant with cabinas for under US$30. Massages and tattoos are reportedly offered. *Albergue de Playa Mamiri* has rooms with private baths for about US$30 and is popular with surfers. Others in this price range are *Cabinas Rodamar* (reportedly about US$20), *Luna Llena Cabins* and *Cabinas 14 de Febrero*. There are plenty of pricier places.

Near the Zully Mar there is the *Jungle Bus*, a hamburger and hot dog stand inside a decrepit bus. Cheap eats are US$2 or US$3. Other, pricier places are nearby.

The popular *Johann's Bakery* has fresh pastries and croissants from about 7 am. They also serve pizzas. Next door *Restaurant Cocodrilo* is a popular bar with tasty bar food, seafood, snacks and bocas. *Soda Frutas Tropicales* is a typical soda with good fruit drinks, and opposite is the *International Deli* serving US-style sandwiches. *Restaurant/Bar El Delfín* is an inexpensive

COSTA RICA

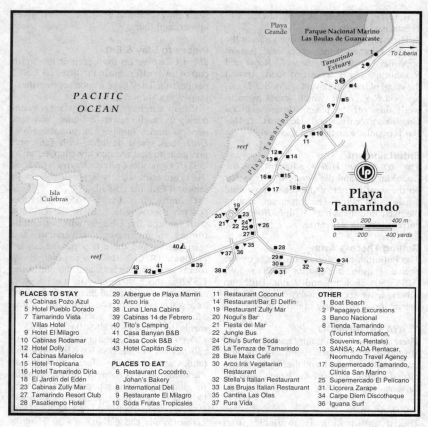

PLACES TO STAY
4 Cabinas Pozo Azul
5 Hotel Pueblo Dorado
7 Tamarindo Vista
  Villas Hotel
9 Hotel El Milagro
10 Cabinas Rodamar
12 Hotel Dolly
14 Cabinas Marielos
15 Hotel Tropicana
16 Hotel Tamarindo Diria
18 El Jardín del Edén
23 Cabinas Zully Mar
27 Tamarindo Resort Club
28 Pasatiempo Hotel
29 Albergue de Playa Mamiri
30 Arco Iris
38 Luna Llena Cabins
39 Cabinas 14 de Febrero
40 Tito's Camping
41 Casa Banyan B&B
42 Casa Cook B&B
43 Hotel Capitán Suizo

PLACES TO EAT
6 Restaurant Cocodrilo,
  Johan's Bakery
8 International Deli
9 Restaurante El Milagro
10 Soda Frutas Tropicales
11 Restaurant Coconut
14 Restaurant/Bar El Delfín
19 Restaurant Zully Mar
20 Nogui's Bar
21 Fiesta del Mar
22 Jungle Bus
24 Chu's Surfer Soda
26 La Terraza de Tamarindo
28 Blue Maxx Café
30 Arco Iris Vegetarian
  Restaurant
32 Stella's Italian Restaurant
34 Las Brujas Italian Restaurant
35 Cantina Las Olas
37 Pura Vida

OTHER
1 Boat Beach
2 Papagayo Excursions
3 Banco Nacional
8 Tienda Tamarindo
  (Tourist Information,
  Souvenirs, Rentals)
13 SANSA; ADA Rentacar,
  Neomundo Travel Agency
17 Supermercado Tamarindo,
  Clínica San Marino
25 Supermercado El Pelícano
31 Licorera Zarape
34 Carpe Diem Discotheque
36 Iguana Surf

local place, and *Chu's Surfer Soda* has cheap eats.

Getting There & Away
Air Travelair (US$88/146) and SANSA (US$50/100) both have several daily flights from San José. Some flights may stop at other airstrips. The Travelair agent is in the Hotel Pueblo Dorado and the SANSA agent (☎ 653-0001) is on the main road. The airport is 2.5 km north of town.

Bus Empresa Alfaro and TRALAPA have daily afternoon buses from San José, returning from Tamarindo at 5:45 and 6:45 am.

There is an 8:30 pm bus from Santa Cruz, returning at 6:45 am.

PARQUE NACIONAL MARINO LAS BAULAS DE GUANACASTE
This includes Playa Grande, an important nesting site for the *baula* (leatherback turtle). This is the world's largest turtle, which can weigh over 500 kg! Nesting season is October to March, and over a hundred turtles may be seen laying their eggs during the course of a night.

Tamarindo hotels and agencies will organize turtle-watching tours in season. Some of these are by boat. Tours cost about US$12 and up, depending on the size of the group, where you start from and the quality of the guide. Turtle watchers pay a US$6 park fee and must watch the activities from specified viewing areas, accompanied by a guide or ranger. No flash photography or lights are allowed, as this disturbs the laying process.

Howler monkeys, raccoons, coatis, otters and a goodly variety of crabs and birds in the mangroves may also be seen.

PLAYA AVELLANA

This popular surfing beach is about 15 km south of Tamarindo by road but closer to 10 km if you walk in along the beaches. The road may require 4WD in the wet season. The relatively difficult access means that this beach is frequented by those who appreciate it, which is mainly surfers.

Places to Stay & Eat

There are several surfers' hangouts. Locals say the best is *Mono Congo Surf Lodge*, where the owner repairs surfboards and cooks food and has double rooms for US$35. *Pablo's Picasso* has hamburgers 'as big as your head,' huge surfing murals and dorms with beds for US$10 or doubles for US$30. *Avellanes Surf Ranch* and *Cabinas Gregorios* are among the other options.

PLAYA JUNQUILLAL

This is a wide and wild beach, with high surf, strong rip currents and few people. The beach is two km long, has tide pools and is pleasant to walk. Sea turtles nest here, but in smaller numbers than at the refuges. There is no village to speak of.

Places to Stay

You can camp by the *Hotel Playa Junquillal* for about US$4 per night, or stay in one of their few basic cabins with hot shower for US$30 for a double; it's often full. Try Coco (☎ /fax 680-0053) in Santa Cruz for reservations. You could probably camp almost anywhere along the beach if you

had your own food and water. *Hospedaje El Malinche* offers a few low-budget rooms and a camping area. There are several pricier places.

Getting There & Away

TRALAPA has a daily bus from San José (five hours) at 2 pm, returning at 5 am, and from Santa Cruz at 6:30 pm, returning at 5 am.

SANTA CRUZ
Population 15,000

This small town, 57 km from Liberia, is a possible overnight stop for people visiting the peninsula. There is an annual rodeo and fiesta during the second week in January.

An interesting excursion is to the village of **Guaitil**, 12 km away, where local families make and sell attractive pottery in the pre-Columbian Chorotega style.

Places to Stay & Eat

Pensión Isabel (☎ 680-0173), 400 meters south and 50 meters east of the Plaza de Los Mangos, has basic rooms for US$5 per person. The family-run *Hospedaje y Restaurante Avellanas* (☎ 680-0808), 150 meters north of the Banco Anglo Costarricense, is US$10 for a double with bath. A block away is the cheaper and friendly *Posada Tu Casa*. Other basic cheapies to try are *Pensión Pampera* (☎ 680-1045), *Hospedaje Amadita* and *Cabinas Tauro*. The *Hotel La Estancia* (☎ 680-0476, 680-1033, fax 680-0348), 100 meters west of the plaza, has 16 clean rooms with fans, TV and private bath for US$17/23.

Check out *La Fabrica de Tortillas*, 700 meters south of the Plaza de Los Mangos. They have inexpensive tico-style country meals cooked in an open kitchen right in front of you.

Getting There & Away

There are two bus terminals. Transportes La Pampa (☎ 680-0111) leaves from the north side of the Plaza de Los Mangos to Nicoya 17 times a day from 6 am to 9:30 pm and to Liberia 16 times a day from 5:30 am to 7:30 pm.

COSTA RICA

The main terminal is 400 meters east of the center. TRALAPA (☎ 680-0392) has buses to San José at 3, 4:30, 6:30, 8:30 and 11:30 am and 1 pm. Alfaro buses between San José and Nicoya stop in Santa Cruz. There are six buses a day to Guaitil. Buses for Playas Conchal, Brasilito, Flamingo and Potrero leave four times a day during the dry season; fewer in the wet. A bus leaves for Junquillal at 6:30 am and Tamarindo at 6:45 am and 8:30 pm. Some TRALAPA beach buses also go via Santa Cruz.

NICOYA
Population 25,000

Nicoya, 23 km south of Santa Cruz, is the most important town on the peninsula. It was named after the Chorotega Indian Chief Nicoya, who welcomed the first Spaniards in 1523. Some locals are partly of Chorotega descent. The shining white church on the pleasant Parque Central dates to the mid-17th century and is worth a look. Nicoya is now the commercial center of the cattle industry as well as the political capital and the transport hub of the peninsula. Banks here will change US dollars.

Places to Stay & Eat
The *Hotel Ali* (☎ 685-5148) has basic rooms for US$3.50 per person. The *Hotel Venecia* (☎ 685-5325) charges US$8 for basic doubles with shared cold shower and US$15 for a double with private shower. The *Hotel Elegancia* (☎ 685-5159) is similarly priced. The clean and popular *Hotel Chorotega* (☎ 685-5245) has basic rooms with fans for US$4 per person and decent rooms with shower and fan for US$7.50 per person.

The *Hotel Las Tinajas* (☎ 685-5081, fax 685-5096) has decent single/double rooms with bath and fans for US$12/17. Larger rooms with private bath sleeping seven people are US$45. The *Hotel Jenny* (☎ 685-5050) is clean, popular and helpful. Air-conditioned rooms with bath and TV are US$14/20.

There are three or four Chinese restaurants in the center. *Café Daniela* serves breakfasts, burgers, pizzas and snacks and is popular. The *Bar/Restaurant Nicoya* is good for standard meals. Stands and sodas around the park sell cheap snacks.

Getting There & Away
Buses for Liberia leave 18 times a day from Transportes La Pampa at Av 1 and Calle 5. Most other buses leave Nicoya from the bus terminal at the south end of Calle 5. There are six to eight buses a day for San José, buses at 5:15 am and 1 pm for Playa Naranjo (connecting with the Puntarenas ferry) and daily service to Playa Sámara, Playa Nosara, Quebrada Honda, Santa Ana, Copal and other local towns.

PARQUE NACIONAL BARRA HONDA
This park protects Costa Rica's most interesting cave system, though it's hard to enter without caving gear.

Information
The ranger station at the southwest corner of the park provides information and takes the US$6 entrance fee. About 350 meters beyond the station is a camping area (US$2) with latrines and water. Trails lead to the top of nearby hills – carry plenty of water.

Just outside the park entrance, the locals have organized *Proyecto Las Delicias*, which has a campsite (US$2), simple restaurant and cabins for US$11 per person. Local guides with gear charge US$50 per group to descend into a cave. The dry season is recommended for caving.

Getting There & Away
There are no buses to the park, but buses go from Nicoya to Santa Ana, Corralillo and Nacaome, which are three-, four- and six-km walks, respectively, from the park.

PLAYA NOSARA
This attractive white-sand beach is backed by a pocket of luxuriant vegetation that attracts birds and wildlife. Foreign (especially North American) retirees live here year round. Note that the village and airport of Nosara are five km inland from the beach. Basic food supplies are available in the village.

The small beaches of Playa Pelada and Playa Guiones, a couple of kilometers south of Playa Nosara, are attractive and worth visiting if you are spending a few days.

Places to Stay & Eat
Cheap hotels are in the village. The basic *Cabinas Chorotega* (☎ 680-0836) is US$8 per person. The clean *Cabinas Agnel* is similar.

El Ranchito serves burgers and beer, and *La Lechuza* is locally popular.

On the beach, camping is possible and there are shelters and water. Beach-area hotels start in the US$40s. *Olga's Restaurant* on Playa Pelada has US$3 casados.

Getting There & Away
Air SANSA (US$50/100) and Travelair (US$88/131 one way/roundtrip) have daily flights from San José.

Bus Transportes Rojas (☎ 685-5352) has a daily bus from Nicoya's main terminal at 1 pm returning to Nicoya at 6 am (2½ to five hours depending on road conditions). Transportes Alfaro has a bus from San José at 6:15 am, returning from Nosara at 4 pm.

REFUGIO NACIONAL DE FAUNA SILVESTRE OSTIONAL
This refuge includes the coastal village of Ostional, eight km northwest of Playa Nosara. The reserve is eight km long but only a few hundred meters wide. The main attraction is the annual nesting of the olive ridley sea turtle, from July to November with a peak from August to October.

Apart from turtles, there are iguanas, crabs, howler monkeys, coatis and many birds to be seen. There is a small mangrove swamp, and the tide pools are teeming with life.

The villagers of Ostional are helpful and will guide you to the best areas.

Camping is permitted, but there are no camping facilities. Ostional has a small store (☎ 680-0467) where you can get basic food supplies. Next door, the *Hospedaje Guacamaya* has a few basic rooms for US$5 per person; bring mosquito coils. Another cheap hotel has recently opened.

A bus runs from Santa Cruz at noon, depending on road conditions. Alternatively, walk from Nosara.

PLAYA SÁMARA
This beautiful, gentle, white-sand beach is one of Costa Rica's safest and prettiest. Former president Oscar Arias has a vacation house near here. It is a favorite beach for tourists, and bus and air service are improving. A paved road arrived in 1996 and a phone system is slated for 1997. Expect changes!

Pulpería Mileth has a public phone and bus information. There is a disco nearby. Hotels arrange horseback riding and diving.

Places to Stay & Eat
Camp near *Soda Yuré*, *Coco's* or *Nicho's* on the beach for US$2.25 per person. *Soda Yuré* has typical food, including casados for US$2.50 and other plates around US$4, but no beer is served. Ask around for other places to camp.

The basic but popular *Hotel Playa Sámara* (☎ 680-0750) charges US$6 per person. A cheap soda and a loud disco are nearby. Other cheap places to try are the *Cabinas Sámara* (☎ 680-0222) with rooms with private baths, the cheaper *Cabinas Magaly* or the *Bar/Cabinas Los Mangos*. *Cabinas & Comedor Arenas* (☎ 680-0445) has doubles with bath and fan for US$29.

About four km southeast of Sámara is the quiet **Playa Carrillo**, where there are basic rooms offered by *Bar Restaurant Chala*. There are a couple of other unsigned places with cheap rooms – ask around. Beach camping is possible.

Getting There & Away
Air The airport is between Sámara and Carrillo and is also called Carrillo. The SANSA agent is at the Hotel Giada and has flights from Monday to Saturday from San José (US$50/100 one way/roundtrip). Travelair has daily flights (US$80/131).

Bus Alfaro in San José has a daily noon bus to Sámara, taking six hours. It leaves Sámara at 4 am. Buses from Nicoya leave at 8 am and 3 pm (two hours, US$1.25). The return is at 6 am and 4:30 pm.

PLAYA NARANJO

This village is the terminal for the Puntarenas ferry, and the beach is not very exciting. Most ferry passengers continue on to Nicoya, about 70 km, three to four hours, to the northwest. There are no cheap hotels at this writing.

All transport is geared to the Puntarenas ferry (☎ 661-1069), which departs three to five times a day. Buses for Nicoya meet incoming ferries.

If you want to go to the south part of the Península de Nicoya, don't come to Playa Naranjo – take the passenger ferry from Puntarenas to Paquera.

PAQUERA

Four km away from the Puntarenas-Paquera passenger ferry terminal, Paquera village is reached by a very crowded truck. In the village there are a couple of basic cabinas. However, most travelers take the bus from the ferry terminal to Montezuma (two hours, US$2.50). The bus is crowded – get off the ferry early to get a seat.

There is a snack bar at the Paquera ferry terminal.

The passenger ferry leaves for Puntarenas daily at 8 am, 12:30 and 5 pm.

There's also a car and passenger ferry from Puntarenas with four departures a day (see Puntarenas, above).

MONTEZUMA

This village, near the tip of the peninsula, has good beaches, friendly residents, a lovely waterfall and swimming hole nearby and a nature reserve a few kilometers away. Montezuma is very popular with younger gringo travelers who enjoy the laid-back atmosphere and affordable prices.

Information

Monte Aventuras (☎ /fax 642-0025) provides international public fax and phone and has tourist information. They can arrange virtually any kind of tour or activity you want, or tell you where to go to do

it. They are closed on Sunday.

El Sano Banano (see Places to Eat) is also a good source of local information and contacts. There are also locally run information booths in the center of town. The staff can help you find places to stay and connect you with locals who rent horses, give tours and provide land and sea transportation (see Things to See & Do).

There are no banks, but you can change cash US dollars or traveler's checks at Monte Aventuras. You might also be able to change cash dollars at either Chico's or El Sano Banano restaurants – if they have enough colones available. There is a laundry and book exchange (see map).

Things to See & Do

Bicycle rentals are US$12.50 per day. Horses are about US$25 a half day. Roger Rojas has been recommended for guided horseback rides. Snorkeling gear and tours are available.

A lovely waterfall with a swimming hole is reached by taking the trail to the right just after the bridge past the Restaurant Cascada. It's a 20-minute walk. A second set of falls is farther upriver. Lovely beaches are strung out along the coast, separated by small rocky headlands and offering great beach-combing and tide-pool studying. (Also see Reserva Natural Absoluta Cabo Blanco).

All-day boat excursions to swim and snorkel at Isla Tortuga are US$30 a person, including light snacks. It's 90 minutes to the island. Bring a sun hat and sunblock. Other boat excursions are available.

Places to Stay

The high season (December to April) sometimes gets crowded, especially if you arrive late Friday afternoon. Single rooms are hard to find. Low-season discounts are common. Budget hotels have cold showers.

Camping in town itself is locally discouraged, although there is a campground with showers reached by walking north along the beach. They charge US$3.

Pensión Jenny has nice balcony views and basic but clean rooms – a fair deal for

US$5.50 per person in dormitories (four bunk beds) or US$11 for double rooms. All bathrooms are shared. Nearby, *Cabinas El Caracol* (☎ 642-0194) has large bare rooms with communal baths for US$6 per person; double rooms with private bath are US$16. A cheap restaurant is attached, though a reader reports gross overcharging.

Pensión Lucy (☎ 642-0273) has ocean views and is a good deal for US$6/11 for a single/double; get an upstairs room. *Cabinas Tucan* (☎ 642-0284, fax 642-0284) is OK for US$8/13. *Pensión Arenas* (☎ 642-0306) is similarly priced and has private showers and a good beachfront setting. There's a family-run restaurant.

The *Hotel Moctezuma* (☎ 642-0258, fax 642-0058) is central and has a restaurant and popular bar with music loud enough to wake light sleepers. Clean, large rooms with fans and shower cost US$12/18 or US$8/11 in a few rooms with shared baths. Triples and quads are available.

Cabinas Capitan (☎ 642-0069) has basic but clean rooms with fans for US$10 for a single (shared showers) or US$15 for a double (private shower). The *Cabinas Mar y Cielo* (☎ 662-0036, 642-0261) is also clean and charges US$20 to US$35 for two to six people in rooms with private bath and fan. Upstairs rooms are breezy with nice views. The *Mochila Inn* (☎ 642-0030) is US$10 per person with shared bathroom. Double rooms with kitchen privileges are US$25.

The good *Hotel La Aurora* (☎ 642-0051, fax 642-0025) has clean rooms, some with private bath, in the US$20s. There is a kitchen and homey touches like free coffee and tea, a library and nice areas to hangout.

Places to Eat
Some places charge 23% tax on top of the bill. Ask first if you are on a budget. *Chico's Bar* is the traditional place for a beer and simple meal and is a popular bar with loud music until 11 pm. Cheap, good-value places that recently didn't add tax include the *Soda La Gemelas* and *Restaurant El Parque*. Fish casado in these places is US$3.50, a little less with chicken, or around US$5 for a full fish dinner. They don't sell alcohol, but you can bring your own. These places are very popular with young travelers – you should go by about 6 pm for the best choice of food and tables. The restaurant at *Cabinas El Caracol* is also similarly priced.

Other places that serve decent meals but are a little pricier include *El Chiringuito Tropical*, which serves seafood, *Restaurant La Casacada*, which is quiet and pleasant next to a stream, and the popular restaurant/bar in the *Hotel Moctezuma*. Next door to the Moctezuma is the *Pizzería del Sol*, which serves pizza slices.

The *El Sano Banano* (☎ /fax 642-0068, net) restaurant serves yogurt, juices, fruit salads, vegetarian meals, seafood and pizzas. It has a big-screen TV and shows movies (US$2.50 minimum consumption). The owners are a good source of information.

Entertainment
Start with a 7:30 movie at *El Sano Banano*, go on to *Chico's Bar* for a beer, and finish up in the *Kali Olin Disco* for dancing until the early hours. The disco is about a kilometer northwest of town, on the road to Cóbano.

Getting There & Away
The Puntarenas-Paquera passenger ferry connects with a bus to Montezuma. The 3 pm ferry gets you into Montezuma well after dark.

Buses leave Montezuma at 5:30, 10 am and 2 pm for Paquera, connecting with the Puntarenas ferry. If you take the 2 pm bus, you can just catch the last Puntarenas to San José bus if you hustle.

MALPAÍS
This small village is popular with surfers. Horses can be rented. Several hotels have opened recently but are rather spread out, so ask for directions. *Frank's Place* charges US$12.50/20 and has a restaurant attached. *Cabinas Bosque Mar* (☎ 226-0475, fax 227-6688) has big rooms with hot showers for US$18/28 and rooms with kitchenette for a few dollars more. Other places at similar prices are the friendly *Cabinas Mar*

Azul, the *Cabinas Laura Mar* and, further north, the *Cabinas Playa Santa Teresita*. The village is reached by two daily buses from Cóbano.

RESERVA NATURAL ABSOLUTA CABO BLANCO

This beautiful reserve encompasses the southern tip of the peninsula. It is 11 km south of Montezuma by dirt road. The reserve has an evergreen forest, a couple of attractive beaches and a host of birds and animals.

A trail leads to the beaches at the tip of the peninsula. The hike takes a couple of hours and you can return by a different trail. Look for boobies, pelicans and frigate birds.

There is a ranger station (☎ /fax 642-0093) where you pay US$6 admission and obtain information. Reserve hours are Wednesday to Sunday 8 am to 4 pm. Camping is not permitted and no food or drink is available.

A 4WD taxi (up to six passengers) from Montezuma to the park costs about US$15, or walk or cycle. Tours are available, though many people don't bother because you can get around yourself. However, guides charge only US$5 per person and you'll see more, so a tour is worthwhile for your first visit.

Panama

It's ironic that Panama is still largely 'undiscovered,' while just across the border Costa Rica is becoming one of the world's most popular tourist destinations. It's especially ironic considering Panama's amazing natural wonders.

Panama has several very apt nicknames: 'the land of contrasts' and 'the crossroads of the world.' Few countries offer such interesting and dramatic contrasts in such a small area: lush tropical rain forests in the central and eastern regions, cool, fresh volcanic mountains in the west, fascinating Caribbean and Pacific islands. And the country's allure is heightened by its mosaic of peoples and cultures. At the center of it all is Panama City, with the most international and cosmopolitan ambiance of any Central American city. Many interesting sites lie in the city and nearby.

Panama's contrasts arise in part from its geographic position. The narrowest land mass between the Atlantic and Pacific Oceans, and the connecting bridge between North and South America, Panama has been a crossroads for centuries – not only for humans, but also for birds, animals and plants migrating between North and South America. Panama is an interesting combination of Spanish, Latin American, North American, Caribbean and indigenous cultural influences, with immigrants from Asia, Europe, the Middle East and other places spicing up the mix.

Despite Panama's attractions, many travelers to Central America bypass it. This unfortunate trend is largely due to the fact that outsiders don't know much about Panama, and the ideas they do have about it are often mistaken. Images of the 1989 US invasion stick in many people's minds, and they expect Panama to be like an armed camp or especially dangerous. Not so – Panama today is a peaceful place. Another misperception is that Panama is expensive. Lodging here may tend to be more expensive than in other parts of Central America, but the prices for everything else – food, transportation, places to visit – are very reasonable indeed. Panama is full of surprises that begin to reveal themselves the moment you arrive.

Facts about Panama

HISTORY
Pre-Columbian History

Archaeological evidence shows that people have been living in Panama for at least around 11,000 years, with agriculture arising as early as 1500 BC.

Archaeologists divide pre-Columbian Panama into three distinct cultural zones – western, central and eastern – based on the types of ceramics (pottery) and other artifacts found at various archaeological sites. None of these zones were culturally isolated; evidence of trading shows ties not only among the zones, but between them and Colombia, other parts of Central America and even Mexico and Peru. In addition to commercial trade, the economies of all of Panama's early societies were based on extensive agriculture, hunting and fishing. It is believed these societies were hierarchical and headed by chiefs *(caciques)*, and that war played a significant role.

In western Panama on the slopes of the giant Volcán Barú, Barriles is an important archaeological center, where finds have included unusual life-size stone statues of human figures, sometimes with one figure bearing another sitting astride his shoulders. Giant *metates* – flat stone platforms used for grinding corn – have also been found here.

Between Penonomé and Natá in the central region, Sitio Conte is an important archaeological zone and ancient ceremonial

Map Index

CARIBBEAN SEA

Panama City
pgs 726-727

San Felipe
(Casco Viejo)
pg 730

Central
Panama City
pg 733

Bocas del Toro
pg 772

Panama City
see inset

COSTA
RICA

Boquete
pg 762

David
pg 758

Panama Canal
pg 741

Darién Gap
pg 783

COLOMBIA

OTHER MAPS
• Panama pgs 702-703
• Provinces of Panama pg 710

PACIFIC OCEAN

0   50   100 km
0   30   60 miles

center where thousands of pieces of pottery, as well as tombs and many other items of interest, have been unearthed.

Another central archaeological zone, Cerro Juan Díaz, near Villa de los Santos on the Península de Azuero, is believed to have been inhabited from around 300 BC until the time of the Spanish conquest. Presently being excavated by the Smithsonian Institute, it is revealing many items of interest including evidence that pottery made here was traded for Columbian goods, including gold. Pre-Columbian pottery and other artifacts have also been found at sites in the Parque Nacional Sarigua, also on the Península de Azuero.

Archeologists estimate that the early civilization represented at Barriles was established around the 4th or 5th century BC when settlers arrived from the west (now Costa Rica). This culture came to an abrupt end when Volcán Barú erupted violently in the 5th century AD. Later on, the region was inhabited once again, this time by two different groups whose archaeological remnants include a great variety of distinctive types of pottery.

Not as much is known about the early peoples of the eastern region of Panama, because archaeologists have yet to conduct extensive studies there. Most of the history of this area and its hierarchical, tribal social structure has been learned from accounts of the first Spaniards, who arrived in the Darién Province.

Pre-Columbian Gold

Gold appeared in Panama suddenly with a sophisticated and completely developed technology. Metallurgy was being practiced in Peru as early as the 2nd century BC; by the 1st century AD it had arrived in Panama. Archaeologists believe it probably arrived in Panama from the Sinu, Quimbaya and Tairona regions of Colombia, with the Urabá area as the point of contact and interchange.

Colombia, Panama and Costa Rica all

became metallurgic provinces, and objects of gold and other metals were exchanged all the way from Mesoamerica to the Andes. Gold was made into ornaments (necklaces, nose rings and so on) and animal, human and other figures. Its use was mostly for ornamentation and ceremonial purposes; it probably did not connote wealth in the same way that it did for the Spanish.

When Spaniards first arrived on the isthmus of Panama in the early 16th century, they found it inhabited by various indigenous peoples. The population may have been as large then as it is now, but it was rapidly decimated by European diseases and Spanish swords.

Spanish Colonization

The first European in the area was the Spanish explorer Rodrigo de Bastidas, who sailed along Panama's Caribbean Coast in 1501 with Vasco Nuñez de Balboa and Juan de la Cosa. The following year, Christopher Columbus sailed along part of this coast on his fourth and final New World voyage. In 1510, the first Spanish settlement, Nombre de Dios, was founded at the mouth of the Río Chagres by another explorer, Diego de Nicuesa.

Not far away on the Gulf of Urabá in what is now Colombia, Alonso de Ojeda founded another settlement, San Sebastian de Urabá. This settlement was later moved to the Panamanian coast under the leadership of Vasco Nuñez de Balboa and renamed Santa María la Antigua del Darién.

Indians told Balboa of a large sea and a wealthy, gold-producing civilization – almost certainly referring to the Inca empire of Peru – across the mountains of the isthmus. Balboa subsequently scaled the mountains and on September 26, 1513, 'discovered' the Pacific Ocean, claiming it for the King of Spain. He called it the *Mar del Sur* – South Sea – because he crossed Panama from north to south.

In 1519 the settlement of Santa María was moved again, this time across the isthmus to the Pacific side near where Panama City stands today. It was named Panamá (meaning 'abundance of fish' in a native language) and became an important Spanish settlement, commercial center and the springboard for further explorations, including the conquest of Peru and expeditions north into Central America. The ruins of this old settlement, Panamá Viejo, remain today.

Las Cruces Trail connected Panamá to Nombre de Dios on the Caribbean side. Goods were carried between the two ports until late in the 16th century, when Nombre de Dios was destroyed by the English pirate Francis Drake. The small bay of Portobelo then became the chief Caribbean connection. Gold from Peru and other colonial products were brought there along El Camino Real (The King's Highway) by mule train from Panamá. The treasure was then held for an annual trading fair that lured Spanish galleons laden with European goods.

All this wealth concentrated in one small bay naturally attracted English, French, Dutch and other pirates who were plying the Caribbean at the time. The Spanish built large stone fortresses to try to ward off attack: the ones at Portobelo and at Fuerte (Fort) San Lorenzo at the mouth of the Río Chagres can still be visited today.

These fortifications weren't enough, however. In 1671 the English pirate Henry Morgan overpowered Fort San Lorenzo, sailed up the Río Chagres and crossed the isthmus. His forces destroyed the city of Panamá, making off with its entire treasure and arriving back on the Caribbean Coast with 200 mules loaded with loot. The town was rebuilt a few years later on a cape several kilometers west of its original site, where the San Felipe District of Panama City is today.

In 1739 Portobelo was also destroyed by British Admiral Edward Vernon, finally forcing Spain to abandon the Panamanian crossing in favor of sailing the long way around Cape Horn to the west coast of South America. Panama declined in importance and in 1739 was made a part of the Viceroyalty of Nueva Andalucía, later Nueva Granada, which eventually became Colombia.

Panama

Independence

In 1821 Colombia, including Panama, gained its independence from Spain. Panama joined Gran Colombia, which included Colombia, Venezuela, Ecuador, Peru and Bolivia, forming the united Latin American nation that had long been the dream of Simón Bolívar. Later Gran Colombia split up, but Panama remained a province of Colombia.

The Panama Railroad

From the moment that the world's major powers learned that the isthmus of Panama was the narrowest point between the Atlantic and Pacific Oceans, they focused attention on the region.

In 1846 Colombia signed a treaty to permit the USA to construct a railway across the isthmus. The treaty guaranteed the USA the right of free transit across the isthmus and the right to protect the line with military force. This was a time of great political turbulence in Panama. Construction of the railroad began in 1850 and concluded in 1855; during that time Panama had 20 governors.

The California gold rush of 1848 helped

to make the railway a profitable venture and it also spurred efforts to construct an interoceanic canal across Central America.

The Panama Canal & the French

The idea of a canal across the isthmus was first mooted in 1524, when King Charles V of Spain ordered a survey to be conducted to determine the feasibility of constructing such a waterway. In 1878, the Colombian government awarded a contract to build a canal to Lucien N B Wyse, who sold the concession to the French diplomat Ferdinand de Lesseps, then basking in his success as the contractor-builder of the Suez Canal.

De Lesseps' Compagnie Universelle du Canal Interocéanique began work in 1880. De Lesseps was determined to build a sea-level canal alongside the interoceanic railway, but the project proved more difficult than anyone had expected. Yellow fever and malaria killed around 22,000 workers, there were insurmountable construction problems, and financial mismanagement drove the company bankrupt by 1889.

One of de Lesseps' chief engineers, Philippe Bunau-Varilla, formed a new

PANAMA

canal company, but at the same time the USA was seriously considering putting its own canal somewhere through Central America. Nicaragua seemed the most likely site (see the Nicaragua chapter), but taking over the canal in Panama was also a possibility. The French, unable to complete the canal, finally agreed to sell the concession to the USA. In 1903 Bunau-Varilla asked the Colombian government for permission to conclude the sale. Colombia refused.

Panama Becomes a Nation
Revolutionary sentiments had been brewing in Panama for many years, but repeated attempts to break away from Colombia had met with no success. In 1903 a civil war in Colombia was breeding fresh discontents, as Panamanians were drafted to fight and Panamanian property was seized by the Colombian government for the war effort.

When the Colombian government refused to allow the transfer of the canal treaty to the USA, it thwarted US and French interests as well as Panama's own. Bunau-Varilla, who had a lot to gain financially if the sale went through, approached the US government to back Panama if it declared its independence from Colombia.

A revolutionary junta declared Panama independent on November 3, 1903, with the support of the USA, which immediately recognized the new government. Colombia sent troops by sea to try to regain control of the province, but US battleships prevented their reaching land.

The First Canal Treaty
Bunau-Varilla, now Panamanian ambassador to the USA, moved quickly to preempt the arrival in Washington, DC, of an official delegation from Panama that was slated to negotiate the treaty terms. On November 18, he signed the Hay-Bunau-Varilla Treaty with US Secretary of State John Hay. It gave the USA far more than had been offered in the original treaty rejected by the Colombian government. The treaty's 26 articles awarded the US 'sovereign rights in perpetuity over the Canal Zone,' an area extending eight km on either side of the canal, and a broad right of intervention in Panamanian affairs. By the time the Panamanian delegation arrived in Washington, DC, the treaty had been signed. It was ratified over their protests.

The treaty led to friction between the USA and Panama for decades, partly because it was overly favorable to the USA at the expense of Panama and partly due to lingering questions about its legality. Colombia did not recognize Panama as a legitimately separate nation until 1921, when the USA paid Colombia US$25 million in 'compensation.'

The USA Builds the Canal
Construction began again on the canal in 1904. The project remains one of the greatest engineering achievements of the 20th century, completed despite disease, landslides and many other difficulties. Over 75,000 workers were employed on it. Canal heroes included Colonel William Crawford Gorgas, who managed a massive campaign to eliminate yellow fever and malaria, and two chief engineers, John F Stevens and Colonel George Washington Goethals.

Construction took 10 years. The first ship sailed through the canal on August 15, 1914.

Rise of the Military
The US military intervened repeatedly in Panama's political affairs until 1936, when the Hay-Bunau-Varilla Treaty was replaced by the Hull-Alfaro Treaty. The USA relinquished its rights to use its troops outside the Canal Zone and to seize land for canal purposes, and the annual sum paid to Panama for use of the Canal Zone was increased.

With the new restrictions on US military activity, the Panamanian army grew more powerful. In 1968 the Guardia Nacional deposed the elected president and took control of the government; the constitution was suspended, the national assembly dissolved and the press censored. The Guardia's General Omar Torrijos Herrera emerged as the new leader.

Torrijos conducted public works programs on a grand scale, including a massive modernization of Panama City, which won him the support of much of the populace but also plunged Panama into huge debt.

1977 Canal Treaty

US dominion over the Canal Zone, and the canal itself, were continuing sources of conflict between Panama and the USA. After years of negotiation that foundered in a series of stalemates, a new treaty was finally accepted by both sides in 1977.

The new treaty provides that US control of the canal will be gradually phased out, with Panama assuming complete ownership and control on December 31, 1999. It also provides for the phasing out of US military bases in Panama. A separate treaty ensures that the canal shall remain open and neutral for all nations, during both peace and war. In 1978, the US Senate attached extenuating conditions that grant the US the right of limited intervention and rights to defend the canal beyond the 1999 date. The treaty finally went into effect on October 1, 1979.

Manuel Noriega

Torrijos was killed in a plane crash in 1981. In September 1983, after a brief period of leadership by Colonel Paredes, Colonel Manuel Antonio Noriega Moreno took control of the Guardia Nacional and then of the country itself.

Noriega, a former head of Panama's secret police and a former CIA operative, quickly consolidated his power. He enlarged the Guardia Nacional and its powers, closed down all media that criticized him and created a paramilitary 'Dignity Battalion' in every city, town and village, armed and ready to inform on any of their neighbors showing less than complete loyalty to the Noriega regime.

The first presidential election in 16 years was held in 1984. Although the count was challenged, Noriega's candidate, respected economist Nicolás Ardito Barletta, was declared the winner. A year later Ardito

Barletta was removed by Noriega for insisting on a top-level investigation into the murder of a popular Panamanian political leader, Dr Hugo Spadafora.

In early 1987 Noriega became the focus of an international scandal. He was publicly accused of involvement in drug trafficking with Colombian drug cartels, murdering his opponents and rigging elections. Panamanians demanded Noriega's dismissal, protesting with general strikes and street demonstrations that resulted in violent clashes with the National Defense Forces.

Relations with the US went from bad to worse. By February 1988, the US had indicted Noriega for drug trafficking and involvement in organized crime. In the same month, Barletta's successor as president, Eric Arturo Delvalle, attempted to dismiss Noriega, but Noriega still held the reins of power, and Delvalle ended up fleeing Panama after being deposed himself. Noriega appointed a substitute president.

Noriega's regime was now an international embarrassment. In March 1988 the USA imposed sanctions against Panama, ending a preferential trade agreement, freezing Panamanian assets and refusing to pay canal fees. Panama's international offshore banking industry, which the USA had asserted was deeply involved with international drug cartels and with laundering money for organized crime, buckled under the strain of the US sanctions.

A few days after the sanctions were imposed, there was an unsuccessful military coup. Noriega responded by stepping up the violent repression of his critics, including the increasing numbers of antigovernment demonstrators.

Presidential elections were held once again in May 1989. When Noriega's candidate failed to win, Noriega simply declared the entire election null and void. Guillermo Endara, the winning candidate, and his two vice-presidential running mates were beaten bloody by Noriega's forces, a scene captured live on national TV, infuriating the nation. An attempted coup in October 1989 was followed by even more repressive measures.

On December 15, 1989, Noriega's legislature declared him president. At the same time, it was announced that Panama was at war with the USA. The following day, an unarmed US marine dressed in civilian clothes was killed by Panamanian soldiers.

'Operation Just Cause'

US reaction was swift. In the first hour of December 20, 1989, Panama City was attacked by aircraft, tanks and 26,000 US troops in an all-out mission called 'Operation Just Cause.' US President George Bush said the invasion had four objectives: to protect US lives, to maintain the security of the Panama Canal, to restore democracy to Panama and to capture Noriega and bring him to justice.

Shortly before the invasion there had been an attempt to kidnap Noriega, but he had gone into hiding. Then on Christmas Day, the fifth day of the invasion, he went to the Vatican Embassy to request asylum. He remained there for 10 days. Outside, the US forces reinforced diplomatic pressure on the Vatican to expel him by setting up loudspeakers outside the embassy, blaring rock music (including the song 'You're No Good'), and the recorded sounds of helicopters and gunfire to wear down the nerves of those inside. Meanwhile, angry public riots near the blocked-off embassy urged Noriega's ousting.

The Vatican Embassy chief finally persuaded Noriega to give himself up by threatening to cancel his asylum. Noriega surrendered to US forces on the evening of January 3, 1991. He was flown immediately to Miami, where he was tried on numerous criminal charges and convicted in April 1992 on eight charges of conspiracy to manufacture and distribute cocaine. In July 1992 he was sentenced to 40 years in prison. He remains under control of the US penal authorities.

Post-Invasion Panama

After Noriega's ouster, Guillermo Endara, the legitimate winner of the 1989 election, was sworn in as president, and Panama City attempted to put itself back together. It had suffered damage not only from the invasion itself, but from widespread looting. Many residential blocks of the district of Chorrillo, near the Panama Defence Force headquarters, burned to the ground in a fire during the invasion.

The death toll from the invasion was a subject of great controversy. The 'official' death toll was put at 540; a human-rights commission later determined that at least 4000 Panamanians had been killed, and other sources gave estimates as high as 7000, asserting that unknown numbers of bodies were buried in mass graves. However, not one mass grave was ever found, and the allegations of mass murder receded into the past.

The Endara government, however, did not turn out to be a panacea. There was public concern over what many considered to be Endara's excessive involvement with the US, his failure to create civil and economic well-being for the country following the ouster of Noriega and his handling of the military. The public was also concerned with the future of the canal.

In the next presidential election, held on May 8, 1994, Ernesto Pérez Ballardes, candidate of a political alliance including the Partido Revolucionario Democrático (PRD) and Partido Laborista (PALA) parties, won by a narrow margin, with 33% of the votes. Rubén Blades, an internationally renowned Panamanian salsa music star, represented the Movimiento Papa Egoró (MPE) party and took third place, receiving 17% of the votes.

Pérez Ballardes will serve a five-year term. Halfway through his term, there are no public displays of dissatisfaction, and signs all over the country point out the president's efforts to aid the citizenry, including everything from housing projects to farming assistance. Many citizens, however, privately wonder if government involvement with illegal activities such as drugs and money-laundering have really changed much.

Panamanian opinion of the USA remains divided. On the one hand, many people are glad the USA got rid of Noriega, admitting that the Panamanians themselves had been unable to do it. Others resent the continuing involvement of the US in Panamanian affairs – a situation that will continue, however, at least until the final transfer of the ownership and control of the canal from the USA to Panama. This is occurring in scheduled stages, with the final transfer scheduled for December 31, 1999. As that deadline approaches, relations between the USA and Panama may continue to be touchy; Panamanians see both gains and losses to be accrued from the transfer, since the canal needs expensive technological upgrading, and salaries and other expenses have long been high, pegged to the US rather than the Panamanian national budget.

GEOGRAPHY

Panama is the southernmost of the Central American countries. It is a long, narrow country in the shape of an S, bordered on the west by Costa Rica, on the east by Colombia, on the north by a 1160-km Caribbean coastline and on the south by a 1690-km Pacific coastline. The total land area is 75,517 sq km.

The isthmus of Panama is the narrowest land mass between the Atlantic and Pacific Oceans. At the narrowest point it is less than 50 km (30 miles) wide. The Panama Canal, which is around 80 km (50 miles) long, effectively divides the country into eastern and western regions.

Two mountain chains run along Panama's spine, one in the east and one in the west. The highest point in the country is 3475-meter Volcán Barú in western Chiriqui Province. Panama's only volcano, it is dormant, although hot springs around its flanks testify to continuing thermal activity underground.

Like all the Central American countries, Panama has large flat coastal lowlands. In some places these lowlands are covered in huge banana plantations.

There are around 500 rivers in Panama and over 1600 islands near its shores. The two main island groups, both just off the Caribbean Coast, are the San Blas and Bocas del Toro Archipelagos, but most of

the islands are in fact on the Pacific side. Even the Panama Canal has islands, including Isla Barro Colorado, which has a world-famous tropical rain forest research station operated by the Smithsonian Institute.

CLIMATE

Like the rest of Central America, Panama has two seasons. The dry season (summer, or *verano*) lasts from around mid-December to mid-April, and the rainy season (winter, or *invierno*) lasts from mid-April to mid-December.

The patterns of precipitation, however, are markedly different on the Caribbean and Pacific sides of the country. The mountains that extend almost all the way along the spine of the country form a barrier against the warm, moist trade winds blowing from the Caribbean. As the warm air rises against the mountains, the moisture it holds falls, frequently and heavily, as rain. The Caribbean Coast receives around 1500 to 3500 mm a year; of course, the rainy season is wetter, but downpours are possible at any time of year. There are lush

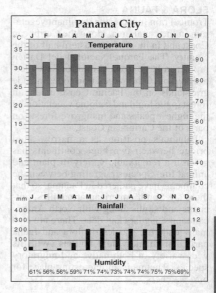

Panama City

tropical rain forests on the Caribbean side, along the Panama Canal and in the Darién Province.

Most people live on the Pacific side of the mountains. Here, the annual rainfall is only 1140 to 2290 mm. This is still no small amount, but the rains are confined almost entirely to the rainy season. This seasonal weather pattern does not support tropical rain forest; the Pacific Coast is lined with broad grasslands, or savanna.

Temperatures are typically hot in the lowlands (day/night temperatures around 32°/21°C) and cool in the mountains (18°/10°C). These remain about the same all year. In Panama City, the heat is tempered by fresh sea breezes.

ECOLOGY & ENVIRONMENT

With 29% of its total land area set aside in protected areas including national parks, forest reserves, wildlife refuges and other designations, Panama is a country that is conscious of its natural resources. For organizations offering information on natural resources, see National Parks below.

FLORA & FAUNA

Tropical rain forest is the dominant vegetation in the canal area, along the Caribbean Coast and in most of the eastern half of the country. The Parque Nacional del Darién protects a large tropical rain forest wilderness region. Other vegetation zones include grasslands on the Pacific Coast, mountain forest in the highlands, alpine vegetation on the highest peaks and mangrove forests on parts of the Caribbean Coast.

Panama's position as a narrow land bridge between two huge continents has given it a remarkable variety of plant and animal life. Species migrating between the continents have gathered in Panama, so that there are South American armadillos, anteaters and sloths along with North American tapirs, jaguars and deer. There are also many endemic species of flora and fauna particular to individual regions. With its wide variety of both native and migratory species, Panama is an interesting place for bird watchers.

Panama also has 81 rare and endangered species. Among them are scarlet macaws, harpy eagles, green iguanas, golden frogs, jaguars, *conejos pintados* (a spotted animal similar to a rabbit) and various species of sea turtles.

National Parks

Information about all of the following national parks, wildlife refuges and other protected areas is available from the offices of the Instituto de Recursos Naturales Renovables (INRENARE). The main office is in Paraíso near Panama City, and there are branch offices in Bocas del Toro, Changuinola, David and other places throughout Panama. A permit from INRENARE, available free from any INRENARE office, is required to camp in any of the parks. More general information about the parks is available from IPAT offices.

The Asociación Nacional para la Conservación de la Naturaleza (ANCON) also has information on Panama's flora and fauna, national parks and other wild areas, and organizes volunteer programs in natural areas (see Work).

Panama has 16 national parks. From west to east, they include:

Parque Internacional La Amistad
  Shared by Panama and Costa Rica, this park contains seven of the 12 classified life zones, with great biodiversity and many endemic species of flora and fauna. It is considered a World Heritage Site. Access is from Cerro Punta (Wetzo entrance) and Changuinola (Bocas del Toro entrance). (207,000 hectares)

Parque Nacional Volcán Barú
  This park contains the giant Volcán Barú, which soars to the highest elevation in Panama (3475 meters). It contains many interesting species, including quetzals and a variety of endemic plants. Access is from Cerro Punta and Boquete. (14,000 hectares)

Parque Nacional Marino Golfo de Chiriquí
  On and around Isla Parida, this park protects insular, marine and coastal areas. Access is from David. (14,740 hectares)

Parque Nacional Marino Isla Bastimentos
  On the Caribbean Coast of western Panama in the Bocas del Toro Province, this park conserves marine and coastal ecosystems

including coral reefs, white-sand beaches and more than 200 species of tropical fish. Access is from Bocas del Toro. (13,266 hectares)

Parque Nacional Isla Coiba
In Veraguas Province, this remote park protects marine and coastal ecosystems with a diversity of flora and fauna in an almost virgin setting. (270,000 hectares)

Parque General de División Omar
Torrijos El Cope
In the center of the isthmus, this forest reserve includes cloud forest, rubber trees and the hydrographic basins of the Bermejo, Marta, Blanco, Guabal and Lajas Rivers. (6000 hectares)

Parque Nacional Cerro Hoya
On the southwest Península de Azuero, this park protects the headwaters of the Tonosí, Portobelo and Pavo Rivers and 30 endemic plant species and fauna including the carato parakeet. (32,557 hectares)

Parque Nacional Sarigua
On the northeast Península de Azuero, this is an unusual tropical desert produced by salinity of water that covers the area for four months of the year, as well as by wind, erosion and human intervention. It includes flora, fauna and an archaeological zone. Access is from Chitré. (8000 hectares)

Parque Nacional Altos de Campana
This park protects the hydrographic basin of the Río Sajalices. Endemic species include golden frogs, the common vampire bat and the colored rabbit; there's also a great variety of native conifers and almost pure fields of certain plants. (4816 hectares)

Parque Nacional Interoceánico de las Americas
Panama's newest national park, established in 1993 and still awaiting legalization, this park protects the hydrographic basin of the west side of the Panama Canal. It includes the old Spanish Fort San Lorenzo. Access is from Panama City. (62,159 hectares)

Parque Nacional Soberanía
In the hydrographic basin of the Panama Canal, this park contains excellent hiking trails including the Camino del Oleoducto (Pipeline Road), good for bird watching, and the short, easy Sendero El Charco nature trail. Access is from Panama City. (22,104 hectares)

Parque Nacional Camino de Cruces
On the old Spanish Camino de Cruces Trail, this park forms an ecological corridor connecting Parque Nacional Soberanía and Parque Nacional Metropolitano. There are

waterfalls and a great variety of flora and fauna, including the titi monkey, armadillo, iguana and three-toed sloth. Access is from Panama City. (4000 hectares)

Parque Nacional Metropolitano
This tropical rain-forest park right in Panama City has nature trails and is the site of scientific tropical rain-forest research. (265 hectares)

Parque Nacional Portobelo
On the north coast of the isthmus, east of Colón, this World Heritage Site park protects 70 km of coastal areas with rich coral reefs and palm trees, and the ruins of the historic Spanish fort and settlement at Portobelo. Access is from Panama City. (35,929 hectares)

Parque Nacional Chagres
This park preserves the hydrographic basin of the Panama Canal. It includes the Río Chagres, Lago de Alajuela, the historic Spanish Camino Real and traditional settlements of Embera Indians. Access is from Panama City. (129,000 hectares)

Parque Nacional del Darién
Categorized as a World Heritage Site and a Biosphere Reserve, Panama's largest national park contains the largest tropical rain-forest wilderness in Central America and forms an effective barrier between Panama and Colombia. Access is from El Real, Yaviza and other places. (579,000 hectares)

GOVERNMENT & POLITICS

Panama is governed as a constitutional democracy. The executive branch is led by a president, elected by popular vote to a five-year term. He is assisted by two elected vice presidents and an appointed cabinet. President Ernesto Pérez Ballardes was elected to a five-year term in May 1994.

The legislative assembly has 72 members, also elected by popular vote to five-year terms. The judiciary consists of a nine-member Supreme Court, appointed to 10-year terms by the president and approved by the legislature and various lower courts.

Panama has nine provinces, plus the autonomous region of San Blas governed by the Kuna Indian tribal leaders *(caciques)*. Each province has a governor appointed by the president, and each is divided into municipal districts.

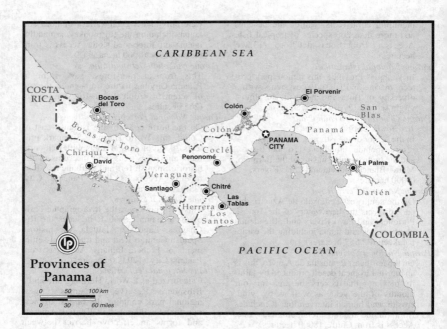

**Provinces of
Panama**

ECONOMY

Panama is much better off economically than the other countries of Central America. With its tall skyscrapers and international banking and trade, Panama City is as modern as any capital city, though like other modern cities it also has its slums, crime and unemployment – officially 11% but probably much higher.

Panama's economy is primarily focused around four principal service industries: offshore banking, which accounts for around 15% of the GNP; the Panama Canal (9%); the Colón Free Zone (the second largest duty-free trading zone in the world after Hong Kong; 8.5%); and merchant shipping. Altogether, the services sector constitutes over 70% of Panama's economy.

Agriculture, including fishing, livestock and forestry, employs about 30% of the work force. The principal crops are bananas, plantains, sugar cane, rice, maize, coffee, beans and tobacco. Cattle, pigs and poultry are farmed; sea products include fish, shrimp and lobster. Industry employs around 16% of the labor force; manufacturing constitutes about 9% of the labor force.

Bananas, produced primarily around the Bocas del Toro and Puerto Armuelles areas, account for almost 40% of Panama's exports; other important exports are shrimp (19%), coffee (5%), sugar (5%) and clothing (5%). The USA is Panama's main trading partner, taking 45% of its exports and providing 40% of its imports. Other important trading partners include Japan, Germany, Costa Rica, Ecuador and Venezuela. Tourism is also a significant growing industry.

POPULATION & PEOPLE

Panama's population was estimated to be 2,655,000 in 1996.

The majority of the population (70%) are mestizos of mixed indigenous and Spanish descent, but there are also a number of other sizable groups. Blacks make up 14% of the population, whites 10% and indigenous peoples 6%.

PANAMA

The blacks are mostly descendants of English-speaking West Indians such as Jamaicans, Bajuns and Trinidadians, who were brought to Panama as cheap labor for various projects. West Indians worked on banana plantations in the Bocas del Toro Province, the trans-isthmian railway in the 1850s, the first French canal project in the 1870s and 1880s, and the US construction of the canal in the early 20th century.

Panama has three major indigenous tribes: the Kuna on the San Blas islands and northeastern Caribbean Coast, the Chocó in the Darién region, and the Guaymí in western Panama. There are also several smaller indigenous groups in the western part of the country, the largest of which are the Teribe and the Bokota. Each of these groups maintains its own language and culture. The Kuna, who govern their ancestral territory as an autonomous region and send representatives to the legislature, are the most organized politically.

Panama City is a cosmopolitan crossroads of the world. The US military bases are like little US colonies.

EDUCATION

The education system is composed of elementary, secondary and university sections, each lasting six years. Education begins at the age of six; children go to elementary school for six years and then undergo two three-year cycles of secondary school. Officially, education is compulsory for six years between the ages of six and 15. Actual enrollment of children in elementary school is high (over 90%), while there's a drop-off at the secondary level (about 50% enrollment). Education is free up to the university level. Panama has three universities, with regional campuses in the interior.

Panama's has one of the lowest adult illiteracy rates in Central America, at around 11%.

ARTS

Panama's arts reflect its ethnic mix. Traditional products include woodcarvings, weaving and textiles, ceramics, masks, straw goods and many other handicrafts. Some of the more famous Panamanian handicrafts include *molas*, colorful hand-stitched appliqué textiles made by the Kuna Indian women, and the *pollera*, the intricately stitched, lacy, Spanish-influenced dress of the Península de Azuero, which is the 'national dress' of Panama for festive occasions.

There is also a magnificent variety of music, dance, theater and other arts. To take music as an example, in one week in Panama City you could hear anything from salsa to calypso, symphony to jazz, heavy metal to reggae to traditional pan-pipe music.

SOCIETY & CONDUCT

Panama's regions are home to ethnic groups as different as if they were on opposite sides of the planet. The diverse Indian tribes; the various West Indian groups; the Spanish-Indian mestizos; the Chinese, Middle-Eastern, Swiss and Croatian immigrants; the North Americans; and others all maintain their own cultures, while some elements of the cultures have mixed to form new combinations. Many come together in Panama City, where there's as much international variety as anywhere on Earth.

Of the various indigenous groups, the Kuna (in the San Blas Archipelago and Panama City) and the Guaymí (in western Panama) are the ones most often noticed by visitors. While the men of both tribes have adopted western dress, the women tend to dress in traditional costume. The women also often have less direct contact with western culture than the men; it's not uncommon for the men to speak Spanish (and even English as well) in their commerce with others. However, sometimes the women may speak only their tribal language and are more shy.

The Kuna are a most attractive people. It may be tempting to take photographs of them. If you wish to do so, be polite and respectful, and ask their permission; it is customary to pay the Kuna a small amount (US$0.25 to US$1) for each photo. Remember, they are doing you a favor.

As elsewhere in the world, standards of conduct and dress are more relaxed in the big city than in more rural areas. In Panama City, almost anything goes; in other parts of the country, it's important to be sensitive to local customs of behavior and dress. As elsewhere in Latin America, women should dress modestly, especially in rural areas (see Women Travelers in the Facts for the Visitor chapter).

Panama City is beautiful, but it has everything from affluent districts to dangerous slums. Keep out of the slums; they're dangerous.

RELIGION

The major faiths are Roman Catholicism (85%), Protestant denominations (5%), Islam (5%) and Baha'i (1%). There are also a small number of Hindus, Jews and other believers.

Religion is especially mixed in Panama City, home to immigrants from all over the world. The city has many Catholic and Protestant churches, a Jewish synagogue, and Hindu, Muslim and Baha'i temples.

LANGUAGE

Spanish is the official language of Panama, but most of the descendants of the West Indian immigrants still speak their original Caribbean-accented English. English is also common as a second language among other ethnic groups due to US influence in Panama City and the areas around the former Canal Zone, and to Panama's role in international business.

The Indian groups still speak their own languages, and many immigrant groups do the same. You may hear Spanish, English, Kuna, Chinese, Serbo-Croat, Italian and Arabic spoken.

Panamanian Spanish is distinctive and may be difficult to understand at first. It has a lot of slang and unusual words and a distinctive accent, and it is spoken very rapidly.

Facts for the Visitor

PLANNING
When to Go

Panama's tourist season is during the dry season from around mid-December to mid-April. The weather can be hot and steamy in the lowlands during the rainy season, when the humidity makes the heat more oppressive than otherwise. But it won't rain nonstop; rain in Panama, as elsewhere in the tropics, tends to come in sudden short downpours that freshen the air and are followed by sunshine. If you'll be doing any long, strenuous hiking, the dry season is the most comfortable time to do it; the Darién Gap can be crossed only at this time. The mountains in western Panama are much cooler than the lowlands.

If you like to party, try to be in Panama City or on the Península de Azuero for Carnaval (Mardi Gras), held each year on the weekend before Ash Wednesday. Panama City's Carnaval celebration is one of the world's largest; on the Península de Azuero it's great fun, too, but the crowds are not as huge. Panama also has a number of other festivals worth catching, especially on the Península de Azuero; see that section for details.

Maps

Free tourist publications including *Focus on Panama, Panama 2000, My Name Is Panama* and *The Best of the Best in Panama* – all available free from IPAT tourist offices and other places – contain fold-out maps of Panama showing the country on one side and maps of Panama City, David and Colón on the other.

The Instituto Geográfico Nacional Tommy Guardia in Panama City sells a tourist map (US$1.50) with a good street map of Panama City on one side and a country map on the other. It also sells 1:50,000 topographical maps, nautical maps, city maps and others (see the Maps section in Panama City).

ITM publishes an excellent color map of Panama, showing the geographical features (mountains, lowlands, rivers), cities, towns and national parks and reserves. It also publishes an excellent 1:1,800,000 color map of Central America as a whole (see Maps in the regional Facts for the Visitor chapter).

What to Bring
You can buy anything you are likely to need in Panama and probably more cheaply than you can back home. But you may need to bring one or more kinds of antimalarial medication depending on which parts of Panama you'll be visiting (see the Health section in the Facts for the Visitor chapter).

HIGHLIGHTS
Panama Canal
Thousands of visitors come to see this engineering wonder. An observation platform, with informative literature, a museum and a bilingual guide, has been set up at Miraflores Locks near Panama City, or you can take a boat tour on the canal itself.

Islands
Panama has 1600 islands; the more accessible ones are among the most interesting and enjoyable places in the country.

On the Caribbean side, great islands to visit include the Archipiélago de San Blas, with its traditional Kuna Indian culture; the Archipiélago de Bocas del Toro, protected by the Isla Bastimentos National Marine Park; and the tiny Isla Grande, just off the Caribbean Coast near Portobelo.

Islands to visit on the Pacific side include Isla Taboga near Panama City; the Archipiélago de Perlas, farther out in the Golfo de Panamá; and Isla Iguana, off the east coast of the Península de Azuero. In the Golfo de Chiriquí near David is another national marine park; Isla Parida and Isla Boca Brava can be accessed from David.

Tropical Rain Forest
Panama has some significant areas of tropical rain forest. The Parque Nacional del

Darién, along the Colombian border, is Panama's largest and protects a large rainforest wilderness. Closer to civilization, Isla Barro Colorado, in the canal itself, and the Parque Nacional Soberanía, beside the canal, can be visited in a few hours from Panama City. Both provide nature trails and literature explaining the basics of tropical rain-forest ecology.

Boquete & Volcán Barú
Boquete is a lovely little town on the slope of Volcán Barú in western Panama. Its 1060-meter elevation makes for a cool, fresh climate. You can enjoy good walks in the hills, visit coffee plantations or a natural hot spring, go bird watching or trout fishing or scale the 3475-meter Volcán Barú.

Boquete's Feria de las Flores y del Café, held annually for 10 days in January, attracts visitors from all over the country. Lodging may be difficult to find at that time.

Volcán Barú's slopes are very fertile; the combination of rich, dark volcanic soil and ideal climate makes Boquete excellent for agriculture.

Festivals
Many annual festivals are celebrated in Panama. Some are large, modern affairs, like Carnaval in Panama City; others preserve centuries-old traditions of folkloric dance, popular outdoor theater, storytelling, music, costumes, masks and handicrafts.

The Península de Azuero is particularly known for its traditional festivals (see Public Holidays & Special Events), but other parts of the country also have some notable celebrations. For more on some of these, see the sections on Isla Taboga and Portobelo.

TOURIST OFFICES
Panama has no tourist offices in other countries, but information is available at Panamanian embassies.

The Instituto Panameño de Turismo (IPAT) has its main office in Panama City at the Atlapa Convention Center, with smaller information counters at the ruins of

Panamá Viejo and at the international airport at Tocumen. It also runs offices in Colón, Portobelo, Bocas del Toro, David, Santiago, Chitré and Cocle, and at Paso Canoas, the principal border crossing between Panama and Costa Rica. These have plenty of printed information about the country, including tourist magazines with fold-out maps of Panama, Panama City, David and Colón.

VISAS & DOCUMENTS

Everyone needs a passport to enter Panama. Citizens of the UK, Germany, the Netherlands, Switzerland, Spain, Finland and Austria, as well as a few South and Central American countries, receive 90 days upon entry, with no visa or tourist card required.

Most other nationals, including US, Canadian, Australian and New Zealand citizens, may enter with either a visa or a US$5 tourist card, available from consulates, embassies and also from airlines, Tica bus or at the airport or border post upon entry. However, those planning to enter Panama overland would be well advised to obtain a normal visa before showing up at the border, even though it is not technically required; the border post may run out of tourist cards, which has happened more than once. Visas and tourist cards are both good for 30 days and can be extended within Panama to 90 days.

Visas must be obtained before entering the country by nationals of many other countries. Visas are issued at Panamanian embassies and consulates within 24 hours of application and cost around US$15, depending on the nationality of the applicant.

If you are heading to Colombia, Venezuela or some other South American country, you may need an onward ticket before you'll be allowed entry or even allowed to board the plane if you're flying. A quick check with the appropriate embassy – easy to do by phone in Panama City – will tell you whether the country you're heading to has an onward-ticket requirement.

Visa Extensions

To extend your stay past the 30 days (or 90 days for those who received 90 days upon entry), go to an office of Migración y Naturalización in Panama City, David, Santiago, Chitré or Changuinola. You must bring your passport along with a photocopy of the page with your personal information and of the stamp of your most recent entry to Panama; you also must bring two passport-size photos, an onward air or bus ticket, and a letter to the director stating your reasons for wishing to extend your visit. You will have to fill out a *Prorroga de Turista* form to request an extension and pay US$10. You will then be issued a plastic photo ID card, good for another 60 days in the country.

If you do extend your time, you must obtain a permit (*permiso de salida*) when you want to leave the country. For this, bring your passport and a *Paz y Salvo* form to the immigration office. Paz y Salvos are issued at Ministerios de Hacienda y Tesoro, found in towns with immigration offices, which simply require that you bring in your passport, fill out a form and pay US$1.

EMBASSIES & CONSULATES
Panamanian Embassies Abroad

If you need a visa, you can obtain one from a Panamanian embassy or consulate in another country. Some countries have several Panamanian consulates; in the USA, Panama has consulates in Atlanta, Chicago, Honolulu, Houston, Los Angeles, Miami, New Orleans, New York, Philadelphia, San Diego and San Francisco, in addition to its embassy in Washington, DC. Panamanian diplomatic missions include:

Belize
    See Embassies & Consulates
    under Belize City.
Canada
    130 Albert St, Suite 300, Ottawa,
    Ontario K1P 5G4 (☎ (613) 236-7177)
Colombia
    Calle 92, No 7-70, Bogotá
    (☎ (1) 257-5067, (1) 257-5068)
Costa Rica
    See Foreign Embassies in Costa Rica.

El Salvador
See Foreign Embassies in El Salvador.
France
145 Avenue de Suffren, 75015 Paris
(☎ (01) 4783-2332, (01) 4566-4244)
Germany
Lutzowstrasse 1, 53173 Bonn
(☎ (228) 363558)
Guatemala
See Embassies in Guatemala City.
Honduras
See Foreign Embassies in Tegucigalpa.
Mexico
Schiller 326, 8th Floor, Colonia
Chapultepec-Morales, CP 11570, México
DF (☎ (5) 250-4229, (5) 250-4045)
Nicaragua
See Foreign Embassies in Managua.
UK
48 Park St, London W1Y 3PD
(☎ (0171) 493-4646)
USA
2862 McGill Terrace NW, Washington, DC
20008 (☎ (202) 483-1407)

Foreign Embassies in Panama

Foreign embassies are in Panama City; see
that section for details. Costa Rica has a
consulate in David as well.

CUSTOMS

You may bring in up to 500 cigarettes, 500
grams of tobacco and three bottles of alcoholic beverages.

MONEY
Costs

Accommodations tend to be more expensive in Panama than in other parts of
Central America; a hotel room that might
cost US$6 in Nicaragua or Guatemala
might cost US$12 here. In Panama City,
you can get a very basic room for US$5,
but it will not be in the best part of town; a
modern room in a better area may cost
around US$15 to US$20 a night. Away
from Panama City, accommodations are
much less expensive; a fine room may cost
around US$10. Die-hard shoestring travel-
ers can still find a room anywhere in the
country for around US$4 or US$5.

In Panama, however, more modern lodgings and better food are available at lower

prices than elsewhere in the region and are
very good values. Prices for everything
else – food, transportation, places to visit –
are very reasonable.

Currency & Exchange

Panama uses the US dollar as its currency.
The official name for it is the Balboa, but
it's exactly the same bill, and in practice
people use the terms '*dólar*' and 'Balboa'
interchangeably.

Panamanian coins are of the same value,
size and metal as US coins; both are used.
Coins include one, five, 10, 25 and 50 centavos; 100 centavos equals one Balboa.

In most of Central America, US dollars
are the only currency exchanged. In
Panama City, however, you can exchange
currencies from almost anywhere in the
world, due to the city's large international
offshore banking industry (see Panama
City for details).

Exchange rates include:

Australia	A$1	=	0.75 Balboas
Canada	C$1	=	0.74 Balboas
Germany	DM1	=	0.61 Balboas
New Zealand	NZ$1	=	0.69 Balboas
UK	UK£1	=	1.60 Balboas
US	US$1	=	1.00 Balboas

Tipping & Bargaining

You can tip some small change, or around
10% of the bill if you're feeling affluent, in
fancier restaurants; in small cafes and more
casual places, tipping is not necessary.
Haggling over prices is not the general
custom in Panama.

Taxes

A tax of 10% is added to the price of hotel
rooms; when you inquire about a hotel
price, be sure to determine whether the
quoted price includes the tax. Hotel prices
given in this book include the 10% tax.

POST & COMMUNICATIONS
Sending Mail

Mail to the USA takes five to 10 days and
costs US$0.35 (postcards US$0.25); to

Europe and Australia it takes 10 days and costs US$0.45 (postcards US$0.35).

Receiving Mail

Poste restante mail can be addressed to '(name), Entrega General, (town and province), República de Panamá.' Be sure the writer calls the country 'República de Panamá' rather than simply 'Panamá,' or the mail may be sent back. The postal service in Panama is more reliable than in many other parts of Central America.

Telephone, Fax & Email

Intel offices throughout Panama offer international telephone, telegraph, fax, and sometimes email and modem services.

Telephone calls to anywhere within Panama can be made from phone boxes. Local calls cost US$0.05 for three minutes. Five, 10 and 25 centavo coins are all accepted. Follow the directions given on the phone; some phones require you insert the coin first, and others instruct you to first wait for the tone, then dial the number. For this latter type, don't deposit the coin until a recorded voice tells you to do so (after the call has been answered at the other end).

When calling internationally, you can connect directly to an operator of that country; this works from any public, residential or business phone. To connect with an operator in the USA, dial 108 (MCI), 109 (ATT), 115 (Sprint) or 117 (TRT). For a Costa Rican operator, dial 107; for a Colombian operator, dial 116.

Panama's country code is 507. There are no local area codes.

The first pages of the telephone directory give information on email connections (☎ 269-7111, ext 229 or 163, División de Ventas, for specific information), modem rental and other specialized services.

BOOKS

Getting to Know Panama by Michele Labrut is a thorough and lively introduction to the country, available everywhere.

The Path Between the Seas: The Creation of the Panama Canal by David McCullough is a readable and exciting account of the building of the Panama Canal. It's 700 pages long and reads like a suspense novel. *The Impossible Dream: The Building of the Panama Canal* by Ian Cameron is also good.

The Panama Canal: The Crisis in Historical Perspective by Walter LaFeber is a good scholarly history of Panama and its relations with the USA.

The Sack of Panamá: Sir Henry Morgan's Adventures on the Spanish Main by Peter Earle is a vivid account of the British pirate's looting and destruction of Panama City in 1671.

On a more recent note, *Our Man in Panama: How General Noriega Used the United States and Made Millions in Drugs and Arms* by John Dinges tells the story of Manuel Noriega. *Panama: The Whole Story* by Kevin Buckley is another fine book about Noriega and the events that led to the 1989 US invasion; 'as readable as a spy thriller,' as the jacket proclaims. For yet another perspective on the Noriega story, look for his memoir *America's Prisoner: The Memoirs of Manuel Noriega*, cowritten with Peter Eisner, who has researched Noriega's claims and footnoted the text.

The Noriega Mess: The Drugs, the Canal, and Why America Invaded by Luis Murillo (Video Books), a 1000-page tome, is highly interesting and quite readable. It's based on a wide variety of sources and information that has come to light in the years since 1989.

Birders should look for *A Guide to the Birds of Panamá* by Robert S Ridgley and John A Gwynne, Jr, a thick, heavy and expensive but very comprehensive volume that also includes the birds of Costa Rica, Honduras and Nicaragua.

Backpacking in Central America by Tim Burford (Bradt Publications, UK) has excellent information on hiking in Panama.

An Adventurer's Guide for Crossing the Darién Gap of Panama and Colombia by Patricia E Upton is a good source of information for anyone wanting to cross this remote region. See the Darién section at the end of this chapter for details on obtaining this booklet.

MEDIA

La Prensa is the most widely circulated daily newspaper in Panama, but there are several other major dailies, including *La Estrella de Panamá, El Panamá América, Universal de Panamá, Crítica* and *La República.*

The *Miami Herald International Edition* is widely available. English-language magazines and newspapers including the *International Herald Tribune* are available at Farmacia Arrocha branches and at Gran Morrison stores.

The local radio and TV stations include a TV channel broadcasting in English for US military personnel, with both local and US programs.

PHOTOGRAPHY & FILM

All types of cameras and film are available in Panama, and they may be cheaper than elsewhere due to the presence of the duty-free zone in Colón. Film processing in Panama City is as advanced as anywhere.

See the Society & Conduct section for advice about photographing the indigenous people.

TIME

Panama time is in line with New York and Miami: five hours behind GMT, and one hour ahead of the rest of Central America. If you're coming from Costa Rica, be sure to check the time when you cross the border.

ELECTRICITY

Beware of variations in electrical currents in Panama. Almost everywhere, voltage will be 110 volts, but there are exceptions – an ordinary socket may be either 110 or 220 volts. Find out which it is before you plug in your appliance! Many travel appliances such as hairdryers can be adjusted for different voltages.

LAUNDRY

Laundromats *(lavamáticos)* are abundant and convenient; usually you drop off your laundry, they wash and dry it for you, and you pick it up a few hours later. Cost per load is US$0.75 to wash, US$0.75 to dry, and about another US$0.25 for soap powder unless you bring your own. Dry cleaners *(lavanderías)* are also widely available.

WEIGHTS & MEASURES

The metric system is the official system for weights and measures, but the US system of pounds, gallons and miles is also used.

HEALTH

Tap water is safe to drink in all areas except in the Bocas del Toros region and in the smallest, most remote towns. This means that washed raw vegetables and ice are OK, too.

Malaria is not a problem in Panama City. The area east of the canal, including the San Blas islands and Darién Province, and the Bocas del Toro area in western Panama, are the only parts of Central America where a chloroquine-resistant strain of malaria is present. If you go to these areas, you should take special precautions; see the Health section in the introductory Facts for the Visitor chapter.

You can protect yourself against the sun's rays with a hat, long sleeves and/or a good sunscreen lotion. Panama is between 7° and 10° from the equator – Panama City is exactly 9° north – so the sun is very strong. Be sure to drink plenty of liquids, preferably water, to avoid becoming dehydrated.

DANGERS & ANNOYANCES

Crime is a problem in certain parts of Panama City. However, the city's upper-class districts are much safer than in many other capitals: witness the all-night restaurants and activity on the streets at night. On the other hand, it is not safe to walk around at night in the Casco Viejo (San Felipe) District, where the cheapest accommodations are found; be careful in the side streets of this district even in the daytime. In general, use common sense, and stay where it's well lit and there are plenty of people around.

Colón is a sad slum known for street crime. If you walk around there, even in the middle of the day, well-meaning residents will inform you that you are in danger. It's probably best to avoid the city altogether.

Most other areas of Panama are rural and quite safe.

BUSINESS HOURS

Business hours are normally Monday to Friday 8 am to noon and 1:30 to 5 pm, and Saturday from 8 am to noon. Government offices are open Monday to Friday from 8 am until 4 or 4:30 pm and don't close for lunch. Most banks are open Monday to Friday, from around 8:30 am until 3 pm; some have Saturday hours as well, from around 8:30 am to noon or 1 pm. Shops are generally open from around 9 or 10 am until 6 or 7 pm.

PUBLIC HOLIDAYS & SPECIAL EVENTS

January 1
  New Year's Day
January 9
  Martyrs' Day
March-April
  Good Friday, Easter Sunday
May 1
  Labor Day
August 15
  Founding of Old Panama
  (celebrated in Panama City only)
October 12
  Hispanic Day
November 1
  National Anthem Day
November 2
  All Souls' Day
November 3
  Independence Day
November 10
  First Call for Independence
November 28
  Independence from Spain
December 8
  Mothers' Day
December 25
  Christmas Day

Carnaval, the Panamanian version of Mardi Gras, is celebrated on the four days before Ash Wednesday, the beginning of Lent. A major holiday in Panama City, it involves costumes, music, dancing, general festivities and a big parade on Shrove Tuesday, the final day. Carnaval is also celebrated on the Península de Azuero

at Las Tablas, Chitré, Villa de Los Santos and Parita. The celebrations in Panama City and Las Tablas are famous and well worth attending.

Semana Santa (Holy Week, the week before Easter) is another occasion for special events throughout the country, including the reenactment of the events surrounding the crucifixion and resurrection of Christ; on Good Friday, religious processions are held all over the country.

The famous Corpus Christi celebrations at Villa de Los Santos, on the Península de Azuero, take place 40 days after Easter. Masked and costumed dancers representing angels, devils, imps and other figures enact dances, acrobatics and dramas.

The Península de Azuero also has a number of other notable festivals; see the Península de Azuero section for details. The Black Christ celebration at Portobelo on October 21 attracts pilgrims from near and far; the celebration for the Virgen del Carmen, which takes place on Isla Taboga on July 16 also attracts jolly crowds. In western Panama, Boquete's Feria de las Flores y del Café, held for 10 days in January, attracts visitors from all over Panama.

Panama's many ethnic groups each have their own cultural events; the Kuna people and the descendants of West Indians and Spanish all have their own special music and dance. If you get a chance to attend any of these occasions, don't miss it.

ACTIVITIES
Snorkeling & Diving

Probably the best place in Panama for snorkeling and diving is the Parque Nacional Marino Isla Bastimentos, in the Bocas del Toro Archipelago on the Caribbean Coast of western Panama. Several dive shops operate out of little Bocas del Toro town, offering both diving and snorkeling tours.

Another national marine park has been established in the Golfo de Chiriquí on the Pacific side of western Panama; the islands of Isla Parida and Boca Brava both offer snorkeling opportunities. Isla Iguana, off the eastern coast of the Península de

Azuero, is another possibility; tours can be arranged from Panama City.

Almost any island offers snorkeling opportunities, however. The Archipiélago de San Blas and Isla Grande, both on the Caribbean Coast east of the canal, are recommended. Isla Taboga, off the coast of Panama City, is not known for its snorkeling but is in fact very interesting.

IPAT can put you in touch with diving operators. Avid snorkelers should bring along their own gear, as it's not always available for hire on the spot.

Fishing

Panama has around 500 rivers, 1600 islands and over 2000 km of coast, so there's no problem finding a fishing spot. Possibilities include deep-sea fishing, fishing for bass in Lago Gatún on the Panama Canal, and trout fishing in the rivers running down Volcán Barú near the towns of Boquete, Volcán, Bambito and Cerro Punta.

Surfing

There are surf beaches along the Pacific Coast. The best three are Playa El Palmar near San Carlos, about 1½ hours west of Panama City and easily accessible; Playa Venado on the south end of the Península de Azuero, which is connected by bus to La Tablas; and the comparatively remote Santa Catalina farther west, which can be reached by a long road turning off from Soná.

White-Water Rafting

Rafting trips are available on the Río Chagres near Panama City and in Chiriquí Province.

Hiking

Opportunities for hiking abound in Panama. From Boquete, you can hike to the top of Volcán Barú, Panama's highest peak and only volcano. There are also plenty of other walks around Boquete, where the narrow roads wind up and down the slopes among the coffee plantations. A trail leads from Boquete over Volcán Barú to Cerro Punta on the other side; it's a five- to six-

hour hike through deep jungle, and since it's almost inevitable you will lose the trail, it's best to go with a guide, which you can find in Boquete.

The little town of El Valle, nestled into the Valle de Anton about a 2½-hour drive west of Panama City, is a fine place for walking. Many trails lead into the hills around the valley; they are well defined, as the local *campesinos* frequently use them.

Near Panama City on the shores of the canal, Parque Nacional Soberanía has a section of the old Las Cruces Trail used by the Spanish to cross between the coasts, as well as a short and easy but interesting nature trail, the Sendero El Charco, which is signed from the highway. The Parque Natural Metropolitano on the outskirts of Panama City also has some good walks including a nature trail and a 'monkey trail.'

Of course, the most famous walk in Panama is the trek of a week or more through the Darién Gap, where the Interamericana comes to a dead end and a wilderness of tropical rain forest stands between Panama and Colombia. This is the only overland route to South America; it can only be undertaken in the dry season and it is currently extremely dangerous. The trek is described in detail in the Darién section.

Backpacking in Central America by Tim Burford (see the Books section) is an excellent resource for hikers in Panama.

Bird Watching

Panama is a magnificent place for bird watching. The Panama Audobon Society, which does a Christmas Bird Count every year, consistently counts more species of birds in Panama than are recorded anywhere else in Latin America. This is due to several factors: Panama's location between two giant continents and its narrow girth. Birds migrating between North and South America tend to be funneled into a small area. Many North and South American species are represented, both native and migratory; Panama also has a number of endemic species.

The famous quetzal, symbol of Central America, is more abundant in western Panama than anywhere else in Central America. It can be seen around Volcán Barú, notably in the hills around Boquete, where it is not all that uncommon depending on the time of year. One well-known guide in Panama observed that 'in Costa Rica there are 20 people out looking for one quetzal; in Panama, one person goes out and sees 20 quetzals.'

Other species of interest in Panama include toucans, macaws, eagles and several species of hummingbirds. All in all, over 900 species (native, migratory and endemic) have been identified in Panama.

To see birds in Panama, just get a good set of binoculars and get out on a trail. The Pipeline Trail near Panama City is a favorite with birders; over 385 species have been sighted here. Most birds are seen around dawn and just after, so avid birders may want to camp out or arrive before daylight.

A Guide to the Birds of Panama is extremely helpful (see the Books section). Helpful organizations include INRENARE, ANCON and the Panama Audobon Society in Panama City (☎ 252-1908, ☎ /fax 224-4740), which organizes birding expeditions. Commercial companies offering birding expeditions include Eco-Tours, Iguana Tours and Panama Paradise, all based in Panama City (see Panama City's Organized Tours section).

WORK

You might be able to pick up some casual labor as a linehandler (deckhand) on a yacht going through the Panama Canal. This is hard, heavy work and the one- to two-day trip pays around US$50. You can check for possibilities at the yacht clubs on both sides of the canal: the Balboa Yacht Club on the Pacific (Panama City) side, the Panama Canal Yacht Club on the Caribbean (Colón) side. Larger ships are pulled through the locks by locomotives.

Teaching English is another possibility. However, English is widely spoken and teachers are not in short supply.

ANCON (the Asociación Nacional para la Conservación de la Naturaleza) offers opportunities for volunteering on projects in national parks and other remote and beautiful natural surroundings. Volunteers might protect nesting sea turtles near Bocas del Toro, do environmental education in the Darién or help to ranger or patrol in a variety of national parks. You can volunteer for anywhere from a week up to several months; you won't get paid, but ANCON will supply your basic necessities such as food and shelter. Contact the ANCON office in Panama City for details.

ACCOMMODATIONS

Accommodations of all kinds are available in Panama. See the Money section above for information about costs and hotel taxes.

FOOD

In keeping with its international and ethnic character, Panama offers a variety of food.

Panama's national dish is *sancocho*, a spicy chicken and vegetable stew. *Ropa vieja* ('old clothes'), a spicy shredded beef combination served over rice, is another common and tasty dish.

Other typical Panamanian dishes include:

carimañola – a roll made from ground and boiled yucca filled with chopped meat and boiled egg, and then deep-fried.

empanadas – corn turnovers filled with ground meat and fried.

patacones – fried green plantains cut crossways in thin pieces and covered in salt, then pressed and fried.

platano maduro – also called *platanos ententación*; ripe plantain cut in slices lengthwise and baked or broiled with butter, brown sugar and cinnamon; served hot.

tajadas – ripe plantain sliced lengthwise and fried.

tamales – made from boiled ground corn with spices, with chicken or pork; the tamale is wrapped in banana leaves and boiled.

tasajo – dried meat, cooked with vegetables.

tortilla de maíz – thick cornmeal tortilla, fried.

Seafood is excellent and abundant in Panama. On the Caribbean Coast and islands, common everyday foods include lobster, shrimp, Caribbean king crab, fish such as corvina (a tender white fish with few bones) and octopus. Often the seafood is mixed with coconut sauce; coconut rice and coconut bread are other Caribbean treats.

The area around Volcán Barú is known for its mountain rainbow trout, coffee, Boquete navel oranges and the many other fruits and vegetables.

In Panama City carts sell *raspadas*, cones of shaved ice with sweet fruit syrup and optional sweetened condensed milk poured over the top. This is no world-class gourmet dish, but on these hot streets it tastes like heaven.

DRINKS
Fresh fruit drinks, sweetened and mixed with water, are called *chicha* and are the most common cold drinks in Panama. (There is no need to worry about the water here.) Soft drinks are called *sodas*, and all the usual brands are available.

Beer and rum are made in Panama. The Carta Vieja rum distillery between David and Concepción gives free tours (see David later in this chapter).

ENTERTAINMENT
Panama City has plenty of nightlife, with everything from casinos and striptease shows to the symphonies and ballets at the opulent turn-of-the-century Teatro Nacional. You can also see presentations of Panamanian music and dance. Concerts, theater and dance performances, and other events are presented in the huge, modern Atlapa Convention Center. The IPAT tourist office is also at the Atlapa Center, and staff can tell you about coming events.

Panama City also has many cinemas, some showing the latest films from the USA. There are horseraces and cockfights. But perhaps the most entertaining events are the festivals, ranging from the giant Carnaval celebrations in Panama City to small towns' celebrations of saints' days (see Cultural Events).

SPECTATOR SPORTS
Panamanians are enthusiastic sports fans. As in all of Latin America, soccer is a favorite; here in Panama, baseball, softball and basketball are also all the rage. Boxing is another popular spectator sport; it has been a source of pride to Panamanians (and to Latin Americans in general) ever since Roberto Durán, a Panama City native and boxing legend, won the world championship lightweight title in 1972. He went on to also become the world champion in the welterweight (1980), light middleweight (1983) and super middleweight (1989) categories.

THINGS TO BUY
A remarkable variety of imported goods, including cameras, electronic equipment and clothing, is sold in Panama, both in the Colón Free Zone and in Panama City. The giant stores in the Colón Free Zone cater mostly to mass buyers, and most of them will not sell individual items. Panama City's Av Central, however, is a mecca for bargain hunters. Shop around and bargain, as there's a lot of competition.

The favorite handicraft souvenir from Panama is the *mola*, a colorful, intricate, multilayered appliqué textile sewn by Kuna Indian women from the Archipiélago de San Blas. Small, simple souvenir molas can be bought for as little as US$5, but the best ones are sold on the islands and can fetch several hundred dollars.

Other handicrafts include woodcarvings, masks, ceramics and clothing. See the section on the Península de Azuero for details of particular villages' specialties in that area; *polleras*, the lacy, frilly, intricately sewn dresses that are considered Panama's national dress, are made there. You can buy a pollera, but they're not cheap – some may cost around US$1000.

All the Gran Morrison chain department stores have handicraft and traditional art sections. Other places to buy handicrafts are mentioned in the Panama City section.

PANAMA

Getting There & Away

Panama sees international visitors and passers-through in great numbers. Sea vessels from all over the Caribbean, Atlantic and Pacific go through the canal. Overland travelers cross the country in droves, and Panama is also a major hub for air travelers.

Air, land and sea travel between Panama and Colombia is covered in the Getting There & Away chapter and in the Darién section.

AIR

Airlines connect Panama with all the other Central American countries, South America, North America and the Caribbean, and you can usually arrange a ticket with one or more free stopovers.

The main air connection points in North America for flights to and from Panama are Miami, Houston, New York, Washington, DC, Dallas and Los Angeles. Miami is the principal one. Fares from the US are competitive and may change seasonally.

COPA is Panama's national airline. Panama City has dozens of travel agents, including one specializing in student travel (see Panama City).

There's a US$20 departure tax at the airport.

LAND

To/From Costa Rica

There are three border crossings between Panama and Costa Rica. Paso Canoas on the Interamericana is the one most travelers use to go to and from Panama City. It's open every day from 6 am to 11 pm. The Instituto Panameño de Turismo (IPAT), Panama's national tourist office, has an office here (☎ 727-6524).

The Río Sereno border crossing is rather remote and not as busy. The northernmost crossing at Guabito (Sixaola on the Costa Rican side) is the closest to Bocas del Toro; it's an interesting option for overland travelers. Both of these are officially open every day from 7 am to 11 pm (closed one hour for lunch and another for dinner).

Bus At all three of these border crossings, you can take local buses up to the border on either side, cross and board the next country's local bus.

Two companies, Panaline and Tica Bus, also operate daily direct buses between San José and Panama City. Both recommend that you make reservations a few days in advance to ensure getting a space; if you show up at the last minute, they'll take you if they have space.

Panaline buses (☎ 262-1618) arrive and depart from Panama City at the Hotel Internacional on Plaza Cinco de Mayo. They depart Panama City every day at 1 pm, arriving in San José the following morning around 4:30 or 5 am. These are good buses, equipped with air con, bathroom and video; riders get free sodas, and students receive a 10% discount with ISIC card. The cost is US$25 one way, double for roundtrip.

Tica Bus (☎ 262-2084, 262-6275) arrives and departs from Panama City at the Hotel Ideal, Calle 17 Oeste, No 15-55, a block west of Av Central. These buses depart Panama City every day at noon, arriving in San José the following morning around 4 or 5 am. The cost is US$20 one way, double for roundtrip. You must bring your passport when you reserve your ticket. Tica Bus also has buses continuing up through Central America as far as Guatemala; see the introductory Getting Around chapter for details.

A direct international bus also operates between San José, Costa Rica and Changuinola near Bocas del Toro. See the Changuinola section for details.

Onward Tickets For years, both Panama and Costa Rica had onward ticket requirements. While this requirement is still officially on the books, an onward ticket is rarely asked for nowadays.

If you want to stay in Panama beyond the initial 30 or 60 days you receive upon entry, you'll have to produce an onward ticket to get an extension. If you don't already have one, the cheapest way to satisfy this requirement is to buy a Tracopa bus ticket from David to San José, Costa Rica; alternatively you could buy a ticket from Panama City to San José with Tica Bus or Panaline. Of course if you plan to fly out of the country, an airline ticket will fill the bill, too.

SEA

The *Crucero Express*, a large, modern ferry carrying passengers and vehicles, was providing convenient transport between Colón (Panama) and Cartagena (Colombia) until service was suspended in mid-1996. A similar service was scheduled to begin, but as of early 1997 it had not. Inquire at the IPAT tourist office whether service has resumed.

Since Panama is one of the world's major shipping bottlenecks, you would think you could find a boat to take you almost anywhere. However, it's not as easy as it might seem. The ships waiting to pass through the canal do not usually berth, so you don't have a chance to ask about going along.

Some cargo boats do occasionally take on passengers. Some will accept passengers accompanying their own freight, such as a car, but others take only the freight itself and you have to make your own way to pick it up at the other end.

The idea of working your way into the sunset on a cargo boat is little more than a dream these days. In addition to the usual international maritime regulations, a Panamanian law states that only their own merchant mariners can sign on in Panama. On the other hand, you could conceivably get a crewing spot on a private yacht. Your chances are considerably improved if you have experience, but often yachties who need crew will take whoever looks a likely prospect at the time. You can ask around and post signs at the yacht clubs on both the Colón and the Panama City (Balboa) ends of the canal.

Another possibility is taking a merchant boat from the San Blas islands to Colombia. This is a very 'unofficial' way to go, but it can be done. See the Eastern Panama section for more about this.

Getting Around

AIR

Panama is served by a good network of domestic flights on several domestic airlines. One-way prices are given here; double these for roundtrip. The following table lists flights on Aeroperlas (☎ 269-4555 in Panama City):

Panama City to	Frequency	Fare
Bocas del Toro	Five times weekly	US$48
Changuinola	Daily	US$51
Chitré	Daily	US$29
Colón	Weekdays only	US$26
David	Daily	US$55
El Real	Thrice weekly	US$37
Garachiné	Wednesday	US$34
Isla Contadora	Daily	US$24
Jaqué	Thrice weekly	US$42
La Palma	Daily	US$35
Sambú	Thrice weekly	US$35
San Miguel	Thrice weekly	US$22
Santiago	Daily	US$33

Other Aeroperlas routes include: David – Changuinola, daily, for US$24; Bocas del Toro – Changuinola, on demand, for US$10; La Palma – El Real, twice weekly, for US$21.

Aerotaxi (☎ 264-8644, 264-2950) and Ansa (☎ 226-7891, 226-6881) fly between Panama City and the San Blas Archipelago, serving 19 of the islands, from Cartí and El Porvenir (nearest Panama City) to Puerto Obaldía (nearest Colombia), with daily early morning flights to El Porvenir and flights thrice weekly all the way to Puerto Obaldía. One-way fares are US$28 to El Porvenir, US$44 to Puerto Obaldía; double for roundtrip. Fares to other islands fall somewhere in between.

BUS

There's a good bus system serving all the accessible parts of the country. Intercity fares are typically within the US$2 to US$5 range, except for long-distance routes, which run from US$9 to US$15.

PANAMA

TRAIN

The famous old passenger train that ran along the canal between Panama City and Colón was destroyed during the 1989 US invasion. It was supposed to be repaired but hadn't been at the time of writing. Check with IPAT.

The train service between the port of Almirante and Guabito/Sixaola on the Costa Rican border is running again after a hiatus caused by the 1991 earthquake. For information, call ☎ 758-3215.

The banana train serving Puerto Armuelles no longer carries passengers.

CAR & MOTORCYCLE

Road rules are generally the same as in the USA. Conditions are good on major highways. More remote areas are served by dirt roads.

Car Rental

Many agencies offer competitive rates on rental cars in Panama City; a few agencies also have offices in David. Average prices are around US$40 per day, but what with price wars and weekly discounts, you may be able to find something for much less. If you have an American Express card, you can forgo paying the extra for insurance, bringing the cost down to as little as around US$15 per day. If you can get a few people together to share the cost, renting a car can be a good deal.

If you want to get into the mountains or off the beaten track, ask for a 4WD vehicle. In Panama these are called '4 by 4' (*'cuatro por cuatro'*).

One company in Panama City rents 125cc motorcycles. See the Panama City section for details.

Bringing Your Own

There's a great deal of paperwork involved in bringing a car into the country.

If you want to take a vehicle between Central and South America, you will have to ship it around the Darién Gap, as the highway does not go through. See the Getting There & Away chapter for suggestions on how to do this.

BICYCLE

You could cycle through Panama easily enough, but it's a very hot country. Panama doesn't have much cool mountainous terrain, as some other Central American countries do. The Interamericana is narrow and overhung with jungle in places, leaving no room to move aside should a car pass by.

In Panama City bicycles are available for long- or short-term rentals; see Panama City for details.

HITCHHIKING

Hitchhiking is not as widespread in Panama as elsewhere in the region; most people travel by bus, and foreigners would do best to follow suit.

BOAT

Boats are the principal means of transport in several parts of Panama, particularly between the islands of the San Blas and Bocas del Toro archipelagos. Kuna Indian merchant boats carry cargo and passengers all along the San Blas coast between Colón and Puerto Obaldía, stopping at up to 48 of the islands to load and unload passengers and cargo. See the Archipiélago de San Blas section and the Getting There & Away chapter for further details on this route.

Bocas del Toro Island is accessible from Almirante and Chiriquí Grande by ferry (slower, but it carries vehicles) or water taxi.

Boat trips from Panama City include those to Isla Taboga just offshore, full and partial crossings of the Panama Canal, trips to Isla Barro Colorado in Lago Gatún in the Panama Canal, and a longer trip to El Real in Darién Province. River boats form important links in the overland route through the Darién Gap.

LOCAL TRANSPORT

Bus

All of Panama's cities and towns are served by cheap local buses; a ride usually costs around US$0.15.

Taxi

Taxis in Panama are not metered; always agree on a price for the ride before you get into the cab. Taxis are usually reasonably priced; a ride across town might cost around US$1.

ORGANIZED TOURS

Tour agencies in Panama City offer many kinds of tours, ranging from local city tours to ecological tours into remote regions of the country. While tours are not cheap, they can be the easiest way to explore many of Panama's natural wonders. The tourist office can give you referrals.

Eco-Tours (☎ 263-3077, fax 263-3089) on Calle Ricardo Arias, No 7, in Panama City (mailing: Apdo Postal 87-2402, Zona 7 Panamá, República de Panamá) offers several ecological tours around Panama. These include tours to the San Blas islands, white-water rafting in the Chiriquí Province, diving and snorkeling trips to Isla Coiba and Bocas del Toro, fishing trips and trips into the Darién. These people are the Darién specialists, offering birding excursions to the gold mine at Cana, a trip up Pirre Mountain (the Darién's highest point) to the Darién cloud forest, and a Darién Explorer journey going into the heart of the Darién mostly by river. Their most ambitious trip is the arduous 14-day Trans-Darién Expedition, crossing the Darién from the Atlantic to the Pacific sides, re-creating the journey Balboa took when he became the first European to sight the Pacific Ocean.

Iguana Tours (☎ 226-8738, fax 226-4736), also in Panama City (mailing: Apdo 6655, Zona 5 Panamá, República de Panamá), offers an array of ecological tours around the country, including trips to the Isla Iguana wildlife refuge off the Península de Azuero, fresh and saltwater fishing trips, Caribbean scuba- and skin-diving trips, trips to the San Blas islands and more.

Then there are white-water rafting tours on the Río Chagres near Panama City and on various rivers in the Chiriquí Province; information for these appears in the Panama City and Chiriquí sections.

See the Panama City and Panama Canal sections for information on tours in those areas.

Panama City

Population 460,000

The capital of Panama is a modern, thriving center for international banking, business, trade and transport, with a cosmopolitan flair. An almost constant sea breeze keeps the air comfortably fresh.

History

Panama City was founded on the site of an Indian fishing village by the Spanish governor Pedro Arias Dávila (Pedrarias) in 1519, not long after Balboa first saw the Pacific.

The Spanish settlement immediately became an important center of government and church authority. It was from here, too, that the gold and other goods from the Pacific Spanish colonies were taken along El Camino Real trail across the isthmus to the Caribbean.

This treasure made Panama City the target of many attacks over the years. In 1671 the city was ransacked and finally destroyed by the English pirate Henry Morgan, leaving only the stone ruins of Panamá Viejo that still stand today.

Two years later, the city was re-established about eight km to the west, down the coast at San Felipe. The Spanish believed the new site, on a small peninsula, would be easier to defend. The sea lapped the city on three sides; a moat was constructed on the land side and a massive stone wall ran around the whole city within these defenses. It was never successfully attacked again.

The overland trade route, however, was attacked repeatedly and the principal Caribbean port at Portobelo was destroyed. In 1746 the Spanish stopped using the route altogether; Panama City subsequently declined in importance. It was not until the 1850s, when the Panama Railroad was completed and gold rushers on their way to California flooded across the isthmus by train, that Panama City returned to prominence.

PANAMA

To Miraflores Locks,
Paraíso, Summit,
Gamboa

Camino de la Amistad

✻ Mirador

**Parque Natural
Metropolitana**

Panama Canal (Canal de Panamá)

Balboa
Harbor

Muelle 18
(Pier 18)

Ferry to Isla Taboga

Carretera Diablo

Carretera Gaillard

Albrook US
Air Force Base

CURUNDU

Camino de la Amistad

Av Juan Pablo II

ℹ Centro de Visitantes
(Visitor Center)

Calle Curundu

BALBOA

Carretera Balboa

Carretera Gaillard

Ancón
Train
Station

Av 1 Norte (José D Espinar)

LA CRESTA

Av Manuel E Batista

EL
CANGREJO

LA BOCA

Bridge of
the Americas
(Puente de las Américas)

Cerro Ancón▲
(Ancón Hill)

ANCÓN

Av Central

Av Central España

LA EXPOSICIÓN

BELLA
VISTA

Via España

Calle Amador

Ave A

Av de los Mártires

Av 3 Sur (Justo Arosemena)

Av Federico Boyd

Balboa
Yacht
Club

Fuerte
Amador

CHORIRILLO

CALIDONIA

Av 6 Sur (Av Balboa)

Av Central

Bahía de Panamá

PUNTA
PAITILLA

see San Felipe
(Casco Viejo) map

To Causeway, Naos Island,
Perico Island, Flamenco Island

Panama was declared independent of Colombia on November 3, 1903 in Panama City's Parque Catedral; the city then became the capital of the new nation. Since the Panama Canal was completed in 1914, the city has grown in importance as a center for international business and trade.

Orientation

Panama City stretches about 10 km along the coast, from the Panama Canal at its western end to the ruins of Panamá Viejo to the east. Buses to most other parts of the country arrive and depart from the Interior bus station on Av Balboa. Everything outside Panama City is referred to as the 'interior.'

Near the canal are the US Albrook Air Force Base, Fort Amador, and the wealthy Balboa and Ancón suburbs built for the US canal and military workers. The Bridge of the Americas arches gracefully over the canal.

The colonial part of the city, called San Felipe or Casco Viejo, juts into the sea on the southwestern side of town.

From San Felipe, two major roads head east through the city. The 'main drag' is

PANAMA

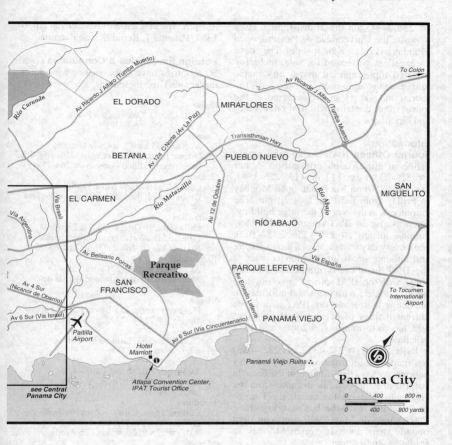

Av Central, which runs past the cathedral in San Felipe, continuing out of San Felipe to Plaza Santa Ana and Plaza Cinco de Mayo; between these two plazas, traffic has been diverted and the avenue is a pedestrian-only shopping street. At a fork farther on, the avenue becomes Av Central España; the section that traverses the business and financial district is called Via España. The other side of the fork becomes Av 1 Norte José D Espinar, Av Simón Bolívar, and finally Via Transístmica as it heads out of town and across the isthmus towards Colón.

Av 6 Sur branches off Av Central, not far out of San Felipe, and undergoes several name changes; it is called Av Balboa as it curves around the edge of the bay to Paitilla, on the bay's eastern point opposite San Felipe; it then continues under various names past La Paitilla airport and the Atlapa convention center to the ruins at Panamá Viejo.

All three main roads are served by frequent buses.

Maps For detailed maps, go to the Instituto Geográfico Nacional Tommy Guardia

(☎ 236-2444), on the Transisthmian Hwy opposite the Universidad de Panamá, open Monday to Friday, 8 am to 4 pm. They have an excellent collection for sale, including detailed topographical maps, city maps, tourist maps and more. Several of the tourist magazines given out free at the tourist office contain small fold-out country and city maps.

Information
Tourist Offices IPAT has an information office at the Atlapa convention center (☎ 226-7000, ext 112 or 113, 226-3544, fax 226-6856) on Via Israel, open Monday to Friday from 8:30 am to 4:30 pm. The entrance is at the rear of the large building. There is also an IPAT counter at the international airport (☎ 238-4356, 238-4102), open every day from around 8 am to 10 pm, and another small information counter at the IPAT handicrafts market in Panamá Viejo. All the IPAT offices give out free tourist booklets with maps and information on things to see and do. IPAT also keeps current listings of hotels and their prices and has information on tours and boat schedules.

INRENARE (☎ 232-4325, fax 232-4083) has maps and information on all Panama's national parks. Their office is at the Escuela Paraíso in Paraíso, a fair distance from the city center, beside the canal; the Paraíso bus, leaving from the bus station behind Plaza Cinco de Mayo, will drop you right outside their door. It's open Monday to Friday, 8 am to 4 pm.

To contact INRENARE before reaching Panama, write to INRENARE, Depto de Parques Nacionales y de Vida Silvestre, Apdo 2016, Paraíso, Corregimiento de Ancón, Panamá, Republica de Panamá.

ANCON (☎ 264-8100, fax 264-1836, net), in the Edificio ANCON, Calle Alberto Navarro in El Cangrejo District, works on environmental protection throughout the country and has information on most natural attractions, as well as volunteer programs in remote natural areas (see the Work section). It's open Monday to Friday from 8 am to 1 pm and 2 to 5 pm, Saturday 9 am to 1 pm. You can write to ANCON at Apdo 1387, Panamá 1, Republica de Panamá.

Foreign Embassies & Consulates Over 50 countries have embassies or consulates in Panama City, including:

Belize
    Calle Quinta, Colonias del Prado, Casa 592 (☎ 266-8939)
Canada
    Av Samuel Lewis and Calle Gerardo Ortega, Edificio Banco Central Hispano, 4th floor, frente Edifico Comosa (☎ 264-9731)
Colombia
    Calle Manuel María Icaza, Edificio Grobman, 6th floor, frente Edificio Comosa (☎ 223-3535)
Costa Rica
    Calle Gerardo Ortega and Vía España, Edificio Miraflores, ground floor, beside Niko's Cafe (☎ 264-2937, fax 264-6348)
El Salvador
    Av Manuel Espinoza Batista, Edificio Metropolis, 4th floor, behind Iglesia del Carmen (☎ 223-3020)
France
    Plaza de Francia, Las Bóvedas, San Felipe District (☎ 228-7824, 228-7835)
Germany
    Calle 50 and 53, Edificio Bancomer, 6th floor (☎ 263-7733)
Guatemala
    Av Federico Boyd and Calle 48, Bella Vista District, over the Colossal store (☎ 269-3475)
Honduras
    Edificio Tapia, Calle 31, entre Av Justo Arosemena y Av México, 2nd floor, Oficina 2-01 (☎ 225-8200, ☎ /fax 225-3283)
Mexico
    Calle 50 and 53, Edificio Bancomer, 5th floor (☎ 263-5021)
Nicaragua
    Calle 50 and Av Federico Boyd, Zona 1, Corregimiento Bella Vista (☎ 223-0981, 269-6721)
UK
    Calle 53, Edificio Swissbank, 4th floor, Marbella District (☎ 269-0866)
USA
    Av Balboa and Calle 37 (☎ 227-1777)

Immigration The Migración y Naturalización office (☎ 227-1077) on the corner of Calle 29 and Av 2 (Av Cuba) is open

Monday to Friday from 8 am to 4 pm. You can come here to extend your visa or get your permit to leave the country.

Money In contrast to other Central American countries, you can change the currencies of most countries here. Panacambios (☎ 223-1800) on the ground floor of the Plaza Regency, 177 Via España, opposite El Rey supermarket in El Cangrejo banking district, buys and sells international currencies. Many banks from around the world have branches in Panama City; most will exchange their home countries' currencies.

Since the US dollar is the official currency of Panama, it is easy to cash US dollar traveler's checks. Banco del Istmo, Banco Exterior and Banco General all sell American Express traveler's checks; Banco del Istmo and Chase Manhattan Bank sell Visa traveler's checks. Cash advances on Visa and MasterCard are available at Banco del Istmo and Chase Manhattan Bank; Banco General gives cash advances on Visa cards only. All of these banks have several branches around Panama City.

The American Express office (☎ 225-5858) is on Av Balboa in the Edificio Banco Exterior, 9th floor; it's open Monday to Friday, 9 am to 1 pm.

Post & Communications There's a post office on Via España, half a block east of Via Argentina; it's open Monday to Friday from 7 am to 5:45 pm, Saturday 7 am to 4:45 pm. Another is on Av Balboa, with several others dotted around the city.

International telephone and fax services are available at the Intel office in the Edificio Di Lido on Calle Manuel María Icaza (☎ 264-6200), half a block from Via España, open every day from 7:30 am to 9:30 pm. Nearby on Via España, email, modem and telex services are available at Intel's Ventas (sales) office, in the Edificio Banco Nacional, Torre 2, 6th floor (☎ 263-8696), open Monday to Friday, 8 am to 4:30 pm. Another Intel office with international telephone and fax services is on Calle Gavilán in Balboa (☎ 262-0894).

Travel Agencies As befits the 'crossroads of the world,' Panama City has a great number of travel agencies. Over 80 are listed in the telephone directory, and some of these have several offices.

Turismo Joven Panamá (☎ 225-2356), Calle 46 and Calle 50 in the Bella Vista District, issues the ISIC card and offers an ISIC discount on certain international flights for students under 31 years old bearing the card. They also distribute a list of over 100 businesses around the city offering discounts, some up to 50%, to ISIC cardholders, including everything from discos, cinemas, shops, restaurants and even a dental clinic.

Bookstores Librería Argosy (☎ 223-5344) on Via Argentina near the corner of Via España, in El Cangrejo District, is a bookstore and cultural institution. Its owner, the interesting and ebullient Greek-born Gerasimos (Gerry) Kanelopulos, offers a fine selection of books (including Lonely Planet) in English, Spanish and French.

There are several Gran Morrison department stores around the city; they carry a selection of postcards, books and magazines in English, including travel books. Farmacia Arrocha, also with several branches around the city, carries a smaller selection of books and magazines in English.

Medical Services Medicine in Panama, especially in Panama City, is of a high standard. Hospitals and clinics are listed in the yellow pages of the telephone directory. Ask your hotel or embassy for a recommendation if you fall ill.

Emergency Emergency phone numbers in Panama City are:

Police	☎ 104
Fire	☎ 103
Ambulance	☎ 225-1436, 228-2187
Hospital Santo Tomás	☎ 225-1436

Walking Tour

The colonial San Felipe District, also called Casco Viejo, is one of the more interesting parts of the city. Sadly, nowadays it isn't one of the more economically affluent districts; it's unsafe to walk here at night, and you must be careful walking down side streets here even in the daytime, though you should be fine as long as you stick to the main streets.

You could start a walking tour in San Felipe at the **Paseo de las Bóvedas**, on the southern tip of the peninsula. A walkway runs along the top of the sea wall built by the Spanish to protect the city. From here you can see the ships lining up to enter the canal, and the Bridge of the Americas arching over the canal.

Below the wall, on the tip of the point, is the **Plaza de Francia**, where large stone tablets tell the story (in Spanish) of the canal's construction and the role of the French. The plaza is dedicated to the memory of the 22,000 workers, most of them from France, Guadeloupe and Martinique, who died working on the canal. Most were killed by yellow fever and malaria, and among the busts of the

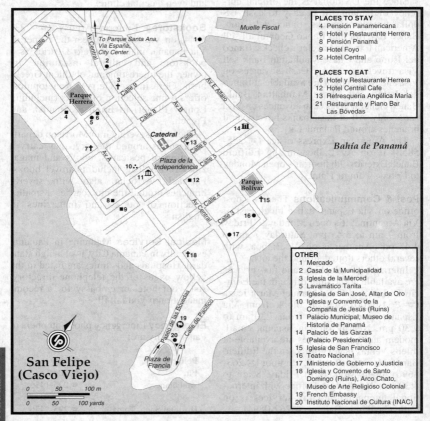

PLACES TO STAY
4 Pensión Panamericana
6 Hotel y Restaurante Herrera
8 Pensión Panamá
9 Hotel Foyo
12 Hotel Central

PLACES TO EAT
6 Hotel y Restaurante Herrera
12 Hotel Central Cafe
13 Refresquería Angélica María
21 Restaurante y Piano Bar Las Bóvedas

Bahía de Panamá

OTHER
1 Mercado
2 Casa de la Municipalidad
3 Iglesia de la Merced
5 Lavamático Tanita
7 Iglesia de San José, Altar de Oro
10 Iglesia y Convento de la Compañía de Jesús (Ruins)
11 Palacio Municipal, Museo de Historia de Panamá
14 Palacio de las Garzas (Palacio Presidencial)
15 Iglesia de San Francisco
16 Teatro Nacional
17 Ministerio de Gobierno y Justicia
18 Iglesia y Convento de Santo Domingo (Ruins), Arco Chato, Museo de Arte Religioso Colonial
19 French Embassy
20 Instituto Nacional de Cultura (INAC)

San Felipe (Casco Viejo)

0   50   100 m
0   50   100 yards

PANAMA

Frenchmen who played important parts in the canal's construction is a monument to Carlos J Finlay, who discovered how mosquitoes transmit yellow fever. His work led to the eradication of the disease in Panama.

On one side of the plaza are some old **dungeons**. Although they now contain an art gallery and an expensive restaurant/piano bar (Las Bóvedas) you can still see the dungeons' original stonework. Also on the plaza are the Instituto Nacional de Cultura (INAC) and the French Embassy.

Leaving the plaza to walk up Av A, you soon come to the **Museo de Arte Religioso Colonial**, beside the ruins of the **Iglesia y Convento de Santo Domingo** on the corner of Calle 3. Just inside the doorway of the ruins is the **Arco Chato**, a long arch that has stood here, unsupported, for centuries. It reputedly played a part in the selection of Panama over Nicaragua as the site for the canal: its stability was taken as evidence that the area was not subject to earthquakes.

Turning north along Calle 3, you pass the **Ministerio de Gobierno y Justicia** building, and behind it the **Teatro Nacional**, built in 1907. The ornate interior has been restored, and it boasts red and gold decorations, a ceiling mural, a big crystal chandelier and several tiers of seats. Performances are still held here; to find out about them, or just to have a look at the theater, go around to the office door at the side of the building.

Opposite the theater is the **Iglesia de San Francisco**, facing onto the **Parque Bolívar**. In 1826 in a schoolroom opposite this plaza, Simón Bolívar held a meeting urging the union of the Latin American countries.

Around the block from this plaza, on Av Alfaro, is the presidential palace, called the **Palacio de las Garzas** for the herons kept there. The president of Panama lives on the upper floor. A few blocks farther west are the **Muelle Fiscal** (the port) and **mercado**.

Two blocks south of the palace, at the center of San Felipe, is the central plaza, **Parque Catedral**, also called the **Plaza de la Independencia**, where Panamanian independence was declared on November 3, 1903. In addition to the cathedral, the plaza is fringed by several other historic buildings. On the south side of the plaza, **Museo de Historia de Panamá** is on the top floor of the **Palacio Municipal** (city hall). Next door is the building that was once the headquarters of the French company that first worked on the canal; the canal officials and other dignitaries stayed at the nearby **Hotel Central**, a very luxurious place in those days.

Half a block south of the plaza on Calle 7 are the ruins of another church, the **Iglesia y Convento de la Compañia de Jesus**. Walk to the end of the block to rejoin Av A, then walk a block west to arrive at the **Iglesia de San José**. There is a colorful story attached to its famous **Altar de Oro** (golden altar), about the only thing of value salvaged after Henry Morgan sacked Panamá Viejo in 1671. When word came of the pirate's impending attack, according to local tales, a priest painted the altar black – some say he covered it with mud – to disguise it. The priest allegedly told Morgan the famous altar had been stolen by another pirate, and even, according to legend, convinced Morgan to donate handsomely for its replacement! Morgan is said to have told the priest, 'I don't know why I think you are more of a pirate than I am.' Whatever the historical fact, the altar was later moved from its original church in the old city to this one, where it only just fits inside.

A block farther is another plaza, the **Parque Herrera**. A block north, on Av Central, two blocks behind the cathedral, is the **Iglesia de La Merced**.

Walking out of the San Felipe District along Av Central, past the **Casa de la Municipalidad**, after a couple of blocks you come to the **Parque Santa Ana**, with its **Iglesia de Santa Ana**. Plaza Santa Ana marks the beginning of the Av Central shopping district; it is surrounded by restaurants and there are buses to the rest of the city.

Walk about five more blocks down Av Central, past all the big air-conditioned stores with hawkers outside, and you come to the large **Plaza Cinco de Mayo**. This part of Av Central, between Parque Santa

Ana and the Plaza Cinco de Mayo, is a pedestrian-only shopping street. On Av Central opposite Plaza Cinco de Mayo are the excellent **Museo Antropológico Reina Torres de Araúz**, which focuses on the anthropology and archaeology of Panama, and behind it, the **Mercado de Buonherías y Artesanías** (handicrafts market).

Plaza Cinco de Mayo is a major bus stop. Buses leave here for the canal area (including the Miraflores Locks), the Ancón area (including the causeway and the Balboa Yacht Club), and the Tocumen international airport. Any Vía España bus will take you into the business and banking district of **El Cangrejo**, but not along Av Central (later Vía España) itself, which is a one-way avenue heading towards San Felipe; the bus mostly runs along Av Perú, one block to the south. In El Cangrejo, the fancy white French-Gothic style **Iglesia del Carmen** at the corner of Vía España and Av Federico Boyd is one of the city's most distinctive buildings.

Panamá Viejo

At the east end of the city by the sea, are the ruins of the first city the Spanish built here. The ruins cover a large area and you can still see the cathedral with its stone tower, the plaza beside it, the Santo Domingo and San José convents, the San Juan de Dios hospital and the city hall. The bridge which marked the beginning of El Camino Real, on which the booty from Peru and other Pacific colonies was taken by mule train to Portobelo on the Caribbean, is still standing.

The ruins are not fenced and you can visit them any time; Panamá Viejo buses coming from Plaza Cinco de Mayo will take you there. The IPAT tourist office operates a fine two-story mercado de artesanías near the ruins, open every day from 9 am to 6 pm.

Museums

A couple of museums have already been mentioned but there are several more. Here's a complete list:

Museo de Historia de Panamá (☎ 228-6231)
   Palacio Municipal, on Parque Catedral, Calle 7, San Felipe; open Monday to Friday, 8 am to noon and 12:30 to 4 pm; admission free. Exhibits on the history of Panama, mostly since its European discovery.
Museo de Arte Religioso Colonial
   Av A and Calle 3, in the Santo Domingo chapel, next to the church and convent of the same name in the San Felipe District; open Tuesday to Saturday, 9 am to 4:15 pm; admission US$0.75 (children US$0.25). Colonial-era religious art.
Museo Antropológico Reina Torres de Araúz (☎ 262-8338) Plaza Cinco de Mayo, Av Central; open Tuesday to Saturday, 9 am to 4 pm; admission US$1.50 (children US$0.50). Fascinating museum of Panamanian anthropology, archaeology and pre-Columbian history.
Museo de Arte Contemporaneo (☎ 262-8012)
   Av de los Mártires, near Calle J; open Monday to Friday, 9 am to 4 pm, Saturday 9 am to noon, Sunday 9 am to 3 pm; admission free. Permanent and changing exhibitions.
Museo Afro-Antilleano (☎ 262-5348)
   Av Justo Arosemena and Calle 24; open Tuesday to Saturday, 9 am to 4 pm; admission US$1 (children US$0.25). Exhibits on the history of Panama's West Indian community.
Museo de Ciencias Naturales (☎ 225-0645)
   Av Cuba, between Calle 29 and 30, behind Hotel Soloy; open Tuesday to Saturday, 9 am to 4 pm, Sunday 9 am to 1 pm; admission US$1 (children US$0.25). Natural sciences, flora, fauna, geology and paleontology of Panama.
Casa-Museo del Banco Nacional (☎ 225-0640)
   Calle 34 and Av Cuba; open Tuesday to Friday, 8 am to 12:30 pm and 1:30 to 4 pm, Saturday 7:30 am to noon; admission free. Coins and bills circulated in Panama from the 16th century to the present; stamps and other objects related to the history of the Panamanian postal service.

Causeway

At the Pacific entrance to the Panama Canal, a *calzada* (causeway) connects the three small islands of Naos, Perico and Flamenco to the Amador section of the city. Solidaridad, the beach on Naos, is one of the most popular in the area.

Many people come to the causeway in the early morning and late afternoon to

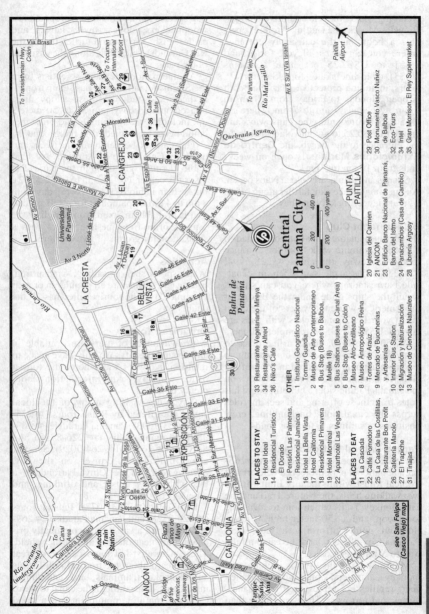

Central Panama City

PLACES TO STAY
3 Hotel Ideal
14 Residencial Turístico El Dorado
15 Pensión Las Palmeras, Residencial Jamaica
16 Hotel La Bella Vista
17 Hotel California
18 Residencial Primavera
19 Hotel Montreal
22 Aparthotel Las Vegas

PLACES TO EAT
11 La Cascada
25 Caffé Pomodoro
25 La Casa de las Costillitas, Restaurante Bon Profit
26 Cafetería Manolo
27 El Trapiche
31 Tinajas

33 Restaurante Vegetariano Mireya
34 Restaurante Alfred
36 Niko's Cafe

OTHER
1 Instituto Geográfico Nacional Tommy Guardia
2 Museo de Arte Contemporáneo
4 Bus Stop (Buses to Balboa, Muelle 18)
5 Bus Station (Buses to Canal Area)
6 Bus Stop (Buses to Colón)
7 Museo Afro-Antillano
8 Museo Antropológico Reina Torres de Araúz
9 Mercado de Buonherías y Artesanías
10 Interior Bus Station
12 Migración y Naturalización
13 Museo de Ciencias Naturales

20 Iglesia del Carmen
21 ANCON
23 Edificio Banco Nacional de Panamá, Banco del Istmo
24 Panacambios (Casa de Cambio)
28 Librería Argosy

29 Post Office
30 Monumento Vasco Núñez de Balboa
32 Eco-Tours
34 Intel
35 Gran Morrison, El Rey Supermarket

see San Felipe (Casco Viejo) map

PANAMA

walk, jog, skate, bicycle and drive along it. Bicycles Moses (see Getting Around) operates a booth at the causeway entrance where you can rent a bicycle for around US$1 to US$2.25 per hour (tandems US$3), or in-line skates for US$5 for 1½ hours, including protective gear; the booth is open Monday to Friday from 10 am to 7 pm, weekends 7 am to 7 pm. There's a US$0.25 fee to enter the causeway, and another US$0.25 to go onto Naos beach. At the entrance to the beach, the **Centro de Exhibiciones Marinas** is open on weekends from 10 am to 5 pm.

Snacks and drinks are sold at Naos beach. An open-air terrace cafe farther along offers a great view of the city and bay.

Balboa Yacht Club
Beside the Panama Canal at Fort Amador, about a 15-minute walk from the entrance to the causeway, the club (☎ 228-5794, 228-2313) has a pleasant open-air canalside bar/restaurant where you can sit and watch the ships glide under the Bridge of the Americas while the waters of the canal lap at your feet. Sandwiches with fries are around US$2 to US$3, complete dinners US$7.50 to US$10, or it's a fine place to come just for a drink. Yachts waiting to cross the canal are anchored in front of the club. This is the place to meet yachties on the canal's Pacific side; a bulletin board has notes from those offering and seeking rides across the canal, jobs linehandling, crew positions or sailings to faraway lands.

Parque Natural Metropolitano
Up on a hill behind the city, this 265-hectare national park protects a wild area of tropical forest within the city limits. It has two walking trails, the Nature Trail and the Tití Monkey Trail, which join to form one long loop, and a 150-meter-high *Mirador* (lookout point) affording a view over Panama City, the bay, and the canal all the way to Miraflores Locks.

Mammals in the park include tití monkeys, anteaters, sloths and white-tailed deer; reptiles are represented by iguanas, turtles and tortoises. There are more than 200 species of birds including oropéndolas, woodpeckers, doves, owls, hawks and eagles. Fish, shrimp and turtles live in the Río Curundu which runs along the east side of the park.

An international team of scientists from the Smithsonian Institute has set up a crane in the park to study the forest canopy; there is a complete ecosystem 30 to 50 meters up, including many animals and birds that could never be studied from the ground.

The park is bordered on the west and north by Camino de la Amistad; Av Juan Pablo II runs right through the park. The visitors' center (☎ 232-5516, 232-5552), on Av Juan Pablo II, is open every day from 8 am to 4 pm. A pamphlet for a self-guided tour is available in Spanish and English; the rangers offer free one-hour tours with a slide show for groups of five or more.

Activities
Water sports such as sailing, windsurfing, fishing and surfing are all popular in or near Panama City. The tourist office has all the details.

Organized Tours
A great number of tours are available in and around the city. We only have space to mention a few of them here; the tourist office can give you information about plenty of others.

City tours visiting many of the local sights are offered by Reisa Tours (☎ 225-4721, 263-7693), Panama Paradise (☎ 269-9861), Iguana Tours (☎ 226-8738) and Servitur (☎ 264-3014, 264-3029). Servitur also offers lunch cruises on the bay, evening tours on the 'Chiva Parrandera,' a bus with lively music and drinking, and others.

Eco-Tours (☎ 263-3077), Iguana Tours (☎ 226-8738) and Panama Paradise (☎ 269-9861) operate a variety of ecologically oriented tours near the city and farther afield. These naturalist-led tours can be a great way to learn about the tropical rain forests and their plants, animals, birds and human inhabitants. Trips through the canal to Barro Colorado natural monument are a good alternative to trips to Barro Colorado island, seeing the same wildlife and jungle.

Other trips offered by these companies include bird watching on the Pipeline Road in Soberanía National Park, visits to remote Chocó and Embera Indian villages, salt and freshwater fishing trips, trips to Portobelo, Fort San Lorenzo, El Valle, Isla Taboga, Isla Contadora, and trips farther afield in Panama.

An air-conditioned train travels between the Ancón section of Panama City and the Summit Botanical Gardens & Zoo on Sundays. It departs from the Ancón train station (☎ 232-6018) on Carretera Gaillard at 9:30 am, 11:25 am and 1:50 pm, arriving at Summit an hour later. Cost is US$1.50 one way (children US$0.75), double for roundtrip.

Aventuras Panamá (☎ 260-0044) offers The 'Chagres Challenge,' a full-day white-water rafting trip on the Chagres river, which includes 1½ hours of hiking through tropical rain forest to get there.

See the Panama Canal section for details on boat tours through the canal, and to the Smithsonian nature reserve on Isla Barro Colorado in the canal's Lago Gatún. See also Panama, Getting Around, above.

Special Events
Carnaval, on the four days preceding Ash Wednesday, is a magnificent festival in Panama City. See the Special Events section for more details.

Places to Stay – budget
San Felipe (Casco Viejo) The historic San Felipe (Casco Viejo) District is where the city's lowest-priced lodgings are found. Their quality is nothing to write home about, though budget backpackers will probably find them adequate. It's dangerous to walk around this district at night; keep your eyes open in the side streets even in daytime.

Hotel Central (☎ 262-8044, 262-8096), on the plaza opposite the cathedral, was very grand around the turn of the century; illustrious figures in the canal's history lodged here in its early days. The hotel has

been allowed to deteriorate, but the rooms still have their high ceilings and arched French doors opening onto private balconies overlooking the plaza. Singles/doubles are US$7.50/8.50 with shared bath, US$8.50/10.50 with private bath. A small cafe is on the ground floor.

A block and a half from the cathedral, at 6 Calle, No 8-25, *Hotel Foyo* (☎ 262-8023) is basic but clean, with rooms for US$6/11 with shared/private bath; a few smaller rooms adequate for one person are US$4.50. Some of the rooms of the same price are better than others; ask to see several.

Opposite the Foyo, the *Pensión Panamá* (☎ 262-8053) has single/double rooms with shared bath for US$4/6.

On Parque Herrera, on 9 Calle, the *Hotel y Restaurante Herrera* (☎ 228-8994) has single/double rooms for US$4/8 with shared bath, or US$11 with private bath; rooms with air con, fridge and TV cost extra.

Other Areas Several other areas of the city have cheap hotels, but aren't recommendable areas. The places mentioned here are in better districts.

Residencial Primavera (☎ 225-1195), simple but clean and well-kept, is in a good location on Av Cuba near the corner of Calle 43, in a residential neighborhood just a block from Via España. All the rooms have private bath and ceiling fans, and cost US$10 a night.

Pensión Las Palmeras (☎ 225-0811) at Av Cuba No 38-29, near Calle 38, is also simple but clean, with rooms for US$10 with shower in the room and toilet down the hall, or US$12 with private bath. Next door, the *Residencial Jamaica* (☎ 225-9870) on Av Cuba at the corner of Calle 38 has rooms with private bath, air con and color TV for US$20.

A block away, the *Residencial Turístico El Dorado* (☎ 227-5767) on Calle 37 between Av Cuba and Av Perú has rooms with private bath for US$10 with fan, US$12 with air con, or US$15 with air con and color TV.

Hotel Ideal (☎ 262-2400, 262-2087) on Calle 17 Oeste, a block from the Av Central pedestrian shopping street, isn't in the best part of town, but it's where all the Peace Corps volunteers stay. It's a large hotel where all the rooms have air con and color cable TV; singles/doubles with shared bath are US$16/18, or US$18/20 with private bath. Downstairs is a 24-hour restaurant. Local buses stop nearby, and the Tica bus to Costa Rica comes and goes from here.

Places to Stay – middle
A couple of hotels on Via España offer a higher standard of accommodations, at good value. The *Hotel California* (☎ 263-7736, 263-7844) on Via España near the corner of Calle 43 has good, clean rooms with private bath, telephone and color TV for US$25, with a restaurant/bar downstairs and free coffee in the lobby.

The *Hotel Montreal* (☎ 263-4422) on Via España at the corner of Av Justo Arosemena has all the same amenities, plus a rooftop swimming pool and parking; rooms are US$22 with a single bed, US$27.50 with a double bed.

Aparthotel Las Vegas (☎ 269-0722, fax 223-0047), at the corner of Calle 55 Oeste and Av Eusebio A Morales in El Cangrejo District, is a modern, well-kept apartment/hotel with studios or suites with air con, private kitchen and bath, color satellite TV and phone. The rooms on the upper floors have a good view. The listed rate for studio apartments is US$55 per day, but if you stay for seven to 29 days the rate drops to US$25 per day, and it's US$20 per day if you stay by the month; suites are US$10 more. A 'mini-studio' without kitchen or air con costs US$15/12/10 per day by the day/week/month; with air con they're US$5 more. Las Vegas is two blocks from Via España and convenient to the 24-hour El Rey supermarket, banks, cinemas, a bus stop and a number of decent restaurants, including the fine *Caffé Pomodoro* downstairs.

Places to Eat
Panama City has hundreds of good places to eat, with everything from fast-food joints to the fanciest gourmet restaurants.

International restaurants run the gamut and there are vegetarian restaurants too.

Near Av Balboa *La Cascada* (☎ 262-1297), on the corner of Av Balboa and Calle 25, is a good place for a pleasant evening out. It has a large garden dining patio and a bilingual menu with many choices. The meals are gigantic and very reasonably priced; for US$5.25 you can get an excellent steak or corvina fish, or try the giant seafood platter for US$9.25. It's open Monday to Saturday, 3 to 11 pm.

Near Via España *La Casa de las Costillitas* (☎ 269-6670) at Via Argentina 6, in El Cangrejo District just off Via España, is a branch of La Cascada and offers the same menu; it's open every day except Monday.

Next door, the nouvelle cuisine at *Bon Profit* (☎ 263-9667) on Via Argentina 5 is a splurge, but one well worth the price. The title, which means 'good eating' in Catalán, indicates the Catalán-Mallorcan background of the owner, who offers such delicacies as corvina in a spinach and garlic sauce, with dinners from around US$8 to US$12.

Across the street on Via Argentina are a couple of popular, more economical alternatives. *El Trapiche* offers good, inexpensive traditional Panamanian dishes; among the many selections is a set meal (different each day) including soup, salad, a main dish and dessert, all for US$6.50. Nearby, *Cafetería Manolo* at Via Argentina 12 is popular with locals for its good food at good prices. Both restaurants have tables outdoors under covered verandahs as well as inside in air-conditioned coolness, and are open every day from 7 am until 11 pm (Manolo's until 1 am).

Another economical choice in this same area is *Niko's Cafe* on Calle 51 Este, half a block south of Via España. Niko's is open 24 hours every day, and is a favorite with locals on a budget; you can easily fill up here for around US$3 to US$5.

Caffé Pomodoro on the ground floor of the Aparthotel Las Vegas (see Places to Stay) is good for Italian food, with tables inside in an attractive air-conditioned restaurant as well as outdoors in a pleasant courtyard, shady in daytime and softly lit in the evening. It's open every day from 7 am to 11 pm.

The *Napoli Ristorante e Pizzeria* on Calle 57, 1½ blocks south of Via España, is another fine place for Italian food; it's a large, popular, air-conditioned restaurant with a good reputation. Pasta dishes are US$3.25 to US$5.50; pizza, seafood and meats are also served. It's open Tuesday to Sunday, 11 am to 11:30 pm. This is just off our city map; heading east on Via España, Calle 57 is the next street on the south side, after passing Via Argentina.

Opposite the Napoli, *Athen's* serves excellent Greek food and pizza. Prices are very reasonable, and there are tables inside (where there's air con) or outside on the covered verandah. It's open every day except Tuesday, 11 am to 11:30 pm.

For Chinese food, the *Restaurante Alfred* on Calle Manuel María Icaza, half a block south of Via España, has no atmosphere at all – but it has good, authentic Chinese food, and other foods besides, all at very cheap prices. This is where the Chinese people come to eat. It's open every day from 11:30 am to midnight.

To satisfy vegetarians, the *Restaurante Vegetariano Mireya* on the corner of Calle 50 Este and Av 3 Sur, a block south of Via España, serves a wide selection of cafeteria-style meals. It's a pleasant place, with tables inside where there's air con, as well as outside on a covered verandah. Whole grain bread and natural yogurt are also sold here. It's open Monday to Saturday, 6 am to 7 pm.

If you want to spend up, *Tinajas* (☎ 269-3840, 263-7890) at Calle 51, No 22, in the Bella Vista District, is one of the city's more famous places. A folkloric show with traditional music and dance performances is presented on Tuesday, Thursday, Friday and Saturday nights at 9 pm, with a cover charge of US$5; phone for reservations. A dinner of authentic Panamanian dishes, including soup, main dish, dessert and coffee, might come to around

US$16, with an extra US$5 if you want to see the folkloric show. Tinajas is open Monday to Saturday, 11:30 am to 11 pm.

Parque Santa Ana A few blocks from the Casco Viejo District, at the corner of Av Central and Calle 12, Parque Santa Ana has many inexpensive restaurants to choose from, some open-air, some air con. The cool *Café Coca-Cola* on a far corner of the plaza is an old favorite for inexpensive food as well as local color; it's open every day from 7:30 am to 11:30 pm. You'll find plenty of other restaurants and cafés as you head down Av Central from this plaza, but beware at night.

Entertainment

Dance, music, theater and other performances are presented at the historic *Teatro Nacional* (☎ 262-3582) in the San Felipe District, and at the two modern theaters in the *Atlapa* convention center (☎ 226-7000). Other venues include *Teatro La Cúpula* (☎ 264-1989) in El Cangrejo District, the *Guild de Ancón* (☎ 252-6786) in Ancón, and the *Teatro En Círculo* (☎ 261-5375, 261-5259). Many air-conditioned cinemas around the city show current US films, usually in English with Spanish subtitles (admission US$3).

Popular discos include *Bacchus* (☎ 263-9004) on Via España opposite the large Hotel Panamá; *My Place* (☎ 223-9924) on Via Venetto, beside the Hotel Panamá, popular with *norteamericanos*; *Cubares* (☎ 264-8905) at Calle 52 and Via España, featuring Latin music such as salsa and merengue; *Dreams* (☎ 263-4248) on Via España, popular for its economical open bar nights, when the cover includes all you can drink; *Mabuhay* (☎ 226-2755) at Calle 50 and Via Cincuentenario; *Rock Cafe* (☎ 264-5364) in the Plaza La Florida; *Patatús* (☎ 264-8467) in the Plaza New York on Calle 50; and the *Patatús Caribe No 2* (☎ 264-8467) in the Centro Comercial Los Pueblos on the road to Tocumen.

Several of the larger hotels offer 'Noches Típicas' featuring traditional Panamanian dancing and floor shows; the tourist office has current information. Traditional dancing is also presented at the *Tinajas* restaurant (see Places to Eat), and at the lottery draws on Wednesday and Sunday afternoons.

Gambling is legal; about 20 casinos, including some at the larger hotels, are listed in the telephone directory.

Spectator Sports

Horse races, soccer, baseball and boxing are all popular in or near Panama City. The tourist office has all the details.

Things to Buy

Merchandise from around the world is sold very cheaply in Panama. Walk along Av Central and take your pick.

The IPAT tourist office operates a handicrafts market at the ruins of Panama Viejo; the excellent quality handicrafts here include Kuna molas and other textile arts, woodwork, tile and ceramics, basketry, Panama hats, leatherwork, beadwork, soapstone carvings and more, representing regions all around Panama. The market (☎ 221-8221) is open every day from 9 am to 6 pm.

Just off Plaza Cinco de Mayo, behind the large Museo Antropológico Reina Torres de Araúz, the Mercado de Buonherías y Artesanías also has handicrafts. There are many other artesanías shops around Panama City; the tourist office has a complete list.

Gran Morrison department stores sell a variety of Panamanian handicrafts, including molas, ceramics, woodcarvings, woven hats and basketry; they also sell postcards, and books and magazines in English.

Getting There & Away

Air A number of airlines provide services between Panama City and other parts of the country; see Panama's Getting Around section, above. Domestic flights arrive and depart from La Paitilla airport, in the city.

International flights arrive and depart from the Omar Torrijos airport at Tocumen, 25 km from the city center. See Panama's Getting There & Away section for more information.

Bus Buses to most other parts of the country arrive and depart from the 'Interior bus station' on Av Balboa. On Av Balboa itself is the station for buses to David; directly behind this is the station for buses to other parts of the country.

These are some of the major bus routes. There are also buses to many small towns.

Chitré and Los Santos
    (255 km, four hours US$6) Hourly, 7 am to 9 pm.
Darién
    Departs at 6:30, 8:30 and 10:30 am, and at noon; January to April it goes as far as Yaviza (10 hours, US$14); the rest of the year the rain makes the last part of the road impassable and the bus only goes as far as Metetí (seven hours, US$9). Travel times are approximate, depending on the condition of the road.
David
    (438 km) Regular bus departs every 45 minutes from 7 am to 11:30 am, then every 1¼ hours until last bus at 8 pm (6½ to seven hours, US$11); express bus departs at midnight (5½ to six hours, US$15).
El Valle
    (123 km, 2½ hours, US$3.50) Hourly, 7 am to 7 pm.
Las Tablas
    (282 km, 4½ hours, US$7) Goes when bus is full (around every two hours), 6 am to 6 pm.

Buses departing from other locations include:

Canal Zone
    Buses to everywhere in the Canal Zone (Miraflores and Pedro Miguel Locks, Paraíso, Gamboa and more) depart from the bus station at Plaza Cinco de Mayo, on Av Central.
Colón (76 km, 1¾ hours)
    Departs from Calle P (opposite Calle 26) at the corner of Av Central. Regular and express buses depart every 20 minutes from around 5 am to 9 pm, with the last bus going at 1 am. The express bus is air-conditioned and costs US$0.50 extra, but doesn't get there much faster.
Costa Rica
    Panaline (☎ 262-1618) and Tica Bus (☎ 262-2084, 262-6275) both offer direct bus services between Panama City and San José, Costa Rica. See Panama's Getting There & Away section for details.

Train The train which used to take the famously scenic route to Colón along the canal was damaged during the 1989 US invasion. Check with IPAT to see if it has been repaired.

Boat Passenger boats go from Panama City to Isla Taboga; tour boats go along part of the Panama Canal. See the Around Panama City section for details.

Cargo boats to Colombia depart from the docks near San Felipe. See the introductory Getting There & Away chapter for more information on boats to Colombia.

Getting Around
To/From the Airport The international airport Omar Torrijos is at Tocumen, 25 km northeast of the city center. Local Tocumen buses depart every 15 minutes from the bus stop opposite the Plaza Cinco de Mayo; they cost US$0.35 and take an hour to reach the airport.

A taxi to the Tocumen airport costs US$20. When arriving at Tocumen, look for the 'Transportes Turísticos' desk at the airport exit. Beside it is a taxi stand, with posted prices. Taxi drivers will assail you offering rides into town for US$20, but the staff at the desk will inform you that you can take a *colectivo* for US$8 per person (for three or more passengers) or US$12 per person (for two passengers). For two or more people traveling together, a taxi can be cheaper.

La Paitilla airport, within the city, handles domestic flights. City bus No 2 that runs along Av Balboa stops there; the ride costs US$0.15.

Bus Panama City has an excellent network of local buses, which run every day from around 5 am to 11 pm. A ride costs US$0.15.

Car & Motorcycle Rental car companies in Panama City include:

Avis
    ☎ 264-0722, 213-0555;
    airport 238-4056, 238-4037
Barriga
    ☎ 269-0221, 269-0283; airport 238-4495

Budget
    ☎ 263-8777, 263-9190; airport 238-4069
Central
    airport ☎ 230-0447
Dollar
    ☎ 269-7542, 269-7514; airport 238-4032
Hertz
    ☎ 264-1111, 263-6511; airport 238-4081
International
    ☎ 264-4540, 264-8643; airport 238-4404
National
    ☎ 264-8277, 269-1921; airport 238-4144
Thrifty
    ☎ 264-2613, 264-3085; airport 238-4955
Toyota
    ☎ 223-6085, 223-6087
Vantage
    ☎ 226-8122, 263-3745; airport 238-4500

As always, it pays to shop around to compare rates and special promotions. At the time of writing, rates ranged from US$30 to US$45 per day for the most economical cars, with insurance and unlimited kilometers.

Motos Minsk (☎ 213-0618) at Via Brasil, Final No 53, rents 125cc motorcycles for US$10 per day, plus US$3 for helmet; a US$100 deposit is refunded when you return the bike in good condition. A special motorcycle driver's license is not required; your ordinary driver's license will do.

Taxi Taxis are plentiful. They are not metered but there is a list of standard fares which they are supposed to charge, measured by zones. The fare for one zone is a minimum of US$0.75; the maximum fare within the city is US$2. An average ride, crossing a couple of zones, would cost US$1 or US$1.50, plus US$0.25 for each additional passenger. Always agree on a fare before you get into the cab.

Watch out for unmarked, large-model US cars serving hotels as cabs. Their prices are up to four times that of regular street taxis. You can phone for a taxi:

Ama	☎ 221-1865
America	☎ 223-7694
El Parador	☎ 238-9111
Latino	☎ 226-7313
San Cristóbal	☎ 221-8704
Unico	☎ 221-4074

Bicycle Alquiler de Bicicletas Moses (☎ 228-0116) has two shops in Panama City, one by the entrance to the bridge, the other near the Officers Club in Fuerte Amador. Both are open Monday to Friday from 10 am to 7 pm, Saturday and Sunday 7 am to 7 pm. They hire bicycles for short or long term; mountain bikes are US$2.25 per hour, five-speed and children's bikes US$1 per hour, and tandems US$3 per hour, with more economical daily, weekly and monthly rates available. They also rent in-line skates, at US$5 for 1½ hours.

Ferry Ferries connect Panama City with Isla Taboga, out in the bay. See the Isla Taboga section, below.

Around Panama City

Not far from Panama City, the Panama Canal is the first attraction for most visitors. It is also easy to make a day trip across the isthmus to the Atlantic side, to visit Portobelo and Isla Grande on the east side of the canal, and Fort San Lorenzo on the west side; all are only a couple of hours away by road.

Offshore in the Bahía de Panama, Isla Taboga and Isla Contadora are also just a short distance from the city.

PANAMA CANAL

The canal is one of the most significant waterways on Earth, and is truly an engineering marvel, stretching 80 km (50 miles) from Panama City on the Pacific side to Colón on the Atlantic side, cutting right through the Great Divide. In 1992, over 12,600 ocean-going vessels passed through the canal; ships are crossing 24 hours a day, waiting in line on both sides for their turn. Ships worldwide are built with the dimensions of the Panama Canal's locks in mind: 305 meters long and 33.5 meters wide.

The canal has three sets of double locks: Miraflores and Pedro Miguel Locks on the Pacific side, and Gatún Locks on the

Atlantic side. Between the locks, ships pass through a huge artificial lake, Lago Gatún, created by the Gatún Dam across the Río Chagres (when created they were the largest dam and the largest artificial lake on earth), and the Gaillard Cut, a 14-km cut through the rock and shale of the isthmian mountains. The cut was called the Culebra Cut, because of its snake-like appearance, before it was renamed for the engineer in charge of its construction. Construction was an extreme challenge – in the wet climate the loose soil was subject to horrendous landslides even after the canal opened.

Ships' fees bring millions of dollars into Panama every year. Ships pay according to their weight, with the average fee around US$30,000 for commercial ships. The highest was US$141,344.97, paid on May 2, 1993, by *Crown Princess*, the largest passenger ship to transit the canal; the lowest was 36¢, in 1928 by Richard Halliburton, who swam through.

The more you learn about the Panama Canal, the more interesting it becomes, both in terms of the monumental construction project, and the associated political intrigues.

Things to See & Do

Miraflores Locks The easiest and best way to visit the canal is to go to the Miraflores Locks, the locks closest to Panama City, where a viewing platform gives you a good view of the locks in operation. A bilingual guide and bilingual illustrated pamphlets give information about the canal, and there's a museum with a model and film about the canal.

Entrance is free, every day from 9 am to 5 pm. To get there, take any Paraíso or Gamboa bus from the Plaza Cinco de Mayo bus terminal in Panama City. These buses, passing along the canal-side highway to Gamboa, will let you off at the Miraflores Locks sign on the highway, 12 km from the city center, from where it's about a 15-minute walk to the locks.

Other Locks Further on past the Miraflores Locks are the Pedro Miguel Locks. You

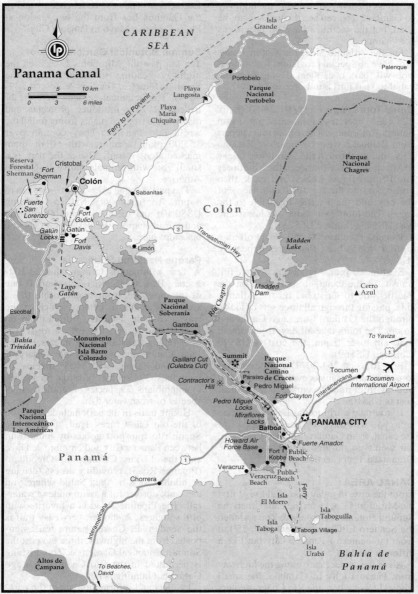

Panama Canal

| 0 | 5 | 10 km |
| 0 | 3 | 6 miles |

CARIBBEAN SEA

Isla Grande

Palenque

Ferry to El Porvenir

Portobelo

Parque Nacional Portobelo

Playa Langosta

Playa María Chiquita

Reserva Forestal Sherman

Fort Sherman

Cristobal

Colón

Fuerte San Lorenzo

Gatún Locks

Fort Gulick

Gatún

Fort Davis

Colón

Sabanitas

3

Transisthmian Hwy

Parque Nacional Chagres

Limón

Madden Lake

Lago Gatún

Escobal

Cerro Azul

Madden Dam

Río Chagres

Bahía Trinidad

Monumento Nacional Isla Barro Colorado

Parque Nacional Soberanía

Gamboa

To Yaviza

1

Gaillard Cut (Culebra Cut)

Summit

Parque Nacional Camino de Cruces

Tocumen

Contractor's Hill

Paraíso

Pedro Miguel

Tocumen International Airport

Interamericana

Parque Nacional Interoceánico Las Américas

Pedro Miguel Locks

Miraflores Locks

Fort Clayton

PANAMA CITY

Balboa

Panamá

Howard Air Force Base

Fuerte Amador

Fort Kobbe

Public Beach

Chorrera

Veracruz

Veracruz Beach

Public Beach

Ferry

Isla El Morro

Isla Taboguilla

Interamericana

Isla Taboga

Taboga Village

Altos de Campana

To Beaches, David

Isla Urabá

Bahía de Panamá

PANAMA

will pass them if you're taking the highway to Gamboa. You can see the locks from the road, but the facilities have no provisions for visitors.

On the Atlantic side, the Gatún Locks also have no special provisions for visitors. You will pass over them if you cross the canal to visit Fort San Lorenzo.

Canal Tours Argo Tours (☎ 228-6069, fax 228-1234) operates partial canal transits on Saturday mornings. These boat tours depart from Balboa, a western suburb of Panama City, and go through the Miraflores Locks to Miraflores Lake (between the Miraflores and Pedro Miguel Locks) and back, then cruise out into the bay for scenic views of the city and the Pacific approach to the canal. The tours last about 4½ hours and cost US$45 (children US$25).

Panama Paradise (☎ 269-9861) offers a similar tour, but it's more expensive (US$65).

Six times a year, Argo Tours operate full transits of the canal, from Balboa on the Pacific side to Cristóbal on the Atlantic side, passing through all three sets of locks, through the Gaillard Cut, Lago Gatún and so on. The tours take all day, from around 7:30 am to 5:30 pm; the cost is US$90 (children US$69).

Eco-Tours (☎ 263-3077) operates ocean-to-ocean canal transits every Saturday and Sunday from mid-December to mid-April; cost is US$109.

If you take a trip to the Barro Colorado area, you will travel by boat along part of the canal, from Gamboa to Barro Colorado, but won't go through any locks (see the Organized Tours section, above).

CANAL AREA

From the city, in a day you could visit first the Miraflores Locks on the canal, then the Summit Botanical Gardens & Zoo and then the Sendero El Charco nature trail, 25 km from the center of Panama City but like a different world.

All of these places are along the highway from Panama City to Gamboa, the small tropical town where the Río Chagres enters

Lago Gatún. They can be reached by taking the Gamboa bus from the bus station at Plaza Cinco de Mayo in Panama City.

Summit Botanical Gardens & Zoo

Ten km past the Miraflores Locks, on the highway heading to Gamboa, are the Summit Botanical Gardens & Zoo (☎ 232-4854). The botanical gardens were established in 1923 to introduce, propagate and disseminate tropical plants from around the world into Panama. They contain over 15,000 plant species, with 50 of them marked along a trail. Also at the park is a small zoo with animals native to Central America.

The park is open every day from 8 am to 4 pm. Admission is US$0.25 (children US$0.10) and includes some information and a trail map of the park. The Gamboa bus stops here.

Parque Nacional Soberanía

A few kilometers farther, the 22,104-hectare Parque Nacional Soberanía is one of the most accessible tropical rain forest areas in Panama. It extends much of the way across the isthmus, from Limón on Lago Gatún to just above Paraíso. It features hiking trails, the Río Chagres, part of Lago Gatún, and a remarkable variety of flora and fauna, with 105 species of mammals, 394 species of birds, 55 species of amphibians, 79 species of reptiles and 36 species of freshwater fish.

Hiking trails in the park include a section of the old Las Cruces Trail, used by the Spanish to transport goods by mule train between Panama City and Nombre de Dios, and the 17-km Camino de Oleoducto (Pipeline Road), providing access (driving or hiking) to Río Agua Salud where you can walk upriver for a swim under a waterfall. The Pipeline Road is a favorite with bird watchers. A shorter, very easy trail is the Sendero El Charco nature trail, signposted from the highway, three km past the Summit Botanical Gardens & Zoo. Fishing is permitted in the Río Chagres or Lago Gatún, but hunting is not.

Leaflets and information about the park,

including a self-guiding brochure for the nature trail, are available from the INRENARE and ANCON offices (see Panama City), or from the Soberanía National Park Headquarters in Gamboa (☎ 276-6370). If you want to camp in the park, you must first get permission from INRENARE or from the park headquarters.

Contractors Hill

On the west side of the canal, Contractors Hill was originally 123 meters above sea level. It was one of the highest points the Culebra (Gaillard) Cut had to cut through. There were landslides along the Cut, and Contractors Hill was reduced to its present height of 111 meters in 1954, in an effort to stabilize it.

Contractors Hill is one of the most accessible points from which to see the Gaillard Cut, but only if you have a private vehicle. The hill is pretty remote and is not served by public transport.

ISLA BARRO COLORADO

The Smithsonian Tropical Research Institute is on Isla Barro Colorado, in the middle of Lago Gatún in the Panama Canal. A lush tropical rain forest, it is completely protected since only scientists and only a limited number of visitors are allowed onto the island. It makes an interesting day trip from Panama City, with a boat ride down a good part of the canal, from Gamboa over Lago Gatún to the island. The institute is known worldwide, and some important scientific studies have been conducted here.

The island has over 40 km of trails, but visitors stay on a special 2.5-km nature trail, which has been marked with information about the forest. Self-guiding booklets are available. If you have time, the staff can show you other trails on the map.

Visitors are allowed on the island only on Saturdays and Sundays, in groups of 15. Make a reservation as far in advance as possible – to have a chance of getting a spot, you'll probably need to book at least six months in advance, a year is even better! If you don't have a complete group

of 15, the institute will match you with others to complete the number.

A visit to the island takes a full day and costs US$22 per person, which includes a guide, the boat ride there and back, and lunch at the research station cafeteria. Children under 12 are not allowed on the island. The island has many ticks so you should wear long pants, socks and closed shoes, and use insect repellent.

To arrange a visit to the island, contact the Smithsonian Tropical Research Institute (☎ 227-6022, fax 232-5978, net) at the Tapper Building on Av Roosevelt, opposite the Legislative Palace, in the Ancón District of Panama City. It's open Mondays, Wednesdays and Fridays from 8 am to noon and 1 to 5 pm, with a research library open to the public.

If you haven't managed to secure a reservation to visit the island, a good alternative is to take a tour to the Monumento Natural de Barro Colorado, also administered by the Smithsonian, and very similar to the island (see Panama's Organized Tours section). Full-day tours are offered by Eco-Tours and Iguana Tours for around US$85 per person.

CERRO AZUL

About an hour's drive east of Panama City is Cerro Azul, which is part of the Parque Nacional Chagres, a mountainous area of natural forest and mountain streams.

Within the park, Altos de Cerro Azul (☎ 260-4813, 260-0290) has built nature trails and other resources for visitors. The 1600-meter El Cantar nature trail passes through the forest and over streams; there's a free booklet on the trail.

Cerro Azul can't be reached by bus, but if you telephone, they may be able to help you get out there. If you have a vehicle, take the highway heading towards Tocumen and turn left at the intersection with the Hotel Riande.

BAHA'I & HINDU TEMPLES

On the outskirts of Panama City, 11 km from the city center on the Transisthmian Highway, the white-domed Baha'i Temple sits on the crest of a hill. It looks much like an egg from the outside but inside it is surprisingly beautiful, with a fresh breeze always blowing through. This is the Baha'i House of Worship serving all of Latin America. Information about the faith is available at the temple (☎ 231-1137, 231-1191) in English and Spanish; readings from the Baha'i writings (in English and Spanish) are held Sunday mornings at 10 am.

It's open every day from 10 am to 6 pm. Any bus to Colón can let you off on the highway, but it's a long walk up the hill. A taxi from Panama City costs around US$5.

On the way to the Baha'i Temple, also on a hill, is the magnificent Hindu Temple, open daily from 7:30 to 11 am and again from 4:30 to 7:30 pm.

BEACHES
Kobbe & Veracruz Beaches
Just across the canal from Panama City, Kobbe is a popular beach. Part of it is the Kobbe Beach Club (☎ 263-6885); at the entrance you pay US$7 for coupons good for food and drink at the club's restaurant/bar. The beach is safe and protected, has lifeguards, and has windsurfers and boats for hire, and other recreation.

Buses to Kobbe beach leave from the bus station at Plaza Cinco de Mayo. If you're driving, go over the Bridge of the Americas, take the first exit and follow the signs to the beach. About one km past the entrance to Kobbe beach is the signposted entrance to Veracruz, a free public beach. Food is available, and it is popular, especially on weekends.

Beaches near San Carlos
A couple of hours' drive west of the city, a strip of excellent beaches stretches along the Pacific Coast from **Playa Chame** to **Playa Farallón**.

About in the middle of this strip, 92 km from Panama City, **San Carlos** is one of the best and most popular beaches in the country. Nearby, **Playa El Palmar** is one of the country's more famous surf breaks. Other good beaches along this part of the

coast include **Playa Gorgona**, **Playa Coronado**, **Playa Río Mar**, **Playa Corona**, and **Playa Santa Clara**.

The Interamericana runs near the coast along here, so it is easy to reach these beaches. From the Interior bus terminal on Av Balboa in Panama City, you could take just about any bus heading west along this part of the coast.

EL VALLE
Population 5600

Just past San Carlos, a road takes off inland into the mountains. After 28 km of winding up through the mountains, with good views back over the coastline, it reaches the small, pretty village of El Valle, known for its flora and fauna. The village is nestled into the Valle de Anton, which is the crater of a volcano with peaks rising all around it; it's a good area for hiking in the mountain air, a refreshing change from the city and the lowlands. With an elevation of 600 meters above sea level, the climate stays fresh and relatively cool.

Every Sunday, Indians come down from the surrounding mountain villages to sell their wares. This handicrafts market is known throughout Panama; Sunday is when most visitors come to El Valle, and there's plenty of pleasant activity. If you come on any other day, you won't see many visitors.

Information
IPAT, the national tourist office, publishes a free 10-page color booklet about El Valle. It's worth stopping by IPAT (in Panama City or elsewhere) to pick up a copy; it contains a good map of El Valle and its natural features, information in English and Spanish and plenty of photos.

Things to See & Do
On Sundays, the main attraction is the **handicrafts market**, where excellent quality fiber baskets and hats, woodwork, ceramics, soapstone carvings, flowers and plants (including orchids) and a variety of fresh produce are sold. It's held in the marketplace in the center of town,

starting at 7 am and running until late afternoon.

Also in the center of town, beside the church, a small **museum** is open on Sunday mornings from around 9 am until noon, with exhibits on the interesting geologic and human history of the valley; admission is US$0.25.

Near the center of town, beside the Río Anton, are **hot springs**, called the Pozos Termales. It's a beautiful spot; the large, shady grounds have trails and picnic areas. Scattered around the grounds are several small outdoor pools with warm water said to cure arthritis, rheumatism and skin ailments; in one of the pools, you can take a mud bath. Entrance is US$0.25; sitting in the pools costs US$1 for half an hour. It's open every day from around 7 or 8 am to 5 or 6 pm.

Signs with directions to the following are prominently posted on the roads.

El Nispero, a large, beautiful garden and zoo of exotic plants, birds and animals, is another enchanting place worth visiting. Tours take about 45 minutes to an hour, and cost US$2 (children US$1); it's open every day from 7 am to 5 pm.

El Valle's famous **golden frogs** can be seen in grottos at El Nispero, or at the Hotel Campestre. The **square trees**, El Valle's other unusual native species, can be seen up behind the Hotel Campestre.

Look up from town towards the west and you'll see the outline of **La India Dormida**, the sleeping Indian girl. Ask someone to tell you the legend.

The hills around El Valle are excellent for walking and horseback riding. Trails are well defined, since they are used all the time by the locals. **Piedra El Sapo** ('toad stone'), near La India Dormida, is said to have some of the most beautiful trails. Also in the same direction as La India Dormida, at La Pintada, are some unusual ancient **petroglyphs** representing humans, animals and other shapes difficult to decipher.

El Macho waterfall is one of the valley's most beautiful spots. The 35-meter waterfall pools at the bottom; it's surrounded by lush vegetation, and protected as an ecological refuge. The waterfall is on the road to La Mesa village, about 500 meters past the Doña Chabela bridge. **Las Mozas** is another beautiful waterfall.

Organized Tours

Day tours coming from Panama City are offered by several companies, including Eco-Tours (☎ 263-3077), Iguana Tours (☎ 226-8738), Panama Paradise (☎ 269-9861) and others.

Aventuras Panamá (☎ 260-0044) offers the 'Canopy Tour,' where you can ascend into the forest canopy in the ecological refuge at El Macho waterfall for a view of the forest canopy, traveling from tree to tree and from platform to platform by a network of cables (you sit in a harness). The tour involves picking you up in Panama City, traveling to El Valle, a one-hour forest walk to the site, the tour through the canopy, descending by rappelling and then visiting other sights around El Valle before returning to the city.

Places to Stay & Eat

You can get from Panama City to El Valle in 2½ hours, so it's a manageable day trip, but the place is so idyllic, you may want to stay over.

For backpackers there's a hostel, the *Cabañas-Hostal Valle Chiquito* (☎ 236-4632), but it's rather remote: five km before you reach El Valle, you'll see a sign pointing down a steep dirt road heading off to the right, saying the hostel is five km by 4WD ('4×4') vehicle.

More accessible, the *Hotel El Greco* (☎ 983-6149), on your right as you enter the town, offers rooms for US$19.50.

Cabañas Las Mozas (☎ 983-6071) and *Cabañas Potosí* (☎ 983-6181) each offer cabins (small houses) where you can fit several people and do your own cooking; the cost is around US$30 or US$35 per night.

Hotel Campestre (☎ 983-6146) is the luxury place to stay in El Valle, with single/double rooms for US$45/50, including breakfast. The large grounds are home to

El Valle's famous square-trunked trees, and there's also a grotto with golden frogs.

In town, there's a restaurant opposite the marketplace.

Getting There & Away
From Panama City, buses to El Valle depart from the Interior bus station hourly from 7 am to 7 pm (123 km, 2½ hours). Or you can get to San Carlos on any bus heading west from Panama City, and take a bus up the hill from there (every half-hour from 6 am to 6:30 pm, 45 minutes).

Another way to come to El Valle is on a tour from Panama City.

Getting Around
The center of town is small, but many of El Valle's attractions are a distance from the center. If you have your own vehicle and the IPAT brochure with a map of the town, you can find all the places yourself – signs point the way. If you have plenty of time and like walking, this is a great way to get around, too.

Otherwise, horses and bicycles are available for rent, and there are taxis. Most of the locals get around by bicycle.

ISLA TABOGA
About 20 km offshore and an hour's ferry ride from Panama City, Taboga is a small, peaceful island with a good beach and swimming, and an attractive village with only one narrow road, like a footpath, with no traffic. It is known as the Island of Flowers, because at certain times of the year it is covered with sweet-smelling blossoms, the aroma filling the air. Taboga is a favorite retreat from the city.

Taboga has a long history. It was settled by the Spanish in 1515, just two years after Balboa first sighted the Pacific, and before Panama City was built. The village of Taboga has a small church, said to be the second oldest in the Western Hemisphere; the island's graveyard dates back to the 16th century.

The island has a sheltered deep-water port and it was from here that Pizarro took off for Peru in 1524. Ships coming from South America anchored at this port during the colonial era; at that time, before the mainland port was built, the large tidal variations meant that ships could not anchor too close to the mainland.

Taboga also saw its share of piracy; Henry Morgan visited the island after sacking Panama City in 1671.

El Morro, the small island in front of the Hotel Taboga, is joined to Isla Taboga at low tide. In the 1860s it was the headquarters of the Pacific Steamship Navigation Company. The ruins of some of the walls and the wharf can still be seen, though no buildings remain. Some of the company workers are buried in a small cemetery there.

Information
INRENARE (☎ 250-2082) has an office on Taboga near the ferry dock, open Monday to Friday, 8 am to 4 pm. It has information on the island's natural features, good snorkeling spots and a big topographical map.

Things to See & Do
Most people come to Taboga to go to the beach. There are fine beaches going in either direction from the ferry dock. All the beaches are free to visit. Many visitors head straight for the Hotel Taboga, to your right as you walk off the ferry dock; the hotel faces onto the island's most popular beach, arcing between Taboga and the tiny Isla El Morro. A day entrance fee of US$5 includes food and beverages at the hotel restaurant, dressing room and showers, use of the large garden grounds, and they also rent paddle boats, beach umbrellas, hammocks, mats, snorkeling and diving gear and the like. There's no need to pay the hotel simply to use the beach, however; from the entrance to the hotel, you can get to the beach by going down between the little restaurants.

On weekends, when most people visit Taboga, small boats will take you around the island to see it from all sides and to reach some good snorkeling spots. There are some caves on the island's west side, rumored (of course) to hold golden treasure left there by pirates. During the week, when the small boats aren't taking people around, you can still snorkel around Isla El Morro, and see some large fish and other interesting things.

The **old church** in Taboga village is worth visiting. Even if it's closed, you can probably find someone to get the key for you. There's some beautiful old artwork inside.

Also interesting is the **shell house** ('La Concha'), where the friendly old fisherman, shell diver and artist Jesús Heballo has spent years decorating the outside of his house with shells he collected when diving. He has some beautiful shells for sale; when we last paid a visit to him, in 1996, he was 86 years old and still diving. Stop by for a visit.

For a fine view, you can walk up the hill on the east side of the island, Cerro de la Cruz, which has a cross on the top. Another trail leads to a *mirador* (lookout point) at the top of Cerro El Vigia, on the west side of the island; a large wooden sign posted near the dock shows a map of the island, including the trail. If you're not up to the hike, the Hotel Taboga takes visitors up to the lookout point by car for US$5 (or US$2, walking). There are many other trails for walks around the island.

A wildlife refuge, the **Refugio de Vida Silvestre Taboga Uraba**, covers about a third of the island – the north and northwest sides – as well as the island of Uraba just off the east side of Taboga. You can see the **pelican colony** on Taboga's far side. May is the height of the nesting season, but pelicans can be seen at any time from January to June.

Special Events

Taboga's annual festival takes place on July 16, the day of its patron saint, the Virgen del Carmen. A statue of the Virgin on a boat filled with flowers is sailed around the island, followed by a procession of fishing boats, motorboats, yachts and any other boats around at the time.

Places to Stay & Eat

There are two hotels on the island, but they are not cheap; most people just come over to the island for the day. The *Hotel Chu* (☎ 250-2035) has single/double rooms for around US$20/25; it's a simple old wooden hotel, but clean and well kept, with upstairs rooms with balconies overlooking the sea. The *Hotel Taboga* (☎ 250-2122, 264-6096) is larger, more modern and more expensive, with rooms starting at US$50.

The Hotel Chu has an open-air restaurant overlooking the sea, and there are a few other restaurants, little shops and snack stands around town. The restaurant at the fancier Hotel Taboga is more expensive.

Getting There & Away

The one-hour boat trip to Taboga is part of the island's attraction. The *Calypso Queen* ferry (☎ 232-5736, 264-6096) departs from Muelle (Pier) 18 in Balboa, passing under the Bridge of the Americas, along the Balboa port, and along the last part of the Panama Canal channel on its way out to sea, past the causeway linking Fuerte Amador to the three small offshore islands. Tuesday to Friday the ferry leaves Balboa at 8:30 am, departing Taboga for the return trip at 4 pm (3:30 pm on Friday). On Saturday, Sunday and holidays it departs Balboa at 7:45 am, 10:30 am and 4:30 pm, and Taboga at 9 am, 3 pm and 5:45 pm. There's no service on Monday. The ferry costs US$2.50 one way, US$5 roundtrip, half price for children. Phone to check the schedule.

Argo Tours (☎ 228-6069) operates two ferries to the island: the 200-passenger MV *Isla Morada*, and the 600-passenger MV *Fantasia del Mar*. Ferries depart from Panama City's Muelle 18 Monday to Friday at 8:30 am and 3 pm, returning from the island at 10 am and 4:30 pm. On Saturdays and Sundays, the boats depart Muelle 18 at 8:30 am, 11:30 am and 4 pm, returning from Taboga at 10 am, 2 pm and 5 pm. Cost is US$3 one way, US$6 roundtrip.

To get to Muelle 18, take one of the squat little Balboa buses leaving from Plaza Cinco de Mayo.

PANAMA

ARCHIPIÉLAGO DE LAS PERLAS & ISLA CONTADORA

The archipelago, about 70 km out from Panama City, is named for the large pearls that were once found in its waters.

Contadora is the best known island of the group and the easiest to get to. It is a lovely island with white-sand beaches, turquoise waters, excellent fishing and a luxury resort, the *Hotel Contadora Resort & Casino* (☎ 227-2904).

Getting There & Away

The resort on Contadora is expensive, so if you want to visit Contadora you may want to make it a day trip. There may be a boat from Panama City; check with the tourist office. The journey takes three hours. Otherwise, you can fly to the island with Aeroperlas (☎ 269-4555), which has daily roundtrip flights going in the morning and returning in the afternoon for US$48.

Veraguas Province

Continuing west from Panama City's beachy suburbs, the Interamericana cuts inland and passes through several small towns, including Penonomé and Aguadulce, before reaching **Divisa**, 214 km west of Panama City. Divisa is a small crossroads town and it's here that you turn south if you're heading for the Península de Azuero.

Thirty-five km west from Divisa, and 248 km from Panama City, is **Santiago**, Panama's fourth largest city (population 50,000) and capital of the large province of Veraguas – the only province with both Pacific and Caribbean Coasts. Santiago is a pleasant town, but unremarkable. The town center is about one km from the highway. Most of the town's commerce and services, including shops, banks, fuel stations, places to eat and a few hotels, are along Av Central, the town's main drag.

Continuing west towards David you will start to see Guaymí people; the Guaymí women are easy to recognize, dressed in long, loose, brightly colored dresses. Along the highway you'll pass roadside stands where these dresses are for sale, along with wide, beaded necklaces. The villages of **Tolé** and **San Félix**, each a kilometer or two north off the Interamericana, are home to many Guaymí people.

Colón & Around

Colón is the capital of the large province of the same name, which extends over 200 km along the Caribbean Coast from Veraguas Province in the west to San Blas Province in the east. Most of the region is undeveloped and inaccessible.

It's probably best to avoid the city of Colón, but Portobelo and Fuerte San Lorenzo, two historic Spanish fortresses, are impressive and worth seeing. On the way to Portobelo are a couple of good beaches. Just beyond it, Isla Grande, a beautiful little island just off the coast, is an idyllic retreat busy on weekends and holidays; the rest of the time it's isolated, quiet and peaceful.

All of these places can easily be visited as day trips from Panama City, only a couple of hours away across the isthmus.

COLÓN

Population 59,000

On the Caribbean entrance to the Panama Canal, Colón is Panama's second largest city and the country's principal Caribbean port.

Warning Colón is a dangerous slum, and if you don't have a pressing reason to come here, do yourself a favor and give it a miss. Crime is a serious problem. It is not only possible but likely that you will get mugged, even in broad daylight, and even if you take every precaution. If you must go somewhere in Colón, take a taxi from the bus station; don't walk.

History

Colón was founded in 1850 as the Caribbean terminus of the Panama Railroad. It was originally called Aspinwall, after a builder who worked on the railway.

Around the turn of the century, when controversy over independence from Colombia was intense, the city was burned down in a political melee. It was rebuilt in a turn-of-the-century French style, as the French were the dominant force in the area at that time. They were attempting to start construction on the canal, and the port of Cristóbal was built to accommodate materials shipped in for the project. Many of the wooden houses built at the turn of the century are now on the verge of collapsing, with people still living inside them.

Things to See & Do

There are only a few reasons travelers would want to come to Colón.

One reason would be the **Zona Libre** (Free Zone), a huge fortress-like walled-off area of giant international stores selling things at duty-free prices; it's the world's second largest duty-free port after Hong Kong. However, most of these stores only deal in bulk merchandise; they aren't set up to sell to individual tourists. Many travelers have been disappointed. Nevertheless, if you want to enter the Free Zone, you can. When you enter you must present your passport, or a tourist card with official identification, at the security office. The Zone is open Monday to Friday from 8 am to 5 pm; a few shops are open Saturday morning, and the whole Zone closes on Sunday.

Another reason to visit Colón might be to catch a boat. The **Panama Canal Yacht Club** (☎ 441-5882, 441-6970) on Calle 16 in Cristóbal is a safe haven for yachties heading through the canal. It has a restaurant, bar, showers and a bulletin board with notices from people offering or seeking positions as crew, rides to exotic places, and passage through the canal, whether for the simple thrill of it or as a linehandler. Boats heading along the coast past the San Blas islands depart from the Coco Solo

pier; see the Archipiélago de San Blas section below.

The Gatún Locks are accessible by taxi, bus or private vehicle, but have no special provisions for visitors. You'll drive over them if you go to Fuerte San Lorenzo.

Getting There & Away

Bus The bus station is on the corner of Av del Frente and Calle 12.

From Colón to Panama City (76 km) there are two buses, the regular and the express, but there's not much difference in price or travel time between the two. The regular buses depart every day, every 20 minutes from 4 am to 1 am (two hours). The express buses have air con and depart every 20 minutes from 5 am to 9 pm Monday to Friday, hourly on Saturday; they don't run on Sunday (1¾ hours).

Buses to Portobelo depart from Colón every day, hourly from 6:30 am to 6 pm (44 km, one hour). These same buses can be boarded at Sabanitas, the turnoff for Portobelo, thus avoiding a trip into Colón.

Train Check with IPAT, the national tourist office, to see if the passenger train passing alongside the Panama Canal has been restarted. Cargo trains still ply the route.

FUERTE SAN LORENZO

On a promontory to the west of the canal, Fuerte (fort) San Lorenzo is perched at the mouth of the Río Chagres. It was on this river that the British pirate Henry Morgan gained access to the interior in 1671, enabling him to sack and destroy the original Panama City, today the ruins of Panamá Viejo.

Like the fortresses at Portobelo that date from the same period, the Spanish fortress here is built of stone and displays rows of old cannons. A British cannon among the Spanish ones is evidence of the times when British pirates overcame the fort. Much of the fort is very well preserved, including the moat, the cannons and the arched stone rooms. The fort commands a wide view of the river and bay far below.

There is no public transport to Fort San Lorenzo. To get there, drive over the Gatún Locks and pass through the security gate of the US base, Fort Sherman, presenting identification to pass. Fort San Lorenzo is in a military zone, about 10 km past Fort Sherman.

PORTOBELO
Population 3300

Portobelo, 44 km east of Colón, is one of Panama's most important historic places. The extensive ruins of Spanish stone fortresses erected centuries ago make for some interesting exploration.

There are no places to stay in Portobelo, but there are various little restaurants. Visitors come as a day trip from Panama City.

History

Portobelo, the 'beautiful port,' was named by Columbus in 1502 when he stopped here on his fourth New World voyage. It was the principal Spanish Caribbean port in Central America for around 200 years, to the 18th century. Gold and other treasure from Peru was shipped to Panama City and carried overland by mule. The goods were stored in fortresses at Portobelo until the annual trade fair, when galleons laden with goods from Spain arrived to trade for gold and other goods from the New World.

British and other pirates made repeated attacks on all the strategic points of the Spanish treasure route; in 1739 Portobelo was destroyed by an attack led by the British Admiral Edward Vernon. In 1746 the Spanish gave up and stopped using the overland Panama route altogether, instead sailing the long way around Cape Horn to and from the west coast of South America.

Portobelo was rebuilt in 1751, but it never achieved its former importance. In time, it became a virtual ruin. Much of the outermost fortress was dismantled during construction of the Panama Canal, and the stones used in building the Gatún Locks. There are still considerable parts of the town and fortresses left, however, and today Portobelo is protected as a national park and historic place.

Information

The national tourist office, IPAT, has an office in the Alcaldía building (☎ 448-2073); it's open Monday to Friday from 8:30 am to 4:30 pm.

Things to See & Do

In addition to the famous fort and line of cannons (featured on Panama's tourist literature) the site extends outward with stone walls and other ruins visible for some distance if you look for them. The present-day town of Portobelo is built among the ruins of the Spanish settlement. Yet more fortress ruins stand on either side of the harbor entrance.

The other notable feature of Portobelo is its large colonial church, built in 1776. It contains a famous life-size statue, the Black Christ, said to have miraculous powers. On October 21 each year, the **Festival of the Black Christ** attracts hundreds of pilgrims from near and far, many dressed in the same royal purple color as the statue's clothes. The statue is paraded through the streets, people attach symbols to it in thanks for miracles performed and the celebrations continue all day and all night.

On the way to Portobelo, the black-sand **Playa María Chiquita** and the white-sand **Playa Langosta** are two attractive beaches.

Getting There & Away

Buses run between Colón and Portobelo hourly from 6:30 am to 6 pm (one hour).

If you're coming by bus from Panama City, take the bus heading for Colón and get off at Sabanitas, 10 km before Colón, about a 1½-hour ride from Panama City. Then catch the bus coming from Colón to Portobelo when it passes through Sabanitas. You don't have to go to Colón at all.

ISLA GRANDE

East of Portobelo, the road continues as a narrow dirt track until it reaches La Guayra, from where small boats go to Isla Grande, just offshore. This island, five km long and 1½ km wide, is remote and beautiful, with white-sand beaches, palm trees and crystal-clear turquoise water.

About 300 people of African descent live on the island, making a living from fishing and producing coconuts. Seafood and coconut milk are the principal ingredients of the food on the island, which includes *fufu*, seafood soups, *ceviche*, Caribbean king crab, lobster, shrimp, octopus, sea turtle, shad and corvina. The island has several places to eat, and a few places to stay. Facilities are available for diving, snorkeling and fishing.

Visitors primarily come to the island on weekends, holidays and for a number of annual celebrations. San Juan Bautista is celebrated on June 24, with swimming and canoe races. The day of the Virgen del Carmen is July 16, with a land and sea procession, baptisms and masses. Carnaval is also celebrated; they dance the conga with ribbons and mirrors in their hair, the women wearing the traditional, lacy pollera dresses, and the men in ragged pants, inside out and tied at the waist with old sea rope. Together with the dancing there are actions and songs about current events, and a lot of joking in the Caribbean calypso tradition.

The French built a lighthouse here in 1893, which sent red, green and white light over 100 km out to sea. Today the lighthouse still functions, but with just a white light visible for only 70 km.

Places to Stay

Places to stay on the island include *Cabañas Jackson, Cabañas La Cholita,* the *Posada Villa Ensueño* and the more expensive *Hotel Isla Grande*. Most of them charge around US$30 or more. The cabañas can accommodate several people, and they come with kitchens so you can do your own cooking. Camping on the island is another fine option. On the mainland at La Guayra is the *Cabañas Turicentro Montecarlo* (☎ 441-1917).

Contacting the island by phone isn't always successful. You can find a place to stay without an advance reservation at any time of year, except during busy holidays when Panamanians will have probably reserved all the hotels weeks in advance.

Península de Azuero

The Península de Azuero hangs into the Pacific in a wide bulge. This area, settled by the Spanish in the 16th century, maintained many Spanish colonial traditions for centuries due to its relative isolation.

Today the region has an economy based on agriculture, but is primarily known for its many traditional festivals and handicrafts. The intricate pollera dress is produced in this region. The region is also known for its excellent beaches.

Parts of the peninsula are still as isolated as they ever were, but a paved road now serves much of the eastern and southern area. Turning south from the Interamericana at Divisa, the road passes through Chitré, capital of Herrera Province, and Las Tablas, capital of Los Santos Province. If you want to stay on the peninsula, Chitré has the most facilities for travelers.

Many other small towns are dotted around the peninsula where they were founded by the Spanish four centuries ago, and are not much bigger than they were then. Most still have their original, well-preserved colonial churches.

National Parks & Wildlife Refuges

The **Humboldt Ecological Station**, at Playa Agallito near Chitré, is a research center specializing in migratory birds; you're welcome to visit.

In the northeast part of the peninsula, near Parita and Chitré, the 8000-hectare **Parque Nacional Sarigua** protects an unusual and eerie tropical desert, where a significant pre-Columbian archaeological site has been preserved (you can visit it). Salt water covers much of the park from around July to October; during the dry season, it's so dry that there can be sandstorms. The park is just a 15-minute drive from Chitré, but it feels like a remote other world.

The **Refugio de Vida Silvestre Cenegón del Mangle**, near Parita, protects a mangrove forest at the mouths of the

PANAMA

Parita and Santa María rivers, an important wildlife area and nesting ground for herons – its primary attraction is for bird watching. Small thermal pools are said to contain health-giving waters; they're too small to jump into, but people come to lift the water out with cups or small buckets and use it on their skin. The refuge is about a 45-minute drive from Chitré.

The **Ciénaga de las Macanas** in the Rincón de Santa María District of Herrera is a 2000-hectare wetland with a great biodiversity of flora and fauna, an important area for native and migratory birds. It's about a 35-minute drive from Chitré.

The **Reserva Forestal El Montuoso**, in the district of Las Minas, is more remote; it's off the Las Minas-Chepo road, but can only be reached by 4WD vehicle. Its abundant flora includes Panama's only insectivorous plant; also here are petroglyphs from prehistoric times.

On the southeast corner of the peninsula, the **Refugio de Vida Silvestre Isla Iguana** (Isla Iguana Wildlife Refuge) is an important reserve, not only for the iguanas the island is named for, but also for its coral reefs, forest and birdlife. The reef covers 15 hectares, contains 13 of the 20 eastern Pacific coral species and hosts over 200 species of fish. Swimming, snorkeling, diving, lazing on the white sandy beach, bird watching, hiking, fishing and camping are all possibilities here. The island itself is 53 hectares.

Humpback whales inhabit the waters around Isla Iguana from around June to November. These large sea mammals, 15 to 20 meters long, mate and bear their young here, and then teach them to dive. The humpbacks are the famous 'singing whales' that you may have heard on recordings; occasionally if you're diving here, you can hear their underwater sounds.

Isla Iguana is so remote that it gets few visitors, but getting there is not difficult. Go to the Alcaldía (town hall; ☎ 995-2154) in Pedasí (see Beaches & Balnearios, below); they will connect you with a cooperative of fishermen, who will take you on an all-day trip to the island for US$40 for the whole

lancha. If you want to go snorkeling, you must bring your own gear.

Iguana Tours (☎ 226-8738, 226-4516) operates skin diving and snorkeling tours to the island from Panama City.

The southwest corner of the peninsula is protected by the **Parque Nacional Cerro Hoya**. This is a remote area; you can drive in, but only during the dry season, from around December to April. Or you could get there by boat all year round, departing from Guanico Abajo, Tonosí; ask for Sr Roberto Diaz.

The IPAT office in Chitré has more information about all of these places.

Beaches & Balnearios

There are dozens of good beaches around the peninsula. Some of the best are near Chitré; **Playa Agallito** where migratory birds are studied (see below), **Playa Monagre** and **Playa El Rompío** (both served by buses from town).

Another fine beach is **Playa El Uverito**, near Las Tablas. There's no bus to this one, but you can hitch or take a taxi from Las Tablas.

At the southern end of the peninsula, **Playa Venado** is famous for surfing. It's way off the beaten track. There are cabins costing around US$8 a night during the week, or US$20 for a weekend, but they're pretty basic; you're probably better off staying in Pedasí, or you could camp out on the beach at Playa Venado. Playa Venado also has a bar and restaurant. A bus operates once a day between Playa Venado and Las Tablas; the trip takes two hours down a long dirt road. They say that it will take only 45 minutes if the new road ever goes through.

Pedasí (population 3000) makes a convenient base for visits to Isla Iguana and Playa Venado. Buses connect Pedasí and Chitré; the trip takes an hour. Pedasí's annual festival, the Patronales de San Pablo, is held on June 29. Places to stay include the *Residencial Moscoso* (☎ 995-2203), where rooms with fan are US$12 (US$15 with air con). The *Residencial Pedasí* (☎ 995-2322) has singles/doubles for US$16.50/22, all with air con.

Balnearios on the peninsula include the **Balneario Las Trancas**, two km from Las Minas, and the **Balneario Río Santa María**, near the conjunction of Herrera, Coclé and Veraguas, about a 25-minute drive from Chitré.

Special Events
Festivals on the Península de Azuero are famous throughout Panama for their traditional costumes and celebration. Some have survived intact for centuries; the 'dance of the little devils,' the 'penitent of the other life' and the 'peasant wedding' are dances and skits which show aspects of life in the times of the early Spaniards.

You can get details about these and other celebrations from any office of IPAT, the national tourist office. Some of the peninsula's best known festivals, attracting visitors from all over Panama, include:

January 20
    Festival of San Sebastián; in Ocú
February/March
    Carnaval; the four days before Ash Wednesday, in Las Tablas, Chitré, Villa de Los Santos and Parita
March/April
    Semana Santa; in Villa de Los Santos and Pesé
Late April/early May
    Feria de Azuero; in Villa de los Santos
May/June
    Fiesta de Corpus Christi; Thursday to Sunday, 40 days after Easter, in Villa de Los Santos; one of Panama's most famous celebrations, with medieval dances and traditional costumes
June 24
    Fiesta de San Juan Bautista; in Chitré
June 29
    Patronales de San Pablo; in Pedasí
July 20
    Fiesta de Santa Librada, Festival de la Pollera; in Las Tablas
August 15
    Festival del Manito; Fiesta Popular; Matrimonio Campesino; El Duelo del Tamarindo; El Penitente de la Otra Vida; all celebrated in Ocú with traditional costumes
September 24
    Festival de la Mejorana, Festival de la Virgen de las Mercedes; in Guararé with folkloric dance and music

October 19
    Founding of District of Chitré (1848); parades, historical costumes and celebrations in Chitré
November 10
    First Cry for Independence (1821); in Villa de Los Santos

Artesanías
The Península de Azuero is also known for its traditional handicrafts, some of which have been made in the same places for hundreds of years.

Some of the best known handicrafts, and the towns where they're made, include:

Polleras (dresses)
    Santo Domingo (near Las Tablas); La Enea (near Guararé)
Masks
    Parita; Villa de Los Santos
Musical instruments
    San José de Las Tablas (near Santo Domingo, which is near Las Tablas)
Ceramics
    La Arena (near Chitré)
Woven hats
    Ocú, Los Pozos
Woven mats, carpets and wall hangings
    Chitré

CHITRÉ
Population 24,000
Capital of the province of Herrera, Chitré is the largest town on the peninsula, and it makes a convenient base. It's also the home of some of the area's best known festivals.

Information
The IPAT tourist office (☎ /fax 996-4331) is a bit out of the way, off the road to Los Santos on the outskirts of town, in the Ministerio de Comercio e Industria building, beside Seguro Social. Consequently, not many tourists drop in, but it has useful information, including an interesting booklet on festivals and things to see and do on the peninsula. The office is open Monday to Friday, 8:30 am to noon and 12:45 to 4:30 pm.

In addition to being very friendly and eager to help, if they're not too busy, the

IPAT staff will even offer to go along with you to show you the sights of the area, some of which are much easier to find when you have a guide. They charge nothing for this service; these people are tops. Please give our regards to Sr Generino Barrios, a consummate guide.

On our last visit, IPAT was constructing a new office on the highway to Las Tablas; coming from Chitré you'll see it on your right, six km south of Chitré and two km south of Los Santos. When they move in their phone number will change.

Things to See & Do

Chitré has a fine **cathedral**, and an interesting provincial museum, the **Museo de Herrera** (☎ 996-0077), which is worth a visit. It's on Calle Manuel M Correa beside a little park; to find it, start from the cathedral, walk one block straight ahead, turn left and walk another three blocks. The museum is open Tuesday to Saturday from 9 am to 12:30 pm and 1:30 to 4 pm, Sunday from 9 am to noon, closed Monday; admission US$1 (children US$0.25).

In the vicinity of Chitré are the Parque Nacional Sarigua, the Monagre and El Rompío beaches, the Humboldt Ecological Station at Agallito beach and, a short walk or bus ride away, the village of La Arena, three km from Chitré, where you can see ceramics being made. The town of Villa de los Santos, where some of the peninsula's most important festivals take place, is four km to the south (see below).

Places to Stay & Eat

Halfway down the block directly in front of the cathedral, the *Hotel El Prado* (☎ 996-4620, 996-6859), at 3946 Av Herrera, is a clean, well-kept hotel with a 2nd-floor restaurant, sitting area and open balcony over the street, and an off-street car park. The rooms are back from the street so they're not too noisy; each has private bath, TV and telephone. Single/double rooms with fan are US$11/20, or US$16/26 with air conditioning.

Around the corner to the left heading away from the cathedral, the *Hotel Santa Rita* (☎ 996-4610), on Calle Manuel María Correa near the corner of Av Herrera, has a restaurant at street level serving Chinese and regular food, and clean, modern rooms upstairs for US$11/15.40 with overhead fan and private cold bath. Rooms with air conditioning, TV and hot water are US$14.30/19.80.

Pensión Herrerana (☎ 996-4356), 4072 Av Herrera, two blocks in front of the cathedral, is a clean but basic place with some of the cheapest rooms in town. Three rooms have private bath, the rest share facilities and a communal sitting area; there's private parking in the rear. Prices are flexible.

In the same block as the museum, on Calle Manuel M Correa about three blocks from the cathedral, the *Pensión Chitré* (☎ 996-1856) has rooms with private bath and fan for US$8/12.

There are plenty of restaurants in the district around the cathedral. The mercado is beside the cathedral.

Getting There & Away

Air Aeroperlas (☎ 996-4021) operates daily flights between Panama City and Chitré; cost is US$29 one way, double roundtrip. A taxi to the airport costs around US$1.50.

Bus Chitré is a center for bus transport in the region. Buses arrive and depart from a central bus terminal, the Terminal de Transportes de Herrera, about a kilometer from the center of town. To get from the center to the terminal, take a 'Terminal' bus from the corner behind the cathedral for US$0.10, or a taxi for US$0.75. The terminal has a restaurant open 24 hours.

Tuasa (☎ 996-5619) has buses departing Chitré for Panama City at 1:30, 2:30, 4, 5 and 6 am, then every 45 minutes until the last bus departs at 6 pm. Transportes Inazun (☎ 996-4177) also has buses to the capital, departing hourly from 6 am to 3 pm. Both charge US$6 (255 km, four hours). Other buses from Chitré include:

Buses to	Distance	Duration
La Arena	3 km	five minutes
Villa de Los Santos	4 km	10 minutes
Playa El Aguillito,		
Playa Monagre, and		
Playa El Rompío		20 minutes
Las Tablas	31 km	30 minutes
Pedasí	73 km	1 hour
Tonosí	48 km	3 hours
Las Minas	51 km	1 hour
Ocú	46 km	1 hour
Divisa	37 km	30 minutes
Santiago	71 km	1¼ hours

VILLA DE LOS SANTOS
Population 6900

Villa de Los Santos (often called simply Los Santos) is four km south of Chitré.

This was where Panama's first 'cry for independence' from Spain was heard on November 10, 1821. The small **Museo de la Nacionalidad** (☎ 966-8192), opposite Parque Simón Bolívar, has been established in the house where Panama's Declaration of Independence was signed. It's open Tuesday to Saturday from 9 am to 4:30 pm, Sunday 9 am to 1 pm, closed Monday; admission US$1 (children US$0.25).

The 18th-century **Iglesia de San Atanacio**, with a number of ornate and colorful 17th- and 18th-century altars, is also worth a visit.

The Parque de Simón Bolívar, with the museum and the church, is three blocks east of the Chitré-Las Tablas highway. Chitré-Las Tablas buses stop on the highway; Chitré-Los Santos buses stop on the plaza.

Three km from Los Santos, the Smithsonian Institute is excavating an archaeological site at **Cerro Juan Diaz**, where evidence shows people lived from around 300 BC until the time of the Spanish conquest. It's fascinating to see the archaeologists at work, unearthing pottery, shells and other items. You're welcome to visit the site, but you'll probably have a hard time finding it on your own. A taxi from the taxi stand behind the church will bring you from Los Santos for US$1.50. Ask the taxi to return for you, as there is no other transport out there in the boonies.

The anniversary of the Cry for Independence is celebrated in Los Santos on November 10 every year. Other notable festivals include Carnaval, Semana Santa, the Feria de Azuero and Corpus Christi.

GUARARÉ
Population 3500

The tiny town of Guararé, on the main road between Chitré and Las Tablas, is very small and there's nothing much to see. The single attraction is the **Museo Manuel F Zárate** (☎ 994-5644). Zárate was a folklorist who appreciated and tried to conserve the traditions and folklore of the Azuero region. The museum, in Zárate's former home, contains pollera dresses, masks, *diablito* (little devil) costumes and other exhibits. The museum is two blocks behind the church, about six short blocks from the main road (turn off at the Delta fuel station). It's open Tuesday to Saturday from 8 am to noon and 12:45 to 4 pm, Sunday 8 am to noon; admission is US$0.75 (children US$0.25).

The Festival de la Mejorana is celebrated in Guararé on September 24.

La Enea, a small village near Guararé, is known for the fine polleras made there.

Places to Stay

Just off the Chitré-Las Tablas highway, the *Residencial La Mejorana* (☎ 994-5794, 994-5796) is a large, clean hotel, new in 1994. The rooms are in great condition; each has air con, TV, telephone and private hot-water bath. Prices range from US$16 up to US$50, but the US$16 rooms are just fine. There's a restaurant here, and parking.

LAS TABLAS
Population 7200

Las Tablas is the capital of Los Santos Province and has one of the finest colonial churches in the area: **Santa Librada**, with its ornate gold-painted altar, has been declared a national historical monument. It's on the central plaza, in the heart of Las Tablas.

Also on the central plaza is the **Museo Belisario Porras** (☎ 994-6326), dedicated to this Las Tablas statesman who was three times president of Panama. The museum is open Tuesday to Saturday from 8 am to noon and 12:45 to 4 pm, Sunday 8 am to noon; admission US$0.75 (children US$0.25).

In the countryside a few kilometers from town, **El Pausílipo** is the former country estate of Belisario Porras. It's said the name means 'tranquillity' in Greek; it's easy to see how the statesman would have treasured the tranquillity here. El Pausílipo and the grounds around it are open Tuesday to Saturday from 9 am to 4 pm, Sunday 8 am to noon; admission is free, but you can make a donation.

Las Tablas hosts annual festivals including Carnaval and the Fiesta de Santa Librada, with its accompanying Festival de la Pollera.

The small town of **Santo Domingo**, about 10 minutes from Las Tablas, is known for its fine pollera dresses; polleras are also made in the nearby towns of **San José**, **El Carate**, **La Tiza** and **El Cocal**. The best beach in the vicinity is **Playa El Uverito**.

Places to Stay & Eat
Hotel Hospedaje Zafiro (☎ 994-8200), right on the plaza and opposite Santa Librada church, is an upstairs hotel – the entrance is around the corner from the plaza, on Av Central. It's clean and cheerful, with an upstairs balcony where guests can look out over the plaza. The nine rooms, all with private bath, air con and color TV, cost US$14.30/16.50 for singles/doubles, with larger rooms for up to five people also available.

Several little restaurants are found around the plaza.

Getting There & Away
Buses connect Las Tablas with Santo Domingo (10 minutes), Chitré (31 km, 30 minutes), Panama City (282 km, 4½ hours), Playa Venado (68 km, two hours), Tonosí (79 km, 2½ hours) and other places. There is no bus to Playa El Uverito; a taxi to the beach costs about US$4.

Chiriquí

Chiriquí is Panama's beautiful southwest province.

The giant Volcán Barú, Panama's only volcano, is protected as a national park and at 3475 meters is the highest point in the country. The flanks of the volcano, with rich black volcanic soil and a cool mountain climate, are home to a number of small farming communities including Boquete and Cerro Punta.

Chiriquí also has hot springs, beaches (Las Lajas is the best known) and opportunities for trout fishing, hiking, mountain climbing and bird watching. The Golfo de Chiriquí has a national marine park and a couple of islands accessible to visitors, Isla Parida and Isla Boca Brava.

David, Panama's third largest city, is the capital of the province and a major stopover point between Panama and Costa Rica; the border at Paso Canoas is 53 km (an hour) west of David on the Interamericana.

Both the highlands and lowlands of Chiriquí are fertile and productive. The province's most important products include coffee, citrus fruit, bananas, sugar cane, rum, vegetables, livestock, thoroughbred racehorses and rainbow trout.

Chiriquí Province is home to the Guaymí people. Guaymí women are easily recognized, wearing full, long, brightly colored dresses.

Chiriquí White-Water Rafting
White-water rafting trips on Chiriquí rivers are offered by several companies including Chiriquí River Rafting (☎ 236-5217 in Panama City, 774-0204 in David), which has a great reputation and does trips on various rivers all year round. Panama Rafting (☎ 774-2845) and Aventuras Panamá (☎ 260-0044) also do rafting trips here. ■

DAVID

Population 75,000

David is Panama's third largest city, capital of Chiriquí Province, and the center of a rich agricultural region. It has plenty of places to stay and eat. Many travelers stop here overnight on their way to or from the Costa Rican border at Paso Canoas. It is also used as a base to visit Boquete or Volcán, near the Parque Nacional Volcán Barú, and the islands in the Golfo de Chiriquí.

David is about halfway between San José (Costa Rica) and Panama City – about seven hours by road from either place.

While David's climate tends to be hot, it's much cooler at the higher elevations around Volcán Barú, just a short distance away.

Orientation

The Interamericana does not enter the town, but skirts around it on the north and west sides. The city's heart is its fine central plaza, called Parque de Cervantes, about a kilometer in from the highway.

Information

Tourist Offices IPAT (☎ /fax 775-4120) has a tourist information office upstairs in the Edificio Galherna, the building beside the church, right on the central plaza; a small sign is posted beside the stairway going up. It's open Monday to Friday from 8:30 am to 4:30 pm, and has information on the whole of Chiriquí Province.

INRENARE (☎ 775-7840, 775-3163) has an office near the airport, where you can get information and free permits to camp in the national parks. It's open Monday to Friday, 8 am to 4 pm.

Consulates The Costa Rican consulate (☎ /fax 774-7725) is about 100 meters behind the Hospital Mae Lewis, which is on the Interamericana; you'll recognize it by the flag in front of the house. Office hours are Monday to Friday, 9 am to 2 pm. Please give our regards to the elegant consul, Sr Gerardo Madriz Cortés.

Immigration Migración y Naturalización (☎ 775-4515), on Calle C Sur near the corner of Av Central, is the place to extend your Panamanian visa or get permission to leave Panama (if you need it because you've been in Panama for over 30 days). The office is open Monday to Friday from 8 am to 3 pm.

Post & Communications The post office is on Calle C Norte, a block behind the central plaza. It's open Monday to Friday from 7 am to 5:30 pm, Saturday 7 am to 4:30 pm.

Intel, for international phone calls, is a block away. It's open Monday to Saturday from 8 am to 9:30 pm, Sunday 9 am to 8 pm, with fax service Monday to Friday from 8 am to 4:30 pm. Calls to anywhere within Panama can be made from the telephone boxes on the footpath in front of the office.

Laundry Lavamática Crystal (☎ 775-9339) on Calle D Norte between Av 1a and 2a Oeste will wash, dry and fold your laundry in a few hours (US$0.75 to wash, US$0.75 to dry). It's open Monday to Saturday from 7 am to 7 pm, Sunday 8 am to 1 pm.

Things to See & Do

David's small **Museo de Historia y de Arte José de Obaldía**, is in an old two-story house on Av 8 Este, near the corner of Calle A Norte. It's in the former home of José de Obaldía Orejuela, founder of Chiriquí Province.

There's not much to do in David itself, but there are many good places to visit within about an hour's drive, including Boquete, the Caldera hot springs, Volcán, Cerro Punta and Playa Las Lajas. There's also the Carta Vieja rum distillery and Los Delfines (see Around David).

Ask at the IPAT tourist office to see if the medicinal sulphur springs, **Pozo de Agua Sulfurosa**, on the outskirts of David, are open yet. The springs are off the road to the Universidad Santa María la Antigua (USMA). Last time we asked, they told us the springs were on private property and

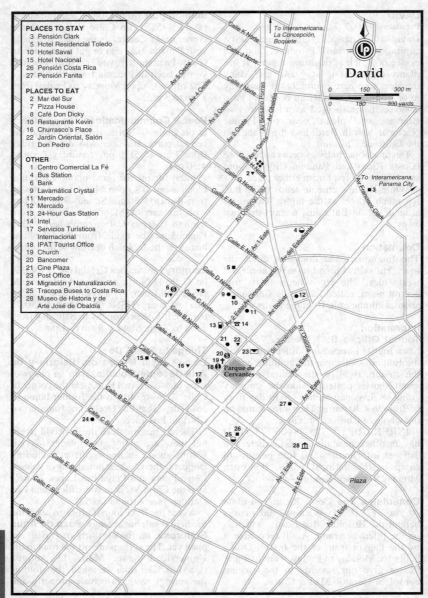

David

To Interamericana,
La Concepción,
Boquete

To Interamericana,
Panama City

0   150   300 m
0   150   300 yards

PLACES TO STAY
3   Pensión Clark
5   Hotel Residencial Toledo
10 Hotel Saval
15 Hotel Nacional
26 Pensión Costa Rica
27 Pensión Fanita

PLACES TO EAT
2   Mar del Sur
7   Pizza House
8   Café Don Dicky
10 Restaurante Kevin
16 Churrasco's Place
22 Jardín Oriental, Salón
    Don Pedro

OTHER
1   Centro Comercial La Fé
4   Bus Station
6   Bank
9   Lavamática Crystal
11 Mercado
12 Mercado
13 24-Hour Gas Station
14 Intel
17 Servicios Turísticos
    Internacional
18 IPAT Tourist Office
19 Church
20 Bancomer
21 Cine Plaza
23 Post Office
24 Migración y Naturalización
25 Tracopa Buses to Costa Rica
28 Museo de Historia y de
    Arte José de Obaldía

Parque de
Cervantes

Plaza

PANAMA

not officially open to the public, but that people were going there anyway.

Special Events
The Feria de San José de David, held for 10 days each March, is a big international fair. In Concepción, half an hour west of David, the Feria de la Candelaria is celebrated in the first days of February; the saint's day is February 2.

Places to Stay – budget
Central David has two old, bottom-of-the-budget hotels that are none too fancy. Several other places, all quite nice, cost slightly more. The best are a few blocks from the center of town – a five-minute, US$1 taxi ride, or a 15-minute walk. Except for the Fanita, all places mentioned have areas for parking.

Town Center *Pensión Fanita* (☎ 775-3718), on Calle B Norte two blocks southeast of the plaza, is a big two-story wooden hotel with no sign out front. It's very basic but it's cheap, with single/double rooms with shared bath for US$2.75/5.50, with private bath for US$4.40/8.80, or with private bath and air con for US$6.60/13.20.

Pensión Costa Rica (☎ 775-1241), on Av 5 Este near the corner of Calle A Sur, is another cheapie; singles/doubles with fan are US$3.85/6.60 with shared bath, or US$6/11 with private bath. Buses to Costa Rica depart from the Tracopa office next door.

The *Hotel Saval* (☎ 775-3543), on Calle D Norte between Av Cincuentenario and Av 1 Este, is simple but quiet and clean. It has rooms with up to six beds, a sitting area outdoors under a covered patio, and an economical little open-air restaurant in front selling breakfast and lunch. Singles/doubles, all with private bath, are US$8/10 with fan, US$10/12 with air con.

A Few Blocks Out *Pensión Clark* (☎ 774-3452) is on Av Francisco Clark, about a kilometer northeast of the plaza, the fourth house from the Av del Estudiante corner. It's a pleasant little family-run place, clean,

quiet and respectable, with six rooms, four with private bath, all priced at US$7.70. Ask for a room in the rear – each has a private balcony overlooking the lush green yard.

Pensión Don Juan (☎ 775-1895) at Av 3a Oeste and Calle G Sur, a block from the Mercado San Mateo and a block from Calle F Sur, near the fairgrounds, is an upstairs hotel with clean rooms with fan for US$6.60, or US$10 with air con.

Pensión Castrejón (☎ 775-4447) on Calle F Sur, is another good place. It's quite large, with clean rooms with private bath and ceiling fan encircling a shady interior garden courtyard with plenty of trees, a place you can wash and hang your clothes, and safe parking. Outdoor seats are provided for each room, or you can sit in the open-air covered sitting area and watch TV. Singles/doubles are US$10/15; larger rooms have up to five beds for US$25.

Places to Stay – middle
Hotel Nacional (☎ 775-2222, 775-2223), on the corner of Av Central and Calle Central, is a large hotel with a restaurant, pizzeria, casino, a large swimming pool with diving board and slide, and safe parking. The 75 rooms, all with air con, telephone and private hot-water bath, are US$15/21 for singles/doubles; a few dollars extra gets you color cable TV.

The *Hotel Residencial Toledo* (☎ 774-6732, 774-6733) on Av 1 Este, an upstairs hotel built in 1995, has clean rooms with air con, private hot-water bath, color TV and phone for US$16.50. Ask for a room with windows.

Places to Eat
Town Center The *Jardín Oriental – Salón Don Pedro* on the north corner of the plaza offers Chinese as well as Panamanian food, an economical 'meal of the day' for US$2, and some of the coolest air conditioning in town. It's open every day from 9:30 am until 10 pm.

A block from the plaza, *Churrasco's Place* on Av 2a Este is popular with locals for its good, inexpensive food. Downstairs is a covered, open-air restaurant; a slightly more expensive air-con bar/restaurant section is upstairs in the rear. Churrasco's is open 24 hours, every day.

Café Don Dicky on Calle C Norte is also open 24 hours. From the front it looks like a cheap open-air diner, but they make good food and there's a more attractive dining area at the rear.

A pleasant little place for an inexpensive breakfast or lunch is the small open-air *Restaurante Kevin* in the front of the Hotel Saval. Service is friendly, and meals go for US$1.50.

The small open-air *Pizza House*, three blocks northwest of the plaza on Av Domingo Diaz, serves inexpensive pizza and offers delivery (☎ 775-0680). It's open every day until 11 pm.

A Few Blocks Out *Mar del Sur*, behind the large La Fé shopping center on Av Obaldía, is known for its Peruvian food and good seafood. It's open every day for lunch and dinner.

La Cacerola, in the rear of the large *Super Barú* supermarket building on the corner of Av Obaldía and the Interamericana, is an unassuming cafeteria but it's popular with locals for its good, cheap food and probably its air conditioning too.

Mariscos y Steak House on the Interamericana, two buildings west of the Av Obaldía intersection, is more expensive but it has excellent seafood, meats and Chinese food. It's open every day, 11 am to 11 pm.

Entertainment

The cinema, *Cine Plaza*, is half a block west of the plaza. *Jorón Zebede*, half a kilometer from the Interamericana on the road to Boquete, is a popular disco for dancing on weekends, sometimes featuring live music. In town, *Copacabana* is another popular disco.

Getting There & Away

Air David's airport, the Aeropuerto Enrique Malek, is about five km from town. There are no buses to the airport; use a taxi.

Aeroperlas (☎ 721-1195, 721-1084) offers daily flights connecting David with Panama City (US$55) and Changuinola (US$24); double for roundtrip. The Changuinola flight goes three times daily; their weekday morning flight continues on from Changuinola to Bocas del Toro (US$34).

Buses within Panama The bus station is on Av del Estudiante, about 600 meters north of the central plaza. It has a small office where you can leave luggage for US$0.25, and a restaurant open from 5 am to midnight.

David is the hub of bus transport for western Panama and has buses to many places, including:

Boquete (35 km, one hour, US$1.20) Every half-hour, 6 am to 9 pm.
Caldera (20 km, 45 minutes, US$1.50) Six buses daily, 10:15 am to 4:45 pm.
Cerro Punta (79 km, 2¼ hours, US$2.65) The Volcán bus continues to Bambito (10 minutes from Volcán) and to Cerro Punta, half an hour further.
Chiriquí Grande (106 km, three hours, US$6) Hourly, 6 am to 9 pm.
Horconcitos (45 km, 45 minutes, US$1.50) Four buses daily, 11:15 am to 5 pm.
Las Lajas (100 km, 1½ hours, US$2) Six buses daily, 11:45 am to 6:30 pm.
Panama City
  Regular bus (438 km, 6½ to seven hours, US$10.60) Every 45 minutes, 7 am to 8 pm. Express bus (5½ to six hours, US$15); one bus at midnight.
Paso Canoas (Costa Rican border, 53 km, 1½ hours, US$1.50) Buses every 10 minutes, 5 am to 5:20 pm.
Puerto Armuelles (88 km, 2½ hours, US$2.65) Every 15 minutes, 4:30 am to 8:30 pm.
Río Sereno (Costa Rican border, 104 km, 2½ hours, US$2.30) Every 45 minutes, 7 am to 10 am, then hourly until last bus at 5 pm, via Volcán.
Volcán (57 km, 1¾ hours, US$2.30) Every 15 minutes, 5:30 am to 6 pm.

Buses to/from Costa Rica As well as the regular buses to the borders at Paso Canoas and Río Sereno, Tracopa (☎ 775-0585) operates direct buses between David and San José, the Costa Rican capital. Buses depart every day at 8:30 am and 12:30 pm from their office at the corner of Av 5 Este and Calle A Sur, beside the Pensión Costa Rica, arriving in San José about eight hours later. From San José, they depart for the return trip to David at 7:30 am and noon. The fare is US$12.50 one way.

You can buy your ticket when you show up for the bus, or up to two days in advance. The Tracopa office is open Monday to Saturday from 7:30 am to noon and from 2 to 4:30 pm (closing at 4 pm on Saturday), and Sunday from 7:30 am to 12:30 pm.

Getting Around
David has local buses and plenty of taxis. Taxi fares within the city are US$0.65 to US$1; fare to the airport is US$2.

Rental car companies in David include:

Avis	☎ 774-7075/6
Budget	☎ 775-1667
Chiriquí	☎ 774-3464
Hertz	☎ 775-6828/9
Hilary	☎ 775-5459
Mike's	☎ 775-4963

If you want to get off the beaten track, ask about renting a 4WD vehicle (known here as '4x4,' or 'cuatro por cuatro').

AROUND DAVID
The **Carta Vieja rum distillery**, just off the Interamericana west of David, gives tours. Phone the office in David (☎ 772-7083) for information, or just stop at the distillery; it operates Monday to Friday, 7:30 am to noon and 12:30 to 4 pm. To get there, turn south (left if you're coming from David) at the crossroads to Boquerón, as if you're heading for Alanje; the turnoff is between David and Concepción. It's about a 20-minute drive from David.

Also west of David, just north of the Interamericana between David and Concepción, the **Hotel Centro Turístico Los Delfines** (☎ 722-4029/30/32) in Boquerón is an expensive hotel (rooms are US$44 a night), but you don't have to stay there to use the facilities; for US$5 you can come and use the swimming pool, hot tub, sauna, gym, tennis courts, billiards, table tennis, and there's also a restaurant and a bar/disco.

GOLFO DE CHIRIQUÍ
South of David, the Golfo de Chiriquí is home to the **Parque Nacional Marino Golfo de Chiriquí**, a national marine park with an area of 14,740 hectares protecting 25 islands, 19 coral reefs and abundant wildlife. Attractions include bird watching, big game fishing, beaches, swimming, snorkeling, diving, and surfing.

Nearest David, **Isla Parida** is at the heart of the marine park. A boat to the island departs about three times a week from the port at Pedregal, a few kilometers south of David, and takes two hours to reach the island. The boat trip costs US$25 roundtrip; schedules and tickets are available from the Servicios Turísticos Internacional travel agency (☎ 775-4644, 774-0968) on Calle Central in David. The boat makes a roundtrip to the island only on Sundays; other days it stays overnight.

On the island, the *Hotel Cabañas Parida* (☎ 775-6006, código 6138, or 774-8166), operated by Canadians Sharon and Dave Simpson, offers cottages for US$40 a night; make a reservation before you show up, either directly or through Servicios Turísticos Internacional. They may operate a camping area in the future.

Isla Boca Brava is farther east in the gulf; to reach it, you must first drive or take a bus to Horconcitos, off the Interamericana about an hour east of David, then get from there to Boca Chica, a small fishing village about 15 minutes from Horconcitos. On the island, German-born Frank Kolher operates the *Restaurante Boca Brava* (☎ 775-6006, código 8731, or 775-4996, código 8731); phone him and he'll come in a small boat to pick you up at Boca Chica for US$1.

PLAYA LAS LAJAS
About 100 km east of David, several km south of the Interamericana, Playa Las Lajas is one of several beaches along this stretch of the Pacific Coast. With a broad white-sand beach, Las Lajas is most people's favorite.

PANAMA

This is probably the best place to stop over between David and Santiago, if you want to break the journey. There's a village, Las Lajas, with places to stay if you want to spend the night. One English bicyclist highly recommended a 'friendly no-name restaurant-pensión-laundromat' in Las Lajas village, with about six rooms for US$6 a single or double (but necessary to bargain) and good, cheap food.

Six buses a day run between Las Lajas and David (1½ hours, US$2); the first one leaves Las Lajas at around 10 am, the last at around 5 pm.

BOQUETE
Population 2800

Just 35 km north (one hour by bus) from David, Boquete is so different it feels like it's in another country. Nestled into a craggy mountain valley at 1060 meters, with the rocky Río Caldera running through it, Boquete is known for its cool, fresh climate and pristine natural environment. It's a fine place for walking, bird watching, and enjoying a respite from the heat of the lowlands. Boquete is a healthy place; it's claimed that several residents have lived to over 115 years of age.

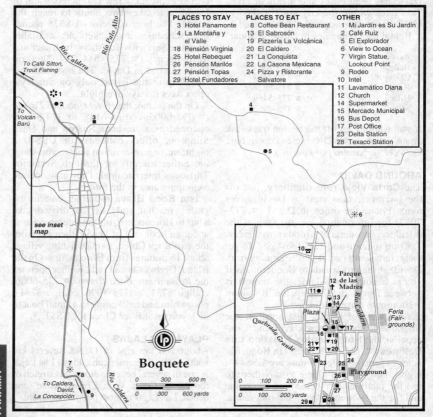

PLACES TO STAY	PLACES TO EAT	OTHER
3 Hotel Panamonte	8 Coffee Bean Restaurant	1 Mi Jardín es Su Jardín
4 La Montaña y el Valle	13 El Sabrosón	2 Café Ruiz
18 Pensión Virginia	19 Pizzería La Volcánica	5 El Explorador
25 Hotel Rebequet	20 El Caldero	6 View to Ocean
26 Pensión Marilós	21 La Conquista	7 Virgin Statue, Lookout Point
27 Pensión Topas	22 La Casona Mexicana	9 Rodeo
29 Hotel Fundadores	24 Pizza y Ristorante Salvatore	10 Intel
		11 Lavamático Diana
		12 Church
		14 Supermarket
		15 Mercado Municipal
		16 Bus Depot
		17 Post Office
		23 Delta Station
		28 Texaco Station

To Café Sitton, Trout Fishing

To Volcán Barú

Río Caldera

Río Palo Alto

see inset map

Boquete

To Caldera, David, La Concepción

| 0 | 300 | 600 m |
| 0 | 300 | 600 yards |

Parque de las Madres

Plaza

Feria (Fairgrounds)

Quebrada Grande

Playground

| 0 | 100 | 200 m |
| 0 | 100 | 200 yards |

Flowers, coffee, vegetables and citrus fruits are grown around Boquete. Navel orange season, from November to February, is a popular time to visit Boquete – the oranges here are known for their fine flavor.

Orientation

Boquete's central area is only a few blocks. The main road, coming up from David, passes along the west side of the plaza and continues up the hill past the church.

Information

The post office, on the east side of the plaza, is open Monday to Friday from 7 am to 6 pm, Saturday 7 am to 5 pm. Telephone calls to anywhere within Panama can be made from the coin phone outside the post office. For international calls, go to Intel, uphill and a couple of blocks west of the church; it's open Monday to Friday, 8 am to noon and 1 to 4:30 pm.

The laundry, Lavamático Diana, is on the main road, opposite and a little downhill from the church. They'll wash, dry and fold your clothes Monday to Saturday, 7 am to 6 pm.

Things to See & Do

There is a lot to see and do around Boquete. Several good paved roads lead out of town into the surrounding hills, passing coffee plantations, agricultural and cattle farms, gardens and virgin forest. **Coffee plantations** include Café Sitton, one of the largest with big processing barns, Café Princesa Janca and Café Ruíz. You can visit to see how the coffee is grown and processed; at Café Ruíz you can see how flavored coffees are made.

Boquete is a great place for **walking and hiking**. Walk around the roads and trails, up the river, or, for the ambitious, climb to the summit of 3475-meter Volcán Barú, in the nearby national park. There are several entrances to the park but the easiest access is from Boquete (see the section on the park).

Stroll around town and visit the **Parque de las Madres** with its flowers, fountain and children's playground, the fairgrounds and the river.

Mi Jardín es Su Jardín, just uphill from Café Ruiz, is a magnificent garden surrounding a luxurious private estate. You're welcome to visit; if you see a caretaker, ask permission. There's no admission charge.

El Explorador offers a large garden with picnic areas, hiking trails, fine views, classical music and a small open-air cafe. It's open only on weekends and holidays, from 9 am to 6 pm; admission US$1.

Orchids are grown in a greenhouse on a local farm. If you're an orchid buff, contact Frank at Pensión Marilós (see Places to Stay) and he can arrange a visit.

Cockfights are held in the center of town on weekends. **Rodeos** are held from time to time in Boquete and other towns in the area, put together by a 'rodeo club' of local farmers and cattle ranchers. They welcome visitors. Boquete's rodeo ring is near the Coffee Bean Restaurant, on the south side of town.

Other activities include **bird watching** (there are many species of birds here, including the quetzal), **trout fishing** in the river (bring your own tackle), and **horse riding**. Plenty of people around Boquete have horses for hire; you could ask the Coffee Bean Restaurant, the Pensión Marilós or the Pensión Topas to put you in touch with someone. Further afield, you can visit the Caldera hot springs.

At the entrance to town, where the 'Bienvenidos a Boquete' sign stretches over the highway, there's a statue of the Virgin, and a great view over the whole town and valley. Also here is the Coffee Bean Restaurant (☎ 720-3203), which offers a number of tours, including trips to the hot springs and coffee plantations, an all-day 4WD trip to the summit of Volcán Barú, camping trips on Volcán Barú, or longer trips by 4WD over the mountains to Chiriquí Grande or into the forest to see wildlife. English and Spanish are spoken, and the friendly owners, Nelly and Roberto, do everything they can to be helpful to travelers.

Special Events

The town's annual festival, the Feria de las Flores y del Café, held for 10 days each January, draws people from near and far.

Organized Tours

The folks at the Coffee Bean Restaurant offer half-day local tours for US$15 per person, and some interesting longer trips (see above). The owners of the Pensión Marilós can put you in touch with someone to take you around in a private car; if you get a group together, this is not expensive.

Places to Stay

Camping *La Montaña y el Valle* (☎ /fax 720-2211, net), a mountainside retreat 2.5 km from town, opposite El Explorador and overlooking town, has large, attractive 2.5-hectare grounds with nature trails and great views. Three tent sites, each on a concrete platform for protection from dampness, are US$7 each. Facilities for campers include hot showers, flush toilets, electricity, a covered cooking area, a 1000-volume Spanish/English library, and gourmet foods from their take-out kitchen.

Hotels Because of the cool climate, all the places to stay in Boquete have hot showers. *Pensión Marilós* (☎ 720-1380) on the corner of Av A Este and Calle 6 Sur, two blocks south of the plaza and two blocks in from the main road, is a favorite with budget travelers from around the world. It's a great place to stay – family-run, clean and comfortable. You can cook in the kitchen here, do your laundry (US$1 a big load), and they serve you free coffee each morning. Single/double rooms are US$6.60/9.90 with shared bath, or US$9.90/15.40 with private bath. Ask Frank for advice about Boquete – he's full of helpful suggestions (in English or Spanish) on where to see quetzals, how to get up the volcano for free, where to find the best food in town, and other tips.

Pensión Topas (☎ /fax 720-1005), on Av Belisario Porras, three blocks south of the plaza and one block in from the main road, is another great place to stay, new in 1995. It

has a swimming pool, organic garden (help yourself), a large garden grounds, a great view of Volcán Barú, and just five rooms. Four rooms have private hot-water baths and are US$14/18 single/double in winter (mid-May to November), US$18/28 in summer (December to mid-May), higher for two larger rooms. One room, with an outside, solar-heated bath, is cheaper at US$8/10 in summer, US$10/14 in winter. A wonderful breakfast is available for US$3.80. The gracious hostess, Lorenza, speaks English, Spanish, German and French.

Pensión Virginia (☎ 720-1260) on the central plaza is an older hotel with singles/doubles for US$8.80/18.50 with shared bath, or US$12.50/22.50 with private bath. They have a restaurant downstairs, and a piano and color TV in the upstairs sitting room.

Several other places to stay in Boquete are a bit more expensive. Opposite the Pensión Marilós, the *Hotel Rebequet* (☎ 720-1365) has attractive rooms with private bath at US$20/30 for singles/doubles. Each room has private bath, TV and fridge; guests are welcome to cook in the kitchen, play billiards or use the TV room. *Hotel Fundadores* (☎ 720-1298) on the main road charges US$22 per room.

La Montaña y el Valle (see Camping) has three luxury cabins, new in 1996, each with a well-equipped kitchen, spacious living room/dining area, separate bedroom, hot water bath and private terrace. The cabins hold three or five people; cost is US$55 for single nights, but US$40 per night if you stay three nights or more.

The *Hotel Panamonte* (☎ 720-1327) is another beautiful old favorite in Boquete, great for peace and quiet. The owners, the Collins family, deal with many visiting naturalists; rooms are US$38 to US$50.

Places to Eat

Boquete has many inexpensive restaurants to choose from. *La Conquista*, on the main road near the plaza, has typical food including *trucha* (local rainbow trout). Opposite this, the *Pizzería La Volcánica* has pizza and Italian dishes. *Pizza y Ristorante Salvatore*, two blocks south and one block east of the plaza, has a pleasant environment with tables inside and out; it's a little more expensive. There's a Chinese restaurant on the corner of the plaza and the main road.

On the main road a block south of the plaza, *El Caldero*, operated by a Frenchman, has a good selection of dishes to choose from, on a cafeteria line where you can walk along and see all the food; fish, chicken, meats, vegetables, European desserts and espresso drinks are all delicious and inexpensive.

On the main road opposite El Caldero, *La Casona Mexicana* has good Mexican food.

El Sabrosón, on the main road uphill from the plaza, is a simple place but it's popular with locals, serving typical food of the region.

The *Coffee Bean Restaurant*, at the entrance to town where the 'Bienvenidos a Boquete' sign arches over the road, is a bit more expensive than other restaurants in town, but it's an attractive place with great atmosphere, good food, a splendid view of the town and an English book exchange. The owners, who offer tours of the area, are happy to give information about the town and its environs.

The area's fresh produce is sold at the *Mercado Municipal*, on the northeast corner of the plaza.

Getting There & Away

Buses to David, and local buses that will take you around the Boquete area, depart from the west side of the plaza. A bus runs between Boquete and David every half-hour from 5 am to 6:30 pm. The 35-km trip on a good paved road takes an hour and costs US$1.20.

Getting Around

Boquete is a small town and you can easily walk around the center in a short time. Walking is a great way to see the area, if you have plenty of time. See also Organized Tours, above.

The local 'urbano' buses, winding around through the hills among coffee plantations, farms and forest, cost just US$0.50 and are a good way to get oriented. There are also taxis.

Getting around on horseback is another option.

LOS POZOS DE CALDERA

These natural hot springs are famous for their health-giving properties, especially for rheumatism sufferers. The springs are on private land near the town of **Caldera**, and have not been developed for visitors. The owners, the Collins family who own the Panamonte Hotel in Boquete, don't mind people visiting the springs as long as they respect the property, and take their rubbish out with them.

Getting There & Away

Caldera is 14 km off the road from David to Boquete; a sign marks the turnoff. There's a bus from David to Caldera, or you could take any bus between David and Boquete, get off at the turnoff, and hitch the rest of the way (though there may not be much traffic).

The springs are about a 45-minute walk from Caldera, where the paved road passes through town. In a 4WD vehicle you can drive up to within about a 10-minute walk from the springs. You'll need to ask the way; there are no signs. The people at the Coffee Bean Restaurant in Boquete sometimes make trips there.

PARQUE NACIONAL VOLCÁN BARÚ

The giant Volcán Barú, Panama's only volcano, is the dominant geographical feature of western Panama. Its fertile volcanic soil and the temperate climate of its mid-altitude slopes support some of Panama's most productive agriculture, especially in the areas around Cerro Punta and Boquete. On the volcano's upper slopes, the large trees of the lower slopes give way to smaller plants, bushes, scrub and abundant alpine wildflowers.

Volcán Barú is no longer active and there is no record of its most recent eruption. It has not one, but seven craters.

The 14,300-hectare Parque Nacional Volcán Barú provides ample possibilities for hiking, mountain climbing and camping, with many walking trails. A climb to the top, though quite steep, is not technically difficult, and no special climbing equipment is required. The summit is the highest point in Panama (3478 meters) and on a clear day it affords views to both the Pacific and the Caribbean coasts.

The park is home to abundant wildlife including puma, jaguar, tapir and the spotted conejo pintado. It's also a good place for bird watching, with a great variety of species; the famous quetzal is often seen here, especially during the dry season from November to April.

The park has entrances on different sides of the volcano. The easiest access to the summit is from Boquete, about 16 km from the summit, but it's a strenuous – some would say painful – uphill hike along a dirt road full of scree. One hiker suggested it would be better as a two-day trip. If you drive (or take a taxi, about US$5) as far up as you can and then walk the rest of the way, it takes about five or six hours to reach the summit from the park gate; walking from town would take about 10 hours. Still, locals say this is the best side from which to attempt the summit climb, not the Cerro Punta side.

Another park entrance is just outside the town of Volcán, on the road to Cerro Punta. The road into the park here goes only to the foot of the volcano, not far off the main road. The view of the peaks from this entrance is impressive.

The Sendero Los Quetzales, a trail connecting Cerro Punta and Boquete, is best done in the direction from Cerro Punta to Boquete. It's recommended you go with a guide, because the trail goes through deep jungle and it's extremely easy to lose the trail (and yourself). Guides are available in Volcán, or from the Coffee Bean Restaurant in Boquete.

AROUND VOLCÁN BARÚ

A road branches off the Interamericana at Concepción, and climbs steadily through the towns of Volcán (1500 meters) and Bambito until it stops at **Guadalupe** (2130 meters), just past **Cerro Punta**, on the west side of Volcán Barú. It's a good, paved road the entire way, frequently traversed by buses coming from David.

As in Boquete, the climate up here is cool and the air is brisk. The agricultural lands around Cerro Punta also have rich, black volcanic soil and are very fertile. It is a great area for walking.

As you ascend towards Cerro Punta, everything starts to look more and more European, with meticulously tended agricultural plots and European-style houses with steep-pitched tin roofs. A Swiss colony was founded here (one farm is named Nueva Suiza). Later immigrants included Croatians, and you may still hear their language spoken in the area.

This area produces not only abundant cool-climate crops, including vegetables, fruits, strawberries, flowers and coffee, but also trout, livestock and thoroughbred racehorses. You'll pass several *haras* (stables) where racehorses are bred, along the Cerro Punta road.

It's pricier to stay on this side of the volcano than on the Boquete side; this side doesn't have the extremely low-budget accommodations that Boquete has. Nevertheless, there are places to stay in all of the tiny towns, or you could camp in the national park or in the Parque Internacional La Amistad (PILA), which is more remote. Or you can easily visit this area as a day trip from David; buses run frequently between David and Cerro Punta, via Volcán and Bambito.

VOLCÁN
Population 8400

From Concepción, this little town, also sometimes called Hato del Volcán, is the first you'll come to, 32 km uphill from the Interamericana turnoff. Clinging to the flanks of the giant Volcán Barú, it's almost dwarfed by its namesake.

Orientation & Information
In the center of town, there's a fork in the road coming up from Concepción, with one arrow pointing left to Río Sereno (Costa

Rican border, 47 km), the other pointing right to Cerro Punta (16 km).

Before you reach this fork, on the left side of the road as you're coming from Concepción, you'll see a small building marked 'Guias de Turismo' (☎ 771-4755); the actual name is 'Guideco Siglo XXI.' These friendly people, a cooperative of nine student guides, offer a number of very reasonably priced tours (in English and Spanish) around the area. They offer half-price discounts for students, scientists, journalists, investigators, backpackers and groups. Students and backpackers might like to take advantage of a great opportunity: if you want to work with them, helping out, they'll offer you free food and a place to stay.

You're also welcome to stop in here just to ask information about the area; they offer a map and plenty of helpful information, including directions to places of interest, if you want to go on your own.

A similar associated tourism cooperative is based in a small office beside the Shell station, at the fork in the road in the center of town; it's marked 'Información al Turista' (☎ 771-4036). It, too, offers information, maps of the area, tours and guides.

Things to See & Do

Three km before reaching the town, on the west side of the road, **Arte Cruz** (☎ 775-7101, código 16) is where the famous artist José de la Cruz González makes woodcarvings, sculptures, furniture and other wood products, and etchings on crystal and glass; his work is known all over Panama. Visitors are welcome, and he is happy to demonstrate and explain his craft. Small items are for sale, or he will make you a personal souvenir in just a few minutes.

Just past Volcán, on the way to Bambito, is one of the entrances to the Parque Nacional Volcán Barú. A rugged road enters the park, soon becoming too rough for anything but a 4WD vehicle. The view of the volcanic peaks from here is impressive.

The ruins of the pre-Columbian culture at **Barriles** are about a five-minute drive from the center of town. The ruins are on private land, but the family who lives on the land are very gracious, allowing visitors to see the ruins and answering any questions about them. In 1996 they were beginning a small museum, with artifacts from the ruins. Major artifacts (statues, metates, pottery, jewelry) from the archaeological site here are displayed at the Museo Antropológico Reina Torres de Araúz in Panama City.

Other attractions around Volcán include springs, rivers, lakes (Las Lagunas), trout fishing, a botanical garden, coffee plantations (Cafetales Durán, with a million coffee bushes!), racehorse ranches and habitats of the quetzal and other interesting birds. Hiking trails include one to the top of Cerro Punta, another across the national park to Boquete (the 'Sendero Los Quetzales'), a 'Sendero del Tapir' to a place where many tapirs live, and a number of others.

On weekends, a market is held at the San Benito school; handicrafts are sold, as well as ordinary items at good prices. All proceeds go to benefit the school.

Places to Stay & Eat

Cabañas Reina (☎ 771-4338) is off the main road in a residential section of town. A sign marks the turnoff; go to the end of the block, turn right, and follow the road for about half a kilometer as it winds around. Six two-bedroom cabins, each with six beds, fully equipped kitchen, bathroom, sitting area and TV, are set around a spacious lawn. Daily rates are US$27.50 for two.

More places to stay are on the road to Río Sereno. Closest in, the *Motel California* (☎ 771-4272) is run by José Zizic, a friendly old Croatian guy who speaks English and Spanish. Clean cabins with private hot bath are US$20, and there's a restaurant and bar.

Farther along, a sign points the way to *Antojitos La Nona* (☎ 771-4284), 400 meters off the road. Behind the little restaurant are four clean cabins, each with private hot bath. A two-room cabin with kitchen, sleeping three people, is US$35 a night; three three-room cabins without kitchen, sleeping five, are US$40.

Farther along, the *Hotel y Restaurante Don Tavo* (☎ 771-4258), new in 1996, has 17 rooms for US$25 and up.

Next, you come to *Cabañas Las Huacas* (☎ 771-4363), where five two-story A-frame cottages, each with kitchen and hot-water bath, are set around attractive grounds. Prices range from US$40 for one or two people, up to US$85 for eight.

Farthest from town, 2½ km from the center, the *Hotel Dos Ríos* (☎ 771-4271) is a nice-looking hotel with a restaurant, bar and 16 rooms for US$27.50/33.

In the center of Volcán are a food market and a number of restaurants.

BAMBITO

Seven km past Volcán on the way to Cerro Punta, Bambito is barely a town at all. The only noticeable feature is the large Hotel Bambito. Opposite this, the Truchas de Bambito rainbow trout farm is worth a stop, with thousands of trout being raised in outdoor ponds with frigid water from the nearby river surging through. You can buy fresh trout here, or hire some tackle and catch your own.

Places to Stay & Eat

The large, five-star *Hotel Bambito* (☎ 771-4265, fax 771-4207, in Panama City ☎ 223-1660) is expensive, with singles/doubles for US$104/115, but if you want a real splurge, you couldn't find a more beautiful place for it. It has every luxury – swimming pool, sauna, hot tub, tennis courts, horseback riding, mountain bikes, restaurant, lounge and more.

If you can't afford to stay here, you can still stop in for a drink in the lounge or a meal at the restaurant, enjoying the beautiful surroundings and view. It's not cheap, but not as expensive as you'd expect; you can get fresh trout for US$8.75, a pasta dish for US$6.25, a delicious potato or onion soup for US$4 or even just a coffee or tea for US$1. On Sundays, a big buffet for US$12.50 is served from noon to 3 pm.

Past the trout farm, *Cabañas Kucikas* (☎ 771-4245, in Panama City ☎ 269-0623) has 17 spacious cottages set around large,

peaceful, park-like grounds with children's play areas, BBQ areas and the river running alongside (good for trout fishing). Cottages of various sizes, sleeping two to 10 people, have a complete kitchen and hot-water bath. Cost is around US$58 for two, but not that much higher for up to six people.

CERRO PUNTA
Population 6000

This small town, only a few blocks long at 1970 meters, is surrounded by beautiful, rich agricultural lands. The town offers spectacular views across a fertile valley to the peaks of the Parque Internacional La Amistad, a few kilometers away. This is a great place for walking.

Visitors come here primarily during the dry season, from around November to April, to visit the two nearby national parks (Volcán Barú and La Amistad) and to enjoy the beauty of the surroundings. During this time, quetzals are often seen right on the road; though they can be seen here all year round, they tend to live farther up in the mountains during the rainy season. The Finca Fernández, five minutes from town, is a good place to see quetzals.

Other attractions in Cerro Punta include Fresa Cerro Punta, where strawberries are grown, and Panaflores and Plantas y Flores, where flowers are grown; you can visit all of these places. Racehorse and prize cattle farms are also here.

The main road continues through Cerro Punta and on to Guadalupe, three km farther, which is the end of the road. Another road takes off to the west, heading for the Las Nubes entrance to the Parque Internacional La Amistad, 6.8 km away; the turnoff is marked by a large wooden sign. Cerro Punta is the end of the line for buses coming from David.

One km past Cerro Punta, heading towards Guadalupe, a sign points the way to the *Sendero Los Quetzales* (Quetzal Trail). Keep following the 'Los Quetzales' signs all the way through Guadalupe, to reach the trail. This trail goes six km to Boquete, crossing back and forth over the Río Caldera. Though you could probably start on part of the trail by yourself, go with a guide if you want to go all the way through to Boquete; see the Parque Nacional Volcán Barú section for more on this trail.

Places to Stay & Eat

The *Hotel Cerro Punta* (☎ 771-2020) on the main road offers 10 rooms, each with private hot bath, for US$22/27.50 for singles/doubles. Also here are a restaurant and bar.

Pensión Eterna Primavera (☎ in David 775-3860) is half a kilometer down the road to Las Nubes, opposite the Delca store. This is a much more basic place, with just five rooms; two with cold water are US$12.50 per room, and three with hot water are US$15.

At either place, it's a good idea to make reservations during the tourist season, from around November to April. The Pensión Eterna Primavera sometimes closes at other times of year.

Getting There & Away

A bus runs from David to Cerro Punta every 15 minutes from 5:30 am to 6 pm daily (79 km, 2¼ hours), stopping at Volcán (1¾ hours) and Bambito. You could catch this bus at the turnoff from the Interamericana in Concepción, if you're coming from Costa Rica.

GUADALUPE

Three km past Cerro Punta, Guadalupe is at the end of the road. It's a beautiful area for walking among the meticulously tended farms and gardens, and enjoying the cool climate. Last time we were there, signs were posted, saying things like 'Esteemed Visitor: We are making all Guadalupe a garden – please don't pick the flowers.' The little community is full of flowers, and the agricultural plots curling up the steep, rich hillsides are as beautiful as any garden in the world.

Places to Stay & Eat

In the center of town, the *Hotel y Cabañas Los Quetzales* (☎ 771-2182, 771-4036, fax 771-2226, in Panama City, ☎ /fax 272-2384) is a 10-room hotel, new in 1996, with a restaurant, bar/lounge, cafeteria, bakery and pizzeria. Single/double rooms, all with private hot baths, are US$18/25, or US$30 for larger rooms. Operated in conjunction with Los Quetzales chalets (see Parque Internacional La Amistad), the hotel rate includes free transport into the rain forest of the national park, ponchos, boots, guides and horses.

A couple of other tiny restaurants are also in town.

Getting There & Away

The bus goes only as far as Cerro Punta. You can walk to Guadalupe from Cerro Punta, or take a taxi.

PARQUE INTERNACIONAL LA AMISTAD

This large, 207,000-hectare (2070 sq km) park, established jointly in 1988 by Panama and Costa Rica, has territory in both countries – hence its name, 'Friendship.' It also has territory in both the Chiriquí and Bocas del Toro Provinces of Panama. Locally, the park is referred to by its acronym, 'PILA.'

The park is known for its pristine rain forest and its abundant species of flora and fauna.

Most of the park's area is rather remote, in the Talamanca mountain range, but you can get there; it's probably this very remoteness that has kept the park so pure, and so full of wildlife.

On the Panama side, there are two main entrances to the park staffed with helpful rangers always on duty: Las Nubes (on the Chiriquí side, near Cerro Punta) and Wetzo (on the Bocas del Toro side, near Changuinola). Not only do rangers provide park information, they also conduct guided tours on interesting trails near the ranger station.

Both stations also have dormitories where you can stay for free, cook in the kitchen and use the showers; bring your own bedding and food. Camping permits are required to camp in the park; they're available for free at the park entrance stations, or from any INRENARE office.

At 2280 meters above sea level, the climate on the Las Nubes side is cool, usually around 75°F in the daytime, dropping to around 38°F at night. It's warmer on the Wetzo side.

Information

The INRENARE offices are in David (for the Las Nubes side) and in Changuinola (for the Wetzo side). The people at Los Quetzales cabins in Guadalupe, and the tour guides in Volcán, also provide park information.

Places to Stay

In addition to their hotel in Guadalupe, *Los Quetzales* (see the Guadalupe section) also has three chalets nearby in the park, at the border of PILA and the Parque Nacional Volcán Barú. The chalets are beautiful, each with a fully equipped kitchen and bedrooms, hot bath, fireplace, kerosene lanterns and large terraces. Best of all, they're out in the rain forest, a great setting for walking and seeing animal and birdlife. Here you experience the forest at its best – or just enjoy complete relaxation. Built in 1996, these cabins are famous all over Panama for making the rain forest accessible to visitors.

The chalets hold five, eight or 14 people. Cost for an entire cabin is US$90 per night (with off-season discounts), but individual rooms are also available, with access to the entire house, for US$18/20 single/double. If no one else is there, you'll have the whole house to yourself. These nightly rates include transport to get there, wildlife and trail guides for exploring the forest, horses, ponchos and boots. It's a great deal. All you supply is your food. It's a good idea to reserve in advance, especially during the dry season, from November to April.

Other park accommodations are basic. The park entrance stations at Las Nubes and Wetzo have similar setups: two dormitories, each with six beds (bunks), where you can stay for free. The price is certainly fine, but we'd encourage you to make a donation for the maintenance of the station. Bring your own bedding (a sleeping bag is fine) and food. Also here are a hot-water bathroom and a kitchen where you can cook. Otherwise, you can camp out on the lawn here, or farther into the park; you must get a camping permit, which the ranger here will give you for free.

Getting There & Away

On the Chiriquí side, the entrance station for Las Nubes park is about 7 km from Cerro Punta; a sign on the main road in Cerro Punta marks the turnoff. The road starts out good and paved, but by the time you reach the park, it's a rutted track suitable only for 4WD vehicles. A taxi will bring you from Cerro Punta for US$1.50 per person; some of the taxis here are 4WD pickup trucks.

On the Bocas del Toro side, Wetzo is accessible from Changuinola (see Bocas del Toro map). It involves first traveling by vehicle to El Silencio, about 20 minutes south from Changuinola (minibuses go frequently), then a 45-minute boat ride on the Río Teribe from El Silencio to Wetzo. The INRENARE office in Changuinola can help you arrange transport.

RÍO SERENO

At Volcán a road turns off and heads west for 47 km to Río Sereno, on the Costa Rican border. The road to get there is long and slow, though beautiful, winding through mountains; mudslides onto the road can sometimes occur during the rainy season.

The border crossing at Río Sereno is officially open every day from 8 am to 11 pm, closing for about an hour each for lunch and dinner. As this is not a major border crossing, don't be too surprised if hours vary. If you need to stay over, the *Pensión Los Andes* above the pharmacy is OK.

A bus connects Río Sereno with David, passing through Volcán on the way. The bus takes about 1¾ hours from David to Volcán, from where it's about another hour (or more) to Río Sereno. You can meet this bus at the crossroads of the Interamericana at Concepción if you're coming from Costa Rica, or you could catch it in Volcán. If you're coming by private vehicle, travel time will be shortened: about 45 minutes from David to Volcán, and another hour or so to reach Río Sereno.

On the Costa Rica side of the border, you can bus or take a taxi to San Vito, about a 15-minute ride (see Costa Rica chapter).

PUERTO ARMUELLES

Puerto Armuelles is Panama's second Pacific port, used mainly for loading bananas from the area's plantations. You can visit the banana plantations to see how the bananas are grown and packed for shipping. They're owned by the Chiriquí Land Company (☎ 770-7243, 770-7245), and cover much of the land around Puerto Armuelles. There are some good beaches just south of town.

Puerto Armuelles has restaurants and hotels. *Hotel Koco's Place* (☎ 770-7049) offers rooms for US$16.50 with fan, or US$27.50 with air con.

A passenger train once operated between Puerto Armuelles and Concepción, but now the trains carry only bananas.

Buses go to Puerto Armuelles from David every 15 minutes or so, from 4:30 am to 8:30 pm (88 km, 2½ hours, US$2.65).

Bocas del Toro Province

Bocas del Toro Province is bordered by Costa Rica to the west, the Caribbean Sea to the north, and the Cordillera de Talamanca and Cordillera Central to the south.

The main reason travelers go to Bocas is to visit the pristine islands of the Archipiélago de Bocas del Toro and the Parque Nacional Marino Isla Bastimentos. The archipelago, in the Laguna de Chiriquí just 32 km from the Costa Rican border, has nine major islands, 59 cays (smaller islands) and many even smaller mangrove cays.

More remotely, the Wetzo entrance to the Parque Internacional La Amistad, the large park shared by Panama and Costa Rica, is accessible from Changuinola; see Parque Internacional La Amistad in the Chiriquí section.

PARQUE NACIONAL MARINO ISLA BASTIMENTOS

Parque Nacional Bastimentos was established in 1988 as Panama's first marine park. Protecting various parts of the Archipiélago de Bocas del Toro, including parts of the large Isla Bastimentos (especially Playa Larga) and the Cayos Zapatillas, the park is an important nature reserve for many species of Caribbean wildlife. Its beaches are used as a nesting ground by carey, canal and green sea turtles; the abundant coral reefs, great for snorkeling and diving, support countless species of fish, lobster and other forms of sea life; lagoons are home to other wildlife including freshwater turtles and caymans; and there is still more wildlife in the forests.

You can get current park information from the IPAT office in Bocas del Toro, or from any INRENARE office. The aprk entrance fee is US$10. The diving operators and boatmen in Bocas del Toro are also good sources of information about the park and its attractions. As in all the rest of Panama's national parks, if you want to camp out anywhere in the park you must first get a free permit from INRENARE.

BOCAS DEL TORO
Population 5800

The town of Bocas del Toro, on the southeast tip of Isla Colón, is the provincial capital on the Archipiélago de Bocas del Toro and a pleasant and convenient base for exploring the Parque Nacional Bastimentos. The town, the archipelago, and the province as a whole all share the same name – Bocas del Toro. Isla Colón and Bocas del Toro town are often referred to as Bocas Isla.

Bocas del Toro is a peaceful little town of English-speaking black people of West Indian descent; there are many Spanish-speaking Latinos as well, making it practically a bilingual town. Guari-guari, a mixture of Afro-Antillean English, Spanish and Guaymi, is also spoken, especially by the residents of Isla Bastimentos, to the south.

Bocas is a great place to hang out for a few days. On the local islands and reefs are

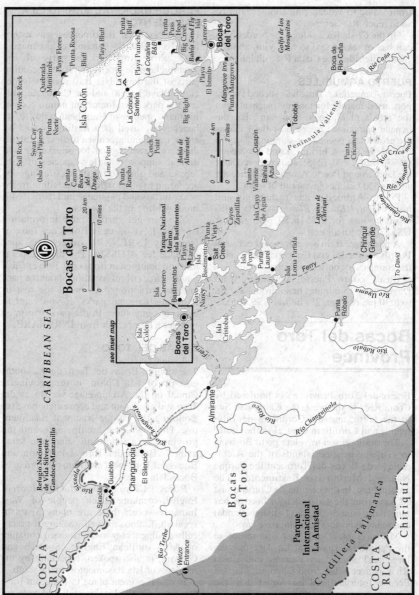

great opportunities for swimming, snorkeling and diving, lounging on white sandy beaches fringed by pipas and coconut palms. The town's relaxed, friendly atmosphere seems to rub off on everyone who visits; it's especially easy here to meet locals and travelers.

Relaxed as it is right now, Bocas is beginning to experience a tourist boom; land prices have skyrocketed in the last year or two, with foreign investors buying up land and preparing to build fancy resorts and the like. By the time you read this book, the town will probably have undergone a lot of changes.

Information

The IPAT tourist office (☎ /fax 757-9642) on the main road is a great source of information. They hand out the free magazine *Islas de Bocas*, available in both English and Spanish, which has maps of Bocas town, the islands and plenty of good information about the area. The office is open Monday to Friday, 8:30 am to 4:30 pm, sometimes closing for an hour at lunchtime.

INRENARE (☎ 757-9244) has an office on 1st St, open Monday to Friday from 8 am to noon and 1 to 4 pm. It's not really set up as a tourist information office, though if you have questions about the national park they can answer them; they have information here about all four of the protected areas in Bocas del Toro Province. If you want to camp out in any of the protected areas, you must first get a free permit from this or any other INRENARE office.

The post office and immigration office are in the large government building on the main road, beside Simón Bolívar Park. Behind this building on Av F, the Banco Nacional de Panamá changes traveler's checks; it's open Monday to Friday from 8 am to 3 pm, Saturday 9 am to noon. International telephone calls can be made from the Intel office on 1st St, open Monday to Friday from 8 am to noon and 1 to 4 pm.

Warning Unlike in most other places in Panama, tap water is not safe to drink in the Bocas del Toro area. Bottled water is readily available, though expensive – almost US$2 for a 1.5 liter bottle.

Diving, Snorkeling & Other Tours

Diving and snorkeling trips are offered by the Bocas Dive Shop (☎ /fax 757-9541) and Turtle Divers (☎ /fax 757-9594), both on the main road; Turtle Divers is based at the Mangrove Roots Shop, beside the park. Both offer full-day snorkeling tours to the Cayos Zapatillas for US$15, including lunch, a laze on the beach and a jungle walkabout on the island; this is the most popular trip. Diving trips cost around US$30 for one tank/one site, US$40 or US$50 for two tanks/two sites; PADI open-water and advanced courses are also available. Diving is still pretty virginal around here, with new dive spots being discovered all the time.

Both dive shops also offer basic gear rental, and other tours around the area. The Bocas Dive Shop offers boat trips upriver to see manatees, jungle walks on Isla Bastimentos, trips to waterfalls and to see red frogs, sailboat trips, beach picnics and camping trips to Second Beach (Playa Segunda) on Isla Bastimentos. Turtle Divers offer a historic tour to Hospital and Mangrove points, an 'Indian Tour' to a Guaymi village (both of these include snorkeling spots), and a 'Birds Tour' to Swan Cay and Boca del Drago.

Starfleet Eco Adventures (☎ /fax 757-9630) offers sailing, diving and snorkeling trips on a 29-foot catamaran, plus windsurfer and other gear rentals, and a sunset cruise. Happy Tours (☎ 757-9516) offers sailboat trips to various places.

If you have your own snorkeling gear (or if you rent it), you can also get the local boatmen to take you to many good snorkeling spots around the area in their small motorized *botes*. They know many good spots, and this can work out cheaper than the dive companies; agree on a price before you go.

Beaches

Bocas del Drago & La Gruta Across the island, Bocas del Drago is a beautiful, remote beach, one of the best on Isla Colón. The *Restaurant Joany* provides basic meals, and a pensión is under construction.

Halfway to Bocas del Drago, right in the center of the island, is a cave known as La Gruta; it's also called the 'Santuario Natural de la Virgen del Carmen' or the 'Santuario Natural de Nuestra Señora de la Gruta,' for the statue of the Virgen del Carmen there at the cave. The cave has stalactites, stalagmites and bats; you can enter it at one end, and come out the other end. A small village, La Colonia, is near the cave.

A bus operates from Boca del Drago to Bocas del Toro, leaving Boca del Drago in the early morning (around 7:30 am) and returning in the late afternoon, for people who live there and work in town. In Bocas del Toro it parks in front of the mercado, between the Hotel Las Brisas and the fire station. Check with the bus driver at about 8:30 or 9 am to ask about making a trip across the island to Boca del Drago; if a few people want to go, the bus will take you across, stopping at La Gruta on the way and bringing you back to town in the afternoon. It takes about half an hour or 45 minutes to get there; the roundtrip costs about US$2.25.

Other Beaches There are plenty of beaches around Isla Colón; there's no public transport but a taxi or bote will take you and you can arrange for them to come back for you at an appointed time.

A road skirts up the eastern coast from town. **Playa El Istmito**, also called **Playa La Cabaña**, is the closest to town; it's on Sand Fly Bay and it has not only sandflies but also *chitras*, a biting insect even smaller than a sandfly and with a bite even itchier. (Repellent is available in town.) This is not the most attractive beach; better ones are farther along.

Farther up the coast are **Big Creek**, **Punta Puss Head** and **Playa Paunch**, which is dangerous for swimming but good for surfing. A hole in the reef near La Coralina B&B is like a natural jacuzzi, and there's good snorkeling there. After you

round **Punta Bluff**, the road passes along the long **Playa Larga**, also called **Playa Bluff**, stretching all the way to **Punta Rocosa**. Endangered sea turtles nest on Playa Larga during their nesting season, from around May to September (see PROMAR, below).

Other good beaches are on islands nearby, especially Isla Bastimentos.

Bocas Sea Turtle Protection & Volunteer Projects
During sea turtle nesting season, from around May to September, ANCON (☎/fax 757-9226) offers a volunteer program for the protection of nesting sea turtles on Playa Larga, on Isla Bastimentos. Other year-round ANCON volunteer projects include patrolling the national marine park, reforestation in Bahía Honda on Isla Bastimentos, a demonstration farming project at Boca del Drago, and environmental education around the local area. You don't get paid, but they'll take care of your basic needs. Details are available at the ANCON offices here in Bocas or at the main office in Panama City.

PROMAR, a conglomerate of local businesses and individuals interested in preserving the natural area, also works to protect nesting sea turtles. They go up to Playa Bluff, on Isla Colón; they'll take you up to stay all night and work with the turtles (the turtles make their nests at night), or just for a short time to see the turtles. They also do other projects with marine life, and can use volunteers; contact them at the Mangrove Roots shop (☎/fax 757-9594) on the main road, next to the park.

Language Courses
La Escuelita de Bocas del Toro (☎ 757-9435, net), upstairs over the Todo Tropical restaurant/bar, offers language classes in Spanish and English. It's a branch of another language school, in Costa Rica.

Special Events
Bocas celebrates all Panama's holidays, with a few enjoyable local ones besides.

Annual events celebrated on Bocas and Bastimentos include:

May 1
> *May Day* – While the rest of Panama is celebrating the *Día del Trabajador*, *Palo de Mayo* (a Maypole dance) is done by young girls in Bocas del Toro and on Isla Bastimentos.

Third Sunday in July
> *Día de la Virgen del Carmen* – Everyone on Bocas island makes a pilgrimage to La Gruta, in the middle of the island, for a mass in honor of the Virgen del Carmen.

September
> *Feria del Mar* – The 'fair of the sea' is a festival and fair held on Playa El Istmita (also called Playa La Cabaña), a few kilometers north of Bocas town, for four days each September.

November
> *Fundación de la Provincia de Bocas del Toro* – Celebrating the foundation of the province in 1904, this day is celebrated by parades and other events; it's a big affair, attracting people from all over the province, and the Panamanian president also attends.
> *Día de Bastimentos* – Bastimentos Day is celebrated with a parade and drums on Isla Bastimentos.

Places to Stay

When we visited the island, there were only six places to stay on Bocas Isla, which was keeping tourism down to an unobtrusive level. With so few hotels, make a reservation in advance; sometimes visitors show up and find all the hotels full, especially during the busy tourist season from December to April.

A number of other places to stay are under construction; the IPAT tourist office will have current information. A couple of other places to stay are on Isla Bastimentos, a short boat ride from Bocas.

In Town The *Hotel Las Brisas* (☎ 757-9248, 757-9555, fax 757-9247) on the north end of the main road, formerly called the Botel Thomas, is a very popular spot, mostly for its terrace right over the water. Guests congregate here in the evening, making it easy to meet fellow travelers. The rooms all have private bath with hot water, but they are very

basic; only some have windows. Singles/doubles are US$16.50/17.50 with fan, or US$18.70/19.80 with air con; larger rooms for three or four people are also available. The hotel also offers bicycle and kayak rental.

The stately old wooden *Hotel Bahía* (☎/fax 757-9626) on the south end of the main road has an upstairs verandah overlooking the sea and an open-air Italian restaurant on the ground floor. Rooms for one to three people are US$16.50 with fan, or US$19.50 with air con; the newer rooms in the rear are quite pleasant.

Las Delicias (☎ 757-9318), also on the main road, is a simpler place with singles/doubles for US$5.50/10 with shared bath, or US$10/13.20 with private bath. Larger rooms with private bath are available for US$6.60 per person; all the rooms have fans. The hotel is upstairs over Las Delicias restaurant.

Hospedaje Sagitarius offers rooms with private bath, color TV and fan for US$14. *Hospedaje Alexandra* is another new, inexpensive place.

The *Bocabanana* bar (☎ 757-9425) has a few rooms upstairs over the bar, where beds (single or double) are rented for US$5 per person; as in a hostel, you may end up sharing a room with others. This place is for people who like to stay up late and party; the bar downstairs is the main party spot on the island for young international travelers, and it stays open every night until around 1 or 3 am. The bar serves breakfast from 9 am to 1 pm, seafood and snacks from 8 pm on.

Around the Island *La Coralina B&B* (☎/fax 757-9458) is on a hill overlooking the sea, four km north of town (about a 20-minute drive). In a luxurious formerly private estate, it's quiet here and close to nature – parrots and congo monkeys can be seen in the trees, and there's much other wildlife, various trails and a freshwater spring you can dip into. With six rooms, all different, it holds a maximum of 20 guests. Small single rooms are US$25, double rooms are US$30; larger rooms for US$50 and US$60

PANAMA

are quite luxurious. All prices include a continental breakfast. A taxi will bring you from town for US$4.

The *Mangrove Inn Eco-Dive Resort* (☎/fax 757-9594), a 10-minute boat ride from town (they provide transport), includes several wooden cabins and a restaurant/bar, all built on concrete stilts right over the water and reached by wooden walkways. A protected reef here offers good snorkeling. Each cabin has a private bath, and holds four to six people. The prices of US$110/85 for divers/non-divers include all meals, scheduled dives (or snorkeling tours for non-divers), and boat transport to/from town.

Places to Eat

Bocas is small but has several excellent places to eat. *Happy Italy Pomodoro*, upstairs over the Mangrove Roots shop, serves delicious Italian food with a pleasant atmosphere and a balcony overlooking the street. Pizza, pasta, seafood and lobster are the specialties.

The open-air *Restaurant Bahía*, in front of the Hotel Bahía, also serves Italian food. Both of these places are operated by Italians.

The *Todo Tropical* restaurant/bar on 1st St has a congenial atmosphere, with tables inside or outside under a palapa roof with a view of the sea. They serve delicious seafood, as well as inexpensive meals of beans, rice and salad; you can even bring your own fish and barbecue it on the grill. In the evening this is a pleasant place for a drink, with soft music playing and a relaxed atmosphere.

Lako's Place on Av H is another good spot for seafood, often recommended by locals.

The locals' favorite spot to eat is *Don Chicho's*, on the main road; it's actually named *El Lorito*, but no one ever calls it that. It's open from early in the morning to late in the evening.

The *Hong Kong* restaurant opposite the Hotel Las Brisas and *Kun Ja* on the main road are both good for Chinese food.

Just across the water on Isla Carenero,

Spice! (☎ 757-9364) is a good vegetarian and seafood restaurant, built half on land and half out in the water; they offer free boat transport between islands every half hour. There's also a restaurant at the *Mangrove Inn* (☎ 757-9594), a 10-minute boat ride from town, with a good snorkeling spot right in front.

Entertainment

The little cinema on the main road shows two different movies nightly, at 7 and 9 pm, for US$1.50 a pop (children half price). The *Bocabanana* bar is the party spot; it's open every night except Tuesday, till around 1 or 3 am. The *Restaurant/Bar Todo Tropical* is a more peaceful place for a quiet drink and friendly socializing, with a bar and tables inside or out under the palapa roof.

Getting There & Away

There are three ways to get to Bocas del Toro: from David by bus to Chiriquí Grande, and boat from there; from the Costa Rica border at Sixaola/Guabito through Changuinola to Almirante and by boat from there (see Changuinola, below); and from David, Changuinola, Panama City or San José, Costa Rica, by plane.

Air Bocas del Toro has a good new airport that's the pride of the town. Aeroperlas (☎ 757-8341) offers flights five times weekly connecting Bocas with Panama City (US$48). A weekday morning flight from David to Changuinola (US$24) takes on passengers and continues on to Bocas (US$10). All fares are double for roundtrip.

TACA is planning to initiate direct flights between Bocas and San José, Costa Rica; they will probably be operating by the time you are reading this book.

Water Taxi Between Almirante and Bocas, two companies, Taxi Marino Dela-Tours (☎ 358-3357) and Empresa Taxi 25 (☎ 758-3498) operate frequent water taxis (*taxis marinos* or *taxis acuáticos*). Their offices/docks are near one another in both towns;

you can easily walk from one to the other to ask which has a taxi leaving soonest. Both companies' taxis leave hourly, 6:30 am to 4:30 pm; the last taxi of the day, leaving Almirante at 5:30 pm, is operated by Dela-Tours. The trip takes about 20 minutes and costs US$3.

A water taxi route between Almirante and Chiriquí Grande will make a stop at Bocas if there are passengers wanting to go to Chiriquí Grande. Walk down to the dock at the '?' sign and tell them you want to go; they'll radio that there are passengers, and tell you when a taxi will stop by for you. The water taxi ride to Chiriquí Grande takes about an hour and costs US$6.

Ferry Ferries operating between Almirante and Chiriquí Grande stop at Bocas on Fridays and Sundays. These are slower and cheaper than the water taxis, and they carry both passengers and vehicles. See the Chiriquí Grande & Almirante section below for schedules and fares.

Getting Around

Bicycles can be rented from several places around town, including the Farmacia Chen (☎ 757-9280), the Todo Tropical restaurant/bar (☎ 757-9435) and the Hotel Las Brisas. Cost is about US$1.50 per hour, US$5 per half-day or US$7.50 per day. Farmacia Chen also rents small motorcycles for US$5 per hour, US$15 per half-day or US$25 per day, and jet skis.

Kayaks can be rented from Todo Tropical or the Hotel Las Brisas for around US$10 per day. Todo Tropical also rents snorkeling gear and fishing gear.

For getting to nearby islands, boatmen operate long motorized canoes *(botes)* from the '?' sign at the dock on the main road. Their services don't cost much and they'll take you not only to other islands, but to some good snorkeling spots.

ISLA BASTIMENTOS

A short hop by *bote* from Bocas del Toro, Isla Bastimentos is a beautiful island. The small village of Bastimentos has no roads,

only a footpath; there are a couple of places to stay and eat here. On the far side of the island, a Guaymi Indian village at Salt Creek is remote. Tropical forest covers the interior of the island; you can go exploring, but go only with a guide, as it's very easy to get lost. There's also a lake, called Laguna Bastimentos.

The island has beautiful beaches. You can walk across the island to **Playa Wizard** from town in about 15 minutes. Plenty of other beautiful beaches are also along the north side of the island, including **Playa Segunda** and the long **Playa Larga**, where sea turtles nest in season (see Turtle Protection, above). Playa Larga, and much of the west side of the island, is protected by the national marine park.

Places to Stay & Eat

Restaurante Ila (☎ /fax 757-9018) has a couple of clean, simple rooms. It charged US$7.50 for singles, US$10 for doubles, just off the restaurant. *Sylvia de Bryan* (☎ 757-9455) rents a room in the family home for the same price. Up on a small hill, with a view of the sea and islands, the *Restaurant & Pensión Calypso Club* was closed on our last visit; you could check to see if it's reopened.

The Bocas Dive Shop on Isla Colón does picnics and camping trips on Playa Segunda.

Getting There & Away

It's easy to get to Isla Bastimentos from Bocas del Toro; just walk down to the dock and ask a boatman to take you over. It doesn't cost much.

OTHER ISLANDS

The archipelago also has many other beautiful islands, all with good snorkeling spots. Just across the water from Bocas town, **Isla Carenero** has a village with a good vegetarian restaurant; it will soon be possible to stay over there, too, as some family cabins are under construction.

Cayo Nancy, sometimes called **Cayo Solarte**, has Hospital Point, named for the hospital of the United Fruit Company which was established there in 1900, when the United Fruit Company had its headquarters in Bocas town. The hospital was established there to isolate the diseased; the island briefly became known as Quarantine Island. This was before it was known that malaria and yellow fever, both rampant in the area at that time, were transmitted by mosquitoes. The hospital complex eventually included 16 buildings. It was there for only two decades, however; when a fungus killed the banana plants United Fruit was growing on the islands, the banana operations were moved to the mainland, the hospital buildings were dismantled and the forest reclaimed the site. There's good snorkeling in front of Hospital Point.

Swan Cay, also called **Isla de los Pájaros**, is on the north side of Isla Colón, 20 minutes by boat from Boca del Drago. A great number of tropical birds are here, and the island makes a popular excursion for birders. Nearby are **Wreck Rock** and **Sail Rock**.

The **Cayos Zapatillas**, south past Isla Bastimentos, are one of the most popular destinations for snorkeling and diving trips; the two cays, Cayo Zapatilla Norte and Cayo Zapatilla Sur, have beautiful white-sand beaches surrounded by pristine reefs, plus forests for exploring. The national park ranger station is on the south cay.

On the way to the Cayos Zapatillas, **Cayo Crawl**, in the channel between Isla Bastimentos and Isla Popa, makes a popular stopover. It has a restaurant, *El Paso del Marisco*, and good snorkeling; the island is about half an hour by boat from Bocas town.

CHIRIQUÍ GRANDE & ALMIRANTE
Population 12,000 & 15,550

A port town on Laguna de Chiriquí, Chiriquí Grande is a jumping-off point for trips to Bocas del Toro. Try to schedule yourself to pass through Chiriquí Grande early enough in the day so you won't have to stay overnight; this is easy to achieve. There are places to stay if you must spend

the night, but the town is not the most pleasant and you'll be much happier staying over in Bocas del Toro or David.

On Laguna de Chiriquí's northern coast, Almirante is the jumping-off point for water taxis and ferries to Bocas del Toro. Overland connections (bus, taxi and train) between Almirante, Changuinola and the Costa Rican/Panamanian border at Sixaola/Guabito are mentioned in the Changuinola section.

Getting There & Away
Bus From David, buses depart for Chiriquí Grande every 1½ hours from 6:30 am to 4 pm (106 km, three hours, US$6). The coast-to-coast trip over the Cordillera Central mountain range is a beautiful journey.

Water Taxi Service from Almirante to Bocas is frequent; see Getting There & Away under Bocas, above.

Between Almirante and Chiriquí Grande, direct water taxis operate frequently, taking about 1½ hours and costing US$8. They will stop at Bocas del Toro upon request.

Ferry Ferries carrying passengers and vehicles operate between Almirante and Chiriquí Grande, with scheduled stops at Bocas del Toro on Fridays and Sundays.

At ferry offices in Almirante (☎ 758-3731), Bocas del Toro (☎ 757-9560) and Chiriquí Grande (☎ 757-9767), you can buy tickets and ask current schedules. At the time of writing, the schedule was as follows:

From Almirante
    Tuesday to Sunday: departing Almirante at 8 am, arriving at Chiriquí Grande at noon. Friday & Sunday: this ferry stops over in Bocas del Toro at 9:30 am, arriving at Chiriquí Grande at 1 pm; another departs Almirante at 1:30 pm, arriving in Chiriquí Grande at 6:40 pm.

From Chiriquí Grande
    Daily except Tuesday: departing Chiriquí Grande at 9 am, arriving in Almirante at 1:30 pm. Friday & Sunday: departing Chiriquí Grande at 2 pm, arriving at Bocas del Toro at 5:30 pm, and at Almirante at

7:30 pm. Tuesday, Wednesday, Thursday & Saturday: afternoon ferry departs Chiriquí Grande at 1 pm, arriving in Almirante at 5:30 pm, with no stop at Bocas.

From Bocas
Daily: departing for Chiriquí Grande at 9:30 am and for Almirante at 5 pm.

Ferry fares on these routes are:

Route	Person	Vehicle
Almirante–Chiriquí Grande	US$4	US$33
Bocas del Toro–Almirante	US$1	US$10
Bocas del Toro–Chiriquí Grande	US$4	US$33

CHANGUINOLA
Population 47,000

Headquarters of the Chiriquí Land Company, who bring you Chiquita bananas, Changuinola is a small, hot, rather dusty town surrounded by a sea of banana plantations, north of Almirante.

Changuinola is mainly a transit point on the way to or from Bocas del Toro. It's also the access point for the Wetzo entrance to the Parque International La Amistad; see the Chiriquí section. INRENARE (☎ 758-6822), at Swiche 4, has information on the Wetzo entrance to Parque Internacional La Amistad, and they can help you arrange transport. The office is open Monday to Friday, 8 am to 4 pm.

Changuinola is the best place to stay overnight between Bocas del Toro and the border. The last water taxi from Almirante to Bocas del Toro departs at 5:30 pm; if you won't make it on time, break your journey here.

The border crossing at **Guabito** (Sixaola on the Costa Rica side) is open every day from 7 am to 11 pm; from either side, buses to the border run only until around 7 pm. See the Changuinola section above, for details.

Places to Stay & Eat
The best hotel in Changuinola is the *Hotel Ejecutivo Taliali* (☎ 758-6010), on the main road two blocks from the bus station. It's a good place to stay; the 15 clean rooms all have air con, private hot bath, TV, telephone and fridge, and cost US$28/33/35 for singles/doubles/triples. *Hotel Carol* (☎ 758-8731), a few doors down, has singles/doubles for US$11/14, all with air con and private hot bath.

The *Restaurant/Bar Chiquita Banana* on the main road opposite the bus station is a good place for a meal, with tables inside and out on the patio. Plenty of other places to eat are also along the main road.

Getting There & Away
Air Aeroperlas (☎ 758-7521, 758-6097) offers daily flights connecting Changuinola with Panama City (US$51) and David (US$24), double for roundtrip.

The 45-minute flights between David and Changuinola operate three times each day. The morning flight coming from David continues on from Changuinola to Bocas del Toro for an extra US$10. These are especially convenient, since the same route by bus and boat takes several hours and ends up costing almost the same.

Bus The bus station is on the main road, right in the center of town. Remember there's a one-hour time change between Costa Rica and Panama. Bus services include:

Almirante (21 km, 35 minutes, US$1) Buses every 20 or 25 minutes, 6:15 am to 9 pm.
El Silencio (20 minutes, US$0.50) Frequent minibuses, 6 am to 8:30 pm.
Guabito (border with Sixaola, Costa Rica; 17 km, 30 minutes, US$0.75) Buses every half hour, 6 am to 7 pm, going up to the bridge at the border, from where you transfer to another bus on the Costa Rica side.
San José, Costa Rica (281 km, 5½ to 6½ hours, US$8) A direct express bus operates once a day between Changuinola and San José. In Changuinola it departs from the bus station at 10 am; in San José it also departs at 10 am, from the Coca-Cola terminal. Coming from San José, the bus arrives in time for you to continue on to Almirante and catch the water taxi for Bocas del Toro.

Train The Chiriquí Land Company (☎ 758-8481) operates a train between the border and Almirante, taking Chiquita bananas for shipping, and offering free transport for the workers on the banana plantations. The train stops everywhere, loading bananas. You can take the train for free; it's slow, but the price is right.

The train leaves from El Empalme, just south of Changuinola, every day at 5 am, arriving at Guabito (the border) at 6 am. It then leaves Guabito, arriving at Almirante around 7:30 or 8 am. It leaves Almirante at about 1 or 1:30 pm, arriving back in Guabito around 4 pm. Finally it returns to El Empalme, arriving there at around 6 or 7 pm, where it spends the night.

Taxi A taxi from Changuinola to Almirante takes about 20 minutes and costs US$12; if you're arriving in Changuinola by bus or plane, you can often find a few other passengers to share the ride and cost.

A taxi from Changuinola to the Costa Rican border at Guabito takes about 15 minutes and costs US$5.

You can taxi all the way from the border to Almirante, passing through Changuinola, for about US$15; the ride takes around 45 minutes and saves a lot of waiting for buses.

Eastern Panama

Panama's eastern area is composed of two provinces. The San Blas Province is a narrow, 200-km long strip on the Caribbean Coast. The large Darién Province covers all the rest of the eastern side of the country.

Eastern Panama is sparsely inhabited, has vast wilderness areas and is not much visited by travelers; this is about as 'off the beaten path' as you can get.

ARCHIPIÉLAGO DE SAN BLAS

The islands of the San Blas archipelago are strung out along the coast of Panama from the Golfo de San Blas nearly all the way to the Colombian border. The tourist literature says there are 365 San Blas islands, one for every day of the year, but the Kuna Indians who live there say there are even more – 378 islands, which the Kuna people call Kuna Yala. They range in size from tiny, uninhabited sand cays, with just a few coconut palms, to islands with large villages with so many people that there's only enough room for their palm huts, and the narrow walkways between them.

The islands are home to the Kuna, who run San Blas as an autonomous province, with minimal interference from the national government, using their own system of governance, consultation and decision-making. They maintain their own economic system, language, customs, and culture, with distinctive dress, legends, music and dance. Given that their area has been in contact with Europeans ever since Columbus sailed along here in 1502, this is no mean achievement and has required remarkable tenacity, wisdom, foresight and practical organization by the Kuna, who still zealously guard their traditional way of life.

The economy of the San Blas islands is based primarily on coconuts and fishing. No one knows why, but the coconuts from the San Blas islands are particularly good, and many are sold to Colombia. Seafood includes fish, lobster, shrimp, Caribbean king crab and octopus; these are not usually sold for cash, but are traded among the Kuna. Other food crops, including rice, yams, yucca, bananas and pineapples, are not grown on the islands themselves, but in plots on the mainland, a short distance away.

Kuna women make the intricately hand-stitched, many-layered appliqué molas, the most famous of Panamanian traditional handicrafts. Buyers come here from many countries. It takes a long time and a lot of skill to make the best molas, so they are not cheap. You can find a tiny, simple souvenir mola for around US$5, but a high-quality mola can cost anywhere from US$50 to several hundred dollars. Molas are also sold in handicrafts *(artesanías)* shops and specialty shops in Panama City.

The Kuna women usually wear traditional dress: a colorful short-sleeved blouse with a red patterned mola sewn onto the front and back, a red and yellow printed scarf placed on the head but not tied, a colorful printed cloth tied around the waist to make a long skirt, dozens of bracelets on both arms and legs, and pure gold nose rings, earrings and sometimes necklaces. The heavy gold necklaces, which cover the whole chest, are not worn every day, but all the rest is daily attire. The women cut their shiny black hair short, and often have a black line tattooed down the middle of the nose. They are small people, but very striking in appearance. Kuna men usually wear Western dress, which in these warm islands often means shorts and a singlet.

Information
El Porvenir, a small island, is the principal airport for the small planes coming from Panama City. It also has a post office and telephone station.

If you want to take photos of people on the islands, bring plenty of small change. It is customary to pay Kuna Indians US$0.25 for each photo you take of them.

Things to See & Do
Swimming and fishing are good on the islands, as are snorkeling and diving in some places. You may be able to hire snorkeling and diving gear, though serious snorkelers should bring their own. Diving conditions are fine except in April, May and June.

In the area around El Porvenir, some of the most interesting islands are Achutupu (dog island), which has a shipwreck offshore, and Kagantupu and Coco Blanco, with good beaches; all are good for snorkeling or diving. Or you can visit the island where the Smithsonian Institute operates a research station for marine and nature research.

Places to Stay & Eat
If you want to make arrangements other than hotels to stay on the islands, you will have to ask the Kuna elders. One traveler suggested that you may be able to arrange to stay with a private family, which works out much cheaper than a hotel. The Kuna are a kind people, but they are very particular about what outsiders do on their islands.

Since there are no restaurants, each of the few hotels provides all the meals for its guests. The meals are usually based on seafood, with lobster a specialty, but other food is available. Hotel rates include three meals a day, plus a guide and boat to take you snorkeling, swimming, to visit neighboring islands or other activities.

Near El Porvenir, the *Hotel San Blas* (☎ 262-5410) on the island of Nalunega is the most economical hotel in the San Blas archipelago. If you like the simple life, this is a great place to enjoy it. The hotel consists of 10 simple but pleasant Kuna-style palm cabins with sand floors, served by communal showers, kitchen and hammocks. The daily rate of US$27 per person includes three meals a day and boat tours. You can stay cheaper if you supply your own food, but the food they provide is delicious. If you supply all your own needs and want to camp out, you may be able to string up a hammock there for as little as US$5.

Also near El Porvenir, the *Hotel Anai* (☎ 239-3025, 239-3128) on the island of Wichub-Wala is more up-market, with a swimming pool and rooms with private bath. The cost of US$55 per person includes three meals and boat transport.

Other places to stay are farther east along the coast. The *Hotel Kuannidup* (☎ 227-0872) on Kuannidup Island charges US$60 per person; to get here, you'll fly in to Río Sidra island. Also near Río Sidra is the *Hotel Turenega*, charging US$35 per person; bookings can be made through Aerotaxi for this and other hotels in the islands. On Kwadule Island, the *Hotel Kwadule* (☎ 269-6313, fax 269-6309) is more expensive. The *Hotel Ikusas* (☎ 224-9694) on the island of Ailigandí, halfway down the coast towards Colombia, belongs to the town cooperative society and charges US$50 per person. Eco-Tours (☎ 263-3077, fax 263-3089), based in Panama City, offers trips to the *Dolphin Island Lodge* on the island of Uaguitupo.

Getting There & Away

Air Aerotaxi (☎ 264-8644, 264-2950) and Ansa (☎ 226-6881) operate small planes (10-seaters or so) between Panama City and the islands. They depart from La Paitilla airport in Panama City every day at 6 am, arriving at El Porvenir airport at 6:30 am. Return flights leave El Porvenir at 7 am.

Though El Porvenir is the principal stop, many other islands in the archipelago also have airports, and your plane may stop at a number of them while loading and unloading passengers or cargo. The airlines offer service to islands along the north coast all the way from El Porvenir to Puerto Obaldía, near the Colombian border.

Flying between Panama City and El Porvenir costs US$27.50 one way, double for roundtrip. Between Panama City and Puerto Obaldía it's US$44 one way, double roundtrip. Fares for islands between these two places will fall somewhere in between.

Land You can drive to Cartí Suitupo, on the coast of the Golfo San Blas, and take a boat from there. It takes about three hours on a rough road to reach Cartí from Panama City. Until the road is improved there will be no bus along this route; a 4WD vehicle is needed, and the road may be impassable altogether in the rainy season. Hitching is difficult because there's not much traffic.

Motorboats, which will take up to eight people, can take you to one of the islands: to El Porvenir, Nalunega or Wichub-Wala it takes 45 minutes and costs about US$10.

Sea Kuna merchant ships to the San Blas islands depart from Coco Solo Pier in Colón, and they act as the islands' buses and taxis. The boats depart from the pier at around midnight, to reach El Porvenir in the morning (eight hours, around US$6.50).

The boats continue east along the coast, stopping at about 48 islands along the way, until they reach Puerto Obaldía, near the Colombian border, where they turn around to come back. The trip from Colón all the way to Puerto Obaldía takes five days and costs around US$25, including all meals. These boats are nothing luxurious, but they let you see the whole archipelago, and stop at many of the islands while goods and passengers are being loaded and unloaded. You'll have to make your own sleeping arrangements on deck; a hammock is very useful. You might be able to stay on one or two of the islands along the way.

The IPAT tourist office in Panama City told us they do not recommend these boats for tourists; the boats do not leave at any particular time (you may have to wait around for days to catch one), and there's no guarantee about either the quality of the boat (some have been known to sink) or the character of the people on it (some boats may be carrying contraband).

Nevertheless, if you want to try it, the thing to do would be to go to the Coco Solo Pier in Colón (see Colón, above), find the captain of one of these boats, and make the arrangements directly.

If you want to continue on to Colombia, you may encounter a Colombian merchant ship as you make your way through the islands. One Dutch traveler told us he recently took a Kuna merchant boat from Colón to Ustupo (the end of the line for that boat) for US$20, where he transferred to a Colombian merchant boat and continued on to Cartagena for another US$30, all meals included. He stressed that this wouldn't be the thing to do if you're in a hurry; do it only if you have no time pressure.

DARIÉN

The Interamericana does not go all the way through Panama but terminates in the middle of the jungle near a town called Yaviza in a vast wilderness region called the Darién. This transport gap between Central and South America is known to travelers as the Darién Gap. (Despite the occasional announcements by international

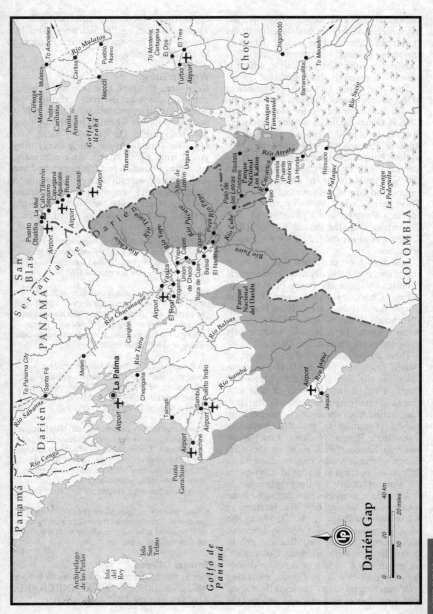

Darién Gap

PANAMA

authorities, it is extremely unlikely that the Interamericana will be pushed through the Darién. In addition to ecological and social concerns, Panama is extremely fearful of foot-and-mouth disease in cattle, which is presently limited to South America.)

The large Darién Province occupies most of the eastern side of Panama. This a region of pristine tropical rain forest which UNESCO has declared a World Heritage Site. It is also designated a Biosphere Reserve. Panama has established the 5790-sq km Parque Nacional Darién, one of Central America's largest national parks and wilderness areas, to protect both the natural and human resources of the region. This park covers 90% of the border between Panama and Colombia. On the Colombian side, the Parque Nacional Los Katíos was also established for wilderness protection.

Scientists have described this region as one of the most naturally diverse in tropical America, with many types of flora and fauna. Chocó, Emberá, and Uainana peoples inhabit the region, living traditionally, mostly along the rivers. The Kuna are better known; they also live traditionally along the north coast of the Darién.

There are basically two ways through the Darién Gap. The first skirts the northern coast via the San Blas Archipelago and Puerto Obaldía, making use of boat services and involving a minimum of walking. The second goes through the jungle from Yaviza (Panama) to the Río Atrato in Colombia's Parque Nacional Los Katíos, and you have to walk most of the way. Either of these routes can be done in as little as a week, but you should allow twice this time, especially for the jungle route.

A trickle of travelers pass through on the roadless, challenging trip. Tim Burford, in his section on crossing the Darién in the book *Backpacking in Central America*, asks a very good question: 'But why give in to this fixation with reaching Colombia?' He points out a variety of other enjoyable things to do while in the Darién, including bird watching at Cana (an excellent spot, with a number of endemic species) and the

coast-to-coast crossing offered by Eco-Tours, re-creating the journey taken by Balboa when he became the first European to sight the Pacific.

What to Bring

Keep your baggage to a minimum, especially on the overland routes through the jungle; you'll appreciate having as light a pack as possible when hiking through the hot, wet jungle. On the other hand, you must be sure to bring along everything you'll truly need. A tent isn't necessary, according to quite a few travelers who have done the trek; several have suggested that a hammock with a very tight-fitting mosquito net. You might make the journey in eight days but it's best to plan for a longer trek.

- Take dried food with you; there are very few places where you can buy food, though in villages you can usually find someone to cook a hot meal for you for around US$5.

- Be sure you have plenty of water and drink lots of it – this is a very hot region. You'll need to carry some drinking water, and be equipped to purify more as required. Since you'll be doing a lot of sweating, it's a good idea to take along oral rehydration salts.

- A compass and a sharp machete are also essential equipment, and army surplus jungle boots are a very good idea – holes in the sides allow water to drain out, and their canvas uppers don't take forever to dry.

- Insect repellent is another essential; the jungle is home to millions of biting insects, especially mosquitoes. The mosquitoes of eastern Panama are resistant to chloroquine, so you'll need to be on a regimen of Mefloquine or some other non-chloroquine antimalarial drug. Ticks are also plentiful along certain parts of the journey.

- Some fluency in Spanish is desirable – almost essential – to minimize the risk of getting lost and to avoid misunderstandings with the locals in this isolated area.

Tourist Offices

Get as much information as you can before taking off into the Darién. INRENARE, ANCON and the IPAT tourist office, all in

Panama City, are good places to ask for information. You must get a free permit from INRENARE to enter Darién National Park.

In the past few years, a couple of adventure tour companies have initiated tours into the Darién. Information on these is given in the Organized Tours section in the Getting There & Away chapter. Eco-Tours, based in Panama City, is the grandfather of them all; they offer a variety of tours into the Darién region and they can also help plan an independent journey.

The South American Explorers Club (see Useful Organizations in the Facts for the Visitor chapter) is also a storehouse of information about crossing the Darién region. Many of their members have written trip reports about their adventures, accessible to you if you become a member.

ANCON This agency has environmental education centers in the Darién at Punta Patiño and at Cana. They offer a program for visits to the centers; US$75 per night includes lodging, three meals a day, and guided trips around the areas. They also have a volunteer program in which you can volunteer to help out, usually for a minimum of a week, in which case it costs you nothing and they will take care of your basic needs (food, lodging). Contact the ANCON office in Panama City to ask about this.

INRENARE This national organization, in Paraíso near Panama City, is a good source for current information. There's also an office in El Real with more local, on-the-spot information, where you can hire a dependable guide or arrange boats and pack animals as needed. Lodging is free, whether you use their guides or not, but you must bring your own food.

IPAT This tourist office in Panama City has information about the Darién.

Books & Maps

A good source of written information is the detailed, 40-page booklet *An Adventurer's Guide for Crossing the Darién Gap of Panama and Colombia* by Patricia E Upton (1996); it's available for US$12 by contacting her at PO Box 803, Salmon, ID 83467 USA (fax (208) 756-2544, net). Patricia and her husband Loren have crossed the Darién several times.

The book *Backpacking in Central America* by Tim Burford (1996) has a good 13-page section on crossing the Darién. He points out that there is not only one route for crossing the Darién, but rather a network of routes, and suggests a variety of possibilities.

The Insituto Geográfico Nacional Tommy Guardia in Panama City sells detailed topographical maps of the region. Reportedly these maps contain slight errors, but they are the best maps available.

Visas & Documents

Remember that both Panama and Colombia officially demand an onward ticket before they'll allow you to enter the country, so get one, and a visa if you need one, before you set out. Many travelers have been turned back at the border for lack of an onward ticket, and it's a long trip back to buy one. Visas are not available at border crossings, but rather from embassies and consulates.

A Word of Warning

The information given here is intended only as a general guideline. Crossing the Darién is a serious journey; don't depend only on what you read here to be sufficient to get you through. Anything may have changed since the time this was written. There's no substitute for good on-the-spot information.

We recommend you seek reliable local advice before setting out, and that you use guides along the way, not just to find the right trail (though this is part of it) but also for safety. Use one of the offices listed above to find a guide; local guides should be available as far south as Boca de Cupe.

In addition to such natural hazards as high rivers and mudslides (the Darién is a

PANAMA

zone of serious seismic activity), the human dangers to travelers in the area must not be underestimated. An unaccompanied foreigner might be assumed to be either a drug trafficker or a US Drug Enforcement Agency operative. There are also bandits who prey on jungle travelers.

The Darién is not unpopulated; there are a fair number of people crossing the region by small boat and on foot. The indigenous inhabitants get around on the trails and by river, and there's a mine at Cana to which miners walk from both the Panamanian and Colombian sides. The mine is controlled by the Panamanian government environmental agency, ANCON. Many freelance miners are undocumented immigrants, and are subject to arrest by the indigenous Kuna authorities. There are also a lot of Peruvians heading north to the USA, as well as smugglers of drugs and other contraband. As a result, the route is getting more dangerous.

In addition, the Darién has become a major area of activity for guerrillas from the neighboring Colombian province of Antioquia. In January 1993, three US missionaries, who had been working among the Kuna and who were known for their aid to travelers through the region, were kidnapped from the town of Púcuro; it's said they were kidnapped by Colombian guerrillas, reportedly affiliated with the Colombian Revolutionary Armed Forces (FARC). The FARC demanded US$5 million for the three missionaries. They were never ransomed or released, and they are now presumed dead.

There have been other foreigners kidnapped by FARC. Apparently kidnapping people and demanding exorbitant ransoms is one way the guerillas make money.

The guerrillas are said to have a camp in the Altos de Limón mountain area on the Panama-Colombian border, due east of Púcuro overlooking the trail from Yaviza to Palo de las Letras, and to dominate the entire area. Don't underestimate the dangers you will face from them in this region.

Local Indian guides are reportedly willing to conduct travelers to but not across the Colombian border, for fear of kidnapping by guerrillas for forced labor. In another recent disturbing incident, a young Canadian hiker who attempted to cross the Darién alone disappeared, and his body was found after a search. He was shot to death, apparently by guerrillas.

Having said all that, many people complete this route without major problems. Those who have done so describe it as a unique and rewarding experience.

Along the North Coast

Thanks to Carlton Lee (USA), Krzysztof Dydynski (Poland), Juan Amado Iglesias (Panama), Hernán Araúz of Eco-Tours (Panama), Jaime Troyano of IPAT (Panama) and various Colombian and Panamanian travelers for providing us with information.

This route starts at Puerto Obaldía (Panama), then goes to Capurganá (Colombia), Acandí and on to Turbo. The whole journey between El Porvenir and Turbo can be done in as little as a week, but it could easily take double that or even longer, especially if you have to wait around for boats between El Porvenir and Puerto Obaldía, or if you stay awhile somewhere on the way. The San Blas archipelago, Sapzurro and Capurganá are the most pleasant places to break the journey.

The first thing to do is to get to Puerto Obaldía, in Panama near the Colombian border. The simplest way to do this is to fly there from Panama City; see the Getting Around section of the Panama chapter for details on domestic flights.

Alternatively, you might find a cargo boat heading for Puerto Obaldía via El Porvenir in the San Blas archipelago. (You may also encounter Colombian merchant boats, and you can often negotiate a ride with them to take you to Colombia.) From El Porvenir to Puerto Obaldía, a boat costs around US$25, meals included. It takes about five days, depending on how many stops the boat makes; it may stop at 48 islands along the way – take this route only if you have no time pressure. This is detailed in the San Blas section, above.

Puerto Obaldía is a small tropical waystation for traffic between Colombia and Panama. It has good beaches, palms and clear blue sea. If you're on a tight budget you can sleep on the beach south of the town, though there are a few hotels – a basic hotel near the airstrip costs about US$5 per bed (anyone can direct you there).

If you're heading south you need to check with the immigration inspector here for an exit stamp or, if you're heading north, an entry stamp. Make sure you have all the necessary papers, visas and onward tickets, as well as sufficient funds. Though you may not be asked for these, it's a very long backtrack if you show up short.

Once you have your exit stamp, you can continue on to Colombia. There are two options: boat or walk. Boats depart irregularly, when they collect enough passengers, to Sapzurro (US$4, 45 minutes) and Capurganá (US$6, one hour). The boatmen often try to make foreign travelers pay more – by claiming it's an 'international route' or saying that your backpack is heavy. Alternatively, you can negotiate a boat for your party to La Miel, the last Panamanian village before the Colombian border. There are always fishermen around eager to get a little extra money, so the fare isn't too high: around US$10 per person if there are two people, less if there are more passengers. A boat to Sapzurro shouldn't cost much more.

The other alternative is to walk. You can walk from Puerto Obaldía to Sapzurro, a small Colombian fishing village, in about 2½ hours.

The first part of the trail goes from Puerto Obaldía to La Miel, the last Panamanian village, a two-hour walk. Locals in both Puerto Obaldía and La Miel say this track is unsafe for walking. So far, we have not received confirmed reports about robberies (though this does not mean they have not occurred), but we have received letters from travelers saying the trails were so indistinct that they were lost for days. There are many misleading trails branching off inland, so it's easy to get lost. You may want to hire a responsible guide to take you

through, who will act both as a guide and as protection – guides are available in Puerto Obaldía. The soldiers at the military post can also supply current information on the route. Otherwise, it may be best to do the Puerto Obaldía-La Miel portion by boat.

Once you reach La Miel, there are no further problems. From the village, you climb a small hill, pass the border marker on the top and descend to Sapzurro – all that in half an hour.

Sapzurro is a small, pleasant fishing village, beautifully set on the shore of a deep horseshoe-shaped bay. There are a couple of hospedajes and several restaurants, a narrow but clean white-sand beach shaded by coconut palms and a Panamanian consulate – your last chance to get a visa for Panama if you're heading north.

From Sapzurro the footpath climbs again, then drops to the next coastal village, Capurganá. This portion can be easily done in 1½ or two hours – go at a leisurely pace, to take in the splendid scenery. There is no road, only a footpath.

Capurganá is the most touristy place of the whole area and gets pretty crowded from mid-December to the end of January (the Colombian holiday season), but at other times it's quiet and easy-going. It has a choice of budget hotels and restaurants and is a pleasant place to spend a day or two. You can make a trip to El Cielo, a lovely nature spot an hour's walk upstream alongside the small river passing through Capurganá. Several hotels have horses for hire. A few places in the village change US dollars, though at a poor rate.

From Capurganá there are several ways to continue the journey. If you want to go quickly, you can fly from Capurganá to Medellín for about US$77; flights operate twice daily. Or you can take a boat to Turbo (US$12, 2½ to three hours). If there's no direct boat to Turbo, take a boat to Acandí (US$4, one hour) and continue on another boat to Turbo (US$9, around two hours). If you are not in a hurry, though, it's worthwhile to continue from Capurganá to Acandí on foot. It's a lovely walk; allow yourself the best part of a day.

Start along the beach and follow the path, which doesn't always stick to the coast. Sometimes it goes a bit inland, climbing the hills to avoid the high rocky cliffs. An hour's walk brings you to Aguacate, which is nothing more than several huts with a local-style house functioning as an hospedaje. Follow the footpath for a bit over an hour to Rufino, a cluster of houses. From there the path turns inland. It climbs the extensive coastal ridge, passes it, and drops into the valley of the Acandí River (another hour to get to this point). Follow the river downstream; it is a leisurely three-hour walk to Acandí. The path does not always follow the river and includes several crossings; be prepared to wet your shoes. This part of the track is often muddy.

Acandí is a fair-sized village with a church, several small hotels and guest houses, and a number of cafés and small *tiendas* selling mostly bottled and canned goods of limited variety and quantity. Some of the shops here will change US dollars into Colombian pesos, and will probably give a better rate than you'll get in Capurganá, or even in Turbo, your next stop.

A launch operates every morning between Acandí and Turbo; most of the time it makes a stop at Titumate. The journey between Acandí and Turbo takes two to four hours and costs around US$10. The boat service is only reliable during the first six months of the year, when the sea is not too rough; at other times you might have to wait for good weather before the boat will go. It is never a very smooth journey; be prepared to get soaked through. Anything you want to keep dry should be wrapped up in plastic. Try to get one of the seats in the rear of the boat. Alternatively, you can fly between Acandí and Turbo for US$25; Aces operates four flights a week.

Capurganá and Acandí are also jumping off points for inland, east-west trekking through Darién to the Interamericana.

Turbo is an uninteresting and unsafe port on the Golfo de Urabá. There's a variety of fresh and canned foods available, so if you're heading north then this is a good place to stock up.

Whether you're heading north or south, you need to call at the Policía Distrito Especial, two blocks from the harbor in Turbo, to obtain an exit or entry stamp. It's very informal and quick as long as your papers are in order. Travelers have been fined for entering Colombia via Turbo without an entry stamp, intending to get one in Cartagena.

There's no bank in Turbo to change either cash or traveler's checks, but many shops and the more expensive hotels will exchange cash dollars. They usually give a poor rate, so only change enough to get to Medellín or Cartagena. If you need to spend the night in Turbo, try the *Residencias Marcela* at Carrera 14B, No 100-54, one block from the church, with comfortable rooms for US$3 per person. If they're full you could try the *Residencias Turbo* next door or the *Residencias El Viajero* just round the corner, both for similar prices.

There is no Panamanian consulate in Turbo, so if you're heading to Panama, get your Panamanian visa beforehand. You still have a chance to get one in Sapzurro, but if the consulate there is closed for some reason, you will have to go a long, long way back to Medellín or Barranquilla to get one.

There are several buses daily from Turbo to Medellín (355 km, 13 hours, US$15). The journey can take much longer, twisting and winding along rugged mountain roads; one traveler reported it went on for over 30 hours! The road can be chilly, and if you're prone to motion sickness it can be quite an ordeal. Most of the buses depart in the late afternoon or early evening for the overnight trip.

If you're heading from Turbo to Cartagena, take a jeep from the market square to Montería (six hours, US$10) and then continue by bus to Cartagena. Alternatively, you can take a cargo boat from Turbo to Cartagena for around US$15; these boats depart a few times a week. Once again, time is relative; you may be told the journey will take around 18 hours, and find it takes days! Or you can boat from Turbo to the Los Katíos National Park – take the boat heading for Riosucio, which departs from Turbo daily at 8 am and takes 1½ hours to reach Sautatá, the entrance to the park (US$10).

There's an airport in Turbo, about four km from town on the beach road near the customs building; Aces operates three flights daily to Medellín (US$52) and four flights a week to Acandí (US$25). Bookings can be made at the Aces office, in town at Calle 101, No 14-10. They provide free transport to/from the airport.

Through the Jungle

The original information about this journey comes from Lilian Wordell (Ireland), updated with recent advice from, amongst others, David Wilson (England), Jaime Troyano (IPAT in Panama City), eleven Peruvians, two Swiss bikers, and a Panamanian who has made the journey many times. Thanks also to Patricia E Upton (author of *An Adventurer's Guide for Crossing the Darién Gap of Panama and Colombia*) for allowing us to pass on her comments about Púcuro and Paya, and to Tim Burford (author of *Backpacking in Central America*) for his very helpful letter.

This trip should only be undertaken in the dry season, from December to March (or possibly in July and August if little rain has fallen) and never without preparation. The rest of the time the trails are almost impossibly waterlogged and the rivers are raging torrents full of broken trees and the like. On the other hand, towards the end of the dry season the rivers get low and it's often difficult to find boats.

Going through the jungle, the total cost of crossing from Panama to Colombia won't be any less than flying between the two countries, by the time you add up the cost of buses, boats, accommodations, food and guides; be prepared to spend about US$200 for the Panama City-Turbo route. But the experience will be incomparable.

From Panama City there are two ways to start the trek: via Yaviza (the more popular route) or via El Real.

To Boca de Cupe via Yaviza You can get to Yaviza from Panama City by bus on the Interamericana (10 to 12 hours, US$14); the bus departs Panama City from the bus terminal on Av B (☎ 262-8256, 262-9971). It's a long, hard bus trip on a dirt road, and even the bus trip can only be accomplished in the dry season; the rest of the year the last stretch of the road becomes impassable and the bus goes only as far as Metetí (seven hours, US$9), from where you could probably find a 4WD vehicle to take you the rest of the way. If you need to spend the night in Metetí there is one hotel, the *Hotel Mi Felicidad* (☎ 262-4272).

Flights used to operate between Panama City and Yaviza, but last time we checked, they were no longer operating. Check with Aeroperlas (☎ 269-4555 in Panama City) to see if they've been resumed. Otherwise the nearest place you could fly into would be El Real.

Yaviza is principally a trading center, with produce coming through on the way to Panama City. In Yaviza there's one hotel, the *Hotel América*, which costs US$7 per person. There's also a ruin of an old Spanish fort, built to guard the entrance to the gold mines at Cana.

To continue from Yaviza you first have to trek to Unión de Chocó on the Río Tuira, which will take about a day. To get there, first cross the river by canoe (US$0.25), then walk 1½ hours to Pinogana. Wade through the river here or cross by dugout (US$1) and then walk for three to four hours along a jeep track to Aruza. Chocó Indians live in the area, and you'll encounter quite a few along the way. Cross the river at Aruza by wading through it again and then walk for about 45 minutes to Unión de Chocó. From there, continue on the same side of the river to Yape, Capetí and finally cross the river to Boca de Cupe. It's a very pleasant walk which will take about five hours.

Alternatively, you may be able to find a boat going from Yaviza to Boca de Cupe. It never hurts to ask around.

To Boca de Cupe via El Real You can get to El Real from Panama City either by air or by banana boat. Aeroperlas (☎ 269-4555 in Panama City) offers flights three times a week for US$37 one way, double for roundtrip; phone to check the schedule. Banana boats depart from Panama City's Muelle Fiscal (☎ 262-2762) and take between 12 and 36 hours. They cost about US$25 per person, including the simple meals which are provided on board. There's no fixed schedule for these boats but, if possible, try to get a passage on a larger and more comfortable one.

On the way to El Real you will pass La Palma, capital of the Darién Province, at the mouth of the Río Tuira. It's mainly a trading center, not very large, with only about 5000 people, and you probably won't need to stop there. If you do need to, there are two lodges where you could spend the night.

The port at El Real is some distance away from the town itself, so you first have to go about five km upstream to the Mercadero, where you pick up a boat heading upstream to Boca de Cupe. The best place to inquire about these is the general store; most provisions arrive by boat so the owner is generally clued up about what's going on. Prices for the two- to four-hour boat trip to Boca de Cupe are negotiable, as are all the boat trips on this route. The fare can cost anywhere between US$10 and US$20 per person. If you need to spend the night in El Real there is one place to stay, or you can camp either at the port or at the Mercadero.

Boca de Cupe to Púcuro Boca de Cupe, a Chocó Indian village on the Río Tuira, is the last town of any size you'll see until you're near the end of the trail. It's here that you must get your Panamanian exit or entry stamp from a shop alongside the river. Ask for Antonio, the shop owner, and you will be directed there. According to recent reports, the immigration formalities have moved to Púcuro, but you still have to present yourself at the shop to have your passport details recorded.

You can stay overnight in Boca de Cupe with a local family, or ask for the *casa comunal*, a small community house with four double rooms (US$5 per person). Locals will soon approach you to ask if you want meals cooked for you.

From Boca de Cupe you must find a boat going to Púcuro, a five- or six-hour trip (US$30). You may have to wait two or three days for a boat. Or you may be able to arrange a motorized dugout via the school-teacher (three hours, US$7.50 per person).

Púcuro is the first Kuna Indian village you'll encounter. When the river is high you'll find yourself landing right at the village but otherwise it takes about half an hour to walk there. Ask someone where you can stay for the night. The *cacique* (village chief) may let you sleep in the meeting hall for a fee (with all the village taking an interest in you), but there are other possibilities. If you want to keep moving, ask where the trail to Paya starts.

Note, however, that Púcuro has been the site of recent guerrilla activity; it's the place where the missionaries were kidnapped in 1993, and other travelers have had problems there too. In early 1995, Patricia Upton was alone in camp after dark (after having been shown where to camp by the village chief) when a group of 15 to 20 angry Kuna men raided the camp, demanded their motorcycle, and chained the bike to a post. They held it for US$500 ransom.

The Uptons eventually negotiated the release of their bike, but Patricia advises avoiding both Púcuro and Paya. She suggests that before arriving in Púcuro you could check at the friendly Chocó village of Balsal, on the Río Tuira, and ask about 'a land route going farther up the Tuira River towards the village of Punusa, then across the mountains and into Colombia, coming out somewhere near the village of Boca Limón.'

Púcuro to Paya From Púcuro, the 18-km walk to Paya, the next Kuna village, can be done in a day and involves four river crossings (all the rivers are fordable). You need to look hard for the trail after the third crossing. There are good camping sites just before the third crossing and just after the last. Guides can be hired in Púcuro for this section of the trail for about US$30, but don't pay in advance. The walk should take about six to eight hours.

When you get to Paya, you must go to the military barracks, about two km away, for a passport (and most probably luggage) inspection. This involves wading across the river; the locals will show you the path to take to the crossing point. The soldiers will probably offer to let you stay the night in the barracks, but no food is available.

Ask the village chief where you can stay before you go to the barracks. He is likely to let you sleep in his home and his family will cook for you. Pay a reasonable fee for these services, even though he probably won't bring up the subject of payment.

Paya was once the site of the Kuna 'university' where Kunas from all over the area came to study the traditional arts of magic, medicine and history. It fell on hard times about 100 years ago as European technology and European diseases gradually penetrated the area.

Travelers' reports about Paya are mixed. Some find it interesting, while others have found the locals' attitude toward outsiders to be rather hostile, and recommend keeping a close eye on your belongings. Be discreet with your camera, and ask permission before you take photographs; some travelers have reported the Kuna here demand an exorbitant price to allow you to photograph them. As mentioned earlier, Patricia Upton recommends avoiding both Púcuro and Paya altogether.

There's a foot-and-mouth disease control station in the barracks. If you're coming from Colombia, your baggage will be inspected and anything made of leather, or even vaguely resembling leather, will be dipped in a mild antiseptic to kill any pathogens.

Paya to Cristales The next part of the trail goes to Cristales via **Palo de las Letras**, the border marker between Panama and Colombia. It is the most difficult stage, being very steep, and usually takes one or two days, though you can do it in eight to 10 hours under the right conditions. It's also the part where you're most likely to get lost, so you'll appreciate a guide. In 1992 a party of six were lost here for nine days, according to rangers.

Guides can be found in Paya – ask the chief. A pair of guides (they won't like to go on their own) for the route to Cristales will cost about US$70. Be sure you clarify with your guides exactly how far they will take you; some travelers have reported that the Kuna will go only up to the border post, but no farther, fearing kidnapping by the guerrillas.

The first part of the trail to Palo de las Letras is uphill; this is perhaps the most difficult portion. A British Army expedition came through here in 1972 and cut the trail about three meters wide, but recently we've heard that this trail is overgrown. You'll appreciate having those guides; there's guerrilla activity around here. You should reach Palo de las Letras in about three hours.

It's said that Palo de las Letras got its name from a tree that used to stand here, on which travelers carved their initials. There's no evidence of this tree today. The Colombian government erected a concrete marker in its place to mark the border, but by recent reports, even the concrete marker has not managed to survive in one piece.

At Palo de las Letras, you leave behind Panama's Parque Nacional del Darién and enter Colombia's Parque Nacional Los Katíos.

From the border marker it's downhill about 20 km to Cristales; it should take about five to seven hours. After about an hour of tramping downhill through thick forest you come to the Río Tule; follow it downstream. Quite a few travelers have had adventures (some would call them ordeals) getting lost on this leg, as the trails are either a maze or indistinct, being difficult to locate after many of the river crossings. Perhaps the best bet is to follow the river, even wading in it if necessary, to avoid

PANAMA

getting lost. After a couple of hours, the Río Tule meets the Río Cacarica; follow this river downstream for two or three hours to Cristales.

When you reach Cristales, carry on another half an hour downstream to the headquarters of the Parque Nacional Los Katíos. At the Cristales ranger station, shout to be taken across the river, which is quite deep, to the headquarters. The staff are very friendly and helpful, and will probably let you sleep in the station free of charge.

Cristales to Turbo The last part of the trip, from Cristales to Turbo, is by a combination of motorized dugouts and banana boats. This river trip is one of the most beautiful parts of the entire journey; you'll see plenty of birds and other wildlife.

If the park workers are going for supplies in Turbo then the trip from Cristales can be done in one haul, but if not you'll first have to find a boat to Bijao and then, possibly, another to Travesía, also known as Puente América, on the Río Atrato. A regular boat from Cristales to Bijao will cost about US$40; you can walk instead in five hours but getting lost is highly likely unless you hire someone to guide you.

Bijao is just a collection of poor huts. The best person to ask about boats in Bijao is the store owner. You may have to wait a few days before a boat turns up.

Hiring a motorized dugout from Bijao to Travesía may cost around US$45 (three hours). If you decide to take one of the cargo boats which ply up and down the Río Atrato, allow a whole day for the journey; your boat may stop en route several times to load, unload, fix the engine, fish, rest, fix

the engine, visit the family, fix the engine, or for a hundred other unexpected reasons.

Once at Travesía you'll have no difficulty finding transport to Turbo. There are fast passenger motorboats coming through from Riosucio every morning, which continue downriver to Turbo (US$10, two hours). Travesía is not the most pleasant place to wait around for a boat; travelers have called it unfriendly and expensive, and recommended keeping a close eye on your gear. If you do need to wait overnight for a boat, there's a basic place to stay, or you can sleep overnight in the town's communal hall for free. There is a shop with expensive food, soft drinks and beer; purified water is also sold here.

For information about Turbo see Along the North Coast, above.

Instead of going straight to Turbo, though, it's well worth stopping off in Sautatá, the visitors' center of Los Katíos National Park, to rest for a couple of days after the trek. Near the visitors' center are a number of fine places to visit including three waterfalls (Salto del Tilupo, Salto del Tendal and Salto de la Tigra), four lakes (Ciénagas de Tumarandó) and an old cemetery.

From the Sautatá wharf it's a 20-minute trek to the park visitors' center, where there's a pleasant, spacious house with a capacity for about 20 visitors (US$6 per person); if you have your own hammock you can string it under the roof for a nominal fee or even for nothing. Camping is also possible (US$2 per tent). The park's kitchen sometimes serves meals (US$3), but only if there are not too many visitors. As everything has to be shipped in from Turbo, food is limited, so it's best to bring your own.

Glossary

abajo – down

adiós – greeting used when passing someone in the street (Costa Rica); good-bye

aguardiente – a clear liquor made from sugar cane, with an alcohol content even higher than that of vodka

alfombra – carpet

almacene – big store

alquiler de automóviles – car rental

antigeño – citizen of Antigua Guatemala

apartado – post office box

arriba – up

artesanías – handicrafts

Av – abbreviation for avenida (avenue)

bahía – bay

baleada – filled tortilla (Honduras)

balneario – public bathing or swimming spot

barba amarilla – literally 'yellow beard'; the poisonous fer-de-lance snake

barrio – neighborhood

bistec – grilled or fried beef

bocas – little side dishes served with drinks

bomba – gasoline (petrol) station

bote – motorized boat (Panama)

cabaña – cabin

cacique – Indian tribal elder; provincial warlord or strongman

cafetería – literally 'coffee-shop'; any informal restaurant with waiter service, not a self-service place

cafetín – small cafeteria

calzada – causeway

calzones – long baggy shorts

cama matrimonial – double bed

camarotes – smaller rooms

camión – truck; bus

camionetas – pickup trucks

caracol – seashell; snail

carnet de passage – (French) literally 'card of passage'; official paper for vehicles going to South America

carretera – highway

casa de cambio – place to exchange money

casa de huespedes – guesthouse

casa de la mujer – women's center

casado – a cheap set meal, usually served at lunchtime

cay, caye or **cayo** – small island of sand or coral fragments

cayuca – dugout canoe

cerro – hill

cerveza – beer

ceviche – seafood marinated in lime juice

chamarras – thick, heavy woolen blankets (Guatemala)

chapín – a citizen of Guatemala; Guatemalan

chicha – fruit juice mixed with sugar and water (Panama)

chuletas de puerco – pork chops

churrasco – Guatemalan-style beef

cine – movie theater

ciudad – city

cocina – literally 'kitchen'; small, cheap cookshop of the kind found near markets

cofradía – traditional religious brotherhood

colectivo – van or minibus operating as a shared taxi

Colón – Spanish spelling of Columbus; also the unit of currency in Costa Rica and El Salvador

comedor – a small, simple, cheap restaurant

comida corrida – a set meal of several courses, usually offered at lunchtime

comida corriente – a mixed plate of different foods typical of the local region

comida típica – similar to a comida corriente

completo – complete, fully booked

conjunto – combined; also an ensemble, a musical group

conquistador – Spanish conqueror of Latin America

Contras – counterrevolutionaries fighting against the Sandinista government in Nicaragua in the 1980s

cordillera – mountain range
correo aéreo – air mail
costa – coast
criollo – Creole, born in Latin America of Spanish descent; on the Caribbean coast it refers to someone of mixed Black and European descent
cuadra – city block
cueva – cave

Día de los Muertos – Day of the Dead, or All Souls' Day, November 1

encomienda – Spanish colonial practice of putting Indians under the 'guardianship' of landowners, a form of serfdom
enredo – a wraparound skirt
esquadrones de muerte – death squads, supported by Somoza in El Salvador
estación ferrocarril – railway station

faja – waist sash that binds garments and holds what would otherwise be put in pockets
farmacia de turno – the 'on-duty' pharmacy in the revolving system that keeps one pharmacy at a time open 24 hours
filibustero – filibuster, an irregular military adventurer, freebooter
finca – plantation, ranch
fresco – drink made of fruit juice, sugar and water
frijoles con arroz – beans with rice

gallo pinto – blend of rice and beans, with cooking water from the beans added; a common meal, especially in Nicaragua
galón, galones – US gallon (3.79 liters)
Garífuna, plural **Garinagu** – also called Black Caribs; mixed-race descendants of Africans and Carib Indians from the Caribbean island of St Vincent, who came to Central America in the late 18th century
gaseosa – soda, soft drink
gibnut – small, brown-spotted rodent similar to a guinea pig; also called a paca
golfo – gulf
gringo/gringa – non-Latin American, especially from the USA; sometimes, not always, derogatory
guacamole – a salad of mashed or chopped avocadoes, onions and tomatoes

guaro – the local firewater in Costa Rica
guayabera – embroidered men's dress shirt, worn outside the pants

hacienda – estate; also 'Treasury,' as in *Departamento de Hacienda* (Treasury Department)
hamburguesas – hamburgers
hospedaje – guesthouse
huipil – a long, woven, white sleeveless tunic from the Maya regions, with intricate, colorful embroidery

iglesia – church
Internacionalistas – volunteers from around the world who came to Nicaragua after the revolution to assist the Sandinistas
invierno – winter; in Central America, the wet season, roughly from April to November
ISIC – International Student Identity Card, can be useful for obtaining student airfares or other discounts
IVA – *impuesto al valor agregado* (or 'ee-vah'), a value-added tax

jejenes – sandflies
junco – type of basket weaving

ladino – Indian or mestizo who speaks Spanish and lives a modern lifestyle
lago – lake
laguna – lagoon, lake
lancha – small motorboat
Lempira – Honduran unit of currency
leng – colloquial Maya term for coins (Guatemalan highlands)
libra – pound weight, 0.45 kg
licuado – fresh fruit drink, blended with milk or water
lista de correos – poste restante (general delivery)

machismo – the exaggerated masculine pride of the Latin American male
malecón – pier or jetty; waterside walkway
mamey – a fruit
manzana – literally 'apple,' but also a term for a city block
mar – sea

mariachi – (adj & noun) traditional Mexican acoustic musical group

MCO – miscellaneous charges order

mercado – market

mestizo – person of mixed Spanish and Indian descent

metate – flat stone on which corn is ground

migración – immigration, office of an immigration department

milla – mile (1.61 km)

milpa – cornfield

mirador – lookout

mola – Cuna Indian fabric appliqué

mordida – literally 'little bite'; a small bribe of the kind that keeps the wheels of bureaucracy turning

morería – storehouse for the ceremonial masks, costumes and regalia used in religious festivals

muchacho – boy; also used as 'mate' or 'pal'

muelle – pier

municipalidad – town hall

Nahuatl – the language of the Aztecs in Mexico

Navidad – Christmas

NGO – non-governmental organization

nuevo/nueva – new

oficina de correos – post office

onza – ounce (28 g)

paca – gibnut

PADI – international diving organization

palacio de gobierno – colonial government headquarters

palapa – an open-air structure with a palm-thatched roof and no walls (Panama)

pan de coco – coconut bread

panga – small motorboat

panqueques – pancakes

parque – park; sometimes also used for plaza

pavo silvestre – wild turkey

peña – a folkloric club; an evening of music, song and dance

pensión – guesthouse

peso – nickname for Nicaraguan córdoba

petate – plant material used for basketry and mats (Nicaragua)

pie, pies – foot, feet (0.3 meters)

pisto – colloquial Maya term for money, quetzals (Guatemalan highlands)

platillo chapín – dish of Guatemalan specialities

plato del día – plate (or meal) of the day

plato típico – a mixed plate of various foods typical of a place or region

playa – beach

pollera – lacy Panamanian national dress for women

pollo asado – grilled chicken

propina – tip (not a bribe)

puente – bridge

puerto – port, harbor

punta – point; Garífuna dancing involving much hip movement

pupusa – a small, hot corn tortilla stuffed with meat, beans or cheese (El Salvador)

pupusería – restaurant selling pupusas

quebrada – ravine, brook

quechiquémitl – a shoulder cape

refresco – soda, soft drink

río – river

rockola – jukebox

ropa vieja – literally 'old clothes'; spicy shredded beef and rice dish (Panama)

rosticería – restaurant selling roast meats

ruletero – jitney, public minibus

sacbé – ceremonial limestone avenue between Maya cities

salchichas – sausages, like hot dogs

salsa – modern Latin dance music

sancocho – spicy meat and vegetable stew, the national dish of Panama

Semana Santa – Holy Week, the week before Easter

sendero – path

servicios sanitarios – toilets

sierra – mountain range; a saw

soda – place that serves a counter lunch; soft drink (Panama)

sorbetería – ice-cream parlor

sorpresa – literally 'surprise'; a tiny ceramic scene inside a ceramic cover

stela – carved stone monument of the ancient Maya

supermercado – supermarket

tajaditas – crisp, fried banana chips
tamales – steamed corn dough rolls, perhaps with a meat or other stuffing
teléfono monedero – coin-operated telephone
temblor – earthquake
tico/tica – inhabitant of Costa Rica
tienda – small shop
trucha – trout
Turicentro – literally 'tourist center'; outdoor recreation center with swimming facilities, restaurants and camping (El Salvador)

vegetariano – vegetarian
venado – deer; venison
ventanillas especiales – special teller windows for changing money
verano – summer; in Central America, the dry season, roughly from November to April
viajero/viajera – traveler
viejo/vieja – old
villa – village, settlement
vinchuca – a bug that carries Chagas' disease; a smooth, oval, brownish insect, with two antennae curving under the narrow conical head
volcán – volcano

Spanish for Travelers

The language patterns of Central America follow the patterns of colonization. Spanish is the primary language of most of the Central American countries, with the exception of Belize, which was colonized by the British. There the official language is English.

The patterns of British and US influence have left other English-speaking pockets in Central America, notably among the blacks on the Caribbean Coast. English is an important language in Panama, not only because of the English-speaking descendants of Jamaican and West Indian settlers, but also because of the US influence in connection with the canal, and the tendency of more affluent families to send their children to study in the USA.

Throughout Central America there are groups of people who speak native Indian languages and dialects – at least 30 languages and even more dialects are spoken. But in most of Central America, Spanish is the predominant language.

Hints for the Traveler

Fortunately, Spanish is a relatively easy language for an English speaker to learn. If you have no background in the language, you could begin by taking an evening class or by borrowing a record/cassette course from the local library. Try to find a Spanish speaker to practice with.

There are a few places in Central America, notably Antigua and Quetzaltenango in Guatemala, that specialize in Spanish language courses. A few weeks spent studying Spanish at the beginning of your trip could make an enormous difference in your experience of Central America and any other Spanish-speaking countries you may ever visit.

A pocket-size book of Spanish grammar and phrases can help you tremendously. Lonely Planet's *Latin American Spanish Phrasebook* is very useful and compact.

Also be sure to take along a pocket-size Spanish-English dictionary. Many are available, so you might want to compare several. It's best to bring your own as they are not widely available in Central America, though you might find one in an occasional bookstore or in the gift shop of a major hotel.

Spanish-speakers often have remarkable patience with those who are attempting to learn the language. Even if you feel like an idiot at first, your efforts to communicate in Spanish will most often be met with warm smiles and helpfulness by local people. So don't be shy about practicing your Spanish.

Central American Spanish

As with Spanish everywhere, Central American Spanish has lots of regional variations in words and slang. For example, a soft drink is called a *refresco* in Guatemala and Honduras, but a *gaseosa* in El Salvador and Nicaragua, and it's a *soda* in Panama. A bus is often called a *camioneta* in Guatemala, but in other parts of Central America it's a *bus* (pronounced 'boos'). If you're heading south from Mexico, don't call the bus a *camión* as in Mexico – in Central America, a *camión* is a truck!

Since a lot of travel takes place between the small Central American republics, people are familiar with the various words used in different places, and most of the time there is no problem with understanding.

Another peculiarity of Central American Spanish, with a number of regional variations, concerns the use of the formal/informal verb forms *tú* and *usted*. In Honduras, the more formal *usted* is used almost exclusively – you'll even hear sweethearts and married couples refer to one another as *usted*, a practice that would seem comical in many other Spanish-speaking countries. In both Honduras and Guatemala, you'll rarely hear the more informal *tú*. These countries do have a slangy informal term, though – *vos*, which you won't hear in many other places.

Panamanian Spanish is spoken very fast, with a unique accent and many slang words that are used only in Panama.

Pronunciation

Most of the sounds in Spanish have equivalents in English, and written Spanish is largely phonetic. Once you've learned how to pronounce all the letters, and certain groups of letters, and you know which syllable to stress, you can read any word or sentence and pronounce it more or less correctly.

Vowels There is not much variation in the length of vowels in Spanish. Each vowel is consistently pronounced the same way except if it's in a specific vowel combination.

a   as the 'u' in nut or a shorter sound than the 'a' in 'father'
e   as the 'e' in 'met'; at the end of a word as in 'they'
i   similar to the 'i' in 'marine' but not as strong or drawn out; between that sound and the 'i' in 'flip'
o   similar to the 'o' in 'for'
u   as the 'oo' in 'fool'

Diphthongs Vowel combinations (diphthongs) are best pronounced by just running the two vowel sounds together into one syllable.

ai   as the 'i' in 'hide'
au   as the 'ow' in 'how'
ei   as the 'ay' in 'hay'
ia   as the 'ya' in 'yard'
ie   as the 'ye' in 'yes'
oi   as the 'oy' in 'boy'

Consonants Many Spanish consonants are pronounced similarly to their English counterparts. The pronunciation of a consonant varies according to which vowel follows it and also according to what part of Central America you happen to be in.

c   when followed by 'a,' 'o' or 'u,' a hard 'c' as in 'cat'; before 'e' or 'i,' as an 's'

ch   as 'ch' in 'choose'
d   in the initial position, as the 'd' in 'dog'; elsewhere as the 'th' in 'the'
g   before 'a,' 'o,' 'u,' 'ua' or 'uo,' as the 'g' in 'gate'; before 'e' or 'i,' it is a throaty sound, like the 'h' in 'hit'; when 'g' is followed by 'ue' or 'ui,' the 'g' is pronounced as the 'g' in 'gate' but the 'u' is silent, unless it's a 'ü'
h   never pronounced, silent
j   most closely resembles English 'h' as in 'hot' but is slightly more guttural
ll   as the 'y' in 'yes'
ñ   a nasal sound like the 'ni' in 'onion'
q   as the 'c' in 'cat'; 'q' is always followed by a silent 'u' and either 'e' or 'i'
r   a rolled 'r' sound, longer and stronger for a double 'r' or if it's at the start of the word
s   as the 's' in 'send'
v   as the 'b' in 'book'
x   as the 'ks' in 'thinks' with a weaker 'k' sound
y   a semiconsonant, pronounced as the Spanish 'i' when it's by itself or in the middle of a word; at the start or end of a word it is pronounced between the 'y' in 'yonder' and the 'g' in 'beige'
z   as the 's' in 'sat'

Stress As a general rule the stress goes on the second to last (penultimate) syllable of a word. Words ending in an 'r' (usually verbs) have the stress on the last syllable. If an accent appears on any vowel, the stress is on that syllable.

amigo – a-MI-go
comer – com-ER
aquí – a-QUI

Grammar

This section, though brief, aims to explain the basic rules that should enable you to construct your own sentences.

Word Order The word order of Spanish sentences is similar to English sentence word order, that is, subject-verb-object. When the subject of the sentence is a pronoun, it is usually omitted.

The girl works in a restaurant.
  La chica trabaja en un restaurante.
She works in a restaurant.
  Trabaja en un restaurante.
Central Americans speak Spanish.
  Los centroamericanos hablan español.
We speak English.
  Hablamos inglés.

Verbs There are three types of verbs in Spanish, with infinitives ending in *-ar*, *-er* and *-ir*. They each have a standard set of endings for first, second and third person, singular and plural, and if you follow those, you will manage very well. The verb *hablar*, 'to speak,' is a regular *-ar* verb:

I speak	*(yo) hablo*
you speak (familiar)	*(tú) hablas*
you speak (formal)	*(usted) habla*
he/she/it speaks	*(él/ella) habla*
we speak	*(nosotros)hablamos*
you speak (plural)	*(ustedes) hablan*
they speak	*(ellos/ellas) hablan*

The verb *comer*, 'to eat,' is a regular *-er* verb:

I eat	*(yo) como*
you eat (familiar)	*(tú) comes*
you eat (formal)	*(usted) come*
he/she/it eats	*(él/ella) come*
we eat	*(nosotros) comemos*
you eat (plural)	*(ustedes) comen*
they eat	*(ellos/ellas) comen*

The verb *vivir*, 'to live,' is a regular *-ir* verb:

I live	*(yo) vivo*
you live (familiar)	*(tú) vives*
you live (formal)	*(usted) vive*
he/she/it lives	*(él/ella) vive*
we live	*(nosotros) vivimos*
you live (plural)	*(ustedes) viven*
they live	*(ellos/ellas) viven*

In addition there are quite a few irregular verbs, and the only way to learn is to memorize them. However, the verb endings are more or less common to all regular and most irregular verbs.

In general, the familiar form of 'you' (singular), *tú*, and the verb forms that go with it, are used with family and friends, particularly among young people. The more formal *usted* should be used to address officials and to show respect to older or more senior people.

Nouns Spanish nouns are either masculine or feminine. Nouns ending in 'o,' 'e' or 'ma' are usually masculine. Nouns ending in 'a,' 'ión' or 'dad' are usually feminine.

masculine

book	*libro*
glass	*vaso*
bridge	*puente*
problem	*problema*
traveler	*viajero*

feminine

house	*casa*
song	*canción*
city	*ciudad*
reality	*realidad*
traveler	*viajera*

Plurals As a general rule you make a plural by adding 's' to the noun or adding 'es' if the noun ends in a consonant.

house, houses	*casa, casas*
election, elections	*elección, elecciones*

Articles The definite article (the) and the indefinite article (a, some) must agree with the noun in gender and number, so there are four forms of each.

the boy	*el chico*
the boys	*los chicos*
the girl	*la chica*
the girls	*las chicas*
the bed	*la cama*
the beds	*las camas*
a boy	*un chico*
some boys	*unos chicos*
a girl	*una chica*
some girls	*unas chicas*
a bed	*una cama*
some beds	*unas camas*

Adjectives An adjective follows the noun it describes and, like the definite or indefinite article, must agree with it in gender and number.

the pretty house	la casa bonita
some pretty rooms	unos cuartos bonitos
a good boy	un chico bueno
the good girls	las chicas buenas

Greetings & Civilities

Greetings are used more frequently in Latin America than in English-speaking countries. For example, it is polite to greet people when you walk into a shop or a bar.

hello	hola
good morning	buenos días
good afternoon	buenas tardes
good evening or good night	
	buenas noches

The last three are frequently shortened to *buenos/as*. This is used in Central America, accompanied by a slight nod of the head.

How are you?	¿Cómo está? (formal)
	or ¿Cómo estás? (informal)
How are things going?	¿Qué tal?
Well, thanks.	Bien, gracias.
Very well.	Muy bien.
Very badly.	Muy mal.
Good-bye.	Adiós (rarely used).
Bye, see you soon.	Hasta luego (sometimes just 'sta luego').
please	por favor
thank you	gracias
many thanks	muchas gracias
you're welcome	de nada
excuse me	permiso
sorry	perdón
excuse me, forgive me	
	disculpe, discúlpeme
Good luck!	¡Buena suerte!
Mr, Sir	Señor (formal)
Madam, Mrs	Señora (formal)
unmarried woman	Señorita
pal, friend	compañero/a, amigo/a

Small Talk

I'd like to introduce you to . . .	
	Le presento a . . .
A pleasure (to meet you).	
	Mucho gusto.
What is your name?	
	¿Cómo se llama usted? (formal)
	¿Cómo te llamas? (informal)
My name is . . .	Me llamo . . .

Where are you from?	
	¿De dónde es usted? (formal)
	¿De dónde vienes? (familiar)
I am from . . .	Soy de . . .
Australia	Australia
Canada	Canadá
England	Inglaterra
Germany	Alemania
Israel	Israel
Italy	Italia
Japan	Japón
New Zealand	Nueva Zelanda
Norway	Noruega
Scotland	Escocia
Sweden	Suecia
the United States	los Estados Unidos
What do you do?	¿Qué hace?
What's your profession?	
	¿Cuál es su profesión?
I am a . . .	Soy . . .
student	estudiante
teacher	profesor/a
nurse	enfermero/a
lawyer	abogado/a
engineer	ingeniero/a
mechanic	mecánico/a
Can I take a photo?	
	¿Puedo sacar una foto?
Of course/Why not/Sure.	
	Por supuesto/Cómo no/Claro.
How old are you?	
	¿Cuántos años tiene?
Do you speak English?	
	¿Habla inglés?
I speak a little Spanish.	
	Hablo un poquito de español.
I don't understand.	
	No entiendo.
Could you repeat that?	
	¿Puede repetirlo?
Could you speak more slowly please?	
	¿Puede hablar más despacio por favor?
How does one say . . . ?	
	¿Cómo se dice . . . ?
What does . . . mean?	
	¿Que significa . . . ?

Families are very important in Central America and people will generally ask you all about yours.

Are you married? *¿Es casado/a?*
I am single. *Soy soltero/a.*
I am married. *Soy casado/a.*
Is your husband/wife here?
    ¿Está su esposo/a aquí?

If the conversation is more personal, the 'familiar' form is used:

How many children do you have?
    ¿Cuántos niños tienes?
How many brothers/sisters do you have?
    ¿Cuántos hermanos/hermanas tienes?
Do you have a boyfriend/girlfriend?
    ¿Tienes novio/a?

Feelings

Spanish usually uses the irregular verb *tener* (to have) to express feelings.

I am . . . *Tengo . . .*
    cold *frío*
    hot *calor*
We are . . . *Tenemos . . .*
    sleepy *sueño*
    thirsty *sed*
    hungry *hambre*

Accommodations

Where is . . . ? *¿Dónde hay . . . ?*
    a hotel *un hotel*
    a boarding house *una pensión*
    a guesthouse *un hospedaje*
I am looking for . . . *Estoy buscando . . .*
    a cheap hotel *un hotel barato*
    a good hotel *un hotel bueno*
    a nearby hotel *un hotel cercano*
    a clean hotel *un hotel limpio*
Are there any rooms available?
    ¿Hay habitaciones libres?
Where are the toilets?
    ¿Dónde están los servicios/baños?
I would like a . . . *Quisiera un . . .*
    single room *cuarto sencillo*
    double room *cuarto doble*
    room with a bath *cuarto con baño*
Can I see it? *¿Puedo verlo?*
Are there others? *¿Hay otros?*
How much is it? *¿Cuánto cuesta?*
It's too expensive. *Es demasiado caro.*
your name *su nombre*
your surname *su apellido*
room number *el número de cuarto*

Transportation

Where is . . . ? *¿Dónde está . . . ?*
    the central bus station
        la estación central de autobuses
    the railway station *la estación de trenes*
    the airport *el aeropuerto*
    the ticket office *la boletería*
    the bus *el bus/la camioneta*
When does the bus/train/plane leave?
    ¿Cuándo sale el bus/tren/avión?
I want to go to . . . *Quiero ir a . . .*
What time do they leave?
    ¿A qué hora salen?
Can you take me to . . . ?
    ¿Puede llevarme a . . . ?
Could you tell me where . . . is located?
    ¿Podría decirme dónde está . . . ?
Is it far? *¿Está lejos?*
Is it close to here? *¿Está cerca de aquí?*
Stop! *¡Pare!*
Wait! *¡Espere!*
north *norte*
south *sur*
east *este*
west *oeste*

Around Town

I'm looking for . . . *Estoy buscando . . .*
    the post office *el correo*
    the . . . embassy *la embajada de . . .*
    the museum *el museo*
    the police *la policía*
    the market *el mercado*
    the bank *el banco*

Money

I want to change some money.
    Quiero cambiar dinero.
I want to change traveler's checks.
    Quiero cambiar cheques viajeros.
What is the exchange rate?
    ¿Cuál es el tipo de cambio?
How many colones/pesos/quetzales
per dollar?
    ¿Cuántos colones/pesos/quetzales
por dólar?
cashier *caja*
credit card *tarjeta de crédito*
the black market *el mercado negro*
bank notes *billetes de banco*
exchange houses *casas de cambio*

Emergencies

Watch out!	¡Cuidado!
Help!	¡Socorro!
	or ¡Auxilio!
Fire!	¡Fuego!
Thief!	¡Ladrón!
I've been robbed.	Me han robado.
They took . . .	Se llevaron . . .
my money	mi dinero
my passport	mi pasaporte
my bag	mi bolsa
Where is . . . ?	¿Dónde hay . . . ?
a policeman	un policía
a doctor	un doctor
a hospital	un hospital
Leave me alone!	¡Déjeme!
Don't bother me!	¡No me moleste!
Get lost!	¡Váyase!

Time

What time is it?	¿Qué hora es?
It is 1 o'clock.	Es la una.
It is 7 o'clock.	Son las siete.

Days

Monday	lunes
Tuesday	martes
Wednesday	miércoles
Thursday	jueves
Friday	viernes
Saturday	sábado
Sunday	domingo

Months

January	enero
February	febrero
March	marzo
April	abril
May	mayo
June	junio
July	julio
August	agosto
September	septiembre
October	octubre
November	noviembre
December	diciembre

Past, Present, Future

today	hoy
this morning	esta mañana
this afternoon	esta tarde
tonight	esta noche
yesterday	ayer
last night	anoche
tomorrow	mañana
week/month/year	semana/mes/año
last week	la semana pasada
next month	el próximo mes
always	siempre
it's early/late	es temprano/tarde
now	ahora
before/after	antes/después

Ordinal Numbers

Masculine forms are given; the feminine form ends with an 'a' instead of an 'o.'

first	primero
second	segundo
third	tercero
fourth	cuarto
fifth	quinto
sixth	sexto
seventh	séptimo
eighth	octavo
ninth	noveno, nono
tenth	décimo
eleventh	undécimo
twelfth	duodécimo
twentieth	vigésimo

Cardinal Numbers

0	*cero*	30	*treinta*
1	*uno, una*	31	*treinta y uno*
2	*dos*	40	*cuarenta*
3	*tres*	50	*cincuenta*
4	*cuatro*	60	*sesenta*
5	*cinco*	70	*setenta*
6	*seis*	80	*ochenta*
7	*siete*	90	*noventa*
8	*ocho*	100	*cien*; when followed
9	*nueve*		by a noun, *ciento*
10	*diez*	101	*ciento uno*
11	*once*	102	*ciento dos*
12	*doce*	193	*ciento noventa y tres*
13	*trece*	200	*doscientos*
14	*catorce*	300	*trescientos*
15	*quince*	500	*quinientos*
16	*dieciséis*	600	*seiscientos*
17	*diecisiete*	900	*novecientos*
18	*dieciocho*	1000	*mil*
19	*diecinueve*	2000	*dos mil*
20	*veinte*	100,000	*cien mil*
21	*veintiuno*	1,000,000	*un millón*
22	*veintidós*	2,000,000	*dos millones*

Online Resources

FACTS FOR THE VISITOR
Useful Organizations
Latin American Bureau
  lab@gn.apc.org
South American Explorers Club
  in the USA: explorer@samexplo.org
  in Quito: explorer@saec.org.ec
  in Lima: montague@amauta.rcp.net.pe
  www.samexplo.org
Citizens Emergency Center,
  US State Department,travel advisories
  www.travel.state.gov

GETTING THERE & AWAY
International Association of Air Travel Couriers
  iaatc@courier.org
STA Travel
  help@statravelgroup.co.uk
Travel CUTS/Voyages Campus
  mail@travelcuts.com
  www.travelcuts.com

GETTING AROUND
Green Tortoise
  tortoise@greentortoise.com
  www.greentortoise.com

GUATEMALA
Newspapers & Magazines
Guatemala Weekly
  gweekly@pronet.net.gt
  www.pronet.net.gt/gweekly/
The Siglo News
  sales@sigloxxi.com
  www.sigloxxi.com
Revue
  Revue@guate.net
CERIGUA
  cerigua@guate.net
Central America Report
  inforpre@guate.net
Guatemala News and Information Bureau (GNIB)
  gnib@igc.apc.org

Language Courses
Kermit Frazier, the Kuinik Ta'ik Language School
  momos@guate.net

Work
ADIFAM
  momos@guate.net
ARCAS
  arcas@pronet.net.gt

Guatemala City
Hotel Ajau
  hotajau@gua.gbm.net

Antigua Guatemala
Conexion
  Conex@ibm.net

Escuela de Español San José el Viejo
  spanish@guate.net
  www.guate.net/spanish/

Santiago Atitlán
Posada de Santiago
  posdesantiago@guate.net

Quetzaltenango
Casa Internacional
  estrella@c.net.gt
Centro de Estudios de Español Pop Wuj
  popwujxel@pronet.net.gt
  for US contact: PopWuj@aol.com
Escuela de Español Sakribal
  sakribal@aol.com
Juan Sisay Spanish School
  bufetej@pronet.net.gt

Momostenango
Kuinik Ta'ik Language School
  momos@guate.net
ADIFAM
  momos@guate.net

Tikal
The Adventure Travel Center
  viareal@guate.net

Río Dulce
Hollymar Restaurant
  HollymarG@aol.com

BELIZE

For a small country with a primitive telephone system, Belize has embraced the Internet with surprising speed and success. Many Belizean businesses are reachable by electronic mail (often in the format *businessname*@btl.net), and there are several useful World Wide Web sites, including:

General & Commercial Information

www.belize.com
www.belizeit.com
www.belizenet.com

Tourist & Commercial Information on
    Ambergris Caye
    www.ambergriscaye.com

El Pilar Archaeological reserve near
    San Ignacio, Cayo
    alishaw.sscf.ucsb.edu/~ford/index.html

Maya Research Project excavations at Blue Creek
    www.qvision.com/MRP

Media

Equator Publishing
    74763.2254@compuserve.com

Transportation

Maya Airways
    mayair@btl.net

Tour Belize Auto Rental
    tourbelize@btl.net

Belize City

Belize Tourist Board
    btb@btl.net

Belize Tourism Industry Association
    btia@btl.net

Atlantic Bank Limited
    atlantic@btl.net

Belize Bank
    bbankisd@btl.net

Colton House (hotel)
    coltonhse@btl.net

Ambergris Caye

Blue Hole Dive Center
    bluehole@btl.net

Coral Beach Hotel & Dive Club
    forman@btl.net

Bermudian Landing
Community Baboon Sanctuary

Belize Audubon Society
    base@btl.net

Corozal Town

Corozal Central Guesthouse
    Vince@btl.net

San Ignacio (Cayo)

Eva's Restaurant & Bar
    evas@btl.net

Midas Eco-Resort
    evas@btl.net (ATTN: MIDAS)

Venus Hotel
    daniels@btl.net

Toledo District

Toledo Ecotourism Association
    ttea@btl.net

HONDURAS
Tourist Offices

Instituto Hondureño de Turismo, US office
    104202.3433@compuserve.com

Books

Honduras Travel Guide by Brad Martin
    Honduras1@aol.com

La Mosquitia: A Guide to the Savannas, Rain Forest, and Turtle Hunters by Derek Parent
    derekp@vir.com
    www.cir.com/~derekp/index.html

Media

El Tiempo
    www.tiempo.hn

Honduras This Week
    hontweek@hondutel.hn
    www.marrder.com/htw/

Honduras Tips
    www.globalnet.hn/hondutip.htm

La Prensa
    www.laprensahn.com

Coconut Telegraph
    cocotel@globalnet.hn
    www.bayislands.com

Tegucigalpa

Email service: Telemática
    www.hondutel.hn

Shakespeare & Co Books
    tataylor@ns.gbm.hn

San Pedro Sula

Javier Pinel
    mayaeco@globalnet.hn

Cambio Centroamérica
    cambio@mayanet.hn

Parque National Cusuco

Fundación Héctor Rodrigo Pastor Fasquelle
fehrpf@globalnet.hn

La Ceiba

Euro Honduras Tours
eurotour@hondutel.hn

Ríos Honduras
73241.3240@compuserve.com
riosrios@globalnet.hn

Roatán

Waterloo Design & Communications
waterloo@globalnet.hn
www.best/roatanet.com

Coconut Telegraph
cocotel@globalnet.hn
www.bayislands.com

Ocean Divers
oceandivers@globalnet.hn

Cayos Cochinos

Plantation Beach Resort
hkinett@hondutel.hn

EL SALVADOR
Useful Organizations

Centro Internacional de Solidaridad (CIS)
cis@nicarao.apc.org

San Salvador

Oasis Guest House
oasisdam@es.com.sv

Isla Montecristo

Cordes
cordes@itinet.net

COSTA RICA

Some Website addresses in Costa Rica are case sensitive: they must be typed exactly as shown.

General Information

Costa Rica's TravelNet
www.centralamerica.com/cr/

Instituto Costarricence de Turismo (ICT, Costa Rican Tourist Board)
info@tourism-costarica.com
www.tourism-costarica.com

Travelin' Woman Newsletter
travliw@aol.com

Triángulo Rosa (gay support group in San José)
rastern@sol.racsa.co.cr

Canadian Organization for Tropical Education and Rain Forest Conservation (COTERC)
coterc@maple.net

Caribbean Conservation Corporation (CCC)
US Office: cccorp@nervm.nerdc.ufl.edu
Tortuguero CCC Research Station:
ccctort@expreso.co.cr

Costa Rican Outlook Newsletter
sagcm@electriciti.com

Tour & Travel Agencies

Americana Fishing Services
fishing@sol.racsa.co.cr

Aventuras Naturales
avenat@sol.racsa.co.cr

Blue Wing International (the *Rain Goddess*)
bluewing@ticonet.cr

Calypso Tours
calypso@centralamerica.com
www.calypsotours.com/cr/calypso/index.htm

Canopy Tour, San José
canopy@sol.racsa.co.cr
canopytour.co.cr

Costa Rica Expeditions
costaric@expeditions.co.cr.co.cr
www.crexped.co.cr

Cotur
cotour@sol.racsa.co.cr

Horizontes
horizont@sol.racsa.co.cr
www.horizontes.com

Lynch Tourist Service, Quepos
lyntur@sol.racsa.co.cr

Mitur
mitour@sol.racsa.co.cr

Outward Bound (Costa Rica School)
crrobs@sol.racsa.co.cr
centralamerica.com/cr/crrobs

Ríos Tropicales
info@riostro.com
rios@centralamerica.com
www.riostro.com
centralamerica.com/cr/raft/rios.htm

Selva Mar, San Isidro & Dominical
selvamar@sol.racsa.co.cr

Tico Travel
tico@gate.net

Spanish Schools in Costa Rica

Central American Institute for Intl Affairs
    icai@expreso.co.cr

Centro Linguistico Conversa
    conversa@sol.racsa.co.cr
    www.centralamerica.com/cr/school/con-
    versa.htm

Centro Panamericano de Idiomas
    anajarro@sol.racsa.co.cr
    www.westnet.com/costarica/cpi.html

Forester Instituto Nacional
    forester@sol.racsa.co.cr
    www.cool.co.cr/forester

ILISA
    info@langlink.com
    www.langlink.com

Instituto de Lenguaje Pura Vida, Heredia
    BS7324@aol.com
    www.arweb.com/puravida

Intercultura of Heredia
    see ILISA

ASLS
    span1@aol.com
    ISLSCR@sol.racsa.co.cr
    www.ISLS.com

Universidad Veritas
    veritas@sol.racsa.co.cr

Other Businesses

Arco Iris Ecolodge, Monteverde
    arcoiris@sol.racsa.co.cr
    www.bbb.or.cr/Lodges/ArcoIris/
    ArcoIris.htm

Bill Beard's Diving Safaris, Playa Hermosa
    diving@sol.racsa.co.cr

The Butterfly Farm
    bflyfarm@sol.racsa.co.cr

Café Britt Coffeetour
    britt@sol.racsa.co.cr

El Sano Banano, Montezuma
    elbanano@sol.racsa.co.cr
    www.efn.org/~timbl/cr/elbanano.html

La Buena Nota, Manuel Antonio
    buennota@sol.racsa.co.cr

La Selva Biological Station
    laselva@ns.ots.ac.cr
    see Organization for Tropical Studies

Maiden Voyages Magazine
    info@maiden-voyages.com
    www.maiden-voyages.com

Monteverde Conservation League
    acmmcl@sol.racsa.co.cr

Monteverde Institute
    mviimv@sol.racsa.co.cr

Organization of Tropical Studies, San José
    Reservations Office
    reservas@ns.ots.ac.cr

Rainforest Aerial Tram
    doselsa@sol.racsa.co.cr
    www.rainforest.co.cr

Rich Coast Diving, Playa del Coco
    richcoas@sol.racsa.co.cr
    scuba@divecostarica.com
    www.divecostarica.com

Wilson Botanical Gardens, San Vito
    lcruces@ns.ots.ac.cr
    see Organization for Tropical Studies

PANAMA
Books & Maps

Patricia E Upton
    patricia@dmi.net

Panama City

ANCON
    ancon2@ancon.up.ac.pa

Isla Barro Colorado

Smithsonian Tropical Research Institute
    stri.tivoli.arosemo@ic.si.edu

Boquete

La Montaña y el Valle
    montana@chiriqui.com

Bocas del Toro

La Escuelita de Bocas del Toro
    domini@sol.racsa.co.cr
    www.westnet/costarica/edu/escuelita.html

Index

ABBREVIATIONS

B – Belize
C – Costa Rica
Col – Colombia
E – El Salvador

G – Guatemala
H – Honduras
Mex – Mexico
N – Nicaragua

P – Panama
PN – Parque Nacional
   (National Park)

MAPS

Central America between
   pp 16 & 17

Belize 256
   districts 259
   Map Index 255
   Parks & Protected Areas 258
Belize City 266
   Central Belize City 268-269
Belmopan 290
Benque Viejo del Carmen 297
Caye Caulker 275
Cayo District 295
Corozal Town 287
Dangriga 300
Orange Walk Town 285
Placencia 303
Punta Gorda 305
San Ignacio (Cayo) 292
San Pedro (Ambergris Caye)
   279

Costa Rica 590-591
   Map Index 589
   Parks & Protected Areas 596
Cahuita 658
Central Valley & Highlands
   630-631
Golfito 670-671
Jacó Area 678
Jacó Center 679
Liberia 645
Manuel Antonio Area 684-685
Monteverde & Santa Elena
   640-641
Península de Nicoya 688-689
Península de Osa & Golfo Dulce
   668
Playa del Coco 690
Playa Tamarindo 692
Puerto Limón 653
Puerto Viejo de Talamanca 662
Puntarenas 676

Quepos 681
San Isidro de El General 666
San José 614-615
San Vito 674
Turrialba 637

El Salvador 458
   Map Index 457
La Libertad 493
La Unión 510
San Miguel 507
San Salvador 476
   Blvd de los Héroes 482
   City Center 478
Santa Ana 498

Guatemala 98-99
   Map Index 96
   Parks & Protected Areas 103
Antigua Guatemala 136-137
Chichicastenango 165
Chiquimula 211
Cobán 205
El Petén 232
Flores 234
Guatemala City 120-121
Huehuetenango 187
Lago de Atitlán 150
Lago de Petén Itzá 233
Lívingston 227
Panajachel 152
Puerto Barrios 223
Quetzaltenango 175
   Central Quetzaltenango 178
Retalhuleu 192
Santa Elena 236
Santa Lucía Cotzumalguapa 195
Tikal 242-243

Honduras 310-311
   Map Index 309
   Parks & Protected Areas 317
Bay Islands (Islas de la Bahía)
   418

Choluteca 453
Comayagua 356
Copán 377
Copán Ruinas 372
Gracias 384
Guanaja 442
Juticalpa 446
La Ceiba 401
Puerto Cortés 390
Roatán 424-425
San Pedro Sula 363
Santa Rosa de Copán 381
Siguatepeque 359
Tegucigalpa 340-341
Tela 394
Trujillo 410
Utila 436

Nicaragua 518-519
   Map Index 517
Bluefields 586
Estelí 556
Granada 570
Isla de Ometepe 578
León 561
Managua 539
   Barrio Martha Quezada 544
   Around Managua 549
Masaya 566
Matagalpa 552
Rama 585
San Juan del Sur 576

Panama 702-703
   Map Index 700
   provinces 710
Bocas del Toro 772
Boquete 762
Darién Gap 783
David 758
Panama Canal 741
Panama City 726-727
   San Felipe (Casco Viejo) 730
   Central Panama City 733

TEXT

Map references are in **bold** type.

Abaj Takalik (G) 194
Acajutla (ES) 503-504
Acandí (P) 788
accommodations 70-71
Agua Caliente (H) 388
Aguacate (P) 788
Agustín de Iturbide 19
Ahuachapán (ES) 502
Ahuas (H) 449
air passes 85-86
air travel
    Belize 264-265, 272
    Central America 74-81,
        85-86
    Costa Rica 610, 625-626
    El Salvador 472-474
    Guatemala 130
    Honduras 334-335
    Nicaragua 535
    Panama 722-723
airfares 74-81, 85-86
airlines 85
airports, international 74
Alajuela (CR) 629
Alemán, Arnoldo 524
Almirante (P) 778-779
Altagracia (N) 581
Altun Ha (B) 282-283
Alvarado, Pedro de 18, 171
Álvaro, Enrique Arzú Irigoyen
    100
Amapala (H) 452
Ambergris Caye (B) 278-282
Andino, General Tiburcio Carías
    314
Anguiatú (ES) 213
Antigua Guatemala 134-148,
    136-137
    accommodations 143-144
    entertainment 146
    organized tours 143
    orientation 135-138
    restaurants 144-146
    things to see & do 139-143
    tourist office 138
    transportation to/from
        147-148
    transportation within 148
Apaneca (ES) 502
Aquino, Anastasio 459
ARCAS 235
archaeology 33, 358, 584, 755
Archbishop Romero 480

Archipiélago de Bocas del Toro
    (P) 771-778, **772**
Archipiélago de las Perlas (P)
    748
Archipiélago de San Blas (P)
    780-784
Archipiélago de Solentiname
    (N) 581-582
Area de Conservación
    Guanacaste (ACG) 647
artesanías 28, 565, 753
arts 28
Asociación del Medio Ambiente
    y Rehabilitación de Aves
    Silvestres (AMARAS) 409
Asociación Talamanqueña de
    Ecoturismo y Conservación
    (ATEC) 661
Atecozol (ES) 503
Atiquizaya (ES) 502
Augusto C Sandino International
    Airport (N) 535, 547
Avalon Reserve (CR) 665

backpacking 45, 69, 608
Baha'i Temple (P) 743
Bahía Drake (CR) 669
Baird's tapir (B) 258
Baja Mar (H) 391-392
Balboa, Vasco Nuñez de 18,
    701
Balboa Yacht Club (P) 734
Ballet Folklórico Garífuna 399
Balneario Aguas Termales (H)
    386
Balneario Bahr (H) 362
Balneario Chio (G) 208
Balneario Las Islas (G) 208
balnearios 753
Bambito (P) 768
banana republic 313
Barbareta Island (H) 434-435
bargaining 42
Barra del Colorado (CR)
    656-657
Barra Plátano (H) 448-449
Barriles (P) 767
Barva (CR) 633
Basílica de Suyapa (H) 351-352
Bay Islands (Islas de la Bahía)
    (H) 418-444, **418**
beaches 34, 68
    Belize 301

Costa Rica 659-661, 664-
    665, 672-679, 683, 688,
    691, 694-698
    See also playa
El Salvador 492-493, 495,
    509, 511
Honduras 389, 403, 406-411
Nicaragua 550-551, 575-576,
    581-588
Panama 744, 746-747, 750-
    753, 762, 774
Belén Gualcho (H) 386
Belize 255-308, **256**, **258-259**
    accommodations 263
    highlights 260
    history 255-257
    money 261-262
    tourist offices 260-261
    transportation to/from 264
    transportation within 264-265
    visas 261
Belize Audubon Society 282
Belize City (B) 265-274, **266**,
    268-269
    accommodations 271-272
    entertainment 272
    information 270
    orientation 267
    restaurants 272
    things to see & do 270-271
    tourist offices 267
    transportation to/from
        272-273
    transportation within
        273-274
Belize Zoo (B) 289
Belmopan (B) 289-291, **290**
Benemérito (Mex) 252
Benque Viejo (B) 251
Benque Viejo del Carmen (B)
    297, **297**
Bermudian Landing Community
    Baboon Sanctuary 282
Bethel (G) 251
bicycling 45, 92-93, 142, 395
Bijao (P) 792
Bilbao (G) 196-197
Biotopo Cerro Cahuí (G) 240
Biotopo del Quetzal (G) 203-
    204
Biotopo Mario Dary Rivera
    Nature Reserve. *See* Biotopo
    del Quetzal

bird watching
  Belize 303
  Costa Rica 595, 608, 643-
    644, 651, 654
  Guatemala 115, 236
  Honduras 331, 361, 375
  Nicaragua 553
  Panama 719-720, 742, 752
black Caribs. See Garifunas
black Creoles 259, 583
black market 41-42
Bliss, Baron 271
Bliss Institute 270
Blue Creek (B) 308
Blue Hole National Park (B)
  299
Bluefields (N) 36, 585-587, **586**
Bluff (N) 585
boat travel 93-94
  Belize 273, 278-280, 291
  Honduras 337-338
Boca de Cupe (P) 790
Bocas del Drago (P) 774
Bocas del Toro province (P)
  771-779, **772**
Bocas del Toro town (P)
  771-777
Bocas Isla (P) 773
books 44-46
Boquerón (ES) 490
Boquete (P) 763-765, **762**
border crossings 88
Boruca 27
Borucas (CR) 598
Bribri (CR) 27, 598
Brus Laguna (H) 449
Bryan-Chamorro Treaty 521
Buenos Aires (H) 370
bus stations 87
bus travel 81, 86-88
  Belize 272-273
  Costa Rica 611-612, 626-628
  El Salvador 472-474
  Guatemala 131-132,
    147-148, 158, 181-182
  Honduras 334-337
  Nicaragua 546-547
  Panama 723

Cabulco (G) 203
Cahal Pech (B) 291
Cahuita (CR) 657-660, **658**
Cakchiquel Maya (G) 150
Caldera (P) 765
camping 70
Cañas (CR) 643-644

canoeing 331
Capurganá (Col) 786-788
car & motorcycle travel 88-92
  Belize 265
  Costa Rica 612
  El Salvador 474-475
Caracol (B) 296
carnaval 753
Carretera de Occidente (H) 370
Carretera del Litoral (ES)
  505-506
Carta Vieja Rum Distillery (P)
  761
Cartago (CR) 634-636
Casa de la Cultura
  Totonicapense (G) 173-174
Casa K'ojom (G) 140
Casa Popenoe (G) 141
Catacamas (H) 447
Catarina (N) 568
CATIE 636
caves 360
Caye Caulker (B) 274-278, **275**
Cayo. See San Ignacio (B)
Cayo District (B) 294-296, **295**
Cayo Nancy (P) 778
Cayos Blancos (H) 417
Cayos Cochinos (Hog Islands)
  (H) 408, 443-444
Cayos Zapatillas (P) 778
CCC 655
Cedeño (H) 452
Ceibal (G) 252
Cerro Azul (P) 743
Cerro Calentura (H) 415
Cerro Chirripó (CR) 667-669
Cerro de la Cruz (G) 148
Cerro de la Muerte (CR) 665
Cerro Juan Díaz Archaelogical
  Site (P) 700-755
Cerro Punta (P) 766-769
Cerro Verde (ES) 496-497
Cerros Archaeological Site (B)
  287-288
Cerros Quemados (Burnt Hills)
  Islands (ES) 490
Chalate. See Chalatenango
Chalatenango (ES) 513-514
Chamorro, Pedro Joaquín 522
Champerico (G) 194
Changuinola (P) 611, 779-780
Chechem Ha (B) 294
Chichicastenango (G) 164-170,
  165
Chimaltenango (G) 149
Chinandega (N) 564

Chiquimula (G) 211-213, **211**
Chiriquí (P) 756-771
Chiriquí Grande (P) 778-779
Chitré (P) 753-755
Chocó Indians (P) 790
Choluteca (H) 452-455, **453**
Chorotegas (N) 568, 578
Chorti (H) 321
Ciénaga de las Macanas (P) 752
cigars 334
CINCAP 235
Ciudad Hidalgo (Mex) 191
Ciudad Quesada (CR) 648-649
Ciudad Segundo Montes (ES)
  512
Ciudad Tecún Umán (G) 191
Ciudad Vieja (G) 148
climate 21-22
cloud forest 24
Cobán (G) 204-208, **205**
Coca-Cola bus terminal (CR)
  626
Cockscomb Basin Wildlife
  Sanctuary (B) 302
coffee
  Costa Rica 592, 633
  El Salvador 459
  Panama 763
cofradías 166
COHDEFOR 339
Cojutepeque (ES) 504
Colombian Revolutionary
  Armed Forces (FARC) 786
Colón (P) 748-749
Columbus, Christopher 17-18,
  410
Comarca coffee cooperative (H)
  359
Comayagua (H) 356-358, **356**
comida corriente 535
Conchagua (ES) 510
Contractors Hill (P) 743
Contras 356, 523-524
Copán archaeological site (H)
  376-381, **377**
Copán Ruinas (H) 371-375, **372**
coral conservation 429
Cordillera de Guanacaste (CR)
  638
Cordillera de Tilarán (CR) 638
Corn Islands (Islas del Maíz) (N)
  525, 588
Coronado (CR) 634
Corozal (H) 407
Corozal Town (B) 286-288, **287**

Cortés, Hernán 18
Costa del Sol (ES) 492-493
Costa Rica 589-698, **590-591,
   596, 630-631**
   accommodations 608-609
   health 606
   highlights 600
   history 589-593
   tourist offices 600-601
   transportation to/from
      610-611
   transportation within
      611-613
   visas 601
courier flights 77
Coxen Hole (H) 423-427
Coyotepe (N) 567
Creoles 19, 585
crime. See dangers &
   annoyances
Cristales (P) 792
Cristóbal (P) 749
Crooked Tree Wildlife
   Sanctuary (B) 283
Cuatro Caminos (G) 173
Cuello Archaeological Site (B)
   285-286
Cuero y Salado Wildlife Refuge
   (H) 408
Cuevas de Taulabé (H) 360-361
culture 28-29, 35-36

dangers & annoyances 65-68,
   263
Dangriga (B) 299-301, **300**
Danlí (H) 451
Dantio (H) 406
Darién Gap (P) 36, 784, **783**
Darién Province (P) 784-792
Darío, Rubén (N) 527, 560, 562
David (P) 757-761, **758**
deforestation 22-23, 316, 594
Dem Dats Doin (B) 307
Diriamba (N) 568
diving, scuba 34, 69
   Belize 274, 276, 278, 280,
      303
   Costa Rica 608, 688
   Guatemala 163
   Honduras 330, 395, 418,
      420-429, 438, 441
   Panama 718, 752, 773-774,
      778
Divisa (P) 748
Dominical (CR) 686
Douglas da Silva (formerly

Augustine) forest ranger
   station (B) 296
drinks 72
driving regulations. See car &
   motorcycle travel
drug trade. See dangers &
   annoyances
drugs 68
Dulce Nombre de Maria (ES)
   514

ecology 22-23
economy 26
ecotourism 375
El Amatillo (H) 455
El Carmen (G) 191
El Castillo (H) 411
El Castillo (N) 583
El Castillo de San Felipe (G)
   220-221
El Cristo Negro (G) 214
El Cuco (ES) 509-510
El Espino (H) 455
El Estor (G) 221
El Florido (G) 216-217
El Manzano (ES) 514
El Mozote (ES) 513
El Naranjo (G) 251
El Paraíso (H) 451
El Petén (G) 231, **232**
El Porvenir (H) 407
El Poy (H) 388
El Real (P) 790
El Remate (G) 240-241
El Rosario (H) 354-355
El Rubí waterfall (H) 375
El Salvador 457-515, **458**
   accommodations 470-471
   health 468
   highlights 465
   history 457-461
   money 466-467
   organized tours 475
   tourist offices 465
   transportation to/from
      472-474
   transportation within
      474-475
   visas 465
El Subín (G) 251
El Tamarindo (ES) 511-512
El Tránsito (N) 551
El Trapiche (N) 543
El Triunfo de la Cruz (H) 399
El Valle (P) 744-746
El Viejo (N) 564

El Zarco Junction (G) 192
email. See Online Resources
   appendix
environment 22-23
Escuintla (G) 199
Esquipulas (G) 213-216
Estanzuela (G) 210-211
Estelí (N) 555-558, **556**

fauna 24-25
faxing 43
Feria de Suyapa (H) 346
Finca del Eddie Serrano (CR)
   665
Finca El Baúl (G) 197
Finca El Paraíso (G) 221
Finca Las Ilusiones (G) 197-198
fishing 34
   Belize 274-276, 278-280,
      303
   Costa Rica 656, 680
   Honduras 361, 395, 424
   Nicaragua 534
   Panama 719
Flamenco (island) (P) 732
flora 23-24
Flores (G) 233-240, 251, **234**
Flour Camp Cave (B) 294
FMLN 459
Fonseca, Carlos 522, 552
food 71-72
Fort Sherman (P) 750
Fortuna (CR) 649-650
French Harbour (H) 427
Frontera Corozal (Mex) 251
FSLN 521-524
Fuentes Georginas (G) 183-184
Fuerte (Fort) San Lorenzo (P)
   749-750
FUCAGUA 415

Gaillard Cut (P) 740
Gandoca-Manzanillo Wildlife
   Refuge (CR) 665
Garífunas (Garinagus) 28, 298-
   259, 263, 321, 388, 393-395,
   398-400, 407, 416-419, 526,
   583, 585
Gatún Locks (P) 742
gay & lesbian travelers 64-65
geography 20-21
geology 21
Glover's Atoll (B) 301
Golfito (CR) 669-672, **670-671**
Golfo de Chiriquí (P) 761-762
Golfo de Fonseca (H) 451-452

Gracias (H) 383-385, **384**
Granada (N) 569-573, **570**
Green Tortoise (tours) 94
Grutas Actun-Can (G) 235
Grutas de Lanquín (G) 209
Guabito (CR) 611
Guabito (N) 665
Guabito (P) 779
Guadalupe (P) 766-769
Guaitil (CR) 693
Guanacaste National Park (B)
    289
Guanaja (H) 441-443, **442**
Guararé (P) 755
Guasaule (H) 455
Guatemala 95-254, **98-99, 103**
    accommodations 116
    health 113
    highlights 108
    history 95-101
    money 109-110
    tourist offices 108
    transportation to/from
        117-118
    transportation within
        118-119
    visas 108-109
Guatemala City (G) 119-133,
    120-121
    accommodations 127-128
    entertainment 129
    orientation 122-123
    restaurants 128-129
    things to see & do 125-127
    tourist offices 123
    transportation to/from
        130-133
    transportation within 133
Guaymí (people) 27, 748, 757
Guerra de Fútbol (H) 314

Hacienda Santa Rosa (CR) 647
handicrafts 146-147. *See also*
    artesanías
Hato del Volcán. *See* Volcán
health 48-62
    insurance 48-49
    women's 62
Heredia (CR) 632-633
highlands 134-191
highlights, regional 33-36
history 17-20
HIV/AIDS 58
hiking 45, 69
    Costa Rica 608, 634, 639,
        659, 673

El Salvador 497, 514
Guatemala 115, 163, 203
Honduras 330, 353
Nicaragua 533, 579
Panama 719, 742, 763, 766
hitchhiking 93
Hog Islands. *See* Cayos
    Cochinos
Honduras 309-456, **310-311,
    317**
    accommodations 331-332
    health 328
    highlights 322-323
    history 312-316
    money 324-325
    organized tours 338
    tourist offices 323
    transportation to/from
        334-335
    transportation within
        335-338
    visas 323
Hopkins (B) 301-302
horseback riding
    Guatemala 141
    Belize 331, 372, 376
    Honduras 608, 639, 659, 687
    Panama 745
hospedajes 71
Huehuetenango (G) 186-190,
    187
Huellas de Acahualinca (N) 543
Humboldt Ecological Station (P)
    751
Hummingbird Hwy (B) 298-299

Iglesia de San Francisco (G)
    140
Iglesia de Santo Tomás (G) 167
Iglesia y Convento de la
    Recolección (G) 141
Iglesia y Convento de Nuestra
    Señora de La Merced (G)
    140
Ilobasco (ES) 505
immunizations 49-50
Indian Church (B) 283
Indians 27
Instituto Clodomiro Picado 634
Iran-Contra Affair 523
Isla Ballena (CR) 687
Isla Barro Colorado (P) 743
Isla Bastimentos (P) 777-778
Isla Boca Brava (P) 761
Isla Colón (P) 771
Isla Conchagüita (ES) 511

Isla Contadora (P) 748
Isla de los Pájaros (P) 778
Isla de Ometepe (N) 578-581,
    578
Isla el Morro (N) 573
Isla el Tigre (H) 511
Isla Grande (P) 750-751
Isla Martín Pérez (ES) 511
Isla Meanguera (ES) 511
Isla Montecristo (ES) 506
Isla Parida (P) 761
Isla Taboga (P) 746-747
Isla Zacatillo (ES) 511
Isla Zapatera (N) 573
Islas de la Bahía. *See* Bay
    Islands
Islas del Maíz. *See* Corn Islands
Isleñas (H) 419
itineraries 33
Iximché (G) 150-151
Izalco (ES) 503
Iztapa (G) 199

Jacó (CR) 679-680, **678-679**
jade 147
Jaguar Reserve. *See* Cockscomb
    Basin Wildlife Sanctuary
jet lag 54
Jicaque (or Xicaque). *See*
    Tolupanes
Jinotega (N) 554-555
Jinotepe (N) 568
Joya de Cerén (ES) 459, 491
Juan Santamaría International
    Airport (CR) 610-611, 625
Juigalpa (N) 584
Jungle Trail (H) 335
Jutiapa (H) 354-355
Juticalpa (H) 445-447, **446**

K'umarcaaj (G) 171
Kaminaljuyú (G) 127
kayaking
    El Salvador 470
    Honduras 331, 438-439
KéköLdi Reserve (CR) 661
Kobbe beach (P) 744
Kuna Indians 790-791

La Aurora International Airport
    (G) 133
La Basílica de Nuestra Señora
    de los Angeles (CR) 635
La Campa (H) 386
La Ceiba (H) 400-406, 450, **401**
La Costa del Bálsamo (ES) 495

814   Index

La Cruz (CR) 648
La Cueva de la Serpiente (G)
    235
La Democracia (G) 198-199
La Ensenada (H) 398
La Entrada (H) 370-371
La Esperanza (H) 360
La Guayra (P) 750
La Libertad (ES) 493-495, **493**
La Libertad (G) 251
La Meseta Central (CR)
    628-637
La Mesilla (G) 190
La Negrita (CR) 635
La Palma (ES) 514
La Palma (G) 251
La Palma (P) 790
La Puntita (ES) 492
La Selva Biological Station (CR)
    651
La Unión (ES) 510-511, **510**
La Unión (H) 444-445
Lago de Amatitlán (G) 201
Lago de Apanás (N) 555
Lago de Atitlán (G) 34,
    149-164, **150**
Lago de Cachí (CR) 635
Lago de Coatepeque (ES)
    495-496
Lago de Güija (ES) 500
Lago de Ilopango (ES) 490
Lago de Izabal (G) 219-221
Lago de Nicaragua (N)
    571-572, 577-578
Lago de Petén Itzá (G) 236, **233**
Lago de Yojoa (H) 361
Lago Gatún (P) 740
Laguna Caldera Volcano (ES)
    459
Laguna de Apoyo (N) 568
Laguna de Asososca (N) 543
Laguna de los Micos (H) 398
Laguna de Masaya (N) 567
Laguna de Perlas (N) 587
Laguna de Xiloá (N) 543
Laguna el Jocotál (ES) 506
Laguna Guaimoreto (H) 416
Lamanai (B) 283-284
Lancetilla Jardín Botánico (H)
    397-398
language courses 69
    Costa Rica 608, 633, 641
    El Salvador 483
    Guatemala 115, 142, 154,
        177-179, 185, 227
    Honduras 331, 373, 412
    Nicaragua 534

Panama 775
Lankester Gardens (CR) 635
Las Isletas (N) 573-574
Las Manos (H) 451
Las Marías (H) 448
Las Pailas (CR) 647
Las Siete Altares (G) 231
Las Tablas (P) 755
Las Vueltas (ES) 513
Latin American Bureau (LAB)
    63
Lempira (H) 312
Lenca (H) 321
León (N) 560-564, **561**
León Viejo (N) 550
Liberia (CR) 644-646, **645**
Likín (G) 199
Limón (CR). *See* Puerto Limón
Limón (H) 418
literature 46, 327, 527, 560, 569
Lívingston (G) 226-230, **227**
Lomas Barbudal (CR) 644
Los Ausoles (ES) 502
Los Chiles (CR) 611, 651
Los Chorros (ES) 491
Los Chorros (H) 407
Los Encuentros (G) 149
Los Naranjos (H) 355, 361
Los Planes de Renderos (ES)
    491-492
Los Pozos de Caldera (P) 765
Los Sapos (H) 373
Los Vahos (H) 182-183
Lubaantun (B) 307

malaria 58-60
Malpaís (CR) 697-698
Managua 538-548, **539, 544,**
    549
    accommodations 544-545
    entertainment 546
    organized tours 543-544
    orientation 540
    restaurants 545-546
    things to see & do 542-543
    tourist offices 540
    transportation to/from
        546-547
    transportation within
        547-548
Mangrove Bight (H) 441
Manuel Antonio (CR) 682-683,
    684-685
Manzanillo (CR) 665
maps 32
    Belize 260
    Costa Rica 600

El Salvador 464
Guatemala 108
Honduras 322
Panama 712-713, 727
maquila industry 462
Marcala (H) 359
Mariscos (G) 221
Martí, Augustín Farabundo (ES)
    459
Masaya (N) 565-568, **566**
Matagalpa (N) 551-554, **552**
Maya people 17, 27, 33, 45-46
    Belize 259
    El Salvador 457, 491,
        501-502
    Guatemala 105-107
    Honduras 360, 444
Maya Center (B) 302
Maya ruins 33, 46
    Belize 282-288, 291-294,
        296, 307
    Guatemala 150, 171, 196-
        197, 218, 241, 249-250
    Honduras 312, 371-375
Mayan airpass 74, 85
Mazatenango (G) 194
Medellín (P) 789
Melchor de Mencos (G) 250,
    298
Menchú, Rigoberta 172
Méndez, Modesto 221
Mennonites 260, 283-284, 293
Mercado Roberto Huembes (N)
    543
Mercado San Isidro (H) 345
Mestizos 526
Metapán (ES) 500
Miami (H) 399
Miraflores Locks (P) 740
Miskito Indians 27, 321, 526,
    583-585, 587
Momostenango (G) 185-186
Moncagua (ES) 508
money 38-42
Montaña de Celaque (H) 386
Monte Sky (CR) 635
Monterrico (G) 200-201
Monteverde (CR) 638-643,
    640-641
Monteverde Cloud Forest
    Reserve (CR) 638-639
Monteverde Music Festival (CR)
    642
Montezuma (CR) 696-697
Monumento Nacional Guayabo
    (CR) 637
Mopan Maya (B) 308

Morazán, Francisco 95
Morgan, Captain Henry 701
Mosquitia region (H) 447-450.
   See also Mosquito Coast
Mosquito Coast (N) 525,
   583-584
motorcycle travel. *See* car &
   motorcycle travel
Moyogalpa (N) 580-581
Museo Colonial (H) 357
Museo de Antropología (N) 574
Museo de Arqueología e
   Historia (H) 365
Museo de Arqueología Maya
   (H) 371
Museo de Arte Costarricense
   (CR) 618-619
Museo de Arte y Diseño
   Contemporaneo (CR) 619
Museo de Jade (CR) 618
Museo de Oro Precolombino
   (CR) 618
Museo Garífuna (G) 226
Museo Nacional (CR) 618
Museo Nacional de Arqueología
   y Etnología (G) 127
Museo Popol Vuh (G) 126

Nahuatl (N) 517
Nahuizalco (ES) 503
Naos (island) (P) 732
national parks 25. *See also* PN
Native American civilizations
   17-18
Nebaj (G) 172
Neily (CR) 673
New River (B) 283
Nicaragua 517-588, **518-519**
   accommodations 534
   health 532
   highlights 528-529
   history 517-524
   money 530-531
   tourist offices 529
   transportation to/from
      535-537
   transportation within
      537-538
   visas 529
Nicaraos (N) 517, 526, 568
Nicoya (CR) 694
Nim Li Punit (B) 307
Nindirí (N) 568
Niquinohomo (N) 568
Nohmul Archaeological Site (B)
   285-286
Noriega, Manuel 705-706

Nueva España 19
Nueva Ocotepeque (H) 209,
   387-388
Nueva San Salvador (ES).
   See Santa Tecla

Oak Ridge (H) 427-428
Ocotal (N) 559
Ojojona (H) 355
Olmec people 457
Omoa (H) 392-393
online services 43. *See also*
   Online Resources appendix
onward tickets 37-38, 76
Orange Walk Town (B)
   284-286, **285**
organized tours 94
Orosi (CR) 635
Ortega, Daniel 523-524
Ostional (CR) 695
OTS 651

Pacbitun (B) 294
Pacific Slope (G) 191-201
PADI certification 420
Padre Miguel Junction (G) 213
Palacios (H) 449
Palenque (Mex) 251-252
Palmar Norte (CR) 669
Palmar Sur (CR) 669
Palo de las Letras (P) 791-792
Panajachel (G) 151-159, **152**
Panama 699-792, **702-703**, **710**
   highlights 713
   history 699-707
   money 715
   organized tours 725
   tourist offices 713-714
   transportation to/from
      722-723
   transportation within
      723-725
   visas 714
Panama Canal (P) 33, 703-705,
   740-742, **741**
Panama Canal Yacht Club (P)
   749
Panama City (P) 725-740,
   726-727, **730**, **733**
   accommodations 735-736
   entertainment 737-738
   information 728
   organized tours 734-735
   orientation 726-728
   restaurants 736-737
   things to see & do 730-734

transportation to/from
   738-739
transportation within
   739-740
Panamá Viejo (P) 701, 732
Panchimalco (ES) 492
Paquera (CR) 696
Paraíso (CR) 635
Parque Balboa (ES) 491
Parque de las Naciones Unidas
   (H) 346
Parque de las Piedrecitas (N)
   543
Parque Internacional la Amistad
   (P) 768-770
parque nacional. *See* PN
Parque Zoológico Simón Bolívar
   (CR) 619
Partido Liberación Nacional
   (PLN) 593
Paso Canoas (CR) 611, 675
Pavones (CR) 672
Paya (P) 791
Pech (also called Paya) (H) 321
Pedasí (P) 752
Pedro Miguel Locks (P) 740
Peñas Blancas (CR) 610, 648
Peñas Blancas (N) 575
Península de Azuero (P)
   751-756
Península de Nicoya (CR) 687,
   688-689
Peninsula de Osa (CR) 672, **668**
People's United Party (PUP)
   259
Perico (island) (P) 732
Perquín (ES) 512
photography 47-48
Pipil (ES) 457
Placencia (B) 302-304, **303**
Playa Avellana (CR) 693
Playa Chiquita (CR) 664
Playa Cocles (CR) 664
Playa del Coco (CR) 688-691,
   690
Playa el Espino (ES) 506
Playa Hermosa (CR) 679
Playa Junquillal (CR) 693
Playa las Lajas (P) 762
Playa Naranjo (CR) 696
Playa Nosara (CR) 694-695
Playa Sámara (CR) 695-696
Playa Tamarindo (CR) 691-692,
   692
Playa Venado (P) 752
Playa Zancudo (CR) 672
PN Barra Honda (CR) 694

PN Braulio Carrillo (CR) 633-634
PN Cahuita (CR) 657, 660-661
PN Capiro-Calentura (H) 415
PN Celaque (H) 383, 386-387
PN Cerro Azul Meambar (H) 361
PN Cerro Hoya (P) 752
PN Chagres (P) 743
PN Chirripó (CR) 667-669
PN Corcovado (CR) 672-673
PN Cusuco (H) 369-370
PN de Béisbol (ES) 488
PN el Imposible (ES) 504
PN Guanacaste (CR) 648
PN La Muralla (H) 445
PN La Tigra (H) 353-355
PN Las Victorias (G) 206
PN Los Katíos (Col) 784, 793
PN Manuel Antonio (CR) 683-686
PN Marino Ballena (CR) 687
PN Marino Golfo de Chiriquí (P) 761
PN Marino Isla Bastimentos (P) 771
PN Marino Las Baulas de Guanacaste (CR) 692-693
PN Marino Punta Sal (H) 398
PN Montecristo-El Trifinio (ES) 500-501
PN Nancuchiname (ES) 506
PN Palo Verde (CR) 644
PN Pico Bonito (H) 408-409
PN Rincón de la Vieja (CR) 646-647
PN Santa Bárbara (H) 361
PN Santa Rosa (CR) 647-648
PN Sarigua (P) 751
PN Soberanía (P) 742-743
PN Tapantí (CR) 635
PN Tikal (G) 241-249
PN Tortuguero (CR) 654-655
PN Volcán Arenal (CR) 649
PN Volcán Barú (P) 765-766
PN Volcán Irazú (CR) 635-636
PN Volcán Masaya (N) 548-550
PN Volcán Poás (CR) 632
Pochomil (N) 550
politics 25
Poneloya (N) 564
Poptún (G) 221-222
population & people 27-28
Portobelo (P) 750
post 42-43
pre-Columbian history 17, 312, 355, 376, 574

Provincias Unidas del Centro de América 20
Púcuro (P) 790-791
Puerta del Diablo (ES) 491
Puerto Armuelles (P) 771
Puerto Asese (N) 573
Puerto Barrios (G) 222-226, **223**
Puerto Cabezas (N) 587-588
Puerto Castilla (H) 416
Puerto Cortés (H) 389-391, **390**
Puerto Jiménez (CR) 672-673
Puerto Lempira (H) 449
Puerto Limón (CR) 652-654, **653**
Puerto Obaldía (P) 786-787
Puerto San José (G) 199
Puerto Viejo de Sarapiquí (CR) 651-652
Puerto Viejo de Talamanca (CR) 661-664, **662**
Pulhapanzak (H) 361-362
Punta (H) 399
Punta Gorda (B) 304-306, **305**
Punta Ratón (H) 452
Punta Uva (CR) 664
Puntarenas (CR) 675-678, **676**
Purisil (CR) 635

Quepos (CR) 680-682, **681**
quetzal 24, 369
Quetzaltenango (G) 174-182, **175, 178**
Quiché, Departamento del (G) 164-173
Quiriguá (G) 217-219

Rabin Ajau (G) 204
Rabinal (G) 203
Rabinal Maya (G) 204
rain forest 22-23, 45
Rain Forest Aerial Tram 634
Rain Forest Canopy Tours 608
Rain Forest Medicine Trail (B) 294
Rama (N) 583-585, **585**
Ramas (N) 526, 585
Reagan, Ronald 522-523
Refugio de Vida Silvestre Cenegón del Mangle (P) 752
Refugio de Vida Silvestre Isla Iguana (P) 752
Refugio de Vida Silvestre Punta Izopo (H) 398
Refugio de Vida Silvestre Taboga Uraba (P) 747
Refugio Nacional de Fauna

Silvestre Golfito (CR) 669-672
Refugio Nacional de Fauna Silvestre Ostional (CR) 695
Refugio Nacional de Vida Silvestre Caño Negro (CR) 651
religion 30
Reserva Biológica Bosque Nuboso Monteverde (CR) 638
Reserva Biológica Carara (CR) 678
Reserva Biológica Lomas Barbudal (CR) 644
Reserva Biológica Oro Verde (CR) 687
Reserva Forestal el Montuoso (P) 752
Reserva Natural Absoluta Cabo Blanco (CR) 698
Reserva Santa Elena (CR) 639, **640-641**
Retalhuleu (G) 192-194, **192**
Río Agua Caliente (G) 221
Río Cangrejal (H) 407-408
Río Dulce (G) 36, 219-220, 230-231
Río Frío (CR) 651
Río Hondo (G) 209-210
Río María (H) 407
Río Orosi Valley (CR) 635
Río Plátano Biosphere Reserve (H) 447-449
Río San Juan 36, 582-583
Río Sereno (P) 770-771
Río Tinto (H) 399
rip tide safety 68
Rivas (N) 574-575, 610
Roatán (H) 423-435, **424-425**
Rock Harbour (H) 438
Roman Catholicism 30
Romero, Rafael Leonardo Callejas 315
Ruinas de Quelepa (ES) 508
Ruinas de San Andrés (ES) 491
Ruinas de Tazumal (ES) 501-502
ruins 411, 637, 767
  Spanish 750
  See also Maya ruins

Sabanitas (P) 750
Sacramento (CR) 634
sailboarding 278-280
sailing 303
St Herman's Cave (B) 298

St John's Cathedral (B) 271
Salamá (G) 202-203
Sambo Creek (H) 407
San Andrés (Col) 78-79
San Andrés (G) 241
San Antonio (B) 294, 308
San Antonio Aguas Calientes
 (G) 148
San Antonio de Oriente (H) 451
San Antonio Los Ranchos (ES)
 513
San Antonio Palopó (G) 159
San Benito (G) 233-240
San Carlos. See Ciudad Quesada
 (CR)
San Carlos (N) 582, 611, 651
San Felipe (G) 220-221
San Félix (P) 748
San Francisco El Alto (G)
 184-185
San Gerardo de Rivas (CR) 667
San Ignacio (Cayo) (B) 291, **292**
San Isidro de Coronado. See
 Coronado (CR)
San Isidro de El General (CR)
 666-667, **666**
San Jerónimo (G) 203
San José (CR) 613-628,
 614-616
 accommodations 621-623
 entertainment 624-625
 organized tours 620-621
 orientation 613
 restaurants 623-624
 things to see & do 618-621
 tourist offices 613
 transportation to/from
  625-628
 transportation within 628
San José Las Flores (ES) 513
San José Succotz (B) 296
San Juan (H) 399
San Juan Chamelco (G) 208
San Juan de Oriente (N) 568
San Juan del Sur (N) 575-577,
 576
San Juan Sacatepéquez (G) 203
San Juancito (H) 353
San Lorenzo (H) 452
San Lucas Tolimán (G) 159
San Manuel Colohete (H) 386
San Marcos (N) 569
San Marcos de Colón (H) 455
San Marcos La Laguna (G)
 162-163
San Miguel (ES) 506-509, **507**

San Miguel Chicaj (G) 203
San Miguel Totonicapán (G)
 173-174
San Pablo Island (N) 573
San Pedro 278, **279**
San Pedro Carcha (G) 208
San Pedro La Laguna (G)
 161-162
San Pedro Sula (H) 362-369,
 363
San Salvador 475-489, **476**,
 479, **482**
 accommodations 483-485
 entertainment 487-488
 orientation 477-479
 restaurants 485-487
 things to see & do 480-483
 tourist offices 479
 transportation to/from
  488-489
 transportation within 489
San Sebastián (ES) 505
San Vicente (ES) 505
San Vito (CR) 673-675, **674**
Sandinistas. See FSLN
Sandino, Augusto C 521, 568
Sandy Bay (H) 433-434
Santa Ana (ES) 497-500, **498**
Santa Bárbara (H) 362
Santa Catarina Palopó (G) 159
Santa Cruz del Quiché (G)
 170-172
Santa Cruz La Laguna (G)
 163-164
Santa Elena (CR) 638-643,
 640-641
Santa Elena (G) 233-240, **236**
Santa Lucía (H) 352
Santa Lucía Cotzumalguapa (G)
 195-198, **195**
Santa María (CR) 647
Santa María (G) 149
Santamaría, Juan (CR) 592
Santa Rita Archaeological Site
 (B) 287
Santa Rita de Copán (H) 375
Santa Rosa de Aguán (H)
 417-418
Santa Rosa de Copán (H)
 381-383, **381**
Santa Rosa de Lima (ES) 512
Santa Tecla (ES) 490
Santiago (P) 748
Santiago Atitlán (G) 159-161
Santo Domingo beach area (N)
 581

Sapoá (N) 575
Sapzurro (P) 787
Sarchí (CR) 629-632
Sautatá (Col) 793
Sautatá (P) 789
Savannah Bight (H) 441
Sayaxché (G) 252
scuba diving. See diving, scuba
sea kayaking 534, 608
sea travel 83-84, 335, 723
seasons. See climate
Sébaco (N) 553
Selva Negra (N) 551, 553
Semana Santa (Holy Week)
 114, 143
Semuc-Champey (G) 209
Seven Altars. See Las Siete
 Altares
sexually transmitted diseases 58
Sierpe (CR) 669
Siguatepeque (H) 359-360, **359**
Sipacate (G) 199
Siren (CR) 673
Sittee River (B) 302
Sixaola (CR) 611, 665, 779
Smithsonian Tropical Research
 Institute 743
snorkeling 34, 69, 429
 Belize 274-276, 278-280,
  303
 Costa Rica 608, 659, 665,
  691
 Honduras 395, 417-418, 423,
  438, 441
 Nicaragua 534
 Panama 718, 752, 773-774
Sololá (G) 151
Somoto (N) 559
Somoza García, Anastasio
 521-522
Sonsonate (ES) 497, 503
sorpresas 505
South American Explorers Club
 63
Southern Highway (B) 301-302
Spanish language 797-803. See
 also language courses
special events 330
Spirogyra Jardín de Mariposas
 (CR) 619
Standard Fruit (H) 313
student travel agencies 86
Suchitoto (ES) 490
Summit Botanical Gardens &
 Zoo (P) 742
Sumo (N) 583

Sumos (N) 526
surfing 69
    Costa Rica 608, 661, 664,
        672, 679, 686, 691, 693
    El Salvador 493
    Nicaragua 534
    Panama 719
Suyapa (H) 352
Swan Cay (P) 778
swimming 68
    Belize 278, 280
    Costa Rica 672
    Guatemala 115
    Nicaragua 534, 550, 557,
        564, 579

Talismán (Mex) 191
Tanah Maya Art Museum (B)
    293
taxes 42
Teatro Nacional (CR) 620
Tecpán Guatemala (G) 150-151
Tegucigalpa (H) 338-351,
    340-341
    accommodations 346-348
    entertainment 348-349
    organized tours 346
    orientation 338-339
    restaurants 348
    tourist offices 339
    transportation to/from
        349-351
    transportation within 351
Tela (H) 393-397, **394**
telephone 43
Tenampua (H) 355-360
Tenosique (G) 251
Tikal (G) 241-249, **242-243**
Tilarán (CR) 650
time 48
tipping 42
Tobías Bolaños Airport (CR)
    611, 625
Todos Santos Cuchumatán (G)
    190-191
toilets 62
Tolé (P) 748
Toledo Ecotourism Association
    307

Toltecs 492
Tolupanes (H) 27, 321
Tornabé (H) 399
Toro Guaco festivals 533
Tortuguero (CR) 655-656
train travel 88
Travesía (H) 391-392
Travesía (P) 792
Trinidad (CR) 652
Trujillo (H) 410-415, **410**
Turbo (Col) 792
Turbo (P) 788-792
Turrialba (CR) 636-637, **637**
turtles, sea 302, 648, 654-655,
    692, 774

Uaxactún (G) 249-250
Ujarrás (CR) 635
Unión Nacional Opositora
    (UNO) 523
United Democratic Party (UDP)
    259
United Fruit (H) 313
Uspantán (G) 172-173
Usulután (ES) 506
Utila (H) 435-441, **436**
Uvita (CR) 687
Uxbenka (B) 308

vaccinations. See
    immunizations
Vado Hondo (G) 216
Valle de Angeles (H) 352-353
Valle de Comayagua (H) 355
Valle de Sula (H) 362
value-added tax. See money
vegetarian food 72
Veracruz beach (P) 744
Villa. See Neily (CR)
Villa de los Santos (P) 755
Villa Rhina (H) 407
Violeta Barrios de Chamorro (N)
    522-523
visas 36-37
Vívero Verapaz (G) 206
Volcán (P) 767-768
Volcán Acatenango (G) 149
Volcán Agua (G) 149
Volcán Arenal (CR) 649-650

Volcán Barú (P) 699, 765-766
Volcán Barva (CR) 633
Volcán Concepción (N) 578
Volcán Fuego (G) 149
Volcán Irazú (CR) 635-636
Volcán Izalco (ES) 496-497
Volcán Madera (N) 578
Volcán Masaya (N) 548-550,
    567
Volcán Mombacho (N) 574
Volcán Momotombo (N) 550
Volcán Pacaya (G) 148-149
Volcán Poás (CR) 632
Volcán Rincón de la Vieja (CR)
    646-647
Volcán Santiago. See Volcán
    Masaya (N)
volcanoes 34

Walker, William 313, 411, 520,
    592
water 50-51
weaving courses 115, 179
West End (H) 428-433
Wetzo (P) 770
white-water rafting 115, 142,
    331, 470, 608, 719, 756
Wilson Botanical Gardens (CR)
    674
windsurfing 395, 534, 608, 650,
    691
women travelers 63-64
work 69-70

Xela. See Quetzaltenango
Xunantunich (B) 296

Yarumela (H) 355, 358
Yaviza (P) 784, 789-790
Yuscarán (H) 451

Zacapa (G) 211
Zacatecoluca (ES) 506
Zelaya, José Santos 521
Zona Libre (Free Zone) (P) 749
zoomorphs 218
Zunil (G) 183

THANKS

Thanks to all the many travelers who wrote in with comments about our last edition and with tips and comments about Central America:

Bob Agnew, Giuseppe Anzalone, Wilfred Ariëns, Jan Bailey & Ezra Doron, B & S Baumeister, Taylor Beavers, Rob Bell, Frederick Belland, Charles Bennett, Brian Betts, Hans Bevers, Jessica Bjorklund, Carla Black, Jane Bode, Nicole Boogaers, Theo Borst, Erik Botsford, Christian Boulay, Annemarie Breeve, Stefano Briscini, Kay & Nathan Brooks, Allison Brown, Heather Brown, Thierry Brun, Ben Budnitz, Tim Burford, John Bushby, Claude Bussires, Judith Butler, Mark Camp, Miguel A Cauhépé, Myléne Chalifoux, Trevor Charles, Robyn Christie & Mark Dellar, Bess Cocke, David J Connor, Michelle Cooper, Pascale Courrieu, Steve Creamer, Fernando Sanchez Cuenca, Ben Davis, Luc & Jose de Vries, Michael Derby, Celia Diephuis, Alon Diller, C Djossor, Ulrike Dorrie, Stéphane Doutriaux, Roel Duijf, Rona Fergusson, Dr Gerhard Fiala, Daniel Finkbeiner, Sandi Fisher, Tom Fletcher Jr, Fernando Capitán Flores, Harmony Folz, Annick Forest, Reto & Heike Furger, Claus Gaasvig, Ulf Gäbler, Christer Garbis & Christina Eriksson, Nacho Garcia, Terry Gardner, Hans Gerd, Huber Gerhard, Clive Giddings, Jenny Gill, Tracy R Glass, Uwe Goehl, Elke Ditscheid Göller, Wolf Gotthilf, Line Gregoire, Michael Greig, Rokus Groeneveld, Ulf Gubler, A B Guevui, E I Haaijer, Hubert Haas, Mary Anne Hamer, Mabel Haourt, Langdon W Harris, Colin Harvey, Tricia Hausman, Steve Herrick, Matthias Herrlein, Michael Hogen, Abigail Hogg, Dorsey & Hal Holappa, Nancy Humber, Marianne Hummel, Alexander Hunter, Cameron Hutchison, Andrew Hyde, Gill Irvin, Dores Jay-Pang, Tim Jeffries, Martin Jirman, Jeroen Jongkind, Tim San Jule,

Alexander Jurk, Hugo Kaelen, Rikke Kamstrup & Anders Aarkrog, Tom Kegelman, David Kerkhoff, Mario Kerri, Samyra Keus, Jochen Kick, Jeff & Kelly Klempen, Ingo Koeker, Marieke Koerselman, Leslie Korn, Raghu Krishnan, Randall R Krueger, Rainer Kugler, Eve Lafferty, Katalijne Lens, Steve Lidguy, Dawn Louck, Jurgen Maisch, Douglas Margolis, Anna Soler Marti, Brent Masuda, Andrew May, Patrick McGarry, Twid McGrath, Kim McMaken, Ross Melles, Ludo Mevissen, Stephanie Mills, Brenda Minis, L C Murray, Paula Nanson, Juraj Neidel, Salena Noel, Graham Norris, Lynne Oakerbee, David Olsen, Dean Oman, Karin Oyevaar, Alberte Pagán, Ann Pagles, Louise Palmer, Louise Parker, Jennifer Payne, Jane Pedersen, Brian Pederson, Karen Petersen, Stephan Philip, Javier Pinel, Briggitte Poels, Andreas Poethen, Richard Procter, Aleesha Pruett, Alison Pugsley, Jeannine Pulsfort-Mendel, Ben Radford, Genevieve Ragule, Brett Rallings, Hanna Ramberg, Dave Redmond, Sanne Reijs, Simone Remijnse, James Renn, Tim Richey, Lisa Roberts, Ingrid Robeyns, Tim Rodsham, Jenni Romaniuk, Jeff Rothman, Senta Rudi, Sia Rumpff, John F Ryan, April Schlenk, Stephen Schmidt, Wanda Schooley, Devin Scott, Brian & Susan Scowcroft, Holly Shaffer, Aisha Siddiqi, Bobby Singh, Bo Sjoholm, Dr John Sloss, Angie Smith, Donald M Smith, Mde Solis, Garry R Sprague, Giulleame Stephane, Michael Stock, Lisa Stocking, Anja Stoltenborg, Anouk Studer, Teresa Taylor, Hilary Tempest, Tim C Thatcher, Loretta Thorpe, Lisette Thresh, Gabriel Tojo, Monica Trabattoni, E & J P Tremblay, Mike & Pauline Truman, Karena Uledc, Martin Uzelac, Juan Ramon Vallarino, Stefi van de Graaf, Willy van Heeli, Nancie-Ann Watson, Wolfgang Weigomd, John T Widdowson, Julie Williamson, Eldon R Wilson, Tris Winfield, C Wrenthore, Mario Xerri.

LONELY PLANET

Phrasebooks

L onely Planet phrasebooks are packed with essential words and phrases to help travellers communicate with the locals. With colour tabs for quick reference, an extensive vocabulary and use of script, these handy pocket-sized language guides cover day-to-day travel situations.

- handy pocket-sized books
- easy to understand Pronunciation chapter
- clear & comprehensive Grammar chapter
- romanisation alongside script to allow ease of pronunciation
- script throughout so users can point to phrases for every situation
- full of cultural information and tips for the traveller

'...vital for a real DIY spirit and attitude in language learning'
— *Backpacker*

'the phrasebooks have good cultural backgrounders and offer solid advice for challenging situations in remote locations'
— *San Francisco Examiner*

Arabic (Egyptian) • Arabic (Moroccan) • Australian *(Australian English, Aboriginal and Torres Strait languages)* • Baltic States *(Estonian, Latvian, Lithuanian)* • Bengali • Brazilian • British • Burmese • Cantonese • Central Asia • Central Europe *(Czech, French, German, Hungarian, Italian, Slovak)* • Eastern Europe *(Bulgarian, Czech, Hungarian, Polish, Romanian, Slovak)* • Ethiopian (Amharic) • Fijian • French • German • Greek • Hebrew phrasebook • Hill Tribes • Hindi/Urdu • Indonesian • Italian • Japanese • Korean • Lao • Latin American Spanish • Malay • Mandarin • Mediterranean Europe *(Albanian, Croatian, Greek, Italian, Macedonian, Maltese, Serbian, Slovene)* • Mongolian • Nepali • Pidgin • Pilipino (Tagalog) • Quechua • Russian • Scandinavian Europe *(Danish, Finnish, Icelandic, Norwegian, Swedish)* • South-East Asia *(Burmese, Indonesian, Khmer, Lao, Malay, Tagalog Pilipino, Thai, Vietnamese)* • South Pacific Languages • Spanish (Castilian) *(also includes Catalan, Galician and Basque)* • Sri Lanka • Swahili • Thai • Tibetan • Turkish • Ukrainian • USA *(US English, Vernacular, Native American languages, Hawaiian)* • Vietnamese • Western Europe *(Basque, Catalan, Dutch, French, German, Greek, Irish)*

Lonely Planet Journeys

JOURNEYS is a unique collection of travel writing – published by the company that understands travel better than anyone else. It is a series for anyone who has ever experienced – or dreamed of – the magical moment when they encountered a strange culture or saw a place for the first time. They are tales to read while you're planning a trip, while you're on the road or while you're in an armchair in front of a fire.

These outstanding titles explore our planet through the eyes of a diverse group of international writers. JOURNEYS books catch the spirit of a place, illuminate a culture, recount a crazy adventure or introduce a fascinating way of life. They always entertain, and always enrich the experience of travel.

FULL CIRCLE
A South American Journey
Luis Sepúlveda (translated by Chris Andrews)

'A journey without a fixed itinerary' with Chilean writer Luis Sepúlveda. Extravagant characters and extraordinary situations are memorably evoked: gauchos organising a tournament of lies, a scheming heiress on the lookout for a husband, a pilot with a corpse on board his plane ... *Full Circle* brings us the distinctive voice of one of South America's most compelling writers.

WINNER 1996 Astrolabe – Etonnants Voyageurs award for the best work of travel literature published in France.

GREEN DREAMS
Travels in Central America
Stephen Benz

On the Amazon, in Costa Rica, Honduras and on the Mayan trail from Guatemala to Mexico, Stephen Benz describes his encounters with water, mud, insects and other wildlife – and not least with the ecotourists themselves. With witty insights into modern travel, *Green Dreams* discusses the paradox of cultural and 'green' tourism.

DRIVE THRU AMERICA
Sean Condon

If you've ever wanted to drive across the USA but couldn't find the time (or afford the gas), *Drive Thru America* is perfect for you.

In his search for American myths and realities – along with comfort, cable TV and good, reasonably priced coffee – Sean Condon paints a hilarious road-portrait of the USA.

'entertaining and laugh-out-loud funny' – *Alex Wilber, Travel editor, Amazon.com*

SEAN & DAVID'S LONG DRIVE
Sean Condon

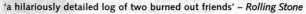

Sean and David are young townies who have rarely strayed beyond city limits. One day, for no good reason, they set out to discover their homeland, and what follows is a wildly entertaining adventure that covers half of Australia.

'a hilariously detailed log of two burned out friends' – *Rolling Stone*

Lonely Planet Travel Atlases

Lonely Planet has long been famous for the number and quality of its guidebook maps. Now we've gone one step further and produced a handy companion series: Lonely Planet travel atlases – maps of a country produced in book form.

Unlike other maps, which look good but lead travellers astray, our travel atlases have been researched on the road by Lonely Planet's experienced team of writers. All details are carefully checked to ensure the atlas corresponds with the equivalent Lonely Planet guidebook.

- full-colour throughout
- maps researched and checked by Lonely Planet authors
- place names correspond with Lonely Planet guidebooks
- no confusing spelling differences
- legend and travelling information in English, French, German, Japanese and Spanish
- size: 230 x 160 mm

Available now: Chile & Easter Island • Egypt • India & Bangladesh • Israel & the Palestinian Territories • Jordan, Syria & Lebanon • Kenya • Laos • Portugal • South Africa, Lesotho & Swaziland • Thailand • Turkey • Vietnam • Zimbabwe, Botswana & Namibia

Lonely Planet TV Series & Videos

Lonely Planet travel guides have been brought to life on television screens around the world. Like our guides, the programs are based on the joy of independent travel, and look honestly at some of the most exciting, picturesque and frustrating places in the world. Each show is presented by one of three travellers from Australia, England or the USA and combines an innovative mixture of video, Super-8 film, atmospheric soundscapes and original music.

Videos of each episode – containing additional footage not shown on television – are available from good book and video shops, but the availability of individual videos varies with regional screening schedules.

Video destinations include: Alaska • American Rockies • Australia – The South-East • Baja California & the Copper Canyon • Brazil • Central Asia • Chile & Easter Island • Corsica, Sicily & Sardinia – The Mediterranean Islands • East Africa (Tanzania & Zanzibar) • Ecuador & the Galapagos Islands • Greenland & Iceland • Indonesia • Israel & the Sinai Desert • Jamaica • Japan • La Ruta Maya • Morocco • New York • North India • Pacific Islands (Fiji, Solomon Islands & Vanuatu) • South India • South West China • Turkey • Vietnam • West Africa • Zimbabwe, Botswana & Namibia

The Lonely Planet TV series is produced by: Pilot Productions
The Old Studio
18 Middle Row
London W10 5AT, UK

LONELY PLANET

Guides by Region

Lonely Planet is known worldwide for publishing practical, reliable and nononsense travel information in our guides and on our Web site. The Lonely Planet list covers just about every accessible part of the world. Currently there are thirteen series: travel guides, shoestring guides, walking guides, city guides, phrasebooks, audio packs, city maps, travel atlases, diving & snorkeling guides, restaurant guides, first-time travel guides, healthy travel and travel literature.

AFRICA Africa on a shoestring ● Africa – the South ● Arabic (Egyptian) phrasebook ● Arabic (Moroccan) phrasebook ● Cairo ● Cape Town ● Cape Town city map● Central Africa ● East Africa ● Egypt ● Egypt travel atlas ● Ethiopian (Amharic) phrasebook ● The Gambia & Senegal ● Healthy Travel Africa ● Kenya ● Kenya travel atlas ● Malawi, Mozambique & Zambia ● Morocco ● North Africa ● South Africa, Lesotho & Swaziland ● South Africa, Lesotho & Swaziland travel atlas ● Swahili phrasebook ● Tanzania, Zanzibar & Pemba ● Trekking in East Africa ● Tunisia ● West Africa ● Zimbabwe, Botswana & Namibia ● Zimbabwe, Botswana & Namibia travel atlas
Travel Literature: The Rainbird: A Central African Journey ● Songs to an African Sunset: A Zimbabwean Story ● Mali Blues: Traveling to an African Beat

AUSTRALIA & THE PACIFIC Auckland ● Australia ● Australian phrasebook ● Bushwalking in Australia ● Bushwalking in Papua New Guinea ● Fiji ● Fijian phrasebook ● Healthy Travel Australia, NZ and the Pacific ● Islands of Australia's Great Barrier Reef ● Melbourne ● Melbourne city map ● Micronesia ● New Caledonia ● New South Wales & the ACT ● New Zealand ● Northern Territory ● Outback Australia ● Out To Eat – Melbourne ● Out to Eat – Sydney ● Papua New Guinea ● Pidgin phrasebook ● Queensland ● Rarotonga & the Cook Islands ● Samoa ● Solomon Islands ● South Australia ● South Pacific Languages phrasebook ● Sydney ● Sydney city map ● Sydney Condensed ● Tahiti & French Polynesia ● Tasmania ● Tonga ● Tramping in New Zealand ● Vanuatu ● Victoria ● Western Australia
Travel Literature: Islands in the Clouds ● Kiwi Tracks: A New Zealand Journey ● Sean & David's Long Drive

CENTRAL AMERICA & THE CARIBBEAN Bahamas, Turks & Caicos ● Bermuda ● Central America on a shoestring ● Costa Rica ● Cuba ● Dominican Republic & Haiti ● Eastern Caribbean ● Guatemala, Belize & Yucatán: La Ruta Maya ● Jamaica ● Mexico ● Mexico City ● Panama ● Puerto Rico
Travel Literature: Green Dreams: Travels in Central America

EUROPE Amsterdam ● Amsterdam city map ● Andalucía ● Austria ● Baltic States phrasebook ● Barcelona ● Berlin ● Berlin city map ● Britain ● British phrasebook ● Brussels, Bruges & Antwerp ● Budapest city map ● Canary Islands ● Central Europe ● Central Europe phrasebook ● Corsica ● Croatia ● Czech & Slovak Republics ● Denmark ● Dublin ● Eastern Europe ● Eastern Europe phrasebook ● Edinburgh ● Estonia, Latvia & Lithuania ● Europe on a shoestring ● Finland ● France ● French phrasebook ● Germany ● German phrasebook ● Greece ● Greek Islands ● Greek phrasebook ● Hungary ● Iceland, Greenland & the Faroe Islands ● Ireland ● Italian phrasebook ● Italy ● Krakow ● Lisbon ● London ● London city map ● London Condensed ● Mediterranean Europe ● Mediterranean Europe phrasebook ● Norway ● Paris ● Paris city map ● Poland ● Portugal ● Portugal travel atlas ● Prague ● Prague city map ● Provence & the Côte d'Azur ● Romania & Moldova ● Rome ● Russia, Ukraine & Belarus ● Russian phrasebook ● Scandinavian & Baltic Europe ● Scandinavian Europe phrasebook ● Scotland ● Slovenia ● Spain ● Spanish phrasebook ● St Petersburg ● Switzerland ● Trekking in Spain ● Ukrainian phrasebook ● Vienna ● Walking in Britain ● Walking in Ireland ● Walking in Italy ● Walking in Spain ● Walking in Switzerland ● Western Europe ● Western Europe phrasebook
Travel Literature: The Olive Grove: Travels in Greece

INDIAN SUBCONTINENT Bangladesh ● Bengali phrasebook ● Bhutan ● Delhi ● Goa ● Hindi & Urdu phrasebook ● India ● India & Bangladesh travel atlas ● Indian Himalaya ● Karakoram Highway ● Kerala ● Mumbai (Bombay) ● Nepal ● Nepali phrasebook ● Pakistan ● Rajasthan ● Read This First: Asia & India ● South India ● Sri Lanka ● Sri Lanka phrasebook ● Trekking in the Indian Himalaya ● Trekking in the Karakoram & Hindukush ● Trekking in the Nepal Himalaya
Travel Literature: In Rajasthan ● Shopping for Buddhas

LONELY PLANET

Mail Order

Lonely Planet products are distributed worldwide. They are also available by mail order from Lonely Planet, so if you have difficulty finding a title please write to us. North and South American residents should write to 150 Linden St, Oakland, CA 94607, USA; European and African residents should write to 10a Spring Place, London NW5 3BH, UK; and residents of other countries to PO Box 617, Hawthorn, Victoria 3122, Australia.

ISLANDS OF THE INDIAN OCEAN Madagascar & Comoros • Maldives • Mauritius, Réunion & Seychelles

MIDDLE EAST & CENTRAL ASIA Arab Gulf States • Central Asia • Central Asia phrasebook • Hebrew phrasebook • Iran • Israel & the Palestinian Territories • Israel & the Palestinian Territories travel atlas • Istanbul • Istanbul to Cairo • Jerusalem • Jordan & Syria • Jordan, Syria & Lebanon travel atlas • Lebanon • Middle East on a shoestring • Syria • Turkey • Turkey travel atlas • Turkish phrasebook • Yemen
Travel Literature: The Gates of Damascus • Kingdom of the Film Stars: Journey into Jordan

NORTH AMERICA Alaska • Backpacking in Alaska • Baja California • California & Nevada • Canada • Chicago • Chicago city map • Deep South • Florida • Hawaii • Honolulu • Las Vegas • Los Angeles • Miami • New England • New Orleans • New York City • New York city map • New York, New Jersey & Pennsylvania • Pacific Northwest USA • Puerto Rico • Rocky Mountain • San Francisco • San Francisco city map • Seattle • Southwest USA • Texas • USA • USA phrasebook • Vancouver • Washington, DC & the Capital Region • Washington DC city map
Travel Literature: Drive Thru America

NORTH-EAST ASIA Beijing • Cantonese phrasebook • China • Hong Kong • Hong Kong city map • Hong Kong, Macau & Guangzhou • Japan • Japanese phrasebook • Japanese audio pack • Korea • Korean phrasebook • Kyoto • Mandarin phrasebook • Mongolia • Mongolian phrasebook • North-East Asia on a shoestring • Seoul • South-West China • Taiwan • Tibet • Tibetan phrasebook • Tokyo
Travel Literature: Lost Japan

SOUTH AMERICA Argentina, Uruguay & Paraguay • Bolivia • Brazil • Brazilian phrasebook • Buenos Aires • Chile & Easter Island • Chile & Easter Island travel atlas • Colombia • Ecuador & the Galapagos Islands • Healthy Travel Central & South America • Latin American Spanish phrasebook • Peru • Quechua phrasebook • Rio de Janeiro • Rio de Janeiro city map • South America on a shoestring • Trekking in the Patagonian Andes • Venezuela
Travel Literature: Full Circle: A South American Journey

SOUTH-EAST ASIA Bali & Lombok • Bangkok • Bangkok city map • Burmese phrasebook • Cambodia • Hanoi • Healthy Travel Asia & India • Hill Tribes phrasebook • Ho Chi Minh City • Indonesia • Indonesia's Eastern Islands • Indonesian phrasebook • Indonesian audio pack • Jakarta • Java • Laos • Lao phrasebook • Laos travel atlas • Malay phrasebook • Malaysia, Singapore & Brunei • Myanmar (Burma) • Philippines • Pilipino (Tagalog) phrasebook • Singapore • South-East Asia on a shoestring • South-East Asia phrasebook • Thailand • Thailand's Islands & Beaches • Thailand travel atlas • Thai phrasebook • Thai audio pack • Vietnam • Vietnamese phrasebook • Vietnam travel atlas

ALSO AVAILABLE: Antarctica • The Arctic • Brief Encounters: Stories of Love, Sex & Travel • Chasing Rickshaws • Lonely Planet Unpacked • Not the Only Planet: Travel Stories from Science Fiction • Sacred India • Travel with Children • Traveller's Tales

The Lonely Planet Story

Lonely Planet published its first book in 1973 in response to the numerous 'How did you do it?' questions Maureen and Tony Wheeler were asked after driving, bussing, hitching, sailing and railing their way from England to Australia.

Written at a kitchen table and hand collated, trimmed and stapled, *Across Asia on the Cheap* became an instant local bestseller, inspiring thoughts of another book.

Eighteen months in South-East Asia resulted in their second guide, *South-East Asia on a shoestring*, which they put together in a backstreet Chinese hotel in Singapore in 1975. The 'yellow bible', as it quickly became known to backpackers around the world, soon became *the* guide to the region. It has sold well over half a million copies and is now in its 9th edition, still retaining its familiar yellow cover.

Today there are over 350 titles, including travel guides, walking guides, language kits & phrasebooks, travel atlases, diving guides and travel literature. The company is the largest independent travel publisher in the world. Although Lonely Planet initially specialised in guides to Asia, today there are few corners of the globe that have not been covered.

The emphasis continues to be on travel for independent travellers. Tony and Maureen still travel for several months of each year and play an active part in the writing, updating and quality control of Lonely Planet's guides.

They have been joined by over 120 authors and 280 staff at our offices in Melbourne (Australia), Oakland (USA), London (UK) and Paris (France). Travellers themselves also make a valuable contribution to the guides through the feedback we receive in thousands of letters each year and on our web site.

The people at Lonely Planet strongly believe that travellers can make a positive contribution to the countries they visit, both through their appreciation of the countries' culture, wildlife and natural features, and through the money they spend. In addition, the company makes a direct contribution to the countries and regions it covers. Since 1986 a percentage of the income from each book has been donated to ventures such as famine relief in Africa; aid projects in India; agricultural projects in Central America; Greenpeace's efforts to halt French nuclear testing in the Pacific; and Amnesty International.

LONELY PLANET OFFICES

Australia
PO Box 617, Hawthorn, Victoria 3122
☎ 03 9819 1877 fax 03 9819 6459
email: talk2us@lonelyplanet.com.au

USA
150 Linden St, Oakland, CA 94607
☎ 510 893 8555 TOLL FREE: 800 275 8555
fax 510 893 8572
email: info@lonelyplanet.com

UK
10a Spring Place, London NW5 3BH
☎ 020 7428 4800 fax 020 7428 4828
email: go@lonelyplanet.co.uk

France
1 rue du Dahomey, 75011 Paris
☎ 01 55 25 33 00 fax 01 55 25 33 01
email: bip@lonelyplanet.fr
www.lonelyplanet.fr

World Wide Web: www.lonelyplanet.com *or* AOL keyword: lp
Lonely Planet Images: lpi@lonelyplanet.com.au